THE GREEK HISTORIANS

HERODOTUS
THUCYDIDES
XENOPHON
ARRIAN

The Greek Historians

THE COMPLETE AND UNABRIDGED
HISTORICAL WORKS OF

Herodotus

TRANSLATED BY GEORGE RAWLINSON

Thucydides

TRANSLATED BY BENJAMIN JOWETT

Xenophon

TRANSLATED BY HENRY G. DAKYNS

Arrian

TRANSLATED BY EDWARD J. CHINNOCK

*Edited, with an introduction, revisions
and additional notes, by*

FRANCIS R. B. GODOLPHIN

*Associate Professor of Classics and Acting Chairman of the
Department of Classics, Princeton University*

IN TWO VOLUMES

2

RANDOM HOUSE · NEW YORK · PUBLISHER

Contents

VOLUME ONE

VOLUME TWO

APPENDIX

XENOPHON:

THE HELLENICA
AND
THE ANABASIS OF CYRUS

THE HELLENICA OF XENOPHON

BOOK I

1. A few days after these events[1] Thymochares arrived from Athens with a few ships, when another sea-fight between the Lacedaemonians and Athenians at once took place, in which the former, under the command of Agesandridas, gained the victory.

After a short interval, in early winter, Dorieus, the son of Diagoras, was entering the Hellespont with fourteen ships from Rhodes at daybreak. The Athenian day-watch seeing him, signalled to the generals, and they, with twenty sail, put out to sea to attack him. Dorieus made good his escape, and, as he shook himself free of the narrows, ran his triremes aground off Rhoeteum. When the Athenians had come to close quarters, the fighting commenced, and was sustained at once from ships and shore, until at length the Athenians retired to their main camp at Madytus, having achieved nothing.

Meanwhile Mindarus, while sacrificing to Athena at Ilium, had observed the battle. He at once hastened to the sea, and getting his own triremes afloat, sailed out to pick up the ships with Dorieus. The Athenians on their side put out to meet him, and engaged him off Abydos. From early morning till the afternoon the fight was kept up close to the shore. Victory and defeat hung still in even balance, when Alcibiades came sailing up with eighteen ships. Thereupon the Peloponnesians fled towards Abydos, where, however, Pharnabazus brought them timely assistance. Mounted on horseback, he pushed forward into the sea as far as his horse would let him, doing battle himself, and encouraging his troopers and the infantry alike. Then the Peloponnesians, ranging their ships in close-packed order, and drawing up their battle line close to the land, kept up the fight. At length the Athenians, having captured thirty of the enemy's vessels without their crews, and having recovered those of their own which they had previously lost, set sail for Sestos. Here the fleet, with the exception of forty vessels, dispersed in different directions outside the Hellespont, to collect money; while Thrasylus, one of the generals, sailed to Athens to report what had happened, and

[1] The author refers to the closing chapter of Thucydides, viii. 109. The scene of this sea-fight is the Hellespont.

3

to beg for a reinforcement of troops and ships. After the above incidents, Tissaphernes arrived in the Hellespont, and received a visit from Alcibiades, who presented himself with a single ship, bringing with him tokens of friendship and gifts, whereupon Tissaphernes seized him and shut him up in Sardis, giving out that the king's orders were to go to war with the Athenians. Thirty days later Alcibiades, accompanied by Mantitheus, who had been captured in Caria, managed to procure horses and escaped by night to Clazomenae.

And now the Athenians at Sestos, hearing that Mindarus was planning an attack upon them with a squadron of sixty sail, gave him the slip, and under cover of night escaped to Cardia. Hither also Alcibiades repaired from Clazomenae, having with him five triremes and a light skiff; but on learning that the Peloponnesian fleet had left Abydos and was sailing for Cyzicus, he set off himself by land to Sestos, giving orders to the fleet to sail round and join him there. Presently the vessels arrived, and he was on the point of putting out to sea with everything ready for action, when Theramenes, with a fleet of twenty ships from Macedonia, entered the port, and at the same instant Thrasybulus, with a second fleet of twenty sail from Thasos, both squadrons having been engaged in collecting money. Bidding these officers also follow him with all speed, as soon as they had taken off their large sails and cleared for action, Alcibiades set sail himself for Parium. During the following night the united squadron, consisting now of eighty-six vessels, stood out to sea from Parium, and reached Proconnesus next morning, about the hour of breakfast. Here they learned that Mindarus was in Cyzicus, and that Pharnabazus, with a body of infantry, was with him. Accordingly they waited the whole of this day at Proconnesus. On the following day Alcibiades summoned an assembly, and addressing the men in terms of encouragement, warned them that a threefold service was expected of them; that they must be ready for a sea-fight, a land-fight, and a wall-fight all at once, "For look you," said he, "we have no money, but the enemy has unlimited supplies from the king."

Now, on the previous day, as soon as they had anchored, he had collected all the ships, big and little alike, under his own control, that no one might report the number of his squadron to the enemy, and he had further caused a proclamation to be made, that any one caught sailing across to the opposite coast would be punished with death. When the meeting was over, he got his ships ready for action, and stood out to sea towards Cyzicus in a heavy rain. Off Cyzicus the sky cleared, and the sun shone out and revealed to him the spectacle of Mindarus's vessels, sixty in number, exercising at some distance from the harbour, and, in fact, intercepted by himself. The Peloponnesians, perceiving at a glance the greatly increased number of the Athenian galleys, and noting their proximity to the port, made haste to reach the land, where they brought their vessels to anchor in a body, and prepared to engage the enemy as he sailed to the attack. But Alcibiades, sailing round with twenty of his vessels, came to land and disembarked. Seeing this, Mindarus also landed, and in the engagement which ensued he fell fighting, whilst those who were with him took to flight. As for the enemy's ships, the Athenians succeeded in capturing the whole of them (with the exception of the Syracusan vessels, which were burned by their crews), and made off with their prizes to Proconnesus. From thence on the following day they sailed to attack Cyzicus. The men of that place, seeing that the Peloponnesians and Pharnabazus had evacuated the town, admitted the Athenians. Here Alcibiades remained twenty days, obtaining large sums of money from the Cyzicenes, but otherwise inflicting no damage on the community. He then sailed back to Proconnesus, and from there to Perinthus and Selybria. The inhabitants of the former place welcomed his troops into their city, but the Selybrians preferred to give money, and so escape the admission of the troops. Continuing the voyage the squadron reached Chrysopolis in Calchedonia, where they built a fort, and established a custom-house to collect the ten per cent. tax which they levied on all merchantmen passing through the Straits from the Black Sea. Besides this, a detachment of thirty ships was left there under the two generals, Theramenes and Eubulus, with instructions not only to keep a look-out on the port itself and on all traders passing through the channel, but generally to injure the enemy in any way which might present itself. This done, the rest of the generals hastened back to the Hellespont.

Now a despatch from Hippocrates, Mindarus's vice-admiral, had been intercepted on its way to Lacedaemon, and taken to Athens. It ran as follows, "Ships gone; Mindarus dead; the men starving; at our wits' end what to do."

Pharnabazus, however, was ready to meet with encouragement the despondency which afflicted the whole Peloponnesian army and their allies. "As long as their own bodies were safe and sound, why need they take to heart the loss of a few wooden hulls? Was there not timber enough and to spare in the king's territory?" And so he presented each man with a cloak and maintenance for a couple of months, after which he armed the sailors and formed them into a coastguard for the security of his own seaboard.

He next called a meeting of the generals and trierarchs of the different States, and instructed them to build just as many new ships in the dockyards of Antandrus as they had respectively lost. He himself was to furnish the funds, and he told them to bring down timber from Mount Ida. While the ships were building, the Syracusans helped the men of Antandrus to finish a section of their walls, and made themselves very popular on garrison duty; and that is why the Syracusans to this day enjoy the privilege of citizens and benefactors at Antandrus. Having so arranged these matters, Pharnabazus proceeded at once to the rescue of Calchedon.

It was at this date that the Syracusan generals received news from home of their banishment by the democratic party.[2] Accordingly they called a meeting of their separate divisions, and putting forward Hermocrates[3] as their spokesman, proceeded to deplore their misfortune, insisting upon the injustice and the illegality of their banishment. "And now let us admonish you," they added, "to be eager and willing in the future, even as in the past: whatever the word of command may be, show yourselves good men and true: let[4] not the memory of those glorious sea-fights fade. Think of those victories you have won, those ships you have captured by your own unaided efforts; forget not that long list of achievements shared by yourselves with others, in all which you proved yourselves invincible under our generalship. By a happy combination of our skill and your enthusiasm, displayed alike on land and sea, you have had the post of honour in the battle-line."

With these words they called upon the men to choose other commanders, who should undertake the duties of their office, until the arrival of their successors. Thereupon the whole assembly, and more particularly the captains and masters of vessels and marines, insisted with loud cries on their continuance in command. The generals replied, "It was not for them to indulge in faction against the State, but rather it was their duty, in case any charges were forthcoming against themselves, at once to render an account." When, however, no one had any kind of accusation to prefer, they yielded to the general demand, and were content to await the arrival of their successors. The names of these were—Demarchus, the son of Epidocus; Myscon, the son of Menecrates; and Potamis, the son of Gnosis.

The captains, for the most part, swore to restore the exiled generals as soon as they themselves should return to Syracuse. At present with a general vote of thanks they despatched them to their several destina-

---

[2] Syracuse was a democracy but the generals belonged to the oligarchic party.
[3] Hermocrates, the son of Hermon. We first hear of him as the chief agent in bringing the Sicilian States together in conference at Gela 424 B.C. In 415 B.C., when the attack came, he was again the master spirit in rendering it abortive. In 412 B.C. it was he who urged the Sicilians to assist in completing the overthrow of Athens, by sending a squadron to co-operate with the Peloponnesian navy.
[4] The rest of this speech appears in the following paragraph in the manuscripts.

tions. In particular those who had associated with Hermocrates recalled his virtues with regret, his thoroughness and enthusiasm, his frankness and affability, the care with which every morning and evening he was wont to gather in his quarters a group of the best naval captains and marines and master mariners whom he knew. These were his confidants, to whom he communicated what he intended to say or do: they were also his pupils, whom he instructed, now calling upon them to speak extempore, and now again after deliberation. By these means Hermocrates had gained a wide reputation at the council board, where his mastery of language was no less felt than the wisdom of his advice. Appearing at Lacedaemon as the accuser of Tissaphernes, he had carried his case, not only by the testimony of Astyochus, but by the obvious sincerity of his statements, and on the strength of this reputation he now betook himself to Pharnabazus. The latter did not wait to be asked, but at once gave him money, which enabled him to collect friends and triremes, with a view to his ultimate recall to Syracuse. Meanwhile the successors of the Syracusans had arrived at Miletus, where they took charge of the ships and the army.

It was at this same season that a revolution occurred in Thasos, involving the expulsion of the philo-Laconian party, with the Laconian governor Eteonicus. The Laconian Pasippidas was charged with having brought the business about in conjunction with Tissaphernes, and was banished from Sparta in consequence. The naval force which he had collected from the allies was handed over to Cratesippidas, who was sent out to take his place in Chios.

About the same period, while Thrasylus was still in Athens, Agis made a foraging expedition up to the very walls of the city. But Thrasylus led out the Athenians with the rest of the inhabitants of the city, and drew them up by the side of the Lyceum, ready to engage the enemy if they approached; seeing which, Agis beat a hasty retreat, not however without the loss of some of his supports, a few of whom were cut down by the Athenian light troops. This success disposed the citizens to take a still more favourable view of the objects for which Thrasylus had come; and they passed a decree empowering him to call out 1,000 hoplites, 100 cavalry, and fifty triremes.

Meanwhile Agis, as he looked out from Deceleia, and saw vessel after vessel laden with corn reaching Piraeus, declared that it was useless for his troops to go on for so long a time excluding the Athenians from their own land, while no one stopped the source of their corn supply by sea: the best plan would be to send Clearchus, the son of Rhamphius, who was proxenus of the Byzantines, to Calchedon and Byzantium. The suggestion was approved, and with fifteen vessels duly manned from Megara, or furnished by other allies, Clearchus set out. These were troop-ships rather than swift-sailing men-of-war. Three of them, on reaching the Hellespont, were destroyed by the nine Athenian ships employed to convoy merchant craft in those waters. The other twelve escaped to Sestos, and thence finally reached Byzantium in safety.

[So closed the year—a year notable also for the expedition against Sicily of the Carthaginians under Hannibal with 100,000 men, and the capture, within three months, of the two Hellenic cities of Selinus and Himera.] [5]

2. Next year [the first of Olympiad ninety-three, celebrated as the year in which the newly added two-horse race was won by Evagoras the Eleian, and the 200 yard foot-race by the Cyrenaean Eubotas, when Evarchippus was ephor at Sparta and Euctemon archon at Athens], the Athenians fortified Thoricus; and Thrasylus, taking the vessels lately voted him and 5,000 of his seamen armed to serve as peltasts, set sail for Samos at the beginning of summer. At Samos he stayed three days, and then continued his voyage to Pygela, where he proceeded to ravage the territory and attack the fortress. Presently a detachment from Miletus came to the rescue of the men of Pygela, and attacking the scattered bands of the Athenian light troops, put them to flight. But to the aid of the light troops came the naval brigade of peltasts, with two companies of heavy infantry, and all but annihilated the whole detachment from Miletus. They captured about 200 shields, and set up a trophy. Next day they sailed to Notium, and from Notium, after due preparation, marched upon Colophon. The Colophonians capitulated without a blow. The following night they made an incursion into Lydia, where the corn crops were ripe, and burnt several villages, and captured money, slaves, and other booty in large quantity. But Stages, the Persian, who was employed in this neighbourhood, fell in with a reinforcement of cavalry sent to protect the scattered pillaging parties from the Athenian camp, while occupied with their individual plunder, and took one trooper prisoner, killing seven others. After this Thrasylus led his troops back to the sea, intending to sail to Ephesus. Meanwhile Tissaphernes, who learned of this plan, began collecting a large army and despatching cavalry with a summons to the inhabitants all to rally to the defence of Artemis at Ephesus.

On the seventeenth day after the incursion above mentioned Thrasylus sailed to Ephesus. He disembarked his troops in two divisions, his heavy infantry in the neighbourhood of Mount Coressus; his cavalry, peltasts, and marines, with the remainder of his force, near the marsh on the

[5] The consensus among scholars is that all passages in the *Hellenica* enclosed within brackets are interpolations and are frequently inaccurate.—Ed.

other side of the city. At daybreak he pushed forward both divisions. The citizens of Ephesus, on their side, were not slow to protect themselves. They had to aid them the troops brought up by Tissaphernes, as well as two detachments of Syracusans, consisting of the crews of their former twenty vessels and those of five new vessels which had opportunely arrived quite recently under Eucles, the son of Hippon, and Heracleides, the son of Aristogenes, together with two Selinuntian vessels. All these several forces first attacked the heavy infantry near Coressus; these they routed, killing about 100 of them, and driving the remainder down into the sea. They then turned to deal with the second division on the marsh. Here, too, the Athenians were put to flight, and about 300 of them perished. On this spot the Ephesians erected a trophy, and another at Coressus. The valour of the Syracusans and Selinuntians had been so conspicuous that the citizens presented many of them, both publicly and privately, with prizes for distinction in the field, besides offering the right of residence in their city with certain immunities to all who at any time might wish to live there. To the Selinuntians, indeed, as their own city had lately been destroyed, they offered full citizenship.

The Athenians, after picking up their dead under a truce, set sail for Notium, and having there buried the slain, continued their voyage towards Lesbos and the Hellespont. Whilst lying at anchor in the harbour of Methymna, in that island, they caught sight of the Syracusan vessels, twenty-five in number, coasting along from Ephesus. They put out to sea to attack them, and captured four ships with their crews, and chased the remainder back to Ephesus. The prisoners were sent by Thrasylus to Athens, with one exception. This was an Athenian, Alcibiades, who was a cousin and fellow-exile of Alcibiades. Him Thrasylus stoned to death. From Methymna Thrasylus set sail to Sestos to join the main body of the army, after which the united forces crossed to Lampsacus. And now winter was approaching. It was the winter in which the Syracusan prisoners who had been immured in the stone quarries of Piraeus dug through the rock and escaped one night, some to Deceleia and others to Megara. At Lampsacus Alcibiades was anxious to marshal the whole military force there collected in one body, but the old troops refused to be incorporated with those of Thrasylus, for they said they had never yet been beaten, while these newcomers had just suffered a defeat. So they devoted the winter to fortifying Lampsacus. They also made an expedition against Abydos, where Pharnabazus, coming to the rescue of the place, encountered them with numerous cavalry, but was defeated and forced to flee, Alcibiades pursuing hard with his cavalry and 120 infantry under the command of Menander,

till darkness intervened. After this battle the soldiers came together of
their own accord, and freely fraternised with the troops of Thrasylus.
This expedition was followed by other incursions during the winter
into the interior, where they found plenty to do in ravaging the king's
territory.

It was at this period also that the Lacedaemonians allowed their revolted Helots from Malea, who had found an asylum at Coryphasium,
to depart under a flag of truce. It was also about the same period that
the Achaeans betrayed the colonists of Heracleia Trachinia, when they
were all drawn up in battle to meet the hostile Oetaeans, whereby about
700 of them were lost, together with the governor from Lacedaemon,
Labotas. [Thus the year came to its close—a year marked further by
a revolt of the Medes from Darius, the king of Persia, followed by renewed submission to his authority.]

3. The year following is the year in which the temple of Athena, in
Phocaea, was struck by lightning and set on fire [in the ephorate of
Pantacles and the archonship of Antigenes, twenty-two years from the
beginning of the war.] With the cessation of winter, in early spring,
the Athenians set sail with their whole force to Proconnesus, and thence
advanced upon Calchedon and Byzantium, encamping near the former
town. The men of Calchedon, aware of their approach, had taken the
precaution to deposit all their pillageable property with their neighbours,
the Bithynian Thracians; whereupon Alcibiades put himself at the
head of a small body of heavy infantry with the cavalry, and giving
orders to the fleet to follow along the coast, marched against the Bithynians and demanded back the property of the Calchedonians, threatening them with war in case of refusal. The Bithynians delivered up the
property. Returning to camp, not only thus enriched, but with the further satisfaction of having secured pledges of good behaviour from the
Bithynians, Alcibiades set to work with the whole of his troops to draw
lines of circumvallation round Calchedon from sea to sea, so as to include as much of the river as possible within his wall, which was made
of timber. Thereupon the Lacedaemonian governor, Hippocrates, led
his troops out of the city and offered battle, and the Athenians, on their
side, drew up their forces opposite to receive him; while Pharnabazus,
from without the lines of circumvallation, was still advancing with his
army and large bodies of horse. Hippocrates and Thrasylus engaged
each other with their heavy infantry for a long while, until Alcibiades,
with a detachment of infantry and the cavalry, intervened. Presently
Hippocrates fell, and the troops under him fled into the city; at the
same instant Pharnabazus, unable to effect a junction with the Lacedaemonian leader, owing to the circumscribed nature of the ground and

the close proximity of the river to the enemy's lines, retired to the
Heracleium, belonging to the Calchedonians, where his camp lay. After
this success Alcibiades set off to the Hellespont and the Chersonese to
raise money, and the remaining generals came to terms with Pharnabazus
in respect of Calchedon; according to these, the Persian satrap agreed
to pay the Athenians twenty talents in behalf of the town, and to grant
their ambassadors a safe conduct to the king. It was further stipulated
by mutual consent and under oaths provided, that the Calchedonians
should continue the payment of their customary tribute to Athens, being also bound to discharge all outstanding debts. The Athenians, on
their side, were bound to desist from hostilities until the return of their
ambassadors from the king. These oaths were not witnessed by Alcibiades, who was now in the neighbourhood of Selybria. Having taken that
place, he presently appeared before the walls of Byzantium at the head
of the men of Chersonese, who came out with their whole force; he was
aided further by troops from Thrace and more than 300 horse. Accordingly Pharnabazus, insisting that he too must take the oath, decided to remain in Calchedon, and to await his arrival from Byzantium.
Alcibiades came, but was not prepared to bind himself by any oaths, unless Pharnabazus would, on his side, take oaths to himself. After this,
oaths were exchanged between them by proxy. Alcibiades took them at
Chrysopolis in the presence of two representatives sent by Pharnabazus
—namely, Mitrobates and Arnapes. Pharnabazus took them at Calchedon in the presence of Euryptolemus and Diotimus, who represented
Alcibiades. Both parties bound themselves not only by the general oath,
but also interchanged personal pledges of good faith.

This done, Pharnabazus left Calchedon at once, with injunctions
that those who were going up to the king as ambassadors should meet
him at Cyzicus. The representatives of Athens were Dorotheus, Philo-
dices, Theogenes, Euryptolemus, and Mantitheus; with them were two
Argives, Cleostratus and Pyrrholochus. An embassy from the Lacedaemonians was also about to make the journey. This consisted of Pasippidas and his fellows, with whom were Hermocrates, now an exile from
Syracuse, and his brother Proxenus. So Pharnabazus put himself at
their head. Meanwhile the Athenians prosecuted the siege of Byzantium;
lines of circumvallation were drawn; and they diversified the blockade
by sharpshooting at long range and occasional assaults upon the walls.
Inside the city lay Clearchus, the Lacedaemonian governor, and a body
of Perioeci with a small detachment of Neodamodes. There was also a
body of Megarians under their general Helixus, a Megarian, and another body of Boeotians, with their general Coeratadas. The Athenians,
finding presently that they could effect nothing by force, worked upon

some of the inhabitants to betray the place. Clearchus, meanwhile never dreaming that any one would be capable of such an act, had crossed over to the opposite coast to visit Pharnabazus; he had left everything in perfect order, entrusting the government of the city to Coeratadas and Helixus. His mission was to obtain pay for the soldiers from the Persian satrap, and to collect vessels from various quarters. Some were already in the Hellespont, where they had been left as guardships by Pasippidas, or else at Antandrus. Others formed the fleet which Age-sandridas, who had formerly served as a marine under Mindarus, now commanded on the Thracian coast. Others Clearchus planned to have built, and with the whole united squadron so to injure the allies of the Athenians as to draw off the besieging army from Byzantium. But no sooner was he fairly gone than those who were minded to betray the city set to work. Their names were Cydon, Ariston, Anaxicrates, Lycurgus, and Anaxilaus. The last-named was afterwards impeached for treachery in Lacedaemon on the capital charge, and acquitted on the plea that, to begin with, he was not a Lacedaemonian, but a Byzantine, and, so far from having betrayed the city, he had saved it, when he saw women and children perishing of starvation; for Clearchus had given away all the corn in the city to the Lacedaemonian soldiers. It was for these reasons, as Anaxilaus himself admitted, he had introduced the enemy, and not for the sake of money, nor out of hatred to Lacedaemon.

As soon then as everything was ready, these people opened the gates leading to the Thracian Square, as it is called, and admitted the Athenian troops with Alcibiades at their head. Helixus and Coeratadas, in complete ignorance of the plot, hastened to the Agora with the whole of the garrison, ready to confront the danger; but finding the enemy in occupation, they could do nothing but give themselves up. They were sent off as prisoners to Athens, where Coeratadas, in the midst of the crowd and confusion of disembarkation at Piraeus, gave his guards the slip, and made his way in safety to Deceleia.

4. Pharnabazus and the ambassadors were passing the winter at Gordium in Phrygia, when they heard of the occurrences at Byzantium. Continuing their journey to the king's court in the commencement of spring, they were met by a former embassy, which was now on its return journey. These were the Lacedaemonian ambassadors, Boeotius and his party, with the other envoys; who told them that the Lacedaemonians had obtained from the king all they wanted. One of the company was Cyrus, the new governor of all the seaboard districts, who was prepared ·to co-operate with the Lacedaemonians in war. He was the bearer, more-over, of a letter with the royal seal attached. It was addressed to all the populations of Lower Asia, and contained the following words, "I send

down Cyrus as Karanos"—that is to say, supreme lord—"over all those who muster at Castolus." The ambassadors of the Athenians, even while listening to this announcement, and indeed after they had seen Cyrus, were still desirous, if possible, to continue their journey to the king, or, failing that, to return home. Cyrus, however, urged upon Pharnabazus either to deliver them up to himself, or to defer sending them home at present; his object being to prevent the Athenians learning what was going on. Pharnabazus, wishing to escape all blame, for the time being detained them, telling them, at one time, that he would presently escort them up country to the king, and at another time that he would send them safe home. But when three years had elapsed, he prayed Cyrus to let them go, declaring that he had taken an oath to bring them back to the sea, in default of escorting them up to the king. Then at last they received safe conduct to Ariobarzanes, with orders for their further transportation. The latter conducted them to Cius in Mysia; and from Cius they set sail to join their main armament.

Alcibiades, whose chief desire was to return home to Athens with the troops, immediately set sail for Samos; and from that island, taking twenty of the ships, he sailed to the Ceramic Gulf of Caria, where he collected 100 talents, and so returned to Samos.

Thrasybulus had gone Thrace-wards with thirty ships. In this quarter he reduced various places which had revolted to Lacedaemon, including the island of Thasos, which was in a bad plight, the result of wars, revolutions, and famine.

Thrasylus, with the rest of the army, sailed back straight to Athens. On his arrival he found that the Athenians had already chosen as their general Alcibiades, who was still in exile, and Thrasybulus, who was also absent, and as a third, from among those at home, Conon.

Meanwhile Alcibiades, with the money lately collected and his fleet of twenty ships, left Samos and visited Paros. From Paros he stood out to sea across to Gytheum, to take a look at the thirty ships of war which, as he was informed, the Lacedaemonians were equipping in that arsenal. Gytheum would also be a favourable point of observation from which to gauge the disposition of his fellow-countrymen and the prospects of his recall. When at length their good disposition seemed to him established, not only by his election as general, but by the messages of invitation which he received in private from his friends, he sailed home, and entered Piraeus on the very day of the festival of the Plynteria,[6]

---

[6] The feast of washings, held on the 25th of the month Thargelion, when the image of the goddess Athena was stripped in order that her clothes might be washed by the Praxiergidae; neither assembly nor court was held on that day, and the Temple was closed.

when the statue of Athena is veiled and screened from public gaze. This was a coincidence, as some thought, of evil omen, and unpropitious alike to himself and the State, for no Athenian would transact serious business on such a day.

As he sailed into the harbour, two great crowds—one from the Piraeus, the other from the city—flocked to meet the vessels. Wonderment, mixed with a desire to see Alcibiades, was the prevailing sentiment of the multitude. Of him they spoke; some asserting that he was the best of citizens, and that in his sole instance banishment had been ill-deserved. He had been the victim of plots, hatched in the brains of people less able than himself, however much they might excel in pestilent speech; men whose one principle of statecraft was to look to their private gains; whereas this man's policy had ever been to uphold the common weal, as much by his private means as by all the power of the State. His own choice, eight years ago, when the charge of impiety in the matter of the mysteries was still fresh, would have been to submit to trial at once. It was his personal foes, who had succeeded in postponing that undeniably just procedure; who waited till his back was turned, and then robbed him of his fatherland. Then it was that, being made the very slave of circumstance, he was driven to court the men he hated most; and at a time when his own life was in daily peril, he must see his dearest friends and fellow-citizens, nay, the very State itself, bent on a suicidal course, and yet, in the exclusion of exile, be unable to lend a helping hand. "It is not men of this stamp," they averred, "who desire changes in affairs and revolution: had he not already guaranteed to him by the democracy a position higher than that of his equals in age, and scarcely if at all inferior to his seniors? How different was the position of his enemies. It had been the fortune of these, though they were known to be the same men they had always been, to use their lately acquired power for the destruction in the first instance of the better classes; and then, being alone left surviving, to be accepted by their fellow-citizens in the absence of better men."

Others, however, insisted that for all their past miseries and misfortunes Alcibiades alone was responsible, "If more trials were still in store for the State, here was the master mischief-maker ready at his post to precipitate them."

When the vessels came to their moorings, close to the land, Alcibiades, from fear of his enemies, was unwilling to disembark at once. Mounting on the quarterdeck, he scanned the multitude, anxious to make certain of the presence of his friends. Presently his eyes lit upon Euryptolemus, the son of Peisianax, who was his cousin, and then on the rest of his relations and other friends. Upon this he landed, and so, in the midst of

an escort ready to put down any attempt upon his person, made his way
to the city.

In the Senate and Public Assembly he made speeches, defending
himself against the charge of impiety, and asserting that he had been
the victim of injustice, with other like topics, which in the present temper of the assembly no one ventured to gainsay.

He was then formally declared leader and chief of the State, with
full powers, as being the sole individual capable of recovering the ancient power and prestige of Athens. Armed with this authority, his first
act was to institute anew the processional march to Eleusis; for of late
years, owing to the war, the Athenians had been forced to conduct the
mysteries by sea. Now, at the head of the troops, he caused them to be
conducted once again by land. This done, his next step was to muster
an armament of 1,500 heavy infantry, 150 cavalry, and 100 ships; and
lastly, within three months of his return, he set sail for Andros, which
had revolted from Athens.

The generals chosen to co-operate with him on land were Aristocrates
and Adeimantus, the son of Leucophilides. He disembarked his troops
on the island of Andros at Gaurium, and routed the Andrian citizens
who sallied out from the town to resist the invader; forcing them to
return and keep close within their walls, though the number who fell
was not large. This defeat was shared by some Lacedaemonians who
were in the place. Alcibiades erected a trophy, and after a few days set
sail himself for Samos, which became his base of operations in the future
conduct of the war.

5. At a date not much earlier than that of the incidents just described,
the Lacedaemonians had sent out Lysander as their admiral, in the
place of Cratesippidas, whose period of office had expired. The new
admiral first visited Rhodes, where he got some ships, and sailed to Cos
and Miletus, and from the latter place to Ephesus. At Ephesus he waited
with seventy sail, expecting the advent of Cyrus in Sardis, when he at
once went up to pay the prince a visit with the ambassadors from Lacedaemon. And now an opportunity was given to denounce the proceedings of Tissaphernes, and at the same time to beg Cyrus himself to
show as much zeal as possible in the prosecution of the war. Cyrus replied that not only had he received express injunctions from his father
to the same effect, but that his own views coincided with their wishes,
which he was determined to carry out to the letter. He had, he informed
them, brought with him 500 talents; and if that sum failed, he had still
the private revenue, which his father allowed him, to fall back upon,
and when this resource was in its turn exhausted, he would coin the gold
and silver throne on which he sat, into money for their benefit.

His audience thanked him for what he said, and further begged him to fix the rate of payment for the seamen at one Attic drachma per man, explaining that should this rate of payment be adopted, the sailors of the Athenians would desert, and in the end there would be a saving of expenditure. Cyrus complimented them on the soundness of their arguments, but said that it was not in his power to exceed the injunctions of the king. The terms of agreement were precise, thirty minae a month per vessel to be given, whatever number of vessels the Lacedaemonians might choose to maintain.

To this rejoinder Lysander at the moment said nothing. But after dinner, when Cyrus drank to his health, asking him, "What he could do to gratify him most?" Lysander replied, "Add an obol to the sailors' pay." After this the pay was raised to four instead of three obols, as it hitherto had been. Nor did the liberality of Cyrus end here; he not only paid up all arrears, but further gave a month's pay in advance, so that, if the enthusiasm of the army had been great before, it was greater than ever now. The Athenians when they heard the news were proportionately depressed, and by help of Tissaphernes despatched ambassadors to Cyrus. That prince, however, refused to receive them, nor were the prayers of Tissaphernes of any avail, however much he insisted that Cyrus should adopt the policy which he himself, on the advice of Alcibiades, had persistently acted on. This was simply not to suffer any single Hellenic state to grow strong at the expense of the rest, but to keep them all weak alike, distracted by internecine strife.

Lysander, now that the organisation of his navy was arranged to his satisfaction, beached his squadron of ninety vessels at Ephesus, and sat with hands folded, whilst the vessels dried and underwent repairs. Alcibiades, being informed that Thrasybulus had come south of the Hellespont and was fortifying Phocaea, sailed across to join him, leaving his own pilot Antiochus in command of the fleet, with orders not to attack Lysander's fleet. Antiochus, however, was tempted to leave Notium and sail into the harbour of Ephesus with a couple of ships, his own and another, past the prows of Lysander's squadron. The Spartan at first contented himself with launching a few of his ships, and started in pursuit of the intruder; but when the Athenians came out with other vessels to assist Antiochus, he formed his whole squadron into line of battle, and bore down upon them, whereupon the Athenians followed suit, and getting their remaining triremes under weigh at Notium, stood out to sea as fast as each vessel could clear the point. Thus it befell in the engagement which ensued, that while the enemy was in due order, the Athenians came up in scattered detachments and without concert, and in the end were put to flight with the loss of fifteen ships of war.

Of the crews, indeed, the majority escaped, though a certain number fell into the hands of the enemy. Then Lysander collected his vessels, and having erected a trophy on Cape Notium, sailed across to Ephesus, whilst the Athenians retired to Samos.

On his return to Samos a little later, Alcibiades put out to sea with the whole squadron in the direction of the harbour of Ephesus. At the mouth of the harbour he marshalled his fleet in battle order, and tried to tempt the enemy to an engagement; but as Lysander, conscious of his inferiority in numbers, refused to accept the challenge, he sailed back again to Samos. Shortly after this the Lacedaemonians captured Delphinium and Eion.

But now the news of the late disaster at Notium had reached the Athenians at home, and in their indignation they turned upon Alcibiades, to whose negligence and lack of self-command they attributed the destruction of the ships. Accordingly they chose ten new generals— namely Conon, Diomedon, Leon, Pericles, Erasinides, Aristocrates, Archestratus, Protomachus, Thrasylus, and Aristogenes. Alcibiades, who was moreover in bad odour in the camp, sailed away with a single trireme to his private fortress in the Chersonese.

After this Conon, in obedience to a decree of the Athenian people, set sail from Andros with the twenty vessels under his command in that island to Samos, and took command of the whole squadron. To fill the place thus vacated by Conon, Phanosthenes was sent to Andros with four ships. That captain was fortunate enough to intercept and capture two Thurian ships of war, crews and all, and these captives were all imprisoned by the Athenians, with the exception of their leader Dorieus. He was the Rhodian, who some while back had been banished from Athens and from his native city by the Athenians, when sentence of death was passed upon him and his family. This man, who had once enjoyed the right of citizenship among them, they now took pity on and released him without ransom.

When Conon had reached Samos he found the armament in a state of great despondency. Accordingly his first measure was to man seventy ships with their full complement, instead of the former hundred and odd vessels. With this squadron he put to sea accompanied by the other generals, and confined himself to making descents first at one point and then at another of the enemy's territory, and to collecting plunder.

And so the year drew to its close: a year signalised further by an invasion of Sicily by the Carthaginians, with 120 ships of war and a land force of 120,000 men, which resulted in the capture of Agrigentum. The town was finally reduced by famine after a siege of seven months, the invaders having previously been worsted in battle.

6. In the following year—the year of the evening eclipse of the moon, and the burning of the old temple of Athena[7] at Athens [in the ephorate of Pityas and the archonship of Callias at Athens]—the Lacedaemonians sent out Callicratidas to replace Lysander, whose period of office had now expired [with the twenty-fourth year of the war].[8] Lysander, when surrendering the squadron to his successor, spoke of himself as the winner of a sea-fight, which had left him in undisputed mastery of the sea, and with this boast he handed over the ships to Callicratidas, who retorted, "If you will convey the fleet from Ephesus, keeping Samos to your right" (that is, past where the Athenian navy lay) "and hand it over to me at Miletus, I will admit that you are master of the sea." But Lysander had no mind to interfere in the province of another officer. Thus Callicratidas assumed responsibility. He first manned, in addition to the squadron which he received from Lysander, fifty new vessels furnished by the allies from Chios and Rhodes and elsewhere. When all these contingents were assembled, they formed a total of 140 sail, and with these he began making preparations for engagement with the enemy. But it was impossible for him not to note the strong current of opposition which he encountered from the friends of Lysander. Not only was there lack of zeal in their service, but they openly disseminated an opinion in the cities, that it was the greatest possible blunder on the part of the Lacedaemonians so to change their admirals. Of course, they must from time to time get officers altogether unfit for the post—men whose nautical knowledge dated from yesterday, and who, moreover, had no notion of dealing with human beings. It would be very odd if this practice of sending out people ignorant of the sea and unknown to the folk of the country did not lead to some catastrophe. Callicratidas at once summoned the Lacedaemonians there present, and addressed them in the following terms:

"For my part," he said, "I am content to stay at home: and if Lysander or any one else claim greater experience in nautical affairs than I possess, I have no desire to block his path. Only, being sent out by the State to take command of this fleet, I do not know what is left to me, save to carry out my instructions to the best of my ability. For yourselves, all I beg of you, in reference to my personal ambitions and the kind of charges brought against our common city, and of which you are as well aware as I am, is to state what you consider to be the best course: am I to stay where I am, or shall I sail back home, and explain the position of affairs out here?"

No one ventured to suggest any other course than that he should obey

[7] Probably the old temple of Athena Polias on the Acropolis.
[8] The correct date should be twenty-fifth.

the authorities, and do what he was sent out to do. Callicratidas then
went up to the court of Cyrus to ask for further pay for the sailors, but
the answer he got from Cyrus was that he should wait for two days.
Callicratidas was annoyed at the rebuff: to dance attendance at the
palace gates was little to his taste. In a fit of anger he cried out at the
sorry condition of the Hellenes, thus forced to flatter the barbarian for
the sake of money. "If ever I get back home," he added, "I will do what
in me lies to reconcile the Athenians and the Lacedaemonians." And so
he turned and sailed back to Miletus. From Miletus he sent some
triremes to Lacedaemon to get money, and convoking the public assembly of the Milesians, addressed them thus:

"Men of Miletus, necessity is laid upon me to obey the rulers at
home; but for yourselves, whose neighbourhood to the barbarians has
exposed you to many evils at their hands, I only ask you to let your
zeal in the war bear some proportion to your former sufferings. You
should set an example to the rest of the allies, and show us how to inflict
the sharpest and swiftest injury on our enemy, while we await the return
from Lacedaemon of my envoys with the necessary funds. Since one
of the last acts of Lysander, before he left us, was to hand back to
Cyrus the funds already on the spot, as though we could well dispense
with them. I was thus forced to turn to Cyrus, but all I got from him
was a series of rebuffs; he refused me an audience, and, for my part, I
could not induce myself to hang about his gates like a mendicant. But
I give you my word, men of Miletus, that in return for any assistance
which you can render us while waiting for these aids, I will reward you
richly. Only by the gods' help let us show these barbarians that we do
not need to worship them, in order to punish our foes."

The speech was effective; many members of the assembly arose, and
not the least eagerly those who were accused of opposing him. These,
in some terror, proposed a vote of money, backed by offers of further
private contributions. Furnished with these sums, and having procured
from Chios a further remittance of five drachmas apiece as outfit for
each seaman, he set sail to Methymna in Lesbos, which was in the hands
of the enemy. But as the Methymnaeans were not disposed to come over
to him (since there was an Athenian garrison in the place, and the men
at the head of affairs were partisans of Athens), he assaulted and took
the place by storm. All the property within accordingly became the
spoil of the soldiers. The prisoners were collected for sale by Callicratidas
in the market-place, where, in answer to the demand of the allies, who
called upon him to sell the Methymnaeans also, he made answer, that
as long as he was in command, not a single Hellene should be enslaved
if he could help it. The next day he set at liberty the free-born cap-

tives; the Athenian garrison with the captured slaves he sold. To Conon he sent word that he would put a stop to his adultery with the sea.[9] And catching sight of him, as he put out to sea, at break of day, he gave chase, hoping to cut him off from his passage to Samos, and prevent his taking refuge there.

But Conon, aided by the sailing qualities of his fleet, the rowers of which were the pick of several ships' companies, concentrated in a few vessels, made good his escape, seeking shelter within the harbour of Mytilene in Lesbos, and with him two of the ten generals, Leon and Erasinides. Callicratidas, pursuing him with 170 sail, entered the harbour simultaneously; and Conon thus hindered from further or final escape by the too rapid movements of the enemy, was forced to engage inside the harbour, and lost thirty of his ships, though the crews escaped to land. The remaining, forty in number, he hauled up under the walls of the town. Callicratidas, on his side, came to moorings in the harbour; and, having command of the exit, blockaded the Athenian within. His next step was to send for the Methymnaeans in force by land, and to transport his army across from Chios. Money also came to him from Cyrus.

Conon, finding himself besieged by land and sea, without means of providing himself with corn from any quarter, the city crowded with inhabitants, and aid from Athens, whither no news of the late events could be conveyed, impossible, launched two of the fastest sailing vessels of his squadron. These he manned, before daybreak, with the best rowers whom he could pick out of the fleet, stowing away the marines at the same time in the hold of the ships and closing the port shutters. Every day for four days they held out in this fashion, but at evening as soon as it was dark he disembarked his men, so that the enemy might not suspect what they were after. On the fifth day, having got in a small stock of provisions, when it was already mid-day and the blockaders were paying little or no attention, and some of them even were taking their siesta, the two ships sailed out of the harbour: the one directing her course towards the Hellespont, whilst her companion made for the open sea. Then, on the part of the blockaders, there was a rush to the scene of action, as fast as the several crews could get clear of land, in bustle and confusion, cutting away the anchors, and rousing themselves from sleep, for, as chance would have it, they had been breakfasting on shore. Once on board, however, they were soon in hot pursuit of the ship which had started for the open sea, and ere the sun dipped they overhauled her, and after a successful engagement attached her by cables and towed her back into harbour, crew and all. Her comrade,

[9] The sea was Sparta's bride.

making for the Hellespont, escaped, and eventually reached Athens with news of the blockade. The first relief was brought to the blockaded fleet by Diomedon, who anchored with twelve vessels in the Mytilenaean Narrows. But a sudden attack of Callicratidas, who bore down upon him without warning, cost him ten of his vessels, Diomedon himself escaping with his own ship and one other.

Now that the position of affairs, including the blockade, was fully known at Athens, a vote was passed to send out a reinforcement of 110 ships. Every man of military age, whether slave or free, was impressed for this service, so that within thirty days the whole 110 vessels were fully manned and weighed anchor. Amongst those who served in this fleet were also many of the knights. The fleet at once stood out across to Samos, and picked up the Samian vessels in that island. The muster-roll was swelled by the addition of more than thirty others from the rest of the allies, to whom the same principle of conscription applied, as also it did to the ships already engaged on foreign service. The actual total, therefore, when all the contingents were collected, was over 150 vessels.

Callicratidas, hearing that the relief squadron had already reached Samos, left fifty ships, under command of Eteonicus, in the harbour of Mytilene, and setting sail with the other 120, hove to for the evening meal off Cape Malea in Lesbos, opposite Mytilene. It so happened that the Athenians on this day were supping on the islands of Arginusae, which lie opposite Lesbos. In the night the Spartan not only saw their watch-fires, but received positive information that these were the Athenians; and about midnight he got under weigh, intending to fall upon them suddenly. But a violent downpour of rain with thunder and lightning prevented him putting out to sea. By daybreak it had cleared, and he sailed towards Arginusae. On their side, the Athenian squadron stood out to meet him, with their left wing facing towards the open sea, and drawn up in the following order: Aristocrates, in command of the left wing, with fifteen ships, led the van; next came Diomedon with fifteen others, and immediately in rear of Aristocrates and Diomedon respectively, as their supports, came Pericles and Erasinides. Parallel with Diomedon were the Samians, with their ten ships drawn up in single line, under the command of a Samian officer named Hippeus. Next to these came the ten vessels of the taxiarchs, also in single line, and supporting them, the three ships of the nauarchs, with any other allied vessels in the squadron. The right wing was entrusted to Protomachus with fifteen ships, and next to him (on the extreme right) was Thrasylus with another division of fifteen. Protomachus was supported by Lysias with an equal number of ships, and Thrasylus by Aristogenes. The object of this formation was to prevent the enemy from manoeuvring so

as to break their line by striking them amidships, since they were inferior in sailing power.

The Lacedaemonians, on the contrary, trusting to their superior seamanship, were formed opposite with their ships all in single line, with
the special object of manoeuvring so as either to break the enemy's line
or to wheel round them. Callicratidas commanded the right wing in
person. Before the battle the officer who acted as his pilot, the Megarian
Hermon, suggested that it might be well to withdraw the fleet as the
Athenian ships were far more numerous. But Callicratidas replied that
Sparta would be no worse off even if he personally should perish, but
to flee would be disgraceful. And now the fleets approached, and fought
for a long time. At first the vessels were engaged in crowded masses,
and later on in scattered groups. At length Callicratidas, as his vessel
dashed her beak into her antagonist, was hurled off into the sea and
disappeared. At the same instant Protomachus, with his division on the
right, had defeated the enemy's left, and then the flight of the Peloponnesians began towards Chios, though a very considerable body of
them made for Phocaea, whilst the Athenians sailed back again to
Arginusae. The losses on the side of the Athenians were twenty-five
ships, crews and all, with the exception of the few who contrived to reach
dry land. On the Peloponnesian side, nine out of the ten Lacedaemonian
ships, and more than sixty belonging to the rest of the allied squadron,
were lost.

After consultation the Athenian generals agreed that two captains of
triremes, Theramenes and Thrasybulus, accompanied by some of the
taxiarchs, should take forty-seven ships and sail to the assistance of the
disabled fleet and of the men on board, while the rest of the squadron
proceeded to attack the enemy's blockading squadron under Eteonicus
at Mytilene. In spite of their desire to carry out this resolution, the wind
and a violent storm which arose prevented them. So they set up a trophy,
and took up their quarters for the night. As to Eteonicus, the details of
the engagement were faithfully reported to him by the express despatch-
boat in attendance. On receipt of the news, however, he sent the despatch-boat out again the way she came, with an injunction to those on
board of her to sail off quickly without exchanging a word with any
one. Then on a sudden they were to return garlanded with wreaths of
victory and shouting, "Callicratidas has won a great sea-fight, and the
whole Athenian squadron is destroyed." This they did, and Eteonicus,
on his side, as soon as the despatch-boat came sailing in, proceeded to
offer sacrifice of thanksgiving in honour of the good news. Meanwhile
he gave orders that the troops were to take their evening meal, and that
the masters of the trading ships were silently to stow away their goods

on board the merchant ships and make sail as fast as the favourable
breeze could speed them to Chios. The ships of war were to follow suit
with what speed they might. This done, he set fire to his camp, and
led off the land forces to Methymna. Conon, finding the enemy had
made off, and the wind had grown comparatively mild, got his ships
afloat, and so fell in with the Athenian squadron, which had by this
time set out from Arginusae. To these he explained the proceedings of
Eteonicus. The squadron put into Mytilene, and from Mytilene stood
across to Chios, and thence, without effecting anything further, sailed
back to Samos.

7. All the above-named generals, with the exception of Conon, were
presently deposed by the home authorities. In addition to Conon two
new generals were chosen, Adeimantus and Philocles. Of those concerned in the late victory two never returned to Athens: these were
Protomachus and Aristogenes. The other six sailed home. Their names
were Pericles, Diomedon, Lysias, Aristocrates, Thrasylus, and Erasinides. On their arrival Archidemus, the leader of the democracy at that
date, who had charge of the two-obol fund, inflicted a fine on Erasinides,
and accused him before the court of having appropriated money derived
from the Hellespont, which belonged to the people. He brought a further
charge against him of misconduct while acting as general, and the court
sentenced him to imprisonment.

These proceedings in the law court were followed by the statement of
the generals before the senate touching the late victory and the magnitude of the storm. Timocrates then proposed that the other five generals
should be put in custody and handed over to the public assembly. Whereupon the senate committed them all to prison. Then came the meeting
of the public assembly, in which others, and more particularly Theramenes, formally accused the generals. He insisted that they ought to
show cause why they had not picked up the shipwrecked crews. To
prove that there had been no attempt on their parts to attach blame to
others, he might point, as conclusive testimony, to the despatch sent by
the generals themselves to the senate and the people, in which they attributed the whole disaster to the storm, and nothing else. After this
the generals each in turn made a defence, which was necessarily limited
to a few words, since no right of addressing the assembly at length was
allowed by law. Their explanation of the occurrences was that, in order
to be free to sail against the enemy themselves, they had devolved the
duty of picking up the shipwrecked crews upon certain competent captains of men-of-war, who had themselves been generals in their time, to
wit Theramenes and Thrasybulus, and others of like stamp. If blame
could attach to any one at all with regard to the duty in question, those

to whom their orders had been given were the sole persons they could hold responsible. "But," they went on to say, "we will not, because these very persons have denounced us, invent a lie, and say that Theramenes and Thrasybulus are to blame, when the truth of the matter is that the magnitude of the storm alone prevented the burial of the dead and the rescue of the living." In proof of their contention, they produced the pilots and numerous other witnesses from among those present at the engagement. By these arguments they were in a fair way to persuade the people of their innocence. Indeed many private citizens rose wishing to become bail for the accused, but it was resolved to defer decision till another meeting of the assembly. It was indeed already so late that it would have been impossible to see to count the show of hands. It was further resolved that the senate meanwhile should prepare a measure, to be introduced at the next assembly, as to the mode in which the accused should take their trial.

Then came the festival of the Aparturia, with its family gatherings of fathers and kinsfolk. Accordingly the party of Theramenes procured numbers of people clad in black apparel, and close-shaven, who were to go in and present themselves before the public assembly in the middle of the festival, as relatives, presumably, of the men who had perished; and they persuaded Callixenus to accuse the generals in the senate. The next step was to convoke the assembly, when the senate laid before it the proposal just passed by their body, at the instance of Callixenus, which ran as follows, "Seeing that both the parties to this case, to wit, the prosecutors of the generals on the one hand, and the accused themselves in their defence on the other, have been heard in the late meeting of the assembly; we propose that the people of Athens now record their votes, one and all, by their tribes; that a couple of voting urns be placed for the convenience of each several tribe; and the public crier in the hearing of each several tribe proclaim the mode of voting as follows, 'Let every one who finds the generals guilty of not rescuing the heroes of the late sea-fight deposit his vote in one urn. Let him who is of the contrary opinion deposit his vote in the other urn. Further, in the event of the aforesaid generals being found guilty, let death be the penalty. Let the guilty persons be delivered over to the eleven. Let their property be confiscated to the State, with the exception of one tithe, which falls to the goddess.' "

Now there came forward in the assembly a man, who said that he had escaped drowning by clinging to a meal tub. The poor fellows perishing around him had commissioned him, if he succeeded in saving himself, to tell the people of Athens how bravely they had fought for their fatherland, and how the generals had left them there to drown.

Presently Euryptolemus, the son of Peisianax, and others served a notice of indictment on Callixenus, insisting that his proposal was unconstitutional, and this view of the case was applauded by some members of the assembly. But the majority kept crying out that it was monstrous if the people were to be hindered by any stray individual from doing what seemed to them right. And then Lyciscus, embodying the spirit of those cries, formally proposed that if these persons would not abandon their actions, they should be tried by the same vote along with the generals: a proposition to which the mob gave vociferous assent; and so these were compelled to abandon their summonses. Again, when some of the Prytanes objected to put a resolution to the vote which was in itself unconstitutional, Callixenus again got up and accused them in the same terms, and the shouting began again to summon all who refuse, until the Prytanes, in alarm, all agreed with one exception to permit the voting. This obstinate dissentient was Socrates, the son of Sophroniscus, who insisted that he would do nothing except in accordance with the law. After this Euryptolemus rose and spoke in behalf of the generals. He said:

"I stand here, men of Athens, partly to accuse Pericles, though he is a close and intimate connection of my own, and Diomedon, who is my friend, and partly to urge certain considerations on their behalf, but chiefly to press upon you what seems to me the best course for the State collectively. I hold them to blame in that they dissuaded their colleagues from their intention to send a despatch to the senate and this assembly, which should have informed you of the orders given to Theramenes and Thrasybulus to take forty-seven ships of war and pick up the shipwrecked crews, and of the neglect of the two officers to carry out those orders. And it follows that though the offence was committed by one or two, the responsibility must be shared by all; and in return for kindness in the past, they are in danger at present of sacrificing their lives to the machinations of these very men, and others whom I could mention. In danger, do I say, of losing their lives? No, not so, if you will suffer me to persuade you to do what is just and right; if you will only adopt such a course as shall enable you best to discover the truth and shall save you from too late repentance, when you find you have transgressed irremediably against heaven and your own selves. In what I urge there is no trap nor plot whereby you can be deceived by me or any other man; it is a straightforward course which will enable you to discover and punish the offender by whatever process you like, collectively or individually. Let them have, if not more, at any rate one whole day to make what defence they can for themselves; and trust to your own unbiased judgment to guide you to a right conclusion.

"You know, men of Athens, the exceeding stringency of the decree of Cannonus, which orders that man, whosoever he be, who is guilty of treason against the people of Athens, to be put in irons, and so to meet the charge against him before the people. If he be convicted, he is to be thrown into the Barathrum and perish, and the property of such an one is to be confiscated, with the exception of the tithe which falls to the goddess. I call upon you to try these generals in accordance with this decree. Yes, and so help me Zeus—if it please you, begin with my own kinsman Pericles for base would it be on my part to make him of more account than the whole of the State. Or, if you prefer, try them by that other law, which is directed against robbers of temples and betrayers of their country, which says: if a man betray his city or rob a sacred temple of the gods, he shall be tried before a law court, and if he be convicted, his body shall not be buried in Attica, and his goods shall be confiscated. Take your choice as between these two laws, men of Athens, and let the prisoners be tried by one or other. Let three portions of a day be assigned to each respectively, one portion wherein they shall listen to their accusation, a second wherein they shall make their defence, and a third wherein you shall meet and give your votes in due order on the question of their guilt or innocence. By this procedure the malefactors will receive the desert of their misdeeds in full, and those who are innocent will owe to you, men of Athens, the recovery of their liberty, in place of unmerited destruction.

"On your side, in trying the accused by recognised legal procedure, you will show that you obey the dictates of pious feeling, and can regard the sanctity of an oath, instead of joining hands with our enemies the Lacedaemonians and fighting their battles. For is it not to fight their battles, if you take their conquerors, the men who deprived them of seventy vessels, and send them to destruction untried and in violation of the law? What are you afraid of, that you press forward with such hot haste? Do you imagine that you may be robbed of the power of life and death over whom you please, should you condescend to a legal trial? But that you are safe if you take shelter behind an illegality, like the illegality of Callixenus, when he worked upon the senate to propose to this assembly to deal with the accused by a single vote? But consider, you may actually put to death an innocent man, and then repentence will one day visit you too late. Think how painful and unavailing remorse will then be, and more particularly if your error has cost a fellow-creature his life. What a travesty of justice it would be if in the case of a man like Aristarchus, who first tried to destroy the democracy and then betrayed Oenoe to our enemy the Thebans, you granted him a day for his defence, consulting his wishes, and conceded to him all the other benefits of the law; whereas now you are proposing to deprive of these same privileges your own generals, who in every way conformed to your views and defeated your enemies. Do not you, of all men, I implore you, men of Athens, act thus. Why, these laws are your own, to them, beyond all else you owe your greatness. Guard them jealously; in nothing, I implore you, act without their sanction.

"But now, turn for a moment and consider with me the actual occurrences which have created the suspicion of misconduct on the part of our late generals. The sea-fight had been fought and won, and the ships had returned to land, when Diomedon urged that the whole squadron should sail out in line and pick up the wrecks and floating crews. Erasinides was in favour of all the vessels sailing as fast as possible to deal with the enemy's forces at Mytilene. And Thrasylus represented that both objects could be effected, by leaving one division of the fleet there, and with the rest sailing against the enemy; and if this resolution were agreed to, he advised that each of the eight generals should leave three ships of his own division with the ten vessels of the taxiarchs, the ten Samian vessels, and the three belonging to the nauarchs. These added together make forty-seven, four for each of the lost vessels, twelve in number. Among the taxiarchs left behind, two were Thrasybulus and Theramenes, the man who in the late meeting of this assembly undertook to accuse the generals. With the remainder of the fleet they were to sail to attack the enemy's fleet. Everything, you must admit, was duly and admirably planned. It is only common justice, therefore, that those whose duty it was to attack the enemy should render an account for all miscarriage of operations against the enemy; while those who were commissioned to pick up the dead and dying should, if they failed to carry out the instructions of the generals, be put on trial to explain the reasons of the failure. This indeed I may say in behalf of both parties. It was really the storm which, in spite of what the generals had planned, prevented anything being done. There are witnesses ready to attest the truth of this: the men who escaped as by a miracle, and among these one of these very generals, who was on a sinking ship and was saved. And this man, who needed picking up as much as anybody at that moment, is, they insist, to be tried by one and the same vote as those who neglected to perform their orders! Once more, I beg you, men of Athens, to accept your victory and your good fortune, instead of behaving like the desperate victims of misfortune and defeat. Recognise the finger of divine necessity; do not incur the reproach of stony-heartedness by discovering treason where there was merely powerlessness, and condemning as guilty those who were prevented by the storm from carrying out their instructions. Nay! you will better satisfy the demands of justice by crowning these conquerors with wreaths of victory than by punishing them with death at the instigation of wicked men."

At the conclusion of his speech Euryptolemus proposed, as an amendment, that the prisoners should, in accordance with the decree of Cannonus, be tried each separately, as against the proposal of the senate to try them all by a single vote.

At the show of hands the tellers gave the majority in favour of Euryptolemus's amendment, but upon the application of Menecles, who took formal exception to this decision, the show of hands was gone through again, and now the verdict was in favour of the resolution of the senate. At a later date the balloting was made, and by the votes recorded the eight generals were condemned, and the six who were in Athens were put to death.

Not long after, repentance seized the Athenians, and they passed a decree authorising the public prosecution of those who had deceived the people, and the appointment of proper securities for their persons until the trial was over. Callixenus was one of these committed for trial. There were, besides Callixenus, four others against whom true bills were declared, and they were all five imprisoned by their sureties. But all subsequently effected their escape before the trial, at the time of the sedition in which Cleophon[10] was killed. Callixenus eventually came back when the party in Piraeus returned to the city, at the date of the amnesty,[11] but only to die of hunger, an object of universal detestation.

---

[10] Cleophon, the well-known demagogue. For his character, as popularly conceived, cf. Aristophanes, *Frogs,* 677.

[11] 403 B.C.

BOOK II

1. To return to Eteonicus and his troops in Chios. During summer they were well able to support themselves on the fruits of the season, or by labouring for hire in different parts of the island, but with the approach of winter these means of subsistence began to fail. Ill-clad at the same time, and ill-shod, they fell to caballing and arranging plans to attack the city of Chios. It was agreed among them, that in order to gauge their numbers, every member of the conspiracy should carry a reed. Eteonicus learned of the design, but was at a loss how to deal with it, considering the number of these reed-bearers. To make an open attack upon them seemed dangerous. It would probably lead to a rush to arms, in which the conspirators would seize the city and commence hostilities, and, in the event of their success, everything hitherto achieved would be lost. Or again, the destruction on his part of many fellow-creatures and allies was a terrible alternative, which would place the Spartans in an unenviable light with regard to the rest of Hellas, and render the soldiers ill-disposed to the cause in hand. Accordingly he took with him fifteen men, armed with daggers, and marched through the city. Falling in with one of the reed-bearers, a man suffering from ophthalmia, who was returning from the surgeon's house, he put him to death. This led to some uproar, and people asked why the man was thus slain. By Eteonicus's orders the answer was because he carried a reed. As the explanation circulated, one reed-bearer after another threw away the symbol, each one saying to himself, as he heard the reason given, "I had better not be seen with this." After a while Eteonicus called a meeting of the Chians, and imposed upon them a contribution of money, on the ground that with pay in their pockets the sailors would have no temptation to revolutionary projects. The Chians acquiesced. Whereupon Eteonicus promptly ordered his crews to get on board their vessels. He then rowed alongside each ship in turn, and addressed the men at some length in terms of encouragement and cheery admonition, just as though he knew nothing of what had taken place, and so distributed a month's pay to every man on board.

After this the Chians and the other allies held a meeting in Ephesus, and, considering the present state of affairs, determined to send ambassadors to Lacedaemon with a statement of the facts, and a request that

Lysander might be sent out to take command of the fleet. Lysander's high reputation among the allies dated back to his former period of office, when as admiral he had won the naval victory of Notium. The ambassadors accordingly were despatched, accompanied by envoys also from Cyrus, charged with the same message. The Lacedaemonians responded by sending them Lysander as second in command, with Aracus as admiral, since it was contrary to their custom that the same man should be admiral twice. At the same time the fleet was entrusted to Lysander. [At this date the war had lasted five-and-twenty years.]

It was in this year that Cyrus put Autoboesaces and Mitraeus to death. These were sons of the sister of Dariaeus[1] [the daughter of Xerxes, the father of Darius.] He put them to death for neglecting, when they met him, to thrust their hands into the sleeve (or *kore*), which is a tribute of respect paid to the king alone. This *kore* is longer than the ordinary sleeve, so long in fact that a man with his hand inside is rendered helpless. In consequence of this act on the part of Cyrus, Hieramenes and his wife urged upon Dariaeus the danger of overlooking such excessive insolence on the part of the young prince, and Dariaeus, on the plea of sickness, sent a special embassy to summon Cyrus to his bedside.

In the following year [during the ephorate of Archytas and the archonship at Athens of Alexias,] Lysander arrived at Ephesus, and sent for Eteonicus with his ships from Chios, and collected all other vessels elsewhere to be found. His time was now devoted to refitting the old ships and having new ones built in Antandrus. He also made a journey to the court of Cyrus with a request for money. All Cyrus could say was, that not only the money sent by the king was spent, but much more besides; and he pointed out the various sums which each of the admirals had received, but at the same time he gave him what he asked for. Furnished with this money, Lysander appointed captains to the different triremes, and paid the sailors their wages. Meanwhile the Athenian generals, on their side, were devoting their energies to the improvement of their navy at Samos.

It was now Cyrus's turn to send for Lysander. It was the moment at which the envoy from his father had arrived with the message, "Your father is on his sick-bed and desires your presence." The king lay at Thamneria, in Media, near the territory of the Cadusians, against whom he had marched to put down a revolt. When Lysander presented himself, Cyrus was urgent with him not to engage the Athenians at sea unless he had many more ships than they. "The king," he added, "and I have

---

[1] Dariaeus, *i.e.* Darius, but the spelling of the name is correct, and occurs in Ctesias, though in the *Anabasis* we have the spelling Darius.

plenty of wealth, so that, as far as money goes, you can man plenty
of vessels." He then consigned to him all the tributes from the several
cities which belonged to him personally, and gave him the money which
he had on hand; and finally, reminding him of the sincere friendship he
entertained towards the state of Lacedaemon, as well as to himself personally, he set out up country to visit his father. Lysander, finding
himself thus left with the complete control of the property of Cyrus
(during the absence of that prince, so summoned to the bedside of his
father), was able to distribute pay to his troops, after which he set sail
for the Ceramic Gulf of Caria. Here he stormed a city in alliance with
the Athenians named Cedreae, and on the following day's assault took
it, and reduced the inhabitants to slavery. These were of a mixed
Hellene and barbarian stock. From Cedreae he continued his voyage to
Rhodes. The Athenians meanwhile, using Samos as their base of operations, were employed in devastating the king's territory, or in swooping
down upon Chios and Ephesus, and in general were preparing for a
naval battle, having but lately chosen three new generals in addition to
those already in office, whose names were Menander, Tydeus, and
Cephisodotus. Now Lysander, leaving Rhodes, and coasting along Ionia,
made his way to the Hellespont, to block the passage of vessels through
the Straits, and to attack the cities which had revolted from Sparta. The
Athenians also set sail from Chios, but stood out to the open sea, since
the seaboard of Asia was hostile to them.

Lysander was again on the move; leaving Abydos, he passed up channel to Lampsacus, which town was allied with Athens; the men of
Abydos and the rest of the troops advancing by land, under the command of the Lacedaemonian Thorax. They then attacked and took by
storm the town, which was wealthy, and with its stores of wine and
wheat and other commodities was pillaged by the soldiery. All freeborn
persons, however, were without exception released by Lysander. And
now the Athenian fleet, following close on his heels, came to moorings
at Elaeus, in the Chersonesus, 180 sail in all. It was not until they had
reached this place, and were getting their early meal, that the news of
what had happened at Lampsacus reached them. Then they instantly
set sail again to Sestos, and, having halted long enough merely to take
in stores, sailed on further to Aegospotami, a point facing Lampsacus,
where the Hellespont is not quite two miles broad. Here they took their
evening meal.

The night following, or rather early next morning, with the first
streak of dawn, Lysander gave the signal for the men to take their
breakfasts and get on board their vessels; and so, having got all ready for
a naval engagement, with his ports closed and movable bulwarks at-

tached, he issued the order that no one was to stir from his post or put out to sea. As the sun rose the Athenians drew up their vessels facing the harbour, in line of battle ready for action; but Lysander declining to come out to meet them, as the day advanced they retired again to Aegospotami. Then Lysander ordered the swiftest of his ships to follow the Athenians, and as soon as the crews had disembarked, to watch what they did, sail back, and report to him. Until these look-outs returned he would permit no disembarkation from his ships. This performance he repeated for four successive days, and each day the Athenians put out to sea and challenged an engagement.

But now Alcibiades, from his fortress, could see the position of his fellow-countrymen, moored on an open beach beyond reach of any city, and forced to send for supplies to Sestos, which was nearly two miles distant, while their enemies were safely lodged in a harbour, with a city adjoining, and everything within reach. The situation did not please him, and he advised them to shift their anchorage to Sestos, where they would have the advantage of a harbour and a city. "Once there," he concluded, "you can engage the enemy whenever it suits you." But the generals, and more particularly Tydeus and Menander, bade him go about his business. "We are generals now—not you," they said; and so he went away. And now for five days in succession the Athenians had sailed out to offer battle, and for the fifth time retired, followed by the same swift sailers of the enemy. But this time Lysander's orders to the vessels so sent in pursuit were, that as soon as they saw the enemy's crew fairly disembarked and dispersed along the shores of the Chersonesus (a practice, it should be mentioned, which had grown upon them from day to day owing to the distance at which eatables had to be purchased, and out of sheer contempt, no doubt, of Lysander, who refused to accept battle), they were to begin their return voyage, and when in mid-channel to hoist a shield. The orders were punctually carried out, and Lysander at once signalled to his whole squadron to put across with all speed, while Thorax, with the troops, went with the fleet. Aware of the enemy's fleet, which he could see bearing down upon him, Conon had only time to signal to the crews to join their ships and rally to the rescue with all their might. But the men were scattered far and wide, and some of the vessels had only two out of their three banks of rowers, some only a single one, while others again were completely empty. Conon's own ship, with seven others in attendance on him and the Paralus, put out to sea, a little cluster of nine vessels, with their full complement of men; but every one of the remaining 171 vessels were captured by Lysander on the beach. As to the men themselves, the large majority of them were easily made prisoners on shore, a few only escaping to the small fortresses of the neighbourhood. Meanwhile Conon and his nine vessels made good their escape. For himself, knowing that the fortune of Athens was ruined, he put into Abarnis, the promontory of Lampsacus, and there picked up the great sails of Lysander's ships, and then with eight ships set sail himself to seek refuge with Evagoras in Cyprus, while the Paralus started for Athens with tidings of what had taken place.

Lysander, on his side, conveyed the ships and prisoners and all other spoil back to Lampsacus, having on board some of the Athenian generals, notably Philocles and Adeimantus. On the very day of these achievements he despatched Theopompus, a Milesian privateer, to Lacedaemon to report what had taken place. This envoy arrived within three days and delivered his message. Lysander's next step was to convene the allies and bid them deliberate as to the treatment of the prisoners. Many were the accusations here levied against the Athenians. There was talk of crimes committed against the law of Hellas, and of cruelties sanctioned by popular decrees; which, had they conquered in the late sea-fight, would have been carried out; such as the proposal to cut off the right hand of every prisoner taken alive, and lastly the ill-treatment of two captured men-of-war, a Corinthian and an Andrian vessel, when every man on board had been hurled overboard. Philocles was the very general of the Athenians who had so ruthlessly destroyed those men. Many other tales were told; and at length a resolution was passed to put all the Athenian prisoners, with the exception of Adeimantus, to death. He alone, it was pleaded, had taken exception to the proposal to cut off the prisoners' hands. On the other hand, he was himself accused by some people of having betrayed the fleet. As to Philocles, Lysander put to him one question, as the officer who had thrown the Corinthians and Andrians overboard: What fate did the man deserve to suffer who had embarked on so cruel a course of illegality against Hellenes? and so delivered him to the executioner.

2. When he had set the affairs of Lampsacus in order, Lysander sailed to Byzantium and Calchedon, where the inhabitants, having first dismissed the Athenian garrison under a truce, admitted him within their walls. Those citizens of Byzantium, who had betrayed Byzantium into the hands of Alcibiades, fled as exiles into Pontus, but subsequently betaking themselves to Athens, became Athenian citizens. In dealing with the Athenian garrisons, and indeed with all Athenians wheresoever found, Lysander made it a rule to give them safe conduct to Athens, and to Athens only, in the certainty that the larger the number collected within the city and Piraeus, the more quickly the want of necessaries of life would make itself felt. And now, leaving Sthenelaus, a Laconian,

as governor-general of Byzantium and Calchedon, he sailed back himself to Lampsacus and devoted himself to refitting his ships.

It was night when the Paralus reached Athens with her evil tidings, and a bitter wail of woe broke forth. From Piraeus, following the line of the long walls up to the heart of the city, it swept and swelled, as each man to his neighbour passed on the news. On that night no man slept. There was mourning and sorrow for those that were lost, but the lamentation for the dead was merged in even deeper sorrow for themselves, as they pictured the evils they were about to suffer, the like of which they had themselves inflicted upon the men of Melos, who were colonists of the Lacedaemonians, when they mastered them by siege. Or on the men of Histiaea; on Scione and Torone; on the Aeginetans, and many another Hellenic city. On the following day the public assembly met, and, after debate, it was resolved to block up all the harbours save one, to put the walls in a state of defence, to post guards at various points, and to make all other necessary preparation for a siege. Such were the concerns of the men of Athens.

Lysander presently left the Hellespont with 200 ships and arrived at Lesbos, where he arranged things in Mytilene and the other cities of the island. Meanwhile he despatched Eteonicus with a squadron of ten ships to the Thracian coast, where that officer brought the whole region into the hands of Lacedaemon. Indeed, in a moment of time, after the sea-fight, the whole of Hellas had revolted from Athens, with the exception of the Samians. These, having massacred the nobles, held the state under their control. After a while Lysander sent messages to Agis at Deceleia, and to Lacedaemon, announcing his approach with a squadron of 200 ships.

In obedience to command of Pausanias, the other king of Lacedaemon, a levy in force of the Lacedaemonians and all the rest of Peloponnesus, except the Argives, was set in motion for a campaign. As soon as the several contingents had arrived, the king put himself at their head and marched against Athens, encamping in the Academy, as it is called. Lysander had now reached Aegina, where, having got together as many of the former inhabitants as possible, he formally reinstated them in their city; and what he did in behalf of the Aeginetans, he did also in behalf of the Melians, and of the rest who had been deprived of their countries. He then pillaged the island of Salamis, and anchored at Piraeus with 150 ships, and established a blockade against all merchant ships entering that harbour.

The Athenians, finding themselves besieged by land and sea, were at a loss what to do. Without ships, without allies, without provisions, the belief gained hold upon them that there was no way of escape. They must now, in their turn, suffer what they had themselves inflicted upon others; not in retaliation, indeed, for ills received, but out of sheer insolence, overriding the citizens of small states, and for no better reason than that these were allies of the very men now at their gates. In this frame of mind they enfranchised those who at any time had lost their civil rights, and schooled themselves to endurance; and, although many were dying of starvation, they refused to treat for peace. But when the stock of corn was absolutely insufficient, they sent an embassage to Agis, proposing to become allies of the Lacedaemonians on the sole condition of keeping their fortification walls and Piraeus; and to draw up articles of treaty on these terms. Agis bade them betake themselves to Lacedaemon, seeing that he had no authority to act himself. With this answer the ambassadors returned to Athens, and were forthwith sent on to Lacedaemon. On reaching Sellasia, a town in Laconian territory, they waited till they got their answer from the ephors, who, having learnt their terms (which were identical with those already proposed to Agis), bade them instantly to be gone, and, if they really desired peace, to come with other proposals, the fruit of happier reflection. Thus the ambassadors returned home, and reported the result of their embassy, whereupon despondency fell upon all. It was a painful reflection that in the end they would be sold into slavery; and meanwhile, pending the return of a second embassy, many must fall victims to starvation. The razing of their fortifications was not a solution which any one cared to recommend. A senator, Archestratus, had indeed put the question in the senate, whether it were not best to make peace with the Lacedaemonians on such terms as they were willing to propose; but he was thrown into prison. The Laconian proposals referred to involved the destruction of both long walls for a space of more than a mile. And a decree had been passed, making it illegal to submit any such proposition about the walls. Things having reached this pass, Theramenes made a proposal in the public assembly as follows: If they chose to send him as an ambassador to Lysander, he would go and find out why the Lacedaemonians were so unyielding about the walls; whether it was they really intended to enslave the city, or merely that they wanted a guarantee of good faith. Despatched accordingly, he lingered on with Lysander for three whole months and more, watching for the time when the Athenians, at the last pinch of starvation, would be willing to accede to any terms that might be offered. At last, in the fourth month, he returned and reported to the public assembly that Lysander had detained him all this while, and had ended by bidding him betake himself to Lacedaemon, since he had no authority himself to answer his questions, which must be addressed directly to the ephors. After this Theramenes was chosen with nine others to go to Lacedaemon as ambassadors with full powers. Meanwhile Lysander had sent an Athenian exile, named Aristoteles, in company of certain Lacedaemonians, to Sparta to report to the board of ephors how he had answered Theramenes, that they, and they alone, had supreme authority in matters of peace and war.

Theramenes and his companions presently reached Sellasia, and being here questioned as to the reason of their visit, replied that they had full powers to treat of peace. After which the ephors ordered them to be summoned to their presence. On their arrival a general assembly was convened, in which the Corinthians and Thebans more particularly, though their views were shared by many other Hellenes also, urged the meeting not to come to terms with the Athenians, but to destroy them. The Lacedaemonians replied that they would never reduce to slavery a city which was itself an integral portion of Hellas, and had performed a great and noble service to Hellas in the most perilous of emergencies. On the contrary, they were willing to offer peace on the terms now specified—namely, "That the long walls and the fortifications of Piraeus should be destroyed; that the Athenian fleet, with the exception of twelve vessels, should be surrendered; that the exiles should be restored; and lastly, that the Athenians should acknowledge the headship of Sparta in peace and war, leaving to her the choice of friends and foes, and following her lead by land and sea." Such were the terms which Theramenes and the rest who acted with him were able to report on their return to Athens. As they entered the city, a vast crowd met them, trembling lest their mission should have proved fruitless. For indeed delay was no longer possible, so long already was the list of victims daily perishing from starvation. On the day following, the ambassadors delivered their report, stating the terms upon which the Lacedaemonians were willing to make peace. Theramenes acted as spokesman, insisting that they ought to obey the Lacedaemonians and pull down the walls. A small minority raised their voice in opposition, but the majority were strongly in favour of the proposition, and the resolution was passed to accept the peace. After that, Lysander sailed into the Piraeus, and the exiles were readmitted. And so they fell to levelling the fortifications and walls with much enthusiasm, to the accompaniment of female flute-players, deeming that day the beginning of liberty to Greece.

[Thus the year drew to its close—during its middle months took place the accession of Dionysius, the son of Hermocrates the Syracusan, to the tyranny of Syracuse; an incident itself preceded by a victory gained over the Carthaginians by the Syracusans; the reduction of Agrigentum through famine by the Carthaginians themselves; and the exodus of the Siciliots from that city.]

3. In the following year [that year of the Olympiad cycle in which Crocinas, a Thessalian, won the Stadium; when Endius was ephor at Sparta, and Pythodorus archon at Athens, though the Athenians indeed do not call the year by that archon's name, since he was elected during the oligarchy, but prefer to speak of the year without archons] the aforesaid oligarchy originated thus: the people passed a resolution to choose thirty men who were to draft a constitution based on the ancestral laws of the State. The following were chosen to act on this committee: Polychares, Critias, Melobius, Hippolochus, Eucleides, Hiero, Mnesilochus, Chremo, Theramenes, Aresias, Diocles, Phaedrias, Chaereleos, Anaetius, Piso, Sophocles, Eratosthenes, Charicles, Onomacles, Theognis, Aeschines, Theogenes, Cleomedes, Erasistratus, Pheido, Dracontides, Eumathes, Aristoteles, Hippomachus, Mnesitheides. After these transactions, Lysander set sail for Samos; and Agis withdrew the land force from Deceleia and disbanded the troops, dismissing the contingents to their several cities.

It was at this date, about the time of the solar eclipse,[2] that Lycophron of Pherae, who was ambitious of ruling over the whole of Thessaly, defeated those sections of the Thessalians who opposed him, such as the men of Larissa and others, and slew many of them. It was also about this date that Dionysius, now tyrant of Syracuse, was defeated by the Carthaginians, and lost Gela and Camarina. And again, a little later, the men of Leontini, who previously had been amalgamated with the Syracusans, separated themselves from Syracuse and Dionysius, and asserted their independence, and returned to their native city. Another incident of this period was the sudden despatch and introduction of Syracusan horse into Catana by Dionysius.

Now the Samians, though besieged by Lysander on all sides, were at first unwilling to come to terms. But at the last moment, when Lysander was on the point of assaulting the town, they accepted the terms, which allowed every free man to leave the island, but not to carry away any part of his property, except the clothes upon his back. On these conditions they marched out. The city and all it contained was then delivered over to its ancient citizens by Lysander, who finally appointed ten governors to garrison the island. After which, he disbanded the allied fleet, dismissing them to their respective cities, while he himself, with the Lacedaemonian squadron, set sail for Laconia, bringing with him the prows of the conquered vessels and the whole navy of Piraeus, with the exception of twelve ships. He also brought the crowns which he had received from the cities as private gifts, and a sum of 470 talents in silver (the surplus of the tribute money which Cyrus had assigned to

[2] This took place on 2 September 404 B.C.

him for the prosecution of the war), besides other property, the fruit of
his military exploits. All these things Lysander delivered to the Lacedaemonians in the latter end of summer,[3] [a summer, the close of which
coincided with the termination of a war which had lasted twenty-eight
and a half years, as the list of annual ephors, appended in order, serves
to show. Aenesias is the first name. The war began during his ephorate,
in the fifteenth year of the thirty years' truce after the capture of
Euboea. His successors were Brasidas, Isanor, Sostratidas, Exarchus,
Agesistratus, Angenidas, Onomacles, Zeuxippus, Pityas, Pleistolas, Clei-
nomachus, Ilarchus, Leon, Chaerilas, Patesiadas, Cleosthenes, Lycarius,
Eperatus, Onomantius, Alexippidas, Misgolaidas, Isias, Aracus, Euar-
chippus, Pantacles, Pityas, Archytas, and lastly, Endius, during whose
year of office Lysander sailed home in triumph, after performing the
exploits above recorded.]

The Thirty had been chosen almost immediately after the long walls
and the fortifications round Piraeus had been razed. They were chosen
for the express purpose of compiling a code of laws for the future constitution of the State. The laws were always on the point of being published, yet they were never forthcoming; and the thirty compilers contented themselves meanwhile with appointing a senate and the other
magistracies as suited their fancy best. That done, they turned their
attention, in the first instance, to such persons as were known to have
made their living as informers under the democracy, and to have been
troublesome to the aristocrats. These they laid hold on and prosecuted
on the capital charge. The new senate gladly voted them guilty; and
the rest, as many as were not similar to them, seemed scarcely vexed.
But the Thirty did not stop there. Presently they began to deliberate by
what means they could get the city under their absolute control, in
order that they might work their will upon it. Here again they proceeded
tentatively; in the first instance, they sent Aeschines and Aristoteles,
to Lacedaemon, and persuaded Lysander to support them in getting a
Lacedaemonian garrison despatched to Athens. They only needed it
until they had got the "malignants" out of the way, and had established
the constitution; and they would undertake to maintain these troops at
their own cost. Lysander was not deaf to their persuasions, and by his
co-operation their request was granted. A bodyguard, with Callibius as
governor, was sent.

And now that they had got the garrison, they fell to flattering Callib-

---

[3] This marks the point at which Xenophon is generally believed to have laid aside
the *Hellenica* for many years, the remainder showing evidence of a considerable
alteration in his style. See M. MacLaren, "On the Composition of Xenophon's
Hellenica," *American Journal of Philology* 55 (1934) 121-139, 249-262.

ius with all servile flattery, in order that he might give countenance to
their doings. Thus they prevailed on him to allow some of the guards to
accompany them, while they proceeded to lay hands on whom they
would; no longer confining themselves to base folk and people of no
account, but boldly laying hands on those who they felt sure would least
easily brook being thrust aside, or, if a spirit of opposition seized them,
could command the largest number of partisans.

These were early days; as yet Critias was of one mind with Theramenes, and the two were friends. But the time came when, in proportion as Critias was ready to rush headlong into wholesale carnage, like
one who thirsted for the blood of the democracy, which had banished
him, Theramenes blocked and thwarted him. It was not reasonable, he
argued, to put people to death who had never done a wrong to respectable people in their lives, simply because they had enjoyed influence
and honour under the democracy. "Why, you and I, Critias," he said,
"have said and done many things ere now for the sake of popularity."
To which the other (for the terms of friendly intimacy still subsisted)
would retort, "There is no choice left to us, since we intend to obtain
control, but to get rid of those who are best able to hinder us. If you
imagine, because we are thirty instead of one, our government requires
less careful guarding than an actual tyranny, you are a fool."

So things went on. Day after day the list of persons put to death for
no just reason grew longer. Day after day the signs of resentment were
more significant in the groups of citizens banding together and fore-
casting the character of this future constitution; till at length Theramenes spoke again, protesting: There was no help for it but to associate
with themselves a sufficient number of persons in the conduct of affairs,
or the oligarchy would certainly come to an end. Critias and the rest of
the Thirty, whose fears had already converted Theramenes into a
dangerous popular idol, proceeded at once to draw up a list of 3,000
citizens; fit and proper persons to have a share in the conduct of affairs. But Theramenes was not wholly satisfied, "indeed he must say,
for himself, he regarded it as ridiculous, that in their effort to associate
the better classes with themselves in power, they should fix on just that
particular number, 3,000, as if that figure had some necessary connection with the exact number of gentlemen in the State, making it impossible to discover any respectability outside or rascality within the magic
number. And in the second place," he continued, "I see we are trying
to do two things, diametrically opposed; we are setting up a government, which is based on force, and at the same time inferior in strength
to those whom we propose to govern." That was what he said, but
what his colleagues did, was to institute a military inspection or review.

The Three Thousand were drawn up in the Agora, and the rest of the citizens, who were not included in the list, elsewhere in various quarters of the city. The order to stack arms was given; but while the men were away, at the bidding of the Thirty, the Laconian guards, with those of the citizens who shared their views, appeared on the scene and took away the arms of all except the Three Thousand, carried them up to the Acropolis, and safely deposited them in the temple.

The ground being thus cleared, as it were, and feeling that they had it in their power to do what they pleased, they embarked on a course of wholesale butchery, in which many were sacrificed to the merest hatred, many to the accident of possessing riches. Presently the question rose, How they were to get money to pay their guards? and to meet this difficulty a resolution was passed empowering each of the committee to seize on one of the resident aliens apiece, to put his victim to death, and to confiscate his property. Theramenes was invited, or rather told to seize some one or other. "Choose whom you will, only let it be done." To which he answered that it hardly seemed to him a noble or worthy course on the part of those who claimed to be the *élite* of society to go beyond the informers in injustice. "Yesterday they, to-day we; with this difference, the victim of the informer must live as a source of income; our innocents must die that we may get their wealth. Surely their method was innocent in comparison with ours."

The rest of the Thirty, who had come to regard Theramenes as an obstacle to any course they might wish to adopt, proceeded to plot against him. They addressed themselves to the members of the senate in private, here a man and there a man, and denounced him as the mar-plot of the constitution. Then they issued an order to some young men, picking out the most audacious characters they could find, to be present, each with a dagger hidden in the hollow of the armpit; and so called a meeting of the senate. When Theramenes had taken his place, Critias got up and addressed the meeting:

"If," said he, "any member of this council, here seated, imagines that an undue amount of blood has been shed, let me remind him that with changes of constitutions such things can not be avoided. It is the rule everywhere, but more particularly at Athens it was inevitable there should be found a specially large number of persons sworn foes to any constitutional change in the direction of oligarchy, and this for two reasons. First, because the population of this city, compared with other Hellenic cities, is enormously large; and again, owing to the length of time during which the people has been bred up on liberty. Now, as to two points we are clear. The first is that democracy is a form of government detestable to persons like ourselves—to us and to you; the next is that the people of Athens could never be got to be friendly to our friends and saviours, the Lacedaemonians. But on the loyalty of the better classes the Lacedaemonians can count. And that is our reason for establishing an oligarchical constitution with their concurrence. That is why we do our best to rid us of every one whom we perceive to be opposed to the oligarchy; and, in our opinion, if one of ourselves should elect to undermine this constitution of ours, he would deserve punishment. Do you not agree? And the case," he continued, "is no imaginary one. The offender is here present—Theramenes. And what we say of him is, that he is bent upon destroying yourselves and us by every means in his power. These are not baseless charges; but if you will consider it, you will find them amply established in his unmeasured censure of the present posture of affairs, and his persistent opposition to us, his colleagues, if ever we seek to get rid of any of these demagogues. Had this been his guiding principle of action from the beginning, in spite of hostility, at least he would have escaped all imputation of villainy. Why, this is the very man who originated our friendly and confidential relations with Lacedaemon. This is the very man who authorised the abolition of the democracy, who urged us on to inflict punishment on the earliest batch of prisoners brought before us. But to-day all is changed; now you and we are hated by the people, and he accordingly has ceased to be pleased with our proceedings. The explanation is obvious. In case of a catastrophe, how much pleasanter for him once again to light upon his legs, and leave us to render account for our past performances.

"I contend that this man is fairly entitled to render his account also, not only as an ordinary enemy, but as a traitor to yourselves and us. And let us add, not only is treason more formidable than open war, in proportion as it is harder to guard against a hidden assassin than an open foe, but it bears the impress of a more enduring hostility, inasmuch as men fight their enemies and come to terms with them again and are fast friends; but whoever heard of reconciliation with a traitor? There he stands unmasked; he has forfeited our confidence for evermore. But to show you that these are no new tactics of his, to prove to you that he is a traitor in grain, I will recall to your memories some points in his past history.

"He began by being held in high honour by the democracy; but like his father Hagnon, he next showed a most headlong anxiety to transform the democracy into the Four Hundred, and, in fact, for a time held the first place in that body. But presently, detecting the formation of a rival power to the oligarchs, round he shifted; and we find him next a ringleader of the popular party in assailing them. It must be admitted, he has well earned his nickname Buskin. [The buskin seems to fit both legs equally, he faces both ways.] Yes, Theramenes! clever you may be, but the man who deserves to live should not show his cleverness in leading on his associates into trouble, and when some obstacle presents itself, at once veer round; but like a pilot on shipboard, he ought then to redouble his efforts, until the wind is fair. Else, how in the world are those mariners to reach the haven where they would be, if at the first contrary wind or tide they turn about and sail in the opposite direction? Death and destruction are concomitants of constitutional changes and revolution, no doubt; but you are such an impersonation of change, that, as you twist and turn and double, you deal destruction on all sides. At one swoop you are the ruin of many oligarchs at the hands of the people, and at another of many democrats at the hands of the better classes. Why, sirs, this is the man to whom the orders were given by the generals, in the sea-fight off Lesbos, to pick up the crews of the disabled vessels; and who, neglecting to obey orders, turned round and accused the generals; and to save himself murdered them! What, I ask you, of a man who so openly studies the art of self-seeking, deaf alike to the pleas of honour and to the claims of friendship? Would not leniency towards such a creature be misplaced? Can it be our duty at all to spare him? Ought we not rather, when we know the doublings of his nature, to guard against them, lest we enable him presently to practise on ourselves? The case is clear. We therefore hereby cite this man before you, as a conspirator and traitor against yourselves and us. The reasonableness of our conduct, one further reflection may make clear. No one, I take it, will dispute the splendour, the perfection of the Laconian constitution. Imagine one of the ephors there in Sparta, in lieu of obedience to the majority, taking on himself to find fault with the government and to oppose all measures. Do you not think that the ephors themselves, and the whole commonwealth besides, would hold this renegade worthy of the greatest punishment? So, too, by the same token, if you are wise, do you spare yourselves, not him. For what does the alternative mean? I will tell you. His preservation will cause the courage of many who hold opposite views to your own to rise; his destruction will cut off the last hopes of all your enemies, whether within or without the city."

With these words he sat down, but Theramenes rose and said, "Sirs, with your permission I will first touch upon the charge against me which Critias has mentioned last. The assertion is that as the accuser of the generals I was their murderer. Now certainly it was not I who began the attack upon them, but it was they who asserted that in spite of the orders given me I had neglected to pick up the unfortunates in the sea-fight off Lesbos. All I did was to defend myself. My defence was that the storm was too violent to permit any vessel to ride at sea, much more therefore to pick up the men, and this defence was accepted by my fellow-citizens as highly reasonable, while the generals seemed to be condemned out of their own mouths. For while they kept on asserting that it was possible to save the men, the fact still remained that they abandoned them to their fate, set sail, and were gone.

"However, I am not surprised, I confess, at this grave misconception on the part of Critias, for at the date of these occurrences he was not in Athens. He was away in Thessaly, laying the foundations of a democracy with Prometheus, and arming the serfs against their masters. Heaven forbid that any of his transactions there should be re-enacted here. However, I must say, I do heartily concur with him on one point. Whoever desires to exclude you from the government, or to strengthen the hands of your secret foes, deserves and ought to meet with condign punishment; but who is most capable of so doing? That you will best discover, I think, by looking a little more closely into the past and the present conduct of each of us. Well then, up to the moment at which you were formed into a senatorial body, when the magistracies were appointed, and certain notorious 'informers' were brought to trial, we all held the same views. But later on, when our friends yonder began to hale respectable honest men to prison and to death, I, on my side, began to differ from them. From the moment when Leon of Salamis, a man of high and well-deserved reputation, was put to death, though he had not committed any sort of a crime, I knew that all men like him must tremble for themselves, and, so trembling, be driven into opposition to the new constitution. In the same way, when Niceratus, the son of Nicias, was arrested; a wealthy man, who like his father, had never done anything that could be called demagogic in his life; it did not require much insight to discover that those like him would become our foes. But to go a step further: when it came to Antiphon falling at our hands—Antiphon, who during the war contributed two fast-sailing men-of-war out of his own resources, it was then plain to me, that all who had been zealous must eye us with suspicion. Once more I could not help speaking out in opposition to my colleagues when they suggested that each of us ought to seize some one resident alien. For what could be more certain than that their death-warrant would turn the whole resident foreign population into enemies of the constitution. I spoke out again when they insisted on depriving the populace of their arms; it being no part of my creed that we ought to take the strength out of the city; nor, indeed, as far as I could see, had the Lacedaemonians stepped between us and destruction merely that we might become a handful of people, powerless to aid them in the day of need.

Had that been their object, they might have swept us away to the last man. A little while longer would have sufficed to extinguish us by famine. Nor, again, can I say that the importation of mercenary foreign guards was altogether to my taste, when it would have been so easy for us to add to our own body a sufficient number of fellow-citizens to ensure our supremacy as governors over those we essayed to govern. But when I saw what an army of malcontents this government had raised up within the city walls, besides another daily increasing host of exiles without, I could not but regard the banishment of people like Thrasybulus and Anytus and Alcibiades as impolitic. Had our object been to strengthen the rival power, we could hardly have set about it better than by providing the populace with the competent leaders whom they needed, and the would-be leaders themselves with an army of willing adherents.

"I ask then is the man who tenders such advice in the full light of day justly to be regarded as a traitor, and not as a benefactor? Surely, Critias, the peacemaker, the man who hinders the creation of many enemies, whose counsels tend to the acquisition of yet more friends, cannot be accused of strengthening the hands of the enemy. Much more truly may the imputation be retorted on those who wrongfully appropriate their neighbour's goods and put to death those who have done no wrong. These are they who cause our adversaries to grow and multiply, and who in very truth are traitors, not to their friends only, but to themselves, spurred on by sordid love of gain.

"I might prove the truth of what I say in many ways, but I beg you to look at the matter thus. With which condition of affairs here in Athens do you think will Thrasybulus and Anytus and the other exiles be the better pleased? That which I have pictured as desirable, or that which my colleagues yonder are producing? For my part I cannot doubt but that, as things now are, they are saying to themselves, 'Our allies muster thick and fast.' But were the real strength of the city kindly disposed to us, they would find it an uphill task even to get a foothold anywhere in the country.

"Then, with regard to what he said of me and my propensity to be for ever changing sides, let me draw your attention to the following facts. Was it not the people itself, the democracy, who voted the constitution of the Four Hundred? This they did, because they had learned to think that the Lacedaemonians would trust any other form of government rather than a democracy. But when the efforts of Lacedaemon were not a whit relaxed, when Aristoteles, Melanthius, and Aristarchus, and the rest of them acting as generals, were plainly constructing a fortress on the mole for the purpose of admitting the enemy, and so getting the city under the power of themselves and their associates; because I got wind of these schemes, and prevented them, is that to be a traitor to one's friends?

"Then he threw in my teeth the nickname 'Buskin,' as descriptive of an endeavour on my part to fit both parties. But what of the man who pleases neither? What in god's name are we to call him? Yes, you —Critias? Under the democracy you were looked upon as the most arrant hater of the people, and under the aristocracy you have proved yourself the bitterest foe of everything respectable. Yes! Critias, I am, and ever have been, a foe of those who think that a democracy cannot reach perfection until slaves and those who, from poverty, would sell the city for a drachma, can share in the government. But not less am I, and ever have been, a pronounced opponent of those who do not think there can possibly exist a perfect oligarchy until the State is subjected to the despotism of a few. On the contrary, my own ambition has been to combine with those who are rich enough to possess a horse and shield, and to use them for the benefit of the State. That was my ideal in old days, and I hold to it still. If you can mention when and where, in conjunction with despots or demagogues, I have set to my hand to deprive honest gentlefolk of their citizenship, pray speak. If you can convict me of such crimes at present, or can prove my perpetration of them in the past, I admit that I deserve to die, and by the worst of deaths."

With these words he ceased, and the loud murmur of applause which followed marked the favourable impression produced upon the senate. It was plain to Critias, that if he allowed his adversary's fate to be decided by formal voting, Theramenes would escape, and this would be intolerable. Accordingly he stepped forward and spoke a word or two in the ears of the Thirty. This done, he went out and gave an order to the men with the daggers to stand close to the bar in full view of the senators. Again he entered and addressed the senate thus, "I hold it to be the duty of a good leader, when he sees the friends about him being made dupes, to intervene. That at any rate is what I propose to do. Indeed our friends here standing by the bar say that if we propose to acquit a man so openly bent upon the ruin of the oligarchy, they do not mean to let us do so. Now there is a clause in the new code forbidding any of the Three Thousand to be put to death without your vote; but the Thirty have power of life and death over all outside that list. Accordingly," he proceeded, "I herewith strike this man, Theramenes, off the list; and this with the concurrence of my colleagues. And now," he continued, "we condemn him to death."

Hearing these words Theramenes sprang upon the altar exclaiming, "And I, sirs, supplicate you for the barest forms of law and justice. Let it not be in the power of Critias to strike off either me, or any one of you whom he will. But in my case, in what may be your case, if we are tried, let our trial be in accordance with the law they have made concerning those on the list. By the gods, I know," he added, "but too well, that this altar will not protect me; but I will make it plain that these men are as impious towards the gods as they are nefarious towards men. Yet I do marvel, good sirs and honest gentlemen, for so you are, that you will not help yourselves, and that too when you must see that the name of every one of you is as easily erased as mine."

But when he had got so far, the voice of the herald was heard giving the order to the Eleven to seize Theramenes. They at that instant entered with their attendants, at their head Satyrus, the boldest and most shameless of the body, and Critias exclaimed, addressing the Eleven, "We deliver over to you Theramenes yonder, who has been condemned according to the law. Do you take him and lead him away to the proper place, and do there with him what remains to do." As Critias uttered the words, Satyrus laid hold upon Theramenes to drag him from the altar, and the attendants lent their aid. But he, as was natural, called upon gods and men to witness what was happening. The senators the while kept silence, seeing the companions of Satyrus at the bar, and the whole front of the senate house crowded with the foreign guards, nor did they need to be told that they had daggers.

And so Theramenes was dragged through the Agora, in vehement and loud tones proclaiming the wrongs that he was suffering. One statement of his I cite. It is this: Satyrus bade him, "Be silent, or he would suffer;" to which he answered, "And if I am silent, shall I not suffer?" Also, when they brought him the hemlock, and the time was come to drink the fatal draught, they tell how he playfully jerked out the dregs from the bottom of the cup, like one who plays Cottabos,[4] with the words, "This to the lovely Critias." These are sayings too slight, perhaps, to deserve record; yet I must deem it an admirable trait in this man's character, if at such a moment, when death confronted him, neither his wits forsook him, nor could the childlike sportiveness vanish from his soul.

4. So Theramenes met his death; and, now that this obstacle was removed, the Thirty, feeling that they had it in their power to play the tyrant without fear, issued an order forbidding all, whose names were not on the list, to set foot within the city. They evicted them from their estates that their farms might fall to the possession of the Thirty and their friends. Even Piraeus was not safe; of those who sought refuge

---

[4] A Sicilian game in which each threw the wine left in his cup so as to strike smartly in a metal basin, at the same time invoking his beloved; if all fell into the basin and the sound was clear, it was a sign he stood well.

there, many were driven forth in similar fashion, until Megara and Thebes overflowed with the crowd of refugees.

Presently Thrasybulus, with about seventy followers, sallied out from Thebes, and took the fortress of Phyle. The weather was brilliant, and the Thirty marched out of the city to repel the invader; with them were the Three Thousand and the Knights. When they reached the place, some of the young men, in the foolhardiness of youth, made a dash at the fortress, but without effect; all they got was wounds, and so retired. The intention of the Thirty now was to blockade the place; by shutting off all the avenues of supplies, they thought to force the garrison to capitulate. But this project was interrupted by a steady downfall of snow that night and the following day. In the snow they retreated to the city, but not without the sacrifice of many of their camp-followers, who fell a prey to the men in Phyle. The next anxiety of the government in Athens was to secure the farms against the plundering to which they would be exposed, if there were no armed force to protect them. With this object a protecting force was despatched to the boundary estates, about two miles this side of Phyle. This corps consisted of the Lacedaemonian guards, or nearly all of them, and two divisions of horse. They encamped in a wild district, and stood guard.

But by this time there were about 700 men collected in Phyle; and with these Thrasybulus one night descended. When he was not quite half a mile from the enemy's encampment he grounded arms, and a deep silence was maintained until it drew towards day. In a little while the men opposite, one by one, were getting to their legs or leaving the camp for necessary purposes, while a din arose, caused by the grooms currying and combing their horses. At this moment Thrasybulus and his men snatched up their arms and dashed at the enemy's position. Some they felled on the spot; and routing the whole body, pursued them six or seven furlongs, killing 120 hoplites and more. Of the cavalry, Nicostratus, "the beautiful," as men called him, and two others besides were slain; they were caught while still in their beds. Returning from the pursuit, the victors set up a trophy, got together all the arms they had taken, besides baggage, and retired again to Phyle. A reinforcement of horse sent from the city could not discover the vestige of a foe; but waited on the scene of battle until the bodies of the slain had been picked up by their relatives, when they withdrew again to the city.

After this the Thirty, who had begun to realise the insecurity of their position, were anxious to appropriate Eleusis, so that a refuge might be ready for them if needed. With this view an order was issued to the Knights; and Critias, with the rest of the Thirty, visited Eleusis. There they held a review of the Eleusinians in the presence of the Knights;

and, on the pretext of wishing to discover how many they were, and how large a garrison they would further require, they ordered the townsfolk to enter their names. As each man did so he had to retire by a postern leading to the sea. But on the sea-beach this side there were lines of cavalry drawn up in waiting, and as each man appeared he was bound by the servants of the Thirty. When all had so been seized, they gave orders to Lysimachus, the commander of the cavalry, to take them off to the city and deliver them over to the Eleven. Next day they summoned the heavy-armed who were on the list, and the rest of the Knights to the Odeum, and Critias rose and addressed them. He said, "Sirs, the constitution which we are establishing, is a work undertaken in your interests no less than ours; you must therefore participate in its dangers, even as you will partake of its honours. We expect you therefore, in reference to these Eleusinians, who have been seized, to vote their condemnation, so that our hopes and fears may be identical." Then, pointing to a particular spot, he said peremptorily, "You will please deposit your votes there within sight of all." It must be understood that the Laconian guards were present at this scene, fully armed, and filling one-half of the Odeum. As to the proceedings themselves, they found acceptance with those members of the State, besides the Thirty, who could be satisfied with a simple policy of self-aggrandisement.

But now Thrasybulus at the head of his followers, by this time about 1,000 strong, descended from Phyle and reached Piraeus in the night. The Thirty, on their side, informed of this new move, were not slow to rally to the rescue, with the Laconian guards, supported by their own cavalry and hoplites. And so they advanced, marching down along the carriage road which leads into Piraeus. The men from Phyle seemed at first inclined to dispute their passage, but as the wide circuit of the walls needed a defence beyond the reach of their still scanty numbers, they fell back in a compact body upon Munychia. Then the troops from the city poured into the Agora of Hippodamus.[5] Here they formed in line, stretching along and filling the street which leads to the temple of Artemis and the temple of Bendis. This line must have been at least fifty shields deep; and in this formation they at once began to march up. As to the men of Phyle, they too blocked the street at the opposite end, and facing the foe. They presented only a thin line, not more than ten deep, though behind these, certainly, were ranged a body of targeteers and light-armed javelin-men, who were again supported by an artillery of stone-throwers—a numerous division drawn from the popu-

---

[5] Named after the famous architect Hippodamus, who built the town. It was situated near where the two long walls joined the wall of Piraeus; a broad street led from it up to the citadel of Munychia.

lation of the port and district itself. While his antagonists were still advancing, Thrasybulus gave the order to ground their heavy shields, and having done so himself, whilst retaining the rest of his arms, he stood in the midst, and thus addressed them, "Men and fellow-citizens, I wish to inform some, and to remind others of you, that of the men you see advancing beneath us there, the right division are the very men we routed and pursued only four days ago; while on the extreme left there you see the Thirty. These are the men who have not spared to rob us of our city, though we did no wrong; who have hounded us from our homes; who have set the seal of proscription on our dearest friends. But to-day that has come about which least of all they looked for, which most of all we prayed for. Here we stand with our arms in our hands, face to face with our foes; and the gods themselves are with us, seeing that we were arrested in the midst of our peaceful pursuits; at any moment, whilst we supped, or slept, or marketed, sentence of banishment was passed upon us: we had done no wrong, nay, many of us were not even resident in the country. To-day, therefore, I repeat, the gods do visibly fight upon our side; the great gods, who raise a storm even in fair weather for our benefit, and when we lay to our hand to fight, enable our little company to set up the trophy of victory over the multitude of our foes. On this day they have brought us to a place where the steep ascent hinders our foes from hurling spear or javelin over the heads of their own front ranks; but we with our volleys of spears and javelins and stones cannot fail to reach them with terrible effect. Had we been forced to meet their front ranks on an equal footing, who could have been surprised? But as it is, let fly your missiles with a will in brave style. No one can miss his mark when the road is full of them. To avoid our darts they must be for ever skulking beneath their shields; but we will rain blows upon them in their blindness; we will leap upon them and lay them low. But, men, let me call upon you so to bear yourselves that each shall be conscious to himself that the victory was won by him and him alone. Victory—which, god willing, shall this day restore to us the land of our fathers, our homes, our freedom, and the rewards of civic life, our children, if children we have, and our wives! Happy those among us who as conquerors shall look upon this gladdest of all days. Nor less fortunate the man who falls to-day. Not all the wealth in the world shall purchase him a monument so glorious. At the right instant I will strike up the paean; then, with an invocation to the god of battle, and in return for the wanton insults they put upon us, let us with one accord wreak vengeance on yonder men."

Having so spoken, he turned round, facing the enemy, and kept quiet, for the order passed by the soothsayer enjoined on them, not to charge before one of their side was slain or wounded. "As soon as that happens," said the seer, "we will lead you onwards, and the victory shall be yours; but for myself, if I err not, death is waiting." And herein he spoke truly, for they had barely resumed their arms when he himself, as though he were driven by some fatal hand, leapt out in front of the ranks, and so springing into the midst of the foe, was slain, and lies now buried at the passage of the Cephisus. But the rest were victorious, and pursued the routed enemy down to the level ground. There fell in this engagement, out of the number of the Thirty, Critias himself and Hippomachus, and with them Charmides, the son of Glaucon, one of the ten archons in Piraeus, and of the rest about seventy men. The arms of the slain were taken; but, as fellow-citizens, the conquerors forebore to despoil them of their tunics. This being done, they proceeded to give back the dead under cover of a truce, when the men, on either side, in numbers stepped forward and conversed with one another. Then Cleocritus, the Herald of the Initiated,[6] who had a very fine voice, silenced them and said, "Fellow-citizens—Why do you drive us forth? Why would you slay us? What evil have we wrought you at any time? We have shared with you in the most solemn rites and sacrifices, and in festivals of the fairest: we have been companions in the chorus, the school, the army. We have braved a thousand dangers with you by land and sea in behalf of our common safety, our common liberty. By the gods of our fathers, by the gods of our mothers, by the hallowed names of kinship, intermarriage, comradeship, those three bonds which many of us share, bow in reverence before god and man, and cease to sin against the land of our fathers: cease to obey these most unhallowed Thirty, who for the sake of private gain have in eight months slain almost more men than the Peloponnesians together in ten years of warfare. See, we have it in our power to live as citizens in peace; it is only these men, who lay upon us this most foul burden, this hideous horror of fratricidal war, loathed of god and man. Ah, be well assured, for these men slain by our hands this day, you are not the sole mourners. There are among them some whose deaths have wrung from us also many a bitter tear."

So he spoke, but the officers and leaders of the defeated army who were left, unwilling that their troops should listen to such topics at that moment, led them back to the city. But the next day the Thirty, in deep down-heartedness and desolation, sat in the council chamber. The Three Thousand, wherever their several divisions were posted, were everywhere a prey to discord. Those who were implicated in deeds of vio-

[6] *I.e.* of the Eleusinian mysteries. He had not only a loud voice, but a big body. Cf. Aristoph. *Frogs*, 1237.

lence, and whose fears could not sleep, protested violently against yielding to the party in Piraeus. Those on the other hand who had faith in their own innocence, argued in their own minds, and tried to convince their neighbours that they could well dispense with most of their present evils. "Why yield obedience to these Thirty?" they asked, "Why assign to them the privilege of destroying the State?" In the end they voted a resolution to depose the government, and to elect another. This was a board of ten, elected one from each tribe.

As to the Thirty, they retired to Eleusis; but the Ten, assisted by the cavalry officers, had enough to do to keep watch over the men in the city, whose anarchy and mutual distrust were rampant. The Knights did not return to quarters at night, but slept out in the Odeum, keeping their horses and shields close beside them; indeed the distrust was so great that from evening onwards they patrolled the walls on foot with their shields, and at break of day mounted their horses, at every moment fearing some sudden attack upon them by the men in Piraeus. These latter were now so numerous, and of so mixed a company, that it was difficult to find arms for all. Some had to be content with shields of wood, others of wicker-work, which they spent their time in coating with whitening. Before ten days had elapsed guarantees were given, securing equality of taxation to all, even foreigners, who would take part in the fighting. Thus they were presently able to take the field, with large detachments both of heavy infantry and light-armed troops, besides a division of cavalry, about seventy in number. Their system was to push forward foraging parties in quest of wood and fruits, returning at nightfall to Piraeus. Of the city party no one ventured to take the field under arms; only, from time to time, the cavalry would capture stray pillagers from Piraeus or inflict some damage on the main body of their opponents. Once they fell in with a party belonging to the deme Aexone, marching to their own farms in search of provisions. These, in spite of many prayers for mercy and the strong disapprobation of many of the knights, were slaughtered by Lysimachus, the general of cavalry. The men of Piraeus retaliated by putting to death a horseman, named Callistratus, of the tribe Leontis, whom they captured in the country. Indeed their courage ran so high at present that they even meditated an assault upon the city walls. And here perhaps the reader will pardon the record of a device on the part of the city engineer, who, aware of the enemy's intention to advance his batteries along the racecourse, which slopes from the Lyceum, had all the carts and waggons which were to be found laden with blocks of stone, each one a cartload in itself, and so had them dropped at random on the course. The annoyance created by these separate blocks of stone was considerable.

The Thirty despatched one set of ambassadors from Eleusis to Lacedaemon, while another set representing the government of the city, that is to say the men on the list, was despatched to summon the Lacedaemonians to their aid, on the plea that the people had revolted from Sparta. At Sparta, Lysander taking into account the possibility of speedily reducing the party in Piraeus by blockading them by land and sea, and so cutting them off from all supplies, supported the application, and negotiated the loan of 100 talents to his clients, backed by the appointment of himself as governor on land, and of his brother, Libys, as admiral of the fleet. And so proceeding to the scene of action at Eleusis, he got together a large body of Peloponnesian hoplites, whilst his brother, the admiral, kept guard by sea to prevent the importation of supplies into Piraeus by water. Thus the men in Piraeus were soon again reduced to their former helplessness, while the ardour of the city folk rose to a proportionally high pitch under the auspices of Lysander.

Things were progressing after this sort when King Pausanias intervened. Touched by a certain envy of Lysander (who seemed, by a final stroke of achievement, about to reach the pinnacle of popularity, with Athens as his own) the king persuaded three of the ephors to support him, and forthwith led out an army. With him marched contingents of all the allied states, except the Boeotians and Corinthians. These maintained, that to undertake such an expedition against the Athenians, in whose conduct they saw nothing contrary to the treaty, was inconsistent with their oaths. But they did this because they thought the Lacedaemonians wished to make the soil of the Athenians their own. Pausanias encamped on the Halipedon, as the sandy flat is called, with his right wing resting on Piraeus, and Lysander and his mercenaries forming the left. His first act was to send an embassage to the party in Piraeus, calling upon them to retire peaceably to their homes; when they refused to obey, he made, as far as mere noise went, the semblance of an attack, with sufficient show of fight to prevent his kindly disposition being too apparent. But gaining nothing by the feint, he was forced to retire. Next day he took two Laconian regiments, with three tribes of Athenian horse, and crossed over to the Mute Harbour, examining the lie of the ground to discover how and where it would be easiest to draw lines of circumvallation round Piraeus. As he turned his back to retire, a party of the enemy sallied out and caused him annoyance. Angered, he ordered the cavalry to charge at the gallop, supported by the younger infantry, while he himself, with the rest of the troops, followed close, holding quietly back in reserve. They cut down about thirty of the enemy's light troops and pursued the rest hotly to the theatre in Piraeus. Here, as chance would have it, the whole light and heavy infantry of the

Piraeus men were getting under arms; and in an instant their light troops rushed out and dashed at the assailants; thick and fast flew missiles of all sorts—javelins, arrows, and sling stones. The Lacedaemonians finding the number of their wounded increasing every minute, and hard pressed, slowly fell back step by step, facing their opponents. These meanwhile resolutely pressed on. Here fell Chaeron and Thibrachus, both polemarchs, here also Lacrates, an Olympic victor, and other Lacedaemonians, all of whom now lie buried before the city gates in the Ceramicus.

Watching how matters went, Thrasybulus began his advance with the whole of his heavy infantry to support his light troops and quickly fell into line eight deep, acting as a screen to the rest of his troops. Pausanias, on his side, had retired, sorely pressed, about half a mile towards a bit of rising ground, where he sent orders to the Lacedaemonian and the other allied troops to bring up reinforcements. Here, on this slope, he reformed his troops, giving his phalanx the full depth, and advanced against the Athenians, who did not hesitate to receive him at close quarters, but presently had to give way; one portion being forced into the mud and clay at Halae, while the others wavered and broke their line; 150 of them were left dead on the field, whereupon Pausanias set up a trophy and retired. Not even so, were his feelings embittered against his adversary. On the contrary he sent secretly and instructed the men of Piraeus, what sort of terms they should propose to himself and the ephors in attendance. To this advice they listened. He also fostered a division in the party within the city. He ordered a deputation, as large as possible, to seek an audience of him and the ephors and to say that they had no desire or occasion to look upon the men of Piraeus as enemies; they would prefer a general reconciliation and the friendship of both sides with Lacedaemon. Nauclidas also was pleased to hear this. He was present as ephor, in accordance with the custom which obliges two members of that board to serve on all military expeditions with the king, and with his colleague shared the political views represented by Pausanias, rather than those of Lysander and his party. Thus the authorities were quite ready to despatch to Lacedaemon the representatives of Piraeus, carrying their terms of truce with the Lacedaemonians, as also two private individuals belonging to the city party, whose names were Cephisophon and Meletus. This double deputation, however, had no sooner set out to Lacedaemon than the *de facto* government of the city followed suit, by sending a third set of representatives to state on their behalf: that they were prepared to deliver up themselves and the fortifications in their possession to the Lacedaemonians, to do with them what they liked. "Are the men of Piraeus," they asked, "prepared to surrender Piraeus and Munychia in the same way? If they are sincere in their profession of friendship to Lacedaemon, they ought to do so." The ephors and the members of assembly at Sparta gave audience to these several parties, and sent out fifteen commissioners to Athens empowered, in conjunction with Pausanias, to discover the best settlement possible. The terms arrived at were that a general peace between the rival parties should be established, liberty to return to their own homes being granted to all, with the exception of the Thirty, the Eleven, and the Ten who had been governors in Piraeus; but a proviso was added, enabling any of the city party who feared to remain at Athens to find a home in Eleusis.

And now that everything was happily concluded, Pausanias disbanded his army, and the men from Piraeus marched up under arms into the Acropolis and offered sacrifice to Athena. When they were come down, the generals called a meeting of the Assembly, and Thrasybulus made a speech in which, addressing the city party, he said, "Men of the city, I have one piece of advice; it is that you should learn to know yourselves, and towards the attainment of that self-knowledge I would have you make a careful computation of your good qualities and satisfy yourselves on the strength of which of these it is that you claim to rule over us. Is it that you are more just than ourselves? Yet the people, who are poorer—have never wronged you for the purposes of plunder; but you, whose wealth would outweigh the whole of ours, have wrought many a shameful deed for the sake of gain. If, then, you have no monopoly of justice, can it be on the score of courage that you are warranted to hold your heads so high? If so, what fairer test of courage will you propose than the arbitrament of war—the war just ended? Or do you claim superiority of intelligence?—you, who with all your wealth of arms and walls, money and Peloponnesian allies, have been defeated by men who had none of those things to aid them! Or is it on these Laconian friends of yours that you pride yourselves? What! when these same friends have dealt by you as men deal by vicious dogs. You know how that is. They put a heavy collar round the neck of the brutes and hand them over muzzled to their masters. So too have the Lacedaemonians handed you over to the people, this very people whom you have injured; and now they have turned their backs and are gone. But" (turning to the mass) "do not misconceive me. It is not for me to beg of you, in no respect to violate your solemn oaths. I go further; I beg you, to crown your list of exploits by one final display of virtue. Show the world that you can be faithful to your oaths, and flawless in your conduct." By these and other kindred arguments he impressed upon them that there was no need for anarchy or disorder, seeing that there were the ancient laws ready for use. And so he broke up the assembly.

At this auspicious moment, then, they reappointed the several magistrates; the constitution began to work afresh, and civic life was recommenced. At a subsequent period,[7] on receiving information that the party at Eleusis were collecting a body of mercenaries, they marched out with their whole force against them, and put to death their generals, who came out to parley. These removed, they introduced to the others their friends and connections, and so persuaded them to come to terms and be reconciled. The oath they bound themselves by consisted of a simple asseveration: "We will remember past offences no more;" and to this day the two parties live amicably together as good citizens, and the democracy is steadfast to its oaths.

[7] 401 B.C.

BOOK III

1. Thus the civil strife at Athens had an end. At a subsequent date Cyrus sent messengers to Lacedaemon, claiming requital in kind for the service which he had lately rendered in the war with Athens. The demand seemed to the ephorate just and reasonable. Accordingly they ordered Samius, who was admiral at the time, to put himself at the disposition of Cyrus for any service which he might require. Samius himself needed no persuasion to carry out the wishes of Cyrus. With his own fleet, accompanied by that of Cyrus, he sailed round to Cilicia, and so made it impossible for Syennesis, the ruler of that province, to oppose Cyrus by land in his advance against the king his brother.

The particulars of the expedition are to be found in the pages of the Syracusan Themistogenes,[1] who describes the mustering of the armament, and the advance of Cyrus at the head of his troops; and then the battle, and death of Cyrus himself, and the consequent retreat of the Hellenes while effecting their escape to the sea.[2]

It was in recognition of the service which he had rendered in this affair, that Tissaphernes was despatched to Lower Asia by the king his master. He came as satrap, not only of his own provinces, but of those which had belonged to Cyrus; and he at once demanded the absolute submission of the Ionic cities, without exception, to his authority. These communities, partly from a desire to maintain their freedom, and partly from fear of Tissaphernes himself, whom they had rejected in favour of Cyrus during the lifetime of that prince, refused to admit the satrap within their gates. They thought it better to send an embassy to the Lacedaemonians, calling upon them as representatives and leaders of the Hellenic world to look to the interests of their petitioners, who were Hellenes also, albeit they lived in Asia, and not to suffer their country to be ravaged and themselves enslaved.

In answer to this appeal, the Lacedaemonians sent out Thibron as governor, providing him with a body of troops, consisting of 1,000 enfranchised Helots and 4,000 Peloponnesians. In addition to these, Thibron himself applied to the Athenians for a detachment of 300 horse, for whose service-money he would hold himself responsible. The Athe-

---

[1] Themistogenes is apparently the pseudonym under which Xenophon published his *Anabasis*.
[2] At Trapezus, 10 March, 400 B.C.

nians in answer sent him some of the knights who had served under the Thirty, thinking that the people of Athens would be well rid of them if they went abroad and perished there.

On their arrival in Asia, Thibron further collected contingents from the Hellenic cities on the continent; for at this time the word of a Lacedaemonian was law. He had only to command, and every city must needs obey. But although he had this armament, Thibron, when he saw the cavalry, had no mind to descend into the plain. If he succeeded in protecting from pillage the particular district in which he chanced to be, he was quite content. It was only when the troops who had taken part in the expedition of Cyrus had joined him on their safe return, that he assumed a bolder attitude. He was now ready to confront Tissaphernes, army against army, on the level ground, and won over a number of cities. Pergamum came in of her own accord. So did Teuthrania and Halisarna. These were under the government of Eurysthenes and Procles, the descendants of Demaratus the Lacedaemonian, who in days of old had received this territory as a gift from the Persian monarch in return for his share in the campaign against Hellas. Gorgion and Gongylus, two brothers, also gave in their adhesion; they were lords, the one of Gambreum and Palae-Gambreum, the other of Myrina and Gryneum, four cities which, like those above named, had originally been gifts from the king to an earlier Gongylus—the sole Eretrian who joined the Mede, and in consequence was banished. Other cities which were too weak to resist, Thibron took by force of arms. In the case of one he was not so successful. This was the Egyptian Larisa, as it is called, which refused to capitulate, and was forthwith invested and subjected to a regular siege. When all other attempts to take it failed, he set about digging a tank, and in connection with the tank an underground channel, by means of which he proposed to draw off the water supply of the inhabitants. In this he was baffled by frequent sallies of the besieged, and a continual discharge of timber and stones into the cutting. He retaliated by the construction of a wooden shed which he erected over the tank; but once more the shed was burnt in a successful night attack on the part of the men of Larisa. These ineffectual efforts induced the ephors to send a despatch bidding Thibron give up Larisa and march upon Caria.

He had already reached Ephesus, and was on the point of marching into Caria, when Dercylidas arrived to take command of his army. The new general was a man whose genius for invention had won him the nickname of Sisyphus. Thus it was that Thibron returned home, where on his arrival he was fined and banished, the allies accusing him of allowing his troops to plunder their friends.

Dercylidas was not slow to perceive and turn to account the jealousy which subsisted between Tissaphernes and Pharnabazus. Coming to terms with the former, he marched into the territory of the latter, preferring, as he said, to be at war with one of the pair at a time, rather than the two together. His hostility, indeed, to Pharnabazus was an old story, dating back to a period during the naval command of Lysander, when he was himself governor in Abydos; where, thanks to Pharnabazus, he had got into trouble with his superior officer, and had been made to stand with his shield on his arm—a stigma on his honour which no true Lacedaemonian would forgive, since this is the punishment of insubordination. For this reason, doubtless, Dercylidas had the greater satisfaction in marching against Pharnabazus. From the moment he assumed command there was a marked difference for the better between his methods and those of his predecessor. Thus he contrived to conduct his troops into that portion of the Aeolid which belonged to Pharnabazus, through the heart of a friendly territory without injury to the allies.

This district of Aeolis belonged to Pharnabazus, but had been held as a satrapy under him by a Dardanian named Zenis while he was alive; but when Zenis fell sick and died, Pharnabazus made preparation to give the satrapy to another. Then Mania the wife of Zenis, herself also a Dardanian, fitted out an expedition, and taking with her gifts wherewith to make a present to Pharnabazus himself, and to gratify his concubines and those whose power was greatest with Pharnabazus, set forth on her journey. When she had obtained audience of him she spoke as follows, "O Pharnabazus, you know that your servant my husband was in all respects friendly to you; moreover, he paid you the tributes which were your due, so that you praised and honoured him. Now therefore, if I serve you as faithfully as my husband, why need you appoint another satrap? If in any matter I please you not, is it not in your power to take from me the government on that day, and to give it to another?" When he had heard her words, Pharnabazus decided that the woman ought to be satrap. She, as soon as she was mistress of the territory, never ceased to render the tribute in due season, even as her husband before her had done. Moreover, whenever she came to the court of Pharnabazus she brought him gifts continually, and whenever Pharnabazus went down to visit her provinces she welcomed him with all fair and courteous entertainment beyond what his other viceroys were wont to do. The cities also which had been left to her by her husband, she guarded safely for him; while of those cities that owed her no allegiance, she acquired, on the seaboard, Larisa and Hamaxitus and Colonae—attacking their walls by aid of Hellenic mercenaries, while she

herself sat in her carriage and watched the spectacle. Nor was she sparing of her gifts to those who won her admiration; and thus she furnished herself with a mercenary force of exceptional splendour. She also
went with Pharnabazus on his campaigns, even when, on pretext of some
injury done to the king's territory, Mysians or Pisidians were the object
of attack. In requital, Pharnabazus paid her magnificent honour, and at
times invited her to assist him with her counsel.

Now when Mania was more than forty years old, the husband of her
own daughter, Meidias—flustered by the suggestions of certain people
who said that it was monstrous a woman should rule and he remain a
private person—found his way into her presence, as the story goes, and
strangled her. For Mania, albeit she carefully guarded herself against
all ordinary comers, as was proper in the exercise of her tyranny, trusted
in Meidias, and, as a woman might her own son-in-law, was ready to
greet him at all times with open arms. He also murdered her son, a youth
of marvellous beauty, who was about seventeen years of age. He next
seized upon the strong cities of Scepsis and Gergithes, in which lay for
the most part the property and wealth of Mania. As for the other cities
of the satrapy, they would not receive the usurper, their garrisons keeping them safely for Pharnabazus. Thereupon Meidias sent gifts to
Pharnabazus, and claimed to hold the district even as Mania had held
it; to whom the other answered, "Keep your gifts and guard them safely
till that day when I shall come in person and take both you and them
together," adding, "What care I to live longer if I avenge not myself
for the murder of Mania!"

Just at the critical moment Dercylidas arrived, and in a single day
received the adhesion of the three seaboard cities Larisa, Hamaxitus, and
Colonae—which threw upon their gates to him. Then he sent messengers
to the cities of the Aeolid also, offering them freedom if they would receive him within their walls and become allies. Accordingly the men of
Neandria and Ilium and Cocylium lent willing ears; for since the death
of Mania their Hellenic garrisons had been treated but ill. But the commander of the garrison in Cebrene, a place of some strength, bethink-
ing him that if he should succeed in guarding that city for Pharnabazus,
he would receive honour at his hands, refused to admit Dercylidas.
Whereupon the latter, in a rage, prepared to take the place by force;
but when he came to sacrifice, on the first day the victims would not
yield good omens; on the second, and again upon the third day, it was
the same story. Thus for as many as four days he persevered in sacrificing, cherishing wrath the while—for he was in haste to become master of the whole Aeolid before Pharnabazus came to the rescue of the
district.

Meanwhile a certain Sicyonian captain, Athenadas by name, said to himself, "Dercylidas does but trifle to waste his time here, while I with my own hand can draw off their water from the men of Cebrene"; wherewith he ran forward with his division and essayed to choke up the spring which supplied the city. But the garrison sallied out and covered the Sicyonian himself with wounds, besides killing two of his men. Indeed, they plied their swords and missiles with such good effect that the whole company was forced to beat a retreat. Dercylidas was not a little annoyed, thinking that now the spirit of the besiegers would certainly die away; but while he was in this mood, there arrived from the beleaguered fortress emissaries of the Hellenes, who stated that the action taken by the commandant was not to their taste; for themselves, they would far rather be joined in bonds of fellowship with Hellenes than with barbarians. While the matter was still under discussion there came a messenger also from the commandant, to say that whatever the former deputation had proposed he, on his side, was ready to endorse. Accordingly Dercylidas, who, it so happened, had at length obtained favourable omens on that day, marched his force without more ado up to the gates of the city, which were flung open by those within; and so he entered. Here, then, he established a garrison, and advanced at once upon Scepsis and Gergithes.

And now Meidias, partly expecting the hostile advance of Pharnabazus, and partly mistrusting the citizens, sent to Dercylidas, proposing to meet him in conference provided he might take security of hostages. In answer to this suggestion the other sent him one man from each of the cities of the allies, and bade him take his pick of these, whichsoever and how many soever he chose, as hostages for his own security. Meidias selected ten, and so went out. In conversation with Dercylidas, he asked him on what terms he would accept his alliance. The other answered, "The terms are that you grant the citizens freedom and self-government." The words were scarcely out of his mouth before he began marching upon Scepsis. Whereupon Meidias, perceiving it was vain to hinder him in the teeth of the citizens, allowed him to enter. That done, Dercylidas offered sacrifice to Athena in the citadel of the Scepsians, turned out the bodyguards of Meidias, and handed over the city to the citizens. And so, having admonished them to regulate their civic life as Hellenes and free men ought, he left the place and continued his advance against Gergithes. On this last march he was escorted by many of the Scepsians themselves; such was the honour they paid him and so great their satisfaction at his exploits. Meidias also followed close at his side, petitioning that he would hand over the city of the Gergithians to himself. To whom Dercylidas only made reply, that

he should not fail to obtain any of his just rights. And while the words
were yet upon his lips he was drawing close to the gates, with Meidias
at his side. Behind him followed the troops, marching two and two in
peaceful fashion. The defenders of Gergithes from their towers—which
were extraordinarily high—espied Meidias in company of the Spartan,
and abstained from shooting. And Dercylidas said, "Bid them open
the gates, Meidias, when you shall lead the way, and I will enter the
temple along with you and do sacrifice to Athena." And Meidias, though
he shrank from opening the gates, yet in terror of finding himself suddenly seized, gave the order to open the gates. As soon as he was entered in, the Spartan, still taking Meidias with him, marched up to the
citadel and there ordered the main body of his soldiers to take up their
position round the walls, while he with those about him did sacrifice to
Athena. When the sacrifice was ended he ordered Meidias's bodyguard
to pile arms in the van of his troops. Here for the future they would
serve as mercenaries, since Meidias their former master stood no longer
in need of their protection. The latter, being at his wits' end what to do,
exclaimed, "Look you, I will now leave you; I go to make preparation
for my guest." But the other replied, "Heaven forbid! Ill were it that
I who have offered sacrifice should be treated as a guest by you. I
rather should be the entertainer and you the guest. Pray stay with us,
and while the supper is preparing, you and I can consider our obligations, and perform them."

When they were seated Dercylidas put certain questions, "Tell me,
Meidias, did your father leave you heir to his estates?" "Certainly he
did," answered the other. "And how many dwelling-houses have you?
What landed estates? How much pasturage?" The other began running
off an inventory, while some of the Scepsians who were present kept
interposing, "He is lying to you, Dercylidas." "Nay, you take too minute
a view of matters," replied the Spartan. When the inventory of the paternal property was completed, he proceeded, "Tell me, Meidias, to
whom did Mania belong?" A chorus of voices rejoined, "To Pharnabazus." "Then her property must have belonged to Pharnabazus too."
"Certainly," they answered. "Then it must now be ours," he remarked,
"by right of conquest, since Pharnabazus is at war with us. Will some
one of you escort me to the place where the property of Mania and
Pharnabazus lies?" So the rest led the way to the dwelling-place of
Mania which Meidias had taken from her, and Meidias followed too.
When he was entered, Dercylidas summoned the stewards, and bidding
his attendants seize them, gave them to understand that, if detected
stealing anything which belonged to Mania, they would lose their heads
on the spot. The stewards proceeded to point out the treasures, and he,

when he had looked through the whole store, bolted and barred the doors, affixing his seal and setting a watch. As he went out he found at the doors certain of the generals and captains, and said to them, "Here, sirs, we have pay ready made for the army—nearly a year's pay for 8,000 men—and if we can win anything besides, there will be so much the more." This he said, knowing that those who heard it would be all the more amenable to discipline, and would yield him a more flattering obedience. Then Meidias asked, "And where am I to live, Dercylidas?" "Where you have the very best right to live," replied the other, "in your native town of Scepsis, and in your father's house."

2. Such were the exploits of Dercylidas: nine cities taken in eight days. Two considerations now began to occupy his mind: how was he to avoid falling into the fatal error of Thibron and becoming a burden to his allies, while wintering in a friendly country? How, again, was he to prevent Pharnabazus from overriding the Hellenic states in pure contempt with his cavalry? Accordingly he sent to Pharnabazus and put it to him point-blank, "Which will you have, peace or war?" Whereupon Pharnabazus, who could not but perceive that the whole Aeolid had now been converted practically into a fortified base of operations, which threatened his own homestead of Phrygia, chose peace.

This being so, Dercylidas advanced into Bithynian Thrace, and there spent the winter; nor did Pharnabazus exhibit a shadow of annoyance, since the Bithynians were perpetually at war with himself. For the most part, Dercylidas continued to harry Bithynia in perfect security, and found provisions without stint. Presently he was joined from the other side of the straits by some Odrysian allies sent by Seuthes; they numbered 200 horse and 300 peltasts. These fellows pitched upon a site a little more than a couple of miles from the Hellenic force, where they entrenched themselves; then having got from Dercylidas some heavy infantry soldiers to act as guards of their encampment, they devoted themselves to plundering, and succeeded in capturing an ample store of slaves and other wealth. Presently their camp was full of prisoners, when one morning the Bithynians, having ascertained the actual numbers of the marauding parties as well as of the Hellenes left as guards behind, collected in large masses of light troops and cavalry, and attacked the garrison, who were not more than 200 strong. As soon as they came close enough, they began discharging spears and other missiles on the little body, who on their side continued to be wounded and shot down, but were quite unable to retaliate, cooped up as they were within a palisading barely six feet high, until in desperation they tore down their defences with their own hands, and dashed at the enemy. These had nothing to do but to draw back from the point of egress, and being light troops easily escaped beyond the grasp of heavy-armed men, while ever and again, from one point of vantage or another, they poured their shower of javelins, and at every sally laid many a man low, till at length, like sheep penned in a fold, the defenders were shot down almost to a man. A remnant, it is true, did escape, consisting of some fifteen who, seeing the turn affairs were taking, had already made off in the middle of the fighting. Slipping away, to the small concern of the Bithynians, they reached the main Hellenic camp in safety. The Bithynians, satisfied with their achievement, part of which consisted in cutting down the tent guards of the Odrysian Thracians and recovering all their prisoners, made off without delay; so that by the time the Hellenes got wind of the affair and rallied to the rescue, they found nothing left in the camp save only the stripped corpses of the slain. When the Odrysians themselves returned, they fell to burying their own dead, drinking quantities of wine in their honour and holding horse-races; but for the future they deemed it advisable to camp along with the Hellenes. Thus they harried and burned Bithynia the winter through.

With the commencement of spring Dercylidas turned his back upon the Bithynians and came to Lampsacus. While there, envoys reached him from the home authorities. These were Aracus, Naubates, and Antisthenes. They were sent to inquire generally into the condition of affairs in Asia, and to inform Dercylidas of the extension of his office for another year. They had been further commissioned by the ephors to summon a meeting of the soldiers and inform them that the ephors held them to blame for their former doings, though for their present avoidance of evil conduct they must needs praise them; and for the future they must understand that while no repetition of misdoing would be tolerated, all just and upright dealing by the allies would receive praise. The soldiers were therefore summoned, and the envoys delivered their message, to which the leader of the Cyreians[3] answered, "Men of Lacedaemon, listen; we are the same to-day as we were last year; only our general of to-day is different from our general in the past. If to-day we have avoided our offence of yesterday, the cause is not far to seek; you may discover it for yourselves."

Aracus and the other envoys shared the hospitality of Dercylidas's tent, and one of the party chanced to mention how they had left an embassy from the men of Chersonese in Lacedaemon. According to their statement, he added, it was impossible for them to till their lands nowadays, so perpetually were they robbed and plundered by the Thracians; whereas the peninsula needed only to be walled across from sea to sea, and there would be abundance of good land to cultivate—enough for

[3] Probably Xenophon himself.

themselves and as many others from Lacedaemon as cared to come. "So that it would not surprise us," continued the envoys, "if a Lacedaemonian were actually sent out from Sparta with a force to carry out the project." Dercylidas kept his ears open but his counsel close, and so sent forward the commissioners to Ephesus. It pleased him to picture their progress through the Hellenic cities, and the spectacle of peace and prosperity which would everywhere greet their eyes. When he knew that his stay was to be prolonged, he sent again to Pharnabazus and offered him once more as an alternative either the prolongation of the winter truce or war. And once again Pharnabazus chose truce. It was thus that Dercylidas was able to leave the cities in the neighbourhood of the satrap in peace and friendship. Crossing the Hellespont himself he brought his army into Europe, and marching through Thrace, which was also friendly, was entertained by Seuthes, and so reached the Chersonese.

This district, he soon discovered, not only contained something like a dozen cities, but was singularly fertile. The soil was of the best, but ruined by the ravages of the Thracians, precisely as he had been told. Accordingly, having measured and found the breadth of the isthmus barely four miles, he no longer hesitated. Having offered sacrifice, he commenced his line of wall, distributing the area to the soldiers in detachments, and promising to award them prizes for their industry—a first prize for the section first completed, and to the rest as each detachment of workers might deserve. By this means the whole wall begun in spring was finished before autumn. Within these lines he established eleven cities, with numerous harbours, abundance of good arable land, and plenty of land under plantation, besides magnificent grazing grounds for sheep and cattle of every kind.

Having finished the work, he crossed back again into Asia, and on a tour of inspection, found the cities for the most part in a thriving condition; but when he came to Atarneus he discovered that certain exiles from Chios had got possession of the stronghold, which served them as a convenient base for pillaging and plundering Ionia; and this, in fact, was their means of livelihood. Being further informed of the large supplies of grain which they had inside, he proceeded to draw entrenchments round the place with a view to a regular investment, and by this means he reduced it in eight months. Then having appointed Draco of Pellene commandant, he stocked the fortress with an abundance of provisions of all sorts, to serve him as a halting-place when he chanced to pass that way, and so withdrew to Ephesus, which is three days' journey from Sardis.

Up to this date peace had been maintained between Tissaphernes and

Dercylidas, as also between the Hellenes and barbarians in those parts. But the time came when an embassy arrived at Lacedaemon from the Ionic cities, protesting that Tissaphernes might, if he chose, leave the Hellenic cities independent. "Our idea," they added, "is, that if Caria, the home of Tissaphernes, felt the pinch of war, the satrap would very soon agree to grant us independence." The ephors, on hearing this, sent a despatch to Dercylidas, and bade him cross the frontier with his army into Caria, while Pharax the admiral coasted round with the fleet. These orders were carried out. Meanwhile a visitor had reached Tissaphernes. This was no less a person than Pharnabazus. His coming was partly owing to the fact that Tissaphernes had been appointed general-in-chief, and partly in order to testify his readiness to make common cause with his brother satrap in fighting and expelling the Hellenes from the king's territory; for if his heart was stirred by jealousy on account of the generalship bestowed upon his rival, he was not the less aggrieved at finding himself robbed of the Aeolid. Tissaphernes, lending willing ears to the proposal, had answered, "First cross over with me into Caria, and then we will take counsel on these matters." But being arrived in Caria, they determined to establish garrisons of some strength in the various fortresses, and so crossed back again into Ionia.

Hearing that the satraps had recrossed the Maeander, Dercylidas grew apprehensive for the district which lay there unprotected. "If Tissaphernes and Pharnabazus," he said to Pharax, "chose to make a descent, they could harry the country right and left." In this mind he followed suit, and recrossed the frontier too. And now as they marched on, preserving no sort of battle order—on the supposition that the enemy had got far ahead of them into the district of Ephesus—suddenly they caught sight of his scouts perched on some monumental structures facing them. To send up scouts into similar edifices and towers on their own side was the work of a few moments, and before them lay revealed the long lines of troops drawn up just where their road lay. These were the Carians, with their white shields, and the whole Persian troops there present, with all the Hellenic contingents belonging to either satrap. Besides these there was a great cloud of cavalry: on the right wing the squadrons of Tissaphernes, and on the left those of Pharnabazus.

Seeing how matters lay, Dercylidas ordered the generals of brigade and captains to form into line as quickly as possible, eight deep, placing the light infantry on the fringe of battle, with the cavalry—such cavalry, that is, and of such numerical strength, as he chanced to have. Meanwhile, as general, he sacrificed. During this interval the troops from Peloponnese kept quiet in preparation as for battle. Not so the troops from Priene and Achilleum, from the islands and the Ionic cities, some of whom left their arms in the corn, which stood thick and deep in the plain of the Maeander, and took to their heels; while those who remained at their posts gave evident signs that their steadiness would not last. Pharnabazus, it was reported, had given orders to engage; but Tissaphernes, who recalled his experience of his own military exploits with the Cyreian army, and assumed that all other Hellenes were of similar mettle, had no desire to engage, but sent to Dercylidas saying, he should be glad to meet him in conference. So Dercylidas, attended by the best of his troops, horse and foot, went forward to meet the envoys. He told them that for his own part he had made his preparations to engage, as they themselves might see, but still, if the satraps were minded to meet him in conference, he had nothing to say against it, "Only, in that case, there must be a mutual exchange of hostages and other pledges."

When this proposal had been agreed to and carried out, the two armies retired for the night—the Asiatics to Tralles in Caria, the Hellenes to Leucophrys, where was a temple of Artemis of great sanctity, and a sandy-bottomed lake more than a furlong in extent, fed by a spring of ever-flowing water fit for drinking and warm. For the moment so much was effected. On the next day they met at the place appointed, and it was agreed that they should mutually ascertain the terms on which either party was willing to make peace. On his side, Dercylidas insisted that the king should grant independence to the Hellenic cities; while Tissaphernes and Pharnabazus demanded the evacuation of the country by the Hellenic army, and the withdrawal of the Lacedaemonian governors from the cities. After this interchange of ideas a truce was entered into, so as to allow time for the reports of the proceedings to be sent by Dercylidas to Lacedaemon, and by Tissaphernes to the king.

While such was the conduct of affairs in Asia under the guidance of Dercylidas, the Lacedaemonians at home were at the same time no less busily employed with other matters. They cherished a long-standing embitterment against the Eleians, the grounds of which were that the Eleians had once[4] contracted an alliance with the Athenians, Argives, and Mantineans; moreover, on pretence of a sentence registered against the Lacedaemonians, they had excluded them from the horse-race and gymnastic contests. Nor was that the sum of their offending. They had taken and scourged Lichas, under the following circumstances: Being a Spartan, he had formally consigned his chariot to the Thebans, and when the Thebans were proclaimed victors he stepped forward to crown his charioteer; whereupon, in spite of his gray hairs, the Eleians put those indignities upon him and expelled him from the festival. Again, at a date subsequent to that occurrence, Agis being sent to offer sacrifice to

---

[4] In 421 B.C.

Olympian Zeus in accordance with the bidding of an oracle, the Eleians would not suffer him to offer prayer for victory in war, asserting that the ancient law and custom forbade Hellenes to consult the god for war with Hellenes; and Agis was forced to go away without offering the sacrifice.

In consequence of all these annoyances the ephors and the Assembly determined to bring the men of Elis to their senses. Thereupon they sent an embassy to that state, announcing that the authorities of Lacedaemon deemed it just and right that they should leave the country townships in the territory of Elis free and independent. This the Eleians flatly refused to do. The cities in question were theirs by right of war. Thereupon the ephors called out the army. The leader of the expedition was Agis. He invaded Elis through Achaia by the Larisus; but the army had hardly set foot on the enemy's soil and the work of devastation begun, when an earthquake took place, and Agis, taking this as a sign from heaven, marched back again out of the country and disbanded his army. Thereat the men of Elis were much more emboldened, and sent embassies to various cities which they knew to be hostile to the Lacedaemonians.

The year was not over before the ephors again called out the army against Elis, and the invading host of Agis was this time swelled by the rest of the allies, including the Athenians; the Boeotians and Corinthians alone excepted. The Spartan king now entered through Aulon, and the men of Lepreum at once revolted from the Eleians and gave in their adhesion to the Spartan, and simultaneously with these the Macistians and their next-door neighbours the Epitalians. As he crossed the river further adhesions followed, on the part of the Letrinians, the Amphidolians, and the Marganians.

Upon this he pushed on into Olympian territory and did sacrifice to Olympian Zeus. There was no attempt to stay his proceedings now. After sacrifice he marched against the capital, devastating and burning the country as he went. Multitudes of cattle, multitudes of slaves, were the fruits of conquest yielded, insomuch that the fame thereof spread, and many more Arcadians and Achaeans flocked to join the standard of the invader and to share in the plunder. In fact, the expedition became one enormous foray. Here was the chance to fill all the granaries of Peloponnese with corn. When he had reached the capital, the beautiful suburbs and gymnasia became a spoil to the troops; but the city itself, though it lay open before him a defenceless and unwalled town, he kept aloof from. He would not, rather than could not, take it. Such was the explanation given. Thus the country was a prey to devastation, and the invaders massed round Cyllene.

Then the friends of a certain Xenias—a man of whom it was said that

he might measure the silver coin inherited from his father by the bushel
—wishing to be the leading instruments in bringing over the state to
Lacedaemon, rushed out of the house, sword in hand, and began a work
of butchery. Amongst other victims they killed a man who strongly resembled the leader of the democratic party, Thrasydaeus. Every one
believed it was really Thrasydaeus who was slain. The popular party
were panic-stricken, and stirred neither hand nor foot. On their side the
cut-throats fondly imagined all was over; and their sympathisers poured
their armed bands into the market-place. But Thrasydaeus was still
asleep where he had gotten drunk. When the people came to discover
that their hero was not dead, they crowded round his house this side
and that, like a swarm of bees clinging to their leader; and as soon as
Thrasydaeus had put himself in the van, with the people at his back, a
battle was fought, and the people won. And those who had laid their
hands to deeds of butchery went as exiles to the Lacedaemonians.

After a while Agis himself retired, recrossing the Alpheus; but he was
careful to leave a garrison in Epitalium near that river, with Lysippus as
governor, and the exiles from Elis along with him. Having so done, he
disbanded his army and returned home himself.

During the rest of the summer and the ensuing winter the territory of
the Eleians was ravaged and ransacked by Lysippus and his troops, until
Thrasydaeus, the following summer, sent to Lacedaemon and agreed
to dismantle the walls of Phea and Cyllene, and to grant autonomy to
the Triphylian townships—together with Phrixa and Epitalium, the
Letrinians, Amphidolians, and Marganians; and besides these to the
Acroreians and to Lasion, a place claimed by the Arcadians. With regard
to Epeium, a town midway between Heraea and Macistus, the Eleians
claimed the right to keep it, on the plea that they had purchased the
whole district from its then owners, for thirty talents, which sum they
had actually paid. But the Lacedaemonians, acting on the principle that
a purchase which forcibly deprives the weaker party of his possession is
no more justifiable than a seizure by violence, compelled them to emancipate Epeium also. From the presidency of the temple of Olympian Zeus,
however, they did not oust them; not that it belonged to Elis of ancient
right, but because the rival claimants, it was felt, were villagers, hardly
equal to the exercise of the presidency. After these concessions, peace
and alliance between the Eleians and the Lacedaemonians were established, and the war between Elis and Sparta ceased.

3. After this Agis came to Delphi and offered as a sacrifice a tenth
of the spoil. On his return journey he fell ill at Heraea—being by this
time an old man—and was carried back to Lacedaemon. He survived

the journey, but being there arrived, death speedily overtook him. He was buried in solemnity beyond the lot of ordinary mortals.

When the holy days of mourning were accomplished, and it was necessary to choose another king, there were rival claimants to the throne. Leotychides claimed it as the son, Agesilaus as the brother, of Agis. Then Leotychides protested, "Yet consider, Agesilaus, the law bids not the king's brother, but the king's son to be king; only if there chance to be no son, in that case shall the brother of the king be king." "Then I should be king." "How so, seeing that I am not dead?" "Because he whom you call your father denied you, saying, 'Leotychides is no son[5] of mine.'" "Nay, but my mother, who would know far better than he, said, and still to-day says, I am." "Nay, but the god himself, Poseidon, laid his finger on thy falsity when by his earthquake he drove forth thy father from the bridal chamber into the light of day; and time, that tells no lies, as the proverb has it, bare witness to the witness of the god; for just ten months from the moment at which he fled and was no more seen within that chamber, you were born." So they reasoned together.

Diopeithes, a great authority upon oracles, supported Leotychides. There was an oracle of Apollo, he urged, which said, "Beware of the lame reign." But Diopeithes was met by Lysander, who in behalf of Agesilaus demurred to this interpretation put upon the language of the god. If they were to beware of a lame reign, it meant not, beware lest a man stumble and halt, but rather, beware of him in whose veins flows not the blood of Heracles; most assuredly the kingdom would halt, and that would be a lame reign in very deed, whensoever the descendants of Heracles should cease to lead the state. Such were the arguments on either side, after hearing which the city chose Agesilaus to be king.

Now Agesilaus had not been seated on the throne one year when, as he sacrificed one of the appointed sacrifices in behalf of the city, the soothsayer warned him, saying, "The gods reveal a conspiracy of the most fearful character." When the king sacrificed a second time, he said, "The aspect of the victims is now even yet more terrible." When he had sacrificed for the third time, the soothsayer exclaimed, "O Agesilaus, the sign is given to me, even as though we were in the very midst of the enemy." Thereupon they sacrificed to the deities who avert evil and work salvation, and so barely obtained good omens and ceased sacrificing. Nor had five days elapsed after the sacrifices were ended, ere one came bringing information to the ephors of a conspiracy, and named Cinadon as the ringleader, a young man robust of body as of soul, but not one of the peers. Accordingly the ephors questioned their informant,

[5] Alcibiades was reputedly the father of Leotychides.

"How say you the occurrence is to take place?" He who gave the information answered, "Cinadon took me to the limit of the market-place, and bade me count how many Spartans there were in the market-place; and I counted—king, and ephors, and elders, and others—maybe forty. 'But tell me, Cinadon,' I said to him, 'why have you bidden me count them?' and he answered me, 'Those men, I would have you know, are your sworn foes; and all those others, more than 4,000, congregated there are your natural allies.' Then he took and showed me in the streets, here one and there two of our enemies, as we chanced to come across them, and all the rest our natural allies; and so again running through the list of Spartans to be found in the country districts, he still kept harping on that string, 'Look you, on each estate one foeman—the master—and all the rest allies.' " The ephors asked, "How many do you reckon are in the secret of this matter?" The informant answered, "On that point also he gave me to understand that there were by no means many in their secret who were prime movers of the affair, but those few to be depended on. 'And to make up,' said he, 'we ourselves are in their secret, all the rest of them—Helots, enfranchised, inferiors, provincials, one and all. Note their demeanour when Spartans chance to be the topic of their talk. Not one of them can conceal the delight it would give him if he might eat up every Spartan raw.' " Then, as the inquiry went on, the question came, "And where did they propose to find arms?" The answer followed, "He explained that those of us, of course, who are enrolled in regiments have arms of our own already, and as for the mass —he led the way to the war foundry, and showed me scores and scores of knives, of swords, of spits, hatchets, and axes, and reaping-hooks. 'Anything or everything,' he told me, 'which men use to delve in earth, cut timber, or quarry stone, would serve our purpose; nay, the instruments used for other arts would in nine cases out of ten furnish weapons enough and to spare, especially in dealing with unarmed antagonists.' " Once more being asked what time the affair was to come off, he replied his orders were not to leave the city.

As the result of their inquiry the ephors were persuaded that the man's statements were based upon things he had really seen, and they were so alarmed that they did not even venture to summon the Little Assembly, as it was named; but holding informal meetings among themselves —a few senators here and a few there—they determined to send Cinadon and others of the young men to Aulon, with instructions to apprehend certain of the inhabitants and Helots, whose names were written on the scytale. He had further instructions to capture another resident in Aulon; this was a woman, the most beautiful in the place—supposed to be the arch-corruptress of all Lacedaemonians, young and old, who vis-

ited Aulon. It was not the first mission of the sort on which Cinadon
had been employed by the ephors. It was natural, therefore, that the
ephors should entrust him with the scytale on which the names of the
suspects were inscribed; and in answer to his inquiry which of the young
men he was to take with him, they said, "Go and order the eldest of the
commanders of horse to let you have six or seven who chance to be
there." But they had taken care to let the commander know whom he
was to send, and that those sent should also know that their business
was to capture Cinadon. Further, the authorities instructed Cinadon
that they would send three waggons to save bringing back his captives
on foot—concealing as deeply as possible the fact that he, and he alone,
was the object of the mission. Their reason for not securing him in the
city was that they did not really know the extent of the mischief; and
they wished, in the first instance, to learn from Cinadon who his accomplices were before these latter could discover they were informed against
and effect their escape. His captors were to secure him first, and having
learned from him the names of his confederates, to write them down
and send them as quickly as possible to the ephors. The ephors, indeed,
were so much concerned about the whole occurrence that they further
sent a company of cavalry to assist those going to Aulon. As soon as the
capture was effected, and one of the horsemen was back with the list
of names taken down on the information of Cinadon, they lost no time
in apprehending the soothsayer Tisamenus and the rest who were the
principals in the conspiracy. When Cinadon himself was brought back
and cross-examined, and had made a full confession of the whole plot,
his plans, and his accomplices, they put to him one final question, "What
was your object in undertaking this business?" He answered, "I wished
to be inferior to no man in Lacedaemon." Let that be as it might, his
fate was to be taken out forthwith in irons, just as he was, and to be
placed with his two hands and his neck in the collar, and so under
scourge and goad to be driven, himself and his accomplices, round the
city. Thus upon the heads of those was visited the penalty of their
offences.

4. It was after the incidents just recorded that a Syracusan named
Herodas brought news to Lacedaemon. He had chanced to be in Phoenicia with a certain shipowner, and was struck by the number of Phoenician triremes which he observed, some coming into harbour from other
ports, others already there with their ships' companies complete, while
others again were still completing their equipments. Nor was it only
what he saw, but he had heard say further that there were to be 300
of these vessels all told; whereupon he had taken passage home on
the first sailing ship bound for Hellas. He was in haste to lay this in-

formation before the Lacedaemonians, feeling sure that the king and Tissaphernes were concerned in these preparations—though where the fleet was to act, or against whom, he would not venture to predict.

These reports threw the Lacedaemonians into a flutter of expectation and anxiety. They summoned a meeting of the allies, and began to deliberate as to what ought to be done. Lysander, convinced of the enormous superiority of the Hellenic navy, and with regard to land forces drawing an obvious inference from the safe return of the troops with Cyrus, persuaded Agesilaus to undertake a campaign into Asia, provided the authorities would furnish him with thirty Spartans, 2,000 of the enfranchised Helots, and contingents of the allies amounting to 6,000 men. Apart from these calculations, Lysander had a personal object: he wished to accompany the king himself, and by his aid to re-establish the decarchies originally set up by himself in the different cities, but at a later date expelled through the action of the ephors, who had issued a proclamation re-establishing the old order of constitution.

To this offer on the part of Agesilaus to undertake such an expedition the Lacedaemonians responded by presenting him with all he asked for, and six months' provisions besides. When the hour of departure came he offered all such sacrifices as are necessary, and lastly those before crossing the border, and so set out. This done, he despatched to the several states messengers with directions as to the numbers to be sent from each, and the points of rendezvous; but for himself he was minded to go and do sacrifice at Aulis, even as Agamemnon had offered sacrifice in that place ere he set sail for Troy. But when he had reached the place and had begun to sacrifice, the Boeotarchs, being apprised of his design, sent a body of cavalry and bade him desist from further sacrificing; and lighting upon victims already offered, they hurled them from off the altars, scattering the fragments. Then Agesilaus, calling the gods to witness, got on board his trireme in bitter indignation, and sailed away. Arrived at Geraestus, he there collected as large a portion of his troops as possible, and sailed for Ephesus.

When he had reached that city the first move was made by Tissaphernes, who sent asking, "With what purpose he was come thither?" And the Spartan king answered, "With the intention that the cities in Asia shall be independent even as are the cities in our quarter of Hellas." In answer to this Tissaphernes said, "If you on your part choose to make a truce while I send ambassadors to the king, I think you may well arrange the matter, and sail back home again, if so you will." "Willing enough should I be," replied Agesilaus, "were I not persuaded that you are cheating me." "Nay, but it is open to you," replied the satrap, "to exact a surety for the execution of the terms . . . 'Provided always that you, Tissaphernes, carry out what you say without deceit, we on our side will abstain from injuring your dominion in any respect whatever during the truce.' " Accordingly in the presence of three commissioners —Herippidas, Dercylidas, and Megillus—Tissaphernes took an oath in the words prescribed, "Verily and indeed, I will effect peace honestly and without guile." To which the commissioners, on behalf of Agesilaus, swore a counter-oath, "Verily and indeed, provided Tissaphernes so acts, we on our side will observe the truce."

Tissaphernes at once gave the lie to what he had sworn. Instead of adhering to peace he sent up to demand a large army from the king, in addition to that which he already had. But Agesilaus, though he was fully alive to these proceedings, adhered as rigidly as ever to the truce.

To keep quiet and enjoy leisure was his duty, in the exercise of which he wore away the time at Ephesus. But in reference to the organisation of the several states it was a season of vehement constitutional disturbance in the several cities; that is to say, there were neither democracies as in the old days of the Athenians, nor yet were there decarchies as in the days of Lysander. But here was Lysander back again. Every one recognised him, and flocked to him with petitions for one favour or another, which he was to obtain for them from Agesilaus. A crowd of suitors danced attendance on his heels, and formed so conspicuous a retinue that Agesilaus, any one would have supposed, was the private person and Lysander the king. All this was maddening to Agesilaus, as was presently plain. As to the rest of the Thirty, jealousy did not suffer them to keep silence, and they put it plainly to Agesilaus that the super-regal splendour in which Lysander lived was a violation of the constitution. So when Lysander took upon himself to introduce some of his petitioners to Agesilaus, the latter turned them a deaf ear. Their being aided and abetted by Lysander was sufficient; he sent them away discomfited. At length, as time after time things turned out contrary to his wishes, Lysander himself perceived the position of affairs. He now no longer suffered that crowd to follow him, and gave those who asked his help in anything plainly to understand they would gain nothing, but rather be losers, by his intervention. But being bitterly annoyed at the degradation put upon him, he came to the king and said to him, "Ah, Agesilaus, how well you know the art of humbling your friends!" "Ay, indeed," the king replied, "those of them whose one idea it is to appear greater than myself; if I did not know also how to requite with honour those who work for my good, I should be ashamed." And Lysander said, "Maybe there is more reason in your doings than ever guided my conduct. Grant me for the rest one favour, so shall I cease to blush at the loss of my influence with you, and you will cease to be embarrassed by my presence. Send me off on a mission somewhere; wherever I am I will strive to be of service to you." Such was the proposal of Lysander. Agesilaus resolved to act upon it, and despatched Lysander to the Hellespont. And this is what befell. Lysander, being made aware of a slight which had been 'put upon Spithridates the Persian by Pharnabazus, got into conversation with the injured man, and so worked upon him that he was persuaded to bring his children and his personal belongings, and with about 200 troopers to revolt. The next step was to deposit all the goods safely in Cyzicus, and the last to get on shipboard with Spithridates and his son, and so to present himself with his Persian friends to Agesilaus. Agesilaus, on his side, was delighted at the transaction, and set himself at once to get information about Pharnabazus, his territory and his government.

Meanwhile Tissaphernes grew bolder. A large body of troops had been sent down by the king. On the strength of that he declared war against Agesilaus, if he did not instantly withdraw his troops from Asia. The Lacedaemonians there present, no less than the allies, received the news with profound vexation, persuaded as they were that Agesilaus had no force capable of competing with the king's grand armament. But a smile lit up the face of Agesilaus as he bade the ambassadors return to Tissaphernes and tell him that he was much in his debt for the perjury by which he had made the very gods themselves allies of Hellas. He at once issued a general order to the troops to equip themselves for a forward movement. He warned the cities through which he must pass in an advance upon Caria, to have markets in readiness, and lastly, he despatched a message to the Ionian, Aeolian, and Hellespontine communities to send their contingents to join him at Ephesus.

Tissaphernes, putting together the facts that Agesilaus had no cavalry and that Caria was a region unadapted to that arm, and persuaded in his own mind also that the Spartan could not but cherish wrath against himself personally for his deceit, felt convinced that he was really intending to invade Caria, and that the satrap's palace was his final goal. Accordingly he transferred the whole of his infantry into that province, and proceeded to lead his cavalry round into the plain of the Maeander. Here he conceived himself capable of trampling the Hellenes under foot with his horsemen before they could reach the craggy districts where no cavalry could operate.

But, instead of marching straight into Caria, Agesilaus turned sharp off in the opposite direction towards Phrygia. Picking up various detachments of troops which met him on his march, he steadily advanced, laying cities prostrate before him, and by the unexpectedness of his

attack reaping a great harvest of spoil. As a rule the march was prosecuted safely; but not far from Dascylium his advanced guard of cavalry
were pushing on towards a knoll to take a survey of the state of things
in front, when, as chance would have it, a detachment of cavalry sent
forward by Pharnabazus—the corps, in fact, of Rhathines and his bastard brother Bagaeus—just about equal to the Hellenes in number,
also came galloping up towards the very knoll in question. The two
bodies found themselves face to face not 150 yards apart, and for the
first moment or two stood stock still. The Hellenic horse were drawn up
like an ordinary phalanx four deep, the barbarians presenting a narrow
front of twelve or thereabouts, and a very disproportionate depth. There
was a moment's pause, and then the barbarians, taking the initiative,
charged. There was a hand-to-hand tussle, in which any Hellene who
succeeded in striking his man shivered his lance with the blow, while
the Persian troopers, armed with cornel-wood javelins, speedily despatched a dozen men and a couple of horses. At this point the Hellenic
cavalry turned and fled. But as Agesilaus came up to the rescue with
his heavy infantry, the Asiatics were forced in their turn to withdraw,
with the loss of one man slain. This cavalry engagement gave them
pause. Agesilaus on the day following it offered sacrifice. "Was he to
continue his advance?" But the victims proved hopeless. After this
manifestation he turned and marched towards the sea. It was clear
enough to his mind that without a proper calvary force it would be impossible to conduct a campaign in the flat country. Cavalry, therefore,
he must get, or be driven to a mere guerilla warfare. With this view he
drew up a list of all the wealthiest inhabitants belonging to the several
cities of those parts. Their duty would be to support a body of cavalry,
with the proviso, however, that any one contributing a horse, arms,
and rider, up to the standard, would be exempted from personal service.
The effect was instantaneous. The zeal with which the recipients of
these orders responded could hardly have been greater if they had been
seeking substitutes to die for them.

After this, at the first indication of spring, he collected the whole
of his army at Ephesus. But the army needed training. With that object
he proposed a series of prizes—prizes to the several heavy infantry regiments, to be won by those who presented their men in the best condition; prizes for the cavalry regiments which could ride best; prizes for
those divisions of peltasts and archers which proved most efficient in
their respective duties. And now the gymnasiums were a sight to see,
thronged as they were, one and all, with warriors stripped for exercise;
or again, the hippodrome crowded with horses and riders performing
their evolutions; or the javelin men and archers going through their

peculiar drill. In fact, the whole city where he lay presented under his hands a spectacle not to be forgotten. The market-place literally teemed with horses, arms, and accoutrements of all sorts for sale. The bronze-worker, the carpenter, the smith, the leather-cutter, the painter and embosser, were all busily engaged in fabricating the implements of war; so that the city of Ephesus itself was fairly converted into a military workshop. One would have been cheered to see the lines of soldiers with Agesilaus at their head, as they stepped garlanded from the gymnasiums to dedicate their wreaths to the goddess Artemis. Here it was natural for the place to be filled with high hopes. Here were reverence and piety towards heaven; here practice in war and military training; here discipline with habitual obedience to authority. But contempt for one's enemy will infuse a kind of strength in battle. So the Spartan leader argued; and with a view to its production he ordered the quartermasters to put up the prisoners who had been captured by his foraging bands for auction, stripped naked; so that his Hellene soldiery, as they looked at the white skins which had never been bared to sun and wind, the soft limbs unused to toil through constant riding in carriages, came to the conclusion that war with such adversaries would differ little from a fight with women.

By this date a full year had elapsed since the embarkation of Agesilaus, and the time had come for the Thirty with Lysander to sail back home, and for their successors, with Herippidas, to arrive. Among these Agesilaus appointed Xenocles and another to the command of the cavalry, Scythes to that of the heavy infantry of the enfranchised Helots, Herippidas to that of the Cyreians, and Migdon to that of the contingents from the states. Agesilaus told them that he intended to lead them immediately by the most expeditious route against the stronghold of the country, so that without further ceremony they might prepare their minds and bodies for the battle. Tissaphernes, however, was firmly persuaded that this was only talk intended to deceive him; Agesilaus would this time certainly invade Caria. Accordingly he repeated his former tactics, transporting his infantry bodily into Caria and posting his cavalry in the valley of the Maeander. But Agesilaus was as good as his word, and at once invaded the district of Sardis. A three days' march through a region denuded of the enemy threw large supplies into his hands. On the fourth day the cavalry of the enemy approached. Their general ordered the officer in charge of his baggage-train to cross the Pactolus and encamp, while his troopers, catching sight of stragglers from the Hellenic force scattered in pursuit of booty, killed many of them. Perceiving which, Agesilaus ordered his cavalry to the rescue; and the Persians on their side, seeing their advance, collected together in battle order to receive them, with dense squadrons of horse, troop upon troop. The Spartan, reflecting that the enemy had as yet no infantry to support him, while he had all branches of the service to depend upon, concluded that the critical moment had arrived to risk an engagement. In this mood he sacrificed, and began advancing his main line of battle against the lines of cavalry in front of him, at the same time ordering the flower of his heavy infantry—the younger men—to close with them at a run, and the peltasts to bring up their supports at the double. The order passed to his cavalry was to charge in confidence that he and the whole body of his troops were close behind them. The cavalry charge was received by the Persians without flinching, but presently finding themselves environed by the full tide of war they swerved. Some found a speedy grave within the river, but the mass of them gradually made good their escape. The Hellenes followed close on the heels of the flying foe and captured his camp. Here the peltasts not unnaturally fell to pillaging; whereupon Agesilaus planted his troops so as to form a cordon enclosing the property of friends and foes alike. The spoil taken was considerable; it brought more than seventy talents, not to mention the famous camels, subsequently brought over by Agesilaus into Hellas, which were captured here. At the moment of the battle Tissaphernes lay in Sardis. Hence the Persians argued that they had been betrayed by the satrap. And the king of Persia, coming to a like conclusion himself that Tissaphernes was to blame for the evil turn of his affairs, sent down Tithraustes and beheaded him.

This done, Tithraustes sent an embassy to Agesilaus with a message as follows, "The author of all our trouble, yours and ours, Agesilaus, has paid the penalty of his misdoings; the king therefore asks of you first that you should sail back home in peace; secondly, that the cities in Asia secured in their autonomy should continue to render him the ancient tribute." To this proposition Agesilaus made answer that without the authorities at home he could do nothing in the matter. "Then do you, at least," replied Tithraustes, "while awaiting advice from Lacedaemon, withdraw into the territory of Pharnabazus. Have I not avenged you of your enemy?" "While, then, I am on my way thither," rejoined Agesilaus, "will you support my army with provisions?" Accordingly, Tithraustes handed him thirty talents, which the other took, and began his march into Phrygia (the Phrygia of Pharnabazus). He lay in the plain district above Cyme, when a message reached him from the home authorities, giving him absolute disposal of the naval forces, with the right to appoint the admiral of his choice. This course the Lacedaemonians were led to adopt by the following considerations: If, they argued, the same man were in command of both services, the land force would be greatly strengthened through the concentration of the double force at any point necessary; and the navy likewise would be far more useful through the immediate presence and co-operation of the land force where needed. Apprised of these measures, Agesilaus in the first instance sent an order to the cities on the islands and the seaboard to fit out as many ships of war as they severally might deem desirable. The result was a new navy, consisting of the vessels thus voluntarily furnished by the states, with others presented by private persons out of courtesy to their commander, and amounting in all to a fleet of 120 triremes. The admiral whom he selected was Peisander, his wife's brother, a man of genuine ambition and of a vigorous spirit, but not sufficiently expert in the details of equipment to achieve a great naval success. Thus while Peisander set off to attend to naval matters, Agesilaus continued his march whither he was bound to Phrygia.

5. But now Tithraustes seemed to have discovered in Agesilaus a disposition to despise the fortunes of the Persian monarch—he evidently had no intention to withdraw from Asia; on the contrary, he was cherishing hopes vast enough to include the capture of the king himself. Being at his wits' end how to manage matters, he resolved to send Timocrates the Rhodian to Hellas with a gift of gold worth fifty silver talents, and enjoined upon him to endeavour to exchange solemn pledges with the leading men in the several states, binding them to undertake a war against Lacedaemon. Timocrates arrived and began to dole out his presents. In Thebes he gave gifts to Androcleidas, Ismenias, and Galaxidorus; in Corinth to Timolaus and Polyanthes; in Argos to Cylon and his party. The Athenians, though they took no share of the gold, were none the less eager for the war, being of opinion that empire was theirs by right. The recipients of the moneys forthwith began to defame the Lacedaemonians in their respective states, and, when they had brought these to a sufficient pitch of hatred, bound together the most important of them in a confederacy.

But it was clear to the leaders in Thebes that, unless some one struck the first blow, the Lacedaemonians would never be brought to break the truce with the allies. They therefore persuaded the Opuntian Locrians to levy money on a debatable district, jointly claimed by the Phocians and themselves, when the Phocians would be sure to retaliate by an attack on Locris. These expectations were fulfilled. The Phocians immediately invaded Locris and seized much more valuable property. Then Androcleidas and his friends lost no time in persuading the Thebans to assist the Locrians, on the ground that it was no debatable district which had been entered by the Phocians, but the admittedly

friendly and allied territory of Locris itself. The counter-invasion of
Phocis and pillage of their country by the Thebans promptly induced
the Phocians to send an embassy to Lacedaemon. In claiming assistance
they explained that the war was not of their own seeking, but that they
had attacked the Locrians in self-defence. On their side the Lacedaemonians were glad enough to seize a pretext for marching upon the
Thebans, against whom they cherished a long-standing bitterness. They
had not forgotten the claim which the Thebans had set up to a tithe for
Apollo in Deceleia, nor yet their refusal to support Lacedaemon in the
attack on Piraeus; and they accused them further of having persuaded
the Corinthians not to join that expedition. Nor did they fail to call to
mind some later proceedings of the Thebans—their refusal to allow
Agesilaus to sacrifice in Aulis; their snatching the victims already offered and hurling them from the altars; their refusal to join the same
general in a campaign directed even against Asia. The Lacedaemonians
further reasoned that now, if ever, was the favourable moment to conduct an expedition against the Thebans, and once for all to put a stop
to their insolent behaviour towards them. Affairs in Asia were pros-
pering under the strong arm of Agesilaus, and in Hellas they had no
other war on hand to hamper their movements. Such, therefore, being
the general view of the situation adopted at Lacedaemon, the ephors
proceeded to call out the army. Meanwhile they despatched Lysander to
Phocis with orders to put himself at the head of the Phocians along with
the Oetaeans, Heracleotes, Melians, and Aenianians, and to march upon
Haliartus; before the walls of which place Pausanias, the destined leader
of the expedition, undertook to present himself at the head of the Lacedaemonians and other Peloponnesian forces by a specified date. Lysander not only carried out his instructions to the letter, but, going a
little beyond them, succeeded in detaching Orchomenus from Thebes.
Pausanias, on the other hand, after finding the sacrifices for crossing
the frontier favourable, sat down at Tegea and set about despatching
to and fro the commandants of allied troops while contentedly awaiting
the soldiers from the provincial districts of Laconia.

And now that it was fully plain to the Thebans that the Lacedaemonians would invade their territory, they sent ambassadors to Athens, who
spoke as follows:

"Men of Athens, it is a mistake on your part to blame us for certain
harsh resolutions concerning Athens at the conclusion of the war. That
vote was not authorised by the state of Thebes. It was the utterance
merely of one man, who was at that time seated in the congress of the
allies. A more important fact is that when the Lacedaemonians summoned us to attack Piraeus the collective state of Thebes passed a resolu-

tion refusing to join in the campaign. As then you are to a large extent the cause of the resentment which the Lacedaemonians feel towards us, we consider it only fair that you in your turn should assist us. Still more do we demand of you who were of the city party at that date, to enter heart and soul into war with the Lacedaemonians. For what were their services to you? They first deliberately converted you into an oligarchy and placed you in hostility to the democracy, and then they came with a great force under guise of being your allies, and delivered you over to the majority, so that, for any service they rendered you, you were all dead men; and you owe your lives to our friends here, the people of Athens.

"But to pass on—we all know, men of Athens, that you would like to recover the empire which you formerly possessed; and how can you compass your object better than by coming to the aid yourselves of the victims of Lacedaemonian injustice? Is it their wide empire of which you are afraid? Let not that make cowards of you—much rather let it embolden you as you lay to heart and ponder your own case. When your empire was widest then the crop of your enemies was thickest. Only so long as they found no opportunity to revolt did they keep their hatred of you dark; but no sooner had they found a champion in Lacedaemon than they at once showed what they really felt towards you. So too to-day. Let us show plainly that we mean to stand shoulder to shoulder embattled against the Lacedaemonians; and haters enough of them— whole armies—never fear, will be forthcoming. To prove the truth of this assertion you need only to count upon your fingers. How many friends have they left to them to-day? The Argives have been, are, and ever will be, hostile to them. Of course. But the Eleians? Why, the Eleians have quite lately been robbed of so much territory and so many cities that their friendship is converted into hatred. And what shall we say of the Corinthians? the Arcadians? the Achaeans? In the war which Sparta waged against you, there was no toil, no danger, no expense, which those peoples did not share, in obedience to the coaxings and persuasions of that power. The Lacedaemonians gained what they wanted, and then not one fractional portion of empire, honour, or wealth did these faithful followers come in for. That is not all. They have no scruple in appointing their Helots as governors, and on the free necks of their allies, in the day of their good fortune, they have planted the tyrant's heel.

"Take again the case of those whom they have detached from your- selves. In the most patent way they have cajoled and cheated them; in place of freedom they have presented them with a twofold slavery. The allies are tyrannised over by the governor and tyrannised over by the ten commissioners set up by Lysander over every subject city. And to come lastly to the great king. In spite of all the contributions with which he aided them to gain a mastery over you, is the lord of Asia one whit better off to-day than if he had taken exactly the opposite course and joined you in reducing them?

"Is it not clear that you have only to step forward once again as the champions of this crowd of sufferers from injustice, and you will attain to a pinnacle of power quite unprecedented? In the days of your old empire you were leaders of the maritime powers merely—that is clear; but your new empire to-day will be universal. You will have at your backs not only your former subjects, but ourselves, and the Peloponnesians, and the king himself, with all that mighty power which is his. We do not deny that we were serviceable allies enough to Lacedaemon, as you will bear us witness; but this we say: If we helped the Lacedaemonians vigorously in the past, everything tends to show that we shall help you still more vigorously to-day; for our swords will be unsheathed, not in behalf of islanders, or Syracusans, or men of alien stock, as happened in the late war, but of ourselves, suffering under a sense of wrong. And there is another important fact which you ought to realise: this selfish system of organised greed which is Sparta's will fall more readily to pieces than your own late empire. Yours was the proud assertion of naval empire over subjects powerless by sea. Theirs is the selfish sway of a minority asserting dominion over states equally well armed with themselves, and many times more numerous. Here our remarks end. Do not forget, however, men of Athens, that as far as we can understand the matter, the field to which we invite you is destined to prove far richer in blessings to your own state of Athens than to ours, Thebes."

With these words the speaker ended. Among the Athenians, speaker after speaker spoke in favour of the proposition, and finally a unanimous resolution was passed voting assistance to the Thebans. Thrasybulus, in an answer communicating the resolution, pointed out with pride that in spite of the unfortified condition of Piraeus, Athens would not shrink from repaying her debt of gratitude to Thebes with interest. "You," he added, "refused to join in a campaign against us; we are prepared to fight your battles with you against the enemy, if he attacks you." Thus the Thebans returned home and made preparations to defend themselves, while the Athenians made ready to assist them.

And now the Lacedaemonians no longer hesitated. Pausanias the king advanced into Boeotia with the home army and the whole of the Peloponnesian contingents, saving only the Corinthians, who declined to serve. Lysander, at the head of the army supplied by the Phocians and Orchomenus and the other strong places in those parts, had already reached Haliartus, in front of Pausanias. Having arrived, he refused to sit quietly and await the arrival of the army from Lacedaemon, but at once marched with what troops he had against the walls of Haliartus; and in the first instance he tried to persuade the citizens to detach themselves from Thebes and to assume autonomy, but the intention was cut short by certain Thebans within the fortress. Whereupon Lysander attacked the place. The Thebans were made aware, and hurried to the rescue with heavy infantry and cavalry. Then, whether it was that the army of relief fell upon Lysander unawares, or that with clear knowledge of his approach he preferred to await the enemy, with intent to crush him, is uncertain. This only is clear: a battle was fought beside the walls, and a trophy still exists to mark the victory of the townsfolk before the gates of Haliartus. Lysander was slain, and the rest fled to the mountains, the Thebans hotly pursuing. But when the pursuit had led them to some considerable height, and they were hemmed in by difficult ground and narrow space, then the heavy infantry turned and greeted them with a shower of darts and missiles. First two or three men dropped who had been foremost of the pursuers, and then upon the rest they poured volleys of stones down the precipitous incline, and pressed on their late pursuers with much zeal, until the Thebans turned tail and quitted the deadly slope, leaving behind them more than 200 corpses.

On this day, therefore, the Thebans were discouraged as they counted their losses and found them equal to their gains; but the next day they discovered that during the night the Phocians and the rest of them had made off to their several homes, whereupon they fell to pluming themselves highly on their achievement. But presently Pausanias appeared at the head of the Lacedaemonian army, and once more their dangers seemed to thicken round them. Deep, we are told, was the silence and despondency in their army. It was not until the next day, when the Athenians arrived, and were duly drawn up beside them, while Pausanias neither attacked nor offered battle, that at length the confidence of the Thebans took a larger range. Pausanias, on his side, having summoned his generals and commanders of fifties, deliberated whether to give battle or to content himself with picking up the bodies of Lysander and of those who fell with him, under cover of a truce.

The considerations which weighed on the minds of Pausanias and the other high officers of the Lacedaemonians seem to have been that Lysander was dead and his defeated army in retreat; while, as far as they themselves were concerned, the Corinthian contingent was absolutely wanting, and the zeal of the troops there present at the lowest ebb. They further reasoned that the enemy's cavalry was numerous and theirs the reverse; while, weightiest of all, there lay the dead right under the walls, so that if they had been ever so much stronger it would have been no easy task to pick up the bodies within range of the towers of Haliartus. On all these grounds they determined to ask for a truce, in order to pick up the bodies of the slain. These, however, the Thebans were not disposed to give back unless they agreed to retire from their territory. The terms were gladly accepted by the Lacedaemonians, who at once picked up the corpses of the slain, and prepared to quit the territory of Boeotia. The preliminaries were transacted, and the retreat commenced. Despondent indeed was the demeanour of the Lacedaemonians, in contrast with the insolent bearing of the Thebans, who visited the slightest attempt to trespass on their private estates with blows and chased the offenders back on to the high roads, unflinchingly. Such was the conclusion of the campaign of the Lacedaemonians.

As for Pausanias, on his arrival at home he was tried on the capital charge. The heads of indictment set forth that he had failed to reach Haliartus as soon as Lysander, in spite of his undertaking to be there on the same day; that, instead of using any endeavour to pick up the bodies of the slain by force of arms, he had asked for a truce; that at an earlier date, when he had got the popular government of Athens fairly in his grip at Piraeus, he had suffered it to slip through his fingers and escape. Besides this, he failed to present himself at the trial, and a sentence of death was passed upon him. He escaped to Tegea and there died of an illness while still in exile. Thus closes the chapter of events enacted on the soil of Hellas. To return to Asia and Agesilaus.

BOOK IV

1. With the fall of the year Agesilaus reached Phrygia—the Phrygia of Pharnabazus—and proceeded to burn and harry the district. City after city was taken, some by force and some by voluntary surrender. To a proposal of Spithridates to lead him into Paphlagonia, where he would introduce the king of the country to him in conference and obtain his alliance, he readily acceded. It was a long-cherished ambition of Agesilaus to alienate some one of the subject nations from the Persian monarch, and he pushed forward eagerly.

On his arrival in Paphlagonia, King Otys[1] came, and an alliance was made. (The fact was, he had been summoned by the king to Susa and had not gone up.) More than that, through the persuasion of Spithridates he left behind as a parting gift to Agesilaus 1,000 cavalry and 2,000 peltasts. Agesilaus was anxious in some way to show his gratitude to Spithridates for such help, and spoke as follows, "Tell me," he said to Spithridates, "would you not like to give your daughter to King Otys?" "Much more would I like to give her," he answered, "than he to take her—I an outcast wanderer, and he lord of a vast territory and forces." Nothing more was said at the time about the marriage; but when Otys was on the point of departure and came to bid farewell, Agesilaus, having taken care that Spithridates should be out of the way, in the presence of the thirty Spartans broached the subject, "Can you tell me, Otys, to what sort of family Spithridates belongs?" "To one of the noblest in Persia," replied the king. Agesilaus said, "Have you observed how beautiful his son is?" "To be sure; last evening I dined with him." "And they tell me that his daughter is yet more beautiful." "That may well be; beautiful she is." Otys answered, "For my part, as you have proved so good a friend to us, I should like to advise you to take this girl to wife. Not only is she very beautiful—and what more should a husband ask for?—but her father is of noble family, and has a force at his back large enough to retaliate on Pharnabazus for an injury. He has made the satrap, as you see, a fugitive and a vagabond in his own vast territory. I need not tell you," he added, "that a man who can so chastise an enemy is well able to benefit a friend; and of this be assured: by such an alliance you will gain not the connection

[1] Elsewhere he is called Cotys.

84

of Spithridates alone, but of myself and the Lacedaemonians, and, as we are the leaders of Hellas, of the rest of Hellas also. And what a wedding yours will be! Were ever nuptials celebrated on so grand a scale before? Was ever bride led home by such an escort of cavalry and light-armed troops and heavy infantry, as shall escort your wife home to your palace?" Otys asked, "Is Spithridates of one mind with you in this proposal?" Agesilaus answered, "By the gods he did not bid me make it for him. And for my own part in the matter, though it is, I admit, a rare pleasure to requite an enemy, yet I had far rather at any time discover some good fortune for my friends." "Why not ask," said he, "if your project pleases Spithridates too?" Then Agesilaus, turning to Herippidas and the rest of the thirty, bade them go to Spithridates. "Give him such good instruction," he added, "that he shall wish what we wish." They rose and retired to administer their lesson. But they seemed to tarry a long time, and Agesilaus asked, "What say you, King Otys—shall we summon him hither ourselves? You, I feel certain, are better able to persuade him than all the rest put together." Thereupon Agesilaus summoned Spithridates and the others. As they came forward, Herippidas promptly delivered himself thus, "I spare you the details, Agesilaus. To make a long story short, Spithridates says, 'He will be glad to do whatever pleases you.'" Then Agesilaus turned first to one and then to the other. "What pleases me," said he, "is that you should wed a daughter—and you a wife—so happily. But," he added, "I do not see how we can well bring home the bride by land till spring." "No, not by land," the suitor answered, "but you might, if you chose, conduct her home at once by sea." Thereupon they exchanged pledges to ratify the compact; and so sent Otys on his way.

Agesilaus, who had not failed to note the king's impatience, at once fitted out a ship of war and gave orders to Callias, a Lacedaemonian, to escort the maiden to her new home; after which he himself began his march on Dascylium. Here was the palace of Pharnabazus. It lay in the midst of numerous villages, which were large and well stocked with abundant supplies. Here, too, were most fair hunting grounds, offering the hunter choice between enclosed parks and a wide expanse of field and fell; and all around there flowed a river full of fish of every sort; and for the sportsman versed in fowling, winged game in abundance.

In these quarters the Spartan king passed the winter, collecting supplies for the army either on the spot or by a system of forage. On one of these occasions the troops, who had grown reckless and scornful of the enemy through long immunity from attack, while engaged in collecting supplies, were scattered over the flat country, when Pharnabazus fell upon them with two scythe-chariots and about 400 horse. Seeing him thus advancing, the Hellenes ran together, mustering possibly 700 men. The Persian did not hesitate, but placing his chariots in front, supported by himself and the cavalry, he gave the command to charge. The scythe-chariots charged and scattered the compact mass, and speedily the cavalry had laid low in the dust about 100 men, while the rest retreated hastily, under cover of Agesilaus and his hoplites, who were fortunately near.

It was the third or fourth day after this that Spithridates made a discovery: Pharnabazus lay encamped in Caue, a large village not more than eighteen miles away. This news he lost no time in reporting to Herippidas. The latter, who was longing for some brilliant exploit, begged Agesilaus to furnish him with 2,000 hoplites, an equal number of peltasts, and some cavalry—the latter to consist of the horsemen of Spithridates, the Paphlagonians, and as many Hellene troopers as he might perchance persuade to follow him. Having got the promise of them from Agesilaus, he proceeded to take the auspices. Towards late afternoon he obtained favourable omens and broke off the sacrifice. Thereupon he ordered the troops to get their evening meal, after which they were to present themselves in front of the camp. But by the time darkness had closed in, not one half of them had come out. To abandon the project was to call down the ridicule of the rest of the thirty Spartans. So he set out with the force to hand, and about daylight, falling on the camp of Pharnabazus, put many of his advanced guard of Mysians to the sword. The men themselves made good their escape in different directions, but the camp was taken, and with it many goblets and other gear such as a man like Pharnabazus would have, not to speak of much baggage and many baggage animals. It was the dread of being surrounded and besieged, if he should establish himself for long at any one spot, which induced Pharnabazus to flee in gipsy fashion from point to point over the country, carefully obliterating his encampments. Now as the Paphlagonians and Spithridates brought back the captured property, they were met by Herippidas with his brigadiers and captains, who stopped them and relieved them of all they had; the object being to have as large a list as possible of captures to deliver over to the officers who superintended the sale of booty. This treatment the Asiatics found intolerable. They deemed themselves at once injured and insulted, got their kit together in the night, and made off in the direction of Sardis to join Ariaeus without mistrust, seeing that he too had revolted and gone to war with the king. On Agesilaus himself no heavier blow fell during the whole campaign than the desertion of Spithridates and Megabates and the Paphlagonians.

Now there was a certain man of Cyzicus, Apollophanes by name;

he was an old friend of Pharnabazus, and at this time had become a friend also of Agesilaus. This man informed Agesilaus that he thought he could bring about a meeting between him and Pharnabazus, which might tend to friendship; and having so got ear of him, he obtained pledges of good faith between his two friends, and presented himself with Pharnabazus at the meeting place, where Agesilaus with the thirty Spartans around him awaited their coming, reclining on the grass. Pharnabazus presently arrived clad in costliest apparel; but just as his attendants were about to spread at his feet the carpets on which the Persians delicately seat themselves, he was touched with a sense of shame at his own luxury in sight of the simplicity of Agesilaus, and he also without further ceremony seated himself on the bare ground. And first the two bade one another hail, and then Pharnabazus stretched out his right hand and Agesilaus his to meet him, and the conversation began. Pharnabazus, as the elder of the two, spoke first. "Agesilaus," he said, "and all you Lacedaemonians here present, while you were at war with the Athenians I was your friend and ally; it was I who furnished the wealth that made your navy strong on sea; on land I fought on horseback by your side, and pursued your enemies into the sea. As to duplicity like that of Tissaphernes, I challenge you to accuse me of having played you false by word or deed. Such have I ever been; and in return how am I treated by yourselves to-day? In such sort that I cannot even sup in my own country unless, like the wild animals, I pick up the scraps you chance to leave. The beautiful palaces which my father left me as an heirloom, the parks full of trees and beasts of the chase in which my heart rejoiced, lie before my eyes hacked to pieces, burnt to ashes. Maybe I do not comprehend the first principles of justice and righteousness; do you then explain to me how all this resembles the conduct of men who know how to repay a simple debt of gratitude." He ceased, and the thirty Spartans were ashamed before him and kept silence.

At length, after some pause, Agesilaus spoke. "I think you are aware," he said, "Pharnabazus, that within the states of Hellas the folk of one community contract relations of friendship and hospitality with one another; but if these states should go to war, then each man will side with his fatherland, and friend will find himself pitted against friend in the field of battle, and, if it so happen, the one may even deal the other his death-blow. So too we to-day, being at war with your sovereign lord the king, must needs regard as our enemy all that he calls his; not but that with yourself personally we should esteem it our high fortune to be friends. If indeed it were merely an exchange of service, were you asked to give up your lord the king and to take us as your masters in his stead, I could not so advise you; but the fact is, by joining with us it is in your power to-day to bow your head to no man, to call no man master, to reap the produce of your own domain in freedom—freedom, which to my mind is more precious than all riches. Not that we bid you to become a beggar for the sake of freedom, but rather to use our friendship to increase not the king's authority, but your own, by subduing those who are your fellow-slaves to-day, and who to-morrow shall be your willing subjects. Well, then, freedom given and wealth added—what more would you desire to fill the cup of happiness to overflowing?" Pharnabazus replied, "Shall I tell you plainly what I will do?" "That were but kind and courteous on your part," he answered. "Thus it stands with me, then," said Pharnabazus. "If the king should send another general, and if he should wish to rank me under this new man's orders, I, for my part, am willing to accept your friendship and alliance; but if he offers me the supreme command—why, then, I plainly tell you, there is a certain something in the very name ambition which whispers me that I shall war against you to the best of my ability." When he heard that, Agesilaus seized the satrap's hand, exclaiming, "Ah, best of mortals, may the day arrive which sends us such a friend! Of one thing rest assured. This instant I leave your territory with what haste I may, and for the future—even in case of war—as long as we can find foes elsewhere our hands shall hold aloof from you and yours."

And with these words he broke up the meeting. Pharnabazus mounted his horse and rode away, but his son by Parapita, who was still in the bloom of youth, lingered behind; then, running up to Agesilaus, he exclaimed, "See, I choose you as my friend." "And I accept you," replied the king. "Remember, then," the lad answered, and with the word presented the beautiful javelin in his hand to Agesilaus, who received it, and unclasping a splendid trapping which his secretary, Idaeus, had round the neck of his horse, he gave it in return to the youth; whereupon the boy leaped on his horse's back and galloped after his father. At a later date, during the absence of Pharnabazus abroad, this same youth, the son of Parapita, was deprived of the government by his brother and driven into exile. Then Agesilaus took great interest in him, and as he had a strong attachment to the son of Eualces, an Athenian, Agesilaus did all he could to have this friend of his, who was the tallest of the boys, admitted to the 200 yard race at Olympia.

But to return to the actual moment. Agesilaus was as good as his word, and at once marched out of the territory of Pharnabazus. The season verged on spring. Reaching the plain of Thebe, he encamped in the neighbourhood of the temple of Artemis of Astyra, and there employed himself in collecting troops from every side, in addition to those which he already had, so as to form a complete armament. These preparations were pressed forward with a view to penetrating as far as possible into the interior. He was persuaded that every tribe or nation placed in his rear might be considered as alienated from the king.

2. Such were the concerns and projects of Agesilaus. Meanwhile the Lacedaemonians at home were quite alive to the fact that money had been sent into Hellas, and that the bigger states were leagued together to declare war against them. It was hard to avoid the conclusion that Sparta herself was in actual danger and that a campaign was inevitable. While busy, therefore, with preparations themselves, they lost no time in despatching Epicydidas to bring Agesilaus. That officer, on his arrival, explained the position of affairs, and concluded by delivering a peremptory summons of the state recalling him to the assistance of the fatherland without delay. The announcement could not but come as a grievous blow to Agesilaus, as he reflected on the vanished hopes, and the honours plucked from his grasp. Still, he summoned the allies and announced to them the contents of the despatch from home. "To aid our fatherland," he added, "is an imperative duty. If, however, matters turn out well on the other side, rely upon it, friends and allies, I will not forget you, but I shall be back anon to carry out your wishes." When they heard the announcement many wept, and they passed a resolution, one and all, to join Agesilaus in assisting Lacedaemon; if matters turned out well there, they undertook to take him as their leader and come back again to Asia; and so they made preparations to follow him.

Agesilaus, on his side, determined to leave behind him in Asia Euxenus as governor, and with him a garrison numbering no less than 4,000 troops, which would enable him to protect the states in Asia. But for himself, as on the one hand he could see that the majority of the soldiers would far rather stay behind than undertake service against fellow-Hellenes, and on the other hand he wished to take as fine and large an army with him as he could, he offered prizes first to that state or city which should contribute the best corps of troops, and secondly to that captain of mercenaries who should join the expedition with the best equipped battalion of heavy infantry, archers, and light infantry. On the same principle he informed the chief cavalry officers that the general who succeeded in presenting the best equipped and best mounted regiment would receive from himself some victorious distinction. "The final adjudication," he said, "would not be made until they had crossed from Asia into Europe and had reached the Chersonese." And this was with a view to impress upon them that the prizes were not for show but for real campaigners. These consisted for the most part of infantry or cavalry arms and accoutrements beautifully finished, besides which there were chaplets of gold. The whole, useful and ornamental alike, must have cost at least four talents, but as the result of this outlay, no doubt, arms of great value were procured for the expedition. When the Hellespont was crossed the judges were appointed. The Lacedaemonians were represented by Menascus, Herippidas, and Orsippus, and the allies by one member from each state. As soon as the adjudication was complete, the army commenced its march with Agesilaus at its head, following the very route taken by the great king when he invaded Hellas.

Meanwhile the ephors had called out the army, and as Agesipolis was still a boy, the state called upon Aristodemus, who was of the royal family and guardian of the young king, to lead the expedition; and now that the Lacedaemonians were ready to take the field and the forces of their opponents were also duly mustered, the latter met to consider the most advantageous method of doing battle.

Timolaus of Corinth spoke, "Soldiers of the allied forces," he said, "the growth of Lacedaemon seems to me just like that of some mighty river—at its sources small and easily crossed, but as it farther and farther advances, other rivers discharge themselves into its channel, and its stream grows ever more formidable. So is it with the Lacedaemonians. Take them at the starting-point and they are but a single community, but as they advance and attach city after city they grow more numerous and more resistless. I observe that when people wish to take wasps' nests—if they try to capture the creatures on the wing, they are liable to be attacked by half the hive; whereas, if they apply fire to them ere they leave their homes, they will master them without scathe themselves. On this principle I think it best to bring about the battle within the hive itself, or, short of that, as close to Lacedaemon as possible."

The arguments of the speaker were considered sound, and a resolution was passed in that sense; but before it could be carried out there were various arrangements to be made. There was the question of leadership. Then, again, what was the proper depth of line to be given to the different army corps? For if any particular state or states gave too great a depth to their battle line they would enable the enemy to turn their flank. Whilst they were debating these points, the Lacedaemonians had incorporated the men of Tegea and the men of Mantinea, and were ready to march into the sea-girt region.[2] And as the two armies advanced almost at the same time, the Corinthians and the rest reached the district of Nemea, and the Lacedaemonians and their allies occupied Sicyon. The Lacedaemonians entered by Epieiceia, and at first were severely handled by the light-armed troops of the enemy, who discharged stones and arrows from the vantage-ground on their right; but

---

[2] The text is corrupt; no satisfactory interpretation has been proposed.

as they dropped down upon the Gulf of Corinth they advanced steadily
onwards through the flat country, felling timber and burning the fair
land. Their rivals, on their side, after a certain forward movement,
paused and encamped, placing the ravine in front of them; but still the
Lacedaemonians advanced, and it was only when they were within about
a mile of the hostile position that they followed suit and encamped, and
then they remained quiet.

And here I may state the numbers on either side. The Lacedaemonian heavy-armed infantry levies amounted to 6,000 men. Of Eleians,
Triphylians, Acroreians, and Lasionians there must have been nearly
3,000, with 1,500 Sicyonians, while Epidaurus, Troezen, Hermione, and
Halieis contributed at least another 3,000. To these heavy infantry
troops must be added 600 Lacedaemonian cavalry, a body of Cretan
archers about 300 strong, besides another force of slingers, at least 400
in all, consisting of Marganians, Letrinians, and Amphidolians. The men
of Phlius were not represented. Their plea was they were keeping a
holy truce. That was the total of the forces on the Lacedaemonian side.
There were collected on the enemy's side 6,000 Athenian heavy infantry,
with about, as was stated, 7,000 Argives, and in the absence of the men
of Orchomenus something like 5,000 Boeotians. There were besides
3,000 Corinthians, and again from the whole of Euboea at least 3,000.
These formed the heavy infantry. Of cavalry the Boeotians, again in
the absence of the Orchomenians, furnished 800, the Athenians 600, the
Chalcidians of Euboea 100, the Opuntian Locrians fifty. Their light
troops, including those of the Corinthians, were more numerous, as the
Ozolian Locrians, the Melians, and Acarnanians helped to swell their
numbers.

Such was the strength of the two armies. The Boeotians, as long as
they occupied the left wing,[3] showed no anxiety to join battle but, after
a rearrangement which gave them the right, placing the Athenians opposite to the Lacedaemonians, and themselves opposite the Achaeans,
at once they said that the sacrifices were favourable, and the order was
passed along the lines to prepare for immediate action. The Boeotians,
in the first place, abandoning the rule of sixteen deep, chose to give their
division the fullest possible depth, and, moreover, kept veering more
and more to their right, with the intention of overlapping their opponents' flank. The consequence was that the Athenians, to avoid being
absolutely severed, were forced to follow suit, and edged towards the
right, though they recognised the risk they ran of having their flank
turned. For a while the Lacedaemonians had no idea of the advance
of the enemy, owing to the rough nature of the ground, but the notes of

[3] Opposite the Lacedaemonians.

the paean at length announced to them the fact, and without an instant's delay the order to prepare for battle ran along the different
sections of their army. As soon as their troops were drawn up, according to the tactical disposition of the various generals of foreign brigades,
the order was passed to follow the lead, and then the Lacedaemonians
on their side also began edging to their right, and eventually stretched
out their wing so far that only six out of the ten regimental divisions
of the Athenians confronted the Lacedaemonians, the other four finding
themselves face to face with the men of Tegea. And now when they
were less than a furlong apart, the Lacedaemonians sacrificed in customary fashion a kid to the huntress goddess, and advanced upon their
opponents, wheeling round their overlapping columns to outflank his
left. As the two armies closed, the allies of Lacedaemon were as a rule
fairly borne down by their opponents. The men of Pellene alone, steadily
confronting the Thespiaeans, held their ground, and the dead of either
side strewed the position. As to the Lacedaemonians themselves: crushing that portion of the Athenian troops which lay immediately in front
of them, and at the same time encircling them with their overlapping
right, they slew man after man of them; and, absolutely unscathed themselves, their unbroken columns continued their march, and so passed
behind the four remaining divisions of the Athenians before these latter
had returned from their own victorious pursuit. Whereby the four divisions in question also emerged from battle intact, except for the casual-
ties inflicted by the Tegeans in the first clash of the engagement. The
troops next encountered by the Lacedaemonians were the Argives retiring. These they fell foul of, and the senior polemarch was just on the
point of closing with them in front when some one, it is said, shouted,
"Let their front ranks pass." This was done, and as the Argives raced
past, their enemies thrust at their unprotected sides, and killed many
of them. The Corinthians were caught in the same way as they retired,
and when their turn had passed, once more the Lacedaemonians lit upon
a portion of the Theban division retiring from the pursuit, and strewed
the field with their dead. The end of it all was that the defeated troops
in the first instance made for safety to the walls of their city, but the
Corinthians within closed the gates, whereupon the troops took up
quarters once again in their old encampment. The Lacedaemonians on
their side withdrew to the point at which they first closed with the
enemy, and there set up a trophy of victory. So the battle ended.

3. Meanwhile Agesilaus was rapidly hastening with his reinforcements from Asia. He had reached Amphipolis when Dercylidas brought
the news of this fresh victory of the Lacedaemonians; their own loss
had been eight men, that of the enemy considerable. It was his business

at the same time to explain that not a few of the allies had fallen also. Agesilaus asked, "Would it not be opportune, Dercylidas, if the cities that have furnished us with contingents could hear of this victory as soon as possible?" And Dercylidas replied, "The news at any rate is likely to put them in better heart." Then said the king, "As you were an eye-witness there could hardly be a better bearer of the news than yourself." To this proposal Dercylidas lent a willing ear—to travel abroad was his special delight, and he replied, "Yes, under your orders." "Then you have my orders," the king said. "And you may further inform the states from myself that we have not forgotten our promise; if all goes well over here we shall be with them again before long." So Dercylidas set off on his travels, in the first instance to the Hellespont; while Agesilaus crossed Macedonia and arrived in Thessaly. And now the men of Larissa, Crannon, Scotussa, and Pharsalus, who were allies of the Boeotians—and in fact all the Thessalians except the exiles for the time being—hung on his heels and did him damage.

For some while he marched his troops in a hollow square, posting half his cavalry in front and half on his rear; but finding that the Thessalians checked his passage by repeated charges from behind, he strengthened his rearguard by sending round the cavalry from his van, with the exception of his own personal escort. The two armies stood confronted in battle order; but the Thessalians, not liking the notion of a cavalry engagement with heavy infantry, turned, and step by step retreated, while the others followed them with considerable caution. Agesilaus, perceiving the error under which both alike laboured, now sent his own personal guard of stalwart troopers with orders that both they and the rest of the horsemen should charge at full gallop, and not give the enemy the chance to recoil. The Thessalians were taken aback by this unexpected onslaught, and half of them never thought of wheeling about, whilst those who did essay to do so presented the flanks of their horses to the charge, and were made prisoners. Still Polycharmus of Pharsalus, the general in command of their cavalry, rallied his men for an instant, and fell, sword in hand, with his immediate followers. This was the signal for a flight so precipitate on the part of the Thessalians, that their dead and dying lined the road, and prisoners were taken; nor was any halt made until they reached Mount Narthacius. Here, then, midway between Pras and Narthacius, Agesilaus set up a trophy, halting for the moment, in unfeigned satisfaction at the exploit. It was from antagonists who prided themselves on their cavalry beyond everything that he had wrested victory, with a body of cavalry of his own mustering. Next day he crossed the mountains of Achaea Phthiotis, and for the future continued his march through friendly territory until he reached the confines of Boeotia.

Here, at the entrance of that territory, the sun (in partial eclipse)[4] seemed to appear in a crescent shape, and the news reached him of the defeat of the Lacedaemonians in a naval engagement, and of the death of the admiral Peisander. Details of the disaster were not wanting. The engagement of the hostile fleets took place off Cnidus. Pharnabazus, the Persian admiral, was present with the Phoenician fleet, and in front of him were ranged the ships of the Hellenic squadron under Conon.[5] Peisander had ventured to draw out his squadron to meet the combined fleets, though the numerical inferiority of his fleet to that of the Hellenic navy under Conon was conspicuous, and he had the mortification of seeing the allies who formed his left wing take to flight immediately. He himself came to close quarters with the enemy, and was driven on shore, on board his trireme, under pressure of the hostile rams. The rest, as many as were driven to shore, deserted their ships and sought safety as best they could in the territory of Cnidus. The admiral alone stuck to his ship, and fell sword in hand.

It was impossible for Agesilaus not to feel depressed by those tidings at first; on further reflection, however, it seemed to him that the moral quality of more than half his troops well entitled them to share in the sunshine of success, but in the day of trouble, when things looked black, he was not bound to take them into his confidence. Accordingly he turned round and gave out that he had received news that Peisander was dead, but that he had fallen in the arms of victory in a sea-fight; and suiting his action to the word, he proceeded to offer sacrifice in return for good tidings, distributing portions of the victims to a large number of recipients. So it befell that in the first skirmish with the enemy the troops of Agesilaus gained the upper hand, in consequence of the report that the Lacedaemonians had won a victory by sea.

To confront Agesilaus stood an army composed of the Boeotians, Athenians, Argives, Corinthians, Aenianians, Euboeans, and both divisions of the Locrians. Agesilaus on his side had with him a division of Lacedaemonians, which had crossed from Corinth, also half the division from Orchomenus; besides which there were the neodamodes from Lacedaemon, on service with him already; and in addition to these the foreign contingent under Herippidas; and again the quota furnished by the Hellenic cities in Asia, with others from the cities in Europe which he had brought over during his progress; and lastly, there were additional levies from the spot—Orchomenian and Phocian heavy

---

[4] August 14, 394 B.C.
[5] Conon and the Greeks were serving the Persians as mercenaries.

infantry. In light-armed troops, indeed, the numbers told heavily in favour of Agesilaus, but the cavalry on both sides were fairly balanced.

Such were the forces of either party. I will describe the battle itself, if only on account of certain features which distinguish it from the battles of our time. The two armies met on the plain of Coronea—the troops of Agesilaus advancing from the Cephisus, the Thebans and their allies from the slopes of Helicon. Agesilaus commanded his own right in person, with the men of Orchomenus on his extreme left. The Thebans formed their own right, while the Argives held their left. As they drew together, for a while deep silence reigned on either side; but when they were not more than a furlong apart, with a loud hurrah the Thebans, quickening to a run, rushed furiously to close quarters; and now there was barely a hundred yards breadth between the armies, when Herippidas with his foreign brigade, and with them the Ionians, Aeolians, and Hellespontines, darted out from the Spartans' battle-lines to greet their onset. One and all of the above played their part in the first rush forward; in another instant they were within spear-thrust of the enemy, and had routed the section immediately before them. As to the Argives, they actually declined to receive the attack of Agesilaus, and betook themselves in flight to Helicon. At this moment some of the foreign division were already in the act of crowning Agesilaus with the wreath of victory, when some one brought him word that the Thebans had cut through the Orchomenians and were in among the baggage train. At this the Spartan general immediately turned his army right about and advanced against them. The Thebans, on their side, catching sight of their allies withdrawn in flight to the base of Helicon, and anxious to get across to their own friends, formed in close order and tramped forward stoutly.

At this point no one will dispute the valour of Agesilaus, but he certainly did not choose the safest course. It was open to him to make way for the enemy to pass, which done, he might have hung upon his heels and mastered his rear. This, however, he refused to do, preferring to crash full front against the Thebans. Thereupon, with close interlock of shield wedged in with shield, they shoved, they fought, they killed and were killed. At last a portion of the Thebans broke their way through towards Helicon, but paid for that departure by the loss of many lives. And now the victory of Agesilaus was fairly won, and he himself, wounded, had been carried back to the main line, when a party of horse came galloping up to tell him that something like eighty of the enemy, under arms, were sheltering under the temple, and they asked what they ought to do. Agesilaus, though he was covered with wounds, did not, for all that, forget his duty to god. He gave orders to let them retire unscathed, and would not suffer any injury to be done to them. And now, seeing it was already late, they took their suppers and retired to rest.

But with the morning Gylis the polemarch received orders to draw up the troops in battle order, and to set up a trophy, every man crowned with a wreath in honour of the god, and all the pipers piping. Thus they busied themselves in the Spartan camp. On their side the Thebans sent heralds asking to bury their dead, under a truce; and in this wise a truce was made. Agesilaus withdrew to Delphi, where on arrival he offered to the god a tithe of the produce of his spoils—no less than 100 talents. Gylis the polemarch meanwhile withdrew into Phocis at the head of his troops, and from that district made a hostile advance into Locris. Here nearly a whole day was spent by the men in freely helping themselves to goods and chattels out of the villages and pillaging the corn; but as it drew towards evening the troops began to retire, with the Lacedaemonians in the rear. The Locrians hung upon their heels with a heavy pelt of stones and javelins. Thereupon the Lacedaemonians turned short round and gave chase, laying some of their assailants low. Then the Locrians ceased clinging to their rear, but continued their volleys from the vantage-ground above. The Lacedaemonians again made efforts to pursue their persistent foes even up the slope. At last darkness descended on them, and as they retired man after man dropped, succumbing to the sheer difficulty of the ground; some in their inability to see what lay in front, or else shot down by the enemy's missiles. It was then that Gylis the polemarch met his end, as also Pelles, who was on his personal staff, and the whole of the Spartans present without exception—eighteen or thereabouts—perished, either crushed by stones or succumbing to other wounds. Indeed, except for timely aid brought from the camp where the men were supping, the chances are not a man would have escaped.

4. This incident ended the campaign. The army as a whole was disbanded, the contingents retiring to their several cities, and Agesilaus home across the Gulf by sea.

Subsequently the war between the two parties recommenced. The Athenians, Boeotians, Argives, and the other allies made Corinth the base of their operations; the Lacedaemonians and their allies held Sicyon as theirs. As to the Corinthians, they had to face the fact that, owing to their proximity to the seat of war, it was their territory which was ravaged and their people who perished, while the rest of the allies abode in peace and reaped the fruits of their lands in due season. Hence the majority of them, including the better class, desired peace, and gathering into knots they indoctrinated one another with these views.

On the other hand, it could hardly escape the notice of the allied powers, the Argives, Athenians, and Boeotians, as also those of the Corinthians themselves who had received a share of the king's moneys, or for whatever reason were most directly interested in the war, that if they did not promptly put the peace party out of the way, probably the state would go over to Sparta again. It seemed there was nothing for it but a general slaughter. There was a refinement of wickedness in the plan adopted. With most people the life even of a legally condemned criminal is held sacred during a solemn season, but these men deliberately selected the last day of the Eucleia,[6] when they might reckon on capturing more victims in the crowded market-place, for their murderous purposes. Their agents were supplied with the names of those to be got rid of, the signal was given, and then, drawing their daggers, they fell to work. Here a man was struck down standing in the centre of a group of talkers, and there another seated; a third while peaceably enjoying himself at the play; a fourth actually while officiating as a judge at some dramatic contest. When what was taking place became known, there was a general flight on the part of the better classes. Some fled to the images of the gods in the market-place, others to the altars; and here these unhallowed miscreants, ringleaders and followers alike, utterly regardless of duty and law, fell to butchering their victims even within the sacred precincts of the gods; so that even some of those against whom no hand was lifted—honest, law-abiding folk—were filled with sore amazement at sight of such impiety. In this way many of the elder citizens, as mustering more thickly in the market-place, were done to death. The younger men, acting on a suspicion conceived by one of their number, Pasimelus, as to what was going to take place, kept quiet in the Kraneion; but hearing screams and shouting, and being joined anon by some who had escaped from the affair, they took the hint, and, running up along the slope of the Acrocorinthus, succeeded in repelling an attack of the Argives and the rest. While they were still deliberating what they ought to do, down fell a capital from its column—without assignable cause, whether of earthquake or wind. Also, when they sacrificed, the aspect of the victims was such that the soothsayers said it was better to descend from the position.

So they retired, in the first instance prepared to go into exile beyond the territory of Corinth. It was only upon the persuasion of their friends and the earnest entreaties of their mothers and sisters who came out to them, supported by the solemn assurance of the men in power themselves, who swore to guarantee them against evil consequences, that some of them finally consented to return home. Presented to their eyes

[6] The festival of Artemis Eucleia.

was the spectacle of a tyranny in full exercise, and to their minds the consciousness of the obliteration of their city, seeing that boundaries were plucked up and the land of their fathers had come to be re-entitled by the name of Argos instead of Corinth; and furthermore, compulsion was put upon them to share in the constitution in vogue at Argos, for which they had little appetite, while in their own city they wielded less power than the resident aliens. So that a party sprang up among them whose creed was, that life was not worth living on such terms: their endeavour must be to make their fatherland once more the Corinth of old days—to restore freedom to their city, purified from the murderer and his pollution and fairly rooted in good order and legality. It was a design worth the venture: if they succeeded they would become the saviours of their country; if not—why, in the effort to grasp the fairest flower of happiness, they would but overreach, and find instead a glorious termination to existence.

It was in furtherance of this design that two men—Pasimelus and Alcimenes—undertook to creep through a watercourse and effect a meeting with Praxitas the polemarch of the Lacedaemonians, who was on garrison duty with his own division in Sicyon. They told him they could give him ingress at a point in the long walls leading to Lechaeum. Praxitas, knowing from previous experience that the two men might be relied upon, believed their statement; and having arranged for the further detention in Sicyon of the division which was on the point of departure, he busied himself with plans for the enterprise. When the two men, partly by chance and partly by contrivance, came to be on guard at the gate where the trophy now stands, without further ado Praxitas presented himself with his division, taking with him also the men of Sicyon and the whole of the Corinthian exiles. Having reached the gate, he had a qualm of misgiving, and hesitated to step inside until he had first sent in a man on whom he could rely to take a look at things within. The two Corinthians introduced him, and made so simple and straightforward a representation that the visitor was convinced, and reported everything as free of pitfalls as the two had asserted. Then the polemarch entered, but owing to the wide space between the double walls, as soon as they came to form in line within, the intruders were impressed by the paucity of their numbers. They therefore erected a stockade, and dug as good a trench as they could in front of them, pending the arrival of reinforcements from the allies. In their rear, moreover, lay the guard of the Boeotians in the harbour. Thus they passed the whole day which followed the night of ingress without striking a blow.

On the next day, however, the Argive troops arrived in all haste, hurrying to the rescue, and found the enemy duly drawn up. The Lacedaemonians were on their own right, the men of Sicyon next, and leaning against the eastern wall the Corinthian exiles, 150 strong. Their opponents marshalled their lines face to face in correspondence: Iphicrates with his mercenaries abutting on the eastern wall; next to them the Argives, while the Corinthians of the city held their left. In the pride inspired by numbers they began advancing at once. They overpowered the Sicyonians, and tearing asunder the stockade, pursued them to the sea and here slew numbers of them. At that instant Pasimachus, the cavalry general, at the head of a handful of troopers, seeing the Sicyonians hard pressed, made fast the horses of his troopers to the trees, and relieving the Sicyonians of their heavy infantry shields, advanced with his volunteers against the Argives. The latter, seeing the *Sigmas* on the shields and taking them to be Sicyonians, had not the slightest fear. Whereupon, as the story goes, Pasimachus, exclaiming in his broad Doric, "By the twin gods,[7] these Sigmas will cheat you, you Argives," came to close quarters, and in that battle of a handful against a host, was slain himself with all his followers. In another quarter of the field, however, the Corinthian exiles had got the better of their opponents and worked their way up, so that they were now touching the wall around the city.

The Lacedaemonians, on their side, perceiving the discomfiture of the Sicyonians, sprang out with timely aid, keeping the palisade-work on their left. But the Argives, discovering that the Lacedaemonians were behind them, wheeled round and came racing back, pouring out of the palisade at full speed. Their extreme right, with unprotected flanks exposed, fell victims to the Lacedaemonians; the rest, hugging the wall, made good their retreat in dense masses towards the city. Here they encountered the Corinthian exiles, and, discovering that they had fallen upon foes, swerved aside in the reverse direction. In this predicament some mounted by the ladders of the city wall, and, leaping down from its summit, were destroyed; others perished, thrust through, as they jostled at the foot of the steps; others again were literally trampled under one another's feet and suffocated.

The Lacedaemonians had no difficulty in the choice of victims; for at that instant a work was assigned to them to do, such as they could hardly have prayed for. To find delivered into their hands a mob of helpless enemies, in an ecstasy of terror, presenting their unarmed sides in such sort that none turned to defend himself, but each victim rather seemed to contribute what he could towards his own destruction,—if that was not a divine interposition, I know not what to call it. At any

[7] Castor and Pollux.

rate, in that little space so many fell, and the corpses lay piled so thick, that eyes familiar with the stacking of corn or wood or piles of stones were called upon to gaze at layers of human bodies. Nor did the guard of the Boeotians in the port itself escape death: some were slain upon the ramparts, others on the roofs of the dock-houses, which they had scaled for refuge. Nothing remained but for the Corinthians and Argives to carry away their dead under a truce; while the allies of Lacedaemon poured in their reinforcements. When these were collected, Praxitas decided in the first place to raze enough of the walls to allow a free passage for an army on march. This done, he put himself at the head of his troops and advanced on the road to Megara, taking by assault, first Sidus and next Crommyon. Leaving garrisons in these two fortresses, he retraced his steps, and finally fortifying Epieiceia as a garrison outpost to protect the territory of the allies, he at once disbanded his troops and himself withdrew to Lacedaemon.

After this the great armaments of both belligerents had ceased to exist. The states merely furnished garrisons—the one set at Corinth, the other set at Sicyon—and were content to guard the walls. Though even so, a vigorous war was carried on by dint of the mercenary troops with which both sides were furnished.

A signal incident of the period was the invasion of Phlius by Iphicrates. He laid an ambuscade, and with a small body of troops adopting a system of guerilla war, took occasion of an unguarded sally of the citizens of Phlius to inflict such losses on them, that though they had never previously received the Lacedaemonians within their walls, they received them now. They had hitherto feared to do so lest it might lead to the restoration of the banished members of the community, who gave out that they owed their exile to their Lacedaemonian sympathies; but they were now in such abject fear of the Corinthian party that they sent to fetch the Lacedaemonians, and delivered the city and citadel to their safe keeping. These latter, however well disposed to the exiles of Phlius, did not, all the time they held the city, so much as breathe the thought of bringing back the exiles; on the contrary, as soon as the city seemed to have recovered its confidence, they took their departure, leaving city and laws precisely as they had found them on their entry.

To return to Iphicrates and his men: they frequently extended their incursions even into Arcadia in many directions, following their usual guerilla tactics, but also making assaults on fortified posts. The heavy infantry of the Arcadians positively refused to face them in the field, so profound was the terror in which they held these light troops. In compensation, the light troops themselves entertained a wholesome dread of the Lacedaemonians, and did not venture to approach even within javelin-range of their heavy infantry. They had been taught a lesson when, within that distance, some of the younger hoplites had made a dash at them, catching and putting some of them to the sword. But however profound the contempt of the Lacedaemonians for these light troops, their contempt for their own allies was deeper. (On one occasion a reinforcement of Mantineans had sallied from the walls between Corinth and Lechaeum to engage the peltasts, and had no sooner come under attack than they swerved, losing some of their men as they made good their retreat. The Lacedaemonians were unkind enough to poke fun at these unfortunates. "Our allies," they said, "stand in as much awe of these peltasts as children of the hobgoblins of their nurses." For themselves, starting from Lechaeum, they found no difficulty in marching right round the city of Corinth with a single Lacedaemonian division and the Corinthian exiles.)

The Athenians, on their side, who felt the power of the Lacedaemonians to be dangerously close, now that the walls of Corinth had been laid open, and even apprehended a direct attack upon themselves, determined to rebuild the portion of the wall severed by Praxitas. Accordingly they set out with their whole force, including stonelayers, masons, and carpenters, and within a few days erected a quite splendid wall on the side facing Sicyon towards the west, and then proceeded with more leisure to the completion of the eastern portion.

To turn once more to the other side: the Lacedaemonians, indignant at the notion that the Argives should be gathering the produce of their lands in peace at home, as if war were a pastime, marched against them. Agesilaus commanded the expedition, and after ravaging their territory from one end to the other, crossed their frontier at Tenea and swooped down upon Corinth, taking the walls which had been lately rebuilt by the Athenians. He was supported on the sea side by his brother Teleutias with a naval force of about twelve triremes, and the mother of both was able to congratulate herself on the joint success of both her sons; one having captured the enemy's walls by land and the other his ships and naval arsenal by sea, on the same day. These achievements sufficed Agesilaus for the present; he disbanded the army of the allies and led the state troops home.

5. Subsequently the Lacedaemonians made a second expedition against Corinth. They heard from the exiles that the citizens contrived to preserve all their cattle in Peiraeum; indeed, large numbers derived their subsistence from the place. Agesilaus was again in command of the expedition. In the first instance he advanced upon the Isthmus. It

was the month of the Isthmian games,[8] and here he found the Argives engaged in conducting the sacrifice to Poseidon, as if Corinth were Argos. So when they perceived the approach of Agesilaus, the Argives and their friends left the offerings as they lay, including the preparations for the breakfast, and retired with undisguised alarm into the city by the Cenchrean road. Agesilaus, though he observed the movement, refrained from giving chase, but taking up his quarters in the temple, there proceeded to offer victims to the god himself, and waited until the Corinthian exiles had celebrated the sacrifice to Poseidon, along with the games. But no sooner had Agesilaus turned his back and retired, than the Argives returned and celebrated the Isthmian games afresh; so that in this particular year there were cases in which the same competitors were twice defeated in this or that contest, or conversely, the same man was proclaimed victor twice over.

On the fourth day Agesilaus led his troops against Peiraeum, but finding it strongly defended, he made a sudden retreat after the morning meal in the direction of the capital, as though he calculated on the betrayal of the city. The Corinthians, in apprehension of some such catastrophe, sent to summon Iphicrates with the larger portion of his light infantry. These passed by duly in the night, not unobserved, however, by Agesilaus, who at once turned round at break of day and advanced on Peiraeum. He himself kept to the low ground by the hot springs, sending a division to scale the top of the pass. That night he encamped at the hot springs, while the division bivouacked in the open, in possession of the pass. Here Agesilaus distinguished himself by an invention as seasonable as it was simple. Among those who carried provisions for the division not one had thought of bringing fire. The altitude was considerable; there had been a fall of rain and hail towards evening and the temperature was low; besides which, the scaling party were clad in thin garments suited to the summer season. There they sat shivering in the dark, with scarcely heart to attack their suppers, when Agesilaus sent up to them as many as ten porters carrying fire in earthen pots. One found his way up one way, one another, and presently there were many bonfires blazing—magnificently enough, since there was plenty of wood to hand; so that all fell to oiling themselves and many supped over again. The same night the sky was lit up by the blaze of the temple of Poseidon—set on fire no one knows how.

When the men in Peiraeum perceived that the pass was occupied, they at once abandoned all thought of self-defence and fled for refuge to the Heraeum—men and women, slaves and free-born, with the greater part

[8] The Isthmian games were celebrated about April in the first and third Olympic years.

of their flocks and herds. Agesilaus, with the main body, meanwhile pursued his march by the sea-shore, and the division, simultaneously descending from the heights, captured the fortified position of Oenoe, appropriating its contents. Indeed, all the troops on that day reaped a rich harvest in the supplies they brought in from various farmsteads. Presently those who had escaped into the Heraeum came out, offering to leave it to Agesilaus to decide what he would do with them. He decided to deliver up to the exiles all those concerned with the late butchery, and that all else should be sold. And so from the Heraeum streamed out a long line of prisoners, while from other sides embassies arrived in numbers; and amongst these a deputation from the Boeotians, anxious to learn what they should do to obtain peace. These latter Agesilaus, with a certain loftiness of manner, affected not even to see, although Pharax, their proxenus, stood by their side to introduce them. Seated in a circular edifice on the margin of the lake, he surveyed the host of captives and valuables as they were brought out. Beside the prisoners, to guard them, stepped the Lacedaemonian warriors from the camp, carrying their spears—and were much admired, so readily will success and the transient fortune of the moment rivet attention. But even while Agesilaus was still thus seated, wearing a look betokening satisfaction at some great achievement, a horseman came galloping up; the flanks of his charger streamed with sweat. To the many inquiries what news he brought, the rider responded never a word; but being now close beside Agesilaus, he leaped from his horse, and running up to him with gloomy visage narrated the disaster of the Spartan division at Lechaeum. At these tidings the king sprang instantly from his seat, clutching his spear, and bade his herald summon to a meeting the generals, captains of fifties, and commanders of foreign brigades. When these had rapidly assembled he bade them, seeing that the morning meal had not yet been tasted, to swallow hastily what they could, and with all possible speed to overtake him. But for himself, he, with the officers of the royal staff, set off at once without breakfast. His bodyguard, with their heavy arms, accompanied him with all speed—himself in advance, the officers following behind. In this fashion he had already passed beyond the warm springs, and was well within the plateau of Lechaeum, when three horsemen rode up with further news: the dead bodies had been picked up. When he heard this he commanded the troops to order arms, and having rested them a little, led them back again to the Heraeum. The next day he spent in disposing of the captured property.

The ambassadors of the Boeotians were then summoned, and, being asked to explain the object of their coming, made no further mention of peace, but replied that, if there was nothing to hinder it, they wished to have a pass to their own soldiers within the capital. The king answered

104   *Xenophon*   [390 B.C.]

with a smile, "I know your desire is not so much to see your soldiers as to feast your eyes on the good fortune of your friends, and to measure its magnitude. Wait then, I will conduct you myself; with me you will be better able to discover the true value of what has taken place." And he was as good as his word. Next day he sacrificed, and led his army up to the gates of Corinth. The trophy he respected, but not one tree else did he leave standing—chopping and burning, as proof positive that no one dared to face him in the field. And having so done, he encamped about Lechaeum; and as to the Theban ambassadors, in lieu of letting them pass into the city, he sent them off by sea across to Creusis.

But since such a calamity was unusual for the Lacedaemonians, a widespread mourning fell upon the whole Laconian army, those alone excepted whose sons or fathers or brothers had died at their post. The bearing of these resembled that of conquerors, as with bright faces they moved freely to and fro, glorying in their domestic sorrow. Now the disaster to the division happened this way: It was the unvaried custom of the men of Amyclae to return home at the Hyacinthia,[9] to join in the sacred paean, a custom not to be interrupted either by active service or absence from home or for any other reason. So, too, on this occasion, Agesilaus had left behind all the Amyclaeans serving in any part of his army at Lechaeum. At the right moment the general in command of the garrison at that place had posted the garrison troops of the allies to guard the walls during his absence, and put himself at the head of his division of heavy infantry with that of the cavalry, and led the Amyclaeans past the walls of Corinth. Arrived at a point within three miles or so of Sicyon, the polemarch turned back himself in the direction of Lechaeum with his heavy infantry regiment, 600 strong, giving orders to the cavalry commandant to escort the Amyclaeans with his division as far as they required, and then to turn and overtake him. It cannot be said that the Lacedaemonians were ignorant of the large number of light troops and heavy infantry inside Corinth, but owing to their former successes they arrogantly presumed that no one would attack them. Within the capital of the Corinthians, however, their scant numbers— a thin line of heavy infantry unsupported by light infantry or cavalry —had been noted; and Callias, the son of Hipponicus, who was in command of the Athenian hoplites, and Iphicrates at the head of his peltasts, saw no risk in attacking with the light brigade. Since if the enemy continued his march by the high road, he would be cut up by showers of javelins on his exposed right flank; or if he were tempted to take the offensive, they with their peltasts, the nimblest of all light troops, would easily slip out of the grasp of his hoplites.

[9] Observed on three days of the month Hecatombaeon (July).

With this clearly-conceived idea they led out their troops; and while Callias drew up his heavy infantry in line at no great distance from the city, Iphicrates and his peltasts made a dash at the returning division.

The Lacedaemonians were presently within range of the javelins. Here a man was wounded, and there another killed. Each time orders were given to the attendant shield-bearers to pick up the men and bear them into Lechaeum; and these indeed were the only members of the regiment who were, strictly speaking, saved. Then the polemarch ordered the younger men to charge and drive off their assailants. Charge, however, as they might, they took nothing by their pains—not a man could they come at within javelin range. Being heavy infantry opposed to light troops, before they could get to close quarters the enemy's word of command sounded, "Retire!" while as soon as their own ranks fell back, scattered as they were in consequence of a charge where each man's individual speed had told, Iphicrates and his men turned right about and renewed the javelin attack, while others, running alongside, harassed their exposed flank. At the very first charge the assailants had shot down nine or ten, and, encouraged by this success, pressed on with increasing audacity. These attacks told so severely that the polemarch a second time gave the order (and this time for more of the younger men) to charge. The order was promptly obeyed, but on retiring they lost more men than on the first occasion, and it was not until the pick and flower of the division had succumbed that they were joined by their returning cavalry, in whose company they once again attempted a charge. The light infantry gave way, but the attack of the cavalry was feebly enforced. Instead of pressing home the charge until at least they had killed some of the enemy, they kept their horses abreast of their infantry skirmishes, charging and wheeling side by side.

Again and again the monotonous tale of doing and suffering repeated itself, except that as their own ranks grew thinner and their courage ebbed, the courage of their assailants grew bolder and their numbers increased. In desperation they massed compactly upon the narrow slope of a hillock, distant a quarter of a mile or so from the sea, and a couple of miles perhaps from Lechaeum. Their friends in Lechaeum, perceiving them, embarked in boats and sailed round until they were immediately under the hillock. And now, in despair, being so sorely troubled as man after man dropped dead, and unable to strike a blow, to crown their distress they saw the enemy's heavy infantry advancing. Then they took to flight; some of them threw themselves into the sea; others —a mere handful—escaped with the cavalry into Lechaeum. The death-roll, including those who fell in the second fight and the final fight, must have numbered 250 slain, or thereabouts. Such is the tale of the destruction of the Lacedaemonian regiment.

Subsequently, with the mutilated fragment of the division, Agesilaus turned his back upon Lechaeum, leaving another division behind to garrison that port. On his passage homewards, as he wound his way through the various cities, he made a point of arriving at each as late in the day as possible, renewing his march as early as possible next morning. Leaving Orchomenus at the first streak of dawn, he passed Mantinea still under cover of darkness. The spectacle of the Mantineans rejoicing at their misfortune would have been too severe an ordeal for his soldiers.

But Iphicrates had not yet reached the summit of his good fortune. Success followed upon success. Lacedaemonian garrisons had been placed in Sidus and Crommyon by Praxitas when he took these fortresses, and again in Oenoe, when Peiraeum was taken quite lately by Agesilaus. All of these now fell into the hands of Iphicrates. Lechaeum still held out, garrisoned as it was by the Lacedaemonians and their allies; while the Corinthian exiles, unable since the disaster of the regiment any longer to pass freely by land from Sicyon, had the sea passage still open to them, and using Lechaeum as their base, kept up a game of mutual annoyance with the party in the capital.

6. At a later date the Achaeans, being in possession of Calydon, a town from old times belonging to Aetolia, and having further incorporated the Calydonians as citizens, were under the necessity of garrisoning their new possessions. The reason was, that the Acarnanians were threatening the place with an army, and were aided by contingents from Athens and Boeotia, who were anxious to help their allies. Under the strain of this combined attack the Achaeans despatched ambassadors to Lacedaemon, who on arrival complained of the unfair conduct of Lacedaemon towards themselves. "We, sirs," they said, "are ever ready to serve in your armies, in obedience to whatever orders you choose to issue; we follow you wherever you think fit to lead; but when it comes to our being besieged by the Acarnanians, with their allies the Athenians and Boeotians, you show not the slightest concern. Understand, then, that if things go on thus we cannot hold out; but either we must give up all part in the war in Peloponnesus and cross over in full force to engage the Acarnanians, or we must make peace with them on whatever terms we can." This language was a tacit threat that if they failed to obtain the assistance they felt entitled to from Lacedaemon they would quit the alliance.

The ephors and the assembly concluded that there was no alternative but to assist the Achaeans in their campaign against the Acarnanians.

Accordingly they sent out Agesilaus with two divisions and the proper complement of allies. The Achaeans none the less marched out in full force themselves. No sooner had Agesilaus crossed the gulf than there was a general flight of the population from the country districts into the towns, while the flocks and herds were driven into remote districts that they might not be captured by the troops. Arriving on the frontier of the enemy's territory, Agesilaus sent to the general assembly of the Acarnanians at Stratus, warning them that unless they chose to give up their alliance with the Boeotians and Athenians, and to take instead themselves and their allies, he would ravage their territory through its length and breadth, and not spare a single thing. When they turned a deaf ear to this summons, the other proceeded to do what he threatened, systematically laying the district waste, felling the timber and cutting down the fruit-trees, while slowly moving on at the rate of a mile or so a day. The Acarnanians, owing to the slow progress of the enemy, were lulled into a sense of security. They even began bringing down their cattle from the mountains, and devoted themselves to the tillage of far the greater portion of their fields. But Agesilaus only waited till their rash confidence reached its climax; then on the fifteenth or sixteenth day after he had first entered the country he sacrificed at early dawn, and before evening had traversed eighteen miles or so of country to the lake round which were collected nearly all the flocks and herds of the Acarnanians, and so captured a vast quantity of cattle, horses, and grazing stock of all kinds, besides numerous slaves.

Having secured this prize, he stayed on the spot the whole of the following day, and devoted himself to disposing of the captured property by public sale. While he was thus engaged, a large body of Acarnanian light infantry appeared, and availing themselves of the position in which Agesilaus was encamped against the mountain side, assailed him with volleys of sling-stones and rocks from the ridge of the mountain, without suffering any harm themselves. By this means they succeeded in dislodging and forcing his troops down into the level plain, and that too at an hour when the whole camp was engaged in preparations for the evening meal. As night drew on, the Acarnanians retired; sentinels were posted, and the troops slept in peace.

Next day Agesilaus led off his army. The exit from the plain and meadow-land round the lake was a narrow opening through a close encircling range of hills. In occupation of this mountain barrier the Acarnanians, from the vantage-ground above, poured down stones and other missiles, or, creeping down to the fringes, dogged and annoyed them so much that the army was no longer able to proceed. If the heavy infantry or cavalry made sallies from the main line they did no harm to their assailants, for the Acarnanians had only to retire and they had quickly gained their strongholds. It was too severe a task, Agesilaus thought, to force his way through the narrow pass so sorely beset. He made up his mind, therefore, to charge that portion of the enemy who dogged his left, though these were pretty numerous. The range of hills on this side was more accessible to heavy infantry and horse alike. During the interval needed for the inspection of victims, the Acarnanians kept pressing them with javelins and stones, and, coming into close proximity, wounded man after man. But presently came the word of command, "Advance!" and the first two ranks of the heavy infantry ran forward, accompanied by the cavalry, at a round pace, the general himself steadily following with the rest of the column. Those of the Acarnanians who had crept down the mountainside at that instant in the midst of their sharpshooting turned and fled, and as they climbed the steep, man after man was slain. When, however, the top of the pass was reached, there stood the hoplites of the Acarnanians drawn up in battle line, and supported by the mass of their light infantry. There they steadily waited, keeping up a continuous discharge of missiles the while, or launching their long spears; whereby they dealt wounds to the cavalry troopers and death in some cases to the horses. But when they were all but within the clutches of the advancing heavy infantry of the Lacedaemonians their firmness forsook them; they swerved and fled, and there died of them on that day about 300. So ended the affair.

Agesilaus set up a trophy of victory, and afterwards making a tour of the country, he visited it with axe and fire. Occasionally, in obedience to pressure put upon him by the Achaeans, he would assault some city, but did not capture a single one. And now, as the season of autumn rapidly approached, he prepared to leave the country; whereupon the Achaeans, who looked upon his exploits as abortive, seeing that not a single city, willingly or unwillingly, had as yet been detached from their opponents, begged him, as the smallest service he could render them, at any rate to stay long enough in the country to prevent the Acarnanians from sowing their corn. He answered that the course they suggested ran counter to expediency. "You forget," he said, "that I mean to invade your enemies again next summer; and therefore the larger their sowing now, the stronger will be their appetite for peace hereafter." With this retort he withdrew overland through Aetolia, and by roads, moreover, which no army, small or great, could possibly have traversed without the consent of the inhabitants. The Aetolians, however, were only too glad to yield the Spartan king a free passage, cherishing hopes as they did that he would aid them to recover Naupactus. On reaching Rhium he crossed the gulf at that point and returned homewards, the

more direct passage from Calydon to Peloponnesus being effectually
barred by an Athenian squadron stationed at Oeniadae.

7. On the expiration of winter, and in fulfilment of his promise to
the Achaeans, Agesilaus called out the army once more with early spring
to invade the Acarnanians. The latter were apprised of his intention,
and, being persuaded that owing to the midland situation of their cities
they would just as truly be blockaded by an enemy who chose to destroy their corn as they would be if besieged with entrenchments in regular form, they sent ambassadors to Lacedaemon, and made peace with
the Achaeans and alliance with the Lacedaemonians. Thus closes this
page of history concerning the affairs of Acarnania.

To turn to the next. There was a feeling on the part of the Lacedaemonians that no expedition against Athens or Boeotia would be safe
so long as a state so important and so close to their own frontier as Argos remained in open hostility behind them. Accordingly they called out
the army against Argos. Now when Agesipolis learnt that the duty of
leadership devolved on him, and, moreover, that the sacrifices before
crossing the frontier were favourable, he went to Olympia and consulted
the will of the god. "Would it be lawful to him," he inquired, "not to
accept the holy truce, on the ground that the Argives made the season
for it [10] depend not on a fixed date, but on the prospect of a Lacedaemonian invasion?" The god indicated to the inquirer that he might lawfully repudiate any holy truce which was fraudulently dated. Not content with this, the young king, on leaving Olympia, went at once to
Delphi, and at that shrine put the same question to Apollo, "Were his
views in accord with his Father's as touching the holy truce?" The son
of Zeus answered, "Yea, altogether in accordance."

Then, without further hesitation, picking up his army at Phlius
(where, during his absence to visit the temples, the troops had been
collecting), he advanced by Nemea into the enemy's territory. The Argives, on their side, perceiving that they would be unable to hinder his
advance, in accordance with their custom sent a couple of heralds, garlanded, and presented their usual plea of a holy truce. Agesipolis answered them curtly that the gods were not satisfied with the justice of
their plea, and, refusing to accept the truce, pushed forward, causing
thereby great perplexity and consternation throughout the rural districts and in the capital itself.

But while he was getting his evening meal that first evening in the Argive territory—just at the moment when the after-dinner libation had
been poured out—the god sent an earthquake; and with one consent the

[10] Variation in the calendar made it easy for Greek cities to shift the times of
festivals.

Lacedaemonians, beginning with the officers of the royal quarters, sang the sacred hymn of Poseidon. The soldiers, in general, expected to retreat, arguing that, on the occurrence of an earthquake once before, Agis had retired from Elis. But Agesipolis held another view: if the god had sent his earthquake at the moment when he was meditating invasion, he should have understood that the god forbade his entrance; but now, when the invasion was a thing effected, he must needs take it as a signal of his approval. Accordingly next morning he sacrificed to Poseidon, and advanced a short distance farther into the country.

The late expedition of Agesilaus into Argos was still fresh in men's minds, and Agesipolis was eager to ascertain from the soldiers how close his predecessor had advanced to the fortification walls; or again, how far he had gone in ravaging the open country—not unlike a competitor in the pentathlon, eager to cap the performance of his rival in each event. On one occasion it was only the discharge of missiles from the towers which forced him to recross the trenches round the walls; on another, profiting by the absence of the majority of the Argives in Laconian territory, he came so close to the gates that their defenders actually shut out their own Boeotian cavalry on the point of entering, in terror lest the Lacedaemonians might pour into the town in company; and these Boeotian troopers were forced to cling, like bats to a wall, under the walls beneath the battlements. Had it not been for the accidental absence of the Cretans, who had gone off on a raid to Nauplia, without a doubt numbers of men and horses would have been shot down. At a later date, while encamping in the neighbourhood of the Enclosures,[11] a thunderbolt fell into his camp. One or two men were struck, while others died from the effect of the concussion on their brains. At a still later period he was anxious to fortify some sort of garrison outpost in the pass of Celusa, but upon offering sacrifice the livers of the victims proved lobeless, and he was constrained to lead back and disband his army—not without serious injury inflicted on the Argives, as the result of an invasion which had taken them wholly by surprise.

8. Such were the land operations in the war. Meanwhile another series of events was being enacted on the sea and within the seaboard cities; and these I will now narrate in detail. But I shall confine my pen to the more memorable incidents, and others of less account I shall pass over.

In the first place, then, Pharnabazus and Conon, after defeating the Lacedaemonians in the naval engagement off Cnidus, commenced a tour of inspection round the islands and the maritime states, expelling from them, as they visited them, one after another, the Spartan gov-

---

[11] What these were is unknown.

ernors. Everywhere they gave consolatory assurances to the citizens that
they had no intention of establishing fortress citadels within their walls,
or in any way interfering with their self-government. Such words fell
soothingly upon the ears of those to whom they were addressed; the
proposals were courteously accepted; all were eager to present Pharnabazus with gifts of friendship and hospitality. The satrap, indeed, was
only applying the instructions of his master Conon on these matters—
who had taught him that if he acted thus all the states would be friendly
to him, whereas, if he showed any intention to enslave them, the smallest of them would, as Conon insisted, be capable of causing a world of
trouble, and the chances were, if apprehensions were once excited, he
would find himself face to face with a coalition of united Hellas. To
these admonitions Pharnabazus lent a willing ear.

Accordingly, when disembarking at Ephesus, he presented Conon
with a fleet of forty triremes, and having further instructed him to meet
him at Sestos, set off himself by land along the coast to visit his own
provinces. For here it should be mentioned that his old enemy Dercylidas chanced to be in Abydos at the time of the sea-fight; nor had he
at a later date suffered eclipse with the other governors, but, on the contrary, had kept tight hold of Abydos and still preserved it in attachment to Lacedaemon. The course he had adopted was to summon a
meeting of the Abydenians, when he made them a speech as follows,
"Gentlemen, to-day it is possible for you, who have before been friends
to my city, to appear as benefactors of the Lacedaemonians. For a man
to prove faithful to his friends in the heyday of their good fortune is
no great marvel; but to prove steadfast when his friends are in misfortune—that is a service monumental for all time. But do not mistake me.
It does not follow that, because we have been defeated in a great sea-
fight, we are therefore annihilated. Certainly not. Even in old days,
you will admit, when Athens was mistress of the sea, our state was not
powerless to benefit friends or chastise enemies. Moreover, in proportion
as the rest of the cities have joined hands with fortune to turn their
backs upon us, so much the more certainly will the grandeur of your fidelity shine forth. Or, is any one haunted by the fear that we may find
ourselves blockaded by land and sea? Let him consider that at present
there is no Hellenic navy whatever on the seas, and if the barbarian attempts to clutch the empire of the sea, Hellas will not sit by and suffer
it; so that, if only in self-defence, she must inevitably take your side."

To this the Abydenians lent no deaf ears, but rather responded with
willingness approaching enthusiasm—extending the hand of fellowship
to the ex-governors, some of whom were already flocking to Abydos as
a harbour of refuge, while others they sent to summon from a distance.

So when a number of efficient and serviceable men had been collected, Dercylidas ventured to cross over to Sestos—lying, as it does, not more than a mile distant, directly facing Abydos. There he not only set about collecting those who held lands in the Chersonese through Lacedaemonian influence, but extended his welcome also to the governors who had been driven out of European states. He insisted that, if they came to think of it, not even was their case desperate, reminding them that even in Asia, which originally belonged to the Persian monarch, places were to be found—such as the little state of Temnos, or Aegae, and others, capable of administering their affairs, unsubjected to the king of Persia. "But," he added, "if you want a strong impregnable position, I cannot conceive what better you can find than Sestos. Why, it would need a combined naval and military force to invest that port." By these and such like arguments he rescued them from the lethargy of despair.

Now when Pharnabazus found Abydos and Sestos so conditioned, he gave them to understand that unless they chose to eject the Lacedaemonians, he would make war upon them; and when they refused to obey, having first assigned to Conon as his business to keep the sea closed against them, he proceeded in person to ravage the territory of the men of Abydos. Presently, finding himself no nearer the fulfilment of his object—which was their reduction—he set off home himself and left it to Conon the while so to conciliate the Hellespontine states that as large a naval power as possible might be mustered against the coming spring. In his wrath against the Lacedaemonians, in return for the treatment he had received from them, his paramount object was to invade their territory and exact what vengeance he could.

The winter was thus fully taken up with preparations; but with the approach of spring, Pharnabazus and Conon, with a large fleet fully manned, and a foreign mercenary brigade to boot, threaded their way through the islands to Melos. This island was to serve as a base of operations against Lacedaemon. And in the first instance he sailed down to Pherae and ravaged that district, after which he made successive descents at various other points on the seaboard, and did what injury he could. But in apprehension of the harbourless character of the coast, coupled with the enemy's facility of reinforcement and his own scarcity of supplies, he very soon turned back and sailed away, until finally he came to moorings in the harbour of Phoenicus in Cythera. The occupants of the city of the Cytherians, in terror of being taken by storm, evacuated the walls. To dismiss these under a truce across to Laconia was his first step; his second was to repair the fortress in question and to leave a garrison in the island under an Athenian governor—Nicophemus. After this he set sail to the Isthmus of Corinth, where he de-

livered an exhortation to the allies begging them to prosecute the war
vigorously, and to show themselves faithful to the Great King, and so,
having left them all the money he had with him, set off on his voyage
home.

But Conon had a proposal to make: If Pharnabazus would allow
him to keep the fleet, he would undertake, in the first place, to support it free of expense from the islands; besides which, he would sail
to his own country and help his fellow-citizens the Athenians to rebuild
their long walls and the fortifications round Piraeus. No heavier blow,
he insisted, could well be inflicted on Lacedaemon. "In this way, I can
assure you," he added, "you will win the eternal gratitude of the Athenians and wreak consummate vengeance on the Lacedaemonians, since
at one stroke you will render null and void that on which they have bestowed their utmost labour." These arguments so far weighed with
Pharnabazus that he despatched Conon to Athens with alacrity, and
further supplied him with funds for the restoration of the walls. Thus
it was that Conon, on his arrival at Athens, was able to rebuild a large
portion of the walls—partly by lending his own crews, and partly by
giving pay to carpenters and stone-masons, and meeting all the necessary expenses. There were other portions of the walls which the Athenians and Boeotians and other states raised as a joint voluntary undertaking.

Nor must it be forgotten that the Corinthians, with the funds left
them by Pharnabazus, manned a fleet—the command of which they
entrusted to their admiral Agathinus—and so were undisputed masters
of the sea within the gulf round Achaia and Lechaeum.

The Lacedaemonians, in opposition, fitted out a fleet under the command of Podanemus. That officer, in an attack of no great moment, lost
his life, and Pollis, his second in command, was presently in his turn
obliged to retire, being wounded, whereupon Herippidas took command
of the vessels. On the other hand, Proaenus the Corinthian, who had relieved Agathinus, evacuated Rhium, and the Lacedaemonians recovered
that post. Subsequently Teleutias succeeded to Herippidas's fleet, and
it was then the turn of that admiral to dominate the gulf.

The Lacedaemonians were well informed of the proceedings of Conon. They knew that he was not only restoring the fortifications of
Athens by help of the king's gold, but maintaining a fleet at his expense
besides, and conciliating the islands and seaboard cities towards Athens.
If, therefore, they could indoctrinate Tiribazus—who was a general of
the king—with their sentiments, they believed they could not fail either
to draw him aside to their own interests, or, at any rate, to put a stop
to his feeding Conon's navy. With this intention they sent Antalcidas to

Tiribazus: his orders were to carry out this policy and, if possible, to arrange a peace between Lacedaemon and the king. The Athenians, getting wind of this, sent a counter-embassy, consisting of Hermogenes, Dion, Callisthenes, and Callimedon, with Conon himself. They at the same time invited the attendance of ambassadors from the allies, and there were also present representatives of the Boeotians, of Corinth, and of Argos. When they had arrived at their destination, Antalcidas explained to Tiribazus the object of his visit: he wished, if possible, to cement a peace between the state he represented and the king—a peace, moreover, exactly suited to the aspirations of the king himself; in other words, the Lacedaemonians gave up all claim to the Hellenic cities in Asia as against the king, while for their own part they were content that all the islands and other cities should be independent. "Such being our unbiased wishes," he continued, "for what earthly reason should [the Hellenes or] the king go to war with us? or why should he expend his money? The king is guaranteed against attack on the part of Hellas, since the Athenians are powerless apart from our leadership, and we are powerless so long as the separate states are independent." The proposals of Antalcidas sounded very pleasantly in the ears of Tiribazus, but to the opponents of Sparta they were the merest talk. The Athenians were apprehensive of an agreement which provided for the independence of the cities in the islands, whereby they might be deprived of Lemnos, Imbros, and Scyros. The Thebans, again, were afraid of being compelled to let the Boeotian states go free. The Argives did not see how such treaty contracts and covenants were compatible with the realisation of their own great object—the absorption of Corinth by Argos. And so it came to pass that this peace proved abortive, and the representatives departed each to his own home.

Tiribazus, on his side, thought it hardly consistent with his own safety to adopt the cause of the Lacedaemonians without the concurrence of the king—a scruple which did not prevent him from privately presenting Antalcidas with a sum of money, in hopes that when the Athenians and their allies discovered that the Lacedaemonians had the wherewithal to furnish a fleet, they might perhaps be more disposed to desire peace. Further, accepting the statements of the Lacedaemonians as true, he took on himself to secure the person of Conon, as guilty of wrongdoing towards the king, and shut him up. That done, he set off up country to the king to recount the proposals of Lacedaemon, with his own subsequent capture of Conon as a wrong-doer man, and to ask for further guidance on all these matters.

On the arrival of Tiribazus at the palace, the king sent down Struthas to take charge of the seaboard district. The latter, however, was a strong

partisan of Athens and her allies, since he found it impossible to forget
the long list of evils which the king's country had suffered at the hands
of Agesilaus; so that the Lacedaemonians, contrasting the hostile disposition of the new satrap towards themselves with his friendliness to
the Athenians, sent Thibron to deal with him by force of arms.

That general crossed over and established his base of operations in
Ephesus and the towns in the plain of the Maeander—Priene, Leucophrys, and Achilleum—and proceeded to harry the king's territory, sparing neither live nor dead chattel. But as time went on, Struthas, who
could not but note the disorderly, and indeed recklessly scornful manner
in which the Lacedaemonian brought up his supports on each occasion,
despatched a body of cavalry into the plain. Their orders were to gallop
down and scour the plain, making a clean sweep of all they could lay
their hands on. Thibron, as it befell, had just finished breakfast, and
was returning from the mess with Thersander the flute-player. The latter was not only a good flute-player, but, as affecting Lacedaemonian
manners, laid claim to personal prowess. Struthas, then, seeing the disorderly advance of the supports and the paucity of the vanguard, appeared suddenly at the head of a large body of cavalry, all in orderly
array. Thibron and Thersander were the first to be cut down, and when
these had fallen the rest of the troops were easily turned. A mere chase
ensued, in which man after man was struck down, though a remnant
contrived to escape into the friendly cities; still larger numbers owed
their safety to their late discovery of the business on hand. Nor, indeed,
was this the first time the Spartan commander had rushed to the field,
without even issuing a general order. So ends the history of these events.

A party of Rhodian exiles expelled by the popular party arrived at
Lacedaemon. They insisted that it was not equitable to allow the Athenians to subjugate Rhodes and thus build up so vast a power. The Lacedaemonians were alive to the fact that the fate of Rhodes depended on
which party in the state prevailed: if the democracy were to dominate,
the whole island must fall into the hands of Athens; if the wealthier
classes, into their own. Accordingly they fitted out for them a fleet of
eight vessels, and put Ecdicus in command of it as admiral.

At the same time they despatched another officer on board these vessels named Diphridas, on a separate mission. His orders were to cross
over into Asia and to secure the states which had received Thibron. He
was also to pick up the survivors of Thibron's army, and with these
troops, aided by a second army which he would collect from any other
quarter open to him, he was to prosecute the war against Struthas.
Diphridas followed out his instructions, and amongst other achievements was fortunate enough to capture Tigranes, the son-in-law of

Struthas, with his wife, on their road to Sardis. The sum paid for their ransom was so large that he at once had the money to pay his mercenaries. Diphridas was no less attractive than his predecessor Thibron; but he was of a more orderly temperament, steadier, and incomparably more enterprising as a general; the secret of this superiority being that he was a man over whom the pleasures of the body exercised no sway. He became readily absorbed in the business before him—whatever he had to do he did with a will.

Ecdicus, having reached Cnidus, there learned that the democracy in Rhodes were entirely masters of the situation. They were dominant by land and sea; indeed they possessed a fleet twice the size of his own. He was therefore content to keep quiet in Cnidus until the Lacedaemonians, perceiving that his force was too small to allow him to benefit their friends, determined to relieve him. With this view they ordered Teleutias to take the twelve ships which formed his squadron (at present in the gulf adjoining Achaia and Lechaeum), and to feel his way round to Ecdicus: that officer he was to send home. For himself, he was to undertake personally to protect the interests of all who cared to be their friends, while injuring the enemy by every possible means.

So then Teleutias, having reached Samos, where he added some vessels to his fleet, set sail to Cnidus. At this point Ecdicus returned home, and Teleutias, continuing his voyage, reached Rhodes, at the head now of twenty-seven vessels. It was during this portion of the voyage that he fell in with Philocrates, the son of Ephialtes, who was sailing from Athens to Cyprus with ten triremes, in aid of their ally Evagoras. The whole flotilla fell into the Spartan's hands—a curious instance, it may be added, of cross purposes on the part of both belligerents. Here were the Athenians, supposed to be on friendly terms with the king, engaged in sending an allied force to support Evagoras, who was at open war with him; and here again was Teleutias, the representative of a people at war with Persia, engaged in crippling a fleet which had been despatched on a mission hostile to their adversary. Teleutias put back into Cnidus to dispose of his captives, and so eventually reached Rhodes, where his arrival brought timely aid to the party in favour of Lacedaemon.

And now the Athenians, fully impressed with the belief that their rivals were laying the basis of a new naval supremacy, despatched Thrasybulus the Steirian to check them, with a fleet of forty ships. That officer set sail, but abstained from bringing aid to Rhodes, and for good reasons. In Rhodes the Lacedaemonian party had hold of the fortress, and would be out of reach of his attack, especially as Teleutias was close at hand to aid them with his fleet. On the other hand, his own friends ran no danger of succumbing to the enemy, as they held the cities and were numerically much stronger, and they had established their superiority in the field. Consequently he made for the Hellespont, where, in the absence of any rival power, he hoped to achieve some stroke of good fortune for his city. Thus, in the first place, having detected the rivalries existing between Amedocus, the king of the Odrysians, and Seuthes, the rival ruler of the seaboard, he reconciled them to each other, and made them friends and allies of Athens, in the belief that if he secured their friendship the Hellenic cities on the Thracian coast would show greater favour to Athens. Such being the happy state of affairs not only in Europe but as regards the states in Asia also, thanks to the friendly attitude of the king to his fellow-citizens, he sailed into Byzantium and sold the tithe-duty levied on vessels arriving from the Euxine. By another stroke he converted the oligarchy of Byzantium into a democracy. The result of this was that the Byzantine common people were no longer sorry to see as many Athenians in their city as possible. Having so done, and having further won the friendship of the men of Calchedon, he set sail south of the Hellespont. Arrived at Lesbos, he found all the cities devoted to Lacedaemon with the exception of Mytilene. He therefore attacked none of the former until he had organised a force within the latter. This force consisted of 400 hoplites, furnished from his own vessels, and a corps of exiles from the different cities who had sought shelter in Mytilene; to which he added a stout contingent, the pick of the Mytileneian citizens themselves. He stirred the ardour of the several contingents by suitable appeals: representing to the men of Mytilene that by their capture of the cities they would at once become the chiefs and patrons of Lesbos; to the exiles he made it appear that if they would but unite to attack each several city in turn, they might all reckon on their particular restoration; while he needed only to remind his own warriors that the acquisition of Lesbos meant not only the attachment of a friendly city, but the discovery of a mine of wealth. The exhortations ended and the contingents organised, he advanced against Methymna.

Therimachus, who chanced to be the Lacedaemonian governor at the time, on hearing of the meditated attack of Thrasybulus, had taken a body of marines from his vessels, and, aided by the citizens of Methymna themselves, along with all the Mytileneian exiles to be found in that place, advanced to meet the enemy on their borders. A battle was fought and Therimachus was slain, a fate shared by several of the exiles of his party.

As a result of his victory the Athenian general succeeded in winning the adhesion of some of the states; or, where adhesion was refused, he could at least raise supplies for his soldiers by freebooting expeditions, and so hastened to reach his goal, which was the island of Rhodes. His chief concern was to support as powerful an army as possible in those parts, and with this object he proceeded to collect money, visiting various cities, till he finally reached Aspendus, and came to moorings in the river Eurymedon. The money was safely collected from the Aspendians, and the work completed, when, taking occasion of some depredations of the soldiers on the farms, the people of the place in a fit of irritation burst into the general's quarters at night and butchered him in his tent.

So perished Thrasybulus, a good and great man by all admission. In his place the Athenians chose Agyrrhius, who was despatched to take command of the fleet. And now the Lacedaemonians—alive to the fact that the sale of the Euxine tithe-dues had been negotiated in Byzantium by Athens; aware also that as long as the Athenians kept hold on Calchedon the loyalty of the other Hellespontine cities was secured to them (at any rate while Pharnabazus remained their friend)—felt that the state of affairs demanded their serious attention. They attached no blame indeed to Dercylidas. Anaxibius, however, through the friendship of the ephors, contrived to get himself appointed as governor, on a mission to Abydos. With the requisite funds and ships, he promised to exert such hostile pressure upon Athens that at least her prospects in the Hellespont would cease to be so good. His friends the ephors granted him in return for these promises three ships of war and funds to support 1,000 mercenaries, and so they despatched him on his mission. Reaching Abydos, he set about improving his naval and military position. First he collected a foreign brigade, by help of which he drew off some of the Aeolid cities from Pharnabazus. Next he set on foot a series of retaliatory expeditions against the states which attacked Abydos, marching upon them and ravaging their territories; and lastly, manning three vessels besides those which he already held in the harbour of Abydos, he intercepted and brought into port all the merchant ships of Athens or of her allies which he could lay hands on.

Learning of these proceedings, the Athenians, fearing lest the fair foundations laid for them by Thrasybulus in the Hellespont should be ruined, sent out Iphicrates with eight vessels and 1,200 peltasts. The majority of them consisted of troops which he had commanded at Corinth. In explanation it may be stated that the Argives, when once they had appropriated Corinth and incorporated it with Argos, gave out they had no further need of Iphicrates or his troops; the real fact being that he had put to death some of the partisans of Argos. And so it was he turned his back on Corinth and found himself at home in Athens at the present crisis.

When Iphicrates first reached the Chersonese he and Anaxibius carried on war against each other by sending guerilla bands across the straits. But as time wore on, information reached him of the departure of Anaxibius to Antandrus, accompanied by his mercenaries and his own bodyguard of Laconians and 200 Abydenian hoplites. Hearing further that Anaxibius had won the friendship of Antandrus, Iphicrates conjectured that after establishing a garrison in that place he would make the best of his way back, if only to bring the Abydenians home again. He therefore crossed in the night, selecting a desert point on the Abydene coast, from which he scaled the hills above the town and planted himself in ambuscade within their folds. The triremes which brought him across had orders at break of day to coast up northwards along the Chersonese, which would suggest the notion that he was only out on one of his customary voyages to collect money. The sequel more than fulfilled his expectations. Anaxibius began his return march, and if report speaks truly, he did so notwithstanding that the sacrifices were against his marching that day; contemptuously disregarding the warning, and satisfied that his march lay all along through a friendly country and was directed to a friendly city. Besides which, those whom he met assured him that Iphicrates was off on a voyage to Proconnesus: hence the unusual absence of precaution on the march. On his side Iphicrates saw the chance, but, so long as the troops of Anaxibius lingered on the level bottoms, refused to spring from his lair, waiting for the moment when the Abydenian division in the van was safely landed in the plain of Cremaste, at the point where the gold mines stand; the main column following on the downward slope, and Anaxibius with his Laconians just beginning the descent. At that instant Iphicrates set his ambuscade in motion, and dashed against the Spartan at full speed. The latter quickly discerned that there was no hope of escape as he scanned the long straggling line of his attenuated column. The troops in advance, he was persuaded, would never be able to come back to his aid up the face of that acclivity; besides which, he observed the utter bewilderment of the whole body at sight of the ambuscade. He therefore turned to those next him, and spoke as follows, "Men, it is good for me to die on this spot, where honour bids me; but you hurry and save yourselves before the enemy can close with us." When he had spoken, he took his shield from his shield-bearer, and there died fighting; not quite alone, for by his side a favourite youth stood, and of the Lacedaemonian governors who had rallied to Abydos from their several cities yet other twelve fought and fell beside the pair. The rest fled, dropping one by one as the army pursued them to the walls of the city. The death-roll amounted to something like fifty hoplites of the Abydenians, and of the rest 200. After this exploit Iphicrates returned to the Chersonese.

BOOK V

1. Such was the state of affairs in the Hellespont, so far at least as Athens and Sparta are concerned. Eteonicus was once more in Aegina; and notwithstanding that the Aeginetans and Athenians had up to this time held commercial intercourse, yet now that the war was plainly to be fought out on the sea, that officer, with the concurrence of the ephorate, gave permission to any one who liked to plunder Attica. The Athenians retaliated by despatching a body of hoplites under their general Pamphilus, who constructed a fort against the Aeginetans, and proceeded to blockade them by land and sea with ten warships. Teleutias, however, while threading his way among the islands in quest of contributions, had chanced to reach a point where he received information of the turn in affairs with regard to the construction of the fortress, whereupon he came to the rescue of the beleaguered Aeginetans, and so far succeeded that he drove off the enemy's blockading squadron. But Pamphilus kept a firm hold on the offensive fortress, and was not to be dislodged.

After this the new admiral, Hierax, arrived from Lacedaemon. The naval force was transferred into his successor's hands, and under the happiest auspices Teleutias set sail for home. As he descended to the seashore to start on his homeward voyage there was not one among his soldiers who had not a warm shake of the hand for their old admiral. Here one presented him with a crown, and there another with a victor's wreath; and those who arrived too late, still, as the ship weighed anchor, threw garlands into the sea and prayed for many blessings for him. I am well aware that in the above incident I have no memorable story of munificence, peril, or invention to narrate, but in all sincerity I protest that a man may find food for reflection in the inquiry what Teleutias had done to create such a disposition in his subordinates. Here we are brought face to face with a true man's work more worthy of account than multitudes of riches or adventure.

The new admiral, Hierax, taking with him the larger portion of the fleet, set sail once more for Rhodes. He left behind him twelve vessels in Aegina under his vice-admiral Gorgopas, who was now installed as governor of that island. In consequence of this change the Athenian troops inside the fortress were more blockaded than the Aeginetans themselves, so much so that a vote was passed by the Athenian assembly, in obedience to which a large fleet was manned, and the garrison, after four months' sojourn in Aegina, were brought back. But this was no sooner done than they began to be harassed by Gorgopas and the privateers again. To operate against these they fitted out thirteen vessels, choosing Eunomus as admiral in command. Hierax was still at Rhodes when the Lacedaemonians sent out a new admiral, Antalcidas; they believed that they could not find a better mode of gratifying Tiribazus. Accordingly Antalcidas, after visiting Aegina in order to pick up the vessels under Gorgopas, set sail for Ephesus. At this point he sent back Gorgopas with his twelve ships to Aegina, and appointed his vice-admiral Nicolochus to command the remainder of the fleet.

Nicolochus was to relieve Abydos, and thither set sail; but in the course of the voyage turned aside to Tenedos, where he ravaged the territory, and, with the money so secured, sailed on to Abydos. The Athenian generals on their side, collecting from Samothrace, Thasos, and the fortresses in that quarter, hastened to the relief of Tenedos; but, finding that Nicolochus had continued his voyage to Abydos, they selected the Chersonese as their base, and proceeded to blockade him and his fleet of twenty-five vessels with the thirty-two vessels under their joint command.

Meanwhile Gorgopas, returning from Ephesus, fell in with the Athenian admiral Eunomus, and, shunning an encounter at the moment, sought shelter in Aegina, which he reached a little before sunset; and at once disembarking his men, set them down to their evening meal; while Eunomus on his side, after hanging back for a little while, sailed away. Night fell, and the Athenian, showing the customary signal light to prevent his squadron straggling, led the way in the darkness. Gorgopas instantly got his men on board again, and, taking the lantern for his guide, followed the Athenians, craftily lagging behind a little space, so as not to show himself or raise any suspicion of his presence. In place of the usual cry the boatswains timed the rowers by a clink of stones, and they slid the oars. When the squadron of Eunomus was touching the coast, off Cape Zoster in Attica, the Spartan sounded the bugle-note for the charge. Some of Eunomus's vessels were in the act of discharging their crews, others were still getting to their moorings, while others were as yet only bearing down to land. The engagement was fought by the light of the moon, and Gorgopas captured four triremes, which he tied astern, and so set sail with his prizes in tow towards Aegina. The rest of the Athenian squadron made their escape into the harbour of Piraeus.

It was after these events that Chabrias commenced his voyage to Cyprus, bringing relief to Evagoras. His force consisted at first of 800 light troops and ten triremes, but was further increased by other vessels from Athens and a body of heavy infantry. Thus reinforced, the admiral chose a night and landed in Aegina; and secreted himself in ambuscade with his light troops in hollow ground some way beyond the temple of Heracles. At break of day, as prearranged, the Athenian hoplites made their appearance under command of Demaenetus, and began mounting up between two and three miles beyond the Heracleium at Tripurgia, as it is called. The news soon reached Gorgopas, who sallied out to the rescue with the Aeginetans and the marines of his vessels, being further accompanied by eight Spartans who happened to be with him. Not content with these he issued orders inviting any of the ships' crews, who were free men, to join the relief party. A large number of these sailors responded. They armed themselves as best they could, and the advance commenced. When the vanguard were well past the ambuscade, Chabrias and his men sprang up from their hiding-place, and poured a volley of javelins and stones upon the enemy. At the same moment the hoplites, who had disembarked, were advancing, so that the Spartan vanguard, in the absence of anything like collective action, were speedily cut down, and among them fell Gorgopas with the Lacedaemonians. At their fall the rest of course turned and fled. One hundred and fifty Aeginetans were numbered among the slain, while the loss incurred by the foreigners, metics, and sailors who had joined the relief party, reached a total of 200. After this the Athenians sailed the sea as freely as in the times of actual peace. Nor would anything induce the sailors to row a single stroke for Eteonicus—even under pressure—since he had no pay to give.

Subsequently the Lacedaemonians despatched Teleutias once again to take command of the squadron, and when the sailors saw it was he who had come, they were overjoyed. He summoned a meeting and addressed them thus, "Soldiers, I am back again, but I bring with me no money. Yet if god be willing, and your zeal flag not, I will endeavour to supply you with provisions without stint. Be well assured, as often as I find myself in command of you, I have but one prayer—that your lives may be spared no less than mine; and as for the necessaries of existence, perhaps it would astonish you if I said that I would rather you should have them than I. Yet by the gods I swear I would welcome two days' starvation in order to spare you one. Was not my door open in old days to every comer? Open again it shall stand now; and so it shall be: when your own board overflows, you shall look in and mark the luxury of your general; but if at other times you see him bearing up against cold and heat and sleepless nights, you must apply the lesson to yourselves and study to endure those evils. I do not bid you do this for self-mortification's sake, but that you may derive some benefit from it. Soldiers, let Lacedaemon, our own mother-city, be to you an example. Her good fortune is reputed to stand high. That you know; and you know too, that she purchased her glory and her greatness not by faint-heartedness, but by choosing to suffer pain and incur dangers in the day of need. You, too, as I can bear you witness, have been in times past brave; but to-day must we strive to be better than ourselves. So shall we share our pains without repining, and when fortune smiles, mingle our joys; for indeed the sweetest thing of all surely is to flatter no man, Hellene or barbarian, for the sake of hire; we will suffice to ourselves, and from a source to which honour pre-eminently invites us; since, I need not remind you, abundance won from the enemy in war furnishes forth not bodily nutriment only, but glory everywhere."

So he spoke, and with one voice they all shouted to him to issue what orders he thought fit; they would not fail him in willing service. The general's sacrifice was just concluded, and he answered, "Good, then, my men; go now, as you intended, and take your evening meal, and next provide yourselves, please, with one day's food. After that repair to your ships without delay, for we have a voyage on hand, whither god wills, and must arrive in time." So then, when the men returned, he embarked them on their ships, and sailed under cover of night for the great harbour of Piraeus: at one time he gave the rowers rest, passing the order to take a snatch of sleep; at another he pushed forward towards his goal with rise and fall of oars. If any one supposes that there was a touch of madness in such an expedition—with but twelve triremes to attack an enemy possessed of a large fleet—he should consider the calculations of Teleutias. He was under the firm persuasion that the Athenians were more careless than ever about their navy in the harbour since the death of Gorgopas; and in case of finding warships riding at anchor—even so, there was less danger, he conjectured, in attacking twenty ships in the port of Athens than ten elsewhere; for, whereas, anywhere outside the harbour the sailors would certainly be quartered on board, at Athens it was easy to divine that the captains and officers would be sleeping at their homes, and the crews located here and there in different quarters.

Thus minded he set sail, and when he was five or six furlongs distant from the harbour he lay on his oars and rested. But with the first streak of dawn he led the way, the rest following. The admiral's orders to the crews were explicit. They were on no account to sink any merchant vessel; they were equally to avoid damaging their own vessels, but if at any point they espied a warship at her moorings they must try and cripple her. The trading vessels, provided they had got their cargoes on board, they must seize and tow out of the harbour; those of larger tonnage they were to board wherever they could and capture the crews. Some of his men actually jumped on to the Deigma quay, where they seized hold of various traders and pilots and deposited them bodily on board ship. So the Spartan admiral carried out his program.

As to the Athenians, meanwhile, some of them who got wind of what was happening rushed from indoors outside to see what the commotion meant, others from the streets home to get their arms, and others again were off to the city with the news. The whole of Athens rallied to the rescue at that instant, heavy infantry and cavalry alike, the apprehension being that Piraeus was taken. But the Spartan sent off the captured vessels to Aegina, telling off three or four of his triremes to convoy them thither; with the rest he followed along the coast of Attica, and emerging from the harbour, captured a number of fishing smacks, and passage boats laden with passengers crossing to Piraeus from the islands; and finally, on reaching Sunium he captured some merchantmen laden with corn or other merchandise. After these performances he sailed back to Aegina, where he sold his prizes, and with the proceeds was able to provide his troops with a month's pay, and for the future was free to cruise about and make what reprisals chance cast in his way. By such procedure he was able to support a full quota of mariners on board his squadron, and procured to himself the prompt and enthusiastic service of his troops.

Antalcidas had now returned from the Persian court with Tiribazus. The negotiations had been successful. He had secured the alliance of the Persian king and his military co-operation in case the Athenians and their allies refused to abide by the peace which the king dictated. But learning that his second in command, Nicolochus, was being blockaded with his fleet by Iphicrates and Diotimus in Abydos, he set off at once by land for that city. From there he took the fleet one night and put out to sea, having first spread a story that he had invitations from a party in Calchedon; but as a matter of fact he came to anchorage in Percote and there kept quiet. Meanwhile the Athenian forces under Demaenetus and Dionysius and Leontichus and Phanias learned of his movement, and were in hot pursuit towards Proconnesus. As soon as they were well past, the Spartan veered round and returned to Abydos, trusting to information brought him of the approach of Polyxenus with the Syracusan and Italian squadron of twenty ships, which he wished to pick up and incorporate with his own.

A little later the Athenian Thrasybulus of Collytus was making his way up with eight ships from Thrace, his object being to effect a junction with the main Athenian squadron. The scouts signalled the approach

of eight triremes, whereupon Antalcidas, embarking his marines on board
twelve of the fastest ships of his fleet, ordered them to make up their
full complements, where defective, from the remaining vessels, and so
lay to, skulking in his lair with all possible secrecy. As soon as the enemy's vessels came sailing past he gave chase; and they catching sight
of him took to flight. With his swiftest sailers he speedily overhauled
their laggards, and ordering his vanguard to let these alone, he followed
hard on those ahead. But when the foremost had fallen into his clutches,
the enemy's hinder vessels, seeing their leaders taken one by one, out of
sheer despondency fell an easy prey to the slower sailers of the foe, so
that not one of the eight vessels escaped.

Presently the Syracusan squadron of twenty vessels joined him, and
again another squadron from Ionia, or rather so much of that district
as lay under the control of Tiribazus. The full quota of the contingent
was further made up from the territory of Ariobarzanes (with whom
Antalcidas kept up a friendship of long standing), in the absence of
Pharnabazus, who by this date had already been summoned up country
on the occasion of his marriage with the king's daughter. With this fleet,
which, from whatever sources derived, amounted to more than eighty
ships, Antalcidas ruled the seas, and was in a position not only to cut
off the passage of vessels bound to Athens from the Euxine, but to convoy them into the harbours of Sparta's allies.

The Athenians could not but watch with alarm the growth of the enemy's fleet, and began to fear a repetition of their former misfortune.
To be trampled under foot by the hostile power seemed indeed no remote possibility, now that the Lacedaemonians had procured an ally in
the person of the Persian monarch, and they were in little less than a
state of siege themselves, pestered as they were by privateers from
Aegina. On all these grounds the Athenians became passionately desirous of peace. The Lacedaemonians were equally disgusted with the war
for various reasons—what with their garrison duties, one detachment
at Lechaeum and another at Orchomenus, and the necessity of keeping
watch and ward on the states, if loyal not to lose them, if disaffected
to prevent their revolt; not to mention that reciprocity of annoyance
of which Corinth was the centre. So again the Argives had a strong appetite for peace; they knew that the army had been called out against
them, and, it was plain, that no fictitious alteration of the calendar
would any longer stand them in good stead. Hence, when Tiribazus issued a summons calling on all who were willing to listen to the terms
of peace sent down by the king to present themselves, the invitation was
promptly accepted. When they had gathered, Tiribazus pointed to the

king's seal attached to the document, and proceeded to read the contents, which ran as follows:

"The king, Artaxerxes, deems it just that the cities in Asia, with the islands of Clazomenae and Cyprus, should belong to himself; the rest of the Hellenic cities he thinks it just to leave independent, both small and great, with the exception of Lemnos, Imbros, and Scyros, which three are to belong to Athens as of old. Should any of the parties concerned not accept this peace, I, Artaxerxes, will war against him or them, with those who share my views. This will I do by land and by sea, with ships and with money."

After listening to the above declaration the ambassadors from the several states proceeded to report the same to their respective governments. One and all of these took the oaths to ratify and confirm the terms unreservedly, with the exception of the Thebans, who claimed to take the oaths in behalf of all Boeotians. This claim Agesilaus repudiated: unless they chose to take the oaths in precise conformity with the words of the king's edict, which insisted on the future autonomy of each state, small or great, he would not admit them. To this the Theban ambassadors made no other reply, except that the instructions they had received were different. "Pray go, then," Agesilaus retorted, "and ask the question; and you may inform your countrymen that if they will not comply, they will be excluded from the treaty." The Theban ambassadors departed, but Agesilaus, out of hatred to the Thebans, took active measures at once. Having got the consent of the ephors he forthwith offered sacrifice. The offerings for crossing the frontier were propitious, and he pushed on to Tegea. From Tegea he despatched some of the knights right and left to visit the Perioeci and hasten their mobilisation, and at the same time sent commanders of allied brigades to the various cities on a similar errand. But before he had started from Tegea the answer from Thebes arrived: the point was yielded, they would suffer the states to be independent. Under these circumstances the Lacedaemonians returned home, and the Thebans were forced to accept the truce unconditionally, and to recognise the autonomy of the Boeotian cities. But now the Corinthians would not dismiss the garrison of the Argives. Accordingly Agesilaus had a word of warning for both. To the former he said that if they did not dismiss the Argives, and to the latter, if they did not quit Corinth, he would march an army into their territories. The terror of both was so great that the Argives marched out of Corinth, and Corinth was once again left to herself; whereupon the butchers and their accomplices in the deed of blood determined to retire from Corinth, and the rest of the citizens welcomed back their late exiles voluntarily.

Now that the transactions were complete, and the states were bound by their oaths to abide by the peace sent down to them by the king, the immediate result was a general disarmament, military and naval forces being alike disbanded; and so it was that the Lacedaemonians and Athenians, with their allies, found themselves in the enjoyment of peace for the first time since the period of hostilities subsequent to the demolition of the walls of Athens. From a condition which, during the war, can only be described as a sort of even balance with their antagonists, the Lacedaemonians now emerged; and reached preeminence consequent upon the Peace of Antalcidas, so called. As guarantors of the peace presented to Hellas by the king, and as administrators personally of the autonomy of the states, they had added Corinth to their alliance; they had obtained the independence of the states of Boeotia at the expense of Thebes, which meant the gratification of an old ambition; and lastly, by calling out the army in case the Argives refused to evacuate Corinth, they had put a stop to the appropriation of that city by the Argives.

2. Indeed the late events had so entirely shaped themselves in conformity with the wishes of the Lacedaemonians, that they determined to go a step farther and chastise those of their allies who either had been hostile to them during the war, or otherwise had shown themselves less favourable to Lacedaemon than to her enemies. Chastisement was not all; they must lay down such secure foundations for the future as should render the like disloyalty impossible again. As the first step towards this policy they sent a dictatorial message to the Mantineans, and ordered them to raze their fortifications, on the ground that they could not otherwise trust them not to side with their enemies. Many things in their conduct, they alleged, from time to time, had not escaped their notice: their frequent despatches of corn to the Argives while at war with Lacedaemon; at other times their refusal to furnish contingents during a campaign, on the pretext of some holy truce or other; or if they did reluctantly take the field—the miserable inefficiency of their service. "But, more than that," they added, "we note your envy of our good fortune and the extravagant pleasure you exhibit at any disaster."

This very year, moreover, it was commonly said, saw the expiration, as far as the Mantineans were concerned, of the thirty years' truce, consequent upon the battle of Mantinea.[1] On their refusal, therefore, to raze their fortification walls the army was called out against them. Agesilaus begged the state to absolve him from the conduct of this war on the plea that the city of Mantinea had done frequent service to his

[1] 418 B.C.

father [2] in his Messenian wars. Accordingly Agesipolis led the expedition—in spite of the cordial relations of his father Pausanias with the leaders of the popular party in Mantinea.

The first move of the invader was to subject the enemy's territory to devastation; but failing by such means to induce them to raze their walls, he proceeded to draw lines of circumvallation round the city, keeping half his troops under arms to screen the entrenching parties while the other half pushed on the work with the spade. As soon as the trench was completed, he experienced no further difficulty in building a wall round the city. Aware, however, of the existence of a large supply of corn inside the town, the result of the bountiful harvest of the preceding year, and averse to the notion of wearing out the city of Lacedaemon and her allies by tedious campaigning, he dammed up the river which flowed through the town.

It was a stream of no inconsiderable size. By erecting a barrier at its exit from the town he caused the water to rise above the basements of the private dwellings and the foundations of the fortification walls. Then, as the lower layers of bricks became saturated and refused their support to the rows above, the wall began to crack and soon to totter to its fall. The citizens for some time tried to prop it with pieces of timber, and used other devices to avert the imminent ruin of their tower; but finding themselves overmatched by the water, and in dread lest the fall at some point of the encircling wall might deliver them captive to the enemy, they signified their consent to raze their walls. But the Lacedaemonians now steadily refused any form of truce, except on the further condition that the Mantineans would suffer themselves to be broken up and distributed into villages. They, looking the necessity in the face, consented to do even that. The sympathisers with Argos among them, and the leaders of their democracy, thought that their fate was sealed. Then the father treated with the son, Pausanias with Agesipolis, in their behalf, and obtained immunity for them—sixty in number—on condition that they should quit the city. The Lacedaemonian troops stood lining the road on both sides, beginning from the gates, and watched the outgoers; and with their spears in their hands, in spite of bitter hatred, kept aloof from them with less difficulty than the Mantineans of the better classes themselves—a weighty testimony to the power of Spartan discipline, be it said. In conclusion, the wall was razed, and Mantinea split up into four parts, assuming once again its primitive condition as regards inhabitants. The first feeling was one of annoyance at the necessity of pulling down their present houses and building others, yet when the owners found themselves located so much nearer their

[2] Archidamus.

estates round about the villages, in the full enjoyment of aristocracy, and rid for ever of the troublesome demagogues, they were delighted with the turn which affairs had taken. It became the custom for Sparta to send them, not one commander of contingents, but four, one for each village; and the zeal displayed, now that the quotas for military service were furnished from the several village centres, was far greater than it had been under the democratic system. So the transactions in connection with Mantinea were brought to a conclusion, and thereby one lesson of wisdom was taught mankind—not to conduct a river though a fortress town.

The party in exile from Phlius, seeing the severe scrutiny to which the behaviour of the allies of Lacedaemon during the late war was being subjected, felt that their opportunity had come. They repaired to Lacedaemon, and laid great emphasis on the fact that, so long as they had been in power themselves at home, their city used to welcome Lacedaemonians within her walls, and her citizens flocked to the campaign under their leadership; but no sooner had they been driven into exile than a change had come. The men of Phlius now flatly refused to follow Lacedaemon anywhere; the Lacedaemonians, alone of all men living, must not be admitted within their gates. After listening to their story the ephors agreed that the matter demanded attention. Then they sent to the state of Phlius a message to this effect: the Phliasian exiles were friends of Lacedaemon; nor did it appear that they owed their exile to any misdoing. Under the circumstances, Lacedaemon claimed their recall from banishment, not by force, but as a concession voluntarily granted. When the matter was thus stated, the Phliasians were not without alarm that an army might march upon Phlius, and a party inside the town might admit the enemy within the walls; for within the walls of Phlius were to be found many who, either as blood relations or for other reasons, were partisans of the exiles, and as so often happens, at any rate in the majority of states, there was a revolutionary party who, in their ardour for reform, would welcome gladly their restoration. Owing to fears of this character, a formal decree was passed: to welcome home the exiles, and to restore to them all undisputed property, the purchasers of the same being indemnified from the treasury of the state; and in the event of any ambiguity or question arising between the parties, the same to be determined before a court of justice. Such was the position of affairs in connection with the Phliasian exiles at the date in question.

And now from yet another quarter ambassadors arrived at Lacedaemon: that is to say, from Acanthus and Apollonia, the two largest and most important states of the Olynthian confederacy. The ephorate, after learning from them the object of their visit, presented them to the assembly and the allies, in presence of whom Cleigenes of Acanthus made a speech to this effect, "Men of Lacedaemon and of the allied states, are you aware of a portentous growth within the bosom of Hellas? Few here need to be told that for size and importance Olynthus now stands at the head of the Thracian cities. But are you aware that the citizens of Olynthus have already brought over several states by the bribe of joint citizenship and common laws; that they have forcibly annexed some of the larger states; and that, so encouraged, they have taken in hand further to free the cities of Macedonia from Amyntas the king of the Macedonians; that, as soon as their immediate neighbours had shown compliance, they at once proceeded to attack larger and more distant communities; so much so, that when we started to come hither, we left them masters not only of many other places, but of Pella itself, the capital of Macedonia. Amyntas, we saw plainly, must soon withdraw from his cities, and was in fact already all but in name an outcast from Macedonia.

"The Olynthians have actually sent to ourselves and to the men of Apollonia a joint embassy, warning us of their intention to attack us if we refuse to present ourselves at Olynthus with a military contingent. Now, for our parts, men of Lacedaemon, we desire nothing better than to abide by our ancestral laws and institutions, to be free and independent citizens; but if aid from without is going to fail us, we too must follow the rest and coalesce with the Olynthians. Why, even now they muster no less than 800 heavy infantry and a considerably larger body of light infantry, while their cavalry, when we have joined them, will exceed 1,000 men. At the date of our departure we left embassies from Athens and Boeotia in Olynthus, and we were told that the Olynthians themselves had passed a formal resolution to return the compliment. They were to send an embassy on their side to the aforesaid states to treat of an alliance. And yet, if the power of the Athenians and the Thebans is to be further increased by such an accession of strength, look to it," the speaker added, "whether hereafter you will find things so easy to manage in that quarter.

"They hold Potidaea, the key to the isthmus of Pallene, and therefore, you can well believe, they can command the states within that peninsula. If you want any further proof of the abject terror of those states, you have it in the fact that notwithstanding the bitter hatred which they bear to Olynthus, not one of them has dared to send ambassadors along with us to apprise you of these matters.

"Reflect, how you can reconcile your anxiety to prevent the unification of Boeotia with your neglect to hinder the solidifying of a far larger power—a power destined, moreover, to become formidable not on land only, but by sea? For what is to stop it, when the soil itself supplies timber for shipbuilding, and there are rich revenues derived from numerous harbours and commercial centers?—it cannot but be that abundance of food and abundance of population will go hand in hand. Nor have we yet reached the limits of Olynthian expansion; there are their neighbours to be thought of—the kingless or independent Thracians. These are already to-day the devoted servants of Olynthus, and when it comes to their being actually under her, that means at once another vast accession of strength to her. With the Thracians in her train, the gold mines of Pangaeus will stretch out to her the hand of welcome.

"In making these assertions, we are but uttering remarks ten thousand times repeated in the democracy of Olynthus. And as to their confident spirit, who shall attempt to describe it? It is god, for aught I know, who, with the growth of a new capacity, gives increase also to the proud thoughts and vast designs of humanity. For ourselves, men of Lacedaemon and of the allied states, our task is completed. We have played our parts in announcing to you how things stand there. To you it is left to determine whether what we have described is worthy of your concern. One only thing further you ought to recognise: the power we have spoken of as great is not as yet invincible, for those states which are involuntary participators in the citizenship of Olynthus will, in prospect of any rival power appearing in the field, speedily fall away. On the contrary, let them be once closely knit and welded together by the privileges of intermarriage and reciprocal rights of holding property in land—which have already become enactments; let them discover that it is a gain to them to follow in the wake of conquerors (just as the Arcadians, for instance, find it profitable to march in your ranks, whereby they save their own property and pillage their neighbours'); let these things come to pass, and perhaps you may find the knot no longer so easy to unloose."

At the conclusion of this address, the Lacedaemonians requested the allies to speak, bidding them give their joint advice as to the best course to be pursued in the interests of Peloponnese and the allies. Thereupon many members, and especially those who wished to gratify the Lacedaemonians, agreed in counselling active measures; and it was resolved that the states should severally send contingents to form a total of 10,000 men. Proposals were also made to allow any state, so wishing, to give money instead of men, at the rate of three Aeginetan obols a day per man; or where the contingent consisted of cavalry, the pay given for one horseman was to be equivalent to that of four hoplites; while, in the event of any state defaulting in service, the Lacedaemonians should be allowed to fine the said state of a stater per day for each man. These resolutions were passed, and the deputies from Acanthus rose again. They argued that, though excellent, these resolutions were not of a nature to be rapidly carried into effect. Would it not be better, they asked, pending the mobilisation of the troops, to despatch an officer at once in command of a force from Lacedaemon and the other states, not too large to start immediately. The effect would be instantaneous, for the states which had not yet given in their adhesion to Olynthus would be brought to a standstill, and those already forcibly enrolled would be shaken in their alliance. These further resolutions being also passed, the Lacedaemonians despatched Eudamidas, accompanied by a body of neodamodes, with perioeci and Sciritae, to the number of about 2,000. Eudamidas lost no time in setting out, having obtained leave from the ephors for his brother Phoebidas to follow later with the remainder of the troops assigned to him. Pushing on himself to the Thracian territory, he set about despatching garrisons to various cities at their request. He also secured the voluntary adhesion of Potidaea, although already a number of the Olynthian alliance; and this town now served as his base of operations for carrying on war on a scale adapted to his somewhat limited armament.

Phoebidas, when the remaining portion of his brother's forces was duly mustered, put himself at their head and commenced his march. On reaching Thebes the troops encamped outside the city, round the gymnasium. Faction was rife within the city. The two polemarchs in office, Ismenias and Leontiades, were diametrically opposed, being the respective heads of antagonistic political clubs. Hence it was that, while Ismenias, ever inspired by hatred to the Lacedaemonians, would not come anywhere near the Spartan general, Leontiades, on the other hand, was assiduous in courting him; and when a sufficient intimacy was established between them, he made a proposal as follows, "You have it in your power," he said, addressing Phoebidas, "this very day to confer supreme benefit on your country. Follow me with your hoplites, and I will introduce you into the citadel. That done, you may rest assured Thebes will be completely under the control of Lacedaemon and of us, your friends. At present, as you see, there is a proclamation forbidding any Theban to take service with you against Olynthus, but we will change all that. You have only to act with us as we suggest, and we shall at once be able to furnish you with large supplies of infantry and cavalry, so that you will join your brother with a magnificent reinforcement, and pending his proposed reduction of Olynthus, you will have accomplished the reduction of a far larger state than that—to wit, this city of Thebes."

The imagination of Phoebidas was kindled as he listened to the tempting proposal. To do a brilliant deed was far dearer to him than life; on the other hand, he had no reasoning capacity, and would seem to have been deficient altogether in sound sense. The consent of the Spartan secured, Leontiades bade him set his troops in motion, as if everything were ready for his departure. "And, when the proper moment comes," added the Theban, "I will be with you, and show you the way myself."

The senate was seated in the arcade in the market-place, since the Cadmeia was in possession of the women who were celebrating the Thesmophoria.[3] It was noon of a hot summer's day; scarcely a soul was stirring in the streets. This was the moment for Leontiades. He mounted on horseback and galloped off to overtake Phoebidas. He turned him back, and led him without further delay into the acropolis. Having posted Phoebidas and his soldiers inside, he handed him the key of the gates, and warning him not to suffer any one to enter into the citadel without a pass from himself, he straightway betook himself to the senate. Arrived there, he spoke as follows, "Gentlemen, the Lacedaemonians are in possession of the citadel; but that is no cause for despondency, since, as they assure us, they have no hostile intention, except, indeed, towards any one who has an appetite for war. For myself, and acting in obedience to the law, which empowers the polemarch to apprehend all persons suspected of capital crimes, I hereby seize the person of Ismenias as an arch-fomenter of war. I call upon you who are captains of companies, and you who are ranked with them, to do your duty. Arise and secure the prisoner, and lead him away to the place appointed."

Those who were privy to the affair, it will be understood, presented themselves, and the orders were promptly carried out. Of those not in the secret, but opposed to the party of Leontiades, some sought refuge at once outside the city in terror for their lives; while the rest retired to their houses at first; yet when they found that Ismenias was imprisoned in the Cadmeia, and further delay seemed dangerous, retreated to Athens. These were the men who shared the views of Androcedas and Ismenias, and they must have numbered about 300.

Now that the transactions were concluded, another polemarch was chosen in place of Ismenias, and Leontiades at once set out to Lacedaemon. There he found the ephors and the mass of the community highly incensed against Phoebidas, who had failed to execute the orders assigned him by the state. Against this general indignation, however, Agesilaus protested. If mischief had been wrought to Lacedaemon by this deed, it was just that the doer of it should be punished; but, if

---

[3] An ancient festival held by women in honour of Demeter and Persephone.

good, it was a time-honoured custom to allow full scope for impromptu acts of this character. "The sole point you have to look to," he urged, "is whether what has been done is good or evil." After this, however, Leontiades presented himself to the assembly and addressed the members as follows, "Lacedaemonians, the hostile attitude of Thebes towards you, before the occurrence of late events, was a topic constantly on your lips, since time upon time your eyes were called upon to witness her friendly bearing to your foes in contrast with her hatred of your friends. Can it be denied that Thebes refused to take part with you in the campaign against your direst enemy, the democracy in Piraeus; and balanced that lukewarmness by an onslaught on the Phocians, whose sole crime was cordiality to yourselves? Nor is that all. In full knowledge that you were likely to be engaged in war with Olynthus, she proceeded at once to make an alliance with that city. So that up to the last moment you were in constant expectation of hearing some day that the whole of Boeotia was laid at the feet of Thebes. With the late incidents all is changed. You need fear Thebes no longer. One brief despatch in cipher will procure support for your every wish in that quarter, provided only you will take as kindly an interest in us as we in you."

This appeal told upon the meeting, and the Lacedaemonians resolved formally, now that the citadel had been taken, to keep it, and to put Ismenias on trial. In consequence of this resolution a body of commissioners was despatched, three Lacedaemonians and one for each of the allied states, great and small alike. The court of inquiry thus constituted, the sittings commenced, and an indictment was preferred against Ismenias. He was accused of playing into the hands of the barbarian; of seeking amity with the Persian to the detriment of Hellas; of accepting sums of money as bribes from the king; and, finally, of being, along with Androcleidas, the prime cause of the whole intestine trouble to which Hellas was a prey. Each of these charges was met by the defendant, but to no purpose, since he failed to disabuse the court of their conviction that the grandeur of his designs was only equalled by their wickedness. The verdict was given against him, and he was put to death. The party of Leontiades thus possessed the city; and went beyond the injunctions given them in the eager performance of their services.

As a result of these transactions the Lacedaemonians pressed on the combined campaign against Olynthus with still greater enthusiasm. They not only sent out Teleutias as governor, but by their united efforts furnished him with an aggregate army of 10,000 men. They also sent despatches to the allied states, calling upon them to support Teleutias in accordance with the resolution of the allies. All the states were ready to display devotion to Teleutias, and to do him service, since he was a

man who never forgot a service rendered him. Nor was Thebes an exception; for was not the governor a brother of Agesilaus? Thebes, therefore, was enthusiastic in sending her contribution of heavy infantry and
cavalry. The Spartan conducted his march slowly and surely, taking
the utmost pains to avoid injuring his friends, and to collect as large a
force as possible. He also sent a message in advance to Amyntas, begging him, if he were truly desirous of recovering his empire, to raise a
body of mercenaries, and to distribute sums of money among the neighbouring kings with a view to their alliance. Nor was that all. He sent also
to Derdas, the ruler of Elimia, pointing out to him that the Olynthians,
having laid at their feet the great power of Macedonia, would certainly
not suffer his lesser power to escape unless they were stayed by force
of arms in their career of insolence. Proceeding thus, by the time he
had reached the territory of the allied powers, he was at the head of
a very considerable army. At Potidaea he halted to make the necessary
disposition of his troops, and thence advanced into the territory of the
enemy. As he approached the hostile city, he abstained from felling and
firing alike, being persuaded that to do so was only to create difficulties
in his own path, whether advancing or retreating; it would be time
enough, when he retired from Olynthus, to fell the trees and lay them
as a barrier in the path of any assailant in the rear.

Being now within a mile or so of the city he came to a halt. The left
division was under his personal command, for it suited him to advance
in a line opposite the gate from which the enemy sallied; the other division of the allies stretched away to the right. The cavalry were thus
distributed: the Laconians, Thebans, and all the Macedonians present
were posted on the right. With his own division he kept Derdas and his
troopers, 400 strong. This he did partly out of genuine admiration for
this body of horse, and partly as a mark of courtesy to Derdas, which
should make him not regret his coming.

Presently the enemy issued forth and formed in line opposite, under
cover of their walls. Then their cavalry formed in close order and
commenced the attack. Dashing down upon the Laconians and Boeotians
they dismounted Polycharmus, the Lacedaemonian cavalry general, inflicting many wounds on him as he lay on the ground, and cut down
others, and finally put to flight the cavalry on the right wing. The
flight of these troopers infected the infantry in close proximity to them,
who in turn swerved; and it looked as if the whole army was about to
be worsted, when Derdas at the head of his cavalry dashed straight at
the gates of Olynthus, Teleutias supporting him with the troops of his
division. The Olynthian cavalry, seeing how matters were going, and in
dread of finding the gates closed upon them, wheeled round and retired

swiftly. Thus it was that Derdas had his chance to cut down man after man as their cavalry ran the gauntlet past him. In the same way, too, the infantry of the Olynthians retreated within their city, though, owing to the closeness of the walls in their case, their loss was trifling. Teleutias claimed the victory, and a trophy was duly erected, after which he turned his back on Olynthus and devoted himself to felling the fruit-trees. This was the campaign of the summer. He now dismissed both the Macedonian army and the cavalry force of Derdas. Incursions, however, on the part of the Olynthians themselves against the states allied to Lacedaemon were frequent; lands were pillaged, and people put to the sword.

3. With the beginning of spring the Olynthian cavalry, 600 strong, had swooped into the territory of Apollonia—about the middle of the day—and dispersing over the district, were employed in pillaging; but as luck would have it, Derdas had arrived that day with his troopers, and was breakfasting in Apollonia. He noted the enemy's incursion, but kept quiet; his horses were ready saddled, and his troopers fully armed. As the Olynthians came galloping up contemptuously, not only into the suburbs, but to the very gates of the city, he seized his opportunity, and with his compact and well-ordered squadron dashed out; whereupon the invaders took to flight. Having once turned them, Derdas gave them no respite, pursuing and slaughtering them for ten miles or more, until he had driven them for shelter within the very ramparts of Olynthus. Report said that Derdas slew something like eighty men in this affair. After this the Olynthians were more disposed to keep to their walls, contenting themselves with tilling the merest corner of their territory.

Time advanced, and Teleutias was in conduct of another expedition against the city of Olynthus. His object was to destroy any timber still left standing, or fields still cultivated in the hostile territory. This brought out the Olynthian cavalry, who, stealthily advancing, crossed the river which washes the walls of the town, and again continued their silent march right up to the adversary's camp. At sight of an audacity which nettled him, Teleutias at once ordered Tlemonidas, the officer commanding his light infantry division, to charge the assailants at the run. On their side the men of Olynthus, seeing the rapid approach of the light infantry, wheeled and quietly retired until they had recrossed the river, drawing the enemy on, who followed with conspicuous hardihood. Rashly assuming the position of pursuers towards fugitives, they did not hesitate to cross the river which stood between them and their prey. Then the Olynthian cavalry, choosing a favourable moment, when those who had crossed seemed easy to deal with, wheeled and attacked them, putting Tlemonidas himself to the sword with more than

100 of his company. Teleutias, when he saw what was happening, snatched up his arms in a fit of anger and began leading his hoplites swiftly forward, ordering at the same time his peltasts and cavalry to give chase and not to slacken. Their fate was the fate of many before and since, who, in the ardour of pursuit, have come too close to the enemy's walls and found it hard to get back again. Under a hail of missiles from the walls they were forced to retire in disorder and with the necessity of guarding themselves against the missiles. At this juncture the Olynthians sent out their cavalry at full gallop, backed by supports of light infantry; and finally their heavy infantry reserves poured out and fell upon the enemy's lines, now in thorough confusion. Here Teleutias fell fighting, and when that happened, without further pause the troops immediately about him swerved. Not one soul longer cared to make a stand, but the flight became general, some fleeing towards Spartolus, others in the direction of Acanthus, a third set seeking refuge within the walls of Apollonia, and the majority within those of Potidaea. At the tide of fugitives broke into several streams, so also the pursuers divided the work between them; this way and that they poured, dealing death wholesale. So perished the best part of the army.

Such calamities are not indeed without a moral. The lesson they are meant to teach mankind, I think, is plain. If in a general sense one ought not to punish any one, even one's own slave, in anger, since the master in his wrath may easily incur worse evil himself than he inflicts, so, in the case of antagonists in war, to attack an enemy under the influence of passion rather than of judgment is an absolute error. For wrath is but a blind impulse devoid of foresight, whereas to the reason a blow parried may be better than a wound inflicted.

When the news of what had happened reached Lacedaemon it was agreed, after due deliberation, that a force should be sent, and of no trifling description, if only to quench the victors' pride, and to prevent their own achievements from becoming worthless. In this determination they sent out King Agesipolis as general, attended, like Agesilaus on his Asiatic campaign, by thirty Spartans. Volunteers flocked to his standard. They were partly the pick and flower of the provincials, partly foreigners of the class called foster-children,[4] or lastly, bastard sons of Spartans, comely and beautiful of limb, and well versed in the lore of Spartan discipline. The ranks of this invading force were further swelled by volunteers from the allied states, the Thessalians notably contributing a corps of cavalry. All were animated by the desire of becoming known to Agesipolis, so that even Amyntas and Derdas in zeal of service out-

[4] Xenophon's own sons educated at Sparta would belong to this class.

did themselves. With this promise of success Agesipolis marched forward against Olynthus.

Meanwhile the state of Phlius, complimented by Agesipolis on the amount of the funds contributed by them to his expedition and the celerity with which the money had been raised, and in full belief that while the one king was in the field they were secure against the hostile attack of the other (since it was hardly to be expected that both kings should be absent from Sparta at one moment), boldly desisted from doing justice by her lately reinstated citizens. On the one hand, these exiles claimed that points in dispute should be determined before an impartial court of justice; the citizens, on the other, insisted on the claimants submitting the cases for trial in the city itself. And when the latter asked, "What sort of trial that would be where the offenders were also the judges?" they appealed to deaf ears. Consequently the restored party appeared at Sparta, to prefer a complaint against their city. They were accompanied by other members of the community, who stated that many of the Phliasians themselves besides the appellants recognised the injustice of their treatment. The state of Phlius was indignant at this manoeuvre, and retaliated by imposing a fine on all who had betaken themselves to Lacedaemon without orders from the state. Those who incurred the fine hesitated to return home; they preferred to stay where they were and enforce their views, "It is quite plain now who were the perpetrators of all the violence—the very people who originally drove us into exile, and shut their gates upon Lacedaemon; the confiscators of our property one day, the ruthless opponents of its restoration the next. Who else but they have now brought it about that we should be fined for appearing at Lacedaemon? and for what purpose but to deter any one else for the future from venturing to expose the proceedings at Phlius?" Thus far the appellants. And indeed the conduct of the men of Phlius did seem insolent; so much so that the ephors called out the army against them.

Nor was Agesilaus dissatisfied with this decision, not only on the ground of old relations of friendly hospitality between his father Archidamus and the party of Podanemus, who were numbered among the restored exiles at this time, but because personally he was bound by similar ties himself towards the adherents of Procles, son of Hipponicus. The border sacrifices proving favourable, the march commenced at once. As he advanced, embassy after embassy met him, and tried by presents of money to avert invasion. But the king answered that the object of his march was not to commit wrongdoing, but to protect the victims of injustice. Then the petitioners offered to do anything, only they begged him to forgo invasion. Again he replied—How could he trust to their

words when they had lied to him already? He must have the warrant
of acts, not promises. And being asked, "What act would satisfy him?"
he answered once more, saying, "The same which you performed afore-
time, and suffered no wrong at our hands"—in other words, the surrender of the Acropolis. But to this they could not bring themselves.
Whereupon he invaded the territory of Phlius, and promptly drawing
lines of circumvallation, commenced the siege. Many of the Lacedaemonians objected, for the sake of a mere handful of wretched people, so to
embroil themselves with a state of over 5,000 men. For, indeed, to leave
no doubt on this score, the men of Phlius met regularly in assembly in
full view of those outside. But Agesilaus was not to be beaten by this
move. Whenever any of the townsmen came out, drawn by friendship
or kinship with the exiles, in every case the king's instructions were
to place the public messes at the service of the visitors, and, if they
were willing to go through the course of gymnastic training, to give them
enough to procure necessaries. All members of these classes were, by
the general's strict injunctions, further to be provided with arms, and
loans were to be raised for the purpose without delay. Presently the
superintendents of this branch of the service were able to turn out a
detachment of over 1,000 men, in the prime of bodily perfection, well
disciplined and splendidly armed, so that in the end the Lacedaemonians affirmed, "Fellow-soldiers of this stamp are too good to lose." Such
were the concerns of Agesilaus.

Meanwhile Agesipolis on leaving Macedonia advanced straight upon
Olynthus and took up a strategical position in front of the town. Finding that no one came out to oppose him, he occupied himself for the
present with pillaging any remnant of the district still intact, and with
marching into the territory allied with the enemy, where he destroyed
the corn. The town of Torone he attacked and took by storm. But
while he was so engaged, in the height of mid-summer he was attacked
by a burning fever. In this condition his mind reverted to a scene once
visited, the temple of Dionysus at Aphytis, and a longing for its cool
and sparkling waters and shady places seized him. To this spot accordingly he was carried, still living, but only to breathe his last outside the
sacred shrine, within a week of the day on which he sickened. His body
was laid in honey and conveyed home to Sparta, where he obtained royal
burial.

When the news reached Agesilaus he displayed none of the satisfaction which might possibly have been expected at the removal of an
antagonist. On the contrary, he wept and pined for the companionship
so severed, it being the fashion at Sparta for the kings when at home to
mess together and to share the same quarters. Moreover, Agesipolis

was admirably suited to Agesilaus, sharing with the merriment of youth
in tales of the chase and horsemanship and boyish loves; while, to
crown all, the touch of reverence due from younger to elder was not
wanting in their common life. In place of Agesipolis, the Lacedaemonians despatched Polybiades as governor to Olynthus.

Agesilaus had already exceeded the time during which the supplies of
food in Phlius were expected to last. The difference, in fact, between
self-command and mere appetite is so great that the men of Phlius had
only to pass a resolution to cut down the food expenditure by one half,
and by doing so were able to prolong the siege for twice the calculated
period. But if the contrast between self-restraint and appetite is so
great, no less startling is that between boldness and faint-heartedness.
A Phliasian named Delphion, a real hero, it would seem, took to himself
300 Phliasians, and not only succeeded in preventing the peace-party
from carrying out their wishes, but was equal to the task of incarcerat-
ing and keeping safely under lock and key those whom he mistrusted.
Nor did his ability end here. He succeeded in forcing the mob of citizens
to perform garrison duty, and by vigorous patrolling kept them constant to the work. Over and over again, accompanied by his personal
attendants, he would dash out of the walls and drive in the enemy's
outposts, first at one point and then at another of the beleaguering
circle. But the time eventually came when, search as they might by
every means, these picked defenders could find no further store of food
within the walls, and they were forced to send to Agesilaus, requesting
a truce for an embassy to visit Sparta, adding that they were resolved
to leave it to the discretion of the authorities at Lacedaemon to do with
their city what they liked. Agesilaus granted a pass to the embassy, but,
at the same time, he was so angry at their setting his personal authority
aside, that he sent to his friends at home and arranged that the fate of
Phlius should be left to his discretion. Meanwhile he proceeded to
tighten the cordon of investment, so as to render it impossible that a
single soul inside the city should escape. In spite of this, however,
Delphion, with one comrade, a branded dare-devil, who had often
stolen the arms of the besieging parties, escaped by night. Presently
the deputation returned with the answer from Lacedaemon that the state
left it entirely to the discretion of Agesilaus to decide the fate of Phlius
as seemed to him best. Then Agesilaus pronounced his verdict. A board
of 100—fifty taken from the restored exiles, fifty from those within the
city—were in the first place to inquire as to who deserved to live and
who to die, after which they were to lay down laws as the basis of a
new constitution. Pending the carrying out of these transactions, he left
a detachment of troops to garrison the place for six months, with pay

for that period. After this he dismissed the allied forces, and led the state division home. Thus the transactions concerning Phlius were brought to a conclusion, having occupied altogether one year and eight months.

Meanwhile Polybiades had reduced the citizens of Olynthus to the last stage of misery through famine. Unable to supply themselves with corn from their own land, or to import it by sea, they were forced to send an embassy to Lacedaemon to sue for peace. The plenipotentiaries on their arrival accepted articles of agreement by which they bound themselves to have the same friends and the same foes as Lacedaemon, to follow her lead, and to be enrolled among her allies; and so, having taken an oath to abide by these terms, they returned home.

On every side the affairs of Lacedaemon had signally prospered: Thebes and the rest of the Boeotian states lay absolutely at her feet; Corinth had become her most faithful ally; Argos, unable longer to avail herself of the subterfuge of a movable calendar, was humbled to the dust; Athens was isolated; and, lastly, those of her own allies who displayed a hostile feeling towards her had been punished; so that, to all outward appearance, the foundations of her empire were at length absolutely well and firmly laid.

4. Abundant examples might be found, alike in Hellenic and in foreign history, to prove that the gods mark what is done amiss, winking neither at impiety nor at the commission of unhallowed acts; but at present I confine myself to the facts before me. The Lacedaemonians, who had pledged themselves by oath to leave the states independent, had laid violent hands on the Acropolis of Thebes, and were eventually punished by the victims of that iniquity single-handed, the Lacedaemonians, be it noted, who had never before been mastered by living man; and not they alone, but those citizens of Thebes who introduced them into their Acropolis, and who wished to enslave their city to Lacedaemon, that they might play the tyrant themselves—how fared it with them? A bare seven of the exiles were sufficient to destroy their government. How this happened I will now narrate in detail.

There was a man named Phyllidas—he was secretary to Archias, that is, to the polemarchs. Beyond his official duties, he had rendered his chief other services, and all apparently in an exemplary fashion. A visit to Athens in pursuance of some business brought this man into contact with a former acquaintance of his own, Melon, one of the exiles who had fled for safety to Athens. Melon had various questions to ask touching the sort of tyranny practised by Archias in the exercise of the polemarchy, and by Philip. He soon discovered that affairs at home were still more detestable to Phyllidas than to himself. It only remained to exchange pledges, and to arrange the details of what was to be done. After a certain interval Melon, accompanied by six of the trustiest comrades he could find among his fellow-exiles, set off for Thebes. They were armed with nothing but daggers, and first of all crept into the neighbourhood under cover of night. The whole of the next day they lay concealed in a desert place, and drew near to the city gates in the guise of labourers returning home with the latest comers from the fields. Having got safely within the city, they spent the whole of that night at the house of a man named Charon, and again the next day in the same fashion. Phyllidas meanwhile was busily taken up with the concerns of the polemarchs, who were to celebrate a feast of Aphrodite on going out of office. Amongst other things, the secretary was to take this opportunity of fulfilling an old undertaking, which was the introduction of certain women to the polemarchs. They were to be the most majestic and the most beautiful to be found in Thebes. The polemarchs, on their side (and the character of the men is sufficiently marked), were looking forward to the pleasures of the night with joyful anticipation. Supper was over, and, thanks to the zeal with which the master of the ceremonies responded to their mood, they were speedily intoxicated. To their oft-repeated orders to introduce their mistresses, he went out and fetched Melon and the rest, three of them dressed up as women and the rest as their attendant maidens. Having brought them into the treasury of the polemarchs' residence, he returned himself and announced to Archias and his friends that the women would not present themselves as long as any of the attendants remained in the room; whereupon they promptly bade all withdraw, and Phyllidas, furnishing the servants with wine, sent them off to the house of one of them. And now at last he introduced the mistresses, and led them to their seats beside their respective lords. It was preconcerted that as soon as they were seated they were to throw aside their veils and strike home. That is one version of the death of the polemarchs. According to another, Melon and his friends came in as revellers, and so despatched their victims.

That over, Phyllidas, with three of the band, set off to the house of Leontiades. Arrived there, he knocked at the door, and sent in word that he had a message from the polemarchs. Leontiades, as chance befell, was still reclining in privacy after dinner, and his wife was seated beside him working wools. The fidelity of Phyllidas was well known to him, and he gave orders to admit him at once. They entered, slew Leontiades, and with threats silenced his wife. As they went out they ordered the door to be shut, threatening that if they found it open they would kill every one in the house. And now that this deed was done, Phyllidas, with two of the band, presented himself at the prison, telling the gaoler he had brought a man from the polemarchs to be locked up. The gaoler opened the door, and was at once despatched, and the prisoners were released. These they speedily supplied with arms taken from the armoury in the stoa, and then led them to the shrine of Amphion, and bade them take up a position there, after which they at once made a proclamation calling on all Thebans to come out, horse and foot, seeing that the tyrants were dead. The citizens, indeed, as long as it was night, not knowing whom or what to trust, kept quiet, but when day dawned and revealed what had occurred, the summons was responded to with alacrity, heavy infantry and cavalry under arms alike sallying forth. Horsemen were also despatched by the now restored exiles to the two Athenian generals on the frontier; and they, being aware of the object of the message [promptly responded].[5]

On the other hand, the Lacedaemonian governor in the citadel, as soon as that night's proclamation reached his ears, was not slow to send to Plataea[6] and Thespiae for reinforcements. The approach of the Plataeans was perceived by the Theban cavalry, who met them and killed a score of them and more, and after that achievement returned to the city, to find the Athenians from the frontier already arrived. Then they assaulted the Acropolis. The troops within recognised the paucity of their own numbers, while the zeal of their opponents (one and all advancing to the attack) was plainly visible, and loud were the proclamations, promising rewards to those who should be first to scale the walls. All this so worked upon their fears that they agreed to evacuate the place if the citizens would allow them a safe-conduct to retire with their arms. To this request the others gladly yielded, and they made a truce. Oaths were taken on the terms aforesaid, and the citizens dismissed their adversaries. For all that, as the garrison retired, those of them who were recognised as personal foes were seized and put to death. Some were rescued through the good offices of the Athenian reinforcements from the frontier, who smuggled them across and saved them. The Thebans were not content with putting the men to death; if any of them had children, these also were sacrificed to their vengeance.

When the news of these proceedings reached Sparta the first thing the Lacedaemonians did was to put to death the governor, who had abandoned the Cadmeia instead of awaiting reinforcements, and the next was to call out the army against Thebes. Agesilaus had little taste to head the expedition; he pointed out that he had seen more than forty years' service, and that the exemption from foreign duty applicable to others at that age was applicable on the same principle to the king.

[5] There is a lacuna in the manuscripts at this point.
[6] This city had been refounded in 386 B.C.

Such were the ostensible grounds on which he excused himself from the present expedition, but his real objections lay deeper. He felt certain that if he led the expedition his fellow-citizens would say, "Agesilaus caused all this trouble to the state in order to aid and abet tyrants." Therefore he preferred to leave his countrymen to settle the matter themselves as they liked. Accordingly the ephors, instructed by the Theban exiles who had escaped the late massacres, despatched Cleombrotus. He had not commanded before, and it was the depth of winter.

Now while Chabrias, with a body of Athenian peltasts, kept watch and ward over the road through Eleutherae, Cleombrotus made his way up by the direct route to Plataea. His column of light infantry, pushing forward in advance, fell upon the men who had been released from the Theban prison, guarding the summit, to the number of about 150. These, with the exception of one or two who escaped, were cut down by the peltasts, and Cleombrotus descended in person upon Plataea, which was still friendly to Sparta. Presently he reached Thespiae, and that was the base for an advance upon Cynoscephalae, where he encamped on Theban Territory. Here he halted sixteen days, and then again fell back upon Thespiae. At this latter place he now left Sphodrias as governor, with a third portion of each of the contingents of the allies, handing over to him all the money he had brought with him from home, with directions to supplement his force with a contingent of mercenaries.

Whilst Sphodrias was so employed, Cleombrotus himself commenced his homeward march, following the road through Creusis at the head of his own troops, who indeed were in considerable perplexity to discover whether they were at war with the Thebans or at peace, seeing that the general had led his army into Theban territory, had inflicted the minimum of mischief, and again retired. No sooner, however, was his back turned than a violent wind storm assailed him in his rear, which some construed as an omen clearly significant of what was about to take place. Many a blow this assailant dealt them, and as the general and his army, crossing from Creusis, scaled that face of the mountain[7] which stretches seaward, the blast hurled headlong from the precipices a string of asses, baggage and all; countless arms were wrested from the bearers' grasp and whirled into the sea; finally, numbers of the men, unable to march with their arms, deposited them at different points of the pass, first filling the hollow of their shields with stones. For the moment, then, they halted at Aegosthena, on Megarian soil, and supped as best they could. Next day they returned and recovered their arms. After this adventure the contingents lost no time in returning to their several homes, as Cleombrotus disbanded them.

[7] Mt. Cithaeron.

Meanwhile at Athens and Thebes alike fear reigned. To the Athenians the strength of the Lacedaemonians was unmistakable: the war was plainly no longer confined to Corinth; on the contrary, the Lacedaemonians had ventured to skirt Athenian territory and to invade Thebes. They were so worked upon by their alarm that the two generals who had been privy to the insurrection of Melon against Leontiades and his party had to suffer: the one was formally tried and put to death; the other, refusing to stand trial, was banished.

The apprehensions of the Thebans were of a different sort: their fear was rather lest they should find themselves in single-handed war with Lacedaemon. To prevent this they hit upon the following expedient. They worked upon Sphodrias, the Spartan governor left in Thespiae, by offering him, as at least was suspected, a substantial sum, in return for which he was to make an incursion into Attica; their great object being to involve Athens and Lacedaemon in hostilities. Sphodrias lent a willing ear, and, pretending that he could easily capture Piraeus in its present gateless condition, gave his troops an early evening meal and marched out of Thespiae, saying that he would reach Piraeus before daybreak. As a matter of fact day overtook him at Thria, nor did he take any pains even to conceal his intentions; on the contrary, being forced to turn aside, he seized cattle and sacked houses. Meanwhile some who chanced upon him in the night had fled to the city and brought news to the men of Athens that a large body of troops was approaching. They swiftly armed the cavalry and heavy infantry and stood on guard to protect the city. As chance befell, there were some Lacedaemonian ambassadors in Athens at the moment, at the house of Callias their proxenus; their names were Etymocles, Aristolochus, and Ocyllus. Immediately on receipt of the news the Athenians seized these three and imprisoned them, as not improbably concerned in the plot. Utterly taken aback by the affair themselves, the ambassadors pleaded that, had they been aware of an attempt to seize Piraeus, they would hardly have been so foolish as to put themselves into the power of the Athenians, or have selected the house of their proxenus for protection, where they were so easily to be found. It would, they further urged, soon be plain to the Athenians themselves that the state of Lacedaemon was quite as little cognisant of these proceedings as they. "You will hear before long" —such was their confident prediction—"that Sphodrias has paid for his behaviour by his life." Accordingly, the ambassadors were acquitted of all concern in the matter and dismissed. Sphodrias himself was recalled and indicted by the ephors on the capital charge, and, in spite of his refusal to face the trial, he was acquitted. This miscarriage of justice, as it seemed to many, who described it as unprecedented in Lacedaemon, has an explanation.

Sphodrias had a son named Cleonymus. He was just at the age when youth emerges from boyhood, very handsome and of high repute among his fellows. To this youth Archidamus, the son of Agesilaus, was passionately attached. Now the friends of Cleombrotus, as comrades of Sphodrias, were disposed to acquit him; but they feared Agesilaus and his friends, not to mention the intermediate party, for the enormity of his proceeding was clear. So then Sphodrias addressed his son Cleonymus, "You have it in your power, my son, to save your father, if you will, by begging Archidamus to dispose Agesilaus favourably to me at my trial." Thus instructed, the youth did not shrink from visiting Archidamus, and implored him for his sake to save his father. Now when Archidamus saw how Cleonymus wept, he too was melted to tears as he stood beside him, but to his petition he answered thus, "Nay, Cleonymus, it is the bare truth I tell you, I cannot so much as look my father in the face; if I wished anything transacted for me in the city I would beg assistance from the whole world sooner than from my father. Still, since it is you who bid me, rest assured I will do my best to bring this about for you as you desire." He then left the common hall and retired home to rest, but with dawn he arose and kept watch that his father might not go out without his knowledge. Presently, when he saw him ready to go forth, first some citizen was present, and then another and another; and in each case he stepped aside, while they held his father in conversation. By and by a stranger would come, and then another; and so it went on until he even found himself making way for a string of petitioning attendants. At last, when his father had turned his back on the Eurotas, and was entering his house again, he went away without so much as approaching him. The next day he fared no better: all happened as on the previous day. Now Agesilaus, although he had his suspicions why his son went to and fro in this way, asked no questions, but left him to take his own course. Archidamus, on his side, was longing, as was natural, to see his friend Cleonymus; but how he was to visit him, without having held the desired conversation with his father, he knew not. The friends of Sphodrias, observing that he who was once so frequent a visitor had ceased coming, were in agony; he must surely have been deterred by the reproaches of his father. At last, however, Archidamus dared to go to his father, and said, "Father, Cleonymus bids me ask you to save his father; grant me this boon, if possible, I beg you." He answered, "For yourself, my son, I can make excuse, but how shall my city make excuse for me if I fail to condemn that man who, for his own purpose, traffics to the injury of the state?" For the moment the other made no reply, but retired crestfallen before the verdict of justice. Afterwards, whether the thought was his own or that he was prompted by some other, he came and said, "Father, if Sphodrias had done no wrong you would have released him, that I know; but now, if he has done something wrong, may he not be excused by you for our sakes?" And the father answered, "If it can be done without loss of honour on our parts, so shall it be." At that word the young man, in deep despondency, turned and went. Now one of the friends of Sphodrias, conversing with Etymocles, remarked to him, "You are all bent on putting Sphodrias to death, I take it, you friends of Agesilaus?" And Etymocles replied, "If that be so, we all are bent upon one thing, and Agesilaus on another, since in all his conversations he still harps upon one string: that Sphodrias has done a wrong there is no denying, yet Sphodrias is a man who, from boyhood to manhood, was ever constant to the call of honour. To put such a man as that to death is hard; nay, Sparta needs such soldiers." The other accordingly went off and reported what he had just heard to Cleonymus; and he in the joy of his heart went straightway to Archidamus and said, "Now we know that you care for us; rest assured, Archidamus, that we in turn will take great pains that you shall never have cause to blush for our friendship." Nor did his acts belie his words; but so long as he lived he was ever faithful to the code of Spartan honour; and at Leuctra, fighting in front of the king side by side with Deinon the polemarch, thrice fell before he died, the first of the citizens in the midst of the enemy. And so, although he caused his friend the bitterest sorrow, yet to that which he had promised he was faithful, seeing he wrought Archidamus no shame, but contrariwise brought honour to him. In this way Sphodrias obtained his acquittal.

At Athens the friends of Boeotia were not slow to instruct the people that his countrymen, so far from punishing Sphodrias, had even applauded him for his designs on Athens; and in consequence of this the Athenians not only furnished Piraeus with gates, but set to work to build a fleet, and displayed great zeal in sending aid to the Boeotians. The Lacedaemonians, on their side, called out the army against the Thebans; and being persuaded that in Agesilaus they would find a more prudent general than Cleombrotus had proved, they begged the former to undertake the expedition. He, replying that the wish of the state was for him law, began making preparations to take the field.

Now he had come to the conclusion that without the occupation of Mount Cithaeron any attack on Thebes would be difficult. Learning then that the men of Cletor were just now at war with the men of Orchomenus, and were maintaining a foreign brigade, he came to an understanding with the Cletorians that in the event of his needing it, this force would be at his service; and as soon as the sacrifices for crossing the frontier proved favourable, he sent to the commander of the Cletorian mercenaries, and handing him a month's pay, ordered him to occupy Cithaeron with his men. This was before he himself reached Tegea. Meanwhile he sent a message to the men of Orchomenus that so long as the campaign lasted they must cease from war. If any city during his campaign abroad took on itself to march against another city, his first duty, he declared, would be to march against such offending city in accordance with a decree of the allies.

Thus crossing Cithaeron he reached Thespiae, and from that base made the territory of Thebes his objective. Finding the great plain fenced round with ditch and palisade, as also the most valuable portions of the country, he adopted the plan of shifting his encampment from one place to another. Regularly each day, after the morning meal, he marched out his troops and ravaged the territory, confining himself to his own side of the palisadings and trench. The appearance of Agesilaus at any point whatever was a signal to the enemy, who within the circuit of his entrenchment kept moving in parallel line to the invader, and was ever ready to defend the threatened point. On one occasion, the Spartan king having retired and being well on the road back to camp, the Theban cavalry, hitherto invisible, suddenly dashed out, following one of the regularly constructed roads out of the entrenchment. Taking advantage of the enemy's position—his light troops breaking off to supper or busily preparing the meal, and the cavalry, some of them still dismounted, and others in the act of mounting,—on they rode, pressing the charge home. Man after man of the light troops was cut down; and three cavalry troopers besides—two Spartans, Cleas and Epicydidas by name, and the third a provincial named Eudicus, who had not had time to mount their horses, and whose fate was shared by some Theban exiles. But presently Agesilaus wheeled about and advanced with his heavy infantry to the rescue; his cavalry dashed at the enemy's cavalry, and the flower of the heavy infantry, the younger men, charged by their side. The Theban cavalry at that instant looked like men who had been drinking too freely in the noontide heat—that is to say, they awaited the charge long enough to hurl their spears; but they were still out of range, and yet wheeling about at that distance they left twelve of their number dead upon the field.

Agesilaus had not failed to note with what regularity the enemy presented himself after the morning meal. Turning the observation to account, he offered sacrifice at dawn, and marched with all possible speed, and so crossed within the palisadings, through what might have been a desert, as far as defence went. Once well inside, he proceeded to cut down and set on fire everything up to the city gates. After this exploit he beat a retreat, retiring into Thespiae, where he fortified their citadel for them. Here he left Phoebidas as governor, while he himself crossed the passes back into Megara. Arrived here he disbanded the allies, and led the city troops homewards.

After the departure of Agesilaus, Phoebidas devoted himself to harrying the Thebans by sending out robber bands, and laid waste their land by a system of regular incursions. The Thebans, on their side, desiring to retaliate, marched out with their whole force into the territory of Thespiae. But once well inside the district they found themselves closely beset by Phoebidas and his light troops, who would not give them the slightest chance to scatter from their main body, so that the Thebans, heartily vexed at the turn their foray had taken, beat a retreat quicker than they had come. The muleteers threw away with their own hands the fruits they had captured, in their anxiety to get home as quickly as possible; so dire a dread had fallen upon the invading army. This was the chance for the Spartan to press home his attack boldly, keeping his light division in close attendance on himself, and leaving the heavy infantry under orders to follow him in battle order. He was in hopes even that he might put the enemy to complete rout, so valiantly did he lead the advance, encouraging the light troops to come to a close grip with the invaders, or summoning the heavy infantry of the Thespiaeans to bring up their supports. Presently the Theban cavalry as they retired found themselves face to face with an impassable ravine, where in the first instance they collected in a mob, and next wheeled right-about-face not knowing where to cross. The handful of light troops who formed the Spartan vanguard took fright at the Thebans and fled, and the Theban horsemen, seeing this, put in practice the lesson of attack which the fugitives taught them. As for Phoebidas himself, he and two or three with him fell sword in hand, whereupon his mercenary troops all took to their heels.

When the stream of fugitives reached the Thespiaean heavy infantry reserves, they too, in spite of much boasting beforehand that they would never yield to Thebans, took to flight, though there was absolutely no pursuit whatever, for it was now late. The number slain was not large, but, for all that, the men of Thespiae did not stop until they were inside their walls. As a sequel, the hopes and spirit of the Thebans were again kindled into new life, and they made campaigns against Thespiae and the other provincial cities of Boeotia. In each case, however, the democratic party retired from these cities to Thebes; since absolute governments had been established in all of them on the pattern previously adopted at Thebes; and the result was that the friends of Lacedaemon in these cities also needed her assistance. After the death of Phoebidas the Lacedaemonians despatched a polemarch with a division by sea to form the garrison of Thespiae.

With the advent of spring the ephors again called out the army against Thebes, and requested Agesilaus to lead the expedition, as on the former campaign. He, holding to his former theory with regard to the invasion, even before sacrificing the customary frontier sacrifice, sent a despatch to the polemarch at Thespiae, with orders to seize the pass which commands the road over Cithaeron, and to guard it against his arrival. Then, having once more crossed the pass and reached Plataea, he again made a feint of marching first into Thespiae, and so sent a despatch ordering supplies to be in readiness, and all embassies to be waiting his arrival there; so that the Thebans concentrated their attention on the approaches from Thespiae, which they strongly guarded. Next morning, however, Agesilaus sacrificed at daybreak and set out on the road to Erythrae, and completing in one day what was a good two days' march for an army, gave the Thebans the slip, and crossed their palisade-work at Scolus before the enemy had arrived from the closely-guarded point at which he had effected his entrance formerly. This done he proceeded to ravage the eastward districts of the city of Thebes as far as the territory of Tanagra, for at that date Tanagra was still in the hands of Hypatodorus and his party, who were friends of the Lacedae-monians. After that he turned to retire, keeping the walls of Thebes on his left. But the Thebans, who had stolen, as it were, upon the scene, drew up at the spot called The Old Wife's Breast, keeping the trench and palisading in their rear: they were persuaded that here, if anywhere, lay their chance to risk a decisive engagement, the ground at this point being somewhat narrow and difficult to traverse. Agesilaus, however, in view of the situation, refused to accept the challenge. Instead of marching upon them he turned sharp off in the direction of the city; and the Thebans, in alarm for the city in its undefended state, abandoned the favourable ground on which they were drawn up in battle line and retired at the double towards the city along the road to Potniae, which seemed the safer route. This last move of Agesilaus may be described as a clever one: while it allowed him to retire to a distance, it forced the enemy themselves to retreat at the double. In spite of this, however, one or two of the polemarchs, with their divisions, charged the foe as he raced past. But again the Thebans, from the vantage-ground of their heights, sent volleys of spears upon the assailants, which cost one of the pole-marchs, Alypetus, his life. He fell pierced by a spear. But again from this particular crest the Thebans on their side were forced to turn in flight; so much so that the Sciritae, with some of the cavalry, scaled up and speedily cut down the rearmost ranks of the Thebans as they galloped past into the city. When, however, they were close under cover of their walls the Thebans turned, and the Sciritae, seeing them, retreated at more than a steady walking pace. No one, it is true, was slain; but the Thebans all the same set up a trophy in record of the incident at the point where the scaling party had been forced to retreat.

And now, since the hour was come, Agesilaus fell back and encamped on the very site on which he had seen the enemy drawn up in battle array. Next day he retired by the road to Thespiae. The light troops, who formed a free corps in the pay of the Thebans, hung audaciously on his heels. Their shouts could be heard calling out to Chabrias for not bringing up his supports; when the cavalry of the Olynthians (who now contributed a contingent in accordance with their oaths) wheeled round on them, caught the pursuers in the heat of their pursuit, and drove them uphill, putting large numbers of them to the sword, so quickly are infantry overhauled by cavalry on steep ground which can be ridden over. Being arrived within the walls of Thespiae, Agesilaus found the citizens in a state of party feud, the men of Lacedaemonian proclivities desiring to put their political opponents, one of whom was Menon, to death—a proceeding which Agesilaus would not sanction. After having healed their differences and bound them over by solemn oath to keep the peace with one another, he at once retired, taking his old route across Cithaeron to Megara. Here once more he disbanded the allies, and at the head of the city troops himself marched back to Sparta.

The Thebans had not gathered in the fruits of their soil for two years now, and began to be sorely pinched for want of corn; they therefore sent a body of men on board a couple of triremes to Pagasae, with ten talents in hand for the purchase of corn. But while these commissioners were engaged in effecting their purchases, Alcetas, the Lacedaemonian who was garrisoning Oreus, fitted out three triremes, taking precautions that no rumour of his proceedings should leak out. As soon as the corn was shipped and the vessels under way, he captured not only the corn but the triremes, escort and all, numbering no less than 300 men. This done he locked up his prisoners in the citadel, where he himself was also quartered. Now there was a youth, the son of a native of Oreus, fair of mien and of gentle breeding, who attended the commandant: and the latter left the citadel and went down to busy himself with this youth. This was a piece of carelessness which the prisoners observed and turned to good account by seizing the citadel, whereupon the town revolted, and the Thebans experienced no further difficulty in obtaining corn supplies.

At the return of spring Agesilaus lay sick in bed. The history of the case is this: During the withdrawal of his army from Thebes the year before, when at Megara, while mounting from the Aphrodisium to the government house he ruptured a vein or other vessel of the body. This was followed by a rush of blood to his sound leg. The knee was much swelled, and the pain intolerable, until a Syracusan surgeon made an incision in the vein near the ankle. The blood thus let flowed night and day; do what they could to stop the discharge, all failed, till the patient fainted away; then it ceased. In this plight Agesilaus was conveyed home on a litter to Lacedaemon, and remained an invalid the rest of that summer and throughout the winter.

But to resume: at the first burst of spring the Lacedaemonians again called out the army, and gave orders to Cleombrotus to lead the expedition. The king found himself presently with his troops at the foot of Cithaeron, and his light infantry advanced to occupy the pass which commands the road. But here they found a detachment of Thebans and Athenians already in occupation of the desired height, who for a while let them approach; but when they were close upon them, sprang from their position and charged, putting about forty to the sword. This incident was sufficient to convince Cleombrotus that to invade Thebes by this mountain passage was out of the question, and he led back and disbanded his troops.

The allies met in Lacedaemon, and arguments were adduced on the part of the allies to show that faintheartedness would very soon lead to their being absolutely worn out by the war. They had it in their power, it was urged, to fit out a fleet far outnumbering that of Athens, and to reduce that city by starvation; it was open to them, in the same ships, to carry an army across into Theban territory, and they had a choice of routes—the road into Phocis, or, if they preferred, by Creusis. After thus carefully considering the matter they manned a fleet of sixty triremes, and Pollis was appointed admiral in command. Nor indeed were their expectations altogether belied. The Athenians were soon so closely blockaded that their corn vessels could get no farther than Geraestus; there was no inducing them to coast down farther south, with a Lacedaemonian navy hovering about Aegina and Ceos and Andros. The Athenians, making a virtue of necessity, manned their ships in person, gave battle to Pollis under the leadership of Chabrias, and came out of the sea-fight[8] victorious.

Then the corn supplies flowed freely into Athens. The Lacedaemonians, on their side, were preparing to transport an army across the water into Boeotia, when the Thebans sent a request to the Athenians urging

[8] Battle of Naxos, 376 B.C.

them to despatch an armament round Peloponnesus, under the persuasion that if this were done the Lacedaemonians would find it impossible at once to guard their own or the allied territory in that part of the world, and at the same time to convey an army of any size to operate against Thebes. The proposals fell in with the present temper of the Athenians, irritated with Lacedaemon on account of the exploit of Sphodrias. Accordingly they eagerly manned a fleet of sixty vessels, appointing Timotheus as admiral in command, and despatched it on a cruise round Peloponnesus.

The Thebans, seeing that there had been no hostile invasion of their territory for so long (neither during the campaign of Cleombrotus nor now, while Timotheus prosecuted his coasting voyage), boldly carried out a campaign of their own account against the provincial cities;[9] and one by one they again recovered them.

Timotheus in his cruise reached Corcyra, and reduced it at a blow. That done, he neither enslaved the inhabitants nor drove them into exile, nor changed their laws. And of this conduct he reaped the benefit in the increased cordiality[10] of all the cities of those parts. The Lacedaemonians thereupon fitted out and despatched a counter fleet, with Nicolochus in command, an officer of consummate boldness. This admiral no sooner caught sight of Timotheus's fleet than without hesitation, and in spite of the absence of six Ambraciot vessels which formed part of his squadron, he gave battle, with fifty-five ships to the enemy's sixty. The result was a defeat at the moment, and Timotheus set up a trophy at Alyzia. But as soon as the six missing Ambraciot vessels had reinforced him—the ships of Timotheus meanwhile being docked and undergoing repairs—he bore down upon Alyzia in search of the Athenian, and as Timotheus refused to put out to meet him, the Lacedaemonian in his turn set up a trophy on the nearest group of islands.

Timotheus, after repairing his original squadron and manning more vessels from Corcyra, found himself at the head of more than seventy ships. His naval superiority was undisputed, but he was forced to send to Athens for money, seeing his fleet was large and his wants great.

[9] Xenophon has omitted the fight at Tegyra where Pelopidas and the Sacred Band defeated a superior force of Spartans.
[10] The Corcyraeans, Acarnanians, and Cephallenians join the alliance 375 B.C.

BOOK VI

1. The Athenians and Lacedaemonians were thus engaged. But to return to the Thebans. After the subjugation of the cities in Boeotia, they extended the area of aggression and marched into Phocis. The Phocians, on their side, sent an embassy to Lacedaemon, and pleaded that without assistance from that power they must inevitably yield to Thebes. The Lacedaemonians in response conveyed by sea into the territory of Phocis their king Cleombrotus, at the head of four regiments[1] and proportionate contingents of the allies.

About the same time Polydamas of Pharsalus arrived from Thessaly to address the general assembly of Lacedaemon. He was a man of high repute throughout the whole of Thessaly, while in his native city he was regarded as so honourable that the faction-ridden Pharsalians were content to entrust the citadel to his keeping, and to allow their revenues to pass through his hands. It was his privilege to disburse the money needed for sacred rites or other expenditure, within the limits of their written law and constitution. Out of these funds this faithful steward of the state was able to garrison and guard in safety for the citizens their capital. Every year he rendered an account of his administration in general. If there was a deficit he made it up out of his own pocket, and when the revenues expanded he paid himself back. For the rest, his hospitality to foreigners and his magnificence were on a true Thessalian scale. Such was the style and character of the man who now arrived in Lacedaemon and spoke as follows:

"Men of Lacedaemon, it is in my capacity as proxenus and benefactor (titles borne by my ancestry from time immemorial) that I claim, or rather am bound, in case of any difficulty to come to you, and, in case of any complication dangerous to your interests in Thessaly, to give you warning. The name of Jason, I feel sure, is not unknown to Lacedaemonian ears. His power as a prince is sufficiently large, and his fame widespread. It is of Jason I have to speak. Under cover of a treaty of peace he has lately conferred with me, and this is the substance of what he urged, 'Polydamas,' he said, 'if I chose I could lay your city at my feet, even against its will, as the following considerations will prove to you. See,' he went on, 'the majority and the most important of the

[1] Two-thirds of the Spartan army.

154

states of Thessaly are my allies. I subdued them in campaigns in which you took their side in opposition to myself. Again, you do not need to be told that I have 6,000 mercenaries who are a match in themselves, I take it, for any single state. It is not the mere numbers on which I insist. No doubt as large an army could be raised in other quarters; but these citizen armies have this defect—they include men who are already advanced in years, with others whose beards are scarcely grown. Again, it is only a fraction of the citizens who attend to bodily training in a state, whereas with me no one takes mercenary service who is not as capable of endurance as myself.'

"And here, Lacedaemonians, I must tell you what is the bare truth. This Jason is a man stout of limb and robust of body, with an insatiable appetite for toil. Equally true is it that he tests the mettle of those with him day by day. He is always at their head, whether on a field-day under arms, or in the gymnasium, or on some military expedition. The weak members of the corps he weeds out, but those whom he sees bear themselves stout-heartedly in the face of war, like true lovers of danger and of toil, he honours with double, treble, and quadruple pay, or with other gifts. On the bed of sickness they will not lack attendance, nor honour in their graves. Thus every foreigner in his service knows that his valour in war may obtain for him a livelihood—a life replete at once with honour and abundance.

"Then with some parade he pointed out to me what I knew before, that the Maracians, and the Dolopians, and Alcetas the ruler in Epirus, were already subject to his sway; 'so that I may fairly ask you, Polydamas,' he proceeded, 'what I have to apprehend that I should not look on your future subjugation as mere child's play. Perhaps some one who did not know me, and what manner of man I am, might put it to me: "Well, Jason, if all you say be true, why do you hesitate? Why do you not march at once against Pharsalia?" For the good reason, I reply, that it suits me better to win you voluntarily than to annex you against your wills. Since, if you are forced, you will always be planning all the mischief you can against me, and I on my side shall be striving to diminish your power; whereas if you throw in your lot with mine trustfully and willingly, it is certain we shall do what we can to help each other. I see and know, Polydamas, that your country fixes her eyes on one man only, and that is yourself; what I guarantee you, therefore, is that, if you will dispose her lovingly to myself, I on my side will raise you up to be the greatest man in Hellas next to me. Listen, while I tell you what it is in which I offer you the second prize. Listen, and accept nothing which does not approve itself as true to your own reasoning. First, is it not plain to us both, that with the adhesion of Pharsalus and the swarm of pettier states dependent on yourselves, I shall with infinite ease become Tagus[2] of all the Thessalians; and then the corollary—Thessaly so united—6,000 cavalry and more than 10,000 heavy infantry leap into life. Indeed, when I contemplate the physique and proud carriage of these men, I cannot but persuade myself that, with proper handling, there is not a nation or tribe of men to which Thessalians would deign to yield submission. Look at the broad expanse of Thessaly and consider: when once a Tagus is established here, all the tribes in a circle round will lie in subjection; and almost every member of each of these tribes is an archer born, so that in the light infantry division of the service our power would excel. Furthermore, the Boeotians and all the rest of the world in arms against Lacedaemon are my allies; they clamour to follow my banner, if only I will free them from Sparta's yoke. So again the Athenians, I am sure, will do all they can to gain our alliance; but with them I do not think we will make friends, for my persuasion is that empire by sea will be even easier to acquire than empire by land; and to show you the justice of this reasoning I would have you weigh the following considerations. With Macedonia, which is the timber-yard of the Athenian navy, in our hands we shall be able to construct a far larger fleet than theirs. That stands to reason. And as to men, which will be the better able to man vessels, think you—Athens, or ourselves with our stalwart and numerous serfs? Which will better support mariners—a nation which, like our own, out of her abundance exports her corn to foreign parts, or Athens, which, but for foreign purchases, has not enough to support herself? And so as to wealth in general it is only natural, is it not, that we, who do not look to a string of little islands for supplies, but gather the fruits of continental peoples, should find our resources more copious? As soon as the scattered powers of Thessaly are gathered into a principality, all the tribes around, I repeat, will become our tributaries. I need not tell you that the king of Persia reaps the fruits, not of islands, but of a continent, and he is the wealthiest of men. But the reduction of Persia will be still more practicable, I imagine, than that of Hellas, for there the men, save one, are better versed in slavery than in prowess. Nor have I forgotten, during the advance of Cyrus, and afterwards under Agesilaus, how scant the force was before which the Persian quailed.'

"Such, Lacedaemonians, were the glowing arguments of Jason. In answer I told him that what he urged was well worth weighing, but that we, the friends of Lacedaemon, should so, without a quarrel, desert her and rush into the arms of her opponents, seemed to me sheer madness.

[2] The Tagus of Thessaly was not a King, because his office was not hereditary; neither was he a Tyrant, because his office had some sort of legal sanction.

Whereat he praised me, and said that now must he needs cling all the closer to me if that were my disposition, and so charged me to come to you and tell you the plain truth, which is, that he intends to march against Pharsalus if we will not yield to him. Accordingly he bade me demand assistance from you. 'And if they suffer you,' he added, 'so to work upon them that they will send you a force sufficient to do battle with me, it is well: we will abide by war's decision, nor quarrel with the consequence; but if in your eyes that aid is insufficient, look to yourself. How shall you longer be held blameless before that fatherland which honours you and in which you fare so well?'

"These are the matters," Polydamas continued, "which have brought me to Lacedaemon. I have told you the whole story; it is based partly on what I see to be the case, and partly on what I have heard from yonder man. My firm belief is, men of Lacedaemon, that if you are likely to despatch a force sufficient, not in my eyes only, but in the eyes of all the rest of Thessaly, to cope with Jason in war, the states will revolt from him, for they are all in alarm as to the future development of the man's power; but if you think a company of newly-enfranchised slaves and any amateur general will suffice, I advise you to rest in peace. You may take my word for it, you will have a great power to contend against, and a man who is so prudent a general that, in all he essays to do, be it an affair of secrecy, or speed, or force, he is wont to hit the mark of his endeavours: one who is skilled, should occasion serve, to make the night of equal service to him with the day; or, if speed be needful, will labour on while breakfasting or taking an evening meal. And as for repose, he thinks that the time for it has come when the goal is reached or the business on hand accomplished. And to this same practice he has accustomed those about him. Right well he knows how to reward the expectations of his soldiers, when by the extra toil which makes the difference they have achieved success; so that in his school all have laid to heart that maxim, 'Pain first and pleasure after.' And in regard to pleasure of the senses, of all the men I know, he is the most continent; so that these also are powerless to make him idle at the expense of duty. You must consider the matter then and tell me, as befits you, what you can and will do."

Such were the representations of Polydamas. The Lacedaemonians, for the time being, deferred their answer; but after calculating the next day and the day following how many divisions they had on foreign service, and how many ships on the coast of Laconia to deal with the foreign squadron of the Athenians, and taking also into account the war with their neighbours, they gave their answer to Polydamas, "For the present they would not be able to send him a sufficient aid: under the circumstances they advised him to go back and make the best settlement he could of his own affairs and those of his city." He, thanking the Lacedaemonians for their straightforwardness, withdrew.

The citadel of Pharsalus he begged Jason not to force him to give up: his desire was to preserve it for those who had entrusted it to his safe keeping; his own sons Jason was free to take as hostages, and he would do his best to procure for him the voluntary adhesion of his city by persuasion, and in every way to further his appointment as Tagus of Thessaly. Accordingly, after interchange of solemn assurances between the pair, the Pharsalians were let alone in peace, and soon Jason was, by general consent, appointed Tagus of all the Thessalians. Once fairly vested with that authority, he drew up a list of the cavalry and heavy infantry which the several states were capable of furnishing as their quota, with the result that his cavalry, inclusive of allies, numbered more than 8,000, while his infantry force was computed at not less than 20,000; and his light troops would have been a match for those of the whole world—the mere enumeration of their cities would be a labour in itself. His next act was a summons to all the dwellers round to pay as tribute exactly the amount imposed in the days of Scopas.[3] And here in this state of accomplishment we may leave these matters. I return to the point reached when this digression into the affairs of Jason began.

2. The Lacedaemonians and their allies were collecting in Phocis, and the Thebans, after retreating into their own territory, were guarding the approaches. At this juncture the Athenians, seeing the Thebans growing strong at their expense without contributing a single penny to the maintenance of the fleet, while they themselves, what with money contributions, and piratical attacks from Aegina, and the garrisoning of their territory, were being pared to the bone, conceived a desire to cease from war. In this mood they sent an embassy to Lacedaemon and concluded peace.

Two of the ambassadors, in obedience to a decree of the state, set sail at once from Laconian territory, bearing orders to Timotheus to sail home, since peace was established. That officer, while obeying his orders, availed himself of the homeward voyage to land certain Zacynthian exiles on their native soil, whereupon the Zacynthian city party sent to Lacedaemon and complained of the treatment they had received from Timotheus; and the Lacedaemonians, without further consideration, decided that the Athenians were in the wrong, and proceeded to equip another navy, and at length collected from Laconia itself, from Corinth, Leucas, Ambracia, Elis, Zacynthus, Achaia, Epidaurus, Troe-

[3] Scopas ruled at Crannon in the earlier half of the fifth century B.C.

zen, Hermione, and Halieis, a force amounting to sixty ships. In command of this squadron they appointed Mnasippus admiral, with orders to attack Corcyra, and in general to look after their interests in those seas. They, moreover, sent an embassy to Dionysius, showing him that his interests would be advanced by the withdrawal of Corcyra from Athenian hands.

Accordingly Mnasippus set sail, as soon as his squadron was ready, direct to Corcyra; he took with him, besides his troops from Lacedaemon, a body of mercenaries, making a total in all of no less than 1,500 men. He disembarked, and soon became master of the island, the country district falling a prey to the spoiler. It was in a high state of cultivation, and rich with fruit-trees, not to speak of magnificent dwelling-houses and wine-cellars fitted up on the farms: so that, it was said, the soldiers reached such a pitch of luxury that they refused to drink wine which had not a fine bouquet. A crowd of slaves, too, and fat beasts were captured on the estates.

The general's next move was to encamp with his land forces about three-quarters of a mile from the city, on rising ground, which commanded the rural district, so that any Corcyraean who attempted to leave the city to go into the country would be certainly cut off on that side. The fleet he stationed on the other side of the city, at a point where he calculated on detecting and preventing the approach of convoys. Besides which he established a blockade in front of the harbour when the weather permitted. In this way the city was completely invested.

The Corcyraeans, on their side, were in the sorest straits. They could get nothing from their soil owing to the vise in which they were gripped by land, while owing to the predominance of the enemy at sea nothing could be imported. Accordingly they sent to the Athenians and begged for their assistance. They urged upon them that it would be a great mistake if they suffered themselves to be robbed of Corcyra. If they did so, they would not only throw away a great advantage to themselves, but add a considerable strength to their enemy; since, with the exception of Athens, no state was capable of furnishing a larger fleet or revenue. Moreover, Corcyra was favourably placed for commanding the Corinthian gulf and the cities which line its shores; it was splendidly situated for injuring the rural districts of Laconia, and still more splendidly in relation to the opposite shores of the continent of Epirus, and the passage between Peloponnesus and Sicily.

This appeal did not fall on deaf ears. The Athenians were persuaded that the matter demanded their most serious attention, and they at once despatched Ctesicles as general, with about 600 peltasts. They also requested Alcetas to help them in getting their troops across. Thus under cover of night the whole body were conveyed across to a point in the open country, and found their way into the city. Nor was that all. The Athenians passed a decree to man sixty ships of war, and elected Timotheus admiral. The latter, being unable to man the fleet on the spot, set sail on a cruise to the islands and tried to make up the complements of his crews from those quarters. He evidently looked upon it as no light matter to sail round Peloponnesus as if on a voyage of pleasure, and to attack a fleet in the perfection of training. To the Athenians, however, it seemed that he was wasting the precious time seasonable for the coasting voyage, and they were not disposed to condone such an error, but deposed him, appointing Iphicrates in his stead. The new general was no sooner appointed than he set about getting his vessels manned with the utmost activity, putting pressure on the trierarchs. He further procured from the Athenians for his use not only any vessels cruising on the coast of Attica, but the Paralus and Salaminia also, remarking that, if things turned out well yonder, he would soon send them back plenty of ships. Thus his numbers grew to something like seventy sail.

Meanwhile the Corcyraeans were hard pressed with famine: desertion became every day more frequent, so much so that Mnasippus caused proclamation to be made by herald that all deserters would be sold there and then; and when that had no effect in lessening the stream of runaways, he ended by driving them back with the lash. Those within the walls, however, were not disposed to receive these miserable slaves within the lines, and numbers died outside. Mnasippus, not blind to what was happening, soon persuaded himself that he had as good as got the city into his possession: and he began to try experiments on his mercenaries. Some of them he had already paid off; others still in his service had as much as two months' pay owing to them by the general, who, if report spoke true, had no lack of money, since the majority of the states, not caring for a campaign across the seas, sent him hard cash instead of men. But now the beleaguered citizens seeing from their towers that the outposts were less carefully guarded than formerly, and the men scattered about the rural districts, made a sortie, capturing some and cutting down others. Mnasippus, perceiving the attack, donned his armour, and, with all the heavy troops he had, rushed to the rescue, giving orders to the captains and brigadiers to lead out the mercenaries. Some of the captains answered that it was not so easy to command obedience when the necessaries of life were lacking; at that the Spartan struck one man with his staff, and another with the butt of his spear. Without spirit and full of resentment against their general, the men mustered—a condition very unfavourable to success in battle. Having drawn up the troops, the general in person repulsed the division of the enemy which was opposite the gates, and pursued them closely; but these, rallying close under their walls, turned right about, and from under cover of the tombs kept up a continuous discharge of darts and other missiles; other detachments, dashing out at other gates, meanwhile fell heavily on the flanks of the enemy. The Lacedaemonians, being drawn up eight deep, and thinking that the wing of their phalanx was of inadequate strength, essayed to wheel round; but as soon as they began the movement the Corcyraeans attacked them as if they were fleeing, and they were then unable to recover themselves, while the troops next in position abandoned themselves to flight. Mnasippus, unable to aid those who were being pressed owing to the attack of the enemy immediately in front, found himself left from moment to moment with decreasing numbers. At last the Corcyraeans collected, and with one united effort made a final rush upon Mnasippus and his men, whose numbers were now considerably reduced. At the same instant the townsmen, seeing the state of affairs, rushed out to play their part. First Mnasippus was slain, and then the pursuit became general; nor could the pursuers well have failed to capture the camp, barricade and all, had they not caught sight of the mob of traffickers with a long array of attendants and slaves, and thinking that here was a prize indeed, desisted from further chase.

The Corcyraeans were well content for the moment to set up a trophy and to give back the enemy's dead under a truce; but the after-consequences were even more important to them in the revival of strength and spirits which the citizens experienced, in proportion as the foreign invaders were sunk in despondency. The rumour spread that Iphicrates would soon be there—he was even at the doors; and in fact the Corcyraeans themselves were manning a fleet. So Hypermenes, who was second in command to Mnasippus and the bearer of his despatches, manned every vessel of the fleet as full as it would hold, and then sailing round to the entrenched camp, filled all the transports with prisoners and valuables and other stock, and sent them off. He himself, with his marines and the survivors of the troops, kept watch over the entrenchments; but at last even this remnant in the excess of panic and confusion got on board the men-of-war and sailed off, leaving behind them vast quantities of corn and wine, with numerous prisoners and invalided soldiers. The fact was, they were terribly afraid of being caught by the Athenians in the island, and so they made safely off to Leucas.

Meanwhile Iphicrates had commenced his voyage of circumnavigation, partly voyaging and partly making every preparation for an engagement. He at once left his large sails behind him, as the voyage was only to be the prelude of a battle; his small sails, even if there was a good breeze, were but little used, since by making his progress depend on sheer rowing he hoped at once to improve the physique of his men and the speed of his attack. Often when the squadron was about to put in to shore for the purpose of breakfast or supper, he would seize the moment, and draw back the leading wing of the column from the land off the point in question; and then facing round again with the triremes posted well in line, prow for prow, at a given signal let loose the whole fleet in a stoutly contested race for the shore. Great was the triumph in being the first to take in water or whatever else they might need, or the first to breakfast; just as it was a heavy penalty on the last-comers, not only to come short in all these objects of desire, but to have to put out to sea with the rest as soon as the signal was given; since the first-comers had altogether a quiet time of it, while the hindmost must get through the whole business in haste. So again, in the matter of outposts, if he chanced to be getting the morning meal on hostile territory, pickets would be posted, as was right and proper, on the land; but, apart from these, he would raise his masts and keep look-out men on the maintops. These commanded of course a far wider prospect from their lofty perches than the outposts on the level ground. So too, when he dined or slept he had no fires burning in the camp at night, but only a beacon kindled in front of the encampment to prevent any unseen approach; and frequently in fine weather he put out to sea immediately after the evening meal, when, if the breeze favoured, they ran along and took their rest simultaneously, or if they depended on oars he rested his mariners by turns. During the voyage in daytime he would at one time signal to sail in column, and at another signal to sail in line of battle. So that while they prosecuted the voyage they at the same time became (both as to theory and practice) well versed in all the details of an engagement before they reached the open sea—a sea, as they imagined, occupied by their foes. For the most part they breakfasted and dined on hostile territory; but as he confined himself to bare necessaries he was always too quick for the enemy. Before the hostile reinforcement would come up he had finished his business and was out to sea again.

At the date of Mnasippus's death he chanced to be off Sphagiae in Laconian territory. Reaching Elis, and coasting past the mouth of the Alpheus, he came to moorings under Cape Fish, as it is called. The next day he put out from that port for Cephallenia, so drawing up his line and conducting the voyage that he might be prepared in every detail to engage if necessary. The tale about Mnasippus and his demise had reached him, but he had not heard it from an eye-witness, and suspected that it might have been invented to deceive him and throw him off his guard. He was therefore on the look-out. It was, in fact, only on

arrival in Cephallenia that he learned the news in an explicit form, and
gave his troops rest.

I am well aware that all these details of practice and manoeuvring
are customary in anticipation of a sea-fight, but what I single out for
praise in the case before us is the skill with which the Athenian admiral attained a twofold object. Bearing in mind that it was his duty
to reach a certain point at which he expected to fight a naval battle
without delay, it was a happy discovery on his part not to allow tactical
skill, on the one hand, to be sacrificed to the pace of sailing, nor, on the
other, the need of training to interfere with the date of arrival.

After reducing the towns of Cephallenia, Iphicrates sailed to Corcyra.
There the first news he heard was that the triremes sent by Dionysius
were expected to relieve the Lacedaemonians. On receipt of this information he set off in person and surveyed the country, in order to find a
spot from which it would be possible to see the vessels approaching
and to signal to the city. Here he stationed his look-out men. Signals
were agreed upon to signify vessels in sight, mooring, etc.; which done
he gave his orders to twenty of his captains of men-of-war who were to
follow him at a given word of command. Any one who failed to follow him must not grumble at the penalty; that he warned them. Presently the vessels were signalled approaching; the word of command
was given, and then the enthusiasm was a sight to see—every man of
the crews told off for the expedition racing to join his ship and embark.
Sailing to the point where the enemy's vessels lay, he had no difficulty
in capturing the crews, who had disembarked from all the ships with
one exception. The exception was that of Melanippus the Rhodian,
who had advised the other captains not to stop at this point, and had
then manned his own vessel and sailed off. Thus he encountered the
ships of Iphicrates, but contrived to slip through his fingers, while the
whole of the Syracusan vessels were captured, crews and all.

Having cut the beaks off the prows, Iphicrates bore down into the
harbour of Corcyra with the captured triremes in tow. With the captive
crews themselves he came to an agreement that each should pay a fixed
sum as ransom, with one exception, that of Crinippus, their commander.
Him he kept under guard, with the intention apparently of exacting
a handsome sum in his case or else of selling him. The prisoner, however, from vexation, put an end to his own life. The rest were sent about
their business by Iphicrates, who accepted the Corcyraeans as sureties
for the money. His own sailors he supported for the most part as labourers on the lands of the Corcyraeans, while at the head of his light
infantry and the hoplites of the contingent he crossed over into Acarnania, and there lent his aid to any friendly state that needed his serv-

ices; besides which he went to war with the Thyrians, a sturdy race of warriors in possession of a strong fortress.

Having attached to his squadron the navy also of Corcyra, with a fleet numbering now about ninety ships he set sail, in the first instance to Cephallenia, where he exacted money—which was in some cases voluntarily paid, in others forcibly extorted. In the next place he began making preparations partly to harass the territory of the Lacedaemonians, and partly to win over voluntarily the other states in that quarter which were hostile to Athens; or in case of refusal to go to war with them.

The whole conduct of the campaign reflects, I think, the highest credit on Iphicrates. If his strategy was admirable, so too was the instinct which led him to advise the association with himself of two such colleagues as Callistratus and Chabrias, the former a popular orator but no great friend of himself politically, the other a man of high military reputation. Either he looked upon them as men of unusual sagacity, and wished to profit by their advice, in which case I commend the good sense of the arrangement, or they were, in his belief, antagonists, in which case the determination to approve himself a consummate general, neither indolent nor incautious, was bold, I admit, but indicative of a laudable self-confidence. These, then, were his actions.

3. The Athenians, forced to witness the expatriation from Boeotia of their friends the Plataeans (who had sought an asylum with themselves), forced also to listen to the supplications of the Thespiaeans (who begged them not to suffer them to be robbed of their city), could no longer regard the Thebans with favour; though, when it came to a direct declaration of war, they were checked in part by a feeling of shame, and partly by considerations of expediency. Still, to go hand in hand with them, to be a party to their proceedings, this they absolutely refused, now that they saw them marching against time-honoured friends of the city like the Phocians, and blotting out states whose loyalty in the great Persian war was conspicuous no less than their friendship to Athens. Accordingly the people passed a decree to make peace; but in the first instance they sent an embassy to Thebes, inviting that state to join them if it pleased them on an embassy which they proposed to send to Lacedaemon to treat of peace. In the next place they despatched such an embassy on their own account. Among the commissioners appointed were Callias the son of Hipponicus, Autocles the son of Strombichides, Demostratus the son of Aristophon, Aristocles, Cephisodotus, Melanopus, and Lycaethus.

[These were formally introduced to the Deputies of the Lacedaemonians and the allies.] Nor ought the name of Callistratus to be omitted. That statesman and orator was present. He had obtained furlough from Iphicrates on an undertaking either to send money for the fleet or to arrange a peace. Hence his arrival in Athens and transactions in behalf of peace. After being introduced to the assembly of the Lacedaemonians and to the allies, Callias, who was the torch-bearer in the mysteries, made the first speech. He was a man just as well pleased to praise himself as to hear himself praised by others. He spoke somewhat as follows:

"Lacedaemonians, the duty of representing you as proxenus at Athens is a privilege which I am not the first member of my family to enjoy; my father's father held it as an heirloom of our family and handed it down as a heritage to his descendants. If you will permit me, I should like to show you the disposition of my fatherland towards us. If in times of war she chooses us as her generals, so when her heart is set upon quiet she sends us out as her messengers of peace. I myself have twice already stood here to treat for the conclusion of war, and on both embassies succeeded in arranging a mutually agreeable peace. Now for the third time I am come, and I flatter myself that to-day again I shall obtain a reconciliation, and on grounds exceptionally just. My eyes bear witness that our hearts are in accord: you and we alike are pained at the effacement of Plataea and Thespiae. Is it not then reasonable that out of agreement should spring concord rather than discord? It is never the part, I take it, of wise men to raise the standard of war for the sake of petty differences; but where there is nothing but unanimity they must be marvellous folk who refuse the bond of peace. But I go further. It were just and right on our parts even to refuse to bear arms against each other; since, as the story runs, the first strangers to whom our forefather Triptolemus showed the unspeakable mystic rites of Demeter and Core, the mother and the maiden, were your ancestors; I speak of Heracles, the first founder of your state, and of your two citizens, the great twin sons of Zeus—and to Peloponnesus first he gave as a gift the seed of Demeter's corn-fruits. How, then, can it be just or right either that you should come and ravage the corn crops of those from whom you got the sacred seed of corn, or that we should not desire that they to whom the gift was given should share abundantly of this boon? But if, as it would seem, it is a fixed decree of heaven that war shall never cease among men, yet ought we—your people and our people—to be as slow as possible to begin it, and being in it, as swift as possible to bring it to an end."

After him Autocles spoke: he was of repute as a shrewd orator, and addressed the meeting as follows, "Lacedaemonians, I do not conceal from myself that what I am about to say is not calculated to please you, but it seems to me that, if you wish the friendship which we are cementing to last as long as possible, we are wise to show each other the underlying causes of our wars. Now, you are perpetually saying that the states ought to be independent; but it is you yourselves who most of all stand in the way of independence, your first and last stipulation with the allied states being that they should follow you wherever you choose to lead; and yet what has this principle got to do with independent action? Again, you pick quarrels without consulting your allies, and lead them against those whom you account enemies; so that in many cases, with all their vaunted independence, they are forced to march against their greatest friends; and, what is still more opposed to independence than all else, you are for ever setting up here your decarchies and there your thirty commissioners, and your chief aim in appointing these officers and governors seems to be, not that they should fulfil their office and govern legally, but that they should be able to keep the cities under their heels by sheer force. So that it looks as if you delighted in despotisms rather than free constitutions. Let us go back to the date[4] at which the Persian king enjoined the independence of the states. At that time you made no secret of your conviction that the Thebans, if they did not suffer each state to govern itself and to use the laws of its own choice, would be failing to act in the spirit of the king's rescript. But no sooner had you got hold of the Cadmeia than you would not allow the Thebans themselves to be independent. Now, if the maintenance of friendship be an object, it is no use for people to claim justice from others while they themselves are doing all they can to prove the selfishness of their aims."

These remarks were received in absolute silence, yet in the hearts of those who were annoyed with Lacedaemon they stirred pleasure. After Autocles spoke Callistratus, "Trespasses, men of Lacedaemon, have been committed on both sides, yours and ours, I am free to confess; but still it is not my view that because a man has done wrong we can never again have dealings with him. Experience tells me that no man can go very far without a slip, and it seems to me that sometimes the transgressor by reason of his transgression becomes more tractable, especially if he be chastened through the error he has committed, as has been the case with us. And so in your own case I see that ungenerous acts have sometimes reaped their own proper reward: blow has been met by counter-blow; and as a specimen I take the seizure of the Cadmeia in Thebes. To-day, at any rate, the very cities whose independence you strove for have, since your unrighteous treatment of Thebes, fallen one and all of them again into her power. We are schooled now, both of

[4] 387 B.C.

us, to know that grasping brings not gain. We are prepared, I hope, to be once more moderate under the influence of a mutual friendship. Some, I know, in their desire to render our peace abortive accuse us falsely, as though we had come here, not seeking friendship, but because we dread the arrival of some Antalcidas with money from the king. But consider, what arrant nonsense they talk! Was it not, pray, the great king who demanded that all the states in Hellas should be independent? What have we Athenians, who are in full agreement with the king, both in word and deed, to fear from him? Or is it conceivable that he prefers spending money in making others great to finding his favourite projects realised without expense?

"Well, what is it really that has brought us here? No especial need or difficulty in our affairs. That you may discover by a glance at our maritime condition, or, if you prefer, at the present state of our affairs on land. Well, then, how does the matter stand? It is obvious that some of our allies please us no better than they please you;[5] and, possibly, in return for your former preservation of us, we may be credited with a desire to point out to you the soundness of our policy.

"But, to revert once more to the topic of expediency and common interests. It is admitted, I presume, that, looking at the states collectively, half support your views, half ours; and in every single state one party is for Sparta and another for Athens. Suppose, then, we were to shake hands, from what quarter can we reasonably anticipate danger and trouble? To put the case in so many words, so long as you are our friends no one can vex us by land; no one, while we are your supporters, can injure you by sea. Wars like tempests gather and grow to a head from time to time, and again they are dispelled. That we all know. Some future day, if not to-day, we shall crave, both of us, for peace. Why, then, need we wait for that moment, holding on until we expire under the multitude of our ills, rather than make peace quickly before some irremediable disaster befalls us? I cannot admire the man who, because he has entered the lists and has scored many a victory and obtained to himself renown, is so eaten up with the spirit of rivalry that he must needs go on until he is beaten and all his training is made futile. Nor again do I praise the gambler who, if he wins once, insists on doubling the stakes. Such conduct in the majority of cases must end in absolute collapse. Let us lay the lesson of these to heart, and forbear to enter into any such lists as theirs for life or death, but, while we are still strong and successful, become each other's friend. So assuredly shall we through you and you through us attain to an unprecedented pinnacle of glory throughout Hellas."

[5] This passage is corrupt.

The arguments of the speakers were approved, and the Lacedaemonians passed a resolution to accept peace on a threefold basis: the withdrawal of the governors from the cities, the disbanding of armaments naval and military, and the guarantee of independence to the states. "If any state transgressed these stipulations, it lay at the option of any power whatsoever to aid the states so injured, while, conversely, to bring such aid was not compulsory on any power against its will." On these terms the oaths were administered and accepted by the Lacedaemonians on behalf of themselves and their allies, and by the Athenians and their allies separately state by state. The Thebans had entered their individual name among the states which accepted the oaths, but their ambassadors came the next day with instructions to alter the name of the signatories, substituting for Thebans Boeotians.[6] But Agesilaus answered to this demand that he would alter nothing of what they had in the first instance sworn to and subscribed. If they did not wish to be included in the treaty, he was willing to erase their name at their bidding. So it came to pass that the rest of the world made peace, the sole point of dispute being confined to the Thebans; and the Athenians came to the conclusion that there was a fair prospect of the Thebans being now literally decimated. As to the Thebans themselves, they retired from Sparta in utter despondency.

4. In consequence of the peace the Athenians proceeded to withdraw their garrisons from the different states, and sent to recall Iphicrates with his fleet; besides which they forced him to restore everything captured subsequent to the oaths taken at Lacedaemon. The Lacedaemonians acted differently. Although they withdrew their governors and garrisons from the other states, in Phocis they did not do so. Here Cleombrotus was quartered with his army, and had sent to ask directions from the home authorities. A speaker, Prothous, maintained that their business was to disband the army in accordance with their oaths, and then to send round invitations to the states to contribute what each felt individually disposed, and lay such sum in the temple of Apollo; after which, if any attempt to hinder the independence of the states on any side were manifested, it would be time enough then again to invite all who cared to protect the principle of autonomy to march against its opponents. "In this way," he added, "I think the good-will of heaven will be secured, and the states will suffer least annoyance." But the Assembly, on hearing these views, agreed that this man was talking nonsense. An unseen power, as it would seem, was already driving them onwards; so they sent instructions to Cleombrotus not to disband the army, but to march straight against the Thebans if they refused to rec-

[6] In accordance with the usual claim of the Thebans to supremacy in Boeotia.

ognise the autonomy of the states. [Cleombrotus, it is understood, had, on hearing the news of the establishment of peace, sent to the ephorate to ask for guidance; and then they sent him the above instructions, bidding him under the circumstances named to march upon Thebes.][7]

The Spartan king soon perceived that, so far from leaving the Boeotian states their autonomy, the Thebans were not even preparing to disband their army, clearly in view of a general engagement; he therefore felt justified in marching his troops into Boeotia. The point of entry which he adopted was not that which the Thebans anticipated from Phocis, and where they were keeping guard at a defile; but, marching through Thisbae by a mountainous and unsuspected route, he arrived before Creusis, taking that fortress and capturing twelve Theban warvessels besides. After this achievement he advanced from the seaboard and encamped in Leuctra on Thespian territory. The Thebans encamped on a rising ground immediately opposite at no great distance, and were supported by no allies except the Boeotians.

At this juncture the friends of Cleombrotus came to him and urged upon him strong reasons for delivering battle. "If you let the Thebans escape without a battle," they said, "you will run great risks of suffering the extreme penalty at the hands of the state. People will call to mind against you the time when you reached Cynoscephalae and did not ravage a square foot of Theban territory; and again, a subsequent expedition when you were driven back foiled in your attempt to make an entry into the enemy's country—while Agesilaus on each occasion found his entry by Mount Cithaeron. If then you have any care for yourself, or any attachment to your fatherland, you must march against the enemy." That was what his friends urged. As to his opponents, what they said was, "Now our fine friend will show whether he really is so concerned on behalf of the Thebans as he is said to be."

Cleombrotus, hearing these words, felt driven to join battle. On their side the leaders of Thebes calculated that, if they did not fight, their provincial cities would hold aloof from them and Thebes itself would be besieged; while, if the people of Thebes failed to get supplies, there was every prospect that the city itself would turn against them; and, seeing that many of them had already tasted the bitterness of exile, they came to the conclusion that it was better for them to die on the field of battle than to renew that experience. Besides this they were somewhat encouraged by the recital of an oracle which predicted that the Lacedaemonians would be defeated on the spot where the monument of the virgins stood, who, as the story goes, being raped by certain Lacedae-

[7] This passage reads like an earlier version for which the above was substituted by the author.

monians, had slain themselves. This sepulchral monument the Thebans decked with ornaments before the battle. Furthermore, tidings were brought them from the city that all the temples had opened of their own accord; and the priestesses asserted that the gods revealed victory. Again, from the Heracleium men said that the arms had disappeared, as though Heracles himself had sallied forth to battle. It is true that another interpretation of these marvels made them out to be one and all the artifices of the leaders of Thebes. However this may be, everything in the battle turned out adverse to the Lacedaemonians; while fortune herself lent aid to the Thebans and crowned their efforts with success. Cleombrotus held his last council whether to fight or not, after the morning meal. In the heat of noon a little wine goes a long way; and people said that it had a somewhat provocative effect on their spirits.

Both sides were now arming, and there were the unmistakable signs of approaching battle, when, as the first incident, there issued from the Boeotian lines a long train bent on departure—these were the furnishers of the market, a detachment of baggage bearers, and in general such people as had no inclination to join in the fight. These were met on their retreat and attacked by the mercenary troops under Hiero, who got round them by an encircling movement. The mercenaries were supported by the Phocian light infantry and some squadrons of Heracleot and Phliasian cavalry, who fell upon the retiring train and turned them back, pursuing them and driving them into the camp of the Boeotians. The immediate effect was to make the Boeotian portion of the army more numerous and closer packed than before. The next feature of the combat was that in consequence of the flat space of plain between the opposing armies, the Lacedaemonians posted their cavalry in front of their squares of infantry, and the Thebans followed suit. Only there was this difference; the Theban cavalry was in a high state of training and efficiency, owing to their war with the Orchomenians and again their war with Thespiae, while the cavalry of the Lacedaemonians was at its worst at this period. The horses were reared and kept by the wealthiest members of the state; but whenever the army was called out, an appointed trooper appeared who took the horse with any sort of arms which might be presented to him, and set off on the expedition at a moment's notice. Moreover, these troopers were the least able-bodied of the men: raw recruits set simply astride their horses, and devoid of soldierly ambition. Such was the cavalry of either antagonist.

The heavy infantry of the Lacedaemonians, it is said, advanced by sections three files abreast, allowing a total depth to the whole line of not more than twelve. The Thebans were formed in close order of not less than fifty shields deep, calculating that victory gained over the king's division of the army implied the easy conquest of the rest.

Cleombrotus had hardly begun to lead his division against the foe when, before in fact the troops with him were aware of his advance, the cavalry had already come into collision, and that of the Lacedaemonians was speedily worsted. In their flight they became involved with their own heavy infantry; and to make matters worse, the Theban regiments were already attacking vigorously. Still strong evidence exists for supposing that Cleombrotus and his division were, in the first instance, victorious in the battle, if we consider the fact that they could never have picked him up and brought him back alive unless his vanguard had been masters of the situation for the moment.

When, however, Deinon the polemarch and Sphodrias, a member of the king's council, with his son Cleonymus, had fallen, then it was that the cavalry and the polemarch's adjutants, as they are called, with the rest, under pressure of the mass against them, began retreating; and the left wing of the Lacedaemonians, seeing the right borne down in this way, also swerved. Still, in spite of the numbers slain, and broken as they were, as soon as they had crossed the trench which protected their camp in front, they grounded arms on the spot whence they had rushed to battle. This camp, it must be borne in mind, did not lie at all on the level, but was pitched on a somewhat steep incline. At this juncture there were some of the Lacedaemonians who, looking upon such a disaster as intolerable, maintained that they ought to prevent the enemy from erecting a trophy, and try to recover the dead not under a truce but by another battle. The polemarchs, however, seeing that nearly 1,000 men of the total Lacedaemonian troops were slain; seeing also that of the 700 Spartans themselves who were on the field something like 400 lay dead; aware, further, of the despondency which reigned among the allies, and the general disinclination on their parts to fight longer (a frame of mind not far removed in some instances from positive satisfaction at what had taken place) under the circumstances, I say, the polemarchs called a council of the ablest representatives of the shattered army and deliberated as to what should be done. Finally the unanimous opinion was to pick up the dead under a truce, and they sent a herald to treat for terms. The Thebans after that set up a trophy and gave back the bodies under a truce.

After these events, a messenger was despatched to Lacedaemon with news of the calamity. He reached his destination on the last day of the festival of the Naked Youths, just when the chorus of grown men had entered the theatre. The ephors heard the mournful tidings with grief and pain, as was inevitable; but for all that they did not dismiss the chorus, but allowed the contest to run out its natural course. What they

did was to deliver the names of those who had fallen to their friends
and families, with a word of warning to the women not to make any
loud lamentation but to bear their sorrow in silence; and the next day
it was a striking spectacle to see those who had relations among the
slain moving to and fro in public with bright and radiant looks, while
of those whose friends were reported to be living barely a man was to
be seen, and these went about with lowered heads and scowling brows,
as if in humiliation.

After this the ephors proceeded to call out the army, including the
forty-years-service men of the two remaining regiments; and they proceeded further to despatch the reserves of the same age belonging to the
six regiments already on foreign service. Hitherto the Phocian campaign
had only drawn upon the thirty-five-years-service list. Besides these they
now ordered out on active service the troops retained at the beginning
of the campaign in attendance on the magistrates at the government
offices. Agesilaus being still disabled by his infirmity, the city imposed
the duty of command upon his son Archidamus. The new general found
eager cooperators in the men of Tegea. The friends of Stasippus at this
date were still living, and they were loyal to Lacedaemon, and wielded
considerable power in their state. Not less stoutly did the Mantineans
from their villages under their aristocratic form of government flock to
the Spartan standard. Besides Tegea and Mantinea, the Corinthians
and Sicyonians, the Phliasians and Achaeans were equally enthusiastic
in joining the campaign, while other states sent out soldiers. Then came
the fitting out and manning of ships of war on the part of the Lacedaemonians themselves and of the Corinthians, while the Sicyonians were
requested to furnish a supply of vessels on board which it was proposed
to transport the army across the gulf. And so, finally, Archidamus was
able to offer the sacrifices usual at the moment of crossing the frontier.
But to return to Thebes.

Immediately after the battle the Thebans sent a messenger to Athens
wearing a chaplet. While insisting on the magnitude of the victory they
at the same time called upon the Athenians to send them aid, for now
the opportunity had come to take vengeance on the Lacedaemonians
for all the evil they had done to Athens. As it chanced, the senate of
the Athenians was holding a session on the Acropolis. As soon as the
news was reported, the annoyance caused by its announcement was unmistakable. They neither invited the herald to accept their hospitality
nor replied to the request for assistance. And so the herald turned his
back on Athens and departed.

But there was Jason still to look to, and he was their ally. To him
then the Thebans sent, and earnestly besought his aid, their thoughts

running on the possible turn which events might take. Jason on his side at once proceeded to man a fleet, with the apparent intention of sending assistance by sea, besides which he got together his foreign brigade and his own cavalry; and although the Phocians and he were implacable enemies, he marched through their territory to Boeotia. Appearing like a vision to many of the states before his approach was even announced —at any rate before levies could be mustered from a dozen different points—he had stolen a march upon them and was a long way ahead, giving proof that expedition is sometimes a better tool to work with than sheer force.

When he arrived in Boeotia the Thebans urged upon him that now was the right moment to attack the Lacedaemonians: he with his foreign brigade from the upper ground, they face to face in front; but Jason dissuaded them from their intention. He reminded them that after a noble achievement won it was not worth their while to play for so high a stake, involving a still higher achievement or else the loss of victory already gained. "Do you not see," he urged, "that your success followed close on the heels of necessity? You ought then to reflect that the Lacedaemonians in their distress, with a choice between life and death, will fight it out with reckless desperation. Providence, as it seems, often delights to make the little ones great and the great ones small."

By such arguments he diverted the Thebans from the desperate adventure. But for the Lacedaemonians also he had words of advice, insisting on the difference between an army defeated and an army flushed with victory. "If you wish," he said, "to forget this disaster, my advice to you is to take time to recover breath and recruit your energies. When you have grown stronger then give battle to these unconquered veterans. At present," he continued, "you know without my telling you that among your own allies there are some who are already discussing terms of friendship with your foes. My advice is: by all means endeavour to obtain a truce. This," he added, "is my own ambition: I want to save you, on the ground of my father's friendship with yourselves, and as being myself your representative." Such was the tenor of his speech, but the secret of action was perhaps to be found in a desire to make these mutual antagonists put their dependence on himself alone. Whatever his motive, the Lacedaemonians took his advice, and commissioned him to procure a truce.

As soon as the news arrived that the terms were arranged, the polemarchs passed an order round: the troops were to take their evening meal, get their kit together, and be ready to set off that night, so as to scale the passes of Cithaeron by next morning. After supper, before the hour of sleep, the order to march was given, and with the generals at their head the troops advanced as the shades of evening fell, along the road to Creusis, trusting rather to the chance of their escaping notice, than to the truce itself. It was weary marching in the dead of night, making their retreat in fear, and along a difficult road, until at length they reached Aegosthena in the Megaris. Here they fell in with Archidamus's army of relief. At this point, then, Archidamus waited till all the allies had arrived, and so led the whole of the united armies back to Corinth, from which point he dismissed the allies and led his fellow-citizens home.

Jason took his departure from Boeotia through Phocis, where he captured the suburbs of Hyampolis and ravaged the country districts, putting many to the sword. Content with this, he traversed the rest of Phocis without meddling. Arrived at Heraclea, he knocked down the fortress of the Heracleots, showing that he was not troubled by any apprehension lest when the pass was thrown open somebody or other might march against his own power at some future date. Rather was he haunted by the notion that some one or other might one day seize Heraclea, which commanded the pass, and bar his passage into Hellas—should Hellas ever be his goal. At the moment of his return to Thessaly he had reached the zenith of his greatness. He was the lawfully constituted Tagus of Thessaly, and he had under him a large mercenary force of infantry and cavalry, and all in the highest perfection of training. For this twofold reason he might claim the title great. But he was still greater as the head of a vast alliance. Those who were prepared to fight his battles were numerous, and he might still count upon the help of many more eager to do so; but I call Jason greatest among his contemporaries, because not one among them could afford to look down upon him.

The Pythian games were now approaching, and an order went round the cities from Jason to make preparation for the solemn sacrifice of oxen, sheep and goats, and swine. It was reported that although the requisitions upon the several cities were moderate, the number of cattle did not fall short of 1,000, while the rest of the sacrificial beasts exceeded ten times that number. He issued a proclamation also to this effect: a golden wreath of victory should be given to whichever city could produce the best-bred bull to head the procession in honour of the god. And lastly there was an order issued to all the Thessalians to be ready for a campaign at the date of the Pythian games. His intention, as people said, was to act as manager of the solemn assembly and games in person. What the thought was that passed through his mind with reference to the sacred money, remains to this day uncertain; only, a tale is rife to the effect that in answer to an inquiry of the Delphians,

"What ought we to do, if he takes any of the treasures of the god?" the god made answer, "He would see to that himself." This great man, his brain teeming with vast designs of this high sort, came now to his end. He had ordered a military inspection. The cavalry of the Pheraeans were to pass muster before him. He was already seated, delivering answers to all petitioners, when seven striplings approached, quarrelling, as it seemed, about some matter. Suddenly he was struck down and killed by these seven. Stoutly the guard rushed to the rescue with their long spears, and one of the seven, while still in the act of aiming a blow at Jason, was thrust through with a lance and died; a second, in the act of mounting his horse, was caught, and dropped dead, the recipient of many wounds. The rest leaped on the horses which they had ready waiting and escaped. To whatever city of Hellas they came honours were almost universally accorded them. The whole incident proves clearly that the Hellenes stood in much alarm of Jason. They looked upon him as a tyrant in embryo.

So Jason was dead; and his brothers Polydorus and Polyphron were appointed princes in his place. But of these two, as they journeyed together to Larissa, Polydorus was slain in the night, as he slept, by his brother Polyphron, it was thought; since a death so sudden, without obvious cause, could hardly be otherwise accounted for.

Polyphron governed for a year, and by the year's end he had refashioned the office of Tagus into the likeness of a tyranny. In Pharsalus he put to death Polydamas and eight other of the best citizens; and from Larissa he drove many into exile. But while he was thus employed, he, in his turn, was done to death by Alexander, who slew him to avenge Polydorus and to destroy the tyranny. This man now assumed the reins of office, and had no sooner done so than he showed himself a harsh Tagus to the Thessalians: harsh too and hostile to the Thebans and Athenians, and an unprincipled freebooter everywhere by land and by sea. But if that was his character, he too was doomed to perish shortly. The perpetrators of the deed were his wife's brothers. The counsellor of it was the wife herself. She it was who reported to them that Alexander had designs against them; who hid them within the house a whole day; who welcomed home her husband deep in his cups and laid him to rest, and then while the lamp still burned brought out the prince's sword. It was she also who, perceiving that her brothers shrank back, fearing to go in and attack Alexander, said to them, "If you do not be quick and do the deed, I will wake him up." After they had gone in, she, too, it was who caught and pulled to the door, clinging fast to the knocker till the breath was out of her husband's body. Her fierce hatred against the man is variously explained. By some it was said to date from the day when Alexander, having imprisoned his own favourite—who was a fair young stripling—when his wife supplicated him to release the boy, brought him forth and stabbed him. Others say it originated through his sending to Thebes and seeking the hand of the wife of Jason in marriage, because his own wife bore him no children. These are the various causes assigned to explain the treason of his wife against him. Of the brothers who executed it, the eldest, Tisiphonus, in virtue of his seniority accepted, and up to the date of this history[8] succeeded in holding, the government.

5. The above is a sketch of Thessalian affairs, including the incidents connected with Jason, and those subsequent to his death, down to the government of Tisiphonus. I now return to the point at which we digressed.

Archidamus, after the relief of the army defeated at Leuctra, had led back the united forces. When he was gone, the Athenians, impressed by the fact that the Peloponnesians still felt under an obligation to follow the Lacedaemonians to the field, while Sparta herself was by no means as yet reduced to a condition resembling that to which she had reduced Athens, sent invitations to those states which cared to participate in the peace authorised by the great king. A congress met, and they passed a resolution in conjunction with those who wished to make common cause with them to bind themselves by oath as follows:

"I will abide by the treaty terms as conveyed in the king's rescript, as also by the decrees of the Athenians and the allies. If any one marches against any city among those which have accepted this oath, I will render assistance to that city with all my strength." The oath gave general satisfaction, the Eleians alone opposing its terms and protesting that it was not right to make either the Marganians or the Scilluntians or the Triphylians independent, since these cities belonged to them, and were a part of Elis. The Athenians, however, and the others passed the decree in the language of the king's rescript: that all states—great and small alike—were to be independent; and they sent out administrators of the oath, and enjoined upon them to administer it to the highest authorities in each state. This oath they all, with the exception of the Eleians, swore to.

As an immediate consequence of this agreement, the Mantineans, on the assumption that they were now absolutely independent, met in a body and passed a decree to make Mantinea into a single state and to fortify the town. The proceeding was not overlooked by the Lacedaemonians, who thought it would be hard if this were done without their consent. Accordingly they despatched Agesilaus as ambassador to the

[8] This is the last event (358 B.C.) mentioned by Xenophon.

Mantineans, choosing him as the recognised ancestral friend of that people. When the ambassador arrived, however, the chief magistrates had
no inclination to summon a meeting of the commons to listen to him,
but urged him to make a statement of his wishes to themselves. He, on
his side, was ready to undertake for himself and in their interests that,
if they would at present desist from their fortification work, he would
bring it about that the defensive walls should be built with the sanction of Lacedaemon and without cost. Their answer was, that it was impossible to hold back, since a decree had been passed by the whole state
of Mantinea to build at once. Whereupon Agesilaus went off in rage;
though as to sending troops to stop them, the idea seemed impracticable,
as the peace was based upon the principle of autonomy. Meanwhile
the Mantineans received help from several of the Arcadian states in the
building of their walls; and the Eleians contributed actually three talents of silver to cover the expense of their construction. And here leaving the Mantineans thus engaged, we will turn to the men of Tegea.

There were in Tegea two political parties. The one was the party of
Callibius and Proxenus, who were for drawing together the whole Arcadian population in a confederacy,[9] in which all measures carried in
the common assembly should be held valid for the individual component
states. The program of Stasippus' party was to leave Tegea undisturbed
and in the enjoyment of the old national laws. Defeated in the Sacred
College, the party of Callibius and Proxenus were persuaded that if only
the commons met they would gain an easy victory by an appeal to the
multitude; and in this faith they proceeded to march out the citizen
soldiers. At sight of this Stasippus and his friends on their side armed
in opposition, and proved not inferior in numbers. The result was a collision and battle, in which Proxenus and some few others with him were
slain and the rest put to flight; though the conquerors did not pursue,
for Stasippus was a man who did not care to stain his hands with the
blood of his fellow-citizens.

Callibius and his friends had retired under the fortification walls and
gates facing Mantinea; but, as their opponents made no further attempts against them, they here collected together and remained quiet.
Some while ago they had sent messages to the Mantineans demanding
assistance, but now they were ready to discuss terms of reconciliation
with the party of Stasippus. Presently they saw the Mantineans advancing; whereupon some of them sprang to the walls, and began calling
to them to bring succour with all speed. With shouts they urged upon
them to make haste, while others threw open wide the gates to them.

---

[9] Although the historian does not recount the foundation of Megalopolis, the
mention of the common assembly of the League in this passage implies it.

Stasippus and his party, perceiving what was happening, poured out by the gates leading to Pallantium, and, outspeeding their pursuers, succeeded in reaching the temple of Artemis, where they found shelter, and, shutting the doors, kept quiet. Following close upon their heels, however, their foes scaled the temple, tore off the roof, and began striking them down with the tiles. They, recognising that there was no choice, called upon their assailants to desist, and undertook to come forth. Then their opponents, capturing them, bound them with chains, threw them on to the prisoners' van, and led them off to Tegea. Here with the Mantineans they sentenced and put them to death.

The outcome of these proceedings was the banishment to Lacedaemon of the Tegeans who formed the party of Stasippus, numbering 800; but as a sequel to what had taken place, the Lacedaemonians determined that they were bound by their oaths to aid the banished Tegeans and to avenge the slain. With this purpose they marched against the Mantineans, on the ground that they had violated their oaths in marching against Tegea with an armed force. The ephors called out the army and the state commanded Agesilaus to head the expedition.

Meanwhile most of the Arcadian contingents were mustering at Asea. The Orchomenians not only refused to take part in the Arcadian league, on account of their personal hatred to Mantinea, but had actually welcomed within their city a mercenary force under Polytropus, which had been collected at Corinth. The Mantineans themselves were forced to stay at home to keep an eye on these. The men of Heraea and Lepreum made common cause with the Lacedaemonians in a campaign against Mantinea.

Finding the frontier sacrifices favourable, Agesilaus began his march at once upon Arcadia. He began by occupying the border city of Eutaea, where he found the old men, women, and children dwelling in their houses, while the rest of the population of a military age were off to join the Arcadian league. In spite of this he did not stir a finger unjustly against the city, but suffered the inhabitants to continue in their homes undisturbed. The troops took all they needed, and paid for it in return; if any pillage had occurred on his first entrance into the town, the property was hunted up and restored by the Spartan king. While awaiting the arrival of Polytropus's mercenaries, he repaired such portions of their walls as necessity demanded.

Meanwhile the Mantineans had taken the field against Orchomenus; but from the walls of that city the invaders had some difficulty in retiring, and lost some of their men. On their retreat they found themselves in Elymia; here the heavy infantry of the Orchomenians ceased to follow them; but Polytropus and his troops continued to assail their rear with much audacity. At this juncture, seeing at a glance that either they must beat back the foe or suffer their own men to be shot down, the Mantineans turned right about and met the assailant in a hand-to-hand encounter. Polytropus fell fighting on that battlefield; and of the rest who took to flight, many would have shared his fate, but for the opportune arrival of the Phliasian cavalry, who swooped round to the conqueror's rear and checked him in his pursuit.

Content with this achievement, the Mantineans retired homewards; while Agesilaus, to whom the news was brought, no longer expecting that the Orchomenian mercenaries could effect a junction with himself, determined to advance without further delay. On the first day he encamped for the evening meal in the open country of Tegea, and the day following crossed into Mantinean territory. Here he encamped under the westward mountains of Mantinea, and employed himself in ravaging the country district and sacking the farms; while the troops of the Arcadians who were mustered in Asea stole by night into Tegea. The next day Agesilaus shifted his position, encamping about two miles from Mantinea; and the Arcadians, issuing from Tegea and clinging to the mountains between Mantinea and that city, appeared with large bodies of heavy infantry, wishing to effect a junction with the Mantineans. The Argives, it is true, supported them, but they were not in full force. And here counsellors were to be found who urged on Agesilaus to attack these troops separately; but fearing lest, in proportion as he pressed on to engage them, the Mantineans might issue from the city behind and attack him on flank and rear, he decided it was best to let the two bodies coalesce, and then, if they would accept battle, to engage them on an open and fair field.

And so shortly the Arcadians effected their object and united with the Mantineans. The next incident was the sudden appearance at daybreak, as Agesilaus was sacrificing in front of the camp, of a body of troops. These proved to be the light infantry from Orchomenus, who in company with the Phliasian cavalry had during the night made their way across past the town of Mantinea; and so caused the mass of the army to rush to their ranks, and Agesilaus himself to retire within the lines. Presently, however, the newcomers were recognised as friends; and as the sacrifices were favourable, Agesilaus led his army forward a stage farther after breakfast. As the shades of evening descended he encamped unobserved within the fold of the hills behind the Mantinean territory, with mountains in close proximity all round.

On the next morning, as day broke, he sacrificed in front of the army; and observing a mustering of men from the city of Mantinea on the hills which overhung the rear of his army, he decided that he must lead his troops out of the hollow by the quickest route. But he feared that, if he himself led off, the enemy might fall upon his rear. In this dilemma he kept quiet; presenting a hostile front to the enemy, he sent orders to his rear to face about to the right, and so getting into line behind his main body, to move forward upon him; and in this way he at once extricated his troops from their cramped position and kept continually adding to the weight and solidity of his line. As soon as the phalanx was doubled in depth he emerged upon the level ground, with his heavy infantry battalions in this order, and then again extended his line till the troops were once more nine or ten shields deep. But the Mantineans were no longer so ready to come out. The arguments of the Eleians who had lent them their cooperation had prevailed: that it was better not to engage until the arrival of the Thebans. The Thebans, it was certain, would soon be with them; for had they not borrowed ten talents from Elis in order to be able to send aid? The Arcadians with this information before them kept quiet inside Mantinea. On his side Agesilaus was anxious to lead off his troops, seeing it was midwinter; but, to avoid seeming to hurry his departure out of fear, he preferred to remain three days longer at no great distance from Mantinea. On the fourth day, after an early morning meal, the retreat commenced. His intention was to encamp on the same ground which he had made his starting-point on leaving Eutaea. But as none of the Arcadians appeared, he marched with all speed and reached Eutaea itself, although very late, that day; being anxious to lead off his heavy troops without catching a glimpse of the enemy's watch-fires, so that no one could say that he withdrew in flight. His main object was in fact achieved. To some extent he had recovered the state from its late despondency, since he had invaded Arcadia and ravaged the country without any one caring to offer him battle. But, once arrived on Laconian soil, he dismissed the Spartan troops to their homes and disbanded the provincials to their several cities.

The Arcadians, now that Agesilaus had retired, realising that he had disbanded his troops, while they themselves were fully mustered, marched upon Heraea, the citizens of which town had not only refused to join the Arcadian league, but had joined the Lacedaemonians in their invasion of Arcadia. For this reason they entered the country, burning the homesteads and cutting down the fruit-trees.

Meanwhile news came of the arrival of the Theban reinforcements at Mantinea, on the strength of which they left Heraea and hastened to join their Theban friends. When they met together, the Thebans, on their side, were well content with the state of affairs: they had duly brought aid, and no enemy was any longer to be discovered in the country; so they made preparations to return home. But the Arcadians, Ar-

gives, and Eleians were eager in urging them to lead the united forces
forthwith into Laconia: they dwelt proudly on their own numbers, extolling above measure the armament of Thebes. And, indeed, the Boeotians one and all were resolute in their military manoeuvres and devotion to arms, exulting in the victory of Leuctra. In the wake of Thebes
followed the Phocians, who were now their subjects, Euboeans from all
the townships of the island, both sections of the Locrians, the Acarnanians, and the men of Heraclea and of Melis; while their force was
further swelled by Thessalian cavalry and light infantry. With the full
consciousness of facts like these, and further justifying their appeal by
dwelling on the desolate condition of Lacedaemon, deserted by her troops,
they entreated them not to turn back without invading the territory of
Laconia. But the Thebans, while they listened to their prayers, urged
arguments on the other side. In the first place, Laconia was by all accounts most difficult to invade; and their belief was that garrisons were
posted at all the points most easily approached. (As a matter of fact,
Ischolaus was posted at Oeum in the Sciritid, with a garrison of neodamodes and about 400 of the youngest of the Tegean exiles; and there
was a second outpost on Leuctrum above Maleatis.) Again it occurred
to the Thebans that the Lacedaemonian forces, though disbanded, would
not take long to muster, and once collected they would fight nowhere
better than on their own native soil. Putting all these considerations together, they were by no means eager to march upon Lacedaemon. A
strong counter-impulse, however, was presently given by the arrival of
messengers from Caryae, giving positive information as to the defenceless
condition of the country, and offering to act as guides themselves; they
were ready to lose their lives if they were convicted of perfidy. A further
impulse in the same direction was given by the presence of some of
the Perioeci, with invitations and promises of revolt, if only they would
appear in the country. These people further stated that even at the present moment, on a summons of the Spartans proper, the Perioeci did not
care to render them assistance. With all these arguments and persuasions
echoing from all sides, the Thebans at last yielded, and invaded. They
chose the Caryan route themselves, while the Arcadians entered by
Oeum in Sciritis.

By all accounts Ischolaus made a mistake in not advancing to meet
them on the difficult ground above Oeum. Had he done so, not a man,
it is believed, would have scaled the passes there. But for the present,
wishing to turn the help of the men of Oeum to good account, he waited
down in the village; and so the invading Arcadians scaled the heights
in a body. At this crisis Ischolaus and his men, as long as they fought
face to face with their foes, held the superiority; but, presently, when

the enemy, from rear and flank, and even from the dwelling-houses up which they scaled, rained blows and missiles upon them, then and there Ischolaus met his end, and every man besides, save only one or two who, failing to be recognised, effected their escape.

After these achievements the Arcadians marched to join the Thebans at Caryae, and the Thebans, hearing what wonders the Arcadians had performed, commenced their descent with far greater confidence. Their first exploit was to burn and ravage the district of Sellasia, but soon finding themselves in the flat land within the sacred enclosure of Apollo, they encamped for the night, and the next day continued their march along the Eurotas. When they came to the bridge they made no attempt to cross it to attack the city, for they caught sight of the heavy infantry in the temple of Alea ready to meet them. So, keeping the Eurotas on their right, they tramped along, burning and pillaging homesteads stocked with numerous stores. The feelings of the citizens may well be imagined. The women who had never set eyes upon a foe could scarcely contain themselves as they beheld the cloud of smoke. The Spartan warriors, inhabiting a city without fortifications, posted at intervals, here one and there another, were in truth what they appeared to be—the veriest handful. And these kept watch. The authorities passed a resolution to announce to the Helots that whosoever among them chose to take arms and join a regiment should have his freedom guaranteed to him by solemn pledges in return for assistance in the common war. More than 6,000 Helots, it is said, enrolled themselves, so that a new terror was excited by the very incorporation of these men, whose numbers seemed to be excessive. But when it was found that the mercenaries from Orchomenus remained faithful, and reinforcements came to Lacedaemon from Phlius, Corinth, Epidaurus, and Pellene, and some other states, the dread of these new levies was speedily diminished.

The enemy in his advance came to Amyclae. Here he crossed the Eurotas. The Thebans wherever they encamped at once formed a stockade of the fruit-trees they had felled, as thickly piled as possible, and so kept on their guard. The Arcadians did nothing of the sort. They left their camping-ground and took themselves off to attack the homesteads and loot. On the third or fourth day after their arrival the cavalry advanced, squadron by squadron, as far as the racecourse, within the sacred enclosure of Poseidon the Earth-upholder. These consisted of the entire Theban cavalry and the Eleians, with as many of the Phocian or Thessalian or Locrian cavalry as were present. The cavalry of the Lacedaemonians, looking a mere handful, were drawn up to meet them. They had posted an ambuscade chosen from their heavy infantry, the younger men, about 300 in number, in the house of the Tyndaridae; and while the cavalry charged, out rushed the 300 at the same instant at full pace. The enemy did not wait to receive the double charge, but swerved, and at sight of that, many also of the infantry took to headlong flight. But the pursuers presently paused; the Theban army remained motionless; and both parties returned to their camps. And now the hope, the confidence strengthened that an attack upon the city itself would never come; nor did it. The invading army broke up from their ground, and marched off on the road to Helos and Gytheum. The unwalled cities were consigned to the flames, but Gytheum, where the Lacedaemonians had their naval arsenal, was subjected to assault for three days. Certain of the provincials also joined in this attack, and shared the campaign with the Thebans and their friends.[10]

The news of these proceedings set the Athenians deeply pondering what they ought to do concerning the Lacedaemonians, and they held an assembly in accordance with a resolution of the senate. It chanced that the ambassadors of the Lacedaemonians and the allies still faithful to Lacedaemon were present. The Lacedaemonian ambassadors were Aracus, Ocyllus, Pharax, Etymocles, and Olontheus, and from the nature of the case they all used, roughly speaking, similar arguments. They reminded the Athenians how they had often in old days stood happily together, shoulder to shoulder, in more than one great crisis. They (the Lacedaemonians), on their side, had helped to expel the tyrant from Athens, and the Athenians, when Lacedaemon was besieged by the Messenians, had heartily lent her a helping hand. Then they fell to enumerating all the blessings that marked the season when the two states shared a common policy, hinting how in common they had warred against the barbarians, and more boldly recalling how the Athenians with the full consent and advice of the Lacedaemonians were chosen by united Hellas leaders of the common navy and guardians of the common treasure, while they themselves were selected by all the Hellenes as confessedly the rightful leaders on land; and this also not without the full consent and concurrence of the Athenians.

One of the speakers ventured on a remark somewhat in this strain, "If you and we can only agree, there is hope to-day that the old saying may be fulfilled, and Thebes be decimated." The Athenians, however, were not in the humour to listen to that style of argument. A sort of suppressed murmur ran through the assembly which seemed to say, "That language may be well enough now; but when they were well off they pressed hard enough on us." But of all the pleas put forward by the Lacedaemonians, the weightiest appeared to be this: that when they

[10] Xenophon fails to mention that Epaminondas, the Theban general, freed Messene which had been subject to Sparta for centuries.

had reduced the Athenians by war, and the Thebans wished to wipe Athens off the face of the earth, they (the Lacedaemonians) themselves had opposed the measure. If that was the argument of most weight, the reasoning which was most commonly urged was to the effect that the solemn oaths necessitated the aid demanded. Sparta had done no wrong to justify this invasion on the part of the Arcadians and their allies. All she had done was to assist the men of Tegea when the Mantineans had marched against that township contrary to their solemn oaths. Again, for the second time, at these expressions a confused din ran through the assembly, half the audience maintaining that the Mantineans were justified in supporting Proxenus and his friends, who were put to death by the party with Stasippus; the other half that they were wrong in bringing an armed force against the men of Tegea.

Whilst these distinctions were being drawn by the assembly itself, Cleiteles the Corinthian got up and spoke as follows, "I daresay, men of Athens, there is a double answer to the question, 'Who began the wrongdoing?' But take the case of ourselves. Since peace began, no one can accuse us either of wantonly attacking any city, or of seizing the wealth of any, or of ravaging a foreign territory. In spite of which the Thebans have come into our country and cut down our fruit-trees, burnt our houses to the ground, filched and torn to pieces our cattle and our goods. How then, I put it to you, will you not be acting contrary to your solemn oaths if you refuse your aid to us, who are so manifestly the victims of wrongdoing? Yes; and when I say solemn oaths, I speak of oaths and undertakings which you yourselves took great pains to exact from all of us." At that point a murmur of applause greeted Cleiteles, the Athenians feeling the truth and justice of the speaker's language.

He sat down, and then Procles of Phlius got up and spoke as follows, "What would happen, men of Athens, if the Lacedaemonians were well out of the way? The answer to that question is obvious. You would be the first object of Theban invasion. Clearly; for they must feel that you and you alone stand in the path between them and empire over Hellas. If this be so, I do not consider that you are more supporting Lacedaemon by a campaign in her behalf than you are helping yourselves. For imagine the Thebans, your own sworn foes and next-door neighbours, masters of Hellas! You will find it a painful and onerous exchange indeed for the distant antagonism of Sparta. As a mere matter of self-interest, now is the time to help yourselves, while you may still reckon upon allies, instead of waiting until they are lost, and you are forced to fight a life-and-death battle with the Thebans single-handed. But the fear suggests itself, that should the Lacedaemonians escape now, they will live to cause you trouble at some future date. Lay this maxim to heart, then, that it is not the potential greatness of those we benefit, but of those we injure, which causes apprehension. And this other also, that it behoves individuals and states alike so to better their position while yet in the zenith of their strength that, in the day of weakness, when it comes, they may find some succour and support in what their former labours have achieved. To you now, at this time, a heaven-sent opportunity is presented. In return for assistance to the Lacedaemonians in their need, you may win their sincere, unhesitating friendship for all time. Yes, I say it deliberately, for the acceptance of these benefits at your hands will not be in the presence of one or two chance witnesses. The all-seeing gods, in whose sight to-morrow is even as to-day, will be cognisant of these things. The knowledge of them will be jointly attested by allies and enemies; nay, by Hellenes and barbarians alike, since to not one of them is what we are doing a matter of unconcern. If, then, in the presence of these witnesses, the Lacedaemonians should prove base towards you, no one will ever again be eager in their cause. But our hope, our expectation should rather be that they will prove themselves good men and not base; since they beyond all others would seem persistently to have cherished a high endeavour, reaching forth after true praise, and holding aloof from ugly deeds.

"But there are further considerations which it were well you should lay to heart. If danger were ever again to visit Hellas from the barbarian world outside, in whom would you place your confidence if not in the Lacedaemonians? Whom would you choose to stand at your right hand in battle if not these, whose soldiers at Thermopylae to a man preferred to fall at their posts rather than save their lives by giving the barbarian free passage into Hellas? Is it not right, then, considering for what thing's sake they displayed that bravery in your companionship, considering also the good hope there is that they will prove the like again— is it not just that you and we should lend them all countenance and goodwill? Nay, even for us their allies' sake, who are present, it would be worth your while to manifest this goodwill. Need you be assured that precisely those who continue faithful to them in their misfortunes would in like manner be ashamed not to requite you with gratitude? And if we seem to be but small states, who are willing to share their dangers with them, lay to heart that there is a speedy cure for this defect: with the accession of your city the reproach that, in spite of all our assistance, we are but small cities, will cease to be.

"For my part, men of Athens, I have hitherto on hearsay admired and envied this great state, whither, I was told, every one who was wronged or stood in terror of aught needed only to betake himself and he would obtain assistance. To-day I no longer hear, I am present myself and see these famous citizens of Lacedaemon here, and by their side their trustiest friends, who have come to you, and ask you in their day of need to give them help. I see Thebans also, the same who in days bygone failed to persuade the Lacedaemonians to reduce you to absolute slavery, to-day asking you to allow those who saved you to be destroyed.

"That was a great deed and of fair renown, attributed in old story to your ancestors, that they did not suffer those Argives who died on the Cadmeia[11] to lie unburied; but a fairer wreath of glory would you weave for your own brows if you suffer not these still living Lacedaemonians to be trampled under the heel of insolence and destroyed. Fair, also, was that achievement when you stayed the insolence of Eurystheus and saved the sons of Heracles;[12] but fairer still than that will your deed be if you rescue from destruction, not the primal authors merely, but the whole city which they founded; fairest of all, if because yesterday the Lacedaemonians won you your preservation by a vote which cost them nothing, you to-day shall bring them help with arms, and at the price of peril. It is a proud day for some of us to stand here and give what aid we can in pleading for assistance to brave men. What, then, must you feel, who in very deed are able to render that assistance! How generous on your parts, who have been so often the friends and foes of Lacedaemon, to forget the injury and remember only the good they have done! How noble of you to repay, not for yourselves only, but for the sake of Hellas, the debt due to those who proved themselves good men and true in her behalf!"

After these speeches the Athenians deliberated, and though there was opposition, the arguments of objectors fell upon deaf ears. The assembly finally passed a decree to send assistance to Lacedaemon in force, and they chose Iphicrates general. Then followed the preliminary sacrifices, and then the general's order to his troops to take the evening meal in the grove of the Academy. But the general himself, it is said, was in no hurry to leave the city; many were found at their posts before him. Presently, however, he put himself at the head of his troops, and the men followed cheerily, in firm persuasion that he was about to lead them to some noble exploit. On arrival at Corinth he wasted some days, and there was a momentary outburst of discontent at so much waste of precious time; but as soon as he led the troops out of Corinth there was an obvious rebound. The men responded to all orders with enthusiasm, heartily following their general's lead, and attacking whatever fortified place he might confront them with.

[11] In reference to the Seven against Thebes.
[12] According to the legend the Athenians restored the Heracleidae when they were driven from the Peloponnese.

And now reverting to the hostile forces on Laconian territory, we find that the Arcadians, Argives, and Eleians had retired in large numbers. They had every inducement so to do since their homes bordered on Laconia; and off they went, driving or carrying whatever they had looted. The Thebans and the rest were no less anxious to get out of the country, though for other reasons, partly because the army was melting away under their eyes day by day, partly because the necessaries of life were growing daily scantier, so much had been either fairly eaten up and pillaged or else recklessly squandered and reduced to ashes. Besides this, it was winter; so that on every ground there was a general desire by this time to get away home.

As soon as the enemy began his retreat from Laconian soil, Iphicrates imitated his movement, and began leading back his troops out of Arcadia into Corinth. Iphicrates exhibited much good generalship, no doubt, with which I have no sort of fault to find. But it is not so with that final feature of the campaign to which we are now come. Here I find his strategy either meaningless in intent or inadequate in execution. He made an attempt to keep guard at Oneion, in order to prevent the Boeotians making their way out homewards; but left meanwhile far the best passage through Cenchreae unguarded. Again, when he wished to discover whether or not the Thebans had passed Oneion, he sent out on a reconnaissance the whole of the Athenian and Corinthian cavalry; whereas, for the object in view, the eyes of a small detachment would have been as useful as a whole regiment; and when it came to falling back, clearly the smaller number had a better chance of hitting on a good road, and so effecting the desired movement quietly. But the height of folly seems to have been reached when he threw into the path of the enemy a large body of troops which were still too weak to cope with him. As a matter of fact, this body of cavalry, owing to their very numbers, could not help covering a large space of ground; and when it became necessary to retire, had to cling to a series of difficult positions in succession, so that they lost not fewer than twenty horsemen. It was thus the Thebans effected their object and retired from Peloponnese.

BOOK VII

1. In the following year plenipotentiary ambassadors from the Lacedaemonians and the allies arrived at Athens to consider and take counsel about the terms of the alliance between Athens and Lacedaemon. It was urged by many speakers, foreigners and Athenians also, that the alliance ought to be based on the principle of absolute equality, when Procles of Phlius put forward the following argument:

"Since you have decided, men of Athens, that it is good to secure the friendship of Lacedaemon, the point, as it appears to me, which you ought now to consider is, by what means this friendship may be made to last as long as possible. The probability is, that we shall hold together best by making a treaty which shall suit the best interests of both parties. On most points we have, I believe, a tolerable unanimity, but there remains the question of leadership. The preliminary decree of your senate anticipates a division, crediting you with the chief maritime power, Lacedaemon with the chief power on land; and to me, personally, I confess, that seems a division not more established by human invention than preordained by some divine naturalness or happy fortune. For, in the first place, you have a geographical position pre-eminently adapted for naval supremacy; most of the states to whom the sea is important are massed round your own, and all of these are inferior to you in strength. Besides, you have harbours and roadsteads, without which it is not possible to turn a naval power to account. Again, you have many ships of war. To extend your naval empire is a traditional policy; all the arts and sciences connected with these matters you possess as home products, and, what is more, in skill and experience of nautical affairs you are far ahead of the rest of the world. The majority of you derive your livelihood from the sea, or things connected with it; so that in the very act of minding your own affairs you are training yourselves to enter the lists of naval combat. Again, no other power in the world can send out a larger collective fleet, and that is no insignificant point in reference to the question of leadership. The nucleus of strength first gained becomes a rallying-point, round which the rest of the world will gladly congregate. Furthermore, your good fortune in this department must be looked upon as a definite gift of god: for, consider among the numberless great sea-fights which you have fought how few you have lost, how many you have won. It is only rational, then, that your allies should much prefer to share this particular risk with you. Indeed, to show you how natural and vital to you is this maritime study, the following reflection may serve. For several years the Lacedaemonians, when at war with you in old days, dominated your territory, but they made no progress towards destroying you. At last god granted them one day to push forward their dominion on the sea, and then in an instant you completely succumbed to them. Is it not self-evident that your safety altogether depends upon the sea? The sea is your natural element—your birthright; it would be base indeed to entrust the hegemony of it to the Lacedaemonians, and the more so, since, as they themselves admit, they are far less acquainted with this business than yourselves; and, secondly, your risk in naval battles would not be for equal stakes—theirs involving only the loss of the men on board their ships, but yours, that of your children and your wives and the entire state.

"And if this is a fair statement of your position, turn, now, and consider that of the Lacedaemonians. The first point to notice is, that they are an inland power; as long as they are dominant on land it does not matter how much they are cut off from the sea—they can carry on existence happily enough. This they so fully recognise, that from boyhood they devote themselves to training for a soldier's life. The keystone of this training is obedience to command, and in this they hold the same pre-eminence on land which you hold on the sea. Just as you with your fleets, so they on land can, at a moment's notice, put the largest army in the field; and with the like consequence, that their allies, as is only rational, attach themselves to them with the greatest courage. Further, god has granted them to enjoy on land a like good fortune to that vouchsafed to you on sea. Among all the many contests they have entered into, it is surprising in how few they have failed, in how many they have been successful. The same unflagging attention which you pay to maritime affairs is required from them on land, and, as the facts reveal, it is no less indispensable to them. Thus, although you were at war with them for several years and gained many a naval victory over them, you never advanced a step nearer reducing them. But once worsted on land, in an instant they were confronted with a danger affecting the very lives of child and wife, and vital to the interests of the entire state. We may very well understand, then, the strangeness, not to say monstrosity, in their eyes, of surrendering to others the military leadership on land, in matters which they have made their special study for so long and with such eminent success. I end where I began. I agree absolutely with the preliminary decree of your own senate, which I consider the solution most advantageous to both parties. My prayer is that you may be guided in your deliberations to that conclusion which is best for each and all of us."

Such were the words of the orator, and the sentiments of his speech were vehemently applauded by the Athenians no less than by the Lacedaemonians who were present. Then Cephisodotus stepped forward and said, "Men of Athens, do you not see how you are being deluded? Listen to me, and I will prove it to you in a moment. There is no doubt about your leadership by sea: it is already secured. But suppose the Lacedaemonians in alliance with you: it is plain they will send you admirals and captains, and possibly marines, of Laconian breed; but who will the sailors be? Helots obviously, or mercenaries of some sort. These are the folk over whom you will exercise your leadership. Reverse the case. The Lacedaemonians have issued a general order summoning you to join them in the field; it is plain again, you will be sending your heavy infantry and your cavalry. You see what follows. You have invented a pretty machine, by which they become leaders of your very selves, and you become the leaders either of their slaves or of the dregs of their state. I should like to put a question to the Lacedaemonian Timocrates seated yonder. Did you not say just now that you came to make an alliance on terms of absolute equality, share and share alike? Answer me." "I did say so." "Well, then, here is a plan by which you get the perfection of equality. I cannot conceive anything more fair and impartial than that turn and turn about each of us should command the navy, each the army; whereby whatever advantage there may be in maritime or military command we may each of us share."

These arguments were successful. The Athenians were converted, and passed a decree vesting the command in either state for periods of five days alternately.

The campaign was commenced by both Athenians and Lacedaemonians with their allies, marching upon Corinth, where it was resolved to keep watch and ward over Oneion jointly. On the advance of the Thebans and their allies the troops were drawn out to defend the pass. They were posted in detachments at different points, the most assailable of which was assigned to the Lacedaemonians and the men of Pellene.

The Thebans and their allies, finding themselves within three or four miles of the troops guarding the pass, encamped on the flat ground below; but presently, after a careful calculation of the time it would take to start and reach the goal at dawn, they advanced against the Lacedaemonian outposts. They timed their movements perfectly, and fell upon the Lacedaemonians and Pellenians just at the interval when the night pickets were turning in and the men were leaving their shakedowns and retiring for necessary purposes. This was the instant for the Thebans to fling themselves upon them; they plied their weapons with good effect, blow upon blow. Order was pitted against disorder, preparation against disarray. When, however, those who escaped from the thick of the business had retired to the nearest rising ground, the Lacedaemonian polemarch, who might have taken as many heavy, or light, infantry of the allies as he wanted, and thus have held the position (no bad one, since it enabled him to get his supplies safely enough from Cenchreae), failed to do so. On the contrary, and in spite of the great perplexity of the Thebans as to how they were to get down from the high level facing Sicyon or else retire the way they came, the Spartan general made a truce, which, in the opinion of the majority, seemed more in favour of the Thebans than himself, and so he withdrew his division and fell back.

The Thebans were now free to descend without hindrance, which they did; and, effecting a junction with their allies the Arcadians, Argives, and Eleians, at once attacked Sicyon and Pellene, and, marching on Epidaurus, laid waste the whole territory of that people. Returning from that exploit with a consummate disdain for all their opponents, when they found themselves near the city of Corinth they advanced at the double against the gate facing towards Phlius; intending if they found it open to rush in. However, a body of light troops sallied out of the city to the rescue, and met the advance of the Theban picked corps not 150 yards from the walls. Mounting on the monuments and commanding eminences, with volleys of sling stones and arrows they laid low a pretty large number in the van of the attack, and routing them, gave chase for three or four furlongs' distance. After this incident the Corinthians dragged the corpses of the slain to the wall, and finally gave them up under a truce, erecting a trophy to record the victory. As a result of this occurrence the allies of the Lacedaemonians took fresh heart.

At the date of the above transactions the Lacedaemonians were cheered by the arrival of a naval reinforcement from Dionysius, consisting of more than twenty warships, which conveyed a body of Celts and Iberians and about fifty cavalry. The day following, the Thebans and the rest of the allies, posted, at intervals, in battle order, and completely filling the flat land down to the sea on one side, and up to the knolls on the other which form the buttresses of the city, proceeded to destroy everything precious they could lay their hands on in the plain. The Athenian and Corinthian cavalry, eyeing the strength, physical and numerical, of their antagonists, kept at a safe distance from their armament. But the little body of cavalry lately arrived from Dionysius spread out in a long thin line, and one at one point and one at another galloped along the front, discharging their missiles as they dashed forward, and when the enemy rushed against them, retired, and again wheeling about, showered another volley. Even while so engaged they would dismount from their horses and take breath; and if their foemen galloped up while they were so dismounted, in an instant they had leapt on their horses' backs and were in full retreat. Or if, again, a party pursued them some distance from the main body, as soon as they turned to retire, they would press upon them, and discharging volleys of missiles, made terrible work, forcing the whole army to advance and retire, merely to keep pace with the movements of fifty horsemen.

After this the Thebans remained only a few more days and then turned back homewards; and the rest likewise to their several homes. Thereupon the troops sent by Dionysius attacked Sicyon. Engaging the Sicyonians in the flat country, they defeated them, killing about seventy men and capturing by assault the fortress of Derae. After these achievements this first reinforcement from Dionysius re-embarked and set sail for Syracuse.

Up to this time the Thebans and all the states which had revolted from Lacedaemon had acted together in perfect harmony, and were content to campaign under the leadership of Thebes; but now a certain Lycomedes, a Mantinean, broke the spell. Inferior in birth and position to none, while in wealth superior, he was for the rest a man of high ambition. This man was able to inspire the Arcadians with high thoughts by reminding them that to Arcadians alone the Peloponnese was in a literal sense a fatherland; since they and they alone were the indigenous inhabitants of its sacred soil, and the Arcadian stock the largest among the Hellenic tribes—a good stock, moreover, and of incomparable physique. And then he declared that they were the bravest, adducing as evidence the fact that every one in need of help turned to the Arcadians. Never in old days had the Lacedaemonians yet invaded Athens without their help; nor could the Thebans nowadays approach Lacedaemon without the Arcadians. "If then," he added, "you are wise, you will be somewhat slow to follow anybody. As when you marched in the train of Sparta you only enhanced her power, so to-day, if you follow Theban guidance without thought or purpose instead of claiming a division of the headship, you will speedily find, perhaps, in her only a second edition of Lacedaemon."

These words, uttered in the ears of the Arcadians, were sufficient to puff them up with pride. They were lavish in their love of Lycomedes, and thought there was no one his equal. He became their hero; he had only to give his orders, and they appointed their magistrates at his bidding. But, indeed, a series of brilliant exploits entitled the Arcadians to magnify themselves. The first of these arose out of an invasion of Epidaurus by the Argives, which seemed likely to end in their finding their escape barred by Chabrias and his foreign brigade with the Athenians and Corinthians. Only, at the critical moment the Arcadians came to the rescue and extricated the Argives, who were closely besieged, and this in spite not only of the enemy, but of the savage nature of the ground itself. Again, they marched on Asine in Laconian territory, and defeated the Lacedaemonian garrison, putting the polemarch Geranor, who was a Spartan, to the sword, and sacking the suburbs of the town. Indeed, whenever or wherever they had a mind to send an invading force, neither night nor wintry weather, nor length of road nor mountain barrier could stay their march. So that at this date they regarded their prowess as invincible. The Thebans, it will be understood, could not but feel a touch of jealousy at these pretensions, and their former friendship to the Arcadians had lost its ardour. With the Eleians, indeed, matters were worse. The revelation came to them when they demanded back from the Arcadians certain cities of which the Lacedaemonians had deprived them. They discovered that their views were held of no account, but that the Triphylians and the rest who had revolted from them were to be made much of, because they claimed to be Arcadians. Hence, as contrasted with the Thebans, the Eleians cherished feelings towards their late friends which were positively hostile.

Self-esteem amounting to arrogance—such was the spirit which animated each section of the allies, when a new phase was introduced by the arrival of Philiscus of Abydos from Ariobarzanes with large sums of money. This agent's first step was to assemble a congress of Thebans, allies, and Lacedaemonians at Delphi to treat of peace. On their arrival, without attempting to communicate or take counsel with the god as to how peace might be re-established, they fell to deliberating unassisted; and when the Thebans refused to acquiesce in the dependency of Messene upon Lacedaemon, Philiscus set about collecting a large foreign brigade to side with Lacedaemon and to prosecute the war.

Whilst these matters were still pending, the second reinforcement from Dionysius arrived. There was a difference of opinion as to where the troops should be employed, the Athenians insisting that they ought to march into Thessaly to oppose the Thebans, the Lacedaemonians being in favour of Laconia; and among the allies this latter opinion carried the day. The reinforcement from Dionysius accordingly sailed round to Laconia, where Archidamus incorporated them with the state troops and opened the campaign. Caryae he took by storm, and put every one captured to the sword, and from this point marching straight upon the Parrhasians of Arcadia, he set about ravaging the country along with his Syracusan supporters.

Presently, when the Arcadians and Argives arrived with assistance, he retreated, and encamped on the knolls above Melea. While he was here, Cissidas, the officer in charge of the reinforcement from Dionysius, made the announcement that the period for his stay abroad had elapsed; and immediately he set off on the road to Sparta. The march itself, however, was not effected without delays, for he was met and cut off by a body of Messenians at a narrow pass, and was forced to send to Archidamus and beg for assistance, which the latter tendered. When they had got as far as the bend on the road to Eutresia, there were the Arcadians and Argives advancing upon Laconia and apparently intending, like the Messenians, to shut the Spartan off from the homeward road.

Archidamus, debouching upon a flat space of ground where the roads to Eutresia and Melea converge, drew up his troops and offered battle. What happened then is thus told: He passed in front of the regiments and addressed them in terms of encouragement thus, "Fellow-citizens, the day has come which calls upon us to prove ourselves brave men and look the world in the face with level eyes. Now are we to deliver to those who come after us our fatherland intact as we received it from our fathers; now will we cease hanging our heads in shame before our children and wives, our old men and our foreign friends, in sight of whom in days of old we shone forth conspicuous beyond all other Hellenes."

The words were scarcely uttered (so runs the tale), when out of the clear sky came lightnings and thunderings, a good omen to him; and it so happened that on his right wing there stood a sacred enclosure and a statue of Heracles, [his great ancestor]. As the result of all these things, so deep a strength and courage came into the hearts of his soldiers, as they tell, that the generals had hard work to restrain their men as they pushed forward to the front. Presently, when Archidamus led the advance, a few only of the enemy cared to await them at the spear's point, and were slain; the mass of them fled, and fleeing fell. Many were cut down by the cavalry, many by the Celts. When the battle ceased and a trophy had been erected, the Spartan at once despatched home Demoteles, the herald, with the news. He had to announce not only the greatness of the victory, but the startling fact that, while the enemy's dead were numerous, not one single Lacedaemonian had been slain.[1] Those in Sparta to whom the news was brought, as says the story, when they heard it, one and all, beginning with Agesilaus, and, after him, the elders and the ephors, wept for joy—so close akin are tears to joy and pain alike. There were others hardly less pleased than the Lacedaemonians themselves at the misfortune which had overtaken the Arcadians: these were the Thebans and Eleians—so offensive to them had the boastful behaviour of these men become.

[1] According to Diodorus (xv. 72) 10,000 of the enemy fell.

The problem perpetually working in the minds of the Thebans was how they were to obtain the leadership of Hellas; and they persuaded themselves that, if they sent an embassy to the King of Persia, they could not but gain some advantage by his help. Accordingly they did not delay, but called together the allies, on the plea that Euthycles the Lacedaemonian was already at the Persian court. The commissioners sent up were, on the part of the Thebans, Pelopidas; on the part of the Arcadians, Antiochus, the pancratiast; and on that of the Eleians, Archidamus. There was also an Argive in attendance. The Athenians, learning of the matter, sent up two commissioners, Timagoras and Leon.

When they arrived at the Persian court the influence of Pelopidas was preponderant with the Persian. He could point out that, besides the fact that the Thebans alone among all the Hellenes had fought on the king's side at Plataea, they had never subsequently engaged in military service against the Persians; nay, the very ground of Lacedaemonian hostility to them was that they had refused to march against the Persian king with Agesilaus, and would not even suffer him to sacrifice to Artemis at Aulis (where Agamemnon sacrificed before he set sail for Asia and captured Troy). In addition, there were two things which contributed to raise the prestige of Thebes, and redounded to the honour of Pelopidas. These were the victory of the Thebans at Leuctra, and the indisputable fact that they had invaded and laid waste the territory of Laconia. Pelopidas went on to point out that the Argives and Arcadians had lately been defeated in battle by the Lacedaemonians, when his own countrymen were not there to assist. The Athenian Timagoras supported all these statements of the Theban by independent testimony, and stood second in honour after Pelopidas.

At this point of the proceedings Pelopidas was asked by the king what special clause he desired inserted in the royal rescript. He replied as follows, "Messene to be independent of Lacedaemon, and the Athenians to lay up their ships of war. Should either power refuse compliance in these respects, such refusal to be a *casus belli;* and any state refusing to take part in the military proceedings consequent, to be herself the first object of attack." These clauses were drawn up and read to the ambassadors, when Leon, in the hearing of the king, exclaimed, "By Zeus, Athenians, it strikes me it is time you looked for some other friend than the great king." The secretary reported the comment of the Athenian envoy, and produced presently an altered copy of the document, with a clause inserted, "If the Athenians have any better and juster views to propound, let them come to the Persian court and explain them."

Thus the ambassadors returned each to his own home and were variously received. Timagoras, on the indictment of Leon, who proved that his fellow-commissioner not only refused to lodge with him at the king's court, but in every way played into the hands of Pelopidas, was put to death. Of the other joint commissioners, the Eleian, Archidamus, was loud in his praises of the king and his policy, because he had shown a preference to Elis over the Arcadians; while for a converse reason, because the Arcadian league was slighted, Antiochus not only refused to accept any gift, but brought back as his report to the general assembly of the Ten Thousand,[2] that the king appeared to have a large army of confectioners and pastry-cooks, butlers and doorkeepers; but as for men capable of doing battle with Hellenes, he had looked carefully, and could not discover any. Besides all which, even the report of his wealth seemed to him, he said, bombastic nonsense. "Why, the golden plane-tree that is so belauded is not big enough to furnish shade to a single grasshopper."

At Thebes a conference of the states had been convened to listen to the great king's letter. The Persian who bore the missive merely pointed to the royal seal, and read the document; whereupon the Thebans invited all, who wished to be their friends, to take an oath to what they had just heard, as binding on the king and on themselves. To which the ambassadors from the states replied that they had been sent to listen to a report, not to take oaths; if oaths were wanted, they recommended the Thebans to send ambassadors to the several states. The Arcadian Lycomedes, moreover, added that the congress ought not to be held at Thebes at all, but at the seat of war, wherever that might be. This remark brought down the wrath of the Thebans on the speaker; they exclaimed that he was bent on breaking up the alliance. Whereupon the Arcadian refused to take a seat in the congress at all, and got up and betook himself off there and then, accompanied by all the Arcadian envoys. Since, therefore, the assembled representatives refused to take the oath at Thebes, the Thebans sent to the different states, one by one in turn, urging each to undertake solemnly to act in accordance with the great king's rescript. They were persuaded that no individual state would venture to quarrel with themselves and the Persian monarch at once. As a matter of fact, however, when they arrived at Corinth—which was the first state visited—the Corinthians stood out and gave as their answer, that they had no desire for any common oath or undertaking with the king. The rest of the states followed suit, giving answers of a similar tenor, so that this striving after empire on the part of Pelopidas and the Thebans melted into air.

But Epaminondas was bent on one more effort. With a view to forcing the Arcadians and the rest of the allies to pay better heed to Thebes,

[2] The Arcadian assembly at Megalopolis.

he desired first to secure the adhesion of the Achaeans, and decided to march an army into Achaea. Accordingly, he persuaded the Argive Peisias, who was at the head of military affairs in Argos, to seize and occupy Oneion in advance. Peisias, having ascertained that only a careless guard was maintained over Oneion by Naucles, the general commanding the Lacedaemonian foreign brigade, and by Timomachus the Athenian, under cover of night seized and occupied with 2,000 heavy infantry the rising ground above Cenchreae, taking with him provisions for seven days. Within the interval the Thebans arrived and surmounted the pass of Oneion; whereupon the allied troops, with Epaminondas at their head, advanced into Achaea. The result of the campaign was that the better classes of Achaea gave in their adhesion to him; and on his personal authority Epaminondas insisted that there should be no driving of the aristocrats into exile, nor any modification of the constitution. He was content to take a pledge from the Achaeans to this effect, "Verily we will be your allies, and follow wherever the Thebans lead."

So he departed home. The Arcadians, however, and the partisans of the opposite faction in Thebes were ready with an indictment against him: "Epaminondas," they said, "had merely organised Achaea for the Lacedaemonians, and then gone off." The Thebans accordingly resolved to send governors into the states of Achaea; and those officers on arrival joined with the commons and drove out the aristocrats, and set up democracies throughout Achaea. On their side, these exiles coalesced, and, marching upon each separate state in turn, for they were pretty numerous, speedily won their restoration and dominated the states. As the party thus reinstated no longer steered a middle course, but went heart and soul into an alliance with Lacedaemon, the Arcadians found themselves hard pressed between the Lacedaemonians and the Achaeans.

At Sicyon, hitherto, the constitution was based on the ancient laws; but at this date Euphron (who during the Lacedaemonian days had been the greatest man in Sicyon, and whose ambition it was to hold a like pre-eminence under their opponents) addressed himself to the Argives and Arcadians as follows, "If the wealthiest classes should ever come into power in Sicyon, without a doubt the city would take the first opportunity of readopting a Laconian policy; whereas, if a democracy be set up," he added, "you may rest assured Sicyon will hold fast by you. All I ask you is to stand by me; I will do the rest. It is I who will call a meeting of the people; and by that selfsame act I shall give you a pledge of my good faith and present you with a state firm in its alliance. All this, be assured," he added, "I do because, like yourselves, I have long detested the pride of Lacedaemon, and shall be glad to escape the yoke of bondage."

These proposals found favour with the Arcadians and the Argives, who gladly gave the assistance demanded. Euphron straightway, in the market-place, in the presence of the two powers concerned, proceeded to convene the Demos, as if there were to be a new constitution, based on the principle of equality. When the convention met, he bade them appoint generals: they might choose whom they liked. Whereupon they elected Euphron himself, Hippodamus, Cleander, Acrisius, and Lysander. When these matters were arranged he appointed Adeas, his own son, over the foreign brigade, in place of the former commander, Lysimenes, whom he removed. His next step was promptly to secure the fidelity of the foreign mercenaries by various acts of kindness, and to attach others; and he spared neither the public nor the sacred moneys for this object. He had, to aid him, further, the property of all the citizens whom he exiled as pro-Spartan, and of this he availed himself. As for his colleagues in office, some he treacherously put to death, others he exiled, by which means he got everything under his own power, and was now a tyrant without disguise. The method by which he got the allies to connive at his doings was twofold. Partly he worked on them by pecuniary aid, partly by the readiness with which he lent the support of his foreign troops on any campaign to which they might invite him.

2. Matters had so far progressed that the Argives had already fortified the Tricaranon above the Heraeum as an outpost to threaten Phlius, while the Sicyonians were engaged in fortifying Thyamia on their frontier; and between the two the Phliasians were severely pinched. They began to suffer from dearth of necessaries; but, in spite of all, remained unshaken in their alliance. It is the habit of historians, I know, to record with admiration each noble achievement of the larger powers, but to me it seems a still more worthy task to bring to light the great exploits of even a little state found faithful in the performance of noble deeds.

Now these Phliasians were friends of Lacedaemon while at the zenith of her power. After her disaster on the field of Leuctra, when many of the Perioeci, and the Helots to a man, revolted; when, more than that, the allies, save only a few, forsook her; and when united Hellas, so to speak, was marching on her; these Phliasians remained staunch in their allegiance; and, in spite of the hostility of the most powerful states of Peloponnese, the Arcadians and the Argives, they insisted on coming to her aid. It fell to their lot to cross into Prasiae as the rearguard of the reinforcements, which consisted of the men of Corinth, of Epidaurus and of Troezen, of Hermione, Halieis, and Sicyon and Pellene, in the days before any of these had revolted. Not even when the commander of the foreign brigade, picking up the divisions already across, left them behind and was gone—not even so did they flinch or turn back, but hired a guide from Prasiae, and though the enemy was massed round Amyclae, slipped through his ranks, as best they could, and so reached Sparta. It was then that the Lacedaemonians, besides other honours conferred upon them, sent them an ox as a gift of hospitality.

Later on, when the enemy had retired from Laconia, the Argives, angered at so much zeal for Lacedaemon on the part of Phlius, marched in full force against the little state, and fell to ravaging their territory. Even then they remained undaunted; and when the enemy turned to retire, destroying all that he could lay hands upon, out dashed the cavalry of the Phliasians and dogged his retreat. And notwithstanding that the Argive's rear consisted of the whole of his cavalry, with some companies of infantry to support them, they attacked him, sixty in number, and routed his whole rearguard. They slew, indeed, but a few of them; but, having so slain that handful, they paused and erected a trophy in full sight of the Argive army with as little concern as if they had cut down their enemies to a man.

Once again the Lacedaemonians and their allies were guarding Oneion, and the Thebans were threatening to scale the pass. The Arcadians and Eleians were moving forwards through Nemea to effect a junction with the Thebans, when a hint was conveyed to them by some Phliasian exiles, "Only show yourselves before Phlius and the town is yours." An agreement was made, and in the dead of night a party consisting of the exiles themselves and others with them, about 600 in number, planted themselves close under the walls with scaling-ladders. Presently the scouts from the Tricaranon signalled to the city that the enemy was advancing. The citizens were all attention; their eyes were fixed upon their scouts. Meanwhile the traitors within were likewise signalling to those in ambush to scale the walls; and these, scaling up, seized the arms of the guards, which they found abandoned, and fell to pursuing the day sentinels, ten in number (one out of each squad of five being always left on day duty). One of these was put to the sword as he lay asleep, and a second as he was escaping to the Heraeum; but the other eight day-pickets leaped down the wall on the side towards the city, one after another. The scaling party now found themselves in undisputed possession of the citadel. But the shouting had reached the city below: the citizens rallied to the rescue; and the enemy began by sallying forth from the citadel, and did battle in front of the gate leading down to the city. By and by, being strongly beleaguered by the ever-increasing reinforcements of the citizens, they retired, falling back upon the citadel; and the citizens along with the enemy forced their way in. The centre of the citadel was speedily deserted; for the enemy scaled the walls and towers, and showered blows and missiles upon the citizens below. These defended themselves from the ground, or pressed the encounter home by climbing the ladders which led to the walls. Once masters of certain towers on this side and the other of the invaders, the citizens came to close quarters with them with reckless desperation. The invaders, pushed by such audacity and hard hitting, were cooped up into narrower and narrower space. But at that critical moment the Arcadians and the Argives were circling round the city, and had begun to dig through the walls of the citadel from its upper side. Of the citizens inside some were beating down their assailants on the wall; others, those of them who were climbing up from outside and were still on the scaling-ladders; while a third set were delivering battle against those who had mounted the towers. These last had found fire in the men's quarters, and were engaged in setting the towers and all ablaze, bringing up sheaves of corn, as luck would have it, garnered off the citadel itself. Thereupon the occupants of the towers, in terror of the flames, leaped down one by one, while those on the walls, under the blows of the defenders, tumbled off with similar expedition; and as soon as they had once begun to yield, the whole citadel, in almost less time than it takes to tell, was cleared of the enemy. In an instant out dashed the cavalry, and the enemy, seeing them, beat a hasty retreat, leaving behind scaling-ladders and dead, besides some comrades hopelessly maimed. In fact, the enemy, what between those who were slain inside and those who leapt from the walls, lost not less than eighty men. And now it was a goodly sight to see the brave men grasp one another by the hand and pledge each other on their preservation, while the women brought them drink and cried for joy. Not one there present but indeed was overcome by laughter mixed with tears.[3]

Next year also Phlius was invaded by the Argives and all the Arcadians. The reason of this perpetually-renewed attack on Phlius is not far to seek: partly it was the result of anger, partly the little township stood midway between them, and they cherished the hope that through want of the necessaries of life they would bring it over. During this invasion the cavalry and the picked troop of the Phliasians, assisted by some Athenian knights, made another famous charge at the crossing of the river.[4] They made it so hot for the enemy that for the rest of that day he was forced to retire under the mountain ridges, and to hold aloof as if afraid to trample down the corn-crops of a friendly people on the plain below.

Again another time the Theban commander in Sicyon marched out against Phlius, taking with him the garrison under his personal com-

[3] In true Homeric fashion; see Homer, *Iliad,* vi. 484.
[4] The Asopus.

mand, with the Sicyonians and Pellenians (for at the date of the incident these states followed in the wake of Thebes). Euphron was there also with his mercenaries, about 2,000 in number, to share the fortunes of the field. The mass of the troops began their descent on the Heraeum by the Tricaranon, intending to ravage the flat bottom below. At the gate leading to Corinth the Theban general left his Sicyonians and Pellenians on the height, to prevent the Phliasians getting behind him at this point and so over the heads of his troops as they lay at the Heraeum beneath. As soon as the citizens of Phlius found that hostile troops were advancing on their corn-land, out dashed the cavalry with the chosen band of the Phliasians and gave battle, not allowing the enemy to penetrate into the plain. The best part of the day was spent in taking long shots at one another on that field, Euphron pushing his attack down to the point where cavalry could operate, the citizens retaliating as far as the Heraeum. Presently the time to withdraw had come, and the enemy began to retire, following the circle of the Tricaranon; the short cut to reach the Pellenians being barred by the ravine which runs in front of the walls. The Phliasians escorted their retreating foes a little way up the steep, and then turning off dashed along the road beside the walls, making for the Pellenians and those with them; whereupon the Theban, perceiving the haste of the Phliasians, began racing with his infantry to outspeed them and aid the Pellenians. The cavalry, however, arrived first and fell to attacking the Pellenians, who received and withstood the shock, and the cavalry drew back. A second time they charged, and were supported by some infantry detachments which had now come up. It ended in a hand-to-hand fight; and eventually the enemy gave way. On the field lay dead some Sicyonians, and of the Pellenians many a good man. In record of the feat the Phliasians began to raise a trophy, as well they might; and loud the paean rang. As to the Theban and Euphron, they and all their men stood by and stared at the proceedings, like men who had raced to see a sight. After all was over the one party retired to Sicyon and the other withdrew into their city.

That too was another noble exploit of the Phliasians, when they took the Pellenian Proxenus prisoner and, although suffering from scarcity at the time, sent him back without a ransom. "As generous as brave," such is their well-earned title who were capable of such performance.

The heroic resolution with which these men maintained their loyalty to their friends is manifest. When excluded from the fruits of their own soil, they contrived to live, partly by helping themselves from the enemy's territory, partly by purchasing from Corinth, though to reach that market they ran many risks; and having reached it their troubles began afresh. There were difficulties in providing payment, difficulties in arranging with the sellers, and it was barely possible to find sureties for the very beasts which should carry home their marketing. They had reached the depth of despair, and were absolutely at a loss what to do, when they arranged with Chares to escort their convoy. Once safe inside Phlius, they begged him to help them to convey their useless and sick folk to Pellene. These they left at that place; and after making purchases and packing as many beasts of burden as they could, they set off to return in the night, not in ignorance that they would be laid in wait for by the enemy, but persuaded that the want of provisions was a worse evil than fighting.

The men of Phlius pushed forward with Chares; presently they stumbled on the enemy and at once grappled to their work. Pressing hard on the foe, they cheered each other on and shouted at the same time to Chares to bring up his aid. In short, the victory was theirs; and the enemy was driven off the road; and so they got themselves and their supplies safely home. The long night-watching caused them to sleep well into the next day. But Chares was no sooner out of bed than he was accosted by the cavalry and the pick of the heavy infantry with the following appeal, "Chares, to-day you have it in your power to perform the noblest deed of arms. The Sicyonians are fortifying an outpost on our borders, they have plenty of stone-masons but a mere handful of hoplites. We the knights of Phlius and we the flower of our infantry force will lead the way; and you shall follow after with your mercenaries. Perhaps when you appear on the scene you will find the whole thing finished, or perhaps your coming will send the enemy flying, as happened at Pellene. If you do not like the sound of these proposals, sacrifice and take counsel of the gods. Our belief is that the gods will bid you yet more emphatically than we to take this step. Only this, Chares, you must well consider, that if you do take it you will have established an outpost on the enemy's frontier; you will have saved a friendly city; you will win great glory in your own fatherland; and among friends and foes alike no name will be heralded with louder praise than that of Chares."

Chares was persuaded, and proceeded to offer sacrifice. Meanwhile the Phliasian cavalry were donning their breastplates and bridling their horses, and the heavy infantry made every preparation for the march. Then they took their arms, fell into line, and tramped off to the place of sacrifice. Chares with the soothsayer stepped forward to meet them, announcing that the victims were favourable. "Only wait for us," they exclaimed; "we will sally forth with you at once." The heralds' cry "To arms!" was sounded, and with a zeal which was miraculous the mercenaries themselves rushed out. As soon as Chares began the march,

the Phliasian cavalry and infantry got in front of him. At first they led
off at a smart pace; presently they began to run along more quickly,
and finally the cavalry were tearing over the ground at top speed, while
the infantry, at the greatest pace compatible with keeping their ranks,
tore after them; and behind them, again, came Chares zealously following up in their rear. There only remained a brief interval of daylight
before the sun went down, and they came upon the enemy in the fortress,
some washing, some cooking, others kneading their bread, others making
their beds. These, when they saw the vehemence of the attack, at once,
in utter panic, took to flight, leaving behind all their provisions for the
brave fellows who took their place. They, as their reward, made a fine
supper off these stores and others which had come from home, pouring
out libations for their good fortune and chanting the battle-hymn; after
which they posted pickets for the night and slept well. The messenger
with the news of their success at Thyamia arrived at Corinth in the
night. The citizens of that state with hearty friendship at once ordered
out by herald all the oxen and beasts of burden which they loaded with
food and brought to Phlius; and all the while the fortress was building
day by day these convoys of food were duly despatched.

3. But on this topic enough, perhaps, has been said to demonstrate
the loyalty of the men of Phlius to their friends, their bravery in war,
and lastly, their steadfastness in maintaining their alliance in spite of
famine.

It seems to have been somewhere about this date that Aeneas the
Stymphalian, who had become general of the Arcadians, finding that the
state of affairs in Sicyon was intolerable, marched up with his army into
the Acropolis. Here he summoned a meeting of the Sicyonian aristocrats
already within the walls, and sent to fetch those others who had been
banished without a decree of the people. Euphron, taking fright at these
proceedings, fled for safety to the harbour-town of Sicyon. Hither he
summoned Pasimelus from Corinth, and through him handed over the
harbour to the Lacedaemonians. Once more reappearing in his old
character, he began to pose as an ally of Sparta. He asserted that his
fidelity to Lacedaemon had never been interrupted; for when the votes
were given in the city whether Sicyon should give up her allegiance to
Lacedaemon, "I, with one or two others," said he, "voted against the
measure; but afterwards these people betrayed me, and in my desire to
avenge myself on them I set up a democracy. At present all traitors to
yourselves are banished—I have seen to that. If only I could get the
power into my own hands, I would go over to you, city and all, at
once. All that I can do at present, I have done; I have surrendered to
you this harbour." That was what Euphron said to his audience there,

but of the many who heard his words, how many really believed him is by no means evident. However, since I have begun the story of Euphron, I desire to bring it to its close.

Faction and party strife ran high in Sicyon between the upper classes and the people, when Euphron, getting a body of foreign troops from Athens, once more obtained his restoration. The city, with the help of the commons, he was master of, but the Theban governor held the citadel. Euphron, perceiving that he would never be able to dominate the state while the Thebans held the Acropolis, collected money and set off to Thebes, intending to persuade the Thebans to expel the aristocrats and once again to hand over the city to himself. But the former exiles, having got wind of this journey of his, and of the whole intrigue, set off themselves to Thebes in front of him. When, however, they saw the terms of intimacy on which he associated with the Theban authorities, in terror of his succeeding in his mission some of them staked their lives on the attempt and stabbed Euphron in the Cadmeia, where the magistrates and senate were seated. The magistrates, indeed, could not but indict the perpetrators of the deed before the senate, and spoke as follows:

"Fellow-citizens, it is our duty to arraign these murderers of Euphron, the men before you, on the capital charge. Mankind may be said to fall into two classes: there are the wise and temperate, who are incapable of any wrong and unhallowed deed; and there are the base, the bad, who do indeed such things, but try to escape the notice of their fellows. The men before you are exceptional. They have so far exceeded all the rest of men in audacity and villainy that, in the very presence of the magistrates and of yourselves, who alone have power of life and death, they have taken the law into their own hands, and have slain this man. But they stand now before the bar of justice, and they must pay the extreme penalty; for, if you spare them, what visitor will have courage to approach the city? Nay, what will become of the city itself, if license is to be given to any one who chooses to murder those who come here, before they have even explained the object of their visit? It is our part, then, to prosecute these men as arch-villains and miscreants, whose contempt for law and justice is only matched by the supreme indifference with which they treat this city. It is your part, now that you have heard the charges, to impose upon them that penalty which seems to be the measure of their guilt."

Such were the words of the magistrates. Among the men thus accused, all save one denied immediate participation in the act. It was not their hands had dealt the blow. This one not only confessed the deed, but made a defence in words somewhat as follows:

"As to treating you with indifference, men of Thebes, that is not possible for a man who knows that with you lies the power to deal with him as you list. Ask rather on what I based my confidence when I slew the man; and be well assured that, in the first place, I based it on the conviction that I was doing right; next, that your verdict also will be right and just. I knew assuredly how you dealt with Archias and Hypates and that company whom you detected in conduct similar to that of Euphron: you did not stay for formal voting, but at the first opportunity within your reach you guided the sword of vengeance, believing that by the verdict of mankind a sentence of death has already been passed against the conspicuously profane person, the manifest traitor, and him who tries to become a tyrant. See, then, what follows. Euphron was liable on each of these several counts: he was a conspicuously profane person, who took into his keeping temples rich in votive offerings of gold and silver, and swept them bare of their sacred treasures; he was an arrant traitor—for what treason could be more manifest than Euphron's? First he was the bosom friend of Lacedaemon, but presently chose you in their stead; and, after exchange of solemn pledges between yourselves and him, once more turned round and played the traitor to you, and delivered up the harbour to your enemies. Lastly, he was most undisguisedly a tyrant, who made not free men only, but free fellow-citizens his slaves; who put to death, or drove into exile, or robbed of their wealth and property, not malefactors, not you, but the mere victims of his whim; and these were ever the better folk. Once again restored by the help of your sworn foes and antagonists, the Athenians, to his native town of Sicyon, the first thing he did was to take up arms against the governor from Thebes; but, finding himself powerless to drive him from the Acropolis, he collected money and came hither. Now, if it were proved that he had mustered armed bands to attack you, I venture to say, you would have thanked me that I slew him. What then, when he came furnished with money to corrupt you, to bribe you to make him once more lord and master of the state? How shall I, who dealt justice upon him, justly suffer death at your hands? For to be overcome in arms implies injury certainly, but of the body only: the defeated man is not proved to be dishonest by his loss of victory. But he who is corrupted by money, contrary to the standard of what is best, is at once injured and involved in shame.

"Now if he had been your friend, however much he was my foe, I confess it would have been scarcely honourable of me to have stabbed him to death in your presence: but why, I should like to ask, should the man who betrayed you be less your enemy than mine? 'Ah, but,' I hear some one retort, 'he came of his own accord.' I presume then you mean that had he chanced to be slain by somebody at a distance from your state, that somebody would have won your praise; but now, on the ground that he came back here to work mischief on the top of mischief, he was wrongfully slain. In what part of Hellas, tell me, do Hellenes keep a truce with traitors, double-dyed deserters, and tyrants? Moreover, I must remind you that you passed a resolution—if I mistake not, it stands recorded in your parliamentary minutes—that renegades are liable to be apprehended in any of the allied cities. Now, here is a renegade restoring himself without any common decree of the allied states: will any one tell me on what ground this person did not deserve to die? What I maintain is that if you put me to death, by so doing you will be aiding and abetting your bitterest foe; while, by a verdict sanctioning the justice of my conduct, you will prove your willingness to protect the interests not of yourselves only, but of the whole body of your allies."

The Thebans on hearing this decided that Euphron had only suffered the fate which he deserved. His own countrymen, however, conveyed away the body with the honours due to a brave and good man, and buried him in the market-place, where they still pay pious reverence to his memory as a founder of the state. So strictly, it would seem, do the mass of mankind confine the term brave and good to those who are the benefactors of themselves.

4. And so ends the history of Euphron. I return to the point reached at the commencement of this digression.[5] The Phliasians were still fortifying Thyamia, and Chares was still with them, when Oropus was seized by the banished citizens of that place. The Athenians in consequence despatched an expedition in full force to the point of danger, and recalled Chares from Thyamia; whereupon the Sicyonians and the Arcadians seized the opportunity to recapture the harbour of Sicyon. Meanwhile the Athenians, forced to act single-handed, with none of their allies to assist them, retired from Oropus, leaving that town in the hands of the Thebans as a deposit till the case at issue could be formally adjudicated.

Now Lycomedes had discovered that the Athenians were harbouring a grievance against their allies, as follows: They felt it hard that, while Athens was put to vast trouble on their account, yet in her need not a man among them stepped forward to render help. Accordingly he persuaded the assembly of Ten Thousand to open negotiations with Athens for the purpose of forming an alliance. At first some of the Athenians were vexed that they, being friends of Lacedaemon, should become allied to her opponents; but on further reflection they discovered it was no less

[5] See above, VII. ii. 23.

desirable for the Lacedaemonians than for themselves that the Arcadians should become independent of Thebes. That being so, they were quite ready to accept an Arcadian alliance. Lycomedes himself was still engaged on this transaction when, taking his departure from Athens, he died, in a manner which looked like a divine intervention.

Out of the many vessels at his service he had chosen the one he liked best, and by the terms of contract was entitled to land at any point he might desire; but, for some reason, selected the exact spot where a body of Mantinean exiles lay. Thus he died; but the alliance on which he had set his heart was already consummated.

Now an argument was advanced by Demotion in the Assembly of Athens, approving highly of the friendship with the Arcadians, which to his mind was an excellent thing, but arguing that the generals should be instructed to see that Corinth was kept safe for the Athenian people. The Corinthians, hearing this, lost no time in despatching garrisons of their own large enough to take the place of the Athenian garrisons at any point where they might have them, with orders to these latter to retire. "We have no further need of foreign garrisons," they said. The garrisons did as they were bid.

As soon as the Athenian garrison troops were met together in the city of Corinth, the Corinthian authorities caused proclamation to be made inviting all Athenians who felt themselves wronged to enter their names and cases upon a list, and they would recover their dues. While things were in this state, Chares arrived at Cenchreae with a fleet. Learning what had been done, he told them that he had heard there were designs against the state of Corinth, and had come to render assistance. The authorities, while thanking him politely for his zeal, were not any the more ready to admit the vessels into the harbour, but bade him sail away; and after rendering justice to the infantry troops, they sent them away likewise. Thus the Athenians were quit of Corinth. To the Arcadians, to be sure, they were forced by the terms of their alliance to send an auxiliary force of cavalry, in case of any foreign attack upon Arcadia. At the same time they were careful not to set foot on Laconian soil for the purposes of war.

The Corinthians had begun to realise on how slender a thread their political existence hung. They were overmastered by land still as ever, with the further difficulty of Athenian hostility now added. They resolved to collect bodies of mercenary troops, both infantry and horse. At the head of these they were able at once to guard their state and to inflict much injury on their neighbouring foes. To Thebes, indeed, they sent ambassadors to ascertain whether they would have any prospect of peace if they came to seek it. The Thebans bade them come, "Peace they should have." Whereupon the Corinthians asked that they might be allowed to visit their allies; in making peace they would like to share it with those who cared for it, and would leave those who preferred war to war. This course also the Thebans sanctioned; and so the Corinthians came to Lacedaemon and said:

"Men of Lacedaemon, we, your friends, are here to present a petition, and on this wise. If you can discover any safety for us while we persist in warlike courses, we beg that you will show it us; but if you recognise the hopelessness of our affairs, we would, in that case, proffer this alternative: if peace is alike conducive to your interests, we beg that you would join us in making peace, since there is no one with whom we would more gladly share our safety than with you; if, on the other hand, you are persuaded that war is more to your interest, permit us at any rate to make peace for ourselves. So saved to-day, perhaps we may live to help you in days to come; whereas, if to-day we be destroyed, plainly we shall never at any time be serviceable again."

The Lacedaemonians, on hearing these proposals, counselled the Corinthians to arrange a peace on their own account; and as for the rest of their allies, they permitted any who did not care to continue the war along with them to take a respite and recruit themselves. "As for ourselves," they said, "we will go on fighting and accept whatever god has in store for us," adding, "never will we submit to be deprived of the territory of Messene, which we received as an heirloom from our fathers."

Satisfied with this answer, the Corinthians set off to Thebes to make peace. The Thebans, indeed, asked them to agree on oath, not to peace only but an alliance; to which they answered, "An alliance meant, not peace, but merely an exchange of war. If they liked, they were ready there and then," they repeated, "to establish a just and equitable peace." And the Thebans, admiring the manner in which, in spite of danger, they refused to undertake war against their benefactors, conceded to them and the Phliasians and the rest who came with them to Thebes, peace on the principle that each should hold their own territory. On these terms the oaths were taken.

Thereupon the Phliasians, in obedience to the compact, at once retired from Thyamia; but the Argives, who had taken the oath of peace on precisely the same terms, finding that they were unable to procure the continuance of the Phliasian exiles in the Tricaranon as a point held within the limits of Argos, took over and garrisoned the place, asserting now that this land was theirs—land which only a little while before they were ravaging as hostile territory. Further, they refused to submit the case to arbitration in answer to the challenge of the Phliasians.

It was nearly at the same date that the son of Dionysius (his father,

Dionysius the first, being already dead) sent a reinforcement to Lacedaemon of twelve triremes under Timocrates, who on his arrival helped
the Lacedaemonians to recover Sellasia, and after that exploit sailed
away home.

Not long after this the Eleians seized Lasion, a place which in old
days was theirs, but at present was attached to the Arcadian league.
The Arcadians did not make light of the matter, but immediately summoned their troops and rallied to the rescue. Counter-reliefs came also
on the side of Elis—their Three Hundred, and again their Four Hundred.[6] The Eleians lay encamped during the day face to face with the
invader, but on a somewhat more level position. The Arcadians were
thereby induced under cover of night to mount on to the summit of the
hill overhanging the Eleians, and at day-dawn they began their descent
upon the enemy. The Eleians soon caught sight of the enemy advancing
from the vantage-ground above them, many times their number; but
a sense of shame forbade retreat at such a distance. Presently they came
to close quarters; there was a hand-to-hand encounter; the Eleians
turned and fled, and in retiring down the difficult ground lost many
men and many arms.

Flushed with this achievement the Arcadians began marching on the
cities of the Acroreia, which, with the exception of Thraustus, they
captured, and so reached Olympia. There they made an entrenched
camp on the hill of Cronus, established a garrison, and held control
over the Olympian hill-country. Margana also, by help of a party inside
who gave it up, next fell into their hands.

These successive advantages gained by their opponents reacted on
the Eleians, and threw them altogether into despair. Meanwhile the
Arcadians were steadily advancing upon their capital. At length they
arrived, and penetrated into the market-place. Here, however, the
cavalry and the rest of the Eleians made a stand, drove the enemy out
with some loss, and set up a trophy.

It should be mentioned that the city of Elis had previously been in a
state of disruption. The party of Charopus, Thrasonidas, and Argeius
were for converting the state into a democracy; the party of Eualcas,
Hippias, and Stratolas were for oligarchy. When the Arcadians, backed
by a large force, appeared as allies of those who favoured a democratic
constitution, the party of Charopus were at once emboldened; and,
having obtained the promise of assistance from the Arcadians, they
seized the Acropolis. The Knights and the Three Hundred did not hesitate, but at once marched up and dislodged them; with the result that

---

[6] From the sequel it would appear that the former were a picked corps of infantry and the latter of cavalry.

about 400 citizens, with Argeius and Charopus, were banished. Not long afterwards these exiles, with the help of some Arcadians, seized and occupied Pylus; where many of the commons withdrew from the capital to join them, attracted not only by the beauty of the position, but by the great power of the Arcadians, in alliance with them.

There was subsequently another invasion of the territory of the Eleians on the part of the Arcadians, who were influenced by the representations of the exiles that the city would come over to them. But the attempt proved abortive. The Achaeans, who had now become friends with the Eleians, kept firm guard on the capital, so that the Arcadians had to retire without further exploit than that of ravaging the country. Immediately, however, on marching out of Eleian territory they were informed that the men of Pellene were in Elis; whereupon they executed a marvellously long night march and seized the Pellenian township of Olurus (the Pellenians at the date in question having already reverted to their old alliance with Lacedaemon). And now the men of Pellene, in their turn getting wind of what had happened at Olurus, made their way round as best they could, and got into their own city of Pellene; after which there was nothing for it but to carry on war with the Arcadians in Olurus and the whole body of their own commons; and in spite of their small numbers they did not cease till they had reduced Olurus by siege.

The Arcadians were presently engaged on another campaign against Elis. While they were encamped between Cyllene and the capital the Eleians attacked them, but the Arcadians made a stand and won the battle. Andromachus, the Eleian cavalry general, who was regarded as responsible for the engagement, committed suicide; and the rest withdrew into the city. This battle cost the life also of another there present —the Spartan Socleides; since, it will be understood, the Lacedaemonians had by this time become allies of the Eleians. Consequently the Eleians, being hard pressed on their own territory, sent an embassy and begged the Lacedaemonians to organise an expedition against the Arcadians. They were persuaded that in this way they would best arrest the progress of the Arcadians, who would thus be placed between two foes. In accordance with the suggestion Archidamus marched out with a body of the city troops and seized Cromnus. Here he left a garrison— three out of the twelve regiments—and so withdrew homewards. The Arcadians had just ended their Eleian campaign, and, without disbanding their levies, hastened to the rescue, surrounded Cromnus with a double line of trenches, and having so secured their position, proceeded to lay siege to those inside the place. The city of Lacedaemon, annoyed at the siege of their citizens, sent out an army, again under the command of Archidamus, who, when he had come, set about ravaging Arcadia to the best of his power, as also Sciritis, and did all he could to draw off, if possible, the besieging army. The Arcadians, for all that, were not to be stirred; they disregarded his proceedings.

Presently espying a certain rising ground, across which the Arcadians had drawn their outer line of circumvallation, Archidamus proposed to take it. If he were once in command of that knoll, the besiegers at its foot would be forced to retire. Accordingly he set about leading a body of troops round to the point in question, and during this movement the light infantry in advance of Archidamus, advancing at the double, caught sight of the Arcadian Eparitoi[7] outside the stockade and attacked them, while the cavalry made an attempt to enforce their attack simultaneously. The Arcadians did not swerve: in compact order they waited impassively. The Lacedaemonians charged a second time: a second time they swerved not, but on the contrary began advancing. Then, as the hoarse roar and shouting deepened, Archidamus himself advanced in support of his troops. To do so he turned aside along the carriage-road leading to Cromnus, and moved onward in column two abreast, which was his natural order. When they came into close proximity to one another—Archidamus's troops in column, seeing they were marching along a road; the Arcadians in compact order with shields interlinked—at this conjuncture the Lacedaemonians were not able to hold out for any length of time against the numbers of the Arcadians. Before long Archidamus had received a wound which pierced through his thigh, while death was busy with those who fought in front of him, Polyaenidas and Chilon, who was wedded to the sister of Archidamus, included. The whole of these, numbering no less than thirty, perished in this action. Presently, falling back along the road, they emerged into the open ground, and now with a sense of relief the Lacedaemonians got themselves into battle order, facing the foe. The Arcadians, without altering their position, stood in compact line, and though falling short in actual numbers, were in better spirits—the result of an attack on a retreating enemy and the severe loss inflicted on him. The Lacedaemonians, on the other hand, were sorely down-hearted; Archidamus lay wounded before their eyes; in their ears rang the names of those who had died, the fallen being not only brave men, but, practically the most distinguished. The two armies were now close together, when one of the elder men lifted up his voice and cried, "Why need we fight, sirs? Why not rather make truce and part friends?" Joyously the words fell on the ears of either host, and they made a truce. The Lacedaemonians picked up their dead and retired; the Arcadians withdrew to the point

[7] So the troops of the Arcadian Federation were named.

where their advance originally began, and set up a trophy of victory.

Now, as the Arcadians lay at Cromnus, the Eleians from the capital, advancing in the first instance upon Pylus, fell in with the men of that place, who had been beaten back from Thalamae. Galloping along the road, the cavalry of the Eleians, when they caught sight of them, did not hesitate, but dashed at them at once, and put some to the sword, while others of them fled for safety to a rising knoll. Soon the Eleian infantry arrived, and succeeded in dislodging this remnant on the hillock also; some they slew, and others, nearly 200 in number, they took alive, all of whom were either sold, if foreigners, or, if Eleian exiles, put to death. After this the Eleians captured the men of Pylus and the place itself, as no one came to their rescue, and recovered the Marganians.

The Lacedaemonians presently made a second attempt upon Cromnus by a night attack, got possession of the part of the palisading facing the Argives, and at once began summoning their besieged fellow-citizens to come out. Out accordingly came all who happened to be within easy distance, and who hurried. The rest were not quick enough; a strong Arcadian reinforcement cut them off, and they remained shut up inside, and were eventually taken prisoners and distributed. One portion of them fell to the lot of the Argives, one to the Thebans, one to the Arcadians, and one to the Messenians. The whole number taken, whether true-born Spartans or Perioeci, amounted to more than 100.

And now that the Arcadians had leisure on the side of Cromnus, they were again able to occupy themselves with the Eleians, and to keep Olympia still more strongly garrisoned. In anticipation of the approaching Olympic year, they began preparations to celebrate the Olympian games in conjunction with the men of Pisa, who claim to be the original presidents of the Temple. Now, when the month of the Olympic Festival —and not the month only, but the very days, during which the solemn assembly meets, were come, the Eleians, in pursuance of preparations and invitations to the Achaeans, of which they made no secret, at length proceeded to march along the road to Olympia. The Arcadians had never imagined that they would really attack them; and they were themselves just now engaged with the men of Pisa in carrying out the details of the solemn assembly. They had already completed the chariot-race, and the foot-race of the pentathlon. The competitors entitled to enter for the wrestling match had left the racecourse, and were getting through their bouts in the space between the racecourse and the great altar.

It must be understood that the Eleians under arms were already close at hand within the sacred enclosure. The Arcadians, without advancing farther to meet them, drew up their troops on the river Cladaus, which flows past the Altis and discharges itself into the Alpheus. Their allies, consisting of 200 Argive hoplites and about 400 Athenian cavalry, were there to support them. Presently the Eleians formed into line on the opposite side of the stream, and, having sacrificed, at once began advancing. Though heretofore in matters of war despised by Arcadians and Argives, by Achaeans and Athenians like, still on this day they led the van of the allied force like the bravest of the brave. Coming into collision with the Arcadians first, they at once put them to flight, and next receiving the attack of the Argive supports, mastered these also. Then having pursued them into the space between the senate-house, the temple of Hestia, and the theatre adjoining, they still kept up the fighting as fiercely as ever, pushing the retreating foe towards the great altar. But now being exposed to missiles from the porticoes and the senate-house and the great temple, while battling with their opponents on the level, some of the Eleians were slain, and amongst others the commander of the Three Hundred himself, Stratolas. At this stage of the proceedings they retired to their camp.

The Arcadians and those with them were so terrified at the thought of the coming day that they gave themselves neither respite nor repose that night, but fell to chopping up the carefully-compacted booths and constructing them into palisades; so that when the Eleians did again advance the next day and saw the strength of the barriers and the number mounted on the temples, they withdrew to their city. They had proved themselves to be warriors of such mettle as a god indeed by the breath of his spirit may raise up and bring to perfection in a single day, but into which it were impossible for mortal men to convert a coward even in a lifetime.

The employment of the sacred treasures of the temple by the Arcadian magistrates as a means of maintaining the Eparitoi aroused protest. The Mantineans were the first to pass a resolution forbidding such use of the sacred property. They set the example themselves of providing the necessary quota for the troop in question from their state exchequer, and this sum they sent to the federal government. The latter, affirming that the Mantineans were undermining the Arcadian league, retaliated by citing their leading statesmen to appear before the assembly of Ten Thousand; and on their refusal to obey the summons, passed sentence upon them, and sent the Eparitoi to apprehend them as convicted persons. The Mantineans, however, closed their gates, and would not admit the Troop within their walls. Their example was speedily followed: others among the Ten Thousand began to protest against the enormity of so applying the sacred treasures; it was doubly wrong to leave as a perpetual heirloom to their children the imputation of a crime so heinous against the gods. But no sooner was a resolution passed in the general assembly forbidding the use of the sacred moneys for profane purposes than those (members of the league) who could not have afforded to serve as Eparitoi without pay began speedily to melt away; while those of more independent means, with mutual encouragement, began to enrol themselves in the ranks of the Eparitoi—the feeling being that they ought not to be a mere tool in the hands of the corps, but rather that the corps itself should be their instrument. Those members of the government who had manipulated the sacred money soon saw that when they came to render an account of their stewardship, in all likelihood they would lose their heads. They therefore sent an embassy to Thebes, with instructions to the Theban authorities warning them that, if they did not open a campaign, the Arcadians would in all probability again veer round to Lacedaemon.

The Thebans, therefore, began making preparations for opening a campaign, but the party who consulted the best interests of Peloponnese persuaded the general assembly of the Arcadians to send an embassy and tell the Thebans not to advance with an army into Arcadia, unless they sent for them; and while this was the language they addressed to Thebes, they reasoned among themselves that they could dispense with war altogether. The presidency over the temple of Zeus, they were persuaded, they might easily dispense with; indeed, it would at once be a more upright and a holier proceeding on their parts to give it back, and with such conduct the god, they thought, would be better pleased. As these were also the views and wishes of the Eleians, both parties agreed to make peace, and a truce was established.

The oaths were ratified; and among those who swore to them were included not only the parties immediately concerned, but the men of Tegea, and the Theban general himself, who was inside Tegea with 300 heavy infantry of the Boeotians. Under these circumstances the Arcadians in Tegea remained behind feasting and keeping holy day, with outpouring of libations and songs of victory, to celebrate the establishment of peace. Here was an opportunity for the Theban and those of the government who regarded the forthcoming inquiry with apprehension. Aided by the Boeotians and those of the Eparitoi who shared their sentiments, they first closed the gates of the fortress of Tegea, and then set about sending to the various quarters to apprehend those of the better class. But, inasmuch as there were Arcadians present from all the cities, and there was a general desire for peace, those apprehended must needs be many. So much so, that the prison-house was presently full to overflowing, and the town-hall was full also. Besides the number lodged in prison, a number had escaped by leaping down the walls, and there were others who were suffered to pass through the gates (a laxity easily explained, since no one, excepting those who were anticipating their own downfall, cherished any wrathful feeling against anybody). But what was a source of still graver perplexity to the Theban commander and those acting with him,—of the Mantineans, the very people whom they had set their hearts on catching, they had got but very few. Nearly all of them, owing to the proximity of their city, had, in fact betaken themselves home. Now, when day came and the Mantineans learned what had happened, they immediately sent and forewarned the other Arcadian states to be ready in arms, and to guard the passes; and they set the example themselves by so doing. They sent at the same time to Tegea and demanded the release of all Mantineans there detained. With regard to the rest of the Arcadians they further claimed that no one should be imprisoned or put to death without trial. If any one had any accusation to bring against any, then by the mouth of their messengers there present they gave notice that the state of Mantinea was ready to offer bail, "Verily and indeed to produce before the general assembly of the Arcadians all who might be summoned into court." The Theban accordingly, on hearing this, was at a loss what to make of the affair, and released his prisoners. Next day, summoning a congress of all the Arcadians who chose to come, he explained, with some show of apology, that he had been altogether deceived; he had heard, he said, that the Lacedaemonians were under arms on the frontier, and that some of the Arcadians were about to betray Tegea into their hands. His auditors acquitted him for the moment, although they knew that he was lying about them. They sent, however, an embassy to Thebes and there accused him as deserving of death. Epaminondas (who was at that time the general at the head of the war department) is reported to have maintained that the Theban commander had acted far more rightly when he seized than when he let go the prisoners. "Thanks to you," he argued, "we have been brought into a state of war, and then you, without our advice or opinion asked, make peace on your own account; would it not be reasonable to retort upon you the charge of treason in such conduct? Anyhow, be assured," he added, "we shall bring an army into Arcadia, and along with those who share our views carry on the war which we have undertaken."

5. This answer was duly reported to the general assembly of the Arcadians, and throughout the several states of the league. Consequently the Mantineans, along with those of the Arcadians who had the interests of Peloponnesus at heart, as also the Eleians and the Achaeans, came to the conclusion that the policy of the Thebans was plain. They wished Peloponnesus to be reduced to such an extremity of weakness that it might fall an easy prey into their hands who were minded to

enslave it. "Why else," they asked, "should they wish us to fight, except that we may tear each other to pieces, and both sides be driven to look to them for support? or why, when we tell them that we have no need of them at present, do they insist on preparing for a foreign campaign? Is it not plain that these preparations are for an expedition which will do us some mischief?"

In this mood they sent to Athens, calling on the Athenians for military aid. Ambassadors went also to Lacedaemon on behalf of the Eparitoi, summoning the Lacedaemonians, if they wished to give a helping hand, to put a stop to the proceedings of any power approaching to enslave Peloponnesus. As regards the headship, they came to an arrangement at once, on the principle that each of the allied states should exercise the generalship within its own territory.

While these matters were in progress, Epaminondas was prosecuting his march at the head of all the Boeotians, with the Euboeans, and a large body of Thessalians, furnished both by Alexander[8] and by his opponents. The Phocians were not represented. Their special agreement only required them to render assistance in case of an attack on Thebes; to assist in a hostile expedition against others was not in the bond. Epaminondas, however, reflected that inside Peloponnesus itself they might count upon the Argives and the Messenians, with that section of the Arcadians which shared their views. These latter were the men of Tegea and Megalopolis, of Asea and Pallantium, with any townships which owing to their small size or their position in the midst of these larger cities were forced to follow their lead.

Epaminondas advanced with rapid strides; but on reaching Nemea he slackened speed, hoping to catch the Athenians as they passed, and reflecting on the magnitude of such an achievement, whether in stimulating the courage of his own allies, or in plunging his foes into despondency; since, to state the matter concisely, any blow to Athens would be a gain to Thebes. But during his pause at Nemea those who shared the opposite policy had time to converge on Mantinea. Presently the news reached Epaminondas that the Athenians had abandoned the idea of marching by land, and were preparing to bring their supports to Arcadia by sea through Lacedaemon. This being so, he abandoned his base of Nemea and pushed on to Tegea.

That the strategy of the Theban general was fortunate I will not pretend to assert, but in the particular combination of prudence and daring which stamps these exploits, I look upon him as consummate. In the first place, I cannot but admire the sagacity which led him to form his camp within the walls of Tegea, where he was in greater security

[8] Alexander of Pherae.

than he would have been if entrenched outside, and where his future movements were more completely concealed from the enemy. Again, the means to collect material and furnish himself with other necessaries were readier to his hand inside the city; while, thirdly, he was able to keep an eye on the movements of his opponents marching outside, and to watch their successful dispositions as well as their mistakes. More than this: in spite of his sense of superiority to his antagonists, over and over again, when he saw them gaining some advantage in position, he refused to be drawn out to attack them. It was only when he saw plainly that no city was going to give him its adhesion, and that time was slipping by, that he made up his mind that a blow must be struck, failing which, he had nothing to expect save a vast ingloriousness, in place of his former fame. He had ascertained that his antagonists held a strong position round Mantinea, and that they had sent to fetch Agesilaus and the whole Lacedaemonian army. He was further aware that Agesilaus had commenced his advance and was already at Pellene. Accordingly he passed the word of command to his troops to take their evening meal, put himself at their head and advanced straight upon Sparta. Had it not been for the arrival (by some providential chance) of a Cretan, who brought the news to Agesilaus of the enemy's advance, he would have captured the city of Sparta like a nest absolutely empty of defenders. As it was, Agesilaus, being forewarned, had time to return to the city before the Thebans came, and here the Spartans made distribution of their scanty force and maintained watch, although few enough in numbers, since the whole of their cavalry were away in Arcadia, and so was their foreign brigade, and so were three out of their twelve regiments.

Arrived within the city of Sparta, Epaminondas abstained from gaining an entry at a point where his troops would have to fight on level ground and under attack from the houses above; where also their large numbers would give them no superiority over the small numbers of the foemen. But, singling out a position which he conceived would give him the advantage, he occupied it and began his advance against the city upon a downward instead of an upward incline.

With regard to what subsequently took place, two possible explanations suggest themselves: either it was miraculous, or it may be maintained that there is no resisting the fury of desperation. Archidamus, advancing at the head of but 100 men, and crossing the one thing which might have been expected to form an obstacle to the enemy, began marching uphill against his antagonists. At this crisis these fire-breathing warriors, these victorious heroes of Leuctra, with their superiority at every point, aided, moreover, by the advantage of their position, did not withstand the attack of Archidamus and those with him, but swerved in flight.

The vanguard of Epaminondas's troops was cut down; when, however, flushed with the glory of their victory, the citizens followed up their pursuit beyond the right point, they in turn were cut down,—so plainly was the demarking line of victory drawn by the finger of god. So then Archidamus set up a trophy to note the limit of his success, and gave back those who had there fallen of the enemy under a truce. Epaminondas, on his side, reflecting that the Arcadians must already be hastening to the relief of Lacedaemon, and being unwilling to engage them in conjunction with the whole of the Lacedaemonian force, especially now that the star of Sparta's fortune shone, while theirs had suffered some eclipse, turned and marched back the way he came with all speed possible into Tegea. There he gave his heavy infantry pause and refreshment, but his cavalry he sent on to Mantinea; he begged them to have courage and hold on, instructing them that in all likelihood they would find the flocks and herds of the Mantineans and the entire population itself outside their walls, especially as it was the moment for carrying the corn. So they set off.

The Athenian cavalry, starting from Eleusis, had made their evening meal at the Isthmus, and passing through Cleonae, as chance befell, had arrived at Mantinea and had encamped within the walls in the houses. As soon as the enemy were seen galloping on with evidently hostile intent, the Mantineans fell to praying the Athenian knights to lend them all the aid they could, and they showed them all their cattle outside, and all their labourers, and among them were many children and graybeards who were free-born citizens. The Athenians were touched by this appeal, and, though they had not yet eaten, neither the men themselves nor their horses, went out eagerly to the rescue. And here we must pause to admire the valour of these men also. The enemy whom they had to cope with far outnumbered them, as was plain to see, and the former misadventure of the cavalry in Corinth was not forgotten. But none of these things entered into their calculations now— nor yet the fact that they were on the point of engaging Thebans and Thessalians, the finest cavalry in the world by all repute. The only thing they thought of was the shame and the dishonour, if, being there, they did not lend a helping hand to their allies. In this mood, so soon as they caught sight of the enemy, they fell with a crash upon him in passionate longing to recover the old ancestral glory. Nor did they fight in vain— the blows they struck enabled the Mantineans to recover all their property outside, but among those who dealt them died some brave heroes; brave heroes also, it is evident, were those whom they slew, since on either side the weapons wielded were not so short but that they could lunge at one another with effect. The dead bodies of their own men they refused to abandon; and there were some of the enemy's slain whom they restored to him under a truce.

The thoughts now working in the mind of Epaminondas were such as these: that within a few days he would be forced to retire, as the period of the campaign was drawing to a close; if it ended in his leaving in the lurch those allies whom he came out to assist, they would be besieged by their antagonists. What a blow would that be to his own fair fame, already somewhat tarnished! Had he not been defeated in Lacedaemon, with a large body of heavy infantry, by a handful of men? defeated again at Mantinea, in the cavalry engagement, and himself the main cause finally of a coalition between five great powers—that is to say, the Lacedaemonians, the Arcadians, the Achaeans, the Eleians, and the Athenians? On all grounds it seemed to him impossible to steal past without a battle. And the more so as he computed the alternatives of victory or death. If the former were his fortune, it would resolve all his perplexities; if death, his end would be noble. How glorious a thing to die in the endeavour to leave behind him, as his last legacy to his fatherland, the empire of Peloponnesus! That such thoughts should pass through his brain strikes me as by no means wonderful, since these are thoughts distinctive of all men of high ambition. Far more wonderful to my mind was the pitch of perfection to which he had brought his army. There was no labour which his troops would shrink from, either by night or by day; there was no danger they would flinch from; and, with the scantiest provisions, their discipline never failed them.

And so, when he gave his last orders to them to prepare for impending battle, they obeyed with alacrity. He gave the word; the cavalry fell to whitening their helmets, the heavy infantry of the Arcadians began inscribing clubs as the crest on their shields, as though they were Thebans, and all were engaged in sharpening their lances and swords and polishing their heavy shields. When the preparations were complete and he had led them out, his next movement is worthy of attention. First, as was natural, he paid heed to their formation, and in so doing seemed to give clear evidence that he intended battle; but no sooner was the army drawn up in the formation which he preferred, than he advanced, not by the shortest route to meet the enemy, but towards the westward-lying mountains which face Tegea, and by this movement created in the enemy an expectation that he would not do battle on that day. In keeping with this expectation, as soon as he arrived at the mountain-region, he extended his phalanx in long line and piled arms under the high cliffs; and to all appearance he was there encamping.

The effect of this manoeuvre on the enemy in general was to relax the prepared bent of their souls for battle, and to weaken their tactical arrangements. Presently, however, wheeling his regiments (which were marching in column) to the front, with the effect of strengthening the beak-like attack which he proposed to lead himself, at the same instant he gave the order, "Shoulder arms, forward," and led the way, the troops following.

When the enemy saw them so unexpectedly approaching, not one of them was able to maintain tranquillity: some began running to their divisions, some fell into line, some might be seen bitting and bridling their horses, some donning their cuirasses, and one and all were like men about to receive rather than to inflict a blow. He, the while, with steady impetus pushed forward his armament, like a ship-of-war prow forward. Wherever he brought his solid wedge to bear, he meant to cleave through the opposing mass, and crumble his adversary's host to pieces. With this design he prepared to throw the brunt of the fighting on the strongest half of his army, while he kept the weaker portion of it in the background, knowing certainly that if worsted it would only cause discouragement to his own division and add force to the foe. The cavalry on the side of his opponents were disposed like an ordinary phalanx of heavy infantry, regular in depth and unsupported by foot-soldiers interspersed among the horses. Epaminondas again differed in strengthening the attacking point of his cavalry, besides which he interspersed footmen between their lines in the belief that, when he had once cut through the cavalry, he would have wrested victory from the antagonist along his whole line; so hard is it to find troops who will care to keep their ground when once they see any of their own side flying. Lastly, to prevent any attempt on the part of the Athenians, who were on the enemy's left wing, to bring up their reliefs in support of the portion next them, he posted bodies of cavalry and heavy infantry on certain hillocks in front of them, intending to create in their minds an apprehension that, in case they offered such assistance, they would be attacked on their own rear by these detachments. Such was the plan of encounter which he formed and executed; nor was he cheated in his hopes. He had so much the mastery at his point of attack that he caused the whole of the enemy's troops to take to flight.

But after he himself had fallen, the rest of the Thebans were not able any longer to turn their victory rightly to account. Though the main battle line of their opponents had given way, not a single man afterwards did the victorious hoplites slay, not an inch forward did they advance from the ground on which the collision took place. Though the cavalry had fled before them, there was no pursuit; not a man, horseman or hoplite did the conquering cavalry cut down; but, like men who have suffered a defeat, as if panic-stricken they slipped back through the ranks of the fleeing foemen. Only the footmen fighting amongst the cavalry and the light infantry, who had together shared in the victory of the cavalry, found their way round to the left wing as masters of the field, but it cost them dear; here they encountered the Athenians, and most of them were cut down.

The effective result of these achievements was the very opposite of that which the world at large anticipated. Here, where well-nigh the whole of Hellas was met together in one field, and the combatants stood rank against rank confronted, there was no one who doubted that, in the event of battle, the conquerors this day would rule; and that those who lost would be their subjects. But god so ordered it that both belligerents alike set up trophies as claiming victory, and neither interfered with the other in the act. Both parties alike gave back their enemy's dead under a truce, and in right of victory; both alike, in symbol of defeat, under a truce took back their dead. And though both claimed to have won the day, neither could show that he had thereby gained any accession of territory, or state, or empire, or was better situated than before the battle. Uncertainty and confusion, indeed, had gained ground, being tenfold greater throughout the length and breadth of Hellas after the battle than before.

At this point I lay aside my pen: the sequel of the story may haply commend itself to another.

20°   22°   24°

MACEDONIA

Pella

Amphipolis
Eion
Pangaeus M.
Apollonia
Acanthus

Sinus Thermaicus

Elimia

Spartolus
Olynthus
Potidaea
Aphytis
Scione
Torone

Pallene

MARE

Dodona

Larisa
Crannon
Pherae
Pharsalus
Narthacius M.
ACHAIA
PHTHIOTIS

Scotussa
Phylace
Pagasae
Pagasaeus
Sinus

Paparae
Peparethus

Scyros

Ambracia

Dolopes Oeniadae AENIS

Oreus Histiaea

Leucas

Alyzia
Stratus
ACARNANI

Heraclea
Trachinia
OETAEA
PHOCIS
Thermopylae
Hyampolis

Thyrium

Oeniadae Calydon AETOLIA

LOCRIS OZOLIS
Naupactus
Rhium Pr.

Orchomenus
Delphi Haliartus
Coronea Thespiae Thebae
Creusis Scolus
Thisbae Leuctra

Chalcis
Eretria
Oropus

EUBOEA

Ithaca

Sinus Corinthiacus
Leontium

Pellene
Sicyon Oenoe
Epieicia
Phlius Cleonae

Decelea
Aegina Eleusis
Megara
COR. Salamis
ATHENAE
Phyle

Geraestus

Cephallenia

Larissa F.
Cyllene
Thalamae
Pylus
Elis

Thraustus
Olympia
Stymphalus

Piraeus
Zoster Pr.

Stiria
Thoricus
Laurium M.
Aegina

Ceos
Cynossus

Zacynthus

Amphidoli
Letrini
Ichthys Pr.
Epitalium

Lamon
Margana
Olympia

Drochomenus
Mantinea
Ormenie
ARCADIA Argos
Heraea Eutaea
Maenalus Tegea
Lepreum Megalopolis
Asea
Caryae

ARG.
Midea
Nauplia
Asine
Hermione
Eion
Mases
Spiraeum
Epidaurus
Troezen
Sunium Pr.

Sunium Pr.

Cythnos

Syros
Seriphos

Paros

PELOPONNESOS

Messene
Sparta
Gytheaeon
Amyclae

Sellasia
LACONIA

Skiatis
Sinus Argolicus

Coryphasium
Sphagia I.

Helos
Gytheum

Sinus
Laconicus

Melos

Taenarum
Prom.

Malea Prom.

Scales
0 200 400 600 800 Olympic Stades
0 20 40 60 80 100 English Miles

36°

Cythera

22°   Longitude East of Greenwich   24°

38°

THE AEGEAN

THE ANABASIS OF CYRUS

BOOK I

1. Darius and Parysatis had two sons: the elder was named Artaxerxes, and the younger Cyrus. Now, as Darius lay sick and suspected that the end of life drew near, he wished both his sons to be with him. The elder, as it chanced, was already there, but Cyrus he must send for from the province over which he had made him satrap, having appointed him general moreover of all the forces that muster in the plain of the Castolus. Thus Cyrus went up, taking with him Tissaphernes as his friend, and accompanied also by a body of Hellenes, 300 heavy armed men, under the command of Xenias the Parrhasian.

Now when Darius was dead, and Artaxerxes was established in the kingdom, Tissaphernes brought slanderous accusation against Cyrus before his brother, the king, of harbouring designs against him. And Artaxerxes, listening to the words of Tissaphernes, laid hands upon Cyrus, desiring to put him to death; but his mother made intercession for him, and sent him back again in safety to his province. He then, having so escaped through peril and dishonour, fell to considering, not only how he might avoid ever again being in his brother's power, but how, if possible, he might become king in his stead. Parysatis, his mother, was his first resource; for she had more love for Cyrus than for Artaxerxes upon his throne. Moreover Cyrus's behaviour towards all who came to him from the king's court was such that, when he sent them away again, they were better friends to himself than to the king his brother. Nor did he neglect the barbarians in his own service; but trained them, at once to be capable as warriors and devoted adherents of himself. Lastly, he began collecting his Hellenic armament, but with the utmost secrecy, so that he might take the king as completely unprepared as possible.

The manner in which he contrived the levying of the troops was as follows: First, he sent orders to the commandants of garrisons in the cities (so held by him), bidding them to get together as large a body of picked Peloponnesian troops as they severally were able, on the plea that Tissaphernes was plotting against their cities; and truly these cities

222

of Ionia had originally belonged to Tissaphernes, being given to him by the king; but at this time, with the exception of Miletus, they had all revolted to Cyrus. In Miletus, Tissaphernes, having become aware of similar designs, had forestalled the conspirators by putting some to death and banishing the remainder. Cyrus, on his side, welcomed these fugitives, and having collected an army, laid siege to Miletus by sea and land, endeavouring to reinstate the exiles; and this gave him another pretext for collecting an armament. At the same time he sent to the king, and claimed, as being the king's brother, that these cities should be given to himself rather than that Tissaphernes should continue to govern them; and in furtherance of this end, the queen, his mother, co-operated with him, so that the king not only failed to see the design against himself, but concluded that Cyrus was spending his money on armaments in order to make war on Tissaphernes. Nor did it pain him greatly to see the two at war together, and the less so because Cyrus was careful to remit the tribute due to the king from the cities which belonged to Tissaphernes.

A third army was being collected for him in the Chersonese, over against Abydos, the origin of which was as follows: There was a Lacedaemonian exile, named Clearchus, with whom Cyrus had become associated. Cyrus admired the man, and made him a present of 10,000 darics. Clearchus took the gold, and with the money raised an army, and using the Chersonese as his base of operations, set to work to fight the Thracians north of the Hellespont, in the interests of the Hellenes, and with the result that the Hellespontine cities, of their own accord, were eager to contribute funds for the support of his troops. In this way, again, an armament was being secretly maintained for Cyrus.

Then there was the Thessalian Aristippus, Cyrus's friend, who, under pressure of the rival political party at home, had come to Cyrus and asked him for pay for 2,000 mercenaries, to be continued for three months, which would enable him, he said, to gain the upper hand of his antagonists. Cyrus replied by presenting him with six months' pay for 4,000 mercenaries—only stipulating that Aristippus should not come to terms with his antagonists without final consultation with himself. In this way he secured to himself the secret maintenance of a fourth armament.

Further, he bade Proxenus, a Boeotian, who was another friend, get together as many men as possible, and join him on an expedition which he meditated against the Pisidians, who were causing annoyance to his territory. Similarly two other friends, Sophaenetus the Stymphalian, and Socrates the Achaean, had orders to get together as many men as possible and come to him, since he was on the point of opening a campaign, along with the Milesian exiles, against Tissaphernes. These orders were duly carried out by the officers in question.

2. But when the right moment seemed to him to have come, at which he should begin his march into the interior, the pretext which he put forward was his desire to expel the Pisidians utterly out of the country; and he began collecting both his Asiatic and his Hellenic armaments, avowedly against that people. From Sardis in each direction his orders sped: to Clearchus, to join him there with the whole of his army; to Aristippus, to come to terms with those at home, and to despatch to him the troops in his employ; to Xenias the Arcadian, who was acting as general-in-chief of the foreign troops in the cities, to present himself with all the men available, excepting only those who were actually needed to garrison the citadels. He next summoned the troops at present engaged in the siege of Miletus, and called upon the exiles to follow him on his intended expedition, promising them that if he were successful in his object, he would not pause until he had reinstated them in their native city. They gladly obeyed; for they believed in him; and with their arms they presented themselves at Sardis. So, too, Xenias arrived at Sardis with the contingent from the cities, 4,000 hoplites; Proxenus, also, with 1,500 hoplites and 500 light-armed troops; Sophaenetus the Stymphalian, with 1,000 hoplites; Socrates the Achaean, with 500 hoplites; while the Megarian Pasion came with 300 hoplites and 300 peltasts. This latter officer, as well as Socrates, belonged to the force engaged against Miletus. These all joined him at Sardis.

But Tissaphernes did not fail to note these proceedings. An equipment so large pointed to something more than an invasion of Pisidia: so he argued; and with what speed he might, he set off to the king, attended by about 500 horse. The king, on his side, had no sooner heard from Tissaphernes of Cyrus's great armament, than he began to make counter-preparations.

Thus Cyrus, with the troops which I have named, set out from Sardis,[1] and marched on and on through Lydia three days,[2] seventy-three miles,[3] to the river Maeander. That river is 200 feet broad, and was spanned by a bridge consisting of seven boats. Crossing it, he marched through Phrygia a single day, twenty-six miles, to Colossae, an inhabited city,[4] prosperous and large. Here he remained seven days, and was joined by Menon the Thessalian, who arrived with 1,000 hoplites and 500 peltasts, Dolopes, Aenianes, and Olynthians. From this place he

---

[1] The date was probably March 6, 401 B.C.
[2] Literally, a stopping place, hence a day's journey.
[3] Although the parasang is not an exact measure of distance, see Appendix, I have approximated the distances in miles.
[4] Many of the cities of Asia being then as now deserted.

marched three days, sixty-six miles in all, to Celaenae, a populous city of Phrygia, large and prosperous. Here Cyrus owned a palace and a large park full of wild beasts, which he used to hunt on horseback, whenever he wished to give himself or his horses exercise. Through the midst of the park flows the river Maeander, the sources of which are within the palace buildings, and it flows through the city of Celaenae. The great king also has a palace in Celaenae, a strong place, on the sources of another river, the Marsyas, at the foot of the Acropolis. This river also flows through the city, discharging itself into the Maeander, and is twenty-five feet broad. Here is the place where Apollo is said to have flayed Marsyas, when he had conquered him in the contest of skill. He hung up the skin of the conquered man, in the cavern where the spring wells forth, and hence the name of the river, Marsyas. It was on this site that Xerxes, as tradition tells, built this very palace, as well as the citadel of Celaenae itself, on his retreat from Hellas, after he had lost the famous battle. Here Cyrus remained for thirty days, during which Clearchus the Lacedaemonian arrived with 1,000 hoplites and 800 Thracian peltasts and 200 Cretan archers. At the same time, also, came Sosis the Syracusan wth 3,000 hoplites, and Sophaenetus the Arcadian with 1,000 hoplites; and here Cyrus held a review, and numbered his Hellenes in the park, and found that they amounted in all to 11,000 hoplites and about 2,000 peltasts.

From this place he continued his march two days—thirty-three miles —to the populous city of Peltae, where he remained three days; while Xenias, the Arcadian, celebrated the Lycaea[5] with sacrifice, and instituted games. The prizes were head-bands of gold; and Cyrus himself was a spectator of the contest. From this place the march was continued two days—forty miles—to Ceramon-agora, a populous city, the last on the confines of Mysia. Thence a march of three days—ninety-nine miles—brought him to Caystru-pedion, a populous city. Here Cyrus halted five days; and the soldiers, whose pay was now more than three months in arrear, came several times to the palace gates demanding their dues; while Cyrus put them off with expectations, but could not conceal his vexation, for it was not his fashion to stint payment, when he had the means. At this point Epyaxa, the wife of Syennesis, the king of the Cilicians, arrived on a visit to Cyrus; and it was said that Cyrus had received a large gift of money from the queen. At this date, at any rate, Cyrus gave the army four months' pay. The queen was accompanied by a bodyguard of Cilicians and Aspendians; and, if report speaks truly, Cyrus had intercourse with the queen.

From this place he marched two days—thirty-three miles—to Thym-

[5] The Lycaea, an Arcadian festival in honour of Zeus.

brium, a populous city. Here, by the side of the road, is the spring of
Midas, the king of Phrygia, as it is called, where Midas, as the story
goes, caught the satyr by drugging the spring with wine. From this place
he marched two days—thirty-three miles—to Tyriaeum, a populous city.
Here he halted three days; and the Cilician queen, according to the
popular account, begged Cyrus to exhibit his army for her amusement.
The latter being only too glad to make such an exhibition, held a review of the Hellenes and barbarians in the plain. He ordered the Hellenes to draw up their lines and post themselves in their customary
battle order, each general marshalling his own battalion. Accordingly
they drew up four-deep. The right was held by Menon and those with
him; the left by Clearchus and his men; the centre by the remaining generals with theirs. Cyrus first inspected the barbarians, who
marched past in troops of horse and companies of infantry. He then
inspected the Hellenes, driving past them in his chariot, with the queen
in her carriage. And they all had brass helmets and purple tunics, and
greaves, and their shields uncovered.

After he had driven past the whole body, he drew up his chariot
in front of the centre of the battle-line, and sent his interpreter Pigres
to the generals of the Hellenes, with orders to present arms and to
advance along the whole line. This order was repeated by the generals
to their men; and at the sound of the trumpet, with shields forward
and spears in rest, they advanced to meet the enemy. The pace quickened, and with a shout the soldiers spantaneously fell into a run, making
in the direction of the camp. Great was the panic of the barbarians.
The Cilician queen in her carriage turned and fled; the people in the
market place[6] left their wares and took to their heels; and the Hellenes
meanwhile came into camp with a roar of laughter. What astounded
the queen was the brilliancy and order of the armament; but Cyrus was
pleased to see the terror inspired by the Hellenes in the hearts of the
Asiatics.

From this place he marched on three days—sixty-six miles—to Ico-
nium, the last city of Phrygia, where he remained three days. Thence he
marched through Lycaonia five days—ninety-nine miles. This was hostile country, and he gave it over to the Hellenes to pillage. At this point
Cyrus sent back the Cilician queen into her own country by the quickest
route; and to escort her he sent the soldiers of Menon, and Menon
himself. With the rest of the troops he continued his march through
Cappadocia four days—eighty-three miles—to Dana, a populous city,
large and flourishing. Here they halted three days, within which in-

---

[6] Greek troops were not supplied with rations but bought their own provisions
in the market each day.

terval Cyrus put to death, on a charge of conspiracy, a Persian noble-
man named Megaphernes, a wearer of the royal purple; and along with
him another high dignitary among his subordinate commanders.

From this place they endeavoured to force a passage into Cilicia. Now
the entrance was by an exceedingly steep cart-road, impracticable for
an army in face of a resisting force; and report said that Syennesis was
on the summit of the pass guarding the approach. Accordingly they
halted a day in the plain; but next day came a messenger informing
them that Syennesis had left the pass; doubtless, after perceiving that
Menon's army was already in Cilicia on his own side of the mountains;
and he had further been informed that ships of war, belonging to the
Lacedaemonians and to Cyrus himself, with Tamos on board as admiral,
were sailing round from Ionia to Cilicia. Whatever the reason might be,
Cyrus made his way up into the hills without hindrance, and came in
sight of the tents where the Cilicians were on guard. From that point he
descended gradually into a large and beautiful plain country, well watered, and thickly covered with trees of all sorts and vines. This plain
produces sesame plentifully, as also panic and millet and barley and
wheat; and it is shut in on all sides by a steep and lofty wall of mountains from sea to sea. Descending through this plain country, he advanced four days—eighty-three miles—to Tarsus, a large and prosperous city of Cilicia. Here stood the palace of Syennesis, the king of the
country; and through the middle of the city flows a river called the
Cydnus, 200 feet broad. They found that the city had been deserted by
its inhabitants, who had betaken themselves, with Syennesis, to a strong
place on the hills. All had gone, except the tavern-keepers. The seaboard inhabitants of Soli and Issi also remained. Now Epyaxa, Syennesis's queen, had reached Tarsus five days in advance of Cyrus. During their passage over the mountains into the plain, two companies of
Menon's army were lost. Some said they had been cut down by the
Cilicians, while engaged on some pillaging affair; another account was
that they had been left behind, and being unable to overtake the main
body, or discover the route, had gone astray and perished. However it
was, they numbered 100 hoplites; and when the rest arrived, being in a
fury at the destruction of their fellow-soldiers, they vented their spleen
by pillaging the city of Tarsus and the palace to boot. Now when Cyrus
had marched into the city, he sent for Syennesis to come to him; but
the latter replied that he had never yet put himself into the hands of any
one who was his superior, nor was he willing to accede to the proposal
of Cyrus now; until, in the end, his wife persuaded him, and he accepted
pledges of good faith. After this they met, and Syennesis gave Cyrus
large sums in aid of his army; while Cyrus presented him with the cus-

tomary royal gifts—a horse with a gold bit, a necklace of gold, a gold bracelet, and a gold scimitar, a Persian dress, and lastly, the exemption of his territory from further pillage, with the privilege of taking back the slaves that had been seized, wherever they might chance to come upon them.

3. At Tarsus Cyrus and his army halted for twenty days; the soldiers refusing to advance further, since the suspicion ripened in their minds, that the expedition was in reality directed against the king; and as they insisted, they had not been hired for that. Clearchus set the example of trying to force his men to continue their march; but he had no sooner started at the head of his troops than they began to pelt him and his baggage train, and Clearchus had a narrow escape of being stoned to death there and then. Later on, when he perceived that force was useless, he summoned an assembly of his own men; and for a long while he stood and wept, while the men gazed in silent astonishment. At last he spoke as follows, "Fellow-soldiers, do not marvel that I am sorely distressed on account of the present troubles. Cyrus has been no ordinary friend to me. When I was in banishment he honoured me in various ways, and made me also a present of 10,000 darics. These I accepted, but not to lay them up for myself for private use; not to squander them in pleasure, but to expend them on yourselves. And, first of all, I went to war with the Thracians, and with you to aid, I wreaked vengeance on them in behalf of Hellas; driving them out of the Chersonese, when they wanted to deprive its Hellenic inhabitants of their lands. But as soon as Cyrus summoned me, I took you with me and set out, so that, if my benefactor had any need of me, I might requite him for the good treatment I myself had received at his hands. But since you are not willing to continue the march with me, either I must renounce you for the sake of my friendship with Cyrus, or I must go with you at the cost of deceiving him. Whether I am about to do right or not, I cannot say, but I choose yourselves; and, whatever may happen, I mean to share your fate. Never shall it be said of me by any one that, having led Greek troops against the barbarians, I betrayed the Hellenes, and chose the friendship of the barbarian. No! since you do not choose to obey and follow me, I will follow after you. Whatever may happen, I will share your fate. I look upon you as my country, my friends, my allies; with you I think I shall be honoured, wherever I be; without you I do not see how I can help a friend or hurt a foe. My decision is taken. Wherever you go, I go also."

Such were his words. But the soldiers, not only his own, but the rest also, when they heard what he said, and how he had scouted the idea of going up to the great king's palace, expressed their approval; and more than 2,000 men deserted Xenias and Pasion, and took their arms and baggage-train, and came and encamped with Clearchus. But Cyrus, in despair and vexation at this turn of affairs, sent for Clearchus. He refused to come; but, without the knowledge of the soldiers, sent a message to Cyrus, bidding him keep a good heart, for that all would arrange itself in the right way; and bade him keep on sending for him, while he himself refused to go. After that he got together his own men, with those who had joined him, and of the rest any who chose to come, and spoke as follows, "Fellow soldiers, it is clear that the relations of Cyrus to us are identical with ours to him. We are no longer his soldiers, since we have ceased to follow him; and he, on his side, is no longer our paymaster. He, however, no doubt considers himself wronged by us; and though he goes on sending for me, I cannot bring myself to go to him: for two reasons, chiefly from a sense of shame, for I am forced to admit to myself that I have altogether deceived him; but partly, too, because I am afraid of his seizing me and inflicting a penalty on me for the wrongs which he conceives that I have done him. In my opinion, then, this is no time for us to go to sleep and forget all about ourselves, rather it is high time to deliberate on our next move; and as long as we do remain here, we had better think how we are to abide in security; or, if we are resolved to turn our backs at once, what will be the safest means of retreat; and, further, how we are to procure supplies, for without supplies there is no profit whatsoever either in the general or the private soldier. The man with whom we have to deal is an excellent friend to his friends, but a very dangerous enemy to his foes. And he is backed by a force of infantry and cavalry and ships such as we all alike very well see and know, since we can hardly be said to have posted ourselves at any great distance from him. If, then, any one has a suggestion to make, now is the time to speak." With these words he ceased.

Then various speakers stood up; some of their own motion to propound their views; others inspired by Clearchus to dilate on the hopeless difficulty of either staying, or going back without the goodwill of Cyrus. One of these, in particular, with a make-believe of anxiety to commence the homeward march without further pause, called upon them instantly to choose other generals, if Clearchus were not himself prepared to lead them back, "Let them at once purchase supplies" (the market being in the Asiatic camp), "let them pack up their baggage, let them," he added, "go to Cyrus and ask for some ships in order to return by sea; if he refused to give them ships, let them demand of him a guide to lead them back through a friendly district; and if he would not so much as give them a guide, they could but put themselves, without more ado, in marching order, and send on a detachment to occupy the pass—before Cyrus and the Cilicians, whose property," the speaker added, "we have so plentifully pillaged, can anticipate us." Such were the remarks of that speaker; he was followed by Clearchus, who merely said, "As to my acting personally as general at this season, pray do not propose it. I can see numerous obstacles to my doing so. Obedience, in the fullest, I can render to the man of your choice, that is another matter: and you shall see and know that I can play my part, under command, with the best of you."

After Clearchus another spokesman stood up, and proceeded to point out the simplicity of the speaker, who proposed to ask for vessels, just as if Cyrus were minded to renounce the expedition and sail back again. "And let me further point out," he said, "what a simple-minded notion it is to beg a guide of the very man whose designs we are marring. If we can trust any guide whom Cyrus may vouchsafe to give us, why not order Cyrus at once to occupy the pass for us? For my part, I should think twice before I set foot on any ships that he might give us, for fear lest he should sink them with his men-of-war; and I should equally hesitate to follow any guide of his: he might lead us into some place out of which we should find it impossible to escape. I should much prefer, if I am to return against the will of Cyrus at all, to give him the slip, and so be gone: which indeed is impossible. But these schemes are simply nonsensical. My proposal is that a deputation of fit persons, with Clearchus, should go to Cyrus: let them go to Cyrus and ask him what use he proposes to make of us; if the business is at all similar to that on which he once before employed a body of foreigners—let us by all means follow: let us show that we are the equals of those who accompanied him on his march up formerly. But if the design should turn out to be of larger import than the former one—involving more toil and more danger—we should ask him, either to give us good reasons for following his lead, or else consent to send us away into a friendly country. In this way, whether we follow him, we shall do so as friends, and with heart and soul, or whether we go back, we shall do so in security. The answer to this shall be reported to us here, and when we have heard it, we will advise as to our best course."

This resolution was carried, and they chose and sent a deputation with Clearchus, who put to Cyrus the questions which had been agreed upon by the army. Cyrus replied as follows: That he had received news that Abrocomas, an enemy of his, was posted on the Euphrates, twelve days off; his object was to march against this aforesaid Abrocomas: and if he were still there, he wished to inflict punishment on him, "or if he be fled" (so the reply concluded), "we will there deliberate on the best course." The deputation received the answer and reported it to the soldiers. The suspicion that he was leading them against the king was not dispelled; but it seemed best to follow him. They only demanded an increase of pay, and Cyrus promised to give them half as much again as they had hitherto received,—that is to say, a daric and a half a month to each man, instead of a daric. Was he really leading them to attack the king? Not even at this moment was any one apprised of the fact, at any rate in any open and public manner.

4. From this point he marched two days—thirty-three miles—to the river Psarus, which is 200 feet broad, and from the Psarus he marched a single day—sixteen miles—to the river Pyramus, which is about 200 yards broad, and from the Pyramus two days—fifty miles—to Issi, the last city in Cilicia. It lies on the seaboard—a prosperous, large, and flourishing town. Here they halted three days, and here Cyrus was joined by his fleet. There were thirty-five ships from Peloponnesus, with the Lacedaemonian admiral Pythagoras on board. These had been piloted from Ephesus by Tamos the Egyptian, who himself had another fleet of twenty-five ships belonging to Cyrus. These had formed Tamos's blockading squadron at Miletus, when that city sided with Tissaphernes; he had also used them in other military services rendered to Cyrus in his operations against that satrap. There was a third officer on board the fleet, the Lacedaemonian Cheirisophus, who had been sent for by Cyrus, and had brought with him 700 hoplites, over whom he was to act as general in the service of Cyrus. The fleet lay at anchor opposite Cyrus's tent. Here too another reinforcement presented itself. This was a body of 400 hoplites, Hellenic mercenaries in the service of Abrocomas, who deserted him for Cyrus, and joined in the campaign against the king.

From Issi, he marched a single day—sixteen miles—to the gates of Cilicia and Syria. This was a double fortress: the inner and nearer one, which protects Cilicia, was held by Syennesis and a garrison of Cilicians; the outer and further one, protecting Syria, was reported to be garrisoned by a body of the king's troops. Through the gap between the two fortresses flows a river named the Carsus, which is 100 feet broad, and the whole space between was scarcely more than 600 yards. To force a passage here would be impossible, so narrow was the pass itself, with the fortification walls stretching down to the sea, and precipitous rocks above; while both fortresses were furnished with gates. It was the existence of this pass which had induced Cyrus to send for the fleet, so as to enable him to lead a body of hoplites inside and outside the gates; and so to force a passage through the enemy, if he were guarding the Syrian gate, as he fully expected to find Abrocomas doing with a large army. This, however, Abrocomas had not done; but as soon as he learned that Cyrus was in Cilicia, he had turned round and made his exit from

Phoenicia, to join the king with an army amounting, as report said, to 300,000 men.

From this point Cyrus pursued his march through Syria a single day—sixteen miles—to Myriandus, a city inhabited by Phoenicians, on the sea-coast. This was a commercial port, and numerous merchant vessels were riding at anchor in the harbour. Here they halted seven days, and here Xenias the Arcadian general, and Pasion the Megarian got on board a trader, and having stowed away their most valuable effects, set sail for home; most people explained the act as the outcome of a fit of jealousy, because Cyrus had allowed Clearchus to retain their men, who had deserted to him, in hopes of returning to Hellas instead of marching against the king; when the two had so vanished, a rumour spread that Cyrus was after them with some ships of war, and some hoped the cowards might be caught, others pitied them, if that should be their fate.

But Cyrus summoned the generals and addressed them, "Xenias and Pasion," he said, "have taken leave of us; but they need not flatter themselves that in so doing they have stolen into hiding. I know where they are gone; nor will they owe their escape to speed; I have men-of-war to capture their craft, if I like. But heaven help me! if I mean to pursue them: never shall it be said of me, that I turn people to account as long as they stay with me; but as soon as they are minded to be off, I seize and maltreat them, and strip them of their wealth. Not so! let them go with the consciousness that our behaviour to them is better than theirs to us. And yet I have their children and wives safe under lock and key in Tralles; but they shall not be deprived even of these. They shall receive them back in return for their former goodness to me." So he spoke, and the Hellenes, even those who had been out of heart at the thought of marching up the country, when they heard of the nobleness of Cyrus, were happier and more eager to follow him on his path.

After this Cyrus marched onwards four days—sixty-six miles—to the river Chalus. That river is 100 feet broad, and is stocked with large tame fish which the Syrians regard as gods, and will not suffer to be injured—and so too the pigeons of the place. The villages in which they encamped belonged to Parysatis, as part of her girdle money. From this point he marched on five days—ninety-nine miles—to the sources of the river Dardas, which is 100 feet broad. Here stood the palace of Belesys, the late ruler of Syria, with its park—which was a very large and beautiful one, and full of the products of all the seasons in their course. But Cyrus cut down the park and burned the palace. Thence he marched on three days—fifty miles—to the river Euphrates, which is nearly half a mile broad. A large and flourishing city, named Thapsacus, stands on its banks. Here they halted five days, and here Cyrus sent for the generals of the Hellenes, and told them that the advance was now to be upon Babylon, against the great king; he bade them communicate this information to the soldiers and persuade them to follow. The generals called an assembly, and announced the news to the soldiers. The latter were indignant and angry with the generals, accusing them of having kept secret what they had long known; and refused to go, unless such a bribe of money were given them as had been given to their predecessors, when they went up with Cyrus to the court of his father, not as now to fight a battle, but on a peaceful errand—the visit of a son to his father by invitation. The demand was reported to Cyrus by the generals, and he undertook to give each man five silver minae as soon as Babylon was reached, and their pay in full, until he had safely conveyed them back to Ionia again. In this manner the Hellenic force were persuaded, that is to say, the majority of them. Menon, indeed, before it was clear what the rest of the soldiers would do—whether, in fact, they would follow Cyrus or not—collected his own troops apart and made them the following speech, "Men," he said, "if you will listen to me, there is a method by which, without risk or toil, you may win the special favour of Cyrus beyond the rest of the soldiers. You ask what it is I would have you to do? I will tell you. Cyrus at this instant is begging the Hellenes to follow him to attack the king. I say then: Cross the Euphrates at once, before it is clear what answer the rest will make; if they vote in favour of following, you will get the credit of having set the example, and Cyrus will be grateful to you. He will look upon you as being the heartiest in his cause; he will repay, as of all others he best knows how; while, if the rest vote against crossing, we shall all go back again; but as the sole adherents, whose fidelity he can altogether trust, it is you whom Cyrus will turn to account, as commandants of garrisons or captains of companies. You need only ask him for whatever you want, and you will get it from him, as being the friends of Cyrus."

The men heard and obeyed, and before the rest had given their answer, they were already across. But when Cyrus perceived that Menon's troops had crossed, he was well pleased, and he sent Glus to the division in question, with this message, "Soldiers, accept my thanks at present; eventually you shall thank me. I will see to that, or my name is not Cyrus." The soldiers therefore could not but pray heartily for his success; so high their hopes ran. But to Menon, it was said, he sent gifts with lordly liberality. This done, Cyrus proceeded to cross; and in his wake followed the rest of the armament to a man. As they forded, never a man was wetted above the chest: nor ever until this moment, said the men of Thapsacus, had the river been so crossed on foot, boats had always been required; but these, at the present time, Abrocomas, in his desire to hinder Cyrus from crossing, had burned. Thus the passage was looked upon as a thing miraculous; the river had manifestly retired before the face of Cyrus, like a courtier bowing to his future king. From this place he continued his march through Syria nine days—165 miles— and they reached the river Araxes. Here were several villages full of corn and wine; in which they halted three days, and provisioned the army.

5. Thence he marched on through Arabia, keeping the Euphrates on the right, five days across desert—115 miles. In this region the ground was one long level plain, stretching far and wide like the sea, full of absinth; while all the other vegetation, whether wood or reed, was sweet scented like spice or sweet herb; there were no trees; but there was wild game of all kinds—wild asses in greatest abundance, with plenty of ostriches; besides these, there were bustards and antelopes. These creatures were occasionally chased by the cavalry. The asses, when pursued, would run forward a space, and then stand still—their pace being much swifter than that of horses; and as soon as the horses came close, they went through the same performance. The only way to catch them was for the riders to post themselves at intervals, and to hunt them in relays, as it were. The flesh of those they captured was not unlike venison, only more tender. No one was lucky enough to capture an ostrich. Some of the troopers did give chase, but it had soon to be abandoned; for the bird, in its effort to escape, speedily put a long interval between itself and its pursuers; plying its legs at full speed, and using its wings the while like a sail. The bustards were not so hard to catch when started suddenly; for they take only short flights, like partridges, and are soon tired. Their flesh is delicious.

As the army wended its way through this region, they reached the river Mascas, which is 100 feet in breadth. Here stood a big deserted city called Corsote, almost literally surrounded by the stream, which flows round it in a circle. Here they halted three days and provisioned themselves. Hence they continued their march thirteen days across desert— 297 miles—with the Euphrates still on their right, until they reached the Gates. On these marches several of the baggage animals perished of hunger, for there was neither grass nor green herb, or tree of any sort; but the country throughout was barren. The inhabitants make their living by quarrying millstones on the river banks, which they work up and take to Babylon and sell, purchasing corn in exchange for their goods. Corn failed the army, and was not to be got for money, except in the Lydian market open in Cyrus's Asiatic army; where a capithe of wheat or barley cost four sigli; the sigli being equal to seven and a half

Attic obols, whilst the capithe is the equivalent of two Attic choenices,[7] dry measure, so that the soldiers subsisted on meat alone for the whole period. Some of the days' journeys were very long, whenever they had to push on to find water or fodder; and once they found themselves involved in a narrow way, where the deep clay presented an obstacle to the progress of the wagons. Cyrus, with the nobles about him, halted to superintend the operation, and ordered Glus and Pigres to take a body of barbarians and to help in extricating the wagons. As they seemed to be slow about the business, he turned round angrily to the Persian nobles and bade them lend a hand to force the wagons out. Then, if ever, what goes to constitute one branch of good discipline, was to be witnessed. Each of those addressed, just where he chanced to be standing, threw off his purple cloak, and flung himself into the work with as much eagerness as if it had been a charge for victory. Down a steep hill side they flew, with their costly tunics and embroidered trousers,—some with the circlets round their necks, and bracelets on their arms—in an instant, they had sprung into the miry clay, and in less time than one could have conceived, they had landed the wagons safe on dry land.

Altogether it was plain that Cyrus was bent on pressing on the march, and averse to stopping, except where he halted for the sake of provisioning or some other necessary object; being convinced that the more rapidly he advanced, the less prepared for battle would he find the king; while the slower his own progress, the larger would be the hostile army which he would find collected. Indeed, the attentive observer could see, at a glance, that if the king's empire was strong in its extent of territory and the number of inhabitants, that strength is compensated by an inherent weakness, dependent upon the length of roads and the inevitable dispersion of defensive forces, where an invader insists upon pressing home the war by forced marches.

On the opposite side of the Euphrates to the point reached on one of these desert stages, was a large and flourishing city named Charmande. From this town the soldiers made purchases of provisions, crossing the river on rafts, in the following fashion: They took the skins which they used as tent coverings, and filled them with light grass; they then compressed and stitched them tightly together by the ends, so that the water might not touch the hay. On these they crossed and got provisions: wine made from the date-nut, and millet or panic-corn, the common staple of the country. Some dispute or other here occurred between the soldiers of Menon and Clearchus, in which Clearchus sentenced one of Menon's men, as the delinquent, and had him flogged. The man went back to his

---

[7] The choenix equals one quart. The prices were about fifty times normal prices in Athens.

own division and told them. Hearing what had been done to their comrade, his fellows fumed, and were highly incensed against Clearchus. The same day Clearchus visited the passage of the river, and after inspecting the market there, was returning with a few followers, on horseback, to his tent, and had to pass through Menon's quarters. Cyrus had not yet come up, but was riding up in the same direction. One of Menon's men, who was splitting wood, caught sight of Clearchus as he rode past, and aimed a blow at him with his axe. The aim took no effect; when another hurled a stone at him, and a third, and then several, with a great outcry. Clearchus made a rapid retreat to his own troops, and at once ordered them to get under arms. He bade his hoplites remain in position with their shields resting against their knees, while he, at the head of his Thracians and horsemen, of which he had more than forty in his army—Thracians for the most part—advanced against Menon's soldiers, so that the latter, with Menon himself, were panicstricken, and ran to seize their arms; some even stood riveted to the spot, in perplexity at the occurrence. Just then Proxenus came up from behind, as chance would have it, with his division of hoplites, and without a moment's hesitation marched into the open space between the rival parties, and grounded arms; then he fell to begging Clearchus to desist. The latter was not too well pleased to hear his trouble lightly spoken of, when he had barely escaped being stoned to death; and he bade Proxenus retire and leave the intervening space open. At this juncture Cyrus arrived and inquired what was happening. There was no time for hesitation. With his javelins firmly grasped in his hands he galloped up, escorted by some of his faithful bodyguard, who were present—and was soon in the midst, exclaiming, "Clearchus, Proxenus, and you other Hellenes yonder, you know not what you do. As surely as you come to blows with one another, our fate is sealed—this very day I shall be cut to pieces, and so will you: your turn will follow close on mine. Let our fortunes once take an evil turn, and these barbarians whom you see around will be worse foes to us than those who are at present serving with the king." At these words Clearchus came to his senses. Both parties paused from battle, and retired to their quarters: order reigned.

6. As they advanced from this point (opposite Charmande), they came upon the hoof-prints and dung of horses at frequent intervals. It looked like the trail of some 2,000 horses. Keeping ahead of the army, these fellows burned up the grass and everything else that was good for use. Now there was a Persian, named Orontas; he was closely related to the king by birth: and in matters pertaining to war reckoned among the best of Persian warriors. Having formerly been at war with Cyrus, and afterwards reconciled to him, he now made a conspiracy to destroy

him. He made a proposal to Cyrus: if Cyrus would furnish him with
1,000 horsemen, he would deal with these troopers, who were burning
down everything in front of them; he would lay an ambuscade and cut
them down, or he would capture a host of them alive; in any case, he
would put a stop to their aggressiveness and burnings; he would see to
it that they did not ever get a chance of setting eyes on Cyrus's army
and reporting its advent to the king. The proposal seemed plausible to
Cyrus, who accordingly authorised Orontas to take a detachment from
each of the generals, and be gone. He, thinking that he had got his
horsemen ready to his hand, wrote a letter to the king, announcing that
he would soon join him with as many troopers as he could bring; he bade
him, at the same time, instruct the royal cavalry to welcome him on arrival as a friend. The letter further contained certain reminders of his
former friendship and fidelity. This despatch he delivered into the hands
of one who was a trusty messenger, as he thought; but the bearer took
and gave it to Cyrus. Cyrus read it. Orontas was arrested. Then Cyrus
summoned to his tent seven of the noblest Persians among his personal
attendants, and sent orders to the Hellenic generals to bring up a body
of hoplites. These troops were to take up a position round his tent. This
the generals did, bringing up about 3,000 hoplites. Clearchus was also
invited inside, to assist at the court-martial; a compliment due to the
position he held among the other generals, in the opinion not only of
Cyrus, but also of the rest of the court. When he came out, he reported
the circumstances of the trial (as to which, indeed, there was no mystery) to his friends. He said that Cyrus opened the inquiry with these
words, "I have invited you hither, my friends, that I may take advice
with you, and carry out whatever, in the sight of god and man, it is
right for me to do, as concerning the man before you, Orontas. The prisoner was, in the first instance, given to me by my father, to be my faithful subject. In the next place, acting, to use his own words, under the
orders of my brother, and having hold of the Acropolis of Sardis, he
went to war with me. I met war with war, and forced him to think it
more prudent to desist from war with me: whereupon we shook hands,
exchanging solemn pledges. After that," and at this point Cyrus turned
to Orontas, and addressed him personally, "after that, did I do you any
wrong?" He answered, "Never." Again, another question, "Then later
on, having received, as you admit, no injury from me, did you revolt to
the Mysians and injure my territory, as far as in you lay?" "I did,"
was the reply. "Then, once more having discovered the limits of your
power, did you flee to the altar of Artemis, crying out that you repented?
And did you thus work upon my feelings, that we a second time shook
hands and made interchange of solemn pledges? Are these things so?"

Orontas again assented. "Then what injury have you received from me," Cyrus asked, "that now for the third time, you have been detected in a treasonous plot against me?" "No injury," Orontas replied. And Cyrus asked once more, "You plead guilty to having sinned against me?" "I must do so," he answered. Then Cyrus put one more question, "But the day may come, may it not, when you will once again be hostile to my brother, and a faithful friend to myself?" The other answered, "Even if I were, you could never be brought to believe it, Cyrus."

At this point Cyrus turned to those who were present and said, "Such has been the conduct of the prisoner in the past: such is his language now. I now call upon you, and you first, Clearchus, to declare your opinion—what think you?" And Clearchus answered, "My advice to you is to put this man out of the way as soon as may be, so that we may be saved the necessity of watching him, and have more leisure, as far as he is concerned, to requite the services of those whose friendship is sincere." "To this opinion," he told us, "the rest of the court adhered." After that, at the bidding of Cyrus, each of those present, in turn, including the kinsmen of Orontas, took him by the girdle; which is as much as to say, "Let him die the death," and then those appointed led him out; and they who in old days were wont to do obeisance to him, could not refrain, even at that moment, from bowing down before him, although they knew he was being led forth to death.

After they had conducted him to the tent of Artapates, the trustiest of Cyrus's wand-bearers, none set eyes upon him ever again, alive or dead. No one, of his own knowledge, could declare the manner of his death; though some conjectured one thing and some another. No tomb to mark his resting-place, either then or since, was ever seen.

7. From this place Cyrus marched through Babylonia three days— forty miles. Now, on the third day, about midnight, Cyrus held a review of the Hellenes and Asiatics in the plain, expecting that the king would arrive the following day with his army to offer battle. He gave orders to Clearchus to take command of the right wing, and to Menon the Thessalian of the left, while he himself undertook the disposition of his own forces in person. After the review, with the first approach of day, deserters from the great king arrived, bringing Cyrus information about the royal army. Then Cyrus summoned the generals and captains of the Hellenes, and held a council of war to arrange the plan of battle. He took this opportunity also to address the following words of compliment and encouragement to the meeting, "Men of Hellas," he said, "it is certainly not from lack of barbarians to fight my battles that I put myself at your head as my allies; but because I hold you to be better and stronger than many barbarians. That is why I took you. See then that

you prove yourselves to be men worthy of the liberty which you possess, and which I envy you. Liberty—it is a thing which, be well assured, I would choose in preference to all my other possessions, multiplied many times. But I would like you to know into what sort of struggle you are going: learn its nature from one who knows. Their numbers are great, and they come on with much noise; but if you can hold out against these two things, I confess I am ashamed to think, what a sorry set of folk you will find the inhabitants of this land to be. But you are men, and brave you must be, being men: it is agreed; then if you wish to return home, any of you, I undertake to send you back, in such sort that your friends at home shall envy you; but I flatter myself I shall persuade many of you to accept what I will offer you here, in lieu of what you left at home."

Here Gaulites, a Samian exile, and a trusty friend of Cyrus, being present, exclaimed, "And yet, Cyrus, some say you can afford to make large promises now, because you are in the crisis of impending danger; but let matters go well with you, will you recollect? They shake their heads. Indeed, some add that, even if you did recollect, and were ever so willing, you would not be able to make good all your promises, and repay." When Cyrus heard that, he answered, "You forget, men, my father's empire stretches southwards to a region where men cannot dwell by reason of the heat, and northwards to a region uninhabitable through cold; but all the intervening space is mapped out in satrapies belonging to my brother's friends: so that if the victory be ours, it will be ours also to put our friends in possession in their place. On the whole my fear is, not that I may not have enough to give to each of my friends, but lest I may not have friends enough on whom to bestow what I have to give, and to each of you Hellenes I will give a crown of gold."

So they, when they heard these words, were more elated than ever themselves, and spread the good news among the rest outside. And there came into his presence both the generals and some of the other Hellenes also, claiming to know what they should have in the event of victory; and Cyrus satisfied the expectation of each and all, and so dismissed them. Now the advice and admonition of all who came into conversation with him was, not to enter the battle himself, but to post himself in rear of themselves; and at this moment Clearchus put a question to him, "But do you think that your brother will give battle to you, Cyrus?" and Cyrus answered, "Not without a battle, be assured, shall the prize be won; if he be the son of Darius and Parysatis, and a brother of mine."

In the final arming for battle at this juncture, the numbers were as follows: Of Hellenes there were 10,400 heavy infantry with 2,500 targeteers, while the barbarians with Cyrus reached a total of 100,000.

He had too about twenty scythe-chariots. The enemy's forces[8] were reported to number 1,200,000, with 200 scythe-chariots, besides which he had 6,000 cavalry under Artagerses. These formed the immediate vanguard of the king himself. The royal army was marshalled by four generals or field-marshals, each in command of 300,000 men. Their names were Abrocomas, Tissaphernes, Gobryas, and Arbaces. (But of this total not more than 900,000 were engaged in the battle, with 150 scythe-chariots; since Abrocomas, on his march from Phoenicia, arrived five days too late for the battle.) Such was the information brought to Cyrus by deserters who came in from the king's army before the battle, and it was corroborated after the battle by those of the enemy who were taken prisoners.

From this place Cyrus advanced one day—ten miles—with the whole body of his troops, Hellenic and barbarian alike in order of battle. He expected the king to give battle the same day, for in the middle of this day's march a deep sunk trench was reached, thirty feet broad, and eighteen feet deep. The trench was carried inland through the plain, forty miles' distance, to the wall of Media. [Here are canals, flowing from the river Tigris; they are four in number, each 100 feet broad, and very deep, with corn ships plying upon them; they empty themselves into the Euphrates, and are at intervals of three miles apart, and are spanned by bridges.][9]

Between the Euphrates and the trench was a narrow passage, twenty feet only in breadth. The trench itself had been constructed by the great king upon hearing of Cyrus's approach, to serve as a line of defence. Through this narrow passage then Cyrus and his army passed, and found themselves safe inside the trench. So there was no battle to be fought with the king that day; only there were numerous unmistakable traces of horse and infantry in retreat. Here Cyrus summoned Silanus, his Ambraciot soothsayer, and presented him with 3,000 darics; because eleven days back, when sacrificing, he had told him that the king would not fight within ten days, and Cyrus had answered, "Well, then, if he does not fight within that time, he will not fight at all; and if your prophecy comes true, I promise you ten talents." So now, that the ten days were passed, he presented him with the above sum.

But as the king had failed to hinder the passage of Cyrus's army at the trench, Cyrus himself and the rest concluded that he must have abandoned the idea of offering battle, so that next day Cyrus advanced with less than his former caution. On the third day he was conducting the march, seated in his carriage, with only a small body of troops

[8] These numbers are undoubtedly much exaggerated.
[9] This passage is generally regarded as an interpolation.

drawn up in front of him. The mass of the army was moving on in no
kind of order, the soldiers having consigned their heavy arms to be carried in the wagons or on the backs of beasts.

8. It was already about full market time.[10] and the halting-place at
which the army was to take up quarters was nearly reached, when Pa-
tegyas, a Persian, a trusty member of Cyrus's personal staff, came galloping up at full speed on his horse, which was bathed in sweat, and at
once to every one he met he shouted in Greek and Persian, "The king is
advancing with a large army ready for battle." Then ensued a scene of
wild confusion. The Hellenes and all alike were expecting to be attacked
on the instant, and before they could form their lines. Cyrus sprang from
his carriage and donned his breastplate; then leaping on to his charger's back, with the javelins firmly clutched, he passed the order to the
rest, to arm themselves and fall into their several ranks.

The orders were carried out with alacrity; the ranks shaped themselves. Clearchus held the right of the wing resting on the Euphrates,
Proxenus was next, and after him the rest, while Menon with his troops
held the Hellenic left. Of the Asiatics, a body of Paphlagonian cavalry,
1,000 strong, were posted beside Clearchus on the right, and with them
stood the Hellenic peltasts. On the left was Ariaeus, Cyrus's second in
command, and the rest of the barbarian host. Cyrus was with his body-
guard of cavalry about 600 strong, all armed with breastplates like
Cyrus, and thigh-guards and helmets; but not so Cyrus: he went into
battle with head unhelmeted. [To expose oneself to the risks of war
bareheaded is, it is said, a practice common to the Persians.] So too
all the horses with Cyrus wore forehead-pieces and breast-pieces, and the
troopers carried short Hellenic swords.

It was now mid-day, and the enemy was not yet in sight; but with
the approach of afternoon was seen dust like a white cloud, and after
a considerable interval a black pall as it were spread far and high over
the plain. As they came nearer, very soon was seen here and there a glint
of bronze and spear-points; and the ranks could plainly be distinguished.
On the left were troopers wearing white cuirasses. That is Tissaphernes
in command, they said, and next to these a body of men bearing wicker-
shields, and next again heavy-armed infantry, with long wooden shields
reaching to the feet. These were the Egyptians, they said, and then other
cavalry, other bowmen; all were in national divisions, each nation
marching in densely-crowded squares. And all along their front was a
line of chariots at considerable intervals from one another, the famous
scythe-chariots, as they were named, having their scythes fitted to the
axle-trees and stretching out slantwise, while others protruded under

[10] Between nine and ten o'clock in the morning.

the chariot-seats, facing the ground, so as to cut through all they encountered. The design was to let them dash full speed into the ranks of the Hellenes and cut them through.

The anticipation of Cyrus, when at the council of war he admonished the Hellenes not to mind the shouting of the Asiatics, was not justified. Instead of shouting, they came on in deep silence, softly and slowly, with even tread. At this instant, Cyrus, riding past in person, accompanied by Pigres, his interpreter, and three or four others, called aloud to Clearchus to advance against the enemy's centre, for there the king was to be found. "And if we strike home at this point," he added, "our work is finished." Clearchus, though he could see the compact body at the centre, and had been told by Cyrus that the king lay outside the Hellenic left (for, owing to numerical superiority, the king, while holding his own centre, could well overlap Cyrus's extreme left), still hesitated to draw off his right wing from the river, for fear of being turned on both flanks; and he simply replied, assuring Cyrus that he would take care all went well.

At this time the barbarian army was evenly advancing, and the Hellenic division was still riveted to the spot, completing its formation as the various contingents came up. Cyrus, riding past at some distance from the lines, glanced his eye first in one direction and then in the other, so as to take a complete survey of friends and foes; when Xenophon the Athenian, seeing him, rode up from the Hellenic quarter to meet him, asking whether he had any orders to give. Cyrus, pulling up his horse, begged him to make the announcement generally known that the omens from the victims, internal and external alike, were good. While he was still speaking, he heard a confused murmur passing through the ranks, and asked what it meant. The other replied that it was the watchword being passed down for the second time. Cyrus wondered who had given the order, and asked what the watchword was. On being told it was "Zeus our Saviour and Victory," he replied, "I accept it; so let it be," and with that remark rode away to his own position. And now the two battle lines were no more than three or four furlongs apart, when the Hellenes began chanting the paean, and at the same time advanced against the enemy.

But with the forward movement a certain portion of the line billowed onwards in advance, and the portion left behind quickened to a run; and simultaneously a thrilling cry burst from all lips, like that in honour of the war-god—Eleleu! Eleleu! and the running became general. Some say they clashed their shields and spears, thereby causing terror to the horses; and before they had got within arrowshot the barbarians swerved and took to flight. And now the Hellenes gave chase with all their might, checked only by shouts to one another not to race, but to keep their ranks. The enemy's chariots, without their charioteers, swept onwards, some through the enemy themselves, others past the Hellenes. They, as they saw them coming, opened a gap and let them pass. One fellow, like some dumbfounded mortal on a race-course, was caught by the heels, but even he, they said, received no hurt; nor indeed, with the single exception of some one on the left wing who was said to have been wounded by an arrow, did any Hellene in this battle suffer a single hurt.

Cyrus, seeing the Hellenes conquering, as far as they at any rate were concerned, and in hot pursuit, was well content; but in spite of his joy and the salutations offered him at that moment by those about him, as though he were already king, he was not led away to join in the pursuit, but keeping his squadron of 600 horsemen in close order, waited and watched to see what the king himself would do. The king, he knew, held the centre of the Persian army. Indeed it is the fashion for the Asiatic monarch to occupy that position during action, for this twofold reason: he holds the safest place, with his troops on either side of him, while, if he has occasion to despatch any necessary order along the lines, his troops will receive the message in half the time. The king accordingly on this occasion held the centre of his army, but for all that, he was outside Cyrus's left wing; and seeing that no one offered him battle in front, nor yet the troops in front of him, he wheeled as if to encircle the enemy. It was then that Cyrus, in apprehension lest the king might get round to the rear and cut to pieces the Hellenic body, charged to meet him. Attacking with his 600, he mastered the line of troops in front of the king, and put to flight the 6,000, cutting down, as is said, with his own hand their general, Artagerses.

But as soon as the rout commenced, Cyrus's own 600 themselves, in the ardour of pursuit, were scattered, with the exception of a handful who were left with Cyrus himself—chiefly his table companions, so-called. Left alone with these, he caught sight of the king and the close throng about him. Unable longer to contain himself, with a cry, "I see the man," he rushed at him and dealt a blow at his chest, wounding him through the breastplate. So says Ctesias the physician,[11] who further states that he himself healed the wound. As Cyrus delivered the blow, some one struck him with a javelin under the eye severely; and in the struggle which then ensued between the king and Cyrus and those about them to protect one or other, we have the statement of Ctesias

---

[11] Ctesias was a physician of Cnidos. Seventeen years of his life were passed at the court of Persia; he returned to Greece in 398 B.C. He wrote a history of Persian affairs.

as to the number slain on the king's side, for he was by his side. On the other, Cyrus himself fell, and eight of his bravest companions lay on the top of him. The story says that Artapates, the trustiest squire among his wand-bearers, when he saw that Cyrus had fallen to the ground, leaped from his horse and threw his arms about him. Then, as one account says, the king bade one slay him as a worthy victim to his brother: others say that Artapates drew his scimitar and slew himself by his own hand, A golden scimitar it is true, he had; he wore also a collar and bracelets and the other ornaments such as the noblest Persians wear; for his kindliness and fidelity had won him honours at the hands of Cyrus.

9. So died Cyrus; a man the kingliest[12] and most worthy to rule of all the Persians who have lived since the elder Cyrus: according to the concurrent testimony of all who are reputed to have known him intimately. To begin from the beginning, when still a boy, and while being brought up with his brother and the other lads, his unrivalled excellence was recognised. For the sons of the noblest Persians, it must be known, are brought up, one and all, at the king's court. Here lessons of sobriety and self-control may be learned, while there is nothing base to see or hear. There is the daily spectacle ever before the boys of some receiving honour from the king, and again of others receiving dishonour; and the tale of all this is in their ears, so that from earliest boyhood they learn how to rule and to be ruled.

In this training Cyrus was held to be first a paragon of modesty among his fellows, rendering an obedience to his elders which exceeded that of many of his own inferiors; and next he bore away the palm for skill in horsemanship and for love of the animal itself. Likewise in matters of war, in the use of the bow and the javelin, he was held by men in general to be at once the aptest of learners and the most eager practiser. As soon as his age permitted, the same pre-eminence showed itself in his fondness for the chase, not without a certain appetite for perilous adventure in facing the wild beasts themselves. Once a bear made a furious rush at him, and without wincing he grappled with her, and was pulled from his horse, receiving wounds the scars of which were visible through life; but in the end he slew the creature, nor did he forget him who first came to his aid, but made him enviable in the eyes of many.

After he had been sent down by his father to be satrap of Lydia and Great Phrygia and Cappadocia, and had been appointed general of the forces, whose business it is to muster in the plain of the Castolus, noth-

[12] The character now to be drawn is afterwards elaborated into the Cyrus of the *Cyropaedeia*.

ing was more noticeable in his conduct than the importance which he
attached to the faithful fulfilment of every treaty or compact or undertaking entered into with others. He would tell no lies to any one.
Thus doubtless it was that he won the confidence alike of individuals
and of the communities entrusted to his care; or in case of hostility, a
treaty made with Cyrus was a guarantee sufficient to the combatant that
he would suffer nothing contrary to its terms. Therefore, in the war
with Tissaphernes, all the states of their own accord chose Cyrus rather
than Tissaphernes, except only the men of Miletus, and these were
only alienated through fear of him, because he refused to abandon their
exiled citizens; and his deeds and words bore emphatic witness to his
principle: even if they were weakened in number or in fortune, he would
never abandon those who had once become his friends.

He made no secret of his endeavour to outdo his friends and his foes
alike in reciprocity of conduct. The prayer has been attributed to him,
"God grant I may live long enough to recompense my friends and requite my foes with a strong arm." However this may be, no one, at
least in our days, ever drew together so ardent a following of friends,
eager to lay at his feet their money, their cities, their own lives and persons; nor is it to be inferred from this that he suffered the malefactor
and the wrongdoer to laugh him to scorn; on the contrary, these he
punished most unflinchingly. It was no rare sight to see on the well-
trodden highways, men who had forfeited hand or foot or eye; the result
being that throughout the satrapy of Cyrus any one, Hellene or barbarian, provided he were innocent, might fearlessly travel wherever he
pleased, and take with him whatever he felt disposed. However, as all
allowed, it was for the brave in war that he reserved especial honour.
To take the first instance to hand, he had a war with the Pisidians and
Mysians. Being himself at the head of an expedition into those territories, he could observe those who voluntarily encountered risks; these
he made rulers of the territory which he subjected, and afterwards honoured them with other gifts. So that, if the good and brave were set on
a pinnacle of fortune, cowards were recognised as their natural slaves;
and so it befel that Cyrus never had lack of volunteers in any service of
danger, whenever it was expected that his eye would be upon them.

So again, wherever he might discover any one ready to distinguish
himself in the service of uprightness, his delight was to make this man
richer than those who seek for gain by unfair means. On the same principle, his own administration was in all respects uprightly conducted,
and, in particular, he secured the services of an army worthy of the
name. Generals, and Captains alike, came to him from across the seas,
not merely to make money, but because they saw that loyalty to Cyrus

was a more profitable investment than so much pay a month. Let any man whatsoever render him willing service, such enthusiasm was sure to win its reward. And so Cyrus could always command the service of the best assistants, it was said, whatever the work might be.

Or if he saw any skilful and just steward who furnished well the country over which he ruled, and created revenues, so far from robbing him at any time, to him who had, he delighted to give more. So that toil was a pleasure, and gains were amassed with confidence, and least of all from Cyrus would a man conceal the amount of his possessions, seeing that he showed no jealousy of wealth openly avowed, but his endeavour was rather to turn to account the riches of those who kept them secret. Towards the friends he had made, whose kindliness he knew, or whose fitness as fellow-workers with himself, in anything which he might wish to carry out, he had tested, he showed himself in turn an adept in the arts of courtesy. Just in proportion as he felt the need of this friend or that to help him, so he tried to help each of them in return in whatever seemed to be their desire.

Many were the gifts bestowed on him, for many and diverse reasons; no one man, perhaps, ever received more; no one, certainly, was ever more ready to bestow them on others, with an eye ever to the taste of each, so as to gratify what he saw to be the individual requirement. Many of these presents were sent to him to serve as personal adornments of the body or for battle; and as touching these he would say, "How am I to deck myself out in all these? To my mind a man's chief ornament is the adornment of nobly-adorned friends." Indeed, that he should triumph over his friends in the great matters of welldoing is not surprising, seeing that he was much more powerful than they, but that he should go beyond them in minute attentions, and in an eager desire to give pleasure, seems to me, I must confess, more admirable. Frequently when he had tasted some specially excellent wine, he would send the half remaining flagon to some friend with a message to say, "Cyrus says, this is the best wine he has tasted for a long time, that is his excuse for sending it to you. He hopes you will drink it up to-day with a choice party of friends." Or, perhaps, he would send the remainder of a dish of geese, half loaves of bread, and so forth, the bearer being instructed to say, "This is Cyrus's favourite dish, he hopes you will taste it yourself." Or, perhaps, there was a great dearth of fodder, when, through the number of his servants and his own careful forethought, he was enabled to get supplies for himself; at such times he would send to his friends in different parts, bidding them feed their horses on his hay, since it would not do for the horses that carried his friends to go starving. Then, on any long march or expedition, where the crowd of lookers-on would be large, he would call his friends to him and entertain them with serious talk, as much as to say, "These I delight to honour."

So that, for myself, and from all that I can hear, I should be disposed
to say that no one, Greek or barbarian, was ever so beloved. In proof
of this, I may cite the fact that, though Cyrus was the king's vassal and
slave, no one ever forsook him to join his master, if I may except the attempt of Orontas. That man, indeed, had to learn that Cyrus was
closer to the heart of him on whose fidelity he relied than he himself
was. On the other hand, many a man revolted from the king to Cyrus,
after they went to war with one another; nor were these nobodies, but
rather persons high in the king's affection; yet for all that, they believed
that their virtues would obtain a reward more adequate from Cyrus
than from the king. Another great proof at once of his own worth and of
his capacity rightly to discern all loyal, loving, and firm friendship is afforded by an incident which belongs to the last moment of his life. He
was slain, but fighting for his life beside him fell also every one of his
faithful bodyguard of friends and table-companions, with the sole exception of Ariaeus, who was in command of the cavalry on the left, and
he no sooner perceived the fall of Cyrus than he betook himself to
flight, with the whole body of troops under his lead.

10. Then the head of Cyrus and his right hand were severed from
the body. But the king and those about him pursued and fell upon the
Cyreian camp, and the troops of Ariaeus no longer stood their ground,
but fled through their own camp back to the halting-place of the night
before—a distance of thirteen miles, it was said. So the king and those
with him fell to ravaging right and left, and amongst other spoil he captured the Phocaean woman, who was a concubine of Cyrus, witty and
beautiful, it is said. The Milesian, who was the younger, was also seized
by some of the king's men; but, letting go her outer garment, she made
good her escape to the Hellenes, who had been left among the camp followers on guard. These fell at once into line and put to the sword many
of the pillagers, though they lost some men themselves; they stuck to
the place and succeeded in saving not only the woman, but all else,
whether chattels or human beings, which lay within their reach.

At this point the king and the Hellenes were something like three
miles apart; the one set were pursuing their opponents just as if their
conquest had been general; the others were pillaging as merrily as if
their victory were already universal. But when the Hellenes learned that
the king and his troops were in the baggage camp; and the king, on his
side, was informed by Tissaphernes that the Hellenes were victorious
in their quarter of the field, and had gone forward in pursuit, the effect

was instantaneous. The king massed his troops and formed into line. Clearchus summoned Proxenus, who was next him, and debated whether to send a detachment or to go in a body to the camp to save it.

Meanwhile the king was seen again advancing, as it seemed, from the rear; and the Hellenes, turning right about, prepared to receive his attack then and there. But, instead of advancing upon them at that point, he drew off, following the line by which he had passed earlier in the day, outside the left wing of his opponent, and so picked up in his passage those who had deserted to the Hellenes during the battle, as also Tissaphernes and his division. The latter had not fled in the first shock of the encounter; he had charged parallel to the line of the Euphrates into the Greek peltasts, and through them. But charge as he might, he did not lay low a single man. On the contrary, the Hellenes made a gap to let them through, hacking them with their swords and hurling their javelins as they passed. Episthenes of Amphipolis was in command of the peltasts, and he showed himself a sensible man, it was said. Thus it was that Tissaphernes, having got through haphazard, with rather the worst of it, failed to wheel round and return the way he came, but reaching the camp of the Hellenes, there fell in with the king; and falling into order again, the two divisions advanced side by side.

When they were parallel with the (original) left wing of the Hellenes, fear seized the latter lest they might take them in flank and enfold them on both sides and cut them down. In this apprehension they determined to extend their line and place the river on their rear. But while they deliberated, the king passed by and ranged his troops in line to meet them, in exactly the same position in which he had advanced to offer battle at the commencement of the engagement. The Hellenes, now seeing them in close proximity and in battle order, once again raised the paean and began the attack with still greater enthusiasm than before: and once again the barbarians did not wait to receive them, but took to flight, even at a greater distance than before. The Hellenes pressed the pursuit until they reached a certain village, where they halted, for above the village rose a mound, on which the king and his party rallied and reformed; they had no infantry any longer, but the crest was crowded with cavalry, so that it was impossible to discover what was happening. They did see, they said, the royal standard, a kind of golden eagle, with wings extended, perched on a bar of wood and raised upon a lance.

But as soon as the Hellenes again moved onwards, the hostile cavalry at once left the hillock—not in a body any longer, but in fragments— some streaming from one side, some from another; and the crest was gradually stripped of its occupants, till at last the company was gone. Accordingly, Clearchus did not ascend the crest, but posting his army at its base, he sent Lycius of Syracuse and another to the summit, with orders to inspect the condition of things on the other side, and to report results. Lycius galloped up and investigated, bringing back news that they were fleeing headlong. Almost at that instant the sun set. There the Hellenes halted; they grounded arms and rested, marvelling the while that Cyrus was not anywhere to be seen, and that no messenger had come from him. For they were in complete ignorance of his death, and conjectured that either he had gone off in pursuit, or had pushed forward to occupy some point. Left to themselves, they now deliberated, whether they should stay where they were and have the baggage train brought up, or should return to camp. They resolved to return, and about supper time reached the tents. Such was the conclusion of this day.

They found the larger portion of their property pillaged, eatables and drinkables alike, not excepting the waggons laden with corn and wine, which Cyrus had prepared in case of some extreme need overtaking the expedition, to divide among the Hellenes. There were 400 of these waggons, it was said, and these had now been ransacked by the king and his men; so that the greater number of the Hellenes went supperless, having already gone without their breakfasts, since the king had appeared before the usual halt for breakfast. Accordingly, in this situation they passed the night.

BOOK II

[In the previous book will be found a full account of the method by which Cyrus collected a body of Greeks when meditating an expedition against his brother Artaxerxes; as also of various occurrences on the march up; of the battle itself, and of the death of Cyrus; and lastly, a description of the arrival of the Hellenes in camp after the battle, and as to how they betook themselves to rest, supposing that they were altogether victorious and that Cyrus lived.][1]

I. At daybreak the generals met, and were surprised that Cyrus should not have appeared himself, or at any rate have sent some one to tell them what to do. Accordingly, they resolved to put what they had together, to get under arms, and to push forward until they effected junction with Cyrus. Just as they were on the point of starting, with the rising sun came Procles the ruler of Teuthrania. He was a descendant of Damaratus[2] the Laconian, and with him also came Glus the son of Tamos. These two told them, first, that Cyrus was dead; next, that Ariaeus had retreated with the rest of the barbarians to the halting-place whence they had started at dawn on the previous day; and wished to inform them that, if they intended to come, he would wait for this one day, but on the morrow he should return home again to Ionia, whence he came.

When they heard these tidings, the generals were sorely distressed; so too were the rest of the Hellenes when they were informed of it. Then Clearchus spoke as follows, "Would that Cyrus were yet alive! But since he is dead, take back this answer to Ariaeus, that we, at any rate, have conquered the king; and, as you yourselves may see, there is not a man left in the field to meet us. Indeed, had you not arrived, we should now have begun our march upon the king. Now, we can promise to Ariaeus that, if he will join us here, we will place him on the king's throne. Surely the rule belongs to those who conquer." With these words he sent back the messengers, and with them he sent Cheirisophus the Laconian, and Menon the Thessalian. That was what Menon himself wished, being, as he was, a friend and intimate of Ariaeus, and bound

[1] This summary, as well as those prefixed to other books, seems to be the work of a late editor.
[2] The Spartan king who was deposed in 491 B.C., whereupon he fled to King Darius, and settled in south-western Mysia.

by mutual ties of hospitality. So these set off, and Clearchus waited for them.

The soldiers furnished themselves with food as best they might—falling back on the baggage animals, and cutting up oxen and asses. There was no lack of firewood; they need only step forward a few paces from the line where the battle was fought, and they would find arrows to hand in abundance, which the Hellenes had forced the deserters from the king to throw away. There were arrows and wicker shields also, and the huge wooden shields of the Egyptians. There were many light shields also, and empty waggons left to be carried off. Here was a store which they were not slow to make use of to cook their meat and serve their meals that day.

It was now about full market hour when heralds from the king and Tissaphernes arrived. These were barbarians with one exception. This was a certain Phalinus, a Hellene who lived at the court of Tissaphernes, and was held in high esteem. He claimed to be an expert in tactics and the art of fighting with heavy arms. These were the men who now came up, and having summoned the generals of the Hellenes, they delivered the following message, "The great king having won the victory and slain Cyrus, bids the Hellenes to surrender their arms, to betake themselves to the gates of the king's palace, and there obtain for themselves what terms they can." That was what the heralds said, and the Hellenes listened with annoyance; but Clearchus spoke, and his words were few, "Conquerors do not, as a rule, give up their arms." Then turning to the others he added, "I leave it to you, my fellow-generals, to make the best and noblest answer, that you may, to these gentlemen. I will rejoin you presently." At the moment an official had summoned him to come and look at the entrails which had been taken out, for, as it chanced, he was engaged in sacrificing. As soon as he was gone, Cleanor the Arcadian, by right of seniority, answered, "They would sooner die than give up their arms." Then Proxenus the Theban said, "For my part, I marvel if the king demands our arms as our master, or for the sake of friendship merely, as presents. If as our master, why need he ask for them rather than come and take them? But if he wants to wheedle us out of them by fine speeches, he should tell us what the soldiers will receive in return for such kindness." In answer to him Phalinus said, "The king claims to have conquered, because he has put Cyrus to death; and who is there now to claim the kingdom as against himself? He further flatters himself that you also are in his power, since he holds you in the heart of his country, hemmed in by impassable rivers; and he can at any moment bring against you a multitude so vast that even if leave were given to rise and slay you could not kill them." After him Theopompus

the Athenian spoke. "Phalinus," he said, "at this instant, as you yourself can see, we have nothing left but our arms and our valour. If we
keep the former we imagine we can make use of the latter; but if we
deliver up our arms we shall presently be robbed of our lives. Do not
suppose then that we are going to give up to you the only good things
which we possess. We prefer to keep them; and by their help we will do
battle with you for the good things which are yours." Phalinus laughed
when he heard those words, and said, "Spoken like a philosopher, my
fine young man, and very pretty reasoning too; yet, let me tell you,
your wits are somewhat scattered if you imagine that your valour will
get the better of the king's power." There were one or two others, it was
said, who with a touch of weakness in their tone or argument, answered,
"They had proved good and trusty friends to Cyrus, and the king might
find them no less valuable. If he liked to be friends with them, he might
turn them to any use that pleased his fancy, say for a campaign against
Egypt. Their arms were at his service; they would help to lay that country at his feet."

Just then Clearchus returned, and wished to know what answer they
had given. The words were barely out of his mouth before Phalinus interrupting, answered, "As for your friends here, one says one thing
and one another; will you please give us your opinion." He replied,
"The sight of you, Phalinus, caused me much pleasure; and not only
me, but all of us, I feel sure; for you are a Hellene even as we are—
every one of us whom you see before you. In our present plight we
would like to take you into our counsel as to what we had better do
touching your proposals. I beg you then solemnly, in the sight of heaven,
—do you tender us such advice as you shall deem best and worthiest,
and such as shall bring you honour in after time, when it will be said of
you how once on a time Phalinus was sent by the great king to bid certain Hellenes yield up their arms, and when they had taken him into
their counsel, he gave them such and such advice. You know that whatever advice you do give us cannot fail to be reported in Hellas."

Clearchus threw out these leading remarks in hopes that this man,
who was the ambassador from the king, might himself be led to advise
them not to give up their arms, in which case the Hellenes would be
still more sanguine and hopeful. But, contrary to his expectation, Phalinus turned round and said, "I say that if you have one chance, one
hope in ten thousand to wage a war with the king successfully, do not
give up your arms. That is my advice. If, however, you have no chance
of escape without the king's consent, then I say save yourselves in the
only way you can." And Clearchus answered, "So, then, that is your deliberate view? Well, this is our answer, take it back. We conceive that

in either case, whether we are expected to be friends with the king, we shall be worth more as friends if we keep our arms than if we yield them to another; or whether we are to go to war, we shall fight better with them than without." And Phalinus said, "That answer we will repeat; but the king bade me tell you this besides, 'While you remain here there is truce; but one step forward or one step back, the truce ends; there is war.' Will you then please inform us as to that point also? Are you minded to stop and keep truce, or is there to be war? What answer shall I take from you?" And Clearchus replied, "Pray answer that we hold precisely the same views on this point as the king." "How say you the same views?" asked Phalinus. Clearchus answered, "As long as we stay here there is truce, but a step forward or a step backward, the truce ends; there is war." The other again asked, "Peace or war, what answer shall I make?" Clearchus returned answer once again in the same words, "Truce if we stop, but if we move forwards or backwards war." But what he really intended to do, that he refused to make further manifest.

2. Phalinus and those that were with him turned and went. But the messengers from Ariaeus, Procles, and Cheirisophus came back. As to Menon, he stayed behind with Ariaeus. They brought back this answer from Ariaeus, " 'There are many Persians,' he says, 'better than himself who will not suffer him to sit upon the king's throne; but if you wish to go back with him, you must join him this very night, otherwise he will set off himself to-morrow on the homeward route.' " And Clearchus said, "It had best stand thus between us then. If we come, well and good, be it as you propose; but if we do not come, do whatever you think most conducive to your interests." And so he kept these also in the dark as to his real intention.

After this, when the sun was already sinking, he summoned the generals and officers, and made the following statement, "Sirs, I sacrificed and found the victims unfavourable to an advance against the king. After all, it is not so surprising perhaps, for, as I now learn, between us and the king flows the river Tigris, navigable for big vessels, and we could not possibly cross it without boats, and boats we have none. On the other hand, to stop here is out of the question, for there is no possibility of getting provisions. However, the victims were quite agreeable to our joining the friends of Cyrus. This is what we must do then. Let each go away and sup on whatever he has. At the first sound of the horn to turn in, get kit and baggage together; at the second signal, place them on the baggage animals; and at the third, fall in and follow the lead, with the baggage animals on the inside protected by the river, and the troops outside." After hearing the orders, the generals and officers retired and did as they were bid; and for the future Clearchus led, and the rest followed in obedience to his orders, not that they had expressly chosen him, but they saw that he alone had the sense and wisdom requisite in a general, while the rest were inexperienced. [The total distance of the route, taking Ephesus in Ionia as the starting point up to the field of battle, consisted of ninety-three days' marches, 535 parasangs, or 16,050 furlongs; from the battle-field to Babylon (reckoned a three days' journey) would have been another 360 furlongs.]

Here, under cover of the darkness which descended, the Thracian Miltocythes, with forty horsemen and 300 Thracian infantry, deserted to the king; but the rest of the troops—Clearchus leading and the rest following in accordance with the orders promulgated—took their departure, and about midnight reached their first stage, having come up with Ariaeus and his army. They grounded arms just as they stood in rank, and the generals and officers of the Hellenes met in the tent of Ariaeus. There they exchanged oaths—the Hellenes on the one side and Ariaeus with his principal officers on the other—not to betray one another, but to be true to each other as allies. The Asiatics further solemnly pledged themselves by oath to lead the way without treachery. The oaths were ratified by the sacrifice of a bull, [a wolf] a boar, and a ram over a shield. The Hellenes dipped a sword, the barbarians a lance, into the blood of the victims.

As soon as the pledge was taken, Clearchus said, "And now, Ariaeus, since you and we have one expedition in prospect, will you tell us what you think about the route; shall we return the way we came, or have you devised a better?" He answered, "To return the same way is to perish to a man by hunger; for at this moment we have no provisions whatsoever. During the seventeen last days' marches, even on our way hither, we could extract nothing from the country; or, if there was now and again anything, we passed over and utterly consumed it. At this time our project is to take another and a longer journey certainly, but we shall not lack provisions. The earliest marches must be very long, as long as we can make them; the object is to put as large a space as possible between us and the royal army; once we are two or three days' journey off, the danger is over. The king will never overtake us. With a small army he will not dare to dog our heels, and with a vast equipment he will lack the power to march quickly. Perhaps he, too, may even find a scarcity of provisions. There," said he, "you asked for my opinion, see, I have given it."

Here was a plan of the campaign, which was equivalent to a stampede: they were to run away, or get into hiding somehow; but fortune proved a better general. For as soon as it was day they recommenced the journey, keeping the sun on their right, and calculating that at sunset they would have reached villages in the territory of Babylonia, and in this hope they were not deceived. While it was yet afternoon, they thought they caught sight of some of the enemy's cavalry; and those of the Hellenes who were not in rank ran to their ranks; and Ariaeus, who was riding in a waggon to nurse a wound, got down and donned his breastplate, the rest of his party following his example. While they were arming themselves, the scouts, who had been sent forward, came back with the information that they were not cavalry but baggage animals grazing. It was at once clear to all that they must be somewhere in the neighbourhood of the king's encampment. Smoke could actually be seen rising, evidently from villages not far ahead. Clearchus hesitated to advance upon the enemy, knowing that the troops were tired and hungry; and indeed it was already late. On the other hand he had no mind either to swerve from his route—guarding against any appearance of flight. Accordingly he marched straight ahead, and with sunset entered the nearest villages with his vanguard and took up quarters.

These villages had been thoroughly sacked and dismantled by the royal army—down to the very woodwork and furniture of the houses. Still, the vanguard contrived to take up their quarters in some sort of fashion; but the rear division, coming up in the dark, had to bivouac as best they could, one detachment after another; and a great noise they made, with hue and cry to one another, so that the enemy could hear them; and those in their immediate proximity actually took to their heels, left their quarters, and decamped, as was plain enough next morning, when not a beast was to be seen, nor sign of camp or wreath of smoke anywhere in the neighbourhood. The king, as it would appear, was himself quite taken aback by the advent of the army, as he fully showed by his proceedings next day.

During the progress of this night the Hellenes had their turn of scare, a panic seized them, and there was a noise and clatter, hardly to be explained except by the visitation of some sudden terror. But Clearchus had with him the Eleian Tolmides, the best herald of his time; him he ordered to proclaim silence, and then to give out this proclamation of the generals, "Whoever will give any information as to who let an ass into the camp shall receive a talent of silver in reward." On hearing this proclamation the soldiers made up their minds that their fear was baseless, and their generals safe and sound. At break of day Clearchus gave the order to the Hellenes to get under arms in line of battle, and take up exactly the same position as they held on the day of the battle.

3. And now comes the proof of what I stated above—that the king was utterly taken aback by the sudden apparition of the army; only

the day before, he had sent and demanded the surrender of their arms—and now, with the rising sun, came heralds sent by him to arrange a truce. These, having reached the advanced guard, asked for the generals. The guard reported their arrival; and Clearchus, who was busy inspecting the ranks, sent back word to the heralds that they must await his leisure. Having carefully arranged the troops so that from every side they might present the appearance of a compact battle line without a single unarmed man in sight, he summoned the ambassadors, and himself went forward to meet them with the soldiers, who for equipment and appearance were the best of his force, a course which he had told the other generals also to adopt.

And now, being face to face with the ambassadors, he questioned them as to what their wishes were. They replied that they had come to arrange a truce, and were persons competent to carry proposals from the king to the Hellenes and from the Hellenes to the king. He answered them, "Take back word then to your master, that we need a battle first, for we have had no breakfast; and he will be a brave man who will dare mention the word truce to Hellenes without providing them with breakfast." With this message the heralds rode off, but were back again in no time, which was a proof that the king, or some one appointed by him to transact the business, was hard by. They reported that the message seemed reasonable to the king; they had now come bringing guides who, if a truce were arranged, would conduct them where they would get provisions. Clearchus inquired whether the truce was offered to the individual men merely as they went and came, or to all alike. "To all," they replied, "until the king receives your final answer." When they had so spoken, Clearchus, having removed the ambassadors, held a council; and it was resolved to make a truce at once, and then quietly to go and secure provisions; and Clearchus said, "I agree to the resolution; still I do not propose to announce it at once, but to delay until the ambassadors begin to fear that we have decided against the truce; though I suspect," he added, "the same fear will operate on the minds of our soldiers also." As soon as the right moment seemed to have arrived, he delivered his answer in favour of the truce, and bade the ambassadors at once conduct them to the provisions.

So these led the way; and Clearchus, without relaxing precaution, in spite of having secured a truce, marched after them with his army in line and himself in command of the rearguard. Over and over again they encountered trenches and conduits so full of water that they could not be crossed without bridges; but they contrived well enough for these by means of trunks of palm trees which had fallen, or which they cut down for the occasion. And here Clearchus's system of command was

a study in itself; as he stood with a spear in his left hand and a stick
in the other; and when it seemed to him there was any dawdling among
the parties told off to the work, he would pick out the right man and
down would come the stick; nor, at the same time, was he above plunging into the mud and lending a hand himself, so that every one else was
forced for very shame to display equal alacrity. The men told off for
the business were the men up to thirty years of age; but even the elder
men, when they saw the energy of Clearchus, could not resist lending
their aid also. What stimulated the haste of Clearchus was the suspicion
in his mind that these trenches were not, as a rule, so full of water, since
it was not the season to irrigate the plain; and he fancied that the king
had let the water on for the express purpose of vividly presenting to the
Hellenes the many dangers with which their march was threatened at
the very start.

Proceeding on their way they reached some villages, where their guides
indicated to them that they would find provisions. They were found to
contain plenty of corn, and wine made from palm dates, and a sour beverage extracted from the same fruit by boiling. As to the palm nuts or
dates themselves, it was noticeable that the sort which we are accustomed to see in Hellas were set aside for the domestic servants; those
put aside for the masters are picked specimens, and marvellous for their
beauty and size, looking like lumps of amber; some specimens they dried
and preserved as sweetmeats. Sweet enough they were as an accompaniment of wine, but apt to give headache. Here, too, for the first time in
their lives, the men tasted the crown of the palm. No one could help being struck by the beauty of this object, and the peculiarity of its delicious flavour; but this, like the dried fruits, was exceedingly apt to give
headache. When this cabbage or crown has been removed from the palm
the whole tree withers from top to bottom.

In these villages they remained three days, and a deputation from
the great king arrived—Tissaphernes and the king's brother-in-law and
three other Persians—with a retinue of many slaves. As soon as the generals of the Hellenes had presented themselves, Tissaphernes opened the
proceedings with the following speech, through the lips of an interpreter,
"Men of Hellas, I am your next-door neighbour in Hellas. Therefore
was it that I, when I saw into what a sea of troubles you were fallen,
regarded it as a godsend, if by any means I might obtain, as a boon
from the king, the privilege of bringing you back in safety to your own
country: and that, I take it, will earn me gratitude from you and all
Hellas. In this determination I preferred my request to the king; I
claimed it as a favour which was fairly my due; for was it not I who
first announced to him the hostile approach of Cyrus? who supported

that announcement by the aid I brought; who alone among the officers confronted with the Hellenes in battle did not flee, but charged right through and united my troops with the king inside your camp, where he was arrived, having slain Cyrus; it was I, lastly, who gave chase to the barbarians under Cyrus, with the help of those here present with me at this moment, which also are among the trustiest followers of our lord the king. On hearing my proposals, he promised me to deliberate, and he bade me come, to ask you for what cause you marched against him. Now, I counsel you to give a moderate answer, so that it may be easier for me to carry out my design, if I may obtain from him some good thing in your behalf."

Thereupon the Hellenes retired and took counsel. Then they answered, and Clearchus was their spokesman, "We neither mustered as a body to make war against the king, nor was our march conducted with that object. But it was Cyrus, as you know, who invented many pretexts, that he might take you off your guard, and transport us hither. Yet, after a while, when we saw that he was in sore straits, we were ashamed in the sight of god and man to betray him, whom we had permitted for so long a season to benefit us. But now that Cyrus is dead, we set up no claim to his kingdom against the king himself; there is neither person nor thing for the sake of which we would care to injure the king's country; we would not choose to kill him if we could, rather we would march straight home, if we were not molested; but, god helping us, we will retaliate on all who injure us. On the other hand, if any be found to benefit us, we do not mean to be outdone in kindly deeds, as far as in us lies."

So he spoke, and Tissaphernes listened and replied, "That answer will I take back to the king and bring you word from him again. Until I come again, let the truce continue, and we will furnish you with a market." All next day he did not come back, and the Hellenes were troubled with anxieties, but on the third day he arrived with the news that he had obtained from the king the boon he asked; he was permitted to save the Hellenes, though there were many opponents who argued that it was not seemly for the king to let those who had marched against him depart in peace. And at last he said, "You may now, if you like, take pledges from us, that we will make the countries through which you pass friendly to you, and will lead you back without treachery into Hellas, and will furnish you with a market; and wherever you cannot purchase, we will permit you to take provisions from the district. You, on your side, must swear that you will march as through a friendly country, without damage—merely taking food and drink wherever we fail to supply a market—or, if we afford a market, you shall only obtain provisions by paying for them." This was agreed to, and oaths and pledges exchanged between them—Tissaphernes and the king's brother-in-law upon the one side, and the generals and officers of the Hellenes on the other. After this Tissaphernes said, "And now I go back to the king; as soon as I have transacted what I have a mind to, I will come back, ready equipped, to lead you away to Hellas, and to return myself to my own dominion."

4. After these things the Hellenes and Ariaeus waited for Tissaphernes, being encamped close to one another: for more than twenty days they waited, during which time there came visitors to Ariaeus, his brother and other kinsfolk. To those under him came certain other Persians, encouraging them and bearing pledges to some of them from the king himself—that he would bear no grudge against them on account of the part they bore in the expedition against him with Cyrus, or for aught else of the things which were past. While these overtures were being made, Ariaeus and his friends gave manifest signs of paying less attention to the Hellenes, so much so that, if for no other reason, the majority of the latter were not well pleased, and they came to Clearchus and the other generals, asking what they were waiting for. "Do we not know full well," they said, "that the king would give a great deal to destroy us, so that other Hellenes may take warning and think twice before they march against the king. To-day it suits his purpose to induce us to stop here, because his army is scattered; but as soon as he has got together another armament, he will most certainly attack us. How do we know he is not at this moment digging away at trenches, or running up walls, to make our path impassable. It is not to be supposed that he will desire us to return to Hellas with a tale how a handful of men like ourselves beat the king at his own gates, laughed him to scorn, and then came home again." Clearchus replied, "I too am keenly aware of all this; but I reason thus: if we turn our backs now, they will say, we mean war and are acting contrary to the truce, and then what follows? First of all, no one will furnish us with a market or means of providing ourselves with food. Next, we shall have no one to guide us; moreover, such action on our part will be a signal to Ariaeus to hold aloof from us, so that not a friend will be left to us; even those who were formerly our friends will now be numbered with our enemies. What other river, or rivers, we may find we have to cross, I do not know; but this we know, to cross the Euphrates in face of resistance is impossible. You see, in the event of being driven to an engagement, we have no cavalry to help us, but with the enemy it is the reverse—not only the most, but the best of his troops are cavalry, so that if we are victorious, we shall kill no one, but if we are defeated, not a man of us can escape. For my part, I cannot see why the king, who has so many advantages on his

side, if he desires to destroy us, should swear oaths and tender solemn pledges merely in order to perjure himself in the sight of heaven, to render his word worthless and his credit discreditable the wide world over." These arguments he propounded at length.

Meanwhile Tissaphernes came back, apparently ready to return home; he had his own force with him, and so had Orontas,[3] who was also present, his. The latter brought, moreover, his bride with him, the king's daughter, whom he had just wedded. The journey was now at length fairly commenced. Tissaphernes led the way, and provided a market. They advanced, and Ariaeus advanced too, at the head of Cyrus's Asiatic troops, side by side with Tissaphernes and Orontas, and with these two he also pitched his camp. The Hellenes, holding them in suspicion, marched separately with the guides, and they encamped on each occasion three miles apart, or rather more; and both parties kept watch upon each other as if they were enemies, which hardly tended to lull suspicion; and sometimes, while foraging for wood and grass and so forth on the same ground, blows were exchanged, which occasioned further embitterments. After three days' march they reached the wall of Media, as it is called, and passed within it. It was built of baked bricks laid in asphalt. It was twenty feet broad and 100 feet high, and the length of it was said to be sixty-six miles. It lies at no great distance from Babylon.

From this point they marched two days—twenty-six miles—and crossed two canals, the first by a regular bridge, the other spanned by a bridge of seven boats. These canals issued from the Tigris, and from them a whole system of minor trenches was cut, leading over the country, large ones to begin with, and then smaller and smaller, till at last they become the merest runnels, like those in Hellas used for watering millet fields. They reached the river Tigris. At this point there was a large and thickly populated city named Sittace, at a distance of two miles from the river. The Hellenes accordingly encamped by the side of that city, near a large and beautiful park, which was thick with all sorts of trees.

The Asiatics had crossed the Tigris, but somehow were entirely hidden from view. After supper, Proxenus and Xenophon were walking in front of the place where arms were stacked, when a man came up and demanded of the advanced guard where he could find Proxenus or Clearchus. He did not ask for Menon, and that too though he came from Ariaeus, who was Menon's friend. As soon as Proxenus had said, "I am he, whom you seek," the man replied, "I have been sent by Ariaeus and Artaozus, who have been trusty friends to Cyrus in past

---

[3] Satrap of Armenia.

days, and are your well-wishers. They warn you to be on your guard, in case the barbarians attack you in the night. There is a large body of troops in the neighbouring park. They also warn you to send and occupy the bridge over the Tigris, since Tissaphernes intends to break it down in the night, if he can, so that you may not cross, but be caught between the river and the canal." On hearing this they took the man to Clearchus and acquainted him with his statement. Clearchus, on his side, was much disturbed, and indeed alarmed at the news. But a young fellow who was present, struck with an idea, suggested that the two statements were inconsistent; as to the contemplated attack and the proposed destruction of the bridge. Clearly, the attacking party must either conquer or be worsted: if they conquer, what need of their breaking down the bridge? "Why! if there were many bridges," said he, "we should not be any the more able to save ourselves by flight—there would be no place to flee to; but, in the opposite case, suppose we win, with the bridge broken down, it is they who will not be able to save themselves by flight; and, what is worse for them, not a single one will be able to aid them from the other side, for all their numbers, since the bridge will be broken down."

Clearchus listened to the reasoning, and then he asked the messenger, "How large the country between the Tigris and the canal might be?" "A large district," he replied, "and in it are villages and cities numerous and large." Then it dawned upon them: the barbarians had sent the man with subtlety, in fear lest the Hellenes should cut the bridge and occupy the island territory, with the strong defences of the Tigris on the one side and of the canal on the other; supplying themselves with provisions from the country so included, large and rich as it was, with no lack of hands to till it; in addition to which, a harbour of refuge would be found for any one who wanted to do the king a mischief.

After this they retired to rest in peace, not, however, neglecting to send a guard to occupy the bridge in spite of all; but nothing happened, and there was no attack from any quarter whatsoever; nor did any of the enemy's people approach the bridges: so the guards were able to report next morning. But as soon as it was morning, they proceeded to cross the bridge, which consisted of thirty-seven vessels, and in so doing they used the utmost precaution possible; for reports were brought by some of the Hellenes with Tissaphernes that an attempt was to be made to attack them while crossing. All this turned out to be false, though it is true that while crossing they did catch sight of Glus watching, with some others, so see if they crossed the river; but as soon as he had satisfied himself on that point, he rode off and was gone.

From the river Tigris they advanced four days—sixty-six miles—

to the river Physcus, which is 100 feet broad and spanned by a bridge. Here lay a large and populous city named Opis, close to which the Hellenes were encountered by the bastard brother of Cyrus and Artaxerxes, who was leading a large army from Susa and Ecbatana to assist the king. He halted his troops and watched the Hellenes march past. Clearchus led them in column two abreast: and from time to time he marched and from time to time he halted. But every time the vanguard came to a standstill, just so long the effect repeated itself down along the whole line; so that even to the Hellenes themselves their army seemed enormous; and the Persian was fairly astonished at the spectacle.

From this place they marched through Media six days across desert —ninety-nine miles—to the villages of Parysatis, Cyrus's and the king's mother. These Tissaphernes, in mockery of Cyrus, delivered over to the Hellenes to plunder, except that the folk in them were not to be made slaves. They contained much corn, cattle, and other property. From this place they advanced four days across desert—sixty-six miles—keeping the Tigris on the left. On the first of these stages, on the other side of the river, lay a large city; it was a well-to-do place named Caenae, from which the natives used to carry across loaves and cheeses and wine on rafts made of skins.

5. After this they reached the river Zapatas, which is 400 feet broad, and here they halted three days. During the interval suspicions were rife, though no act of treachery displayed itself. Clearchus accordingly resolved to seek an interview with Tissaphernes, and if possible to bring to an end these feelings of mistrust, before they led to war. Consequently, he sent a messenger to the Persian to say that he desired an interview with him; to which the other readily consented. As soon as they were met, Clearchus spoke as follows, "Tissaphernes, I do not forget that oaths have been exchanged between us, and right hands shaken, in token that we will abstain from mutual injury; but I can see that you watch us narrowly, as if we were foes; and we, seeing this, watch you narrowly in return. But as I fail to discover, after investigation, that you are endeavouring to do us a mischief—and I am quite sure that nothing of the sort has ever entered our heads with regard to you —the best plan seemed to me to come and talk the matter over with you, so that, if possible, we might dispel the mutual distrust on either side. For I have known people before, the victims in some cases of calumny, or possibly of mere suspicion, who in apprehension of one another and eager to deal the first blow, have committed irreparable wrong against those who neither intended nor so much as harboured a thought of mischief against them. I have come to you under a conviction that such misunderstandings may best be put a stop to by personal inter-

course, and I wish to instruct you plainly that you are wrong in mistrusting us. The first and weightiest reason is that the oaths, which we took in the sight of heaven, are a barrier to mutual hostility. I envy not the man whose conscience tells him that he has disregarded these! For in a war with the gods, by what swiftness of foot can a man escape? In what quarter find refuge? In what darkness slink away and be hid? To what strong fortress scale and be out of reach? Are not all things in all ways subject to the gods? Is not their lordship over all alike outspread? As touching the gods, therefore, and our oaths, that is how I view this matter. To their safe keeping we consigned the friendship which we solemnly contracted. But turning to matters human, I look upon you as our greatest blessing in this present time. With you every path is plain to us, every river passable, and of provisions we shall know no stint. But without you, all our way is through darkness; for we know nothing concerning it, every river will be an obstacle, each multitude a terror; but, worst terror of all, the vast wilderness, so full of endless perplexity. Nay, if in a fit of madness we murdered you, what then? In slaying our benefactor should we not have challenged to enter the lists against us a more formidable antagonist in the king himself? Let me tell you, how many high hopes I should rob myself of, were I to take in hand to do you mischief.

"I wanted the friendship of Cyrus; I believed him to be abler than any man of his day to benefit those whom he chose; but now I look and it is you who are in his place; the power which belonged to Cyrus and his territory are yours now. You have them, and your own satrapy besides, safe and sound; while the king's power, which was a thorn in the side of Cyrus, is your support. This being so, it would be madness not to wish to be your friend. But I will go further and state to you the reasons of my confidence, that you on your side will desire our friendship. I know that the Mysians are a cause of trouble to you, and I flatter myself that with my present force I could render them obedient to you. This applies to the Pisidians also; and I am told there are many other such tribes besides. I think I can deal with them all; they shall cease from being a constant disturbance to your peace and prosperity. Then there are the Egyptians.[4] I know your anger against them to-day is very great. Nor can I see what better force you will find to help you in chastising them than this which marches at my back to-day. Again, if you seek the friendship of any of your neighbours round, there shall be no friend so great as you; if any one annoys you, with us as your faithful servitors you shall lord it over him; and such service will we

---

[4] We learn from Diodorus Siculus (xiv. 35) that the Egyptians had revolted from the Persians towards the end of the reign of Darius.

render you, not as hirelings merely for pay's sake, but for the gratitude which we shall rightly feel to you, to whom we owe our lives. As I dwell on these matters, I confess, the idea of your feeling mistrust of us is so astonishing, that I would give much to discover the name of the man, who is so clever of speech that he can persuade you that we harbour designs against you." Clearchus ended, and Tissaphernes responded thus:

"I am glad, Clearchus, to listen to your sensible remarks; for with the sentiments you hold, if you were to devise any michief against me, it could only be out of malevolence to yourself. But if you imagine that you, on your side, have any better reason to mistrust the king and me, than we you, listen to me in turn, and I will undeceive you. I ask you, does it seem to you that we lack the means, if we had the will, to destroy you? Have we not horsemen enough, or infantry, or whatever other arm you like, whereby we may be able to injure you, without risk of suffering in return? Or, possibly, do we seem to you to lack the physical surroundings suitable for attacking you? Do you not see all these great plains, which you find it hard enough to traverse even when they are friendly? And all yonder great mountain chains left for you to cross, which we can at any time occupy in advance and render impassable? And all those rivers, on whose banks we can deal craftily by you, checking and controlling and choosing the right number of you whom we care to fight! Nay, there are some which you will not be able to cross at all, unless we transport you to the other side.

"And if at all these points we were worsted, yet fire, as they say, is stronger than the fruit of the field: we can burn it down and call up famine in arms against you, against which you, for all your bravery, will never be able to contend. Why then, with all these avenues of attack, this machinery of war, open to us, not one of which can be turned against ourselves, why should we select from among them all that method, which alone in the sight of god is impious and of man abominable? Surely it belongs to people altogether without resources, who are helplessly struggling in the toils of fate, and are villains to boot, to seek accomplishment of their desires by perjury to heaven and faithlessness to their fellows. We are not so unreasoning, Clearchus, nor so foolish.

"Why, when we had it in our power to destroy you, did we not proceed to do it? Know well that the cause of this was nothing less than my passion to prove myself faithful to the Hellenes, and that, as Cyrus went up, relying on a foreign force attracted by payment, I in turn might go down strong in the same through service rendered. Various ways in which you Hellenes may be useful to me you yourself have mentioned, but there is one still greater. It is the great king's privilege alone to wear the tiara upright upon his head, yet in your presence it may be given to another mortal to wear it upright, here, upon his heart."

Throughout this speech he seemed to Clearchus to be speaking the truth, and he rejoined, "Then are not those worthy of the worst penalties who, in spite of all that exists to strengthen our friendship, endeavour by slander to make us enemies?" "Even so," replied Tissaphernes, "and if your generals and captains care to come in some open and public way, I will name to you those who tell me that you are plotting against me and the army under me." "Good," replied Clearchus. "I will bring all, and I will show you, on my side, the source from which I derive my information concerning you."

After this conversation Tissaphernes, with kindliest expressions, invited Clearchus to remain with him at the time, and entertained him at dinner. Next day Clearchus returned to the camp, and made no secret of his persuasion that he at any rate stood high in the affections of Tissaphernes, and he reported what he had said, insisting that those invited ought to go to Tissaphernes, and that any Hellene convicted of calumnious language ought to be punished, not only as traitors themselves, but as disaffected to their fellow-countrymen. The slanderer and traducer was Menon; so, at any rate, he suspected, because he knew that he had had meetings with Tissaphernes while he was with Ariaeus, and was factiously opposed to himself, plotting how to win over the whole army to him, as a means of winning the good graces of Tissaphernes. But Clearchus wanted the entire army to give its mind to no one else, and that refractory people should be put out of the way. Some of the soldiers protested: the captains and generals had better not all go; it was better not to put too much confidence in Tissaphernes. But Clearchus insisted so strongly that finally it was arranged for five generals to go and twenty captains. These were accompanied by about 200 of the other soldiers, who took the opportunity of marketing.

On arrival at the doors of Tissaphernes's quarters the generals were summoned inside. They were Proxenus the Boeotian, Menon the Thessalian, Agias the Arcadian, Clearchus the Laconian, and Socrates the Achaean; while the captains remained at the doors. Not long after, at one and the same signal, those within were seized and those without cut down; after which some of the barbarian horsemen galloped over the plain, killing every Hellene they encountered, bond or free. The Hellenes, as they looked from the camp, viewed that strange horsemanship with surprise, and could not explain to themselves what it all meant, until Nicarchus the Arcadian came fleeing for life with a wound in the belly, and clutching his entrails in his hands. He told them all that had happened. Instantly the Hellenes ran to their arms, one and all, in utter consternation, and fully expecting that the enemy would instantly be down upon the camp. However, they did not all come: only Ariaeus came, and Artaozus and Mithridates, who were Cyrus's most faithful friends; but the interpreter of the Hellenes said he saw and recognised the brother of Tissaphernes also with them. They had at their back other Persians also, armed with breastplates, as many as 300. As soon as they were within a short distance, they bade any general or captain of the Hellenes who might be there to approach and hear a message from the king. After this, two Hellene generals went out with all precaution. These were Cleanor the Orchomenian, and Sophaenetus the Stymphalian, attended by Xenophon the Athenian, who went to learn news of Proxenus. Cheirisophus was at the time away in a village with a party getting provisions. As soon as they had halted within earshot, Ariaeus said, "Hellenes, Clearchus being shown to have committed perjury and to have broken the truce, has suffered the penalty, and he is dead; but Proxenus and Menon, in return for having given information of his treachery, are in high esteem and honour. As to yourselves, the king demands your arms. He claims them as his, since they belonged to Cyrus, who was his slave." To this the Hellenes made answer by the mouth of Cleanor of Orchomenus, their spokesman, who said, addressing Ariaeus, "You villain, Ariaeus, and the rest of you, who were Cyrus's friends, have you no shame before god or man, first to swear to us you would have the same friends and the same enemies as we ourselves, and then to turn and betray us, making common cause with Tissaphernes, that most impious and villainous of men? With him you have murdered the very men to whom you gave your solemn oath, and to the rest of us turned traitors; and, having so done, you join hand with our enemies to come against us." Ariaeus answered, "There is no doubt but that Clearchus has been known for some time to harbour designs against Tissaphernes and Orontas, and all of us who side with them." Taking up this assertion, Xenophon said, "Well, then, granting that Clearchus broke the truce contrary to our oaths, he has his deserts, for perjurers deserve to perish; but where are Proxenus and Menon, our generals and your good friends and benefactors, as you admit? Send them back to us. Surely, just because they are friends of both parties, they will try to give the best advice for you and for us."

At this, the Asiatics stood discussing with one another for a long while, and then they went away without saying a word.

6. The generals who were thus seized were taken up to the king and there decapitated. The first of these, Clearchus, was a thorough soldier, and a true lover of fighting. This is the testimony of all who knew him intimately. As long as the war between the Lacedaemonians and Athe-

nians lasted, he could find occupation at home; but after the peace, he persuaded his own city that the Thracians were injuring the Hellenes, and having secured his object, set sail, empowered by the ephorate to make war upon the Thracians north of the Chersonese and Perinthus. But he had no sooner fairly started than, for some reason or other, the ephors changed their minds, and endeavoured to bring him back again from the isthmus. Thereupon he refused further obedience, and went off with sails set for the Hellespont. In consequence he was condemned to death by the Spartan authorities for disobedience to orders; and now, finding himself an exile, he came to Cyrus. Working on the feelings of that prince, in language described elsewhere, he received from his entertainer a present of 10,000 darics. Having got this money, he did not sink into a life of ease and indolence, but collected an army with it, carried on war against the Thracians and conquered them in battle, and from that date onwards harried and plundered them with war incessantly, until Cyrus wanted his army; whereupon he at once went off, in hopes of finding another sphere of warfare in his company.

These, I take it, were the characteristic acts of a man whose affections are set on warfare. When it is open to him to enjoy peace with honour, no shame, no injury attached, still he prefers war; when he may live at home at ease, he insists on toil, if only it may end in fighting; when it is given to him to keep his riches without risk, he would rather lessen his fortune by the pastime of battle. To put it briefly, war was his mistress; just as another man will spend his fortune on a favourite, or to gratify some pleasure, so he chose to squander his substance on soldiering.

But if the life of a soldier was a passion with him, he was none the less a soldier born, as herein appears; danger was a delight to him; he courted it, attacking the enemy by night or by day; and in difficulties he did not lose his head, as all who ever served in a campaign with him would with one consent allow. Was he equally good as a commander? It must be admitted that, as far as was compatible with his quality of temper, he was. Capable to a singular degree of devising how his army was to get supplies, and of actually getting them, he was also capable of impressing upon those about him that Clearchus must be obeyed; and that he brought about by the very hardness of his nature. With a scowling expression and a harshly-grating voice, he chastised with severity, and at times with such fury, that he was sorry afterwards himself for what he had done. Yet it was not without purpose that he punished; he had a theory that there was no good to be got out of an unchastened army. A saying of his is recorded to the effect that the soldier who is to mount guard and keep his hands off his friends, and be ready to dash without a moment's hesitation against the foe—must fear his commander more than the enemy. Accordingly, in any strait, this was the man whom the soldiers were eager to obey, and they would have no other in his place. The cloud which lay upon his brow, at those times lit up with brightness; his face became radiant, and the old sternness was so charged with vigour and knitted strength to meet the foe, that it savoured of salvation, not of cruelty. But when the pinch of danger was past, and it was open to them to go and taste subordination under some other officer, many forsook him. So lacking in grace of manner was he; but was ever harsh and savage, so that the feeling of the soldiers towards him was that of schoolboys to a master. In other words, though it was not his good fortune ever to have followers inspired solely by friendship or goodwill, yet those who found themselves under him, either by State appointment or through want, or other arch necessity, yielded him implicit obedience. From the moment that he led them to victory, the elements which went to make his soldiers efficient were numerous enough. There was the feeling of confidence in facing the foe, which never left them, and there was the dread of punishment at his hands to keep them orderly. In this way and to this extent he knew how to rule; but to play a subordinate part himself he had no great taste; so, at any rate, it was said. At the time of his death he must have been about fifty years of age.

Proxenus, the Boeotian, was of a different temperament. It had been the dream of his boyhood to become a man capable of great achievements. In obedience to this passionate desire it was, that he paid his fee to Gorgias of Leontini.[5] After enjoying that teacher's society, he flattered himself that he must be at once qualified to rule; and while he was on friendly terms with the leaders of the age, he was not to be outdone in reciprocity of service. In this mood he threw himself into the projects of Cyrus, and in return expected to derive from this essay the reward of a great name, large power, and wide wealth. But for all that he pitched his hopes so high, it was none the less evident that he would refuse to gain any of the ends he set before him wrongfully. Righteously and honourably he would obtain them, if he might, or else forego them. As a commander he had the art of leading gentlemen, but he failed to inspire adequately either respect for himself or fear in the soldiers under him. Indeed, he showed a more delicate regard for his soldiers than his subordinates for him, and he was indisputably more apprehensive of incurring their hatred than they were of disobeying him. The one thing needful to real and recognised generalship was, he thought, to praise the virtuous and to withhold praise from the evildoer. It can be easily

[5] The famous rhetorician whose fee was 100 minae.

understood, then, that of those who were brought in contact with him, the good and noble indeed were his well-wishers; but he laid himself open to the machinations of the base, who looked upon him as a person to be dealt with as they liked. At the time of his death he was only thirty years of age.

As to Menon the Thessalian, the mainspring of his action was obvious; what he sought after insatiably was wealth. Rule he sought after only as a stepping-stone to larger spoils. Honours and high estate he craved for simply that he might extend the area of his gains; and if he studied to be on friendly terms with the powerful, it was in order that he might commit wrong with impunity. The shortest road to the achievement of his desires lay, he thought, through false swearing, lying, and cheating; for in his vocabulary simplicity and truth were synonyms of folly. Natural affection he clearly entertained for nobody. If he called a man his friend, it might be looked upon as certain that he was plotting against him. Laughter at an enemy, he considered out of place, but his whole conversation turned upon the ridicule of his associates. In like manner, the possessions of his foes were secure from his designs, since it was no easy task, he thought, to steal from people on their guard; but it was his particular good fortune to have discovered how easy it is to rob a friend in the midst of his security. If it were a perjured person or a wrongdoer, he dreaded him as well armed and intrenched; but the honourable and the truth-loving he tried to practise on, regarding them as weaklings devoid of manhood. And as other men pride themselves on piety and truth and righteousness, so Menon prided himself on a capacity for fraud, on the fabrication of lies, on the mockery and scorn of friends. The man who was not a rogue he ever looked upon as only half educated. Did he aspire to the first place in another man's friendship, he set about his object by slandering those who stood nearest to him in affection. He contrived to secure the obedience of his soldiers by making himself an accomplice in their misdeeds, and the fluency with which he vaunted his own capacity and readiness for enormous guilt was a sufficient title to be honoured and courted by them. Or if any one stood aloof from him, he set it down as a meritorious act of kindness on his part that during their intercourse he had not destroyed him.

As to certain obscure charges brought against his character, these may certainly be fabrications. I confine myself to the following facts, which are known to all. He was in the bloom of youth when he procured from Aristippus the command of his mercenaries; he had not yet lost that bloom when he became exceedingly intimate with Ariaeus, a barbarian, whose passion for fair young men was the explanation; and before he had grown a beard himself, he had contracted a similar relationship with a bearded favourite named Tharypas. When his fellow-generals were put to death on the plea that they had marched with Cyrus against the king, he alone, although he had shared their conduct, was exempted from their fate. But after their deaths the vengeance of the king fell upon him, and he was put to death, not like Clearchus and the others by what would appear to be the speediest of deaths—decapitation—but, as report says, he lived for a year in pain and disgrace and died the death of a felon.

Agias the Arcadian, and Socrates the Achaean were both among those who were put to death. To the credit, be it said, of both, no one ever derided either as cowardly in war: no one ever had a fault to find with either on the score of friendship. They were both about thirty-five years of age.

BOOK III

[In the preceding pages of the narrative will be found a full account, not only of the doings of the Hellenes during the advance of Cyrus till the date of the battle, but of the incidents which befell them after Cyrus's death at the commencement of the retreat, while in company with Tissaphernes during the truce.]

1. After the generals had been seized, and the captains and soldiers who formed their escort had been killed, the Hellenes lay in deep perplexity—a prey to painful reflections. Here were they at the king's gates, and on every side about them were many hostile cities and tribes of men. Who was there now to furnish them with a market? Separated from Hellas by more than a thousand miles, they had not even a guide to point the way. Impassable rivers lay athwart their homeward route, and hemmed them in. Betrayed even by the Asiatics, at whose side they had marched with Cyrus to the attack, they were left in isolation. Without a single mounted trooper to aid them in pursuit: was it not perfectly plain that if they won a battle, their enemies would escape to a man, but if they were beaten themselves, not one soul of them would survive?

Haunted by such thoughts, and with hearts full of despair, but few of them tasted food that evening; but few of them kindled even a fire, and many never came into camp at all that night, but took their rest where each chanced to be. They could not close their eyes for very pain and yearning after their fatherlands or their parents, the wife or child whom they never expected to see again. Such was the plight in which each and all tried to seek repose.

Now there was in the army a certain man, an Athenian, Xenophon,[1] who had accompanied Cyrus, neither as a general, nor as an officer, nor yet as a private soldier, but simply on the invitation of an old friend, Proxenus. This old friend had sent to fetch him from home, promising, if he would come, to introduce him to Cyrus, "whom," said Proxenus, "I consider to be worth my fatherland and more to me."

Xenophon having read the letter, consulted Socrates the Athenian,[2]

[1] Xenophon has been mentioned, of course, more than once before; but he now steps upon the scene as the protagonist.
[2] This is Socrates the philosopher, Xenophon's teacher and friend.

271

whether he should accept or refuse the invitation. Socrates, who had a
suspicion that the State of Athens might in some way look askance at
any friendship with Cyrus, whose zealous co-operation with the Lacedaemonians against Athens in the war was not forgotten, advised Xenophon
to go to Delphi and there to consult the god as to the desirability of
such a journey. Xenophon went and put the question to Apollo, to which
of the gods he must pray and do sacrifice, so that he might best accomplish his intended journey and return in safety, with good fortune. Then
Apollo answered and told him to what gods he must sacrifice, and when
he had returned home he reported to Socrates the oracle. But he, when
he heard, blamed Xenophon that he had not, in the first instance, inquired of the god, whether it were better for him to go or to stay, but
had taken on himself to settle that point affirmatively, by inquiring
straightway, how he might best perform the journey. "Since, however,"
continued Socrates, "you did so put the question, you should do what
the god enjoined." Thus, and without further ado, Xenophon offered
sacrifice to those whom the god had named, and set sail on his voyage.
He overtook Proxenus and Cyrus at Sardis, when they were just ready
to start on the march up country, and was at once introduced to Cyrus.
Proxenus eagerly pressed him to stop—a request which Cyrus with like
ardour supported, adding that as soon as the campaign was over he
would send him home. The campaign referred to was understood to be
against the Pisidians. That is how Xenophon came to join the expedition,
deceived indeed, though not by Proxenus, who was equally in the dark
with the rest of the Hellenes, not counting Clearchus, as to the intended
attack upon the king. However, when they reached Cilicia, it was pretty
plain to all that the expedition was really against the king. Then, though
the majority were in apprehension of the journey, which was not at all
to their minds, yet, for very shame of one another and Cyrus, they continued to follow him, and with the rest went Xenophon.

And now in this season of perplexity, he too, with the rest, was in
great distress, and could not sleep; but presently, getting a little sleep,
he had a dream. It seemed to him in a vision that there was a storm of
thunder and lightning, and a bolt fell on his father's house, and thereupon the house was all in a blaze. He sprung up in terror, and pondering
the matter, decided that in part the dream was good: in that he had
seen a great light from Zeus, while in the midst of toil and danger. But
partly too he feared it, for evidently it had come from Zeus the king.
And the fire kindled all around—what could that mean but that he was
hemmed in by various perplexities, and so could not escape from the
country of the king? The full meaning, however, is to be discovered from
what happened after the dream.

This is what took place. As soon as he was fully awake, the first clear thought which came into his head was, Why am I lying here? The night advances; with the day, it is like enough, the enemy will be upon us. If we are to fall into the hands of the king, what is left us but to face the most horrible of sights, and to suffer the most fearful pains, and then to die, insulted, an ignominious death? To defend ourselves—to ward off that fate—not a hand stirs: no one is preparing, none cares; but here we lie, as though it were time to rest and take our ease. I too! What am I waiting for? A general to undertake the work? And from what city? Am I waiting till I am older myself and of riper age? Older I shall never be, if to-day I betray myself to my enemies.

Thereupon he got up, and called together first Proxenus's officers; and when they met, he said, "I am unable to sleep, nor can you, I fancy, nor lie here longer, when I see in what straits we are. Our enemy, we may be sure, did not open war upon us till he felt he had everything amply ready; yet none of us shows a corresponding anxiety to enter the lists of battle in the bravest style.

"And yet, if we yield ourselves and fall into the king's power, need we ask what our fate will be? This man, who, when his own brother, the son of the same parents, was dead, was not content with that, but severed head and hand from the body, and nailed them to a cross. We, then, who have not even the tie of blood in our favour, but who marched against him, meaning to make a slave of him instead of a king—and to slay him if we could: what is likely to be our fate at his hands? Will he not go all lengths so that, by inflicting on us the extreme of ignominy and torture, he may rouse in the rest of mankind a terror of ever marching against him any more? There is no question but that our business is to avoid by all means getting into his clutches.

"For my part, all the while the truce lasted, I never ceased pitying ourselves and congratulating the king and those with him, as, like a helpless spectator, I surveyed the extent and quality of their territory, the plenteousness of their provisions, the multitude of their dependents, their cattle, their gold, and their apparel. And then to turn and ponder the condition of our soldiers, without part or lot in these good things, except we bought it: few, I knew, had any longer the wherewithal to buy, and yet our oath held us down, so that we could not provide ourselves otherwise than by purchase. I say, as I reasoned thus, there were times when I dreaded the truce more than I now dread war.

"Now, however, that they have abruptly ended the truce, there is an end also to their own insolence and to our suspicion. All these good things of theirs are now set as prizes for the combatants. To whichever of us shall prove the better men, will they fall as prizes; and the gods

themselves are the judges of the strife. The gods, who surely will be on
our side, seeing it is our enemies who have taken their names falsely;
while we, with much to lure us, yet for our oath's sake, and the gods
who were our witnesses, sternly held aloof. So that, it seems to me, we
have a right to enter upon this contest with much more heart than our
foes; and further, we are possessed of bodies more capable than theirs
of bearing cold and heat and labour; souls too we have, by the help of
heaven, better and braver; nay, the men themselves are more vulnerable,
more mortal, than ourselves, if the gods grant us victory once again.

"However, for others are probably thinking the same things, let us
not, in god's name, wait for others to come and challenge us to noble
deeds; let us rather take the lead in stimulating the rest to valour. Show
yourselves to be the bravest of officers, and among generals, the worthiest to command. For myself, if you choose to start forward on this
quest, I will follow; or, if you bid me lead you, my age shall be no excuse
to stand between me and your orders. At least I am of full age, I take
it, to avert misfortune from my own head."

Such were the speaker's words; and the officers, when they heard, all,
with one exception, called upon him to put himself at their head. This
was a certain Apollonides there present, who spoke in the Boeotian dialect. This man's opinion was that it was mere nonsense for any one to
pretend they could obtain safety otherwise than by an appeal to the
king, if he had skill to enforce it; and at the same time he began to
dilate on the difficulties. But Xenophon cut him short. "O most marvellous of men, though you have eyes to see, you do not perceive; though
you have ears to hear, you do not recollect. You were present with the
rest of us now here when, after the death of Cyrus, the king, vaunting
himself on that occurrence, sent dictatorially to bid us lay down our
arms. But when we, instead of giving up our arms, put them on and
went and pitched our camp near him, his manner changed. It is hard
to say what he did not do, he was so at his wit's end, sending us embassies and begging for a truce, and furnishing provisions the while, until
he had got it. Or to take the contrary instance, when just now, acting
precisely on your principles, our generals and captains went, trusting to
the truce, unarmed to a conference with them, what came of it? What
is happening at this instant? Beaten, goaded with pricks, insulted, poor
souls, they cannot even die: though death, I think, would be very sweet.
And you, who know all this, how can you say that it is mere nonsense to
talk of self-defence? How can you bid us go again and try the arts of
persuasion? In my opinion, sirs, we ought not to admit this fellow to the
same rank with ourselves; rather ought we to deprive him of his cap-
taincy, and load him with packs and treat him as such. The man is a

disgrace to his own fatherland and the whole of Hellas, that, being a Hellene, he is what he is."

Here Agasias the Stymphalian broke in, exclaiming, "Nay, this fellow has no connection either with Boeotia or with Hellas, none whatever. I have noted both his ears bored like a Lydian's." And so it was. Him then they banished. But the rest visited the ranks, and wherever a general was left, they summoned the general; where he was gone, the lieutenant-general; and where again the captain alone was left, the captain. As soon as they were all met, they seated themselves in front of the encampment: the assembled generals and officers, numbering about 100. It was nearly midnight when this took place.

Thereupon Hieronymus the Eleian, the eldest of Proxenus's captains, commenced speaking as follows, "Generals and captains, it seemed right to us, in view of the present crisis, ourselves to assemble and to summon you, that we might advise upon some practicable course. Would you, Xenophon, repeat what you said to us?"

Thereupon Xenophon spoke as follows, "We all know only too well, that the king and Tissaphernes have seized as many of us as they could, and it is clear they are plotting to destroy the rest of us if they can. Our business is plain: it is to do all we can to avoid getting into the power of the barbarians; rather, if we can, we will get them into our power. Rely upon this then, all you who are here assembled, now is your great opportunity. The soldiers outside have their eyes fixed upon you; if they think that you are faint-hearted, they will turn cowards; but if you show them that you are making your own preparations to attack the enemy, and setting an example, to the rest—follow you, be assured, they will: imitate you they will. Probably it is but right and fair that you should somewhat excel them, for you are generals, you are commanders of brigades or of regiments; and if, while it was peace, you had the advantage in wealth and position, so now, when it is war, you are expected to rise superior to the common herd—to think for them, to toil for them, whenever there be need.

"At this very moment you would greatly aid the army, if you made it your business to appoint generals and officers to fill the places of those that are lost. For without leaders nothing good or noble, to put it concisely, was ever wrought anywhere; and in military matters this is absolutely true; for if discipline is held to be of saving virtue, the want of it has been the ruin of many ere now. Then, when you have appointed all the commanders necessary, it would only be opportune, I take it, if you were to summon the rest of the soldiers and to speak some words of encouragement. Even now, I daresay you noticed yourselves the crestfallen air with which they came into camp, the despondency with which they fell to picket duty, so that, unless there is a change for the better, I do not know for what service they will be fit; whether by night, if need were, or even by day. The thing is to get them to turn their thoughts to what they mean to do, instead of to what they are likely to suffer. Do that, and their spirits will soon revive wonderfully. You know, I need hardly remind you, it is not numbers or strength that gives victory in war; but, the gods helping them, to one or other of two combatants it is given to dash with stouter hearts to meet the foe, and such onset, in nine cases out of ten, those others refuse to meet. This observation, also, I have laid to heart, that they, who in matters of war seek in all ways to save their lives, are just they who, as a rule, die dishonourably; whereas they who, recognising that death is the common lot and destiny of all men, strive hard to die nobly: these more frequently, as I observe, do after all attain to old age, or, at any rate, while life lasts, they spend their days more happily. This lesson let all lay to heart this day, for we are just at such a crisis of our fate. Now is the season to be brave ourselves, and to stimulate the rest by our example."

With these words he ceased; and after him, Cheirisophus said, "Xenophon, hitherto I knew only so much of you as that you were, I heard, an Athenian, but now I must commend you for your words and for your conduct. I hope that there may be many more like you, for it would prove a public blessing. And now," said he, "let us waste no time; retire at once, I beg you, and choose leaders where you need them. After you have made your elections, come back to the middle of the camp, and bring the newly appointed officers. After that, we will there summon a general meeting of the soldiers. Let Tolmides, the herald," he added, "be in attendance." With these words on his lips he got up, in order that what was needful might be done at once without delay. After this the generals were chosen. These were Timasion the Dardanian, in place of Clearchus; Xanthicles, an Achaean, in place of Socrates; Cleanor, an Arcadian, in place of Agias; Philesius, an Achaean, in place of Menon; and in place of Proxenus, Xenophon the Athenian.

2. By the time the new generals had been chosen, the first glimmer of dawn had hardly commenced, as they met in the centre of the camp, and resolved to post an advance guard and to call a general meeting of the soldiers. Now, when these had come together, Cheirisophus the Lacedaemonian first rose and spoke as follows, "Fellow-soldiers, the present state of affairs is not pleasant, seeing that we are robbed of so many generals and captains and soldiers; and more than that, our former allies, Ariaeus and his men, have betrayed us; still, we must rise above our circumstances to prove ourselves brave men, and not give in, but try to save ourselves by glorious victory if we can; or, if not, at least die

gloriously, and never, while we have breath in our bodies, fall into the hands of our enemies. In which latter case, I fear, we shall suffer things, which I pray the gods may visit rather upon those we hate."

At this point Cleanor the Orchomenian stood up and spoke as follows, "You see, men, the perjury and the impiety of the king. You see the faithlessness of Tissaphernes, professing that he was next-door neighbour to Hellas, and would give a good deal to save us, in confirmation of which he took an oath to us himself, he gave us the pledge of his right hand, and then, with a lie upon his lips, this same man turned round and arrested our generals. He had no reverence even for Zeus, the god of strangers; but, after entertaining Clearchus at his own board as a friend, he used his hospitality to delude and decoy his victims. And Ariaeus, whom we offered to make king, with whom we exchanged pledges not to betray each other, even this man, without a particle of fear of the gods, or respect for Cyrus in his grave, though he was most honoured by Cyrus in lifetime, even he has turned aside to the worst foes of Cyrus, and is doing his best to injure the dead man's friends. Them may the gods requite as they deserve! But we, with these things before our eyes, will not any more be cheated and cajoled by them; we will make the best fight we can, and having made it, whatever the gods think fit to send, we will accept."

After him Xenophon arose; he was arrayed for war in his finest apparel. "For," said he to himself, "if the gods grant victory, the finest attire will match with victory best; or if I must needs die, then for one who has aspired to the noblest, it is well there should be some outward correspondence between his expectation and his end." He began his speech as follows, "Cleanor has spoken of the perjury and faithlessness of the barbarians, and you yourselves know them only too well, I fancy. If then we wish to enter a second time into terms of friendship with them, with the experience of what our generals, who in all confidence entrusted themselves to their power, have suffered, it is inevitable that we should feel deep despondency. If, on the other hand, we intend to take our swords in our hands and to inflict punishment on them for what they have done, and from this time forward will be on terms of downright war with them, then, god helping, we have many a bright hope of safety." The words were scarcely spoken when some one sneezed,[3] and with one impulse the soldiers bowed in worship; and Xenophon proceeded, "I move, gentlemen, since, even as we spoke of safety, an omen from Zeus the Saviour has appeared, we vow a vow to sacrifice to the Saviour thank-offerings for safe deliverance, wheresoever first we reach a friendly country; and let us couple with that vow another of individual assent, that

---

[3] This is an ancient omen of good luck.

we will offer to the rest of the gods according to our ability. Let all those who are in favour of this proposal hold up their hands." They all held up their hands, and there and then they vowed a vow and chanted the battle hymn. But as soon as these sacred matters were duly ended, he began once more thus, "I was saying that many and bright are the hopes we have of safety. First of all, we it is who confirm and ratify the oaths we take by heaven, but our enemies have taken false oaths and broken the truce, contrary to their solemn word. This being so, it is but natural that the gods should be opposed to our enemies, but with ourselves allied; the gods, who are able to make the great ones quickly small, and out of sore perplexity can save the little ones with ease, what time it pleases them. In the next place, let me recall to your minds the dangers of our own forefathers, that you may see and know that bravery is your heirloom, and that by the aid of the gods brave men are rescued even out of the greatest dangers. So was it when the Persians came, and their attendant hosts,[4] with a very great armament, to wipe out Athens from the face of the earth—the men of Athens had the heart to withstand them and conquered them. Then they vowed to Artemis that for every man they slew of the enemy, they would sacrifice to the goddess goats so many; and when they could not find sufficient for the slain, they resolved to offer yearly five hundred; and to this day they perform that sacrifice. And at a somewhat later date, when Xerxes assembled his countless hosts and marched upon Hellas, then[5] too our fathers conquered the forefathers of our foes by land and by sea.

"And proofs of these things are yet to be seen in trophies; but the greatest witness of all is the freedom of our cities, the liberty of that land in which you were born and bred. For you call no man master or lord; you bow your heads to none save to the gods alone. Such were your forefathers, and you are their sons. Think not I am going to say that you put to shame in any way your ancestry—far from it. Not many days since, you too were drawn up in battle face to face with these true descendants of their ancestors, and by the help of heaven you conquered them, though they many times outnumbered you. At that time, it was to win a throne for Cyrus that you showed your bravery; to-day, when the struggle is for your own salvation, what is more natural than that you should show yourselves braver and more zealous still. Nay, it is very right you should be more undaunted still to-day to face the foe. The other day, though you had not tested them, and before your eyes

---

[4] The allusion is to the invasion of Greece by Datis and Artaphernes, and to their defeat at Marathon, 490 B.C. Herodotus estimates the number of those who fell on the Persian side at 6,400 men.

[5] At Salamis, 480 B.C., and at Plataea 479 B.C.

lay their immeasurable host, you had the heart to go against them with the spirit of your fathers. To-day you have made trial of them, and knowing that, however many times your number, they do not care to await your onset, what concern have you now to be afraid of them?

"Nor let any one suppose that herein is a point of weakness, in that Cyrus's troops, who before were drawn up by your side, have now deserted us, for they are even worse cowards still than those we worsted. At any rate they have deserted us, and sought refuge with them. Leaders of the forlorn hope of flight—far better is it to have them brigaded with the enemy than shoulder to shoulder in our ranks. But if any of you is out of heart to think that we have no cavalry, while the enemy have many squadrons to command, lay to heart this doctrine, that 10,000 horse equal only the 10,000 men upon their backs, neither less nor more. Did any one ever die in battle from the bite or kick of a horse? It is the men, the real swordsmen, who do whatever is done in battles. In fact we, on our stout shanks, are better mounted than those cavalry fellows; there they hang on to their horses' necks in mortal dread, not only of us, but of falling off; while we, well planted upon earth, can deal far heavier blows to our assailants, and aim more steadily at whom we will. There is one point, I admit, in which their cavalry have the whip-hand of us; it is safer for them than it is for us to run away.

"Maybe, however, you are in good heart about the fighting, but annoyed to think that Tissaphernes will not guide us any more, and that the king will not furnish us with a market any longer. Now, consider, is it better for us to have a guide like Tissaphernes, whom we know to be plotting against us, or to take our chance of the stray people whom we catch and compel to guide us, who will know that any mistake made in leading us will be a sad mistake for their own lives? Again, is it better to be buying provisions in a market of their providing, in scant measure and at high prices, without even the money to pay for them any longer; or, by right of conquest, to help ourselves, applying such measure as suits our fancy best?

"Or again, perhaps you admit that our present position is not without its advantages, but you feel sure that the rivers are a difficulty, and think that you were never more taken in than when you crossed them; if so, consider whether, after all, this is not perhaps the most foolish thing which the barbarians have done. No river is impassable throughout; whatever difficulties it may present at some distance from its source, you need only make your way up to the springhead, and there you may cross it without wetting more than your ankles. But, granted that the rivers do bar our passage, and that guides are not forthcoming, what care we? We need feel no alarm for all that. We have heard of the

Mysians, a people whom we certainly cannot admit to be better than ourselves; and yet they inhabit numbers of large and prosperous cities in the king's own country without asking leave. The Pisidians are an equally good instance, or the Lycaonians. We have seen with our own eyes how they fare: seizing fortresses down in the plains, and reaping the fruits of these men's territory. As to us, I go so far as to assert, we ought never to have let it be seen that we were bent on getting home: at any rate, not so soon; we should have begun stocking and furnishing ourselves, as if we fully meant to settle down for life somewhere or other hereabouts. I am sure that the king would be thrice glad to give the Mysians as many guides as they like, or as many hostages as they care to demand, in return for a safe conduct out of his country; he would make carriage roads for them, and if they preferred to take their departure in four-horse chariots, he would not say them nay. So too, I am sure, he would be only too glad to accommodate us in the same way, if he saw us preparing to settle down here. But, perhaps, it is just as well that we did not stop; for I fear, if once we learn to live in idleness and in luxury and dalliance with these tall and handsome Median and Persian women and maidens, we shall be like the Lotus-eaters, and forget the road home altogether.

"It seems to me that it is only right, in the first instance, to make an effort to return to Hellas and to revisit our hearths and homes, if only to prove to other Hellenes that it is their own faults if they are poor and needy, seeing it is in their power to give to those now living a pauper life at home a free passage hither, and convert them into rich men at once. Now, sirs, is it not clear that all these good things belong to whoever has strength to hold them?

"Let us look another matter in the face. How are we to march most safely? Or where blows are needed, how are we to fight to the best advantage? That is the question.

"The first thing which I recommend is to burn the waggons we have, so that we may be free to march wherever the army needs, and not, practically, make our baggage train our general. And, next, we should throw our tents into the bonfire also: for these again are only a trouble to carry, and do not contribute one grain of good either for fighting or getting provisions. Further, let us get rid of all superfluous baggage, save only what we require for the sake of war, or meat and drink, so that as many of us as possible may be under arms, and as few as possible doing porterage. I need not remind you that, in case of defeat, the owners' goods are not their own; but if we master our foes, we will make them our baggage bearers.

"It only rests for me to name the one thing which I look upon as the greatest of all. You see, the enemy did not dare to bring war to bear upon us until they had first seized our generals; they felt that while our rulers were there, and we obeyed them, they were no match for us in war; but having got hold of them, they fully expected that the consequent confusion and anarchy would prove fatal to us. What follows? This: Officers and leaders ought to be more vigilant even than their predecessors; subordinates still more orderly and obedient to those in command now than even they were to those who are gone. And you should pass a resolution that, in case of insubordination, any one who stands by is to aid the officer in chastising the offender. So the enemy will be mightily deceived; for on this day they will behold 10,000 Clearchuses instead of one, who will not suffer one man to play the coward. And now it is high time I brought my remarks to an end, for may be the enemy will be here soon. Let those who are in favour of these proposals confirm them with all speed, that they may be realised in fact; or if any other course seem better, let not any one, even though he be a private soldier, shrink from proposing it. Our common safety is our common need."

After this Cheirisophus said, "If there is anything else to be done, beyond what Xenophon has mentioned, we shall be able to carry it out presently; but with regard to what he has already proposed, it seems to me the best course to vote upon the matters at once. Those who are in favour of Xenophon's proposals, hold up their hands." They all held them up. Xenophon rose again and said, "Listen, men, while I tell you what I think we have need of besides. It is clear that we must march where we can get provisions. Now, I am told there are some splendid villages not more than two miles and a half distant. I should not be surprised, then, if the enemy were to hang on our heels and dog us as we retire, like cowardly curs which rush out at the passer-by and bite him if they can, but when you turn upon them they run away. Such will be their tactics, I take it. It may be safer, then, to march in a hollow square, so as to place the baggage animals and our mob of camp-followers in greater security. It will save time to make the appointments at once, and to settle who leads the square and directs the vanguard; who will take command of the two flanks, and who of the rearguard; so that, when the enemy appears, we shall not need to deliberate, but can at once set in motion the machinery in existence.

"If any one has any better plan, we need not adopt mine; but if not, suppose Cheirisophus takes the lead, as he is a Lacedaemonian, and the two eldest generals take in charge the two wings respectively, whilst Timasion and I, the two youngest, will for the present guard the rear. For the rest, we can but make experiment of this arrangement, and

alter it with deliberation, as from time to time any improvement suggests
itself. If any one has a better plan to propose, let him do so." No dissenting voice was heard. Accordingly he said, "Those in favour of this resolution, hold up their hands." The resolution was carried. "And now,"
said he, "it would be well to separate and carry out what we have decreed. If any of you has set his heart on seeing his friends again, let
him remember to prove himself a man; there is no other way to achieve
his heart's wish. Or is mere living an object with any of you, strive to
conquer; if to slay is the privilege of victory, to die is the doom of the
defeated. Or perhaps to gain money and wealth is your ambition, strive
again for mastery; have not conquerors the double gain of keeping what
is their own, while they seize the possessions of the vanquished?"

3. The speaking was ended; they got up and retired; then they burned
the waggons and the tents, and after sharing with one another what each
needed out of their various superfluities, they threw the remnant into
the fire. Having done that, they proceeded to make their breakfasts.
While they were breakfasting, Mithridates came with about thirty horsemen, and summoning the generals within earshot, he thus addressed
them, "Men of Hellas, I have been faithful to Cyrus, as you know well,
and to-day I am your well-wisher; indeed, I am here spending my days
in great fear: if then I could see any salutary course in prospect, I should
be disposed to join you with all my retainers. Please inform me, then,
as to what you propose, regarding me as your friend and well-wisher,
anxious only to pursue his march in your company." The generals held
council, and resolved to give the following answer, Cheirisophus acting
as spokesman, "We have resolved to make our way through the country,
inflicting the least possible damage, provided we are allowed a free passage homewards; but if any one tries to hinder us, he will have to fight
it out with us, and we shall bring all the force in our power to bear."
Thereat Mithridates set himself to prove to them that their deliverance,
except with the king's good pleasure, was hopeless. Then the meaning
of his mission was plain. He was an agent in disguise; in fact, a relation
of Tissaphernes was in attendance to keep a check on his loyalty. After
that, the generals resolved that it would be better to proclaim open war,
without truce or herald, as long as they were in the enemy's country;
for they used to come and corrupt the soldiers, and they were even
successful with one officer—Nicarchus, an Arcadian, who went off in the
night with about twenty men.

After this, they breakfasted and crossed the river Zapatas, marching
in regular order, with the beasts and mob of followers in the middle.
They had not advanced far on their route when Mithridates made his
appearance again, with about 200 horsemen at his back, and bowmen

and slingers twice as many, very nimble and active fellows. He approached the Hellenes as if he were friendly; but when they had got fairly to close quarters, all of a sudden some of them, whether mounted or on foot, began shooting with their bows and arrows, and another set with slings, wounding the men. The rearguard of the Hellenes suffered for a while severely without being able to retaliate, for the Cretans had a shorter range than the Persians, and at the same time, being light-armed troops, they lay cooped up within the ranks of the heavy infantry, while the javelin men again did not shoot far enough to reach the enemy's slingers. This being so, Xenophon thought there was nothing for it but to charge, and charge they did; some of the heavy and light infantry, who were guarding the rear, with him; but for all their charging they did not catch a single man.

The dearth of cavalry told against the Hellenes; nor were their infantry able to overhaul the enemy's infantry, with the long start they had, and considering the shortness of the race, for it was out of the question to pursue them far from the main body of the army. On the other hand, the Asiatic cavalry, even while fleeing, poured volleys of arrows behind their backs, and wounded the pursuers; while the Hellenes must fall back fighting every step of the way they had measured in the pursuit; so that by the end of that day they had not gone much more than three miles; but in the late afternoon they reached the villages.

Here there was a return of the old despondency. Cheirisophus and the eldest of the generals blamed Xenophon for leaving the main body to give chase and endangering himself thereby, while he could not damage the enemy one whit the more. Xenophon admitted that they were right in blaming him: no better proof of that was wanted than the result. "The fact is," he added, "I was driven to pursue; it was too trying to look on and see our men suffer so badly, and be unable to retaliate. However, when we did charge, there is no denying the truth of what you say; we were not a whit more able to injure the enemy, while we had considerable difficulty in beating a retreat ourselves. Thank heaven they did not come upon us in any great force, but were only a handful of men; so that the injury they did us was not large, as it might have been; and at least it has served to show us what we need. At present the enemy shoot and sling beyond our range, so that our Cretan archers are no match for them; our hand-throwers cannot reach as far; and when we pursue, it is not possible to push the pursuit to any great distance from the main body, and within the short distance no foot-soldier, however fleet of foot, could overtake another foot-soldier who has a bow-shot the start of him. If, then, we are to exclude them from all possibility of injuring us as we march, we must get slingers as soon as possible and cavalry. I am told there are in the army some Rhodians, most of whom, they say, know how to sling, and their missile will reach even twice as far as the Persian slings (which, on account of their being loaded with stones as big as one's fist, have a comparatively short range; but the Rhodians are skilled in the use of leaden bullets). Suppose, then, we investigate and find out first of all who among them possess slings, and for these slings offer the owner the money value; and to another, who will plait some more, hand over the money price; and for a third, who will volunteer to be enrolled as a slinger, invent some other sort of privilege, I think we shall soon find people to come forward capable of helping us. There are horses in the army, I know; some few with myself, others belonging to Clearchus's stud, and a good many others captured from the enemy, used for carrying baggage. Let us take the pick of these, supplying their places by ordinary baggage animals, and equipping the horses for cavalry. I should not wonder if our troopers gave some annoyance to these fugitives."

These proposals were carried, and that night 200 slingers were enrolled, and next day as many as fifty horse and horsemen passed muster as duly qualified; buff jackets and breastplates were provided for them, and a commandant of cavalry appointed to command—Lycius, the son of Polystratus, by name, an Athenian.

4. That day they remained inactive, but the next they rose earlier than usual, and set out, for they had a ravine to cross, where they feared the enemy might attack them in the act of crossing. When they were across, Mithridates appeared again with 1,000 horse, and archers and slingers to the number of 4,000. This whole body he had got by request from Tissaphernes, and in return he undertook to deliver up the Hellenes to Tissaphernes. He had grown contemptuous since his late attack, when, with so small a detachment, he had done, as he thought, a good deal of mischief, without the slightest loss to himself.

When the Hellenes were not only right across, but had got about a mile from the ravine, Mithridates also crossed with his forces. An order had been passed down the lines, what light infantry and what heavy infantry were to take part in the pursuit; and the cavalry were instructed to follow up the pursuit with confidence, as a considerable support was in their rear. So, when Mithridates had come up with them, and they were well within arrow and sling shot, the trumpet sounded the signal to the Hellenes; and immediately the detachment under orders rushed to close quarters, and the cavalry charged. There the enemy preferred not to wait, but fled towards the ravine. In this pursuit the Asiatics lost several of their infantry killed, and of their cavalry as many as eighteen were taken prisoners in the ravine. As to those who were slain the Hellenes, acting upon impulse, mutilated their bodies, by way of impressing their enemy with as frightful an image as possible.

So fared the foe and so fell back; but the Hellenes, continuing their march in safety for the rest of that day, reached the river Tigris. Here they came upon a large deserted city, the name of which was Larissa: a place inhabited by the Medes in days of old; the breadth of its walls was twenty-five feet, and the height of them 100, and the circuit of the whole six miles. It was built of clay-bricks, supported on a stone basis twenty feet high. This city the king of the Persians[6] besieged, when the Persians strove to snatch their empire from the Medes, but he could in no way take it; then a cloud hid the face of the sun and blotted out the light thereof, until the inhabitants were gone out of the city, and so it was taken. By the side of this city there was a stone pyramid in breadth 100 feet, and in height 200 feet; in it were many of the barbarians who had fled for refuge from the neighbouring villages.

From this place they marched one stage of twenty miles to a great deserted fortress [which lay over against the city], and the name of that city was Mespila. The Medes once dwelt in it. The basement was made of polished stone full of shells; fifty feet was the breadth of it, and fifty feet the height; and on this basement was reared a wall of brick, the breadth whereof was fifty feet and the height 400; and the circuit of the wall was twenty miles. Hither, as the story goes, Medea,[7] the king's wife, fled when the Medes lost their empire at the hands of the Persians. To this city also the king of the Persians laid siege, but could not take it either by length of days or strength of hand. But Zeus terrified the inhabitants with thunder, and so it was taken.

From this place they marched one day—thirteen miles. But, while still on this march, Tissaphernes made his appearance. He had with him his own cavalry and a force belonging to Orontas, who had the king's daughter to wife; and there were, moreover, with them the Asiatics whom Cyrus had taken with him on his march up; together with those whom the king's brother had brought as a reinforcement to the king; besides those whom Tissaphernes himself had received as a gift from the king, so that the armament appeared to be very great. When they were close, he halted some of his regiments at the rear and wheeled others into position on either flank, but hesitated to attack, having no mind apparently to run any risks, and contenting himself with an order to his slingers to sling and his archers to shoot. But when the Rhodian slingers and the bowmen, posted at intervals, retaliated, and every shot told (for with the utmost pains to miss it would have been hard to do so

[6] Cyrus the Great.
[7] The wife of Astyages, the last king of Media.

under the circumstances), then Tissaphernes with all speed retired out of range, the other regiments following suit; and for the rest of the day the one party advanced and the other followed. But now the Asiatics had ceased to be dangerous with their sharpshooting. For the Rhodians could reach further than the Persian slingers, or, indeed, than most of the bowmen. The Persian bows are of great size, so that the Cretans found the arrows which were picked up serviceable, and persevered in using their enemies' arrows, and practised shooting with them, letting them fly upwards to a great height. There were also plenty of bowstrings found in the villages—and lead, which they turned to account for their slings. As the result of this day, then, the Hellenes chancing upon some villages had no sooner encamped than the barbarians fell back, having had distinctly the worst of it in the skirmishing.

The next was a day of inaction: they halted and took in supplies, as there was much corn in the villages; but on the day following, the march was continued through the plain (of the Tigris), and Tissaphernes still hung on their rear with his skirmishers. And now it was that the Hellenes discovered the defect of marching in a square with an enemy following. As a matter of necessity, whenever the wings of an army so disposed draw together, either where a road narrows, or hills close in, or a bridge has to be crossed, the heavy infantry cannot help being squeezed out of their ranks, and march with difficulty, partly from actual pressure, and partly from the general confusion that ensues; and once thrown into disorder that arm is practically useless. Or, supposing the wings are again extended, the troops have hardly recovered from their former distress before they are pulled asunder, and there is a wide space between the wings, and the men concerned lose confidence in themselves, especially with an enemy close behind. What happened, when a bridge had to be crossed or other passage effected, was, that each unit of the force pressed on in anxiety to get over first, and at these moments it was easy for the enemy to make an attack. The generals accordingly, having recognised the defect, set about curing it. To do so, they made six divisions of 100 men apiece, each of which had its own set of captains and under-officers in command of half and quarter companies. It was the duty of these new companies, during a march, whenever the flanks needed to close in, to fall back to the rear, so as to disencumber the wings. This they did by wheeling clear of them. When the sides of the oblong again extended, they filled up the interstices, if the gap were narrow, by columns of companies, if broader, by columns of half companies, or, if broader still, by columns of quarter companies, so that the space between was always filled up. If again it were necessary to effect a passage by a bridge or otherwise, there was no confusion, the several companies crossing in turns; or, if the occasion arose to form in line of battle, these companies came up to the front and fell in.

In this way they advanced four days, but before the fifth was completed, they came in sight of a palace of some sort, with villages clustered round it; they could further see that the road leading to this place pursued its course over high undulating hillocks, the spur of the mountain range, under which lay the village. These knolls were a welcome sight to the Hellenes, naturally enough, as the enemy were cavalry. However, when they had issued from the plain and ascended the first crest, and were in the act of descending it so as to mount the next, at this juncture the barbarians came upon them. From the high ground down the sheer steep they poured a volley of darts, sling-stones, and arrows, which they discharged under the lash, wounding many, until they got the better of the Hellenic light troops, and drove them for shelter behind the heavy infantry, so that this day that arm was altogether useless, huddling in the mob of sutlers, both slingers and archers alike.

But when the Hellenes, being so pressed, made an attempt to pursue, they could barely scale to the summit, being heavy-armed troops, while the enemy as lightly sprung away; and they suffered similarly in retiring to join the rest of the army. And then, on the second hill, the whole had to be gone through again; so that when it came to the third hillock, they determined not to move the main body of troops from their position until they had brought up a division of light infantry from the right flank of the square to a point on the mountain range. When this detachment were once posted above their pursuers, the latter desisted from attacking the main body in its descent, for fear of being cut off and finding themselves between two assailants. Thus the rest of the day they moved on in two divisions: one set keeping to the road by the hillocks, the other marching parallel on the higher level along the mountains; and thus they reached the villages and appointed eight surgeons to attend to the many wounded.

Here they halted three days for the sake of the wounded chiefly, while a further inducement was the plentiful supply of provisions which they found, wheat and wine, and large stores of barley laid up for horses. These supplies had been collected by the ruling satrap of the country. On the fourth day they began their descent into the plain; but when Tissaphernes with his force overtook them, necessity taught them to camp in the first village they caught sight of, and give over the attempt of marching and fighting simultaneously, as so many were *hors de combat,* being either on the list of wounded themselves, or else engaged in carrying the wounded, or laden with the heavy arms of those so occupied. But when they were once encamped, and the barbarians, advancing upon the village, made an attempt to harass them with their sharp-shooters, the superiority of the Hellenes was pronounced. To sustain a running fight with an enemy constantly attacking was one thing; to keep him at arm's length from a fixed base of action another: and the difference was much in their favour.

But when it was late afternoon, the time had come for the enemy to withdraw, since the habit of the barbarian was never to encamp within seven or eight miles of the Hellenic camp. This he did in apprehension of a night attack, for a Persian army is good for nothing at night. Their horses are haltered, and, as a rule, hobbled as well, to prevent their escaping, as they might if loose; so that, if any alarm occurs, the trooper has to saddle and bridle his horse, and then he must put on his own breastplate, and then mount—all which performances are difficult at night and in the midst of confusion. For this reason they always encamped at a distance from the Hellenes.

When the Hellenes perceived that they were preparing to retire, and that the order was being given, the herald's cry, "Pack up for starting," might be heard before the enemy was fairly out of earshot. For a while the Asiatics paused, as if unwilling to be gone; but as night closed in, off they went, for it did not suit their notions of expediency to set off on a march and arrive by night. And now, when the Hellenes saw that they were really and clearly gone, they too broke up their camp and pursued their march till they had traversed seven and a half miles. Thus the distance between the two armies grew to be so great, that the next day the enemy did not appear at all, nor yet the third day; but on the fourth the barbarians had pushed on by a forced night march and occupied a commanding position on the right, where the Hellenes had to pass. It was a narrow mountain spur overhanging the descent into the plain.

But when Cheirisophus saw that this ridge was occupied, he summoned Xenophon from the rear, bidding him at the same time to bring up the peltasts to the front. That Xenophon hesitated to do, for Tissaphernes and his whole army were coming up and were well within sight. Galloping up to the front himself, he asked, "Why do you summon me?" The other answered him, "The reason is plain; look yonder; this crest which overhangs our descent has been occupied. There is no passing, until we have dislodged these fellows; why have you not brought up the light infantry?" Xenophon explained: —he had not thought it desirable to leave the rear unprotected, with an enemy appearing in the field of view. "However, it is time," he added, "to decide how we are to dislodge these fellows from the crest." At this moment his eye fell on the peak of the mountain, rising immediately above their army, and he could see an approach leading from it to the crest in question where the enemy lay. He exclaimed: "The best thing we can do, Cheirisophus, is to make a dash at the height itself, and with what speed we may. If we take it, the party in command of the road will never be able to stop us. If you like, stay in command of the army, and I will go; or, if you prefer, do you go at the mountain, and I will stay here." "I leave it to you," Cheirisophus answered, "to choose which you like best." Xenophon remarking, "I am the younger," elected to go; but he stipulated for a detachment from the front to accompany him, since it was a long way to fetch up troops from the rear. Accordingly Cheirisophus furnished him with the light infantry from the front, reoccupying their place by those from the centre. He also gave him, to form part of the detachment, the 300 of the picked corps[8] under his own command at the head of the square.

They set out from the low ground with all the haste imaginable. But the enemy in position on the crest no sooner perceived their advance upon the summit of the pass than they themselves set off full tilt in a rival race for the summit too. Hoarse were the shouts from the Hellenic troops as the men cheered their companions forwards, and hoarse the answering shout from the troops of Tissaphernes, urging on theirs. Xenophon, mounted on his charger, rode beside his men, and roused their ardour the while. "Now for it, men; think that the race is for Hellas—now or never—to find your boys, your wives; one small effort, and the rest of the march we shall pursue in peace, without ever a blow to strike; now for it." But Soteridas the Sicyonian said, "We are not on equal terms, Xenophon; you are mounted on a horse; I can hardly get along with my shield to carry;" and he, on hearing the reproach, leaped from his horse. In another instant he had pushed Soteridas from the ranks, snatched from him his shield, and begun marching as quickly as he might under the circumstances, having his horseman's breastplate to carry as well, so that he was sore pressed; but he continued to cheer on the troops: exhorting those in front to lead on and the men toiling behind to follow up. Soteridas was not spared by the rest of the men. They gave him blows, they pelted him, they showered him with abuse, till they compelled him to take back his shield and march on; and the other, remounting, led them on horseback as long as the footing held; but when the ground became too steep, he left his horse and pressed forward on foot, and so they found themselves on the summit before the enemy.

5. There and then the barbarians turned and fled as best they might, and the Hellenes held the summit, while the troops with Tissaphernes and Ariaeus turned aside and disappeared by another road. The main body with Cheirisophus made its way down into the plain and encamped

[8] These 300 are probably three of the detached companies described above.

in a village filled with good things of all sorts. Nor did this village stand alone; there were others not a few in this plain of the Tigris equally overflowing with plenty. It was now afternoon; and all of a sudden the enemy came in sight on the plain, and succeeded in cutting down some of the Hellenes belonging to parties who were scattered over the flat land in quest of spoil. Indeed, many herds of cattle had been caught while being conveyed across to the other side of the river. And now Tissaphernes and his troops made an attempt to burn the villages, and some of the Hellenes were disposed to take the matter deeply to heart, being apprehensive that they might not know where to get provisions if the enemy burned the villages.

Cheirisophus and his men were returning from their sally of defence when Xenophon and his party descended, and the latter rode along the ranks as the rescuing party came up, and greeted them thus, "Do you not see, men of Hellas, they admit that the country is now ours; what they stipulated against our doing when they made the treaty, that we were not to fire the king's country, they are now themselves doing, setting fire to it as if it were not their own. But we will be even with them; if they leave provisions for themselves anywhere, there also shall they see us marching." And, turning to Cheirisophus, he added, "But it strikes me, we should sally forth against these incendiaries and protect our country." Cheirisophus retorted, "That is not quite my view; I say, let us do a little burning ourselves, and they will cease all the quicker."

When they had got back to the villages, while the rest were busy about provisions, the generals and officers met: and here there was deep despondency. For on the one side were exceedingly high mountains; on the other a river of such depth that they failed to reach the bottom with their spears. In the midst of their perplexities, a Rhodian came up with a proposal, as follows, "I am ready to carry you across, 4,000 heavy infantry at a time; if you will furnish me with what I need and give me a talent into the bargain for my pains." When asked, "What shall you need?" he replied, "2,000 wine-skins. I see there are plenty of sheep and goats and asses. They have only to be flayed, and their skins inflated, and they will readily give us a passage. I shall want also the straps which you use for the baggage animals. With these I shall couple the skins to one another; then I shall moor each skin by attaching stones and letting them down like anchors into the water. Then I shall carry them across, and when I have fastened the links at both ends, I shall place layers of wood on them and a coating of earth on the top of that. You will see in a minute that there's no danger of your drowning, for every skin will be able to support a couple of men without sinking, and the wood and earth will prevent your slipping off."

The generals thought it a clever idea, but its realisation impracticable, for on the other side were masses of cavalry posted and ready to bar the passage, who, to begin with, would not suffer the first detachment of crossers to carry out any item of the program.

Under these circumstances, the next day they turned right about face, and began retracing their steps in the direction of Babylon to the unburnt villages, having previously set fire to those they left, so that the enemy did not ride up to them, but stood and stared, all agape to see in what direction the Hellenes would betake themselves and what they intended to do. Here, again, while the rest of the soldiers were busy about provisions, the generals and officers met in council, and after collecting the prisoners together, submitted them to a cross-examination touching the whole country round, the names, and so forth, of each district.

The prisoners informed them that the regions south, through which they had come, belonged to the district towards Babylon and Media; the road east led to Susa and Ecbatana, where the king is said to spend summer and spring; crossing the river, the road west led to Lydia and Ionia; and the part through the mountains facing towards the Great Bear, led, they said, to the Carduchians. They were a people, so said the prisoners, dwelling up on the hills, addicted to war, and not subject to the king; so much so that once, when a royal army 120,000 strong had invaded them, not a man came back, owing to the ruggedness of the country. Occasionally, however, they made truce or treaty with the satrap in the plain, and, for the moment, there would be intercourse: "They will come in and out amongst us, and we will go in and out amongst them," said the captives.

After hearing these statements, the generals seated apart those who claimed to have any special knowledge of the country in any direction; they put them to sit apart without making it clear which particular route they intended to take. Finally the resolution to which they came was that they must force a passage through the hills into the territory of the Carduchians; since, according to what their informants told them, when they had once passed these, they would find themselves in Armenia—the rich and large territory governed by Orontas; and from Armenia, it would be easy to proceed in any direction whatever. Thereupon they offered sacrifice, so as to be ready to start on the march as soon as the right moment appeared to have arrived. Their chief fear was that the high pass over the mountains might be occupied in advance: and a general order was issued, that after supper every one should get his kit together for starting, and repose, in readiness to follow as soon as the word of command was given.

BOOK IV

[In the preceding portion of the narrative a full account is given of the incidents of the march up to the battle, and of the occurrences after the battle during the truce which was established between the king and the Hellenes, who marched up with Cyrus, and thirdly, of the fighting to which the Hellenes were exposed, after the king and Tissaphernes had broken the treaty, while a Persian army hung on their rear. Having finally reached a point at which the Tigris was absolutely impassable owing to its depth and breadth, while there was no passage along the bank itself, and the Carduchian hills hung sheer over the river, the generals took the resolution above mentioned of forcing a passage through the mountains. The information derived from the prisoners taken along the way led them to believe that once across the Carduchian mountains they would have the choice either of crossing the Tigris—if they liked to do so—at its sources in Armenia, or of going round them, if so they preferred. Report further said that the sources of the Euphrates also were not far from those of the Tigris, and this is actually the case. The advance into the country of the Carduchians was conducted with a view partly to secrecy, and partly to speed, so as to effect their entry before the enemy could occupy the heights.]

1. It was now about the last watch, and enough of the night remained to allow them to cross the valley under cover of darkness; when, at the word of command, they rose and set off on their march, reaching the mountains at daybreak. At this stage of the march Cheirisophus, at the head of his own division, with the whole of the light troops, led the van, while Xenophon followed behind with the heavy infantry of the rearguard, but without any light troops, since there seemed to be no danger of pursuit or attack from the rear, while they were making their way up hill. Cheirisophus reached the summit without any of the enemy perceiving him. Then he led on slowly, and the rest of the army followed, wave upon wave, cresting the summit and descending into the villages which nestled in the hollows and recesses of the hills.

Thereupon the Carduchians abandoned their dwelling-places, and with their wives and children fled to the mountains; so there was plenty of provisions to be got for the mere trouble of taking, and the homesteads too were well supplied with a copious store of bronze vessels and utensils which the Hellenes kept their hands off, abstaining at the same time from all pursuit of the folk themselves, gently handling them, in hopes that the Carduchians might be willing to give them friendly passage through their country, since they too were enemies of the king; only they helped themselves to such provisions as fell in their way, which indeed was a sheer necessity. But the Carduchians neither gave ear, when they called to them, nor showed any other friendly sign; and now, as the last of the Hellenes descended into the villages from the pass, they were already in the dark, since, owing to the narrowness of the road, the whole day had been spent in the ascent and descent. At that instant a party of the Carduchians, who had collected, made an attack on the hindmost men, killing some and wounding others with stones and arrows—though it was quite a small body who attacked. The fact was, the approach of the Hellenic army had taken them by surprise; if, however, they had mustered in larger force at this time, the chances are that a large portion of the army would have been annihilated. As it was, they got into quarters, and bivouacked in the villages that night, while the Carduchians kept many watch-fires blazing in a circle on the mountains, and kept each other in sight all round.

But with the dawn the generals and officers of the Hellenes met and resolved to proceed, taking only the necessary number of stout baggage animals, and leaving the weaklings behind. They resolved further to let go free all the lately-captured slaves in the host; for the pace of the march was necessarily rendered slow by the quantity of animals and prisoners, and the number of non-combatants in attendance on these was excessive, while, with such a crowd of human beings to feed, twice the amount of provisions had to be procured and carried. These resolutions passed, they caused a proclamation by herald to be made for their enforcement.

When they had breakfasted and the march recommenced, the generals planted themselves a little to one side in a narrow place, and when they found any of the aforesaid slaves or other property still retained, they confiscated them. The soldiers yielded obedience, except where some smuggler, prompted by desire of a good-looking boy or woman, managed to make off with his prize. During this day they contrived to get along after a fashion, now fighting and now resting. But on the next day they were visited by a great storm, in spite of which they were obliged to continue the march, owing to insufficiency of provisions. Cheirisophus was as usual leading in front, while Xenophon headed the rearguard, when the enemy began a violent and sustained attack. At one narrow place after another they came up quite close, pouring in volleys of arrows and slingstones, so that the Hellenes had no choice but to make sallies in pursuit and then again recoil, making but very little progress. Over and over again Xenophon would send an order to the front to slacken pace, when the enemy were pressing their attack severely. As a rule, when the word was so passed up, Cheirisophus slackened; but once instead of slackening, Cheirisophus quickened, sending down a counter-order to the rear to follow on quickly. It was clear that there was something or other happening, but there was no time to go to the front and discover the cause of the hurry. Under these circumstances the march, at any rate in the rear, became very like a rout, and here a brave man lost his life, Cleonymus the Laconian, shot with an arrow in the ribs right through shield and corselet, as also Basias, an Arcadian, shot clean through the head.

As soon as they reached a halting-place, Xenophon, without more ado, came up to Cheirisophus, and took him to task for not having waited, "Whereby," said he, "we were forced to fight and flee at the same moment; and now it has cost us the lives of two fine fellows; they are dead, and we were not able to pick up their bodies or bury them." Cheirisophus answered, "Look up there," pointing as he spoke to the mountain, "do you see how inaccessible it all is? only this one road, which you see, going straight up, and on it all that crowd of men who have seized and are guarding the single exit. That is why I hastened on, and why I could not wait for you, hoping to be beforehand with them yonder in seizing the pass: the guides we have got say there is no other way." And Xenophon replied, "But I have got two prisoners also; the enemy annoyed us so much that we laid an ambuscade for them, which also gave us time to recover our breaths; we killed some of them, and did our best to catch one or two alive—for this very reason —that we might have guides who knew the country, to depend upon."

The two were brought up at once and questioned separately, "Did they know of any other road than the one visible?" The first said no; and in spite of all sorts of terrors applied to extract a better answer—he persisted. When nothing could be got out of him, he was killed before the eyes of his fellow. This latter then explained, "Yonder man said he did not know, because he has got a daughter married to a husband in those parts. I can take you," he added, "by a good road, practicable even for beasts." And when asked whether there was any point on it difficult to pass, he replied that there was a height which it would be impossible to pass unless it were occupied in advance.

Then it was resolved to summon the officers of the light infantry and some of those of the heavy infantry, and to acquaint them with the state of affairs, and ask them whether any of them were minded to distinguish themselves, and would step forward as volunteers on an expedition. Two or three heavy infantry soldiers stepped forward at once—two Arcadians, Aristonymus of Methydrium, and Agasias of Stymphalus— and in emulation of these, a third, also an Arcadian, Callimachus from Parrhasia, who said he was ready to go, and would get volunteers from the whole army to join him. "I know," he added, "there will be no lack of youngsters to follow where I lead." After that they asked, "Were there any captains of light infantry willing to accompany the expedition?" Aristeas, a Chian, who on several occasions proved his usefulness to the army on such service, volunteered.

2. It was already late afternoon, when they ordered the storming party to take a snatch of food and set off; then they bound the guide and handed him over to them. The agreement was, that if they succeeded in taking the summit they were to guard the position that night, and at daybreak to give a signal by trumpet. At this signal the party on the summit were to attack the enemy in occupation of the visible pass, while the generals with the main body would bring up their aid; making their way up with what speed they might. With this understanding, off they set, 2,000 strong; and there was a heavy downpour of rain, but Xenophon, with his rearguard, began advancing to the visible pass, so that the enemy might fix his attention on this road, and the party creeping round might, as much as possible, elude observation. Now when the rearguard, so advancing, had reached a ravine which they must cross in order to strike up the steep, at that instant the barbarians began rolling down great boulders, each a waggon load, some larger, some smaller; against the rocks they crashed and splintered flying like sling-stones in every direction—so that it was absolutely out of the question even to approach the entrance of the pass. Some of the officers finding themselves baulked at this point, kept trying other ways, nor did they desist till darkness set in; and then, when they thought they would not be seen retiring, they returned to supper. Some of them who had been on duty in the rearguard had had no breakfast (it so happened). However, the enemy never ceased rolling down their stones all through the night, as was easy to infer from the booming sound.

The party with the guide made a circuit and surprised the enemy's guards seated round their fire, and after killing some, and driving out the rest, took their places, thinking that they were in possession of the height. As a matter of fact they were not, for above them lay a breast-like hill skirted by the narrow road on which they had found the guards seated. Still, from the spot in question there was an approach to the enemy, who were seated on the pass before mentioned.

Here then they passed the night, but at the first glimpse of dawn they marched stealthily and in battle order against the enemy. There was a mist, so that they could get quite close without being observed. But as soon as they caught sight of one another, the trumpet sounded, and with a loud cheer they rushed upon the fellows, who did not wait their coming, but left the road and made off; with the loss of only a few lives however, so nimble were they. Cheirisophus and his men, catching the sound of the trumpet, charged up by the well-marked road, while others of the generals pushed their way up by pathless routes, where each division chanced to be; the men mounting as they were best able, and hoisting one another up by means of their spears; and these were the first to unite with the party who had already taken the position by storm. Xenophon, with the rearguard, followed the path which the party with the guide had taken, since it was easiest for the beasts of burden; one half of his men he had posted in rear of the baggage animals; the other half he had with himself. In their course they encountered a crest above the road, occupied by the enemy, whom they must either dislodge or be themselves cut off from the rest of the Hellenes. The men by themselves could have taken the same route as the rest, but the baggage animals could not mount by any other way than this.

Here then, with shouts of encouragement to each other, they dashed at the hill with their storming columns, not from all sides, but leaving an avenue of escape for the enemy, if he chose to avail himself of it. For a while, as the men scrambled up where each best could, the natives kept up a fire of arrows and darts, yet did not receive them at close quarters, but presently left the position in flight. No sooner, however, were the Hellenes safely past this crest, than they came in sight of another in front of them, also occupied, and deemed it advisable to storm it also. But now it struck Xenophon that if they left the ridge just taken unprotected in their rear, the enemy might re-occupy it and attack the baggage animals as they filed past, presenting a long extended line owing to the narrowness of the road by which they made their way. To obviate this, he left some officers in charge of the ridge—Cephisodorus, son of Cephisophon, an Athenian; Amphicrates, the son of Amphidemus, an Athenian; and Archagoras, an Argive exile—while he in person with the rest of the men attacked the second ridge; this they took in the same fashion, only to find that they had still a third knoll left, far the steepest of the three. This was none other than the round hill mentioned as above the outpost, which had been captured over their fire by the volunteer storming party in the night. But when the Hellenes were close, the natives, to the astonishment of all, without a struggle deserted the knoll. It was conjectured that they had left their position from fear of being encircled and besieged, but the fact was that

they, from their higher ground, had been able to see what was going on
in the rear, and had all made off in this fashion to attack the rearguard.

So then Xenophon, with the youngest men, scaled up to the top,
leaving orders to the rest to march on slowly, so as to allow the hindmost companies to unite with them; they were to advance by the road,
and when they reached the level to ground arms. Meanwhile the Argive
Archagoras arrived, in full flight, with the announcement that they had
been dislodged from the first ridge, and that Cephisodorus and Amphicrates were slain, with a number of others besides, all in fact who had not
jumped down the crags and so reached the rearguard. After this achievement the barbarians came to a crest facing the knoll, and Xenophon
held a colloquy with them by means of an interpreter, to negotiate a
truce, and demanded back the dead bodies. These they agreed to restore
if he would not burn their houses, and to these terms Xenophon agreed.
Meanwhile, as the rest of the army filed past, and the colloquy was
proceeding, all the people of the place had time to gather gradually, and
the enemy formed; and as soon as the Hellenes began to descend from
the knoll to join the others where the troops were halted, on rushed the
foe, in full force, with hue and cry. They reached the summit of the
knoll from which Xenophon was descending, and began rolling down
crags. One man's leg was crushed to pieces. Xenophon was left by his
shield-bearer, who carried off his shield, but Eurylochus of Lusia, an
Arcadian hoplite, ran up to him, and threw his shield in front to protect
both of them; so the two together beat a retreat, and so too the rest,
and joined the ranks of the main body.

After this the whole Hellenic force united, and took up their quarters
there in numerous beautiful dwellings, with an ample store of provisions,
for there was wine so plentiful that they had it in cemented cisterns.
Xenophon and Cheirisophus arranged to recover the dead, and in return
restored the guide; afterwards they did everything for the dead, according to the means at their disposal, with the customary honours paid
to brave men.

Next day they set off without a guide; and the enemy, by keeping up
a continuous battle and occupying in advance every narrow place, obstructed passage after passage. Accordingly, whenever the van was
obstructed, Xenophon, from behind, made a dash up the hills and broke
the barricade, and freed the vanguard by endeavouring to get above the
obstructing enemy. Whenever the rear was the point attacked, Cheirisophus, in the same way, made a detour, and by endeavouring to mount
higher than the barricaders, freed the passage for the rear rank; and in
this way, turn and turn about, they rescued each other, and paid un-

flinching attention to their mutual needs. At times it happened that the relief party, having mounted, encountered considerable annoyance in their descent from the barbarians, who were so agile that they allowed them to come up quite close, before they turned back, and still escaped, partly no doubt because the only weapons they had to carry were bows and slings.

They were, moreover, excellent archers, using bows nearly five feet long and arrows more than three feet. When discharging the arrow, they draw the string by getting a purchase with the left foot planted forward on the lower end of the bow. The arrows pierced through shield and breastplate, and the Hellenes, when they got hold of them, used them as javelins, fitting them to their thongs. In these districts the Cretans were highly serviceable. They were under the command of Stratocles, a Cretan.

3. During this day they bivouacked in the villages which lie above the plain of the river Centrites, which is about 200 feet broad. It is the frontier river between Armenia and the country of the Carduchians. Here the Hellenes refreshed themselves, and the sight of the plain filled them with joy, for the river was less than a mile from the mountains of the Carduchians. For the moment then they bivouacked very happily; they had their provisions, they had also many memories of the labours that were now passed; seeing that the last seven days spent in traversing the country of the Carduchians had been one long continuous battle, which had cost them more suffering than the whole of their troubles at the hands of the king and Tissaphernes put together. As though they were truly quit of them for ever, they lay down to rest happily.

But at daybreak they saw horsemen at a certain point across the river, fully armed, as if they meant to dispute the passage. Infantry, too, drawn up in line upon the banks above the cavalry, threatened to prevent them debouching into Armenia. These troops were Armenian and Mardian and Chaldaean mercenaries belonging to Orontas and Artuchas. The last of the three, the Chaldaeans, were said to be a free and brave set of people. They were armed with long wicker shields and lances. The banks before named on which they were drawn up were 100 yards or more from the river, and the single road which was visible was one leading upwards and looking like a regular artificially constructed highway. At this point the Hellenes endeavoured to cross, but on their making the attempt the water proved to be more than breast-deep, and the river bed was rough with great slippery stones, and as to holding their arms in the water, it was out of the question—the stream swept them away—or if they tried to carry them over the head, the body was left exposed to the arrows and other missiles; accordingly they turned back and encamped there by the bank of the river.

At the point where they had themselves been last night, up on the mountains, they could see the Carduchians collected in large numbers and under arms. A shadow of deep despair again descended on their souls, whichever way they turned their eyes—in front lay the river so difficult to ford; over, on the other side, a new enemy threatening to bar the passage; on the hills behind, the Carduchians ready to fall upon their rear should they once again attempt to cross. Thus for this day and night they halted, sunk in perplexity. But Xenophon had a dream. In his sleep he thought that he was bound in fetters, but these, of their own accord, fell from off him, so that he was loosed, and could stretch his legs as freely as he wished.[1] So at the first glimpse of daylight he came to Cheirisophus and told him that he had hopes that all things would go well, and related to him his dream.

The other was well pleased, and with the first faint gleam of dawn the generals all were present and did sacrifice; and the victims were favourable at the first essay. Retiring from the sacrifice, the generals and officers issued an order to the troops to take their breakfasts; and while Xenophon was taking his, two young men came running up to him, for every one knew that, breakfasting or supping, he was always accessible, or that even if asleep any one was welcome to awaken him who had anything to say bearing on the business of war. What the two young men had at this time to say was that they had been collecting brushwood for fire, and had presently espied on the opposite side, in among some rocks which came down to the river's brink, an old man and some women and little girls depositing, as it would appear, bags of clothes in a cavernous rock. When they saw them, it struck them that it was safe to cross; in any case the enemy's cavalry could not approach at this point. So they stripped naked, expecting to have to swim for it, and with their long knives in their hands began crossing, but going forward crossed without being wet up to the genitals. Once across they took the clothes, and came back again.

Accordingly Xenophon at once poured out a libation himself, and bade the two young fellows fill the cup and pray to the gods, who showed to him this vision and to them a passage, to bring all other blessings for them to accomplishment. When he had poured out the libations, he at once led the two young men to Cheirisophus, and they repeated to him their story. Cheirisophus, on hearing it, offered libations also, and when they had performed them, they sent a general order to the troops to pack up ready for starting, while they themselves called a meeting

---

[1] The same Greek verb means also to cross (a river).

of the generals and took counsel how they might best effect a passage, so as to overpower the enemy in front without suffering any loss from the men behind. And they resolved that Cheirisophus should lead the van and cross with half the army, the other half still remaining behind under Xenophon, while the baggage animals and the mob of camp-followers were to cross between the two divisions.

When all was duly ordered the move began, the young men pioneering them, and keeping the river on their left. It was about half a mile to the crossing, and as they moved along the bank, the squadrons of cavalry kept pace with them on the opposite side.

But when they had reached a point in a line with the ford, and the cliff-like banks of the river, they halted under arms, and first Cheirisophus himself placed a wreath upon his brows, and throwing off his cloak, resumed his arms, passing the order to all the rest to do the same, and bade the captains form their companies in open order in deep columns, some to left and some to right of himself. Meanwhile the soothsayers were slaying a victim over the river, and the enemy were letting fly their arrows and slingstones; but as yet they were out of range. As soon as the victims were favourable, all the soldiers began singing the battle hymn, and with the notes of the paean mingled the shouting of the men accompanied by the shriller chant of the women, for there were many courtesans in the camp.

So Cheirisophus with his detachment stepped in. But Xenophon, taking the most active-bodied of the rearguard, began running back at full speed to the passage facing the egress into the hills of Armenia, making a feint of crossing at that point to intercept their cavalry on the river bank. The enemy, seeing Cheirisophus's detachment easily crossing the stream, and Xenophon's men racing back, were seized with the fear of being intercepted, and fled at full speed in the direction of the road which emerges from the stream. But when they were come opposite to it they raced up hill towards their mountains. Then Lycius, who commanded the cavalry, and Aeschines, who was in command of the division of light infantry attached to Cheirisophus, no sooner saw them fleeing so lustily than they were after them, and the soldiers shouted not to fall behind, but to follow them right up to the mountains. Cheirisophus, on getting across, forbore to pursue the cavalry, but advanced by the bluffs which reached to the river to attack the enemy overhead. And these, seeing their own cavalry fleeing, seeing also the heavy infantry advancing upon them, abandoned the heights above the river.

Xenophon, as soon as he saw that things were going well on the other side, fell back with all speed to join the troops engaged in crossing, for

by this time the Carduchians were well in sight, descending into the plain
to attack their rear.

Cheirisophus was in possession of the higher ground, and Lycius, with
his little squadron, in an attempt to follow up the pursuit, had captured
some stragglers of their baggage-bearers, and with them some handsome
apparel and drinking-cups. The baggage animals of the Hellenes and
the mob of noncombatants were just about to cross, when Xenophon
turned his troops right about to face the Carduchians, passing the order
to the captains each to form his company into sections, and to deploy
them into line by the left, the captains of companies and lieutenants in
command of sections to advance to meet the Carduchians, while the
rear leaders would keep their position facing the river. But when the
Carduchians saw the rearguard so stripped of the mass, and looking now
like a mere handful of men, they advanced all the more quickly, singing
certain songs the while. Then, as matters were safe with him, Cheirisophus sent back the peltasts and slingers and archers to join Xenophon,
with orders to carry out his instructions. They were in the act of recrossing, when Xenophon, who saw their intention, sent a messenger
across, bidding them wait there at the river's brink without crossing;
but as soon as he and his detachment began to cross they were to step
in facing him in two flanking divisions right and left of them, as if in the
act of crossing; the javelin men with their javelins on the thong, and
the bowmen with their arrows on the string; but they were not to advance far into the stream. The order passed to his own men was, "Wait
till you are within sling-shot, and the shield rattles, then sound the paean
and charge the enemy. As soon as he turns, and the trumpet from the
river sounds for the attack, you will face about to the right, the rear
rank leading, and the whole detachment falling back and crossing the
river as quickly as possible, every one preserving his original rank, so as
to avoid blocking one another: the bravest man is he who gets to the
other side first."

The Carduchians, seeing that the remnant left was the merest handful (for many even of those whose duty it was to remain had gone off
in their anxiety to protect their beasts of burden, or their personal kit, or
their mistresses), bore down upon them valorously, and opened fire with
slingstones and arrows. But the Hellenes, raising the battle hymn,
dashed at them at a run, and they did not await them; armed well
enough for mountain warfare, and with a view to sudden attack followed by speedy flight, they were not by any means sufficiently equipped
for an engagement at close quarters. At this instant the signal of the
trumpet was heard. Its notes added wings to the flight of the barbarians,
but the Hellenes turned right about in the opposite direction, and be-

took themselves to the river with what speed they might. Some of the enemy, here a man and there another, perceived, and running back to the river, let fly their arrows and wounded a few; but the majority, even when the Hellenes were well across, were still to be seen pursuing their flight. The detachment which came to meet Xenophon's men, carried away by their valour, advanced further than they had need to, and had to cross back again in the rear of Xenophon's men, and of these too a few were wounded.

4. The passage effected, they fell into line about midday, and marched through Armenian territory, one long plain with smooth rolling hillocks, not less than sixteen miles in distance; for owing to the wars of this people with the Carduchians there were no villages near the river. The village eventually reached was large, and possessed a palace belonging to the satrap, and most of the houses were crowned with turrets; provisions were plentiful.

From this village they marched two days—thirty-three miles—until they had surmounted the sources of the river Tigris; and from this point they marched three days—fifty miles—to the river Teleboas. This was a fine stream, though not large, and there were many villages about it. The district was named Western Armenia. The lieutenant-governor of it was Tiribazus, the king's friend, and whenever the latter paid a visit, he alone had the privilege of mounting the king upon his horse. This officer rode up to the Hellenes with a body of cavalry, and sending forward an interpreter, stated that he wished to confer with the leaders. The generals resolved to hear what he had to say; and advancing on their side to within speaking distance, they demanded what he wanted. He replied that he wished to make a treaty with them, in accordance with which he on his side would abstain from injuring the Hellenes, if they would not burn his houses, but merely take such provisions as they needed. This proposal satisfied the generals, and a treaty was made on the terms suggested.

From this place they marched three days—fifty miles—through plain country, Tiribazus the while keeping close behind with his own forces more than a mile off. Presently they reached a palace with villages clustered round about it, which were full of supplies in great variety. But while they were encamping in the night there was a heavy fall of snow, and in the morning it was resolved to billet out the different regiments, with their generals, throughout the villages. There was no enemy in sight, and the proceeding seemed prudent, owing to the quantity of snow. In these quarters they had for provisions all the good things there are—sacrificial beasts, corn, old wines with an exquisite bouquet, dried grapes, and vegetables of all sorts. But some of the

stragglers from the camp reported having seen an army, and the blaze
of many watchfires in the night. Accordingly the generals concluded that
it was not prudent to separate their quarters in this way, and a resolution was passed to bring the troops together again. After that they re-
united, the more so that the weather promised to be fine with a clear
sky; but while they lay there in open quarters, during the night down
came so thick a fall of snow that it completely covered up the stacks of
arms and the men themselves lying down. It cramped and crippled the
baggage animals; and there was great unreadiness to get up, so gently
fell the snow as they lay there warm and comfortable, and formed a
blanket, except where it slipped off the sleeper's shoulders; and it was
not until Xenophon roused himself to get up, and, without his cloak on,
began to split wood, that quickly first one and then another got up, and
taking the log away from him, fell to splitting. Thereat the rest followed suit, got up, and began kindling fires and oiling their bodies, for
there was a scented unguent to be found there in abundance, which
they used instead of oil. It was made from pig's fat, sesame, bitter
almonds, and turpentine. There was a sweet oil also to be found, made
of the same ingredients.

After this it was resolved that they must again separate their quarters and get under cover in the villages. At this news the soldiers, with
much joy and shouting, rushed upon the covered houses and the provisions; but all who in their blind folly had set fire to the houses when
they left them before, now paid the penalty in the poor quarters they
got. From this place one night they sent off a party under Democrates,
a Temenite, up into the mountains, where the stragglers reported having
seen watchfires. The leader selected was a man whose judgment might
be depended upon to verify the truth of the matter. With a happy gift
to distinguish between fact and fiction, he had often been successfully
appealed to. He went and reported that he had seen no watchfires, but
he had got a man, whom he brought back with him, carrying a Persian
bow and quiver, and a battleaxe like those worn by the Amazons. When
asked from what country he came, the prisoner answered that he was a
Persian, and was going from the army of Tiribazus to get provisions.
They next asked him how large the army was, and for what object it
had been collected. His answer was that it consisted of Tiribazus at the
head of his own forces, and aided by some Chalybian and Taochian
mercenaries. Tiribazus had got it together, he added, meaning to attack
the Hellenes on the high mountain pass, in a defile which was the sole
passage.

When the generals heard this news, they resolved to collect the troops,
and they set off at once, taking the prisoner to act as guide, and leaving

a garrison behind with Sophaenetus the Stymphalian in command of those who remained in the camp. As soon as they had begun to cross the hills, the light infantry, advancing in front and catching sight of the camp, did not wait for the heavy infantry, but with a loud shout rushed upon the enemy's entrenchment. The natives, hearing the din and clatter, did not care to stop, but took rapidly to their heels. But, for all their expedition, some of them were killed, and as many as twenty horses were captured, with the tent of Tiribazus, and its contents, silver-footed couches and goblets, besides certain persons calling themselves the butlers and bakers. As soon as the generals of the heavy infantry division had learned the news, they resolved to return to the camp with all speed, for fear of an attack being made on the remnant left behind. The recall was sounded and the retreat commenced; the camp was reached the same day.

5. The next day it was resolved that they should set off with all possible speed, before the enemy had time to collect and occupy the defile. Having got their kit and baggage together, they at once began their march through deep snow with several guides, and, crossing the high pass the same day on which Tiribazus was to have attacked them, got safely into camp. From this point they marched three days across desert —fifty miles—to the river Euphrates, and crossed it in water up to the navel. The sources of the river were reported to be at no great distance. From this place they marched through deep snow over a flat country three days—fifty miles. The last of these marches was trying, with the north wind blowing in their teeth, drying up everything and benumbing the men. Here one of the seers suggested to them to do sacrifice to Boreas, and sacrifice was done. The effect was obvious to all in the diminished fierceness of the blast. But there was six feet of snow, so that many of the baggage animals and slaves were lost, and about thirty of the men themselves.

They got through the night by keeping up a fire of wood; for there was fortunately no dearth of wood at the halting-place; only those who came late into camp had no wood. Accordingly those who had arrived a good while and had kindled fires were not for allowing these late-comers near their fires, unless they would in return give a share of their corn or of any other victuals they might have. Here then a general exchange of goods was set up. Where the fire was kindled the snow melted, and great trenches formed themselves down to the bare earth, and here it was possible to measure the depth of the snow.

Leaving these quarters, they marched the whole of the next day over snow, and many of the men were afflicted with hunger-faintness. Xenophon, who was guarding the rear, came upon some men who had dropt down, and he did not know what ailed them; but some one who was experienced in such matters suggested to him that they evidently had hunger-faintness; and if they got something to eat, they would revive. Then he went the round of the baggage train, and taking any eatables he could see, doled them out with his own hands, or sent off other able-bodied agents to distribute to the sufferers, who as soon as they had taken a mouthful got on their legs again and continued the march.

On and on they marched, and about dusk Cheirisophus reached a village, and surprised some women and girls who had come from the village to fetch water at the fountain outside the stockade. These asked them who they were. The interpreters answered for them in Persian that they were on their way from the king to the satrap; in reply to which the women gave them to understand that the satrap was not at home, but was about three miles farther on. As it was late they entered with the water-carriers within the stockade to visit the headman of the village. Accordingly Cheirisophus and as many of the troops as were able got into quarters there, while the rest of the soldiers—those namely who were unable to complete the march—had to spend the night out, without food and without fire; under the circumstances some of the men perished.

On the heels of the army hung perpetually bands of the enemy, snatching away disabled baggage animals and fighting with each other over the carcasses. And in its track not seldom were left to their fate disabled soldiers, struck down with snow-blindness or with toes mortified by frostbite. As to the eyes, it was some alleviation against the snow to march with something black before them; for the feet, the only remedy was to keep in motion without stopping for an instant, and to loose the sandal at night. If they went to sleep with the sandals on, the thong worked into the feet, and the sandals were frozen fast to them. This was partly due to the fact that, since their old sandals had failed, they wore untanned brogues made of newly-flayed ox-hides. It was owing to some such dire necessity that a party of men fell out and were left behind, and seeing a black-looking patch of ground where the snow had evidently disappeared, they conjectured it must have been melted; and this was actually so, owing to a spring of some sort which was to be seen steaming up in a dell close by. To this they had turned aside and sat down, and refused to go a step further. But Xenophon, with his rearguard, perceived them, and begged and implored them by all manner of means not to be left behind, telling them that the enemy were after them in large packs pursuing; and he ended by growing angry. They merely bade him put a knife to their throats; not one step farther would they stir. Then it seemed best to frighten the pursuing enemy if possible, and prevent their falling upon the invalids. It was already dusk, and the pursuers were advancing with much noise and hubbub, wrangling and disputing over their spoils. Then all of a sudden the rearguard, healthy and strong, sprang up and ran upon the enemy, while the invalids bawled out as loud as their sick throats could sound, and clashed their spears against their shields; and the enemy in terror hurled themselves through the snow into the dell, and not one of them ever uttered a sound again.

Xenophon and his party, telling the sick folk that next day people would come for them, set off, and before they had gone half a mile they fell in with some soldiers who had laid down to rest on the snow with their cloaks wrapped round them, but never a guard was established, and they made them get up. Their explanation was that those in front would not move on. Passing by this group he sent forward the strongest of his light infantry in advance, with orders to find out what the stoppage was. They reported that the whole army lay reposing in the same fashion. That being so, Xenophon's men had nothing for it but to bivouac in the open air also, without fire and supperless, merely posting what pickets they could under the circumstances. But as soon as it drew towards day, Xenophon despatched the youngest of his men to the sick folk behind, with orders to make them get up and force them to proceed. Meanwhile Cheirisophus had sent some of his men quartered in the village to enquire how they fared in the rear; they were overjoyed to see them, and handed over the sick folk to them to carry into camp, while they themselves continued their march forwards, and within three miles reached the village in which Cheirisophus was quartered. As soon as the two divisions met, the resolution was come to that it would be safe to billet the regiments throughout the villages; Cheirisophus remained where he was, while the rest drew lots for the villages in sight, and then, with their several detachments, marched off to their respective destinations.

It was here that Polycrates, an Athenian and captain of a company, asked for leave of absence—he wished to be off on a quest of his own; and putting himself at the head of the active men of the division, he ran to the village which had been allotted to Xenophon. He surprised within it the villagers with their headman, and seventeen young horses which were being reared as a tribute for the king, and, last of all, the headman's own daughter, a young bride only eight days wed. Her husband had gone off to chase hares, and so he escaped being taken with the other villagers. The houses were underground structures with an aperture like the mouth of a well by which to enter, but they were broad and spacious below. The entrance for the beasts of burden was dug out, but the human occupants descended by a ladder. In these dwellings were to be found goats, sheep, cattle, cocks and hens, with their various progeny. The flocks and herds were all reared under cover upon green food. There were stores within of wheat and barley and vegetables, and wine made from barley in large bowls; the grains of barley malt lay floating in the beverage up to the lip of the vessel, and reeds lay in them, some longer, some shorter, without joints; when you were thirsty you must take one of these into your mouth, and suck. The beverage without admixture of water was very strong, and of a delicious flavour to certain palates, but the taste must be acquired.

Xenophon made the headman of the village his guest at supper, and bade him keep a good heart; so far from robbing him of his children, they would fill his house full of good things in return for what they took before they went away; only he must set them an example, and discover some blessing or other for the army, until they found themselves with another tribe. To this he readily assented, and with the utmost cordiality showed them the cellar where the wine was buried. For this night then, having taken up their several quarters as described, they slumbered in the midst of plenty, one and all, with the headman under watch and ward, and his children with him safe in sight.

But on the following day Xenophon took the headman and set off to Cheirisophus, making a round of the villages, and at each place turning in to visit the different parties. Everywhere alike he found them faring sumptuously and merry-making. There was not a single village where they did not insist on setting a breakfast before them, and on the same table were spread half a dozen dishes at least, lamb, kid, pork, veal, fowls, with various sorts of bread, some of wheat and some of barley. When, as an act of courtesy, any one wished to drink his neighbour's health, he would drag him to the big bowl, and when there, he must duck his head and take a long pull, drinking like an ox. The headman, they insisted everywhere, must accept as a present whatever he liked to have. But he would accept nothing, except where he espied any of his relations, when he made a point of taking them off with himself.

When they reached Cheirisophus they found a similar scene. There too the men were feasting in their quarters, garlanded with hay and dry grass, and Armenian boys were playing the part of waiters in barbaric costumes, only they had to point out by gesture to the boys what they were to do, like deaf and dumb. After the first formalities, when Cheirisophus and Xenophon had greeted one another like bosom friends, they interrogated the headman in common by means of the Persian-speaking interpreter, "What was the country?" they asked: he replied, "Armenia." And again, "For whom are the horses being bred?" "They are tribute for the king," he replied. "And the neighbouring country?" "Is the land of the Chalybes," he said; and he described the road which led to it. So for the present Xenophon went off, taking the headman back with him to his household and friends. He also made him a present of an oldish horse which he had got; he had heard that the headman was a priest of the sun, and so he could fatten up the beast and sacrifice him; otherwise he was afraid it might die outright, for it had been injured by the long marching. For himself he took his pick of the colts, and gave a colt apiece to each of his fellow-generals and officers. The horses here were smaller than the Persian horses, but much more spirited. It was here too that their friend the headman explained to them, how they should wrap small bags or sacks round the feet of the horses and other cattle when marching through the snow, for without such precautions the creatures sank up to their bellies.

6. When a week had passed, on the eighth day Xenophon delivered over the guide (that is to say, the village headman) to Cheirisophus. He left the headman's household safe behind in the village, with the exception of his son, a lad in the bloom of youth. This boy was entrusted to Pleisthenes of Amphipolis to guard; if the headman proved himself a good guide, he was to take away his son also at his departure. They finally made his house the repository of all the good things they could contrive to get together; then they broke up their camp and commenced the march, the headman guiding them through the snow unfettered. When they had reached the third stopping-place Cheirisophus flew into a rage with him, because he had not brought them to any villages. The headman pleaded that there were none in this part. Cheirisophus struck him, but forgot to bind him, and the end of it was that the headman ran away in the night and was gone, leaving his son behind him. This was the sole ground of difference between Cheirisophus and Xenophon during the march, this combination of ill-treatment and neglect in the case of the guide. As to the boy, Pleisthenes fell in love with him, and took him home with him, and found in him the most faithful of friends.

After this they marched seven days at the rate of sixteen miles a day, to the banks of the river Phasis, which is 100 feet broad; and thence they marched another two days, thirty-three miles; but at the pass leading down into the plain there appeared in front of them a mixed body of Chalybes and Taochians and Phasianians. When Cheirisophus caught sight of the enemy on the pass at a distance of about three or four miles, he ceased marching, not caring to approach the enemy with his troops in column, and he passed down the order to the others: to deploy their companies to the front, that the troops might form into line. As soon as the rearguard had come up, he assembled the generals and officers, and addressed them, "The enemy, as you see, hold the mountain pass, it is time we should consider how we are to make the best fight to win it. My opinion is, that we should give orders to the troops to take their morning meal, while we deliberate whether we should cross the mountains to-day or to-morrow." "My opinion," said Cleanor, "is, that as soon as we have breakfasted, we should arm for the fight and attack the enemy, without loss of time, for if we fritter away to-day, the enemy who are now content to look at us, will grow bolder, and with their growing courage, depend upon it, others more numerous will join them."

After him Xenophon spoke. "This," he said, "is how I see the matter: if fight we must, let us make preparation to sell our lives dearly, but if we desire to cross with the greatest ease, the point to consider is, how we may get the fewest wounds and throw away the smallest number of good men. Well then, that part of the mountain which is visible stretches nearly seven miles. Where are the men posted to intercept us? Except at the road itself, they are nowhere to be seen. It is much better then to try if possible to steal a point of this deserted mountain unobserved, and before they know where we are, secure the prize, than to fly at a strong position and an enemy thoroughly prepared, since it is much easier to march up a mountain without fighting than to tramp along a level when assailants are on either hand; and provided he does not have to fight, a man will see what lies at his feet much more plainly even at night than in broad daylight in the midst of battle; and a rough road in peace may be pleasanter than a smooth surface with missiles whistling about your ears. Nor is it so impossible, I take it, to steal a march, since it is open to us to go by night, when we cannot be seen, and to fall back so far that they will never notice us. In my opinion, however, if we make a feint of attacking here, we shall find the mountain chain all the more deserted elsewhere, since the enemy will be waiting for us here in thicker swarm.

"But what right have I to be drawing conclusions about stealing in your presence, Cheirisophus? for you Lacedaemonians, as I have often been told, you who belong to the peers, practise stealing from your boyhood up; and it is no disgrace but honourable rather to steal, except such things as the law forbids; and in order, I presume, to stimulate your sense of secretiveness, and to make you master thieves, it is lawful for you further to get a whipping, if you are caught. Now then you have a fine opportunity of displaying your training. But take care we are not caught stealing over the mountain, or we shall catch it ourselves."

"For all that," retorted Cheirisophus, "I have heard that you Athenians are clever hands at stealing the public moneys; and that too though there is fearful risk for the person so employed; but, I am told, it is your best men who are most addicted to it; if it is your best men who are thought worthy to rule. So it is a fine opportunity for yourself also, Xenophon, to exhibit your education." "And I," replied Xenophon, "am ready to take the rear division, as soon as we have eaten, and seize the mountain chain. I already have guides, for the light troops laid an ambuscade, and seized some of the stealing vagabonds who hung on our rear. I am further informed by them that the mountain is not inaccessible, but is grazed by goats and cattle, so that if we can once get hold of any portion of it, there will be no difficulty as regards our animals—they can cross. As to the enemy, I expect they will not even wait for us any longer, when they once see us on a level with themselves on the heights, for they do not even at present care to come down and meet us on fair ground." Cheirisophus answered, "But why should you go and leave your command in the rear? Send others rather, unless a band of volunteers will present themselves." Thereupon Aristonymus the Methydrian came forward with some heavy infantry, and Aristeas the Chian with some light troops, and Nicomachus the Oetean with another body of light troops, and they made an agreement to kindle several watch-fires as soon as they held the heights. The arrangements made, they breakfasted; and after breakfast Cheirisophus advanced the whole army about a mile closer towards the enemy, so as to strengthen the impression that he intended to attack them at that point.

But as soon as they had supped and night had fallen, the party under orders set off and occupied the mountain, while the main body rested where they were. Now as soon as the enemy perceived that the mountain was taken, they banished all thought of sleep, and kept many watch-fires blazing through the night. But at break of day Cheirisophus offered sacrifice, and began advancing along the road, while the detachment which held the mountain advanced along the high ground. The larger mass of the enemy, on his side, remained still on the mountain-pass, but a section of them turned to confront the detachment on the heights. Before the main bodies had time to draw together, the detachment on the height came to close quarters, and the Hellenes were victorious and gave chase. Meanwhile the light division of the Hellenes, issuing from the plain, was rapidly advancing against the lines of the enemy, while Cheirisophus followed up with his heavy infantry at quick march. But the enemy on the road no sooner saw their higher division being worsted than they fled, and some few of them were slain, and a vast number of wicker shields were taken, which the Hellenes hacked

to pieces with their short swords and rendered useless. So when they
had reached the summit of the pass, they sacrificed and set up a trophy,
and descending into the plain, reached villages abounding in good things
of every kind.

7. After this they marched into the country of the Taochians five days
—about 100 miles—and provisions failed; for the Taochians lived in
strong places, into which they had carried up all their stores. Now when
the army arrived before one of these strong places—a mere fortress,
without city or houses, into which a motley crowd of men and women
and numerous flocks and herds were gathered—Cheirisophus attacked
at once. When the first regiment fell back tired, a second advanced, and
again a third, for it was impossible to surround the place in full force, as
it was encircled by a river. Presently Xenophon came up with the rearguard, consisting of both light and heavy infantry, whereupon Cheirisophus hailed him with the words, "You have come in the nick of time;
we must take this place, for the troops have no provisions, unless we
take it." Thereupon they consulted together, and to Xenophon's inquiry, "What it was which hindered their simply walking in?" Cheirisophus replied, "There is just this one narrow approach which you see;
but when we attempt to pass by it they roll down volleys of stones from
yonder overhanging crag," pointing up, "and this is the state in which
you find yourself, if you chance to be caught;" and he pointed to some
poor fellows with their legs or ribs crushed to bits. "But when they
have expended their ammunition," said Xenophon, "there is nothing
else, is there, to hinder our passing? Certainly, except yonder handful
of fellows, there is no one in front of us that we can see; and of them,
only two or three apparently are armed, and the distance to be traversed
under fire is, as your eyes will tell you, about 150 feet as near as can be,
and of this space the first hundred is thickly covered with great pines
at intervals; under cover of these, what harm can come to our men
from stones, flying or rolling? So then, there is only fifty feet left to
cross, during a lull of stones." "Ay," said Cheirisophus, "but with our
first attempt to approach the trees a galling fire of stones commences."
"The very thing we want," said the other, "for they will use up their
ammunition all the quicker; but let us select a point from which we
shall have only a brief space to run across, if we can, and from which it
will be easier to get back, if we wish."

Thereupon Cheirisophus and Xenophon set out with Callimachus the
Parrhasian, the captain in command of the officers of the rearguard
that day; the rest of the captains remained out of danger. That done,
the next step was for a party of about seventy men to get away under
the trees, not in a body, but one by one, every one using his best pre-

caution; and Agasias the Stymphalian, and Aristonymus the Methydrian, who were also officers of the rearguard, were posted as supports outside the trees; for it was not possible for more than a single company to stand safely within the trees. Here Callimachus hit upon a scheme—he ran forward from the tree under which he was posted two or three paces, and as soon as the stones came whizzing, he retired easily, but at each excursion more than ten waggon-loads of rocks were expended. Agasias, seeing how Callimachus was amusing himself, and the whole army looking on as spectators, was seized with the fear that he might miss his chance of being first to run the gauntlet of the enemy's fire and get into the place. So, without a word of summons to his next neighbour, Aristonymus, or to Eurylochus of Lusia, both comrades of his, or to any one else, off he set on his own account, and passed the whole detachment. But Callimachus, seeing him tearing past, caught hold of his shield by the rim, and in the meantime Aristonymus the Methydrian ran past both, and after him Eurylochus of Lusia; for they were one and all aspirants to valour, and in that high pursuit, each was the eager rival of the rest. So in this strife of honour, they took the fortress, and when they had once rushed in, not a stone more was hurled from overhead.

And here a terrible spectacle displayed itself: the women first cast their infants down the cliff, and then they cast themselves after their fallen little ones, and the men likewise. In such a scene, Aeneas the Stymphalian, an officer, caught sight of a man with a fine dress about to throw himself over, and seized hold of him to stop him; but the other caught him to his arms, and both were gone in an instant headlong down the crags, and were killed. Out of this place the merest handful of human beings were taken prisoners, but cattle and asses in abundance and flocks of sheep.

From this place they marched through the Chalybes seven days, 165 miles. These were the bravest men whom they encountered on the whole march, coming to close quarters with them. They wore linen cuirasses reaching to the groin, and instead of the ordinary wings, a thickly-plaited fringe of cords. They were also provided with greaves and helmets, and at the girdle a short sabre, about as long as the Spartan dagger, with which they cut the throats of those they mastered, and after severing the head from the trunk they would march along carrying it, singing and dancing, when they drew within their enemy's field of view. They carried also a spear twenty-two feet long, lanced at one end.[2] This folk stayed in regular towns, and whenever the Hellenes passed by

[2] With a single point or spike only, the Hellenic spear having a spike at the butt end also.

they invariably hung close on their heels fighting. They had dwelling-places in their fortresses, and into them they had carried up their supplies, so that the Hellenes could get nothing from this district, but supported themselves on the flocks and herds they had taken from the Taochians. After this the Hellenes reached the river Harpasus, which was 400 feet broad. Hence they marched through the Scythenians four days—sixty-six miles—through a long level country to more villages, among which they halted three days, and got in supplies.

Passing on from thence sixty-six miles in four days, they reached a large and prosperous well-populated city, which went by the name of Gymnias, from which the governor of the country sent them a guide to lead them through a district hostile to his own. This guide told them that within five days he would lead them to a place from which they would see the sea. He added, "If I fail of my word, you are free to take my life." Accordingly he put himself at their head; but he no sooner set foot in the country hostile to himself than he fell to encouraging them to burn and harry the land; indeed his exhortations were so earnest, it was plain that it was for this he had come, and not out of the good-will he bore the Hellenes.

On the fifth day they reached the mountain, the name of which was Theches. No sooner had the men in front ascended it and caught sight of the sea than a great cry arose, and Xenophon, with the rearguard, catching the sound of it, conjectured that another set of enemies must surely be attacking in front; for they were followed by the inhabitants of the country, which was all aflame; indeed the rearguard had killed some and captured others alive by laying an ambuscade; they had taken also about twenty wicker shields, covered with the raw hides of shaggy oxen.

But as the shout became louder and nearer, and those who from time to time came up, began racing at the top of their speed towards the shouters, and the shouting continually recommenced with yet greater volume as the numbers increased, Xenophon settled in his mind that something extraordinary must have happened, so he mounted his horse, and taking with him Lycius and the cavalry, he galloped to the rescue. Presently they could hear the soldiers shouting and passing on the joyful word, *The sea! the sea!*

Thereupon they began running, rearguard and all, and the baggage animals and horses came galloping up. But when they had reached the summit, then indeed they fell to embracing one another—generals and officers and all—and the tears trickled down their cheeks. And on a sudden, some one, whoever it was, having passed down the order, the soldiers began bringing stones and erecting a great cairn, whereon they dedicated a host of untanned skins, and staves, and captured wicker shields, and with his own hand the guide hacked the shields to pieces, inviting the rest to follow his example. After this the Hellenes dismissed the guide with a present raised from the common store, to wit, a horse, a silver bowl, a Persian dress, and ten darics; but what he most begged to have were their rings, and of these he got several from the soldiers. So, after pointing out to them a village where they would find quarters, and the road by which they would proceed towards the land of the Macrones, as evening fell, he turned his back upon them in the night and was gone.

8. From this point the Hellenes marched through the country of the Macrones three days, thirty-three miles, and on the first day they reached the river, which formed the boundary between the land of the Macrones and the land of the Scythenians. Above them, on their right, they had a country of the sternest and ruggedest character, and on their left another river, into which the frontier river discharges itself, and which they must cross. This was thickly fringed with trees which, though not of any great bulk, were closely packed. As soon as they came up to them, the Hellenes proceeded to cut them down in their haste to get out of the place as soon as possible. But the Macrones, armed with wicker shields and lances and hair tunics, were already drawn up to receive them immediately opposite the crossing. They were cheering one another on, and kept throwing stones into the river, though they failed to reach the other side or do any harm.

At this juncture one of the light infantry came up to Xenophon; he had been, he said, a slave at Athens, and he wished to tell him that he recognised the speech of these people. "I think," said he, "this must be my native country, and if there is no objection I will have a talk with them." "No objection at all," replied Xenophon, "pray talk to them, and ask them first, who they are." In answer to this question they said they were Macrones. "Well, then," said he, "ask them why they are drawn up in battle and want to fight with us." They answered, "Because you are invading our country." The generals bade him say, "If so, it is with no intention certainly of doing it or you any harm: but we have been at war with the king, and are now returning to Hellas, and all we want is to reach the sea." The others asked, "Were they willing to give them pledges to that effect?" They replied, "Yes, they were ready to give and receive pledges to that effect." Then the Macrones gave a barbarian lance to the Hellenes, and the Hellenes a Hellenic lance to them. "For these," they said, "would serve as pledges," and both sides called upon the gods to witness.

After the pledges were exchanged, the Macrones fell to vigorously hewing down trees and constructing a road to help them across, mingling freely with the Hellenes and fraternising in their midst, and they afforded them as good a market as they could, and for three days conducted them on their march, until they had brought them safely to the confines of the Colchians. At this point they were confronted by a great mountain chain, which however was accessible, and on it the Colchians were drawn up for battle. In the first instance, the Hellenes drew up opposite in line of battle, as though they were minded to assault the hill in that order; but afterwards the generals determined to hold a council of war, and consider how to make the fairest fight.

Accordingly Xenophon said, "I am not for advancing in line, but advise to form companies by columns. To begin with, the line," he urged, "would be scattered and thrown into disorder at once; for we shall find the mountain full of inequalities, it will be pathless here and easy to traverse there. The mere fact of first having formed in line, and then seeing the line thrown into disorder, must exercise a disheartening effect. Again, if we advance several deep, the enemy will none the less overlap us, and turn their superfluous numbers to account as best they like; while, if we march in shallow order, we may fully expect our line to be cut through and through by the thick rain of missiles and rush of men, and if this happen anywhere along the line, the whole line will equally suffer. No; my notion is to form columns by companies, covering ground sufficient with spaces between the companies to allow the last companies of each flank to be outside the enemy's flanks. Thus we shall with our extreme companies be outside the enemy's line, and the best men at the head of their columns will lead the attack, and every company will pick its way where the ground is easy; also it will be difficult for the enemy to force his way into the intervening spaces, when there are companies on both sides; nor will it be easy for him to cut in two any individual company marching in column. If, too, any particular company should be pressed, the neighbouring company will come to the rescue, or if at any point any single company succeed in reaching the height, from that moment not one man of the enemy will stand his ground."

This proposal was carried, and they formed into columns by companies. Then Xenophon, returning from the right wing to the left, addressed the soldiers. "Men," he said, "these men whom you see in front of you are the sole obstacles still interposed between us and the haven of our hopes so long deferred. We will swallow them up whole, without cooking, if we can."

The several divisions fell into position, the companies were formed into columns, and the result was a total of something like eighty companies of heavy infantry, each company consisting on an average of 100 men. The light infantry and bowmen were arranged in three divisions—two outside to support the left and the right respectively, and the third in the centre—each division consisting of about 600 men.

Before starting, the generals passed the order to offer prayer; and with the prayer and battle hymn rising from their lips they commenced their advance. Cheirisophus and Xenophon, and the light infantry with them, advanced outside the enemy's line to right and left, and the enemy, seeing their advance, made an effort to keep parallel and confront them, but in order to do so, as he extended partly to right and partly to left, he was pulled to pieces, and there was a large space or hollow left in the centre of his line. Seeing them separate thus, the light infantry attached to the Arcadian battalion, under command of Aeschines, an Acarnanian, mistook the movement for flight, and with a loud shout rushed on, and these were the first to scale the mountain summit; but they were closely followed up by the Arcadian heavy infantry, under command of Cleanor of Orchomenus.

When they began running in that way, the enemy stood their ground no longer, but betook themselves to flight, one in one direction, one in another, and the Hellenes scaled the hill and found quarters in numerous villages which contained supplies in abundance. Here, generally speaking, there was nothing to excite their wonderment, but the numbers of bee-hives were indeed astonishing, and so were certain properties of the honey. The effect upon the soldiers who tasted the combs was, that they all went quite off their heads, and suffered from vomiting and diarrhoea, with a total inability to stand steady on their legs. A small dose produced a condition not unlike violent drunkenness, a large one an attack very like a fit of madness, and some dropped down, apparently at death's door. So they lay, hundreds of them, as if there had been a great defeat, a prey to the cruellest despondency. But the next day, none had died; and almost at the same hour of the day at which they had eaten they recovered their senses, and on the third or fourth day got on their legs again like convalescents after a severe course of medical treatment.

From this place they marched on two days—twenty-three miles—and reached the sea at Trapezus, a populous Hellenic city on the Euxine Sea, a colony of the Sinopeans, in the territory of the Colchians. Here they halted about thirty days in the villages of the Colchians, which they used as a base of operations to ravage the whole territory of Colchis. The men of Trapezus supplied the army with a market, entertained them, and gave them, as gifts of hospitality, oxen and wheat and wine. Further, they negotiated with them in behalf of their neighbours the

Colchians, who dwelt in the plain for the most part, and from this folk also came gifts of hospitality in the shape of cattle. And now the Hellenes made preparation for the sacrifice which they had vowed, and a sufficient number of cattle came in for them to offer thank-offerings for safe guidance to Zeus the Saviour, and to Heracles, and to the other gods, according to their vows. They instituted also a gymnastic contest on the mountain side, just where they were quartered, and chose Dracontius, a Spartan (who had been banished from home when a lad, having unintentionally slain another boy with a blow of his dagger), to superintend the course, and be president of the games.

As soon as the sacrifices were over, they handed over the hides of the beasts to Dracontius, and bade him lead the way to his racecourse. He merely waved his hand and pointed to where they were standing, and said, "There, this ridge is just the place for running, anywhere, everywhere." "But how," it was asked, "will they manage to wrestle on the hard scrubby ground?" "Oh! worse knocks for those who are thrown," the president replied. There was a mile race for boys, the majority being captive lads; and for the long race more than sixty Cretans competed; there was wrestling, boxing, and the pancratium. Altogether it was a beautiful spectacle. There was a large number of entries, and the rivalry, with their companions, male and female, standing as spectators, was immense. There was horse-racing also; the riders had to gallop down a steep incline to the sea, and then turn and come up again to the altar, and on the descent more than half rolled head over heels, and then back they came toiling up the tremendous steep, scarcely out of a walking pace. Loud were the shouts, the laughter, and the cheers.

BOOK V

[In the preceding portion of the narrative a detailed account is given of all that the Hellenes did, and how they fared on the march up with Cyrus; and also of all that befell them on their march subsequently, until they reached the seaboard of the Euxine Sea, or Pontus, and the Hellenic city of Trapezus, where they duly offered the sacrifice for safe deliverance which they had vowed to offer as soon as they set foot on a friendly soil.]

1. After this they met and took counsel concerning the remainder of the march. The first speaker was Antileon of Thurii. He rose and said, "For my part, men, I am weary by this time of getting kit together and packing up for a start, of walking and running and carrying heavy arms, and of tramping along in line, or mounting guard, and doing battle. The sole desire I now have is to cease from all these pains, and for the future, since here we have the sea before us, to sail on and on, stretched out like Odysseus,[1] and so to find myself in Hellas." When they heard these remarks, the soldiers showed their approval with loud cries of well said, and then another spoke to the same effect, and then another, and indeed all present. Then Cheirisophus got up and said, "I have a friend, gentlemen, who, as it happens, is now admiral, Anaxibius. If you like to send me to him, I think I can safely promise to return with some men-of-war and other vessels which will carry us. All you have to do, if you really wish to go home by sea, is to wait here till I come. I will be back soon." The soldiers were delighted at these words, and voted that Cheirisophus should set sail on his mission without delay.

After him Xenophon got up, and spoke as follows, "Cheirisophus, it is agreed, sets out in search of vessels, and we are going to await him. Let me tell you what, in my opinion, it is reasonable to do while we are waiting. First of all, we must provide ourselves with necessaries from hostile territory, for there is not a sufficient market, nor, if there were, have we, with a few solitary exceptions, the means of purchase. Now, the district is hostile, so that if you set off in search of provisions without care and precaution, the chances are that many of us will be lost. To meet this risk, I propose that we should organise foraging parties to

[1] See *Odyssey*, xiii. 116-119.

318

capture provisions, and, for the rest, not roam about the country at random. The organisation of the matter should be left to us." The resolution was passed. "Please listen to another proposal:" he continued, "Some of you, no doubt, will be going out to pillage. It will be best, I think, that whoever does so should in each case before starting inform us of his intent, and in what direction he means to go, so that we may know the exact number of those who are out and of those who stop behind. Thus we shall be able to help in preparing and starting the expedition where necessary; and in case of aid or reinforcements being called for, we shall know in what direction to proceed; or, again, if the attempt is to be undertaken by raw or less expert hands, we may throw in the weight of our experience and advice by endeavouring to discover the strength of those whom they design to attack." This proposal was also carried. "Here is another point," he continued, "to which I would draw your attention. Our enemies will not lack leisure to make raids upon us: nor is it unnatural, that they should lay plots against us; for we have appropriated what is theirs; they are seated over us ever on the watch. I propose then that we should have regular outposts round the camp. If we take it in succession to do picket and outlook duty, the enemy will be less able to harry us. And here is another point for your observation; supposing we knew for certain that Cheirisophus must return with a sufficient number of vessels, there would be no need of the remark, but as that is still problematical, I propose that we should try and get together vessels on the spot also. If he comes and finds us already provided for here, we shall have more ships than we need, that is all; while, if he fails to bring them, we shall have the local supply to fall back upon. I see ships sailing past perpetually, so we have only to ask the loan of some war-ships from the men of Trapezus, and we can bring them into port, and safeguard them with their rudders unshipped, until we have enough to carry us. By this course I think we shall not fail of finding the means of transport requisite." That resolution was also passed. He proceeded, "Consider whether you think it equitable to support by means of a general fund the ships' companies which we so impress, while they wait here for our benefit, and to agree upon a fare, on the principle of repaying kindnesses in kind." That too was passed. "Well then," said he, "in case, after all, our endeavours should not be crowned with success, and we find that we have not vessels enough, I propose that we should enjoin on the cities along the seaboard the duty of constructing and putting in order the roads, which we hear are impassable. They will be only to glad to obey, no doubt, out of mere terror and their desire to be rid of us."

This last proposal was met by loud cries and protestations against the idea of going by land at all. So, perceiving their infatuation, he did not put the question to the vote, but eventually persuaded the cities voluntarily to construct roads by the suggestion, "If you get your roads in good order, we shall all the sooner be gone." They further got a fifty-oared galley from the Trapezuntines, and gave the command of it to Dexippus, a Laconian, one of the Perioeci. This man altogether neglected to collect vessels, but slunk off himself, and vanished, ship and all, out of Pontus. Later on, however, he paid the penalty of his misdeeds. He became involved in some meddling in Thrace at the court of Seuthes, and was put to death by the Laconian Nicander. They also got a thirty-oared galley, the command of which was entrusted to Polycrates, an Athenian, and that officer brought into harbour to the camp all the vessels he could lay his hands on. If these were laden, they took out the freights and appointed guards to keep an eye on their preservation, while they used the ships themselves for transport service on the coast. While matters stood at this point, the Hellenes used to make forays with varying success; sometimes they captured prey and sometimes they failed. On one occasion Cleaenetus led his own and another company against a strong position, and was killed himself, with many others of his party.

2. The time came when it was no longer possible to capture provisions, going and returning to the camp in one day. In consequence of this, Xenophon took some guides from the Trapezuntines and led half the army out against the Drilae, leaving the other half to guard the camp. That was necessary, since the Colchians, who had been ousted from their houses, were assembled thickly, and sat eyeing them from the heights above; on the other hand the Trapezuntines, being friendly to the native inhabitants, were not for leading the Hellenes to places where it was easy to capture provisions. But against the Drilae, from whom they personally suffered, they would lead them with enthusiasm, up into mountainous and scarcely accessible fortresses, and against the most warlike people of any in the Pontus.

But when the Hellenes had reached the uplands, the Drilae set fire to all their fastnesses which they thought could be taken easily, and beat a retreat; and except here and there a stray pig or bullock or other animal which had escaped the fire there was nothing to capture; but there was one fastness which served as their metropolis: into this the different streams of people collected; round it ran a tremendously deep ravine, and the approaches to the place were difficult. So the light infantry ran forward about half a mile in advance of the heavy infantry, and crossed the ravine; and seeing quantities of sheep and other things, proceeded to attack the place. Close at their heels followed a number of those who had set out on the foray armed with spears, so that the storming party across the ravine amounted to more than 2,000. But, finding that they could not take the place by fighting, as there was a trench running round it, mounded up some breadth, with a stockade on the top of the earthwork and a close-packed row of wooden bastions, they made an attempt to run back, but the enemy fell upon them from the rear. To get away by a sudden rush was out of the question, since the descent from the fortress into the ravine only admitted of moving in single file. Under the circumstances they sent to Xenophon, who was in command of the heavy infantry. The messenger came and delivered his message, "There is a stronghold full of all sorts of stores, but we cannot take it, it is too strong; nor can we easily get away; the enemy rush out and deliver battle, and the return is difficult."

On hearing this, Xenophon pushed forward his heavy infantry to the edge of the ravine, and there ordered them to take up a position, while he himself with the officers crossed over to determine whether it were better to withdraw the party already across, or to bring over the heavy infantry also, on the supposition that the fortress might be taken. In favour of the latter opinion it was agreed that the retreat must cost many lives, and the officers were further disposed to think, they could take the place. Xenophon consented, relying on the victims, for the seers had announced, that there would be a battle, but that the result of the expedition would be good. So he sent the officers to bring the heavy troops across, while he himself remained, having drawn off all the light infantry and forbidden all sharp-shooting at long range. As soon as the heavy infantry had arrived, he ordered each captain to form his company, in whatever way he hoped to make it most effective in the coming struggle. Side by side together they stood, these captains, not for the first time to-day competitors for the award of manly virtue. While they were thus employed, he—the general—was engaged in passing down his order along the ranks of the light infantry and archers respectively to march with the javelin on its thong and the arrow to the string, ready at the word shoot to discharge their missiles, while the light troops were to have their wallets well stocked with sling-stones; lastly, he despatched his adjutants to see to the proper carrying out of these orders.

And now the preparations were complete: the officers and lieutenants and all others claiming to be the peers of these, were drawn up in their several places. With a glance each was able to command the rest in the crescent-like disposition which the ground invited. Presently the notes of the battle hymn arose, the trumpet sounded, and with a cry in honour of the warrior-god, commenced a rush of the heavy infantry at full speed under cover of a storm of missiles, lances, arrows, bullets, but most of all stones hurled from the hand, while there were some who brought firebrands to bear. Overwhelmed by this crowd of missiles, the enemy left their stockades and their bastion towers, which gave Agasias the Stymphalian and Philoxenus of Pellene a chance not to be missed; laying aside their heavy arms, up they went in bare tunics only, and one hauled another up, and meantime another had mounted, and the place was taken, as they thought. Then the peltasts and light troops rushed in and began snatching what each man could. Xenophon the while, posted at the gates, kept back as many of the hoplites as he could, for there were other enemies now visible on certain strong citadel heights; and after a lapse of no long time a shout arose within, and the men came running back, some still clutching what they had seized; and presently here and there a wounded man; and mighty was the jostling about the portals. To the questions which were put to them the outpouring fugitives repeated the same story: there was a citadel within and enemies in crowds were making savage sallies and beating the fellows inside.

At that Xenophon ordered Tolmides the herald to proclaim that all who wanted plunder should enter. In poured the surging multitude, and the counter-current of persons elbowing their passage in prevailed over the stream of those who issued forth, until they beat back and cooped up the enemy within the citadel again. So outside the citadel everything was sacked and pillaged by the Hellenes, and the heavy infantry took up their position, some about the stockades, others along the road leading up to the citadel. Xenophon and the officers meantime considered the possibility of taking the citadel, for if so, their safety was assured; but if otherwise, it would be very difficult to get away. As the result of their deliberations they agreed that the place was impregnable. Then they began making preparations for the retreat. Each set of men proceeded to pull down the palisading which faced themselves; further, they sent away all who were useless or who had enough to do to carry their burdens, with the mass of the heavy infantry accompanying them; the officers in each case leaving behind men whom they could severally depend upon.

But as soon as they began to retreat, out rushed upon them from within a throng, armed with wicker shields and lances, greaves and Paphlagonian helmets. Others might be seen scaling the houses on this side and that of the road leading into the citadel. Even pursuit in the direction of the gates leading to the citadel was dangerous, since the enemy kept hurling down on them great beams from above, so that to stop and to make off were alike dangerous, and night approaching was full of terrors. But in the midst of their fighting and their despair some god gave them a means of safety. All of a sudden, by whatsoever hand ignited, a flame shot up; it came from a house on the right hand, and as this gradually fell in, the people from the other houses on the right took to their heels and fled.

Xenophon, laying this lesson of fortune to heart, gave orders to set fire to the left-hand houses also, which being of wood burned quickly, with the result that the occupants of these also took to flight. The men immediately at their front were the sole annoyance now, and these were safe to fall upon them as they made their exit and in their descent. Here then the word was passed for all who were out of range to bring up logs of wood and pile them between themselves and the enemy, and when there was enough of these they set them on fire; they also fired the houses along the trench-work itself, so as to occupy the attention of the enemy. Thus they got off, though with difficulty, and escaped from the place by putting a fire between them and the enemy; and the whole city was burned down, houses, turrets, stockading, and everything belonging to it except the citadel.

Next day the Hellenes were bent on getting back with the provisions; but as they dreaded the descent to Trapezus, which was precipitous and narrow, they laid a false ambuscade, and a Mysian, called after the name of his nation Mysus, took ten of the Cretans and halted in some thick brushy ground, where he made a feint of endeavouring to escape the notice of the enemy. The glint of their light shields, which were of brass, now and again gleamed through the brushwood. The enemy, seeing it all through the thicket, were confirmed in their fears of an ambuscade. But the army meanwhile was quietly making its descent; and when it appeared that they had crept down far enough, the signal was given to the Mysian to flee as fast as he could, and he, springing up, fled with his men. The rest of the party, that is the Cretans, saying, "We are caught if we race," left the road and plunged into a wood, and tumbling and rolling down the gullies, were saved. The Mysian, fleeing along the road, kept crying for assistance, which they sent him, and picked him up wounded. The party of rescue now beat a retreat themselves with their face to the foe, exposed to a shower of missiles, to which some of the Cretan bowmen responded with their arrows. In this way they all reached the camp in safety.

3. Now when Cheirisophus did not arrive, and the supply of ships was insufficient, and to get provisions longer was impossible, they resolved to depart. On board the vessels they embarked the sick, and those above forty years of age, with the boys and women, and all the baggage which the soldiers were not absolutely forced to take for their own use. The two eldest generals, Philesius and Sophaenetus, were put in charge,

and so the party embarked, while the rest resumed their march, for the road was now completely constructed. Continuing their march that day and the next, on the third they reached Cerasus, a Hellenic city on the sea, and a colony of Sinope, in the country of the Colchians. Here they halted ten days, and there was a review and numbering of the troops under arms, when there were found to be 8,600 men. So many had escaped; the rest had perished at the hands of the enemy, or by reason of the snow, or else disease.

At this time and place they divided the money accruing from the captives sold, and a tithe selected for Apollo and Artemis of the Ephesians was divided between the generals, each of whom took a portion to guard for the gods, Neon the Asinaean taking on behalf of Cheirisophus.

Out of the portion which fell to Xenophon he caused a dedicatory offering to Apollo to be made and dedicated among the treasures of the Athenians at Delphi. It was inscribed with his own name and that of Proxenus, his friend, who was killed with Clearchus. The gift for Artemis of the Ephesians was, in the first instance, left behind by him in Asia at the time when he left that part of the world himself with Agesilaus on the march into Boeotia.[2] He left it behind in charge of Megabyzus, the sacristan of the goddess, thinking that the voyage on which he was starting was likely to be dangerous. In the event of his coming out of it alive, he charged Megabyzus to restore to him the deposit; but should any evil happen to him, then he was to cause to be made and to dedicate on his behalf to Artemis, whatsoever thing he thought would be pleasing to the goddess.

In the days of his banishment, when Xenophon was now established by the Lacedaemonians as a colonist in Scillus, a place which lies on the main road to Olympia, Megabyzus arrived on his way to Olympia as a spectator to attend the games, and restored to him the deposit. Xenophon took the money and bought for the goddess a plot of ground at a point indicated to him by the oracle. The plot, it so happened, had its own Selinus river flowing through it, just as at Ephesus the river Selinus flows past the temple of Artemis, and in both streams fish and mussels are to be found. On the estate at Scillus there is hunting and shooting of all sorts of beasts of the chase.

Here with the sacred money he built an altar and a temple, and ever after, year by year, tithed the fruits of the land in their season and did sacrifice to the goddess, while all the citizens and neighbours, men and women, shared in the festival. The goddess herself provided for the ban-

---

[2] In the year 394 B.C. The circumstances under which Agesilaus was recalled from Asia, with the details of his march and the battle of Coronea, are described by Xenophon in the fourth book of the *Hellenica*.

queters meat and loaves and wine and sweetmeats, with portions of the victims sacrificed from the sacred pasture, as also of those which were slain in the chase; for Xenophon's own sons, with the sons of the other citizens, always made a hunting excursion against the festival day, in which any grown men who liked might join. The game was captured partly from the sacred district itself, partly from Pholoe, pigs and gazelles and stags. The place lies on the direct road from Lacedaemon to Olympia, about two and one-half miles from the temple of Zeus in Olympia, and within the sacred enclosure there is meadow-land and wood-covered hills, suited to the breeding of pigs and goats and cattle and horses, so that even the pack-animals of the people passing to the feast fare sumptuously. The shrine is girdled by a grove of cultivated trees, yielding dessert fruits in their season. The temple itself is a facsimile on a small scale of the great temple at Ephesus, and the image of the goddess is like the golden statue at Ephesus, save only that it is made, not of gold, but of cypress wood. Beside the temple stands a column bearing this inscription: THE PLACE IS SACRED TO ARTEMIS. HE WHO HOLDS IT AND ENJOYS THE FRUITS OF IT IS BOUND TO SACRIFICE YEARLY A TITHE OF THE PRODUCE. AND FROM THE RESIDUE THEREOF TO KEEP IN REPAIR THE SHRINE. IF ANY MAN FAIL IN AUGHT OF THIS THE GODDESS HERSELF WILL LOOK TO THE MATTER.

4. From Cerasus they continued the march, the same portion of the troops being conveyed by sea as before, and the rest marching by land. When they had reached the frontiers of the Mossynoecians[3] they sent to them Timesitheus the Trapezuntine, who was the proxenus of the Mossynoecians, to inquire whether they were to pass through their territory as friends or foes. They, trusting in their strongholds, replied that they would not give them passage. It was then that Timesitheus informed them that the Mossynoecians on the farther side of the country were hostile to these members of the tribe; and it was resolved to invite the former to make an alliance, if they wished it. So Timesitheus was sent, and came back with their chiefs. On their arrival there was a conference of the Mossynoecian chiefs and the generals of the Hellenes, and Xenophon made a speech which Timesitheus interpreted. He said, "Men of the Mossynoecians, our desire is to reach Hellas in safety; and since we have no vessels we must needs go by foot, but these people who, as we hear, are your enemies, prevent us. Will you take us for your allies? Now is your chance to exact vengeance for any wrong, which they at any time may have put upon you, and for the future they will be your subjects; but if you send us about our business, consider and ask yourselves from what quarter will you ever again obtain so strong a force

[3] Dwellers in mossyns. or wooden towers.

to help you?" To this the chief of the Mossynoecians answered that the proposal was in accordance with their wishes and they welcomed the alliance. "Good," said Xenophon, "but to what use do you propose to put us, if we become your allies? And what will you in your turn be able to do to assist our passage?" They replied, "We can make an incursion into this country hostile to yourselves and us, from the opposite side, and also send you ships and men to this place, who will aid you in fighting and conduct you on the road."

On this understanding, they exchanged pledges and were gone. The next day they returned, bringing 300 canoes, each hollowed out of a single trunk. There were three men in each, two of whom disembarked and fell into rank, while the third remained. Then the one set took the boats and sailed back again, while the other two-thirds who remained marshalled themselves in the following way. They stood in rows of about 100 each, like the rows of dancers in a chorus, standing opposite one another, and all bearing wicker shields, made of white oxhide, shaggy, and shaped like an ivy leaf; in the right hand they brandished a javelin about nine feet long, with a lance in front, and rounded like a ball at the butt end of the shaft.

Their bodies were clad in short tunics, scarcely reaching to the knees and in texture closely resembling that of a linen bedclothes' bag; on their heads they wore leathern helmets just like the Paphlagonian helmet, with a tuft of hair in the middle, as like a tiara in shape as possible. They carried moreover iron battle-axes. Then one of them gave, as it were, the key-note and started, while the rest, taking up the strain and the step, followed singing and marking time. Passing through the various corps and heavy armed battalions of the Hellenes, they marched straight against the enemy, to what appeared the most assailable of his fortresses. It was situated in front of the city, or mother city, as it is called, which latter contains the high citadel of the Mossynoecians. This citadel was the real bone of contention, the occupants at any time being acknowledged as the masters of all the other Mossynoecians. The present holders (so it was explained) had no right to its possession; for the sake of self-aggrandisement they had seized what was really common property.

Some of the Hellenes followed the attacking party, not under the orders of the generals, but for the sake of plunder. As they advanced, the enemy for a while kept quiet; but as they got near the place, they made a sortie and routed them, killing several of the barbarians as well as some of the Hellenes who had gone up with them; and so pursued them until they saw the Hellenes advancing to the rescue. Then they turned round and made off, first cutting off the heads of the dead men and flaunting them in the face of the Hellenes and of their own private foes, dancing the while and singing in a measured strain. But the Hellenes were much vexed to think that their foes had only been rendered bolder, while the Hellenes who had formed part of the expedition had turned tail and fled, in spite of their numbers; a thing which had not happened previously during the whole expedition. So Xenophon called a meeting of the Hellenes and spoke as follows, "Soldiers, do not in any wise be cast down by what has happened, be sure that good no less than evil will be the result; for to begin with, you now know certainly that those who are going to guide us are in very deed hostile to those with whom necessity drives us to quarrel; and, in the next place, some of our own body, these Hellenes who have made so light of orderly array and joint action with ourselves, as though they could achieve in the company of barbarians all they could with ourselves, have paid the penalty and been taught a lesson, so that another time they will be less likely to leave our ranks. But you must be prepared to show these friendly barbarians that you are of a better sort, and prove to the enemy that battle with the undisciplined is one thing, but with men like yourselves another."

Accordingly they halted, as they were, that day. Next day they sacrificed and finding the victims favourable, they breakfasted, formed the companies into columns, and with the barbarians arranged in similar order on their left, began their march. Between the companies were the archers only slightly retired behind the front of the heavy infantry, on account of the enemy's active light troops, who ran down and kept up volleys of stones. These were held in check by the archers and peltasts; and steadily step by step the mass marched on, first to the position from which the barbarians and those with them had been driven two days back, and where the enemy were now drawn up to meet them. Thus it came to pass that the barbarians first grappled with the peltasts and maintained the battle until the heavy infantry were close, when they turned and fled. The peltasts followed without delay, and pursued them right up to their city, while the heavy troops in unbroken order followed. As soon as they were up at the houses of the capital, there and then the enemy, collecting all together in one strong body, fought valiantly, and hurled their javelins, or else clenched their long stout spears, almost too heavy for a man to wield, and did their best to ward off the attack at close quarters.

But when the Hellenes, instead of giving way, kept massing together more thickly, the barbarians fled from this place also, and in a body deserted the fortress. Their king, who sat in his wooden tower or mossyn, built on the citadel (there he sits and there they maintain him, all at the common cost, and guard him), refused to come forth, as did also those in the fortress first taken, and so were burned up where they were, their mossyns, themselves, and all. The Hellenes, pillaging and ransacking these places, discovered in the different houses treasures and magazines of loaves, pile upon pile, the ancestral stores, as the Mossynoecians told them; but the new corn was laid up apart with the straw-stalk and ear together, and this was for the most part spelt. Slices of dolphin were another discovery, in narrow-necked jars, all properly salted and pickled; and there was blubber of dolphin in vessels, which the Mossynoecians used precisely as the Hellenes use oil. Then there were large stores of nuts on the upper floor, the broad kind without a division.[4] This was also a chief article of food with them—boiled nuts and baked loaves. Wine was also discovered. This, from its rough, dry quality, tasted sharp when drunk pure, but mixed with water was sweet and fragrant.

The Hellenes breakfasted and then started forward on their march, having first delivered the stronghold to their allies among the Mossynoecians. As for the other strongholds belonging to tribes allied with their foes, which they passed, the most accessible were either deserted by their inhabitants or surrendered voluntarily. The following description will apply to the majority of them: the cities were on an average ten miles apart, some more, some less; but so elevated is the country and intersected by such deep clefts that if they chose to shout across to one another, their cries would be heard from one city to another. When, in the course of their march, they came upon a friendly population, these would entertain them with exhibitions of fatted children belonging to the wealthy classes, fed up on boiled chestnuts until they were as white as white can be, of skin plump and delicate, and very nearly as broad as they were long, with their backs variegated and their breasts tattooed with patterns of all sorts of flowers. They sought after the women in the Hellenic army, and wanted to have intercourse with them openly in broad daylight, for that was their custom. The whole community, male and female alike, were fair-complexioned and white-skinned.

It was agreed that this was the most barbaric and outlandish people that they had passed through on the whole expedition, and the furthest removed from Hellenic customs, doing in a crowd precisely what other people would prefer to do in solitude, and when alone behaving exactly as others would behave in company, talking to themselves and laughing at their own expense, standing still and then again capering about, wherever they might chance to be, without rhyme or reason, as if their sole business were to show off to the rest of the world.

5. Through this country, friendly or hostile as the chance might be, the Hellenes marched, eight days in all, and reached the Chalybes. These

[4] Chestnuts.

were a people few in number, and subject to the Mossynoecians. Their livelihood was for the most part derived from mining and forging iron.

Thence they came to the Tibarenians. The country of the Tibarenians was far more level, and their fortresses lay on the seaboard and were less strong, whether by art or nature. The generals wanted to attack these places, so that the army might get some pickings, and they would not accept the gifts of hospitality which came in from the Tibarenians, but bidding them wait till they had taken counsel, they proceeded to offer sacrifice. After several abortive attempts, the seers at last all pronounced an opinion that the gods in no wise countenanced war. Then they accepted the gifts of hospitality, and marching through what was now recognised as a friendly country, in two days reached Cotyora, a Hellenic city, and a colony of Sinope, though situated in the territory of the Tibarenians. [Up to this point the expedition was conducted on land, and the distance traversed on foot from the battle-field near Babylon down to Cotyora amounted to 122 days' marches—that is to say, 620 parasangs, or 18,000 furlongs,[5] or if measured in time, an eight months' march.]

Here they halted forty-five days, during which they first of all sacrificed to the gods, and instituted processions, each set of the Hellenes according to their several tribes, with gymnastic contests. Provisions they got in meanwhile, partly from Paphlagonia, partly from the estates of the Cotyorites, for the latter would neither provide them a market nor receive their sick within their walls.

Meanwhile ambassadors arrived from Sinope, full of fears, not only for the Cotyorites and their city, which belonged to Sinope, and brought in tribute, but also for the territory which, as they had heard, was being pillaged. Accordingly they came to the camp and made a speech. Hecatonymus, who was reported to be a clever orator, acted as their spokesman. "Soldiers," he said, "the city of the Sinopeans has sent us to offer you, as Hellenes, our compliments and congratulations on your victories over the barbarians; and next, to express our joyful satisfaction that you have surmounted all those terrible sufferings of which we have heard, and have reached this place in safety. As Hellenes we claim to receive at your hands, as fellow-Hellenes, kindness and not harm. We have certainly not ourselves set you an example heretofore of evil treatment. Now the Cotyorites are our colonists. It was we who gave them this country to dwell in, having taken it from the barbarians; for which reason also they, with the men of Cerasus and Trapezus, pay us an appointed tribute. So that, whatever mischief you inflict on the men of Cotyora, the city of Sinope takes as personal to herself. At the present

[5] About 2,000 miles.

time we hear that you have made forcible entry into their city, some of
you, and are quartered in the houses, besides taking forcibly from the
Cotyorite estates whatever you need, without asking permission. Now
against these things we enter protest. If you mean to go on so doing,
you will drive us to make friends with Corylas and the Paphlagonians,
or any one else we can find."

To meet these charges Xenophon, in behalf of the soldiers, rose and
said, "As to ourselves, men of Sinope, having got so far, we are well
content to have saved our bodies and our arms. Indeed it was impossible at one and the same moment to keep our enemies at bay and to
despoil them of their goods and chattels. And now, since we have reached
Hellenic cities, how has it fared with us? At Trapezus they gave us a
market, and we paid for our provisions at a fair market price. In return
for the honour they did us, and the gifts of hospitality they gave the
army, we requited them with honour. Where the barbarian was friendly
to them, we stayed our hands from injury; or under their escort, we
did damage to their enemies to the utmost of our power. Ask them,
what sort of people they found us. They are here, some of them, to
answer for themselves. Their fellow-citizens and the state of Trapezus,
for friendship's sake, have sent them with us to act as our guides.

"But wherever we come, be it foreign or Hellenic soil, and find no
market for provisions, we are wont to help ourselves, not out of insolence but from necessity. There have been tribes like the Carduchians,
the Taochians, the Chaldaeans, which, although they were not subject
to the great king, yet were no less formidable than independent. These
we had to bring over by our arms. The necessity of getting provisions
forced us; since they refused to offer us a market. Whereas some other
folk, like the Macrones, in spite of their being barbarians, we regarded
as our friends, simply because they did afford us the best market in
their power, and we took no single thing of theirs by force. But, to come
to these Cotyorites, whom you claim to be your people, if we have taken
anything from them, they have themselves to blame, for they did not
deal with us as friends, but shut their gates in our faces. They would
neither welcome us within nor furnish us with a market without. The
only justification they alleged was that your governor had authorised
this conduct.

"As to your assertion," he continued, turning to Hecatonymus, "that
we have got in by force and have taken up quarters, this is what we
did. We requested them to receive our sick and wounded under cover;
and when they refused to open their gates, we walked in where the place
itself invited us. All the violence we have committed amounts to this,
that our sick folk are quartered under cover, paying for their expenses,

and we keep a sentry at the gates, so that our sick and wounded may not lie at the mercy of your governor, but we may have it in our power to remove them whenever we like. The rest of us, you observe, are camping under the canopy of heaven, in regular rank and file, and we are ready to requite kindness with kindness, but to repel evil vigorously. And as for your threat," he said, once again turning to the spokesman, "that you will, if it suits you, make alliance with Corylas and the Paphlagonians to attack us, for our part, we have no objection to fighting both sets of you, if so be we must; we have already fought others many times more numerous than you. Besides, 'if it suits us,' as you put it, to make the Paphlagonian our friend (report says that he has a hankering after your city and some other places on the seaboard), we can enhance the value of our friendship by helping to win for him what he covets."

Thereupon the ambassadors showed very plainly their annoyance with Hecatonymus, on account of the style of his remarks, and one of them stepped forward to explain that their intention in coming was not at all to raise a war, but on the contrary to demonstrate their friendliness. "And if you come to Sinope itself," the speaker continued, "we will welcome you there with gifts of hospitality. Meanwhile we will enjoin upon the citizens of this place to give you what they can; for we can see that every word of what you say is true." Thereupon the Cotyorites sent gifts of hospitality, and the generals of the Hellenes entertained the ambassadors of the Sinopeans. Many and friendly were the topics of conversation; freely flowed the talk on things in general; and, in particular, both parties were able to make inquiries and satisfy their curiosity concerning the remaining portion of the march.

6. Such was the conclusion of that day. On the following day the generals summoned an assembly of the soldiers, when it was resolved to invite the men of Sinope, and to take advice with them touching the remainder of the journey. In the event of their having to continue it on foot, the Sinopeans through their acquaintance with Paphlagonia would be useful to them; while, if they had to go by sea, the services of the same people would be at a premium; for who but they could furnish ships sufficient for the army? Accordingly, they summoned their ambassadors, and took counsel with them, begging them, on the strength of the sacred ties which bind Hellenes to Hellenes, to inaugurate the good reception they had spoken of, by present kindliness and their best advice.

Hecatonymus rose and wished at once to offer an apology with regard to what he had said about the possibility of making friends with the Paphlagonians. "The words were not intended," he said, "to convey a threat, as though they intended to go to war with the Hellenes, but as meaning rather: although we have it in our power to be friendly with the barbarians, we will choose the Hellenes." Then, being urged to aid them by some advice, with a prayer, he commenced, "If I bestow upon you the best counsel I am able, god grant that blessings in abundance may descend on me; but if the contrary, may evil befall me! 'Sacred counsel,' as the saying goes,—well, sirs, if ever the saying held, it should hold I think to-day; when, if I be proved to have given you good counsel, I shall not lack panegyrists, or if evil, your imprecations will be many-tongued.

"As to trouble, I am quite aware, we shall have much more trouble if you are conveyed by sea, for we must provide the vessels; whereas, if you go by land, all the fighting will devolve on you. Still, let come what may, I must state my views. I have an intimate acquaintance with the country of the Paphlagonians and their power. The country possesses the two features of hill and vale, that is to say, the fairest plains and the highest mountains. To begin with the mountains, I know the exact point at which you must make your entry. It is precisely where the horns of a mountain tower over both sides of the road. Let the merest handful of men occupy these and they can hold the pass with ease; for when that is done not all the enemies in the world could effect a passage. I could point out the whole with my finger, if you like to send any one with me to the scene.

"So much for the mountain barrier. But the next thing I know is that there are plains and a cavalry which the barbarians themselves hold to be superior to the entire cavalry of the great king. Why, only the other day these people refused to present themselves to the summons of the king; their chief is too proud for that.

"But now, supposing you were able to seize the mountain barrier, by stealth or expedition, before the enemy could stop you; supposing further, you were able to win an engagement in the plain against not only their cavalry but their more than 120,000 infantry,—you will only find yourself face to face with the rivers, a series of them. First the Thermodon, 300 feet broad, which I take it will be difficult to pass, especially with a host of foes in front and another host following behind. Next comes the Iris river, 300 feet broad; and thirdly, the Halys, at least a quarter of a mile broad, which you could not possibly cross without vessels, and who is going to supply you with vessels? In the same way too the Parthenius is impassable, which you will reach if you cross the Halys. For my part, then, I consider the land-journey, I will not say difficult, but absolutely impossible for you. Whereas if you go by sea, you can coast along from here to Sinope, and from Sinope to Heraclea.

From Heraclea onwards there is no difficulty, whether by land or by sea; for there are plenty of vessels at Heraclea."

After he had finished his remarks, some of his hearers thought they detected a certain bias in them. He would not have spoken so, but for his friendship with Corylas, whose official representative he was. Others guessed he had an itching palm, and that he was hoping to receive a present for his advice. Others again suspected that his object was to prevent their going by foot and doing some mischief to the country of the Sinopeans. However that might be, the Hellenes voted in favour of continuing the journey by sea. After this Xenophon said, "Sinopeans, the army has chosen that method of procedure which you advise, and thus the matter stands. If there are sure to be vessels enough to make it impossible for a single man to be left behind, go by sea we will; but if part of us are to be left while part go by sea, we will not set foot on board the vessels. One fact we plainly recognise, strength is everything to us. So long as we have the mastery, we shall be able to protect ourselves and get provisions; but if we are once caught at the mercy of our foes, it is plain, we shall be reduced to slavery." On hearing this the ambassadors bade them send an embassy. They sent Callimachus the Arcadian, and Ariston the Athenian, and Samolas the Achaean.

So these set off, but meanwhile a thought shaped itself in the mind of Xenophon, as there before his eyes lay that vast army of Hellene hoplites, and that other array of peltasts, archers, and slingers, with cavalry to boot, and all in a state of thorough efficiency from long practice, hardened veterans, and all collected in Pontus, where to raise so large a force would cost a mint of money. Then the idea dawned upon him: how noble an opportunity to acquire new territory and power for Hellas, by the founding of a colony—a city of no mean size, moreover, said he to himself, as he reckoned up their own numbers—and besides themselves a population planted on the shores of Pontus. Thereupon he summoned Silanus the Ambraciot, the soothsayer of Cyrus above mentioned, and before breathing a syllable to any of the soldiers, he consulted the victims by sacrifice.

But Silanus, in apprehension lest these ideas might embody themselves, and the army be permanently halted at some point or other, set a tale going among the men, to the effect that Xenophon wanted to detain the army and found a city in order to win himself a name and acquire power, Silanus himself wishing to reach Hellas with all possible speed, for the simple reason that he still had the 3,000 darics presented to him by Cyrus on the occasion of the sacrifice when he hit the truth so happily about the ten days. Silanus's story was variously received, some few of the soldiers thinking it would be an excellent thing to stay in that country; but the majority were strongly averse. The next incident was that Timasion the Dardanian with Thorax the Boeotian, addressed themselves to some Heracleot and Sinopean traders who had come to Cotyora, and told them that if they did not find means to furnish the army with pay sufficient to keep them in provisions on the homeward voyage, all that great force would most likely settle down permanently in Pontus. "Xenophon has a pet idea," they continued, "which he urges upon us. We are to wait until the ships come, and then we are suddenly to turn round to the army and say, 'Soldiers, we now see the straits we are in, unable to keep ourselves in provisions on the return voyage, or to make our friends at home a little present at the end of our journey. But if you like to select some place on the inhabited seaboard of the Black Sea which may take your fancy and there put in, this is open to you to do. Those who like to go home, go; those who care to stay here, stay. You have vessels now, so that you can make a sudden attack upon any point you choose.' "

The merchants went off with this tale and reported it to every city they came to in turn, nor did they go alone, but Timasion the Dardanian sent a fellow-citizen of his own, Eurymachus, with the Boeotian Thorax, to repeat the same story. So when it reached the ears of the men of Sinope and the Heracleots, they sent to Timasion and pressed him to accept a payment, in return for which he was to arrange for the departure of the troops. Timasion was only too glad to hear this, and he took the opportunity when the soldiers were convened in meeting to make the following remarks, "Soldiers, do not set your thoughts on staying here; let Hellas, and Hellas only, be the object of your affection, for I am told that certain persons have been sacrificing on this very question, without saying a word to you. Now I can promise you, if you once leave these waters, to furnish you with regular monthly pay, dating from the first of the month, at the rate of one cyzicene a head per month. I will bring you to the Troad, from which part I am an exile, and my own state is at your service. They will receive me with open arms. I will be your guide personally, and I will take you to places where you will get plenty of money. I know every corner of the Aeolid, and Phrygia, and the Troad, and indeed the whole satrapy of Pharnabazus, partly because it is my birthplace, partly from campaigns in that region with Clearchus and Dercylidas." [6]

No sooner had he ceased than up got Thorax the Boeotian. This was a man who had a standing battle with Xenophon about the generalship of the army. What he said was that, if they once got fairly out of the

[6] Dercylidas was governor of Abydos in 411 B.C.; in 399 B.C. he superseded Thimbron in Asia Minor; and was himself superseded by Agesilaus in 396 B.C.

Euxine, there was the Chersonese, a beautiful and prosperous country, where they could settle or not, as they chose. Those who liked could stay; and those who liked could return to their homes; how ridiculous then, when there was so much territory in Hellas and to spare, to be poking about in the land of the barbarian. "But until you find yourselves there," he added, "I, no less than Timasion, can guarantee you regular pay." This he said, knowing what promises had been made Timasion by the men of Heraclea and Sinope to induce them to set sail.

Meanwhile Xenophon held his peace. Then up got Philesius and Lycon, two Achaeans. "It was monstrous," they said, "that Xenophon should be privately persuading people to stop there, and consulting the victims for that end, without letting the army into the secret, or breathing a syllable in public about the matter." When it came to this, Xenophon was forced to get up, and speak as follows, "Men, you are well aware that my habit is to sacrifice at all times; whether in your own behalf or my own, I strive in every thought, word, and deed to be directed as is best for yourselves and me. And in the present instance my sole object was to learn whether it were better even so much as to broach the subject, and so take action, or to have absolutely nothing to do with the project. Now Silanus the soothsayer assured me by his answer of what was the main point, that the victims were favourable. No doubt Silanus knew that I was not unversed myself in his lore, as I have so often assisted at the sacrifice; but he added that there were symptoms in the victims of some guile or conspiracy against me. That was a happy discovery on his part, seeing that he was himself conspiring at the moment to traduce me before you; since it was he who set the tale going that I had actually made up my mind to carry out these projects without procuring your consent. Now, for my part, if I saw that you were in any difficulties, I should set myself to discover how you might capture a city, on the understanding of course that all who wished might sail away at once, leaving those who did not wish, to follow at a later date, with something perhaps in their pockets to benefit their friends at home. Now, however, as I see that the men of Heraclea and Sinope are to send you ships to assist you to sail away, and more than one person guarantees to give you regular monthly pay, it is, I admit, a rare chance to be safely piloted to the haven of our hopes, and at the same time to receive pay for our preservation. For myself I have done with that dream, and to those, who came to me to urge these projects, my advice is to have done with them. In fact, this is my view. As long as you stay together united as to-day, you will command respect and procure provisions; for might certainly exercises a right over what belongs to the weaker. But once broken up, with your force split into little bits, you will neither be able to get subsistence, nor indeed will you get off without paying dearly for it. In fact, my resolution coincides precisely with yours. It is that we should set off for Hellas, and if any one stops behind, or is caught deserting before the whole army is in safety, let him be judged as an evil-doer. Pray let all who are in favour of this proposition hold up their hands."

They all held them up; only Silanus began shouting and vainly striving to maintain the right of departure for all who liked to depart. But the soldiers would not suffer him, threatening him that if he were himself caught attempting to run away they would inflict the aforesaid penalty. After this, when the Heracleots learned that the departure by sea was resolved upon, and that the measure itself emanated from Xenophon, they sent the vessels indeed; but as to the money which they had promised to Timasion and Thorax as pay for the soldiers, they were not as good as their word, in fact they cheated them both. Thus the two who had guaranteed regular monthly pay were utterly confounded, and stood in terror of the soldiers. What they did then, was to take to them the other generals to whom they had communicated their former transactions (that is to say, all except Neon the Asinaean, who, as lieutenant-general, was acting for Cheirisophus during his continued absence). This done they came in a body to Xenophon and said that their views were changed. As they had now got the ships, they thought it best to sail to the Phasis, and seize the territory of the Phasians (whose present king was a descendant of Aeetes). Xenophon's reply was curt: Not one syllable would he have to say himself to the army in this matter, "But," he added, "if you like, you can summon an assembly and say your say." Thereupon Timasion the Dardanian set forth as his opinion: It were best to hold no assembly at present, but first to go and conciliate, each of them, his own officers. Thus they went away and proceeded to execute their plans.

7. Presently the soldiers came to learn what was in course of agitation, and Neon gave out that Xenophon had persuaded the other generals to adopt his views, and had a plan to cheat the soldiers and take them back to the Phasis. The soldiers were highly indignant; meetings were held; little groups gathered ominously; and there seemed an alarming probability that they would repeat the violence with which they had lately treated the heralds of the Colchians and the clerks of the market; when all who did not save themselves by jumping into the sea were stoned to death. So Xenophon, seeing what a storm was brewing, resolved to anticipate matters so far as to summon a meeting of the men without delay, and thus prevent their collecting of their own accord, and he ordered the herald to announce an assembly. The voice of the

herald was no sooner heard than they rushed with great readiness to the place of meeting. Then Xenophon, without accusing the generals of having come to him, made the following speech, "I hear that a charge is brought against me. It is I apparently who am going to cheat you and carry you off to Phasis. I beg you by the gods to listen to me; and if there be found any guilt in me, let me not leave this place till I have paid the penalty of my misdoing; but if my accusers are found guilty, treat them as they deserve. I presume you know where the sun rises and where he sets, and that he who would go to Hellas must journey towards the sunset; whereas he who seeks the land of the barbarian must contrariwise fix his face towards the dawn. Now is that a point in which a man might hope to cheat you? Could any one make you believe that the sun rises here and sets there, or that he sets here and rises there? And doubtless you know this too, that it is Boreas, the north wind, who bears the mariner out of Pontus towards Hellas, and the south wind inwards towards the Phasis, whence the saying—

> When the North wind doth blow
> Home to Hellas we will go.

"He would be a clever fellow who could fool you into embarking with a south wind blowing. That sounds all very well, you think, only I may get you on board during a calm. Granted, but I shall be on board my one ship, and you on board another hundred at least, and how am I to constrain you to voyage with me against your will, or by what cajolery shall I carry you off? But I will imagine you so far fooled and bewitched by me, that I have got you to the Phasis; we proceed to disembark on dry land. At last it will come out, that wherever you are, you are not in Hellas, and the inventor of the trick will be one sole man, and you who have been caught by it will number something like 10,000 with swords in your hands. I do not know how a man could better ensure his own punishment than by embarking on such a policy with regard to himself and you.

"Nay, these tales are the invention of silly fellows who are jealous of the honour you bestow on me. A most uncalled-for jealousy! Do I hinder any of them from speaking any word of import in his power? Of striking a blow in your behalf and his own, if that is his choice? Or, finally, of keeping his eyes and ears open to secure your safety? What is it? In your choice of leaders do I stand in the way of any one, is that it? Let him step forward, I yield him place; he shall be your general; only he must prove that he has your good at heart.

"For myself, I have done; but for yourselves, if any of you conceive either that he himself could be the victim of a fraud, or that he could victimise any one else in such a thing as this, let him open his lips and explain to us how. Take your time, but when you have sifted the matter to your hearts' content, do not go away without suffering me to tell you of something which I see looming. If it should burst upon us and prove in fact anything like what it gives signs of being now, it is time for us to take counsel for ourselves and see that we do not prove ourselves to be the worst and basest of men in the sight of gods and men, be they friends or be they foes." The words moved the curiosity of the soldiers. They marvelled what this matter might be, and bade him explain. Thereupon he began again, "You will not have forgotten certain places in the hills—barbaric fastnesses, but friendly to the Cerasuntines—from which people used to come down and sell us large cattle and other things which they possessed, and if I mistake not, some of you went to the nearest of these places and made purchases in the market and came back again. Clearetus the captain learned of this place, that it was but a little one and unguarded. Why should it be guarded since it was friendly? So the folk thought. Thus he stole upon it in the dead of night, and meant to sack it without saying a word to any of us. His design was, if he took the place, not to return again to the army, but to mount a vessel which, with his messmates on board her, was sailing past at the time, and stowing away what he had seized, to set sail and begone beyond the Euxine. All this had been agreed upon and arranged with his comrades on board the vessel, as I now discover. Accordingly, he summoned to his side all whom he could persuade, and set off at their head against the little place. But dawn overtook him on his march. The men collected out of their strongholds, and whether from a distance or close quarters, made such a fight that they killed Clearetus and a good many of the rest, and only a few of them got safe back to Cerasus.

"These things took place on the day on which we started to come hither on foot; while some of those who were to go by sea were still at Cerasus, not having as yet weighed anchor. After this, according to what the Cerasuntines state, there arrived three inhabitants of the place which had been attacked; three elderly men, seeking an interview with our public assembly. Not finding us, they addressed themselves to the men of Cerasus, and told them, they were astonished that we should have thought it right to attack them; however, when, as the Cerasuntines assert, they had assured them that the occurrence was not authorised by public consent, they were pleased, and proposed to sail here, not only to state to us what had occurred, but to offer that those who were interested should take up and bury the bodies of the slain.

"But among the Hellenes still at Cerasus were some of those who had escaped. They found out in which direction the barbarians intended to

go, and not only had the face themselves to pelt them with stones, but
vociferously encouraged their neighbours to do the same. The three men
—ambassadors, mark you—were slain, stoned to death. After this occurrence, the men of Cerasus came to us and reported the affair, and we
generals, on being informed, were annoyed at what had taken place,
and took counsel with the Cerasuntines how the dead bodies of the Hellenes might be buried. While seated in conclave outside the camp, we
suddenly were awere of a great hubbub. We heard cries, 'Strike! Strike!
Shoot! Shoot!' And presently we caught sight of a mass of people racing towards us with stones in their hands, and others picking them up.
The Cerasuntines, naturally enough, considering the incident they had
lately witnessed, retired in terror to their vessels, and, upon my word,
some of us did not feel too comfortable. All I could do was to go to them
and inquire what it all meant. Some of them had not the slightest notion,
although they had stones in their hands, but chancing on some one who
was better informed, I was told by him that the clerks of the market
were treating the army most scandalously. Just then some one got sight
of the market clerk, Zelarchus, making his way off towards the sea, and
shouted, and the rest responding to the cry as if a wild boar or a stag
had been started, they rushed upon him.

"The Cerasuntines, seeing a rush in their direction, thought that,
without a doubt, it was directed against themselves, and fled with all
speed and threw themselves into the sea, in which proceeding they were
imitated by some few of our own men, and all who did not know how to
swim were drowned. But now, what do you think of their case, these
men of Cerasus? They had done no wrong. They were simply afraid
that some madness had seized us, like that to which dogs are liable.

"I say then, if proceedings like this are to be the order of the day,
you had better consider what the ultimate condition of the army is like
to be. As a body you will not have it in your power to undertake war
against whom you like, or to conclude peace. But in private any one
who chooses will conduct the army on any quest which takes his fancy.
And when ambassadors come to you to demand peace, or whatever it
may be, officious people will put them to death and prevent your hearing the proposals which brought them to you. The next step will be that
those whom you as a body may choose as generals will be of no account;
but any one who likes to elect himself general, and will adopt the for-
mula 'Shoot him! shoot him!' will be competent to cut down whomsoever he pleases untried, be it general or private soldier, if only he have
sufficient followers, as was the case just now. But just consider what
these self-appointed generals have achieved for you. Zelarchus, the clerk
of the market, may possibly have done you a wrong; if so, he has sailed

off and is gone without paying you any penalty; or he may be guiltless, in which case we have driven him from the army in terror of perishing unjustly without even a trial. While those who stoned the ambassadors have contrived so cleverly that we alone of all Hellenes cannot approach Cerasus safely without a strong force, and the corpses which the very men who slew them themselves invited us to bury, we cannot now pick up with safety even under a flag of truce. Who indeed would care to carry a flag of truce, or go as a herald with the blood of heralds upon his hands? All we could do was to implore the Cerasuntines to bury them.

"If then you approve of such doings, have a resolution passed to that effect, so that, with a prospect of like occurrences in the future, a man may privately set up a guard and do his best to fix his tent where he can find a strong position with a commanding site. If, however, these seem to you to be the deeds rather of wild beasts than of human beings, think of some means by which to stop them; or else, in heaven's name, how shall we do sacrifice to the gods gladly, with impious deeds to answer for? Or how shall we, who lay the knife to each other's throats, give battle to our enemies? What friendly city will receive us when they see rampant lawlessness in our midst? Who will have the courage to afford us a market, when we prove our worthlessness in these weightiest concerns? And what becomes of the praise we expect to win from the mouths of men? Who will praise us, if this is our behaviour? Should we not ourselves bestow the worst of names on the perpetrators of like deeds?"

After this they rose, and, as one man, proposed that the ringleaders in these matters should be punished; and that for the future, to set an example of lawlessness should be forbidden. Every such ringleader was to be prosecuted on the capital charge; the generals were to bring all offenders to the bar of justice; prosecutions for all other misdemeanours committed since the death of Cyrus were to be instituted; and they ended by constituting the officers into a board of jurors; and upon the strong representation of Xenophon, with the concurrence of the soothsayers, it was resolved to purify the army, and this purification was made.

8. It was further resolved that the generals themselves should undergo a judicial examination in reference to their conduct in past time. In course of investigation, Philesius and Xanthicles respectively were condemned to pay a sum of twenty minae, to meet a deficiency to that amount incurred during the guardianship of the cargoes of the merchantmen. Sophaenetus was fined ten minae for inadequate performance of his duty as one of the chief officers selected. Against Xenophon a charge was brought by certain people, who asserted that they had been beaten

by him, and framed the indictment as one of personal outrage with violence. Xenophon got up and demanded that the first speaker should
state where and when it was he had received these blows. The other,
so challenged, answered, "When we were perishing of cold and there was
a great depth of snow." Xenophon said, "Upon my word, with weather
such as you describe, when our provisions had run out, when we could
not even get a smell of wine, when numbers were dropping down dead
beat, so acute was the suffering, with the enemy close on our heels; certainly, if at such a season as that I was guilty of outrage, I plead guilty
to being a more outrageous brute than the ass, which is too wanton,
they say, to feel fatigue. Still, I wish you would tell us," said he, "what
led to my striking you. Did I ask you for something and, on your refusing it to me, did I proceed to beat you? Was it a debt, for which I
demanded payment? Or a quarrel about some boy or other? Was I the
worse for liquor, and behaving like a drunkard?" When the man met
each of these questions with a negative, he questioned him further, "Are
you a heavy infantry soldier?" "No," said he. "A peltast, then?" "No,
nor yet a peltast." But he had been ordered by his messmates to drive a
mule, although he was a free man. Then at last he recognised him, and
inquired, "Are you the fellow who carried home the sick man?" "Yes,
I am," said he, "thanks to your driving; and you made havoc of my
messmates' kit." "Havoc!" said Xenophon, "Nay, I distributed it; some
to one man, some to another to carry, and bade them bring the things
safely to me; and when I got them back I delivered them all safely to
you, when you, on your side, had rendered an account to me of the man.
Let me tell you," he continued, turning to the court, "what the circumstances were; it is worth hearing.

"A man was left behind from inability to proceed farther; I recognised the poor fellow sufficiently to see that he was one of ours, and I
forced you to carry him to save his life. For, if I am not much mistaken,
the enemy were close at our heels?" The fellow assented to this. "Well
then," said Xenophon, "after I had sent you forward, I overtook you
again, as I came up with the rearguard; you were digging a trench with
intent to bury the man; I pulled up and said something in commendation; as we stood by the poor fellow twitched his leg, and the bystand-
ers all cried out, 'Why, the man's alive!' Your remark was, 'Alive or not
as he likes, I am not going to carry him.' Then I struck you. Yes! you
are right, for it looked very much as if you knew him to be alive."
"Well," said he, "was he any the less dead when I reported him to you?"
"Nay," retorted Xenophon, "by the same token we shall all one day be
dead, but that is no reason why meantime we should all be buried alive."
Then there was a general shout, "If Xenophon had given the fellow a

few more blows, it might have been better." The others were now called upon to state the grounds on which they had been beaten in each case; but when they refused to get up, he proceeded to state them himself.

"I confess, sirs, to having struck certain men for failure in discipline. These were men who were quite content to owe their safety to us. While the rest of the world marched on in rank and did whatever fighting had to be done, they preferred to leave the ranks, and rush forward to loot and enrich themselves at our expense. Now, if this conduct were to be the rule, general ruin would be the result. I do not deny that I have given blows to this man or the other who played the weakling and refused to get up, helplessly abandoning himself to the enemy; and so I forced them to march on. For once in the severe wintry weather I myself happened to sit down for a long time, while waiting for a party who were getting their kit together, and I discovered how difficult it was to get up again and stretch one's legs. After this personal experience, whenever I saw any one else seated in slack and lazy mood, I tried to spur him on. The mere movement and effort to play the man caused warmth and moisture, whereas it was plain that sitting down and keeping quiet helped the blood to freeze and the toes to mortify, calamities which really befell several of the men, as you yourselves are aware.

"I can imagine a third case, that of some straggler stopping behind, merely to rest for rest's sake, and hindering you in front and us behind alike from pressing on the march. If he got a blow with the fist from me it saved him a thrust with the lance from the enemy. In fact, the opportunity they enjoy to-day of taking vengeance on me for any treatment which I put upon them wrongfully, is derived from their salvation then; whereas, if they had fallen into the enemy's hands, let them ask themselves for what outrage, however great, they could expect to get satisfaction now. My defence," he continued, "is simple: if I chastised any one for his own good, I claim to suffer the same penalties as parents pay their children or masters their boys. Does not the surgeon also cauterise and cut us for our good? But if you really believe that these acts are the outcome of wanton insolence, I beg you to observe that although to-day, thank god! I am heartier than formerly, I wear a bolder front now than then, and I drink more wine, yet I never strike a soul; no, for I see that you have reached smooth water. When storm arises, and a great sea strikes the vessel amidships, a mere shake of the head will make the look-out man furious with the crew in the forecastle, or the helmsman with the men in the stern sheets, for at such a crisis even a slight slip may ruin everything. But I appeal to your own verdict, already recorded, in proof that I was justified in striking these men. You stood by with swords, not voting tablets, in your hands, and it was in your power to aid the fellows if you liked; but, to speak the honest truth, you neither aided them nor did you join me in striking the disorderly. In other words, you enabled any evilly disposed person among them to give rein to his wantonness by your passivity. For if you will be at pains to investigate, you will find that those who were then most cowardly are the ringleaders to-day in brutality and outrage.

"There is Boiscus the boxer, a Thessalian, what a battle he fought then to escape carrying his shield, so tired was he, and to-day I am told he has stripped several citizens of Cotyora of the clothes on their backs. If then you are wise, you will treat this person in a way the contrary to that in which men treat dogs. A savage dog is tied up in the day and loosed at night, but if you are wise you will tie this fellow up at night and only let him loose in the day.

"But really," he added, "it does surprise me with what keenness you remember and recount the times when I incurred the hatred of some one; but some other ocasions when I eased the burden of winter and storm for any of you, or beat off an enemy, or helped to minister to you in sickness and want, not a soul of you remembers these. Or when for any noble deed done by any of you I praised the doer, and according to my ability did honour to this brave man or that; these things have slipped from your memories, and are clean forgotten. Yet it were surely more noble, just, and holy, sweeter and kindlier to treasure the memory of good rather than of evil."

He ended, and then one after another of the assembly got up and began recalling incidents of the kind suggested, and things ended pleasantly after all.

BOOK VI

1. After this, while waiting, they lived partly on supplies from the market, partly on the fruit of raids into Paphlagonia. The Paphlagonians, on their side, showed much skill in kidnapping stragglers, wherever they could lay hands on them, and in the night time tried to do mischief to those whose quarters were at a distance from the camp. The result was that their relations to one another were exceedingly hostile, so much so that Corylas, who was the chief of Paphlagonia at that date, sent ambassadors to the Hellenes, bearing horses and fine apparel, and charged with a proposal on the part of Corylas to make terms with the Hellenes on the principle of mutual forbearance from injuries. The generals replied that they would consult with the army about the matter. Meanwhile they gave them a hospitable reception, to which they invited certain members of the army whose claims were obvious. They sacrificed some of the captive cattle and other sacrificial beasts, and with these they furnished forth a sufficiently festal entertainment, and reclining on their couches, fell to eating and drinking out of beakers made of horn which they happened to find in the country.

But as soon as the libation was ended and they had sung the hymn, up got first some Thracians, who performed a dance under arms to the sound of a flute, leaping high into the air with much nimbleness, and brandishing their swords, till at last one man struck his fellow, and every one thought he was really wounded, so skilfully and artistically did he fall, and the Paphlagonians screamed out. Then he that gave the blow stripped the other of his arms, and marched off chanting the Sitalcas,[1] while others of the Thracians bore off the other, who lay as if dead, though he had not received even a scratch.

After this some Aenianians and Magnesians got up and fell to dancing the Carpaea, as it is called, under arms. This was the manner of the dance: one man lays aside his arms and proceeds to drive a yoke of oxen, and while he drives he sows, turning him about frequently, as though he were afraid of something; up comes a cattle-lifter, and no sooner does the ploughman catch sight of him afar, than he snatches up his arms and confronts him. They fight in front of his team, and all in rhythm to the sound of the flute. At last the robber binds the countryman and

---

[1] The Thracian hymn in honour of Sitalcas the king, a national hero.

344

drives off the team. Or sometimes the cattle-driver binds the robber, and then he puts him under the yoke beside the oxen, with his two hands tied behind his back, and off he drives.

After this a Mysian came in with a light shield in either hand and danced, at one time going through a pantomime, as if he were dealing with two assailants at once; at another plying his shields as if to face a single foe, and then again he would whirl about and throw somersaults, keeping the shields in his hands, so that it was a beautiful spectacle. Last of all he danced the Persian dance, clashing the shields together, crouching down on one knee and springing up again from earth; and all this he did in measured time to the sound of the flute. After him the Mantineans stepped upon the stage, and some other Arcadians also stood up; they had accoutred themselves in all their warlike finery. They marched with measured tread, flutes playing, to the tune of the warriors' march; the notes of the paean rose, lightly their limbs moved in dance, as in solemn procession to the holy gods. The Paphlagonians looked upon it as something truly strange that all these dances should be under arms; and the Mysians, seeing their astonishment, persuaded one of the Arcadians who had a dancing girl to let him introduce her, which he did after dressing her up magnificently and giving her a light shield. When, lithe of limb, she danced the Pyrrhic,[2] loud clapping followed; and the Paphlagonians asked, "If these women fought by their side in battle?" They answered, "To be sure, it was the women who routed the great King, and drove him out of camp." So ended the night.

But next day the generals introduced the embassy to the army, and the soldiers passed a resolution in the sense proposed: between themselves and the Paphlagonians there was to be a mutual abstinence from injuries. After this the ambassadors went their way, and the Hellenes, as soon as it was thought that sufficient vessels had arrived, went on board ship, and voyaged a day and a night with a fair breeze, keeping Paphlagonia on their left. And on the following day, arriving at Sinope, they came to moorings in the harbour of Harmene, near Sinope. The Sinopeans, though inhabitants of Paphlagonia, are really colonists of the Milesians. They sent gifts of hospitality to the Hellenes, 3,000 measures of barley with 1,500 jars of wine. At this place Cheirisophus rejoined them with a man-of-war. The soldiers certainly expected that, having come, he would have brought them something, but he brought them nothing, except complimentary phrases, on the part of Anaxibius, the high admiral, and the rest, who sent them their congratulations, coupled with a promise on the part of Anaxibius that, as soon as they were outside the Euxine, pay would be forthcoming.

[2] A famous war dance.

At Harmene the army halted five days; and now that they seemed to be so close to Hellas, the question how they were to reach home not empty-handed presented itself more forcibly to their minds than heretofore. The conclusion they came to was to appoint a single general, since one man would be better able to handle the troops, by night or by day, than was possible while the generalship was divided. If secrecy were desirable, it would be easier to keep matters dark, or if again expedition were an object, there would be less risk of arriving a day too late, since mutual explanations would be avoided, and whatever approved itself to the single judgment would at once be carried into effect, whereas previously the generals had done everything in obedience to the opinion of the majority.

With these ideas working in their minds, they turned to Xenophon, and the officers came to him and told him that this was how the soldiers viewed matters; and each of them, displaying a warmth of kindly feeling, pressed him to accept the office. Xenophon partly would have liked to do so, in the belief that by so doing he would win to himself a higher repute in the esteem of his friends, and that his name would be reported to the city written large; and by some stroke of fortune he might even be the discoverer of some blessing to the army collectively.

These and the like considerations elated him; he had a strong desire to hold the supreme command. But then again, as he turned the matter over, the conviction deepened in his mind that the issue of the future is to every man uncertain; and hence there was the risk of losing perhaps such reputation as he had already acquired. He was in sore straits, and, not knowing how to decide, it seemed best to him to lay the matter before the gods. Accordingly, he led two victims to the altar and made sacrifice to Zeus the King, for it was he and no other who had been named by the oracle at Delphi, and his belief was that the vision which he beheld when he first essayed to undertake the joint administration of the army was sent to him by that god. He also recalled to mind a circumstance which befell him still earlier, when setting out from Ephesus to associate himself with Cyrus; how an eagle screamed on his right hand from the east, and still remained perched, and the soothsayer who was escorting him said that it was a great and royal omen, indicating glory and yet suffering; for the birds only attack the eagle when seated. "Yet," added he, "it bodes not gain in money; for the eagle seizes his food, not when seated, but on the wing."

Thus Xenophon sacrificed, and the god as plainly as might be gave him a sign, neither to demand the generalship, nor, if chosen, to accept the office. And that was how the matter stood when the army met, and the proposal to elect a single leader was unanimous. After this resolution was passed, they proposed Xenophon for election, and when it seemed quite evident that they would elect him, if he put the question to the vote, he got up and spoke as follows:

"I am but mortal, soldiers, and must be happy to be honoured by you. I thank you, and am grateful, and my prayer is that the gods may grant me to be an instrument of blessing to you. Still, when I consider it closer, thus, in the presence of a Lacedaemonian, to be preferred by you as general, seems to me but ill conducive either to your interests or to mine, since you will the less readily obtain from them hereafter anything you may need, while for myself I look upon acceptance as even somewhat dangerous. Do I not see and know with what persistence these Lacedaemonians prosecuted the war till finally they forced our State to acknowledge the leadership of Lacedaemon? This confession once extorted from their antagonists, they ceased warring at once, and the siege of the city was at an end. If, with these facts before my eyes, I seem to be doing all I can to neutralise their high self-esteem, I cannot escape the reflection that personally I may be taught wisdom by a painful process. But with regard to your own idea that under a single general there will be less factiousness than when there were many, be assured that in choosing some other than me you will not find me factious. I hold that whosoever sets up factious opposition to his leader factiously opposes his own safety. While if you determine to choose me, I should not be surprised were that choice to entail upon you and me the resentment of other people."

After those remarks on Xenophon's part, many more got up, one after another, insisting on the propriety of his undertaking the command. One of them, Agasias the Stymphalian, said that it was really ridiculous, if things had come to this pass that the Lacedaemonians are to fly in a rage because a number of friends have met together to dinner, and omitted to choose a Lacedaemonian to sit at the head of the table. "Really, if that is how matters stand," said he, "I do not see what right we have to be officers even, we who are only Arcadians." That sally brought down the plaudits of the assembly; and Xenophon, seeing that something more was needed, stepped forward again and spoke, "Pardon, sirs," he said, "let me make a clean breast of it. I swear to you by all the gods and goddesses; verily and indeed, I no sooner perceived your purpose, than I consulted the victims, whether it was better for you to entrust this leadership to me, and for me to undertake it, or the reverse. And the gods gave me a sign so plain that even a common man might understand it, and perceive that I should hold myself aloof from sole command."

Under these circumstances they chose Cheirisophus, who, after his

election, stepped forward and said, "Well, be assured of this, that had
you chosen some one else, I for my part should not have set up factious opposition. As to Xenophon, I believe you have done him a good
turn by not appointing him; for even now Dexippus has gone some
way in traducing him to Anaxibius, as far as it lay in his power to
do so, and that, in spite of my attempts to silence him. What he said was
that he believed Xenophon would rather share the command of Clearchus's army with Timasion, a Dardanian, than with himself, a Laconian.
But," continued Cheirisophus, "since your choice has fallen upon me, I
will make it my endeavour to do you all the good in my power; so make
your preparations to weigh anchor to-morrow; wind and weather per-
mitting, we will voyage to Heraclea; every one must endeavour, therefore, to put in at that port; and for the rest we will consult, when we
are come thither."

2. The next day they weighed anchor and set sail from Harmene with
a fair breeze, two days' voyage along the coast. [As they coasted along
they came in sight of Jason's beach, where, as the story says, the ship
Argo came to moorings; and then the mouths of the rivers, first the
Thermodon, then the Iris, then the Halys, and next to it the Parthenius.] [3] Coasting past [the latter], they reached Heraclea, a Hellenic
city and a colony of the Megarians, situated in the territory of the Mari-
andynians. So they came to anchorage off the Acherusian Chersonese,
where Heracles is said to have descended to bring up the dog Cerberus,
at a point where they still show the marks of his descent, a deep cleft
more than a quarter of a mile down. Here the Heracleots sent the Hellenes, as gifts of hospitality, 3,000 measures of barley and 2,000 jars
of wine, twenty beeves and 100 sheep. Through the flat country here
flows the Lycus river, as it is called, about 200 feet in breadth.

The soldiers held a meeting, and took counsel about the remainder
of the journey, whether they should make their exit from the Pontus
by sea or by land. And Lycon the Achaean got up and said, "I am astonished, men, that the generals do not endeavour to provide us more
efficiently with provisions. These gifts of hospitality will not afford three
days' victuals for the army; nor do I see from what region we are to
provide ourselves as we march. My proposal, therefore, is to demand of
the Heracleots at least 3,000 cyzicenes." (Another speaker suggested
not less than 10,000.) "Let us at once, before we break up this meeting, send ambassadors to the city and ascertain their answer to the demand and take counsel accordingly." Thereupon they proceeded to put

---

[3] This passage involves a topographical error on the part of whoever wrote it.
Jason's beach and the three first-named rivers lie between Cotyora and Sinope.

up as ambassadors, first and foremost Cheirisophus, as he had been chosen general-in-chief; others also named Xenophon.

But both Cheirisophus and Xenophon stoutly declined, maintaining both alike that they could not compel a Hellenic city, actually friendly, to give anything which they did not spontaneously offer. So, since these two appeared to be backward, the soldiers sent Lycon the Achaean, Callimachus the Parrhasian, and Agasias the Stymphalian. These three went and announced the resolutions passed by the army. Lycon, it was said, even went so far as to threaten certain consequences in case they refused to comply. The Heracleots said they would deliberate; and, without more ado, they got together their goods and chattels from their farms and fields outside, and dismantled the market outside and transferred it within, after which the gates were closed, and arms appeared at the battlements of the walls.

At that check, the authors of these tumultuary measures fell to accusing the generals, as if they had marred the proceeding; and the Arcadians and Achaeans banded together, chiefly under the auspices of the two ringleaders, Callimachus the Parrhasian and Lycon the Achaean. The language they held was to this effect: It was outrageous that a single Athenian and a Lacedaemonian, who had not contributed a soldier to the expedition, should rule Peloponnesians; scandalous that they themselves should bear the toils while others pocketed the spoils, and that too though the preservation of the army was due to themselves; for, as every one must admit, to the Arcadians and Achaeans the credit of that achievement was due, and the rest of the army went for nothing (which was indeed so far true that the Arcadians and Achaeans did form numerically the larger part of the whole army). What then did common sense suggest? Why, that they, the Arcadians and Achaeans, should make common cause, choose generals for themselves independently, continue the march, and try somewhat to better their condition. This proposal was carried. All the Arcadians and Achaeans who chanced to be with Cheirisophus left him and Xenophon, setting up for themselves and choosing ten generals of their own. These ten, it was decreed, were to put into effect such measures as approved themselves to the majority. Thus the absolute authority vested in Cheirisophus was terminated there and then, within less than a week of his appointment.

Xenophon however was minded to prosecute the journey in their company, thinking that this would be a safer plan than for each to start on his own account. But Neon threw in his weight in favour of separate action. "Every one for himself," he said, for he had heard from Cheirisophus that Cleander, the Spartan governor-general at Byzantium, talked of coming to Calpe Haven with some war vessels. Neon's advice was due to his desire to secure a passage home in these war vessels for themselves and their soldiers, without allowing any one else to share in their good fortune. As for Cheirisophus, he was at once so out of heart at the turn things had taken, and soured with the whole army, that he left it to his subordinate, Neon, to do just what he liked. Xenophon, on his side, would still have been glad to be quit of the expedition and sail home; but on offering sacrifice to Heracles the Leader, and seeking advice, whether it were better and more desirable to continue the march in charge of the soldiers who had remained faithful, or to take his departure, the god indicated to him by the victims that he should adopt the former course.

In this way the army was now split up into three divisions. First, the Arcadians and Achaeans, over 4,500 men, all heavy infantry. Secondly, Cheirisophus and his men, 1,400 heavy infantry and the 700 peltasts, (Clearchus's Thracians). Thirdly, Xenophon's division of 1,700 heavy infantry, and 300 peltasts; but then he alone had the cavalry—about forty troopers.

The Arcadians, who had bargained with the Heracleots and got some vessels from them, were the first to set sail; they hoped, by pouncing suddenly on the Bithynians, to make as large a haul as possible. With that object they disembarked at Calpe Haven, pretty nearly at a middle point in Thrace. Cheirisophus setting off straight from Heraclea, commenced a land march through the country; but having entered into Thrace, he preferred to cling to the seaboard, health and strength failing him. Xenophon, lastly, took vessels, and disembarking on the confines of Thrace and the Heracleotid, pushed forward through the heart of the country.

3. The Arcadians, disembarking under cover of night at Calpe Haven, marched against the nearest villages about four miles from the sea; and as soon as it was light, each of the ten generals led his company to attack one village, or if the village were large, a couple of companies advanced under their combined generals. They further agreed upon a certain knoll, where they were all eventually to assemble. So sudden was their attack that they seized a number of captives and enclosed a multitude of small cattle. But the Thracians who escaped began to collect again; for being light-armed troops they had slipped in large numbers through the hands of the heavy infantry; and now that they were got together they first attacked the company of the Arcadian general, Smicres, who had done his work and was retiring to the appointed meeting-place, driving along a large train of captives and cattle. For a good while the Hellenes maintained a running fight; but at the passage of a gorge the enemy routed them, slaying Smicres himself and those with

him to a man. The fate of another company under command of Hegesander, another of the ten, was nearly as bad; only eight men escaped,
Hegesander being one of them. The remaining companies eventually
met, some with somewhat to show for their pains, others empty-handed.

The Thracians, having achieved this success, kept up a continual
shouting and clatter of conversation to one another during the night; but
with daybreak they marshalled themselves right round the knoll on
which the Hellenes were encamped—both cavalry in large numbers and
light-armed troops—while every minute the stream of newcomers grew
greater. Then they commenced an attack on the heavy infantry in all
security; for the Hellenes had not a single bowman, javelin-man, or
mounted trooper amongst them; while the enemy rushed forward on
foot or galloped up on horseback and let fly their javelins. It was vain
to attempt to retaliate, so lightly did they spring back and escape; and
ever the attack renewed itself from every point, so that on one side man
after man was wounded, on the other not a soul was touched; the result
being that they could not stir from their position, and the Thracians
ended by cutting them off even from their water. In their despair they
began to parley about a truce, and finally various concessions were made
and terms agreed to between them; but the Thracians would not hear
of giving hostages in answer to the demand of the Hellenes; at that point
the matter rested. So fared it with the Arcadians.

As to Cheirisophus, that general prosecuted his march along the seaboard, and without check reached Calpe Haven. Xenophon advanced
through the heart of the country; and his cavalry pushing on in front,
came upon some old men pursuing their road somewhere, who were
brought to him, and in answer to his question, whether they had caught
sight of another Hellenic army anywhere, told him all that had lately
taken place, adding that at present they were being besieged upon a knoll
with all the Thracians in close circle round them. Thereupon he kept the
old men under strict guard to serve as guides in case of need; next, having appointed outposts, he called a meeting of the soldiers, and addressed
them, "Soldiers, some of the Arcadians are dead and the rest are being
besieged upon a certain knoll. Now my own belief is, that if they are to
perish, with their deaths the seal is set to our own fate: since we must
reckon with an enemy at once numerous and emboldened. Clearly our
best course is to hasten to their rescue, in the hope that we may find
them still alive, and do battle by their side rather than suffer isolation,
confronting danger single-handed.

"As[4] for ourselves," he continued, "we need not look to find cover
in any direction; for it is a long step back to Heraclea and a long leap

_____

[4] The following sections are arranged according to the transposition of Rehdantz.

across to Chrysopolis, and the enemy is at the door. The shortest road is to Calpe Haven, where we suppose Cheirisophus, if safe, to be; but then, when we get there, at Calpe Haven there are no vessels for us to sail away in; and if we stop here, we have not provisions for a single day. Suppose the beleaguered Arcadians left to their fate, we shall find it but a sorry alternative to run the gauntlet with Cheirisophos's detachment alone; better to save them if we can, and with united forces work out our deliverance in common. But if so, we must set out with minds prepared, since to-day either a glorious death awaits us or the achievement of a deed of noblest emprise in the rescue of so many Hellene lives. Maybe it is god who leads us thus, god who chooses to humble the proud boaster, boasting as though he were exceeding wise, but for us, the beginning of whose every act is by heaven's grace, that same god reserves a higher grade of honour. One duty I would recall to you, to apply your minds to the execution of the orders with promptitude.

"Let us then at once push forward as far as may seem opportune till supper-time, and then encamp. As long as we are marching, let Timasion, with the cavalry, gallop on in front, but without losing sight of us; and let him examine all closely in front, so that nothing may escape our observation."

With these words he led the way. (At the same time too, he sent out some active fellows of the light-armed troops to the flanks and to the high tops, who were to give a signal if they espied anything anywhere; ordering them to burn everything inflammable which lay in their path.) The cavalry, scattering as far in advance as was prudent, wherever they set foot, set fire. The peltasts moving parallel on the high ground were similarly employed, burning everything combustible they could discover. While the main army, wherever they came upon anything which had accidentally escaped, completed the work, so that the whole country looked as if it were ablaze; and the army might easily pass for a larger one. When the hour had come, they turned aside to a knoll and took up quarters; and there they saw the enemy's watch-fires. He was about five miles distant. On their side also they kindled as many watch-fires as possible; but as soon as they had dined the order was passed to quench all the fires. So during the night they posted guards and slept. But at day-break they offered prayers to the gods, and drawing up in order of battle, began marching with what speed they might. Timasion and the cavalry, who had the guides with them, and were moving on briskly in front, found themselves without knowing it at the very knoll upon which the Hellenes had been beleaguered. But no army could they discover, whether of friend or foe; only some starveling old women and men, with a few sheep and oxen which had been left behind. This news they re-

ported to Xenophon and the main body. At first the marvel was what
had happened; but soon they found out by inquiries from the folk who
had been left behind, that the Thracians had set off immediately after
sundown, and were gone; the Hellenes had waited till morning before
they made off, but in what direction, they could not say.

On hearing this, Xenophon's troops first breakfasted, and then getting
their kit together began their march, desiring to unite with the rest at
Calpe's Haven without loss of time. As they continued their march, they
came across the track of the Arcadians and Achaeans along the road to
Calpe, and both divisions arriving eventually at the same place, were
overjoyed to see one another again, and they embraced each other like
brothers. Then the Arcadians inquired of Xenophon's officers why they
had quenched the watch-fires. "At first," said they, "when we lost sight
of your watch-fires, we expected you to attack the enemy in the night;
and the enemy, so at least we imagined, must have been afraid of that
and so set off. The time at any rate at which they set off would corre-
spond. But when the requisite time had elapsed and you did not come,
we concluded that you must have learned what was happening to us,
and in terror had made a bolt for it to the seaboard. We resolved not
to be left behind by you; and that is how we also came to march hither."

4. During this day they contented themselves with bivouacking there
on the beach at the harbour. The place which goes by the name of Calpe
Haven is in Asiatic Thrace, the name given to a region extending from
the mouth of the Euxine all the way to Heraclea, which lies on the right
hand as you sail into the Euxine. It is a long day's voyage for a warship, using her three banks of oars, from Byzantium to Heraclea, and
between these two there is not a single Hellenic or friendly city, but only
these Bithynian Thracians, who have a bad reputation for the savagery
with which they treat any Hellenes cast ashore by shipwreck or otherwise thrown into their power.

Now the haven of Calpe lies exactly midway, halving the voyage between Byzantium and Heracleia. It is a long promontory running out into
the sea; the seaward portion being a rocky precipice, at no point less
than 120 feet high; but on the landward side there is a neck about 400
feet wide; and the space inside the neck is capable of accommodating
10,000 inhabitants, and there is a harbour immediately under the crag
with a beach facing the west. Then there is a copious spring of fresh
water flowing on the shore of the sea commanded by the stronghold.
Again, there is plenty of wood of various sorts; but most plentiful of
all, fine shipbuilding timber down to the very edge of the sea. The up-
land stretches into the heart of the country for about two and one-half
miles. It is good loamy soil, free from stones. For a still greater distance

the seaboard is thickly grown with large timber trees of every description. The surrounding country is beautiful and spacious, containing numerous well populated villages. The soil produces barley and wheat, and pulse of all sorts, millet and sesame, figs in ample supply, with numerous vines producing sweet wines, and indeed everything else except olives. Such is the character of the country.

The tents were pitched on the seaward-facing beach, the soldiers being altogether averse to camping on ground which might so easily be converted into a city. Indeed, their arrival at the place at all seemed very like the crafty design of some persons who wished to found a city. The aversion was not unnatural, since the majority of the soldiers had not left their homes on so long a voyage from scantiness of subsistence, but attracted by the fame of Cyrus's virtues; some of them bringing followers, while others had expended money on the expedition. And among them was a third set who had run away from fathers and mothers; while a different class had left children behind, hoping to return to them with money or other gains. Other people with Cyrus won great success, they were told; why should it not be so with them? Being persons then of this description, the one longing of their hearts was to reach Hellas safely.

It was on the day after their meeting that Xenophon sacrificed as a preliminary to a military expedition; for it was needful to march out in search of provisions, besides which he designed burying the dead. As soon as the victims proved favourable they all set out, the Arcadians following with the rest. The majority of the dead, who had lain already five days, they buried just where they had fallen, in groups; to remove their bodies now would have been impossible. Some few, who lay off the roads, they got together and buried with what splendour they could, considering the means in their power. Others they could not find, and for these they erected a great cenotaph, and covered it with wreaths. When it was all done, they returned home to camp. At that time they supped, and went to rest.

Next day there was a general meeting of the soldiers, collected chiefly by Agasias the Stymphalian, a captain, and Hieronymus, an Eleian, also a captain, and other seniors of the Arcadians; and they passed a resolution that, for the future, whoever revived the idea of breaking up the army should be punished by death. And the army, it was decided, would now resume its old position under the command of its former generals, though Cheirisophus, indeed, had already died under medical treatment for fever; and Neon the Asinaean had taken his place.

After these resolutions Xenophon got up and said, "Soldiers, the journey must now, I presume, be conducted on foot; indeed this is clear, since we have no vessels; and we are driven to commence it at once, for we have no provisions if we stop. We then," he continued, "will sacrifice, and you must prepare yourselves to fight now, if ever, for the spirit of the enemy has revived."

Thereupon the generals sacrificed, in the presence of the Arcadian seer, Arexion; for Silanus the Ambraciot had chartered a vessel at Heraclea and made his escape before this. Sacrificing with a view to departure, the victims proved unfavourable to them. Accordingly they waited that day. Certain people were bold enough to say that Xenophon, out of his desire to colonise the place, had persuaded the seer to say that the victims were unfavourable to departure. Consequently he proclaimed by herald next morning that any one who liked should be present at the sacrifice; or if he were a seer he was bidden to be present and help to inspect the victims. Then he sacrificed, and there were numbers present; but though the sacrifice on the question of departure was repeated as many as three times, the victims were persistently unfavourable. Thereat the soldiers were angry, for the provisions they had brought with them had reached the lowest ebb, and there was no market to be had.

Consequently there was another meeting, and Xenophon spoke again. "Men," said he, "the victims are, as you may see for yourselves, not yet favourable to the march; but meanwhile, as I can see for myself, you are in need of provisions; accordingly we must narrow the sacrifice to the particular point." Some one got up and said, "Naturally enough the victims are unfavourable, for, as I learned from some one on a vessel which arrived here yesterday by accident, Cleander, the governor at Byzantium, intends to come here with ships and men-of-war." Thereat they were all in favour of stopping; but they had to go out for provisions, and with this object he again sacrificed three times, and the victims remained adverse. Things had now reached such a pass that the men actually came to Xenophon's tent to proclaim that they had no provisions. His sole answer was that he would not lead them out till the victims were favourable.

So again the next day he sacrificed; and nearly the whole army, so strong was the general anxiety, flocked round the victims; and now the very victims themselves failed. So the generals, instead of leading out the army, called the men together. Xenophon, as was incumbent on him, spoke, "It is quite possible that the enemy are collected in a body, and we shall have to fight. If we were to leave our baggage in the strong place and sally forth prepared for battle, the victims might favour us." But the soldiers, on hearing this proposal, cried out, "No need to take us inside that place; better sacrifice with all speed." Now sheep there were none any longer. So they purchased oxen from under a wagon

and sacrificed; and Xenophon begged Cleanor the Arcadian to superintend the sacrifice on his behalf, in case there might be some change
now. But even so there was no improvement.

Now Neon was general in place of Cheirisophus, and seeing the men
suffering so cruelly from want, he was willing to do them a good turn.
So he got hold of some Heracleot or other who said he knew of villages
close by from which they could get provisions, and proclaimed by herald,
"If any one liked to come out and get provisions, be it known that he,
Neon, would be their leader." So out came the men with spears, and
wine skins and sacks and other vessels—2,000 strong in all. But when
they had reached the villages and began to scatter for the purpose of
foraging, Pharnabazus's cavalry were the first to fall upon them. They
had come to the aid of the Bithynians, wishing, if possible, in conjunction with the latter, to hinder the Hellenes from entering Phrygia. These
troopers killed no less than 500 of the men; the rest fled for their lives
up into the hill country.

News of the catastrophe was presently brought into camp by one of
those who had escaped, and Xenophon, seeing that the victims had not
been favourable on that day, took a wagon bullock, in the absence of
other sacrificial beasts, offered it up, and started for the rescue, he and
the rest under thirty years of age to the last man. Thus they picked up
the remnant of Neon's party and returned to camp. It was now about
sunset; and the Hellenes in deep despondency were making their evening meal, when all of a sudden, through the bushes, a party of Bithynians fell upon the pickets, cutting down some and chasing the rest into
camp. In the midst of screams and shouts the Hellenes ran to their
arms, one and all; yet to pursue or move the camp in the night seemed
hardly safe, for the ground was thickly grown with bush; all they could
do was to strengthen the outposts and keep watch under arms the whole
night.

5. And so they spent the night, but with dawn the generals led the
way into the stronghold, and the others picked up their arms and baggage and followed the lead. Before the breakfast-hour arrived, they had
fenced off with a ditch the only approach to the place, and had palisaded
off the whole, leaving only three gates. And a ship from Heraclea arrived
bringing barleymeal, victim animals, and wine.

Xenophon was up early, and made the usual offering before starting
on an expedition, and at the first victim the sacrifice was favourable.
Just as the sacrifice ended, the seer, Arexion the Parrhasian, caught sight
of an eagle, which boded well, and bade Xenophon lead on. So they
crossed the trench and grounded arms. Then proclamation was made by
herald for the soldiers to breakfast and start on an expedition under

arms; the mob of camp-followers and the captured slaves would be left
in camp. Accordingly the mass of the troops set out. Neon alone remained; for it seemed best to leave that general and his men to guard
the contents of the camp. But when the officers and soldiers left him in
the lurch, because they were so ashamed to stop in camp while the rest
marched out, the generals left behind only those above forty-five years
of age.

These then stayed, while the rest set out on the march. Before they
had gone two miles, they stumbled upon dead bodies, and when they
had brought up the rear of the column in a line with the first bodies
to be seen, they began digging graves and burying all included in the
column from end to end. After burying the first batch, they advanced,
and again bringing the rear even with the first unburied bodies which
appeared, they buried in the same way all which the line of troops included. Finally, reaching the road that led out of the villages where the
bodies lay thick together, they collected them and laid them in a common grave.

It was now about midday, when pushing forward the troops up to the
villages without entering them, they proceeded to seize provisions, laying hands on everything they could set eyes on under cover of their
lines; when suddenly they caught sight of the enemy cresting certain
hillocks in front of them, duly marshalled in line—a large body of cavalry and infantry. It was Spithridates and Rhathines, sent by Pharnabazus with their force at their backs. As soon as the enemy caught
sight of the Hellenes, they stood still, about two miles distant. Then
Arexion the seer sacrificed, and at the first essay the victims were favourable. Whereupon Xenophon addressed the other generals, "I would advise that we should detach one or more reserve columns to support our
main attack, so that in case of need at any point we may have reserves
in readiness to assist our main body, and the enemy, in the confusion
of battle, may find himself attacking the unbroken lines of troops not
hitherto engaged." These views approved themselves to all. "Do you
then," said he, "lead on the vanguard straight at the enemy. Do not let
us stand parleying here, now that we have caught sight of him and he
of us. I will detach the hindmost companies in the way we have decided
upon and follow you." After that they quietly advanced, and he, withdrawing the rear-rank companies in three brigades consisting of 200
men apiece, commissioned the first on the right to follow the main body
at the distance of 100 feet. Samolas the Achaean was in command of
this brigade. The duty of the second, under the command of Pyrrhias
the Arcadian, was to follow in the centre. The last was posted on the
left, with Phrasias, an Athenian, in command. As they advanced, the

vanguard reached a large and difficult woody glen, and halted, not knowing whether the obstacle needed to be crossed or not. They passed down the word for the generals and officers to come forward to the front. Xenophon, wondering what it was that stopped the march, and presently hearing the above order passed along the ranks, rode up with all speed. As soon as they were met, Sophaenetus, as the eldest general, stated his opinion that the question, whether a gully of that kind ought to be crossed or not, was not worth discussing. Xenophon, with some ardour, retorted, "You know, men, I have not been in the habit hitherto of introducing you to danger which you might avoid. It is not your reputation for courage surely that is at stake, but your safe return home. But now the matter stands thus: It is impossible to retire from this point without a battle; if we do not advance against the enemy ourselves, he will follow us as soon as we have turned our backs and attack us. Consider, then; is it better to go and meet the foe with arms advanced, or with arms reversed to watch him as he assails us on our rear? You know this at any rate, that to retire before an enemy has nothing glorious about it, whereas attack engenders courage even in a coward. For my part, I would rather at any time attack with half my men than retreat with twice the number. As to these fellows, if we attack them, I am sure you do not really expect them to await us; though, if we retreat, we know for certain they will be emboldened to pursue us. Nay, if the result of crossing is to place a difficult gully behind us when we are on the point of engaging, surely that is an advantage worth seizing. At least, if it were left to me, I would choose that everything should appear smooth and passable to the enemy, which may invite retreat; but for ourselves we may bless the ground which teaches us that except in victory we have no deliverance. It astonishes me that any one should deem this particular gully a whit more terrible than any of the other barriers which we have successfully passed. How impassable was the plain, had we failed to conquer their cavalry! How insurmountable the mountains already traversed by us, with all their peltasts in hot pursuit at our heels! Nay, when we have safely reached the sea, the Pontus will present a somewhat formidable gully, when we have neither vessels to convey us away nor corn to keep us alive whilst we stop. But we shall no sooner be there than we must be off again to get provisions. Surely it is better to fight to-day after a good breakfast than to-morrow on an empty stomach. Sirs, the offerings are favourable to us, the omens are propitious, the victims more than promising; let us attack the enemy! Now that they have had a good look at us, these fellows must not be allowed to enjoy their dinners or choose a camp wherever they please."

After that the officers bade him lead on. None gainsaid, and he led the way. His orders were to cross the gully, where each man chanced to find himself. By this method, as it seemed to him, the troops would more quickly mass themselves on the far side than was possible, if they defiled along the bridge which spanned the gully. But once across he passed along the line and addressed the troops, "Soldiers, call to mind what by help of the gods you have already done. Think of the battles you have won at close quarters with the foe; of the fate which awaits those who flee before their foes. Forget not that we stand at the very doors of Hellas. Follow in the steps of Heracles, our guide, and cheer each the other onwards by name. Sweet were it surely by some brave and noble word or deed, spoken or done this day, to leave the memory of oneself in the hearts of those one loves."

These words were spoken as he rode past, and simultaneously he began leading on the troops in battle line; and, placing the peltasts on either flank of the main body, they moved against the enemy. Along the line the order had sped to keep their spears at rest on the right shoulder until the trumpet signal; then lower them for the charge, slow march, and even pace, no one to quicken into a run. Lastly, the watch-word was passed, "Zeus the Saviour, Heracles our Guide." The enemy waited their approach, confident in the excellence of his position; but as they drew closer the Hellene light troops, with a loud battle-cry, without waiting for the order, dashed against the foe. The latter, on their side, came forward eagerly to meet the charge, both the cavalry and the mass of the Bithynians; and these turned the peltasts. But when with counter-wave the phalanx of the heavy infantry rapidly advancing, faced them, and at the same time the trumpet sounded, and the battle hymn rose from all lips, and after this a loud cheer rose, and at the same instant they couched their spears—at this conjuncture the enemy no longer welcomed them, but fled. Timasion with his cavalry followed close, and, considering their scant numbers, they did great execution. It was the left wing of the enemy, in a line with which the Hellene cavalry were posted, that was so speedily scattered. But the right, which was not so hotly pursued, collected upon a knoll; and when the Hellenes saw them standing firm, it seemed the easiest and least dangerous course to go against them at once. Raising the battle hymn, they straightway fell upon them, but the others did not await their coming. Thereupon the peltasts gave chase until the right of the enemy was in its turn scattered, though with slight loss in killed; for the enemy's cavalry was numerous and threatening.

But when the Hellenes saw the cavalry of Pharnabazus still standing in compact order, and the Bithynian horsemen massing together as if to join it, and like spectators gazing down from a knoll at the occurrences below; though weary, they determined to attack the enemy as best they could, and not suffer him to recover breath with reviving courage. So they formed in compact line and advanced. Thereupon the hostile cavalry turned and fled down the steep as swiftly as if they had been pursued by cavalry. In fact they sought the shelter of a gully, the existence of which was unknown to the Hellenes. The latter accordingly turned aside too soon and gave up the chase, for it was late. Returning to the point where the first encounter took place they erected a trophy, and went back to the sea about sunset. It was something like seven miles to camp.

6. After this the enemy confined themselves to their own concerns, and removed their households and property as far away as possible. The Hellenes, on their side, were still awaiting the arrival of Cleander with the ships of war and transports, which ought to be there soon. So each day they went out with the baggage animals and slaves and fearlessly brought in wheat and barley, wine and vegetables, millet and figs; since the district produced all good things, the olive alone excepted. When the army stayed in camp to rest, pillaging parties were allowed to go out, and those who went out appropriated the spoils; but when the whole army went out, if any one went off apart and seized anything, it was voted to be public property. Before long there was an ample abundance of supplies of all sorts, for marketables arrived from Hellenic cities on all sides, and marts were established. Mariners coasting by, and hearing that a city was being founded and that there was a harbour, were glad to put in. Even the hostile tribes dwelling in the neighbourhood presently began to send envoys to Xenophon. It was he who was forming the place into a city, as they understood, and they would be glad to learn on what terms they might secure his friendship. He made a point of introducing these visitors to the soldiers.

Meanwhile Cleander arrived with two ships of war, but not a single transport. At the moment of his arrival, as it happened, the army had taken the field, and a separate party had gone off on a pillaging excursion into the hills and had captured a number of small cattle. In their apprehension of being deprived of them, these same people spoke to Dexippus (this was the man who had made off from Trapezus with the fifty-oared galley), and urged him to save their sheep for them. "Take some for yourself," said they, "and give the rest back to us." So, without more ado, he drove off the soldiers standing near, who kept repeating that the spoil was public property. Then off he went to Cleander. "Here is an attempt," said he, "at robbery." Cleander bade him to bring up the culprit to him. Dexippus seized on some one, and was for hauling him to the Spartan governor. Just then Agasias came across him and rescued the man, who was a member of his company; and the rest of the soldiers present set to work to stone Dexippus, calling him traitor. Things looked so ill that a number of the crew of the ships of war took fright and fled to the sea, and with the rest Cleander himself. Xenophon and the other generals tried to hold the men back, assuring Cleander that the affair signified nothing at all, and that the origin of it was a decree passed by the army. That was to blame, if anything. But Cleander, goaded on by Dexippus, and personally annoyed at the fright which he had experienced, threatened to sail away and publish an interdict against them, forbidding any city to receive them, as being public enemies. For at this date the Lacedaemonians held sway over the whole Hellenic world.

Thereat the affair began to wear an ugly look, and the Hellenes begged and implored Cleander to reconsider his intention. He replied that he would be as good as his word, and that nothing should stop him, unless the man who set the example of stoning, with the other who rescued the prisoner, were given up to him. Now, one of the two whose persons were thus demanded—Agasias—had been a friend to Xenophon throughout; and that was just why Dexippus was all the more anxious to accuse him. In their perplexity the generals summoned a full meeting of the soldiers, and some speakers were disposed to make very light of Cleander and set him at naught. But Xenophon took a more serious view of the matter; he rose and addressed the meeting thus, "Soldiers, I cannot say that I feel disposed to make light of this business, if Cleander be allowed to go away, as he threatens to do, in his present temper towards us. There are Hellenic cities close by; but then the Lacedaemonians are the lords of Hellas, and they can, any one of them, carry out whatever they like in the cities. If then the first thing this Lacedaemonian does is to close the gates of Byzantium, and next to pass an order to the other governors, city by city, not to receive us because we are a set of lawless ruffians disloyal to the Lacedaemonians; and if, further, this report of us should reach the ears of their admiral, Anaxibius, to stay or to sail away will alike be difficult. Remember, the Lacedaemonians at the present time are lords alike on land and on sea. For the sake then of a single man, or for two men's sake, it is not right that the rest of us should be debarred from Hellas; but whatever they enjoin we must obey. Do not the cities which gave us birth yield them obedience also? For my own part, inasmuch as Dexippus, I believe, keeps telling Cleander that Agasias would never have done this had not I, Xenophon, bidden him, I absolve you of all complicity, and Agasias too, if Agasias himself states that I am in any way a prime mover in this matter. If I have set the fashion of stone-throwing or any other sort of violence I condemn myself—I say that I deserve the extreme penalty, and I will submit to undergo it. I further say that if any one else is accused, that man is bound to surrender himself to Cleander for judgment, for by this means you will be absolved entirely from the accusation. But as the matter now stands, it is cruel that just when we were aspiring to win praise and honour throughout Hellas, we are destined to sink below the level of the rest of the world, banned from the Hellenic cities whose common name we boast."

After him Agasias got up, and said, "I swear to you, men, by the gods and goddesses, verily and indeed, neither Xenophon nor any one else among you bade me rescue the man. I saw an honest man—one of my own company—being taken up by Dexippus, the man who betrayed you, as you know full well. That I could not endure; I rescued him, I admit the fact. Do not you deliver me up. I will surrender myself, as Xenophon suggests, to Cleander to pass what verdict on me he thinks right. Do not, for the sake of such a matter, make foes of the Lacedaemonians; rather act so that each of you may safely reach the goal of his desire. Only do you choose from among yourselves and send with me to Cleander those who, in case of any omission on my part, may by their words and acts supply what is lacking." Thereupon the army granted him to choose for himself whom he would have go with him and to go; and he at once chose the generals. After this they all set off to Cleander—Agasias and the generals and the man who had been rescued by Agasias—and the generals spoke as follows, "The army has sent us to you, Cleander, and this is their bidding, 'If you have fault to find with all, they say, you ought to pass sentence on all, and do with them what seems best; or if the charge is against one man or two, or possibly several, what they expect of these people is to surrender themselves to you for judgment.' Accordingly, if you lay anything to the charge of us generals, here we stand at your bar. Or do you impute the fault to some one not here? Tell us whom. Short of flying in the face of our authority, there is no one who will absent himself."

At that point Agasias stepped forward and said, "It was I, Cleander, who rescued the man before you yonder from Dexippus, when the latter was carrying him off, and it was I who gave the order to strike Dexippus. My plea is that I know the prisoner to be an honest man. As to Dexippus, I know that he was chosen by the army to command a fifty-oared galley, which we had obtained by request from the men of Trapezus for the express purpose of collecting vessels to carry us safely home. But this same Dexippus betrayed his fellow-soldiers, with whom he had been delivered from so many perils, and made off into hiding like a runaway slave, whereby we have robbed the Trapezuntines of their ship, and must appear as knaves in their eyes for this man's sake. As to ourselves, as far as he could, he has ruined us; for, like the rest of us, he had heard how all but impossible it was for us to retreat by foot across the rivers and to reach Hellas in safety. That is the stamp of man whom I robbed of his prey. Now, had it been you yourself who carried him off, or one of your emissaries, or indeed any one short of a runaway from ourselves, be sure that I should have acted far otherwise. Be assured that if you put me to death at this time you are sacrificing a good, honest man for the sake of a coward and a scamp."

When he had listened to these remarks, Cleander replied that if such had been the conduct of Dexippus he could not congratulate him. "But still," he added, turning to the generals, "were Dexippus ever so great a scamp he ought not to suffer violence; but in the language of your own demand he was entitled to a fair trial, and so to obtain his deserts. What I have to say at present therefore is: leave your friend here and go your way, and when I give the order be present at the trial. I have no further charge against the army or any one, since the prisoner himself admits that he rescued the man." Then the man who had been rescued said, "In behalf of myself, Cleander, if possibly you think that I was being taken up for some misdeed, it is not so; I neither struck nor shot; I merely said that the sheep were public property; for it was a resolution of the soldiers that whenever the army went out as a body any booty privately obtained was to be public property. That was all I said, and thereupon yonder fellow seized me and began dragging me off. He wanted to stop our mouths, so that he might have a share of the things himself, and keep the rest for these buccaneers, contrary to the ordinance." In answer to that Cleander said, "Very well, if that is your disposition you can stay behind too, and we will take your case into consideration also."

Thereupon Cleander and his party proceeded to breakfast; but Xenophon collected the army in assembly, and advised their sending a deputation to Cleander to intercede in behalf of the men. Accordingly it was resolved to send some generals and officers with Dracontius the Spartan, and of the rest those who seemed best fitted to go. The deputation was to request Cleander by all means to release the two men. Accordingly Xenophon came and addressed him thus, "Cleander, you have the men; the army has bowed to you and assented to do what you wished with respect to these two members of their body and themselves in general. But now they beg and pray you to give up these two men, and not to put them to death. Many a good service have these two wrought for our army in past days. Let them but obtain this from you, and in return the army promises that, if you will put yourself at their head and the gracious gods approve, they will show you how orderly they are, how apt to obey their general, and, with the gods' help, to face their foes unflinchingly. They make this further request to you, that you will present yourself and take command of them and make trial of them. 'Test us ourselves,' they say, 'and test Dexippus, what each of us is like, and afterwards assign to each his due.' " When Cleander heard these things, he answered, "Well, by the twin gods,[5] I will answer you quickly enough. Here I make you a present of the two men, and I will as you say present myself, and then, if the gods grant it, I will put myself at your head and lead you into Hellas. Very different is your language from the tale I used to hear concerning you from certain people, that you wanted to withdraw the army from allegiance to the Lacedaemonians."

After this the deputation thanked him and retired, taking with them the two men; then Cleander sacrificed as a preliminary to marching, and associated with Xenophon in friendly fashion, and the two struck up an alliance. When the Spartan saw with what good discipline the men carried out their orders, he was still more anxious to become their leader. However, in spite of sacrifices repeated on three successive days, the victims steadily remained unfavourable. So he summoned the generals and said to them, "The victims are not favourable to me, they suffer me not to lead you home; but be not out of heart at that. To you it is given, as it would appear, to bring your men safe home. Forward then, and for our part, whenever you come yonder, we will bestow on you as warm a welcome as we may."

Then the soldiers resolved to make him a present of the public cattle, which he accepted, but again gave back to them. So he sailed away; but the soldiers made division of the corn which they had collected and of the other captured property, and commenced their homeward march through the territory of the Bithynians.

At first they confined themselves to the main road; but not chancing upon anything whereby they might reach a friendly territory with something in their pockets for themselves, they resolved to turn sharp round, and marched for one day and night in the opposite direction. By this proceeding they captured many slaves and much small cattle; and on the sixth day reached Chrysopolis in Calchedonia. Here they halted seven days while they disposed of their booty by sale.

[5] Castor and Pollux.

BOOK VII

[In the earlier portion of the narrative will be found a detailed history of the fortunes of the Hellenes during their march up country with Cyrus down to the date of the battle; and, subsequently to his death, until they reached the Euxine; as also of all their doings in their efforts to escape from the Euxine, partly by land marches and partly under sail by sea, until they found themselves outside the mouth of the Black Sea at Chrysopolis in Asia.]

1. At this point Pharnabazus, who was afraid that the army might undertake a campaign against his satrapy, sent to Anaxibius, the Spartan high admiral, who chanced to be in Byzantium, and begged him to convey the army out of Asia, undertaking to comply with his wishes in every respect. Anaxibius accordingly sent to summon the generals and officers to Byzantium, and promised that the soldiers should not lack pay for service, if they crossed the strait. The officers said that they would deliberate and return an answer. Xenophon individually informed him that he was about to quit the army at once, and was only anxious to set sail. Anaxibius pressed him not to be in so great a hurry. "Cross over with the rest," he said, "and then it will be time enough to think about quitting the army." This the other undertook to do.

Now Seuthes the Thracian sent Medosades and begged Xenophon to use his influence to get the army across. "Tell Xenophon, if he will do his best for me in this matter, he will not regret it." Xenophon answered, "The army is in any case going to cross; so that, as far as that is concerned, Seuthes is under no obligation to me or to any one else; but as soon as it is once across, I personally shall be quit of it. Let Seuthes therefore, as far as he may deem consistent with prudence, apply to those who are going to remain and will have a voice in affairs."

After this the whole body of troops crossed to Byzantium. But Anaxibius, instead of proceeding to give pay, made proclamation that, the soldiers were to take up their arms and baggage and go forth, as if all he wished were to ascertain their numbers and send them on their way at the same moment. The soldiers were not well pleased at that, because they had no money to furnish themselves with provisions for the march; and they sluggishly set about getting their baggage together. Xenophon meanwhile, being on terms of intimacy with the governor, Cleander, came to pay his host a final visit, and bid him adieu, being on the point of setting sail. But the other protested, "Do not do so, or else," said he, "you will be blamed, for even now certain people are disposed to hold you to account because the army is so slow in getting under way." The other answered, "Why, I am not to blame for that. It is the men themselves, who are in want of provisions; that is why they are out of heart at their departure." "All the same," he replied, "I advise you to go out, as if you intended to march with them, and when you are well outside, it will be time enough to take yourself off." "Well, then," said Xenophon, "we will go and arrange all this with Anaxibius." They went and stated the case to the admiral, who insisted that they must do as he had said, and march out, bag and baggage, by the quickest road; and as an appendix to the former edict, he added, "Any one absenting himself from the review and the muster will have himself to blame for the consequences." This was peremptory. So out marched the generals first, and then the rest; and now, with the exception of here a man and there, they were all outside; and Eteonicus stood posted near the gates, ready to close them, as soon as the men were fairly out, and to thrust in the bolt pin.

Then Anaxibius summoned the generals and captains, and addressed them, "Provisions you had better get from the Thracian villages; you will find plenty of barley, wheat, and other necessaries in them; and when you have got them, off with you to the Chersonese, where Cyniscus will take you into his service." Some of the soldiers overheard what was said, or possibly one of the officers was the medium of communication; however it was, the news was handed on to the army. As to the generals, their immediate concern was to try and gain some information as to whether Seuthes was hostile or friendly; also whether they would have to march through the Sacred Mountain, or round about through the middle of Thrace.

While they were discussing these points, the soldiers snatched up their arms and made a rush full speed at the gates, with the intention of getting inside the fortification again. But Eteonicus and his men, seeing the heavy infantry coming up at a run promptly closed the gates and thrust in the bolt pin. Then the soldiers fell to battering the gates, exclaiming that it was iniquitous to thrust them forth in this fashion into the jaws of their enemies. "If you do not of your own accord open the gates," they cried, "we will split them in half." Another set rushed down to the sea, and so along the breakwater and over the wall into the city; while a third set, consisting of those few who were still inside, having never left the city, seeing the affair at the gates, severed the bars with axes and flung the portals wide open; and the rest came pouring in.

Xenophon, seeing what was happening, was seized with alarm lest the army should betake itself to pillage, and ills incurable be wrought to the city, to himself and to the soldiers. Then he set off, and, plunging into the throng, was swept through the gates with the crowd. The Byzantines no sooner saw the soldiers forcibly rushing in than they left the open square, and fled, some to the shipping, others to their homes, while those already indoors came racing out, and some fell to dragging down their ships of war, hoping possibly to be safe on board these; while there was not a soul who doubted but that the city was taken, and they were all undone. Eteonicus made a swift retreat to the citadel. Anaxibius ran down to the sea, and, getting on board a fisherman's smack, sailed round to the citadel, and at once sent off for the garrison troops from Calchedon, since those already in the citadel seemed hardly sufficient to keep the men in check.

The soldiers, catching sight of Xenophon, threw themselves upon him, crying, "Now, Xenophon, is the time to prove yourself a man. You have a city, you have triremes, you have money, you have men; to-day, if you only choose, you can do us a good turn, and we will make you a great man." He replied, "Certainly, I like what you say, and I will do it all; but if that is what you have set your hearts on, fall into rank and take up position at once." This he said, wishing to quiet them, and so passed the order along the lines himself, while bidding the rest to do the same, "Take up position; stand easy." But the men themselves, by a species of self-marshalling, fell into rank, and were soon formed, the heavy infantry eight deep, while the light infantry had run up to cover either wing. The Thracian Square, as it is called, is a fine site for manoeuvring, being bare of buildings and level. As soon as the arms were stacked and the men's tempers cooled, Xenophon called a general meeting of the soldiers, and made the following speech:

"Soldiers, I am not surprised at your wrath, or that you consider it monstrous treatment so to be cheated; but consider what will be the consequences if we gratify our indignation, and in return for such deception, avenge ourselves on the Lacedaemonians here present, and plunder an innocent city. We shall be declared enemies of the Lacedaemonians and their allies; and what sort of war that will be, we need not go far to conjecture. I take it, you have not forgotten some quite recent occurrences. We Athenians entered into war against the Lacedaemonians and their allies with a fleet consisting of not less than 300 triremes, including those in docks as well as those afloat. We had vast treasures stored up in the city, and a yearly income which, derived from home or foreign sources, amounted to no less than 1,000 talents. Our empire included all the islands, and we were possessed of numerous cities both in Asia and in Europe. Among others, this very Byzantium, where we now are, was ours; and yet in the end we were vanquished, as you all very well know.

"What, must we anticipate, will now be our fate? The Lacedaemonians have not only their old allies, but the Athenians and those who were at that time allies of Athens are added to them. Tissaphernes and all the rest of the Asiatics on the seaboard are our foes, not to speak of our arch-enemy, the king himself, up yonder, whom we came to deprive of his empire, and to kill, if possible. I ask then, with all these banded together against us, is there any one so insane as to imagine that we can survive the contest? For god's sake, let us not go mad or loosely throw away our lives in war with our own native cities—nay, our own friends, and our kin; for in one or other of the cities they are all included. Every city will march against us, and not unjustly, if, after refusing to hold one single barbarian city by right of conquest, we seize the first Hellenic city that we come to and make it a ruinous heap. For my part, my prayer is that before I see such things wrought by you, I, at any rate, may lie 10,000 fathoms under ground! My counsel to you, as Hellenes, is to try and obtain your just rights, through obedience to those who stand at the head of Hellas; and if so be that you fail in those demands, why, being more sinned against than sinning, need we rob ourselves of Hellas too? At present, I propose that we should send to Anaxibius and tell him that we have made an entrance into the city, not meditating violence, but merely to discover if he and his will show us any good; for if so, it is well; but if otherwise, at least we will let him see that he does not shut the door upon us as dupes and fools. We know the meaning of discipline; we turn our backs and go."

This resolution was passed, and they sent Hieronymus an Eleian, with two others, Eurylochus an Arcadian and Philesius an Achaean, to deliver the message. So these set off on their errand. But while the soldiers were still seated in conclave, Coeratadas, of Thebes, arrived. He was a Theban not in exile, but with a taste for generalship, who made it his business to go the round of Hellas to see if any city or nation were in need of his services. Thus, on the present occasion, he presented himself, and begged to state that he was ready to put himself at their head, and lead them into the Delta of Thrace, as it is called, where they would find themselves in a land of plenty; but until they got there, he would provide them with meat and drınk enough and to spare. While they were still listening to this tale, the return message from Anaxibius came. His answer was, "The discipline, they had spoken of, was not a thing they would regret; indeed he would report their behaviour to the authorities at home; and for himself, he would take advice and do the best he could for them."

Thereupon the soldiers accepted Coeratadas as their general, and retired without the walls. Their new general undertook to present himself to the troops next day with sacrificial beasts and a soothsayer, with eatables also and drinkables for the army. Now, as soon as they were gone out, Anaxibius closed the gates and issued a proclamation to the effect that any of the soldiers caught inside should be sold at once. Next day, Coeratadas arrived with the victims and the soothsayer. A string of twenty bearers bearing barleymeal followed at his heels, succeeded by other twenty carrying wine, and three laden with a supply of olives, and two others carrying, the one about as much garlic as a single man could lift, and the other a similar load of onions. These various supplies he set down, apparently for distribution, and proceeded to sacrifice.

Now Xenophon sent to Cleander, begging him to arrange matters so that he might be allowed to enter the walls, with a view to starting from Byzantium on his homeward voyage. Cleander came, and this is what he said, "I have come; but I was barely able to arrange what you want. Anaxibius insisted that it was not convenient that Xenophon should be inside while the soldiers are close to the walls without; the Byzantines were suffering from party strife moreover; and no love was lost between the one party of them and the other. Still, he ended by bidding you to come inside, if you really intended to leave the town by sea with himself." Accordingly Xenophon bade the soldiers good-bye, and returned with Cleander within the walls.

To return to Coeratadas. The first day he failed to get favourable signs at the sacrifice, and never a dole of rations did he make to the soldiers. On the second day the victims were standing ready near the altar, and so was Coeratadas, with chaplet crowned, all ready to sacrifice, when up comes Timasion the Dardanian, with Neon the Asinaean, and Cleanor of Orchomenus, forbidding Coeratadas to sacrifice, for he must understand there was an end to his generalship, unless he gave them provisions. The other bade them measure out the supplies. But when he found that he had a good deal short of a single day's provisions for each man, he picked up his paraphernalia of sacrifice and withdrew. As to being general, he would have nothing more to say to it.

2. Now these five were left—Neon the Asinaean, Phryniscus the Achaean, Philesius the Achaean, Xanthicles the Achaean, Timasion the Dardanian—at the head of the army, and they pushed on to some villages of the Thracians facing Byzantium, and there encamped. Now the generals could not agree. Cleanor and Phryniscus wished to march to join Seuthes, who had worked upon their feelings by presenting one with

a horse and the other with a woman. But Neon's object was to come to the Chersonese. "When we are under the wing of the Lacedaemonians," he thought, "I shall step to the front and command the whole army."

Timasion's one ambition was to cross back again into Asia, hoping to be reinstated at home and end his exile. The soldiers shared the wishes of the last general. But, as time dragged on, many of the men sold their arms at different places and set sail as best they could; others became absorbed in the cities. Anaxibius rejoiced to hear of the break-up of the army, since he thought that if it continued Pharnabazus would be greatly pleased.

But Anaxibius, while prosecuting his voyage from Byzantium, was met at Cyzicus by Aristarchus, the new governor, who was to succeed Cleander at Byzantium; and report said that a new admiral, Polus, if he had not actually arrived, would presently reach the Hellespont and relieve Anaxibius. The latter sent a parting injunction to Aristarchus to be sure and sell all the Cyreian soldiers he could lay hands on still lingering in Byzantium; for Cleander had not sold a single man of them; on the contrary, he had made it his business to tend the sick and wounded, pitying them, and insisting on their being received in the houses. Aristarchus changed all that, and was no sooner arrived in Byzantium than he sold no less than 400 of them. Meanwhile Anaxibius, on his coasting voyage, reached Parium, and, according to the terms of their agreement, he sent to Pharnabazus. But the latter, learning that Aristarchus was the new governor at Byzantium, and that Anaxibius had ceased to be admiral, turned upon him a cold shoulder, and set about concocting the same measures concerning the Cyreian army with Aristarchus, as he had lately been at work upon with Anaxibius.

Anaxibius thereupon summoned Xenophon and bade him, by every manner of means, sail to the army with the utmost speed, and keep it together, and also collect the scattered fragments and march them down to Perinthus, and thence convey them across to Asia without loss of time. And herewith he put a thirty-oared galley at his service, and gave him a letter of authority and an officer to accompany him, with an order to the Perinthians to escort Xenophon without delay on horseback to the army. So it was that Xenophon sailed across and eventually reached the army. The soldiers gave him a joyous welcome, and would have been only too glad to cross from Thrace into Asia under his leadership.

But Seuthes, hearing that Xenophon had arrived, sent Medosades again, by sea to meet him, and begged him to bring the army to him; and whatever he thought would make his speech persuasive, he was ready to promise him. But the other replied, that none of these things were open to him to do; and with this answer Medosades departed, and the

Hellenes proceeded to Perinthus. Here on arrival Neon withdrew his troops and encamped apart, having about 800 men; while the remainder of the army lay in one place under the walls of Perinthus.

After this, Xenophon set himself to find vessels, so as to lose no time in crossing. But in the interval Aristarchus, the governor from Byzantium, arrived with a couple of war ships, being moved to do so by Pharnabazus. To make doubly sure, he first forbade the skippers and shipmasters to carry the troops across, and then he visited the camp and informed the soldiers that their passage into Asia was forbidden. Xenophon replied that he was acting under the orders of Anaxibius, who had sent him thither for this express purpose; to which Aristarchus retorted, "For the matter of that, Anaxibius is no longer admiral, and I am governor in this quarter; if I catch any of you at sea, I will sink you." With these remarks he retired within the walls of Perinthus.

Next day, he sent for the generals and officers of the army. They had already reached the fortification walls, when some one brought word to Xenophon that if he set foot inside, he would be seized, and either meet some ill fate there or more likely be delivered up to Pharnabazus. On hearing this Xenophon sent forward the rest of the party, but for himself pleaded that there was a sacrifice which he wished to offer. In this way he contrived to turn back and consult the victims, "Would the gods allow him to try and bring the army over to Seuthes?" On the one hand it was plain that the idea of crossing over to Asia in the face of this man with his ships of war, who meant to bar the passage, was too dangerous. Nor did he altogether like the notion of being blocked up in the Chersonese with an army in dire need of everything; where, besides being at the beck and call of the governor of the place, they would be debarred from the necessaries of life.

While Xenophon was thus employed, the generals and officers came back with a message from Aristarchus, who had told them they might retire for the present, but in the afternoon he should expect them. The former suspicions of a plot had now ripened to a certainty. Xenophon meantime had ascertained that the victims were favourable to his project. He personally, and the army as a whole, might with safety proceed to Seuthes, they seemed to say. Accordingly, he took with him Polycrates, the Athenian captain, and from each of the generals, not including Neon, some one man whom they could in each case trust, and in the night they set off to visit the army of Seuthes, about seven miles distant.

As they approached, they came upon some deserted watch-fires, and their first impression was that Seuthes had shifted his position; but presently perceiving a confused sound (the voices of Seuthes' people signalling to one another), the explanation dawned on him: Seuthes kept his watch-fires kindled in front of, instead of behind, his night pickets, in order that the outposts, being in the dark, might escape notice, their numbers and position being thus a mystery; while any party approaching from the outside, so far from escaping notice, would, through the glare of the fire, stand out conspicuously. Perceiving how matters stood, Xenophon sent forward his interpreter, who was one of the party, and bade him inform Seuthes that Xenophon was there and wished to confer with him. The others asked if he were an Athenian from the army yonder, and no sooner had the interpreter replied, "Yes, the same," than up they leaped and galloped off; and in less time than it takes to tell 200 peltasts had come up who seized and carried off Xenophon and those with him and brought them to Seuthes. The latter was in a tower well guarded, and there were horses round it in a circle, standing all ready bitted and bridled; for his alarm was so great that he gave his horses their provender during the day, and during the nights he kept watch with them thus bitted and bridled. It was stated in explanation that in old days an ancestor of his, named Teres, had been in this very country with a large army, several of whom he had lost at the hands of the native inhabitants, besides being robbed of his baggage train. The inhabitants of the country are Thynians, and they are reputed to be far the most warlike set of fighters—especially at night.

When they drew near, Seuthes bade Xenophon enter, and bring with him any two he might choose. As soon as they were inside, they first greeted one another warmly, and then, according to the Thracian custom, pledged themselves in bowls of wine. There was further present at the elbow of Seuthes, Medosades, who on all occasions acted as his ambassador-in-chief. Xenophon took the initiative and spoke as follows, "You have sent to me, Seuthes, once and again. On the first occasion you sent Medosades yonder, to Calchedon, and you begged me to use my influence in favour of the army crossing over from Asia. You promised me, in return for this conduct on my part, various kindnesses; at least that is what Medosades stated." And before proceeding further he turned to Medosades and asked, "Is not that so?" The other assented. "Again, on a second occasion, the same Medosades came when I had crossed over from Parium to rejoin the army; and he promised me that if I would bring you the army, you would in various respects treat me as a friend and brother. He said especially with regard to certain seaboard places of which you are the owner and lord, that you would make me a present of them." At this point he again questioned Medosades, "Whether the words attributed to him were exact?" And Medosades once more fully assented. "Come now," proceeded Xenophon, "recount what answer I made you, and first at Calchedon." "You answered that the army was, in any case, about to cross over to Byzantium; and as far as that went, there was no need to pay you or any one else anything; and for yourself, you added, that once across you intended to leave the army, which thing came to pass even as you said." "Well, what did I say," he asked, "at your next visit, when you came to me in Selymbria?" "You said that the proposal was impossible; you were all going to Perinthus to cross into Asia." "Good," said Xenophon, "and in spite of all, at the present moment, here I am myself, and Phryniscus, one of my colleagues, and Polycrates yonder, a captain; and outside to represent the other generals (all except Neon the Laconian), the trustiest men they could find to send. So that if you wish to give these transactions the seal of still greater security, you have nothing to do but to summon them also; and do you, Polycrates, go and say from me, that I bid them leave their arms outside, and you can leave your own sword outside before you enter with them on your return."

When Seuthes had heard so far, he interposed, "I should never mistrust an Athenian, for we are relatives already,[1] I know; and the best of friends, I believe, we shall be." After that, as soon as the right men entered, Xenophon first questioned Seuthes as to what use he intended to make of the army, and he replied as follows, "Maesades was my father; his sway extended over the Melanditae, the Thynians, and the Tranipsae. Then the affairs of the Odrysians took a bad turn, and my father was driven out of this country, and later on died himself of sickness, leaving me to be brought up as an orphan at the court of Medocus, the present king. But I, when I had grown to man's estate, could not endure to live with my eyes fixed on another's board. So I seated myself on the seat by him as a suppliant, and begged him to give me as many men as he could spare, that I might wreak what mischief I could on those who had driven us forth from our land; that thus I might cease to live in dependence upon another's board. In answer to my petition, he gave me the men and the horses which you will see at break of day, and nowadays I live with these, pillaging my own ancestral land. But if you would join me, I think, with the help of heaven, we might easily recover my empire. That is what I want of you." "Well, then," said Xenophon, "supposing we came, what should you be able to give to the soldiers, the officers, and the generals? Tell us that these witnesses may report your answer." And he promised to give "to the common soldiers a cyzicene, to a captain twice as much, and to a general four times as much, with as much land as ever they liked, some yoke of oxen, and a

---

[1] Tradition said that the Thracians and Athenians were connected, through the marriage of a former prince Tereus (or Teres) with Procne, the daughter of Pandion.

fortified place upon the seaboard." "But now supposing," said Xenophon, "we fail of success, in spite of our endeavours; suppose any intimidation on the part of the Lacedaemonians should arise; will you receive into your country any of us who may seek to find a refuge with you?" He answered, "Nay, not only so, but I shall look upon you as my brothers, entitled to share my seat, and the joint possessors of all the wealth which we may be able to acquire. And to you, Xenophon, I will give my daughter, and if you have a daughter, I will buy her in Thracian fashion; and I will give you Bisanthe as a dwelling-place, which is the fairest of all my possessions on the seaboard."

3. After listening to these proposals, they gave and accepted pledges of good faith; and so the deputation rode off. Before day they were back again in camp, and severally rendered a report to those who sent them. At dawn Aristarchus again summoned the generals and officers, but the latter resolved to have done with the visit to Aristarchus, and to summon a meeting of the army. In full conclave the soldiers met, with the exception of Neon's men, who remained about a mile off. When they were met together Xenophon rose, and made the following announcement, "Men, Aristarchus with his ships of war hinders us from sailing where we wish to go; it is not even safe to set foot on board a vessel. But if he hinders us here, he hastens us there. 'Be off to the Chersonese,' says he, 'force a passage through the Sacred mountain.' If we master it and succeed in getting to the place, he has something in store for us. He promises that he will not sell you any more, as he did at Byzantium; you shall not be cheated again; you shall have pay; he will no longer, as now, suffer you to remain in want of provisions. That is his proposal. But Seuthes says that if you will go to him he will treat you well. What you have now to consider is, whether you will stay to debate this question, or leave its settlement till we have gone up into a land of provisions. If you ask me my opinion, it is this: Since here we have neither money to buy, nor leave to take without money what we need, why should we not go up into these villages where the right to help ourselves is conferred by might? There, unhampered by the want of bare necessaries, you can listen to what this man and the other wants of you and choose whichever sounds best. Let those," he added, "who agree to this, hold up their hands." They all held them up. "Retire then," said he, "and get your kit together, and at the word of command follow your leader."

After this, Xenophon put himself at the head and the rest followed. Neon, indeed, and other agents from Aristarchus tried to turn them from their purpose, but to the persuasions they turned a deaf ear. They had not advanced much more than three miles, when Seuthes met them;

and Xenophon, seeing him, bade him ride up. He wished to tell him what they felt to be conducive to their interests, and in the presence of as many witnesses as possible. As soon as he had approached, Xenophon said, "We are going where the troops will have enough to live upon; when we are there, we will listen to you and to the emissaries of the Laconian, and choose between you both whatever seems best. If then you will lead us where provisions are to be got in plenty, we shall feel indebted to you for your hospitality." And Seuthes answered, "For the matter of that, I know many villages, close-packed and stocked with all kinds of provisions, just far enough off to give you a good appetite for your breakfasts." "Lead on then!" said Xenophon. When they had reached the villages in the afternoon, the soldiers met, and Seuthes made the following speech, "My request to you, sirs, is that you will take the field with me, and my promise to you is that I will give every man of you a cyzicene, and to the officers and generals at the customary rate; besides this I will honour those who show special merit. Food and drink you will get as now for yourselves from the country; but whatever is captured, I shall claim to have myself, so that by distribution of it I may provide you with pay. Let them flee, let them creep into hiding-places, we shall be able to pursue after them, we will track them out; or if they resist, along with you we will endeavour to subdue them to our hands." Xenophon inquired, "And how far from the sea shall you expect the army to follow you?" "Nowhere more than seven days' journey," he answered, "and in many places less."

After this, permission was given to all who wished to speak, and many spoke, but ever to one and the same tune, "What Seuthes said, was very right. It was winter, and for a man to sail home, even if he had the will to do so, was impossible. On the other hand, to continue long in a friendly country, where they must depend upon what they could purchase, was equally beyond their power. If they were to wear away time and support life in a hostile country, it was safer to do so with Seuthes than by themselves, not to speak of all these good things; but if they were going to get pay into the bargain, that indeed was a godsend." To complete the proceedings, Xenophon said, "If any one opposes the measure, let him state his views; if not, let the officer put the proposition to the vote." No one opposed; they put it to the vote, and the resolution was carried; and without loss of time, he informed Seuthes that they would take the field with him.

After this the troops messed in their separate divisions, but the generals and officers were invited by Seuthes to dinner at a neighbouring village which was in his possession. When they were at the doors, and on the point of stepping in to dinner, they were met by a certain Heracleides, of Maronea. He came up to each guest, addressing himself particularly to those who, as he conjectured, ought to be able to make a present to Seuthes. He addressed himself first to some Parians who were there to arrange a friendship with Medocus, the king of the Odrysians, and were bearers of presents to the king and to his wife. Heracleides reminded them, "Medocus is up country twelve days' journey from the sea; but Seuthes, now that he has got this army, will be lord on the sea-coast; as your neighbour, then, he is the man to do you good or do you ill. If you are wise, you will give him whatever he asks of you. On the whole, it will be laid out at better interest than if you gave it to Medocus, who lives so far off." That was his mode of persuasion in their case. Next he came to Timasion the Dardanian, who, some one had told him, was the happy possessor of certain goblets and oriental carpets. What he said to him was, "It is customary when people are invited to dinner by Seuthes for the guests to make him a present; now if he should become a great person in these parts, he will be able to restore you to your native land, or to make you a rich man here." Such were the solicitations which he applied to each man in turn whom he accosted. Presently he came to Xenophon and said, "You are at once a citizen of no mean city, and with Seuthes also your own name is very great. Maybe you expect to obtain a fort or two in this country, just as others of your countrymen have done,[2] and territory. It is only right and proper therefore that you should honour Seuthes in the most magnificent style. Be sure, I give this advice out of pure friendliness, for I know that the greater the gift that you are ready to bestow on him, the better the treatment you will receive at his hands." Xenophon, on hearing this, was in a sad dilemma, for he had brought with him, when he crossed from Parium, nothing but one boy and just enough to pay his travelling expenses.

As soon as the company, consisting of the most powerful Thracians there present, with the generals and captains of the Hellenes, and any embassy from a state which might be there, had arrived, they were seated in a circle, and the dinner was served. Thereupon three-legged stools were brought in and placed in front of the assembled guests. They were laden with pieces of meat, piled up, and there were huge leavened-loaves fastened on to the pieces of meat with long skewers. The tables, as a rule, were set beside the guests at intervals. That was the custom; and Seuthes set the fashion of the performance. He took up the loaves which lay by his side and broke them into little pieces, and then threw the fragments here to one and there to another as seemed him good; and so with the meat likewise, leaving for himself the merest

---

[2] Notably Alcibiades, who possessed two or three such fortresses.

taste. Then the rest fell to following the fashion set them, those that is who had tables placed beside them.

Now there was an Arcadian, Arystas by name, a huge eater; he soon got tired of throwing the pieces about, and seized a good three-quarter loaf in his two hands, placed some pieces of meat upon his knees, and proceeded to discuss his dinner. Then beakers of wine were brought round, and every one partook in turn; but when the cupbearer came to Arystas and handed him the bowl, he looked up, and seeing that Xenophon had done eating, said, "Give it him," he is more at leisure. I have something better to do at present." Seuthes, hearing a remark, asked the cupbearer what was said, and the cupbearer, who knew how to talk Greek, explained. Then followed a peal of laughter.

When the drinking had advanced somewhat, in came a Thracian with a white horse, who snatched the brimming bowl and said, "Here's a health to you, O Seuthes. Let me present you with this horse. Mounted on him, you shall capture whom you choose to pursue, or retiring from battle, you shall not dread the foe." He was followed by one who brought in a boy, and presented him in proper style with a health to Seuthes. A third had clothes for his wife. Timasion, the Dardanian, pledged Seuthes, and presented a silver bowl and a carpet worth ten minae. Gnesippus, an Athenian, got up and said, "It was a good old custom, and a fine one too, that those who had, should give to the king for honour's sake, but to those who had not, the king should give; whereby, my lord," he added, "I too may one day have the wherewithal to give you gifts and honour." Xenophon the while was racking his brains what he was to do; he was not the happier because he was seated in the seat next Seuthes as a mark of honour; and Heracleides bade the cupbearer hand him the bowl. He had already had a few drinks, as it happened; he rose, and manfully seized the cup, and spoke, "I also, Seuthes, have to present you with myself and these my dear comrades to be your trusty friends, and not one of them against his will. They are more ready, one and all, still more than I, to be your friends. Here they are; they ask nothing from you in return, rather they are forward to labour in your behalf; it will be their pleasure to bear the brunt of battle in voluntary service. With them, god willing, you will gain vast territory; you will recover what was once your fore-fathers'; you will win for yourself new lands; and not lands only, but horses many, and of men a multitude, and many fair women besides. You will not need to seize upon them in robber fashion; it is your friends here who, of their own accord, shall take and bring them to you, they shall lay them at your feet as gifts." Up got Seuthes and drained with him the cup, and with him sprinkled the last drops fraternally.

At this stage entered musicians blowing upon horns such as they use for signal calls, and trumpeting on trumpets, made of raw oxhide, tunes and airs, like the music of the harp. Seuthes himself got up and shouted forth a war song; then he sprang from his place and leaped about as though he would guard himself against a missile, in right nimble style. Then came in a set of clowns and jesters.

But when the sun began to set, the Hellenes rose from their seats. It was time, they said, to place the night sentinels and to pass the watchword; further, they begged of Seuthes to issue an order that none of the Thracians were to enter the Hellenic camp at night, "since between your Thracian foes and our Thracian friends there might be some confusion." As they sallied forth, Seuthes rose to accompany them, like the soberest of men. When they were outside, he summoned the generals apart and said, "Gentlemen, our enemies are not aware as yet of our alliance. If, therefore, we attack them before they take precautions not to be caught, or are prepared to repel assault, we shall make a fine haul of captives and other stock." The generals fully approved of these views, and bade him lead on. He answered, "Prepare and wait; as soon as the right time comes I will be with you. I shall pick up the peltasts and yourselves, and with the help of the gods, I will lead on." "But consider one point," urged Xenophon, "if we are to march by night, is not the Hellenic fashion best? When marching in the daytime that part of the army leads the van which seems best suited to the nature of the country to be traversed—heavy or light infantry, or cavalry; but by night our rule is that the slowest arm should take the lead. Thus we avoid the risk of being pulled to pieces: and it is not so easy for a man to give his neighbour the slip without intending, whereas the scattered fragments of an army are apt to fall foul of one another, and to cause damage or incur it in sheer ignorance." To this Seuthes replied, "You reason well, and I will adopt your custom. I will furnish you with guides chosen from the oldest experts of the country, and I will myself follow with the cavalry in the rear; it will not take me long, if need be, to present myself at the front." Then, for kinship's sake, they chose Athenaia as their watchword. With this, they turned and sought repose.

It was about midnight when Seuthes presented himself with his cavalry troopers armed with breastplates, and his light infantry under arms. As soon as he had handed over to them the promised guides, the heavy infantry took the van, followed by the light troops in the centre, while the cavalry brought up the rear. At daybreak Seuthes rode up to the front. He complimented them on their method: so often had he himself, while marching by night with a mere handful of men, been separated with his cavalry from his infantry. "But now," said he, "we find ourselves at dawn of day all happily together, just as we ought to be. Do you wait for me here," he proceeded, "and rest yourselves. I will take a look round and rejoin you." So saying he took a certain path over hill and rode off. As soon as he had reached deep snow, he looked to see whether there were footprints of human beings leading forward or in the opposite direction; and having satisfied himself that the road was untrodden, back he came, exclaiming, "God willing, men, it will be all right; we shall fall on the fellows, before they know where they are. I will lead on with the cavalry; so that if we catch sight of any one, he shall not escape and give warnings to the enemy. Do you follow, and if you are left behind, keep to the trail of the horses. Once on the other side of the mountains, we shall find ourselves in numerous thriving villages."

By the middle of the day he had already gained the top of the pass and looked down upon the villages below. Back he came riding to the heavy infantry and said, "I will at once send off the cavalry into the plain below, and the peltasts too, to attack the villages. Do you follow with what speed you may, so that in case of resistance you may lend us your aid." Hearing this, Xenophon dismounted, and the other asked, "Why do you dismount just when speed is the thing we want?" The other answered, "But you do not want me alone, I am sure. The hoplites will run all the quicker and more cheerily if I lead them on foot."

Thereupon Seuthes went off, and Timasion with him, taking the Hellene squadron of something like forty troopers. Then Xenophon passed the order: the active young fellows up to thirty years of age from the different companies to the front; and off with these he went himself, running along; while Cleanor led the other Hellenes. When they had reached the villages, Seuthes, with about thirty troopers, rode up, exclaiming, "Well, Xenophon, this is just what you said; the fellows are caught, but now look here. My cavalry have gone off unsupported; they are scattered in pursuit, one here, one there, and upon my word, I am more than half afraid the enemy will collect somewhere and do them a mischief. Some of us must remain in the villages, for they are swarming with human beings." "Well then," said Xenophon, "I will seize the heights with the men I have with me, and do you bid Cleanor extend his line along the level beside the villages." When they had done so, there were enclosed—of captives for the slave market, 1,000; of cattle, 2,000; and of other small cattle, 10,000. For the time being they took up quarters there.

4. But next day Seuthes burned the villages to the ground; he left not a single house, wishing to inspire terror in the rest of his enemies,

and to show them what they also were to expect, if they refused obedience; and so he went back again. As to the booty, he sent off Heracleides to Perinthus to dispose of it, with a view to future pay for the soldiers. But for himself he encamped with the Hellenes in the lowland country of the Thynians, the natives leaving the flats and fleeing to the uplands.

There was deep snow, and cold so intense that the water brought in for dinner and the wine within the jars froze; and many of the Hellenes had their noses and ears frost-bitten. Now they came to understand why the Thracians wear fox-skin caps on their heads and about their ears; and why, on the same principle, they are clothed not only about the chest but so as to cover the thighs as well; and why on horseback they envelop themselves in long shawls which reach down to the feet, instead of the ordinary short rider's cloak. Seuthes sent off some of the prisoners to the hills with a message to say that if they did not come down to their homes, and live quietly and obey him, he would burn down their villages and their corn, and leave them to perish with hunger. Thereupon down they came, women and children and the older men; the younger men preferred to quarter themselves in the villages on the skirts of the hills. On discovering this, Seuthes bade Xenophon take the youngest of the heavy infantry and join him on an expedition. They rose in the night, and by daybreak had reached the villages; but the majority of the inhabitants made good their escape, for the hills were close at hand. Those whom he did catch, Seuthes unsparingly shot down.

Now there was a certain Olynthian, named Episthenes; he was a great lover of boys, and seeing a handsome lad, just in the bloom of youth and carrying a light shield, about to be slain, he ran up to Xenophon and supplicated him to rescue the fair youth. Xenophon went to Seuthes and begged him not to put the boy to death. He explained to him the disposition of Episthenes; how he had once enrolled a company, the only qualification required being that of personal beauty; and with these handsome young men at his side there was none so brave as he. Seuthes put the question, "Would you like to die in his behalf, Episthenes?" Then the other stretched out his neck, and said, "Strike, if the boy bids you, and will thank his preserver." Seuthes, turning to the boy, asked, "Shall I smite him instead of you?" The boy shook his head, imploring him to slay neither the one nor the other, whereupon Episthenes caught the lad in his arms, exclaiming, "It is time you did battle with me, Seuthes, for my boy; never will I yield him up." Seuthes laughed and so consented.

In these villages he decided that they must bivouac, so that the men on the mountains might be still further deprived of subsistence.

Stealthily descending he himself found quarters in the plain; while Xenophon with his picked troops encamped in the highest village on the skirts of the hills; and the rest of the Hellenes hard by, among the highland Thracians, as they are called.

After this, not many days had passed before the Thracians from the mountains came down and wished to arrange with Seuthes for terms of truce and hostages. Simultaneously came Xenophon and informed Seuthes that they were camped in bad quarters, with the enemy next door. "It would be pleasanter too," he added, "to bivouac in a strong position in the open, than under cover on the edge of destruction." The other bade him take heart and pointed to some of their hostages. Parties also from the mountaineers came down and pleaded with Xenophon himself, to help arrange a truce for them. This he agreed to do, bidding them pluck up heart, and assuring them that they would meet with no mischief, if they yielded obedience to Seuthes. All their parleying, however, was, as it turned out, merely to get a closer inspection of things. This happened in the day, and in the following night the Thynians descended from the hill country and made an attack. In each case, the guide was the master of the house attacked; otherwise it would have taxed their powers to discover the houses in the dark, which, for the sake of their flocks and herds, were palisaded all round with great stockades. As soon as they had reached the doors of any particular house, the attack began, some hurling in their spears, others belabouring with their clubs, which they carried, it was said, for the purpose of knocking off the lance points from the shaft. Others were busy setting the place on fire; and they kept calling Xenophon by name, "Come out, Xenophon, and die like a man, or we will roast you alive inside."

By this time too the flames were making their appearance through the roof, and Xenophon and his followers were within, with their coats of mail on, and big shields, swords, and helmets. Then Silanus, a Macistian, a youth of some eighteen years, signalled on the trumpet; and in an instant, out they all leaped with their drawn swords, and the inmates of the other quarters as well. The Thracians took to their heels, according to their custom, swinging their light shields round their backs. As they leapt over the stockade some were captured, hanging on the top with their shields caught in the palings; others missed the way out, and so were slain; and the Hellenes chased them hotly, till they were outside the village.

A party of Thynians turned back, and as the men ran past in bold relief against a blazing house, they let fly a volley of javelins, out of the darkness into the glare, and wounded two captains, Hieronymus, an

Euodean,[3] and Theogenes, a Locrian. No one was killed, only the clothes and baggage of some of the men were consumed in the flames. Presently up came Seuthes to the rescue with seven troopers, the first to hand, and his Thracian trumpeter by his side. Seeing that something had happened, he hastened to the rescue, and ever the while his bugler wound his horn, which music added terror to the foe. Arrived at length, he greeted them with outstretched hand, exclaiming, "I thought to find you all dead men."

After that, Xenophon begged him to hand over the hostages to himself, and if so disposed, to join him on an expedition to the hills, or if not, to let him go alone. Accordingly the next day Seuthes delivered up the hostages. They were men already advanced in years, but the pick of the mountaineers, as they themselves gave out. Not merely did Seuthes do this, but he came himself, with his force at his back (and by this time he had treble his former force, for many of the Odrysians, hearing of his proceedings, came down to join in the campaign); and the Thynians, espying from the mountains the vast array of heavy infantry and light infantry and cavalry, rank upon rank, came down and supplicated him to make terms. "They were ready," they professed, "to do all that he demanded; let him take pledges of their good faith." So Seuthes summoned Xenophon and explained their proposals, adding that he should make no terms with them, if Xenophon wished to punish them for their night attack. The latter replied, "For my part I should think their punishment is great enough already, if they are to be slaves instead of free men; still," he added, "I advise you for the future to take as hostages those who are most capable of doing mischief, and to let the old men bide in peace at home." So to a man they gave in their adhesion in that quarter of the country.

5. Crossing over in the direction of the Thracians above Byzantium, they reached the Delta, as it is called. Here they were no longer in the territory of Maesades, but in the country of Teres the Odrysian [an ancient worthy]. Here Heracleides met them with the proceeds of the spoil, and Seuthes picked out three pairs of mules (there were only three, the other teams being oxen); then he summoned Xenophon and bade him take them, and divide the rest between the generals and officers, to which Xenophon replied that for himself, he was content to receive his share another time, but added, "Make a present of these to my friends here, the generals who have served with me, and to the officers." So of the pairs of mules Timasion the Dardanian received one, Cleanor the Orchomenian one, and Phryniscus the Achaean one. The teams of

---

[3] Possibly the word points to some town or district of Elis; or perhaps the text is corrupt.

oxen were divided among the officers. Then Seuthes proceeded to remit pay due for the month already passed, but all he could give was the equivalent of twenty days. Heracleides insisted that this was all he had got by his trafficking. Whereupon Xenophon in anger exclaimed, "Upon my word, Heracleides, I do not think you care for Seuthes' interest as you should. If you did, you would have been at pains to bring back the full amount of the pay, even if you had had to raise a loan to do so, and, if by no other means, by selling the coat off your own back."

What he said annoyed Heracleides, who was afraid of being ousted from the friendship of Seuthes, and from that day forward he did his best to calumniate Xenophon before Seuthes. The soldiers, on their side, laid the blame of course on Xenophon because they did not receive their pay, and Seuthes was vexed with him for persistently demanding it for them. Up to this date he had frequently referred to what he would do when he got to the seaboard again; how he intended to hand over to him Bisanthe, Ganos, and Neontichos. But from this time forward he never mentioned one of them again. The slanderous tongue of Heracleides had whispered him that it was not safe to hand over fortified towns to a man with a force at his back.

Consequently Xenophon fell to considering what he ought to do as regards marching any further up the country; and Heracleides introduced the other generals to Seuthes, urging them to say that they were quite as well able to lead the army as Xenophon, and promising them that within a day or two they should have full pay for two months, and he again implored them to continue the campaign with Seuthes. To which Timasion replied that for his part he would continue no campaign without Xenophon; not even if they were to give him pay for five months; and what Timasion said, Phryniscus and Cleanor repeated; the views of all three coincided.

Seuthes fell to upbraiding Heracleides in round terms because he had not invited Xenophon with the others, and presently they invited him, but by himself alone. He, perceiving the knavery of Heracleides, and that his object was to calumniate him with the other generals, presented himself; but at the same time he took care to bring all the generals and the officers. After their joint consent had been secured, they continued the campaign. Keeping the Pontus on their right, they passed through the millet-eating Thracians, as they are called, and reached Salmydessus. This is a point at which many trading vessels bound for the Black Sea run aground and are wrecked, owing to a sort of marshy ledge or sandbank which runs out for a considerable distance into the sea. The Thracians, who dwell in these parts, have set up pillars as boundary marks, and each set of them plunders the ships wrecked within its own markers; for in old days, before they set up these landmarks, the wreckers, it is said, used freely to slay one another. Here was a rich treasure, of many beds and boxes, with a mass of written books, and all the various things which mariners carry in their wooden chests. Having reduced this district, they turned round and went back again. By this time the army of Seuthes had grown to be considerably larger than the Hellenic army; for on the one hand, the Odrysians flocked down in still larger numbers, and on the other, the tribes which gave their allegiance from time to time were amalgamated with his armament. They got into quarters on the flat country above Selymbria at about three miles distance from the sea. As to pay, not a penny was as yet forthcoming, and the soldiers were cruelly disaffected to Xenophon, while Seuthes, on his side, was no longer so friendly. If Xenophon ever wished to come face to face with him, want of leisure or some other difficulty always seemed to present itself.

6. At this date, when nearly two months had already passed, an embassy arrived. These were two agents from Thibron—Charminus, a Lacedaemonian, and Polynicus. They were sent to say that the Lacedaemonians had resolved to open a campaign against Tissaphernes, and that Thibron, who had set sail to conduct the war, was anxious to avail himself of the troops. He would guarantee that each soldier should receive a daric a month as pay, the officers double pay, and the generals quadruple. The Lacedaemonian emissaries had no sooner arrived than Heracleides, having learned that they had come in search of the Hellenic troops, goes off himself to Seuthes and says, "The best thing that could have happened; the Lacedaemonians want these troops and you have done with them, so that if you hand over the troops to them, you will do the Lacedaemonians a good turn and will cease to be bothered for pay any more. The country will be quit of them once and for ever."

On hearing this Seuthes bade him introduce the emissaries. As soon as they had stated that the object of their coming was to treat for the Hellenic troops, he replied that he would willingly give them up, that his one desire was to be the friend and ally of Lacedaemon. So he invited them to partake of hospitality, and entertained them magnificantly; but he did not invite Xenophon, nor indeed any of the other generals. Presently the Lacedaemonians asked, "What sort of man is Xenophon?" And Seuthes answered, "Not a bad fellow in most respects; but he is too much the soldiers' friend; and that is why it goes ill with him." They asked, "Does he play the popular leader?" Heracleides answered, "Exactly so." "Well then," said they, "he will oppose our taking away the troops, will he not?" "To be sure he will," said Heracleides, "but you have only to call a meeting of the whole body, and promise them pay, and little further heed will they pay to him; they will run off with you." "How then are we to get them collected?" they asked. "Early to-morrow," said Heracleides, "we will bring you to them; and I know," he added once more, "as soon as they set eyes on you, they will flock to you with alacrity." Thus the day ended.

The next day Seuthes and Heracleides brought the two Laconian agents to the army, and the troops were collected, and the agents made a statement as follows, "The Lacedaemonians have resolved on war with Tissaphernes, who did you so much wrong. By going with us therefore you will punish your enemy, and each of you will get a daric a month, the officers twice that sum, and the generals quadruple." The soldiers lent willing ears, and up jumped one of the Arcadians at once, to find fault with Xenophon. Seuthes also was at hand, wishing to know what was going to happen. He stood within ear shot, and his interpreter by his side; not but what he could understand most of what was said in Greek himself. At this point the Arcadian spoke, "For the matter of that, Lacedaemonians, we should have been by your sides long ago, if Xenophon had not persuaded us and brought us hither. We have never ceased campaigning, night and day, the dismal winter through, but he reaps the fruit of our toils. Seuthes has enriched him privately, but deprives us of our honest earnings; so that, standing here as I do to address you first, all I can say is, that if I might see the fellow stoned to death as a penalty for all the long dance he has led us, I should feel I had got my pay in full, and no longer grudge the pains we have undergone." The speaker was followed by another and then another in the same strain; and after that Xenophon made the following speech:

"True is the old adage; there is nothing which mortal man may not expect to see. Here am I being accused by you to-day, just where my conscience tells me that I have displayed the greatest zeal in your behalf. Was I not actually on my road home when I turned back? Not, god knows, because I learned that you were in luck's way, but because I heard that you were in sore straits, and I wished to help you, if in any way I could. I returned, and Seuthes yonder sent me messenger after messenger, and made me promise upon promise, if only I could persuade you to come to him. Yet, as you yourselves will bear me witness, I was not to be diverted. Instead of setting to my hand to do that, I simply led you to a point from which, with least loss of time, I thought you could cross into Asia. This I believed was the best thing for you, and you I knew desired it.

"But when Aristarchus came with his ships of war and hindered our passage across, you will hardly quarrel with me for the step I then took in calling you together that we might advisedly consider our best course. Having heard both sides,—first Aristarchus, who ordered you to march to the Chersonese, then Seuthes, who pleaded with you to undertake a campaign with himself,—you all proposed to go with Seuthes; and you all gave your votes to that effect. What wrong did I commit in bringing you, whither you were eager to go? If, indeed, since the time when Seuthes began to tell lies and cheat us about the pay, I have supported him in this, you may justly find fault with me and hate me. But if I, who at first was most of all his friend, to-day am more than any one else at variance with him, how can I, who have chosen you and rejected Seuthes, in fairness be blamed by you for the very thing which has been the ground of quarrel between him and me? But you will tell me, perhaps, that I get from Seuthes what is by right yours, and that I deal subtly by you? But is it not clear that, if Seuthes has paid me anything, he has at any rate not done so with the intention of losing by what he gives me, while he is still your debtor? If he gave to me, he gave in order that, by a small gift to me, he might escape a larger payment to yourselves. But if that is what you really think has happened, you can render this whole scheme of ours null and void in an instant by exacting from him the money which is your due. It is clear, Seuthes will demand back from me whatever I have got from him, and he will have all the more right to do so, if I have failed to secure for him what he bargained for when I took his gifts. But indeed I am far removed from enjoying what is yours, and I swear to you by all the gods and goddesses that I have not taken even what Seuthes promised me in private. He is present himself and listening, and he is aware in his own heart whether I swear falsely. And what will surprise you the more, I can swear besides, that I have not received even what the other generals have received, no, nor yet what some of the officers have received. But how so? Why have I managed my affairs no better? I thought the more I helped him to bear his poverty at the time, the more I should make him my friend in the day of his power. Whereas, it is just when I see the star of his good fortune rising, that I have come to divine the secret of his character.

"Some one may say, are you not ashamed to be so taken in like a fool? Yes, I should be ashamed, if it had been an open enemy who had so deceived me. But, to my mind, when friend cheats friend, a deeper stain attaches to the perpetrator than to the victim of deceit. Whatever precaution a man may take against his friend, that we took in full. We certainly gave him no pretext for refusing to pay us what he promised. We were perfectly upright in our dealings with him. We did not dawdle over his affairs, nor did we shrink from any work to which he challenged us.

"But you will say, I ought to have taken security of him at the time, so that had he fostered the wish, he might have lacked the ability to deceive. To meet that retort, I must beg you to listen to certain things, which I should never have said in his presence, except for your utter want of feeling towards me, or your extraordinary ingratitude. Try and recall the state of your affairs, when I extricated you and brought you to Seuthes. Do you not recollect how at Perinthus Aristarchus shut the gates in your faces each time you offered to approach the town, and how you were driven to camp outside under the sky? It was midwinter; you were thrown upon the resources of a market wherein few were the articles offered for sale, and scanty the wherewithal to purchase them. Yet stay in Thrace you must, for there were ships of war riding at anchor in the bay, ready to hinder your passage across; and what did that stay imply? It meant being in a hostile country, confronted by countless cavalry, legions of light infantry. And what had we? A heavy infantry force certainly, with which we could have dashed at villages in a body possibly, and seized a modicum of food at most; but as to pursuing the enemy with such a force as ours, or capturing men or cattle, the thing was out of the question; for when I rejoined you your original cavalry and light infantry divisions had disappeared. In such sore straits you lay!

"Supposing that, without making any demands for pay whatever, I had merely won for you the alliance of Seuthes—whose cavalry and light infantry were just what you needed—would you not have thought that I had planned very well for you? I presume, it was through your partnership with him and his that you were able to find such complete stores of corn in the villages, when the Thracians were driven to take to their heels in such hot haste, and you had so large a share of captives and cattle. Why, from the day on which his cavalry force was attached to us, we never set eyes on a single foeman in the field, though up to that date the enemy with his cavalry and his light infantry used undauntedly to hang on our heels, and effectually prevented us from scattering in small bodies and reaping rich harvest of provisions. But if he who partly gave you this security has failed to pay in full the wages due to you therefrom, is not that a terrible misfortune? So monstrous indeed that you think I ought not to go forth alive.

"But let me ask you, in what condition do you turn your backs on this land to-day? Have you not wintered here in the lap of plenty? Whatever you have got from Seuthes has been surplus gain. Your enemies have had to meet the bill of your expenses, while you led a merry round of existence, in which you have not once set eyes on the dead body of a comrade or lost one living man. Again, if you have achieved any, (or rather many) noble deeds against the Asiatic barbarian, you have them safe. And in addition to these to-day you have won for yourselves a second glory. You undertook a campaign against the European Thracians, and have mastered them. What I say then is, that these very matters which you make a ground of quarrel against myself, are rather blessings for which you ought to show gratitude to heaven.

"Thus far I have confined myself to your side of the matter. Bear with me, I beg you, while we examine mine. When I first set out to journey homewards, I was doubly blest. From your lips I had won some praise, and thanks to you, I had obtained glory from the rest of Hellas. I was trusted by the Lacedaemonians; else would they not have sent me back to you. Whereas to-day I turn to go, calumniated before the Lacedaemonians by yourselves, detested in your behalf by Seuthes, whom I meant so to benefit, by help of you, that I should find in him a refuge for myself and for my children, if children I might have, in after time. And you the whole, for whose sake I have incurred so much hate, the hate of people far superior to me in strength, you, for whom I have not yet ceased to devise all the good I can, entertain such sentiments about me. Why? I am no renegade or runaway slave, you have got hold of. If you carry out what you say, be sure you will have done to death a man who has passed many a vigil in watching over you; who has shared with you many a toil and run many a risk in turn and out of turn; who, thanks to the gracious gods, has by your side set up many a trophy over the barbarian; who, lastly, to save you from becoming the foes of your own countrymen, has strained every nerve in his body to protect you against yourselves. And so it is, that to-day you can move freely, where you choose, by sea or by land, and no one can say you nay; and you, on whom this large liberty dawns, who are sailing to a long desired goal, who are sought after by the greatest of military powers, who have pay in prospect, and for leaders these Lacedaemonians, our acknowledged chiefs—now is the appointed time, you think, to put me to a speedy death. But in the days of our difficulties it was very different, O men of marvellous memory! No, in those days you called me father and you promised you would bear me ever in mind, your benefactor. Not so, however, not so ungracious are those who have come to you to-day; nor, if I mistake not, have you bettered yourselves in their eyes by your treatment of me."

With these words he paused, and Charminus the Lacedaemonian got up and said, "Nay, by the twin gods you are wrong, surely, in your anger against this man; I myself can bear testimony in his favour. When Polynicus and I asked Seuthes, what sort of a man he was, Seuthes answered that he had but one fault to find with him, that he was too much the soldiers' friend, which also was the cause why things went wrong with him, whether as regards us Lacedaemonians or himself, Seuthes."

Upon that Eurylochus of Lusia, an Arcadian, got up and said (addressing the two Lacedaemonians), "Yes, sirs; and what strikes me is that you cannot begin your generalship of us better than by exacting from Seuthes our pay. Whether he like it or no, let him pay in full; and do not take us away before."

Polycrates the Athenian, who was put forward by Xenophon, said, "If my eyes do not deceive me, sirs, there stands Heracleides yonder, the man who received the property won by our toil, who took and sold it, and never gave back either to Seuthes or to us the proceeds of the sale, but kept the money to himself, like the thief he is. If we are wise, we will lay hold of him, for he is no Thracian, but a Hellene; and against Hellenes is the wrong he has committed."

When Heracleides heard these words, he was in great consternation; so he came to Seuthes and said, "If we are wise we will get away from here out of reach of these fellows." So they mounted their horses and were gone, galloping to their own camp. Subsequently Seuthes sent Abrozelmes, his private interpreter, to Xenophon, begging him to stay behind with 1,000 heavy troops; and engaging duly to deliver to him the places on the seaboard, and the other things which he had promised; and then, as a great secret, he told him, that he had heard from Polynicus that if he once got into the clutches of the Lacedaemonians, Thibron was certain to put him to death. Similar messages kept coming to Xenophon by letter or otherwise from several quarters, warning him that he was calumniated, and had best be on his guard. Hearing which, he took two victims and sacrificed to Zeus the King to learn whether it were better and happier to stay with Seuthes on the terms proposed, or depart with the army. The answer he received was, "Depart."

7. After this, Seuthes removed his camp to some considerable distance; and the Hellenes took up their quarters in some villages, selecting those in which they could best supply their commissariat, on the road to the sea. Now these particular villages had been given by Seuthes to Medosades. Accordingly, when the latter saw his property in the villages being expended by the Hellenes, he was not over well pleased; and taking with him an Odrysian, a powerful person amongst those who had come down from the interior, and about thirty mounted troopers, he came and challenged Xenophon to come forth from the Hellenic host. He,

taking some of the officers and others of a character to be relied upon, came forward. Then Medosades, addressing Xenophon, said, "You are doing wrong to pillage our villages; we give you fair warning—I, in behalf of Seuthes, and this man by my side, who comes from Medocus, the king up country—to be gone out of the land. If you refuse, understand, we have no notion of handing it over to you; but if you injure our country we will retaliate upon you as foes."

Xenophon, hearing what they had to say, replied, "Such language addressed to us by you, of all people, is hard to answer. Yet for the sake of the young man with you, I will attempt to do so, that at least he may learn how different your nature is from ours. We," he continued, "before we were your friends, had the free run of this country, moving this way or that, as it took our fancy, pillaging and burning just as we chose; and you yourself, Medosades, whenever you came to us on an embassy, camped with us, without apprehension of any foe. As a tribe collectively you scarcely approached the country at all, or if you found yourselves in it, you bivouacked with your horses bitted and bridled, as being in the territory of your superiors. Presently you made friends with us, and, thanks to us, by god's help you won this country, out of which to-day you seek to drive us; a country which we held by our own strength and gave to you. No hostile force, as you well know, was capable of expelling us. It might have been expected of you personally to speed us on our way with some gift, in return for the good we did you. Not so; even though our backs are turned to go, we are too slow in our movements for you. You will not allow us to take up quarters even, if you can help it, and these words arouse no shame in you, either before the gods, or this Odrysian, in whose eyes to-day you are a man of means, though until you cultivated our friendship you lived a robber's life, as you have told us. However, why do you address yourself to me? I am no longer in command. Our generals are the Lacedaemonians, to whom you and yours delivered over the army for withdrawal; and that, without even inviting me to attend, you most marvellous of men, so that if I lost their favour when I brought you the troops, I might now win their gratitude by restoring them."

As soon as the Odrysian had heard this statement, he exclaimed, "For my part, Medosades, I sink under the earth for very shame at what I hear. If I had known the truth before, I would never have accompanied you. As it is, I return at once. Never would King Medocus applaud me, if I drove forth his benefactors." With these words, he mounted his horse and rode away, and with him the rest of his horsemen, except four or five. But Medosades, still vexed by the pillaging of the country, urged Xenophon to summon the two Lacedaemonians; and

he, taking the pick of his men, came to Charminus and Polynicus and
informed them that they were summoned by Medosades; probably they,
like himself, would be warned to leave the country. "If so," he added,
"you will be able to recover the pay which is owing to the army. You
can say to them, that the army has requested you to assist in exacting
their pay from Seuthes, whether he like it or not; that they have promised, as soon as they get this, cheerfully to follow you; that the demand
seems to you to be only just, and that you have accordingly promised
not to leave, until the soldiers have got their dues." The Lacedaemonians
accepted the suggestion: they would apply these arguments and others
the most forcible they could hit upon; and with the proper representatives of the army, they immediately set off.

On their arrival Charminus spoke, "If you have anything to say to
us, Medosades, say it; but if not, we have something to say to you."
And Medosades submissively answered, "I say," said he, "and Seuthes
says the same: we think we have a right to ask that those who have become our friends should not be ill-treated by you; whatever ill you do
to them you really do to us, for they are a part of us." "Good," replied
the Lacedaemonians, "and we intend to go away as soon as those who
won for you the people and the territory in question have got their pay.
Failing that, we are coming without further delay to assist them and
to punish certain others who have broken their oaths and done them
wrong. If it should turn out that you come under this head, when we
come to exact justice we shall begin with you." Xenophon added,
"Would you prefer, Medosades, to leave it to these people themselves,
in whose country we are (your friends, since that is the designation
you prefer), to decide by ballot, which of the two should leave the
country, you or we?" To that proposal he shook his head, but he trusted
the two Lacedaemonians might be induced to go to Seuthes about the
pay, adding, "Seuthes, I am sure, will lend a willing ear." But if they
could not go, then he prayed them to send Xenophon with himself,
promising to lend the latter all the aid in his power, and finally he
begged them not to burn the villages. Accordingly they sent Xenophon,
and with him a serviceable staff. Being arrived, he addressed Seuthes
thus:

"Seuthes, I am here to advance no claims, but to show you, if I can,
how unjust it was on your part to be angered with me because I zealously
demanded of you on behalf of the soldiers what you promised them.
According to my belief, it was no less to your interest to deliver it up,
than it was to theirs to receive it. I cannot forget that, next to the gods,
it was they who raised you up to a conspicuous eminence, when they
made you king of large territory and many men, a position in which

you cannot escape notice, whether you do good or do evil. For a man so circumstanced, I regarded it as a great thing that he should avoid the suspicion even of ungrateful parting with his benefactors. It was a great thing, I thought, that you should be well spoken of by 6,000 human beings; but the greatest thing of all, that you should by no means discredit the sincerity of your own word. For what of the man who cannot be trusted? I see that the words of his mouth are but vain words, powerless, and unhonoured; but with him who is seen to regard truth, the case is otherwise. He can achieve by his words what another achieves by force. If he seeks to bring the foolish to their senses—his very frown, I perceive, has a more sobering effect than the chastisement inflicted by another. Or in negotiations the very promises of such an one are of equal weight with the gifts of another.

"Try and recall to mind in your own case, what advance of money you made to us to purchase our alliance. You know you did not advance one penny. It was simply confidence in the sincerity of your word which incited all these men to assist you in your campaign, and so to acquire for you an empire, worth many times more than thirty talents, which is all they now claim to receive. Here then, first of all, goes the credit which won for you your kingdom, sold for so mean a sum. Let me remind you of the great importance which you then attached to the acquisition of your present conquests. I am certain that to achieve what stands achieved to-day, you would willingly have foregone the gain of fifty times that paltry sum. To me it seems that to lose your present fortune were a more serious loss than never to have won it; since surely it is harder to be poor after being rich than never to have tasted wealth at all, and more painful to sink to the level of a subject, being a king, than never to have worn a crown.

"You cannot forget that your present vassals were not persuaded to become your subjects out of love for you, but by sheer force; and but for some restraining dread they would endeavour to be free again to-morrow. And how do you propose to stimulate their sense of awe, and keep them in good behaviour towards you? Shall they see our soldiers so disposed towards you that a word on your part would suffice to keep them now, or if necessary would bring them back again tomorrow, while others hearing from us many stories in your praise, hasten to present themselves at your desire? Or will you drive them to conclude adversely, that through mistrust of what has happened now, no second set of soldiers will come to help you, for even these troops of ours are more their friends than yours? And indeed it was not because they fell short of us in numbers that they became your subjects, but from lack of proper leaders. There is a danger, therefore, now lest they should choose as their protectors some of us who regard ourselves as wronged by you, or even better men than us—the Lacedaemonians themselves; supposing our soldiers undertake to serve with more enthusiasm, if the debt you owe to them be first exacted; and the Lacedaemonians, who need their services, consent to this request. It is plain, at any rate, that the Thracians, now prostrate at your feet, would display far more enthusiasm in attacking, than in assisting you; for your mastery means their slavery, and your defeat their liberty.

"Again, the country is now yours, and from this time forward you have to make provision for what is yours; and how will you best secure it an immunity from ill? Either these soldiers receive their dues and go, leaving a legacy of peace behind, or they stay and occupy an enemy's country, while you endeavour, by aid of a still larger army, to open a new campaign and turn them out; and your new troops will also need provisions. Or again, which will be the greater drain on your purse, to pay off your present debt, or, with that still owing, to bid for more troops, and of a better quality?

"Heracleides, as he used to prove to me, finds the sum excessive. But surely it is a far less serious thing for you to take and pay it back to-day than it would have been to pay the tithe of it, before we came to you; since the limit between less and more is no fixed number, but depends on the relative capacity of payer and recipient, and your yearly income now is larger than the whole property which you possessed in earlier days.

"Well, Seuthes, for myself these remarks are the expression of friendly forethought for a friend. They are expressed in the double hope that you may show yourself worthy of the good things which the gods have given you, and that my reputation may not be ruined with the army. For I must assure you that to-day, if I wished to injure a foe, I could not do so with this army. Nor again, if I wished to come and help you, should I be competent to the task; such is the disposition of the troops towards me. And yet I call you to witness, along with the gods who know, that never have I received anything from you on account of the soldiers. Never to this day have I, to my private gain, asked for what was theirs, nor even claimed the promises which were made to myself; and I swear to you, not even had you proposed to pay me my dues, would I have accepted them, unless the soldiers also had been going to receive theirs too; how could I? How shameful it would have been in me, so to have secured my own interests, while I disregarded the disastrous state of theirs, I being so honoured by them. Of course to the mind of Heracleides this is all silly talk; since the one great object is to keep money by whatever means. For my part, Seuthes, I believe that no fairer possession can be given to a man, and most of all a prince, than the threefold grace of valour, justice, and generosity. He that possesses these is rich in the multitude of friends which surround him; rich also in the desire of others to be included in their number. While he prospers, he is surrounded by those who will rejoice with him in his joy; or if misfortune overtake him, he has no lack of sympathisers to give him help. However, if you have failed to learn from my deeds that I was, heart and soul, your friend; if my words are powerless to reveal the fact to-day, I would at least direct your attention to what the soldiers said; you were standing by and heard what those who sought to blame me said. They accused me to the Lacedaemonians, and the point of their indictment was that I set greater store by yourself than by the Lacedaemonians; but, as regards themselves, the charge was that I took more pains to secure the success of your interests than their own. They suggested that I had actually taken gifts from you. Was it, do you suppose, because they detected some ill-will in me towards you that they made the allegation? Was it not rather, that they had noticed my abundant zeal on your behalf?

"All men believe, I think, that a fund of kindly feeling is due to him from whom we accept gifts. But what is your behaviour? Before I had ministered to you in any way, or done you a single service, you welcomed me kindly with your eyes, your voice, your hospitality, and you could not sate yourself with promises of all the fine things that were to follow. But having once achieved your object, and become the great man you now are, as great indeed as I could make you, you can stand by and see me degraded among my own soldiers! Well, time will teach you—that I fully believe—to pay whatever seems to you right, and even without the lessons of that teacher you will hardly care to see those who have spent themselves in benefiting you, become your accusers. Only, when you do pay your debt, I beg of you to use your best endeavour to right me with the soldiers. Leave me at least where you found me; that is all I ask."

After listening to this appeal, Seuthes called down curses on him, whose fault it was, that the debt had not long ago been paid, and, if the general suspicion was correct, this was Heracleides. "For myself," said Seuthes, "I never had any idea of robbing you of your just dues. I will repay." Then Xenophon rejoined, "Since you intend to pay, I only ask that you will do so through me, and will not suffer me on your account to hold a different position in the army from what I held when we joined you." He replied, "As far as that goes, so far from holding a less honoured position among your own men on my account, if you will stay with me, keeping only 1,000 heavy infantry, I will deliver to you the fortified places and everything I promised." The other answered, "On these terms I may not accept them, only let us go free." "Nay, but I know," said Seuthes, "that it is safer for you to stay with me than to go away." Then Xenophon again, "For your forethought I thank you, but I may not stay. Somewhere I may rise to honour, and that, be sure, shall redound to your gain also." Thereupon Seuthes spoke, "Of silver I have but little; that little, however, I give you, one talent; but of cattle I can give you 600 head, and of sheep 4,000, and of slaves 120. Take these, and the hostages besides, who wronged you, and go on your way." Xenophon laughed and said, "But supposing these all together do not amount to the pay; for whom is the talent, shall I say? It is a little dangerous for myself, is it not? I think I had better be on the look-out for stones when I return. You heard the threats?"

So for the moment he stayed there, but the next day Seuthes gave up to them what he had promised, and sent an escort to drive the cattle. The soldiers at first maintained that Xenophon had gone to take up his abode with Seuthes, and to receive what he had been promised; so when they saw him they were pleased, and ran to meet him. And Xenophon, seeing Charminus and Polynicus, said, "Thanks to your intervention, thus much has been saved for the army. My duty is to deliver this fraction over to your keeping; do you divide and distribute it to the soldiers." Accordingly they took the property and appointed official vendors of the booty, and in the end incurred considerable blame. Xenophon held aloof. In fact it was not secret that he was making his preparations to return home, for as yet the vote of banishment had not been passed at Athens.[4] But the authorities in the camp came to him and begged him not to go away until he had conducted the army to its destination, and handed it over to Thibron.

8. From this place they sailed across to Lampsacus, and here Xenophon was met by Eucleides the soothsayer, a Phliasian, the son of Cleagoras, who painted the murals in the Lyceum. Eucleides congratulated Xenophon upon his safe return, and asked him how much gold he had got. Xenophon had to confess, "Upon my word, I shall have barely enough to get home, unless I sell my horse, and what I have about my person." The other could not believe the statement. Now when the Lampsacenes sent gifts of hospitality to Xenophon, and he was sacrificing to Apollo, he requested the presence of Eucleides; and the latter, seeing the victims, said, "Now I believe what you said about having no money. But I am certain," he continued, "if it were ever to come, there

---

[4] The natural inference from these words is that the vote of banishment was presently passed, at any rate considerably earlier than the battle of Coronea in 394 B.C.

is an obstacle in the way. If nothing else, you are that obstacle your-self." Xenophon admitted the force of that remark. Then the other said, "Zeus Meilichios[5] is an obstacle to you, I am sure," adding in another tone of voice, "have you tried sacrificing to that god, as I used to sac-rifice and offer whole burnt offerings for you at home?" Xenophon re-plied that since he had been abroad, he had not sacrificed to that god. Accordingly Eucleides counselled him to sacrifice in the old customary way: he was sure that his fortune would improve. The next day Xeno-phon went on to Ophrynium and sacrificed, offering a holocaust of swine, after the custom of his family, and the signs which he obtained were favourable. That very day Bion and Nausicleides arrived laden with gifts for the army. These two were hospitably entertained by Xeno-phon, and were kind enough to repurchase the horse he had sold in Lampsacus for fifty darics; suspecting that he had parted with it out of need, and hearing that he was fond of the beast they restored it to him, refusing to be remunerated.

From this place they marched through the Troad, and, crossing Mount Ida, arrived at Antandrus, and then pushed along the seaboard of Mysia to the plain of Thebe. Thence they made their way through Adramytium and Certonus by Atarneus, coming into the plain of the Caicus, and so reached Pergamus in Mysia.

Here Xenophon was hospitably entertained at the house of Hellas, the wife of Gongylus the Eretrian, the mother of Gorgion and Gongy-lus. From her he learned that Asidates, a Persian notable, was in the plain. "If you take 300 men and go by night, you will take him pris-oner," she said, "wife, children, money, and all; of money he has a store." And to show them the way to these treasures, she sent her own cousin and Daphnagoras, whom she set great store by. So then Xeno-phon, with these two to assist, did sacrifice; and Basias, an Eleian, the soothsayer in attendance, said that the victims were as promising as could be, and the great man would be an easy prey. Accordingly, after dinner he set off, taking with him the officers who had been his staunch-est friends and confidants throughout; as he wished to do them a good turn. A number of others came thrusting themselves on their company, to the number of 600, but the officers repelled them so that they would not have to share the spoil, just as though the property lay already at their feet."

About midnight they arrived. The slaves occupying the precincts of the tower, with the mass of goods and chattels, slipped through their fingers, their sole anxiety being to capture Asidates and his belongings. Failing to take the tower by assault (since it was high and solid, and

[5] Zeus, the gentle or gracious god.

well supplied with ramparts, besides having a large body of warlike defenders), they endeavoured to undermine it. The wall was eight clay
bricks thick, but by daybreak the passage was effected and the wall
undermined. At the first gleam of light through the opening, one of the
defendants inside, with a large ox-spit, smote right through the thigh
of the man nearest the hole, and the rest discharged their arrows so
hotly that it was dangerous to come anywhere near the passage; and
what with their shoutings and kindling of beacon fires, a relief party
at length arrived, consisting of Itabelius at the head of his force, and
a body of Assyrian heavy infantry from Comania, and some Hyrcanian
cavalry, the latter also being mercenaries of the king. There were eighty
of them, and another detachment of light troops, about 800, and more
from Parthenium, and more again from Apollonia and the neighbouring
places, also cavalry.

It was now high time to consider how they were to beat a retreat.
So seizing all the cattle and sheep to be had, with the slaves, they put
them within a hollow square and proceeded to drive them off. Not that
they had a thought to give to the spoils now, but for precaution's sake
and for fear lest if they left the goods and chattels behind and made
off, the retreat would rapidly degenerate into a stampede, the enemy
growing bolder as the troops lost heart. For the present then they retired as if they meant to do battle for the spoils. As soon as Gongylus
saw how few the Hellenes were and how large the attacking party, out
he came himself, in spite of his mother, with his private force, wishing
to share in the action. Another too joined in the rescue,—Procles, from
Halisarna and Teuthrania, a descendant of Damaratus. By this time
Xenophon and his men were being hard pressed by the arrows and sling-
stones, though they marched in a curve so as to keep their shields facing the missiles, and even so, barely crossed the river Carcasus, nearly
half of them wounded. Here it was that Agasias of Stymphalus, the
captain, received his wound, while keeping up a steady unflagging fight
against the enemy from beginning to end. And so they reached home in
safety with about 200 captives, and sheep enough for sacrifices.

The next day Xenophon sacrificed and led out the whole army under
cover of night, intending to pierce far into the heart of Lydia with a
view to lulling to sleep the enemy's alarm at his proximity, and so in
fact to put him off his guard. But Asidates, hearing that Xenophon had
again sacrificed with the intention of another attack, and was approaching with his whole army, left his tower and took up quarters in some
villages lying under the town of Parthenium. Here Xenophon's party
fell in with him, and took him prisoner, with his wife, his children, his
horses, and all that he had; and so the promise of the earlier victims

was literally fulfilled. After that they returned again to Pergamus and here Xenophon thanked the god, for the Laconians, the officers, the other generals, and the soldiers as a body united to give him the pick of horses and cattle teams, and the rest; so that he was now in a position himself to do another a good turn.

Meanwhile Thibron arrived and received the troops, which he incorporated with the rest of his Hellenic forces, and so proceeded to prosecute a war against Tissaphernes and Pharnabazus. [The following is a list of the governors of the several territories of the king which were traversed by us during the expedition: Artimas, governor of Lydia; Artacamas of Phrygia; Mithridates of Lycaonia and Cappadocia; Syennesis of Cilicia; Dernes of Phoenicia and Arabia; Belesys of Syria and Assyria; Rhoparas of Babylon; Arbacas of Media; Tiribazus of the Phasians and Hesperites. Then some independent tribes—the Carduchians, Chalybes, Chaldaeans, Macrones, Colchians, Mossynoecians, Coetians, and Tibarenians. Then Corylas, the governor of Paphlagonia; Pharnabazus, of the Bithynians; Seuthes, of the European Thracians. The entire journey, ascent and descent, consisted of 215 stages, 1,155 parasangs, 34,650 stades. Computed in time, the length of ascent and descent together amounted to one year and three months.]

ARRIAN:

THE ANABASIS OF ALEXANDER

ARRIAN'S PREFACE

I HAVE admitted into my narrative as strictly authentic all the statements relating to Alexander and Philip which Ptolemy, son of Lagus,[1] and Aristobulus, son of Aristobulus,[2] agreed in making; and from those statements which differ I have selected that which appears to me the more credible and at the same time the more deserving of record. Different authors have given different accounts of Alexander's actions; and there is no one about whom more have written, or more at variance with each other. But in my opinion the narratives of Ptolemy and Aristobulus are more worthy of credit than the rest; Aristobulus, because he served under king Alexander in his expedition, and Ptolemy, not only because he accompanied Alexander in his expedition, but also because being a king himself, the falsification of facts would have been more disgraceful to him than to any other man. Moreover, they are both more worthy of credit, because they compiled their histories after Alexander's death, when neither compulsion was used nor reward offered them to write anything different from what really occurred. Some statements also made by other writers I have incorporated in my narrative, because they seemed to me worthy of mention and not altogether improbable; but I have given them merely as reports of Alexander's proceedings. And if any man wonders why, after so many other men have written of Alexander, the compilation of this history came into my mind, after perusing the narratives of all the rest, let him read this of mine, and then wonder (if he can).

[1] Ptolemy's mother, Arsinoe, had been a concubine of Philip of Macedonia, for which reason it was generally believed that Ptolemy was the offspring of that king. Ptolemy was one of the earliest friends of Alexander before his accession to the throne, and accompanied him throughout his campaigns, being one of his most skilful generals and most intimate friends. On the division of the empire after Alexander's death, Ptolemy obtained the kingdom of Egypt, which he transmitted to his descendants. He wrote a history of the wars of Alexander, which is one of the chief authorities on which Arrian composed his narrative.

[2] Aristobulus of Potidaea, a town in Macedonia, which was afterwards called Cassandrea, served under Alexander, and wrote a history of his wars, which, like that of Ptolemy, was sometimes more panegyrical than the facts warranted. Neither of these histories has survived, but they served Arrian as the groundwork for the composition of his own narrative.

ARRIAN:

THE ANABASIS OF ALEXANDER

BOOK I

1. It is said that Philip died [1] when Pythodemus was archon at Athens, and that his son Alexander,[2] being then about twenty years of age, marched into Peloponnesus as soon as he had secured the regal power. There he assembled all the Greeks who were within the Peloponnesus, and asked from them the supreme command of the expedition against the Persians, an office which they had already conferred upon Philip. He received the honour which he asked from all except the Lacedaemonians, who replied that it was an hereditary custom of theirs, not to follow others but to lead them. The Athenians also attempted to bring about some political change; but they were so alarmed at the very approach of Alexander that they conceded to him even more ample public honours than those which had been bestowed upon Philip. He then returned into Macedonia and busied himself in preparing for the expedition into Asia.

However, at the approach of spring, he marched towards Thrace, into the lands of the Triballians and Illyrians, because he ascertained that these nations were meditating a change of policy; and at the same time, as they were lying on his frontier, he thought it inexpedient, when he was about to start on a campaign so far away from his own land, to leave them behind him without having been entirely subjugated. Setting out then from Amphipolis, he invaded the land of the people who were called independent Thracians, keeping the city of Philippi and Mount Orbelus on the left. Crossing the river Nessus, they say he arrived at Mount Haemus on the tenth day. Here, along the defiles up the ascent to the mountain, he was met by many of the traders equipped

[1] 336 B.C. He was murdered by a young noble named Pausanias, who stabbed him at the festival which he was holding to celebrate the marriage of his daughter with Alexander, king of Epirus. At the time of his assassination Philip was just about to start on an expedition against Persia.

[2] Alexander the Great was the son of Philip II. and Olympias, and was born at Pella October 14, 356 B.C.

with arms, as well as by the independent Thracians, who had made preparations to check the further advance of his expedition by seizing the summit of the Haemus, along which was the route for the passage of his army. They had collected their waggons, and placed them in front of them, not only using them as a rampart from which they might defend themselves, in case they should be forced back, but also intending to let them loose upon the phalanx of the Macedonians, where the mountain was most precipitous, if they tried to ascend. They had come to the conclusion that the denser the phalanx was with which the waggons rushing down came into collision, the more easily would they scatter it by the violence of their fall upon it.

But Alexander formed a plan by which he might cross the mountain with the least danger possible; and since he was resolved to run all risks, knowing that there were no means of passing elsewhere, he ordered the heavy-armed soldiers, as soon as the waggoners began to rush down the declivity, to open their ranks, as many as the road was sufficiently wide to permit to do so and to stand apart, so that the waggons might roll down through the gap; but that those who were hemmed in on all sides should either stoop down together or even fall flat on the ground, and lock their shields compactly together, so that the waggons rushing down upon them, and in all probability by their very impetus leaping over them, might pass on without injuring them. And it turned out just as Alexander had conjectured and exhorted. For some of the men made gaps in the phalanx (and others locked their shields together). The waggons rolled over the shields without doing much injury, not a single man being killed under them. Then the Macedonians regained their courage, inasmuch as the waggons, which they had excessively dreaded, had inflicted no damage upon them. With a loud cry they assaulted the Thracians. Alexander ordered his archers to march from the right wing in front of the rest of the phalanx, because there the passage was easier, and to shoot at the Thracians wherever they advanced. He himself took his own guard, the shield-bearing infantry and the Agrianians, and led them to the left. Then the archers shot at the Thracians who sallied forward, and repulsed them; and the phalanx, coming to close fighting, easily drove away from their position men who were light-armed and badly-equipped barbarians. The consequence was, they no longer waited to receive Alexander marching against them from the left, but casting away their arms they fled down the mountain as each man best could. About 1,500 of them were killed; but only a few were taken prisoners on account of their swiftness of foot and acquaintance with the country. However, all the women who were accompanying them were captured, as were also their children and all their booty.

2. Alexander sent the booty away southward to the cities on the sea-shore, entrusting to Lysanias and Philotas[3] the duty of setting it up for sale. But he himself crossed the summit, and advancing through the Haemus into the land of the Triballians, he arrived at the river Lyginus. This river is distant from the Ister three days' march to one intending to go to the Haemus. Syrmus, king of the Triballians, hearing of Alexander's expedition long before, had sent the women and children of the nation on in advance to the Ister, ordering them to pass over into one of the islands in that river, the name of which was Peuce. To this island also the Thracians, who were neighbours of the Triballians, had fled together for refuge at the approach of Alexander. Syrmus himself likewise, accompanied by his train, had fled for refuge to the same place. But the main body of the Triballians fled back to the river, from which Alexander had started the day before.

When he heard of their starting, he wheeled round again, and, marching against them, surprised them just as they were encamping. And those who were surprised drew themselves up in battle array in a glen along the bank of the river. Alexander drew out his phalanx into a deep column, and led it on in person. He also ordered the archers and sling-ers to run forward and discharge arrows and stones at the barbarians, hoping to provoke them by this to come out of the glen into the ground unencumbered with trees. When they were within reach of the missiles, and were struck by them, they rushed out against the archers, who were undefended by shields, with the purpose of fighting them hand-to-hand. But when Alexander had drawn them thus out of the glen, he ordered Philotas to take the cavalry which came from upper Macedonia, and to charge their right wing, where they had advanced furthest in their sally. He also commanded Heraclides and Sopolis to lead on the cavalry which came from Bottiaea and Amphipolis against the left wing; while he himself extended the phalanx of infantry and the rest of the horse in front of the phalanx and led them against the enemy's centre. And in-deed as long as there was only skirmishing on both sides, the Triballians did not get the worst of it; but as soon as the phalanx in dense array at-tacked them with vigour, and the cavalry fell upon them in various quarters, no longer merely striking them with the javelin, but pushing them with their very horses, then at length they turned and fled through the glen to the river. Three thousand were slain in the flight; few also of these were taken prisoners, both because there was a dense wood in front of the river, and the approach of night deprived the Macedonians of certainty in their pursuit. Ptolemy says that of the Macedonians

[3] This officer was commander of the royal body-guard. His father was Parmenio, the most experienced of Alexander's generals.

themselves eleven horsemen and about forty foot soldiers were killed.

3. On the third day after the battle, Alexander reached the river Ister, which is the largest of all the rivers in Europe, traverses a very great tract of country, and separates very warlike nations. Most of these belong to the Celtic race, in whose territory the sources of the river take their rise. Of these nations the remotest are the Quadi and Marcomanni; then the Iazygians, a branch of the Sauromatians; then the Getae, who hold the doctrine of immortality; then the main body of the Sauromatians; and, lastly, the Scythians, (whose land stretches) as far as the outlets of the river, where through five mouths it discharges its water into the Euxine Sea.[4] Here Alexander found some ships of war which had come to him from Byzantium, through the Euxine Sea and up the river. Filling these with archers and heavy-armed troops, he sailed to the island to which the Triballians and Thracians had fled for refuge. He tried to force a landing; but the barbarians came to meet him at the brink of the river, wherever the ships made an assault. But these were only few in number, and the army in them small. The shores of the island, also, were in most places too steep and precipitous for landing, and the current of the river alongside it was rapid and exceedingly difficult to stem, because it was shut up into a narrow channel by the nearness of the banks.

Alexander therefore led back his ships, and determined to cross the Ister and march against the Getae, who dwelt on the other side of that river; for he observed that many of them had collected on the bank of the river for the purpose of barring his way, if he should try to cross. There were of them about 4,000 cavalry and more than 10,000 infantry. At the same time a strong desire seized him to advance beyond the Ister. He therefore went on board the fleet himself. He also filled with hay the hides which served them as tent-coverings, and collected from the country around all the boats made from single trunks of trees. Of these there was a great abundance, because the people who dwell near the Ister use them for fishing in the river, sometimes also for journeying to each other for traffic up the river; and most of them carry on piracy with them. Having collected as many of these as he could, upon them he conveyed across as many of his soldiers as was possible in such a fashion. Those who crossed with Alexander amounted in number to 1,500 cavalry and 4,000 infantry.

4. They crossed over by night to a spot where the corn stood high; and therefore they reached the bank more secretly. At the approach of

---

[4] Herodotus (iv. 47) says the Danube had five mouths; but Strabo (vii. 3) says there were seven. At the present time it has only three mouths. The Greeks euphemistically called the Black Sea the sea kind to strangers.

dawn Alexander led his men through the field of standing corn, ordering the infantry to lean upon the corn with their pikes held transversely,
and thus to advance into the untilled ground. As long as the phalanx was
advancing through the standing corn, the cavalry followed; but when
they marched out of the tilled land, Alexander himself led the horse
round to the right wing, and commanded Nicanor[5] to lead the phalanx
in a square. The Getae did not sustain even the first charge of the cavalry; for Alexander's audacity seemed incredible to them, in having
thus easily crossed the Ister, the largest of rivers, in a single night, without throwing a bridge over the stream. Terrible to them also was the
closely-locked order of the phalanx, and violent the charge of the cavalry. At first they fled for refuge into their city, which was distant about
three miles from the Ister; but when they saw that Alexander was leading his phalanx carefully along the side of the river, to prevent his infantry being anywhere surrounded by the Getae lying in ambush, but
that he was sending his cavalry straight on, they again abandoned the
city, because it was badly fortified. They carried off as many of their
women and children as their horses could bear, and betook themselves
into the steppes, in a direction which led as far as possible from the
river. Alexander took the city and all the booty which the Getae left
behind. This he gave to Meleager and Philip to carry off. After razing
the city to the ground, he offered sacrifice upon the bank of the river,
to Zeus the preserver, to Heracles, and to Ister himself, because he had
allowed him to cross; and while it was still day he brought all his men
back safe to the camp.

There ambassadors came to him from Syrmus, king of the Triballians, and from the other independent nations dwelling near the Ister.
Some even arrived from the Celts who dwelt near the Ionian gulf. These
people are of great stature, and of a haughty disposition. All the envoys
said that they had come to seek Alexander's friendship. To all of them
he gave pledges of amity, and received pledges from them in return.
He then asked the Celts what thing in the world caused them special
alarm, expecting that his own great fame had reached the Celts and had
penetrated still further, and that they would say that they feared him
most of all things. But the answer of the Celts turned out quite contrary
to his expectation; for, as they dwelt so far away from Alexander, inhabiting districts difficult of access, and as they saw he was about to set
out in another direction, they said they were afraid that the sky would
some time or other fall down upon them. These men also he sent back,
calling them friends, and ranking them as allies, only adding the remark
that the Celts were braggarts.

[5] Son of Parmenio and brother of Philotas.

5. He then advanced into the land of the Agrianians and Paeonians, where messengers reached him, who reported that Clitus, son of Bardylis, had revolted, and that Glaucias, king of the Taulantians, had gone over to him. Others also reported that the Autariatians intended to attack him on his way. He accordingly resolved to commence his march without delay. But Langarus, king of the Agrianians, who, in the lifetime of Philip, had been an open and avowed friend of Alexander, and had gone on an embassy to him in his private capacity, at that time also came to him with the finest and best armed of the shield-bearing troops, which he kept as a body-guard. When this man heard that Alexander was inquiring who the Autariatians were, and what was the number of their men, he said that he need take no account of them, since they were the least warlike of the tribes of that district; and that he would himself make an inroad into their land, so that they might have too much occupation about their own affairs to attack others. Accordingly, at Alexander's order, he made an attack upon them; and not only did he attack them, but he swept their land clean of captives and booty. Thus the Autariatians were indeed occupied with their own affairs. Langarus was rewarded by Alexander with the greatest honours, and received from him the gifts which were considered most valuable in the eyes of the king of the Macedonians. Alexander also promised to give him his sister Cyna in marriage if he came to Pella.[6] But Langarus fell ill and died on his return home.

After this, Alexander marched along the river Erigon, and proceeded to the city of Pelium; for Clitus had seized this city, as it was the strongest in the country. When Alexander arrived at this place, and had encamped near the river Eordaicus, he resolved to make an assault upon the wall the next day. But Clitus held the mountains which encircled the city; moreover they commanded it from their height, and were covered with dense thickets. His intention was to fall upon the Macedonians from all sides, if they assaulted the city. But Glaucias, king of the Taulantians, had not yet joined him. Alexander, however, led his forces towards the city; and the enemy, after sacrificing three boys, an equal number of girls, and three black rams, sallied forth for the purpose of receiving the Macedonians in a hand-to-hand conflict. But as soon as the Macedonians came to close quarters with them, they left the positions which they had occupied, strong as they were, in such haste that even their sacrificial victims were captured still lying on the ground.

On this day he shut them up in the city, and encamping near the wall, he resolved to close them in by a circumvallation; but on the next day Glaucias, king of the Taulantians, arrived with a great force. Then, in-

[6] The capital of Macedonia. Philip and Alexander were born here.

deed, Alexander gave up the hope of capturing the city with his present force, since many warlike troops had fled for refuge into it, and Glaucias with his large army would be likely to follow him up closely if he assailed the wall. But he sent Philotas on a foraging expedition, with the beasts of burden from the camp and a sufficient body of cavalry to serve as a guard. When Glaucias heard of the foray of Philotas he marched out to meet him, and seized the mountains which surrounded the plain, from which Philotas intended to procure forage. As soon as Alexander was informed that his cavalry and beasts of burden would be in danger if night overtook them, taking the shield-bearing troops,[7] the archers, the Agrianians, and about 400 cavalry, he went with all speed to their aid. The rest of the army he left behind near the city, to prevent the men in it from hastening forth to form a junction with Glaucias (as they would have done), if all the Macedonian army had withdrawn. Directly Glaucias perceived that Alexander was advancing, he evacuated the mountains, and Philotas and his forces returned to the camp in safety. But Clitus and Glaucias still imagined that they had caught Alexander in a disadvantageous position; for they were occupying the mountains, which commanded the plain by their height, with a large body of cavalry, javelin-throwers, and slingers, besides a considerable number of heavy-armed infantry. Moreover, the men who had been beleaguered in the city were expected to pursue the Macedonians closely if they made a retreat. The ground also through which Alexander had to march was evidently narrow and covered with wood; on one side it was hemmed in by the river, and on the other there was a very lofty and craggy mountain, so that there would not be room for the army to pass, even if only four shield-bearers marched abreast.

6. Then Alexander drew up his army in such a way that the depth of the phalanx was 120 men; and stationing 200 cavalry on each wing, he ordered them to preserve silence, receiving the word of command quickly. Accordingly he gave the signal to the heavy-armed infantry in the first place to hold their spears erect, and then to couch them at the concerted sign; at one time to incline their spears to the right, closely locked together, and at another time towards the left. He then set the phalanx itself into quick motion forward, and marched it towards the wings, now to the right, and then to the left. After thus arranging and re-arranging his lines many times very rapidly, he at last formed his phalanx into a sort of wedge, and led it towards the left against the enemy, who had long been in a state of amazement at seeing both the or-

---

[7] The Hypaspists—shield-bearers, or guards—were a body of infantry organised by Philip, originally few in number, and employed as personal body-guards of the king, but afterwards enlarged into several distinct brigades.

der and the rapidity of his evolutions. Consequently they did not sustain Alexander's attack, but quitted the first ridges of the mountain. Upon this, Alexander ordered the Macedonians to raise the battle-cry and make a clatter with their spears upon their shields; and the Taulantians, being still more alarmed at the noise, led their army back to the city with all speed.

As Alexander saw only a few of the enemy still occupying a ridge, along which lay his route, he ordered his bodyguards and personal companions to take their shields, mount their horses, and ride to the hill; and when they reached it, if those who had occupied the position awaited them, he said that half of them were to leap from their horses, and to fight as foot-soldiers, being mingled with the cavalry. But when the enemy saw Alexander's advance, they quitted the hill and retreated to the mountains in both directions. Then Alexander, with his companions,[8] seized the hill, and sent for the Agrianians and archers, who numbered 2,000. He also ordered the shield-bearing guards to cross the river, and after them the regiments of Macedonian infantry, with instructions that, as soon as they had succeeded in crossing, they should draw out in rank towards the left, so that the phalanx of men crossing might appear compact at once. He himself, in the vanguard, was all the time observing from the ridge the enemy's advance. They, seeing the force crossing the river, marched down the mountains to meet them, with the purpose of attacking Alexander's rear in its retreat. But, as they were just drawing near, Alexander rushed forth with his own attendants, and the phalanx raised the battle-cry, with the intention of advancing through the river. When the enemy saw all the Macedonians marching against them, they gave way and fled. Upon this, Alexander led the Agrianians and archers at full speed towards the river, and succeeded in being himself the first man to cross it. But when he saw the enemy pressing upon the men in the rear, he stationed his engines of war upon the bank, and ordered the engineers to shoot from them as far forward as possible all sorts of projectiles which are usually shot from military engines. He directed the archers, also, to enter the water, and shoot their arrows from the middle of the river. But Glaucias did not dare advance within range of the missiles; so that the Macedonians passed over in such safety, that not one of them lost his life in the retreat.

Three days after this, Alexander discovered that Clitus and Glaucias lay carelessly encamped; that neither were their sentinels on guard at the posts assigned to them, nor had they protected themselves with a rampart or ditch, imagining he had withdrawn through fear; and that

---

[8] The heavy cavalry, wholly or chiefly composed of Macedonians by birth, was known by the honourable name of Companions, or Brothers in Arms.

they had extended their line to a disadvantageous length. He therefore crossed the river again secretly, at the approach of night, leading with him the shield-bearing guards, the Agrianians, the archers, and the brigades of Perdiccas[9] and Coenus, after having given orders for the rest of the army to follow. As soon as he saw a favourable opportunity for the attack, without waiting for all to be present, he despatched the archers and Agrianians against the foe. These, being arranged in phalanx, fell unawares with the most furious charge upon their flank, where they were likely to come into conflict with their weakest point, and slew some of them still in their beds, others being easily caught in their flight. Accordingly, many were there captured and killed, as were many also in the disorderly and panic-stricken retreat which ensued. Not a few, moreover, were taken prisoners. Alexander kept up the pursuit as far as the Taulantian mountains; and as many of them as escaped preserved their lives by throwing away their arms. Clitus first fled for refuge into the city; then he set it on fire, and withdrew to Glaucias, in the land of the Taulantians.

7. While these events were occurring, some of the exiles who had been banished from Thebes, coming to the city by night, and being brought in by some of the citizens, in order to effect a change in the government, apprehended and slew outside the Cadmea, Amyntas and Timolaus, two of the men who held that fortress, having no suspicion that any hostile attempt was about to be made. Then entering the public assembly, they incited the Thebans to revolt from Alexander, holding out to them as pretexts the ancient and glorious words, liberty and freedom of speech, and urging them now at last to rid themselves of the heavy yoke of the Macedonians. By stoutly maintaining that Alexander had been killed in Illyria they gained more power in persuading the multitude, and what is more, this report was prevalent, and for many reasons gained credit, both because he had been absent a long time, and because no news had arrived from him. Accordingly, as is usual in such cases, not knowing the facts, each man conjectured what was most pleasing to himself.

When Alexander heard what was being done at Thebes, he thought it was a movement not at all to be slighted (inasmuch as he had for a long time suspected the city of Athens and deemed the audacious ac-

---

[9] Perdiccas, son of Orontes, a Macedonian, was one of Alexander's most distinguished generals. The king is said on his death-bed to have taken the royal signet from his finger and to have given it to Perdiccas. After Alexander's death he was appointed regent; but an alliance was formed against him by Antipater, Craterus, and Ptolemy. He marched into Egypt against Ptolemy. Being defeated in his attempts to force the passage of the Nile, his own troops mutinied against him and slew him (321 B.C.).

tion of the Thebans no trivial matter), if the Lacedaemonians, who had long been disaffected in their feelings to him, and the Aetolians and certain other States in the Peloponnese, who were not firm in their allegiance to him, should take part with the Thebans in their revolutionary effort. He therefore led his army through Eordaea and Elimiotis and along the peaks of Stymphaea and Paravaea, and on the seventh day arrived at Pelina in Thessaly. Starting thence, he entered Boeotia on the sixth day; so that the Thebans did not learn that he had passed south of Thermopylae until he was at Onchestus with the whole of his army. Even then the authors of the revolt asserted that Antipater's army had arrived out of Macedonia, stoutly affirming that Alexander himself was dead, and being very angry with those who announced that it was Alexander himself who was advancing. For they said it must be another Alexander, the son of Aeropus, who was coming. On the following day Alexander set out from Onchestus, and advanced towards the city along the territory consecrated to Iolaus, where indeed he encamped, in order to give the Thebans further time to repent of their evil resolutions and to send an embassy to him. But so far were they from showing any sign of wishing to come to an accommodation, that their cavalry and a large body of light-armed infantry, sallying forth from the city right up to the camp, began to skirmish with the Macedonian outposts, and slew a few of their men. Alexander hereupon sent forth a party of his light-armed infantry and archers to repel their sortie; and these men repelled them with ease, just as they were approaching the very camp. The next day he took the whole of his army and marched round towards the gate which led to Eleutherae and Attica. But not even then did he assault the wall itself, but encamped not far away from the Cadmea, in order to be at hand to aid the Macedonians who were occupying that citadel. For the Thebans had blockaded the Cadmea with a double stockade and were guarding it, so that no one from without might be able to assist those who were beleaguered, and that the garrison might not be able, by making a sally, to do them an injury, when they were attacking the enemy outside. But Alexander remained encamped near the Cadmea, for he still wished rather to come to friendly terms with the Thebans than to come to a contest with them. Then those of the Thebans who knew what was for the best interest of the commonwealth were eager to go out to Alexander and obtain pardon for the commonalty of Thebes for their revolt; but the exiles and those who had summoned them home kept on inciting the populace to war by every means in their power, since they despaired of obtaining for themselves any indulgence from Alexander, especially as some of them were also Boeotarchs. However not even for this did Alexander assault the city.

8. But Ptolemy, son of Lagus, tells us that Perdiccas, who had been posted in the advanced guard of the camp with his own brigade, and was not far from the enemy's stockade, did not wait for the signal from Alexander to commence the battle, but of his own accord was the first to assault the stockade, and, having made a breach in it, fell upon the advanced guard of the Thebans. Amyntas, son of Andromenes, followed Perdiccas, because he had been stationed with him. This general also of his own accord led on his brigade when he saw that Perdiccas had advanced within the stockade. When Alexander saw this, he led on the rest of his army, fearing that unsupported they might be intercepted by the Thebans and be in danger of destruction. He gave instructions to the archers and Agrianians to rush within the stockade, but he still retained the guards and shield-bearing troops outside. Then indeed Perdiccas, after forcing his way within the second stockade, fell there wounded with a dart, and was carried back grievously injured to the camp, where he was with difficulty cured of his wound. However the men of Perdiccas, in company with the archers sent by Alexander, fell upon the Thebans and shut them up in the hollow way leading to the temple of Heracles, and followed them in their retreat as far as the temple itself. The Thebans, having wheeled round, again advanced from that position with a shout, and put the Macedonians to flight. Eurybotas the Cretan, the captain of the archers, fell with about seventy of his men; but the rest fled to the Macedonian guard and the royal shield-bearing troops. Now, when Alexander saw that his own men were in flight, and that the Thebans had broken their ranks in pursuit, he attacked them with his phalanx drawn up in proper order, and drove them back within the gates. The Thebans fled in such a panic that being driven into the city through the gates they had not time to shut them; for all the Macedonians, who were close behind the fugitives, rushed with them within the fortifications, inasmuch as the walls also were destitute of defenders on account of the numerous pickets in front of them. When the Macedonians had entered the Cadmea, some of them marched out of it, in company with those who held the fortress, along the temple of Amphion[10] into the other part of the city, but others crossing along the walls, which were now in the possession of those who had rushed in together with the fugitives, advanced with a run into the market-place. Those of the Thebans who had been drawn up opposite the temple of Amphion stood their ground for a short time; but when the Macedonians pressed hard upon them in all directions, Alexander presenting himself now in one place now in another, their cavalry rushed through the city and sallied forth into the plain, and their infantry fled for safety as each

[10] The mythical founder of the walls of Thebes.

man found it possible. Then indeed the Thebans, no longer defending themselves, were slain, not so much by the Macedonians as by the Phocians, Plataeans and other Boeotians, who by indiscriminate slaughter vented their rage against them. Some were even attacked in the houses (a few of whom turned to defend themselves), and others as they were supplicating the protection of the gods in the temples; not even the women and children being spared.

9. This was felt by the Greeks to be a general calamity; for it struck the rest of the Greeks with no less consternation than it did those who had themselves taken part in the struggle, both on account of the magnitude of the captured city and the celerity of the action, the result of which was in the highest degree contrary to the expectation both of the sufferers and the perpetrators. For the disasters which befell the Athenians in relation to Sicily, though in regard to the number of those who perished they brought no less misfortune to the city, yet, because their army was destroyed far away from their own land, being composed for the most part rather of auxiliary troops than of native Athenians, and because their city itself was left to them intact, so that afterwards they held their own in war even for a long time, though fighting against the Lacedaemonians and their allies, as well as the Great King; these disasters, I say, neither produced in the persons who were themselves involved in the calamity an equal sensation of the misfortune, nor did they cause the other Greeks a similar consternation at the catastrophe. Again, the defeat sustained by the Athenians at Aegospotami was a naval one, and the city received no other humiliation than the demolition of the Long Walls, the surrender of most of her ships, and the loss of supremacy. However, they still retained their hereditary form of government, and not long after recovered their former power to such a degree as to be able not only to build up the Long Walls but to recover the rule of the sea, and in their turn to preserve from extreme danger those very Lacedaemonians then so formidable to them, who had come and almost obliterated their city. Moreover, the defeat of the Lacedaemonians at Leuctra and Mantinea filled them with consternation rather by the unexpectedness of the disaster than because of the number of those who perished. And the attack made by the Boeotians and Arcadians under Epaminondas upon the city of Sparta, even this terrified both the Lacedaemonians themselves and those who participated with them in the transactions at that time, rather by the novelty of the sight than by the reality of the danger. The capture of the city of the Plataeans was not a great calamity, by reason of the small number of those who were taken in it; most of the citizens having long before escaped to Athens. Again, the capture of Melos and Scione simply related to

insular States, and rather brought disgrace to those who perpetrated the outrages than produced great surprise among the Grecian community as a whole.

But the Thebans having effected their revolt suddenly and without any previous consideration; the capture of the city being brought about in so short a time and without difficulty on the part of the captors; the slaughter, being great, as was natural, from its being made by men of the same race who were glutting their revenge on them for ancient injuries; the complete enslavement of a city which excelled among those in Greece at that time both in power and warlike reputation; all this was attributed not without probability to the avenging wrath of the deity. It seemed as if the Thebans had after a long time suffered this punishment for their betrayal of the Greeks in the Persian war; for their seizure of the city of Plataea during the truce; and for their complete enslavement of it, as well as for the un-Hellenic slaughter of the men who had surrendered to the Lacedaemonians, which had been committed at the instigation of the Thebans; and for the devastation of the territory in which the Greeks had stood in battle-array against the Medes and had repelled danger from Greece; lastly, because by their vote they had tried to ruin the Athenians when a motion was brought forward among the allies of the Lacedaemonians for the enslavement of Athens. Moreover it was reported that before the disaster many portents were sent from the deity, which indeed at the time were treated with neglect, but afterwards when men called them to remembrance they were compelled to consider that the events which occurred had been long before prognosticated.

The settlement of Theban affairs was entrusted by Alexander to the allies who had taken part in the action. They resolved to occupy the Cadmea with a garrison; to raze the city to the ground; to distribute among themselves all the territory, except what was dedicated to the gods; and to sell into slavery the women and children, and as many of the males as survived, except those who were priests or priestesses, and those who were bound to Philip or Alexander by the ties of hospitality or had been public representatives of the Macedonians. It is said that Alexander preserved the house and the descendants of Pindar the poet, out of respect for his memory. In addition to these things, the allies decreed that Orchomenus and Plataea should be rebuilt and fortified.

10. As soon as news of the calamity which had befallen the Thebans reached the other Greeks, the Arcadians, who had set out from their own land for the purpose of bringing aid to the Thebans, passed sentence of death on those who had instigated them to render aid. The Eleans also received back their exiles from banishment, because they

were Alexander's adherents; and the Aetolians, each tribe for itself, sent embassies to him, begging to receive pardon, because they also had attempted to effect a revolution, on the receipt of the report which had been spread by the Thebans. The Athenians also, who, at the time when some of the Thebans, fresh from the action itself, arrived at Athens, were engaged in celebrating the Great Mysteries, abandoned the sacred rites in great consternation, and began to carry their goods and chattels from the rural districts into the city. The people came together in public assembly, and, on the motion of Demades, elected from all the citizens ten ambassadors, men whom they knew to be Alexander's special adherents, and sent them to signify to him, though somewhat unseasonably, that the Athenian people rejoiced at his safe return from the land of the Illyrians and Triballians, and at the punishment which he had inflicted upon the Thebans for their revolution. In regard to other matters he gave the embassy a courteous reply, but wrote a letter to the people demanding the surrender of Demosthenes and Lycurgus, as well as that of Hyperides, Polyeuctus, Chares, Charidemus, Ephialtes, Diotimus, and Moerocles, alleging that these men were the cause of the disaster which befell the city at Chaeronea, and the authors of the subsequent offensive proceedings after Philip's death, both against himself and his father. He also declared that they had instigated the Thebans to revolt no less than had those of the Thebans themselves who favoured a revolution. The Athenians, however, did not surrender the men, but sent another embassy to Alexander, entreating him to remit his wrath against the persons whom he had demanded. The king did remit his wrath against them, perhaps out of respect for the city of Athens, or perhaps from eagerness to start on the expedition into Asia, not wishing to leave behind him among the Greeks any cause for distrust. However, he ordered Charidemus alone of the men whom he had demanded as prisoners and who had not been given up, to go into banishment. Charidemus therefore went as an exile into Asia to King Darius.

11. Having settled these affairs, he returned into Macedonia. He then offered to the Olympian Zeus the sacrifice which had been instituted by Archaelaus, and had been customary up to that time; and he celebrated the public contest of the Olympic games at Aegae. It is said that he also held a public contest in honour of the Muses. At this time it was reported that the statue of Orpheus, son of Oeagrus the Thracian, which was in Pieris, sweated incessantly. Various were the explanations of this prodigy given by the soothsayers; but Aristander, a man of Telmissus, a soothsayer, bade Alexander take courage; for he said it was evident from this that there would be much labour for the epic and

lyric poets, and for the writers of odes, to compose and sing about Alexander and his achievements.

At the beginning of the spring he marched towards the Hellespont, entrusting the affairs of Macedonia and Greece to Antipater. He led with him not much over 30,000 infantry together with light-armed troops and archers, and more than 5,000 cavalry. His march was past the lake Cercinitis, towards Amphipolis and the mouths of the river Strymon. Having crossed this river he passed by the Pangaean mountain, along the road leading to Abdera and Maronea, Grecian cities built on the coast. Thence he arrived at the river Hebrus, and easily crossed it. Thence he proceeded through Paetica to the river Melas, having crossed which he arrived at Sestus, in twenty days altogether from the time of his starting from home. When he came to Elaeus he offered sacrifice to Protesilaus upon the tomb of that hero, both for other reasons and because Protesilaus seemed to have been the first of the Greeks who took part with Agamemnon in the expedition to Ilium to disembark in Asia. The design of this sacrifice was that disembarking in Asia might be more fortunate to himself than that it had been to Protesilaus. He then committed to Parmenio the duty of conveying the cavalry and the greater part of the infantry across from Sestus to Abydus; and they crossed over in 160 triremes, besides many trading vessels. The prevailing account is that Alexander started from Elaeus and put into the Port of Achaeans, that with his own hand he steered the general's ship across, and that when he was about the middle of the channel of the Hellespont he sacrificed a bull to Poseidon and the Nereids, and poured forth a libation to them into the sea from a golden goblet. They say also that he was the first man to step out of the ship in full armour on the land of Asia, and that he erected altars to Zeus, the protector of people landing, to Athena, and to Heracles, at the place in Europe whence he started, and at the place in Asia where he disembarked. It is also said that he went up to Ilium and offered sacrifice to the Trojan Athena; that he set up his own panoply in the temple as a votive offering, and in exchange for it took away some of the consecrated arms which had been preserved from the time of the Trojan war. It is also said that the shield-bearing guards used to carry these arms in front of him into the battles. A report also prevails that he offered sacrifice to Priam upon the altar of Zeus the household god, deprecating the wrath of Priam against the progeny of Neoptolemus, from whom Alexander himself was descended.

12. When he went up to Ilium, Menoetius the pilot crowned him with a golden crown; after him Chares the Athenian, coming from

Sigeum, as well as certain others, both Greeks and natives, did the same. Alexander then encircled the tomb of Achilles with a garland; and it is said that Hephaestion[11] decorated that of Patroclus in the same way. There is indeed a report that Alexander pronounced Achilles fortunate in getting Homer as the herald of his fame to posterity. And in truth it was meet that Alexander should deem Achilles fortunate for this reason especially; for to Alexander himself this privilege was wanting, a thing which was not in accordance with the rest of his good fortune. His achievements have, therefore, not been related to mankind in a manner worthy of the hero. Neither in prose nor in verse has any one suitably honoured him; nor has he ever been sung of in a lyric poem, in which style of poetry Hiero, Gelo, Thero, and many others not at all comparable with Alexander, have been praised. Consequently Alexander's deeds are far less known than the meanest achievements of antiquity. For instance, the march of the ten thousand with Cyrus up to Persia against King Artaxerxes, the tragic fate of Clearchus and those who were captured along with him, and the march of the same men down to the sea, in which they were led by Xenophon, are events much better known to men through Xenophon's narrative than are Alexander and his achievements. And yet Alexander neither accompanied another man's expedition, nor did he in flight from the Great King overcome those who obstructed his march down to the sea. And, indeed, there is no other single individual among Greeks or barbarians who achieved exploits so great or important either in regard to number or magnitude as he did. This was the reason which induced me to undertake this history, not thinking myself incompetent to make Alexander's deeds known to men. For whoever I may be, this I know about myself, that there is no need for me to assert my name, for it is not unknown to men; nor is it needful for me to say what my native land and family are, or if I have held any public office in my own country. But this I do assert, that this historical work is and has been from my youth up, equivalent to native land, family, and public offices for me; and for this reason I do not deem myself unworthy to rank among the first authors in the Greek language, if Alexander indeed is among the first in arms.

From Ilium Alexander came to Arisbe, where his entire force had encamped after crossing the Hellespont; and on the following day he came to Percote. On the next, passing by Lampsacus, he encamped near the river Practius, which flows from the Idaean mountains and discharges itself into the sea between the Hellespont and the Euxine Sea. Thence passing by the city of Colonae, he arrived at Hermotus. He now sent

[11] Son of Amyntas, a Macedonian of Pella. He was the most intimate friend of Alexander, with whom he had been brought up.

scouts before the army under the command of Amyntas, son of Arrhabaeus, who had the squadron of the Companion cavalry which came
from Apollonia, under the captain Socrates, son of Sathon, and four
squadrons of what were called scouts. In the march he despatched
Panegorus, son of Lycagoras, one of the Companions, to take possession
of the city of Priapus, which was surrendered by the inhabitants.

The Persian generals were Arsames, Rheomithres, Petines, Niphates,
and with them Spithridates, viceroy of Lydia and Ionia, and Arsites,
governor of the Phrygia near the Hellespont. These had encamped near
the city of Zeleia with the Persian cavalry and the Grecian mercenaries. When they were holding a council about the state of affairs, it was
reported to them that Alexander had crossed (the Hellespont). Memnon,
the Rhodian, advised them not to risk a conflict with the Macedonians,
since they were far superior to themselves in infantry, and Alexander
was there in person; whereas Darius was not with them. He advised
them to advance and destroy the fodder, by trampling it down under
their horses' hoofs, to burn the crops in the country, and not even to
spare the very cities. "For then Alexander," said he, "will not be able
to stay in the land from lack of provisions." It is said that in the Persian conference Arsites asserted that he would not allow a single house
belonging to the people placed under his rule to be burned, and that the
other Persians agreed with Arsites, because they had a suspicion that
Memnon was deliberately contriving to protract the war for the purpose of obtaining honour from the king.

13. Meantime Alexander was advancing to the river Granicus, with
his army arranged for battle, having drawn up his heavy-armed troops
in a double phalanx, leading the cavalry on the wings, and having ordered that the baggage should follow in the rear. And Hegelochus at the
head of the cavalry, who were armed with the long pike, and about 500
of the light-armed troops, was sent by him to reconnoitre the proceedings of the enemy. When Alexander was not far from the river Granicus,
some of his scouts rode up to him at full speed and announced that the
Persians had taken up their position on the other side of the Granicus,
drawn up ready for battle. Thereupon Alexander arranged all his army
with the intention of fighting. Then Parmenio approached him and
spoke as follows, "I think, O king, that it is advisable for the present
to pitch our camp on the bank of the river as we are. For I think that
the enemy, being much inferior to us in infantry, will not dare to pass
the night near us, and therefore they will permit the army to cross the
ford with ease at daybreak. For we shall then pass over before they can
put themselves in order of battle; whereas, I do not think that we can
now attempt the operation without evident risk, because it is not pos-

sible to lead the army through the river with its front extended. For it is clear that many parts of the stream are deep, and you see that these banks are very steep and in some places abrupt. Therefore the enemy's cavalry, being formed into a dense square, will attack us as we emerge from the water in broken ranks and in column, in the place where we are weakest. At the present juncture the first repulse would be difficult to retrieve, as well as perilous for the issue of the whole war."

But to this Alexander replied, "I recognize the force of these arguments, O Parmenio; but I should feel it a disgrace, if, after crossing the Hellespont so easily, this paltry stream (for with such an appellation he made light of the Granicus) should bar our passage for a moment. I consider that this would be in accordance neither with the fame of the Macedonians nor with my own eagerness for encountering danger. Moreover, I think that the Persians will regain courage, in the belief that they are a match in war for Macedonians, since up to the present time they have suffered no defeat from me to warrant the fear they entertain."

14. Having spoken thus, he sent Parmenio to take the command upon the left wing, while he led in person on the right. And at the head of the right wing he placed the following officers: Philotas, son of Parmenio, with the cavalry Companions, the archers, and the Agrianian javelin-men; and Amyntas, son of Arrhabaeus, with the cavalry carrying the long pike, the Paeonians, and the squadron of Socrates, was posted near Philotas. Close to these were posted the Companions who were shield-bearing infantry under the command of Nicanor, son of Parmenio. Next to these the brigade of Perdiccas, son of Orontes; then that of Coenus, son of Polemocrates; then that of Craterus, son of Alexander; then that of Amyntas, son of Andromenes; finally, the men commanded by Philip, son of Amyntas. On the left wing first were arranged the Thessalian cavalry, commanded by Calas, son of Harpalus; next to these, the cavalry of the Grecian allies, commanded by Philip, son of Menelaus; next to these the Thracians, commanded by Agatho. Close to these were the infantry, the brigades of Craterus, Meleager, and Philip, reaching as far as the centre of the entire line.

The Persian cavalry were about 20,000 in number, and their infantry, consisting of Grecian mercenaries, fell a little short of the same number. They had extended their horse along the bank of the river in a long phalanx, and had posted the infantry behind the cavalry, for the ground above the bank was steep and commanding. They also marshalled dense squadrons of cavalry upon that part of the bank where they observed Alexander himself advancing against their left wing; for he was conspicuous both by the brightness of his arms and by the respectful attendance of his staff. Both armies stood a long time at the margin of the river, keeping quiet from dread of the result; and profound silence was observed on both sides. For the Persians were waiting till the Macedonians should step into the ford, with the intention of attacking them as they emerged. Alexander leaped upon his steed, ordering those about him to follow, and exhorting them to show themselves valiant men. He then commanded Amyntas, son of Arrhabaeus, to make the first rush into the river at the head of the skirmishing cavalry, the Paeonians, and one regiment of infantry; and in front of these he had placed Ptolemy, son of Philip, in command of the squadron of Socrates, which body of men indeed on that day happened to have the lead of all the cavalry force. He himself led the right wing with sounding of trumpets, and the men raising the war-cry to Enyalius.[12] He entered the ford, keeping his line always extended obliquely in the direction in which the stream turned itself aside, in order that the Persians might not fall upon him as he was emerging from the water with his men in column, but that he himself might, as far as practicable, encounter them with a broad line.

15. The Persians began the contest by hurling missiles from above in the direction where the men of Amyntas and Socrates were the first to reach the bank, some of them casting javelins into the river from their commanding position on the bank, and others stepping down along the flatter parts of it to the very edge of the water. Then ensued a violent struggle on the part of the cavalry, on the one side to emerge from the river, and on the other to prevent the landing. From the Persians there was a terrible discharge of darts; but the Macedonians fought with spears. The Macedonians, being far inferior in number, suffered severely at the first onset, because they were obliged to defend themselves from the river, where their footing was unsteady, and where they were below the level of their assailants; whereas the Persians were fighting from the top of the bank, which gave them an advantage, especially as the best of the Persian horse had been posted there. Memnon himself, as well as his sons, were running every risk with these; and the Macedonians who first came into conflict with the Persians, though they showed great valour. were cut down by them, except those who retreated to Alexander, who was now approaching. For the king was already near, leading with him the right wing. He made his first assault upon the Persians at the place where the whole mass of their horse and the leaders themselves were posted; and around him a desperate conflict raged, during which one rank of the Macedonians after another easily kept on crossing the river. Though they fought on horseback, it seemed more

[12] This is an Homeric name for Ares the war-god.

like an infantry than a cavalry battle; for they struggled for the mastery, horses being jammed with horses and men with men, the Macedonians striving to drive the Persians entirely away from the bank and to force them into the plain, and the Persians striving to obstruct their landing and to push them back again into the river. At last Alexander's men began to gain the advantage, both through their superior strength and military discipline, and because they fought with spears whose shafts were made of cornel-wood, whereas the Persians used only darts.

Then indeed, Alexander's spear being broken to shivers in the conflict, he asked Aretis, one of the royal guards, whose duty it was to assist the king to mount his horse, for another spear. But this man's spear had also been shivered while he was in the thickest of the struggle, and he was conspicuous fighting with the half of his broken spear. Showing this to Alexander, he bade him ask some one else for one. Then Demaratus, a man of Corinth, one of his personal Companions, gave him his own spear; which he had no sooner taken than seeing Mithridates, the son-in-law of Darius, riding far in front of the others, and leading with him a body of cavalry arranged like a wedge, he himself rode on in front of the others, and hitting at the face of Mithridates with his spear, struck him to the ground. But hereupon, Rhoesaces rode up to Alexander and hit him on the head with his scimitar, breaking off a piece of his helmet. But the helmet broke the force of the blow. This man also Alexander struck to the ground, hitting him in the chest through the breastplate with his lance. And now Spithridates from behind had already raised aloft his scimitar against the king, when Clitus, son of Dropidas, anticipated his blow, and hitting him on the arm, cut it off, scimitar and all. Meantime the horsemen, as many as were able, kept on securing a landing in succession all down the river, and were joining Alexander's forces.

16. The Persians themselves, as well as their horses, were now being struck on their faces with the lances from all sides, and were being repulsed by the cavalry. They also received much damage from the light-armed troops who were mingled with the cavalry. They first began to give way where Alexander himself was braving danger in the front. When their centre had given way, the horse on both wings were also naturally broken through, and took to speedy flight. Of the Persian cavalry only about 1,000 were killed; for Alexander did not pursue them far, but turned aside to attack the Greek mercenaries, the main body of whom was still remaining where it was posted at first. This they did rather from amazement at the unexpected result of the struggle than from any steady resolution. Leading the phalanx against these, and ordering the cavalry to fall upon them from all sides, he soon completely

surrounded them and cut them up, so that none of them escaped except such as might have concealed themselves among the dead bodies. About 2,000 were taken prisoners. The following leaders of the Persians also fell in the battle: Niphates, Petines, Spithridates, viceroy of Lydia, Mithrobuzanes, governor of Cappadocia, Mithridates, the son-in-law of Darius, Arbupales, son of Darius the son of Artaxerxes, Pharnaces, brother of the wife of Darius, and Omares, commander of the auxiliaries. Arsites fled from the battle into Phrygia, where he is reported to have committed suicide, because he was deemed by the Persians the cause of their defeat on that occasion.

Of the Macedonians, about twenty-five of the Companions were killed at the first onset, brazen statues of whom we erected at Dium, executed by Lysippus,[13] at Alexander's order. The same sculptor also executed a statue of Alexander himself, being chosen by him for the work in preference to all other artists. Of the other cavalry over sixty were slain, and of the infantry about thirty. These were buried by Alexander the next day, together with their arms and other decorations. To their parents and children he granted exemption from imposts on agricultural produce, and he relieved them from all personal services and taxes upon property. He also exhibited great solicitude in regard to the wounded, for he himself visited each man, looked at their wounds, and inquired how and in the performance of what duty they had received them, allowing them both to speak and brag of their own deeds. He also buried the Persian commanders and the Greek mercenaries who were killed fighting on the side of the enemy. But as many of them as he took prisoners he bound in fetters and sent them away to Macedonia to till the soil, because, though they were Greeks, they were fighting against Greece on behalf of the foreigners in opposition to the decrees which the Greeks had made in their federal council. To Athens also he sent 300 suits of Persian armour to be hung up in the Acropolis as a votive offering to Athena, and ordered this inscription to be fixed over them, "Alexander, son of Philip, and all the Greeks except the Lacedaemonians, present this offering from the spoils taken from the foreigners inhabiting Asia."

17. Having appointed Calas to the post of viceroy of the territory which had been under the rule of Arsites, and having commanded the inhabitants to pay to him the same tribute which they had paid to Darius, he ordered as many of the natives as came down from the mountains and surrendered to him to depart to their several abodes. He also

---

[13] Lysippus of Sicyon was one of the most famous of sculptors. Alexander published an edict that no one should paint his portrait but Apelles, that no one should make a statue of him but Lysippus, and that no one should engrave him on seal-rings but Pyrgoteles.

acquitted the people of Zeleia of blame, because he knew they had been compelled to assist the Persians in the war. He then despatched Parmenio to occupy Dascylium, which he easily performed; for the garrison evacuated it. He himself advanced towards Sardis; and when he was about nine miles from that city, he was met by Mithrines, the commandant of the garrison in the Acropolis, accompanied by the most influential of the citizens of Sardis. The latter surrendered the city into his hands, and the Mithrines the fortress and the money laid up in it. Alexander encamped near the river Hermus, which is about two and one-half miles from Sardis; but he sent Amyntas, son of Andromenes, to occupy the citadel of Sardis. He took Mithrines with him, treating him with honour; and granted the Sardians and other Lydians the privilege of enjoying the ancient laws of Lydia, and permitted them to be free. He then ascended into the citadel, which was garrisoned by the Persians. And the position seemed to him a strong one; for it was very lofty, precipitous on every side, and fenced round by a triple wall. He therefore resolved to build a temple to the Olympian Zeus on the hill, and to erect an altar in it; but while he was considering which part of the hill was the most suitable site, suddenly a winter storm arose, though it was the summer season, loud claps of thunder were heard, and rain fell on the spot where the palace of the kings of Lydia had stood. From this Alexander thought that the deity had revealed to him where the temple to Zeus ought to be built; and he gave orders accordingly. He left Pausanias, one of the Companions, to be superintendent of the citadel of Sardis, Nicias to supervise the collection of the tribute and taxes, and Asander, son of Philotas, to be superintendent of Lydia and the rest of the dominion of Spithridates, giving him as large a number of cavalry and light-armed infantry as seemed sufficient for present emergencies. He also sent Calas and Alexander, son of Aeropus, into the country of Memnon, in command of the Peloponnesians and most of the other Grecian allies, except the Argives, who had been left behind to guard the citadel of Sardis.

Meantime, when the news of the cavalry battle was spread abroad, the Grecian mercenaries who formed the garrison of Ephesus, seized two of the Ephesian triremes and set off in flight. They were accompanied by Amyntas, son of Antiochus, who had fled from Alexander out of Macedonia, not because he had received any injury from the king, but from ill-will to him, and thinking it not unlikely that he should suffer some ill-treatment from him. On the fourth day Alexander arrived at Ephesus, where he recalled from exile all the men who had been banished from the city on account of their adherence to him; and having broken up the oligarchy, he established a democratic form of govern-

ment there. He also ordered the Ephesians to contribute to Artemis all
the tribute which they were in the habit of paying to the Persians.
When the people of Ephesus were relieved of their dread of the oligarchs, they rushed headlong to kill the men who had brought Memnon
into the city, as also those who had pillaged the temple of Artemis, and
those who had thrown down the statue of Philip which was in the temple, and those who had dug up and carried off from the tomb in the market place the bones of Heropythus, the liberator of their city. They also
led Syrphax, and his son Pelagon, and the sons of Syrphax' brothers
out of the temple and stoned them to death. But Alexander prevented
them making any further quest of the rest of the oligarchs for the purpose of wreaking their vengeance upon them; for he knew that if the
people were not checked, they would kill the innocent along with the
guilty, some from hatred, and others for the sake of seizing their property. At this time Alexander gained great popularity both by his general course of action and especially by what he did at Ephesus.

18. Men now came to him both from Magnesia and Tralles, offering
to surrender those cities; and to them he sent Parmenio, giving him
2,500 infantry from the Grecian auxiliaries, an equal number of Macedonians, and about 200 of the Cavalry Companions. He also sent Lysimachus, son of Agathocles, with an equal force to the Aeolic cities, and
to as many of the Ionic cities as were still under the Persians. He was
ordered to break up the oligarchies everywhere, to set up a democratic
form of government, to restore their own laws to each of the cities, and
to remit the tribute which they were accustomed to pay to the foreigners.
But Alexander himself remained behind at Ephesus, where he offered a
sacrifice to Artemis and conducted a procession in her honour with the
whole of his army fully armed and marshalled for battle.

On the following day he took the rest of his infantry, the archers,
the Agrianians, the Thracian cavalry, the royal squadron of the Companions, and three other squadrons in addition, and set out for Miletus.
At his first assault he captured that which was called the outer city;
for the garrison had evacuated it. There he encamped and resolved to
blockade the inner city; for Hegesistratus, to whom the king Darius
had entrusted the command of the garrison in Miletus, kept on sending
letters before this to Alexander, offering to surrender Miletus to him.
But then, having regained his courage from the fact that the Persian
fleet was not far off, he made up his mind to preserve the city for Darius.
But Nicanor, the commander of the Grecian fleet, anticipated the Persians by sailing into the port of Miletus three days before they approached; and with 160 ships he anchored at the island of Lade, which
lies near Miletus. The Persian ships arriving too late, and the admirals

discovering that Nicanor had occupied the anchorage at Lade before them, they took moorings near Mount Mycale. Alexander had forestalled them in seizing the island, not only by mooring his ships near it, but also by transporting into it the Thracians and about 4,000 of the other auxiliary troops. The ships of the foreigners were about 400 in number.

Notwithstanding the superiority of the Persian fleet, Parmenio advised Alexander to fight a sea-battle, expecting that the Greeks would be victorious with their fleet both for other reasons and especially because an omen from the deity made him confident of the result; for an eagle had been seen sitting upon the shore, opposite the sterns of Alexander's ships. He also urged that if they won the battle, they would reap a great advantage from it in regard to their main object in the war; and if they were beaten, their defeat would not be of any great moment; for even as it was, the Persians held the sovereignty of the sea. He added that he was willing to go on board the fleet himself and to share the danger. However, Alexander replied that Parmenio was mistaken in his judgment, and in his improbable interpretation of the sign. For it would be rash for him with a few ships to fight a battle against a fleet far more numerous than his own, and with his unpractised naval force to contend against the disciplined fleet of the Cyprians and Phoenicians. Besides, he did not wish to deliver over to the foreigners on so unstable an element the advantage which the Macedonians derived from their skill and courage; and if they were beaten in a sea-battle, their defeat would be no small damage to their first prestige in the war, both for other reasons, and especially because the Greeks, being animated with courage at the news of his naval defeat, would attempt to effect a revolution. Taking all these things into consideration, he declared that he did not think that it was a suitable time for fighting a sea-battle; and for his part, he expounded the divine omen in a different way. He admitted that the eagle was in his favour; but as it was seen sitting on the land, it seemed to him rather to be a sign that he should get the mastery over the Persian fleet by defeating their army on land.

19. At this time Glaucippus, one of the most notable men in Miletus, was sent out to Alexander by the people and the Grecian mercenaries, to whom rather than to the citizens the town had been entrusted, to tell him that the Milesians were willing to make their walls and harbours free to him and the Persians in common; and on these terms to demand that he should raise the siege. But Alexander ordered Glaucippus to depart without delay into the city, and to tell the citizens to prepare for a battle at daybreak. He then stationed his military engines near the wall, and having in a short time partly broken and partly shaken down

a large piece of it, he led his army near, that the men might enter wherever the wall had been thrown down or shaken. The Persians from Mycale were following close upon them and could almost see their friends and allies being besieged. In the meantime, Nicanor, observing from Lade Alexander's commencement of the attack, began to sail into the harbour of Miletus, rowing along the shore; and mooring his triremes as close as possible together, with their prows facing the enemy, across the narrowest part of the mouth of the harbour, he shut off the Persian fleet from the port and made it impossible for the Persians to aid the Milesians. Then the Macedonians from all sides pressed close upon the citizens and the Grecian mercenaries, who took to flight; some of them, casting themselves into the sea, floated along upon their shields with the hollow upwards to an unnamed islet which lies near the city; others getting into their skiffs and hastening to get the start of the Macedonian triremes, were captured by them at the mouth of the harbour. But the majority of them were slain in the city itself. As soon as Alexander had got possession of the city, he sailed against those who had fled for refuge into the island, ordering the men to carry ladders upon the prows of the triremes, with the intention of effecting a landing along the cliffs of the island, as one would mount a wall. But when he saw that the men on the island were resolved to run every risk, he was moved with pity for them, because they appeared to him both brave and loyal; wherefore he made a truce with them on the condition that they would serve as his soldiers. These Grecian mercenaries were about 300 in number. He likewise pardoned all the citizens of Miletus who had escaped death in the capture of the city, and he granted them their freedom.

The foreigners used to start from Mycale every day and sail up to the Grecian fleet, hoping to induce them to accept the challenge and come forth to a battle; but during the night they used to moor their vessels near Mycale, which was an inconvenient station, because they were under the necessity of fetching water from the mouth of the river Maeander, a great way off. Alexander guarded the harbour of Miletus with his ships, in order to prevent the foreigners from forcing an entrance; and at the same time he sent Philotas to Mycale in command of the cavalry and three regiments of infantry, with instructions to prevent the men in the ships from landing. Accordingly, they, being through the scarcity of fresh water and of the other necessaries of life as good as besieged in their ships, sailed away to Samos; where furnishing themselves with food, they sailed back again to Miletus. They then drew up most of their ships in front of the harbour on the deep sea, with the hope that they might in some way or other induce the Macedonians to come out into the open sea. Five of their ships sailed into the roadstead which lay between the island of Lade and the camp, expecting to surprise Alexander's ships while empty of their crews; for they had ascertained that the sailors for the most part were dispersed from the ships, some to gather fuel, others to collect provisions, and others being arranged in foraging parties. And indeed it happened that a number of the sailors were absent; but as soon as Alexander observed the five Persian ships sailing towards him, he manned ten ships with the sailors who happened to be at hand, and sent them with all speed against them with orders to attack prow to prow. No sooner did the men in the five Persian ships see the Macedonians putting out against them, contrary to their expectation, than they immediately tacked about, though far off, and fled to the rest of their fleet. However, the ship of the Iassians, not being a fast sailer, was captured in the flight, men and all; but the other four succeeded in escaping to their own triremes. After this the Persians sailed away from Miletus without effecting anything.

20. Alexander now resolved to disband his fleet, partly from lack of money at the time, and partly because he saw that his own fleet was not a match in battle for that of the Persians. On this account he was unwilling to run the risk of losing even a part of his armament. Besides, he considered that now he was occupying Asia with his land force he would no longer be in need of a fleet; and that he would be able to break up that of the Persians, if he captured the maritime cities; since they would neither have any ports from which they could recruit their crews, nor any harbour in Asia to which they could bring their ships. Thus he explained the omen of the eagle to signify that he should get the mastery over the enemy's ships by his land force. After doing this, he set forth into Caria, because it was reported that a considerable force, both of foreigners and of Grecian auxiliaries, had collected in Halicarnassus. Having taken all the cities between Miletus and Halicarnassus as soon as he approached them, he encamped near the latter city, at a distance from it of about half a mile, as if he expected a long siege. For the natural position of the place made it strong; and wherever there seemed to be any deficiency in regard to security, it had been entirely supplied long before by Memnon, who was there in person, having now been proclaimed by Darius governor of lower Asia and commander of the entire fleet. Many Grecian mercenary soldiers had been left in the city, as well as many Persian troops; the triremes also were moored in the harbour, so that the sailors might render him valuable aid in the operations. On the first day of the siege, while Alexander was leading his men up to the wall in the direction of the gate leading towards Mylasa, the men in the city made a sortie, and a skirmish took place; but Alexander's

men making a rush upon them repulsed them with ease, and shut them up in the city. A few days after this, the king took the shield-bearing guards, the Cavalry Companions, the infantry regiments of Amyntas, Perdiccas and Meleager, and in addition to these the archers and Agrianians, and went round to the part of the city which is in the direction of Myndus, both for the purpose of inspecting the wall, to see if perchance it could be more easily assaulted there than elsewhere; and at the same time to see if he could get hold of Myndus by a sudden and secret attack. For he thought that if Myndus became his own, it would be no small help in the siege of Halicarnassus; moreover, an offer to surrender had been made by the Myndians if he would approach the town secretly, under the cover of night. About midnight, therefore, he approached the wall, according to the plan agreed on; but as no sign of surrender was made by the men within, and though he had with him no military engines or ladders, inasmuch as he had not set out to besiege the town, but an offer to betray it was made to him, he nevertheless led the Macedonian phalanx near and ordered them to undermine the wall. They threw down one of the towers, which, however, in its fall did not make a breach in the wall. But the men in the city stoutly defending themselves, and at the same time many from Halicarnassus having already come to their aid by sea, made it impossible for Alexander to capture Myndus either by surprise or sudden assault. Wherefore he returned without accomplishing any of the plans for which he had set out, and devoted himself once more to the siege of Halicarnassus.

In the first place he filled up with earth the ditch which the enemy had dug in front of the city, about forty-five feet wide and twenty-two feet deep; so that it might be easy to bring forward the towers, from which he intended to discharge missiles against the defenders of the wall; and that he might bring up the other engines with which he was planning to batter the wall down. He easily filled up the ditch, and the towers were then brought forward. But the men in Halicarnassus made a sally by night with the design of setting fire both to the towers and the other engines which had been brought up to the wall, or were nearly brought up to it. They were, however, easily repelled and shut up again within the walls by the Macedonians who were guarding the engines, and by others who were aroused by the noise of the struggle and who came to their aid. Neoptolemus, the brother of Arrhabaeus, son of Amyntas, one of those who had deserted to Darius, was killed, with about 170 others of the enemy. Of Alexander's soldiers sixteen were killed and 300 wounded; for the sally being made in the night, they were less able to guard themselves from being wounded.

21. A few days after this, two Macedonian hoplites of the brigade of Perdiccas, living in the same tent and being messmates, happened in the course of conversation each to be extolling himself and his own exploits. Hence a quarrel arose between them as to which of them was the braver, and, being somewhat inflamed with wine, they agreed to arm themselves, and of their own accord go and assault the wall facing the citadel, which for the most part was turned towards Mylasa. This they did rather to make a display of their own valour than to engage in a dangerous conflict with the enemy. Some of the men in the city, however, perceiving that there were only two of them, and that they were approaching the wall inconsiderately, rushed out upon them; but they slew those who came near, and hurled darts at those who stood at a distance. At last, however, they were overmatched both by the number of their assailants and the disadvantage of their own position; for the enemy made the attack upon them, and threw darts at them from a higher level. Meanwhile some other men from the brigade of Perdiccas, and others from Halicarnassus, rushed out against each other; and a sharp contest ensued near the wall. Those who had made the sally from the city were driven back, and again shut up within the gates by the Macedonians. The city also narrowly escaped capture; for the walls at that time were not under strict guard, and two towers, with the whole intermediate space, having already fallen to the ground, would have offered an easy entrance within the wall to the army, if the whole of it had undertaken the task. The third tower, which had been thoroughly shaken, would likewise have been easily thrown down if it had been undermined; but the enemy easily succeeded in building inside a crescent-shaped brick wall to take the place of the one which had fallen. This they were able to do so quickly because of the multitude of hands at their disposal. On the following day Alexander brought his engines up to this wall also; and the men in the city made another sally to set them on fire. A part of the wicker-work shed near the wall and a piece of one of the wooden towers were burnt, but the rest were protected by Philotas and Hellanicus, to whom the charge of them had been committed. But as soon as those who were making the sally saw Alexander, the men who had come out to render aid by holding torches threw them away, and the majority of them cast away their arms and fled within the walls of the city. And yet at first they had the advantage from the nature of their position, which was commanding on account of its height; for not only did they cast missiles right in front against the men who were fighting in defence of the engines, but also from the towers which alone had been left standing at each end of the battered-down wall they were able to cast them against the sides, and almost against the backs. of those who

were assaulting the wall which had just been built in place of the ruined one.

22. A few days after this, when Alexander again brought his military engines up to the inner brick wall, and was himself superintending the work, a sortie in mass was made from the city, some advancing by the breach in the wall, where Alexander himself was posted, others by the triple gate, where the Macedonians did not at all expect them. The first party cast torches and other combustibles at the engines, in order to set them on fire and to defy the engineers excessively. But when the men around Alexander attacked them vigorously, hurling great stones with the engines from the towers, and launching darts at them, they were easily put to rout and fled into the city; and as a great number of them had sallied forth and great audacity had been exhibited in the fight, no small slaughter took place. For some of them were slain fighting hand-to-hand with the Macedonians, others were killed near the ruins of the wall, because the breach was too narrow for such a multitude to pass through, and the fallen portions of the wall made their passage difficult. The second party, which sallied forth by the triple gate, was met by Ptolemy,[14] one of the royal body-guards, who had with him the regiments of Addaeus and Timander and some of the light-armed troops. These soldiers likewise easily put the men of the city to rout; but as the latter in their retreat were fleeing over a narrow bridge which had been made over the ditch, they had the misfortune to break it down by the weight of their multitude. Many of them fell into the ditch, some of whom were trampled to death by their own comrades, and others were struck by the Macedonians from above. A very great slaughter was also made at the very gates, because they were shut before the proper time from a feeling of terror. For the enemy, being afraid that the Macedonians, who were close upon the fugitives, would rush in with them, shut many of their friends out, who were slain by the Macedonians near the very walls. The city narrowly escaped capture; indeed it would have been taken, had not Alexander called back his army, to see if some friendly sign of surrender would be made by the Halicarnassians; for he was still desirous of saving their city. Of the men in the city about 1,000 were slain; and of Alexander's men about forty, among whom were Ptolemy, one of the king's body-guards, Clearchus, a captain of the archers, Addaeus, who had the command of 1,000 infantry, and other Macedonians of no mean position.

23. Then Orontobates and Memnon, the commanders of the Persians, met and decided from the state of affairs that they could not hold out

[14] There were at least four generals in Alexander's army of this name. The one here mentioned was probably not the famous son of Lagus.

long against the siege, seeing that part of the wall had already fallen
down and part had been battered and weakened, and that many of their
soldiers had either perished in the sorties or been wounded and disabled.
Taking these things into consideration, about the second watch of the
night they set fire to the wooden tower which they had themselves built
to resist the enemy's military engines, and to the magazines in which
their weapons were stored. They also cast fire into the houses near the
wall; and others were burned by the flames, which were carried with
great fury from the magazines and the tower by the wind bearing in that
direction. Some of the enemy then withdrew to the stronghold in the
island, and others to another fortress called Salmacis. When this was
reported to Alexander by some deserters from the incendiaries, and he
himself could see the raging fire, though the occurrence took place about
midnight, yet he led out the Macedonians and slew those who were still
engaged in setting fire to the city. But he issued orders to preserve all
the Halicarnassians who should be taken in their houses. As soon as
the daylight appeared he could discern the strongholds which the Persians and the Grecian mercenaries had occupied; but he decided not to
besiege these, considering that he would meet with no small delay beleaguering them, owing to the natural strength of the sites, and thinking that they would be of little importance to him now that he had
captured the whole city.

Wherefore, burying the dead in the night, he ordered the men who
had been placed in charge of the military engines to convey them to
Tralles. He himself marched into Phrygia, after razing the city to the
ground, and leaving 3,000 Grecian infantry and 200 cavalry as a guard
both of this place and of the rest of Caria, under the command of Ptolemy. He appointed Ada to act as his viceroy of the whole of Caria.[15]
This queen was daughter of Hecatomnus and wife of Hidrieus, who,
though he was her brother, lived with her in wedlock, according to the
custom of the Carians. When Hidrieus was dying, he confided the administration of affairs to her, for it had been a custom in Asia, ever since
the time of Semiramis, even for women to rule men. But Pixodarus expelled her from the rule, and seized the administration of affairs himself. On the death of Pixodarus, his son-in-law Orontobates was sent
by the king of the Persians to rule over the Carians. Ada retained Alinda
alone, the strongest place in Caria; and when Alexander invaded Caria
she went to meet him, offering to surrender Alinda to him, and adopting

---

[15] Hecatomnus, king of Caria, left three sons, Mausolus, Hidrieus, and Pixodarus;
and two daughters, Artemisia and Ada. Artemisia married Mausolus, and Ada married Hidrieus. All these children succeeded their father in the sovereignty, Pixodarus
being the last surviving son.

him as her son. Alexander confided Alinda to her, and did not think the title of son unworthy of his acceptance; moreover, when he had captured Halicarnassus and become master of the rest of Caria, he granted her the privilege of ruling over the whole country.

24. Some of the Macedonians who served in Alexander's army had married just before he undertook the expedition. He thought that he ought not to treat these men with neglect, and therefore sent them back from Caria to spend the winter in Macedonia with their wives. He placed them under the command of Ptolemy, son of Seleucus, one of the royal body-guards, and of the two generals Coenus, son of Polemocrates, and Meleager, son of Neoptolemus, because they were also newly married. He gave these officers instructions to levy as many horse and foot soldiers as they could from the country, when they returned to him and brought back the men who had been sent away with them. By this act more than by any other Alexander acquired popularity among the Macedonians. He also sent Cleander, son of Polemocrates, to levy soldiers in Peloponnesus, and Parmenio to Sardis, giving him the command of a regiment of the Cavalry Companions, the Thessalian cavalry, and the rest of the Grecian allies. He ordered him also to take the waggons to Sardis and to advance from that place into Phrygia.

He himself marched towards Lycia and Pamphylia, in order to gain command of the coast-land, and by that means render the enemy's fleet useless. The first place on his route was Hyparna, a strong position, having a garrison of Grecian mercenaries; but he took it at the first assault, and allowed the Greeks to depart from the citadel under a truce. Then he invaded Lycia and brought over the Telmissians by capitulation; and crossing the river Xanthus, the cities of Pinara, Xanthus, Patara, and about thirty other smaller towns were surrendered to him. Having accomplished this, though it was now the very depth of winter, he invaded the land called Milyas, which is a part of Great Phrygia, but at that time was tributary to Lycia, according to an arrangement made by the Great King. Hither came envoys from the Phaselites, to treat for his friendship, and to crown him with a golden crown; and the majority of the maritime Lycians also sent heralds to him as ambassadors to treat for the same object. He ordered the Phaselites and Lycians to surrender their cities to those who were despatched by him to receive them; and they were all surrendered. He soon afterwards arrived himself at Phaselis, and helped the men of that city to capture a strong fort which had been constructed by the Pisidians to overawe the country, and sallying forth from which those barbarians used to inflict much damage upon the Phaselites who tilled the land.

25. While the king was still near Phaselis he received information

that Alexander, son of Aeropus, who was not only one of the Companions, but also at that time commander of the Thessalian horse, was conspiring against him. This Alexander was brother of Heromenes and Arrhabaeus, who had taken part in the murder of Philip. At that time King
Alexander pardoned him, though he was accused of complicity with
them, because after Philip's death he was among the first of his friends
to come to him, and, helping him on with his breastplate, accompanied
him to the palace. The king afterwards showed him honour at his court,
sent him as general into Thrace; and when Calas the commander of the
Thessalian horse was sent away to a satrapy he was appointed to that
general's command. The details of the conspiracy were reported as follows: When Amyntas deserted to Darius, he conveyed to him certain
messages and a letter from this Alexander. Darius then sent Sisines, one
of his own faithful Persian courtiers, down to the sea-coast, under pretence of going to Atizyes, viceroy of Phrygia, but really to communicate
with this Alexander, and to give him pledges, that if he would kill king
Alexander, Darius would appoint him king of Macedonia, and would
give him 1,000 talents of gold in addition to the kingdom. But Sisines,
being captured by Parmenio, told him the real object of his mission.
Parmenio sent him immediately under guard to the king, who obtained
the same intelligence from him. The king then, having collected his
friends, proposed to them as a subject for deliberation what decision
he ought to make in regard to this Alexander. The Companions thought
that formerly he had not resolved wisely in confiding the best part of his
cavalry to a faithless man, and that now it was advisable to put him
out of the way as speedily as possible, before he became even more
popular among the Thessalians and should try to effect some revolutionary plan with their aid. Moreover they were terrified by a certain divine
portent. For, while Alexander the king was still besieging Halicarnassus,
it is said that he was once taking rest at mid-day, when a swallow flew
about over his head loudly twittering, and perched now on this side of
his couch and now on that, chirping more noisily than usual. On account
of his fatigue he could not be roused from sleep, but being disquieted
by the sound he brushed her away gently with his hand. But though
struck she was so far from trying to escape, that she perched upon the
very head of the king, and did not desist until he was wide awake. Thinking the affair of the swallow of no trivial import, he communicated it
to a soothsayer, Aristander the Telmissian, who told him that it signified
a plot formed by one of his friends. He said it also signified that the plot
would be discovered, because the swallow was a bird fond of man's society and well disposed to him as well as more loquacious than any other
bird. Therefore, comparing this with the depositions of the Persian, the

king sent Amphoterus, son of Alexander and brother of Craterus, to Parmenio; and with him he sent some Pergaeans to show him the way. Amphoterus, putting on a native dress, so that he should not be recognised on the road, reached Parmenio by stealth. He did not carry a letter from Alexander, because it did not appear to the king advisable to write openly about any such matter; but he reported the message entrusted to him by word of mouth. Consequently this Alexander was arrested and kept under guard.[16]

26. Alexander then, moving from Phaselis, sent part of his army to Perga through the mountains, where the Thracians had levelled a road for him by a route which was otherwise difficult and long. But he himself led his own brigade by the beach along the sea, where there is no route, except when the north wind blows. But if the south wind prevails it is impossible to journey by the beach. At that time, after a strong south wind, the north winds blew, and rendered his passage easy and quick, not without the divine intervention, as both he and his men interpreted. As he was advancing from Perga, he was met on the road by envoys from the Aspendians with full powers, who offered to surrender their city, but begged him not lead a garrison into it. Having gained their request in regard to the garrison, they went back; but he ordered them to give him fifty talents as pay for his army, as well as the horses which they were rearing as tribute to Darius. Having agreed with him about the money, and having likewise promised to hand over the horses, they departed.

Alexander then marched to Side, the inhabitants of which were Cymaeans from Cyme, in Aeolis. These people give the following account of themselves, saying that their ancestors starting from Cyme arrived in that country, and disembarked to found a settlement. They immediately forgot the Grecian language, and forthwith began to utter a foreign speech, not, indeed, that of the neighbouring barbarians, but a speech peculiar to themselves, which had never before existed. From that time the Sidetans used to speak a foreign language unlike that of the neighbouring nations. Having left a garrison in Side, Alexander advanced to Syllium, a strong place, containing a garrison of Grecian mercenaries as well as of native barbarians themselves. But he was unable to take Syllium offhand by a sudden assault, for he was informed on his march that the Aspendians refused to perform any of their agreements, and would neither deliver the horses to those who were sent to receive them, nor pay up the money; but that they had collected their property out of the fields into the city, shut their gates against his men,

[16] He was put to death, 330 B.C., immediately after the execution of Philotas.

and were repairing their walls where they had become dilapidated. Hearing this, he marched off to Aspendus.

27. The greater part of Aspendus had been built upon a strong and precipitous rock, at the very foot of which flows the river Eurymedon; but round the rock, on the low ground, were many of the citizens' houses, surrounded by a small wall. As soon as they ascertained that Alexander was approaching, the inhabitants deserted the wall and the houses situated on the low ground, which they thought they were unable to protect; and they fled in a body to the rock. When he arrived with his forces, he passed within the deserted wall and took up his quarters in the houses which had been abandoned by the Aspendians. When these saw that Alexander himself had come, contrary to their expectation, and that his camp was encircling them on all sides, they sent envoys to him, entreating him to form an agreement with them on the former terms. Alexander, considering the strength of the place, and how unprepared he was to undertake a long siege, entered into an agreement with them, though not on the same terms as before. For he ordered them to give him their most influential men as hostages, to hand over the horses which they had formerly agreed to give him, and 100 talents instead of fifty, to obey the viceroy appointed by him, and to pay an annual tribute to the Macedonians. Moreover he directed an inquiry to be held about the land which they were accused of holding by force, though it belonged of right to their neighbours.

When all these concessions had been made to him, he marched away to Perga, and thence set out for Phrygia, his route leading him past the city of Termessus. The people of this city are foreigners, of the Pisidian race, inhabiting a very lofty place, precipitous on every side; and the road to the city is a difficult one. For a mountain stretches from the city as far as the road, where it suddenly stops short; and over against it rises another mountain, no less precipitous. These mountains form gates, as it were, upon the road; and it is possible for those who occupy these eminences even with a small guard to render the passage impracticable. On this occasion the Termessians had come out in a body, and were occupying both the mountains; seeing which, Alexander ordered the Macedonians to encamp there, armed as they were, imagining that the Termessians would not remain in a body when they saw them bivouacking, but that most of them would withdraw into their city, which was near, leaving upon the mountains only sufficient men to form a guard. And it turned out just as he conjectured; for most of them retired, and only a guard remained. He forthwith took the archers, the regiments of javelin-throwers, and the lighter hoplites, and led them against those who were guarding the pass. When these were attacked with missiles, they did not stand their ground, but abandoned the position. Alexander then passed through the defile, and encamped near the city.

28. While he was there, ambassadors came to him from the Selgians, who are also Pisidian barbarians, inhabiting a large city, and being war-like. Because they happened to be inveterate enemies to the Termessians they had despatched this embassy to Alexander, to treat for his friend-ship. He made a treaty with them, and from this time found them faith-ful allies in all his proceedings. Despairing of being able to capture Termessus without a great loss of time, he marched on to Sagalassus. This was also a large city, inhabited likewise by Pisidians; and though all the Pisidians are warlike, the men of this city were deemed the most so. On this occasion they had occupied the hill in front of the city, because it was no less strong than the walls, from which to ward off the enemy; and there they were awaiting him. But Alexander drew up the phalanx of Macedonians in the following way: on the right wing, where he had himself taken up his position, he held the shield-bearing guards, and next to these he extended the foot Companions as far as the left wing, in the order that each of the generals had precedence in the array that day. On the left wing he stationed Amyntas, son of Arrhabaeus, as commander. In front of his right wing were posted the archers and Agrianians, and in front of the left wing the Thracian javelin-throwers under the command of Sitalces. But the cavalry were no use to him in a place so rough and unfavourable. The Termessians also had come to the aid of the Pisidians, and arrayed themselves with them. Alexander had already made an attack upon the mountain which the Pisidians were occupying, advancing up the most abrupt part of the ascent, when the barbarians in column attacked him on both wings, in a place where it was very easy for themselves to advance, but where the route was very difficult for their enemy. The archers, who were the first to approach, were put to rout, inasmuch as they were insufficiently armed; but the Agrianians stood their ground, for the Macedonian phalanx was already drawing near, at the head of which Alexander himself was seen. When the battle became a hand-to-hand one, though the barbarians were des-titute of armour, they rushed against the Macedonian hoplites, and fell wounded on all sides. Then, indeed, they gave way, after about 500 of them had been killed. As they were nimble and well-acquainted with the locality, they effected their retreat without difficulty; whereas the Mace-donians, on account of the heaviness of their arms and their ignorance of the roads, dared not pursue them vigorously. Alexander therefore held off from the fugitives, and took their city by storm. Of those with him, Cleander, the general of the archers, and about twenty others were slain.

Alexander then marched against the rest of the Pisidians, and took some of their strongholds by force; others he won over to him by granting them terms of capitulation.

29. Thence he went into Phrygia, passing by the lake called Ascania, in which salt is naturally solidified. The natives use this salt, and do not need the sea at all for this article. On the fifth day of his march, he arrived at Celaenae, in which city there was a fortified rock, precipitous on all sides. This citadel was occupied by the viceroy of Phrygia with a garrison of 1,000 Carians and 100 Grecian mercenaries. These men despatched ambassadors to Alexander, promising to surrender the place to him, if help did not reach them by a day which had been agreed upon with them, naming the day. This arrangement seemed to Alexander more advantageous than to besiege the fortified rock, which was inaccessible on all sides to attack. At Celaenae he left a garrison of 1,500 soldiers. Remaining here ten days, he appointed Antigonus, son of Philip,[17] viceroy of Phrygia; placed Balacrus, son of Amyntas, as general over the Grecian allies in place of Antigonus; and then directed his march to Gordium. He sent an order to Parmenio to meet him there with the forces under his command; an order which that general obeyed. The newly-married men also, who had been despatched to Macedonia, now arrived at Gordium, and with them another army which had been levied, and put under the command of Ptolemy, son of Seleucus, Coenus, son of Polemocrates, and Meleager, son of Neoptolemus. This army consisted of 3,000 Macedonian foot-soldiers and 300 horse-soldiers, 200 Thessalian cavalry, and 150 Eleans under the command of Alcias the Elean.

Gordium is in the Phrygia which lies near the Hellespont, and is situated upon the river Sangarius, which takes its rise in Phrygia, but, flowing through the land of the Bithynian Thracians, falls into the Euxine Sea. Here an embassy reached Alexander from the Athenians, beseeching him to release to them the Athenian prisoners who had been captured at the river Granicus, serving in the army of the Persians, and were then in Macedonia serving in chains with the 2,000 others captured in that battle. The envoys departed without obtaining their request on behalf of the prisoners for the present. For Alexander did not think it safe, while the war against the Persian was still going on, to relax in the slightest degree the terror with which he inspired the Greeks, who did not deem it unbecoming for them to serve as soldiers on behalf of the foreigners against Greece. However, he replied that whenever his present enterprise had been successfully achieved, they might then come as ambassadors to treat on behalf of the same persons.

[17] Antigonus, called the One-eyed, was father of Demetrius Poliorcetes. On the division of Alexander's empire he received Phrygia, Lycia, and Pamphylia. He eventually acquired the whole of Asia Minor; but was defeated and slain at Ipsus by the allied forces of Cassander, Lysimachus, Ptolemy, and Seleucus (301 B.C.).

BOOK II

1. Soon after this, Memnon, whom King Darius had appointed commander of the whole fleet and of the entire sea-coast, with the design of moving the seat of war into Macedonia and Greece, acquired possession of Chios, which was surrendered to him by treachery. Thence he sailed to Lesbos and brought over to his side all the cities of the island, except Mytilene, the inhabitants of which gave no heed to him. When he had gained these cities over, he turned his attention to Mytilene; and walling off the city from the rest of the island by constructing a double stockade from sea to sea, he easily got the mastery on the land side by building five camps. A part of his fleet guarded their harbour, and, intercepting the ships passing by, he kept the rest of his fleet as a guard off Sigrium, the headland of Lesbos, where is the best landing-place for trading vessels from Chios, Geraestus, and Malea. By this means he deprived the Mytilenaeans of all hope of aid by sea. But hereupon he himself fell ill and died, and his death at that crisis was exceedingly injurious to the king's interests. Nevertheless Autophradates, and Pharnabazus, son of Artabazus, prosecuted the siege with vigour. To the latter indeed, Memnon, when dying, had entrusted his command, as he was his sister's son, till Darius should come to some decision on the matter. The Mytilenaeans, therefore, being excluded from the land, and being blockaded on the sea by many ships lying at anchor, sent to Pharnabazus and came to the following agreement: That the auxiliary troops which had come to their aid from Alexander should depart, that the citizens should demolish the pillars on which the treaty made by them with Alexander was inscribed, that they should become allies of Darius on the terms of the peace which was made with King Darius at the instigation of Antalcidas,[1] and that their exiles should return from banishment on condition of receiving back half the property which they possessed when they were banished. Upon these terms the compact was made between the Mytilenaeans and the Persians. But as soon as Pharnabazus and Autophradates once got within the city, they introduced a garrison with Lycomedes, a Rhodian, as its commandant. They also appointed Diogenes, one of the exiles, to be despot of the city, and exacted money from the Mytilenaeans, taking part of it by violence for themselves from

[1] This treaty was concluded by the Spartans with the king of Persia, 387 B.C.

438

the wealthy citizens, and laying the rest as a tax upon the community.

2. After accomplishing this, Pharnabazus sailed to Lycia, taking with him the Grecian mercenaries; but Autophradates sailed to the other islands. Meantime Darius sent Thymondas, son of Mentor, down to the maritime districts, to take over the Grecian auxiliaries from Pharnabazus and to lead them up to him; and to tell Pharnabazus to assume the command of all whom Memnon had ruled. So Pharnabazus handed over to him the Grecian auxiliaries and then sailed to join Autophradates and the fleet. When they met, they despatched Datames, a Persian, with ten ships to the islands called Cyclades, while they with 100 sailed to Tenedus. Having sailed into the harbour of Tenedus which is called Boreus, they sent a message to the inhabitants, commanding them to demolish the pillars on which the treaty made by them with Alexander and the Greeks was inscribed, and to observe in regard to Darius the terms of the peace which they had ratified with the king of Persia at the advice of Antalcidas. The Tenedians preferred to be on terms of amity with Alexander and the Greeks; but in the present crisis it seemed impossible to save themselves except by yielding to the Persians, since Hegelochus, who had been commissioned by Alexander to collect another naval force, had not yet gathered so large a fleet as to warrant them in expecting any speedy succour from him. Accordingly Pharnabazus made the Tenedians comply with his demands rather from fear than good-will.

Meantime Proteas, son of Andronicus, by command of Antipater, succeeded in collecting ships of war from Euboea and the Peloponnese, so that there might be some protection both for the islands and for Greece itself, if the foreigners attacked them by sea, as it was reported they intended to do. Learning that Datames with ten ships was moored near Siphnus, Proteas set out by night with fifteen from Chalcis on the Euripus, and touching at the island of Cynthus at dawn, he spent the day there in order to get more certain information of the movements of the ten ships, resolving at the same time to fall upon the Phoenicians by night, when he would be likely to strike them with greater terror. Having discovered with certainty that Datames was moored with his ships at Siphnus, he sailed thither while it was still dark, and just at the very dawn fell upon them when they least expected it, and captured eight of the ships, men and all. But Datames, with the other two triremes, escaped by stealth at the beginning of the attack made by the ships with Proteas, and reached the rest of the Persian fleet in safety.

3. When Alexander arrived at Gordium, he was seized with an ardent desire to go up into the citadel, which contained the palace of Gordius and his son Midas. He was also desirous of seeing the waggon of Gordius and the cord of the yoke of this waggon. There was a great deal of talk

about this waggon among the neighbouring population. It was said that Gordius was a poor man among the ancient Phrygians, who had a small piece of land to till, and two yoke of oxen. He used one of these in ploughing and the other to draw the waggon. On one occasion, while he was ploughing, an eagle settled upon the yoke, and remained sitting there until the time came for unyoking the oxen. Being alarmed at the sight, he went to the Telmissian soothsayers to consult them about the sign from the deity; for the Telmissians were skilful in interpreting the meaning of divine manifestations, and the power of divination has been bestowed not only upon the men, but also upon their wives and children from generation to generation. When Gordius was driving his waggon near a certain village of the Telmissians, he met a maiden fetching water from the spring, and to her he related how the sign of the eagle had appeared to him. As she herself was of the prophetic race, she instructed him to return to the very spot and offer sacrifice to Zeus the king. Gordius requested her to accompany him and direct him how to perform the sacrifice. He offered the sacrifice in the way the girl suggested, and afterwards married her. A son was born to them named Midas. When Midas was grown to be a man, handsome and valiant, the Phrygians were harassed by civil discord, and consulting the oracle, they were told that a waggon would bring them a king, who would put an end to their discord. While they were still deliberating about this very matter, Midas arrived with his father and mother, and stopped near the assembly, waggon and all. They, comparing the oracular response with this occurrence, decided that this was the person whom the god told them the waggon would bring. They therefore appointed Midas king; and he, putting an end to their discord, dedicated his father's waggon in the citadel as a thank-offering to Zeus the king for sending the eagle. In addition to this the following saying was current concerning the waggon, that whosoever could loosen the cord of the yoke of this waggon, was destined to gain the rule of Asia. The cord was made of cornel bark, and neither end nor beginning to it could be seen. It is said by some that when Alexander could find out no way to loosen the cord and yet was unwilling to allow it to remain unloosened, lest this should exercise some disturbing influence upon the multitude, he struck it with his sword and cutting it through, said that it had been loosened. But Aristobulus says that he pulled out the pin of the waggon-pole, which was a wooden peg driven right through it, holding the cord together. Having done this, he drew out the yoke from the waggon-pole. How Alexander performed the feat in connection with this cord, I cannot affirm with confidence. At any rate both he and his troops departed from the waggon as if the oracular prediction concerning the loosening of the cord had been fulfilled. Moveover, that very night, the thunder and lightning were signs of its fulfilment; and for this reason Alexander offered sacrifice on the following day to the gods who had revealed the signs and the way to loosen the cord.

4. The next day he set out to Ancyra in Galatia, where he was met by an embassy from the Paphlagonians, offering to surrender their nation to him and to enter into an alliance with him; but they requested him not to invade their land with his forces. He therefore commanded them to submit to the authority of Calas, the viceroy of Phrygia. Marching thence into Cappadocia, he subjugated all that part of it which lies on this side of the river Halys, and much of that which lies beyond it. Having appointed Sabictas viceroy of Cappadocia, he advanced to the gates of Cilicia, and when he arrived at the camp of Cyrus, who went with Xenophon, and saw that the Gates were occupied by a strong guard, he left Parmenio there with the regiments of infantry which were more heavily armed; and about the first watch, taking the shield-bearing guards, the archers, and the Agrianians, he advanced by night to the Gates, in order to fall upon the guards when they least expected it. However, his advance was not unobserved; but his boldness served him equally well, for the guards, perceiving that Alexander was advancing in person, deserted their post and set off in flight. At dawn next day he passed through the Gates with all his forces and descended into Cilicia. Here he was informed that Arsames had previously intended to preserve Tarsus for the Persians; but that when he heard that Alexander had already passed through the Gates, he resolved to abandon the city; and that the Tarsians were therefore afraid he would turn to plunder their city and afterwards evacuate it. Hearing this, Alexander led his cavalry and the lightest of his light infantry to Tarsus with a forced march; consequently Arsames, hearing of his start, fled with speed from Tarsus to King Darius without inflicting any injury upon the city.

Alexander now fell ill from the toils he had undergone, according to the account of Aristobulus; but other authors say that while very hot and in profuse perspiration he leaped into the river Cydnus and swam, being eager to bathe in its water. This river flows through the midst of the city; and as its source is in mount Taurus and it flows through a clear district, it is cold and its water is clear. Alexander therefore was seized with convulsions, accompanied with high fever and continuous sleeplessness. None of the physicians thought he was likely to survive, except Philip, an Acarnanian, a physician in attendance on the king, and very much trusted by him in medical matters, who also enjoyed a great reputation in the army in general affairs. This man wished to administer a purgative draught to Alexander, and the king ordered him to administer it. While Philip was preparing the cup, a letter was given to the king from Parmenio, warning him to beware of Philip; for he heard that the physician had been bribed by Darius to poison Alexander with medicine. But he, having read the letter, and still holding it in his hand, of his own accord took the cup which contained the medicine and gave Philip the letter to read. While Philip was reading the news from Parmenio, Alexander drank the potion. It was at once evident to the king that the physician was acting honourably in giving the medicine, for he was not alarmed at the letter, but only so much the more exhorted the king to obey all the other prescriptions which he might give, promising that his life would be saved if he obeyed his instructions. Alexander was purged by the draught, and his illness then took a favourable turn. He afterwards proved to Philip that he was a faithful friend to him; and to the rest of those about him he proved that he was sure not to be suspicious of his friends personally; and that he could meet death with dauntless courage.

5. After this he sent Parmenio to the other Gates which separate the land of the Cilicians from that of the Assyrians, in order to occupy them before the enemy could do so, and to guard the pass. He gave him the allied infantry, the Grecian mercenaries, the Thracians who were under the command of Sitalces, and the Thessalian cavalry. He afterwards marched from Tarsus, and on the first day arrived at the city of Anchialus. According to report, this city was founded by Sardanapalus the Assyrian: and both from the circumference and from the foundations of the walls it is evident that a large city had been founded and that it had reached a great pitch of power. Also near the wall of Anchialus was the monument of Sardanapalus, upon the top of which stood the statue of that king with the hands joined to each other just as they are joined for clapping. Assyrian letters had been engraved upon it as an inscription, which the Assyrians asserted to be in metre. The meaning which the words expressed was this, "Sardanapalus, son of Anacyndaraxas, built Anchialus and Tarsus in one day; but do thou, O stranger, eat, drink, and play, since all other human things are not worth this;" referring, as in a riddle, to the empty sound which the hands make in clapping. It was also said that the word translated *play* had been expressed by a more lewd one in the Assyrian language.

From Anchialus Alexander went to Soli, into which city he introduced a garrison, and imposed upon the inhabitants a fine of 200 talents of silver, because they were more inclined to favour the Persians than himself. Then, having taken three regiments of Macedonian infantry, all the archers, and the Agrianians, he marched away thence against the Cilicians, who were holding the mountains; and in seven days in all, having expelled some by force, and having brought the rest over by agreement, he marched back to Soli. Here he ascertained that Ptolemy and Asander had gained the mastery over Orontobates the Persian who was guarding the citadel of Halicarnassus, and was also holding Myndus, Caunus, Thera, and Callipolis. He had also brought Cos and Triopium over to his side. They wrote to inform him that Orontobates had been worsted in a great battle, that about 700 of his infantry and fifty of his cavalry had been killed, and not less than 1,000 taken prisoners. In Soli Alexander offered sacrifice to Asclepius, conducting a procession of the entire army, celebrating a torch race, and superintending a gymnastic and musical contest. He granted the Solians the privilege of a democratic constitution; and then marched away to Tarsus, despatching the cavalry under Philotas to march through the Aleian plain to the river Pyramus. But he himself with the infantry and the royal squadron of cavalry came to Magarsus, where he offered sacrifice to the Magarsian Athena. Thence he marched to Mallus, where he rendered to Amphilochus the sacrificial honours due to a hero. He also arrested those who were creating a sedition among the citizens, and thus put a stop to it. He remitted the tribute which they were paying to King Darius, because the Mallotes were a colony of the Argives, and he himself claimed to have sprung from Argos, being one of the descendants of Heracles.

6. While he was still at Mallus, he was informed that Darius was encamped with all his force at Sochi, a place in the land of Assyria, distant about two days' march from the Assyrian Gates. Then indeed he collected the Companions and told them what was reported about Darius and his army. They urged him to lead them on as they were, without delay. At that time he commended them, and broke up the conference; but next day he led them forward against Darius and the Persians. On the second day he passed through the Gates and encamped near the city of Myriandrus; but in the night a heavy tempest and a violent storm of wind and rain occurred which detained him in his camp. Darius, on the other hand, up to this time was delaying with his army, having chosen a plain in the land of Assyria which stretched out in every direction, suitable for the immense size of his army and convenient for the evolutions of cavalry. Amyntas, son of Antiochus, the deserter from Alexander, advised him not to abandon this position, because the open country was favourable to the great multitude of the Persians and the vast quantity of their baggage. So Darius remained. But as Alexander made a long stay at Tarsus on account of his illness, and not a short one at Soli, where he offered sacrifice and conducted his army in procession, and moreover spent some time in marching against the Cilician mountaineers, Darius was induced to swerve from his resolution. He was

also not unwilling to be led to form whatever decision was most agreeable to his own wishes; and being urged on by those who for the gratification of pleasure associated with him, and will associate for their injury with those who for the time are reigning, he came to the conclusion that Alexander was no longer desirous of advancing further, but was shrinking from an encounter on learning that Darius himself was marching against him. On all sides they were urging him on, asserting that he would trample down the army of the Macedonians with his cavalry. Nevertheless, Amyntas, at any rate, confidently affirmed that Alexander would certainly come to any place where he heard Darius might be; and he exhorted him by all means to stay where he was. But the worse advice, because at the immediate time it was more pleasant to hear, prevailed; moreover perhaps he was led by some divine influence into that locality where he derived little advantage from his cavalry and from the very number of his men, javelins and bows, and where he could not even exhibit the mere magnificence of his army, but surrendered to Alexander and his troops an easy victory. For it was already decreed by fate that the Persians should be deprived of the rule of Asia by the Macedonians, just as the Medes had been deprived of it by the Persians, and still earlier the Assyrians by the Medes.

7. Darius crossed the mountain range by what are called the Amanic Gates, and advancing towards Issus, came without being noticed to the rear of Alexander. Having reached Issus, he captured as many of the Macedonians as had been left behind there on account of illness. These he cruelly mutilated and slew. Next day he proceeded to the river Pinarus. As soon as Alexander heard that Darius was in his rear, because the news did not seem to him trustworthy, he embarked some of the Companions in a ship with thirty oars, and sent them back to Issus, to observe whether the report was true. The men who sailed in the thirty-oared ship discovered the Persians encamped there more easily, because the sea in this part takes the form of a bay. They therefore brought back word to Alexander that Darius was at hand. Alexander then called together the generals, the commanders of cavalry, and the leaders of the Grecian allies, and exhorted them to take courage from the dangers which they had already surmounted, asserting that the struggle would be between themselves who had been previously victorious and a foe who had already been beaten; and that the deity was acting the part of general on their behalf better than himself, by putting it into the mind of Darius to move his forces from the spacious plain and shut them up in a narrow place, where there was sufficient room for themselves to deepen their phalanx by marching from front to rear, but where their vast multitude would be useless to the enemy in the battle. He added that their foes

were similar to them neither in strength nor in courage; for the Macedonians, who had long been practised in warlike toils accompanied with danger, were coming into close conflict with Persians and Medes, men who had become enervated by a long course of luxurious ease; and, to crown all, they, being freemen, were about to engage in battle with men who were slaves. He said, moreover, that the Greeks who were coming into conflict with Greeks would not be fighting for the same objects; for those with Darius were braving danger for pay, and that pay not high; whereas, those on their side were voluntarily defending the interests of Greece. Again, of foreigners, the Thracians, Paeonians, Illyrians, and Agrianians, who were the most robust and warlike of men in Europe, were about to be arrayed against the most sluggish and effeminate races of Asia. In addition to all this, Alexander was commanding in the field against Darius. These things he enumerated as evidences of their superiority in the struggle; and then he began to point out the great rewards they would win from the danger to be incurred. For he told them that on that occasion they would overcome, not merely the viceroys of Darius, nor the cavalry drawn up at the Granicus, nor the 20,000 Grecian mercenaries, but all the available forces of the Persians and Medes, as well as all the other races subject to them dwelling in Asia, and the Great King present in person. After this conflict nothing would be left for them to do, except to take possession of all Asia, and to put an end to their many labours. In addition to this, he reminded them of their brilliant achievements in their collective capacity in days gone by; and if any man had individually performed any distinguished feat of valour from love of glory, he mentioned him by name in commendation of the deed. He then recapitulated as modestly as possible his own daring deeds in the various battles. He is also said to have reminded them of Xenophon and the 10,000 men who accompanied him, asserting that the latter were in no way comparable with them either in number or in general excellence. Besides, they had had with them neither Thessalian, Boeotian, Peloponnesian, Macedonian, or Thracian horsemen, nor any of the other kinds of cavalry which were in the Macedonian army; nor had they any archers or slingers except a few Cretans and Rhodians, and even these were got ready by Xenophon on the spur of the moment in the very crisis of danger. And yet they put the king and all his forces to rout close to Babylon itself, and succeeded in reaching the Euxine Sea after defeating all the races which lay in their way as they were marching down thither. He also adduced whatever other arguments were suitable for a great commander to use in order to encourage brave men in such a critical moment before the perils of battle. They urged him to lead them against the foe without delay, coming from all sides to grasp the king's right hand, and encouraging him by their words.

8. Alexander then ordered his soldiers to take their dinner, and having sent a few of his horsemen and archers forward to the Gates to reconnoitre the road in the rear, he took the whole of his army and marched in the night to occupy the pass again. When about midnight he had again got possession of it, he caused the army to rest the remainder of the night there upon the rocks, having posted vigilant sentries. At the approach of dawn he began to descend from the pass along the road; and as long as the space was narrow everywhere, he led his army in column, but when the mountains parted so as to leave a plain between them, he kept on opening out the column into the phalanx, marching one line of heavy armed infantry after another up into line towards the mountain on the right and towards the sea on the left. Up to this time his cavalry had been ranged behind the infantry; but when they advanced into the open country, he began to draw up his army in order of battle. First, upon the right wing near the mountain he placed his infantry guard and the shield-bearers, under the command of Nicanor, son of Parmenio; next to these the regiment of Coenus, and close to them that of Perdiccas. These troops were posted as far as the middle of the heavy-armed infantry to one beginning from the right. On the left wing first stood the regiment of Amyntas, then that of Ptolemy, and close to this that of Meleager. The infantry on the left had been placed under the command of Craterus; but Parmenio held the chief direction of the whole left wing. This general had been ordered not to abandon the sea, so that they might not be surrounded by the foreigners, who were likely to outflank them on all sides by their superior numbers.

But as soon as Darius was certified of Alexander's approach for battle, he conveyed about 30,000 of his cavalry and with them 20,000 of his light-armed infantry across the river Pinarus, in order that he might be able to draw up the rest of his forces with ease. Of the heavy armed infantry, he placed first the 30,000 Greek mercenaries to oppose the phalanx of the Macedonians, and on both sides of these he placed 60,000 of the men called Cardaces, who were also heavy-armed infantry. For the place where they were posted was able to contain only this number in a single phalanx. He also posted 20,000 men near the mountain on their left and facing Alexander's right. Some of these troops were also in the rear of Alexander's army; for the mountain near which they were posted in one part sloped a great way back and formed a sort of bay, like a bay in the sea, and afterwards bending forwards caused the men who had been posted at the foot of it to be behind Alexander's right wing. The remaining multitude of Darius's light-armed and heavy-armed infantry was marshalled by nations to an unserviceable depth and placed behind the Grecian mercenaries and the Persian army arranged in phalanx. The whole of the army with Darius was said to number about 600,000 fighting men.

As Alexander advanced, he found that the ground spread out a little in breadth, and he accordingly brought up his horsemen, both those called Companions, and the Thessalians as well as the Macedonians, and posted them with himself on the right wing. The Peloponnesians and the rest of the allied force of Greeks he sent to Parmenio on the left. When Darius had marshalled his phalanx, by a pre-concerted signal he recalled the cavalry which he had posted in front of the river for the express purpose of rendering the arranging of his army easy. Most of these he placed on the right wing near the sea facing Parmenio; because here the ground was more suitable for the evolutions of cavalry. A certain part of them also he led up to the mountain towards the left. But when they were seen to be useless there on account of the narrowness of the ground, he ordered most of these also to ride round to the right wing and join their comrades there. Darius himself occupied the centre of the whole army, inasmuch as it was the custom for the kings of Persia to take up that position, the reason of which arrangement has been recorded by Xenophon, son of Gryllus.

9. Meantime when Alexander perceived that nearly all the Persian cavalry had changed their ground and gone to his left towards the sea, and that on his side only the Peloponnesians and the rest of the Grecian cavalry were posted there, he sent the Thessalian cavalry thither with speed, ordering them not to ride along before the front of the whole array, lest they should be seen by the enemy to be shifting their ground, but to proceed without being seen in the rear of the phalanx. In front of the cavalry on the right, he posted the lancers under the command of Protomachus, and the Paeonians under that of Aristo; and of the infantry, the archers under the direction of Antiochus, and the Agrianians under that of Attalus. Some of the cavalry and archers also he drew up so as to form an angle with the centre towards the mountain which was in the rear; so that on the right his phalanx had been drawn up separated into two wings, the one fronting Darius and the main body of Persians beyond the river, and the other facing those who had been posted at the mountain in their rear. On the left wing the infantry consisting of the Cretan archers and the Thracians under command of Sitalces were posted in front; and before these the cavalry towards the left. The Grecian mercenaries were drawn up as a reserve for all of them. When he perceived that the phalanx towards the right was too thin, and

it seemed likely that the Persians would outflank him here considerably, he ordered two squadrons of the Companion cavalry, the Anthemusian, of which Peroedas, son of Menestheus, was captain, and that which was called Leugaean, under the command of Pantordanus, son of Cleander, to proceed from the centre to the right without being seen. Having also marched the archers, part of the Agrianians and some of the Grecian mercenaries up to his right in the front, he extended his phalanx beyond the wing of the Persians. But when those who had been posted upon the mountains did not descend, a charge was made by a few of the Agrianians and archers at Alexander's order, by which they were easily put to the rout from the foot of the mountain. As they fled to the summit he decided that he could make use of the men who had been drawn up to keep these in check, to fill up the ranks of his phalanx. He thought it quite sufficient to post 300 horsemen to watch the men on the mountain.

10. Having thus marshalled his men, he caused them to rest for some time, and then led them forward, as he had resolved that their advance should be very slow. For Darius was no longer leading the foreigners against him, as he had arranged them at first, but he remained in his position, upon the bank of the river, which was in many parts steep and precipitous; and in certain places, where it seemed more easy to ascend, he extended a stockade along it. By this it was at once evident to Alexander's men that Darius had become cowed in spirit. But when the armies were at length close to each other, Alexander rode about in every direction to exhort his troops to show their valour, mentioning with befitting epithets the names, not only of the generals, but also those of the captains of cavalry and infantry, and of the Grecian mercenaries as many as were more distinguished either by reputation or any deed of valour. From all sides arose a shout not to delay but to attack the enemy. At first he still led them on in close array with measured step, although he had the forces of Darius already in distant view, lest by a too hasty march any part of the phalanx should fluctuate from the line and get separated from the rest. But when they came within range of darts, Alexander himself and those around him, being posted on the right wing, dashed first into the river with a run, in order to alarm the Persians by the rapidity of their onset, and by coming sooner to close conflict to avoid being much injured by the archers. And it turned out just as Alexander had conjectured; for as soon as the battle became a hand-to-hand one, the part of the Persian army stationed on the left wing was put to rout; and here Alexander and his men won a brilliant victory. But the Grecian mercenaries serving under Darius attacked the Macedonians at the point where they saw their phalanx especially disordered. For the

Macedonian phalanx had been broken and had disjoined towards the
right wing, because Alexander had dashed into the river with eagerness,
and engaging in a hand-to-hand conflict was already driving back the
Persians posted there; but the Macedonians in the centre had not prosecuted their task with equal eagerness; and finding many parts of the
bank steep and precipitous, they were unable to preserve the front of
the phalanx in the same line. Here then the struggle was desperate; the
Grecian mercenaries of Darius fighting in order to push the Macedonians
back into the river, and regain the victory for their allies who were already flying; the Macedonians struggling in order not to fall short of
Alexander's success, which was already manifest, and not to tarnish the
glory of the phalanx, which up to that time had been commonly proclaimed invincible. Moreover the feeling of rivalry which existed between the Grecian and Macedonian races inspired each side in the conflict. Here fell Ptolemy, son of Seleucus, after proving himself a valiant
man, besides about 120 other Macedonians of no mean repute.

11. Hereupon the regiments on the right wing, perceiving that the
Persians opposed to them had already been put to rout, wheeled round
towards the Grecian mercenaries of Darius and their own hard-pressed
detachment. Having driven the Greeks away from the river, they extended their phalanx beyond the Persian army on the side which had
been broken, and attacking the Greeks on the flank, were already beginning to cut them up. However the Persian cavalry which had been
posted opposite the Thessalians did not remain on the other side of the
river during the struggle, but came through the water and made a vigorous attack upon the Thessalian squadrons. In this place a fierce cavalry
battle ensued; for the Persians did not give way until they perceived that
Darius had fled and the Grecian mercenaries had been cut up by the
phalanx and severed from them. Then at last there ensued a decided
flight and on all sides. The horses of the Persians suffered much injury
in the retreat, because their riders were heavily armed; and the horsemen themselves, being so many in number and retreating in panic terror
without any regard to order along narrow roads, were trampled on and
injured no less by each other than by the pursuing enemy. The Thessalians also followed them up with vigour, so that the slaughter of the
cavalry in the flight was no less than it would have been if they had
been infantry.

But as soon as the left wing of Darius was terrified and routed by
Alexander, and the Persian king perceived that this part of his army
was severed from the rest, without any further delay he began to flee
in his chariot along with the first, just as he was. He was conveyed safely
in the chariot as long as he met with level ground in his flight; but

when he lighted upon ravines and other rough ground, he left the chariot there, divesting himself both of his shield and Median mantle. He even left his bow in the chariot; and mounting a horse continued his flight. The night, which came on soon after, alone rescued him from being captured by Alexander; for as long as there was daylight the latter kept up the pursuit at full speed. But when it began to grow dark and the things before the feet became invisible, he turned back again to the camp, after capturing the chariot of Darius with the shield, the Median mantle, and the bow in it. For his pursuit had been too slow for him to overtake Darius, because, though he wheeled round at the first breaking asunder of the phalanx, yet he did not turn to pursue him until he observed that the Grecian mercenaries and the Persian cavalry had been driven away from the river.

Of the Persians were killed Arsames, Rheomithres, and Atizyes, three of the men who had commanded the cavalry at the Granicus. Sabaces, viceroy of Egypt, and Bubaces, one of the Persian dignitaries, were also killed, besides about 100,000 of the private soldiers, among them being more than 10,000 cavalry. So great was the slaughter that Ptolemy, son of Lagus, who then accompanied Alexander, says that the men who were with them pursuing Darius, coming in the pursuit to a ravine, passed over it upon the corpses. The camp of Darius was taken forthwith at the first assault, containing his mother, his wife, who was also his sister, and his infant son. His two daughters, and a few other women, wives of Persian peers, who were in attendance upon them, were likewise captured. For the other Persians happened to have despatched their women along with the rest of their property to Damascus; because Darius had sent to that city the greater part of his money and all the other things which the Great King was in the habit of taking with him as necessary for his luxurious mode of living, even though he was going on a military expedition. The consequence was, that in the camp no more than 3,000 talents were captured; but soon after, the money in Damascus was also seized by Parmenio, who was despatched thither for that very purpose. Such was the result of this famous battle which was fought in the month Maimacterion, when Nicocrates was archon of the Athenians.[2]

12. The next day, Alexander, though suffering from a wound which he had received in the thigh from a sword, visited the wounded, and having collected the bodies of the slain, he gave them a splendid burial with all his forces most brilliantly marshalled in order of battle. He also spoke with eulogy to those whom he himself had recognized performing any gallant deed in the battle, and also to those whose exploits he had learnt by report fully corroborated. He likewise honoured each of them

[2] 333 B.C.; end of October or beginning of November.

individually with a gift of money in proportion to his desert. He then appointed Balacrus, son of Nicanor, one of the royal body-guards, vice-roy of Cilicia; and in his place among the body-guards he chose Menes, son of Dionysius. In the place of Ptolemy, son of Seleucus, who had been killed in the battle, he appointed Polysperchon, son of Simmias, to the command of a brigade. He remitted to the Solians the fifty talents which were still due of the money imposed on them as a fine, and he gave them back their hostages.

Nor did he treat the mother, wife, and children of Darius with neglect; for some of those who have written Alexander's history say that on the very night in which he returned from the pursuit of Darius, entering the Persian king's tent, which had been selected for his use, he heard the lamentation of women and other noise of a similar kind not far from the tent. Inquiring therefore who the women were, and why they were in a tent so near, he was answered by some one as follows, "O king, the mother, wife, and children of Darius are lamenting for him as slain, since they have been informed that you have his bow and his royal mantle, and that his shield has been brought back." When Alexander heard this, he sent Leonnatus, one of his Companions, to them, with injunctions to tell them, "Darius is still alive; in his flight he left his arms and mantle in the chariot; and these are the only things of his that Alexander has." Leonnatus entered the tent and told them the news about Darius, saying, moreover, that Alexander would allow them to retain the state and retinue befitting their royal rank, as well as the title of queens; for he had not undertaken the war against Darius from a feeling of hatred, but he had conducted it in a legitimate manner for the empire of Asia. Such are the statements of Ptolemy and Aristobulus. But there is another report, to the effect that on the following day Alexander himself went into the tent, accompanied alone by Hephaestion one of his Companions. The mother of Darius, being in doubt which of them was the king (for they had both arrayed themselves in the same style of dress), went up to Hephaestion, because he appeared to her the taller of the two, and prostrated herself before him. But when he drew back, and one of her attendants pointed out Alexander, saying he was the king, she was ashamed of her mistake, and was going to retire. But the king told her she had made no mistake, for Hephaestion was also Alexander.[3] This I record neither being sure of its truth nor thinking it altogether unreliable. If it really occurred, I commend Alexander for his compassionate treatment of the women, and the confidence he felt in his companion, and the honour bestowed on him; but if it merely

[3] According to the old saying, a friend is a second self; friends are one soul in two bodies.

seems probable to historians that Alexander would have acted and spoken thus, even for this reason I think him worthy of commendation.[4]

13. Darius fled through the night with a few attendants; but next day, picking up as he went along the Persians and Grecian mercenaries who had come safely out of the battle, he had in all 4,000 men under his command. He then made a forced march towards the city of Thapsacus and the river Euphrates, in order to put that river as soon as possible between himself and Alexander. But Amyntas, son of Antiochus, Thymondas, son of Mentor, Aristomedes the Pheraean, and Bianor the Acarnanian, all being deserters, fled without delay from the posts assigned them in the battle, with about 8,000 soldiers under their command, and passing through the mountains, they arrived at Tripolis in Phoenicia. There they found the ships hauled up on shore in which they had previously been transported from Lesbos; they launched as many of these vessels as they thought sufficient to convey them, and the rest they burned there in the docks, in order not to supply their enemy with the means of quickly pursuing them. They fled first to Cyprus, thence to Egypt where Amyntas shortly after, meddling in some political dispute, was killed by the natives.

Meantime Pharnabazus and Autophradates were staying near Chios; then having established a garrison in this island they despatched some of their ships to Cos and Halicarnassus, and with 100 of their best sailing vessels they put to sea themselves and landed at Siphnus. And Agis, king of the Lacedaemonians, came to them with one trireme, both to ask for money to carry on the war, and also to urge them to send with him into the Peloponnese as large a force both naval and military as they could. At this time news reached them of the battle which had been fought at Issus; and being alarmed at the report, Pharnabazus started off to Chios with twelve triremes and 1,500 Grecian mercenaries, for fear that the Chians might attempt to effect a revolution when they received the news of the Persian defeat. Agis, having received from Autophradates thirty talents of silver and ten triremes, despatched Hippias to lead these ships to his brother Agesilaus at Taenarum, ordering him also to instruct Agesilaus to give full pay to the sailors and then to sail as quickly as possible to Crete, in order to set things in order there. For a time he himself remained there among the islands, but afterwards joined Autophradates at Halicarnassus.

Alexander appointed Menon, son of Cerdimmas, viceroy of Coele-

---

[4] In a letter written by Alexander to Parmenio, an extract from which is preserved by Plutarch (*Alexander*, 22), he says that he never saw nor entertained the desire of seeing the wife of Darius, who was said to be the most beautiful woman in Asia; and that he would not allow himself to listen to those who spoke about her beauty.

Syria, giving him the cavalry of the Grecian allies to guard the country. He then went in person towards Phoenicia; and on the march he was met by Strato, son of Gerostratus, king of the Aradians and of the people living near Aradus. But Gerostratus himself was serving in the fleet with Autophradates, as were also the other kings both of the Phoenicians and the Cyprians. When Strato fell in with Alexander, he placed a golden crown upon his head, promising to surrender to him both the island of Aradus and the great and prosperous city of Marathus, situated on the mainland right opposite Aradus; also Sigon, the city of Mariamme, and all the other places under his own dominion and that of his father.

14. While Alexander was still in Marathus, ambassadors came from Darius bringing a letter, entreating him to give up to him his mother, wife, and children. They were also instructed to support this petition by word of mouth. The letter pointed out to him that friendship and alliance had subsisted between Philip and Artaxerxes; and that when Arses, son of Artaxerxes, ascended the throne, Philip was the first to practise injustice towards him, though he had suffered no injury from the Persians. Alexander also, from the time when Darius began to reign over the Persians, had not sent any one to him to confirm the friendship and alliance which had so long existed, but had crossed over into Asia with his army and had inflicted much injury upon the Persians. For this reason he had come down in person to defend his country and to preserve the empire of his fathers. As to the battle, it had been decided as seemed good to some one of the gods. And now he, a king, begged his captured wife, mother, and children from a king; and he wished to form a friendship with him and become his ally. For this purpose he requested Alexander to send men to him with Meniscus and Arsimas, the messengers who came from the Persians, to receive pledges of fidelity from him and to give them in behalf of Alexander.

To this Alexander wrote a reply, and sent Thersippus with the men who had come from Darius, with instructions to give the letter to Darius, but not to converse about anything. Alexander's letter ran thus, "Your ancestors came into Macedonia and the rest of Greece and treated us ill, without any previous injury from us. I, having been appointed commander-in-chief of the Greeks, and wishing to take revenge on the Persians, crossed over into Asia, hostilities being begun by you. For you sent aid to the Perinthians, who were dealing unjustly with my father; and Ochus sent forces into Thrace, which was under our rule. My father was killed by conspirators whom you instigated, as you have yourself boasted to all in your letters; and after slaying Arses, as well as Bagoas, and unjustly seizing the throne contrary to the law of the Persians, and ruling your subjects unjustly, you sent unfriendly letters about me to the Greeks, urging them to wage war with me. You have also despatched money to the Lacedaemonians, and certain other Greeks; but none of the States received it, except the Lacedaemonians. As your agents corrupted my friends, and were striving to dissolve the league which I had formed among the Greeks, I took the field against you, because you were the party who commenced the hostility. Since I have vanquished your generals and viceroys in the previous battle, and now yourself and your forces in like manner, I am, by the gift of the gods, in possession of your land. As many of the men who fought in your army as were not killed in the battle, but fled to me for refuge, I am protecting; and they are with me, not against their own will, but they are serving in my army as volunteers. Come to me therefore, since I am lord of all Asia; but if you are afraid you may suffer any harsh treatment from me in case you come to me, send some of your friends to receive pledges of safety from me. Come to me then, and ask for your mother, wife, and children, and anything else you wish. For whatever you ask for you will receive; and nothing shall be denied you. But for the future, whenever you send to me, send to me as the king of Asia, and do not address to me your wishes as to an equal; but if you are in need of anything, speak to me as to the man who is lord of all your territories. If you act otherwise, I shall deliberate concerning you as an evil-doer; and if you dispute my right to the kingdom, stay and fight another battle for it; but do not run away. For wherever you may be, I intend to march against you." This is the letter which he sent to Darius.

15. When Alexander ascertained that all the money which Darius had sent off to Damascus with Cophen, son of Artabazus, was captured, and also that the Persians who had been left in charge of it, as well as the rest of the royal property, were taken prisoners, he ordered Parmenio to take the treasure back to Damascus, and there guard it. When he also ascertained that the Grecian ambassadors who had reached Darius before the battle had likewise been captured, he ordered them to be sent to him. They were Euthycles, a Spartan; Thessaliscus, son of Ismenias, and Dionysodorus, a victor in the Olympic games, Thebans; and Iphicrates, son of Iphicrates the general, an Athenian. When these men came to Alexander, he immediately released Thessaliscus and Dionysodorus, though they were Thebans, partly out of pity for Thebes, and partly because they seemed to have acted in a pardonable manner. For their native city had been reduced to slavery by the Macedonians, and they were trying to find whatever succour they could for themselves and perhaps also for their native city from Darius and the Persians. Thinking thus compassionately about both of them, he released them, saying that he dismissed Thessaliscus individually out of respect for his pedi-

gree, for he belonged to the ranks of the distinguished men of Thebes. Dionysodorus also he released because he had been conqueror at the Olympic games; and he kept Iphicrates in attendance on himself as long as he lived, treating him with special honour both from friendship to the city of Athens and from recollection of his father's glory. When he died soon after of disease, he sent his bones back to his relations at Athens. But Euthycles at first he kept in custody, though without fetters, both because he was a Lacedaemonian, of a city at that time openly and eminently hostile to him, and because in the man as an individual he could find nothing to warrant his pardon. Afterwards, when he met with great success, he released even this man also.

He set out from Marathus and took possession of Byblus on terms of capitulation, as he did also of Sidon, the inhabitants of which spontaneously invited him from hatred of the Persians and Darius. Thence he advanced towards Tyre; ambassadors from which city, despatched by the commonwealth, met him on the march, announcing that the Tyrians had decided to do whatever he might command. He commended both the city and its ambassadors, and ordered them to return and tell the Tyrians that he wished to enter their city and offer sacrifice to Heracles. The son of the king of the Tyrians was one of the ambassadors, and the others were conspicuous men in Tyre; but the king Azemilcus himself was sailing with Autophradates.

16. The reason of this demand was, that in Tyre there existed a temple of Heracles, the most ancient of all those which are mentioned in history. It was not dedicated to the Argive Heracles, the son of Alcmena; for this Heracles was honoured in Tyre many generations before Cadmus set out from Phoenicia and occupied Thebes, and before Semele, the daughter of Cadmus, was born, from whom Dionysus, the son of Zeus, was born. Dionysus would be third from Cadmus, being a contemporary of Labdacus, son of Polydorus, the son of Cadmus; and the Argive Heracles lived about the time of Oedipus, son of Laius. The Egyptians also worshipped another Heracles, not the one which either the Tyrians or Greeks worship. But Herodotus says that the Egyptians considered Heracles to be one of the twelve gods,[5] just as the Athenians worshipped a different Dionysus, who was the son of Zeus and Core; and the mystic chant called Iacchus was sung to this Dionysus, not to the Theban. So also I think that the Heracles honoured in Tartessus by the Iberians, where are certain pillars named after Heracles, is the Tyrian Heracles; for Tartessus was a colony of the Phoenicians, and the temple to the Heracles there was built and the sacrifices offered after the usage of the Phoenicians. Hecataeus the historian says Gery-

[5] See Herodotus (ii. 43-45).

ones, against whom the Argive Heracles was despatched by Eurystheus to drive his oxen away and bring them to Mycenae, had nothing to do with the land of the Iberians; nor was Heracles despatched to any island called Erythia outside the Great Sea; but that Geryones was king of the mainland around Ambracia and the Amphilochians, that Heracles drove the oxen from this Epirus, and that this was deemed no mean task. I know that to the present time this part of the mainland is rich in pasture land and rears a very fine breed of oxen; and I do not think it beyond the bounds of probability that the fame of the oxen from Epirus, and the name of the king of Epirus, Geryones, had reached Eurystheus. But I do not think it probable that Eurystheus would know the name of the king of the Iberians, who were the remotest nation in Europe, or whether a fine breed of oxen grazed in their land, unless some one, by introducing Hera into the account, as herself giving these commands to Heracles through Eurystheus, wished, by means of the fable, to disguise the incredibility of the tale.

To this Tyrian Heracles, Alexander said he wished to offer sacrifice. But when this message was brought to Tyre by the ambassadors, the people passed a decree to obey any other command of Alexander, but not to admit into the city any Persian or Macedonian; thinking that under the existing circumstances, this was the most specious answer, and that it would be the safest course for them to pursue in reference to the issue of the war, which was still uncertain. When the answer from Tyre was brought to Alexander, he sent the ambassadors back in a rage. He then summoned a council of his Companions and the leaders of his army, together with the captains of infantry and cavalry, and spoke as follows:

17. "Friends and allies, I see that an expedition to Egypt will not be safe for us, so long as the Persians retain the sovereignty of the sea; nor is it a safe course, both for other reasons, and especially looking at the state of matters in Greece, for us to pursue Darius, leaving in our rear the city of Tyre itself in doubtful allegiance, and Egypt and Cyprus in the occupation of the Persians. I am apprehensive lest while we advance with our forces towards Babylon and in pursuit of Darius, the Persians should again conquer the maritime districts, and transfer the war into Greece with a larger army, considering that the Lacedaemonians are now waging war against us without disguise, and the city of Athens is restrained for the present rather by fear than by any good-will towards us. But if Tyre were captured, the whole of Phoenicia would be in our possession, and the fleet of the Phoenicians, which is the most numerous and the best in the Persian navy, would in all probability come over to us. For the Phoenician sailors and marines will not dare

to put to sea in order to incur danger on behalf of others, when their own cities are occupied by us. After this, Cyprus will either yield to us without delay, or will be captured with ease at the mere arrival of a naval force; and then navigating the sea with the ships from Macedonia in conjunction with those of the Phoenicians, Cyprus also having come over to us, we shall acquire the absolute sovereignty of the sea, and at the same time an expedition into Egypt will become an easy matter for us. After we have brought Egypt into subjection, no anxiety about Greece and our own land will any longer remain, and we shall be able to undertake the expedition to Babylon with safety in regard to affairs at home, and at the same time with greater reputation, in consequence of having appropriated to ourselves all the maritime provinces of the Persians and all the land this side of the Euphrates."

18. By this speech he easily persuaded his officers to make an attempt upon Tyre. Moreover he was encouraged by a divine admonition, for that very night in his sleep he seemed to be approaching the Tyrian walls, and Heracles seemed to take him by the right hand and lead him up into the city. This was interpreted by Aristander to mean that Tyre would be taken with labour, because the deeds of Heracles were accomplished with labour. Certainly, the siege of Tyre appeared to be a great enterprise; for the city was an island[6] and fortified all round with lofty walls. Moreover naval operations seemed at that time more favourable to the Tyrians, both because the Persians still possessed the sovereignty of the sea and many ships were still remaining with the citizens themselves. However, as these arguments of his had prevailed, he resolved to construct a mole from the mainland to the city. The place is a narrow strait full of pools; and the part of it near the mainland is shallow water and muddy, but the part near the city itself, where the channel was deepest, was about eighteen feet in depth. But there was an abundant supply of stones and wood, which they put on the top of the stones. Stakes were easily fixed down firmly in the mud, which itself served as a cement to the stones to hold them firm. The zeal of the Macedonians in the work was great, and it was increased by the presence of Alexander himself, who took the lead in everything, now rousing the men to exertion by speech, and now by presents of money lightening the labour of those who were toiling more than their fellows from the desire of gaining praise for their exertions. As long as the mole was being constructed near the mainland, the work made easy and rapid progress, as the material was poured into a small depth of water, and there was no one to hinder them; but when they began to approach the

[6] The island was about half a mile from the mainland, and about a mile in length.

deeper water, and at the same time came near the city itself, they suffered severely, being assailed with missiles from the walls, which were lofty, inasmuch as they had been expressly equipped for work rather than for fighting. Moreover, as the Tyrians still retained command of the sea, they kept on sailing with the triremes to various parts of the mole, and made it impossible in many places for the Macedonians to pour in the material. But the latter erected two towers upon the mole, which they had now projected over a long stretch of sea, and upon these towers they placed engines of war. Skins and prepared hides served as coverings in front of them, to prevent them being struck by fire-bearing missiles from the wall, and at the same time to be a screen against arrows to those who were working. It was likewise intended that the Tyrians who might sail near to injure the men engaged in the construction of the mole should not retire easily, being assailed by missiles from the towers.

19. But to counteract this the Tyrians adopted the following contrivance. They filled a vessel, which had been used for transporting horses, with dry twigs and other combustible wood, fixed two masts on the prow, and fenced it round in the form of a circle as large as possible, so that it might contain as much chaff and as many torches as possible. Moreover they placed upon this vessel quantities of pitch, brimstone, and whatever else was calculated to foment a great flame. They also stretched out a double yard-arm upon each mast; and from these they hung caldrons into which they had poured or cast materials likely to kindle flame which would extend to a great distance. They then put ballast into the stern, in order to raise the prow aloft, the vessel being weighed down abaft. Then watching for a wind bearing towards the mole, they fastened the vessel to some triremes which towed it before the breeze. As soon as they approached the mole and the towers, they threw fire among the wood, and at the same time ran the vessel, with the triremes, aground as violently as possible, dashing against the end of the mole. The men in the vessel easily swam away, as soon as it was set on fire. A great flame soon caught the towers; and the yard-arms being twisted round poured out into the fire the materials that had been prepared for kindling the flame. The men also in the triremes tarrying near the mole kept on shooting arrows into the towers, so that it was not safe for the men to approach who were bringing materials to quench the fire. Upon this, when the towers had already caught fire, many men hastened from the city, and embarking in light vessels, and striking against various parts of the mole, easily tore down the stockade which had been placed in front of it for protection, and burned up all the engines of war which the fire from the vessel did not reach. But

Alexander began to construct a wider mole from the mainland, capable of containing more towers; and he ordered the engine-makers to prepare fresh engines. While this was being performed, he took the shield-bearing guards and the Agrianians and set out to Sidon, to collect there all the triremes he could; since it was evident that the successful conclusion of the siege would be much more difficult to attain, so long as the Tyrians retained the superiority at sea.

20. About this time Gerostratus, King of Aradus, and Enylus, King of Byblus, ascertaining that their cities were in the possession of Alexander, deserted Autophradates and the fleet under his command, and came to Alexander with their naval force, accompanied by the Sidonian triremes; so that about eighty Phoenician ships joined him. About the same time triremes also came to him from Rhodes, both the one called Peripolus,[7] and nine others with it. From Soli and Mallus also came three, and from Lycia ten; from Macedonia also a ship with fifty oars, in which sailed Proteas, son of Andronicus. Not long after, too, the kings of Cyprus put into Sidon with about 120 ships, since they had heard of the defeat of Darius at Issus, and were terrified, because the whole of Phoenicia was already in the possession of Alexander. To all these Alexander granted indemnity for their previous conduct, because they seemed to have joined the Persian fleet rather by necessity than by their own choice. While the engines of war were being constructed for him, and the ships were being fitted up for a naval attack on the city and for the trial of a sea-battle, he took some squadrons of cavalry, the Agrianians and archers, and made an expedition towards Arabia into the range of mountains called Anti-Libanus. Having subdued some of the mountaineers by force, and drawn others over to him by terms of capitulation, he returned to Sidon in ten days. Here he found Cleander, son of Polemocrates, just arrived from Peloponnesus, having 4,000 Grecian mercenaries with him.

When his fleet had been arranged in due order, he embarked upon the decks as many of his shield-bearing guards as seemed sufficient for his enterprise, unless a sea-battle were to be fought rather by breaking the enemy's line than by a close conflict. He then started from Sidon and sailed towards Tyre with his ships arranged in proper order, himself being on the right wing which stretched out seaward; and with him were the kings of the Cyprians, and all those of the Phoenicians except Pnytagoras, who with Craterus was commanding the left wing of the whole line. The Tyrians had previously resolved to fight a sea-battle, if Alexander should sail against them by sea. But then with surprise they beheld the vast multitude of his ships; for they had not yet learned that

---

[7] This was a state vessel, or guardship.

Alexander had all the ships of the Cyprians and Phoenicians. At the same time they were surprised to see that he was sailing against them with his fleet arranged in due order; for Alexander's fleet, a little before it came near the city, tarried for a while out in the open sea, with the view of provoking the Tyrians to come out to a battle; but afterwards, as the enemy did not put out to sea against them, though they were thus arranged in line, they advanced to the attack with a great dashing of oars. Seeing this, the Tyrians decided not to fight a battle at sea, but closely blocked up the passage for ships with as many triremes as the mouths of their harbour would contain, and guarded it, so that the enemy's fleet might not find an anchorage in one of the harbours.

As the Tyrians did not put out to sea against him, Alexander sailed near the city, but resolved not to try to force an entrance into the harbour towards Sidon on account of the narrowness of its mouth; and at the same time because he saw that the entrance had been blocked up with many triremes having their prows turned towards him. But the Phoenicians fell upon the three triremes moored furthest out at the mouth of the harbour, and attacking them prow to prow, succeeded in sinking them. However, the men in the ships easily swam off to the land which was friendly to them. Then, indeed, Alexander moored his ships along the shore not far from the mole which had been made, where there appeared to be shelter from the winds; and on the following day he ordered the Cyprians with their ships and their admiral Andromachus to moor near the city opposite the harbour which faces towards Sidon, and the Phoenicians opposite the harbour which looks towards Egypt, situated on the other side of the mole, where also was his own tent.

21. He had now collected many engineers both from Cyprus and the whole of Phoenicia, and many engines of war had been constructed, some upon the mole, others upon vessels used for transporting horses, which he brought with him from Sidon, and others upon the triremes which were not fast sailers. When all the preparations had been completed they brought the engines of war both along the mole that had been made and also from the ships moored near various parts of the wall and attempting to breach it. The Tyrians erected wooden towers on their battlements opposite the mole, from which they might annoy the enemy; and if the engines of war were brought near any other part, they defended themselves with missiles and shot at the very ships with fire-bearing arrows, so that they deterred the Macedonians from approaching the wall. Their walls opposite the mole were about 150 feet high, with a breadth in proportion, and constructed with large stones imbedded in gypsum. It was not easy for the horse-transports and the triremes of

the Macedonians, which were conveying the engines of war up to the
wall, to approach the city, because a great quantity of stones hurled
forward into the sea prevented their near assault. These stones Alexander determined to drag out of the sea; but this was a work accomplished with great difficulty, since it was performed from ships and not
from the firm earth; especially as the Tyrians, covering their ships
with screens, brought them alongside the anchors of the triremes, and
cutting the cables of the anchors underneath, made anchoring impossible for the enemy's ships. But Alexander covered many thirty-oared
vessels with screens in the same way, and placed them athwart in front
of the anchors, so that the assault of the ships was repelled by them.
But, notwithstanding this, divers under the sea secretly cut their
cables. The Macedonians then used chains to their anchors instead of
cables, and let them down so that the divers could do nothing further.
Then, fastening slipknots to the stones, they dragged them out of the
sea from the mole; and having raised them aloft with cranes, they
discharged them into deep water, where they were no longer likely to
do injury by being hurled forward. The ships now easily approached the
part of the wall where it had been made clear of the stones which had
been hurled forward. The Tyrians being now reduced to great straits on
all sides, resolved to make an attack on the Cyprian ships, which were
moored opposite the harbour turned towards Sidon. For a long time they
spread sails across the mouth of the harbour, in order that the manning
of the triremes might not be discernible; and about the middle of the
day, when the sailors were scattered in quest of necessaries, and when
Alexander usually retired to his tent from the fleet on the other side of
the city, they manned three quinqueremes, an equal number of quadriremes and seven triremes with the most expert complement of rowers
possible, and with the best-armed men adapted for fighting from the
decks, together with the men most daring in naval contests. At first
they rowed out slowly and quietly in single file, moving forward the
handles of their oars without any signal from the men who give the
time to the rowers; but when they were already tacking against the
Cyprians, and were near enough to be seen, then indeed with a loud
shout and encouragement to each other, and at the same time with im-
petuous rowing, they commenced the attack.

22. It happened on that day that Alexander went away to his tent,
but after a short time returned to his ships, not tarrying according to
his wont. The Tyrians fell all of a sudden upon the ships lying at their
moorings, finding some entirely empty and others being manned with
difficulty from those who happened to be present at the very time of
the shout and attack. At the first onset they at once sank the quin-

quereme of the king of Pnytagoras, that of Androcles the Amanthusian and that of Pasicrates the Curian; and they shattered the other ships by pushing them ashore. But when Alexander perceived the sailing out of the Tyrian triremes, he ordered most of the ships under his command whenever each was manned, to take position at the mouth of the harbour, so that the rest of the Tyrian ships might not sail out. He then took the quinqueremes which he had and about five of the triremes, which were manned by him in haste before the rest were ready, and sailed round the city against the Tyrians who had sailed out of the harbour. The men on the wall, perceiving the enemy's attack and observing that Alexander himself was in the fleet, began to shout to those in their own ships, urging them to return; but as their shouts were not audible, on account of the noise of those who were engaged in the action, they exhorted them to retreat by various kinds of signals. At last after a long time, the Tyrians, perceiving the impending attack of Alexander's fleet, tacked about and began to flee into the harbour; and a few of their ships succeeded in escaping, but Alexander's vessels assaulted the greater number, and rendered some of them unfit for sailing; and a quinquereme and a quadrireme were captured at the very mouth of the harbour. But the slaughter of the marines was not great; for when they perceived that the ships were in possession of the enemy, they swam off without difficulty into the harbour. As the Tyrians could no longer derive any aid from their ships, the Macedonians now brought up their military engines to the wall itself. Those which were brought near the city along the mole did no damage worth mentioning on account of the strength of the wall there. Others brought up some of the ships conveying military engines opposite the part of the city turned towards Sidon. But when even there they met with no success, Alexander passed round to the wall projecting towards the south wind and towards Egypt, and tried everywhere to make a breach. Here first a large piece of the wall was thoroughly shaken, and a part of it was even broken and thrown down. Then indeed for a short time he tried to make a storm to the extent of throwing a draw-bridge upon the part of the wall where a breach had been made. But the Tyrians without much difficulty beat the Macedonians back.

23. The third day after this, having waited for a calm sea, after encouraging the leaders of the regiments for the action, he led the ships containing the military engines up to the city. In the first place he shook down a large piece of the wall; and when the breach appeared to be sufficiently wide, he ordered the vessels conveying the military engines to retire, and brought up two others, which carried the bridges, which he intended to throw upon the breach in the wall. The shield-

bearing guards occupied one of these vessels, which he had put under the command of Admetus; and the other was occupied by the regiment of Coenus, called the foot Companions. Alexander himself, with the shield-bearing guards, intended to scale the wall where it might be practicable. He ordered some of his triremes to sail against both of the harbours, to see if by any means they could force an entrance when the Tyrians had turned themselves to oppose him. He also ordered those of his triremes which contained the missiles to be hurled from engines, or which were carrying archers upon deck, to sail right round the wall and to run aground wherever it was practicable, and to take up position within shooting range, where it was impossible to run aground, so that the Tyrians, being shot at from all quarters, might become distracted, and not know whither to turn in their distress. When Alexander's ships drew close to the city and the bridges were thrown from them upon the wall, the shield-bearing guards mounted valiantly along these upon the wall; for their captain, Admetus, proved himself brave on that occasion, and Alexander accompanied them, both as a courageous participant in the action itself, and as a witness of brilliant and dangerous feats of valour performed by others. The first part of the wall that was captured was where Alexander had posted himself, the Tyrians being easily beaten back from it, as soon as the Macedonians found firm footing, but at the same time a way of entrance not abrupt on every side. Admetus was the first to mount the wall; but while cheering on his men to mount, he was struck with a spear and died on the spot. After him, Alexander with the Companions got possession of the wall; and when some of the towers and the parts of the wall between them were in his hands, he advanced through the battlements to the royal palace, because the descent into the city that way seemed the easiest.

24. To return to the fleet, the Phoenicians forcing their way into the harbour looking towards Egypt, facing which they happened to be moored, and bursting the bars asunder, shattered the ships in the harbour, attacking some of them in deep water and driving others ashore. The Cyprians also sailed into the other harbour looking towards Sidon, which had no bar across it, and made a speedy capture of the city on that side. The main body of the Tyrians deserted the wall when they saw it in the enemy's possession; and rallying opposite what was called the sanctuary of Agenor, they there turned round to resist the Macedonians. Against these Alexander advanced with his shield-bearing guards, destroyed the men who fought there, and pursued those who fled. Great was the slaughter also made both by those who were now occupying the city from the harbour and by the regiment of Coenus, which had also entered it. For the Macedonians were now for the most

part advancing full of rage, being angry both at the length of the siege and also because the Tyrians, having captured some of their men sailing from Sidon, had conveyed them to the top of their walls, so that the deed might be visible from the camp, and after slaughtering them, had cast their bodies into the sea. About 8,000 of the Tyrians were killed; and of the Macedonians, besides Admetus, who had proved himself a valiant man, being the first to scale the wall, twenty of the shield-bearing guards were killed in the assault on that occasion. In the whole siege about 400 Macedonians were slain. Alexander gave an amnesty to all those who fled for refuge into the temple of Heracles; among them being most of the Tyrian magistrates, including the king Azemilcus, as well as certain envoys from the Carthaginians, who had come to their mother-city to attend the sacrifice in honour of Heracles, according to an ancient custom. The rest of the prisoners were reduced to slavery, all the Tyrians and mercenary troops, to the number of about 30,000, who had been captured, being sold. Alexander then offered sacrifice to Heracles, and conducted a procession in honour of that deity with all his soldiers fully armed. The ships also took part in this religious procession in honour of Heracles. He moreover held a gymnastic contest in the temple, and celebrated a torch race. The military engine, also, with which the wall had been battered down, was brought into the temple and dedicated as a thank-offering; and the Tyrian ship sacred to Heracles, which had been captured in the naval attack, was likewise dedicated to the god. An inscription was placed on it, either composed by Alexander himself or by some one else; but as it is not worthy of recollection, I have not deemed it worth while to describe it. Thus then was Tyre captured in the month Hecatombaion, when Anicetus was archon at Athens.[8]

25. While Alexander was still occupied by the siege of Tyre, ambassadors came to him from Darius, announcing that he would give him 10,000 talents in exchange for his mother, wife, and children; that all the territory west of the river Euphrates, as far as the Grecian Sea, should be Alexander's; and proposing that he should marry the daughter of Darius, and become his friend and ally. When these proposals were announced in a conference of the Companions, Parmenio is said to have told Alexander that if he were Alexander he would be glad to put an end to the war on these terms, and incur no further hazard of success. Alexander is said to have replied, so would he also do, if he were Parmenio, but as he was Alexander he replied to Darius as he did. For he said that he was neither in want of money from Darius, nor would he receive a part of his territory instead of the whole; for that all his money and territory were his; and that if he wished to marry the daugh-

[8] The end of July and beginning of August 332 B.C.

ter of Darius, he would marry her, even though Darius refused her to him. He commanded Darius to come to him if he wished to experience any generous treatment from him. When Darius heard this answer, he despaired of coming to terms with Alexander, and began to make fresh preparations for war.

Alexander now resolved to make an expedition into Egypt. All the other parts of what is called Palestine Syria had already yielded to him; but a certain eunuch, named Batis, who was in possession of the city of Gaza, paid no heed to him; but procuring Arabian mercenaries, and having been long employed in laying up sufficient food for a long siege, he resolved not to admit Alexander into the city, feeling confident that the place would never be taken by storm.

26. Gaza is about two and one-half miles from the sea; the approach to it is sandy and the sand deep, and the sea near the city everywhere shallow. The city of Gaza was large, and had been built upon a lofty mound, around which a strong wall had been carried. It is the last city the traveller meets with going from Phoenicia to Egypt, being situated on the edge of the desert. When Alexander arrived near the city, on the first day he encamped at the spot where the wall seemed to him most easy to assail, and ordered his military engines to be constructed. But the engineers expressed the opinion that it was not possible to capture the wall by force, on account of the height of the mound. However, the more impracticable it seemed to be, the more resolutely Alexander determined that it must be captured. For he said that the action would strike the enemy with great alarm from its being contrary to their expectation; whereas his failure to capture the place would redound to his disgrace when mentioned either to the Greeks or to Darius. He therefore resolved to construct a mound right round the city, so as to be able to bring his military engines up to the walls on the same level on the artificial mound which had been raised. The mound was constructed especially over against the southern wall of the city, where it appeared easiest to make an assault. When he thought that the mound had been raised to the proper level with the walls, the Macedonians placed their military engines upon it, and brought them close to the wall of Gaza. At this time while Alexander was offering sacrifice, and, crowned with a garland, was about to commence the first sacred rite according to custom, a certain carnivorous bird, flying over the altar, let a stone which it was carrying with its claws fall upon his head. Alexander asked Aristander, the soothsayer, what this omen meant. He replied, "O king, you will indeed capture the city, but you must take care of yourself on this day."

27. When Alexander heard this, he kept himself for a time near the military engines, out of the reach of missiles. But when a vigorous sortie

was made from the city, and the Arabs were carrying torches to set fire to the military engines, and from their commanding position above hurling missiles at the Macedonians, who were defending themselves from lower ground, were driving them down from the mound which they had made, then Alexander either wilfully disobeyed the soothsayer, or forgot the prophecy from excitement in the heat of action. Taking the shield-bearing guards, he hastened to the rescue where the Macedonians were especially hard pressed, and prevented them from being driven down from the mound in disgraceful flight. But he was himself wounded by a bolt from a catapult, right through the shield and breastplate into the shoulder. When he perceived that Aristander had spoken the truth about the wound, he rejoiced, because he thought he should also capture the city by the aid of the soothsayer. And yet indeed he was not easily cured of the wound. In the meantime the military engines with which he had captured Tyre arrived, having been sent for by sea; and he ordered the mound to be constructed quite round the city on all sides, 1,200 feet in breadth and 250 feet in height. When his engines had been prepared, and brought up along the mound, they shook down a large extent of wall; and mines being dug in various places, and the earth being drawn out by stealth, the wall fell down in many parts, subsiding into the emptied space. The Macedonians then commanded a large extent of ground with their missiles, driving back the men who were defending the city from the towers. Nevertheless, the men of the city sustained three assaults, though many of their number were killed or wounded; but at the fourth attack, Alexander led up the phalanx of the Macedonians from all sides, threw down the part of the wall which was undermined, and shook down another large portion of it by battering it with his engines, so that he rendered the assault an easy matter through the breaches with his scaling ladders. Accordingly the ladders were brought up to the wall; and then there arose a great emulation among those of the Macedonians who laid any claim to valour, to see who should be the first to scale the wall. The first to do so was Neoptolemus, one of the Companions, of the family of the Aeacidae; and after him mounted one rank after another with their officers. When once some of the Macedonians got within the wall, they split open in succession the gates which each party happened to light upon, and thus admitted the whole army into the city. But though their city was now in the hands of the enemy, the Gazaeans nevertheless stood together and fought; so that they were all slain fighting there, as each man had been stationed. Alexander sold their wives and children into slavery; and having peopled the city again from the neighbouring settlers, he made use of it as a fortified post for the war.

BOOK III

1. Alexander now led his army into Egypt, whither he had set out at first from Tyre; and marching from Gaza, on the seventh day he arrived at Pelusium in Egypt. His fleet coasted along also from Phoenicia to Egypt; and he found the ships already moored at Pelusium. When Mazaces the Persian, whom Darius had appointed viceroy of Egypt, ascertained how the battle at Issus had resulted, that Darius had fled in disgraceful flight, and that Phoenicia, Syria, and most of Arabia were already in Alexander's possession, as he had no Persian force with which he could offer resistance, he admitted Alexander into the cities and the country in a friendly way. Alexander introduced a garrison into Pelusium, and ordering the men in the ships to sail up the river as far as the city of Memphis, he went in person towards Heliopolis, having the river Nile on his right. He reached that city through the desert, after getting possession of all the places on the march through the voluntary surrender of the inhabitants. Thence he crossed the stream and came to Memphis, where he offered sacrifice to Apis and the other gods, and celebrated a gymnastic and musical contest, the most distinguished artists in these matters coming to him from Greece. From Memphis he sailed down the river towards the sea, embarking the shield-bearing guards, the archers, the Agrianians, and of the cavalry the royal squadron of the Companions. Coming to Canobus, he sailed round the Lake Mareotis, and disembarked where now is situated the city of Alexandria, which takes its name from him. The position seemed to him a very fine one in which to found a city, and he thought that it would become a prosperous one. Therefore he was seized by an ardent desire to undertake the enterprise, and he marked out the boundaries for the city himself, pointing out the place where the market place was to be constructed, where the temples were to be built, stating how many there were to be, and to what Grecian gods they were to be dedicated, and specially marking a spot for a temple to the Egyptian Isis. He also pointed out where the wall was to be carried round it. In regard to these matters he offered sacrifice, and the victims appeared favourable.

2. The following story is told, which seems to me not unworthy of belief: that Alexander himself wished to leave behind for the builders

the marks for the boundaries of the fortification, but that there was nothing at hand with which to make a mark on the ground. One of the builders hit upon the plan of collecting in vessels the barley which the soldiers were carrying, and throwing it upon the ground where the king led the way; and thus the circle of the fortification which he was designing for the city was completely marked out. The soothsayers, and especially Aristander the Telmissian, who was said already to have given many other true predictions, pondering this, told Alexander that the city would become prosperous in every respect, but especially in regard to the fruits of the earth.

At this time Hegelochus sailed to Egypt and informed Alexander that the Tenedians had revolted from the Persians and attached themselves to him, because they had gone over to the Persians against their own wish. He also said that the democracy of Chios had introduced Alexander's adherents in spite of those who held the city, being established in it by Autophradates and Pharnabazus. The latter commander had been caught there and kept as a prisoner, as was also the despot Aristonicus, a Methymnaean, who sailed into the harbour of Chios with five piratical vessels, fitted with one and a half banks of oars, not knowing that the harbour was in the hands of Alexander's adherents, but being deceived by the declaration of those who kept the bars of the harbour, that the fleet of Pharnabazus was moored in it. All the pirates were there massacred by Alexander's adherents; and Hegelochus brought to the king as prisoners Aristonicus, Apollonides the Chian, Phisinus, Megareus, and all the others who had taken part in the revolt of Chios to the Persians, and who at that time were holding the government of the island by force. He also announced that he had deprived Chares of the possession of Mytilene, that he had brought over the other cities in Lesbos by a voluntary agreement, and that he had sent Amphoterus to Cos with sixty ships, for the Coans themselves invited him to their island. He said that he himself had sailed to Cos and found it already in the hands of Amphoterus. Hegelochus brought all the prisoners with him except Pharnabazus, who had eluded his guards at Cos and got away by stealth. Alexander sent the despots who had been brought from the cities back to their fellow-citizens, to be treated as they pleased; but Apollonides and his Chian partisans he sent under a strict guard to Elephantine, an Egyptian city.

3. After these transactions, Alexander was seized by an ardent desire to visit Ammon[1] in Libya, partly in order to consult the god, because the oracle of Ammon was said to be exact in its information, and

---

[1] The temple of Zeus Ammon was in the oasis of Siwah, to the west of Egypt, about 220 miles from Alexandria.

Perseus and Heracles were said to have consulted it, the former when he was despatched by Polydectes against the Gorgon, and the latter, when he visited Antaeus in Libya and Busiris in Egypt. Alexander was also partly urged by a desire of emulating Perseus and Heracles, from both of whom he traced his descent. He also deduced his pedigree from Ammon, just as the legends traced that of Heracles and Perseus to Zeus. Accordingly he made the expedition to Ammon with the design of learning his own origin more certainly, or at least that he might be able to say that he had learned it. According to Aristobulus, he advanced along the sea-shore to Paraetonium through a country which was a desert, but not destitute of water, a distance of about 187 miles. Thence he turned into the interior, where the oracle of Ammon was located. The route is desert, and most of it is sand and destitute of water. But there was a copious supply of rain for Alexander, a thing which was attributed to the influence of the deity, as was also the following occurrence. Whenever a south wind blows in that district, it heaps up sand upon the route far and wide, rendering the tracks of the road invisible, so that it is impossible to discover where one ought to direct one's course in the sand, just as if one were at sea; for there are no landmarks along the road, neither mountain anywhere, nor tree, nor permanent hills standing erect, by which travellers might be able to form a conjecture of the right course, as sailors do by the stars. Consequently, Alexander's army lost the way, as even the guides were in doubt about the course to take. Ptolemy, son of Lagus, says that two serpents went in front of the army, uttering a voice, and Alexander ordered the guides to follow them, trusting in the divine portent. He says too that they showed the way to the oracle and back again. But Aristobulus, whose account is generally admitted as correct, says that two ravens flew in front of the army, and that these acted as Alexander's guides. I am able to assert with confidence that some divine assistance was afforded him, for probability also coincides with the supposition; but the discrepancies in the accounts of the various narrators have deprived the story of certainty.

4. The place where the temple of Ammon is located is entirely surrounded by a desert of far-stretching sand, which is destitute of water. The fertile spot in the midst of this desert is not extensive; for where it stretches into its greatest expanse it is only about five miles broad. It is full of cultivated trees, olives and palms; and it is the only place in those parts which is refreshed with dew. A spring also rises from it, quite unlike all the other springs which issue from the earth. For at midday the water is cold to the taste, and still more so to the touch, as cold as cold can be. But when the sun has sunk into the west, it gets warmer, and from the evening it keeps on growing warmer until mid-

night, when it reaches its warmest point. After midnight it goes on getting gradually colder: at day-break it is already cold; but at midday it
reaches the coldest point. Every day it undergoes these alternate
changes in regular succession. In this place also natural salt is procured
by digging, and certain of the priests of Ammon convey quantities of it
into Egypt. For whenever they set out for Egypt they put it into little
boxes plaited out of palm, and carry it as a present to the king, or
some other great man. The lumps of this salt are large, some of them
being longer than three fingers' breadth; and it is clear like crystal. The
Egyptians and others who are respectful to the deity use this salt in
their sacrifices, as it is clearer than that which is procured from the sea.
Alexander then was struck with wonder at the place, and consulted the
oracle of the god. Having heard what was agreeable to his wishes, as
he himself said, he set out on the journey back to Egypt by the same
route, according to the statement of Aristobulus; but according to that
of Ptolemy, son of Lagus, he took another road, leading straight to Memphis.

5. At Memphis, many embassies from Greece reached him; and he
sent away no one disappointed by the rejection of his suit. From Antipater also arrived an army of 400 Grecian mercenaries under the command of Menidas, son of Hegesander: likewise from Thrace 500 cavalry,
under the direction of Asclepiodorus, son of Eunicus. Here he offered
sacrifice to Zeus the King, led his soldiers fully armed in solemn procession, and celebrated a gymnastic and musical contest. He then settled the affairs of Egypt, by appointing two Egyptians, Doloaspis and
Petisis, governors of the country, dividing between them the whole land;
but as Petisis declined his province, Doloaspis received the whole. He
appointed two of the Companions to be commandants of garrisons:
Pantaleon the Pydnaean in Memphis, and Polemo, son of Megacles, a
Pellaean, in Pelusium. He also gave the command of the Grecian auxiliaries to Lycidas, an Aetolian, and appointed Eugnostus, son of Xeno-
phantes, one of the Companions, to be secretary over the same troops.
As their overseers he placed Aeschylus and Ephippus the Chalcidean.
The government of the neighbouring country of Libya he granted to
Apollonius, son of Charinus; and the part of Arabia near Heroopolis he
put under Cleomenes, a man of Naucratis. This last was ordered to
allow the governors to rule their respective districts according to the
ancient custom; but to collect from them the tribute due to him. The
native governors were also ordered to pay it to Cleomenes. He appointed
Peucestas, son of Macartatus, and Balacrus, son of Amyntas, generals
of the army which he left behind in Egypt; and he placed Polemo, son
of Theramenes, over the fleet as admiral. He made Leonnatus, son of

Anteas, one of his body-guards instead of Arrhybas, who had died of disease. Antiochus, the commander of the archers, also died; and in his stead Ombrion the Cretan was appointed. When Balacrus was left behind in Egypt, the allied Grecian infantry, which had been under his command, was put under that of Calanus. Alexander was said to have divided the government of Egypt among so many men, because he was surprised at the natural strength of the country, and he thought it unsafe to intrust the rule of the whole to a single person. The Romans also seem to me to have learned a lesson from him, and therefore keep Egypt under strong guard; for they do not send any of the senators thither as proconsul for the same reason, but only men who have the rank among them of Knights.

6. As soon as spring began to appear, he went from Memphis to Phoenicia, bridging the stream of the Nile near Memphis, as well as the canals issuing from it. When he arrived at Tyre, he found his fleet already there. In this city he again offered sacrifice to Heracles, and celebrated both a gymnastic and musical contest. While there, the state vessel called the Paralus came to him from Athens, bringing Diophantus and Achilleus as envoys to him; and all the crew of the Paralus were joined with them in the embassy. These men obtained all the requests which they were despatched to make, and the king gave up to the Athenians all their fellow-citizens who had been captured at the Granicus. Being informed that revolutionary plans had been carried out in the Peloponnese, he sent Amphoterus thither to assist those of the Peloponnesians who were firm in their support of the war against Persia, and were not under the control of the Lacedaemonians. He also commanded the Phoenicians and Cyprians to despatch to the Peloponnese 100 other ships in addition to those which he was sending with Amphoterus. He now started up into the interior towards Thapsacus and the river Euphrates, after placing Coeranus, a Beroean, over the levy of tribute in Phoenicia, and Philoxenus to collect it in Asia as far as the Taurus. In the place of these men he intrusted the custody of the money which he had with him to Harpalus, son of Machatas, who had just returned from exile. For this man at first had been banished, while Philip was still king, because he was an adherent of Alexander; as also was Ptolemy, son of Lagus, for the same reason; likewise Nearchus, son of Androtimus, Erigyius, son of Larichus, and his brother Laomedon. For Alexander fell under Philip's suspicion when the latter married Eurydice[2] and treated Alexander's mother Olympias with dishonour. But after Philip's death those who had been banished on Alexander's account

---

[2] Other historians call this queen Cleopatra. She was the daughter of a Macedonian named Attalus.

returned from exile and were received into favour. He made Ptolemy one of his confidential body-guards; he placed Harpalus over the money, because his bodily strength was unequal to the fatigues of war. Erigyius was made commander of the allied Grecian cavalry, and his brother Laomedon, because he could speak both the Greek and Persian languages and could read Persian writings, was put in charge of the foreign prisoners. Nearchus also was appointed viceroy of Lycia and of the land adjacent to it as far as mount Taurus. But shortly before the battle which was fought at Issus, Harpalus fell under the influence of Tauriscus, an evil man, and fled in his company. The latter started off to Alexander the Epirote[3] in Italy, where he soon after died. But Harpalus found a refuge in Megaris, whence however Alexander persuaded him to return, giving him a pledge that he should be none the worse on account of his desertion. When he came back, he not only received no punishment, but was even reinstated in the office of treasurer. Menander, one of the Companions, was sent away into Lydia as viceroy; and Clearchus was put in command of the Grecian auxiliaries who had been under Menander. Asclepiodorus, son of Eunicus, was also appointed viceroy of Syria instead of Arimmas, because the latter seemed to have been remiss in collecting the supplies which he had been ordered to collect for the army which the king was about to lead into the interior.

7. Alexander arrived at Thapsacus in the month Hecatombaion,[4] in the archonship of Aristophanes at Athens; and he found that two bridges of boats had been constructed over the stream. But Mazaeus, to whom Darius had committed the duty of guarding the river, with about 3,000 cavalry, 2,000 of which were Grecian mercenaries, was up to that time keeping guard there at the river. For this reason the Macedonians had not constructed the bridge right across as far as the opposite bank, being afraid that Mazaeus might make an assault upon the bridge where it ended. But when he heard that Alexander was approaching, he went off in flight with all his army. As soon as he had fled, the bridges were completed as far as the further bank, and Alexander crossed upon them with his army. Thence he marched up into the interior through the land called Mesopotamia, having the river Euphrates and the mountains of Armenia on his left. When he started from the Euphrates he did not march to Babylon by the direct road; because by going the other route he found all things easier for the march of his army, and it was also possible to obtain fodder for the horses and provisions for the men from

---

[3] This king was brother of Alexander's mother Olympias, the husband of Cleopatra, the daughter of Philip and Olympias. He crossed over into Italy to aid the Tarentines against the Lucanians and Bruttians, but was eventually defeated and slain near Pandosia, 326 B.C. See Livy, viii. 24.

[4] July-August, 331 B.C.

the country. Besides this, the heat was not so scorching on the indirect route. Some of the men from Darius's army, who had been dispersed for the purpose of scouting, were taken prisoners; and they reported that Darius was encamped near the river Tigris, having resolved to prevent Alexander from crossing that stream. They also said that he had a much larger army than that with which he fought in Cilicia. Hearing this, Alexander went with all speed towards the Tigris; but when he reached it he found neither Darius himself nor any guard which he had left. However he experienced great difficulty in crossing the stream, on account of the swiftness of the current, though no one tried to stop him. There he made his army rest, and while so doing, an eclipse of the moon nearly total occurred.[5] Alexander thereupon offered sacrifice to the moon, the sun and the earth, whose deed this was, according to common report. Aristander thought that this eclipse of the moon was a portent favourable to Alexander and the Macedonians; that there would be a battle that very month, and that victory for Alexander was signified by the sacrificial victims. Having therefore decamped from the Tigris, he went through the land of Aturia, having the mountains of the Gordyaeans on the left and the Tigris itself on the right; and on the fourth day after the passage of the river, his scouts brought word to him that the enemy's cavalry were visible there along the plain, but how many of them there were they could not guess. Accordingly he drew his army up in order and advanced prepared for battle. Other scouts again riding forward and taking more accurate observations told him that the cavalry did not seem to them to be more than 1,000 in number.

8. Alexander therefore took the royal squadron of cavalry, and one squadron of the Companions, together with the Paeonian scouts, and marched with all speed, having ordered the rest of his army to follow at leisure. The Persian cavalry, seeing Alexander advancing quickly, began to flee with all their might. Though he pressed close upon them in pursuit, most of them escaped; but a few, whose horses were fatigued by the flight, were slain, others were taken prisoners, horses and all. From these they ascertained that Darius with a large force was not far off. For the Indians who were adjacent to the Bactrians, as also the Bactrians themselves and the Sogdianians had come to the aid of Darius, all being under the command of Bessus, the viceroy of the land of Bactria. They were followed by the Sacians, a Scythian tribe belonging to the Scythians who dwell in Asia. These were not subject to Bessus, but were in alliance with Darius. They were commanded by Mavaces, and were horse-bowmen. Barsaentes, the viceroy of Arachotia, led the Arachotians and the men who were called mountaineer Indians. Satibar-

[5] This eclipse occurred September 20, 331 B.C.

zanes, the viceroy of Areia, led the Areians, as did Phrataphernes the Parthians, Hyrcanians, and Tapurians, all of whom were horsemen. Atropates commanded the Medes, with whom were arrayed the Cadusians, Albanians, and Sacesinians. The men who dwelt near the Red Sea[6] were marshalled by Ocondobates, Ariobarzanes, and Otanes. The Uxians and Susianians acknowledged Oxathres son of Aboulites as their leader, and the Babylonians were commanded by Boupares. The Carians who had been deported into central Asia and the Sitacenians had been placed in the same ranks as the Babylonians. The Armenians were commanded by Orontes and Mithraustes, and the Cappadocians by Ariaces. The Syrians from Coele-Syria and the men of Syria which lies between the rivers[7] were led by Mazaeus. The whole army of Darius was said to contain 40,000 cavalry, 1,000,000 infantry, and 200 scythe-bearing chariots. There were only a few elephants, about fifteen in number, belonging to the Indians who live this side of the Indus. With these forces Darius had encamped at Gaugamela, near the river Bumodus, about seventy miles from the city of Arbela, in a district everywhere level; for whatever ground thereabouts was unlevel and unfit for the evolutions of cavalry had long before been levelled by the Persians, and made fit for the easy rolling of chariots and for the galloping of horses. For there were some who persuaded Darius that he had got the worst of it in the battle fought at Issus from the narrowness of the battle-field; and this he was easily induced to believe.

9. When Alexander had received all this information from the Persian scouts who had been captured, he remained four days in the place where he had received the news; and gave his army rest after the march. He meanwhile fortified his camp with a ditch and stockade, as he intended to leave behind the baggage and all the soldiers who were unfit for fighting, and to go into the contest accompanied by his warriors carrying with them nothing except their weapons. Accordingly he took his forces by night, and began the march about the second watch, in order to come into collision with the foreigners at break of day. As soon as Darius was informed of Alexander's approach, he at once drew out his army for battle; and Alexander led on his men drawn up in like manner. Though the armies were only seven miles from each other, they were not yet in sight of each other, for between the hostile forces some hills intervened. But when Alexander was only three and one-half miles

---

[6] The Red Sea was the name originally given to the whole expanse of sea to the west of India as far as Africa. The name was subsequently given to the Arabian Gulf exclusively. Arrain calls the Persian Gulf by this name, as do also Xenophon and Diodorus. This gulf was unknown to Herodotus.

[7] The Greeks called this country Mesopotamia because it lies between the rivers Euphrates and Tigris.

from the enemy, and his army was already marching down from the
hills just mentioned, catching sight of the foreigners, he caused his
phalanx to halt there. Calling a council of the Companions, generals,
cavalry officers, and leaders of the Grecian allies and mercenaries, he
deliberated with them, whether he should at once lead on the phalanx
without delay, as most of them urged him to do; or, whether, as Parmenio thought preferable, to encamp there for the present, to reconnoitre
all the ground, in order to see if there was anything there to excite suspicion or to impede their progress, or if there were ditches or stakes firmly
fixed in the earth out of sight, as well as to make a more accurate survey of the enemy's tactical arrangements. Parmenio's opinion prevailed,
so they encamped there, drawn up in the order in which they intended
to enter the battle. But Alexander took the light infantry and the cavalry Companions and went all round, reconnoitring the whole country
where he was about to fight the battle. Having returned, he again called
together the same leaders, and said that they did not require to be encouraged by him to enter the contest; for they had been long before
encouraged by their own valour, and by the gallant deeds which they
had already so often achieved. He thought it expedient that each of them
individually should stir up his own men separately; each infantry captain the men of his own company, the cavalry captain his own squadron,
the colonels their various regiments, and each of the leaders of the infantry the phalanx intrusted to him. He assured them that in this battle
they were going to fight, not as before, either for Coele-Syria, Phoenicia,
or Egypt, but for the whole of Asia. For he said this battle would decide
who were to be the rulers of the continent. It was not necessary for him
to stir them up to gallant deeds by many words, since they had this
encouragement by nature; but they should see that each man took care,
so far as in him lay, to preserve discipline in the critical moment of action, and to keep perfect silence when it was expedient to advance in
silence. On the other hand, they should see that each man uttered a
sonorous shout, where it would be advantageous to shout, and to raise as
terrible a battle-cry as possible, when a suitable opportunity occurred
of raising the battle-cry. He told them to take care to obey his orders
quickly, and to transmit the orders they had received to the ranks with
all rapidity, each man remembering that both as an individual and in
the aggregate he was increasing the general danger if he was remiss in
the discharge of his duty, and that he was assisting to gain a victory if
he zealously put forth his utmost exertions.

10. With these words and others like them he briefly exhorted his
officers, and in return was exhorted by them to feel confidence in their
valour. He then ordered the soldiers to take dinner and to rest them-

selves. It is said that Parmenio came to him in his tent, and urged him to make a night attack on the Persians, saying that thus he would fall upon them unprepared and in a state of confusion, and at the same time more liable to a panic in the dark. But the reply which he made to him, as others were listening to their conversation, was, that it would be mean to steal a victory, and that Alexander ought to conquer in open daylight, and without any artifice. This vaunting did not appear any arrogance on his part, but rather to indicate self-confidence amid dangers. To me, at any rate, he seems to have used correct reasoning in such a matter. For in the night many accidents have occurred unexpectedly to those who were sufficiently prepared for battle as well as to those who were deficiently prepared, which have caused the superior party to fail in their plans, and have handed the victory over to the inferior party, contrary to the expectations of both sides. Though Alexander was generally fond of encountering danger in battle, the night appeared to him perilous; and, besides, if Darius were again defeated, a furtive and nocturnal attack on the part of the Macedonians would relieve him of the necessity of confessing that he was an inferior general and commanded inferior troops. Moreover, if any unexpected defeat befell his army, the circumjacent country was friendly to the enemy, and they were acquainted with the locality, whereas the Macedonians were unacquainted with it, and surrounded by nothing but foes, of whom the prisoners were no small party. These would be likely to assist in attacking them in the night, not only if they should meet with defeat, but even if they did not appear to be gaining a decisive victory. For this way of reasoning I commend Alexander; and I think him no less worthy of admiration for his excessive liking for open action.

11. Darius and his army remained drawn up during the night in the same order as that in which they had first arrayed themselves; because they had not surrounded themselves with a completely entrenched camp, and, moreover, they were afraid that the enemy would attack them in the night. The success of the Persians, on this occasion, was impeded especially by this long standing on watch with their arms, and by the fear which usually springs up before great dangers; which, however, was not then suddenly aroused by a momentary panic, but had been experienced for a long time, and had thoroughly cowed their spirits. The army of Darius was drawn up in the following manner, for, according to the statement of Aristobulus, the written scheme of arrangement drawn up by Darius was afterwards captured. His left wing was held by the Bactrian cavalry, in conjunction with the Daans and Arachotians; near these had been posted the Persians, horse and foot mixed together; next to these the Susians, and then the Cadusians. This was the ar-

rangement of the left wing as far as the middle of the whole phalanx. On the right had been posted the men from Coele-Syria and Mesopotamia. On the right again were the Medes; next to them the Parthians and Sacians; then the Tapurians and Hyrcanians, and last the Albanians and Sacesinians, extending as far as the middle of the whole phalanx. In the centre where King Darius was had been posted the king's kinsmen,[8] the Persian guards carrying spears with golden apples at the butt end, the Indians, the Carians who had been forcibly removed to Central Asia, and the Mardian archers. The Uxians, the Babylonians, the men who dwell near the Red Sea, and the Sitacenians had also been drawn up in deep column. On the left, opposite Alexander's right, had been posted the Scythian cavalry, about 1,000 Bactrians and 100 scythe-bearing chariots. In front of Darius's royal squadron of cavalry stood the elephants and fifty chariots. In front of the right wing the Armenian and Cappadocian cavalry with fifty scythe-bearing chariots had been posted. The Greek mercenaries, as alone capable of coping with the Macedonians, were stationed right opposite their phalanx, in two divisions close beside Darius himself and his Persian attendants, one division on each side.

Alexander's army was marshalled as follows: The right wing was held by the cavalry Companions, in front of whom had been posted the royal squadron, commanded by Clitus, son of Dropidas. Near this was the squadron of Glaucias, next to it that of Aristo, then that of Sopolis, son of Hermodorus, then that of Heraclides, son of Antiochus. Near this was that of Demetrius, son of Althaemenes, then that of Meleager, and last one of the royal squadrons commanded by Hegelochus, son of Hippostratus. All the cavalry Companions were under the supreme command of Philotas, son of Parmenio. Of the phalanx of Macedonian infantry, nearest to the cavalry had been posted first the select corps of shield-bearing guards, and then the rest of the shield-bearing guards, under the command of Nicanor, son of Parmenio. Next to these was the brigade of Coenus, son of Polemocrates; after these that of Perdiccas, son of Orontes; then that of Meleager, son of Neoptolemus; then that of Polysperchon, son of Simmias; and last that of Amyntas, son of Andromenes, under the command of Simmias, because Amyntas had been despatched to Macedonia to levy an army. The brigade of Craterus, son of Alexander, held the left end of the Macedonian phalanx, and this general commanded the left wing of the infantry. Next to him was the allied Grecian cavalry under the command of Erigyius, son of Larichus. Next to these, towards the left wing of the army, were the Thessalian cavalry, under the command of Philip, son of Menelaus. But the whole

---

[8] A title of honour. Curtius says that they numbered 15,000.

left wing was led by Parmenio, son of Philotas, round whose person were ranged the Pharsalian horsemen, who were both the best and most numerous squadron of the Thessalian cavalry.

12. In this way had Alexander marshalled his army in front; but he also posted a second array, so that his phalanx might be a double one. Directions had been given to the commanders of these men posted in the rear to wheel round and receive the attack of the foreigners, if they should see their own comrades surrounded by the Persian army. Next to the royal squadron on the right wing, half of the Agrianians, under the command of Attalus, in conjunction with the Macedonian archers under Briso's command, were posted angular-wise in case they should be seized anyhow by the necessity of deepening the phalanx, or of closing up the ranks. Next to the archers were the men called the veteran mercenaries, whose commander was Cleander. In front of the Agrianians and archers were posted the light cavalry used for skirmishing, and the Paeonians, under the command of Aretes and Aristo. In front of all had been posted the Grecian mercenary cavalry under the direction of Menidas; and in front of the royal squadron of cavalry and the other Companions had been posted half of the Agrianians and archers, and the javelin-men of Balacrus who had been ranged opposite the scythe-bearing chariots. Instructions had been given to Menidas and the troops under him to wheel round and attack the enemy in flank, if they should ride round their wing. Thus had Alexander arranged matters on the right wing. On the left the Thracians under the command of Sitalces had been posted angular-wise, and near them the cavalry of the Grecian allies, under the direction of Coeranus. Next stood the Odrysian cavalry, under the command of Agatho, son of Tyrimmas. In this part, in front of all, were posted the auxiliary cavalry of the Grecian mercenaries, under the direction of Andromachus, son of Hiero. Near the baggage the infantry from Thrace were posted as a guard. The whole of Alexander's army numbered 7,000 cavalry and about 40,000 infantry.

13. When the armies drew near each other, Darius and the men around him were observed: the apple-bearing Persians, the Indians, the Albanians, the Carians who had been forcibly transported into Central Asia, the Mardian archers ranged opposite Alexander himself and the royal squadron of cavalry. Alexander led his own army more towards the right, and the Persians marched along parallel with him, far outflanking him upon their left. Then the Scythian cavalry rode along the line, and came into conflict with the front men of Alexander's array; but he nevertheless still continued to march towards the right, and almost entirely got beyond the ground which had been cleared and levelled by the Persians. Then Darius, fearing that his chariots would become

useless, if the Macedonians advanced into the uneven ground, ordered the front ranks of his left wing to ride round the right wing of the Macedonians, where Alexander was commanding, to prevent him from marching his wing any further. This being done, Alexander ordered the cavalry of the Grecian mercenaries under the command of Menidas to attack them. But the Scythian cavalry and the Bactrians, who had been drawn up with them, sallied forth against them, and being much more numerous they put the small body of Greeks to rout. Alexander then ordered Aristo at the head of the Paeonians and Grecian auxiliaries to attack the Scythians; and the barbarians gave way. But the rest of the Bactrians, drawing near to the Paeonians and Grecian auxiliaries, caused their own comrades who were already in flight to turn and renew the battle; and thus they brought about a general cavalry engagement, in which more of Alexander's men fell, not only being overwhelmed by the multitude of the barbarians, but also because the Scythians themselves and their horses were much more completely protected with armour for guarding their bodies. Notwithstanding this, the Macedonians sustained their assaults, and assailing them violently squadron by squadron, they succeeded in pushing them out of rank. Meantime the foreigners launched their scythe-bearing chariots against Alexander himself, for the purpose of throwing his phalanx into confusion; but in this they were grievously deceived. For as soon as they approached, the Agrianians and the javelin-men with Balacrus, who had been posted in front of the Companion cavalry, hurled their javelins at some of the horses; others they seized by the reins and pulled the drivers off, and standing round the horses killed them. Yet some got right through the ranks; for the men stood apart and opened their ranks, as they had been instructed, in the places where the chariots assaulted them. In this way it generally happened that the chariots passed through safely, and the men by whom they were driven were uninjured. But these also were afterwards overpowered by the grooms of Alexander's army and by the royal shield-bearing guards.

14. As soon as Darius began to set his whole phalanx in motion, Alexander ordered Aretes to attack those who were riding completely round his right wing; and up to that time he was himself leading his men in column. But when the Persians had made a break in the front line of their army, in consequence of the cavalry sallying forth to assist those who were surrounding the right wing, Alexander wheeled round towards the gap, and forming a wedge as it were of the Companion cavalry and of the part of the phalanx which was posted here, he led them with a quick charge and loud battle-cry straight towards Darius himself. For a short time there ensued a hand-to-hand fight; but when the Macedonian

cavalry, commanded by Alexander himself, pressed on vigorously, thrusting themselves against the Persians and striking their faces with their spears, and when the Macedonian phalanx in dense array and bristling with long pikes had also made an attack upon them, all things together appeared full of terror to Darius, who had already long been in a state of fear, so that he was the first to turn and flee. The Persians also who were riding round the wing were seized with alarm when Aretes made a vigorous attack upon them. In this quarter indeed the Persians took to speedy flight; and the Macedonians followed up the fugitives and slaughtered them. Simmias and his brigade were not yet able to start with Alexander in pursuit, but causing the phalanx to halt there, he took part in the struggle, because the left wing of the Macedonians was reported to be hard pressed. In this part of the field, their line being broken, some of the Indians and of the Persian cavalry burst through the gap towards the baggage of the Macedonians; and there the action became desperate. For the Persians fell boldly on the men, who were most of them unarmed, and never expected that any men would cut through the double phalanx and break through upon them. When the Persians made this attack, the foreign prisoners also assisted them by falling upon the Macedonians in the midst of the action. But the commanders of the men who had been posted as a reserve to the first phalanx, learning what was taking place, quickly moved from the position which they had been ordered to take, and coming upon the Persians in the rear, killed many of them there collected round the baggage. But the rest of them gave way and fled. The Persians on the right wing, who had not yet become aware of the flight of Darius, rode round Alexander's left wing and attacked Parmenio in flank.

15. At this juncture, the Macedonians being at first in a state of confusion from being attacked on all sides, Parmenio sent a messenger to Alexander in haste, to tell him that their side was in a critical position and that he must send him aid. When this news was brought to Alexander, he turned back again from further pursuit, and wheeling round with the Companion cavalry, led them with great speed against the right wing of the foreigners. In the first place he assaulted the fleeing cavalry of the enemy, the Parthians, some of the Indians, and the most numerous and the bravest division of the Persians. Then ensued the most obstinately contested cavalry fight in the whole engagement. For being drawn up by squadrons, the foreigners wheeled round in deep columns, and falling on Alexander's men face to face, they no longer relied on the hurling of javelins or the dexterous deploying of horses, as is the common practice in cavalry battles, but every one of his own account strove eagerly to break through what stood in his way, as their only

means of safety. They struck and were struck without quarter, as they were no longer struggling to secure the victory for another, but were contending for their own personal safety. Here about sixty of Alexander's Companions fell; and Hephaestion himself, as well as Coenus and Menidas, was wounded. But these troops also were overcome by Alexander; and as many of them as could force their way through his ranks fled with all their might. And now Alexander had nearly come into conflict with the enemy's right wing; but in the meantime the Thessalian cavalry in a splendid struggle, were not falling short of Alexander's success in the engagement. For the foreigners on the right wing were already beginning to fly when he came on the scene of conflict; so that he wheeled round again and started off in pursuit of Darius once more, keeping up the chase as long as there was daylight. Parmenio's brigade also followed in pursuit of those who were opposed to them. But Alexander crossed the river Lycus and pitched his camp there, to give his men and horses a little rest; while Parmenio seized the Persian camp with their baggage, elephants, and camels. After giving his horsemen rest until midnight, Alexander again advanced by a forced march towards Arbela, with the hope of seizing Darius there, together with his money and the rest of his royal property. He reached Arbela the next day, having pursued altogether about seventy miles from the battlefield. But as Darius went on fleeing without taking any rest, he did not find him at Arbela. However the money and all the other property were captured, as was also the chariot of Darius a second time. His spear and bow were likewise taken, as had been the case after the battle of Issus. Of Alexander's men about 100 were killed, and more than 1,000 of his horses were lost either from wounds or from fatigue in the pursuit, nearly half of them belonging to the Companion cavalry. Of the foreigners there were said to have been about 300,000 slain, and far more were taken prisoners than were killed. The elephants and all the chariots which had not been destroyed in the battle were also captured. Such was the result of this battle, which was fought in the archonship of Aristophanes at Athens, in the month Pyanepsion;[9] and thus Aristander's prediction was accomplished, that Alexander would both fight a battle and gain a victory in the same month in which the moon was seen to be eclipsed.

16. Immediately after the battle, Darius marched through the mountains of Armenia towards Media, accompanied in his flight by the Bactrian cavalry, as they had then been posted with him in the battle; also by those Persians who were called the king's kinsmen, and by a few of the men called apple-bearers. About 2,000 of his Grecian mercenaries

[9] September 331 B.C.

also accompanied him in his flight, under the command of Paron the Phocian, and Glaucus the Aetolian. He fled towards Media for this reason, because he thought Alexander would take the road to Susa and Babylon immediately after the battle, inasmuch as the whole of that country was inhabited and the road was not difficult for the transit of baggage; and besides Babylon and Susa appeared to be the prizes of the war; whereas the road towards Media was by no means easy for the march of a large army. In this conjecture Darius was not mistaken; for when Alexander started from Arbela, he advanced straight towards Babylon; and when he was now not far from that city, he drew up his army in order of battle and marched forward. The Babylonians came out to meet him in mass, with their priests and rulers, each of whom individually brought gifts, and offered to surrender their city, citadel, and money. Entering the city, he commanded the Babylonians to rebuild all the temples which Xerxes had destroyed, and especially that of Belus, whom the Babylonians venerate more than any other god. He then appointed Mazaeus viceroy of the Babylonians, Apollodorus the Amphipolitan general of the soldiers who were left behind with Mazaeus, and Asclepiodorus, son of Philo, collector of the revenue. He also sent Mithrines, who had surrendered to him the citadel of Sardis, down into Armenia to be viceroy there. Here also he met with the Chaldaeans; and whatever they directed in regard to the religious rites of Babylon he performed, and in particular he offered sacrifice to Belus according to their instructions. He then marched away to Susa; and on the way he was met by the son of the viceroy of the Susians, and a man bearing a letter from Philoxenus, whom he had despatched to Susa directly after the battle. In the letter Philoxenus had written that the Susians had surrendered their city to him, and that all the money was safe for Alexander. In twenty days the king arrived at Susa from Babylon; and entering the city he took possession of the money, which amounted to 50,-000 talents, as well as the rest of the royal property. Many other things were also captured there, which Xerxes brought with him from Greece, especially the brazen statues of Harmodius and Aristogeiton. These Alexander sent back to the Athenians, and they are now standing at Athens in the Ceramicus, where we go up into the Acropolis, right opposite the temple of Rhea, the mother of the gods, not far from the altar of the Eudanemi. Whoever has been initiated in the mysteries of the two goddesses[10] at Eleusis knows the altar of Eudanemus which is upon the plain. At Susa Alexander offered sacrifice after the custom of his fathers, and celebrated a torch race and a gymnastic contest; and then, leaving Abulites, a Persian, as viceroy of Susiana, Mazarus, one

[10] Demeter and Persephone.

of his Companions, as commander of the garrison in the citadel of Susa, and Archelaus, son of Theodorus, as general, he advanced towards the land of the Persians. He also sent Menes down to the sea, as governor of Syria, Phoenicia, and Cilicia, giving him 3,000 talents of silver to convey to the sea, with orders to despatch as many of them to Antipater as he might need to carry on the war against the Lacedaemonians. There also Amyntas, son of Andromenes, reached him with the forces which he was leading from Macedonia; of whom Alexander placed the horsemen in the ranks of the Companion cavalry, and the foot he added to the various regiments of infantry, arranging each according to nationalities. He also established two companies in each squadron of cavalry, whereas before this time companies did not exist in the cavalry; and over them he set as captains those of the Companions who were preeminent for merit.

17. He now set out from Susa, and, crossing the river Pasitigris, invaded the country of the Uxians. Some of these people who inhabit the plains were under the rule of the viceroy of the Persians, and on this occasion surrendered to Alexander; but those who are called the mountaineers were not in subjection to the Persians, and at this time sent word to Alexander that they would not permit him to march with his forces into Persia, unless they received from him as much as they were in the habit of receiving from the king of the Persians for the passage through their mountains. He sent the messengers back with instructions to come to the defiles, the possession of which made them think that the passage into Persis was in their power, promising them that they should there receive from him the prescribed toll. He then took the royal bodyguards, the shield-bearing infantry, and 8,000 men from the rest of his army, and, under the guidance of the Susians, marched by night along a different road from the frequented one. Advancing by a route rough and difficult, on the same day he fell upon the villages of the Uxians, where he captured much booty and killed many of the people while still in their beds; but others escaped into the mountains. He then made a forced march to the defiles, where the Uxians resolved to meet him in mass in order to receive the prescribed toll. But he had already previously despatched Craterus to seize the heights, to which he thought the Uxians would retire if they were repelled by force; and he himself went with great celerity, and got possession of the pass before their arrival. He then drew up his men in battle array, and led them from the higher and more commanding position against the barbarians. They, being alarmed at Alexander's celerity, and finding themselves deprived by stratagem of the position in which they had especially confided, took to flight without ever coming to close combat. Some of them were killed

by Alexander's men in their flight, and many lost their lives by falling over the precipices along the road; but most of them fled up into the mountains for refuge, and falling in with Craterus, were destroyed by his men. Having received these gifts of honour from Alexander, they with difficulty, after much entreaty, procured from him the privilege of retaining possession of their own land on condition of paying him an annual tribute. Ptolemy, son of Lagus, says that the mother of Darius, on their behalf, entreated Alexander to grant them the privilege of inhabiting the land. The tribute agreed upon was 100 horses, 500 oxen, and 30,000 sheep a year; for the Uxians had no money, nor was their country fit for tillage; but most of them were shepherds and herdsmen.

18. After this, Alexander despatched Parmenio with the baggage, the Thessalian cavalry, the Grecian allies, the mercenary auxiliaries, and the rest of the more heavily armed soldiers, to march into Persis along the carriage road leading into that country. He himself took the Macedonian infantry, the Companion cavalry, the light cavalry used for skirmishing, the Agrianians, and the archers, and made a forced march through the mountains. But when he arrived at the Persian Gates, he found that Ariobarzanes, the viceroy of Persis, with 40,000 infantry and 700 cavalry, had built a wall across the pass, and had pitched his camp there near the wall to block Alexander's passage. Then indeed he pitched his camp there; but next day he marshalled his army, and led it up to the wall. When it was evident that it would be difficult to capture it on account of the rugged nature of the ground, and as many of his men were being wounded, the enemy assailing them with missiles from engines of war placed upon higher ground, which gave them an advantage over their assailants, he retreated to his camp. He was informed by the prisoners that they could lead him round by another route, so that he might get to the other end of the pass; but when he ascertained that this road was rough and narrow, he left Craterus there in command of the camp with his own brigade and that of Meleager, as well as a few archers and 500 cavalry, with orders that when he ascertained that he himself had got right round and was approaching the camp of the Persians (which he would easily ascertain, because the trumpets would give him the signal), he should then assault the wall. Alexander advanced by night, and travelling about twelve miles, he took the shield-bearing guards, the brigade of Perdiccas, the lightest armed of the archers, the Agrianians, the royal squadron of the Companions, and one regiment of cavalry besides these, containing four companies; and wheeling round with these troops, he marched towards the pass in the direction the prisoners led him. He ordered Amyntas, Philotas, and Coenus to lead the rest of the army towards the plain, and to make a bridge over the

river[11] which one must cross to go into Persis. He himself went by a route difficult and rough, along which he nevertheless marched for the most part at full speed. Falling upon the first guard of the barbarians before daylight, he destroyed them, and so he did most of the second; but the majority of the third guard escaped, not indeed by fleeing into the camp of Ariobarzanes, but into the mountains as they were, being seized with a sudden panic. Consequently he fell upon the enemy's camp at the approach of dawn without being observed. At the very time he began to assault the trench, the trumpets gave the signal to Craterus, who at once attacked the advanced fortification. The enemy then, being in a state of confusion from being attacked on all sides, fled without coming to close conflict; but they were hemmed in on all hands, Alexander pressing upon them in one direction and the men of Craterus running up in another. Therefore most of them were compelled to wheel round and flee into the fortifications, which were already in the hands of the Macedonians. For Alexander, expecting the very thing which really occurred, had left Ptolemy there with 3,000 infantry; so that most of the barbarians were cut to pieces by the Macedonians at close quarters. Others perished in the flight which became terrible, hurling themselves over the precipices; but Ariobarzanes himself, with a few horsemen, escaped into the mountains.

Alexander now marched back with all speed to the river, and finding the bridge already constructed over it, he easily crossed with his army. Thence he again continued his march to Persepolis, with such speed that he arrived before the guards of the city could pillage the treasury. He also captured the money which was at Pasargadae in the treasury of the first Cyrus, and appointed Phrasaortes, son of Rheomithres, viceroy over the Persians. He burned down the Persian palace, though Parmenio advised him to preserve it, for many reasons, and especially because it was not well to destroy what was now his own property, and because the men of Asia would not by this course of action be induced to come over to him, thinking that he himself had decided not to retain the rule of Asia, but only to conquer it and depart. But Alexander said that he wished to take vengeance on the Persians, in retaliation for their deeds in the invasion of Greece, when they razed Athens to the ground and burned down the temples. He also desired to punish the Persians for all the other injuries they had done the Greeks. But Alexander does not seem to me to have acted on this occasion with prudence; nor do I think that this was any retributive penalty at all on the ancient Persians.

19. After bringing these matters to a successful issue, he advanced

[11] This was the Araxes.

towards Media; for he ascertained that Darius was there. Now Darius had formed the resolution, if Alexander remained at Susa or Babylon, to stay there among the Medes, in order to see if any change in Alexander's affairs should occur. But if the latter marched against him, he resolved to proceed into the interior towards Parthia and Hyrcania, as far as Bactria, laying waste all the land and making it impossible for Alexander to advance any further. He therefore sent the women and the rest of the property which he still retained, together with the covered carriages, to what were called the Caspian Gates; but he himself stayed at Ecbatana, with the forces which had been collected from those who were at hand. Hearing this, Alexander advanced towards Media, and invading the land of the Paraetacae, he subdued it, and appointed Oxathres, son of Abulites, the former viceroy of Susa, to rule as viceroy. Being informed on the march that Darius had determined to meet him for battle, and to try the fortune of war again (for the Scythians and Cadusians had come to him as allies), he ordered that the beasts of burden, with their guards and the rest of the baggage, should follow; and taking the rest of his army, he led it in order of battle, and on the twelfth day arrived in Media. There he ascertained that the forces of Darius were not fit for battle, and that his allies, the Cadusians and Scythians, had not arrived; but that he had resolved to flee. He therefore marched on with still greater speed; and when he was only three days' journey from Ecbatana, he was met by Bistanes, son of Ochus, who had reigned over the Persians before Darius. This man announced that Darius had fled five days before, taking with him 7,000 talents of money from the Medes, and an army of 3,000 cavalry and 6,000 infantry.

When Alexander reached Ecbatana, he sent the Thessalian cavalry and the other Grecian allies back to the sea, paying them the full hire which had been stipulated, and making them an additional donation from himself of 2,000 talents. He issued an order that if any man of his own accord wished still to continue to serve for hire with him, he should enlist; and those who enlisted in his service were not a few. He then ordered Epocillus, son of Polyeides, to conduct the rest down to the sea, taking other cavalry as a guard for them, since the Thessalians sold their horses there. He also sent word to Menes to take upon himself the duty of seeing that they were conveyed in triremes to Euboea, when they arrived at the sea. He instructed Parmenio to deposit the money which was being conveyed from Persis in the citadel at Ecbatana, and to hand it over to the charge of Harpalus; for he had left this man over the money with a guard of 6,000 Macedonians and a few horsemen and light-armed infantry to take care of it. He told Parmenio himself to take the Grecian mercenaries, the Thracians, and all the other horsemen ex-

cept the Companion cavalry, and march by the land of the Cadusians
into Hyrcania. He also sent word to Clitus, the commander of the royal
squadron of cavalry, who had been left behind at Susa ill, that when he
arrived at Ecbatana from Susa he should take the Macedonians who
had been left there in charge of the money, and go in the direction of
Parthia, where also he himself intended soon to arrive.

20. Then taking the Companion cavalry, the light cavalry used for
skirmishing, the Greek mercenary cavalry, under the command of
Erigyius, the Macedonian phalanx, except the men who had been placed
in charge of the money, the archers, and the Agrianians, he marched
against Darius. In the forced march which he made, many of his soldiers were left behind, worn out with fatigue, and many of the horses
died. He nevertheless pressed on, and on the eleventh day arrived at
Rhagae. This place is distant from the Caspian Gates one day's journey to one marching as Alexander did. But Darius had already passed
through this defile before Alexander came up, though many of those
who were his companions in flight deserted him on the way and retired
to their own abodes. Many also surrendered to Alexander. The latter
now gave up the hope of capturing Darius by close pursuit, and remained there five days to give his troops repose. He appointed Oxodates,
a Persian, who had the ill fortune to have been arrested by Darius and
to be shut up at Susa, to the office of viceroy of Media; for this treatment was an inducement to Alexander to rely on his fidelity. He then
marched towards Parthia; and on the first day encamped near the Caspian Gates, which he passed through on the second day as far as the
country was inhabited. Hearing that the country further on was desert,
he resolved to procure a stock of provisions from the place where he was
encamped, and accordingly sent Coenus out on a foraging expedition
with the cavalry and a small body of infantry.

21. At this time Bagistanes, one of the Babylonian nobles, came to
him from the camp of Darius, accompanied by Antibelus, one of the
sons of Mazaeus. These men informed him that Nabarzanes, the commander of the cavalry which accompanied Darius in his flight, Bessus,
viceroy of the Bactrians, and Barsaentes, viceroy of the Arachotians
and Drangians, had arrested the king. When Alexander heard this, he
marched with still greater speed than ever, taking with him only the
Companions and the skirmishing cavalry, as well as some of the foot-
soldiers selected as the strongest and lightest men. He did not even wait
for Coenus to return from the foraging expedition; but placed Craterus
over the men left behind, with instructions to follow in short marches.
His own men took with them nothing but their arms and provisions for
two days. After marching the whole night and till noon of the next day,

he gave his army a short rest, then went on again all night, and when day began to break reached the camp from which Bagistanes had set out to meet him; but he did not catch the enemy. However, in regard to Darius, he ascertained that he had been arrested and was being conveyed in a covered carriage; that Bessus possessed the command instead of Darius, and had been nominated leader by the Bactrian cavalry and all the other barbarians who were companions of Darius in his flight, except Artabazus and his sons, together with the Grecian mercenaries, who still remained faithful to Darius; but, not being able to prevent what was being done, they had turned aside their march from the public thoroughfare and were marching towards the mountains by themselves, refusing to take part with Bessus and his adherents in their enterprise. He also learned that those who had arrested Darius had come to the decision to surrender him to Alexander, and to procure some advantage for themselves, if they should find that Alexander was pursuing them; but if they should learn that he had gone back again, they had resolved to collect as large an army as they could and to preserve the rule for their common benefit. He also ascertained that for the present Bessus held the supreme command, both on account of his relationship to Darius and because the war was being carried on in his satrapy. Hearing this, Alexander thought it necessary to pursue with all his might; and though his men and horses were already quite fatigued by the incessant severity of their labours, he nevertheless proceeded, and, travelling a long way all through the night and the next day till noon, arrived at a certain village, where those who were leading Darius had encamped the day before. Hearing there that the barbarians had decided to continue their march by night, he inquired of the natives if they knew any shorter road to the fugitives. They said they did know one, but that it ran through a country which was desert through lack of water. He nevertheless ordered them to show him this way, and perceiving that the infantry could not keep up with him if he marched at full speed, he caused 500 of the cavalry to dismount from their horses; and selecting the officers of the infantry and the best of the other foot-soldiers, he ordered them to mount the horses armed just as they were. He also directed Nicanor, the commander of the shield-bearing guards, and Attalus, commander of the Agrianians, to lead their men who were left behind, by the same route which Bessus had taken, having equipped them as lightly as possible; and he ordered that the rest of the infantry should follow in regular marching order. He himself began to march in the afternoon, and led the way with great rapidity.[12] Having trav-

---

[12] Plutarch (*Alexander*, 42) says that Alexander rode about 390 miles, in eleven days. In the next chapter he says that only sixty of his men were able to keep up with him in the pursuit.

elled about forty-seven miles in the night, he came upon the barbarians just before daybreak, going along without any order and unarmed; so that only a few of them rushed to defend themselves, but most of them, as soon as they saw Alexander himself, took to flight without even coming to blows. A few of those who had turned to resist being killed, the rest of these also took to flight. Up to this time Bessus and his party were still conveying Darius with them in a covered carriage; but when Alexander was already close upon them Nabarzanes and Barsaentes wounded him and left him there, and with 600 horsemen took to flight. Darius died from his wounds soon after, before Alexander had seen him.

22. Alexander sent the body of Darius to Persepolis, with orders that it should be buried in the royal sepulchre, in the same way as the other Persian kings before him had been buried. He then proclaimed Amminaspes, a Parthian, viceroy over the Parthians and Hyrcanians. This man was one of those who with Mazaces had surrendered Egypt to Alexander. He also appointed Tlepolemus, son of Pythophanes, one of the Companions, to guard his interests in Parthia and Hyrcania. Such was the end of Darius, in the archonship of Aristophon at Athens, in the month Hecatombaion.[13] This king was a man pre-eminently effeminate and lacking in self-reliance in military enterprises; but as to civil matters he never exhibited any disposition to indulge in arbitrary conduct; nor indeed was it in his power to exhibit it. For it happened that he was involved in a war with the Macedonians and Greeks at the very time he succeeded to the regal power; and consequently it was no longer possible for him to act the tyrant towards his subjects, even if he had been so inclined, standing as he did in greater danger than they. As long as he lived, one misfortune after another befell him; nor did he experience any cessation of calamity from the time when he first succeeded to the rule. In the first place the cavalry defeat was sustained by his viceroys at the Granicus, and forthwith Ionia, Aeolis, both the Phrygias, Lydia, and all Caria except Halicarnassus were occupied by his foe; soon after, Halicarnassus also was captured, and then all the coast-line as far as Cilicia. Then came his own discomfiture at Issus, where he saw his mother, wife, and children taken prisoners. Upon this Phoenicia and the whole of Egypt were lost; and then at Arbela he himself fled disgracefully among the first, and lost a very vast army composed of all the nations of his empire. After this, wandering as an exile from his own kingdom, he died after being betrayed by his personal attendants to the worst treatment possible, being at the same time the Great King and a prisoner ignominiously led in chains; and at last he perished through a conspiracy formed of those most intimately acquainted with

[13] In the year 330 B.C. the first of Hecatombaion fell on the first of July.

him. Such were the misfortunes that befell Darius in his life-time; but after his death he received a royal burial; his children received from Alexander a princely rearing and education, just as if their father were still reigning; and Alexander himself became his son-in-law. When he died he was about fifty years of age.

23. Alexander now took the soldiers whom he had left behind in his pursuit and advanced into Hyrcania, which is the country lying on the left of the road leading to Bactra. On one side it is bounded by lofty mountains densely covered with wood, and on the other it is a plain stretching as far as the Great Sea[14] in this part of the world. He led his army by this route, because he ascertained that the Grecian mercenaries serving under Darius had succeeded in escaping by it into the mountains of Tapuria; at the same time he resolved to subdue the Tapurians themselves. Having divided his army into three parts, he himself led the way by the shortest and most difficult route, at the head of the most numerous and at the same time the lightest division of his forces. He despatched Craterus at the head of his own brigade and that of Amyntas, some of the archers, and a few of the cavalry against the Tapurians; and he ordered Erigyius to take the Grecian mercenaries and the rest of the cavalry, and lead the way by the public thoroughfare, though it was longer, conducting the waggons, the baggage, and the crowd of camp-followers. After crossing the first mountains, and encamping there, he took the shield-bearing guards together with the lightest men in the Macedonian phalanx and some of the archers, and went along a road difficult and hard to travel upon, leaving guards for the roads wherever he thought there was any peril, so that the barbarians who held the mountains might not at those points fall upon the men who were following. Having passed through the defiles with his archers, he encamped in the plain near a small river; and while he was here Nabarzanes, the cavalry commander of Darius, Phrataphernes, the satrap of Hyrcania and Parthia, and the other most distinguished of the Persians in attendance on Darius arrived and surrendered themselves. After waiting four days in the camp, he took up those who had been left behind on the march, all of them advancing in safety except the Agrianians who, while guarding the rear, were attacked by the barbarian mountaineers. But these soon drew off when they got the worst of it in the skirmish. Starting from this place, he advanced into Hyrcania as far as Zadracarta, the capital of the Hyrcanians. In this place he was rejoined by Craterus, who had not succeeded in falling in with the Grecian mercenaries of Darius; but he had thoroughly traversed the whole country, gaining over part of it by force and the other part

[14] The Caspian.

by the voluntary capitulation of the inhabitants. Erigyius also arrived
here with the baggage and waggons; and soon after Artabazus came to
Alexander with three of his sons, Cophen, Ariobarzanes, and Arsames,
accompanied by Autophradates, viceroy of Tapuria, and envoys from
the Grecian mercenaries in the service of Darius. To Autophradates
he restored his satrapy; but Artabazus and his sons he kept near himself in a position of honour, not only because they were among the
first nobles of Persia, but also on account of their fidelity to Darius. To
the envoys from the Greeks, begging him to make a truce with them
on behalf of the whole mercenary force, he replied that he would not
make any agreement with them; because they were acting with great
guilt in serving as soldiers on the side of the barbarians against Greece,
in contravention of the resolution of the Greeks. He commanded them
to come in a body and surrender, leaving it to him to treat them as he
pleased, or to preserve themselves as best they could. The envoys said
that they yielded both themselves and their comrades to Alexander,
and urged him to send some one with them to act as their leader, so
that they might be conducted to him with safety. They said they were
1,500 in number. Accordingly he sent Andronicus, son of Agerrhus, and
Artabazus to them.

24. He then marched forward against the Mardians taking with him
the shield-bearing guards, the archers, the Agrianians, the brigades of
Coenus and Amyntas, half of the Companion cavalry, and the horse-
javelin-men; for he had now a troop of horse-javelin-men. Traversing
the greater part of the land of the Mardians, he killed many of them
in their flight, some indeed having turned to defend themselves; and
many were taken prisoners. No one for a long time had invaded their
land in a hostile manner, not only on account of its ruggedness, but also
because the people were poor, and besides being poor were warlike.
Therefore they never feared that Alexander would attack them, especially as he had already advanced further than their country. For
this reason they were caught more easily off their guard. Many of them,
however, escaped into the mountains, which in their land are very lofty
and craggy, thinking that Alexander would not penetrate to these at
any rate. But when he was approaching them even here, they sent envoys to surrender both the people and their land to him. He pardoned
them, and appointed Autophradates, whom he had also recently placed
over the Tapurians, viceroy over them. Returning to the camp, from
which he had started to invade the country of the Mardians, he found
that the Grecian mercenaries of Darius had arrived, accompanied by
the envoys from the Lacedaemonians who were on an embassy to king
Darius. The names of these men were Callicratidas, Pausippus, Mo-

nimus, Onomas, and Dropides, a man from Athens. These were arrested and kept under guard; but he released the envoys from the Sinopeans, because these people had no share in the commonwealth of the Greeks; and as they were in subjection to the Persians, they did not seem to be doing anything unreasonable in going on an embassy to their own king. He also released the rest of the Greeks who were serving for pay with the Persians before the peace and alliance which had been made by the Greeks with the Macedonians. He likewise released Heraclides, the ambassador from the Calchedonians to Darius. The rest he ordered to serve in his army for the same pay as they had received from the Persian king, putting them under the command of Andronicus, who had led them to him, and had evidently been taking prudent measures to save the lives of the men.

25. Having settled these affairs, he marched to Zadracarta, the largest city of Hyrcania, where also was the seat of the Hyrcanian government. Tarrying here fifteen days, he offered sacrifice to the gods according to his custom, and celebrated a gymnastic contest, after which he began his march towards Parthia; thence to the confines of Areia and to Susia, a city in that province, where Satibarzanes, the viceroy of the Areians, came to meet him. To this man he restored his satrapy, and with him sent Anaxippus, one of the Companions, to whom he gave forty horse-javelin-men so that he might be able to station them as guards of the localities, in order that the Areians might not be injured by the army in its march through their land. At this time came to him some Persians, who informed him that Bessus had his tiara erect[15] and was wearing the Persian dress, calling himself Artaxerxes, instead of Bessus, and asserting that he was king of Asia. They said he had in attendance upon him the Persians who had escaped into Bactra and many of the Bactrians themselves; and that he was expecting the Scythians also to come to him as allies. Alexander, having now all his forces together, went towards Bactra, where Philip son of Menelaus came to him out of Media with the Greek mercenary cavalry which were under his own command, those of the Thessalians who had volunteered to remain, and of the men of Andromachus. Nicanor, the son of Parmenio, the commander of the shield-bearing guards, had already died of disease.[16] While Alexander was on his way to Bactra, he was informed that Satibarzanes, viceroy of Areia, had killed Anaxippus and the horse-javelin-men who were with him, had armed the

[15] The cap of the ordinary Persians was low, loose, and clinging about the head in folds; whereas that of the king was high and erect above the head.

[16] This sentence is out of place here in the Mss., and probably came at the end of the next chapter.

Areians and collected them in the city of Artacoana, which was the capital of that nation. It was also said that he had resolved, as soon as he ascertained that Alexander had advanced, to leave that place and go with his forces to Bessus, with the intention of joining that prince in an attack upon the Macedonians, wherever a chance might occur. When he received this news, he stopped the march towards Bactra, and taking with him the Companion cavalry, the horse-javelin-men, the archers, the Agrianians and the regiments of Amyntas and Coenus, and leaving the rest of his forces there under the command of Craterus, he made a forced march against Satibarzanes and the Areians; and having travelled seventy miles in two days came near Artacoana. Satibarzanes, however, no sooner perceived that Alexander was near, than being struck with terror at the quickness of his arrival, he took to flight with a few Areian horsemen. For he was deserted by the majority of his soldiers in his flight, when they also learned that Alexander was at hand. The latter made rapid marches in pursuit of the men whom he discovered to be guilty of the revolt and who at that time had left their villages, fleeing in various directions; some of them he killed and others he sold into slavery. He then proclaimed Arsames, a Persian, viceroy over the Areians. Being now joined by the men who had been left behind with Craterus, he marched into the land of the Zarangaeans, and reached the place where their seat of government was. But Barsaentes, who at that time had possession of the land, being one of those who had fallen upon Darius in his flight, learning that Alexander was approaching, fled to the Indians who live this side of the river Indus. But they arrested him and sent him back to Alexander, by whom he was put to death on account of his guilty conduct towards Darius.

26. Here also Alexander discovered the conspiracy of Philotas, son of Parmenio. Ptolemy and Aristobulus say that it had already been reported to him before in Egypt; but that it did not appear to him credible, both on account of the long-existing friendship between them, the honour which he publicly conferred upon his father Parmenio, and the confidence he reposed in Philotas himself. Ptolemy, son of Lagus, says that Philotas was brought before the Macedonians, that Alexander vehemently accused him, and that he defended himself from the charges. He says also that the divulgers of the plot came forward and convicted him and his accomplices both by other clear proofs and especially because Philotas himself confessed that he had heard of a certain conspiracy which was being formed against Alexander. He was convicted of having said nothing to the king about this plot, though he visited the royal tent twice a day. He and all the others who had taken part with him in the conspiracy were killed by the Macedonians with their

javelins; and Polydamus, one of the Companions, was despatched to Parmenio, carrying letters from Alexander to the generals in Media, Cleander, Sitalces, and Menidas, who had been placed over the army commanded by Parmenio. By these men Parmenio was put to death, perhaps because Alexander deemed it incredible that Philotas should conspire against him and Parmenio not participate in his son's plan; or perhaps, he thought that even if he had had no share in it, he would now be a dangerous man if he survived, after his son had been violently removed, being held in such great respect as he was both by Alexander himself and by all the army, not only the Macedonian, but also that of the Grecian auxiliaries as well, whom he often used to command in accordance with Alexander's order, both in his own turn and out of his turn, with his sovereign's approbation and satisfaction.

27. They also say that about the same time Amyntas, son of Andromenes, was brought to trial, together with his brothers Polemo, Attalus, and Simmias, on the charge of being accessory to the conspiracy against Alexander, on account of their trust in Philotas and their intimate friendship with him. The belief in their participation in the plot was strengthened among the mass of men by the fact that when Philotas was arrested, Polemo, one of the brothers of Amyntas, fled to the enemy. But Amyntas with his other two brothers stayed to await the trial, and defended himself so vigorously among the Macedonians that he was declared innocent of the charge. As soon as he was acquitted in the assembly, he demanded that permission should be given him to go to his brother and bring him back to Alexander. To this the Macedonians acceded; so he went away and on that very day brought Polemo back. On this account he now seemed free from guilt much more than before. But soon after, as he was besieging a certain village, he was shot with an arrow and died of the wound; so that he derived no other advantage from his acquittal except that of dying with an unsullied reputation.

Alexander appointed two commanders over the Companion cavalry, Hephaestion, son of Amyntor, and Clitus, son of Dropidas, dividing the brigade of the Companions into two parts, because he did not wish any one of his friends to have the sole command of so many horsemen, especially as they were the best of all his cavalry, both in public estimation and in martial discipline. He now arrived in the land of the people formerly called Ariaspians, but afterwards named Euergetae, because they assisted Cyrus, son of Cambyses, in his invasion of Scythia. Alexander honoured these people, for the services which their ancestors had rendered to Cyrus; and when he ascertained that the men not only enjoyed a form of government unlike that of the other barbarians in that part of the world, but laid claim to justice equally with the best of the Greeks, he set them free, and gave them besides as much of the adjacent country as they asked for themselves; but they did not ask for much. Here he offered sacrifice to Apollo, and arrested Demetrius, one of his confidential body-guards, on suspicion of having been implicated with Philotas in the conspiracy. Ptolemy, son of Lagus, was appointed to the post vacated by Demetrius.

28. After the transaction of this business, he advanced towards Bactra against Bessus, reducing the Drangians and Gadrosians to subjection on his march. He also reduced the Arachotians to subjection and appointed Menon viceroy over them. He then reached the Indians, who inhabit the land bordering on that of the Arachotians. All these nations he reached marching through deep snow and his soldiers experiencing scarcity of provisions and severe hardship. Learning that the Areians had again revolted, in consequence of Satibarzanes invading their land with 2,000 cavalry, which he had received from Bessus, he despatched against them Artabazus the Persian with Erigyius and Caranus, two of the Companions, also ordering Phrataphernes, satrap of the Parthians, to assist them in attacking the Areians. An obstinately contested battle then took place between the troops of Erigyius and Caranus and those of Satibarzanes; nor did the barbarians give way until Satibarzanes, encountering Erigyius, was struck in the face with a spear and killed. Then the barbarians gave way and fled with headlong speed.

Meantime Alexander was leading his army towards Mount Caucasus,[17] where he founded a city and named it Alexandreia. Having offered sacrifice here to the gods to whom it was his custom to sacrifice, he crossed Mount Caucasus, after appointing Proexes, a Persian, viceroy over the land, and leaving Neiloxenus, son of Satyrus, one of the Companions, with an army as superintendent. According to the account of Aristobulus, Mount Caucasus is as lofty as any in Asia; and much of it is bare, at any rate in that part where Alexander crossed it. This range of mountains stretches out so far that they say even that Mount Taurus, which forms the boundary of Cilicia and Pamphylia, springs from it, as do other great ranges which have been distinguished from the Caucasus by various names according to the position of each. Aristobulus says that in this part of the Caucasus nothing grew except terebinth trees[18] and silphium;[19] notwithstanding which it was in-

---

[17] This was not the range usually so called, but what was known as the Indian Caucasus, the proper name being Paropamisus. It is now called Hindu-Koosh.

[18] The turpentine-tree, grows to the height of thirty or thirty-five feet, and turpentine is obtained from it by incisions.

[19] There are two kinds of silphium or laserpitium, the Cyrenaic, and the Persian. The latter is usually called asafoetida.

habited by many people, and many sheep and oxen graze there; because
sheep are very fond of silphium. For if a sheep smells it even from a
distance, it runs to it and feeds upon the flower. They also dig up the
root, which is devoured by the sheep. For this reason in Cyrene some
drive their flocks as far as possible away from the places where their
silphium is growing; others even inclose the place with a fence, so that
even if the sheep should approach it they would not be able to get within
the inclosure. For the silphium is very valuable to the Cyrenaeans.

Bessus, accompanied by the Persians who had taken part with him
in the seizure of Darius, and by 7,000 of the Bactrians themselves and
the Daäns who dwell on this side the Tanais, was laying waste the country at the foot of Mount Caucasus, in order to prevent Alexander from
marching any further, both by the desolation of the land between the
enemy and himself and by the lack of provisions. But none the less did
Alexander keep up the march, though with difficulty, both on account
of the deep snow and from the want of necessaries; but yet he persevered
in his journey. When Bessus was informed that Alexander was now
not far off, he crossed the river Oxus, and having burned the boats upon
which he had crossed, he withdrew to Nautaca in the land of Sogdiana.
He was followed by Spitamenes and Oxyartes, with the cavalry from
Sogdiana, as well as by the Daäns from the Tanais. But the Bactrian
cavalry, perceiving that Bessus had resolved to take to flight, all dispersed in various directions to their own abodes.

29. Alexander now arrived at Drapsaca, and having there given his
army a rest, he marched to Aornus and Bactra, which are the largest
cities in the land of the Bactrians. These he took at the first assault;
and left a garrison in the citadel of Aornus, over which he placed Archelaus son of Androcles, one of the Companions. He appointed Artabazus,
the Persian, satrap over the rest of the Bactrians, who were easily reduced to submission. Then he marched towards the river Oxus, which
flows from Mount Caucasus, and is the largest of all the rivers in Asia
which Alexander and his army reached, except the Indian rivers; but
the Indian rivers are the largest in the world. The Oxus discharges its
water into the great sea which is near Hyrcania. When he attempted
to cross the river it appeared altogether impassable; for its breadth
was about three-quarters of a mile, and its depth was much greater
than the proportion of its breadth. The bed of the river was sandy,
and the stream so rapid that stakes fixed deep into the bottom were
easily rooted up from the earth by the mere force of the current, inasmuch as they could not be securely fixed in the sand. Besides this,
there was a scarcity of timber in the locality, and he thought it would
take a long time and cause great delay if they fetched from a distance

the materials needful for making a bridge over the river. Therefore he collected the skins which the soldiers used for tent-coverings, and ordered them to be filled with chaff as dry as possible, and tied and stitched tightly together, so that no water might penetrate into them. When these were filled and stitched together, they were sufficient to convey the army across in five days. But before he crossed the river, he selected the oldest of the Macedonians, who were now unfit for military service, and such of the Thessalians as had volunteered to remain in the army, and sent them back home. He then dispatched Stasanor, one of the Companions, into the land of the Areians, with instructions to arrest Arsames, the viceroy of that people, because he thought him disaffected, and to assume the office of viceroy of Areia himself.

After passing over the river Oxus, he made a forced march to the place where he heard that Bessus was with his forces; but at this time messengers reached him from Spitamenes and Dataphernes, to announce that they would arrest Bessus and hand him over to Alexander if he would send to them merely a small army and a commander for it; since even at that very time they were holding him under guard, though they had not bound him with fetters. When Alexander heard this, he gave his army rest, and marched more slowly than before. But he dispatched Ptolemy, son of Lagus, at the head of three regiments of the Companion cavalry and all the horse-javelin-men, and of the infantry, the brigade of Philotas, one regiment of 1,000 shield-bearing guards, all the Agrianians, and half the archers, with orders to make a forced march to Spitamenes and Dataphernes. Ptolemy went according to his instruction, and completing ten days' march in four days, arrived at the camp where on the preceding day the barbarians under Spitamenes had bivouacked.

30. Here Ptolemy learned that Spitamenes and Dataphernes were not firmly resolved about the betrayal of Bessus. He therefore left the infantry behind with orders to follow him in regular order, and advanced with the cavalry till he arrived at a certain village, where Bessus was with a few soldiers; for Spitamenes and his party had already retired from thence, being ashamed to betray Bessus themselves. Ptolemy posted his cavalry right round the village, which was inclosed by a wall supplied with gates. He then issued a proclamation to the barbarians in the village that they would be allowed to depart uninjured if they surrendered Bessus to him. They accordingly admitted Ptolemy and his men into the village. He then seized Bessus and returned; but sent a messenger on before to ask Alexander how he was to conduct Bessus into his presence. Alexander ordered him to bind the prisoner naked in a wooden collar, and thus to lead him and place him on the

right-hand side of the road along which he was about to march with the army. Thus did Ptolemy. When Alexander saw Bessus, he caused his chariot to stop, and asked him for what reason he had in the first place arrested Darius, his own king, who was also his kinsman and benefactor, and then led him as a prisoner in chains, and at last killed him. Bessus said that he was not the only person who had decided to do this, but that it was the joint act of those who were at the time in attendance upon Darius, with the view of procuring safety for themselves from Alexander. For this Alexander ordered that he should be scourged, and that the herald should repeat the very same reproaches which he had himself made to Bessus in his inquiry. After being thus disgracefully tortured, he was sent away to Bactra to be put to death. Such is the account given by Ptolemy in relation to Bessus; but Aristobulus says that Spitamenes and Dataphernes brought Bessus to Ptolemy, and having bound him naked in a wooden collar betrayed him to Alexander.

Alexander supplied his cavalry with horses from that district, for many of his own horses had perished in the passage of the Caucasus and in the march to and from the Oxus. He then led his army to Maracanda,[20] which is the capital of the land of the Sogdianians. Thence he advanced to the river Tanais. This river, which Aristobulus says the neighbouring barbarians call by a different name, Jaxartes, has its source, like the Oxus, in Mount Caucasus, and also discharges itself into the Hyrcanian Sea.[21] It must be a different Tanais from that of which Herodotus the historian speaks, saying that it is the eighth of the Scythian rivers, that it flows out of a great lake in which it originates, and discharges itself into a still larger lake, called the Maeotis. There are some who make this Tanais the boundary of Europe and Asia, saying that the lake Maeotis, issuing from the further recess of the Euxine Sea, and this river Tanais, which discharges itself into the Maeotis, separate Asia and Europe, just in the same way as the sea near Gadeira and the Nomad Libyans opposite Gadeira separates Libya and Europe. Libya also is said by these men to be divided from the rest of Asia by the river Nile. In this place, at the river Tanais, some of the Macedonians, being scattered in foraging, were cut to pieces by the barbarians. The perpetrators of this deed escaped to a mountain, which was very rugged and precipitous on all sides. In number they were about 30,000. Alexander took the lightest men in his army and marched against these. Then the Macedonians made many ineffectual assaults upon the moun-

[20] The modern Samarkand.
[21] Arrian and Strabo are wrong in stating that the Jaxartes rises in the Caucasus, or Hindu-Koosh. It does not flow into the Hyrcanian, or Caspian Sea, but into the Sea of Aral. It is about 900 miles long.

tain. At first they were beaten back by the missiles of the barbarians, and many of them were wounded, including Alexander himself, who was shot right through the leg with an arrow, and the fibula of his leg was broken. Notwithstanding this, he captured the place, and some of the barbarians were cut to pieces there by the Macedonians, while many also cast themselves down from the rocks and perished; so that out of 30,000 not more than 8,000 got off safely.

BOOK IV

1. A few days after this, envoys reached Alexander from the people called Abian Scythians, whom Homer commended in his poem, calling them the justest of men. This nation dwells in Asia and is independent, chiefly by reason of its poverty and love of justice. Envoys also came from the Scythians of Europe, who are the largest nation dwelling in that continent. Alexander sent some of the Companions with them, under the pretext indeed that they were to conclude a friendly alliance by the embassy; but the real object of the mission was rather to spy into the natural features of the Scythian land, the number of the inhabitants and their customs, as well as the armaments which they possessed for making military expeditions. He formed a plan of founding a city near the river Tanais, which was to be named after himself; for the site seemed to him suitable and likely to cause the city to grow to large dimensions. He also thought it would be built in a place which would serve as a favourable basis of operations for an invasion of Scythia, if such an event should ever occur; and not only so, but it would also be a bulwark to secure the land against the incursions of the barbarians dwelling on the further side of the river. Moreover he thought that the city would become great, both by reason of the multitude of those who would join in colonising it, and on account of the celebrity of the name conferred upon it. Meantime the barbarians dwelling near the river seized upon the Macedonian soldiers who were garrisoning their cities and killed them; after which they began to strengthen the cities for their greater security. Most of the Sogdianians joined them in this revolt, being urged on to it by the men who had arrested Bessus. These men were so energetic that they even induced some of the Bactrians to join in their rebellion, either because they were afraid of Alexander, or because their seducers assigned as a reason for their revolt that he had sent instructions to the rulers of that land to assemble for a conference at Zariaspa, the chief city; which conference, they said, would be for no good purpose.

2. When Alexander was informed of this, he gave instructions to each particular company of infantry to prepare the ladders which were assigned to each company. He then started from the camp and advanced

to the nearest city, the name of which was Gaza; for the barbarians of the land were said to have fled for refuge into seven cities. He sent Craterus to the one called Cyropolis, the largest of them all, into which most of the barbarians had gathered. The orders of Craterus were to encamp near the city, to dig a trench round it, to surround it with a stockade, and to fix together the military engines which were required for use, so that the men in this city, having had their attention drawn to his forces, might be unable to render aid to the other cities. As soon as Alexander arrived at Gaza, without any delay he gave the signal to his men to place the ladders against the wall all round and to take it by assault at once, as it was made merely of earth and was not at all high. Simultaneously with the approach of the infantry, his slingers, archers, and javelin-throwers assailed the defenders on the wall, and missiles were hurled from the military engines, so that the wall was quickly cleared of its defenders by the multitude of the missiles. Then the fixing of the ladders and the mounting of the Macedonians upon the wall were matters soon effected. They killed all the men, according to Alexander's injunctions; but the women, the children, and the rest of the booty they carried off as plunder. Thence he immediately marched to the city situated next to that one; and this he took in the same way and on the same day, treating the captives in the same manner. Then he marched against the third city, and took it on the next day at the first assault. While he was thus occupied by these matters with the infantry, he sent out his cavalry to the two neighbouring cities, with orders to guard the men within them closely, so that when they heard of the capture of the neighbouring cities, and at the same time of his own near approach, they should not betake themselves to flight and render it impossible for him to pursue them. It turned out just as he had conjectured; and his dispatch of the cavalry was made just at the nick of time. For when the barbarians who occupied the two cities still uncaptured saw the smoke rising from the city in front of them which was then on fire (and some men, escaping even from the midst of the calamity itself, became the reporters of the capture which they had themselves witnessed), they began to flee in crowds out of the cities as fast as each man could; but falling in with the dense body of cavalry drawn up in array of battle, most of them were cut to pieces.

3. Having thus captured the five cities and reduced them to slavery in two days, he went to Cyropolis, the largest city in the country. It was fortified with a wall higher than those of the others, as it had been founded by Cyrus. The majority of the barbarians of this district, and at the same time the most warlike of them, had fled for refuge thither, and consequently it was not possible for the Macedonians to capture

it so easily at the first assault. Wherefore Alexander brought his military engines up to the wall with the determination of battering it down in this direction, and of making assaults wherever breaches might be made in it from time to time. But when he observed that the course of the river, which flows through the city when it is swollen by the winter rains, was at that time nearly dry and did not reach up to the wall, and would thus afford his soldiers a passage by which to penetrate into the city, he took the body-guards, the shield-bearing guards, the archers, and Agrianians, and made his way secretly into the city along the channel, at first with a few men, while the barbarians had turned their attention towards the military engines and those who were assailing them in that direction. Having from within broken open the gates which were opposite this position, he gave an easy admittance to the rest of his soldiers. Then the barbarians, though they perceived that their city was already in the hands of the enemy, nevertheless turned against Alexander and his men and made a desperate assault upon them, in which Alexander himself received a violent blow on the head and neck with a stone, and Craterus was wounded with an arrow, as were also many other officers. Notwithstanding this, however, they drove the barbarians out of the market-place. Meantime, those who had made the assault upon the wall took it, as it was now void of defenders. In the first capture of the city about 8,000 of the enemy were killed. The rest fled for refuge into the citadel; for 15,000 warriors in all had gathered together into the city. Alexander encamped around these and besieged them for one day, and then they surrendered through lack of water. The seventh city he took at the first assault. Ptolemy says that the men in it surrendered; but Aristobulus asserts that this city was also taken by storm, and that he slew all who were captured therein. Ptolemy also says that he distributed the men among the army and ordered that they should be kept guarded in chains until he should depart from the country, so that none of those who had effected the revolt should be left behind. Meantime an army of the Asiatic Scythians arrived at the bank of the river Tanais, because most of them had heard that some of the barbarians on the opposite side of the river had revolted from Alexander. They intended to attack the Macedonians, if any revolutionary movement worthy of consideration were effected. News was also brought that Spitamenes was besieging the men who had been left in the citadel at Maracanda. Against him Alexander then dispatched Andromachus, Menedemus, and Caranus with sixty of the Companion cavalry, 800 of the mercenary cavalry under the command of Caranus, and 1,500 mercenary infantry. Over them he placed Pharnuches the interpreter, who, though by birth a Lycian, was skilled in the language of the bar-

barians of this country, and in other respects appeared clever in dealing with them.

4. In twenty days he fortified the city which he was projecting, and
settled in it some of the Grecian mercenaries and those of the neighbouring barbarians who volunteered to take part in the settlement, as
well as some of the Macedonians from his army who were now unfit
for military service. He then offered sacrifice to the gods in his customary manner and celebrated an equestrian and gymnastic contest.
When he saw that the Scythians were not retiring from the river's bank,
but were seen shooting arrows into the river, which was not wide here,
and were uttering audacious words in their barbaric tongue to insult
Alexander, to the effect that he dared not touch Scythians, or if he did,
he would learn what was the difference between them and the Asiatic
barbarians, he was irritated by these remarks, and having resolved to
cross over against them, he began to prepare the skins for the passage
of the river. But when he offered sacrifice with a view to crossing, the
victims proved to be unfavourable; and though he was vexed at their
not being favourable, he nevertheless controlled himself and remained
where he was. But as the Scythians did not desist from their insults,
he again offered sacrifice with a view to crossing; and Aristander the
soothsayer told him that the omens still portended danger to himself.
But Alexander said that it was better for him to come into extreme danger than that, after having subdued almost the whole of Asia, he should
be a laughing-stock to Scythians, as Darius, the father of Xerxes, had
been long ago. Aristander refused to explain the will of the gods contrary to the revelations made by the deity simply because Alexander
wished to hear the contrary. When the skins had been prepared for the
passage, and the army, fully equipped, had been posted near the river,
the military engines, at the signal preconcerted, began to shoot at the
Scythians riding along the river's bank. Some of them were wounded by
the missiles, and one was struck right through the wicker-shield and
breastplate and fell from his horse. The others, being alarmed at the
discharge of missiles from so great a distance, and at the death of their
champion, retreated a little from the bank. But Alexander, seeing them
thrown into confusion by the effect of his missiles, began to cross the
river with trumpets sounding, himself leading the way; and the rest of
the army followed him. Having first got the archers and slingers across,
he ordered them to sling and shoot at the Scythians, to prevent them
approaching the phalanx of infantry stepping out of the water, until
all his cavalry had passed over. When they were upon the bank in dense
mass, he first of all launched against the Scythians one regiment of the
Grecian auxiliary cavalry and four squadrons of pike-men. These the

Scythians received, and in great numbers riding round them in circles, wounded them, as they were few in number, themselves escaping with ease. But Alexander mixed the archers, the Agrianians, and other light troops under the command of Balacrus, with the cavalry, and then led them against the enemy. As soon as they came to close quarters, he ordered three regiments of the cavalry Companions and all the horse-javelin-men to charge them. The rest of the cavalry he himself led, and made a rapid attack with his squadrons in column. Accordingly the enemy were no longer able as before to wheel their cavalry force round in circles, for at one and the same time the cavalry and the light-armed infantry mixed with the horsemen pressed upon them, and did not permit them to wheel about in safety. Then the flight of the Scythians was already apparent. One thousand of them fell, including Satraces, one of their chiefs; and 150 were captured. But as the pursuit was keen and fatiguing on account of the excessive heat, the entire army was seized with thirst; and Alexander himself while riding drank of such water as was procurable in that country. He was seized with an incessant diarrhoea; for the water was bad; and for this reason he could not pursue all the Scythians. Otherwise I think all of them would have perished in the flight, if Alexander had not fallen ill. He was carried back to the camp, having fallen into extreme danger; and thus Aristander's prophecy was fulfilled.

5. Soon after this, arrived envoys from the king of the Scythians, who were sent to apologize for what had been done, and to state that it was not the act of the Scythian State, but of certain men who set out for plunder after the manner of freebooters. They also assured him that their king was willing to obey the commands laid upon him. Alexander sent to him a courteous reply, because it did not seem honourable for him to abstain from marching against him if he distrusted him, and at that time there was not a convenient opportunity to do so. The Macedonians who were garrisoning the citadel at Maracanda, when an assault was made upon it by Siptamenes and his adherents, sallied forth, and killing some of the enemy and repulsing all the rest, retreated into the citadel without any loss. But when Spitamenes was informed that the men dispatched by Alexander to Maracanda were now drawing near, he raised the siege of the citadel, and retired to the capital of Sogdiana. Pharnuches and the generals with him, being eager to drive him out altogether, followed him up as he was retreating towards the frontiers of Sogdiana, and without due consideration made a joint attack upon the Nomad Scythians. Then Spitamenes, having received a reinforcement of 600 Scythian horsemen, was further emboldened by the Scythian alliance to wait and receive the Macedonians who were advancing upon

him. Posting his men in a level place near the Scythian desert, he was not willing either to wait for the enemy or to attack them himself; but rode round and discharged arrows at the phalanx of infantry. When the forces of Pharnuches made a charge upon them, they easily escaped, since their horses were swifter and at that time more vigorous, while the cavalry of Andromachus had been exhausted by the incessant marching, as well as by lack of fodder; and the Scythians pressed upon them with all their might whether they halted or retreated. Many of them then were wounded by the arrows, and some were killed. The leaders therefore arranged the soldiers into the form of a square and retreated to the river Polytimetus, because there was a woody glen near it, and it would consequently no longer be easy for the barbarians to shoot arrows at them, and their infantry would be more useful to them. But Caranus, the commander of the cavalry, without communicating with Andromachus, attempted to cross the river in order to put the cavalry in a place of safety on the other side. The infantry followed him without any word of command, their stepping into the river being made in a panic and without any discipline down precipitous banks. When the barbarians perceived the error of the Macedonians, they charged into the ford here and there, horses and all. Some of them seized and held tight those who had already crossed and were departing; others, being posted right in front of those who were crossing, rolled them over into the river; others shot arrows at them from the flanks; while others pressed upon the men who were just entering the water. The Macedonians, being thus encompassed with difficulty on all sides, fled for refuge into one of the small islands in the river, where they were entirely surrounded by the Scythians and the cavalry of Spitamenes, and all killed with arrows, except a few of them, whom they reduced to slavery. All of these were afterwards killed.

6. But Aristobulus says the greater part of this army was destroyed by an ambuscade, the Scythians having hidden themselves in a park and fallen upon the Macedonians from their place of concealment, when Pharnuches was in the very act of trying to retire from the command in favour of the Macedonians who had been sent with him, on the ground of his not being skilled in military affairs, and of his having been sent by Alexander rather to win the favour of the barbarians than to take the supreme command in battles. He also alleged that the Macedonian officers present were the king's Companions. But Andromachus, Menedemus, and Caranus declined to accept the chief command, partly because it did not seem right to make any alteration on their own responsibility contrary to Alexander's instructions to them, and partly because in the very crisis of danger, they were unwilling, if they met

with any defeat, not only individually to take a share of the blame, but also having exercised the command unsuccessfully to incur the whole of it. In this confusion and disorder the barbarians fell upon them, and cut them all off, so that not more than forty horsemen and 300 foot preserved their lives. When the report of this reached Alexander, he was chagrined at the loss of his soldiers, and resolved to march with all speed against Spitamenes and his barbarian adherents. He therefore took half of the Companion cavalry, all the shield-bearing guards, the archers, the Agrianians, and the lightest men of the phalanx, and went towards Maracanda, where he ascertained Spitamenes had returned and was again besieging the men in the citadel. Having travelled 175 miles in three days, at the approach of dawn on the fourth day he came near the city; but when Spitamenes and his party were informed of Alexander's approach, they did not remain, but abandoned the city and fled. Alexander pursued them closely; and coming to the place where the battle was fought, he buried his soldiers as well as the circumstances permitted, and then followed the fugitives as far as the desert. Returning thence, he laid the land waste, and slew the barbarians who had fled for refuge into the fortified places, because they were reported to have taken part in the attack upon the Macedonians. He traversed the whole country which the river Polytimetus waters in its course; but the country beyond the place where the water of this river disappears is desert; for though it has abundance of water, it disappears into the sand. Other large and perennial rivers in that region disappear in a similar way: the Epardus, which flows through the land of the Mardians; the Areius, after which the country of the Areians is named; and the Etymander, which flows through the territory of the Euergetae. All of these are rivers of such a size that none of them is smaller than the Thessalian river Peneius, which flows through Tempe and discharges itself into the sea. The Polytimetus is much too large to be compared with the river Peneius.

7. When he had accomplished this, he came to Zariaspa, where he remained until the depth of winter arrived. At this time came to him Phrataphernes the viceroy of Parthia, and Stasanor, who had been sent into the land of the Areians to arrest Arsames. Him they brought with them in chains, as also Barzanes, whom Bessus had appointed satrap of the land of the Parthians, and some others of those who at that time had joined Bessus in revolt. At the same time arrived from the sea Epocillus, Melamnidas and Ptolemy, the general of the Thracians, who had convoyed down to the sea the Grecian allies and the money sent with Menes. At this time also arrived Asander and Nearchus at the head of an army of Grecian mercenaries. Asclepiodorus, viceroy of Syria,

and Menes the deputy also arrived from the sea, at the head of another army. Then Alexander gathered a conference of those who were then at hand, and led Bessus in before them. Having accused him of the betrayal of Darius, he ordered his nose and ears to be cut off, and that he should be taken to Ecbatana to be put to death there in the council of the Medes and Persians. I do not commend this excessive punishment of Bessus; on the contrary, I consider that the mutilation of the prominent features of the body is a barbaric custom, and I agree with those who say that Alexander was led on by degrees to indulge his desire of emulating the Median and Persian wealth and to treat his subjects as inferior beings in his intercourse with them according to the custom of the foreign kings. Nor do I by any means commend him for changing the Macedonian style of dress of his fathers for the Median one, being as he was a descendant of Heracles. Besides, he was not ashamed to exchange the head-dress which he the conqueror had so long worn, for that of the conquered Persians. None of these things do I commend; but I consider Alexander's great achievements prove, if anything can, that supposing a man to have a vigorous bodily constitution, to be illustrious in descent, and to be even more successful in war than Alexander himself; even supposing he could sail right round Libya as well as Asia, and hold them both in subjection as Alexander indeed designed; even if he could add the possession of Europe to that of Asia and Libya; all these things would be no furtherance to such a man's happiness, unless at the same time he possess the power of self-control, though he has performed deeds which are supposed to be great.[1]

8. Here then I shall give an account of the tragic fate of Clitus, son of Dropidas, and of Alexander's mishap in regard to it. Though it occurred a little while after this, it will not be out of place here. The Macedonians kept a day sacred to Dionysus, and on that day Alexander used to offer sacrifice to him every year. But they say that on this occasion he was neglectful of Dionysus, and sacrificed to the Dioscuri[2] instead; for he had resolved to offer sacrifice to those deities for some reason or other. When the drinking-party on this occasion had already gone on too long (for Alexander had now made innovations even in regard to drinking, by imitating too much the custom of foreigners), and in the midst of the carouse a discussion had arisen about the Dioscuri, how their procreation had been taken away from Tyndareus and ascribed to Zeus, some of those present, in order to flatter Alexander, maintained that Polydeuces and Castor were in no way worthy to com-

---

[1] Arrian was a pupil of Epictetus, the Stoic; hence we need not wonder at this expression of opinion.
[2] The sons of Zeus, Castor and Pollux.

pare with him and his exploits. Such men have always destroyed and will never cease to ruin the interests of those who happen to be reigning. In their carousal they did not even abstain from comparing him with Heracles, saying that envy stood in the way of the living receiving the honours due to them from their associates. It was well known that Clitus had long been vexed at Alexander for the change in his style of living in excessive imitation of foreign customs, and at those who flattered him with their speech. At that time also, being heated with wine, he would not permit them either to insult the deity or, by depreciating the deeds of the ancient heroes, to confer upon Alexander this gratification which deserved no thanks. He affirmed Alexander's deeds were neither in fact at all so great or marvellous as they represented in their laudation; nor had he achieved them by himself, but for the most part they were the deeds of the Macedonians. The delivery of this speech annoyed Alexander; and I do not commend it, for I think, in such a drunken bout, it would have been sufficient if, so far as he was personally concerned, he had kept silence, and not committed the error of indulging in the same flattery as the others. But when some even mentioned Philip's actions without exercising a just judgment, declaring that he had performed nothing great or marvellous, they herein gratified Alexander; but Clitus being then no longer able to contain himself, began to put Philip's achievements in the first rank, and to depreciate Alexander and his performances. Clitus being now quite intoxicated, made other depreciatory remarks and even vehemently reviled him, because after all he had saved his life, when the cavalry battle had been fought with the Persians at the Granicus. Then indeed, arrogantly stretching out his right hand, he said, "This hand, O Alexander, preserved you on that occasion." Alexander could now no longer endure the drunken insolence of Clitus; but jumped up against him in a great rage. He was however restrained by his boon companions. As Clitus did not desist from his insulting remarks, Alexander shouted out a summons for his shield-bearing guards to attend him; but when no one obeyed him, he said that he was reduced to the same position as Darius, when he was led about under arrest by Bessus and his adherents, and that he now possessed the mere name of king. Then his companions were no longer able to restrain him; for according to some he leaped up and snatched a javelin from one of his confidential body-guards; according to others, a long pike from one of his ordinary guards, with which he struck Clitus and killed him. Aristobulus does not say whence the drunken quarrel originated, but asserts that the fault was entirely on the side of Clitus, who, when Alexander had got so enraged with him as to jump up against him with the intention of making an end of him, was led away by Ptolemy, son of Lagus, the confidential body-guard, through the gateway, beyond the wall and ditch of the citadel where the quarrel occurred. He adds that Clitus could not control himself, but went back again, and falling in with Alexander who was calling out for Clitus, he exclaimed, "Alexander, here am I, Clitus!" Thereupon he was struck with a long pike and killed.

9. I think Clitus deserving of severe censure for his insolent behaviour to his king, while at the same time I pity Alexander for his mishap, because on that occasion he showed himself the slave of two vices, anger and drunkenness, by neither of which is it seemly for a prudent man to be enslaved. But then on the other hand I think his subsequent behaviour worthy of praise, because directly after he had done the deed he recognized that it was a horrible one. Some of his biographers even say that he propped the pike against the wall with the intention of falling upon it himself, thinking that it was not proper for him to live who had killed his friend when under the influence of wine. Most historians do not mention this, but say that he went off to bed and lay there lamenting, calling Clitus himself by name, and his sister Lanice, daughter of Dropidas, who had been his nurse. He exclaimed that having reached man's estate he had certainly bestowed a noble reward on her for her care in rearing him, as she had lived to see her own sons die fighting on his behalf, and he himself had slain her brother with his own hand. He did not cease calling himself the murderer of his friends; and for three days rigidly abstained from food and drink, and paid no attention whatever to his personal appearance. Some of the soothsayers revealed that the avenging wrath of Dionysus had been the cause of his conduct, because he had omitted the sacrifice to that deity. At last with great difficulty he was induced by his companions to touch food and to pay proper attention to his person. He then paid to Dionysus the sacrifice due to him, since he was not at all unwilling that the fatality should be attributed rather to the avenging wrath of the deity than to his own depravity. I think Alexander deserves great praise for this, that he did not obstinately persevere in evil, or still worse become a defender and advocate of the wrong which had been done, but confessed that he had committed a crime, being a man (and therefore liable to err). There are some who say that Anaxarchus the Sophist was summoned into Alexander's presence to give him consolation. Finding him lying down and groaning, he laughed at him, and said that he did not know that the wise men of old for this reason made Justice an assessor of Zeus, because whatever was done by him was justly done; and therefore also that which was done by the Great King ought to be deemed just, in the first place by the king himself, and then by the

rest of men. They say that Alexander was then greatly consoled by these remarks. But I assert that Anaxarchus did Alexander a great injury and one still greater than that by which he was then oppressed, if he really thought this to be the opinion of a wise man, that indeed it is proper for a king to come to hasty conclusions and act unjustly, and that whatever is done by a king must be deemed just, no matter how it is done. There is also a current report that Alexander wished men to prostrate themselves before him (as to a god) entertaining the notion that Ammon was his father, rather than Philip; and that he now showed his admiration of the customs of the Persians and Medes by changing the style of his dress, and by the alteration he made in the general etiquette of his court. There were not wanting those who in regard to these matters gave way to his wishes with the design of flattering him; among others being Anaxarchus, one of the philosophers attending his court, and Agis, an Argive who was an epic poet.

10. But it is said that Callisthenes the Olynthian, who had studied philosophy under Aristotle, and was somewhat brusque in his manner, did not approve of this conduct; and so far as this is concerned I quite agree with him. But the following remark of his, if indeed it has been correctly recorded, I do not think at all proper, when he declared that Alexander and his exploits were dependent upon him and his history, and that he had not come to him to acquire reputation from him, but to make him renowned among men; consequently that Alexander's participation in divinity did not depend on the false assertion of Olympias in regard to his procreation, but on what he might report to mankind in his history of the king. There are some writers also who have said that on one occasion Philotas asked him what man he thought to be held in especial honour by the people of Athens; and that he replied, "Harmodius and Aristogeiton; because they slew one of the two despots, and put an end to the despotism." Philotas again asked, "If a man happened now to kill a despot, to which of the Grecian States would you wish him to flee for preservation?" Callisthenes again replied, "If not among others, at any rate among the Athenians an exile would be able to find preservation; for they waged war on behalf of the sons of Heracles against Eurystheus, who at that time was ruling as a despot over Greece." How he resisted Alexander in regard to the ceremony of prostration, the following is the most received account.[3] An arrangement was made between Alexander and the Sophists in conjunction with the most illustrious of the Persians and Medes who were in at-

---

[3] When Conon the famous Athenian visited Babylon, he would not see Artaxerxes, from repugnance to the ceremony of prostration, which was required from all who approached the Great King.

tendance upon him, that this topic should be mentioned at a wine-party. Anaxarchus commenced the discussion by saying that Alexander would much more justly be deemed a god than either Dionysus or Heracles, not only on account of the very numerous and mighty exploits which he had performed, but also because Dionysus was only a Theban, in no way related to Macedonians; and Heracles was an Argive, not at all related to them, except in regard to Alexander's pedigree; for he was a descendant of Heracles. He added that the Macedonians might with greater justice gratify their king with divine honours, for there was no doubt about this, that when he departed from men they would honour him as a god. How much more just then would it be to reward him while alive, than after his death, when it would be no advantage to him to be honoured.

11. When Anaxarchus had uttered these remarks and others of a similar kind, those who were privy to the plan applauded his speech, and wished at once to begin the ceremony of prostration. Most of the Macedonians, however, were vexed at the speech and kept silence. But Callisthenes interposed and said, "O Anaxarchus, I openly declare that there is no honour which Alexander is unworthy to receive, provided that it is consistent with his being human; but men have made distinctions between those honours which are due to men and those due to gods, in many different ways, as for instance by the building of temples and by the erection of statues. Moreover for the gods sacred inclosures are selected, to them sacrifice is offered, and to them libations are made. Hymns also are composed in honour of the gods, and eulogies for men. But the greatest distinction is made by the custom of prostration. For it is the practice that men should be kissed by those who salute them; but because the deity is located somewhere above, it is not lawful even to touch him, and this is the reason no doubt why he is honoured by prostration. Bands of choral dancers are also appointed for the gods, and paeans are sung in their honour. And this is not at all wonderful, seeing that certain honours are specially assigned to some of the gods and certain others to other gods, and, by Zeus, quite different ones again are assigned to heroes, which are very distinct from those paid to the deity. It is not therefore reasonable to confound all these distinctions without discrimination, exalting men to a rank above their condition by extravagant accumulation of honours, and debasing the gods, as far as lies in human power, to an unseemly level, by paying them honours only equal to those paid to men." He said that Alexander would not endure the affront, if some private individual were to be thrust into his royal honours by an unjust vote, either by show of hands or by ballot. Much more justly then would the gods be indignant at those mortals

who usurp divine honours or suffer themselves to be thrust into them by others. "Alexander not only seems to be, but is in reality beyond any competition the bravest of brave men, of kings the most kingly, and of generals the most worthy to command an army. O Anaxarchus, it was your duty rather than any other man's to become the special advocate of these arguments now adduced by me, and the opponent of those contrary to them, seeing that you associate with him for the purpose of imparting philosophy and instruction. Therefore it was unseemly to begin this discussion, when you ought to have remembered that you are not associating with and giving advice to Cambyses or Xerxes, but to the son of Philip, who derives his origin from Heracles and Aeacus, whose ancestors came into Macedonia from Argos, and have continued to rule the Macedonians, not by force, but by law. Not even to Heracles himself while still alive were divine honours paid by the Greeks; and even after his death they were withheld until a decree had been published by the oracle of the god at Delphi that men should honour Heracles as a god. But if, because the discussion is held in the land of foreigners, we ought to adopt the sentiments of foreigners, I for my part demand, O Alexander, that you should think of Greece, for whose sake the whole of this expedition was undertaken by you, that you might join Asia to Greece. Therefore make up your mind whether you will return thither and compel the Greeks, who are men most devoted to freedom, to pay you the honour of prostration, or whether you will keep aloof from Greeks, and inflict this dishonour on the Macedonians alone, or thirdly whether you will make a difference altogether as to the honours to be paid you, so as to be honoured by the Greeks and Macedonians as a human being and after the manner of the Greeks, and by foreigners alone after the foreign fashion. But if it is said that Cyrus, son of Cambyses, was the first man to whom the honour of prostration was paid and that afterwards this degrading ceremony continued in vogue among the Persians and Medes, we ought to bear in mind that the Scythians, men poor but independent, chastened that Cyrus; that other Scythians again chastened Darius, as the Athenians and Lacedaemonians did Xerxes, as Clearchus and Xenophon with their 10,000 followers did Artaxerxes; and finally, that Alexander, though not honoured with prostration, has chastened this Darius."

12. By making these and other remarks of a similar kind, Callisthenes greatly annoyed Alexander, but spoke the exact sentiments of the Macedonians. When the king perceived this, he sent to prevent the Macedonians from making any further mention of the ceremony of prostration. But after the discussion silence ensued; and then the most honourable of the Persians arose in due order and prostrated their bodies

before him. But when one of the Persians seemed to have performed the ceremony in an awkward way, Leonnatus, one of the Companions, laughed at his posture as mean. Alexander at the time was angry with him for this, but was afterwards reconciled to him. The following account has also been given: Alexander drank from a golden goblet the health of the circle of guests, and handed it first to those with whom he had concerted the ceremony of prostration. The first who drank from the goblet rose up and performed the act of prostration, and received a kiss from him. This ceremony proceeded from one to another in due order. But when the pledging of health came to the turn of Callisthenes, he rose up and drank from the goblet, and drew near, wishing to kiss the king without performing the act of prostration. Alexander happened then to be conversing with Hephaestion, and consequently did not observe whether Callisthenes performed the ceremony completely or not. But when Callisthenes was approaching to kiss him, Demetrius, son of Pythonax, one of the Companions, said that he was doing so without having prostrated himself. So the king would not permit him to kiss him; whereupon the philosopher said, "I am going away only with the loss of a kiss." I by no means approve any of these proceedings, which manifested both the insolence of Alexander on the present occasion and the churlish nature of Callisthenes. But I think that, so far as regards himself, it would have been quite sufficient if he had expressed himself discreetly, magnifying as much as possible the exploits of the king, with whom no one thought it a dishonour to associate. Therefore I consider that not without reason Callisthenes became odious to Alexander on account of the unseasonable freedom of speech in which he indulged, as well as from the egregious fatuity of his conduct. I surmise that this was the reason why such easy credit was given to those who accused him of participating in the conspiracy formed against Alexander by his pages, and to those also who affirmed that they had been incited to engage in the conspiracy by him alone. The facts of this conspiracy were as follows.

13. It was a custom introduced by Philip that the sons of those Macedonians who had enjoyed high office, should, as soon as they reached the age of puberty, be selected to attend the king's court. These youths were entrusted with the general attendance on the king's person and the protection of his body while he was asleep. Whenever the king rode out, some of them received the horses from the grooms, and brought them to him, and others assisted him to mount in the Persian fashion. They were also companions of the king in the emulation of the chase. Among these youths was Hermolaus, son of Sopolis, who seemed to be applying his mind to the study of philosophy, and to be cultivating the society of

Callisthenes for this purpose. There is current a tale about this youth to the effect that, in the chase, a boar rushed at Alexander, and that Hermolaus anticipated him by casting a javelin at the beast, by which it was smitten and killed. But Alexander, having lost the opportunity of distinguishing himself by being too late in the assault, was indignant with Hermolaus, and in his wrath ordered him to receive a scourging in sight of the other pages, and also deprived him of his horse. This Hermolaus, being chagrined at the disgrace he had incurred, told Sostratus, son of Amyntas, who was his equal in age and his lover, that life would be insupportable to him unless he could take vengeance upon Alexander for the affront. He easily persuaded Sostratus to join in the enterprise, since he was fondly attached to him. They gained over to their plans Antipater, son of Asclepiodorus, who had been viceroy of Syria, Epimenes son of Arseas, Anticles son of Theocritus, and Philotas son of Carsis the Thracian. They therefore agreed to kill the king by attacking him in his sleep, on the night when the nocturnal watch came round to Antipater's turn. Some say that Alexander accidently happened to be drinking until day-break; but Aristobulus has given the following account: A Syrian woman, who was under the inspiration of the deity, used to follow Alexander about. At first she was a subject of mirth to Alexander and his courtiers; but when all that she said in her inspiration was seen to be true, he no longer treated her with neglect, but she was allowed to have free access to him both by night and day, and she often took her stand near him even when he was asleep. And indeed on that occasion, when he was withdrawing from the drinking-party she met him, being under the inspiration of the deity at the time, and besought him to return and drink all night. Alexander, thinking that there was something divine in the warning, returned and went on drinking; and thus the enterprise of the pages fell through. The next day, Epimenes, son of Arseas, one of those who took part in the conspiracy, spoke of the undertaking to Charicles, son of Menander, who had become his lover; and Charicles told it to Eurylochus, brother of Epimenes. Eurylochus went to Alexander's tent and related the whole affair to Ptolemy, son of Lagus, one of the confidential body-guards. He told Alexander, who ordered those whose names had been mentioned by Eurylochus to be arrested. These, being put on the rack, confessed their own conspiracy, and mentioned the names of certain others.

14. Aristobulus says that the youths asserted it was Callisthenes who instigated them to make the daring attempt; and Ptolemy says the same.[4] Most writers, however, do not agree with this, but represent

[4] Alexander wrote to Craterus, Attalus, and Alcetas that the pages, though put to the torture, asserted that no one but themselves was privy to the conspiracy.

that Alexander readily believed the worst about Callisthenes, from the hatred which he already felt towards him, and because Hermolaus was known to be exceedingly intimate with him. Some authors have also recorded the following particulars: that Hermolaus was brought before the Macedonians, to whom he confessed that he had conspired against the king's life, because it was no longer possible for a free man to bear his insolent tyranny. He then recounted all his acts of despotism, the illegal execution of Philotas, the still more illegal one of his father Parmenio and of the others who were put to death at that time, the murder of Clitus in a fit of drunkenness, the assumption of the Median garb, the introduction of the ceremony of prostration, which had been planned and not yet relinquished, and the drinking-bouts and lethargic sleep arising from them. He said that, being no longer able to bear these things, he wished to free both himself and the other Macedonians. These same authors say that Hermolaus himself and those who had been arrested with him were stoned to death by those who were present. Aristobulus says that Callisthenes was carried about with the army bound with fetters, and afterwards died a natural death; but Ptolemy, son of Lagus, says that he was stretched upon the rack and then hanged. Thus not even did these authors whose narratives are very trustworthy, and who at the time were in intimate association with Alexander, give accounts consistent with each other of events so well known, and the circumstances of which could not have escaped their notice. Other writers have given many various details of these same proceedings which are inconsistent with each other; but I think I have written quite sufficient on this subject. Though these events took place shortly after, I have described them among those which happened to Alexander in reference to Clitus, because, for the purposes of narrative, I consider them very intimately connected with each other.

15. Another embassy from the European Scythians came to Alexander with the envoys whom he had despatched to those people; for the king who was reigning over them, at the time when he sent these envoys, happened to die, and his brother was reigning in his stead. The object of the embassy was to state that the Scythians were willing to do whatsoever Alexander commanded. They were also bringing to him from their king the gifts which among them are deemed most valuable. They said their monarch was willing to give his daughter to Alexander in marriage, in order to confirm the friendship and alliance with him; but

---

In another letter, written to Antipater the regent of Macedonia, he says that the pages had been stoned to death by the Macedonians, but that he himself would punish the Sophist, and those who sent him out, and those who harboured in their cities conspirators against him. Aristotle had sent Callisthenes out. Alexander refers to him and the Athenians. See Plutarch (*Alexander,* 55).

if Alexander himself deigned not to marry the princess of the Scythians, then he was willing at any rate to give the daughters of the governors of the Scythian territory and of the other mighty men throughout the country of Scythia to the most faithful of Alexander's officers. He also sent word that he would come in person if bidden, in order to hear from Alexander's own mouth what his orders were. At this time also came Pharasmanes, king of the Chorasmians, to Alexander with 1,500 horsemen, who affirmed that he dwelt on the confines of the nations of the Colchians and the women called Amazons, and promised, if Alexander was willing to march against these nations in order to subjugate the races in this district whose territories extended to the Euxine Sea, to act as his guide through the mountains and to supply his army with provisions. Alexander then gave a courteous reply to the men who had come from the Scythians, and one that was adapted to the exigencies of that particular time; but said that he had no desire for a Scythian wedding. He also commended Pharasmanes and concluded a friendship and alliance with him, saying that at present it was not convenient for him to march towards the Euxine Sea. After introducing Pharasmanes as a friend to Artabazus the Persian, to whom he had intrusted the government of the Bactrians, and to all the other viceroys who were his neighbours, he sent him back to his own abode. He said that his mind at that time was engrossed by the desire of conquering the Indians; for when he had subdued them, he should possess the whole of Asia. He added that when Asia was in his power he would return to Greece, and thence make an expedition with all his naval and military forces to the eastern part of the Euxine Sea through the Hellespont and Propontis. He desired Pharasmanes to reserve the fulfillment of his present promises until then.

Alexander then returned to the river Oxus, with the intention of advancing into Sogdiana, because news was brought that many of the Sogdianians had fled for refuge into their strongholds and refused to submit to the viceroy whom he had placed over them. While he was encamping near the river Oxus, a spring of water and near it another of oil rose from the ground not far from Alexander's own tent. When this prodigy was announced to Ptolemy, son of Lagus, the confidential body-guard, he told Alexander, who offered the sacrifices which the prophets directed on account of the phenomenon. Aristander affirmed that the spring of oil was the sign of labours; but it also signified that after the labours there would be victory.

16. He therefore crossed the river with a part of his army and entered Sogdiana, leaving Polysperchon, Attalus, Gorgias, and Meleager there among the Bactrians, with instructions to guard the land, to prevent the

barbarians of that region from making any revolutionary change, and to reduce those who had already rebelled. He divided the army which he had with him into five parts; the first of which he put under the command of Hephaestion, the second under that of Ptolemy, son of Lagus, the confidential body-guard; over the third he put Perdiccas; Coenus and Artabazus commanded the fourth brigade for him, while he himself took the fifth division and penetrated into the land towards Maracanda. The others also advanced as each found it practicable, reducing by force some of those who had fled for refuge into the strongholds, and capturing others who surrendered to them on terms of capitulation. When all his forces reached Maracanda, after traversing the greater part of the land of the Sogdianians, he sent Hephaestion away to plant colonies in the cities of Sogdiana. He also sent Coenus and Artabazus into Scythia, because he was informed that Spitamenes had fled for refuge thither; but he himself with the rest of his army traversed Sogdiana and easily reduced all the places still held by the rebels.

While Alexander was thus engaged, Spitamenes, accompanied by some of the Sogdianian exiles, fled into the land of the Scythians called Massagetians, and having collected 600 horsemen from this nation, he came to one of the forts in Bactria. Falling upon the commander of this fort, who was not expecting any hostile demonstration, and upon those who were keeping guard with him, he destroyed the soldiers, and capturing the commander, kept him in custody. Being emboldened by the capture of this fort, a few days after he approached Zariaspa; but resolving not to attack the city, he marched away after collecting a great quantity of booty. But at Zariaspa a few of the Companion cavalry had been left behind on the score of illness, and with them Peithon, son of Sosicles, who had been placed over the royal household of attendants at Zariaspa, and Aristonicus the harper. These men, hearing of the incursion of the Scythians, and having now recovered from their illness, took their arms and mounted their horses. Then collecting eighty mercenary Grecian horsemen, who had been left behind to guard Zariaspa, and some of the royal pages, they sallied forth against the Massagetians. Falling upon the Scythians, who had no suspicion of such an event, they deprived them of all the booty at the first onset, and killed many of those who were driving it off. But as no one was in command, they returned without any regard to order: and being drawn into an ambush by Spitamenes and other Scythians, they lost seven of the Companions and sixty of the mercenary cavalry. Aristonicus the harper was also slain there, having proved himself a brave man, beyond what might have been expected of a harper. Peithon, being wounded, was taken prisoner by the Scythians.

17. When this news was brought to Craterus, he made a forced march

against the Massagetians, who, when they heard that he was marching against them, fled as fast as they could towards the desert. Following them up closely, he overtook those very men and more than 1,000 other Massagetian horsemen, not far from the desert. A fierce battle ensued, in which the Macedonians were victorious. Of the Scythians, 150 horsemen were slain; but the rest of them easily escaped into the desert, for it was impossible for the Macedonians to pursue them any further. At this time Alexander relieved Artabazus of the satrapy of the Bactrians, at his own request, on the ground of his advanced age; and Amyntas, son of Nicolaus, was appointed viceroy in his stead. Coenus was left there with his own brigade and that of Meleager, 400 of the Companion cavalry, and all the horse-javelin-men, besides the Bactrians, Sogdianians, and others who were under the command of Amyntas. They were all under strict injunctions to obey Coenus and to winter there in Sogdiana, in order to protect the country and to arrest Spitamenes, if anyhow they might be able to draw him into an ambush, as he was wandering about during the winter. But when Spitamenes saw that every place was occupied by the Macedonians with garrisons, and that there was no way of flight left open to him, he turned round against Coenus and the army with him, thinking that he would have a better chance of victory in this way. Coming to Bagae, a fortified place in Sogdiana, situated on the confines of the countries of the Sogdianians and the Massagetian Scythians, he easily persuaded 3,000 Scythian horsemen to join him in an invasion of Sogdiana. It is an easy matter to induce these Scythians to engage in one war after another, because they are pinched by poverty, and at the same time have no cities or settled abodes to give them cause for anxiety about what is most dear to them. When Coenus ascertained that Spitamenes was advancing with his cavalry, he went to meet him with his army. A sharp contest ensued, in which the Macedonians were victorious, so that of the barbarian cavalry over 800 fell in the battle, while Coenus lost twenty-five horsemen and twelve foot-soldiers. The consequence was that the Sogdianians who were still left with Spitamenes, as well as most of the Bactrians, deserted him in the flight, and came to Coenus to surrender. The Massagetian Scythians having met with ill-success in the battle, plundered the baggage of the Bactrians and Sogdianians who were serving in the same army as themselves, and then fled into the desert in company with Spitamenes. But when they were informed that Alexander was already on the start to march into the desert, they cut off the head of Spitamenes and sent it to him, with the hope by this deed of diverting him from pursuing them.

18. Meantime Coenus returned to Alexander at Nautaca, as also did Craterus, Phrataphernes the satrap of the Parthians, and Stasanor the

viceroy of the Areians, after executing all the orders which Alexander had given them. The king then caused his army to rest around Nautaca, because it was now mid-winter; but he despatched Phrataphernes into the land of the Mardians and Tapurians to fetch Autophradates the viceroy, because, though he had often been sent for, he did not obey the summons. He also sent Stasanor as viceroy into the land of the Drangians, and Atropates into Media, with the appointment of viceroy over the Medes, because Oxodates seemed disaffected to him. Stamenes also he despatched to Babylon, because news came to him that Mazaeus the Babylonian governor was dead. Sopolis, Epocillus, and Menidas he sent away to Macedonia, to bring him the army up from that country. At the first appearance of spring, he advanced towards the rock in Sogdiana, to which he was informed many of the Sogdianians had fled for refuge; among whom were said to be the wife and daughters of Oxyartes the Bactrian, who had deposited them for safety in that place, as if it were impregnable. For he also had revolted from Alexander. If this rock was captured, it seemed that nothing would any longer be left to those of the Sogdianians who wished to throw off their allegiance. When Alexander approached it, he found it precipitous on all sides against assault, and that the barbarians had collected provisions for a long siege. The great quantity of snow which had fallen helped to make the approach more difficult to the Macedonians, while at the same time it kept the barbarians supplied with plenty of water. But notwithstanding all this, he resolved to assault the place; for a certain overweening and insolent boast uttered by the barbarians had thrown him into a wrathful state of ambitious pertinacity. For when they were invited to come to terms of capitulation, and it was held out to them as an inducement that, if they surrendered the place, they would be allowed to withdraw in safety to their own abodes, they burst out laughing, and in their barbaric tongue bade Alexander seek winged soldiers, to capture the mountain for him, since they had no apprehension of danger from other men. He then issued a proclamation that the first man who mounted should have a reward of twelve talents, the man who came next to him the second prize, and the third so on in proportion, so that the last reward should be 300 darics to the last prize-taker who reached the top. This proclamation excited the valour of the Macedonians still more, though they were even before very eager to commence the assault.

19. All the men who had gained practice in scaling rocks in sieges, banded themselves together to the number of 300, and provided themselves with the small iron pegs with which their tents had been fastened to the ground, with the intention of fixing them into the snow, wherever it might be seen to be frozen hard, or into the ground, if it should any-

where exhibit itself free from snow. Tying strong ropes made of flax to these pegs, they advanced in the night towards the most precipitous part of the rock, which was on this account most unguarded; and fixing some of these pegs into the earth, where it made itself visible, and others into the snow where it seemed least likely to crumble, they hoisted themselves up the rock, some in one place and some in another. Thirty of them perished in the ascent; and as they fell into various parts of the snow, not even could their bodies be found for burial. The rest, however, reached the top of the mountain at the approach of dawn; and taking possession of it, they waved linen flags towards the camp of the Macedonians, as Alexander had directed them to do. He now sent a herald with instructions to shout to the sentries of the barbarians to make no further delay, but surrender at once; since the winged men had been found, and the summits of the mountain were in their possession. At the same time the herald pointed at the soldiers upon the crest of the mountain. The barbarians, being alarmed by the unexpectedness of the sight, and suspecting that the men who were occupying the peaks were more numerous than they really were, and that they were completely armed, surrendered, so frightened did they become at the sight of those few Macedonians. The wives and children of many important men were there captured, including those of Oxyartes. This chief had a daughter, a maiden of marriageable age, named Roxana, who was asserted by the men who served in Alexander's army to have been the most beautiful of all the Asiatic women whom they had seen, with the single exception of the wife of Darius. They also say that no sooner did Alexander see her than he fell in love with her; but though he was in love with her, he refused to offer violence to her as a captive, and did not think it derogatory to his dignity to marry her. This conduct of Alexander I think worthy rather of praise than blame. Moreover, in regard to the wife of Darius, who was said to be the most beautiful woman in Asia, he either did not entertain a passion for her, or else he exercised control over himself, though he was young, and in the very meridian of success, when men usually act with insolence and violence. On the contrary, he acted with modesty and spared her honour, exercising a great amount of chastity, and at the same time exhibiting a very proper desire to obtain a good reputation.

20. In relation to this subject there is a story current, that soon after the battle which was fought at Issus between Darius and Alexander, the eunuch who was guardian of Darius's wife escaped and came to him. When Darius saw this man, his first inquiry was whether his children, wife, and mother were alive? Ascertaining that they were not only alive, but were called queens, and enjoyed the same personal service and

attention which they had been accustomed to have by direction of
Darius, he thereupon made a second inquiry, whether his wife was still
chaste? When he ascertained that she remained so, he asked again
whether Alexander had not offered any violence to her to gratify his
lust? The eunuch took an oath and said, "O king, your wife is just as
you left her; and Alexander is the best and most chaste of men." Upon
this Darius stretched his hands towards heaven and prayed as follows,
"O King Zeus, to whom power has been assigned to regulate the affairs
of kings among men, do you now protect for me first and above all the
empire of the Persians and Medes, as indeed you gave it to me. But if
I am no longer king of Asia, at any rate do you hand over my power to
no other man but Alexander." Thus not even to enemies are chaste actions a matter of unconcern. Oxyartes, hearing that his children were
in the power of Alexander, and that he was treating his daughter Roxana
with respect, took courage and came to him. He was held in honour at
the king's court, as was natural after such a piece of good fortune.

21. When Alexander had finished his operations among the Sogdianians, and was now in possession of the rock, he advanced into the
land of the Paraetacians, because many of the barbarians were said to
be holding another rock, a strongly fortified place in that country. This
was called the rock of Chorienes; and to it Chorienes himself and many
other chiefs had fled for refuge. The height of this rock was about two
and one-half miles, and the circuit about seven. It was precipitous on
all sides, and there was only one ascent to it, which was narrow and
not easy to mount, since it had been constructed in spite of the nature
of the place. It was therefore difficult to ascend even by men in single
file and when no one barred the way. A deep ravine also enclosed the
rock all round, so that whoever intended to lead an army up to it must
long before make a causeway of earth over this ravine in order that he
might start from level ground, when he led his troops to the assault.
Notwithstanding all this, Alexander undertook the enterprise. To so
great a pitch of audacity had he advanced through his career of success
that he thought every place ought to be accessible to him, and to be
captured by him. He cut down the pines, which were very abundant and
lofty all round the mountain, and made ladders of them, so that by
means of them the soldiers might be able to descend into the ravine;
for otherwise it was impossible for them to do so. During the day-time
he himself superintended the work, keeping half of his army engaged
in it; and during the night his confidential body-guards, Perdiccas, Leonnatus, and Ptolemy, son of Lagus, in turn, with the other half of the
army, divided into three parts, performed the duty which had been assigned to each for the night. But they could complete no more than

thirty feet in a day, and not quite so much in a night, though the whole army engaged in the labour; so difficult was the place to approach and so hard was the work in it. Descending into the ravine, they fastened pegs into the steepest and narrowest part of it, distant from each other as far as was consistent with strength to support the weight of what was placed upon them. Upon these they placed hurdles made of willow and osiers, very much in the form of a bridge. Binding these together, they loaded earth above them, so that there might be an approach to the rock for the army on level ground. At first the barbarians derided, as if the attempt was altogether abortive; but when the arrows began to reach the rock, and they were unable to drive back the Macedonians, though they themselves were on a higher level, because the former had constructed screens to ward off the missiles, that they might carry on their labour under them without receiving injury, Chorienes grew alarmed at what was being done, and sent a herald to Alexander, beseeching him to send Oxyartes up to him. Alexander accordingly sent Oxyartes, who on his arrival persuaded Chorienes to entrust himself and the place to Alexander; for he told him that there was nothing which Alexander and his army could not take by storm; and as he himself had entered into an alliance of fidelity and friendship with him, he commended the king's honour and justice in high terms, adducing other examples, and above all his own case for the confirmation of his arguments. By these representations Chorienes was persuaded and came himself to Alexander, accompanied by some of his relations and companions. When he arrived, the king gave him a courteous answer to his inquiries, and retained him after pledging his fidelity and friendship. But he bade him send to the rock some of those who came down with him to order his men to surrender the place; and it was surrendered by those who had fled to it for refuge. Alexander therefore took 500 of his shield-bearing guards and went up to get a view of the rock; and was so far from inflicting any harsh treatment upon Chorienes that he entrusted that very place to him again, and made him governor of all that he had ruled before. It happened that the army suffered much hardship from the severity of the winter, a great quantity of snow having fallen during the siege; while at the same time the men were reduced to great straits from lack of provisions. But Chorienes said he would give the army food for two months; and he gave the men in every tent corn, wine, and salted meat out of the stores in the rock. When he had given them this, he said he had not exhausted even the tenth part of what had been laid up for the siege. Hence Alexander held him in still greater honour, inasmuch as he had surrendered the rock, not so much from compulsion as from his own inclination.

22. After performing this exploit, Alexander himself went to Bactra; but sent Craterus with 600 of the cavalry Companions and his own brigade of infantry as well those of Polysperchon, Attalus, and Alcetas, against Catanes and Austanes, who were the only rebels still remaining in the land of the Paraetacenians. A sharp battle was fought with them, in which Craterus was victorious; Catanes being killed there while fighting, and Austanes being captured and brought to Alexander. Of the barbarians with them 120 horsemen and about 1,500 foot soldiers were killed. When Craterus had done this, he also went to Bactra, where the tragedy in reference to Callisthenes and the pages befell Alexander. As the spring was now over, he took the army and advanced from Bactra towards India, leaving Amyntas in the land of the Bactrians with 3,500 horse, and 10,000 foot. He crossed the Caucasus in ten days and arrived at the city of Alexandria, which had been founded in the land of the Parapamisadae when he made his first expedition to Bactra. He dismissed from office the governor whom he had then placed over the city, because he thought he was not ruling well. He also settled in Alexandria others from the neighbouring tribes and the soldiers who were now unfit for service in addition to the first settlers, and commanded Nicanor, one of the Companions, to regulate the affairs of the city itself. Moreover he appointed Tyriaspes viceroy of the land of the Parapamisadae and of the rest of the country as far as the river Cophen. Arriving at the city of Nicaea, he offered sacrifice to Athena and then advanced towards the Cophen, sending a herald forward to Taxiles and the other chiefs on this side the river Indus, to bid them come and meet him as each might find it convenient. Taxiles and the other chiefs accordingly did come to meet him, bringing the gifts which are reckoned of most value among the Indians. They said that they would also present to him the elephants which they had with them, twenty-five in number. There he divided his army, and sent Hephaestion and Perdiccas away into the land of Peucelaotis, towards the river Indus, with the brigades of Gorgias, Clitus, and Meleager, half of the Companion cavalry, and all the cavalry of the Grecian mercenaries. He gave them instructions either to capture the places on their route by force, or to bring them over on terms of capitulation; and when they reached the river Indus, to make the necessary preparations for the passage of the army. With them Taxiles and the other chiefs also marched. When they reached the river Indus they carried out all Alexander's orders. But Astes, the ruler of the land of Peucelaotis, effected a revolt, which both ruined himself and brought ruin also upon the city into which he had fled for refuge. For Hephaestion captured it after a siege of thirty days, and Astes himself was killed. Sangaeus, who had some time before fled from Astes and deserted to

Taxiles, was appointed to take charge of the city. This desertion was a pledge to Alexander of his fidelity.

23. Alexander now took command of the shield-bearing guards, the Companion cavalry with the exception of those who had been joined with Hephaestion's division, the regiments of what were called the foot-Companions, the archers, the Agrianians and the horse-javelin-men, and advanced with them into the land of the Aspasians, Guraeans and Assacenians. Marching by a mountainous and rough road along the river called Choes, which he crossed with difficulty, he ordered the main body of his infantry to follow at leisure; while he himself took all the cavalry, and 800 of the Macedonian infantry whom he mounted upon horses with their infantry shields, and made a forced march, because he had received information that the barbarians who inhabited that district had fled for safety into the mountains which extend through the land and into as many of their cities as were strong enough to resist attack. Assaulting the first of these cities which was situated on his route, he routed, at the first attack without any delay, the men whom he found drawn up in front of the city, and shut them up in it. He was himself wounded by a dart which penetrated through the breastplate into his shoulder; but his wound was only a slight one, for the breastplate prevented the dart from penetrating right through his shoulder. Leonnatus and Ptolemy, son of Lagus, were also wounded. Then he encamped near the city at the place where the wall seemed most easy to assault. At dawn on the following day the Macedonians easily forced their way through the first wall, as it had not been strongly built. The city had been surrounded with a double wall. At the second wall the barbarians stood their ground for a short time; but when the scaling ladders were now being fixed, and the defenders were being wounded with darts from all sides, they no longer stayed, but rushed through the gates out of the city towards the mountains. Some of them were killed in the flight, and the Macedonians, being enraged because they had wounded Alexander, slew all whom they took prisoners. Most of them, however, escaped into the mountains, because they were not far from the city. Having levelled this city with the ground, he marched to another, named Andaca, which he got possession of by capitulation. He left Craterus there with the other commanders of the infantry to capture all the remaining cities which would not yield of their own accord, and to set the affairs of the whole country in such order as he should find most convenient under the circumstances.

24. Alexander now took command of the shield-bearing guards, the archers, the Agrianians, the brigades of Coenus and Attalus, the royal body-guard of cavalry, about four regiments of the other Companion cavalry, and half of the horse-archers, and advanced towards the river

Euaspla, where the chieftain of the Aspasians was. After a long journey
he arrived at the city on the second day. When the barbarians ascertained that he was approaching they set fire to the city and fled to the
mountains. But Alexander followed close upon the fugitives as far as the
mountains, and slaughtered many of them before they could manage
to get away into the places which were difficult of access. Ptolemy, son
of Lagus, observing that the leader himself of the Indians of that district
was on a certain hill, and that he had some of his shield-bearing guards
round him, though he had with himself far fewer men, yet he still continued to pursue him on horseback. But as the hill was difficult for his
horse to run up, he left it there, handing it over to one of the shield-
bearing guards to lead. He then followed the Indian on foot without
any delay. When the latter observed Ptolemy approaching, he turned
round, and so did the shield-bearing guards with him. The Indian at
close quarters struck Ptolemy on the chest through the breastplate with
a long spear, but the breastplate checked the violence of the blow. Then
Ptolemy, smiting right through the Indian's thigh, overthrew him, and
stripped him of his arms. When his men saw their leader lying dead,
they stood their ground no longer; but the men on the mountains, seeing
their chieftain's corpse being carried off by the enemy, were seized with
indignation, and running down engaged in a desperate conflict over him
on the hill. For Alexander himself was now on the hill with the infantry
who had dismounted from the horses. These, falling upon the Indians,
drove them away to the mountains after a hard struggle, and remained
in possession of the corpse. Then crossing the mountains he descended to
a city called Arigaeum, and found that this had been set on fire by the
inhabitants, who had afterwards fled. There Craterus with his army
reached him, after accomplishing all the king's orders; and because this
city seemed to be built in a convenient place, he directed that general
to fortify it well, and settle in it as many of the neighbouring people as
were willing to live there, together with any of the soldiers who were unfit
for service. He then advanced to the place where he heard that most
of the barbarians of the district had fled for refuge; and coming to a
certain mountain, he encamped at the foot of it. Meantime Ptolemy,
son of Lagus, being sent out by Alexander on a foraging expedition, and
advancing a considerable distance with a few men to reconnoitre, brought
back word to the king that he had observed many more fires in the
camp of the barbarians than there were in Alexander's. But the latter
did not believe in the multitude of the enemy's fires. Discovering, however, that the barbarians of the district had joined their forces into one
body, he left a part of his army there near the mountain, encamped as
they were, and taking as many men as seemed sufficient, according to

the reports he had received, as soon as they could descry the fires near at hand, he divided his army into three parts. Over one part he placed Leonnatus, the confidential body-guard, joining the brigades of Attalus and Balacrus with his own; the second division he put under the lead of Ptolemy, son of Lagus, including the third part of the royal shield-bearing guards, the brigades of Philip and Philotas, two regiments of archers, the Agrianians, and half of the cavalry. The third division he himself led towards the place where most of the barbarians were visible.

25. When the enemy who were occupying the commanding heights perceived the Macedonians approaching, they descended into the plain, being emboldened by their superiority in numbers and despising the Macedonians, because they were seen to be few. A sharp contest ensued; but Alexander won the victory with ease. Ptolemy's men did not range themselves on the level ground, for the barbarians were occupying a hill. Wherefore Ptolemy, forming his battalions into column, led them to the point where the hill seemed most easily assailable, not surrounding it entirely, but leaving room for the barbarians to flee if they were inclined to do so. A hard contest also ensued with these men, both from the difficult nature of the ground, and because the Indians are not like the other barbarians of this district, but are far stronger than their neighbours. These men also were driven away from the mountain by the Macedonians. Leonnatus had the same success with the third division of the army; for his men also defeated those opposed to them. Ptolemy indeed says that all the men were captured, to a number exceeding 40,000, and that over 230,000 oxen were also taken, of which Alexander picked out the finest, because they seemed to him to excel both in beauty and size, wishing to send them into Macedonia to till the soil. Thence he marched towards the land of the Assacenians; for he received news that these people had made preparations to fight him, having 20,000 cavalry, more than 30,000 infantry, and thirty elephants. When Craterus had thoroughly fortified the city, for the founding of which he had been left behind, he brought the heavier armed men of his army for Alexander as well as the military engines, in case it might be necessary to lay siege to any place. Alexander then marched against the Assacenians at the head of the Companion cavalry, the horse-javelin-men, the brigades of Coenus and Polysperchon, the Agrianians, the light-armed troops, and the archers. Passing through the land of the Guraeans, he crossed the river Guraeus, which gives its name to the land, with difficulty, both on account of its depth, and because its current is swift, and the stones in the river being round caused those who stepped upon them to stumble. When the barbarians perceived Alexander approaching, they dared not take their stand for a battle in close array, but dispersed one by one to

their various cities with the determination of preserving these by fighting from the ramparts.

26. In the first place Alexander led his forces against Massaga, the largest of the cities in that district; and when he was approaching the walls, the barbarians, being emboldened by the mercenaries whom they had obtained from the more distant Indians to the number of 7,000, when they saw the Macedonians pitching their camp, advanced against them with a run. Alexander, seeing that the battle was about to be fought near the city, was anxious to draw them further away from their walls, so that if they were put to rout, as he knew they would be, they might not be able easily to preserve themselves by fleeing for refuge into the city close at hand. When therefore he saw the barbarians running out, he ordered the Macedonians to turn round and retreat to a certain hill distant something about a mile from the place where he had resolved to encamp. The enemy being emboldened, as if the Macedonians had already given way, rushed upon them with a run and with no kind of order. But when the arrows began to reach them, Alexander at once wheeled round at the appointed signal, and led his phalanx against them with a run. His horse-javelin-men, Agrianians, and archers first ran forward and engaged with the barbarians, while he himself led the phalanx in regular order. The Indians were alarmed at this unexpected manoeuvre, and as soon as the battle became a hand-to-hand conflict, they gave way and fled into the city. About 200 of them were killed, and the rest were shut up within the walls. Alexander then led his phalanx up to the wall, from which he was soon after slightly wounded in the ankle with an arrow. On the next day he brought up his military engines and easily battered down a piece of the wall; but the Indians so gallantly kept back the Macedonians who were trying to force an entrance where the breach had been made that he recalled the army for this day. But on the morrow the Macedonians themselves made a more vigorous assault, and a wooden tower was drawn up to the walls, from which the archers shot at the Indians, and missiles were hurled from the military engines which repulsed them to a great distance. But not even thus were they able to force their way within the wall. On the third day he led the phalanx near again, and throwing a bridge from a military engine over to the part of the wall where the breach had been made, by this he led up the shield-bearing guards, who had captured Tyre for him in a similar way. But as many were urged on by their ardour, the bridge received too great a weight, and was snapped asunder, so that the Macedonians fell with it. The barbarians, seeing what was taking place, raised a great shout, and shot at them from the wall with stones, arrows, and whatever else any one happened to have at hand, or whatever any one

could lay hold of at the time. Others issued forth by the small gates which they had between the towers in the wall, and at close quarters struck the men who had been thrown into confusion by the fall.

27. Alexander now sent Alcetas with his own brigade to recover the men who had been severely wounded, and to recall to the camp those who were assailing the enemy. On the fourth day he brought up another bridge against the wall in like manner upon another military engine. The Indians, as long as the ruler of the place survived, defended themselves gallantly; but when he was struck and killed with a missile hurled from an engine, and as some of their number had fallen in the siege, which had gone on without any cessation, while most of them were wounded and unfit for service, they sent a herald to Alexander. He was glad to preserve the lives of brave men; so he came to terms with the Indian mercenaries on this condition, that they should be admitted into the ranks with the rest of his army and serve as his soldiers. They therefore came out of the city with their arms, and encamped by themselves upon a hill which was facing the camp of the Macedonians; but they resolved to arise by night and run away to their own abodes, because they were unwilling to take up arms against the other Indians. When Alexander received intelligence of this, he placed the whole of his army round the hill in the night, and intercepting them in the midst of their flight, cut them to pieces. He then took the city by storm, denuded as it was of defenders; and captured the mother and daughter of Assacenus. In the whole siege twenty-five of Alexander's men were killed. Thence he despatched Coenus to Bazira, entertaining an opinion that the inhabitants would surrender, when they heard of the capture of Massaga. He also despatched Attalus, Alcetas, and Demetrius the cavalry officer to another city, named Ora, with instructions to blockade it until he himself arrived. The men of this city made a sortie against the forces of Alcetas; but the Macedonians easily routed them, and drove them into the city within the wall. But affairs at Bazira were not favourable to Coenus, for the inhabitants showed no sign of capitulating, trusting to the strength of the place, because not only was it situated on a lofty eminence, but it was also thoroughly fortified all round. When Alexander learned this, he started off to Bazira; but ascertaining that some of the neighbouring barbarians were about to get into the city of Ora by stealth, being despatched thither by Abisares for that very purpose, he first marched to Ora. He ordered Coenus to fortify a certain strong position to serve as a basis of operations against the city of Bazira, and then to come to him with the rest of his army, after leaving in that place a sufficient garrison to restrain the men in the city from enjoying the free use of their land. But when the men of Bazira saw Coenus de-

parting with the larger part of his army, they despised the Macedonians, as not being able to contend with them, and sallied forth into the plain. A sharply contested battle ensued, in which 500 of the barbarians fell, and over seventy were taken prisoners. But the rest, fleeing for refuge into the city, were now more securely shut off from the country by the men in the fort. The siege of Ora proved an easy matter to Alexander, for he no sooner attacked the walls than at the first assault he got possession of the city, and captured the elephants which had been left there.

28. When the men in Bazira heard this news, despairing of their own affairs, they abandoned the city about the middle of the night, and fled to the rock as the other barbarians were doing. For all the inhabitants deserted the cities and began to flee to the rock which is in their land, and is called Aornus. For stupendous is this rock in this land, about which the current report is that it was found impregnable even by Heracles, the son of Zeus. I cannot affirm with confidence either way, whether the Theban, Tyrian, or Egyptian Heracles penetrated into India or not; but I am rather inclined to think that he did not penetrate so far; for men usually magnify the difficulty of all difficult enterprises to such a degree as to assert that they would have been impracticable even to Heracles. Therefore, I am inclined to think that in regard to this rock the name of Heracles was mentioned simply to add to the marvellousness of the tale. The circuit of the rock is said to be about twenty-three miles, and its height where it is lowest, about a mile and a quarter. There was only one ascent, which was artificial and difficult; on the summit of the rock there was abundance of pure water, a spring issuing from the ground, from which the water flowed; and there was also timber, and sufficient good arable land for 1,000 men to till. When Alexander heard this, he was seized with a vehement desire to capture this mountain also, especially on account of the legend which was current about Heracles. He then made Ora and Massaga fortresses to keep the land in subjection, and fortified the city of Bazira. Hephaestion and Perdiccas also fortified for him another city, named Orobatis, and leaving a garrison in it marched towards the river Indus. When they reached that river they at once began to carry out Alexander's instructions in regard to bridging it. Alexander then appointed Nicanor, one of the Companions, satrap of the land on this side the river Indus; and in the first place leading his army towards that river, he brought over on terms of capitulation the city of Peucelaotis, which was situated not far from it. In this city he placed a garrison of Macedonians, under the command of Philip, and then reduced to subjection some other small towns situated near the same river, being accompanied by Cophaeus and Assagetes, the chieftains of the land. Arriving at the city of Embolima, which was situated

near the rock Aornus, he left Craterus there with a part of the army, to gather as much corn as possible into the city, as well as all the other things requisite for a long stay, so that, making this their base of operations, the Macedonians might be able by a long siege to wear out the men who were holding the rock, supposing it were not captured at the first assault. He then took the bowmen, the Agrianians, and the brigade of Coenus, and selecting the lightest as well as the best-armed men from the rest of the phalanx, with 200 of the Companion cavalry and 100 horse-bowmen, he advanced to the rock. This day he encamped where it appeared to him convenient; but on the morrow he approached a little nearer to the rock, and encamped again.

29. At this juncture some of the natives came to him, and surrendering themselves, offered to lead him to the part of the rock where it could be most easily assailed, and from which it would be easy for him to capture the place. With these he sent Ptolemy, son of Lagus, the confidential body-guard, in command of the Agrianians and the other light-armed troops, together with picked men from the shield-bearing guards. He gave this officer instructions, as soon as he had got possession of the place, to occupy it with a strong guard, and signal to him that it was held. Ptolemy proceeded along a road which was rough and difficult to pass, and occupied the position without the knowledge of the barbarians. After strengthening this position with a stockade and a ditch all round, he raised a beacon from the mountain, whence it was likely to be seen by Alexander. The flame was at once seen, and on the following day the king led his army forward; but as the barbarians disputed his advance, he could do nothing further on account of the difficult nature of the ground. When the barbarians perceived that Alexander could not make an assault, they turned round and attacked Ptolemy, and a sharp battle ensued between them and the Macedonians, the Indians making great efforts to demolish the stockade, and Ptolemy to preserve his position. But the barbarians, getting the worst of it in the skirmish, withdrew as the night came on. Alexander now selected from the Indian deserters a man who was not only devoted to him but acquainted with the locality, and sent him by night to Ptolemy, carrying a letter, in which it was written that as soon as the king attacked the rock, Ptolemy was to come down the mountain upon the barbarians, and not be contented with holding his position in guard; so that the Indians, being assailed from both sides at once, might be in perplexity what course to pursue. Accordingly, starting from his camp at daybreak, he led his army up the path by which Ptolemy had ascended by stealth, entertaining the opinion that if he could force his way in this direction and join his forces with those of Ptolemy, the work would no longer be difficult for him; and

so it turned out. For until midday a smart battle was kept up between
the Indians and the Macedonians, the latter striving to force a way of
approach, and the former hurling missiles at them as they ascended. But
as the Macedonians did not relax their efforts, advancing one after another, and those who were in advance rested till their comrades came
up, after great exertions they gained possession of the pass early in the
afternoon, and formed a junction with Ptolemy's forces. As the whole
army was now united, Alexander led it on again against the rock itself.
But the approach to it was still impracticable. Such then was the result
of this day's labours. At the approach of the dawn he issued an order
that each soldier individually should cut 100 stakes; and when these
had been cut he heaped up a great mound towards the rock, beginning
from the top of the hill where they had encamped. From this mound he
thought the arrows as well as the missiles launched from the military
engines would be able to reach the defenders of the rock. Every one in
the army assisted him in this work of raising the mound; while he himself superintended it, as an observer, not only commending the man who
completed his task with zeal and alacrity, but also chastising him who
was dilatory in the pressing emergency.

30. On the first day his army constructed the mound the length of
200 yards; and on the following day the slingers shooting at the Indians
from the part already finished, assisted by the missiles which were hurled
from the military engines, repulsed the sallies which they made against
the men who were constructing the mound. He went on with the work
for three days without intermission, and on the fourth day a few of the
Macedonians forcing their way occupied a small eminence which was
on a level with the rock. Without taking any rest, Alexander went on
with the mound, being desirous of connecting his artificial rampart with
the eminence which the few men were now occupying for him. But then
the Indians, being alarmed at the indescribable audacity of the Macedonians, who had forced their way to the eminence, and seeing that the
mound was already united with it, desisted from attempting any longer
to resist. They sent their herald to Alexander, saying that they were
willing to surrender the rock, if he would grant them a truce. But they
had formed the design of wasting the day by continually delaying the
ratification of the truce, and of scattering themselves in the night with
the view of escaping one by one to their own abodes. When Alexander
discovered this plan of theirs, he allowed them time to commence their
retreat, and to remove the guard which was placed all round the place.
He remained quiet until they began their retreat; then taking 700 of
the body-guards and shield-bearing infantry, he was the first to scale
the rock at the part of it abandoned by the enemy; and the Macedonians

ascended after him, one in one place another in another, drawing each other up. These men at the concerted signal turned themselves upon the retreating barbarians, and killed many of them in their flight. Others retreating with panic terror perished by leaping down the precipices; and thus the rock which had been inexpugnable to Heracles was occupied by Alexander. He offered sacrifice upon it, and arranged a fort, committing the superintendence of the garrison to Sisicottus, who long before had deserted from the Indians to Bessus in Bactra, and after Alexander had acquired possession of the country of Bactria, entered his army and appeared to be eminently trustworthy.

He now set out from the rock and invaded the land of the Assacenians; for he was informed that the brother of Assacenus with his elephants and many of the neighbouring barbarians had fled into the mountains in this district. When he arrived at the city of Dyrta, he found none of the inhabitants either in it or in the land adjacent. On the following day he sent out Nearchus and Antiochus, the colonels of the shield-bearing guards, giving the former the command of the Agrianians and the light-armed troops, and the latter the command of his own regiment and two others besides. They were despatched both to reconnoitre the locality and to try if they could capture some of the barbarians anywhere in order to get information about the general affairs of the country; and he was especially anxious to learn news of the elephants. He now directed his march towards the river Indus, and his army going forward made a road, as otherwise this district would have been impassable. Here he captured a few of the barbarians, from whom he learned that the Indians of that land had fled for safety to Abisares, but that they had left their elephants there to pasture near the river Indus. He ordered these men to show him the way to the elephants. Many of the Indians are elephant-hunters, and these Alexander kept in attendance upon him in high honour, going out to hunt the elephants in company with them. Two of these animals perished in the chase, by leaping down a precipice, but the rest were caught and being ridden by drivers were marshalled with the army. He also as he was marching along the river lighted upon a wood, the timber of which was suitable for building ships; this was cut down by the army, and ships were built for him, which were brought down the river Indus to the bridge, which had long since been constructed for him by Hephaestion and Perdiccas.

BOOK V

1. In this country, lying between the rivers Cophen and Indus, which was traversed by Alexander, the city of Nysa is said to be situated. The report is that its foundation was the work of Dionysus, who built it after he had subjugated the Indians. But it is impossible to determine who this Dionysus was, and at what time, or from what quarter he led an army against the Indians. For I am unable to decide whether the Theban Dionysus, starting from Thebes or from the Lydian Tmolus, came into India at the head of an army, and after traversing the territories of so many warlike nations, unknown to the Greeks of that time, forcibly subjugating none of them except that of the Indians. But I do not think we ought to make a minute examination of the legends which were promulgated in ancient times about the deity; for things which are not credible to the man who examines them according to the rule of probability, do not appear to be wholly incredible, if one adds the divine agency to the story. When Alexander came to Nysa the citizens sent out to him their chief, whose name was Acuphis, accompanied by thirty of their most distinguished men as envoys, to entreat Alexander to leave their city free for the sake of the god. The envoys entered Alexander's tent and found him seated in his armour still covered with dust from the journey, with his helmet on his head, and holding his spear in his hand. When they beheld the sight they were struck with astonishment, and falling to the earth remained silent a long time. But when Alexander caused them to rise, and bade them be of good courage, then at length Acuphis began thus to speak, "The Nysaeans beseech you, O king, out of respect for Dionysus, to allow them to remain free and independent; for when Dionysus had subjugated the nation of the Indians, and was returning to the Grecian sea, he founded this city from the soldiers who had become unfit for military service, and were under his inspiration as Bacchanals, so that it might be a monument both of his wandering and of his victory to men of after times; just as you also founded Alexandria near Mount Caucasus, and another Alexandria in the country of the Egyptians. Many other cities you have already founded, and others you will found hereafter, in the course of time, inasmuch as you have achieved more exploits than Dionysus. The god indeed called the city Nysa, and the land Nysaea after his nurse Nysa. The mountain also

which is near the city he named Meros, because, according to the legend, he grew in the thigh of Zeus. From that time we inhabit Nysa, a free city, and we ourselves are independent, conducting our government with constitutional order. And let this be a proof to you that our city owes its foundation to Dionysus; for ivy, which does not grow in the rest of the country of India, grows among us."

2. All this was very pleasant to Alexander to hear; for he wished that the legend about the wandering of Dionysus should be believed, as well as that Nysa owed its foundation to that deity, since he had himself reached the place where Dionysus came, and had even advanced beyond the limits of the latter's march. He also thought that the Macedonians would not decline still to share his labours if he advanced further, from a desire to surpass the achievements of Dionysus. He therefore granted the inhabitants of Nysa the privilege of remaining free and independent; and when he heard about their laws, and that the government was in the hands of the aristocracy he commended these things. He required them to send 300 of their horsemen to accompany him, and to select and send 100 of the aristocrats who presided over the government of the State, who also were 300 in number. He ordered Acuphis to make the selection, and appointed him governor of the land of Nysaea. When Acuphis heard this, he is said to have smiled at the speech; whereupon Alexander asked him why he laughed. Acuphis replied, "How, O king, could a single city deprived of 100 of its good men be still well governed? But if you care for the welfare of the Nysaeans, lead with you the 300 horsemen, and still more than that number if you wish: but instead of the 100 of the best men whom you order me to select lead with you double the number of the others who are bad, so that when you come here again the city may appear in the same good order in which it now is." By these remarks he persuaded Alexander; for he thought he was speaking with prudence. So he ordered them to send the horsemen to accompany him, but no longer demanded the 100 select men, nor indeed others in their stead. But he commanded Acuphis to send his own son and his daughter's son to accompany him. He was now seized with a strong desire of seeing the place where the Nysaeans boasted to have certain memorials of Dionysus. So he went to Mount Merus with the Companion cavalry and the foot guard, and saw the mountain, which was quite covered with ivy and laurel and groves thickly shaded with all sorts of timber, and on it were chases of all kinds of wild animals. The Macedonians were delighted at seeing the ivy, as they had not seen any for a long time; for in the land of the Indians there was no ivy, even where they had vines. They eagerly made garlands of it, and crowned themselves with them, as they were, singing hymns in honour of Diony-

sus, and invoking the deity by his various names. Alexander there offered sacrifice to Dionysus, and feasted in company with his companions. Some authors have also stated, but I do not know if any one will believe it, that many of the distinguished Macedonians in attendance upon him, having crowned themselves with ivy, while they were engaged in the invocation of the deity, were seized with the inspiration of Dionysus, uttered cries of Evoi in honour of the god, and acted as Bacchanals.

3. Any one who receives these stories may believe or disbelieve them as he pleases. But I do not altogether agree with Eratosthenes the Cyrenaean,[1] who says that everything which was attributed to the divine agency by the Macedonians was really said to gratify Alexander by excessive eulogy. For he says that the Macedonians, seeing a cavern in the land of the Parapamisadians, and hearing a certain legend which was current among the natives, or themselves forming a conjecture, spread the report, indeed, that this was the cave where Prometheus had been bound, that an eagle frequented it to feast on his inward parts, that when Heracles arrived there he killed the eagle and set Prometheus free from his bonds. He also says that by their account the Macedonians transferred Mount Caucasus from the Euxine Sea to the eastern parts of the earth, and the land of the Parapamisadians to that of the Indians; calling what was really Mount Parapamisus by the name of Caucasus, in order to enhance Alexander's glory, seeing that he forsooth had gone over the Caucasus. He adds, that when they saw in India itself some oxen marked with the brand of a club, they concluded from this that Heracles had penetrated into India. Eratosthenes also disbelieves the similar tale of the wandering of Dionysus. Let me leave the stories about these matters undecided as far as I am concerned.

When Alexander arrived at the river Indus, he found a bridge made over it by Hephaestion, and two thirty-oared galleys, besides many smaller craft. He moreover found that 200 talents of silver, 3,000 oxen, above 10,000 sheep for sacrificial victims, and thirty elephants had arrived as gifts from Taxiles the Indian; 700 Indian horsemen also arrived from Taxiles as a reinforcement, and that prince sent word that he would surrender to him the city of Taxila, the largest town between the river Indus and Hydaspes. Alexander there offered sacrifice to the gods to whom he was in the habit of sacrificing, and celebrated a gymnastic and horse contest near the river. The sacrifices were favourable to his crossing.

4. The following are statements about the river Indus which are quite

---

[1] The celebrated geographer and mathematician, who was born 276 B.C. and died about 196 B.C. His principal work was one on geography, which was of great use to Strabo. None of his works are extant.

unquestionable, and therefore let me record them. The Indus is the largest of all the rivers in Asia and Europe, except the Ganges, which is also an Indian river. It takes its rise on this side Mount Parapamisus, or Caucasus, and discharges its water into the Great Sea which lies near India in the direction of the south wind. It has two mouths, both of which outlets are full of shallow pools like the five outlets of the Ister (Danube). It forms a delta in the land of the Indians resembling that of Egypt; and this is called Pattala in the Indian language. The Hydaspes, Acesines, Hydraotes, and Hyphasis are also Indian rivers, and far exceed the other rivers of Asia in size; but they are not only smaller but much smaller than the Indus, just as that river itself is smaller than the Ganges. Indeed Ctesias[2] says (if any one thinks his evidence to be depended upon), that where the Indus is narrowest, its banks are five miles apart; where it is broadest, twelve miles; and most of it is the mean between these breadths.[3] This river Indus Alexander crossed at daybreak with his army into the country of the Indians; concerning whom, in this history I have described neither what laws they enjoy, nor what strange animals their land produces, nor how many and what sort of fish and water-monsters are produced by the Indus, Hydaspes, Ganges, or the other rivers of India. Nor have I described the ants which work the gold for them, nor the guardian griffins, nor any of the other tales that have been composed rather to amuse than to be received as the relation of facts; since the falsity of the strange stories which have been fabricated about India will not be exposed by any one. However, Alexander and those who served in his army exposed the falsity of most of these tales; but there were even some of these very men who fabricated other stories. They proved that the Indians whom Alexander visited with his army, and he visited many tribes of them, were destitute of gold; and also that they were by no means luxurious in their mode of living. Moreover, they discovered that they were tall in stature, in fact as tall as any men throughout Asia, most of them being seven and one-half feet in height, or a little less. They were blacker than the rest of men, except the Ethiopians; and in war they were far the bravest of all the races inhabiting Asia at that time. For I cannot with any justice compare the race of the ancient Persians with those of India, though at the head of the former Cyrus, son of Cambyses, set out and deprived the Medes of the empire of Asia, and subdued many other races partly by force and partly by voluntary surrender on their own part. For at that

[2] Ctesias was the Greek physician of Artaxerxes Mnemon. He wrote a history of Persia and a book on India, which he compiled from Persian sources. Aristotle says that he was false and untrustworthy.

[3] The fact is, that the Indus is nowhere more than two and one-half miles broad.

time the Persians were a poor people and inhabitants of a rugged land, having laws and customs very similar to the Laconian discipline. Nor am I able with certainty to conjecture whether the defeat sustained by the Persians in the Scythian land was due to the difficult nature of the country met with or to some other error on the part of Cyrus, or whether the Persians were really inferior in warlike matters to the Scythians of that district.

5. But of the Indians I shall treat in a distinct work,[4] giving the most credible accounts which were compiled by those who accompanied Alexander in his expedition, as well as by Nearchus,[5] who sailed right round the Great Sea which is near India. Then I shall add what has been compiled by Megasthenes[6] and Eratosthenes, two men of distinguished authority. I shall describe the customs peculiar to the Indians and the strange animals which are produced in the country, as well as the voyage itself in the external sea. But now let me describe so much only as appears to me sufficient to explain Alexander's achievements. Mount Taurus divides Asia, beginning from Mycale, the mountain which lies opposite the island of Samos; then, cutting through the country of the Pamphylians and Cilicians, it extends into Armenia. From this country it stretches into Media and through the land of the Parthians and Chorasmians. In Bactria it unites with Mount Parapamisus, which the Macedonians who served in Alexander's army called Caucasus, in order, as it is said, to enhance their king's glory; asserting that he went even beyond the Caucasus with his victorious arms. Perhaps it is a fact that this mountain range is a continuation of the other Caucasus in Scythia, as the Taurus is of the same. For this reason I have on a previous occasion called this range Caucasus, and by the same name I shall continue to call it in the future. This Caucasus extends as far as the Great Sea which lies in the direction of India and the East. Of the rivers in Asia worth consideration which take their rise from the Taurus and Caucasus, some have their course turned towards the north, discharging themselves either into Lake Maeotis, or into the sea called Hyrcanian, which in reality is a gulf of the Great Sea.[7] Others flow towards the south, namely, the Euphrates, Tigris, Indus, Hydaspes, Acesines, Hydraotes, Hyphasis, and all those that lie between these and the river Ganges. All these either discharge their water into the sea, or disappear by pouring themselves out into marshes, as the river Euphrates does.

---

[4] The *Indica*.

[5] Nearchus left an account of his voyage, which is not now extant.

[6] Megasthenes was sent by Seleucus, the king of Syria and one of Alexander's generals, as ambassador to Sandracotus, king of the country near the Ganges. He wrote a very valuable account of India in four books.

[7] Herodotus (i. 203) says decidedly that the Caspian is an inland sea.

6. Whoever arranges the position of Asia in such a way that it is divided by the Taurus and the Caucasus from the west wind to the east wind will find that these two very large divisions are made by the Taurus itself, one of which is inclined towards the south and the south wind, and the other towards the north and the north wind. Southern Asia again may be divided into four parts, of which Eratosthenes and Megasthenes make India the largest. The latter author lived with Sibyrtius, the satrap of Arachosia, and says that he frequently visited Sandracotus, king of the Indians. These authors say that the smallest of the four parts is that which is bounded by the river Euphrates and extends to our inland sea. The other two lying between the rivers Euphrates and Indus are scarcely worthy to be compared with India, if they were joined together. They say that India is bounded towards the east and the east wind as far as the south by the Great Sea, towards the north by Mount Caucasus, as far as its junction with the Taurus; and that the river Indus cuts it off towards the west and the north-west wind, as far as the Great Sea. The greater part of it is a plain, which, as they conjecture, has been formed by the alluvial deposits of the rivers; just as the plains in the rest of the earth lying near the sea are for the most part due to the alluvial action of the rivers by themselves. Consequently, the names by which the countries are called were attached in ancient times to the rivers. For instance, a certain plain was called after the Hermus, which rises in the country of Asia from the mountain of Mother Dindymene, and after flowing past the Aeolian city of Smyrna discharges its water into the sea. Another Lydian plain is named after the Cayster, a Lydian river; another in Mysia from the Caicus; and the Carian plain, extending as far as the Ionian city of Miletus, is named from the Maeander. Both Herodotus and Hecataeus the historians (unless the work about the Egyptian country is by another person, and not by Hecataeus) in like manner call Egypt a gift of the river; and Herodotus has shown by no uncertain proofs that such is the case; so that even the country itself perhaps received its name from the river. For that the river which both the Egyptians and men outside Egypt now name the Nile was in ancient times called Aegyptus, Homer is sufficient to prove; since he says that Menelaus stationed his ships at the outlet of the river Aegyptus. If therefore single rivers by themselves, and those not large ones, are sufficient to form an extensive tract of country, while flowing forward into the sea, since they carry down slime and mud from the higher districts whence they derive their sources, surely it is unbecoming to exhibit incredulity about India, how it has come to pass that most of it is a plain, which has been formed by the alluvial deposits of its rivers. For if the Hermus, the Cayster, the Caicus,

the Maeander, and all the many rivers of Asia which discharge their
waters into this inland sea were all put together, they would not be
worthy of comparison for volume of water with one of the Indian rivers.
Not only do I mean the Ganges, which is the largest, and with which
neither the water of the Egyptian Nile nor the Ister flowing through
Europe is worthy to compare; but if all those rivers were mingled together they would not even then become equal to the river Indus, which
is a large river as soon as it issues from its springs, and after receiving
fifteen rivers, all larger than those in the province of Asia, discharges its
water into the sea, retaining its own name and absorbing those of its
tributaries. Let these remarks which I have made about India suffice for
the present, and let the rest be reserved for my *Description of India*.

7. How Alexander constructed his bridge over the river Indus is explained neither by Aristobulus nor Ptolemy, authors whom I usually
follow; nor am I able to form a decided opinion whether the passage
was bridged with boats, as the Hellespont was by Xerxes and the Bosporus and the Ister were by Darius, or whether he made a continuous
bridge over the river. To me it seems probable that the bridge was made
of boats; for the depth of the water would not have admitted of the construction of a regular bridge, nor could so enormous a work have been
completed in so short a time. If the passage was bridged with boats,
I cannot decide whether the vessels being fastened together with ropes
and moored in a row were sufficient to form the bridge, as Herodotus
the Halicarnassian says the Hellespont was bridged, or whether the
work was effected in the way in which the bridge upon the Ister and that
upon the Celtic Rhine are made by the Romans, and in the way in which
they bridged the Euphrates and Tigris, as often as necessity compelled
them. However, as I know myself, the Romans find the quickest way of
making a bridge to be with vessels; and this method I shall on the
present occasion explain, because it is worth describing. At a preconcerted signal they let the vessels loose down the stream, not with their
prows forward, but as if backing water. As might naturally be expected,
the stream carries them down, but a skiff furnished with oars holds them
back, until it settles them in the place assigned to them. Then pyramidal
wicker-baskets made of willow, full of unhewn stones, are let down into
the water from the prow of each vessel, in order to hold it up against
the force of the stream. As soon as any one of these vessels has been held
fast, another is in the same way moored with its prow against the stream,
distant from the first as far as is consistent with their supporting what
is put upon them. Pieces of timber are quickly put on them, projecting
out from both of them, on which cross-planks are placed to bind them
together; and so proceeds the work through all the vessels which are

required to bridge the river. At each end of this bridge firmly fixed gangways are thrown forward, so that the approach may be safer for the horses and waggons, and at the same time to serve as a bond to the bridge. In a short time the whole is finished with a great noise and bustle; but yet discipline is not relaxed while the work is going on. In each vessel the exhortations of the overseers to the men as they chance to occur, or their censures of sluggishness, neither prevent the orders being heard nor impede the rapidity of the work.

8. This has been the method of constructing bridges, practised by the Romans from olden times; but how Alexander laid a bridge over the river Indus I cannot say, because those who served in his army have said nothing about it. But I should think that the bridge was made as near as possible as I have described, or if it were effected by some other contrivance so let it be. When Alexander had crossed to the other side of the river Indus, he again offered sacrifice there, according to his custom. Then starting from the Indus, he arrived at Taxila, a large and prosperous city, in fact the largest of those situated between the rivers Indus and Hydaspes. He was received in a friendly manner by Taxiles, the governor of the city, and by the Indians of that place; and he added to their territory as much of the adjacent country as they asked for. Thither also came to him envoys from Abisares, king of the mountaineer Indians, the embassy including the brother of Abisares as well as the other most notable men. Other envoys also came from Doxareus, the chief of the province, bringing gifts with them. Here again at Taxila Alexander offered the sacrifices which were customary for him to offer, and celebrated a gymnastic and equestrian contest. Having appointed Philip, son of Machatas, viceroy of the Indians of that district, he left a garrison in Taxila, as well as the soldiers who were invalided by sickness, and then marched towards the river Hydaspes. For he was informed that Porus, with the whole of his army, was on the other side of that river, having determined either to prevent him from making the passage, or to attack him while crossing. When Alexander ascertained this, he sent Coenus, son of Polemocrates, back to the river Indus, with instructions to cut in pieces all the vessels which he had prepared for the passage of that river, and to bring them to the river Hydaspes. Coenus cut the vessels in pieces and conveyed them thither, the smaller ones being cut into two parts, and the thirty-oared galleys into three. The sections were conveyed upon waggons, as far as the bank of the Hydaspes; and there the vessels were fixed together again, and seen as a fleet upon that river. Alexander took the forces which he had when he arrived at Taxila, and the 5,000 Indians under the command of Taxiles and the chiefs of that district, and marched towards the same river.

9. Alexander encamped on the bank of the Hydaspes, and Porus was seen with all his army and his large troop of elephants lining the opposite bank. He remained to guard the passage at the place where he saw Alexander had encamped; and sent guards to all the other parts of the river which were more easily fordable, placing officers over each detachment, being resolved to obstruct the passage of the Macedonians. When Alexander saw this, he thought it advisable to move his army in various directions, to distract the attention of Porus, and render him uncertain what to do. Dividing his army into many parts, he himself led some of his troops now into one part of the land and now into another, at one time ravaging the enemy's property, at another looking out for a place where the river might appear easier for him to ford it. The rest of his troops he intrusted to his different generals, and sent them about in many directions. He also conveyed corn from all quarters into his camp from the land on this side the Hydaspes, so that it might be evident to Porus that he had resolved to remain quiet near the bank until the water of the river subsided in the winter, and afforded him a passage in many places. As his vessels were sailing up and down the river, and skins were being filled with hay, and the whole bank appeared to be covered in one place with cavalry, in another with infantry, Porus was not allowed to keep at rest, or to bring his preparations together from all sides to any one point if he selected this as suitable for the defence of the passage. Besides at this season all the Indian rivers were flowing with swollen and turbid waters and with rapid currents; for it was the time of year when the sun is wont to turn towards the summer solstice.[8] At this season incessant and heavy rain falls in India; and the snows on the Caucasus, whence most of the rivers have their sources, melt and swell their streams to a great degree. But in the winter they again subside, become small and clear, and are fordable in certain places, with the exception of the Indus, Ganges, and perhaps one or two others. At any rate the Hydaspes becomes fordable.

10. Alexander therefore spread a report that he would wait for that season of the year, if his passage was obstructed at the present time; but yet all the time he was waiting in ambush to see whether by rapidity of movement he could steal a passage anywhere without being observed. But he perceived that it was impossible for him to cross at the place where Porus himself had encamped near the bank of the Hydaspes, not only on account of the multitude of his elephants, but also because a large army, and that, too, arranged in order of battle and splendidly accoutred, was ready to attack his men as they emerged from the water. Moreover he thought that his horses would refuse even to mount the op-

[8] About the month of May.

posite bank, because the elephants would at once fall upon them and frighten them both by their aspect and trumpeting; nor even before that would they remain upon the inflated hides during the passage of the river; but when they looked across and saw the elephants on the other side they would become frantic and leap into the water. He therefore resolved to steal a crossing by the following manoeuvre: In the night he led most of his cavalry along the bank in various directions, making a clamour and raising the battle-cry in honour of Enyalius. Every kind of noise was raised, as if they were making all the preparations necessary for crossing the river. Porus also marched along the river at the head of his elephants opposite the places where the clamour was heard, and Alexander thus gradually got him into the habit of leading his men along opposite the noise. But when this occurred frequently, and there was merely a clamour and a raising of the battle-cry, Porus no longer continued to move about to meet the expected advance of the cavalry; but perceiving that his fear had been groundless, he kept his position in the camp. However he posted his scouts at many places along the bank. When Alexander had brought it about that the mind of Porus no longer entertained any fear of his nocturnal attempts, he devised the following stratagem.

11. There was in the bank of the Hydaspes a projecting point, where the river makes a remarkable bend. It was densely covered by a grove of all sorts of trees; and over against it in the river was a woody island without a foot-track, on account of its being uninhabited. Perceiving that this island was right in front of the projecting point, and that both the spots were woody and adapted to conceal his attempt to cross the river, he resolved to convey his army over at this place. The projecting point and island were about eighteen miles from his great camp. Along the whole of the bank, he posted sentries, separated as far as was consistent with keeping each other in sight, and easily hearing when any order should be sent along from any quarter. From all sides also during many nights clamours were raised and fires were burned. But when he had made up his mind to undertake the passage of the river, he openly prepared his measures for crossing opposite the camp. Craterus had been left behind at the camp with his own division of cavalry, and the horsemen from the Arachotians and Parapamisadians, as well as the brigades of Alcetas and Polysperchon from the phalanx of the Macedonian infantry, together with the chiefs of the Indians dwelling this side of the Hyphasis, who had with them 5,000 men. He gave Craterus orders not to cross the river before Porus moved off with his forces against them, or before he ascertained that Porus was in flight and that they were victorious. "If, however," said he, "Porus should take only a part of his

army and march against me, and leave the other part with the elephants
in his camp, in that case you also remain in your present position. But
if he leads all his elephants with him against me, and a part of the rest of
his army is left behind in the camp, then you cross the river with all
speed. For it is the elephants alone," said he, "which render it impossible
for the horses to land on the other bank. The rest of the army can easily
cross."

12. Such were the injunctions laid upon Craterus. Between the island
and the great camp where Alexander had left this general he posted
Meleager, Attalus, and Gorgias, with the Grecian mercenaries, cavalry
and infantry, giving them instructions to cross in detachments, breaking
up the army as soon as they saw the Indians already involved in battle.
He then picked the select body-guard called the Companions, as well
as the cavalry regiments of Hephaestion, Perdiccas and Demetrius, the
cavalry from Bactria, Sogdiana and Scythia, and the Daan horse-
archers; and from the phalanx of infantry the shield-bearing guards, the
brigades of Clitus and Coenus, with the archers and Agrianians, and
made a secret march, keeping far away from the bank of the river, in
order not to be seen marching towards the island and headland, from
which he had determined to cross. There the skins were filled in the
night with the hay which had been procured long before, and they were
tightly stitched up. In the night a furious storm of rain occurred, on account of which his preparations and attempt to cross were still less observed, since the claps of thunder and the storm drowned with their din
the clatter of the weapons and the noise which arose from the orders
given by the officers. Most of the vessels, the thirty-oared galleys included with the rest, had been cut in pieces by his order and conveyed to
this place, where they had been secretly fixed together again and hidden
in the wood. At the approach of daylight, both the wind and the rain
calmed down; and the rest of the army went over opposite the island,
the cavalry mounting upon the skins, and as many of the foot soldiers as
the boats would receive getting into them. They went so secretly that
they were not observed by the sentinels posted by Porus, before they
had already got beyond the island and were only a little way from the
other bank.

13. Alexander himself embarked in a thirty-oared galley and went
over, accompanied by Ptolemy, Perdiccas and Lysimachus, the confidential body-guards, Seleucus, one of the Companions, who was afterwards king,[9] and half of the shield-bearing guards; the rest of these

---

[9] Seleucus Nicator, the most powerful of Alexander's successors, became the
king of Syria and founder of the dynasty of the Seleucidae, which came to an end
in 79 B.C.

troops being conveyed in other galleys of the same size. When the soldiers got beyond the island, they openly directed their course to the bank; and when the sentinels perceived that they had started, they at once rode off to Porus as fast as each man's horse could gallop. Alexander himself was the first to land, and he at once took the cavalry as they kept on landing from his own and the other thirty-oared galleys, and drew them up in proper order. For the cavalry had been arranged to land first; and at the head of these in regular array he advanced. But through ignorance of the locality, without realizing it he had landed on ground which was not a part of the mainland, but an island, a large one indeed so that the fact that it was an island more easily escaped notice. It was cut off from the rest of the land by a part of the river where the water was shallow. However, the furious storm of rain, which lasted the greater part of the night, had swelled the water so much that his cavalry could not find out the ford; and he was afraid that he would have to undergo another labour in crossing as great as the first. But when at last the ford was found, he led his men through it with much difficulty; for where the water was deepest, it reached higher than the breasts of the infantry; and of the horses only the heads rose above the river. When he had also crossed this piece of water, he selected the choice guard of cavalry, and the best men from the other cavalry regiments, and brought them up from column into line on the right wing. In front of all the cavalry he posted the horse-archers, and placed next to the cavalry in front of the other infantry the royal shield-bearing guards under the command of Seleucus. Near these he placed the royal footguard, and next to these the other shield-bearing guards, as each happened at the time to have the right of precedence. On each side, at the extremities of the phalanx, his archers, Agrianians and javelin-throwers were posted.

14. Having thus arranged his army, he ordered the infantry to follow at a slow pace and in regular order, numbering as it did not much under 6,000 men; and because he thought he was superior in cavalry, he took only his horse-soldiers, who were 5,000 in number, and led them forward with speed. He also instructed Tauron, the commander of the archers, to lead them on also with speed to back up the cavalry. He had come to the conclusion that if Porus should engage him with all his forces, he would easily be able to overcome him by attacking with his cavalry, or to stand on the defensive until his infantry arrived in the course of the action; but if the Indians should be alarmed at his extraordinary audacity in making the passage of the river and take to flight, he would be able to keep close to them in their flight, so that, the slaughter of them in the retreat being greater, there would be only a slight

work left for him. Aristobulus says that the son of Porus arrived with
about sixty chariots before Alexander made his later passage from the
large island, and that he could have hindered Alexander's crossing (for
he made the passage with difficulty even when no one opposed him), if
the Indians had leaped down from their chariots and assaulted those who
first emerged from the water. But he passed by with the chariots and
thus made the passage quite safe for Alexander, who on reaching the
bank discharged his horse-archers against the Indians in the chariots,
and these were easily put to rout, many of them being wounded. Other
writers say that a battle took place between the Indians, who came with
the son of Porus, and Alexander at the head of his cavalry when the
passage had been effected, that the son of Porus came with a greater
force, that Alexander himself was wounded by him, and that his horse
Bucephalas, of which he was exceedingly fond, was killed, being wounded
like his master by the son of Porus. But Ptolemy, son of Lagus, with
whom I agree, gives a different account. This author also says that
Porus despatched his son, but not at the head of merely sixty chariots;
nor is it indeed likely that Porus hearing from his scouts that either Alexander himself or at any rate a part of his army had effected the passage of the Hydaspes, would despatch his son against him with only
sixty chariots. These indeed were too many to be sent out as a reconnoitring party, and not adapted for speedy retreat; but they were by
no means a sufficient force to keep back those of the enemy who had
not yet got across, as well as to attack those who had already landed.
Ptolemy says that the son of Porus arrived at the head of 2,000 cavalry
and 120 chariots; but that Alexander had already made even the last
passage from the island before he appeared.

15. Ptolemy also says that Alexander in the first place sent the horse-
archers against these, and led the cavalry himself, thinking that Porus
was approaching with all his forces, and that this body of cavalry was
marching in front of the rest of his army, being drawn up by him as
the vanguard. But as soon as he had ascertained with accuracy the number of the Indians, he immediately made a rapid charge upon them with
the cavalry around him. When they perceived that Alexander himself
and the body of cavalry around him had made the assault, not in line
of battle regularly formed, but by squadrons, they gave way; and 400
of their cavalry, including the son of Porus, fell in the contest. The
chariots also were captured, horses and all, being heavy and slow in the
retreat, and useless in the action itself on account of the muddy ground.
When the horsemen who had escaped from this rout brought news to
Porus that Alexander himself had crossed the river with the strongest
part of his army, and that his son had been slain in the battle, he never-

theless could not make up his mind what course to take, because the men who had been left behind under Craterus were seen to be attempting to cross the river from the great camp which was directly opposite his position. However, at last he preferred to march against Alexander himself with all his army, and to come into a decisive conflict with the strongest division of the Macedonians, commanded by the king in person. But nevertheless he left a few of the elephants together with a small army there at the camp to frighten the cavalry under Craterus from the bank of the river. He then took all his cavalry to the number of 4,000 men, all his chariots to the number of 300, with 200 of his elephants and all the infantry available to the number of 30,000, and marched against Alexander. When he found a place where he saw there was no clay, but that on account of the sand the ground was all level and hard, and thus fit for the advance and retreat of horses, he there drew up his army. First he placed the elephants in the front, the animals being not less than 100 feet apart, so that they might be extended in the front before the whole of the phalanx of infantry, and produce terror everywhere among Alexander's cavalry. Besides he thought that none of the enemy would have the audacity to push themselves into the spaces between the elephants, the cavalry being deterred by the fright of their horses; and still less would the infantry do so, it being likely they would be kept off in front by the heavy-armed soldiers falling upon them, and trampled down by the elephants wheeling round against them. Near these he had posted the infantry, not occupying a line on a level with the beasts, but in a second line behind them, only so far behind that the companies of foot might be thrown forward a short distance into the spaces between them. He had also bodies of infantry standing beyond the elephants on the wings; and on both sides of the infantry he had posted the cavalry, in front of which were placed the chariots on both wings of his army.

16. Such was the arrangement which Porus made of his forces. As soon as Alexander observed that the Indians were drawn up in order of battle, he stopped his cavalry from advancing farther, so that he might take up the infantry as it kept on arriving; and even when the phalanx in quick march had effected a junction with the cavalry, he did not at once draw it out and lead it to the attack, not wishing to hand over his men exhausted with fatigue and out of breath, to the barbarians who were fresh and untired. On the contrary, he caused his infantry to rest until their strength was recruited, riding along round the lines to inspect them. When he had surveyed the arrangement of the Indians, he resolved not to advance against the centre, in front of which the elephants had been posted, and in the gaps between them a dense phalanx of men arranged; for he was alarmed at the very arrangements which Porus had

made here with that express design. But as he was superior in the number of his cavalry, he took the greater part of that force, and marched along against the left wing of the enemy for the purpose of making an attack in this direction. Against the right wing he sent Coenus with his own regiment of cavalry and that of Demetrius, with instructions to keep close behind the barbarians when they, seeing the dense mass of cavalry opposed to them, should ride out to fight them. Seleucus, Antigenes, and Tauron were ordered to lead the phalanx of infantry, but not to engage in the action until they observed the enemy's cavalry and phalanx of infantry thrown into disorder by the cavalry under his own command. But when they came within range of missiles, he launched the horse-archers, 1,000 in number, against the left wing of the Indians, in order to throw those of the enemy who were posted there into confusion by the incessant storm of arrows and by the charge of the horses. He himself with the Companion cavalry marched along rapidly against the left wing of the barbarians, being eager to attack them in flank while still in a state of disorder, before their cavalry could be deployed in line.

17. Meantime the Indians had collected their cavalry from all parts, and were riding along, advancing out of their position to meet Alexander's charge. Coenus also appeared with his men in their rear, according to his instructions. The Indians, observing this, were compelled to make the line of their cavalry face both ways; the largest and best part against Alexander, while the rest wheeled round against Coenus and his forces. This therefore at once threw the ranks as well as the decisions of the Indians into confusion. Alexander, seeing his opportunity, at the very moment the cavalry was wheeling round in the other direction, made an attack on those opposed to him with such vigour that the Indians could not sustain the charge of his cavalry, but were scattered and driven to the elephants, as to a friendly wall, for refuge. Upon this, the drivers of the elephants urged forward the beasts against the cavalry; but now the phalanx itself of the Macedonians was advancing against the elephants, the men casting darts at the riders and also striking the beasts themselves, standing round them on all sides. The action was unlike any of the previous contests; for wherever the beasts could wheel round, they rushed forth against the ranks of infantry and demolished the phalanx of the Macedonians, dense as it was. The Indian cavalry also, seeing that the infantry were engaged in the action, rallied again and advanced against the Macedonian cavalry. But when Alexander's men, who far excelled both in strength and military discipline, got the mastery over them the second time, they were again repulsed towards the elephants and cooped up among them. By this time the whole of Alexander's cavalry had collected into one squadron, not by

any command of his, but having settled into this arrangement by the mere effect of the struggle itself; and wherever it fell upon the ranks of the Indians they were broken up with great slaughter. The beasts being now cooped up into a narrow space, their friends were no less injured by them than their foes, being trampled down in their wheeling and pushing about. Accordingly there ensued a great slaughter of the cavalry, cooped up as it was in a narrow space around the elephants. Most of the keepers of the elephants had been killed by the javelins, and some of the elephants themselves had been wounded, while others no longer kept apart in the battle on account of their sufferings or from being destitute of keepers. But, as if frantic with pain, rushing forward at friends and foes alike, they pushed about, trampled down and killed them in every kind of way. However, the Macedonians, inasmuch as they were attacking the beasts in an open space and in accordance with their own plan, got out of their way whenever they rushed at them; and when they wheeled round to return, followed them closely and hurled javelins at them; whereas the Indians retreating among them were now receiving greater injury from them. But when the beasts were tired out, and were no longer able to charge with any vigour, they began to retire slowly, facing the foe like ships backing water, merely uttering a shrill piping sound. Alexander himself surrounded the whole line with his cavalry, and gave the signal that the infantry should link their shields together so as to form a very densely closed body, and thus advance in phalanx. By this means the Indian cavalry, with the exception of a few men, was quite cut up in the action, as was also the infantry, since the Macedonians were now pressing upon them from all sides. Upon this, all who could do so turned to flight through the spaces which intervened between the parts of Alexander's cavalry.

18. At the same time Craterus and the other officers of Alexander's army who had been left behind on the bank of the Hydaspes crossed the river, when they perceived that Alexander was winning a brilliant victory. These men, being fresh, followed up the pursuit instead of Alexander's exhausted troops, and made no less a slaughter of the Indians in their retreat. Of the Indians little short of 20,000 infantry and 3,000 cavalry were killed in this battle. All their chariots were broken to pieces; and two sons of Porus were slain, as were also Spitaces, the governor of the Indians of that district, the managers of the elephants and of the chariots, and all the cavalry officers and generals of Porus's army. All the elephants which were not killed there were captured. Of Alexander's forces, about eighty of the 6,000 foot-soldiers who were engaged in the first attack were killed; ten of the horse-archers, who were also the first to engage in the action; about twenty of the Companion cav-

alry, and about 200 of the other horsemen fell. When Porus, who exhibited great talent in the battle, performing the deeds not only of a general but also of a valiant soldier, observed the slaughter of his cavalry, and some of his elephants lying dead, others destitute of keepers straying about in a forlorn condition, while most of his infantry had perished, he did not depart as Darius the Great King did, setting an example of flight to his men; but as long as any body of Indians remained compact in the battle, he kept up the struggle. But at last, having received a wound on the right shoulder, which part of his body alone was unprotected during the battle, he wheeled round. His coat of mail warded off the missiles from the rest of his body, being extraordinary both for its strength and the close fitting of its joints, as it was afterwards possible for those who saw him to observe. Then indeed he turned his elephant round and began to retire. Alexander, having seen that he was a great man and valiant in the battle, was very desirous of saving his life. He accordingly sent first to him Taxiles the Indian; who rode up as near to the elephant which was carrying Porus as seemed to him safe, and bade him stop the beast, assuring him that it was no longer possible for him to flee, and bidding him listen to Alexander's message. But when he saw his old foe Taxiles, he wheeled round and was preparing to strike him with a javelin; and perhaps he would have killed him, if he had not quickly driven his horse forward out of the reach of Porus before he could strike him. But not even on this account was Alexander angry with Porus; but he kept on sending others in succession; and last of all Meroes an Indian, because he ascertained that he was an old friend of Porus. As soon as the latter heard the message brought to him by Meroes, being at the same time overcome by thirst, he stopped his elephant and dismounted from it. After he had drunk some water and felt refreshed, he ordered Meroes to lead him without delay to Alexander; and Meroes led him thither.

19. When Alexander heard that Meroes was bringing Porus to him, he rode in front of the line with a few of the Companions to meet Porus; and stopping his horse, he admired his handsome figure and his stature, which reached somewhat above seven and one-half feet. He was also surprised that he did not seem to be cowed in spirit, but advanced to meet him as one brave man would meet another brave man, after having gallantly struggled in defence of his own kingdom against another king. Then indeed Alexander was the first to speak, bidding him say what treatment he would like to receive. The story goes that Porus replied, "Treat me, O Alexander, in a kingly way!" Alexander being pleased at the expression, said, "For my own sake, O Porus, you shall be thus treated; but for your own sake demand what is pleasing to you!"

But Porus said that everything was included in that. Alexander, being still more pleased at this remark, not only granted him the rule over his own Indians, but also added another country to that which he had before, of larger extent than the former. Thus he treated the brave man in a kingly way, and from that time found him faithful in all things. Such was the result of Alexander's battle with Porus and the Indians living beyond the river Hydaspes, which was fought in the archonship of Hegemon at Athens, in the month Munychion.[10]

Alexander founded two cities, one where the battle took place, and the other on the spot whence he started to cross the river Hydaspes; the former he named Nicaea, after his victory over the Indians, and the latter Bucephala in memory of his horse Bucephalas, which died there, not from having been wounded by any one, but from the effects of toil and old age; for he was about thirty years old, and quite worn out with toil. This Bucephalas had shared many hardships and incurred many dangers with Alexander during many years, being ridden by none but the king, because he rejected all other riders. He was both of unusual size and generous in mettle. The head of an ox had been engraved upon him as a distinguishing mark, and according to some this was the reason why he bore that name; but others say, that though he was black he had a white mark upon his head which bore a great resemblance to the head of an ox. In the land of the Uxians this horse vanished from Alexander, who thereupon sent a proclamation throughout the country that he would kill all the inhabitants unless they brought the horse back to him. As a result of this proclamation it was immediately brought back. So great was Alexander's attachment to the horse, and so great was the fear of Alexander entertained by the barbarians. Let so much honour be paid by me to this Bucephalas for the sake of his master.

20. When Alexander had paid all due honours to those who had been killed in the battle, he offered the customary sacrifices to the gods in gratitude for his victory, and celebrated a gymnastic and horse contest upon the bank of the Hydaspes at the place where he first crossed with his army. He then left Craterus behind with a part of the army, to erect and fortify the cities which he was founding there; but he himself marched against the Indians bordering on the dominion of Porus. According to Aristobulus the name of this nation was Glauganicians; but Ptolemy calls them Glausians. I am quite indifferent which name it bore. Alexander traversed their land with half the Companion cavalry, the picked men from each phalanx of the infantry, all the horse-bowmen, the Agrianians, and the archers. All the inhabitants came over to him on terms of capitulation; and he thus took thirty-seven cities, the

[10] April-May, 326 B.C.

inhabitants of which, where they were fewest, amounted to no less than 5,000, and those of many numbered above 10,000. He also took many villages, which were no less populous than the cities. This land also he granted to Porus to rule, and sent Taxiles back to his own abode after effecting a reconciliation between him and Porus. At this time arrived envoys from Abisares, who told him that their king was ready to surrender himself and the land which he ruled. And yet before the battle which was fought between Alexander and Porus, Abisares intended to join his forces with those of the latter. On this occasion he sent his brother with the other envoys to Alexander, taking with them money and forty elephants as a gift. Envoys also arrived from the independent Indians, and from a certain other Indian ruler named Porus. Alexander ordered Abisares to come to him as soon as possible, threatening that unless he came he would see him arrive with his army at a place where he would not rejoice to see him. At this time Phratapherenes, satrap of Parthia and Hyrcania, came to Alexander at the head of the Thracians who had been left with him. Messengers also came from Sisicottus, viceroy of the Assacenians, to inform him that those people had slain their governor and revolted from Alexander. Against these he despatched Philip and Tyriaspes with an army, to arrange and set in order the affairs of their land.

He himself advanced towards the river Acesines. Ptolemy, son of Lagus, has described the size of this river alone of those in India, stating that where Alexander crossed it with his army upon boats and skins the stream was rapid and the channel was full of large and sharp rocks, over which the water being violently carried seethed and dashed. He says also that its breadth amounted to almost two miles; that those who went over upon skins had an easy passage; but that not a few of those who crossed in the boats perished there in the water, many of the boats being wrecked upon the rocks and dashed to pieces. From this description then it would be possible for one to come to a conclusion by comparison that the size of the river Indus has been stated not far from the fact by those who think that its mean breadth is five miles, but that it contracts two miles where it is narrowest and therefore deepest; and that this is the width of the Indus in many places. I come then to the conclusion that Alexander chose a part of the Acesines where the passage was widest, so that he might find the stream slower than elsewhere.

21. After crossing the river, he left Coenus with his own brigade there upon the bank, with instructions to superintend the passage of the part of the army which had been left behind for the purpose of collecting corn and other supplies from the country of the Indians which was al-

ready subject to him. He now sent Porus away to his own abode, commanding him to select the most warlike of the Indians and take all the elephants he had and come to him. He resolved to pursue the other Porus, the bad one, with the lightest troops in his army, because he was informed that he had left the land which he ruled and had fled. For this Porus, while hostilities subsisted between Alexander and the other Porus, sent envoys to Alexander offering to surrender both himself and the land subject to him, rather out of enmity of Porus than from friendship to Alexander. But when he ascertained that the former had been released, and that he was ruling over another large country in addition to his own, then, fearing not so much Alexander as the other Porus, his namesake, he fled from his own land, taking with him as many of his warriors as he could persuade to share his flight. Against this man Alexander marched, and arrived at the Hydraotes, which is another Indian river, not less than the Acesines in breadth, but less in swiftness of current. He traversed the whole country as far as the Hydraotes, leaving garrisons in the most suitable places, in order that Craterus and Coenus might advance with safety, scouring most of the land for forage. Then he despatched Hephaestion into the land of the Porus who had revolted, giving him a part of the army, comprising two brigades of infantry, his own regiment of cavalry with that of Demetrius and half of the archers, with instructions to hand the country over to the other Porus, to win over any independent tribes of Indians which dwelt near the banks of the river Hydraotes, and to give them also into the hands of Porus to rule. He himself then crossed the river Hydraotes, not with difficulty, as he had crossed the Acesines. As he was advancing into the country beyond the banks of Hydraotes, it happened that most of the people yielded themselves up on terms of capitulation; but some came to meet him with arms, while others who tried to escape he captured and forcibly reduced to obedience.

22. Meantime he received information that the tribe called Cathaeans and some other tribes of the independent Indians were preparing for battle, if he approached their land; and that they were summoning to the enterprise all the bordering tribes who were in like manner independent. He was also informed that the city, Sangala by name, near which they were thinking of having the struggle, was a strong one. The Cathaeans themselves were considered very daring and skilful in war; and two other tribes of Indians, the Oxydracians and Mallians, were in the same temper as the Cathaeans. For a short time before, it happened that Porus and Abisares had marched against them with their own forces and had roused many other tribes of the independent Indians to arms, but were forced to retreat without effecting anything

worthy of the preparations they had made. When Alexander was informed of this, he made a forced march against the Cathaeans, and on
the second day after starting from the river Hydraotes he arrived at a
city called Pimprama, inhabited by a tribe of Indians named Adraistaeans, who yielded to him on terms of capitulation. Giving his army a
rest the next day, he advanced on the third day to Sangala, where the
Cathaeans and the other neighbouring tribes had assembled and marshalled themselves in front of the city upon a hill which was not precipitous on all sides. They had posted their waggons all round this hill
and were encamping within them in such a way that they were surrounded by a triple palisade of waggons. When Alexander perceived the
great number of the barbarians and the nature of their position, he drew
up his forces in the order which seemed to him especially adapted to
his present circumstances, and sent his horse-archers at once without
any delay against them, ordering them to ride along and shoot at them
from a distance; so that the Indians might not be able to make any
sortie, before his army was in proper array, and that even before the
battle commenced they might be wounded within their stronghold. Upon
the right wing he posted the guard of cavalry and the cavalry regiment
of Clitus; next to these the shield-bearing guards, and then the Agrianians. Towards the left he had stationed Perdiccas with his own regiment
of cavalry, and the battalions of foot Companions. The archers he divided into two parts and placed them on each wing. While he was marshalling his army, the infantry and cavalry of the rear-guard came up.
Of these, he divided the cavalry into two parts and led them to the
wings, and with the infantry which came up he made the ranks of the
phalanx more dense and compact. He then took the cavalry which had
been drawn up on the right, and led it towards the waggons on the left
wing of the Indians; for here their position seemed to him more easy
to assail, and the waggons had not been placed together so densely.

23. As the Indians did not run out from behind the waggons against
the advancing cavalry, but mounted upon them and began to shoot
from the top of them, Alexander, perceiving that it was not the work for
cavalry, leaped down from his horse, and on foot led the phalanx of infantry against them. The Macedonians without difficulty forced the Indians from the first row of waggons; but then the Indians, taking their
stand in front of the second row, more easily repulsed the attack, because they were posted in denser array in a smaller circle. Moreover
the Macedonians were attacking them likewise in a confined space, while
the Indians were secretly creeping under the front row of waggons, and
without regard to discipline were assaulting their enemy through the
gaps left between the waggons as each man found a chance. But never-

theless even from these the Indians were forcibly driven by the phalanx of infantry. They no longer made a stand at the third row, but fled as fast as possible into the city and shut themselves up in it. During that day Alexander with his infantry encamped round the city, as much of it, at least, as his phalanx could surround; for he could not with his camp completely encircle the wall, so extensive was it. Opposite the part uninclosed by his camp, near which also was a lake, he posted the cavalry, placing them all round the lake, which he discovered to be shallow. Moreover, he conjectured that the Indians, being terrified at their previous defeat, would abandon the city in the night; and it turned out just as he had conjectured; for about the second watch of the night most of them dropped down from the wall, but fell in with the sentinels of cavalry. The foremost of them were cut to pieces by these; but the men behind them perceiving that the lake was guarded all round, withdrew into the city again. Alexander now surrounded the city with a double stockade, except in the part where the lake shut it in, and round the lake he posted more perfect guards. He also resolved to bring military engines up to the wall, to batter it down. But some of the men in the city deserted to him, and told him that the Indians intended that very night to steal out of the city and escape by the lake, where the gap in the stockade existed. He accordingly stationed Ptolemy, son of Lagus, there, giving him three regiments of the shield-bearing guards, all the Agrianians, and one line of archers, pointing out to him the place where he especially conjectured the barbarians would try to force their way. "When you perceive the barbarians forcing their way here," said he, "with the army obstruct their advance, and order the bugler to give the signal. And do you, O officers, as soon as the signal has been given, each being arrayed in battle order with your own men, advance towards the noise, wherever the bugle summons you. Nor will I myself withdraw from the action."

24. Such were the orders he gave; and Ptolemy collected there as many waggons as he could from those which had been left behind in the first flight, and placed them athwart, so that there might seem to the fugitives in the night to be many difficulties in their way; and as the stockade had been knocked down, or had not been firmly fixed in the ground, he ordered his men to heap up a mound of earth in various places between the lake and the wall. This his soldiers effected in the night. When it was about the fourth watch, the barbarians, just as Alexander had been informed, opened the gates towards the lake, and made a run in that direction. However they did not escape the notice of the guards there, nor that of Ptolemy, who had been placed behind them to render aid. But at this moment the buglers gave the signal for him,

and he advanced against the barbarians with his army fully equipped
and drawn up in battle array. Moreover the waggons and the stockade
which had been placed in the intervening space were an obstruction
to them. When the bugle sounded and Ptolemy attacked them, killing the men as they kept on stealing out through the waggons, then
indeed they turned back again into the city; and in their retreat 500
of them were killed. In the meanwhile Porus arrived, bringing with him
the elephants that were left to him, and 5,000 Indians. Alexander had
constructed his military engines and they were being led up to the wall;
but before any of it was battered down, the Macedonians took the city
by storm, digging under the wall, which was made of brick, and placing scaling ladders against it all round. In the capture 17,000 of the Indians were killed, and above 70,000 were captured, besides 300 chariots
and 500 cavalry. In the whole siege a little less than 100 of Alexander's
army were killed; but the number of the wounded was greater than the
proportion of the slain, being more than 1,200, among whom were Lysimachus, the confidential body-guard, and other officers. After burying
the dead according to his custom, Alexander sent Eumenes, the secretary,[11] with 300 cavalry to the two cities which had joined Sangala in
revolt, to tell those who held them about the capture of Sangala, and
to inform them that they would receive no harsh treatment from Alexander if they stayed there and received him as a friend; for no harm
had happened to any of the other independent Indians who had surrendered to him of their own accord. But they had become frightened,
and had abandoned the cities and were fleeing; for the news had already reached them that Alexander had taken Sangala by storm. When
Alexander was informed of their flight he pursued them with speed;
but most of them were too quick for him, and effected their escape,
because the pursuit began from a distant starting-place. But all those
who were left behind in the retreat from weakness, were seized by the
army and killed, to the number of about 500. Then, giving up the design of pursuing the fugitives any further, he returned to Sangala,
and razed the city to the ground. He added the land to that of the Indians who had formerly been independent, but who had then voluntarily submitted to him. He then sent Porus with his forces to the cities
which had submitted to him, to introduce garrisons into them; while he
himself, with his army, advanced to the river Hyphasis, to subjugate
the Indians beyond it. Nor did there seem to him any end of the war,
so long as anything hostile to him remained.

[11] Eumenes, of Cardia in Thrace, was private secretary to Philip and Alexander.
After the death of the latter, he obtained the rule of Cappadocia, Paphlagonia,
and Pontus. He displayed great ability both as a general and statesman; but was
put to death by Antigonus in 316 B.C.

25. It was reported that the country beyond the river Hyphasis was fertile; and that the men were good agriculturists, and gallant in war; and that they conducted their own political affairs in a regular and constitutional manner. For the multitude was ruled by the aristocracy, who governed in no respect contrary to the rules of moderation. It was also stated that the men of that district possessed a much greater number of elephants than the other Indians, and that they were men of very great stature, and excelled in valour. These reports excited in Alexander an ardent desire to advance farther; but the spirit of the Macedonians now began to flag, when they saw the king raising one labour after another, and incurring one danger after another. Conferences were held throughout the camp, in which those who were the most moderate bewailed their lot, while others resolutely declared that they would not follow Alexander any farther, even if he should lead the way. When he heard of this, before the disorder and pusillanimity of the soldiers should advance to a greater degree, he called a council of the officers of the brigades and addressed them as follows, "O Macedonians and Grecian allies, seeing that you no longer follow me into dangerous enterprises with a resolution equal to that which formerly animated you, I have collected you together into the same spot, so that I may either persuade you to march forward with me, or may be persuaded by you to return. If indeed the labours which you have already undergone up to our present position seem to you worthy of disapprobation, and if you do not approve of my leading you into them, there can be no advantage in my speaking any further. But if, as the result of these labours, you hold possession of Ionia, the Hellespont, both the Phrygias, Cappadocia, Paphlagonia, Lydia, Caria, Lycia, Pamphylia, Phoenicia, Egypt together with Grecian Libya, as well as part of Arabia, Hollow Syria, Syria between the rivers, Babylon, the nation of the Susians, Persia, Media, besides all the nations which the Persians and the Medes ruled, and many of those which they did not rule, the land beyond the Caspian Gates, the country beyond the Caucasus, the Tanais, as well as the land beyond that river, Bactria, Hyrcania, and the Hyrcanian Sea; if we have also subdued the Scythians as far as the desert; if, in addition to these, the river Indus flows through our territory, as do also the Hydaspes, the Acesines, and the Hydraotes, why do you shrink from adding the Hyphasis also, and the nations beyond this river, to your empire of Macedonia? Do you fear that your advance will be stopped in the future by any other barbarians? Of whom some submit to us of their own accord, and others are captured in the act of fleeing, while others, succeeding in their efforts to escape, hand

over to us their deserted land, which we add to that of our allies, or
to that of those who have voluntarily submitted to us.

26. "I, for my part, think, that to a brave man there is no end to
labours except the labours themselves, provided they lead to glorious
achievements. But if any one desires to hear what will be the end to
our warfare itself, let him learn that the distance still remaining before
we reach the river Ganges and the Eastern Sea is not great; and I inform you that the Hyrcanian Sea will be seen to be united with this, because the Great Sea encircles the whole earth. I will also demonstrate
both to the Macedonians and to the Grecian allies that the Indian
Gulf is confluent with the Persian, and the Hyrcanian Sea with the Indian Gulf. From the Persian Gulf our expedition will sail round into
Libya as far as the Pillars of Heracles. From the Pillars all the interior of Libya becomes ours, and so the whole of Asia will belong to
us, and the limits of our empire, in that direction, will be those which
god has made also the limits of the earth. But, if we now return, many
warlike nations are left unconquered beyond the Hyphasis as far as
the Eastern Sea, and many besides between these and Hyrcania in the
direction of the north wind, and not far from these the Scythian races.
Wherefore, if we go back, there is reason to fear that the races which
are now held in subjection, not being firm in their allegiance, may be
excited to revolt by those who are not yet subdued. Then our many
labours will prove to have been in vain; or it will be necessary for us
to incur over again fresh labours and dangers, as at the beginning. But,
O Macedonians and Grecian allies, stand firm. Glorious are the deeds
of those who undergo labour and run the risk of danger; and it is delightful to live a life of valour and to die leaving behind immortal glory.
Do you not know that our ancestor[12] reached so great a height of glory
as from being a man to become a god, or to seem to become one, not
by remaining in Tiryns or Argos, or even in the Peloponnese or at
Thebes? The labours of Dionysus were not few, and he was too exalted
a deity to be compared with Heracles. But we, indeed, have penetrated
into regions beyond Nysa; and the rock of Aornus, which Heracles was
unable to capture, is in our possession. Do you also add the parts of
Asia still left unsubdued to those already acquired, the few to the many.
But what great or glorious deed could we have performed, if, sitting
at ease in Macedonia, we had thought it sufficient to preserve our own
country without any labour, simply repelling the attacks of the nations on our frontiers, the Thracians, Illyrians, and Triballians, or even
those Greeks who were unfriendly to our interests? If, indeed, without
undergoing labour and being free from danger I were acting as your

[12] Heracles.

commander, while you were undergoing labour and incurring danger, not without reason would you be growing faint in spirit and resolution, because you alone would be sharing the labours, while procuring the rewards of them for others. But now the labours are common to you and me, we have an equal share of the dangers, and the rewards are open to the free competition of all. For the land is yours, and you act as its viceroys. The greater part also of the money now comes to you; and when we have traversed the whole of Asia, then, by Zeus, not merely having satisfied your expectations, but having even exceeded the advantages which each man hopes to receive, those of you who wish to return home I will send back to their own land, or I will myself lead them back; while those who remain here, I will make objects of envy to those who go back."

27. When Alexander had uttered these remarks, and others in the same strain, a long silence ensued, for the auditors neither had the audacity to speak in opposition to the king without constraint, nor did they wish to acquiesce in his proposal. Hereupon, he repeatedly urged any one who wished it to speak, if he entertained different views from those which he had himself expressed. Nevertheless the silence still continued a long time; but at last, Coenus, son of Polemocrates, plucked up courage and spoke as follows:

"O king, inasmuch as you do not wish to rule Macedonians by compulsion, but say you will lead them by persuasion, or yielding to their persuasion will not use violence towards them, I am going to make a speech, not on my own behalf and that of my colleagues here present, who are held in greater honour than the other soldiers, and most of us have already carried off the rewards of our labours, and from our pre-eminence are more zealous than the rest to serve you in all things; but I am going to speak on behalf of the bulk of the army. On behalf of this army I am not going to say what may be gratifying to the men, but what I consider to be both advantageous to you at present, and safest for the future. I feel it incumbent upon me not to conceal what I think the best course to pursue, both on account of my age, the honour paid to me by the rest of the army at your behest, and the boldness which I have without any hesitation displayed up to the present time in incurring dangers and undergoing labours. The more numerous and the greater the exploits have been, which have been achieved by you as our commander, and by those who started from home with you, the more advantageous does it seem to me that some end should be put to our labours and dangers. For you yourself see how many Macedonians and Greeks started with you, and how few of us have been left. Of our number you did well in sending back home the Thessalians at once from

Bactra, because you perceived that they were no longer eager to undergo labours. Of the other Greeks, some have been settled as colonists in the cities which you have founded; where they remain not indeed all of them of their own free will. The Macedonian soldiers and the other Greeks who still continued to share our labours and dangers have either perished in the battles, become unfit for war on account of their wounds, or been left behind in the different parts of Asia. The majority, however, have perished from disease, so that few are left out of many; and these few are no longer equally vigorous in body, while in spirit they are much more exhausted. All those whose parents still survive feel a great yearning to see them once more; they feel a yearning after their wives and children, and a yearning for their native land itself; which it is surely pardonable for them to yearn to see again with the honour and dignity they have acquired from you, returning as great men, whereas they departed small, and as rich men instead of being poor. Do not lead us now against our will; for you will no longer find us the same men in regard to dangers, since free-will will be wanting to us in the contests. But, rather, if it seem good to you, return of your own accord to your own land, see your mother, regulate the affairs of the Greeks, and carry to the home of your fathers these victories so many and great. Then start afresh on another expedition, if you wish, against these very tribes of Indians situated towards the east; or, if you wish, into the Euxine Sea; or else against Carchedon and the parts of Libya beyond the Carchedonians.[13] It is now your business to manage these matters; and other Macedonians and Greeks will follow you, young men in place of old, fresh men in place of exhausted ones, and men to whom warfare has no terrors, because up to the present time they have had no experience of it; and they will be eager to set out, from hope of future reward. The probability also is, that they will accompany you with still more zeal on this account, when they see that those who in the earlier expedition shared your labours and dangers have returned to their own abodes as rich men instead of being poor, and renowned instead of being obscure as they were before. Self-control in the midst of success is the noblest of all virtues, O king. For you have nothing to fear from enemies, while you are commanding and leading such an army as this; but the visitations of the deity are unexpected, and consequently men can take no precautions against them."

28. When Coenus had concluded this speech, loud applause was given to his words by those who were present; and the fact that many even shed tears made it still more evident that they were disinclined to incur further hazards, and that return would be delightful to them.

[13] Carthage.

Alexander then broke up the conference, being annoyed at the freedom of speech in which Coenus indulged, and the hesitation displayed by the other officers. But the next day he called the same men together again in wrath, and told them that he intended to advance farther, but would not force any Macedonian to accompany him against his will; that he would have those only who followed their king of their own accord; and that those who wished to return home were at liberty to return and carry back word to their relations that they were come back, having deserted their king in the midst of his enemies. Having said this, he retired into his tent, and did not admit any of the Companions on that day, or until the third day from that, waiting to see if any change would occur in the minds of the Macedonians and Grecian allies, as is likely to happen as a general rule among a crowd of soldiers, rendering them more disposed to obey. But on the contrary, when there was a profound silence throughout the camp, and the soldiers were evidently annoyed at his wrath, without being at all changed by it, Ptolemy, son of Lagus, says that he none the less offered sacrifice there for the passage of the river, but the victims were unfavourable to him when he sacrificed. Then indeed he collected the oldest of the Companions and especially those who were friendly to him, and as all things indicated the advisability of his returning, he made known to the army that he had resolved to march back again.

29. Then they shouted as a mixed multitude would shout when rejoicing; and most of them shed tears of joy. Some of them even approached the royal tent, and prayed for many blessings upon Alexander; because by them alone he suffered himself to be conquered. Then he divided the army into brigades, and ordered twelve altars to be prepared, equal in height to very large towers, and in breadth much larger than towers, to serve as thank-offerings to the gods who had led him so far as a conqueror, and also to serve as monuments of his own labours. When the altars were completed, he offered sacrifice upon them according to his custom, and celebrated a gymnastic and equestrian contest. After adding the country as far as the river Hyphasis to the dominion of Porus, he marched back to the Hydraotes. Having crossed this river, he continued his return march to the Acesines, where he found the city which Hephaestion had been ordered to fortify quite built. In this city he settled as many of the neighbouring people as volunteered to live in it, as well as those of the Grecian mercenaries who were now unfit for military service; and then began to make the necessary preparations for a voyage down the river into the Great Sea. At this time Arsaces, the ruler of the land bordering on that of Abisares, and the brother of the latter, with his other relations, came to Alexander, bringing the

gifts which are reckoned most valuable among the Indians, including some elephants from Abisares, thirty in number. They declared that Abisares himself was unable to come on account of illness; and with these men the ambassadors sent by Alexander to Abisares agreed. Readily believing that such was the case, he granted that prince the privilege of ruling his own country as his viceroy, and placed Arsaces also under his power. After arranging what tribute they were to pay, he again offered sacrifice near the river Acesines. He then crossed that river again, and came to the Hydaspes, where he employed the army in repairing the damage caused to the cities of Nicaea and Bucephala by the rain, and put the other affairs of the country in order.

BOOK VI

1. Alexander now resolved to sail down the Hydaspes to the Great Sea, after he had prepared on the banks of that river many thirty-oared galleys and others with one and a half banks of oars, as well as a number of vessels for conveying horses, and all the other things requisite for the easy conveyance of an army on a river. At first he thought he had discovered the origin of the Nile, when he saw crocodiles in the river Indus, which he had seen in no other river except the Nile,[1] as well as beans growing near the banks of the Acesines of the same kind as those which the Egyptian land produces. This conjecture was confirmed when he heard that the Acesines falls into the Indus. He thought the Nile rises somewhere or other in India, and after flowing through an extensive tract of desert country loses the name of Indus there; but afterwards when it begins to flow again through the inhabited land, it is called Nile both by the Aethiopians of that district and by the Egyptians, and finally empties itself into the Inner Sea.[2] In like manner Homer made the river Egypt give its name to the country of Egypt. Accordingly when he wrote to Olympias about the country of India, after mentioning other things, he said that he thought he had discovered the sources of the Nile, forming his conclusions about things so great from such small and trivial premises. However, when he had made a more careful inquiry into the facts relating to the river Indus, he learned the following details from the natives: That the Hydaspes unites its water with the Acesines, as the latter does with the Indus, and that they both yield up their names to the Indus; that the last-named river has two mouths, through which it discharges itself into the Great Sea; but that it has no connection with the Egyptian country. He then removed from the letter to his mother the part he had written about the Nile. Planning a voyage down the rivers as far as the Great Sea, he ordered ships for this purpose to be prepared for him. The crews of his ships were fully supplied from the Phoenicians, Cyprians, Carians, and Egyptians who accompanied the army.

2. At this time Coenus, who was one of Alexander's most faithful

---

[1] Herodotus (iv. 44) says that the Indus is the only river besides the Nile which produces crocodiles. He does not seem to have known the Ganges.
[2] The Mediterranean.

Companions, fell ill and died, and the king buried him with as much magnificence as circumstances allowed. Then collecting the Companions and the Indian envoys who had come to him, he appointed Porus king of the part of India which had already been conquered, seven nations in all, containing more than 2,000 cities. After this he made the following distribution of his army. With himself he placed on board the ships all the shield-bearing guards, the archers, the Agrianians, and the body-guard of cavalry. Craterus led a part of the infantry and cavalry along the right bank of the Hydaspes, while along the other bank Hephaestion advanced at the head of the most numerous and efficient part of the army, including the elephants, which now numbered about 200. These generals were ordered to march as quickly as possible to the place where the palace of Sopeithes was situated, and Philip, the satrap of the country beyond the Indus[3] extending to Bactria, was ordered to follow them with his forces after an interval of three days. He sent the Nysaean cavalry back to Nysa. The whole of the naval force was under the command of Nearchus; but the pilot of Alexander's ship was Onesicritus, who, in the narrative which he composed of Alexander's campaigns, falsely asserted that he was admiral, while in reality he was only a pilot. According to Ptolemy, son of Lagus, whose statements I chiefly follow, the entire number of the ships was eighty thirty-oared galleys; but the whole number of vessels, including the horse transports and boats, and all the other river craft, both those previously plying on the rivers and those built at that time, fell not far short of 2,000.

3. When he had made all the necessary preparations the army began to embark at the approach of the dawn; while according to custom he offered sacrifice to the gods and to the river Hydaspes, as the prophets directed. When he had embarked he poured a libation into the river from the prow of the ship out of a golden goblet, invoking the Acesines as well as the Hydaspes, because he had ascertained that it is the largest of all the rivers which unite with the Hydaspes, and that their confluence was not far off. He also invoked the Indus, into which the Acesines flows after its junction with the Hydaspes. Moreover he poured out libations to his forefather Heracles, to Ammon, and the other gods to whom he was in the habit of sacrificing, and then he ordered the signal for starting seawards to be given with the trumpet. As soon as the signal was given they commenced the voyage in regular order; for directions had been given how many abreast it was necessary for the baggage vessels to be arranged, as also for the vessels conveying the horses and for the ships of war; so that they might not fall foul of each other by sailing down

[3] As Alexander was at this time east of the Indus, the expression, beyond the Indus, means west of it.

the channel at random. He did not allow even the fast-sailing ships to get out of rank by out-stripping the rest. The noise of the rowing was never equalled on any other occasion, inasmuch as it proceeded from so many ships rowed at the same time; also the shout of the boatswains giving the time for beginning and stopping the stroke of the oars, and that of the rowers, when keeping time all together, they made a noise like a battle-cry with the dashing of their oars. The banks of the river also, being in many places higher than the ships, and collecting the sound into a narrow space, sent it back to each other very much increased by its very compression. In some parts too groves of trees on each side of the river helped to swell the sound, both from the solitude and the reverberation of the noise. The horses which were visible on the decks of the transports struck the barbarians who saw them with such surprise that those of them who were present at the starting of the fleet accompanied it a long way from the place of embarkation. For horses had never before been seen on board ships in the country of India; and the natives did not call to mind that the expedition of Dionysus into India was a naval one. The shouting of the rowers and the noise of the rowing were heard by the Indians who had already submitted to Alexander, and these came running down to the river's bank and accompanied him singing their native songs. For the Indians have been eminently fond of singing and dancing since the time of Dionysus and those who under his bacchic inspiration traversed the land of the Indians with him.

4. Sailing thus, he stopped on the third day at the spot where he had instructed Hephaestion and Craterus to encamp on opposite banks of the river at the same place. Here he remained two days, until Philip with the rest of the army came up with him. He then sent this general with the men he brought with him to the river Acesines, with orders to march along the bank of that river. He also sent Craterus and Hephaestion off again with instructions how they were to conduct the march. But he himself continued his voyage down the river Hydaspes, the channel of which is nowhere less than two and one-half miles broad. Wherever he happened to moor his vessels near the banks, he received some of the Indians dwelling near into allegiance by surrender on terms of agreement, while he reduced by force those who came into a trial of strength with him. Then he sailed rapidly towards the country of the Mallians and Oxydracians, ascertaining that these tribes were the most numerous and the most warlike of the Indians in that region; and having been informed that they had put their wives and children for safety into their strongest cities, with the resolution of fighting a battle with him, he made the voyage with the greater speed with the express design of attacking them before they had arranged their plans, and while there was still lack of

preparation and a state of confusion among them. Thence he made his second start, and on the fifth day reached the junction of the Hydaspes and Acesines. Where these rivers unite, one very narrow river is formed out of the two; and on account of its narrowness the current is swift. There are also prodigious eddies in the whirling stream, and the water rises in waves and plashes exceedingly, so that the noise of the swell of waters is distinctly heard by people while they are still far off. These things had previously been reported to Alexander by the natives, and he had told his soldiers; and yet, when his army approached the junction of the rivers, the noise made by the stream produced so great an impression upon them that the sailors stopped rowing, not from any word of command, but because the very boatswains who gave the time to the rowers became silent from astonishment and stood aghast at the noise.

5. When they came near the junction of the rivers, the pilots passed on the order that the men should row as hard as possible to get out of the narrows, so that the ships might not fall into the eddies and be overturned by them, but might by the vigorous rowing overcome the whirlings of the water. Being of a round form, the merchant vessels which happened to be whirled round by the current received no damage from the eddy, but the men who were on board were thrown into disorder and fright. For, being kept upright by the force of the stream itself, these vessels settled again into the onward course. But the ships of war, being long, did not emerge so scatheless from the whirling current, not being raised aloft in the same way as the others upon the plashing swell of water. Those ships which had two ranks of oars on each side had the lower oars only a little out of the water; and the oars of these getting athwart in the eddies were snapped asunder, at any rate those which were caught by the water, the workers of which did not raise them in time. Thus many of the ships were damaged; two indeed fell foul of each other and were destroyed, and many of those sailing in them perished. But when the river widened out, there the current was no longer so rapid, and the eddies did not whirl round with so much violence. Alexander therefore moored his fleet on the right bank, where there was a protection from the force of the stream and a roadstead for the ships. A certain promontory also in the river jutted out conveniently for collecting the wrecks. He preserved the lives of the men who were still being conveyed upon them; and when he had repaired the damaged ships, he ordered Nearchus to sail down the river until he reached the confines of the nation called Mallians. He himself made an inroad into the territories of the barbarians who would not yield to him, and after preventing them from succouring the Mallians, he again formed a junction with the naval armament. Hephaestion, Craterus and Philip had already united their

forces here. Alexander then transported the elephants, the brigade of Polysperchon, the horse-archers, and Philip with his army, across the river Hydaspes, and instructed Craterus to lead them. He sent Nearchus with the fleet with orders to set sail three days before the army started. He divided the rest of his army into three parts, and ordered Hephaestion to go five days in advance, so that if any should flee before the men under his own command and go rapidly forward they might fall in with Hephaestion's brigade and thus be captured. He also gave a part of the army to Ptolemy, son of Lagus, with orders to follow him after the lapse of three days, so that all those who fled from him and turned back again might fall in with Ptolemy's brigade. He ordered those in advance to wait, when they arrived at the confluence of the rivers Acesines and Hydraotes, until he himself came up; and he instructed Craterus and Ptolemy also to form a junction with him at the same place.

6. He then took the shield-bearing guards, the bowmen, the Agrianians, Peithon's brigade of men from those who were called foot Companions, all the horse-bowmen and half the cavalry Companions, and marched through a tract of country destitute of water against the Mallians, a tribe of the independent Indians. On the first day he encamped near a small piece of water which was about twelve miles from the river Acesines. Having dined there and caused his army to rest a short time, he ordered every man to fill whatever vessel he had with water. After travelling the remaining part of that day and all the ensuing night a distance of about forty-eight miles, he at daybreak reached the city into which many of the Mallians had fled for refuge. Most of them were outside the city and unarmed, supposing that Alexander would never come against them through the waterless country. It was evident that he led his army by this route for this very reason, because it was difficult to lead an army this way, and consequently it appeared incredible to the enemy that he would lead his forces in this direction. He therefore fell upon them unexpectedly, and killed most of them without their even turning to defend themselves, since they were unarmed. He cooped the rest up in the city, and posted his cavalry all round the wall, because the phalanx of infantry had not yet come up with him. He thus made use of his cavalry in place of a stockade. As soon as the infantry arrived, he sent Perdiccas with his own cavalry regiment and that of Clitus, as well as the Agrianians, against another city of the Mallians, whither many of the Indians of that region had fled for refuge. He ordered Perdiccas to blockade the men in the city, but not to commence the action until he himself should arrive, so that none might escape from this city and carry news to the rest of the barbarians that Alexander was already approaching. He then began to assault the wall; but the barbarians abandoned

it, finding that they were no longer able to defend it, since many had
been killed in the capture, and others had been rendered unfit for fighting
on account of their wounds. Fleeing for refuge into the citadel, they
defended themselves for some time from a position commanding from
its height and difficult of access. But as the Macedonians pressed on
vigorously from all sides, and Alexander himself appeared now in this
part of the action and now in that, the citadel was taken by storm, and
all the men who had fled into it for refuge were killed, to the number of
2,000. Perdiccas also reached the city to which he had been dispatched
and found it deserted; but learning that the inhabitants had fled from it
not long before, he made a forced march on the track of the fugitives.
The light armed troops followed him as quickly as they could on foot,
so that he took and massacred as many of the fugitives as could not out-
strip him and flee for safety into the river-marshes.

7. After dining and causing his men to rest until the first watch of
the night, Alexander marched forward; and travelling a great distance
through the night, he arrived at the river Hydraotes at daybreak. There
he ascertained that most of the Mallians had already crossed the river;
but coming upon those who were still in the act of crossing, he slew
many of them around the ford itself. Having crossed with them in pursuit without any delay by the same ford, he kept close up with those who
had outstripped him in their retreat. Many also of these he slew; some he
took prisoners; but the majority of them escaped into a place strong by
nature and made more so by fortifications. When the infantry reached
him, Alexander dispatched Peithon against the men in the fortress, giving
him the command of his own brigade of infantry and two regiments of
cavalry. These, attacking the place, took it at the first assault, and
made slaves of all those who had fled thither for safety, at least as
many of them as had not perished in the attack. After accomplishing
this, Peithon returned again to the camp. Alexander in person led his
forces against a certain city of the Brachmans,[4] because he ascertained
that some of the Mallians had fled for refuge into it. When he reached
it, he led his phalanx in serried ranks close up to the wall on all sides.
The enemy, seeing that their walls were being undermined, and being
themselves repulsed by the missiles, abandoned the walls, and having
fled for safety into the citadel, began to defend themselves from thence.
A few Macedonians having rushed in with them, turning round and
drawing together into a close body they drove them out and killed
twenty-five of them in their retreat. Hereupon Alexander ordered the
scaling-ladders to be placed against the citadel on all sides, and the wall
to be undermined; and when one of the towers, being undermined, fell

[4] The Brachmans, or Brahmins, were a religious caste of Indians.

down, and a part of the wall between two towers was breached, and thus rendered the citadel more accessible to assault in this quarter, he was seen to be the first man to scale the wall and get hold of it. The other Macedonians seeing him were ashamed of themselves and mounted the ladders in various places. The citadel was soon in their possession. Some of the Indians began to set fire to the houses, and being caught in them were killed; but most of them were slain fighting. About 5,000 in all were killed; and on account of their valour, only a few were taken prisoners.

8. Having remained there one day to give his army rest, he advanced on the morrow against the other Mallians. He found the cities abandoned, and ascertained that the men had fled into the desert. There he again gave the army one day's rest, and on the next day sent Peithon and Demetrius the cavalry general back to the river, in command of their own troops, giving them in addition as many battalions of the light-armed infantry as were sufficient for the enterprise. Their instructions were to go along the bank of the river, and if they met any of those who had fled for safety into the woods, of which there were many near the river's bank, to kill all who refused to surrender. Peithon and Demetrius captured many of these in the woods and killed them. He himself led his forces against the largest city of the Mallians, whither he was informed many from the other cities had taken refuge. But this also the Indians abandoned when they heard that Alexander was marching against it. Crossing the river Hydraotes, they remained with their forces drawn up upon its bank, because it was high, with the intention of obstructing Alexander's passage. When he heard this, he took all the cavalry which he had with him, and went to the part of the river where he was informed that the Mallians had drawn themselves up for battle; and the infantry was ordered to follow. When he reached the river and beheld the enemy drawn up on the opposite bank, he made no delay, but instantly, without resting from the journey, plunged into the ford with the cavalry alone. When they saw that he was now in the middle of the river, though they were drawn up ready for battle, they withdrew from the bank with all speed; and Alexander followed them with his cavalry alone. But when the Indians perceived only cavalry, they wheeled round and fought with desperate valour, being about 50,000 in number. When Alexander perceived that their phalanx was densely compact, as his own infantry was absent, he rode right round their army and made charges upon them, but did not come to close fighting with them. Meanwhile the archers, the Agrianians and the other select battalions of light-armed infantry, which he was leading with him, arrived, and his phalanx of infantry was seen not far off. As all kinds of danger were threatening

them at once, the Indians now wheeled round again and began to flee with headlong speed into the strongest of their adjacent cities; but Alexander followed them and slew many, while those who escaped into the city were cooped up within it. At first indeed he surrounded the city with the horse-soldiers as they came up from the march; but when the infantry arrived, he encamped all round the wall for this day, because not much of it was left for making the assault, and his army had been exhausted, the infantry by the long march, and the horses by the uninterrupted pursuit, and especially by the passage of the river.

9. On the following day, dividing the army into two parts, he himself assaulted the wall at the head of one, and Perdiccas led on the other. Upon this the Indians did not wait to receive the attack of the Macedonians, but abandoned the walls of the city and fled for safety into the citadel. Alexander and his troops therefore split open a small gate, and got within the city long before the others; for those who had been put under Perdiccas were behind time, having experienced difficulty in scaling the walls, as most of them did not bring ladders, thinking that the city had been captured, when they observed that the walls were deserted by the defenders. But when the citadel was seen to be still in the possession of the enemy, and many of them were observed drawn up in front of it to repel attacks, some of the Macedonians tried to force an entry by undermining the wall, and others by placing scaling ladders against it, wherever it was practicable to do so. Alexander, thinking that the men who carried the ladders were too slow, snatched one from a man who was carrying it, placed it against the wall himself, and began to mount it, crouching under his shield. After him mounted Peucestas, the man who carried the sacred shield which Alexander took from the Temple of the Trojan Athena and used to keep with him, and have it carried before him in all his battles. After Peucestas, by the same ladder ascended Leonnatus the confidential body-guard; and up another ladder went Abreas, one of the soldiers who received double pay for distinguished services. The king was now near the battlement of the wall, and leaning his shield against it was pushing some of the Indians within the fort, and had cleared that part of the wall, by killing others with his sword. The shield-bearing guards, becoming very anxious for the king's safety, pushed each other with ardour up the same ladder and broke it; so that those who were already mounting fell down and made the ascent impracticable for the rest. Alexander then, standing upon the wall, was being assailed all round from the adjacent towers; for none of the Indians dared approach him. He was also being assailed by the men in the city, who were throwing darts at him from no great distance; for a mound of earth happened to have been heaped up there opposite the wall. Alex-

ander was conspicuous both by the brilliancy of his weapons and by his extraordinary display of audacity. He therefore perceived that if he remained where he was, he would be incurring danger without being able to perform anything at all worthy of consideration; but if he leaped down within the fort he might perhaps by this very act strike the Indians with terror, and if he did not, but should only thereby be incurring danger, at any rate he would die not ignobly after performing great deeds of valour worth hearing about by men of after times. Forming this resolution, he leaped down from the wall into the citadel; where, supporting himself against the wall, he struck with his sword and killed some of the Indians who came to close quarters with him, including their leader, who rushed upon him too boldly. Another man who approached him he kept in check by hurling a stone at him, and a third in like manner. Another who advanced nearer to him he again kept off with his sword; so that the barbarians were no longer willing to approach him, but standing round him cast at him from all sides whatever missile any one happened to have or could get hold of at the time.

10. Meantime Peucestas and Abreas, the soldier entitled to double pay, and after them Leonnatus, being the only men who happened to have scaled the walls before the ladders were broken, had leaped down and were fighting in front of the king. Abreas, the man entitled to double pay, fell there, being shot with an arrow in the forehead. Alexander himself also was wounded with an arrow under the breast through his breastplate in the chest, so that Ptolemy says air was breathed out from the wound together with the blood. But although he was faint with exhaustion, he defended himself, as long as his blood was still warm. But, the blood streaming out copiously and without ceasing at every expiration of breath, he was seized with a dizziness and swooning, and bending over fell upon his shield. After he had fallen Peucestas defended him, holding over him in front the sacred shield brought from Troy; and on the other side he was defended by Leonnatus. But both these men were themselves wounded, and Alexander was now nearly fainting away from loss of blood. For the Macedonians had experienced great difficulty in the assault also on this account, because those who saw Alexander being shot at upon the wall and then leaping down into the citadel within, in their ardour arising from fear lest their king should meet with any mishap by recklessly exposing himself to danger, broke the ladders. Then some began to devise one plan and others another to mount upon the wall, as well as they could in their state of embarrassment, some fixing pegs into the wall, which was made of earth, and suspending themselves from these hoisted themselves up with difficulty by their means; others got up by mounting one upon the other. The first man who got up threw himself

down from the wall into the city, and so did they all, with a loud lamentation and howl of grief, where they saw the king lying on the ground. Now ensued a desperate conflict around his fallen body, one Macedonian after another holding his shield in front of him. In the meantime some of the soldiers having shivered in pieces the bar by which the gate in the space of wall between the towers was secured, entered the city a few at the time; while others, putting their shoulders under the gap made by the gate, forced their way into the space inside the wall, and thus laid the citadel open in that quarter.

11. Hereupon some of them began to kill the Indians, all of whom they slew, sparing not even a woman or child. Others carried off the king, who was lying in a faint condition, upon his shield; and they could not yet tell whether he was likely to survive. Some authors have stated that Critodemus, a physician of Cos, an Asclepiad by birth, made an incision into the injured part and drew the weapon out of the wound. Other authors say that as there was no physician present at the critical moment, Perdiccas, the confidential body-guard, at Alexander's bidding, made an incision with his sword into the wounded part and removed the weapon. On its removal there was such a copious effusion of blood that Alexander fainted again; and the effect of the faint was that the effusion of blood was stopped. Many other things concerning this catastrophe have been recorded by the historians; and Rumour having received the statements as they were given by the first falsifiers of the facts, still preserves them even to our times, nor will she desist from handling the falsehoods on to others also in regular succession, unless a stop is put to it by this history. For example, the common account is, that this calamity befell Alexander among the Oxydracians; whereas, it really occurred among the Mallians, an independent tribe of Indians; the city belonged to the Mallians, and the men who wounded him were Mallians. These people, indeed, had resolved to join their forces with the Oxydracians and then to make a desperate struggle; but he forestalled them by marching against them through the waterless country, before any aid could reach them from the Oxydracians, or they could render any help to the latter. Moreover, the common account is, that the last battle fought with Darius was near Arbela, at which battle he fled and did not desist from flight until he was arrested by Bessus and put to death at Alexander's approach; just as the battle before this was at Issus, and the first cavalry battle near the Granicus. The cavalry battle did really take place near the Granicus, and the next battle with Darius near Issus; but those authors who make Arbela most distant say that it is seventy-one miles away from the place where Alexander and Darius fought their last battle, while those who make it least distant say that it is fifty-nine miles off.

But Ptolemy and Aristobulus say that the battle was fought at Gauga-mela near the river Bumodus. As Gaugamela was not a city, but only a large village, the place is not celebrated, nor is the name pleasing to the ear; hence, it seems to me, that Arbela, being a city, has carried off the glory of the great battle. But if it is necessary to consider that that engagement took place near Arbela, being in reality so far distant from it, then it is allowable to say that the sea-battle fought at Salamis occurred near the isthmus of the Corinthians, and that fought at Artemisium, in Euboea, occurred near Aegina or Sunium. Moreover, in regard to those who covered Alexander with their shields in his peril, all agree that Peucestas did so; but they no longer agree in regard to Leonnatus or Abreas, the soldier in receipt of double pay for his distinguished services. Some say that Alexander, having received a blow on the head with a piece of wood, fell down in a fit of dizziness; and that having risen again he was wounded with a dart through the corselet in the chest. But Ptolemy, son of Lagus, says that he received only this wound in the chest. However, in my opinion, the greatest error made by those who have written the history of Alexander is the following. There are some who have recorded that Ptolemy, son of Lagus, in company with Peucestas, mounted the ladder with Alexander; that Ptolemy held his shield over him when he lay wounded, and that he was called Soter (the preserver) on that account.[5] And yet Ptolemy himself has recorded that he was not even present at this engagement, but was fighting battles against other barbarians at the head of another army. Let me mention these facts as a digression from the main narrative, so that the correct account of such great deeds and calamities may not be a matter of indifference to men of the future.

12. While Alexander was remaining in this place until his wound was cured, the first news which reached the camp from which he had set out to attack the Mallians was that he had died of the wound; and at first there arose a sound of lamentation from the entire army, as one man handed the rumour on to another. When they ceased their lamentation, they became spiritless, and felt perplexed as to the man who was to become the leader of the army; for many of the officers seemed to stand in equal rank and merit, both in the opinion of Alexander and in that of the Macedonians. They were also in a state of perplexity how to get back in safety to their own country, being quite enclosed by so many warlike nations, some of whom had not yet submitted, and who they conjectured would fight stoutly for their freedom; while others would

[5] Ptolemy received this appellation from the Rhodians whom he relieved from the assaults of Demetrius. The grateful Rhodians paid him divine honours as their preserver, and he was henceforward known as Ptolemy Soter (304 B.C.).

no doubt revolt as soon as they were relieved of their fear of Alexander. Besides, they seemed then at any rate to be in the midst of impassable rivers, and all things appeared to them uncertain and impracticable now that they were bereft of Alexander. But when at length the news came that he was still alive, they with difficulty acquiesced in it; and did not yet believe that he was even likely to survive. Even when a letter came from the king, saying that he was coming down to the camp in a short time, this did not appear to most of them worthy of credit, on account of their excessive fear; for they conjectured that the letter was concocted by his confidential body-guards and generals.

13. When Alexander became acquainted with this, for fear some attempt at a revolution might be made in the army, he had himself conveyed, as soon as it could be done with safety, to the bank of the river Hydraotes, and placed in a boat to sail down the river. For the camp was at the confluence of the Hydraotes and Acesines, where Hephaestion was at the head of the army, and Nearchus of the fleet. When the ship bearing the king approached the camp, he ordered the tent covering to be removed from the stern, that he might be visible to all. But they were still incredulous, thinking, forsooth, that Alexander's corpse was being conveyed on the vessel; until at length he stretched out his hand to the multitude, when the ship was nearing the bank. Then the men raised a cheer, lifting their hands, some towards the sky and others to the king himself. Many even shed involuntary tears at the unexpected sight. Some of the shield-bearing guards brought a litter for him when he was conveyed out of the ship; but he ordered them to fetch his horse. When he was seen again, mounting his horse, the whole army re-echoed with loud clapping of hands, so that the banks of the river and the groves near them reverberated with the sound. On approaching his tent he dismounted from his horse, so that he might be seen walking. Then the men came near, some on one side, others on the other, some touching his hands, others his knees, others only his clothes. Some only came close to get a sight of him, and went away having chanted his praise, while others threw garlands upon him, or the flowers which the country of India supplied at that season of the year. Nearchus says that some of his friends incurred his displeasure, reproaching him for exposing himself to danger in the front of the army in battle; which they said was the duty of a private soldier, and not that of the general. It seems to me that Alexander was offended at these remarks, because he knew that they were correct, and that he deserved the censure. However, like those who are mastered by any other pleasure, he had not sufficient self-control to keep aloof from danger, through his impetuosity in battle and his passion for glory. Nearchus also says that a certain old Boeotian, whose name

he does not mention, perceiving that Alexander was offended at the censures of his friends and was looking sullenly at them, came near him, and speaking in the Boeotian dialect, said, "O Alexander, it is the part of heroes to perform great deeds;" and repeated a certain iambic verse, the purport of which is, that the man who performs anything great is destined also to suffer. This man was not only acceptable to Alexander at the time, but was afterwards received into his more intimate acquaintance.

14. At this time arrived envoys from the Mallians who still survived, offering the submission of the nation; also from the Oxydracians came both the leaders of the cities and the governors of the provinces, accompanied by the other 150 most notable men, with full powers to make a treaty, bringing the gifts which are considered most valuable among the Indians, and also, like the Mallians, offering the submission of their nation. They said that their error in not having sent an embassy to him before was pardonable, because they excelled other races in the desire to be free and independent, and their freedom had been secure from the time Dionysus came into India until Alexander came; but if it seemed good to him, inasmuch as there was a general report that he also was sprung from gods, they were willing to receive whatever viceroy he might appoint, pay the tribute decreed by him, and give him as many hostages as he might demand. He therefore demanded the thousand best men of the nation, whom he might hold as hostages, if he pleased; and if not, that he might keep them as soldiers in his army, until he had finished the war which he was waging against the other Indians. They accordingly selected the thousand best and tallest men of their number, and sent them to him, together with 500 chariots and charioteers, though these were not demanded. Alexander appointed Philip viceroy over these people and the Mallians who were still surviving. He sent back the hostages to them, but retained the chariots. When he had satisfactorily arranged these matters, since many vessels had been built during the delay arising from his being wounded, he embarked 1,700 of the cavalry Companions, as many of the light-armed troops as before, and 10,000 infantry, and sailed a short distance down the river Hydraotes. But when that river mingled its waters with the Acesines, the latter giving its name to the united stream, he continued his voyage down the Acesines, until he reached its junction with the Indus. For these four large rivers which are all navigable discharge their water into the river Indus, though each does not retain its distinct name, for the Hydaspes discharges itself into the Acesines, and after the juction the whole stream forms what is called the Acesines. Again this same river unites with the Hydraotes, and after absorbing this river, still retains its own name. After this the Acesines

takes in the Hyphasis, and finally flows into the Indus under its own name; but after the junction it yields its name to the Indus. From this point I have no doubt that the Indus proceeds twelve miles, and perhaps more, before it is divided so as to form the Delta; and there it spreads out more like a lake than a river.

15. There, at the confluence of the Acesines and Indus, he waited until Perdiccas with the army arrived, after having routed on his way the independent tribe of the Abastanians. Meantime, he was joined by other thirty-oared galleys and trading vessels which had been built for him among the Xathrians, another independent tribe of Indians who had yielded to him. From the Ossadians, who were also an independent tribe of Indians, came envoys to offer the submission of their nation. Having fixed the confluence of the Acesines and Indus as the limit of Philip's satrapy, he left with him all the Thracians and as many men from the infantry regiments as appeared to him sufficient to provide for the security of the country. He then ordered a city to be founded there at the very junction of the two rivers, expecting that it would become large and famous among men. He also ordered a dockyard to be made there. At this time the Bactrian Oxyartes, father of his wife Roxana, came to him, to whom he gave the satrapy over the Parapamisadians, after dismissing the former viceroy, Tiryaspes, because he was reported to be exercising his authority improperly. Then he transported Craterus with the main body of the army and the elephants to the left bank of the river Indus, both because it seemed easier for a heavy-armed force to march along that side of the river, and the tribes dwelling near were not quite friendly. He himself sailed down to the capital of the Sogdians, where he fortified another city, made another dockyard, and repaired his shattered vessels. He appointed Peithon satrap of the land extending from the confluence of the Indus and Acesines as far as the sea, together with all the coast-land of India.[6] He then again despatched Craterus with his army through the country; and himself sailed down the river into the dominions of Musicanus, which was reported to be the most prosperous part of India. He advanced against this king because he had not yet come to meet him to offer the submission of himself and his land, nor had he sent envoys to seek his alliance. He had not even sent him the gifts which were suitable for a great king, or asked any favour from him. He accelerated his voyage down the river to such a degree that he succeeded in reaching the confines of the land of Musicanus before he had even heard that Alexander had started against him. Musicanus was so greatly alarmed that he went as fast as he could to meet him, bringing with him the

[6] It is evident that the name of Oxyartes has got into Arrian's text here before that of Peithon by mistake.

gifts valued most highly among the Indians, and taking all his elephants. He offered to surrender both his nation and himself, at the same time acknowledging his error, which was the most effectual way with Alexander for any one to get what he requested. Accordingly for these considerations Alexander granted him an indemnity for his offences. He also granted him the privilege of ruling the city and country, both of which Alexander admired. Craterus was directed to fortify the citadel in the capital, which was done while Alexander was still present. A garrison was also placed in it, because he thought the place suitable for keeping the neighbouring tribes in subjection.

16. Then he took the archers, Agrianians, and cavalry sailing with him, and marched against the governor of that country, whose name was Oxycanus, because he neither came himself nor did envoys come from him, to offer the surrender of himself and his land. At the very first assault he took by storm the two largest cities under the rule of Oxycanus, in the second of which that prince himself was captured. The booty he gave to his army, but the elephants he led with himself. The other cities in the same land surrendered to him as he advanced, nor did any one turn to resist him; so cowed in spirit had all the Indians now become at the thought of Alexander and his fortune. He then marched back against Sambus, whom he had appointed viceroy of the mountaineer Indians and who was reported to have fled, because he learned that Musicanus had been pardoned by Alexander and was ruling over his own land. For he was at war with Musicanus. But when Alexander approached the city which the country of Sambus held as its metropolis, the name of which was Sindimana, the gates were thrown open to him at his approach, and the relations of Sambus reckoned up his money and went out to meet him, taking with them the elephants also. They assured him that Sambus had fled, not from any hostile feeling towards Alexander, but fearing on account of the pardon of Musicanus. He also captured another city which had revolted at this time, and slew as many of the Brachmans as had been instigators of this revolt. These men are the philosophers of the Indians, of whose philosophy, if such it may be called, I shall give an account in my book descriptive of India.

17. Meantime he was informed that Musicanus had revolted. He despatched the satrap, Peithon, son of Agenor, with a sufficient army against him, while he himself marched against the cities which had been put under the rule of Musicanus. Some of these he razed to the ground, reducing the inhabitants to slavery; and into others he introduced garrisons and fortified the citadels. After accomplishing this, he returned to the camp and fleet. By this time Musicanus had been captured by Peithon, who was bringing him to Alexander. The king ordered him to

be hanged in his own country, and with him as many of the Brachmans
as had instigated him to the revolt. Then came to him the ruler of the
land of the Patalians, who said that the Delta formed by the river Indus
was still larger than the Egyptian Delta. This man surrendered to him
the whole of his own land and entrusted both himself and his property
to him. Alexander sent him away again in possession of his own dominions, with instructions to provide whatever was needful for the reception
of the army. He then sent Craterus into Carmania with the brigades of
Attalus, Meleager, and Antigenes, some of the archers, and as many of
the Companions and other Macedonians as, being now unfit for military
service, he was despatching to Macedonia by the route through the lands
of the Arachotians and Zarangians. To Craterus he also gave the duty
of leading the elephants; but the rest of the army, except the part of it
which was sailing with himself down to the sea, he put under the command of Hephaestion. He transported Peithon with the horse-javelin-
men and Agrianians to the opposite bank of the Indus, not the one along
which Hephaestion was about to lead the army. Peithon was ordered to
collect men to colonise the cities which had just been fortified, and to
form a junction with the king at Patala, after having settled the affairs
of the Indians of that region, if they attempted any revolutionary proceedings. On the third day of his voyage, Alexander was informed that
the governor of the Patalians had collected most of his subjects and was
going away by stealth, having left his land deserted. For this reason
Alexander sailed down the river with greater speed than before; and
when he arrived at Patala, he found both the country and the city deserted by the inhabitants and tillers of the soil. He however despatched
the lightest troops in his army in pursuit of the fugitives; and when some
of them were captured, he sent them away to the rest, bidding them to
be of good courage and return, for they might inhabit the city and till
the country as before. Most of them accordingly returned.

18. After instructing Hephaestion to fortify the citadel in Patala, he
sent men into the adjacent country, which was waterless, to dig wells
and to render the land fit for habitation. Certain of the native barbarians
attacked these men, and falling upon them unawares slew some of them;
but having lost many of their own men, they fled into the desert. The
work was therefore accomplished by those who had been sent out, another army having joined them, which Alexander had despatched to
take part in the work, when he heard of the attack of the barbarians.
Near Patala the water of the Indus is divided into large rivers, both of
which retain the name of Indus as far as the sea. Here Alexander constructed a harbour and dockyard; and when his works had advanced
towards completion he resolved to sail down as far as the mouth of the

right branch of the river. He gave Leonnatus the command of 1,000 cavalry and 8,000 heavy and light-armed infantry, and sent him to march through the island of Patala opposite the naval expedition; while he himself took the fastest sailing vessels, both those having one and a half banks of oars, and all the thirty-oared galleys, with some of the boats, and began to sail down the right branch of the river. The Indians of that region had fled, and consequently he could get no pilot for the voyage, and the voyage down the river was more difficult. On the day after the start a storm arose, and the wind blowing right against the stream caused a heavy swell in the river and shattered the hulls of the vessels violently, so that most of his ships were injured, and some of the thirty-oared galleys were entirely broken up. But they succeeded in running them aground before they quite fell to pieces in the water; and others were therefore constructed. He then sent the quickest of the light-armed troops into the land beyond the river's bank and captured some Indians, who from this time piloted him down the channel. But when they arrived at the place where the river expands, so that where it was widest it extended about twenty-five miles, a strong wind blew from the outer sea, and the oars could hardly be raised in the swell; they there-fore took refuge again in a canal into which his pilots conducted them.

19. While their vessels were moored here, the phenomenon of the ebb of the tide in the great sea occurred, so that their ships were left upon dry ground. This even in itself caused Alexander and his companions no small alarm, inasmuch as they were previously quite unacquainted with it. But they were much more alarmed when, the time coming round again, the water approached and the hulls of the vessels were raised aloft. The ships which it caught settled in the mud were raised aloft without any damage, and floated again without receiving any injury; but those that had been left on the drier land and had not a firm settlement, when an immense compact wave advanced, either fell foul of each other or were dashed against the land and thus shattered to pieces. When Alex-ander had repaired these vessels as well as his circumstances permitted, he sent some men on in advance down the river in two boats to explore the island at which the natives said he must moor his vessels in his voy-age to the sea. They told him that the name of the island was Cilluta. As he was informed that there were harbours in this island, that it was a large one and had water in it, he made the rest of his fleet put in there; but he himself with the best sailing ships advanced beyond, to see if the mouth of the river afforded an easy voyage out into the open sea. After advancing about twenty-five miles from the first island, they sighted another which was quite out in the sea. Then indeed they returned to the island in the river; and having moored his vessels near the extremity

of it, Alexander offered sacrifice to those gods to whom he said he had been directed by Ammon to sacrifice. On the following day he sailed down to the other island which was in the deep sea; and having come to shore here also, he offered other sacrifices to other gods and in another manner. These sacrifices he also offered according to the oracular instructions of Ammon. Then having gone beyond the mouths of the river Indus, he sailed out into the open sea, as he said, to discover if any land lay anywhere near in the sea; but in my opinion, chiefly that he might be able to say that he had navigated the great outer sea of India. There he sacrificed some bulls to Poseidon and cast them into the sea; and having poured out a libation after the sacrifice, he threw the goblet and bowls, which were golden, into the deep as thank-offerings, praying the god to escort safely for him the fleet, which he intended to despatch with Nearchus to the Persian Gulf and the mouths of the Euphrates and Tigris.

20. Returning to Patala, he found that the citadel had been fortified and that Peithon had arrived with his army, having accomplished everything for which he was despatched. He ordered Hephaestion to prepare what was needful for the fortification of a naval station and the construction of dockyards; for he resolved to leave behind here a fleet of many ships near the city of Patala, where the river Indus divides itself into two streams. He himself sailed down again into the Great Sea by the other mouth of the Indus, to ascertain which branch of the river is easier to navigate. The mouths of the river Indus are about 212 miles from each other.[7] In the voyage down he arrived at a large lake in the mouth of the river, which the river makes by spreading itself out; or perhaps the waters of the surrounding district draining into it make it large, so that it very much resembles a gulf of the sea. For in it were seen fish from the sea, larger indeed than those in this sea of ours. Having moored his ships then in the lake, where the pilots directed, he left there most of the soldiers and all the boats with Leonnatus; but he himself with the thirty-oared galleys and the vessels with one and a half banks of oars passed beyond the mouth of the Indus, and advancing into the sea also this way, ascertained that the outlet of the river on this side was easier to navigate than the other. He moored his ships near the shore, and taking with him some of the cavalry went along the sea-coast three days' journey, exploring what kind of country it was for a coasting voyage, and ordering wells to be dug, so that the sailors might have water to drink. He then returned to the ships and sailed back to Patala; but he sent a part of his army along the sea-coast to effect the same thing, instructing them to return to Patala when they had dug the wells. Sail-

---

[7] The distance is really 130 miles.

ing again down to the lake, he there constructed another harbour and dockyard; and leaving a garrison for the place, he collected sufficient food to supply the army for four months, as well as whatever else he could procure for the coasting voyage.

21. The season of the year was then unfit for voyaging; for the periodical winds prevailed, which at that season do not blow there from the north, as with us, but from the Great Sea, in the direction of the south wind. Moreover it was reported that there the sea was fit for navigation after the beginning of winter, that is, from the setting of the Pleiades[8] until the winter solstice; for at that season mild breezes usually blow from the land, drenched as it has been with great rains; and these winds are convenient on a coasting voyage both for oars and sails. Nearchus, who had been placed in command of the fleet, waited for the coasting season; but Alexander, starting from Patala, advanced with all his army as far as the river Arabius. He then took half of the shield-bearing guards and archers, the infantry regiments called foot Companions, the guard of the Companion cavalry, a squadron of each of the other cavalry regiments, and all the horse-bowmen, and turned away thence on the left towards the sea to dig wells, so that there might be abundance of them for the fleet sailing along on the coasting voyage; and at the same time to make an unexpected attack upon the Oritians, a tribe of the Indians in this region, which had long been independent. This he meditated doing because they had performed no friendly act either to himself or his army. He placed Hephaestion in command of the forces left behind. The Arabitians, another independent tribe dwelling near the river Arabius, thinking that they could not cope with Alexander in battle, and yet being unwilling to submit to him, fled into the desert when they heard that he was approaching. But crossing the river Arabius, which was both narrow and shallow, and travelling by night through the greater part of the desert, he came near the inhabited country at daybreak. Then ordering the infantry to follow him in regular line, he took the cavalry with him, dividing it into squadrons, that it might occupy a very large part of the plain, and thus marched into the land of the Oritians. All those who turned to defend themselves were cut to pieces by the cavalry, and many of the others were taken prisoners. He then encamped near a small piece of water; but when Hephaestion formed a junction with him, he advanced farther. Arriving at the largest village of the tribe of the Oritians, which was called Rhambacia, he commended the place and thought that if he colonized a city there it would become great and prosperous. He therefore left Hephaestion behind to carry out this project.

[8] This occurs at the beginning of November.

22. Again he took half of the shield-bearing guards and Agrianians, the guard of cavalry and the horse-bowmen, and marched forward to the confines of the Gadrosians and Oritians, where he was informed that the passage was narrow, and the Oritians were drawn up with the Gadrosians and were encamping in front of the pass, with the purpose of barring Alexander's passage. They had indeed marshalled themselves there; but when it was reported that he was already approaching, most of them fled from the pass, deserting their guard. The chiefs of the Oritians, however, came to him, offering to surrender both themselves and their nation. He instructed these to collect the multitude of their people together and send them to their own abodes, since they were not about to suffer any harm. Over these people he placed Apollophanes as satrap, and with him he left Leonnatus the confidential body-guard in Ora, at the head of all the Agrianians, some of the bowmen and cavalry, and the rest of the Grecian mercenary infantry and cavalry. He instructed him to wait until the fleet had sailed round the land, to colonise the city, and to regulate the affairs of the Oritians so that they might pay the greater respect to the viceroy. He himself, with the main body of the army (for Hephaestion had arrived at the head of the men who had been left behind), advanced into the land of the Gadrosians by a route most of which was desert. Aristobulus says that in this desert many myrrh-trees grew, larger than the ordinary kind; and that the Phoenicians, who accompanied the army for trafficking, gathered the gum of myrrh, and loading the beasts of burden, carried it away. For there was a great quantity of it, inasmuch as it exuded from large stems and had never before been gathered. He also says that this desert produces many odoriferous roots of nard, which the Phoenicians likewise gathered; but much of it was trampled down by the army, and a sweet perfume was diffused far and wide over the land by the trampling; so great was the abundance of it. In the desert there were also other kinds of trees, one of which had foliage like that of the bay-tree, and grew in places washed by the waves of the sea. These trees were on ground which was left dry by the ebb-tide; but when the water advanced they looked as if they had grown in the sea. Of others the roots were always washed by the sea, because they grew in hollow places, from which the water did not retire; and yet the trees were not destroyed by the sea. Some of these trees in this region were even forty-five feet high. At that season they happened to be in bloom; and the flower was very much like the white violet, but the perfume was far superior to that of the latter. There was also another thorny stalk growing out of the earth, the thorn on which was so strong that, piercing the clothes of some men just riding past, it would pull the horseman down from his horse rather than be itself split

off the stalk. It is also said that when hares run past these bushes, the thorns cling to their fur; and thus these animals are caught, as birds are with bird-lime, or fish with hooks. However they were easily cut through with steel; and when the thorns are cut the stalk gives forth much juice, still more abundantly than fig-trees do in the springtime, and it is more pungent.[9]

23. Thence Alexander marched through the land of the Gadrosians, by a difficult route, which was also destitute of provisions; and in many places there was no water for the army. Moreover they were compelled to march most of the way by night, and a great distance from the sea. However he was very desirous of coming to the part of the country along the sea, both to see what harbours were there, and to make what preparations he could on his march for the fleet, either by employing his men in digging wells, or by making arrangements somewhere for a market and anchorage. But the part of the country of the Gadrosians near the sea was entirely desert. He therefore sent Thoas, son of Mandrodorus, with a few horsemen down to the sea, to reconnoitre and see if there happened to be any haven anywhere near, or whether there was water or any other of the necessaries of life not far from the sea. This man returned and reported that he found some fishermen upon the shore living in stifling huts, which were made by putting together mussel-shells, and the back-bones of fishes were used to form the roofs. He also said that these fishermen used little water, obtaining it with difficulty by scraping away the gravel, and that what they got was not at all fresh. When Alexander reached a certain place in Gadrosia, where corn was more abundant, he seized it and placed it upon the beasts of burden; and marking it with his own seal, he ordered it to be conveyed down to the sea. But while he was marching to the halting stage nearest to the sea, the soldiers paying little regard to the seal, the guards made use of the corn themselves, and gave a share of it to those who were especially pinched with hunger. To such a degree were they overcome by their misery that after mature deliberation they resolved to take account of the visible and already impending destruction rather than the danger of incurring the king's wrath, which was not before their eyes and still remote. When Alexander ascertained the necessity which constrained them so to act, he pardoned those who had done the deed. He himself hastened forward to collect from the land all he could for victualling the army which was sailing round with the fleet; and sent Cretheus the Callatian to convey the supplies to the coast. He also ordered the natives to grind as much corn as they could and convey it down from the in-

[9] This is the well-known catechu, obtained chiefly from the Acacia Catechu. The liquid gum is used for dyeing and for medical purposes.

terior of the country, together with dates and sheep for sale to the soldiers. Moreover he sent Telephus, one of the confidential Companions, down to another place on the coast with a small quantity of ground corn.

24. He then advanced towards the capital of the Gadrosians, which was named Pura; and he arrived there in sixty days after starting from Ora. Most of the historians of Alexander's reign assert that all the hardships which his army suffered in Asia were not worthy of comparison with the labours undergone here. They say that Alexander pursued this route, not from ignorance of the difficulty of the journey (Nearchus, indeed, alone says that he was ignorant of it), but because he heard that no one had ever hitherto passed that way with an army and emerged in safety, except Semiramis, when she fled from India. The natives said that even she emerged with only twenty men of her army; and that Cyrus, son of Cambyses, escaped with only seven of his men. For they say that Cyrus also marched into this region for the purpose of invading India, but that he did not effect his retreat before losing the greater part of his army, from the desert and the other difficulties of this route. When Alexander received this information he is said to have been seized with a desire of excelling Cyrus and Semiramis. Nearchus says that he turned his march this way, both for this reason and at the same time for the purpose of conveying provisions near the fleet. The scorching heat and lack of water destroyed a great part of the army, and especially the beasts of burden; most of which perished from thirst and some of them even from the depth and heat of the sand, because it had been thoroughly scorched by the sun. For they met with lofty ridges of deep sand, not closely pressed and hardened, but such as received those who stepped upon it just as if they were stepping into mud, or rather into untrodden snow. At the same time too the horses and mules suffered still more, both in going up and coming down the hills, from the unevenness of the road as well as from its instability. The length of the marches between the stages also exceedingly distressed the army; for the lack of water often compelled them to make the marches of unusual length. When they travelled by night on a journey which it was necessary to complete, and at daybreak came to water, they suffered no hardship at all; but if, while still on the march, on account of the length of the way, they were caught by the heat, the day advancing, then they did indeed suffer hardships from the blazing sun, being at the same time oppressed by unassuageable thirst.

25. The soldiers killed many of the beasts of burden of their own accord; for when provisions were lacking, they came together, and slaughtered most of the horses and mules. They ate the flesh of these, and said that they had died of thirst or had perished from the heat.

There was no one to divulge the real truth of their conduct, both on account of the men's distress and because all alike were implicated in the same offence. What was being done had not escaped Alexander's notice; but he saw that the best cure for the present state of affairs was to pretend to be ignorant of it, rather than to permit it as a thing known to himself. The consequence was that it was no longer easy to convey the soldiers who were suffering from disease, or those who were left behind on the roads on account of the heat, partly from the want of beasts of burden and partly because the men themselves were knocking the waggons to pieces, not being able to draw them on account of the depth of the sand; and because in the first stages they were compelled on this account to go, not by the shortest routes, but by those which were easiest for the carriages. Thus some were left behind along the roads on account of sickness, others from fatigue or the effects of the heat, or from not being able to bear up against the drought; and there was no one either to lead them or to remain and tend them in their sickness. For the expedition was being made with great urgency; and the care of individual persons was necessarily neglected in the zeal displayed for the safety of the army as a whole. As they generally made the marches by night, some of the men also were overcome by sleep on the road; afterwards rousing up again, those who still had strength followed upon the tracks of the army; but only a few out of many overtook the main body in safety. Most of them perished in the sand, like men getting out of the course at sea. Another calamity also befell the army, which greatly distressed men, horses, and beasts of burden; for the country of the Gadrosians is supplied with rain by the periodical winds, just as that of the Indians is; not the plains of Gadrosia, but only the mountains where the clouds are carried by the wind and are dissolved into rain without passing beyond the summits of the mountains. On one occasion, when the army bivouacked, for the sake of its water, near a small brook which was a winter torrent, about the second watch of the night the brook which flowed there was suddenly swelled by the rains in the mountains which had fallen unperceived by the soldiers. The torrent advanced with so great a flood as to destroy most of the wives and children of the men who followed the army, and to sweep away all the royal baggage as well as all the beasts of burden still remaining. The soldiers, after great exertions, were hardly able to save themselves together with their weapons, many of which they lost beyond recovery. When, after enduring the burning heat and thirst, they lighted upon abundance of water, many of them perished from drinking to excess, not being able to check their appetite for it. For this reason Alexander generally pitched his camp, not near the water itself, but at a distance of about two and one-half miles

from it, to prevent the men and beasts from pressing in crowds into the
river and thus perishing, and at the same time to prevent those who had
no control over themselves from fouling the water for the rest of the
army by stepping into the springs or streams.

26. Here I have resolved not to pass over in silence the most noble
deed perhaps ever performed by Alexander, which occurred either in
this land or, according to the assertion of some other authors, still earlier,
among the Parapamisadians. The army was continuing its march through
the sand, though the heat of the sun was already scorching, because it
was necessary to reach water before halting. They were far on the journey, and Alexander himself, though oppressed with thirst, was nevertheless with great pain and difficulty leading the army on foot, so that his
soldiers also, as is usual in such a case, might more patiently bear their
hardships by the equalization of the distress. At this time some of the
light-armed soldiers, starting away from the army in quest of water,
found some collected in a shallow cleft, a small and mean spring. Collecting this water with difficulty, they came with all speed to Alexander,
as if they were bringing him some great boon. As soon as they approached the king, they poured the water into a helmet and carried it to
him. He took it, and commending the men who brought it, immediately
poured it upon the ground in sight of all. As a result of this action, the
entire army was re-invigorated to so great a degree that any one would
have imagined that the water poured away by Alexander had furnished
a draught to every man. This deed beyond all others I commend as evidence of Alexander's power of endurance and self-control, as well as of
his skill in managing an army. The following adventure also occurred to
the army in that country. At last the guides declared that they no longer
remembered the way, because the tracks of it had been rendered invisible
by the wind blowing the sand over them. Moreover, in the deep sand
which had been everywhere reduced to one level, there was nothing by
which they could conjecture the right way, not even the usual trees growing along it, nor any solid hillock rising up; and they had not practised
themselves in making journeys by the stars at night or by the sun in the
daytime, as sailors do by the constellations of the Bears—the Phoenicians by the Little Bear, and other men by the Greater Bear. Then at
length Alexander perceived that it was necessary for him to lead the way
by declining to the left; and taking a few horsemen with him he advanced in front of the army. But when the horses even of these were
exhausted by the heat, he left most of these men behind, and rode away
with only five men and found the sea. Having scraped away the shingle
on the sea-beach, he lighted upon water fresh and pure, and then went
and fetched the whole army. For seven days they marched along the sea-

coast, supplying themselves with water from the shore. Thence he led his expedition into the interior, for now the guides knew the way.

27. When he arrived at the capital of Gadrosia, he there gave his army a rest. He deposed Apollophanes from the satrapy, because he discovered that he had paid no heed to his instructions. Thoas was appointed satrap over the people of this district; but as he fell ill and died, Sibyrtius succeeded to the office. The same man had also lately been appointed by Alexander viceroy of Carmania; but now the rule over the Arachotians and Gadrosians was given to him, and Tlepolemus, son of Pythophanes, received Carmania. The king was already advancing into Carmania, when news was brought to him that Philip, the viceroy of the country of the Indians, had been plotted against by the mercenaries and treacherously killed; but that Philip's Macedonian bodyguards had caught some of the murderers in the very act and others afterwards, and had put them to death. When he had ascertained this, he sent a letter into India to Eudemus and Taxiles, ordering them to administer the affairs of the land which had previously been subordinated to Philip until he could send a viceroy for it. When he arrived in Carmania, Craterus effected a junction with him, bringing with him the rest of the army and the elephants. He also brought Ordanes, whom he had arrested for revolting and trying to effect a revolution. Thither also came Stasanor, the viceroy of the Areians and Zarangians, accompanied by Pharismanes, son of Phrataphernes, the viceroy of the Parthians and Hyrcanians. There came also the generals who had been left with Parmenio over the army in Media, Cleander, Sitalces, and Heracon, bringing with them the greater part of their army. Both the natives and the soldiers themselves brought many accusations against Cleander and Sitalces, as for example, that the temples had been pillaged by them, old tombs rifled, and other acts of injustice, recklessness, and tyranny perpetrated against their subjects. As these charges were proved, he put them to death, in order to inspire others who might be left as viceroys, governors, or prefects of provinces with the fear of suffering equal penalties with them if they swerved from the path of duty. This was one of the chief means by which Alexander kept in subordination the nations which he had conquered in war or which had voluntarily submitted to him, though they were so many in number and so far distant from each other; because under his regal sway it was not allowed that those who were ruled should be unjustly treated by those who ruled. At that time Heracon was acquitted of the charge, but soon after, being convicted by the men of Susa of having pillaged the temple in that city, he also suffered punishment. Stasanor and Phrataphernes came to Alexander bringing a multitude of beasts of burden

and many camels, when they learned that he was marching by the route
to Gadrosia, conjecturing that his army would suffer the very hardships
which it did suffer. Therefore these men arrived just at the very time
they were required, as also did their camels and beasts of burden. For
Alexander distributed all these animals to the officers man by man, to
all the various squadrons and centuries of the cavalry, and to the various
companies of the infantry, as far as their number allowed him.

28. Certain authors have said (though to me the statement seems incredible) that Alexander led his forces through Carmania lying extended with his Companions upon two covered waggons joined together,
the flute being played to him; and that the soldiers followed him wearing garlands and sporting. Food was provided for them, as well as all
kinds of dainties which had been brought together along the roads by
the Carmanians. They say that he did this in imitation of the Bacchic
revelry of Dionysus, because a story was told about that deity, that
after subduing the Indians he traversed the greater part of Asia in this
manner and received the appellation of Thriambus, and that for the same
reason the processions in honour of victories after war were called
thriambi. This has been recorded neither by Ptolemy, son of Lagus, nor
by Aristobulus, son of Aristobulus, nor by any other writer whose testimony on such points any one would feel to be worthy of credit. It is
sufficient therefore for me to record it as unworthy of belief. But as to
what I am now going to describe I follow the account of Aristobulus. In
Carmania Alexander offered sacrifices to the gods as thank-offerings for
his victory over the Indians, and because his army had been brought in
safety out of Gadrosia. He also celebrated a musical and gymnastic contest. He then appointed Peucestas one of his confidential body-guards,
having already resolved to make him viceroy of Persis. He wished him,
before being appointed to the satrapy, to experience this honour and
evidence of confidence, as a reward for his exploit among the Mallians.
Up to this time the number of his confidential body-guards had been
seven: Leonnatus, son of Anteas, Hephaestion, son of Amyntor, Lysimachus, son of Agathocles, Aristonous, son of Pisaeus, these four being
Pellaeans; Perdiccas, son of Orontes, from Orestis, Ptolemy, son of
Lagus, and Peithon, son of Crateas, the Heordaeans. Peucestas, who
had held the shield over Alexander, was now added to them as an
eighth. At this time Nearchus, having sailed round the coast of Ora and
Gadrosia and that of the Fish-Eaters, put into port in the inhabited
part of the coastland of Carmania, and going up thence into the interior with a few men he reported to Alexander the particulars of the
voyage which he had made along the coasts of the external sea. Nearchus
was then sent down to the sea again to sail round as far as the country

of Susiana, and the outlets of the river Tigris. How he sailed from the river Indus to the Persian Sea and the mouth of the Tigris I shall describe in a separate book, following the account of Nearchus himself. For he also wrote a history of Alexander in Greek. Perhaps I shall be able to compose this narrative in the future, if inclination and the divine influence urge me to it. Alexander now ordered Hephaestion to march into Persis from Carmania along the sea-shore with the larger division of the army and the beasts of burden, taking with him also the elephants; because, as he was making the expedition in the season of winter, the part of Persis near the sea was warm and possessed abundant supplies of provisions.

29. He himself then marched to Pasargadae in Persis, with the lightest of his infantry, the Companion cavalry and a part of the archers; but he sent Stasanor down to his own land. When he arrived at the confines of Persis, he found that Phrasaortes was no longer viceroy, for he happened to have died of disease while Alexander was still in India. Orxines was managing the affairs of the country, not because he had been appointed ruler by Alexander, but because he thought it his duty to keep Persis in order for him, as there was no other ruler. Atropates, the viceroy of Media, also came to Pasargadae, bringing Baryaxes, a Mede, under arrest, because he had assumed the upright head-dress and called himself king of the Persians and Medes. With Baryaxes he also brought those who had taken part with him in the attempted revolution and revolt. Alexander put these men to death.

He was grieved by the outrage committed upon the tomb of Cyrus, son of Cambyses; for according to Aristobulus, he found it dug through and pillaged. The tomb of the famous Cyrus was in the royal park at Pasargadae, and around it a grove of all kinds of trees had been planted. The park was also watered by a stream, and high grass grew in the meadow. The base of the tomb itself had been made of squared stone in the form of a rectangle. Above it there was a stone building surmounted by a roof, with a door leading within, so narrow that even a small man could with difficulty enter, after suffering much discomfort. In the building lay a golden coffin, in which the body of Cyrus had been buried, and by the side of the coffin was a couch, the feet of which were of gold wrought with the hammer. A carpet of Babylonian tapestry with purple rugs formed the bedding; upon it were also a Median coat with sleeves and other tunics of Babylonian manufacture. Aristobulus adds that Median trousers and robes dyed the colour of hyacinth were also lying upon it, as well as others of purple and various other colours; moreover there were collars, sabres, and earrings of gold and precious stones soldered together, and near them stood a table. On the middle of the couch lay the coffin which contained the body of Cyrus. Within the inclosure, near the ascent leading to the tomb, there was a small house built for the Magians who guarded the tomb; a duty which they had discharged ever since the time of Cambyses, son of Cyrus, son succeeding father as guard. To these men a sheep and specified quantities of wheaten flour and wine were given daily by the king; and a horse once a month as a sacrifice to Cyrus. Upon the tomb an inscription in Persian letters had been placed, which bore the following meaning in the Persian language, "O man, I am Cyrus, son of Cambyses, who founded the empire of the Persians, and was king of Asia. Do not therefore grudge me this monument." As soon as Alexander had conquered Persia, he was very desirous of entering the tomb of Cyrus; but he found that everything else had been carried off except the coffin and couch. They had even maltreated the king's body; for they had torn off the lid of the coffin and cast out the corpse. They had tried to make the coffin itself of smaller bulk and thus more portable, by cutting part of it off and crushing part of it up; but as their efforts did not succeed, they departed, leaving the coffin in that state. Aristobulus says that he was himself commissioned by Alexander to restore the tomb for Cyrus, to put into the coffin the parts of the body still preserved, to put the lid on, and to repair the parts of the coffin which had been defaced. Moreover he was instructed to stretch the couch tight with bands, and to deposit all the other things which used to lie there for ornament, both resembling the former ones and of the same number. He was ordered also to do away with the door, building part of it up with stone and plastering part of it over with cement; and finally to put the royal seal upon the cement. Alexander arrested the Magians who were the guards of the tomb, and put them to the torture to make them confess who had done the deed; but in spite of the torture they confessed nothing either about themselves or any other person. In no other way were they proved to have been privy to the deed; they were therefore released by Alexander.

30. Thence he proceeded to the royal palace of the Persians, which he had on a former occasion himself burned down, as I have previously related, expressing my disapprobation of the act; and on his return Alexander himself did not commend it. Many charges were brought by the Persians against Orxines, who ruled them after the death of Phrasaortes. He was convicted of having pillaged temples and royal tombs, and of having unjustly put many of the Persians to death. He was therefore hanged by men acting under Alexander's orders; and Peucestas the confidential body-guard was appointed satrap of Persis. The king placed special confidence in him both for other reasons, and

especially on account of his exploit among the Mallians, where he braved the greatest dangers and helped to save Alexander's life. Besides this, he did not refuse to accommodate himself to the Asiatic mode of living; and as soon as he was appointed to the position of viceroy of Persis, he openly assumed the native garb, being the only man among the Macedonians who adopted the Median dress in preference to the Grecian. He also learned to speak the Persian language correctly, and comported himself in all other respects like a Persian. For this conduct he was not only commended by Alexander, but the Persians also were highly delighted with him, for preferring their national customs to those of his own forefathers.

BOOK VII

1. When Alexander arrived at Pasargadae and Persepolis,[1] he was seized with an ardent desire to sail down the Euphrates and Tigris to the Persian Sea, and to see the mouths of those rivers as he had already seen those of the Indus as well as the sea into which it flows. Some authors also have stated that he was meditating a voyage round the larger portion of Arabia, the country of the Ethiopians, Libya, and Numidia beyond Mount Atlas to Gadeira, inward into our sea; thinking that after he had subdued both Libya and Carchedon, then indeed he might with justice be called king of all Asia. For he said that the kings of the Persians and Medes called themselves Great Kings without any right, since they ruled a comparatively small part of Asia. Some say that he was meditating a voyage thence into the Euxine Sea, to Scythia and the Lake Maeotis; while others assert that he intended to go to Sicily and the Iapygian Cape, for the fame of the Romans spreading far and wide was now exciting his jealousy. For my own part I cannot conjecture with any certainty what were his plans; and I do not care to guess. But this I think I can confidently affirm, that he meditated nothing small or mean; and that he would never have remained satisfied with any of the acquisitions he had made, even if he had added Europe to Asia, or the islands of the Britons to Europe; but would still have gone on seeking for some unknown land beyond those mentioned. I verily believe that if he had found no one else to strive with, he would have striven with himself. And on this account I commend some of the Indian philosophers, who are said to have been caught by Alexander as they were walking in the open meadow where they were accustomed to spend their time. At the sight of him and his army they did nothing else but stamp with their feet on the earth, upon which they were stepping. When he asked them by means of interpreters what was the meaning of their action, they replied as follows, "O king Alexander, every man possesses as much of the earth as this upon which we have stepped; but you being only a man like the rest of us, except in being meddlesome and arrogant, have come over so great a part of the earth from your own land, both having trouble yourself and giving it to others. And yet you also

---

[1] Pasargadae was the ancient capital of Cyrus, but Persepolis was that of the later kings of Persia.

591

will soon die, and possess only as much of the earth as is sufficient for your body to be buried in."

2. On this occasion Alexander commended both the words and the men who spoke them; but nevertheless he did just the opposite to that which he commended. When also in the Isthmus he met Diogenes of Sinope, lying in the sun, standing near him with his shield-bearing guards and foot Companions, he asked if he wanted anything. But Diogenes said that he wanted nothing else, except that he and his attendants would stand out of the sun. Alexander is said to have expressed his admiration of Diogenes. Thus it is evident that Alexander was not entirely destitute of better feelings; but he was the slave of his insatiable ambition. Again, when he arrived at Taxila and saw the naked sect of Indian philosophers, he was exceedingly desirous that one of these men should live with him; because he admired their power of endurance. But the oldest of the philosophers, Dandamis by name, of whom the others were disciples, refused to come himself to Alexander, and would not allow the others to do so. He is said to have replied that he was himself a son of Zeus, if Alexander was; and that he wanted nothing from him, because he was quite contented with what he had. And besides he said that he saw his attendants wandering over so much of the land and sea to no advantage, and that there was no end to their many wanderings. Therefore he had no desire that Alexander should give him anything of which he was possessor, nor on the other hand was he afraid that he should be excluded from anything which Alexander ruled over. For while he lived the country of India, which produces the fruits in their season, was sufficient for him; and when he died he should be released from the body, an uncongenial associate. Alexander therefore did not attempt to force him to come to him, considering that the man was free to do as he pleased. But Megasthenes has recorded that Calanus, one of the philosophers of this region, who had very little power over himself, was induced to do so; and that the philosophers themselves reproached him, for having deserted the happiness existing among them, and serving another lord instead of god.

3. This I have recorded, because in the history of Alexander it is necessary also to speak of Calanus; for when he was in the country of Persis his health became delicate, though he had never before been subject to illness. Accordingly, not being willing to lead the life of a man in infirm health, he told Alexander that in such circumstances he thought it best for him to put an end to his existence, before he came into experience of any disease which might compel him to change his former mode of living. For a long time the king tried to dissuade him; however, when he saw that he was not to be overcome, but would find some other

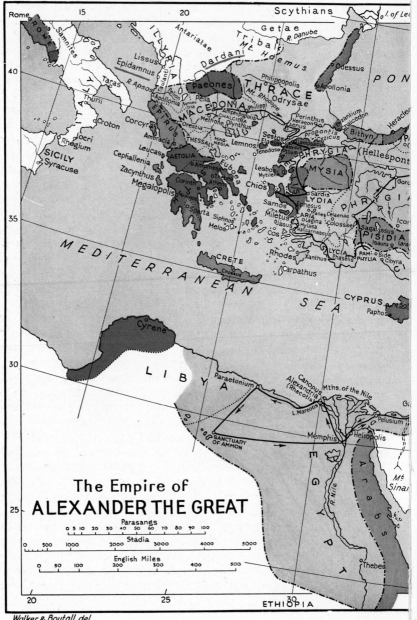

The Empire of
ALEXANDER THE GREAT

Parasangs
0 5 10 20 30 40 50 60 70 80 90 100

Stadia
0   500   1000   2000   3000   4000   5000

English Miles
0   50 100   200   300   400   500

Walker & Boutall, del.

Rome   15   20   Scythians   I. of Le

Getae
ILLYRIA Antariatae Tribali
Dardani Mt. Haemus
Lissus R. Danube
40 Epidamnus
R. Apsos Taulanti
Apollonia Paeones Philippopolis
Pella THRACE Odessus
Lynces Amphipolis Mt. Rhodope Odrysae Apollonia PON
Aria CHALCIDICE Philippi
MACEDONIA Perinthus Byzantium
Corcyra Orestia Heraeon Chalcedon
Methone Olynthus Aenus Propontis Cyzicus Bithyn Heracle
Ambracia Pydna Sestos Lampsacus
EPIRUS THESSALY MAG- Lemnos Abydus Ilium P
Leucas NESIA Tenedos PHRYGIA Hellespont
AETOLIA Lesbos MYSIA
Cephallenia Amphissa Euboea Mytilene
Zacynthus Thebes Athens Chios Sardis LYDIA PHRYGIA
Megalopolis Corinth Ephesus
Sparta Samos Miletus Gord
35 Siphnos CARIA Celaenae Icor
Melos Alabanda Alagina Colossae
Myndus Mylasa Sagalassus PISIDIA
Cos Halicarnassus Isaura Lara
Rhodes LYCIA PAM- Side
Xanthus Phaselis PHYLIA Cibyra C
M E D I T E R R A N E A N
CRETE
Cnossus Carpathus S E A CYPRUS Sol
Paphos

Cyrene

30 L I B Y A Paraetonium Canopus Mths. of the Nile
Alexandria Ga
(Rhacotis) L. Mareotis Pelusium
SANCTUARY Memphis Heliopolis
OF AMMON m Arabs Mt
G Sinai
25 R. Nile Y
P
T
Thebes

20   25   ETHIOPIA 30

SICILY
Syracuse
Croton
Locri
Rhegium
Thurii
Taras
ROME
Samnites
ITALY

way of release, if this were not yielded to him, he ordered a funeral pyre
to be heaped up for him, in the place where the man himself directed,
and gave instructions that Ptolemy, son of Lagus, the confidential body-
guard, should have the charge of it. They say that a solemn procession,
consisting both of horses and men, advanced before him, some of the
latter being armed and others carrying all kinds of incense for the pyre.
They also say that they carried gold and silver goblets and royal apparel; and because he was unable to walk through illness, a horse was
prepared for him. However, not being able to mount the horse, he was
conveyed stretched out upon a litter, crowned with a garland after the
custom of the Indians, and singing in the Indian language. The Indians
say that he sang hymns to the gods and eulogies on his countrymen.
Before he ascended the funeral-pyre he presented the horse which he
should himself have mounted, being a royal steed of the Nisaean breed,
to Lysimachus, one of those who attended him to learn his philosophy.
He distributed among his other disciples the goblets and rugs which
Alexander had ordered to be cast into the pyre as an honour to him.
Then mounting the pyre he lay down upon it in a becoming manner, and
was visible to the whole army. To Alexander the spectacle appeared
unseemly, as it was being exhibited at the cost of a friend; but to the
rest it was a cause of wonder that he did not move any part of his body
in the fire. As soon as the men to whom the duty had been assigned set
fire to the pyre, Nearchus says the trumpets sounded, in accordance
with Alexander's order, and the whole army raised the war-cry as it was
in the habit of shouting when advancing to battle. The elephants also
chimed in with their shrill and warlike cry, in honour of Calanus. Authors upon whom reliance may be placed, have recorded these and
such-like things about Calanus the Indian, facts of great import to
those who are desirous of learning how steadfast and immovable a thing
the human mind is in regard to what it wishes to accomplish.

4. At this time Alexander sent Atropates away to his own satrapy,
after advancing to Susa; where he arrested Abulites and his son Oxathres, and put them to death on the ground that they were governing
the Susians badly. Many outrages upon temples, tombs, and the subjects themselves had been committed by those who were ruling the countries conquered by Alexander in war; because the king's expedition into
India had taken a long time, and it was not thought credible that he
would ever return in safety from so many nations possessing so many
elephants, going to his destruction beyond the Indus, Hydaspes, Acesines, and Hyphasis. The calamities that befell him among the Gadrosians were still greater inducements to those acting as viceroys in this
region to be free from apprehension of his return to his dominions. Not

only so, but Alexander himself is said to have become more inclined at that time to believe accusations which were plausible in every way, as well as to inflict very severe punishment upon those who were convicted even of small offences, because with the same disposition he thought they would be likely to perform great ones.

In Susa also he celebrated both his own wedding and those of his companions. He himself married Barsine, the eldest daughter of Darius, and according to Aristobulus, besides her another, Parysatis, the youngest daughter of Ochus. He had already married Roxana, daughter of Oxyartes the Bactrian. To Hephaestion he gave Drypetis, another daughter of Darius, and his own wife's sister; for he wished Hephaestion's children to be first cousins to his own. To Craterus he gave Amastrine, daughter of Oxyartes the brother of Darius; to Perdiccas, the daughter of Atropates, viceroy of Media; to Ptolemy the confidential body-guard, and Eumenes the royal secretary, the daughters of Artabazus, to the former Artacama, and to the latter Artonis. To Nearchus he gave the daughter of Barsine and Mentor; to Selecus the daughter of Spitamenes the Bactrian. Likewise to the rest of his Companions he gave the choicest daughters of the Persians and Medes, to the number of eighty. The weddings were celebrated after the Persian manner, seats being placed in a row for the bridegrooms; and after the banquet the brides came in and seated themselves, each one near her own husband. The bridegrooms took them by the right hand and kissed them; the king being the first to begin, for the weddings of all were conducted in the same way. This appeared the most popular thing which Alexander ever did; and it proved his affection for his Companions. Each man took his own bride and led her away; and on all without exception Alexander bestowed doweries. He also ordered that the names of all the other Macedonians who had married any of the Asiatic women should be registered. They were over 10,000 in number; and to these Alexander made presents on account of their weddings.

5. He now thought it a favourable opportunity to liquidate the debts of all the soldiers who had incurred them; and for this purpose he ordered that a register should be made of how much each man owed, in order that they might receive the money. At first only a few registered their names, fearing that this had been instituted as a test by Alexander, to discover which of the soldiers found their pay insufficient for their expenses, and which of them were extravagant in their mode of living. When he was informed that most of them were not registering their names, but that those who had borrowed money on bonds were concealing the fact, he reproached them for their distrust of him. For he said that it was not right either that the king should deal otherwise than sin-

cerely with his subjects, or that any of those ruled by him should think
that he would deal otherwise than sincerely with them. Accordingly, he
had tables placed in the camp with money upon them; and he appointed
men to manage the distribution of it. He ordered the debts of all who
showed a money-bond to be liquidated without the debtors' names being
any longer registered. Consequently, the men believed that Alexander
was dealing sincerely with them; and the fact that they were not known
was a greater pleasure to them than the fact that they ceased to be in
debt. This presentation to the army is said to have amounted to 20,000
talents. He also gave presents to particular individuals, according as each
man was held in honour for his merit or valour, if he had become conspicuous in crises of danger. Those who were distinguished for their
personal gallantry he crowned with golden chaplets: first, Peucestas, the
man who had held the shield over him; second, Leonnatus, who also had
held his shield over him, and moreover had incurred dangers in India
and won a victory in Ora. For he had posted himself with the forces
left with him against the Oritians and the tribes living near them, who
were trying to effect a revolution, and had conquered them in battle. He
also seemed to have managed other affairs in Ora with great success. In
addition to these, he crowned Nearchus for his successful voyage
round the coast from the land of the Indians through the Great Sea;
for this officer had now arrived at Susa. Besides these three, he crowned
Onesicritus, the pilot of the royal ship; as well as Hephaestion and the
rest of the confidential body-guards.

6. The viceroys from the newly-built cities and the rest of the territory
subdued in war came to him, bringing with them youths just growing
into manhood to the number of 30,000, all of the same age, whom
Alexander called Epigoni.[2] They had been accoutred with Macedonian
arms, and exercised in military discipline after the Macedonian system.
The arrival of these is said to have vexed the Macedonians, who thought
that Alexander was contriving every means in his power to free himself
from future need of their services. For the same reason also the sight of
his Median dress was no small cause of dissatisfaction to them; and the
weddings celebrated in the Persian fashion were displeasing to most of
them, even including some of those who married, although they had
been greatly honoured by their being put on the same level with the
king in the marriage ceremony. They were offended at Peucestas, the
satrap of Persis, on account of his Persianizing both in dress and in
speech, because the king was delighted by his adopting the Asiatic customs. They were disgusted that the Bactrian, Sogdianian, Arachotian,

[2] The Epigoni, or Afterborn, were the sons of the seven chiefs who fell in the
first war against Thebes.

Zarangian, Arian, and Parthian horsemen, as well as the Persian horsemen called the Evacae, had been distributed among the squadrons of
the Companion cavalry; as many of them at least as were seen to excel
in reputation, fineness of stature, or any other good quality; and that a
fifth cavalry division was added to these troops, not composed entirely of
foreigners; but the whole body of cavalry was increased in number, and
men were picked from the foreigners and put into it. Cophen, son of
Artabazus, Hydarnes and Artiboles, sons of Mazaeus, Sisines and
Phradasmenes, sons of Phrataphernes, viceroy of Parthia and Hyrcania,
Histanes, son of Oxyartes and brother of Alexander's wife, Roxane, as
well as Autobares and his brother Mithrobaeus were picked out and enrolled among the foot-guard in addition to the Macedonian officers.
Over these Hystaspes the Bactrian was placed as commander; and Macedonian spears were given to them instead of the barbarian javelins
which had thongs attached to them. All this offended the Macedonians,
who thought that Alexander was becoming altogether Asiatic in his
ideas, and was holding the Macedonians themselves as well as their customs in a position of contempt.

7. Alexander now ordered Hephaestion to lead the main body of the
infantry as far as the Persian Sea, while he himself, his fleet having
sailed up into the land of Susiana, embarked with the shield-bearing
guards and the body-guard of infantry; and having also put on board a
few of the cavalry Companions, he sailed down the river Eulaeus to the
sea. When he was near the place where the river discharges itself into
the deep, he left there most of his ships, including those which were in
need of repair, and with those especially adapted for fast sailing he
coasted along out of the river Eulaeus through the sea to the mouth of
the Tigris. The rest of the ships were conveyed down the Eulaeus as
far as the canal which had been cut from the Tigris into the Eulaeus,
and by this means they were brought into the Tigris. Of the rivers
Euphrates and Tigris which inclose Syria between them, whence also its
name is called by the natives Mesopotamia, the Tigris flows in a much
lower channel than the Euphrates, from which it receives many canals;
and after taking up many tributaries and its waters being swelled by
them, it falls into the Persian Sea. It is a large river and can be crossed
on foot nowhere as far as its mouth, inasmuch as none of its water is
used up by irrigation of the country. For the land through which it flows
is more elevated than its water, and it is not drawn off into canals or
into another river, but rather receives them into itself. It is nowhere
possible to irrigate the land from it. But the Euphrates flows in an
elevated channel, and is everywhere on a level with the land through
which it passes. Many canals have been made from it, some of which

are always kept flowing, and from which the inhabitants on both banks supply themselves with water; others the people make only when requisite to irrigate the land, when they are in need of water from drought. For this country is usually free from rain. The consequence is, that the Euphrates at last has only a small volume of water, which disappears into a marsh. Alexander sailed over the sea round the shore of the Persian Gulf lying between the rivers Eulaeus and Tigris; and thence he sailed up the latter river as far as the camp where Hephaestion had settled with all his forces. Thence he sailed again to Opis, a city situated on that river. In his voyage up he destroyed the weirs which existed in the river, and thus made the stream quite level. These weirs had been constructed by the Persians, to prevent any enemy having a superior naval force from sailing up from the sea into their country. The Persians had had recourse to these contrivances because they were not a nautical people; and thus by making an unbroken succession of weirs they had rendered the voyage up the Tigris a matter of impossibility. But Alexander said that such devices were unbecoming to men who are victorious in battle; and therefore he considered this means of safety unsuitable for him; and by easily demolishing the laborious work of the Persians, he proved in fact that what they thought a protection was unworthy of the name.

8. When he arrived at Opis, he collected the Macedonians and announced that he intended to discharge from the army those who were useless for military service either from age or from being maimed in the limbs; and he said he would send them back to their own abodes. He also promised to give those who went back as much extra reward as would make them special objects of envy to those at home and arouse in the other Macedonians the wish to share similar dangers and labours. Alexander said this, no doubt, for the purpose of pleasing the Macedonians; but on the contrary they were, not without reason, offended by the speech which he delivered, thinking that now they were despised by him and deemed to be quite useless for military service. Indeed, throughout the whole of this expedition they had been offended at many other things; for his adoption of the Persian dress, thereby exhibiting his contempt for their opinion often caused them grief, as did also his accoutring the foreign soldiers called Epigoni in the Macedonian style, and the mixing of the alien horsemen among the ranks of the Companions. Therefore they could not remain silent and control themselves, but urged him to dismiss all of them from his army; and they advised him to prosecute the war in company with his father, deriding Ammon by this remark. When Alexander heard this (for at that time he was more hasty in temper than heretofore, and no longer, as of old, indulgent to the

Macedonians from having a retinue of foreign attendants), leaping down from the platform with his officers around him, he ordered the most conspicuous of the men who had tried to stir up the multitude to sedition to be arrested. He himself pointed out with his hand to the shield-bearing guards those whom they were to arrest, to the number of thirteen; and he ordered these to be led away to execution. When the rest, stricken with terror, became silent, he mounted the platform again, and spoke as follows:

9. "The speech which I am about to deliver will not be for the purpose of checking your start homeward, for, so far as I am concerned, you may depart wherever you wish; but for the purpose of making you understand when you take yourselves off, what kind of men you have been to us who have conferred such benefits upon you. In the first place, as is reasonable, I shall begin my speech from my father Philip. For he found you vagabonds and destitute of means, most of you clad in hides, feeding a few sheep up the mountain sides, for the protection of which you had to fight with small success against Illyrians, Triballians, and the border Thracians. Instead of the hides he gave you cloaks to wear, and from the mountains he led you down into the plains, and made you capable of fighting the neighbouring barbarians, so that you were no longer compelled to preserve yourselves by trusting rather to the inaccessible strongholds than to your own valour. He made you colonists of cities, which he adorned with useful laws and customs; and from being slaves and subjects, he made you rulers over those very barbarians by whom you yourselves, as well as your property, were previously liable to be carried off or ravaged. He also added the greater part of Thrace to Macedonia, and by seizing the most conveniently situated places on the sea-coast, he spread abundance over the land from commerce, and made the working of the mines a secure employment.[3] He made you rulers over the Thessalians, of whom you had formerly been in mortal fear; and by humbling the nation of the Phocians, he rendered the avenue into Greece broad and easy for you, instead of being narrow and difficult. The Athenians and Thebans, who were always lying in wait to attack Macedonia, he humbled to such a degree, I also then rendering him my personal aid in the campaign, that instead of paying tribute to the former and being vassals to the latter, those States in their turn procure security to themselves by our assistance. He penetrated into the Peloponnese, and after regulating its affairs, was publicly declared commander-in-chief of all the rest of Greece in the expedition against the Persian, adding this glory not more to himself than to

---

[3] The gold and silver mines at Mount Pangaeon near Philippi brought Philip a yearly revenue of more than 1,000 talents.

the commonwealth of the Macedonians. These were the advantages which
accrued to you from my father Philip; great indeed if looked at by
themselves, but small if compared with those you have obtained from
me. For though I inherited from my father only a few gold and silver
goblets, and there were not even sixty talents in the treasury, and
though I found myself charged with a debt of 500 talents owing by
Philip, and I was obliged myself to borrow 800 talents in addition to
these, I started from the country which could not decently support you,
and forthwith laid open to you the passage of the Hellespont, though
at that time the Persians held the sovereignty of the sea. Having overpowered the satraps of Darius with my cavalry, I added to your empire
the whole of Ionia, the whole of Aeolis, both Phrygias and Lydia, and I
took Miletus by siege. All the other places I gained by voluntary surrender, and I granted you the privilege of appropriating the wealth found
in them. The riches of Egypt and Cyrene, which I acquired without
fighting a battle, have come to you. Coele-Syria, Palestine, and Mesopotamia are your property. Babylon, Bactra, and Susa are yours. The
wealth of the Lydians, the treasures of the Persians, and the riches of
the Indians are yours; and so is the External Sea. You are viceroys, you
are generals, you are captains. What then have I reserved to myself after
all these labours, except this purple robe and this diadem? I have appropriated nothing myself, nor can any one point out my treasures,
except these possessions of yours or the things which I am guarding on
your behalf. Individually, however, I have no motive to guard them,
since I feed on the same fare as you do, and I take only the same amount
of sleep. Nay, I do not think that my fare is as good as that of those
among you who live luxuriously; and I know that I often sit up at night
to watch for you, that you may be able to sleep.

10. "But some one may say, that while you endured toil and fatigue,
I have acquired these things as your leader without myself sharing the
toil and fatigue. But who is there of you who knows that he has endured
greater toil for me than I have for him? Come now, whoever of you
has wounds, let him strip and show them, and I will show mine in turn;
for there is no part of my body, in front at any rate, remaining free
from wounds; nor is there any kind of weapon used either for close
combat or for hurling at the enemy, the traces of which I do not bear
on my person. For I have been wounded with the sword in close fight,
I have been shot with arrows, and I have been struck with missiles projected from engines of war; and though oftentimes I have been hit with
stones and bolts of wood for the sake of your lives, your glory, and your
wealth, I am still leading you as conquerors over all the land and sea, all
rivers, mountains, and plains. I have celebrated your weddings with my

own, and the children of many of you will be akin to my children. Moreover I have liquidated the debts of all those who had incurred them,
without inquiring too closely for what purpose they were contracted,
though you received such high pay, and carry off so much booty whenever there is booty to be got after a siege. Most of you have golden
crowns, the eternal memorials of your valour and of the honour you receive from me. Whoever has been killed has met with a glorious end and
has been honoured with a splendid burial. Brazen statues of most of the
slain have been erected at home, and their parents are held in honour,
being released from all public service and from taxation. But no one of
you has ever been killed in flight under my leadership. And now I was
intending to send back those of you who are unfit for service, objects of
envy to those at home; but since you all wish to depart, depart all of
you! Go back and report at home that your king Alexander, the conqueror of the Persians, Medes, Bactrians, and Sacians; the man who has
subjugated the Uxians, Arachotians, and Drangians; who has also acquired the rule of the Parthians, Chorasmians, and Hyrcanians, as far as
the Caspian Sea; who has marched over the Caucasus, through the
Caspian Gates; who has crossed the rivers Oxus and Tanais, and the
Indus besides, which has never been crossed by any one else except
Dionysus; who has also crossed the Hydaspes, Acesines, and Hydraotes,
and who would have crossed the Hyphasis, if you had not shrunk back
with alarm; who has penetrated into the Great Sea by both the mouths
of the Indus; who has marched through the desert of Gadrosia, where
no one ever before marched with an army; who on his route acquired
possession of Carmania and the land of the Oritians, in addition to his
other conquests, his fleet having in the meantime already sailed round
the coast of the sea which extends from India to Persia—report that
when you returned to Susa you deserted him and went away, handing
him over to the protection of conquered foreigners. Perhaps this report of
yours will be both glorious to you in the eyes of men and devout I
ween in the eyes of the gods. Depart!"

11. Having thus spoken, he leaped down quickly from the platform,
and entered the palace, where he paid no attention to the decoration
of his person, nor was any of his Companions admitted to see him.
Not even on the morrow was any one of them admitted to an audience;
but on the third day he summoned the select Persians within, and among
them he distributed the commands of the brigades, and made the rule
that only those whom he proclaimed his kinsmen should have the honour of saluting him with a kiss. But the Macedonians who heard the
speech were thoroughly astonished at the moment, and remained there
in silence near the platform; nor when he retired did any of them ac-

company the king, except his personal Companions and the confidential body-guards. Though they remained most of them had nothing to do or say; and yet they were unwilling to retire. But when the news was reported to them about the Persians and Medes, that the military commands were being given to Persians, that the foreign soldiers were being selected and divided into companies, that a Persian footguard, Persian foot Companions, a Persian regiment of men with silver shields, as well as the cavalry Companions, and another royal guard of cavalry distinct from these, were being called by the Macedonian names, they were no longer able to restrain themselves; but running in a body to the palace, they cast their weapons there in front of the gates as signs of supplication to the king. Standing in front of the gates, they shouted, beseeching to be allowed to enter, and saying that they were willing to surrender the men who had been the instigators of the disturbance on that occasion, and those who had begun the clamour. They also declared they would not retire from the gates either day or night, unless Alexander would take some pity upon them. When he was informed of this, he came out without delay; and seeing them lying on the ground in humble guise, and hearing most of them lamenting with loud voice, tears began to flow also from his own eyes. He made an effort to say something to them, but they continued their importunate entreaties. At length one of them, Callines by name, a man conspicuous both for his age and because he was a captain of the Companion cavalry, spoke as follows, "O king, what grieves the Macedonians is that you have already made some of the Persians kinsmen to yourself, and that Persians are called Alexander's kinsmen, and have the honour of saluting you with a kiss; whereas none of the Macedonians have as yet enjoyed this honour." Then Alexander interrupting him, said, "But all of you without exception I consider my kinsmen, and so from this time I shall call you." When he had said this, Callines advanced and saluted him with a kiss, and so did all those who wished to salute him. Then they took up their weapons and returned to the camp, shouting and singing a song of thanksgiving. After this Alexander offered sacrifice to the gods to whom it was his custom to sacrifice, and gave a public banquet, over which he himself presided, with the Macedonians sitting around him; and next to them the Persians; after whom came the men of the other nations, preferred in honour for their personal rank or for some meritorious action. The king and his guests drew wine from the same bowl and poured out the same libations, both the Grecian prophets and the Magians commencing the ceremony. He prayed for other blessings, and especially that harmony and community of rule might exist between the Macedonians and Persians. The common account is, that those who took part in this banquet were 9,000 in number, that all of them poured out one libation, and after it sang a song of thanksgiving.

12. Then those of the Macedonians who were unfit for service on account of age or any other misfortune went back of their own accord, to the number of about 10,000. To these Alexander gave the pay not only for the time which had already elapsed, but also for that which they would take in returning home. He also gave to each man a talent in addition to his pay. If any of them had children by Asiatic wives, he ordered them to leave them behind with him, lest they should introduce into Macedonia a cause of discord, taking with them children by foreign women who were of a different race from the children whom they had left behind at home born of Macedonian mothers. He promised to take care that they should be brought up as Macedonians, educating them not only in general matters but also in the art of war. He also under- took to lead them into Macedonia when they arrived at manhood, and hand them over to their fathers. These uncertain and obscure promises were made to them as they were departing; and he thought he was giv- ing a most indubitable proof of the friendship and affection he had for them by sending with them, as their guardian and the leader of the ex- pedition, Craterus, the man most faithful to him, and whom he valued equally with himself. Then, having saluted them all, he with tears dis- missed them likewise weeping from his presence. He ordered Craterus to lead these men back, and when he had done so, to take upon himself the government of Macedonia, Thrace, and Thessaly, and to preside over the freedom of the Greeks. He also ordered Antipater to bring to him the Macedonians of manly age as successors to those who were being sent back. He despatched Polysperchon also with Craterus, as his second in command, so that if any mishap befell Craterus on the march (for he was sending him back on account of the weakness of his health), those who were going might not be in need of a general. A secret report was also going about that Alexander was now overcome by his mother's accusations of Antipater, and that he wished to remove him from Mace- donia. This report was current among those who interpret royal actions more jealously the more they are concealed, and who are inclined to construe fidelity into something bad rather than to accept it as real; a course to which they are led by appearances and their own depravity. But perhaps this sending for Antipater was not designed for his dis- honour, but rather to prevent any unpleasant consequences to Antipater and Olympias from their quarrel which he might not himself be able to rectify. For they were incessantly writing to Alexander, the former say- ing that the arrogance, acerbity, and meddlesomeness of Olympias was exceedingly unbecoming to the king's mother; insomuch that Alexander

was related to have used the following remark in reference to the reports which he received about his mother: that she was exacting from him a heavy house-rent for the ten months.[4] The queen wrote that Antipater was overweeningly insolent in his pretensions to sovereignty as well as in the service of his court, no longer remembering the one who had appointed him, but claiming to win and hold the first rank among the Greeks and even the Macedonians. These slanderous reports about Antipater appeared to have more weight with Alexander, since they were more formidable in regard to the regal dignity. However, no overt act or word of the king was reported, from which any one could infer that Antipater was in any way less in favour with him than before.[5]

13. It is said that Hephaestion much against his will yielded to this argument and was reconciled to Eumenes, who on his part wished to settle the dispute. In this journey Alexander is said to have seen the plain which was devoted to the royal mares. Herodotus says that the plain itself was named Nisaean, and that the mares were called Nisaean; adding that in olden times there were 150,000 of these horses. But at this time Alexander found not many above 50,000; for most of them had been carried off by robbers. Here they say that Atropates, the satrap of Media, gave him 100 women, saying that they were of the race of Amazons. These had been equipped with the arms of male horsemen, except that they carried axes instead of spears, and targets instead of shields. They also say that they had the right breast smaller than the left, and that they exposed it in battle. Alexander dismissed them from the army, that no attempt to violate them might be made by the Macedonians or barbarians; and he ordered them to carry word to their queen that he was coming to her in order to procreate children by her. But this story has been recorded neither by Aristobulus nor Ptolemy, nor any other writer who is a trustworthy authority on such matters. I do not even think that the race of Amazons was surviving at that time, or even before Alexander's time; otherwise they would have been mentioned by Xenophon,[6] who mentions the Phasians, Colchians, and all the other barbaric races which the Greeks came upon, when they started from Trapezus or before they marched down to Trapezus. They would certainly have fallen in with the Amazons there, if they were still in ex-

---

[4] The Greeks reckoned according to the lunar months, and therefore they talked of ten months instead of nine as the period of gestation.

[5] Here there is a gap in the manuscripts of Arrian, which probably contained an account of the flight of Harpalus, the viceroy of Babylon, with the treasures committed to his care, and also a description of the dispute between Hephaestion and Eumenes.

[6] This is a mistake, for Xenophon does mention the Amazons in the *Anabasis* (iv. 4, 16).

istence. However it does not seem to me credible that this race of women had no existence at all, because it has been celebrated by so many famous poets. For the general account is, that Heracles marched against them and brought the girdle of their queen Hippolyte into Greece; and that the Athenians under Theseus were the first to conquer and repulse these women as they were advancing into Europe. The battle of the Athenians and Amazons has been painted by Micon, no less than that of the Athenians and Persians. Herodotus also has frequently written about these women; and so have the Athenian writers who have honoured the men who perished in war with orations. They have mentioned the exploit of the Athenians against the Amazons as one of their special glories. If therefore Atropates showed any equestrian women to Alexander, I think he must have shown him some other foreign women trained in horsemanship, and equipped with the arms which were said to be those of the Amazons.

14. In Ecbatana Alexander offered sacrifice according to his custom, for his good fortune; and he celebrated a gymnastic and musical contest. He also held drinking parties with his Companions. At this time Hephaestion fell sick; and they say that the stadium was full of people on the seventh day of his fever, for on that day there was a gymnastic contest for boys. When Alexander was informed that Hephaestion was in a critical state, he went to him without delay, but found him no longer alive. Different authors have given different accounts of Alexander's grief on this occasion; but they all agree in this, that his grief was great. As to what was done in honour of Hephaestion, they make diverse statements, just as each writer was actuated by good-will or envy towards him, or even towards Alexander himself. Of the authors who have made these reckless statements, some seem to me to have thought that whatever Alexander said or did to show his excessive grief for the man who was the dearest to him in the world, redounds to his honour; whereas others seem to have thought that it rather tended to his disgrace, as being conduct unbecoming to any king and especially to Alexander. Some say that he threw himself on his companion's body and lay there for the greater part of that day, bewailing him and refusing to depart from him, until he was forcibly carried away by his Companions. Others that he lay upon the body the whole day and night. Others again say that he hanged the physician Glaucias, for having indiscreetly given the medicine; while others affirm that he, being a spectator of the games, neglected Hephaestion, who was filled with wine. That Alexander should have cut off his hair in honour of the dead man, I do not think improbable, both for other reasons and especially from a desire to imitate Achilles, whom from his boyhood he had an ambi-

tion to rival. Others also say that Alexander himself at one time drove the chariot on which the body was borne; but this statement I by no means believe. Others again affirm that he ordered the shrine of Asclepius in Ecbatana to be razed to the ground; which was an act of barbarism, and by no means in harmony with Alexander's general behaviour, but rather in accordance with the arrogance of Xerxes in his dealings with the deity, who is said to have let fetters down into the Hellespont, in order to punish it. But the following statement, which has been recorded, does not seem to me entirely beyond the range of probability: that when Alexander was marching to Babylon, he was met on the road by many embassies from Greece, among which were some Epidaurian envoys, who obtained from him their requests. He also gave them an offering to be conveyed to Asclepius, adding this remark, "Although Asclepius has not treated me fairly, in not saving the life of my Companion, whom I valued equally with my own head." It has been stated by most writers that he ordered honours to be always paid to Hephaestion as a hero; and some say that he even sent men to Ammon's temple to ask the god if it were allowable to offer sacrifice to Hephaestion as a god; but Ammon replied that it was not allowable. All the authorities, however, agree as to the following facts: that until the third day after Hephaestion's death, Alexander neither tasted food nor paid any attention to his personal appearance, but lay on the ground either bewailing or silently mourning; that he also ordered a funeral pyre to be prepared for him in Babylon at the expense of 10,000 talents; some say at a still greater cost; and that a decree was published throughout all the barbarian territory for the observance of a public mourning. Many of Alexander's Companions dedicated themselves and their arms to the dead Hephaestion in order to show their respect to him; and the first to begin the artifice was Eumenes, whom we a short time ago mentioned as having been at variance with him. This he did that Alexander might not think he was pleased at Hephaestion's death. Alexander did not appoint any one else to be commander of the Companion cavalry in the place of Hephaestion, so that the name of that general might not perish from the brigade; but that division of cavalry was still called Hephaestion's and the figure made from Hephaestion went in front of it. He also resolved to celebrate a gymnastic and musical contest, much more magnificent than any of the preceding, both in the multitude of competitors and in the amount of money expended upon it. For he provided 3,000 competitors in all; and it is said that these men a short time after also competed in the games held at Alexander's own funeral.

15. The mourning was prolonged for many days; and as he was now beginning to recall himself from it, under such circumstances his Com-

panions had less difficulty in rousing him to action. Then at length he
made an expedition against the Cossaeans, a warlike race bordering on
the territory of the Uxians. They are mountaineers, inhabiting strong
positions in separate villages. Whenever a force approached them, they
were in the habit of retiring to the summits of their mountains, either in
a body or separately as each man found it practicable; and thus they escaped, making it difficult for those who attacked them with their forces
to come near them. After the enemy's departure, they used to turn themselves again to marauding, by which occupation they supported themselves. But Alexander subdued this race, though he marched against
them in the winter; for neither winter nor ruggedness of ground was any
impediment either to him or to Ptolemy, son of Lagus, who led a part
of the army in the campaign against them. Thus no military enterprise
which Alexander undertook was ever unsuccessful. As he was marching
back to Babylon, he was met by embassies from the Libyans, who congratulated him and crowned him as conqueror of the kingdom of Asia.
From Italy also came Bruttians, Lucanians, and Tyrrhenians as envoys,
for the same purpose. The Carthaginians are said to have sent an embassy to him at this time; and it is also asserted that envoys came to request his friendship from the Ethiopians, the Scythians of Europe, the
Gauls and Iberians—nations whose names were heard and their accoutrements seen then for the first time by Greeks and Macedonians.
They are also said to have intrusted to Alexander the duty of settling
their disputes with each other. Then indeed it was especially evident
both to himself and to those about him that he was lord of all the land
and sea. Of the men who have written the history of Alexander, Aristus
and Asclepiades alone say that the Romans also sent an embassy to him,
and that when he met their embassy, he predicted something of the future power of Rome, observing both the attire of the men, their love
of labour, and their devotion to freedom. At the same time he made urgent inquiries about their political constitution. This incident I have
recorded neither as certainly authentic nor as altogether incredible; but
none of the Roman writers have made any mention of this embassy having been despatched to Alexander; nor of those who have written an account of Alexander's actions has either Ptolemy, son of Lagus, or Aristobulus mentioned it. With these authors I am generally inclined to
agree. Nor does it seem likely that the Roman republic, which was at
that time remarkable for its love of liberty, would send an embassy to
a foreign king, especially to a place so far away from their own land,
when they were not compelled to do so by fear or any hope of advantage,
being possessed as they were beyond any other people by hatred to the
very name and race of despots.

16. After this, Alexander sent Heracleides, son of Argaeus, into Hyrcania in command of a company of shipwrights, with orders to cut timber from the Hyrcanian mountains and with it to construct a number of ships of war, some without decks and others with decks after the Grecian fashion of ship-building. For he was very desirous of discovering with what sea the one called the Hyrcanian or Caspian unites; whether it communicates with the water of the Euxine Sea, or whether the Great Sea comes right round from the Eastern Sea, which is near India and flows up into the Hyrcanian Gulf; just as he had discovered that the Persian Sea, which was called the Red Sea, is really a gulf of the Great Sea. For the sources of the Caspian Sea had not yet been discovered, although many nations dwell around it, and navigable rivers discharge their waters into it. From Bactria, the Oxus, the largest of Asiatic rivers, those of India excepted, discharges itself into this sea; and through Scythia flows the Jaxartes. The general account is, that the Araxes also, which flows from Armenia, falls into the same sea. These are the largest; but many others flow into these, while others again discharge themselves directly into this sea. Some of these were known to those who visited these nations with Alexander; others are situated towards the farther side of the gulf, as it seems, in the country of the Nomadic Scythians, a district which is quite unknown.

When Alexander had crossed the river Tigris with his army and was marching to Babylon, he was met by the Chaldaean seers; who, having led him away from his Companions, besought him to suspend his march to that city. For they said that an oracular declaration had been made to them by the god Belus, that his entrance into Babylon at that time would not be for his good. But he answered their speech with a line from the poet Euripides to this effect, "He the best prophet is that guesses well." But said the Chaldaeans, "O king, do not at any rate enter the city looking towards the west nor leading the army advancing in that direction; but rather go right round towards the east." But this did not turn out to be easy for him, on account of the difficulty of the ground; for the deity was leading him to the place where entering he was doomed soon to die. And perhaps it was better for him to be taken off in the very acme of his glory as well as of the affection entertained for him by men, before any of the vicissitudes natural to men befell him. Probably this was the reason Solon advised Croesus to look at the end of a long life, and not before pronounce any man happy. Yea indeed, Hephaestion's death had been no small misfortune to Alexander; and I think he would rather have departed before it occurred than have been alive to experience it; no less than Achilles, as it seems to me, would rather have died before Patroclus than have been the avenger of his death.

17. But he had a suspicion that the Chaldaeans were trying to prevent his march into Babylon at that time with reference rather to their own advantage than to the declaration of the oracle. For in the middle of the city of the Babylonians was the temple of Belus, an edifice very great in size, constructed of baked bricks which were cemented together with bitumen. This temple had been razed to the ground by Xerxes, when he returned from Greece; as were also all the other sacred buildings of the Babylonians. Some say that Alexander had formed the resolution to rebuild it upon the former foundations; and for this reason he ordered the Babylonians to carry away the mound. Others say that he intended to build a still larger one than that which formerly existed. But after his departure, the men who had been intrusted with the work prosecuted it without any vigour, so that he determined now to employ the whole of his army in completing it. A great quantity of land as well as gold had been dedicated to the god Belus by the Assyrian kings; and from days of old the temple was kept in repair and sacrifices were offered to the god. But at that time the Chaldaeans were appropriating the property of the god, since nothing existed upon which the revenues could be expended. Alexander suspected that they did not wish him to enter Babylon for this reason, for fear that in a short time the completion of the temple would deprive them of the gains accruing from the money. And yet, according to Aristobulus, he was willing to yield to their persuasions so far at least as to change the direction of his entry into the city. For this purpose, on the first day he encamped near the river Euphrates; and on the next day he marched along the bank, keeping the river on his right hand, with the intention of passing beyond the part of the city turned towards the west, and there wheeling round to lead his army towards the east. But on account of the difficulty of the ground he could not march with his army in this direction; because if a man who is entering the city from the west here changes his direction eastward, he comes upon ground covered with marshes and shoals. Thus, partly by his own will and partly against his will, he disobeyed the god.

18. Moreover Aristobulus has recorded the following story. Apollodorus the Amphipolitan, one of Alexander's Companions, was general of the army which the king left with Mazaeus, the viceroy of Babylon. When he had joined his forces with the king's on the return of the latter from India, and observed that he was severely punishing the viceroys who had been placed over the several countries, he sent to his brother Peithagoras and asked him to divine about his safety. For Peithagoras was a diviner who derived his knowledge of the future from

the inspection of the inward parts of animals. This man sent back to Apollodorus, inquiring of whom he was so especially afraid, as to wish to consult divination. The latter wrote back, "The king himself and Hephaestion." Peithagoras therefore in the first place offered sacrifice with reference to Hephaestion. But as there was no lobe visible upon the liver of the sacrificial victim, he stated this fact in a letter, which he sealed and sent to his brother from Babylon to Ecbatana, explaining that there was no reason at all to be afraid of Hephaestion, for in a short time he would be out of their way. And Aristobulus says that Apollodorus received this epistle only one day before Hephaestion died. Then Peithagoras again offered sacrifice in respect to Alexander, and the liver of the victim consulted in respect to him was also destitute of a lobe. He therefore wrote to Apollodorus to the same purport about Alexander as about Hephaestion. Apollodorus did not conceal the information sent to him, but told Alexander, in order the more to show his good-will to the king, if he urged him to be on his guard lest some danger might befall him at that time. And Aristobulus says that the king commended Apollodorus, and when he entered Babylon, he asked Peithagoras what sign he had met with, to induce him to write thus to his brother. He said that the liver of the victim sacrificed for him was without a lobe. When Alexander asked what the sign meant, he said that it was a very disastrous one. The king was so far from being angry with him, that he even treated him with greater respect, for telling him the truth without any disguise. Aristobulus says that he himself heard this story from Peithagoras; and adds that the same man acted as diviner for Perdiccas and afterwards for Antigonus, and that the same sign occurred for both. It was verified by fact; for Perdiccas lost his life leading an army against Ptolemy,[7] and Antigonus was killed in the battle fought by him at Ipsus against Seleucus and Lysimachus.[8] Also concerning Calanus, the Indian philosopher, the following story has been recorded. When he was going to the funeral pyre to die, he gave the parting salutation to all his other companions; but he refused to approach Alexander to give him the salutation, saying he would meet him at Babylon and there salute him. At the time indeed this remark was treated with neglect; but afterwards, when Alexander had died at Babylon, it came to the recollection of those who had heard it, and they thought forsooth that it was a divine intimation of Alexander's approaching end.

19. As he was entering Babylon, he was met by embassies from the Greeks; but for what purpose each embassy was sent has not been recorded. To me indeed it seems probable that most of them came to

[7] Perdiccas was killed by his own troops at Memphis, 321 B.C.
[8] The battle of Ipsus was fought 301 B.C.

crown and eulogize him on account of his victories, especially the Indian ones, as well as to say that the Greeks rejoiced at his safe return from India. It is said that he greeted these men with the right hand, and after paying them suitable honour sent them back. He also gave the ambassadors permission to take with them all the statues of men and images of gods and the other votive offerings which Xerxes had carried off from Greece to Babylon, Pasargadae, Susa, or any other place in Asia. In this way it is said that the brazen statues of Harmodius and Aristogeiton, as well as the image of the Celcaean Artemis, were carried back to Athens.

Aristobulus says that he found at Babylon the fleet with Nearchus, which had sailed from the Persian Sea up the river Euphrates; and another which had been conveyed from Phoenicia, consisting of two Phoenician quinqueremes, three quadriremes, twelve triremes, and thirty thirty-oared ships. These had been taken to pieces and conveyed to the river Euphrates from Phoenicia to the city of Thapsacus. There they were joined together again and sailed down to Babylon. The same writer says that he cut down the cypresses in Babylonia and with them built another fleet; for in the land of the Assyrians these trees alone are abundant, but of the other things necessary for ship-building this country affords no supply. A multitude of purple-fishers and other seafaring men came to him from Phoenicia and the rest of the seaboard to serve as crews for the ships and perform the other services on board. Near Babylon he made a harbour by excavation large enough to afford anchorage to 1,000 ships of war; and adjoining the harbour he made dockyards. Miccalus the Clazomenian was despatched to Phoenicia and Syria with 500 talents to enlist some men and to purchase others who were experienced in nautical affairs. For Alexander designed to colonise the seaboard near the Persian Gulf, as well as the islands in that sea. For he thought that this land would become no less prosperous than Phoenicia. He made these preparations of the fleet to attack the main body of the Arabs, under the pretext that they were the only barbarians of this region who had not sent an embassy to him or done anything else becoming their position and showing respect to him. But the truth was, as it seems to me, that Alexander was insatiably ambitious of ever acquiring fresh territory.

20. The common report is that he heard that the Arabs venerated only two gods, Uranus and Dionysus; the former because he is himself visible and contains in himself the heavenly luminaries, especially the sun, from which emanates the greatest and most evident benefit to all things human; and the latter on account of the fame he acquired by his expedition into India. Therefore he thought himself quite worthy

to be considered by the Arabs as a third god, since he had performed deeds by no means inferior to those of Dionysus. If then he could conquer the Arabs, he intended to grant them the privilege of conducting their government according to their own customs, as he had already done to the Indians. The fertility of the land was a secret inducement to him to invade it; because he heard that the people obtained cassia from the lakes, and myrrh and frankincense from the trees; that cinnamon was cut from the shrubs, and that the meadows produce spikenard without any cultivation. As to the size of the country, he was informed that the seaboard of Arabia was not less in extent than that of India; that near it lie many islands; that in all parts of the country there were harbours sufficiently commodious to provide anchorage for his fleet, and that it supplied sites for founding cities, which would become flourishing. He was also informed that there were two islands in the sea facing the mouth of the Euphrates, the first of which was not far from the place where the waters of that river are discharged into the sea, being about fourteen miles from the shore and the river's mouth. This is the smaller of the two, and was densely covered with every kind of timber. In it was also a temple of Artemis, around which the inhabitants themselves spent their lives. The island was devoted to the use of wild goats and stags, which were allowed to range at large as being dedicated to Artemis. It was unlawful to chase them unless any one wished to offer sacrifice to the goddess; and for this purpose alone it was lawful to chase them. Aristobulus says that Alexander ordered this island to be called Icarus, after the island so named in the Aegean Sea, on which, as the report goes, Icarus, son of Daedalus fell, when the wax, by which the wings had been fastened to him, melted. For he did not fly near the earth, according to his father's injunctions, but senselessly flying far aloft, he allowed the sun to soften and loosen the wax. Icarus left his name to the island and the sea, the former being called Icarus and the latter the Icarian. The other island was said to be distant from the mouth of the Euphrates about a day and night's voyage for a ship running before the breeze. Its name was Tylus; it was large and most of it neither rugged nor woody, but suitable for producing cultivated fruits and all things in due season. Some of this information was imparted to Alexander by Archias, who was sent with a thirty-oared ship to investigate the course of the coasting voyage to Arabia, and who went as far as the island of Tylus, but dared not pass beyond that point. Androsthenes was despatched with another thirty-oared ship and sailed along a part of the peninsula of Arabia. Hieron of Soli the pilot also received a thirty-oared ship from Alexander and advanced farthest of those whom he despatched to this region; for he had received instructions to sail round the whole Arabian peninsula as far as the Arabian Gulf near Egypt over against Heroopolis. Although he coasted along the country of the Arabs to a great distance, he dared not go as far as he was ordered; but returning to Alexander he reported that the size of the peninsula was marvellous, being only a little smaller than the country of the Indians, and its extremity projected far into the Great Sea. Nearchus indeed in his voyage from India had seen this stretching out not far off, before he turned aside into the Persian Gulf, and he was almost induced to cross over to it. The pilot Onesicritus thought they ought to have gone thither; but Nearchus says that he himself prevented it, so that after sailing right round the Persian Gulf he might be able to give a report to Alexander about the things for which he had sent him. For Nearchus said he had not been despatched to navigate the Great Sea, but to explore the land bordering on the sea, to find out what men inhabit it, to discover the harbours and rivers in it, to ascertain the customs of the people, and to see if any of the country was fertile, and if any was sterile. This was the reason why Alexander's naval expedition returned in safety; for if it had sailed beyond the deserts of Arabia, it would not have returned in safety. This is said also to have been the reason why Hieron turned back.

21. While the triremes were being built for him, and the harbour near Babylon was being excavated, Alexander sailed from Babylon down the Euphrates to what was called the river Pallacopas, which is distant from Babylon about ninety-five miles. This Pallacopas is not a river rising from springs, but a canal cut from the Euphrates. For that river, flowing from the Armenian mountains, proceeds within its banks in the season of winter, because its water is scanty; but when the spring begins to make its appearance, and especially just before the summer solstice, it pours along with mighty stream and overflows its banks into the Assyrian country. For at that season the snow upon the Armenian mountains melts and swells its water to a great degree; and as its stream flows high and on a level with the country, it would flow over the land if some one had not furnished it with an outlet along the Pallacopas and turned it aside into the marshes and pools, which, beginning from this canal, extend as far as the country contiguous to Arabia. Thence it spreads out far and wide into a shallow lake, from which it falls into the sea by many invisible mouths. After the snow has melted, about the time of the setting of the Pleiades, the Euphrates flows with a small stream; but none the less the greater part of it discharges itself into the pools along the Pallacopas. Unless, therefore, some one dammed up the Pallacopas again, so that the water might be turned back within the banks (of the Euphrates) and carried down the channel of the river,

it would drain the Euphrates into itself, and consequently the Assyrian country would not be watered by it. But the outlet of the Euphrates into the Pallacopas used to be dammed up by the satrap of Babylonia with great labour (although it was an easy matter to construct the outlet), because the ground in this region is slimy and most of it mud, so that when it has once received the water of the river it does not allow it to be easily turned back. But more than 10,000 Assyrians used to engage in this labour even until the third month. When Alexander was informed of this, he was induced to confer a benefit upon the land of Assyria. He determined to shut up entirely the outlet by which the stream of the Euphrates was turned into the Pallacopas. When he had advanced about four miles, the earth was seen to be somewhat rocky, so that if it were cut through and a junction made with the old canal along the Pallacopas, on account of the hardness of soil, it would not allow the water to percolate, and there would be no difficulty in turning it back at the appointed season. For this purpose he sailed to the Pallacopas, and then continued his voyage down that canal into the pools towards the country of the Arabs. There seeing a certain admirable site, he founded a city upon it and fortified it. In it he settled as many of the Grecian mercenaries as volunteered to remain, and such as were unfit for military service by reason of age or wounds.

22. Having thus proved the falsity of the prophecy of the Chaldaeans, by not having experienced any unpleasant fortune in Babylon, as they had predicted, but having marched out of that city without suffering any mishap, he grew confident in spirit and sailed again through the marshes, having Babylon on his left hand. Here a part of his fleet lost its way in the narrow branches of the river through want of a pilot, until he sent a man to pilot it and lead it back into the channel of the river. The following story is told. Most of the tombs of the Assyrian kings had been built among the pools and marshes. When Alexander was sailing through these marshes, and, as the story goes, was himself steering the trireme, a strong gust of wind fell upon his broad-brimmed Macedonian hat, and the fillet which encircled it. The hat, being rather heavy, fell into the water; but the fillet, being carried along by the wind, was caught by one of the reeds growing near the tomb of one of the ancient kings. This incident itself was an omen of what was about to occur, and so was the fact that one of the sailors swam off towards the fillet and snatched it from the reed. But he did not carry it in his hands, because it would have been wetted while he was swimming; he therefore put it round his own head and thus conveyed it to the king. Most of the biographers of Alexander say that the king presented him with a talent as a reward for his zeal, and then ordered his head to be cut off; as the

614 *Arrian* [323 B.C.]

prophets had expounded the omen to the effect that he should not permit that head to be safe which had worn the royal fillet. However, Aristobulus says that the man received a talent; but also received a scourging for placing the fillet round his head. The same author says that it was one of the Phoenician sailors who fetched the fillet for Alexander; but there are some who say it was Seleucus, and that this was an omen to Alexander of his death and to Seleucus of his great kingdom. For that, of all those who succeeded to the sovereignty after Alexander, Seleucus became the greatest king, was the most kingly in mind, and ruled over the greatest extent of land after Alexander himself, does not seem to me to admit of question.

23. When he returned to Babylon he found that Peucestas had arrived from Persis, bringing with him an army of 20,000 Persians, as well as many Cossaeans and Tapurians, because these races were reported to be the most warlike of those bordering on Persis. Philoxenus also came to him, bringing an army from Caria; Menander, with another from Lydia, and Menidas with the cavalry which had been put under his command. At the same time arrived embassies from Greece, the members of which, with crowns upon their own heads, approached Alexander and crowned him with golden crowns, as if indeed, they had come to him as special envoys deputed to pay him divine honours; and his end was not far off. Then he commended the Persians for their great zeal towards him, which was shown by their obedience to Peucestas in all things, and Peucestas himself for the prudence which he had displayed in ruling them. He distributed these foreign soldiers among the Macedonian ranks in the following way. Each company was led by a Macedonian commander of ten men, and next to him was a Macedonian receiving double pay for distinguished valour; and then came one who received ten staters, who was so named from the pay he received, being somewhat less than that received by the man with double pay, but more than that of the men who were serving as soldiers without holding a position of honour. Next to these came twelve Persians, and last in the company another Macedonian, who also received the pay of ten staters; so that in each company there were twelve Persians and four Macedonians, three of whom received higher pay, and the fourth was in command of the company. The Macedonians were armed in their hereditary manner; but of the Persians some were archers, while others had javelins furnished with straps, by which they were held. At this time Alexander often reviewed his fleet, had many sham-fights with his triremes and quadriremes in the river, and contests both for rowers and pilots, the winners receiving crowns.

Now arrived the special envoys whom he had despatched to Ammon to inquire how it was lawful for him to honour Hephaestion. They told him that Ammon said it was lawful to offer sacrifice to him as to a hero. Rejoicing at the response of the oracle, he paid respect to him as a hero from that time. He also despatched a letter to Cleomenes, who was a bad man and had committed many acts of injustice in Egypt. For my own part I do not blame him for his friendship to Hephaestion, even when dead, and for his recollection of him; but I do blame him for many other acts. For the letter commanded Cleomenes to prepare chapels for the hero Hephaestion in the Egyptian Alexandria, one in the city itself and another in the island of Pharos, where the tower is situated. The chapels were to be exceedingly large and to be built at lavish expense. The letter also directed that Cleomenes should take care that it should become the custom for them to be named after Hephaestion; and moreover that his name should be engraved on all the legal documents with which the merchants entered into bargains with each other. These things I cannot blame, except that he made so much ado about matters of trifling moment. But the following I must blame severely. "If I find," said the letter, "the sacred rites and chapels of the hero Hephaestion in Egypt well completed, I will not only pardon you any crimes you have committed in the past, but in the future you shall suffer no unpleasant treatment from me, however great may be the crimes you may commit." I cannot commend this message sent from a great king to a man who was ruling a large country and many people, especially as the man was a wicked one.

24. But Alexander's own end was now near. Aristobulus says that the following occurrence was a prognostication of what was about to happen. He was distributing the army which came with Peucestas from Persia, and that which came with Philoxenus and Menander from the sea, among the Macedonian lines, and becoming thirsty he retired from his seat and thus left the royal throne empty. On each side of the throne were couches with silver feet, upon which his personal Companions were sitting. A certain man of obscure condition (some say that he was even one of the men kept under guard without being in chains), seeing the throne and the couches empty, and the eunuchs standing round the throne (for the Companions also rose up from their seats with the king when he retired), walked through the line of eunuchs, ascended the throne, and sat down upon it. According to a Persian law, they did not make him rise from the throne; but rent their garments and beat their breasts and faces as if on account of a great evil.

When Alexander was informed of this, he ordered the man who had sat upon his throne to be put to the torture, with the view of discovering whether he had done this according to a plan concerted by a conspiracy. But the man confessed nothing, except that it came into his mind at the time to act thus. Even more for this reason the diviners explained that this occurrence boded no good to him. A few days after this, after offering to the gods the customary sacrifices for good success, and certain others also for the purpose of divination, he was feasting with his friends, and was drinking far into the night. He is also said to have distributed the sacrificial victims as well as a quantity of wine to the army throughout the companies and centuries. There are some who have recorded that he wished to retire after the drinking party to his bed-chamber; but Medius, at that time the most influential of the Companions, met him and begged him to join a party of revellers at his residence, saying that the revel would be a pleasant one.

25. The Royal Diary[9] gives the following account, to the effect that he revelled and drank at the dwelling of Medius; then rose up, took a bath, and slept; then again supped at the house of Medius and again drank till far into the night. After retiring from the drinking party he took a bath; after which he took a little food and slept there, because he already felt feverish. He was carried out upon a couch to the sacrifices, in order that he might offer them according to his daily custom. After placing the sacrifices upon the altar he lay down in the banqueting hall until dusk. In the meantime he gave instructions to the officers about the expedition and voyage, ordering those who were going on foot to be ready on the fourth day, and those who were going to sail with him to be ready to sail on the fifth day. From this place he was carried upon the couch to the river, where he embarked in a boat and sailed across the river to the park. There he again took a bath and went to rest.

On the following day he took another bath and offered the customary sacrifices. He then entered a tester bed, lay down, and chatted with Medius. He also ordered his officers to meet him at daybreak. Having done this he ate a little supper and was again conveyed into the tester bed. The fever now raged the whole night without intermission. The next day he took a bath; after which he offered sacrifice, and gave orders to Nearchus and the other officers that the voyage should begin on the third day. The next day he bathed again and offered the prescribed sacrifices. After placing the sacrifices upon the altar he did not yet keep quiet though suffering from the fever. Notwithstanding this, he summoned the officers and gave them instructions to have all things ready for the starting of the fleet. In the evening he took a bath, after which he was very ill. The next day he was transferred to the house near the

[9] We learn from Athenaeus (x. p. 434 B) that this Court Journal was kept by the royal secretary, Eumenes, afterwards so famous, and by the historian, Diodotus of Erythrae.

swimming-bath, where he offered the prescribed sacrifices. Though he was now very dangerously ill, he summoned the most responsible of his officers and gave them fresh instructions about the voyage. On the following day he was with difficulty carried out to the sacrifices, which he offered; and none the less gave other orders to the officers about the voyage. The next day, though he was now very ill, he offered the prescribed sacrifices. He now gave orders that the generals should remain in attendance in the hall, and that the colonels and captains should remain before the gates. But being now altogether in a dangerous state, he was conveyed from the park into the palace. When his officers entered the room, he knew them indeed, but no longer uttered a word, being speechless. During the ensuing night and day and the next night and day he was in a very high fever.

26. Such is the account given in the Royal Diary. In addition to this, it states that the soldiers were very desirous of seeing him; some, in order to see him once more while still alive; others, because there was a report that he was already dead, imagined that his death was being concealed by the confidential body-guards, as I for my part suppose. Most of them through grief and affection for their king forced their way in to see him. It is said that when his soldiers passed by him he was unable to speak; yet he greeted each of them with his right hand, raising his head with difficulty and making a sign with his eyes. The Royal Diary also says that Peithon, Attalus, Demophon, and Peucestas, as well as Cleomenes, Menidas, and Seleucus, slept in the temple of Serapis, and asked the god whether it would be better and more desirable for Alexander to be carried into his temple, in order as a suppliant to be cured by him. A voice issued from the god saying that he was not to be carried into the temple, but that it would be better for him to remain where he was. This answer was reported by the Companions; and soon after Alexander died, as if after all, this were now the better thing. Neither Aristobulus nor Ptolemy has given an account differing much from the preceding. Some authors, however, have related that his Companions asked him to whom he left his kingdom; and that he replied, "To the best." Others say, that in addition to this remark, he told them that he saw there would be a great funeral contest held in his honour.

27. I am aware that many other particulars have been related by historians concerning Alexander's death, and especially that poison was sent for him by Antipater, from the effects of which he died. It is also asserted that the poison was procured for Antipater by Aristotle, who was now afraid of Alexander on account of Callisthenes. It is said to have been conveyed by Casander, the son of Antipater, some recording that he conveyed it in the hoof of a mule, and that his younger brother

Iollas gave it to the king. For this man was the royal cup-bearer, and he happened to have received some affront from Alexander a short time before his death. Others have stated that Medius, being a lover of Iollas, took part in the deed; for he it was who induced the king to hold the revel. They say that Alexander was seized with an acute paroxysm of pain over the wine-cup, on feeling which he retired from the drinking bout. One writer has not even been ashamed to record that when Alexander perceived he was unlikely to survive, he was going out to throw himself into the river Euphrates, so that he might disappear from men's sight, and leave among the men of aftertimes a more firmly-rooted opinion that he owed his birth to a god, and had departed to the gods. But as he was going out he did not escape the notice of his wife Roxana, who restrained him from carrying out his design. Whereupon he uttered lamentations, saying that she envied him the complete glory of being thought the offspring of the god. These statements I have recorded rather that I may not seem to be ignorant that they have been made, than because I consider them worthy of credence or even of narration.

28. Alexander died in the 114th Olympiad, in the archonship of Hegesias at Athens.[10] According to the statement of Aristobulus, he lived thirty-two years, and had reached the eighth month of his thirty-third year. He had reigned twelve years and these eight months. He was very handsome in person, and much devoted to exertion, very active in mind, very heroic in courage, very tenacious of honour, exceedingly fond of incurring danger, and strictly observant of his duty to the deity. In regard to the pleasures of the body, he had perfect self-control; and of those of the mind, praise was the only one of which he was insatiable. He was very clever in recognising what was necessary to be done, when others were still in a state of uncertainty; and very successful in conjecturing from the observation of facts what was likely to occur. In marshalling, arming, and ruling an army, he was exceedingly skilful; and very renowned for rousing the courage of his soldiers, filling them with hopes of success, and dispelling their fear in the midst of danger by his own freedom from fear. Therefore even what he had to do in uncertainty of the result he did with the greatest boldness. He was also very clever in getting the start of his enemies, and snatching from them their advantages by secretly forestalling them, before any one even feared what was about to happen. He was likewise very steadfast in keeping the agreements and settlements which he made, as well as very secure from being entrapped by deceivers. Finally, he was very sparing in the expenditure of money for the gratification of his own pleasures;

[10] June, 323 B.C.

but he was exceedingly bountiful in spending it for the benefit of his associates.

29. That Alexander should have committed errors in conduct from impetuosity or from wrath, and that he should have been induced to comport himself like the Persian monarchs to an immoderate degree, I do not think remarkable if we fairly consider both his youth and his uninterrupted career of good fortune; likewise that kings have associates for the gratification of pleasure, and that they will always have associates urging them to do wrong, but caring nothing for their best interests. However, I am certain that Alexander was the only one of the ancient kings who, from nobility of character, repented of the errors which he had committed. The majority of men, even if they have become conscious that they have committed an error, make the mistake of thinking that they can conceal their sin by defending their error as if it had been a just action. But it seems to me that the only cure for sin is for the sinner to confess it, and to be visibly repentant in regard to it. Thus the suffering will not appear altogether intolerable to those who have suffered unpleasant treatment, if the person who inflicted it confesses that he has acted dishonourably; and this good hope for the future is left to the man himself, that he will never again commit a similar sin, if he is seen to be vexed at his former errors. I do not think that even his tracing his origin to a god was a great error on Alexander's part, if it was not perhaps merely a device to induce his subjects to show him reverence. Nor does he seem to me to have been a less renowned king than Minos, Aeacus, or Rhadamanthus, to whom no insolence is attributed by the men of old because they traced their origin to Zeus. Nor does he seem at all inferior to Theseus or Ion, the former being the reputed son of Poseidon, and the latter of Apollo. His adoption of the Persian mode of dressing also seems to me to have been a political device in regard to the foreigners, that the king might not appear altogether alien to them; and in regard to the Macedonians, to show them that he had a refuge from their rashness of temper and insolence. For this reason I think, he mixed the Persian royal guards, who carried golden apples at the end of their spears, among the ranks of the Macedonians, and the Persian peers with the Macedonian body-guards. Aristobulus also asserts that Alexander used to have long drinking parties, not for the purpose of enjoying the wine, as he was not a great wine-drinker, but in order to exhibit his sociality and friendly feeling to his Companions.

30. Whoever therefore reproaches Alexander as a bad man, let him do so; but let him first not only bring before his mind all his actions deserving reproach, but also gather into one view all his deeds of every

620 *Arrian*

kind. Then, indeed, let him reflect who he is himself, and what kind of fortune he has experienced; and then consider who that man was whom he reproaches as bad, and to what a height of human success he attained, becoming without any dispute king of both continents,[11] and reaching every place by his fame; while he himself who reproaches him is of smaller account, spending his labour on petty objects, which, however, he does not succeed in effecting, petty as they are. For my own part, I think there was at that time no race of men, no city, nor even a single individual to whom Alexander's name and fame had not penetrated. For this reason it seems to me that a hero totally unlike any other human being could not have been born without the agency of the deity. And this is said to have been revealed after Alexander's death by the oracular responses, by the visions which presented themselves to various people, and by the dreams which were seen by different individuals. It is also shown by the honour given to him by men up to the present time, and by the remembrance which is still held of him as more than human. Even at the present time, after so long an interval, other oracular responses in his honour have been given to the nation of the Macedonians. In relating the history of Alexander's achievements, there are some things which I have been compelled to censure; but I am not ashamed to admire Alexander himself. Those actions I have branded as bad, both from a regard to my own veracity, and at the same time for the benefit of mankind. For this reason I myself undertook the task of writing this history not without the agency of god.

THE END OF THE HISTORY OF ALEXANDER'S DEEDS.

[11] Europe and Asia. Arrian reckoned Libya, or Africa, as a part of Asia.

APPENDIX

THE BEHISTUN INSCRIPTION OF DARIUS

Behistun is situated on the western frontier of the ancient Media, upon the road from Babylon to the southern Ecbatana, the great thoroughfare between the eastern and the western provinces of the ancient Persia. The precipitous rock, 1,700 feet high, on which the writing is inscribed, forms a portion of the great chain of Zagros, which separates the high plateau of Iran from the vast plain watered by the two streams of the Tigris and Euphrates. The inscription is engraved at the height of 300 feet from the base of the rock, and can only be reached with much exertion and difficulty. It is trilingual: one transcript is in the ancient Persian, one in Babylonian, the other in a Scythic or Tatar dialect. The monument indicates that it was executed in the fifth year of the reign of Darius, 516 B. C.

COLUMN I

1. I (am) Darius, the great king, the king of kings, the king of Persia, the king of the provinces, the son of Hystaspes, the grandson of Arsames, the Achaemenian.

2. Says Darius the king—My father (was) Hystaspes; the father of Hystaspes (was) Arsames; the father of Arsames (was) Ariaramnes; the father of Ariaramnes (was) Teispes; the father (of Teispes) was Achaemenes.

3. Says Darius the king—On that account we have been called Achaemenians; from antiquity we have descended; from antiquity our family have been kings.

4. Says Darius the king—(There are) eight of my race who have been kings before (me); I (am) the ninth; nine of us have been kings in succession.

5. Says Darius the king—By the grace of Ormazd I am king; Ormazd has granted me the empire.

6. Says Darius the king—These are the countries which have come to me; by the grace of Ormazd I have become king of them: Persia, Susiana, Babylonia, Assyria, Arabia, Egypt, those which are of the sea, Saparda, Ionia, Media, Armenia, Cappadocia, Parthia, Zarangia, Aria, Chorasmia, Bactria, Sogdiana, Gandaria, the Sacae, Sattagydia, Arachotia, and Mecia; in all twenty-three provinces.

7. Says Darius the king—These (are) the provinces which have come

to me; by the grace of Ormazd they have become subject to me; they have brought tribute to me. That which has been said to them by me, both by night and by day, it has been done (by them).

8. Says Darius the king—Within these countries, the man who was good, him I have right well cherished. Whoever was evil, him have I utterly rooted out. By the grace of Ormazd, these are the countries by whom my laws have been observed. As it has been said to them by me, so (by them) it has been done.

9. Says Darius the king—Ormazd granted me the empire. Ormazd brought help to me, so that I gained this empire. By the grace of Ormazd I hold this empire.

10. Says Darius the king—This (is) what (was) done by me after that I became king. (A man) named Cambyses, son of Cyrus, of our race, he was here king before me. Of that Cambyses (there was) a brother, Bardes was his name; of the same mother, (and) of the same father with Cambyses. Afterwards Cambyses slew that Bardes. When Cambyses had slain Bardes, it was not known to the people that Bardes had been slain. Afterwards Cambyses proceeded to Egypt. When Cambyses had proceeded to Egypt, then the state became wicked. Then the lie became abounding in the land, both in Persia, and in Media, and in the other provinces.

11. Says Darius the king—Afterwards there was a certain man, a Magian, named Gomates. He arose from Pissiachada, the mountain named Aracadres, from thence. On the 14th day of the month Vayakhna, then it was that he arose. He thus lied to the state, "I am Bardes, the son of Cyrus, the brother of Cambyses." Then the whole state became rebellious. From Cambyses it went over to him, both Persia, and Media, and the other provinces. He seized the empire. On the 9th day of the month Garmapada, then it was he so seized the empire. Afterwards Cambyses, unable to endure, died.

12. Says Darius the king—The empire of which Gomates, the Magian, dispossessed Cambyses, that empire from the olden time had been in our family. After Gomates the Magian had dispossessed Cambyses both of Persia and Media and the dependent provinces, he did according to his desire: he became king.

13. Says Darius the king—There was not a man, neither Persian, nor Median, nor any one of our family, who would dispossess that Gomates the Magian of the crown. The state feared him exceedingly. He slew many people who had known the old Bardes; for that reason he slew them. "Lest they should recognise me that I am not Bardes, the son of Cyrus." No one dared to say anything concerning Gomates the Magian, until I arrived. Then I prayed to Ormazd; Ormazd brought help to me. On the 10th day of the month Bagayadish, then it was, with my faithful

men, I slew that Gomates the Magian, and those who were his chief followers. The fort named Sictachotes in the district of Media called Nisaea, there I slew him. I dispossessed him of the empire. By the grace of Ormazd I became king: Ormazd granted me the sceptre.

14. Says Darius the king—The empire which had been taken away from our family, that I recovered. I established it in its place. As (it was) before, so I made (it). The temples which Gomates the Magian had destroyed, I rebuilt. The sacred offices of the state, both the religious chants and the worship, (I restored) to the people, which Gomates the Magian had deprived them of. I established the state in its place, both Persia, and Media, and the other provinces. As (it was) before, so I restored what (had been) taken away. By the grace of Ormazd I did (this). I arranged so that I established our family in its place. As (it was) before, so I arranged (it), by the grace of Ormazd, so that Gomates the Magian should not supersede our family.

15. Says Darius the king—This (is) what I did, after that I became king.

16. Says Darius the king—When I had slain Gomates the Magian, then a man named Atrines, the son of Opadarmes, he arose; to the state of Susiana thus he said, 'I am king of Susiana.' Then the Susianians became rebellious; they went over to that Atrines; he became king of Susiana. And a man, a Babylonian, Nidintabelus by name, the son of Anires, he arose. To the state of Babylonia he thus falsely declared, 'I am Nabochodrossor, the son of Nabonidus.' Afterwards the whole state of Babylon went over to that Nidintabelus. Babylon became rebellious. He seized the kingdom of Babylonia.

17. Says Darius the king—Then I sent to Susiana; That Atrines was brought to me a prisoner. I slew him.

18. Says Darius the king—Then I went to Babylon against that Nidintabelus, who was called Nabochodrossor. The people of Nidintabelus held the Tigris; there they were posted, and they had boats. There I approached with a detachment in rafts. I brought the enemy into difficulty. (I) carried the enemy's position. Ormazd brought help to me. By the grace of Ormazd I crossed the Tigris. There I slew many of the troops of that Nidintabelus. On the 26th day of the month Atriyata, then it was we so fought.

19. Says Darius the king—Then I went to Babylon. When I arrived near Babylon, at the city named Zazana, on the Euphrates, there that Nidintabelus, who was called Nabochodrossor, came with his forces against me, to do battle. Then we fought a battle. Ormazd brought help to me. By the grace of Ormazd I slew many of the troops of that Nidintabelus—the enemy was driven into the water—the water destroyed them. On the 2nd day of the month Anamaka, then it was we so fought.

Column II

1. Says Darius the king—Then Nidintabelus with the horsemen (that were) faithful (to him) fled to Babylon. Then I went to Babylon. *By the grace of Ormazd* I both took Babylon, and seized that Nidintabelus. Then I slew that Nidintabelus at Babylon.

2. Says Darius the king—While I was at Babylon, these (are) the countries which revolted against me: Persia, Susiana, Media, Assyria, Armenia, Parthia, Margiana, Sattagydia, Sacia.

3. Says Darius the king—A man, named Martius, the son of Sisicres, (in) the city of Persia named Cyganaca, there he dwelt. He arose: to the state of Susiana thus he said, 'I am Imanes, king of Susiana.'

4. Says Darius the king—I was moving a little way (?) in the direction of Susiana. Then the Susianians, fearing from me, seized that Martius. He who was their chief slew him.

5. Says Darius the king—A man, named Phraortes, a Mede, he rose up. To the state of Media thus he said, 'I am Xathrites, of the race of Cyaxares.' Then the Median troops who were at home revolted from me. They went over to that Phraortes: he became king of Media.

6. Says Darius the king—The army of Persians and Medes that was with me, that was faithful to me. Then I sent forth troops. Hydarnes by name, a Persian, one of my subjects, him I appointed their leader. Thus I addressed them, 'Go forth (and) smite that Median state, which does not acknowledge me.' Then that Hydarnes marched with his army. When he reached Media, a city of Media, named Marus, there he fought a battle with the Medes. He who was the leader of the Medes could not at all resist him. Ormazd brought help to me; by the grace of Ormazd, the troops of Hydarnes entirely defeated that rebel army. On the 27th day of the month Anamaka, then it was the battle was thus fought by them. Then that army of mine at (a place) called Capada, a district of Media, waited for me until I arrived in Media.

7. Says Darius the king—Then (a man), Dadarses by name, an Armenian, one of my subjects, him I sent to Armenia. Thus I said to him, 'Go forth; the rebel state, which does not acknowledge me, smite it.' Then Dadarses marched. When he reached Armenia, then the rebels, having collected, came again before Dadarses, to do battle. Zoza by name, a village of Armenia, there they fought a battle. Ormazd brought help to me; by the grace of Ormazd, my forces entirely defeated the rebel army. On the 8th day of the month Thuravahara, then it was a battle was thus fought by them.

8. Says Darius the king—For the second time the rebels, having collected, returned before Dadarses, to do battle. The fort of Armenia named Tigra, there they fought a battle. Ormazd brought help to me; by the

grace of Ormazd, my troops entirely defeated that rebel army. On the 18th day of the month Thuravahara, then it was the battle was thus fought by them.[1]

9. Says Darius the king—For the third time the rebels, having collected, returned before Dadarses, to do battle. The fort of Armenia named Uhyama, there they fought a battle. Ormazd brought help to me; by the grace of Ormazd, my forces entirely defeated the rebel army. On the 9th day of the month Thaigarchish, then it was the battle was thus fought by them. Afterwards Dadarses waited for me there until I reached Media.

10. Says Darius the king—Then (a man) named Vomises, a Persian, one of my subjects, him I sent to Armenia. Thus I said to him, 'Go forth; the rebel state which does not acknowledge me, smite it.' Then Vomises went forth. When he reached Armenia, then the rebels, having collected, came again before Vomises, to do battle. A district of Assyria, named Achidus, there they fought a battle. Ormazd brought help to me; by the grace of Ormazd my troops entirely defeated that rebel army. On the 15th day of the month Anamaka, then it was the battle was thus fought by them.

11. Says Darius the king—For the second time the rebels, having collected, came before Vomises, to do battle. A district of Armenia, named Otiara, there they fought a battle. Ormazd brought help to me; by the grace of Ormazd my troops entirely defeated that rebel army. In the month of Thuravahara, upon the festival (?), the battle was thus fought by them. Afterwards Vomises waited for me in Armenia, until I reached Media.

12. Says Darius the king—Then I went out from Babylon. I proceeded to Media. When I reached Media, a city of Media named Kudrusia, there that Phraortes, who (was) called king of Media, came with an army against me, to do battle. Then we fought a battle. Ormazd brought help to me; by the grace of Ormazd, I entirely defeated the army of Phraortes. On the 26th day of the month Adukanish, then it was we thus fought the battle.

13. Says Darius the king—Then that Phraortes, with his faithful horsemen, fled from thence to a district of Media, called Rhages. Then I sent an army, by which Phraortes was taken (and) brought before me. I cut off both his nose, and his ears, and his tongue, and I put out his eyes. He was kept chained at my door; all the kingdom beheld him. Afterwards I crucified him at Agbatana. And the men, who were his chief followers, I slew within the citadel at Agbatana.

14. Says Darius the king—A man, named Sitrantachmes, a Sagartian, he rebelled against me. To the state thus he said, 'I am the king of

---

[1] The Babylonian transcript adds, "He slew 546 of them, and took 520 of them prisoners."

Sagartia, of the race of Cyaxares.' Then I sent forth an army of Persians and Medes. (A man) named Tachamaspates, a Mede, one of my subjects, him I made their leader. Thus I said to them, 'Go forth, (and) smite that rebel state which does not acknowledge me.' Then Tachamaspates set forth with his army. He fought a battle with Sitrantachmes. Ormazd brought help to me; by the grace of Ormazd, my troops defeated the rebel army, and took Sitrantachmes, and brought (him) before me. Then I cut off both his nose and his ears, and I put out his eyes. He was kept chained at my door. All the kingdom beheld him. Afterwards I crucified him at Arbela.

15. Says Darius the king—This is what (was) done by me in Media.

16. Says Darius the king—Parthia and Hyrcania revolted against me. They declared for Phraortes. Hystaspes, my father, ... Afterwards Hystaspes, with the troops under his orders, set forth. (At a place) called Hyspaostes, a town of Media, there he fought a battle. Ormazd brought help to me; by the grace of Ormazd, Hystaspes entirely defeated that rebel army. On the 22d day of the month Viyakhna, then it was the battle (was) thus fought by them.

Column III

1. Says Darius the king—Then I sent a Persian army to Hystaspes from Rhages. When that army reached Hystaspes, then Hystaspes marched forth with those troops. (At a place) called Patigrabana, a city of Parthia, there he fought a battle with the rebels. Ormazd brought help to me; by the grace of Ormazd, Hystaspes entirely defeated that rebel army. On the 1st day of the month Garmapada, then it was the battle was thus fought by them.[2]

2. Says Darius the king—Then the province submitted to me. This is what (was) done by me in Parthia.

3. Says Darius the king—The province called Margiana, that revolted against me. A man, named Phraortes, a Margian, him they made their leader. Then I sent to him (who was) named Dadarses, (who was) my subject, and satrap of Bactria. Thus I said to him, 'Go forth, (and) smite that people which does not acknowledge me.' Then Dadarses set forth with his forces. He fought a battle with the Margians. Ormazd brought help to me; by the grace of Ormazd my troops entirely defeated that rebel army. On the 23rd day of the month Atriyadiya, then it was the battle was thus fought by them.

4. Says Darius the king—Then the province submitted to me. This is what (was) done by me in Bactria.

[2] The Babylonian adds, "He slew of their number 6,560, and took 4,182 of them prisoners."

5. Says Darius the king—A man, named Veisdates, (in) a city named Tarba, in the district of Persia called Yutiya, there he dwelt. He rose up a second time. To the state of Persia he thus said, 'I am Bardes, the son of Cyrus.' Then the Persian people, who were at home, being at a distance (from me), revolted from me. They went over to that Veisdates. He became king of Persia.

6. Says Darius the king—Then I sent forth the Persian and Median forces which were with me. (A man) named Artabardes, a Persian, one of my subjects, him I made their leader. The other Persian forces accompanied me to Media. Then Artabardes went with his army to Persia. When he reached Persia, (at) a city of Persia called Racha, there that Veisdates, who was called Bardes, came with an army against Artabardes, to do battle. Then they fought a battle. Ormazd brought help to me; by the grace of Ormazd my forces entirely defeated the army of Veisdates. On the 12th day of the month Thuravahara, then it was the battle (was) thus fought by them.

7. Says Darius the king—Then that Veisdates, with his faithful horsemen, fled thence to Pissiachada. From that place he came back again with an army against Artabardes, to do battle. (At) the mountain named Parga, there they fought a battle. Ormazd brought help to me; by the grace of Ormazd my troops entirely defeated the army of Veisdates. On the 6th day of the month Garmapada, then it was the battle (was) so fought by them. They both took that Veisdates, and they took the men who were his chief adherents.

8. Says Darius the king—Then that Veisdates, and the men who were his chief adherents, (at) a city of Persia, named Chodedia, there I crucified them.

9. Says Darius the king—That Veisdates, who was called Bardes, he sent an army to Arachotia, against (a man) named Vibanus, one of my subjects, and the satrap of Arachotia. And he made a certain man their leader. Thus he said to them, 'Go forth, (and) smite Vibanus, and the state which acknowledges king Darius.' Then the army went forth, which Veisdates had sent against Vibanus, to do battle. (At) a fort named Capiscanes, there they fought a battle. Ormazd brought help to me; by the grace of Ormazd my troops entirely defeated the rebel army. On the 13th day of the month Anamaka, then it was the battle was thus fought by them.

10. Says Darius the king—Again the rebels, having collected, returned before Vibanus, to do battle. (In) a district, named Gadytia, there they fought a battle. Ormazd brought help to me; by the grace of Ormazd my troops entirely defeated the rebel army. On the 7th day of the month Viyakhna, then it was the battle (was) thus fought by them.

11. Says Darius the king—Then that man, who was the leader of

those troops which Veisdates had sent against Vibanus, that leader, with the horsemen (who were) faithful (to him), fled away. (At) a fort of Arachotia, named Arshada, in that he took refuge. Then Vibanus with his army set out in pursuit. There he took him, and slew the men who were his chief adherents.

12. Says Darius the king—Then the province submitted to me. This is what (was) done by me in Arachotia.

13. Says Darius the king—While I was in Persia and Media, for the second time the Babylonians revolted from me. A man, named Aracus, an Armenian, the son of Handitis, he arose. A district of Babylon, named Dobana, from thence he arose. Thus he falsely declared, 'I am Nabocho-drossor, the son of Nabonidus.' Then the state of Babylon revolted from me. It went over to that Aracus. He seized on Babylon. He became king of Babylonia.

14. Says Darius the king—Then I sent an army to Babylon. (A man) named Intaphres, a Mede, one of my subjects, him I made (their) leader. Thus I said to them, 'Go forth, (and) smite that Babylonian state, which does not acknowledge me.' Then Intaphres, with his army, marched to Babylon. Ormazd brought help to me; by the grace of Ormazd Intaphres took Babylon. On the 22nd day of the month . . . , then it was he entirely defeated that rebel people.

Column IV

1. Says Darius the king—This is what (was) done by me in Babylonia.

2. Says Darius the king—This is what I have done. By the grace of Ormazd I have accomplished the whole. After that the kings rebelled against me, I fought nineteen battles. By the grace of Ormazd I smote them, and took nine kings (prisoners). One was named Gomates, a Magian. He spake lies. Thus he said, 'I am Bardes, the son of Cyrus.' He caused Persia to revolt. Another (was) named Atrines, a Susianian; he spake lies. Thus he said, 'I am the king of Susiana.' He caused Susiana to revolt from me. Another (was) named Nidintabelus, a Babylonian; he spake lies. Thus he said, 'I am Nabochodrossor, the son of Nabonidus.' He caused Babylon to revolt. Another (was) named Martes, a Persian; he spake lies. Thus he said, 'I am Imanes, the king of Susiana.' He caused Susiana to revolt. Another (was) named Phrortes, a Mede; he spake lies. Thus he said, 'I am Xathrites, of the race of Cyaxares.' He caused Media to revolt. Another (was) named Sitrantachmes, a Sagartian; he spake lies. Thus he said, 'I am the king of Sagartia, of the race of Cyaxares.' He caused Sagartia to revolt. Another (was) named Phraates, a Margian; he spake lies. Thus he said, 'I am king of Margiana.' He caused Margiana to revolt. Another (was) named Veisdates, a Persian; he spake lies. Thus

he said, 'I am Bardes, the son of Cyrus.' He caused Persia to revolt. Another (was) named Aracus, an Armenian; he spake lies. Thus he said, 'I am Nabochodrossor, the son of Nabonidus.' He caused Babylon to revolt.

3. Says Darius the king—These nine kings have I taken in these battles.

4. Says Darius the king—These are the provinces which rebelled. The god Ormazd created lies that they should deceive the people. Afterwards the god Ormazd gave the people into my hand. As I desired, so the god Ormazd did (?).

5. Says Darius the king—Thou who mayest be king hereafter, keep thyself entirely from lies. The man who may be a liar, him destroy utterly. If thou shalt thus observe, my country shall remain in its integrity.

6. Says Darius the king—This is what I have done. By the grace of Ormazd have I achieved the performance of the whole. Thou who mayest hereafter peruse this tablet, let that which has been done by me be a warning (to thee), that thou lie not.

7. Says Darius the king—Ormazd is my witness that I have truly, not falsely, made this record of my deeds throughout.

8. Says Darius the king—By the grace of Ormazd, that which has besides been done by me, (which is) much, I have not inscribed on this tablet. On that account I have not inscribed it, lest he who hereafter might peruse this tablet, to him the many deeds that have been done by me elsewhere might seem to be falsely recorded.

9. Says Darius the king—They who were kings before me, by them it has not been done as by me entirely by the grace of Ormazd.

10. Says Darius the king—Beware, my successor (?), that what has been thus publicly done by me, on that account thou conceal not. If thou conceal not this edict, (but) tell it to the country, may Ormazd be a friend to thee, and may thy offspring be numerous, and mayest thou live long.

11. Says Darius the king—If thou conceal this edict, (and) tell (it) not to the country, may Ormazd be thy enemy, and mayst thou have no offspring.

12. Says Darius the king—This is what I have done. By the grace of Ormazd I have accomplished everything. Ormazd brought help to me, and the other gods which are.

13. Says Darius the king—For this reason Ormazd brought help to me, and the other gods which are, (because) that I was not wicked (heretical?), nor was I a liar, nor was I a tyrant. . . . He who has laboured for my family, him I have cherished and protected; he who has been hostile to me him I have utterly rooted out.

14. Says Darius the king—Thou who mayest be king hereafter, the man who may be a liar, and who may be an evil-doer, do not befriend them. Destroy them with the edge of the sword.

15. Says Darius the king—Thou who mayest hereafter behold this tablet, which I have engraved, and these figures, (beware) lest thou injure (them). As long as thou livest, so long preserve them.

16. Says Darius the king—If thou shalt behold this tablet and these figures, (and) not injure them, and shalt preserve them as long as my seed endures, (then) may Ormazd be thy friend, and may thy seed be numerous, and mayest thou live long; and whatever thou doest, may Ormazd bless it for thee in after times.

17. Says Darius the king—If seeing this tablet, and these images, thou injurest them, and preservest them not as long as my seed endures, (then) may Ormazd be thy enemy, and mayest thou have no offspring, and whatever thou doest, may Ormazd curse it for thee.

18. Says Darius the king—These are the men who alone were there, when I slew Gomates the Magian, who was called Bardes. These men alone laboured in my service; (One) named Intaphernes, the son of Veispares, a Persian; (One) named Otanes, the son of Socris, a Persian; (One) named Gobryas, the son of Mardonius, a Persian; (One) named Hydarnes, the son of Megabignes, a Persian; (One) named Megabyzus, the son of Dadois, a Persian; (One) named Ardomanes, the son of Basuces, a Persian.

19. Says Darius the king—Thou who mayest be king hereafter . . . .

Column V

1. Says Darius the king—This is what I have done; by the grace of Ormazd, I have accomplished all of it . . . . king . . . . This province revolted against me. A man, named . . . imimus, him the Susianians made their chief. Then I sent troops to Susiana. A man, named Gobryas, a Persian, one of my subjects, him I appointed (to be) their leader. Then that Gobryas with (his) troops went to Susiana. He fought a battle with the rebels. Then . . . . and his . . . . and . . . . seized and brought to me . . . . province . . . . there I slew him . . . . .

2. Says Darius the king— . . . . and . . . . Ormazd . . . . by the grace of Ormazd . . . . I have done.

3. Says Darius the king—Whoever may hereafter . . . . this . . . . and of life . . . .

4. Says Darius the king— . . . . I went to Sacia . . . . the Tigris . . . . towards the sea, him . . . I passed over (?) . . . . I slew; the enemy I seized . . . . to me, and . . . . Sacuces by name, him I made prisoner . . . . there the other leader (?) . . . . it was; then . . . .

5. Says Darius the king— . . . . not Ormazd . . . . by the grace of Ormazd . . . . . I have done (it).

6. Says Darius the king— . . . . Ormazd . . . . and of life and . . . .

THE CONSTITUTION OF THE ATHENIANS

By "The Old Oligarch"

Although this treatise is preserved among the works of Xenophon, its authenticity was doubted even in antiquity. Modern scholarship has strengthened the grounds for doubt not only in relation to the general tone and style, which is quite unlike that in any other work of Xenophon, but also because the probable date, about 424 B. C., is too early for Xenophon to have been the author. Many known oligarchs have been suggested as probable authors on insufficient grounds; it is probably best to continue to attribute it to "The Old Oligarch." In any case it is a striking and significant document both for the light it throws on the Athenian constitution and for its evidence of the impartiality tinged with irony with which a fifth century Greek could approach a highly controversial political topic. Despite his fundamental opposition to the Athenian democracy, the author demonstrates the complete consistency with which the constitution implements the principles of Athenian democracy.

1. Now, as for the constitution of the Athenians, and the type or manner of constitution which they have chosen, I praise it not, in so far as the very choice involves the welfare of the baser folk as opposed to that of the better class.[1] I repeat, I withhold my praise so far; but, given the fact that this is the type agreed upon, I propose to show that they set about its preservation in the right way; and that those other transactions in connection with it, which are looked upon as blunders by the rest of the Hellenic world, are the reverse.

In the first place, I maintain, it is only just that the poorer classes and the common people of Athens should be better off than the men of birth and wealth, seeing that it is the people who man the fleet, and have brought the city her power. The steersman, the boatswain, the lieutenant, the look-out-man at the prow, the shipwright—these are the people who supply the city with power far rather than her heavy infantry and men of birth and quality. This being the case, it seems only just that offices of state should be thrown open to every one both in the ballot and the show of hands, and that the right of speech should belong to any one who likes, without restriction. For, observe, there are many of these offices which, according as they are in good or in bad hands, are a source

[1] It should be remembered throughout that the "better" citizens are the friends of the Old Oligarch and that the "worse" are democrats.

633

of safety or of danger to the People, and in these the People prudently abstains from sharing; as, for instance, it does not think it incumbent on itself to share in the functions of the general or of the commander of cavalry. The commons recognises the fact that in forgoing the personal exercise of these offices, and leaving them to the control of the more powerful citizens, it secures the balance of advantage to itself. It is only those departments of government which bring pay and assist the private estate that the People cares to keep in its own hands.

In the next place, in regard to what some people are puzzled to explain—the fact that everywhere greater consideration is shown to the base, to poor people and to common folk, than to persons of good quality,—so far from being a matter of surprise, this, as can be shown, is the keystone of the preservation of the democracy. It is these poor people, this common folk, this worse element, whose prosperity, combined with the growth of their numbers, enhances the democracy. Whereas, a shifting of fortune to the advantage of the wealthy and the better classes implies the establishment on the part of the commons of a strong power in opposition to itself. In fact, all the world over, the cream of society is in opposition to the democracy. Naturally, since the smallest amount of intemperance and injustice, together with the highest scrupulousness in the pursuit of excellence, is to be found in the ranks of the better class, while within the ranks of the People will be found the greatest amount of ignorance, disorderliness, rascality,—poverty acting as a stronger incentive to base conduct, not to speak of lack of education and ignorance, traceable to the lack of means which afflicts the average of mankind.

The objection may be raised that it was a mistake to allow the universal right of speech and a seat in council. These should have been reserved for the cleverest, the flower of the community. But here, again, it will be found that they are acting with wise deliberation in granting to even the baser sort the right of speech, for supposing only the better people might speak, or sit in council, blessings would fall to the lot of those like themselves, but to the commons the reverse of blessings. Whereas now, any one who likes, any base fellow, may get up and discover something to the advantage of himself and his equals. It may be retorted, "And what sort of advantage either for himself or for the People can such a fellow be expected to hit upon?" The answer to which is, that in their judgment the ignorance and the baseness of this fellow, together with his goodwill, are worth a great deal more to them than your superior person's virtue and wisdom, coupled with animosity. What it comes to, therefore, is that a state founded upon such institutions will not be the best state; but, given a democracy, these are the right means to secure its preservation. The People, it must be borne in mind, does not demand that the city should be well governed and itself a slave. It desires to be free and to be master. As to bad legislation it does not concern itself about that. In fact, what you believe to be bad legislation is the very source of the People's strength and freedom. But if you seek for good legislation, in the first place you will see the cleverest members of the community laying down the laws for the rest. And in the next place, the better class will curb and chastise the lower orders; the better class will deliberate in behalf of the state, and not suffer crack-brained fellows to sit in council, or to speak or vote in the assemblies. No doubt; but under the weight of such blessings the People will in a very short time be reduced to slavery.

Another point is the extraordinary amount of license granted to slaves and resident aliens at Athens, where a blow is illegal, and a slave will not step aside to let you pass him in the street. I will explain the reason of this peculiar custom. Supposing it were legal for a slave to be beaten by a free citizen, or for a resident alien or freedman to be beaten by a citizen, it would frequently happen that an Athenian might be mistaken for a slave or an alien and receive a beating; since the Athenian People is not better clothed than the slave or alien, nor in personal appearance is there any superiority. Or if the fact itself that slaves in Athens are allowed to indulge in luxury, and indeed in some cases to live magnificently, be found astonishing, this too, it can be shown, is done of set purpose. Where you have a naval power dependent upon wealth we must perforce be slaves to our slaves, in order that we may get in our slave-rents, and let the real slave go free. Where you have wealthy slaves it ceases to be advantageous that my slave should stand in awe of you. In Lacedaemon my slave stands in awe of you. But if your slave is in awe of me there will be a risk of his giving away his own moneys to avoid running a risk in his own person. It is for this reason then that we have established an equality between our slaves and free men; and again between our resident aliens and full citizens, because the city stands in need of her resident aliens to meet the requirements of such a multiplicity of arts and for the purposes of her navy. That is, I repeat, the justification of the equality conferred upon our resident aliens.

The common people put a stop to citizens devoting their time to athletics and to the cultivation of music, disbelieving in the beauty of such training, and recognising the fact that these are things the cultivation of which is beyond its power. On the same principle, in the case of the choregia,[2] the management of athletics, and the command of ships, the fact is recognised that it is the rich man who trains the chorus, and the People for whom the chorus is trained; it is the rich man who is naval commander or superintendent of athletics, and the People that profits by their labours. In fact, what the People looks upon as its right is to

---

[2] The duties of the choregia consisted in finding maintenance and instruction for the dramatic chorus.

pocket the money. To sing and run and dance and man the vessels is well enough, but only in order that the People may be the gainer, while the rich are made poorer. And so in the courts of justice, justice is not more an object of concern to the jurymen than what touches personal advantage.

To speak next of the allies, and in reference to the point that emissaries from Athens come out, and, according to common opinion, calumniate and vent their hatred upon the better sort of people, this is done on the principle that the ruler cannot help being hated by those whom he rules; but that if wealth and respectability are to wield power in the subject cities the empire of the Athenian People has but a short lease of existence. This explains why the better people are punished with infamy, robbed of their money, driven from their homes, and put to death, while the baser sort are promoted to honour. On the other hand, the better Athenians protect the better class in the allied cities. And why? Because they recognise that it is to the interest of their own class at all times to protect the best element in the cities. It may be urged that if it comes to strength and power the real strength of Athens lies in the capacity of her allies to contribute their money quota. But to the democratic mind it appears a higher advantage still for the individual Athenian to get hold of the wealth of the allies, leaving them only enough to live upon and to cultivate their estates, but powerless to harbour treacherous designs.

Again, it is looked upon as a mistaken policy on the part of the Athenian democracy to compel her allies to voyage to Athens in order to have their cases tried. On the other hand, it is easy to reckon up what a number of advantages the Athenian People derives from the practice impugned. In the first place, there is the steady receipt of salaries throughout the year derived from the court fees. Next, it enables them to manage the affairs of the allied states while seated at home without the expense of naval expeditions. Thirdly, they thus preserve the partisans of the democracy, and ruin her opponents in the law courts. Whereas, supposing the several allied states tried their cases at home, being inspired by hostility to Athens, they would destroy those of their own citizens whose friendship to the Athenian People was most marked. But besides all this the democracy derives the following advantages from hearing the cases of her allies in Athens. In the first place, the one per cent[3] levied in Piraeus is increased to the profit of the state; again, the owner of a lodging-house does better, and so, too, the owner of a pair of beasts, or of slaves to be let out on hire; again, heralds and criers are a class of people who fare better owing to the sojourn of foreigners at Athens. Further still, supposing the allies had not to resort to Athens for the hearing of cases, only the official representative of the imperial state

[3] The text probably should read five per cent.

would be held in honour, such as the general, or trierarch, or ambassador. Whereas now every single individual among the allies is forced to pay flattery to the People of Athens because he knows that he must betake himself to Athens and win or lose his case at the bar, not of any stray set of judges, but of the sovereign People itself, such being the law and custom at Athens. He is compelled to behave as a suppliant in the courts of justice, and when some juryman comes into court, to grasp his hand. For this reason, therefore, the allies find themselves more and more in the position of slaves to the people of Athens.

Furthermore, owing to the possession of property beyond the limits of Attica, and the exercise of magistracies which take them into regions beyond the frontier, they and their attendants have insensibly acquired the art of navigation. A man who is perpetually voyaging is forced to handle the oar, he and his domestic alike, and to learn the terms familiar in seamanship. Hence a stock of skilful mariners is produced, bred upon a wide experience of voyaging and practice. They have learned their business, some in piloting a small craft, others a merchant vessel, while others have been drafted off from these for service on a ship-of-war. So that the majority of them are able to row the moment they set foot on board a vessel, having been in a state of preliminary practice all their lives.

2. As to the heavy infantry, an arm the deficiency of which at Athens is well recognised, this is how the matter stands. They recognise the fact that, in reference to the hostile power, they are themselves inferior, and must be, even if their heavy infantry were more numerous. But relatively to the allies, who bring in the tribute, their strength even on land is enormous. And they are persuaded that their heavy infantry is sufficient for all purposes, provided they retain this superiority. Apart from all else, to a certain extent fortune must be held responsible for the actual condition. The subjects of a power which is dominant by land have it open to them to form contingents from several small states and to muster in force for battle. But with the subjects of a naval power it is different. As far as they are groups of islanders it is impossible for their states to meet together for united action, for the sea lies between them, and the dominant power is master of the sea. And even if it were possible for them to assemble in some single island unobserved, they would only do so to perish by famine. And as to the states subject to Athens which are not islanders, but situated on the continent, the larger are held in check by need and the small ones absolutely by fear, since there is no state in existence which does not depend upon imports and exports, and these she will forfeit if she does not lend a willing ear to those who are masters by sea. In the next place, a power dominant by sea can do certain things which a land power is debarred from doing; as, for instance, ravage the

territory of a superior, since it is always possible to coast along to some point, where either there is no hostile force to deal with or merely a small body; and in case of an advance in force on the part of the enemy they can take to their ships and sail away. Such a performance is attended with less difficulty than that experienced by the relieving force on land. Again, it is open to a power so dominating by sea to leave its own territory and sail off on as long a voyage as you please. Whereas the land power cannot place more than a few days' journey between itself and its own territory, for marches are slow affairs; and it is not possible for an army on the march to have food supplies to last for any great length of time. Such an army must either march through friendly territory or it must force a way by victory in battle. The voyager meanwhile has it in his power to disembark at any point where he finds himself in superior force, or, at the worst, to coast by until he reaches either a friendly district or an enemy too weak to resist. Again, those diseases to which the fruits of the earth are liable as visitations from heaven fall severely on a land power, but are scarcely felt by the naval power, for such sicknesses do not visit the whole earth everywhere at once. So that the ruler of the sea can get in supplies from a thriving district. And if one may descend to more trifling particulars, it is to this same lordship of the sea that the Athenians owe the discovery, in the first place, of many of the luxuries of life through intercourse with other countries. So that the choice things of Sicily and Italy, of Cyprus and Egypt and Lydia, of Pontus or Peloponnese, or wheresoever else it be, are all swept, as it were, into one centre, and all owing, as I say, to their maritime empire. And again, in process of listening to every form of speech, they have selected this from one place and that from another—for themselves. So much so that while the rest of the Hellenes employ each pretty much their own peculiar mode of speech, habit of life, and style of dress, the Athenians have adopted a composite type, to which all sections of Hellas, and the foreigner alike, have contributed.

As regards sacrifices and temples and festivals and sacred enclosures, the People sees that it is not possible for every poor citizen to do sacrifice and hold festival, or to set up temples and to inhabit a large and beautiful city. But it has hit upon a means of meeting the difficulty. They sacrifice —that is, the whole state sacrifices—at the public cost a large number of victims; but it is the People that keeps holiday and distributes the victims by lot among its members. Rich men have in some cases private gymnasia and baths with dressing-rooms, but the People takes care to have built at the public cost a number of palaestras, dressing-rooms, and bathing establishments for its own special use, and the mob gets the benefit of the majority of these, rather than the select few or the well-to-do.

As to wealth, the Athenians are exceptionally placed with regard to Hellenic and foreign communities alike, in their ability to hold it. For, given that some state or other is rich in timber for shipbuilding, where is it to find a market for the product except by persuading the ruler of the sea? Or, suppose the wealth of some state or other to consist of iron, or may be of bronze, or of linen yarn, where will it find a market except by permission of the supreme maritime power? Yet these are the very things, you see, which I need for my ships. Timber I must have from one, and from another iron, from a third bronze, from a fourth linen yarn, from a fifth wax. Besides which they will not suffer their antagonists in those parts to carry these products elsewhere, or they will cease to use the sea. Accordingly I, without one stroke of labour, extract from the land and possess all these good things, thanks to my supremacy on the sea; while not a single other state possesses the two of them. Not timber, for instance, and yarn together, the same city. But where yarn is abundant, the soil will be light and devoid of timber. And in the same way bronze and iron will not be products of the same city. And so for the rest, never two, or at best three, in one state, but one thing here and another thing there. Moreover, above and beyond what has been said, the coastline of every mainland presents, either some jutting promontory, or adjacent island, or narrow strait of some sort, so that those who are masters of the sea can come to moorings at one of these points and wreak vengeance on the inhabitants of the mainland.

There is just one thing which the Athenians lack. Supposing they were the inhabitants of an island, and were still, as now, rulers of the sea, they would have had it in their power to work whatever mischief they liked, and to suffer no evil in return (as long as they kept command of the sea), neither the ravaging of their territory nor the expectation of an enemy's approach. Whereas at present the farming portion of the community and the wealthy landowners are ready to cringe before the enemy overmuch, while the People, knowing full well that, come what may, not one stock or stone of their property will suffer, nothing will be cut down, nothing burnt, lives in freedom from alarm, without fawning at the enemy's approach. Besides this, there is another fear from which they would have been exempt in an island home—the apprehension of the city being at any time betrayed by their oligarchs and the gates thrown open, and an enemy bursting suddenly in. How could incidents like these have taken place if an island had been their home? Again, had they inhabited an island there would have been no stirring of sedition against the People; whereas at present, in the event of faction, those who set it on foot base their hopes of success on the introduction of an enemy by land. But a people inhabiting an island would be free from all anxiety on that score. Since, however, they did not chance to inhabit an island from the first, what they now do is this—they deposit their property in the islands, trusting to their command of the sea, and they suffer the soil of Attica to be ravaged without a sigh. To expend pity on that, they know, would be to deprive themselves of other blessings still more precious.

Further, states oligarchically governed are forced to ratify their alliances and solemn oaths, and if they fail to abide by their contracts, the offence, by whomsoever committed, lies nominally at the door of the oligarchs who entered upon the contract. But in the case of engagements entered into by a democracy it is open to the People to throw the blame on the single individual who spoke in favour of some measure, or put it to the vote, and to maintain to the rest of the world, "I was not present, nor do I approve of the terms of the agreement." Inquiries are made in a full meeting of the People, and should any of these things be disapproved of, they can at once discover countless excuses to avoid doing whatever they do not wish. And if any mischief should spring out of any resolutions which the People has passed in council, the People can readily shift the blame from its own shoulders. "A handful of oligarchs acting against the interests of the People have ruined us." But if any good result ensue, they, the People, at once take the credit of that to themselves.

In the same spirit it is not allowed to caricature on the comic stage or otherwise libel the People, because they do not care to hear themselves ill spoken of. But if any one has a desire to satirise his neighbour he has full leave to do so. And this because they are well aware that, as a general rule, the person caricatured does not belong to the People, or the masses. He is more likely to be some wealthy or well-born person, or man of means and influence. In fact, but few poor people and of the popular stamp incur the comic lash, or if they do they have brought it on themselves by excessive love of meddling or some covetous self-seeking at the expense of the People, so that no particular annoyance is felt at seeing such folk satirised.

What, then, I venture to assert is, that the People of Athens has no difficulty in recognising which of its citizens are of the better sort and which the opposite. And so recognising those who are serviceable and advantageous to itself, even though they be base, the People loves them; but the good folk they are disposed the rather to hate. This virtue of theirs, the People holds, is not engrained in their nature for any good to itself, but rather for its injury. In direct opposition to this, there are some persons who, being born of the People, are yet by natural instinct not commoners. For my part I pardon the People its own democracy, as, indeed, it is pardonable in any one to do good to himself. But the man who, not being himself one of the People, prefers to live in a state democratically governed rather than in an oligarchical state may be said to smooth his own path towards iniquity. He knows that a bad man has a better chance of slipping through the fingers of justice in a democratic than in an oligarchical state.

3. I repeat that my position concerning the constitution of the Athenians is this: the type of constitution is not to my taste, but given that a democratic form of government has been agreed upon, they do seem to me to go the right way to preserve the democracy by the adoption of the particular type which I have set forth.

But there are other objections brought, as I am aware, against the Athenians, by certain people, and to this effect. It not seldom happens, they tell us, that a man is unable to transact a piece of business with the senate or the People, even if he sit waiting a whole year. Now this does happen at Athens, and for no other reason save that, owing to the immense mass of affairs they are unable to work off all the business on hand and dismiss the applicants. And how in the world should they be able, considering in the first place that they, the Athenians, have more festivals to celebrate than any other state throughout the length and breadth of Hellas? [During these festivals, of course, the transaction of any sort of affairs of state is still more out of the question.][4] In the next place, only consider the number of cases they have to decide, what with private suits and public causes and scrutinies of accounts, more than the whole of the rest of mankind put together; while the senate has multifarious points to advise upon concerning peace and war, concerning ways and means, concerning the framing and passing of laws, and concerning the matters affecting the state perpetually occurring, and endless questions touching the allies; besides the receipt of the tribute, the superintendence of dockyards and temples. Can, I ask again, any one find it at all surprising that, with all these affairs on their hands, they are unequal to doing business with all the world?

But some people tell us that if the applicant will only address himself to the senate or the People with a bribe in his hand he will do a good stroke of business. And for my part I am free to confess to these gainsayers that a good many things may be done at Athens by dint of money; and I will add, that a good many more still might be done, if the money flowed still more freely and from more pockets. One thing, however, I know full well, that as to transacting with every one of these applicants all he wants, the state could not do it, not even if all the gold and silver in the world were the inducement offered.

Here are some of the cases which have to be decided on. Some one fails to fit out a ship: judgment must be given. Another puts up a building on a piece of public land: again judgment must be given. Or, to take another class of cases: adjudication has to be made between the patrons of choruses for the Dionysia, the Thargelia, the Panathenaea, the Prome-

[4] This sentence is perhaps a gloss.

theia, and the Hephaestia, year after year. Also as between the trierarchs, 400 of whom are appointed each year, of these, too, any who choose must have their cases adjudicated on, year after year. But that is not all. There are various magistrates to examine and approve and decide between; there are orphans whose status must be examined; and guardians of prisoners to appoint. These, be it borne in mind, are all matters of yearly occurrence; while at intervals there are exemptions and abstentions from military service which call for adjudication, or in connection with some other extraordinary misdemeanour, some case of outrage and violence of an exceptional character, or some charge of impiety. A whole string of others I simply omit; I am content to have named the most important part with the exception of the assessments of tribute which occur, as a rule, at intervals of four years.

I put it to you, then: can any one suppose that all, or any, of these may dispense with adjudication? If so, will any one say which ought, and which ought not, to be adjudicated on, there and then? If, on the other hand, we are forced to admit that these are all fair cases for adjudication, it follows of necessity that they should be decided during the twelve-month; since even now the boards of judges sitting right through the year are powerless to stay the tide of evildoing by reason of the multitude of the people.

So far so good. "But," some one will say, "try the cases you certainly must, but lessen the number of the judges." But if so, it follows of necessity that unless the number of courts themselves are diminished in number there will only be a few judges sitting in each court, with the further consequence that in dealing with so small a body of judges it will be easier for a litigant to present an invulnerable front to the court, and to bribe the whole body, to the great detriment of justice.

But besides this we cannot escape the conclusion that the Athenians have their festivals to keep, during which the courts cannot sit. As a matter of fact these festivals are twice as numerous as those of any other people. But I will reckon them as merely equal to those of the state which has the fewest.

This being so, I maintain that it is not possible for business affairs at Athens to stand on any very different footing from the present, except to some slight extent, by adding here and deducting there. Any large modification is out of the question, short of damaging the democracy itself. No doubt many expedients might be discovered for improving the constitution, but if the problem be to discover some adequate means of improving the constitution, while at the same time the democracy is to remain intact, I say it is not easy to do this, except, as I have just stated, to the extent of some trifling addition here or deduction there.

There is another point in which it is sometimes felt that the Athenians are ill advised, in their adoption, namely, of the less respectable party, in a state divided by faction. But if so, they do it advisedly. If they chose the more respectable, they would be adopting those whose views and interests differ from their own, for there is no state in which the best element is friendly to the people. It is the worst element which in every state favours the democracy—on the principle that like favours like. It is simple enough then. The Athenians choose what is most akin to themselves. Also on every occasion on which they have attempted to side with the better classes, it has not fared well with them, but within a short interval the democratic party has been enslaved, as for instance in Boeotia; or, as when they chose the aristocrats of the Milesians, and within a short time these revolted and cut the people to pieces; or, as when they chose the Lacedaemonians as against the Messenians, and within a short time the Lacedaemonians subjugated the Messenians and went to war against Athens.

I seem to overhear a retort, "No one, of course, is deprived of his civil rights at Athens unjustly." My answer is, that there are some who are unjustly deprived of their civil rights, though the cases are certainly rare. But it will take more than a few to attack the democracy at Athens, since you may take it as an established fact, it is not the man who has lost his civil rights justly that takes the matter to heart, but the victims, if any, of injustice. But how in the world can any one imagine that many are in a state of civil disability at Athens, where the People and the holders of office are one and the same? It is from iniquitous exercise of office, from iniquity exhibited either in speech or action, and the like circumstances, that citizens are punished with deprivation of civil rights in Athens. Due reflection on these matters will serve to dispel the notion that there is any danger at Athens from persons visited with disfranchisement.

WAYS AND MEANS: A PAMPHLET ON REVENUES

By Xenophon

In this little work, written probably toward the end of his life, about 355 B.C., Xenophon sets forth certain proposals for improving the economic situation in Athens. If the public can be induced to subscribe enough capital, Xenophon argues, the state can make great profits out of building lodging-houses, stores, and ships to be rented out to private investors. Above all he argues that a body of state slaves to be used in working the silver mines at Laurium will return a large profit to the state and its citizens, who were unable as individuals to obtain the capital or take the risk involved. A further advantage, says Xenophon, is that such an economic solution to Athens' problem will also greatly improve the political situation. One of the few surviving documents from antiquity specifically oriented to economic problems, it possesses an added interest as the forerunner of countless subsequent efforts to find economic solutions to political problems and to reconcile state control and private capital.

1. For myself I have always believed that the qualities of the leading statesmen in a state are reproduced in the character of the constitution itself.

As, however, it has been maintained by certain leading statesmen in Athens that the recognised standard of right and wrong is as high at Athens as elsewhere, but that, owing to the pressure of poverty on the masses, a certain measure of injustice in their dealing with the allied cities could not be avoided; I set myself to discover whether by any manner of means it were possible for the citizens of Athens to be supported solely from the soil of Attica itself, which was obviously the most equitable solution. For if so, herein lay, as I believed, the antidote at once to their own poverty and to the feeling of suspicion with which they are regarded by the rest of Hellas.

I had no sooner begun my investigation than one fact presented itself clearly to my mind, which is that the country itself is made by nature to provide the amplest resources. And with a view to establishing the truth of this initial proposition I will describe the physical features of Attica.

In the first place, the extraordinary mildness of the climate is proved by the actual products of the soil. Numerous plants which in many parts of the world appear as stunted leafless growths are here fruit-bearing. And as with the soil so with the sea indenting our coasts, the varied productivity of which is exceptionally great. Again with regard to those fruits of earth which the gods bestow on man season by season, one and all they commence earlier and end later in this land. Nor is the supremacy of Attica shown only in those products which year after year flourish and grow old, but the land contains treasures of a more perennial kind. Within its folds lies imbedded by nature a store of marble, out of which are fashioned temples and altars of rarest beauty and the splendour of images sacred to the gods. This marble, moreover, is an object of desire to many foreigners, Hellenes and barbarians alike. Then there is land which, although it yields no fruit to the sower, needs only to be quarried in order to feed many times more mouths than it could as corn-land. Doubtless we owe it to a divine dispensation that our land is veined with silver; if we consider how many neighbouring states lie round us by land and sea and yet into none of them does a single thinnest vein of silver penetrate.

Indeed it would be scarcely irrational to maintain that the city of Athens lies at the centre, not of Hellas merely, but of the habitable world. So true is it, that the farther we remove from Athens the greater the extreme of heat or cold to be encountered; or to use another illustration, the traveller who desires to traverse the confines of Hellas from end to end will find that, whether he voyages by sea or by land, he is describing a circle, the centre of which is Athens.

Once more, this land though not literally sea-girt has all the advantages of an island, being accessible to every wind that blows, and can invite to its bosom or waft from its shore all products, since it is peninsular; while by land it is the emporium of many markets, as being a portion of the continent.

Lastly, while the majority of states have barbarian neighbours, the source of many troubles, Athens has as her next-door neighbours civilised states which are themselves far remote from the barbarians.

2. All these advantages, to repeat what I have said, may, I believe, be traced primarily to the soil and position of Attica itself. But these natural blessings may be added to: in the first place, by a careful handling of our resident alien population. And, for my part, I can hardly conceive of a more splendid source of revenue than lies open in this direction. Here you have a self-supporting class of residents conferring large benefits upon the state, and instead of receiving payment themselves, contributing on the contrary by a special tax. Nor, under the term careful handling, do I demand more than the removal of obligations which, while they confer no benefit on the state, have an air of inflicting various disabilities on the resident aliens. And I would further relieve them from

the obligation of serving as hoplites side by side with the citizen proper; since, beside the personal risk, which is great, the trouble of quitting trades and homesteads is no trifle. Incidentally the state itself would be benefited by this exemption, if the citizens were more in the habit of campaigning with one another, rather than shoulder to shoulder with Lydians, Phrygians, Syrians, and barbarians from all quarters of the world, who form the staple of our resident alien class. Besides the advantage of so weeding the ranks, it would add a positive lustre to our city, were it admitted that the men of Athens, her sons, have reliance on themselves rather than on foreigners to fight her battles. And further, supposing we offered our resident aliens a share in various other honourable duties, including the cavalry service, I shall be surprised if we do not increase the goodwill of the aliens themselves, while at the same time we add distinctly to the strength and grandeur of our city.

In the next place, seeing that there are at present numerous building sites within the city walls as yet devoid of houses, supposing the state were to make free grants of such land to foreigners for building purposes in cases where there could be no doubt as to the respectability of the applicant, if I am not mistaken, the result of such a measure will be that a larger number of persons, and of a better class, will be attracted to Athens as a place of residence.

Lastly, if we could bring ourselves to appoint, as a new government office, a board of guardians of foreign residents like our Guardians of Orphans, with special privileges assigned to those guardians who should show on their books the greatest number of resident aliens, such a measure would tend to improve the goodwill of the class in question, and in all probability all people without a city of their own would aspire to the status of foreign residents in Athens, and so further increase the revenues of the city.

3. At this point I propose to offer some remarks in proof of the attractions and advantages of Athens as a centre of commercial enterprise. In the first place, it will hardly be denied that we possess the finest and safest harbourage for shipping, where vessels of all sorts can come to moorings and be laid up in absolute security as far as stress of weather is concerned. But further than that, in most states the trader is under the necessity of lading his vessel with some merchandise or other in exchange for his cargo, since the current coin has no circulation beyond the frontier. But at Athens he has a choice: he can either in return for his wares export a variety of goods, such as human beings seek after, or, if he does not desire to take goods in exchange for goods, he has simply to export silver, and he cannot have a more excellent freight to export, since wherever he likes to sell it he may look to realise a large percentage on his capital.

Or again, supposing prizes were offered to the magistrates in charge of the market for equitable and speedy settlements of points in dispute to enable any one so wishing to proceed on his voyage without hindrance, the result would be that far more traders would trade with us and with greater satisfaction.

It would indeed be a good and noble institution to pay special marks of honour, such as the privilege of the front seat, to merchants and ship-owners, and on occasion to invite to hospitable entertainment those who, through something notable in the quality of ship or merchandise, may claim to have done the state a service. The recipients of these honours will rush into our arms as friends, not only under the incentive of gain, but of distinction also.

Now the greater the number of people attracted to Athens either as visitors or as residents, clearly the greater the development of imports and exports. More goods will be sent out of the country, there will be more buying and selling, with a consequent increase in rents, dues, and customs. And to secure this augmentation of the revenues, nothing is needed beyond one or two benevolent measures and certain details of supervision.

With regard to the other sources of revenue which I contemplate, I admit, it is different. For these I recognise the necessity of capital to begin with. I am not, however, without good hope that the citizens of this state will contribute heartily to such an object, when I reflect on the large sums subscribed by the state on various late occasions, as, for in-stance, when reinforcements were sent to the Arcadians under the com-mand of Lysistratus,[1] and again at the date of the generalship of Hege-sileos.[2] I am well aware that ships of war are frequently despatched and that too although it is uncertain whether the venture will be for the better or for the worse, and the only certainty is that the contributor will not recover the sum subscribed nor have any further share in the object for which he gave his contribution.

But for a sound investment I know of nothing comparable with the initial outlay to form this fund. Any one whose contribution amounts to ten minae may look forward to a return as high as he would get on bottomry, of nearly one-fifth, as the recipient of three obols a day. The contributor of five minae will on the same principle get more than a third, while the majority of Athenians will get more than 100 per cent on their contribution. That is to say, a subscription of one mina will put the subscriber in possession of nearly double that sum, and that, more-over, without setting foot outside Athens, which, as far as human affairs go, is as sound and durable a security as possible.

Moreover, I am of opinion that if the names of contributors were to

[1] 366 B.C.
[2] 362 B.C.

be inscribed as benefactors for all time, many foreigners would be induced to contribute, and possibly not a few states, in their desire to obtain the right of inscription; indeed I anticipate that some ·kings, tyrants, and satraps will display a keen desire to share in such a favour.

To come to the point. Were such a capital once furnished, it would be a magnificent plan to build lodging-houses for the benefit of shipmasters in the neighbourhood of the harbours, in addition to those which exist; and again, on the same principle, suitable places of meeting for merchants, for the purposes of buying and selling; and thirdly, public lodging-houses for persons visiting the city. Again, supposing dwelling-houses and stores for vending goods were fitted up for retail dealers in Piraeus and the city, they would at once be an ornament to the state and a fertile source of revenue. Also it seems to me it would be a good thing to try to see if, on the principle on which at present the state possesses public warships, it would not be possible to secure public merchant vessels, to be let out on the security of guarantors just like any other public property. If the plan were found feasible this public merchant navy would be a large source of extra revenue.

4. I come to a new topic. I am persuaded that the establishment of the silver mines on a proper footing would be followed by a large increase of wealth apart from the other sources of revenue. And I would like, for the benefit of those who may be ignorant, to point out what the capacity of these mines really is. You will then be in a position to decide how to turn them to better account. It is clear, I presume, to every one that these mines have for a very long time been in active operation; at any rate no one will venture to fix the date at which they first began to be worked. Now in spite of the fact that the silver ore has been dug and carried out for so long a time, I would ask you to note that the mounds of rubbish so shovelled out are but a fractional portion of the series of hillocks containing veins of silver, and as yet unquarried. Nor is the silver-bearing region gradually becoming circumscribed. On the contrary it is evidently extending in wider area from year to year. That is to say, during the period in which the most workers have been employed within the mines no hand was ever stopped for want of work to do. Rather, at any given moment, the work to be done was more than enough for the hands employed. And so it is to-day with the owners of slaves working in the mines; no one dreams of reducing the number of his hands. On the contrary, the object is perpetually to acquire as many additional hands as the owner possibly can. The fact is that with few hands to dig and search, the find of treasure will be small, but with an increase of labour the discovery of the ore itself is more than proportionally increased. So much so, that of all operations with which I am acquainted, this is the only one in which no sort of jealousy is felt at a further devel-

opment of the industry. I may go a step farther; every proprietor of a farm will be able to tell you exactly how many yoke of oxen are sufficient for the estate, and how many farm hands. To send into the field more than the exact number requisite every farmer would consider a dead loss. But in silver mining operations the universal complaint is the want of hands. Indeed there is no analogy between this and other industries. With an increase in the number of bronze-workers articles of bronze may become so cheap that the bronze-worker has to retire from the field. And so again with ironfounders. Or again, in a plethoric condition of the corn and wine market these fruits of the soil will be so depreciated in value that the particular husbandries cease to be remunerative, and many a farmer will give up his tillage of the soil and betake himself to the business of a merchant, or of a shopkeeper, to banking or money-lending. But the converse is the case in the working of silver; there the larger the quantity of ore discovered and the greater the amount of silver extracted, the greater the number of persons ready to engage in the operation. One more illustration: take the case of movable property. No one when he has got sufficient furniture for his house dreams of making further purchases on his head, but of silver no one ever yet possessed so much that he was forced to cry "enough." On the contrary, if ever anybody does become possessed of an immoderate amount he finds as much pleasure in digging a hole in the ground and hoarding it as in the actual employment of it. And from a wider point of view: when a state is prosperous there is nothing which people so much desire as silver. The men want money to expend on beautiful armour and fine horses, and houses, and sumptuous paraphernalia of all sorts. The women betake themselves to expensive apparel and ornaments of gold. Or when states are sick, either through barrenness of corn and other fruits, or through war, the demand for current coin is even more imperative (while the ground lies unproductive), to pay for necessaries or military aid.

And if it be asserted that gold is after all just as useful as silver, without gainsaying the proposition I may note this fact about gold, that, with a sudden influx of this metal, it is the gold itself which is depreciated while causing at the same time a rise in the value of silver.

The above facts are, I think, conclusive. They encourage us not only to introduce as much human labour as possible into the mines, but to extend the scale of operations within, by increase of plant, in full assurance that there is no danger either of the ore itself being exhausted or of silver becoming depreciated. And in advancing these views I am merely following a precedent set me by the state herself. So it seems to me, since the state permits any foreigner who desires it to undertake mining operations on a footing of equality with her own citizens.

But, to make my meaning clearer on the question of maintenance, I will at this point explain in detail how the silver mines may be furnished and extended so as to render them much more useful to the state. Only I would premise that I claim no sort of admiration for anything which I am about to say, as though I had hit upon some recondite discovery. Since half of what I have to say is at the present moment still patent to the eyes of all of us, and as to what belongs to past history, if we are to believe the testimony of our fathers, things were then much the same as now. No, what is really marvellous is that the state, with the fact of so many private persons growing wealthy at her expense, and under her very eyes, should have failed to imitate them. It is an old story, trite enough to those of us who have cared to attend to it, how once on a time Nicias, the son of Niceratus, owned 1,000 men in the silver mines, whom he let out to Sosias, a Thracian, on the following terms. Sosias was to pay him a net obol a day, without charge or deduction, for every slave of the thousand, and be responsible for keeping up the number perpetually at that figure. So again Hipponicus had 600 slaves let out on the same principle, which brought him in a net mina a day without charge or deduction. Then there was Philemonides, with 300, bringing him in half a mina, and others, I make no doubt there were, making profits in proportion to their respective resources and capital. But there is no need to revert to ancient history. At the present moment there are many men in the mines let out on the same principle. And given that my proposal were carried into effect, the only novelty in it is that, just as the individual in acquiring the ownership of a gang of slaves finds himself at once provided with a permanent source of income, so the state, in like fashion, should possess herself of a body of public slaves, to the number, say, of three for every Athenian citizen. As to the feasibility of our proposals, I challenge any one whom it may concern to test the scheme point by point, and to give his verdict.

With regard to the price then of the men themselves, it is obvious that the public treasury is in a better position to provide funds than any private individuals. What can be easier than for the Council to invite by public proclamation all whom it may concern to bring their slaves, and to buy up those produced? Assuming the purchase to be effected, is it credible that people will hesitate to hire from the state rather than from the private owner, and actually on the same terms? People have at all events no hesitation at present in hiring consecrated grounds, sacred victims, houses, or in purchasing the right of farming taxes from the state. To ensure the preservation of the purchased property, the treasury can take the same securities precisely from the lessee as it does from those who purchase the right of farming its taxes. Indeed, fraudulent dealing is easier on the part of the man who has purchased such a right than of the man who hires slaves; since it is not easy to see how the exportation of public money is to be detected, when it differs in no way from private money, whereas it will take a clever thief to make off with these slaves, marked as they will be with the public stamp, and in face of a heavy penalty attached at once to the sale and exportation of them. Up to this point then it would appear feasible enough for the state to acquire property in men and to keep a safe watch over them.

But with reference to an opposite objection which may present itself to the mind of some one: what guarantee is there that, along with the increase in the supply of labourers, there will be a corresponding demand for their services on the part of contractors? It may be reassuring to note, first of all, that many of those who have already embarked on mining operations will be anxious to increase their staff of labourers by hiring some of these public slaves (remember, they have a large capital at stake; and again, many of the actual labourers now engaged are growing old); and secondly, there are many others, Athenians and foreigners alike, who, though unwilling and indeed incapable of working physically in the mines, will be glad enough to earn a livelihood by their wits as superintendents.

Let it be granted, however, that at first a nucleus of 1,200 slaves is formed. It is hardly too sanguine a supposition that out of the profits alone, within five or six years this number may be increased to at least 6,000. Again, out of that number of 6,000—supposing each slave to bring in an obol a day clear of all expenses—we get a revenue of sixty talents a year. And supposing twenty talents out of this sum laid out on the purchase of more slaves, there will be forty talents left for the state to apply to any other purpose it may find advisable. By the time the round number of 10,000 is reached the yearly income will amount to 100 talents.

As a matter of fact, the state will receive much more than these figures represent, as any one here will bear me witness who can remember what the dues derived from slaves realised before the troubles at Decelea. Testimony to the same effect is borne by the fact that, in spite of the countless number of human beings employed in the silver mines within the whole period, the mines present exactly the same appearance to-day as they did within the recollection of our forefathers. And once more everything that is taking place to-day tends to prove that, whatever the number of slaves employed, you will never have more than the works can easily absorb. The miners find no limit of depth in sinking shafts or laterally in piercing galleries. To open cuttings in new directions to-day is just as possible as it was in former times. In fact no one can take on himself to say whether there is more ore in the regions already cut into, or in those where the pick has not yet struck. Well then, it may be asked, why is it that there is not the same rush to make new cuttings now as in former times? The answer is, because the people concerned with the mines are poorer nowadays. The attempt to restart operations is of recent date, and any one who ventures to open up a new area runs a considerable risk. Supposing he hits upon a productive field, he becomes a rich man, but supposing he draws a blank, he loses the whole of his outlay; and that is a danger which people of the present time are shy of facing.

It is a difficulty, but it is one on which, I believe, I can offer some practical advice. I have a plan to suggest which will reduce the risk of opening up new cuttings to a minimum.

The citizens of Athens are divided, as we all know, into ten tribes. Let the state then assign to each of these ten tribes an equal number of slaves, and let the tribes agree to associate their fortunes and proceed to open new cuttings. What will happen? Any single tribe hitting upon a productive lode will be the means of discovering what is advantageous to all. Or, supposing two or three, or possibly the half of them, hit upon a lode, clearly these several operations will proportionally be more remunerative still. That the whole ten will fail is not at all in accordance with what we should expect from the history of the past. It is possible, of course, for private persons to combine in the same way, and share their fortunes and minimise their risks. Nor need you apprehend that a state mining company, established on this principle, will ruin the private owner, or the private owner prove injurious to the state. But rather like allies who render each other stronger the more they combine, so in these silver mines, the greater number of companies at work the larger the riches they will discover and disinter.

This then is a statement, as far as I can make it clear, of the method by which, with the proper state organisation, every Athenian may be supplied with ample maintenance at the public expense. Possibly some of you may be calculating that the capital requisite will be enormous. They may doubt if a sufficient sum will ever be subscribed to meet all the needs. All I can say is, even so, do not despond. It is not as if it were necessary that every feature of the scheme should be carried out at once, or else there is to be no advantage in it at all. On the contrary, whatever number of houses are erected, or ships built, or slaves purchased, these portions will begin to pay at once. In fact, the bit-by-bit method of proceeding will be more advantageous than a simultaneous carrying into effect of the whole plan, to this extent: if we set about erecting buildings wholesale we shall make a more expensive and worse job of it than if we finish them off gradually. Again, if we set about bidding for a great many slaves at once we shall be forced to purchase an inferior type at a higher cost. Whereas, if we proceed tentatively, as we find ourselves able, we can complete any well-devised attempt at our leisure, and, in case of any obvious failure, take warning and not repeat it. Again, if everything were to be carried out at once, it is we who must make the whole provision at our expense. Whereas, if part were proceeded with and part stood over, the portion of revenue in hand will help to furnish what is necessary to go on with. But to come now to what every one probably will regard as a really grave danger, lest the state may become possessed of an over large number of slaves, with the result that the works will be overstocked. That again is an apprehension which we may escape if we are careful not to put into the works more hands from year to year than the works themselves demand. Thus I am persuaded that the easiest method of carrying out this scheme, as a whole, is also the best. If, however, you are persuaded that, owing to the extraordinary property taxes to which you have been subjected during the present war, you will not be equal to any further contributions at present, what you should do is this: during the current year resolve to carry on the financial administration of the state within the limits of a sum equivalent to that which your taxes realised before the peace. That done, you are at liberty to take any surplus sum, whether directly traceable to the peace itself, or to the more courteous treatment of our resident aliens and traders, or to the growth of the imports and exports, coincident with the collecting together of larger masses of human beings, or to an augmentation of harbour and market dues: this surplus, I say, however derived, you should take and invest so as to bring in the greatest revenue.

Again, if there is an apprehension on the part of any that the whole scheme will crumble into nothing on the first outbreak of war, I would only beg these alarmists to note that, under the condition of things which we propose to bring about, war will have more terrors for the attacking party than for this state. Since what possession I should like to know can be more serviceable for war than that of men? Think of the many ships which they will be capable of manning on public service. Think of the number who will serve on land as infantry in the public service and will bear hard upon the enemy. Only we must treat them with courtesy. For myself, my calculation is that even in the event of war we shall be quite able to keep a firm hold of the silver mines. I may take it, we have in the neighbourhood of the mines certain fortresses—one on the southern slope in Anaphlystus; and we have another on the northern side in Thoricus, the two being about seven and a half miles apart. Suppose then a third breastwork were to be placed between these, on the highest point of Besa, that would enable the operatives to collect into one out of all the fortresses, and at the first perception of a hostile movement it would only be a short distance for each to retire into safety. In the event of an enemy advancing in large numbers they might certainly make off with whatever corn or wine or cattle they found outside. But even if they did get hold of the silver ore, it would be little better to them than a heap of stones. But how is an enemy ever to march upon the mines in force? The nearest state, Megara, is distant, I take it, a good deal over sixty miles; and the next closest, Thebes, a good deal nearer seventy. Supposing then an enemy to advance from some such point to attack the mines, he cannot avoid passing Athens; and presuming his force to be small, we may expect him to be annihilated by our cavalry and frontier police. I say, presuming his force to be small, since to march with anything like a large force, and thereby leave his own territory denuded of troops, would be a startling achievement. Why, the fortified city of Athens will be much closer to the states of the attacking parties than they themselves will be by the time they have got to the mines. But, for the sake of argument, let us suppose an enemy to have arrived in the neighbourhood of Laurium; how is he going to stop there without provisions? To go out in search of supplies with a detachment of his force would imply risk, both for the foraging party and for those who have to do the fighting; while, if they are driven to do so in force each time, they may call themselves besiegers, but they will be practically in a state of siege themselves.

But it is not the income derived from the slaves alone to which we look to help the state towards the effective maintenance of her citizens, but with the growth and concentration of a thick population in the mining district various sources of revenue will accrue, whether from the market at Sunium, or from the various state buildings in connection with the silver mines, from furnaces and all the rest; since we must expect a thickly populated city to spring up here, if organised in the way proposed, and plots of land will become as valuable to owners out there as they are to those who possess them in the neighbourhood of the capital.

If, at this point, I may assume my proposals to have been carried into effect, I think I can promise, not only that our city shall be relieved from a financial strain, but that she shall make a great stride in orderliness and in tactical organisation, she shall grow in martial spirit and readiness for war. I anticipate that those who are under orders to go through gymnastic training will devote themselves with a new zeal to the details of the training school, now that they will receive a larger maintenance while under the orders of the trainer in the torch race. So again those on garrison duty in the various fortresses, those enrolled as peltasts, or again as frontier police to protect the rural districts, one and all will carry out their respective duties more ardently when the maintenance appropriate to these several functions is duly forthcoming.

5. But now, if it is evident that, in order to get the full benefit of all these sources of revenue, peace is an indispensable condition, if that is plain, I say, the question suggests itself, would it not be worth while to appoint a board to act as guardians of peace? Since no doubt the election

of such a magistracy would enhance the charm of this city in the eyes
of the whole world, and add largely to the number of our visitors. But if
any one is disposed to take the view that, by adopting a persistent peace
policy, this city will be shorn of her power, that her glory will dwindle
and her good name be forgotten throughout the length and breadth of
Hellas, the view so taken by our friends here is in my poor judgment
somewhat unreasonable. For they are surely the happy states, they, in
popular language, are most fortune-favoured, which endure in peace the
longest season. And of all states Athens is pre-eminently adapted by
nature to flourish and wax strong in peace. The while she abides in peace
she cannot fail to exercise an attractive force on all. From the mariner
and the merchant upwards, all seek her, flocking they come; the wealthy
dealers in corn and wine and oil, the owner of many cattle. And not these
only, but the man who depends upon his wits, whose skill is to do business and make gain out of money and its employment. And here another
crowd, artificers of all sorts, artists and artisans, professors of wisdom,
philosophers, and poets, with those who exhibit and popularise their
works. And next a new train of pleasure-seekers, eager to feast on everything sacred or secular, which may captivate and charm eye and ear.
Or once again, where are all those who seek to effect a rapid sale or purchase of many commodities, to find what they want, if not at Athens?

But if there is no desire to gainsay these views—only that certain
people, in their wish to recover that headship which was once the pride
of our city, are persuaded that the accomplishment of their hopes is to
be found, not in peace but in war, I beg them to reflect on some matters
of history, and to begin at the beginning, the Persian war. Was it by
high-handed violence, or as benefactors of Hellenes, that we obtained
the headship of the naval forces, and the trusteeship of the treasury of
Hellas? Again, when through the too cruel exercise of her presidency, as
men thought, Athens was deprived of her empire, is it not the case that
even in those days, as soon as we held aloof from injustice we were once
more reinstated by the islanders, of their own free will, as presidents of
the naval force? Nay, did not the very Thebans, in return for certain
benefits, grant to us Athenians to exercise leadership over them? And at
another date the Lacedaemonians suffered us Athenians to arrange the
terms of leadership at our discretion, not as driven to such submission,
but in requital of kindly treatment. And to-day, owing to the chaos
which reigns in Hellas, if I mistake not, an opportunity has fallen to this
city of winning back our fellow-Hellenes without pain or peril or expense
of any sort. It is given to us to try to harmonise states which are at war
with one another; it is given to us to reconcile the differences of rival
factions within those states themselves, wherever existing.

Make it but evident that we are minded to preserve the independence of the Delphic shrine in its primitive integrity, not by joining in any war but by the moral force of embassies throughout the length and breadth of Hellas, and I for one shall not be astonished if you find our brother Hellenes of one sentiment and eager under seal of solemn oaths to proceed against those, whoever they may be, who shall seek to step into the place vacated by the Phocians and to occupy the sacred shrine. Make it but evident that you intend to establish a general peace by land and sea, and, if I mistake not, your efforts will find a response in the hearts of all. There is no man but will pray for the salvation of Athens next to that of his own fatherland.

Again, is any one persuaded that, looking solely to riches and money-making, the state may find war more profitable than peace? If so, I cannot conceive a better method to decide that question than to allow the mind to revert to the past history of the state and to note well the sequence of events. He will discover that in times long gone by during a period of peace vast wealth was stored up in the Acropolis, the whole of which was lavishly expended during a subsequent period of war. He will perceive, if he examines closely, that even at the present time we are suffering from its ill effects. Countless sources of revenues have failed, or if they have still flowed in, been lavishly expended on a multiplicity of things. Whereas, now that peace is established by sea, our revenues have expanded and the citizens of Athens have it in their power to turn these to account as they like best.

But if you turn on me with the question, "Do you really mean that even in the event of unjust attacks upon our city on the part of any, we are still resolutely to observe peace towards that offender?" I answer distinctly, "No!" But, on the contrary, I maintain that we shall all the more promptly retaliate on such aggression in proportion as we have done no wrong to any one ourselves. Since that will be to rob the aggressor of his allies.

6. But now if none of these proposals be impracticable or even difficult of execution; if rather by giving them effect we may conciliate further the friendship of Hellas, while we strengthen our own administration and increase our fame; if by the same means the people shall be provided with the necessaries of life, and our rich men be relieved of expenditure on war; if with the large surplus to be counted on, we are in a position to conduct our festivals on an even grander scale than heretofore, to restore our temples, to rebuild our forts and docks, and to reinstate in their ancient privileges our priests, our senators, our magistrates, and our knights—surely it were but reasonable to enter upon this project speedily, so that we too, even in our own day, may witness the unclouded dawn of prosperity in store for our city.

But if you are agreed to carry out this plan, there is one further counsel which I would urge upon you. Send to Dodona and to Delphi, I would beg you, and consult the will of Heaven whether such provision and such a policy on our part be truly to the interest of Athens both for the present and for the time to come. If the consent of Heaven be thus obtained, we ought then, I say, to put a further question: whose special favour among the gods shall we seek to secure with a view to the happier execution of these measures?

And in accordance with that answer, let us offer a sacrifice of happy omen to the deities so named, and commence the work; since if these transactions be so carried out with the will of God, have we not the right to prognosticate some further advance in the path of political progress for this whole state?

THE CONSTITUTION OF THE SPARTANS

By Xenophon

The internal evidence of chapter 14 indicates a date of composition between 378 B.C. and 375 B.C. The work furnishes us with what amounts to the official Spartan view of Lycurgus's institutions, though it can scarcely be considered as genuine history. Of greater interest is the severe criticism of the actual break-down of the traditional institutions in fourth century Sparta. Xenophon's praise of the ideal of Spartan government is in sharp conflict with the actuality as he saw it, and his problem is not unlike that of Plato and the other Athenians who found much to admire in Sparta, although their own lives and beliefs were in many respects quite out of harmony both with the Spartan ideal and the Spartan actuality.

1. I recall the astonishment with which I first noted the unique position of Sparta among the states of Hellas, the relatively sparse population, and at the same time the extraordinary power and prestige of the community. I was puzzled to account for the fact. It was only when I came to consider the peculiar institutions of the Spartans that my wonderment ceased. Or rather, it is transferred to the legislator who gave them those laws, obedience to which has been the secret of their prosperity. This legislator, Lycurgus, I admire, and hold him to have been one of the wisest of mankind. Certainly he was no servile imitator of other states. It was by a stroke of invention rather, and on a pattern much in opposition to the commonly-accepted one, that he brought his fatherland to this pinnacle of prosperity.

Take for example—and it is well to begin at the beginning—the whole topic of the begetting and rearing of children. Throughout the rest of the world the young girl, who will one day become a mother (and I speak of those who may be held to be well brought up), is nurtured on the plainest food attainable, with the scantiest addition of meat or other condiments; while as to wine they train them either to total abstinence or to take it highly diluted with water. And in imitation, as it were, of the handicraft type, since the majority of artificers are sedentary, we, the rest of the Hellenes, are content that our girls should sit quietly and work wools. That is all we demand of them. But how are we to expect that women nurtured in this fashion should produce a splendid offspring?

Lycurgus pursued a different path. Clothes were things, he held, the furnishing of which might well enough be left to female slaves. And, believing that the highest function of a free woman was the bearing of children, in the first place he insisted on the training of the body as incumbent no less on the female than the male; and in pursuit of the same idea instituted rival contests in running and feats of strength for women as for men. His belief was that where both parents were strong their progeny would be found to be more vigorous.

And so again after marriage. In view of the fact that immoderate intercourse is elsewhere permitted during the earlier period of matrimony, he adopted a principle directly opposite. He laid it down as an ordinance that a man should be ashamed to be seen visiting the chamber of his wife, whether going in or coming out. When they did meet under such restraint the mutual longing of these lovers could not but be increased, and the fruit which might spring from such intercourse would tend to be more robust than theirs whose affections are cloyed by satiety. By a farther step in the same direction he refused to allow marriages to be contracted at any period of life according to the fancy of the parties concerned. Marriage, as he ordained it, must only take place in the prime of bodily vigour, this too being, as he believed, a condition conducive to the production of healthy offspring. Or again, to meet the case which might occur of an old man wedded to a young wife. Considering the jealous watch which such husbands are apt to keep over their wives, he introduced a directly opposite custom; that is to say, he made it incumbent on the aged husband to introduce some one whose qualities, physical and moral, he admired, to beget him children. Or again, in the case of a man who might not desire to live with a wife permanently, but yet might still be anxious to have children of his own worthy the name, the lawgiver laid down a law in his behalf. Such an one might select some woman, the wife of some man, well born herself and blest with fair offspring, and, the sanction and consent of her husband first obtained, raise up children for himself through her.

These and many other adaptations of a like sort the lawgiver sanctioned. As, for instance, at Sparta a wife will not object to bear the burden of a double establishment, or a husband to adopt sons as foster-brothers of his own children, with a full share in his family and position, but possessing no claim to his wealth and property.

So opposed to those of the rest of the world are the principles which Lycurgus devised in reference to the production of children. Whether they enabled him to provide Sparta with a race of men superior to all in size and strength I leave to the judgment of whomsoever it may concern.

2. With this exposition of the customs in connection with the birth of children, I wish now to explain the systems of education in fashion here

and elsewhere. Throughout the rest of Hellas the custom on the part of those who claim to educate their sons in the best way is as follows. As soon as the children are of an age to understand what is said to them they are immediately placed under the charge of Paidagogoi (or tutors), who are also attendants, and sent off to the school of some teacher to be taught grammar, music, and the concerns of the palaestra. Besides this they are given shoes to wear which tend to make their feet tender, and their bodies are enervated by various changes of clothing. And as for food, the only measure recognised is that which is fixed by appetite.

But when we turn to Lycurgus, instead of leaving it to each member of the state privately to appoint a slave to be his son's tutor, he set over the young Spartans a public guardian, the Paidonomos, to give him his proper title, with complete authority over them. This guardian was selected from those who filled the highest magistracies. He had authority to hold musters of the boys, and as their overseer, in case of any misbehaviour, to chastise severely. The legislator further provided the pastor with a body of youths in the prime of life, and bearing whips, to inflict punishment when necessary, with this happy result that in Sparta modesty and obedience ever go hand in hand, nor is there lack of either.

Instead of softening their feet with shoe or sandal, his rule was to make them hardy through going barefoot. This habit, if practised, would, as he believed, enable them to scale heights more easily and clamber down precipices with less danger. In fact, with his feet so trained the young Spartan would leap and spring and run faster unshod than another shod in the ordinary way.

Instead of making them effeminate with a variety of clothes, his rule was to habituate them to a single garment the whole year through, thinking that so they would be better prepared to withstand the variations of heat and cold.

Again, as regards food, according to his regulation the prefect, or head of the flock, must see that his messmates gathered to the club meal, with such moderate food as to avoid that heaviness which is engendered by repletion, and yet not to remain altogether unacquainted with the pains of penurious living. His belief was that by such training in boyhood they would be better able when occasion demanded to continue toiling on an empty stomach. They would be all the fitter, if the word of command were given, to remain on the stretch for a long time without extra dieting. The craving for luxuries would be less, the readiness to take any victual set before them greater, and, in general, the regime would be found more healthy. Under it he thought the lads would increase in stature and shape into finer men, since, as he maintained, a dietary which gave suppleness to the limbs must be more conducive to both ends than one which added thickness to the bodily parts by feeding.

On the other hand, in order to guard against a too great pinch of starvation, though he did not actually allow the boys to help themselves without further trouble to what they needed more, he did give them permission to steal this thing or that in the effort to alleviate their hunger. It was not of course from any real difficulty how else to supply them with nutriment that he left it to them to provide themselves by this crafty method. Nor can I conceive that any one will so misinterpret the custom. Clearly its explanation lies in the fact that he who would live the life of a robber must forgo sleep by night, and in the daytime he must employ shifts and lie in ambuscade; he must prepare and make ready his scouts, and so forth, if he is to succeed in capturing the quarry.

It is obvious, I say, that the whole of this education was intended, to make the boys craftier and more inventive in getting in supplies, while at the same time it cultivated their warlike instincts. An objector may retort, "But if he thought it so fine a feat to steal, why did he inflict all those blows on the unfortunate who was caught?" My answer is: for the self-same reason which induces people, in other matters which are taught, to punish the mal-performance of a service. So they, the Lacedaemonians, visit penalties on the boy who is detected thieving as being but a sorry bungler in the art. So to steal as many cheeses as possible [off the shrine of Orthia][1] was a feat to be encouraged; but, at the same moment, others were enjoined to scourge the thief, which would point a moral not obscurely, that by pain endured for a brief season a man may earn the joyous reward of lasting glory. Herein, too, it is plainly shown that where speed is requisite the sluggard will win for himself much trouble and scant good.

Furthermore, and in order that the boys should not want a ruler, even in case the guardian himself were absent, he gave to any citizen who chanced to be present authority to lay upon them injunctions for their good, and to chastise them for any trespass committed. By so doing he created in the boys of Sparta a most rare modesty and reverence. And indeed there is nothing which, whether as boys or men, they respect more highly than the ruler. Lastly, and with the same intention, that the boys must never be reft of a ruler, even if by chance there were no grown man present, he laid down the rule that in such a case the most active of the Leaders or Prefects was to become ruler each of his own division. The conclusion being that under no circumstances whatever are the boys of Sparta destitute of one to rule them.

I ought, as it seems to me, not to omit some remark on the subject of homosexuality, it being a topic in close connection with that of boyhood and the training of boys.

[1] Artemis of the Steep, a title connecting the goddess with Mount Orthion or Orthosion. The words are out of their right place.

We know that the rest of the Hellenes deal with this relationship in different ways, either after the manner of the Boeotians, where man and boy are intimately united by a bond like that of wedlock, or after the manner of the Eleians, where the enjoyment of beauty is gained by favours; while there are others who would absolutely debar the lover from all conversation and discourse with the beloved.

Lycurgus adopted a system opposed to all of these alike. Given that some one, himself being all that a man ought to be, should in admiration of a boy's soul endeavour to discover in him a true friend without reproach, and to consort with him—this was a relationship which Lycurgus commended, and indeed regarded as the noblest type of bringing up. But if, as was evident, it was not an attachment to the soul, but a yearning merely towards the body, he stamped this thing as foul and horrible; and with this result, to the credit of Lycurgus be it said, that in Lacedaemon the relationship of lover and beloved is like that of parent and child or brother and brother where carnal appetite is in abeyance.

That this, however, which is the fact, should be scarcely credited in some quarters does not surprise me, seeing that in many states the laws do not oppose the desires in question.

I have now described the two chief methods of education in vogue; that is to say, the Lacedaemonian as contrasted with that of the rest of Hellas, and I leave it to the judgment of him whom it may concern, which of the two has produced the finer type of men. And by finer I mean the better disciplined, the more modest and reverential, and, in matters where self-restraint is a virtue, the more continent.

3. Coming to the critical period at which a boy ceases to be a boy and becomes a youth, we find that it is just then that the rest of the world proceed to emancipate their children from the private tutor and the schoolmaster, and, without substituting any further ruler, are content to launch them into absolute independence.

Here, again, Lycurgus took an entirely opposite view of the matter. This, if observation might be trusted, was the season when the tide of animal spirits flows fast, and the froth of insolence rises to the surface; when, too, the most violent appetites for pleasures invade the mind. This, then, was the right moment at which to impose constant labours upon the growing youth, and to devise for him a subtle system of absorbing occupation. And by a crowning enactment, which said that he who shrank from the duties imposed on him would forfeit henceforth all claim to the glorious honours of the state, he caused, not only the public authorities, but those personally interested in the youths to take serious pains so that no single individual of them should by an act of cowardice find himself utterly despised within the body politic.

Furthermore, in his desire firmly to implant modesty in them he imposed a special rule. In the streets they were to keep their hands within the folds of the cloak; they were to walk in silence and without turning their heads to gaze, but rather to keep their eyes fixed upon the ground before them. And hereby it would seem to be proved conclusively that, even in the matter of quiet bearing and sobriety, the masculine type may claim greater strength than that which we attribute to the nature of women. At any rate, you might sooner expect a stone image to find voice than one of those Spartan youths; to divert the eyes of some bronze statue were less difficult. And as to quiet bearing, no bride ever stepped in bridal bower with more natural modesty. Note them when they have reached the public table. The plainest answer to the question asked, that is all you need expect to hear from their lips.

4. But if he was thus careful in the education of the stripling, the Spartan lawgiver showed a still greater anxiety in dealing with those who had reached the prime of opening manhood; considering their immense importance to the city in the scale of good, if only they proved themselves the men they should be. He had only to look around to see that wherever the spirit of emulation is most deeply seated, there, too, their choruses and gymnastic contests will present alike a far higher charm to eye and ear. And on the same principle he persuaded himself that he needed only to confront his youthful warriors in the strife of valour, and with like result. They also, in their degree, might be expected to attain to some unknown height of manly virtue.

What method he adopted to engage these combatants I will now explain. Their ephors select three men out of the whole body of the citizens in the prime of life. These three are named masters of the horse. Each of these selects 100 others, being bound to explain for what reason he prefers in honour these and disapproves of those. The result is that those who fail to obtain the distinction are now at open war, not only with those who rejected them, but with those who were chosen in their stead; and they keep ever a jealous eye on one another to detect some slip of conduct contrary to the high code of honour there held customary. And so is set on foot that strife, in truest sense acceptable to heaven, and for the purposes of state most politic. It is a strife in which not only is the pattern of a brave man's conduct fully set forth, but where, too, each against other and in separate camps, the rival parties train for victory. One day the superiority shall be theirs; or, in the day of need, one and all to the last man, they will be ready to aid the fatherland with all their strength.

Necessity, moreover, is laid upon them to study a good habit of the body, coming as they do to blows with their fists for very strife's sake wherever they meet. However, any one present has a right to separate the combatants, and, if obedience is not shown to the peacemaker, the

Guardian of youth hales the delinquent before the ephors, and the ephors inflict heavy damages, since they will have it plainly understood that rage must never override obedience to law.

With regard to those who have already passed the vigour of early manhood, and on whom the highest magistracies henceforth devolve, there is a like contrast. In Hellas generally we find that at this age the need of further attention to physical strength is removed, although the imposition of military service continues. But Lycurgus made it customary for that section of his citizens to regard hunting as the highest honour suited to their age; but not to the exclusion of any public duty. And his aim was that they might be equally able to undergo the fatigues of war with those in the prime of early manhood.

5. The above is a fairly exhaustive statement of the institutions traceable to the legislation of Lycurgus in connection with the successive stages of a citizen's life. It remains that I should endeavour to describe the style of living which he established for the whole body, irrespective of age. It will be understood that, when Lycurgus first came to deal with the question, the Spartans, like the rest of the Hellenes, used to mess privately at home. Tracing more than half the current misdemeanours to this custom, he was determined to drag his people out into the daylight, and so he invented the public mess-rooms. Whereby he expected at any rate to minimise the transgression of orders.

As to food, his ordinance allowed them so much as, while not inducing repletion, should guard them from actual want. And, in fact, there are many exceptional dishes in the shape of game supplied from the hunting field. Or, as a substitute for these, rich men will occasionally garnish the feast with wheaten loaves. So that from beginning to end, till the mess breaks up, the common board is never stinted for viands, nor yet extravagantly furnished.

So also in the matter of drink. While putting a stop to all unnecessary potations, detrimental alike to a firm brain and a steady gait, he left them free to quench thirst when nature dictated; a method which would at once add to the pleasure while it diminished the danger of drinking. And indeed one may fairly ask how, on such a system of common meals, it would be possible for any one to ruin either himself or his family through either gluttony or wine-bibbing.

This too must be borne in mind, that in other states equals in age, for the most part, associate together, and such an atmosphere is little conducive to modesty. Whereas in Sparta Lycurgus was careful so to blend the ages that the younger men must benefit largely by the experience of the elder—an education in itself, and the more so since by custom of the country conversation at the common meal has reference to the honourable acts which this man or that man may have performed in relation to the state. The scene, in fact, but little lends itself to the intrusion of violence or drunken riot; ugly speech and ugly deeds alike are out of place. Among other good results obtained through this out-door system of meals may be mentioned these: There is the necessity of walking home when the meal is over, and a consequent anxiety not to be caught tripping under the influence of wine, since they all know of course that the supper-table must be presently abandoned, and that they must move as freely in the dark as in the day, even the help of a torch to guide the steps being forbidden to all on active service.

In connection with this matter, Lycurgus had not failed to observe the effect of equal amounts of food on different persons. The hardworking man has a good complexion, his muscles are well fed, he is robust and strong. The man who abstains from work, on the other hand, may be detected by his miserable appearance; he is blotched and puffy, and devoid of strength. This observation, I say, was not wasted on him. On the contrary, turning it over in his mind that any one who chooses, as a matter of private judgment, to devote himself to toil may hope to present a very creditable appearance physically, he enjoined upon the eldest for the time being in every gymnasium to see to it that the labours of the class were proportional to the meats. And to my mind he was not out of his reckoning in this matter more than elsewhere. At any rate, it would be hard to discover a healthier or more completely developed human being, physically speaking, than the Spartan. Their gymnastic training, in fact, makes demands alike on the legs, arms and neck equally.

6. There are other points in which this legislator's views run counter to those commonly accepted. Thus: in other states the individual citizen is master over his own children, servants and belongings generally; but Lycurgus, whose aim was to secure to all the citizens a considerable share in one another's goods without mutual injury, enacted that each one should have an equal power over his neighbour's children as over his own. The principle is this. When a man knows that this, that, and the other person are fathers of children subject to his own authority, he must perforce deal by them even as he desires his own children to be dealt by. And, if a boy chance to have received a whipping, not from his own father but some other, and goes and complains to his own father, it would be thought wrong on the part of that father if he did not inflict a second whipping on his son. A striking proof, in its way, how completely they trust each other not to impose dishonourable commands upon their children.

In the same way he empowered them to use their neighbour's servants in case of need. This communism he applied also to dogs used for the chase; in so far that a party in need of dogs will invite the owner to the chase, and if he is not at leisure to attend himself, at any rate he is happy to let his dogs go. The same applies to the use of horses. Some one has fallen sick perhaps, or is in want of a carriage, or is anxious to reach some point or other quickly—in any case he has a right, if he sees a horse anywhere, to take and use it, and restores it safe and sound when he has done with it.

And here is another institution attributed to Lycurgus which scarcely coincides with the customs elsewhere in vogue. A hunting party returns from the chase, belated. They want provisions—they have nothing prepared themselves. To meet this contingency he made it a rule that owners are to leave behind the food that has been dressed; and the party in need will open the seals, take out what they want, seal up the remainder, and leave it. Accordingly, by his system of give-and-take even those with next to nothing have a share in all that the country can supply, if ever they stand in need of anything.

7. There are yet other customs in Sparta which Lycurgus instituted in opposition to those of the rest of Hellas, and the following among them. We all know that in the generality of states every one devotes his full energy to the business of making money: one man as a tiller of the soil, another as a mariner, a third as a merchant, whilst others depend on various arts to earn a living. But at Sparta Lycurgus forbade his freeborn citizens to have anything whatsoever to do with the concerns of money-making. As freemen, he enjoined upon them to regard as their concern exclusively those activities upon which the foundations of civic liberty are based.

And indeed, one may well ask, for what reason should wealth be regarded as a matter for serious pursuit in a community where, partly by a system of equal contributions to the necessaries of life, and partly by the maintenance of a common standard of living, the lawgiver placed so effectual a check upon the desire for riches for the sake of luxury? What inducement, for instance, would there be to make money, even for the sake of wearing apparel, in a state where personal adornment is held to lie not in the costliness of the clothes they wear, but in the healthy condition of the body to be clothed? Nor again could there be much inducement to amass wealth, in order to be able to expend it on the members of a common mess, where the legislator had made it seem far more glorious that a man should help his fellows by the labour of his body than by costly outlay. The latter being, as he finely phrased it, the function of wealth, the former an activity of the soul.

He went a step farther, and set up a strong barrier (even in a society such as I have described) against the pursuance of money-making by wrongful means. In the first place, he established a coinage of so extraordinary a sort, that even a single sum of ten minas could not come into a house without attracting the notice, either of the master himself, or of some member of his household. In fact, it would occupy a considerable space, and need a waggon to carry it. Gold and silver themselves, moreover, are liable to search, and in case of detection, the possessor subjected to a penalty. In fact, to repeat the question asked above, for what reason should money-making become an earnest pursuit in a community where the possession of wealth entails more pain than its employment brings satisfaction?

8. But to proceed. We are all aware that there is no state in the world in which greater obedience is shown to magistrates, and to the laws themselves, than Sparta. But, for my part, I am disposed to think that Lycurgus could never have attempted to establish this healthy condition, until he had first secured the unanimity of the most powerful members of the state. I infer this for the following reasons. In other states the leaders in rank and influence do not even desire to be thought to fear the magistrates. Such a thing they would regard as in itself a symbol of servility. In Sparta, on the contrary, the stronger a man is the more readily does he bow before constituted authority. And indeed, they pride themselves on their humility, and on a prompt obedience, running, or at any rate not crawling with laggard step, at the word of command. Such an example of eager discipline, they are persuaded, set by themselves, will not fail to be followed by the rest. And this is precisely what has taken place. It is reasonable to suppose that it was these same noblest members of the state who combined to lay the foundation of the ephorate, after they had come to the conclusion themselves that of all the blessings which a state, or an army, or a household can enjoy, obedience is the greatest. Since, as they could not but reason, the greater the power with which men fence about authority, the greater the fascination it will exercise upon the mind of the citizen, to the enforcement of obedience.

Accordingly the ephors are competent to punish whomsoever they choose; they have power to exact fines on the spur of the moment; they have power to depose magistrates in mid career, nay, actually to imprison and bring them to trial on the capital charge. Entrusted with these vast powers, they do not, as do the rest of states, allow the magistrates elected to exercise authority as they like, right through the year of office; but, in the style rather of despotic monarchs, or presidents of the games, at the first symptom of an offence against the law they inflict chastisement without warning and without hesitation.

But of all the many beautiful contrivances invented by Lycurgus to kindle a willing obedience to the laws in the hearts of the citizens, none, to my mind, was happier or more excellent than his unwillingness to deliver his code to the people at large, until, attended by the most powerful members of the state, he had betaken himself to Delphi, and there made inquiry of the god whether it were better for Sparta, and conducive to her interests, to obey the laws which he had framed. And not until the divine answer came, "Better will it be in every way," did he deliver them, laying it down as a last ordinance that to refuse obedience to a code which had the sanction of the Pythian god himself was a thing not illegal only, but impious.

9. The following too may well excite our admiration for Lycurgus. I speak of the consummate skill with which he induced the whole state of Sparta to regard an honourable death as preferable to an ignoble life. And indeed if any one will investigate the matter, he will find that by comparison with those who make it a principle to retreat in face of danger, actually fewer of these Spartans die in battle, since, to speak truth, salvation, it would seem, attends on virtue far more frequently than on cowardice—virtue, which is at once easier and sweeter, richer in resource and stronger of arm, than her opposite. And that virtue has another familiar attendant—to wit, glory—needs no showing, since all wish to ally themselves somehow with the good.

Yet the actual means by which he gave currency to these principles is a point which it were well not to overlook. It is clear that the lawgiver set himself deliberately to provide all the blessings of heaven for the good man, and a sorry and ill-starred existence for the coward.

In other states the man who shows himself base and cowardly wins to himself an evil reputation and the nickname of a coward, but that is all. For the rest he buys and sells in the same market-place with the good man; he sits beside him at the play; he exercises with him in the same gymnasium, and all as suits his humour. But at Lacedaemon there is not one man who would not feel ashamed to welcome the coward at the common mess-table, or to try conclusions with such an antagonist in a wrestling bout. Consider the day's round of his existence. The sides are being picked for a game of ball, but he is left out as the odd man: there is no place for him. During the choric dance he is driven away into ignominious quarters. Nay, in the very streets it is he who must step aside for others to pass, or, being seated, he must rise and make room, even for a younger man. At home he will have his maiden relatives to support in their isolation (and they will hold him to blame for their unwedded lives). A hearth with no wife to bless it—that is a condition he must face, and yet he will have to pay damages for incurring it. Let him not roam abroad with a smiling countenance; let him not imitate men whose fame is irreproachable, or he shall feel on his back the blows of his superiors. Such being the weight of infamy which is laid upon all cowards, I, for my part, am not surprised if in Sparta they deem death preferable to a life so steeped in dishonour and reproach.

10. That too was a happy enactment, in my opinion, by which Lycurgus provided for the continual cultivation of virtue, even to old age. By

fixing the election to the council of elders as a last ordeal at the goal of life, he made it impossible for a high standard of virtuous living to be disregarded even in old age. (So, too, it is worthy of admiration in him that he lent his helping hand to virtuous old age. Thus, by making the elders sole arbiters in the trial for life, he contrived to charge old age with a greater weight of honour than that which is accorded to the strength of mature manhood.) And assuredly such a contest as this must appeal to the zeal of mortal man beyond all others in a supreme degree. Fair, doubtless, are contests of gymnastic skill, yet are they but trials of bodily excellence, but this contest for the seniory is of a higher sort—it is an ordeal of the soul itself. In proportion, therefore, as the soul is worthier than the body, so must these contests of the soul appeal to a stronger enthusiasm than their bodily antitypes.

And yet another point may well excite our admiration for Lycurgus largely. It had not escaped his observation that communities exist where those who are willing to make virtue their study and delight fail somehow in ability to add to the glory of their fatherland. That lesson the legislator laid to heart, and in Sparta he enforced, as a matter of public duty, the practice of every virtue by every citizen. And so it is that, just as man differs from man in some excellence, according as he cultivates or neglects to cultivate it, this city of Sparta, with good reason, outshines all other states in virtue; since she, and she alone, has made the attainment of a high standard of noble living a public duty.

And was not this a noble enactment, that whereas other states are content to inflict punishment only in cases where a man does wrong against his neighbour, Lycurgus imposed penalties no less severe on him who openly neglected to make himself as good as possible? For this, it seems, was his principle: in the one case, where a man is robbed, or defrauded, or kidnapped, and made a slave of, the injury of the misdeed, whatever it be, is personal to the individual so maltreated; but in the other case whole communities suffer foul treason at the hands of the base man and the coward. So that it was only reasonable, in my opinion, that he should visit the heaviest penalty upon these latter.

Moreover, he laid upon them, like some irresistible necessity, the obligation to cultivate the whole virtue of a citizen. Provided they duly performed the injunctions of the law, the city belonged to them, each and all, in absolute possession and on an equal footing. Weakness of limb or want of wealth was no drawback in his eyes. But as for him who, out of the cowardice of his heart, shrank from the performance of the law's injunction, the legislator pointed him out as disqualified to be regarded longer as a member of the brotherhood of peers.

It may be added that there is no doubt as to the great antiquity of this code of laws. The point is clear so far, that Lycurgus himself is said to have lived in the days of the Heracleidae. But being of so long standing, these laws, even at this day, still are stamped in the eyes of other men with all the novelty of youth. And the most marvellous thing of all is that, while everybody is agreed to praise these remarkable institutions, there is not a single state which cares to imitate them.

11. The above form a common stock of blessings, open to every Spartan to enjoy, alike in peace and in war. But if any one desires to be informed in what way the legislator improved upon the ordinary machinery of warfare and in reference to an army in the field, it is easy to satisfy his curiosity.

In the first instance, the ephors announce by proclamation the limit of age to which the service applies for cavalry and heavy infantry; and in the next place, for the various handicraftsmen. So that, even on active service, the Lacedaemonians are well supplied with all the conveniences enjoyed by people living as citizens at home. All implements and instruments whatsoever, which an army may need in common, are ordered to be in readiness, some on waggons and others on baggage animals. In this way anything omitted can hardly escape detection.

For the actual encounter under arms, the following inventions are attributed to him. The soldier has a crimson-coloured uniform and a heavy shield of bronze; his theory being that such an equipment has no sort of feminine association, and is altogether most warrior-like. It is most quickly burnished; it is least readily tarnished.

He further permitted those who were above the age of early manhood to wear their hair long. For so, he conceived, they would appear of larger stature, more free and indomitable, and of a more terrible aspect.

So furnished and accoutred, he divided his citizen soldiers into six *morae* (regimental divisions) of cavalry and heavy infantry. Each of these citizen regiments has one polemarch (colonel), four captains of companies, eight lieutenants, each in command of a half company, and sixteen commanders of sections. At the word of command any such regimental division can be formed readily either into single file or into three files abreast, or into six files abreast.

As to the idea, commonly entertained, that the tactical arrangement of the Laconian heavy infantry is highly complicated, no conception could be more opposed to fact. For in the Laconian order the front rank men are all leaders, so that each file has everything necessary to play its part efficiently. In fact, this disposition is so easy to understand that no one who can distinguish one human being from another could fail to follow it. One set have the privilege of leaders, the other the duty of followers. The evolutional orders, by which greater depth or shallowness is given to the battle line, are given by word of mouth by the commander of the section, who plays the part of the herald, and they cannot be mistaken. None of these manoeuvres presents any difficulty whatsoever to the understanding.

But when it comes to their ability to do battle equally well in spite of some confusion which has been set up, and whatever the chapter of accidents may confront them with, I admit that the tactics here are not so easy to understand, except for people trained under the laws of Lycurgus. Even movements which an instructor in heavy-armed warfare might look upon as difficult are performed by the Lacedaemonians with the utmost ease. Thus, the troops, we will suppose, are marching in column; one section of a company is of course stepping up behind another from the rear. Now, if at such a moment a hostile force appears in front in battle order, the word is passed down to the commander of each section, "Deploy into line to the left." And so throughout the whole length of the column, until the line is formed facing the enemy. Or supposing while in this position an enemy appears in the rear. Each file performs a counter-march with the effect of bringing the best men face to face with the enemy all along the line. As to the point that the leader previously on the right finds himself now on the left, they do not consider that they are necessarily losers thereby, but, as it may turn out, even gainers. If, for instance, the enemy attempted to turn their flank, he would find himself wrapping round, not their exposed, but their shielded flank. Or if, for any reason, it be thought advisable for the general to keep the right wing, they turn the corps about, and counter-march by ranks, until the leader is on the right, and the rear rank on the left. Or again, supposing a division of the enemy appears on the right while they are marching in column, they have nothing further to do but to wheel each company to the right, like a trireme, prow forwards, to meet the enemy, and thus the rear company again finds itself on the right. If, however, the enemy should attack on the left, either they will not allow of that and push him aside, or else they wheel their companies to the left to face the antagonist, and thus the rear company once more falls into position on the left.

12. I will now speak of the mode of encampment sanctioned by the regulation of Lycurgus. To avoid the waste incidental to the angles of a square, the encampment, according to him, should be circular, except where there was the security of a hill, or fortification, or where they had a river in their rear. He had sentinels posted during the day along the place of arms and facing inwards; since they are appointed not so much for the sake of the enemy as to keep an eye on friends. The enemy is sufficiently watched by mounted troopers perched on various points commanding the widest prospect.

To guard against hostile approach by night, sentinel duty according to the ordinance was performed by the Sciritae outside the main body. At the present time the rule is so far modified that the duty is entrusted to foreigners, if there be a foreign contingent present, with a leaven of Spartans themselves to keep them company.

The custom of always taking their spears with them when they go their rounds must certainly be attributed to the same cause which makes them exclude their slaves from the place of arms. Nor need we be surprised if, when retiring for necessary purposes, they only withdraw just far enough from one another, or from the place of arms itself, not to create annoyance. The need of precaution is the whole explanation.

The frequency with which they change their encampments is another point. It is done quite as much for the sake of benefiting their friends as of annoying their enemies.

Further, the law enjoins upon all Lacedaemonians, during the whole period of an expedition, the constant practice of gymnastic exercises, whereby their pride in themselves is increased, and they appear freer and of a more liberal aspect than the rest of the world. The walk and the running ground must not exceed in length the space covered by a regimental division, so that no one may find himself far from his own stand of arms. After the gymnastic exercises the senior polemarch gives the order by herald to be seated. This serves all the purposes of an inspection. After this the order is given to get breakfast, and for the outposts to be relieved. After this, again, come pastimes and relaxations before the evening exercises, after which the herald's cry is heard to take the evening meal. When they have sung a hymn to the gods to whom the offerings of happy omen have been performed, the final order, "Retire to rest at the place of arms," is given.

If the story is a little long the reader must not be surprised, since it would be difficult to find any point in military matters omitted by the Lacedaemonians which seems to demand attention.

13. I will now give a detailed account of the power and privilege assigned by Lycurgus to the king during a campaign. To begin with, so long as he is on active service, the state maintains the king and those with him. The polemarchs mess with him and share his quarters, so that by constant intercourse they may be all the better able to consult in common in case of need. Besides the polemarch three other members of the peers share the royal quarters. The duty of these is to attend to all matters of commissariat, in order that the king and the rest may have unbroken leisure to attend to affairs of actual warfare.

But I will resume at a somewhat higher point and describe the manner in which the king sets out on an expedition. As a preliminary step, before leaving home he offers sacrifice in company with his staff to Zeus the Leader, and if the victims prove favourable then and there the priest, who bears the sacred fire, takes thereof from off the altar and leads the way to the boundaries of the land. Here for the second time the king does sacrifice to Zeus and Athena; and as soon as the offerings are accepted by those two divinities he steps across the boundaries of the land. And all the while the fire from those sacrifices leads the way, and is never suffered to go out. Behind follow beasts for sacrifice of every sort.

Invariably when he offers sacrifice the king begins the work before the day has broken, being minded to anticipate the goodwill of the god. And round about the place of sacrifice are present the polemarchs and captains, the lieutenants and sub-lieutenants, with the commandants of the baggage train, and any general of the states who may care to assist. There, too, are to be seen two of the ephors, who never interfere, save only at the summons of the king, yet have they their eyes fixed on the proceedings of each one there and keep all in order, as may well be guessed. When the sacrifices are accomplished the king summons all and issues his orders as to what has to be done. And all with such method that, to witness the proceedings, you might fairly suppose the rest of the world to be but bungling experimenters, and the Lacedaemonians alone true handicraftsmen in the art of soldiering.

Then the king puts himself at the head of the troops, and if no enemy appears he heads the line of march, no one preceding him except the Sciritae, and the mounted troopers exploring in front. If, however, there is any reason to anticipate a battle, the king takes the leading column of the first army corps and wheels to the right until he has got into position with two army corps and two generals of division on either flank. The disposition of the supports is assigned to the eldest of the royal council acting as brigadier, the staff consisting of all peers who share the royal mess and quarters, with the soothsayers, surgeons, and flute-players, whose place is in the front of the troops, with, finally, any volunteers who happen to be present. So that there is no check or hesitation in anything to be done; every contingency is provided for.

The following details also seem to me of high utility among the inventions of Lycurgus with a view to the actual battle. Whenever, the enemy being now close enough to watch the proceedings, the goat is sacrificed; then, says the law, let all the flute-players, in their places, play upon the flutes, and let every Lacedaemonian don a wreath. Then, too, so runs the order, let the shields be brightly polished. The privilege is accorded to the young man to enter battle with his long locks combed. To be of a cheery countenance—that, too, is of good repute. Onwards they pass the word of command to the subaltern in command of his section, since it is impossible to hear along the whole of each section from the particular subaltern posted on the outside. It devolves, finally, on the polemarch to see that all goes well.

When the right moment for encamping has come, the king is responsible for that, and has to point out the proper place. The despatch of embassies, however, whether to friends or to foes, is not the king's affair. Petitioners in general wishing to transact anything treat, in the first instance, with the king. If the case concerns some point of justice, the king despatches the petitioner to the Hellanodicae (who form the court-martial); if of money, to the paymasters. If the petitioner brings booty, he is sent off to the sellers of spoil. This being the mode of procedure, no other duty is left to the king, while he is on active service, except to play the part of priest in matters concerning the gods and of commander-in-chief in his relationship to men.

14. Now, if the question be put to me whether the laws of Lycurgus remain still to this day unchanged, that indeed is an assertion which I should no longer venture to maintain; knowing, as I do, that in former times the Lacedaemonians preferred to live at home on moderate means, content to associate exclusively with themselves rather than to play the part of governor-general in foreign states and to be corrupted by flattery; knowing further, as I do, that formerly they dreaded to be detected in the possession of gold, whereas nowadays there are not a few who make it their glory and their boast to be possessed of it. I am very well aware that in former days alien acts were put in force for this very object. To live abroad was not allowed. And why? Simply in order that the citizens of Sparta might not take the infection of dishonesty and light-living from foreigners; whereas now I am very well aware that those who are reputed to be leading citizens have but one ambition, and that is to live to the end of their days as governors-general on a foreign soil. The days were when their sole anxiety was to fit themselves to lead the rest of Hellas. But nowadays they concern themselves much more to wield command than to be fit themselves to rule. And so it has come to pass that whereas in old days the states of Hellas flocked to Lacedaemon seeking her leadership against the supposed wrongdoer, now numbers are inviting one another to prevent the Lacedaemonians again recovering their empire. Yet, if they have incurred all these reproaches, we need not wonder, seeing that they are so plainly disobedient to the god himself and to the laws of their own lawgiver Lycurgus.

15. I wish to explain with sufficient detail the nature of the covenant between king and state as instituted by Lycurgus; for this, I take it, is the sole type of rule which still preserves the original form in which it was first established; whereas other constitutions will be found either to have been already modified or else to be still undergoing modifications at this moment.

Lycurgus laid it down as law that the king shall offer in behalf of the state all public sacrifices, as being himself of divine descent, and whithersoever the state shall despatch her armies the king shall take the lead. He granted him to receive honorary gifts of the things offered in sacrifice, and he appointed him choice land in many of the provincial cities, enough to satisfy moderate needs without excess of wealth. And in order that the kings also might camp and mess in public he appointed them public quarters; and he honoured them with a double portion each at the evening meal, not in order that they might actually eat twice as much as others, but that the king might have wherewithal to honour whomsoever he desired. He also granted as a gift to each of the two kings to choose two mess-fellows, which same are called Pythii. He also granted them to receive out of every litter of swine one pig, so that the king might never be at a loss for victims if he wished to consult the gods.

Close by the palace a lake affords an unrestricted supply of water; and how useful that is for various purposes they best can tell who lack the luxury. Moreover, all rise from their seats to give place to the king, save only that the ephors rise not from their thrones of office. Monthly they exchange oaths, the ephors in behalf of the state, the king himself in his own behalf. And this is the oath on the king's part, "I will exercise my kingship in accordance with the established laws of the state." And on the part of the State the oath runs, "so long as he (who exercises kingship) shall abide by his oath we will not suffer his kingdom to be shaken."

These then are the honours bestowed upon the king during his lifetime at home, honours by no means much exceeding those of private citizens, since the lawgiver was minded neither to suggest to the kings the pride of the despotic monarch, nor, on the other hand, to engender in the heart of the citizen envy of their power. As to those other honours which are given to the king at his death, the laws of Lycurgus would seem plainly to signify hereby that these kings of Lacedaemon are not mere mortals but heroic beings, and that is why they are preferred in honour.

THE CONSTITUTION OF ATHENS

By Aristotle

We are indebted to the sands of Egypt for this treatise which had been lost for centuries. First published in 1891, it has been much studied by scholars since then and has contributed much that is of value to our knowledge of Athenian history. The sketch of constitutional and political history in the first forty-one chapters has added considerably to our information on many disputed points, and the remaining chapters, on the constitution in the fourth century, provide a clear picture of the Athenian government in Aristotle's own day. Chapter 54, in which the archon of 329 B.C. is mentioned, indicates that the work was written or, more probably, revised after that date. It is one of the 158 constitutions of Greek City States which Aristotle studied in preparation for the writing of the Politics. In a number of passages Aristotle's indebtedness to Herodotus, Thucydides, and Xenophon can be traced, although his efforts to correct them on occasion show that he was never disposed to accept their authority uncritically.

In the sphere of actual politics Aristotle shows a clear preference for aristocracy but he realizes that it does not represent the perfect state, and may be turned into Oligarchy which is inferior to Democracy, the perverted form of true constitutional government.

1. . . . [They[1] were tried] by a court empanelled from among the noble families, and sworn upon the sacrifices. The part of accuser was taken by Myron. They were found guilty of the sacrilege, and their bodies were cast out of their graves and their race banished for ever-

---

[1] The narrative opens with the trial of the Alcmeonidae for sacrilege. Cylon, a young noble, had attempted to seize despotic power by force; but his attempt failed, and his adherents fled to sanctuary, which they were only induced to leave under a safe conduct. This was violated by the archon Megacles, one of the great house of the Alcmeonidae, who caused them all to be put to death; a sacrilege which was supposed to be the cause of the misfortunes which subsequently befell Athens, until the Alcmeonidae submitted themselves to trial. The date of Cylon's attempt to set himself up as tyrant is shown by this treatise to have been before the time of Draco; and, as Cylon was an Olympic victor in 640 B.C., and was apparently still a young man at the time of his attempt, the latter (which took place in an Olympic year) may be assigned to 632 B.C. The expulsion of the Alcmeonidae did not take place till many years afterwards; the visit of Epimenides probably took place about 596 B.C., shortly before the legislation of Solon. Aristotle is here carrying down the story of Cylon's attempt to its conclusion, and he subsequently goes back to the reforms of Draco.

more. In view of this expiation, Epimenides the Cretan performed a purification of the city.

2. After this event there was contention for a long time between the upper classes and the populace. Not only was the constitution at this time oligarchical in every respect, but the poorer classes, men, women, and children, were the serfs of the rich. They were known as Pelatae and also as Hectemori,[2] because they cultivated the lands of the rich at the rent thus indicated. The whole country was in the hands of a few persons, and if the tenants failed to pay their rent they were liable to be haled into slavery, and their children with them. All loans were secured upon the debtor's person, a custom which prevailed until the time of Solon, who was the first to appear as the champion of the people. But the hardest and bitterest part of the constitution in the eyes of the masses was their state of serfdom. Not but what they were also discontented with every other feature of their lot; for, to speak generally, they had no part nor share in anything.

3. Now the ancient constitution, as it existed before the time of Draco, was organised as follows. The magistrates were elected according to qualifications of birth and wealth. At first they governed for life, but subsequently for terms of ten years. The first magistrates, both in date and in importance, were the King, the Polemarch, and the Archon. The earliest of these offices was that of the King, which existed from ancestral antiquity. To this was added, secondly, the office of Polemarch, on account of some of the kings proving feeble in war; for it was on this account that Ion was invited to accept the post on an occasion of pressing need. The last of the three offices was that of the Archon, which most authorities state to have come into existence in the time of Medon. Others assign it to the time of Acastus, and adduce as proof the fact that the nine Archons swear to execute their oaths 'as in the days of Acastus', which seems to suggest that it was in his time that the descendants of Codrus retired from the kingship in return for the prerogatives conferred upon the Archon. Whichever way it be, the difference in date is small; but that it was the last of these magistracies to be created is shown by the fact that the Archon has no part in the ancestral sacrifices, as the King and the Polemarch have, but exclusively in those of later origin. So it is only at a comparatively late date that the office of Archon has become of great importance, through the dignity conferred by these later additions. The Thesmothetae[3] were appointed many years afterwards, when these offices had already become annual, with the object that they might publicly record all legal decisions, and act as guardians of them with a view to determining the issues between litigants. Accordingly

[2] i.e. those who paid a sixth portion.
[3] The six junior Archons.

their office, alone of those which have been mentioned, was never of more than annual duration.

Such, then, is the relative chronological precedence of these offices. At that time the nine Archons did not all live together. The King occupied the building now known as the Bucolium, near the Prytaneum, as may be seen from the fact that even to the present day the marriage of the King's wife to Dionysus[4] takes place there. The Archon lived in the Prytaneum, the Polemarch in the Epilyceum. The latter building was formerly called the Polemarcheum, but after Epilycus, during his term of office as Polemarch, had rebuilt it and fitted it up, it was called the Epilyceum. The Thesmothetae occupied the Thesmotheteum. In the time of Solon, however, they all came together into the Thesmotheteum. They had power to decide cases finally on their own authority, not, as now, merely to hold a preliminary hearing. Such then was the arrangement of the magistracies. The Council of Areopagus had as its constitutionally assigned duty the protection of the laws; but in point of fact it administered the greater and most important part of the government of the state, and inflicted personal punishments and fines summarily upon all who misbehaved themselves. This was the natural consequence of the facts that the Archons were elected under qualifications of birth and wealth, and that the Areopagus was composed of those who had served as Archons; for which latter reason the membership of the Areopagus is the only office which has continued to be a life-magistracy to the present day.

4. Such was, in outline, the first constitution, but not very long after the events above recorded, in the archonship of Aristaichmus,[5] Draco enacted his ordinances. Now his constitution had the following form. The franchise was given to all who could furnish themselves with a military equipment. The nine Archons and the Treasurers were elected by this body from persons possessing an unencumbered property of not less than ten minas, the less important officials from those who could furnish themselves with a military equipment, and the generals (Strategi) and commanders of the cavalry (Hipparchi) from those who could show an unencumbered property of not less than a hundred minas, and had children born in lawful wedlock over ten years of age. These officers were required to hold to bail the Prytanes, the Strategi, and the Hipparchi of the preceding year until their accounts had been audited, taking four securities of the same class as that to which the Strategi and the Hipparchi belonged. There was also to be a Council, consisting of 401 members,

[4] The wife of the King-archon every year went through the ceremony of marriage to the god Dionysus, at the feast of the Anthesteria.
[5] The name of this Archon is not otherwise known, but the traditional date of Draco is 621 B.C.

elected by lot from among those who possessed the franchise. Both for this and for the other magistracies[6] the lot was cast among those who were over thirty years of age; and no one might hold office twice until every one else had had his turn, after which they were to cast the lot afresh. If any member of the Council failed to attend when there was a sitting of the Council or of the Assembly, he paid a fine, to the amount of three drachmas if he was a Pentacosiomedimnus,[7] two if he was a Knight, and one if he was a Zeugites. The Council of Areopagus was guardian of the laws, and kept watch over the magistrates to see that they executed their offices in accordance with the laws. Any person who felt himself wronged might lay an information before the Council of Areopagus, on declaring what law was broken by the wrong done to him. But, as has been said before, loans were secured upon the persons of the debtors, and the land was in the hands of a few.

5. Since such, then, was the organisation of the constitution, and the many were in slavery to the few, the people rose against the upper class. The strife was keen, and for a long time the two parties were ranged in hostile camps against one another, till at last,[8] by common consent, they appointed Solon to be mediator and Archon, and committed the whole constitution to his hands. The immediate occasion of his appointment was his poem, which begins with the words:

I behold, and within my heart deep sadness has claimed its place,
As I mark the oldest home of the ancient Ionian race
Slain by the sword.[9]

In this poem he fights and disputes on behalf of each party in turn against the other, and finally he advises them to come to terms and put an end to the quarrel existing between them. By birth and reputation Solon was one of the foremost men of the day, but in wealth and position he was of the middle class, as is generally agreed, and is, indeed, established by his own evidence in these poems, where he exhorts the wealthy not to be grasping.

But ye who have store of good, who are sated and overflow,
Restrain your swelling soul, and still it and keep it low:
Let the heart that is great within you be trained a lowlier way;
Ye shall not have all at your will, and we will not for ever obey.

---

[6] This does not mean that all the magistrates were at this time elected by lot, which certainly was not the case.

[7] The meanings of these terms are explained in ch. 7, 4.

[8] The traditional date for Solon's legislation is 594 B.C.

[9] A passage of considerable length, which evidently comes from the same poem, is quoted by Demosthenes (*de Fals. Leg.* 255), but this beginning of it is not otherwise known, nor yet the four lines quoted just below.

Indeed, he constantly fastens the blame of the conflict on the rich; and accordingly at the beginning of the poem he says that he fears 'the love of wealth and an overweening mind', evidently meaning that it was through these that the quarrel arose.

6. As soon as he was at the head of affairs, Solon liberated the people once and for all, by prohibiting all loans on the security of the debtor's person; and in addition he made laws by which he cancelled all debts, public and private. This measure is commonly called the Seisachtheia (removal of burdens), since thereby the people had their loads removed from them. In connexion with it some persons try to traduce the character of Solon. It so happened that, when he was about to enact the Seisachtheia, he communicated his intention to some members of the upper class, whereupon, as the partisans of the popular party say, his friends stole a march on him; while those who wish to attack his character maintain that he too had a share in the fraud himself. For these persons borrowed money and bought up a large amount of land, and so when, a short time afterwards, all debts were cancelled, they became wealthy; and this, they say, was the origin of the families which were afterwards looked on as having been wealthy from primeval times. However, the story of the popular party is by far the most probable. A man who was so moderate and public-spirited in all his other actions, that, when it was within his power to put his fellow-citizens beneath his feet and establish himself as tyrant, he preferred instead to incur the hostility of both parties by placing his honour and the general welfare above his personal aggrandisement, is not likely to have consented to defile his hands by such a petty and palpable fraud. That he had this absolute power is, in the first place, indicated by the desperate condition of the country; moreover, he mentions it himself repeatedly in his poems, and it is universally admitted. We are therefore bound to consider this accusation to be false.

7. Next Solon drew up a constitution and enacted new laws; and the ordinances of Draco ceased to be used, with the exception of those relating to murder. The laws were inscribed on the wooden stands, and set up in the King's Porch, and all swore to obey them; and the nine Archons made oath upon the stone, declaring that they would dedicate a golden statue if they should transgress any of them. This is the origin of the oath to that effect which they take to the present day. Solon ratified his laws for 100 years; and the following was the fashion in which he organised the constitution. He divided the population according to property into four classes, just as it had been divided before, namely, Pentacosiomedimni, Knights, Zeugitae, and Thetes. The various magistracies, namely, the nine Archons, the Treasurers, the Commissioners for Public

Contracts, the Eleven,[10] and the Exchequer Clerks,[11] he assigned to the Pentacosiomedimni, the Knights, and the Zeugitae, giving offices to each class in proportion to the value of their rateable property. To those who ranked among the Thetes he gave nothing but a place in the Assembly and in the juries. A man had to rank as a Pentacosiomedimnus if he made, from his own land, 500 measures, whether liquid or solid. Those ranked as Knights who made 300 measures, or, as some say, those who were able to maintain a horse. In support of the latter definition they adduce the name of the class, which may be supposed to be derived from this fact, and also some votive offerings of early times; for in the Acropolis there is a votive offering, a statue of Diphilus, bearing this inscription:

> The son of Diphilus, Anthemion hight,
> Raised from the Thetes and become a Knight,
> Did to the gods this sculptured charger bring,
> For his promotion a thank-offering.

And a horse stands in evidence beside the man, implying that this was what was meant by belonging to the rank of Knight. At the same time it seems reasonable to suppose that this class, like the Pentacosiomedimni, was defined by the possession of an income of a certain number of measures. Those ranked as Zeugitae who made 200 measures, liquid or solid; and the rest ranked as Thetes, and were not eligible for any office. Hence it is that even at the present day, when a candidate for any office is asked to what class he belongs, no one would think of saying that he belonged to the Thetes.

8. The elections to the various offices Solon enacted should be by lot, out of candidates selected by each of the tribes. Each tribe selected ten candidates for the nine archonships, and among these the lot was cast. Hence it is still the custom for each tribe to choose ten candidates by lot, and then the lot is again cast among these. A proof that Solon regulated the elections to office according to the property classes may be found in the law still in force with regard to the Treasurers, which enacts that they shall be chosen from the Pentacosiomedimni.[11a] Such was Solon's legislation with respect to the nine Archons; whereas in early times the Council of Areopagus[11b] summoned suitable persons according to its own

[10] The superintendents of the state prison.

[11] These officers, whose original function was said to have been to 'collect the pieces after a sacrifice', were the Treasury officials in early times, who received the taxes and handed them over to be kept by the Treasurers. In later times the Colacretae seem to have ceased to exist, and they are not mentioned in Aristotle's enumeration of the officials in his own day.

[11a] That this qualification was, in Aristotle's own time, purely nominal appears from ch. 47, 1.

[11b] This statement is of great value, as nothing was previously known concerning the way in which the Archons and other magistrates were appointed previous to the time

judgment and appointed them for the year to the several offices. There were four tribes, as before, and four tribe-kings. Each tribe was divided into Thirds with twelve Naucraries[12] in each; and the Naucraries had officers of their own, called Naucrari, whose duty it was to superintend the current receipts and expenditure. Hence, among the laws of Solon now obsolete, it is repeatedly written that the Naucrari are to receive and to spend out of the Naucraric fund. Solon also appointed a Council of 400—100 from each tribe; but he assigned to the Council of the Areopagus the duty of superintending the laws, acting as before as the guardian of the constitution in general. It kept watch over the affairs of the state in most of the more important matters, and corrected offenders, with full powers to inflict either fines or personal punishment. The money received in fines it brought up into the Acropolis, without assigning the reason for the mulct. It also tried those who conspired for the overthrow of the state, Solon having enacted a process of impeachment to deal with such offenders. Further, since he saw the state often engaged in internal disputes, while many of the citizens from sheer indifference accepted whatever might turn up, he made a law with express reference to such persons, enacting that any one who, in a time of civil factions, did not take up arms with either party, should lose his rights as a citizen and cease to have any part in the state.

9. Such, then, was his legislation concerning the magistracies. There are three points in the constitution of Solon which appear to be its most democratic features: first and most important, the prohibition of loans on the security of the debtor's person; secondly, the right of every person who so willed to claim redress on behalf of any one to whom wrong was being done; thirdly, the institution of the appeal to the jury-courts; and it is to this last, they say, that the masses have owed their strength most of all, since, when the democracy is master of the voting-power, it is master of the constitution. Moreover, since the laws were not drawn up in simple and explicit terms (but like the one concerning inheritances and wards of state), disputes inevitably occurred, and the courts had to decide in every matter, whether public or private. Some persons in fact believe that Solon deliberately made the laws indefinite, in order that the final decision might be in the hands of the people. This, however, is not

---

of Solon. The elections by the Areopagus, which may have begun as early as the first successors of Codrus, apparently lasted till the reforms of Draco, by which the franchise was conferred on all who could furnish a military equipment, and the magistrates were presumably thenceforward elected in the general Ecclesia or Assembly.

[12] It appears from ch. 21, 5 that the Naucraries were local divisions, which, under the constitution of Cleisthenes, were replaced by the demes. The division of tribes into Trittyes and Naucraries existed before the time of Solon, as appears from Herodotus (v. 71), and they are only mentioned here as continuing under Solon's constitution, not as created by him.

probable, and the reason no doubt was that it is impossible to attain ideal perfection when framing a law in general terms; for we must judge of his intentions, not from the actual results in the present day, but from the general tenor of the rest of his legislation.

10. These seem to be the democratic features of his laws; but in addition, before the period of his legislation, he carried through his abolition of debts, and after it his increase in the standards of weights and measures, and of the currency. During his administration the measures were made larger than those of Pheidon, and the mina, which previously had a standard of seventy drachmas, was raised to the full hundred.[13] The standard coin in earlier times was the two-drachma piece. He also made weights corresponding with the coinage, sixty-three minas going to the talent; and the odd three minas were distributed among the staters and the other values.

11. When he had completed his organisation of the constitution in the manner that has been described, he found himself beset by people coming to him and harassing him concerning his laws, criticising here and questioning there, till, as he wished neither to alter what he had decided on nor yet to be an object of ill will to every one by remaining in Athens, he set off on a journey to Egypt, with the combined objects of trade and travel, giving out that he should not return for ten years. He considered that there was no call for him to expound the laws personally, but that every one should obey them just as they were written. Moreover, his position at this time was unpleasant. Many members of the upper class had been estranged from him on account of his abolition of debts, and both parties were alienated through their disappointment at the condition of things which he had created. The mass of the people had expected him to make a complete redistribution of all property, and the upper class hoped he would restore everything to its former position, or, at any rate, make but a small change. Solon, however, had resisted both classes. He might have made himself a despot by attaching himself to whichever party he chose, but he preferred, though at the cost of incurring the enmity of both, to be the saviour of his country and the ideal lawgiver.

12. The truth of this view of Solon's policy is established alike by common consent, and by the mention he has himself made of the matter in his poems. Thus:

I gave to the mass of the people such rank as befitted their need,
I took not away their honour, and I granted naught to their greed;

---

[13] This is a somewhat curious way of expressing the fact that Solon substituted the Euboic for the Aeginetan standard of coinage. Each mina had 100 drachmas in its own standard, but the weight of the Aeginetan mina was only equivalent to seventy Euboic drachmas. The object of the change was to encourage trade with the great commercial cities of Euboea and with Corinth.

While those who were rich in power, who in wealth were glorious and
    great,
I bethought me that naught should befall them unworthy their splendour
    and state;
So I stood with my shield outstretched, and both were safe in its sight,
And I would not that either should triumph, when the triumph was not
    with right.

Again he declares how the mass of the people ought to be treated:

But thus will the people best the voice of their leaders obey,
When neither too slack is the rein, nor violence holdeth the sway;
For indulgence breedeth a child, the presumption that spurns control,
When riches too great are poured upon men of unbalanced soul.

And again elsewhere he speaks about the persons who wished to redis-
tribute the land:

So they came in search of plunder, and their cravings knew no bound,
Every one among them deeming endless wealth would here be found.
And that I with glozing smoothness hid a cruel mind within.
Fondly then and vainly dreamt they; now they raise an angry din,
And they glare askance in anger, and the light within their eyes
Burns with hostile flames upon me. Yet therein no justice lies.
All I promised, fully wrought I with the gods at hand to cheer,
Naught beyond in folly ventured. Never to my soul was dear
With a tyrant's force to govern, nor to see the good and base
Side by side in equal portion share the rich home of our race.

Once more he speaks of the abolition of debts and of those who before
were in servitude, but were released owing to the Seisachtheia:

    Of all the aims for which I summoned forth
    The people, was there one I compassed not?
    Thou, when slow time brings justice in its train,
    O mighty mother of the Olympian gods,
    Dark Earth, thou best canst witness, from whose breast
    I swept the pillars[14] broadcast planted there,
    And made thee free, who hadst been slave of yore.
    And many a man whom fraud or law had sold
    Far from his god-built land, an outcast slave,
    I brought again to Athens; yea, and some,
    Exiles from home through debt's oppressive load,
    Speaking no more the dear Athenian tongue,
    But wandering far and wide, I brought again;
    And those that here in vilest slavery

[14] These were the pillars set up on mortgaged lands, to record the fact of the en-
cumbrance.

> Crouched 'neath a master's frown, I set them free.
> Thus might and right were yoked in harmony,
> Since by the force of law I won my ends
> And kept my promise. Equal laws I gave
> To evil and to good, with even hand
> Drawing straight justice for the lot of each.
> But had another held the goad as I,
> One in whose heart was guile and greediness,
> He had not kept the people back from strife.
> For had I granted, now what pleased the one,
> Then what their foes devised in counterpoise,
> Of many a man this state had been bereft.
> Therefore I showed my might on every side,
> Turning at bay like wolf among the hounds.

And again he reviles both parties for their grumblings in the times that followed:

> Nay, if one must lay blame where blame is due,
> Wer't not for me, the people ne'er had set
> Their eyes upon these blessings e'en in dreams:
> While greater men, the men of wealthier life,
> Should praise me and should court me as their friend.

For had any other man, he says, received his exalted post,

> He had not kept the people back, nor ceased
> Till he had robbed the richness of the milk.
> But I stood forth a landmark in the midst,
> And barred the foes from battle.

13. Such, then, were Solon's reasons for his departure from the country. After his retirement the city was still torn by divisions. For four years, indeed, they lived in peace; but in the fifth year after Solon's government they were unable to elect an Archon on account of their dissensions, and again four years later they elected no Archon for the same reason. Subsequently, after a similar period had elapsed, Damasias was elected Archon;[15] and he governed for two years and two months, until he was forcibly expelled from his office. After this it was agreed, as a compromise, to elect ten Archons, five from the Eupatridae, three from the Agroeci, and two from the Demiurgi;[16] and they ruled for the year following Damasias. It is clear from this that the Archon was at the time the magistrate who possessed the greatest power, since it is always in

[15] Probably in 582 B.C.; but several varieties of calculation are possible, and some editors omit the words 'after a similar period had elapsed'.

[16] Eupatridae, the aristocrats; Agroeci, the country, or agricultural, party; Demiurgi, the handworkers, or labour party.

connection with this office that conflicts are seen to arise. But altogether they were in a continual state of internal disorder. Some found the cause and justification of their discontent in the abolition of debts, because thereby they had been reduced to poverty; others were dissatisfied with the political constitution, because it had undergone a revolutionary change; while with others the motive was found in personal rivalries among themselves. The parties at this time were three in number. First there was the party of the Shore, led by Megacles the son of Alcmeon, which was considered to aim at a moderate form of government; then there were the men of the Plain, who desired an oligarchy and were led by Lycurgus; and thirdly there were the men of the Highlands, at the head of whom was Pisistratus, who was looked on as an extreme democrat. This latter party was reinforced by those who had been deprived of the debts due to them, from motives of poverty, and by those who were not of pure descent, from motives of personal apprehension.[17] A proof of this is seen in the fact that after the tyranny was overthrown a revision was made of the citizen-roll, on the ground that many persons were partaking in the franchise without having a right to it. The names given to the respective parties were derived from the districts in which they held their lands.

14. Pisistratus had the reputation of being an extreme democrat, and he also had distinguished himself greatly in the war with Megara. Taking advantage of this, he wounded himself, and by representing that his injuries had been inflicted on him by his political rivals, he persuaded the people, through a motion proposed by Aristion, to grant him a bodyguard. After he had got these 'club-bearers', as they were called, he made an attack with them on the people and seized the Acropolis. This happened in the archonship of Comeas, thirty-one years after the legislation of Solon. It is related that, when Pisistratus asked for his bodyguard, Solon opposed the request, and declared that in so doing he proved himself wiser than half the people and braver than the rest, wiser than those who did not see that Pisistratus designed to make himself tyrant, and braver than those who saw it and kept silence. But when all his words availed nothing he carried forth his armour and set it up in front of his house, saying that he had helped his country so far as lay in his power (he was already a very old man), and that he called on all others to do the same. Solon's exhortations, however, proved fruitless, and Pisistratus assumed the sovereignty. His administration was more like a constitutional government than the rule of a tyrant; but before his power was firmly established, the adherents of Megacles and Lycurgus made a coalition and drove him out. This took place in the archonship of Hegesias, five years

[17] Lest their right to the franchise should be disputed, as it in fact was after the fall of the Pisistratidae.

after the first establishment of his rule. Eleven years later[18] Megacles, being in difficulties in a party struggle, again opened negotiations with Pisistratus, proposing that the latter should marry his daughter; and on these terms he brought him back to Athens, by a very primitive and simple-minded device. He first spread abroad a rumour that Athena was bringing back Pisistratus, and then, having found a woman of great stature and beauty, named Phye (according to Herodotus, of the deme of Paeania, but as others say a Thracian flower-seller of the deme of Collytus), he dressed her in a garb resembling that of the goddess and brought her into the city with Pisistratus. The latter drove in on a chariot with the woman beside him, and the inhabitants of the city, struck with awe, received him with adoration.

15. In this manner did his first return take place. He did not, however, hold his power long, for about six years after his return he was again expelled. He refused to treat the daughter of Megacles as his wife, and being afraid, in consequence, of a combination of the two opposing parties, he retired from the country. First he led a colony to a place called Rhaicelus, in the region of the Thermaic gulf; and thence he passed to the country in the neighbourhood of Mt. Pangaeus. Here he acquired wealth and hired mercenaries; and not till ten years had elapsed did he return to Eretria and make an attempt to recover the government by force. In this he had the assistance of many allies, notably the Thebans and Lygdamis of Naxos, and also the Knights who held the supreme power in the constitution of Eretria. After his victory in the battle at Pallene he captured Athens, and when he had disarmed the people he at last had his tyranny securely established, and was able to take Naxos and set up Lygdamis as ruler there. He effected the disarmament of the people in the following manner. He ordered a parade in full armour in the Theseum, and began to make a speech to the people. He spoke for a short time, until the people called out that they could not hear him, whereupon he bade them come up to the entrance of the Acropolis, in order that his voice might be better heard. Then, while he continued to

[18] There is some error in Aristotle's chronology of the life of Pisistratus, for while he states below that, of the thirty-three years between his first accession and his death, nineteen were spent in possession of the tyranny and fourteen in exile, in the actual enumeration of years he gives twenty-one years of exile and consequently only twelve of rule, of which only one can be assigned to his last period of government, which is always spoken of as the longest. It is therefore tolerably certain that one of the periods of exile is wrongly dated; and as the ten years of the second exile are confirmed by Herodotus, it may be concluded that the eleven years here assigned to the first exile are wrong, and should be reduced to four. It should be noticed that in the *Politics* it is stated that Pisistratus was actually in power only seventeen years out of the thirty-three; but this would reduce the duration of his third tenure of power lower than is at all probable, unless we suppose that the length of the two earlier terms is wrongly given here. For a statement of the various solutions offered by different commentators, see Sandys *ad loc.*

speak to them at great length, men whom he had appointed for the purpose collected the arms and locked them up in the chambers of the Theseum hard by, and came and made a signal to him that it was done. Pisistratus accordingly, when he had finished the rest of what he had to say, told the people also what had happened to their arms; adding that they were not to be surprised or alarmed, but go home and attend to their private affairs, while he would himself for the future manage all the business of the state.

16. Such was the origin and such the vicissitudes of the tyranny of Pisistratus. His administration was temperate, as has been said before, and more like constitutional government than a tyranny. Not only was he in every respect humane and mild and ready to forgive those who offended, but, in addition, he advanced money to the poorer people to help them in their labours, so that they might make their living by agriculture. In this he had two objects, first that they might not spend their time in the city but might be scattered over all the face of the country, and secondly that, being moderately well off and occupied with their own business, they might have neither the wish nor the time to attend to public affairs. At the same time his revenues were increased by the thorough cultivation of the country, since he imposed a tax of one tenth on all the produce. For the same reasons he instituted the local justices, and often made expeditions in person into the country to inspect it and to settle disputes between individuals, that they might not come into the city and neglect their farms. It was in one of these progresses that, as the story goes, Pisistratus had his adventure with the man of Hymettus, who was cultivating the spot afterwards known as 'Tax-free Farm'. He saw a man digging and working at a very stony piece of ground, and being surprised he sent his attendant to ask what he got out of this plot of land. 'Aches and pains', said the man; 'and that's what Pisistratus ought to have his tenth of'. The man spoke without knowing who his questioner was; but Pisistratus was so pleased with his frank speech and his industry that he granted him exemption from all taxes. And so in matters in general he burdened the people as little as possible with his government, but always cultivated peace and kept them in all quietness. Hence the tyranny of Pisistratus was often spoken of proverbially as 'the age of gold'; for when his sons succeeded him the government became much harsher. But most important of all in this respect was his popular and kindly disposition. In all things he was accustomed to observe the laws, without giving himself any exceptional privileges. Once he was summoned on a charge of homicide before the Areopagus, and he appeared in person to make his defence; but the prosecutor was afraid to present himself and abandoned the case. For these reasons he held power long, and whenever he was expelled he regained his position easily. The

majority alike of the upper class and of the people were in his favour; the former he won by his social intercourse with them, the latter by the assistance which he gave to their private purses, and his nature fitted him to win the hearts of both. Moreover, the laws in reference to tyrants at that time in force at Athens were very mild, especially the one which applies more particularly to the establishment of a tyranny. The law ran as follows, "These are the ancestral statutes of the Athenians; if any persons shall make an attempt to establish a tyranny, or if any person shall join in setting up a tyranny, he shall lose his civic rights, both himself and his whole house."

17. Thus did Pisistratus grow old in the possession of power, and he died a natural death in the archonship of Philoneos,[19] thirty-three years from the time at which he first established himself as tyrant, during nineteen of which he was in possession of power; the rest he spent in exile. It is evident from this that the story is mere gossip which states that Pisistratus was the youthful favourite of Solon and commanded in the war against Megara for the recovery of Salamis. It will not harmonise with their respective ages, as any one may see who will reckon up the years of the life of each of them, and the dates at which they died. After the death of Pisistratus his sons took up the government, and conducted it on the same system. He had two sons by his first and legitimate[20] wife, Hippias and Hipparchus, and two by his Argive consort, Iophon and Hegesistratus, who was surnamed Thessalus. For Pisistratus took a wife from Argos, Timonassa, the daughter of a man of Argos, named Gorgilus; she had previously been the wife of Archinus of Ambracia, one of the descendants of Cypselus. This was the origin of his friendship with the Argives, on account of which 1,000 of them were brought over by Hegesistratus and fought on his side in the battle at Pallene. Some authorities say that this marriage took place after his first expulsion from Athens, others while he was in possession of the government.

18. Hippias and Hipparchus assumed the control of affairs on grounds alike of standing and of age; but Hippias, as being also naturally of a statesmanlike and shrewd disposition, was really the head of the government. Hipparchus was youthful in disposition, amorous, and fond of literature (it was he who invited to Athens Anacreon, Simonides, and the other poets), while Thessalus was much junior in age, and was violent and headstrong in his behaviour. It was from his character that all the evils arose which befell the house.[21] He became enamoured of

---

[19] 527 B.C.

[20] Pisistratus' second wife was a foreigner, and therefore not legitimate according to strict Athenian law.

[21] This is a direct contradiction of the narrative of Thucydides (vi. 54), who makes Hipparchus responsible for the outrage which provoked the plot of Harmodius and Aristogeiton. It is impossible to say positively which is right. The exact details would

Harmodius, and, since he failed to win his affection, he lost all restraint upon his passion, and in addition to other exhibitions of rage he finally prevented the sister of Harmodius from taking the part of a basket-bearer in the Panathenaic procession, alleging as his reason that Harmodius was a person of loose life. Thereupon, in a frenzy of wrath, Harmodius and Aristogeiton did their celebrated deed, in conjunction with a number of confederates.[22] But while they were lying in wait for Hippias in the Acropolis at the time of the Panathenaea (Hippias, at this moment, was awaiting the arrival of the procession, while Hipparchus was organising its dispatch) they saw one of the persons privy to the plot talking familiarly with him. Thinking that he was betraying them, and desiring to do something before they were arrested, they rushed down and made their attempt without waiting for the rest of their confederates. They succeeded in killing Hipparchus near the Leocoreum while he was engaged in arranging the procession, but ruined the design as a whole; of the two leaders, Harmodius was killed on the spot by the guards, while Aristogeiton was arrested, and perished later after suffering long tortures. While under the torture he accused many persons who belonged by birth to the most distinguished families and were also personal friends of the tyrants. At first the government could find no clue to the conspiracy; for the current story,[23] that Hippias made all who were taking part in the procession leave their arms, and then detected those who were carrying secret daggers, cannot be true, since at that time they did not bear arms in the processions, this being a custom instituted at a later period by the democracy. According to the story of the popular party, Aristogeiton accused the friends of the tyrants with the deliberate intention that the latter might commit an impious act, and at the same time weaken themselves, by putting to death innocent men who were their own friends; others say that he told no falsehood, but was betraying the actual accomplices. At last, when for all his efforts he could not obtain release by death, he promised to give further information against a number of other persons; and, having induced Hippias to give him his hand to confirm his word, as soon as he had hold of it he reviled him for giving his hand to the murderer of his brother, till Hippias, in a frenzy of rage, lost control of himself and snatched out his dagger and dispatched him.

19. After this event the tyranny became much harsher. In consequence of his vengeance for his brother, and of the execution and banishment of

be known to few, and the fact that it was Hipparchus who was killed (though Hippias, and not he, was the person aimed at) would cause men to believe that he was the person to blame.

[22] Thucydides states expressly (vi. 56) that the conspirators were few in number. Aristotle probably again intends to correct him, silently but pointedly.

[23] This is the version given by Thucydides (vi. 58), which Aristotle evidently again wishes to correct.

a large number of persons, Hippias became a distrusted and an embittered man. About three years after the death of Hipparchus, finding his position in the city insecure, he set about fortifying Munichia, with the intention of establishing himself there. While he was still engaged on this work, however, he was expelled by Cleomenes, king of Lacedaemon, in consequence of the Spartans being continually incited by oracles to overthrow the tyranny. These oracles were obtained in the following way. The Athenian exiles, headed by the Alcmeonidae, could not by their own power effect their return, but failed continually in their attempts. Among their other failures, they fortified a post in Attica, Lipsydrium, above Mt. Parnes, and were there joined by some partisans from the city; but they were besieged by the tyrants and reduced to surrender. After this disaster the following became a popular drinking song:

> Ah! Lipsydrium, faithless friend!
> Lo, what heroes to death didst send,
> Nobly born and great in deed!
> Well did they prove themselves at need
> Of noble sires a noble seed.

Having failed, then, in every other method, they took the contract for rebuilding the temple at Delphi,[24] thereby obtaining ample funds, which they employed to secure the help of the Lacedaemonians. All this time the Pythia kept continually enjoining on the Lacedaemonians who came to consult the oracle, that they must free Athens; till finally she succeeded in impelling the Spartans to that step, although the house of Pisistratus was connected with them by ties of hospitality. The resolution of the Lacedaemonians was, however, at least equally due to the friendship which had been formed between the house of Pisistratus and Argos. Accordingly they first sent Anchimolus by sea at the head of an army; but he was defeated and killed, through the arrival of Cineas of Thessaly to support the sons of Pisistratus with a force of 1,000 horsemen. Then, being roused to anger by this disaster, they sent their king, Cleomenes, by land at the head of a larger force; and he, after defeating the Thessalian cavalry when they attempted to intercept his march into Attica, shut up Hippias within what was known as the Pelargic wall and blockaded him there with the assistance of the Athenians. While he was sitting down before the place, it so happened that the sons of the Pisistratidae were captured in an attempt to slip out; upon which the tyrants capitulated on condition of the safety of their children, and surrendered the Acropolis to the Athenians, five days being first allowed them to remove their

---

[24] The temple at Delphi had been burnt, as is recorded by Herodotus (ii. 180).

effects. This took place in the archonship of Harpactides,[25] after they had held the tyranny for about seventeen years since their father's death, or in all, including the period of their father's rule, for forty-nine years.

20. After the overthrow of the tyranny, the rival leaders in the state were Isagoras son of Tisander, a partisan of the tyrants, and Cleisthenes, who belonged to the family of the Alcmeonidae. Cleisthenes, being beaten in the political clubs, called in the people by giving the franchise to the masses. Thereupon Isagoras, finding himself left inferior in power, invited Cleomenes, who was united to him by ties of hospitality, to return to Athens, and persuaded him to 'drive out the pollution', a plea derived from the fact that the Alcmeonidae were supposed to be under the curse of pollution. On this Cleisthenes retired from the country, and Cleomenes, entering Attica with a small force, expelled, as polluted, 700 Athenian families. Having effected this, he next attempted to dissolve the Council, and to set up Isagoras and 300 of his partisans as the supreme power in the state. The Council, however, resisted, the populace flocked together, and Cleomenes and Isagoras, with their adherents, took refuge in the Acropolis. Here the people sat down and besieged them for two days; and on the third they agreed to let Cleomenes and all his followers depart, while they summoned Cleisthenes and the other exiles back to Athens. When the people had thus obtained the command of affairs, Cleisthenes was their chief and popular leader. And this was natural; for the Alcmeonidae were perhaps the chief cause of the expulsion of the tyrants, and for the greater part of their rule were at perpetual war with them. But even earlier than the attempts of the Alcmeonidae, one Cedon made an attack on the tyrants; whence there came another popular drinking song, addressed to him:

Pour a health yet again, boy, to Cedon; forget not this duty to do,
If a health is an honour befitting the name of a good man and true.

21. The people, therefore, had good reason to place confidence in Cleisthenes. Accordingly, now that he was the popular leader, three years after the expulsion of the tyrants, in the archonship of Isagoras,[26] his first step was to distribute the whole population into ten tribes in place of the existing four, with the object of intermixing the members of the different tribes, and so securing that more persons might have a share in the franchise.[27] From this arose the saying 'Do not look at the tribes',

[25] The Archon's name was not previously known, but the date is established independently as the year 511-10 B.C. (the Athenian official year beginning in July), apparently in the spring of 510 B.C.

[26] 508 B.C.

[27] It is not at first sight evident why a mere redistribution of the population into ten tribes instead of four should give more persons a share in the franchise. But the

addressed to those who wished to scrutinise the lists of the old families.[28] Next he made the Council to consist of 500 members instead of 400, each tribe now contributing fifty, whereas formerly each had sent 100. The reason why he did not organise the people into twelve tribes was that he might not have to use the existing division into trittyes; for the four tribes had twelve trittyes, so that he would not have achieved his object of redistributing the population in fresh combinations. Further, he divided the country into thirty groups of demes,[29] ten from the districts about the city, ten from the coast, and ten from the interior. These he called trittyes; and he assigned three of them by lot to each tribe, in such a way that each should have one portion in each of these three localities. All who lived in any given deme he declared fellow-demesmen, to the end that the new citizens might not be exposed by the habitual use of family names, but that men might be officially described by the names of their demes;[30] and accordingly it is by the names of their demes that the Athenians speak of one another. He also instituted Demarchs, who had the same duties as the previously existing Naucrari; the demes being made to take the place of the naucraries. He gave names to the demes, some from the localities to which they belonged, some from the persons who founded them, since some of the areas no longer corresponded to localities possessing names. On the other hand he allowed every one to retain his family and clan and religious rites according to ancestral custom. The names given to the tribes were the ten which the Pythia appointed out of the hundred selected national heroes.

22. By these reforms the constitution became much more democratic

object of Cleisthenes was to break down the old family and tribal feelings on which political contests had hitherto been based. To do this, he established a new division into tribes, which corresponded to no existing subdivision of the old ones, and at the same time he introduced a large number of new citizens by the enfranchisement of emancipated slaves and resident aliens. There would have been endless difficulties in the way of introducing them into the old tribes, which were organized into clans and families on the old aristocratic basis; but they were easily included in the new tribes, which had no such associations connected with them.

[28] Apparently this means that it was useless to look at the lists of the tribes if any one wished to examine the rolls of the families. Hence the phrase seems to have become a proverbial one for making useless distinctions or refinements.

[29] The total number of demes, or parishes, is not given, but from Herodotus it appears to have been a hundred. It gradually increased with the growth of population, and in the third century B.C. there were 176 demes. The demes composing each trittys appear to have been contiguous, but each trittys was separate from its two fellows, so that the party feeling of the tribe was spread over three local divisions, and the old feuds between the different districts of Attica became impossible.

[30] If the people continued to speak of one another by their family names as hitherto, newly enfranchised citizens, whose fathers had been slaves or aliens, would be markedly distinguished from the older citizens who belonged to ancient families; but by making the name of the deme part of the necessary description of every citizen he broke down the family tradition; moreover, it was easy for any man to establish his claim to citizenship by naming the deme to which he belonged, even though his father's name might be foreign or unfamiliar.

than that of Solon. The laws of Solon had been obliterated by disuse during the period of the tyranny, while Cleisthenes substituted new ones with the object of securing the goodwill of the masses. Among these was the law concerning ostracism. Four years[31] after the establishment of this system, in the archonship of Hermocreon, they first imposed upon the Council of Five Hundred the oath which they take to the present day. Next they began to elect the generals by tribes, one from each tribe, while the Polemarch was the commander of the whole army. Then, eleven years later, in the archonship of Phaenippus they won the battle of Marathon; and two years after this victory, when the people had now gained self-confidence, they for the first time made use of the law of ostracism. This had originally been passed as a precaution against men in high office, because Pisistratus took advantage of his position as a popular leader and general to make himself tyrant; and the first person ostracized was one of his relatives, Hipparchus son of Charmus, of the deme of Collytus, the very person on whose account especially Cleisthenes had enacted the law, as he wished to get rid of him. Hitherto, however, he had escaped; for the Athenians, with the usual leniency of the democracy, allowed all the partisans of the tyrants, who had not joined in their evil deeds in the time of the troubles, to remain in the city; and the chief and leader of these was Hipparchus. Then in the very next year, in the archonship of Telesinus,[32] they for the first time since the tyranny elected, tribe by tribe, the nine Archons by lot out of the 500[33] candidates selected by the demes, all the earlier ones having been elected by vote;[34] and in the same year Megacles son of Hippocrates, of the deme of Alopece, was

[31] This, if correct, would place this event in 504 B.C. But, in the first place, that year belongs to another Archon; and secondly, it is inconsistent with the statement below, that the battle of Marathon occurred eleven years later. Marathon was fought in 490 B.C., therefore the archonship of Hermocreon should be assigned to 501 B.C., for which year no name occurs in the extant lists of Archons. Whether the mistake in the present passage is due to the author or a copyist it is impossible to say.

[32] 487 B.C. The date here given is valuable, because it had hitherto been a matter of doubt whether Callimachus, the polemarch at Marathon, on whose casting vote the fighting of that battle depended, was elected by lot or by open vote. The words of Herodotus (vi. 109), strictly interpreted, imply the former; but it is repugnant to common sense to suppose that an officer holding so important a position was elected by lot, and it is now clear that, until three years after Marathon, the Archons were still elected by direct vote, and, as stated above in this same chapter, the polemarch was the chief of the army, the ten generals (who subsequently became the chief military commanders) being his subordinates.

[33] It is probable that there is a mistake in this number. It appears from ch. 8, 1 that under the Solonian constitution the number of candidates nominated by each tribe was ten, and that the same was the number in the writer's own day; and it is hardly likely that the higher number of fifty ever prevailed at an intermediate period. The Greek numerals for 100 and 500 are easily confused.

[34] This statement can only apply to the period after the expulsion of the tyrants and the reforms of Cleisthenes, since under the Solonian constitution (ch. 8, 1) the Archons were elected by lot out of forty candidates selected by the tribes.

ostracised. Thus for three years they continued to ostracise the friends of the tyrants, on whose account the law had been passed; but in the following year they began to remove others as well, including any one who seemed to be more powerful than was expedient. The first person unconnected with the tyrants who was ostracised was Xanthippus son of Ariphron. Two years later, in the archonship of Nicodemus,[35] the mines of Maroneia were discovered, and the state made a profit of 100 talents from the working of them. Some persons advised the people to make a distribution of the money among themselves, but this was prevented by Themistocles. He refused to say on what he proposed to spend the money, but he bade them lend it to the hundred richest men in Athens, one talent to each, and then, if the manner in which it was employed pleased the people, the expenditure should be charged to the state, but otherwise the state should receive the sum back from those to whom it was lent. On these terms he received the money and with it he had 100 triremes built, each of the hundred individuals building one; and it was with these ships that they fought the battle of Salamis against the barbarians. About this time Aristides the son of Lysimachus was ostracised. Three years later, however, in the archonship of Hypsichides,[36] all the ostracised persons were recalled, on account of the advance of the army of Xerxes; and it was laid down for the future that persons under sentence of ostracism must live between Geraestus and Scyllaeum,[37] on pain of losing their civic rights irrevocably.

23. So far, then, had the city progressed by this time, growing gradually with the growth of the democracy; but after the Persian wars the Council of Areopagus once more developed strength and assumed the control of the state. It did not acquire this supremacy by virtue of any formal decree, but because it had been the cause of the battle of Salamis being fought. When the generals were utterly at a loss how to meet the crisis and made proclamation that every one should see to his own safety, the Areopagus provided a donation of money, distributing eight drachmas to each member of the ships' crews, and so prevailed on them to go on board. On these grounds people bowed to its prestige; and during this period Athens was well administered. At this time they devoted themselves to the prosecution of the war and were in high repute among the Greeks, so that the command by sea was conferred upon them, in spite of the opposition of the Lacedaemonians. The leaders of the people during this period were Aristides, son of Lysimachus, and Themistocles, son of Neocles, of whom the latter appeared to devote himself to the

---

[35] 483 B.C.
[36] 481 B.C. The name of this Archon is new.
[37] So the MS., but one of the grammarians, who probably drew from this passage, says that ostracised persons were compelled to live *outside* these boundaries.

conduct of war, while the former had the reputation of being a clever statesman and the most upright man of his time. Accordingly the one was usually employed as general, the other as political adviser. The rebuilding of the fortifications they conducted in combination, although they were political opponents; but it was Aristides who, seizing the opportunity afforded by the discredit brought upon the Lacedaemonians by Pausanias, guided the public policy in the matter of the defection of the Ionian states from the alliance with Sparta. It follows that it was he who made the first assessment of tribute from the various allied states, two years after the battle of Salamis, in the archonship of Timosthenes;[38] and it was he who took the oath of offensive and defensive alliance with the Ionians, on which occasion they cast the masses of iron into the sea.

24. After this, seeing the state growing in confidence and much wealth accumulated, he advised the people to lay hold of the leadership of the league, and to quit the country districts and settle in the city. He pointed out to them that all would be able to gain a living there, some by service in the army, others in the garrisons, others by taking a part in public affairs; and in this way they would secure the leadership. This advice was taken; and when the people had assumed the supreme control they proceeded to treat their allies in a more imperious fashion, with the exception of the Chians, Lesbians, and Samians. These they maintained to protect their empire, leaving their constitutions untouched, and allowing them to retain whatever dominion they then possessed. They also secured an ample maintenance for the mass of the population in the way which Aristides had pointed out to them. Out of the proceeds of the tributes and the taxes and the contributions of the allies more than 20,000 persons were maintained. There were 6,000 jurymen, 1,600 bowmen, 1,200 Knights, 500 members of the Council, 500 guards of the dockyards, besides fifty guards in the Acropolis. There were some 700 magistrates at home, and some 700[39] abroad. Further, when they subsequently went to war, there were in addition 2,500 heavy-armed troops, twenty guardships, and other ships which collected the tributes, with crews amounting to 2,000 men, selected by lot; and besides these there were the persons maintained at the Prytaneum, and orphans, and gaolers, since all these were supported by the state.

25. Such was the way in which the people earned their livelihood. The supremacy of the Areopagus lasted for about seventeen years after the Persian wars, although gradually declining. But as the strength of the masses increased, Ephialtes, son of Sophonides, a man with a reputation for incorruptibility and public virtue, who had become the leader of the people, made an attack upon that Council. First of all he ruined many of

[38] 478 B.C.
[39] The number seems to be repeated by mistake on the part of the copyist.

its members by bringing actions against them with reference to their administration. Then, in the archonship of Conon,[40] he stripped the Council of all the acquired prerogatives from which it derived its guardianship of the constitution, and assigned some of them to the Council of Five Hundred, and others to the Assembly and the law-courts. In this revolution he was assisted by Themistocles,[41] who was himself a member of the Areopagus, but was expecting to be tried before it on a charge of treasonable dealings with Persia. This made him anxious that it should be overthrown, and accordingly he warned Ephialtes that the Council intended to arrest him, while at the same time he informed the Areopagites that he would reveal to them certain persons who were conspiring to subvert the constitution. He then conducted the representatives delegated by the Council to the residence of Ephialtes, promising to show them the conspirators who assembled there, and proceeded to converse with them in an earnest manner. Ephialtes, seeing this, was seized with alarm and took refuge in suppliant guise at the altar. Every one was astounded at the occurrence, and presently, when the Council of Five Hundred met, Ephialtes and Themistocles together proceeded to denounce the Areopagus to them. This they repeated in similar fashion in the Assembly, until they succeeded in depriving it of its power. Not long afterwards, however, Ephialtes was assassinated by Aristodicus of Tanagra. In this way was the Council of Areopagus deprived of its guardianship of the state.

26. After this revolution the administration of the state became more and more lax, in consequence of the eager rivalry of candidates for popular favour. During this period the moderate party, as it happened, had no real chief, their leader being Cimon son of Miltiades, who was a comparatively young man,[42] and had been late in entering public life; and at the same time the general populace suffered great losses by war. The soldiers for active service were selected at that time from the roll of citizens, and as the generals were men of no military experience, who owed their position solely to their family standing, it continually hap-

---

[40] 462 B.C.

[41] This is one of the most striking of the new views of history brought to light by the reappearance of Aristotle's work. The current opinion (based mainly on Thucydides) is that Themistocles was ostracised about 471 B.C., that the charge of complicity with Pausanias in his intrigues with Persia was brought against him about 466 B.C., and that he reached Persia in his flight about 465 B.C., the year in which Artaxerxes succeeded Xerxes. It now appears (if the evidence of this work is to be accepted) that he was in Athens in 462 B.C., and his ostracism cannot, therefore, be placed earlier than 461 B.C., and his flight to Persia may have occurred in 460 B.C. This statement is irreconcilable with the narrative of Thucydides (i. 137) that in his flight he was nearly captured by the Athenian fleet then engaged in the siege of Naxos, which is generally assigned to the year 466 B.C.; and most critics reject it. It is evident, however, that Thucydides' system of chronology for this period was not the only one current in antiquity.

[42] This is inconsistent with the received chronology, and also with the words which immediately follow.

pened that some two or three thousand of the troops perished on an expedition; and in this way the best men alike of the lower and the upper classes were exhausted. Consequently in most matters of administration less heed was paid to the laws than had formerly been the case. No alteration, however, was made in the method of election of the nine Archons, except that five years after the death of Ephialtes it was decided that the candidates to be submitted to the lot for that office might be selected from the Zeugitae as well as from the higher classes. The first Archon from that class was Mnesitheides.[43] Up to this time all the Archons had been taken from the Pentacosiomedimni and Knights, while the Zeugitae were confined to the ordinary magistracies, save where an evasion of the law was overlooked. Four years later, in the archonship of Lysicrates,[44] the thirty 'local justices', as they were called, were re-established; and two years afterwards, in the archonship of Antidotus,[45] in consequence of the great increase in the number of citizens, it was resolved, on the motion of Pericles, that no one should be admitted to the franchise who was not of citizen birth by both parents.

27. After this Pericles came forward as popular leader, having first distinguished himself while still a young man by prosecuting Cimon on the audit of his official accounts as general. Under his auspices the constitution became still more democratic. He took away some of the privileges of the Areopagus, and, above all, he turned the policy of the state in the direction of sea power, which caused the masses to acquire confidence in themselves and consequently to take the conduct of affairs more and more into their own hands. Moreover, forty-eight years after the battle of Salamis, in the archonship of Pythodorus,[46] the Peloponnesian war broke out, during which the populace was shut up in the city and became accustomed to gain its livelihood by military service, and so, partly voluntarily and partly involuntarily, determined to assume the administration of the state itself. Pericles was also the first to institute pay for service in the law-courts, as a bid for popular favour to counterbalance the wealth of Cimon. The latter, having private possessions on a regal scale, not only performed the regular public services magnificently, but also maintained a large number of his fellow-demesmen. Any member of the deme of Laciadae could go every day to Cimon's house and there receive a reasonable provision; while his estate

---

[43] The archonship of Mnesitheides was in 457 B.C.; and as the death of Ephialtes was in 462 B.C., and it has just been stated that the alteration in the law was made five years later, it follows that a Zeugites was elected for the first year in which the members of that order were eligible.

[44] 453 B.C.

[45] 451 B.C.

[46] 432-1 B.C.; and as the war broke out four months before the end of Pythodorus' year of office (Thuc. ii. 2), the actual date falls in the spring of 431 B.C.

was guarded by no fences, so that any one who liked might help himself to the fruit from it. Pericles' private property was quite unequal to this magnificence and accordingly he took the advice of Damonides of Oia (who was commonly supposed to be the person who prompted Pericles in most of his measures, and was therefore subsequently ostracised), which was that, as he was beaten in the matter of private possessions, he should make gifts to the people from their own property; and accordingly he instituted pay for the members of the juries. Some critics accuse him of thereby causing a deterioration in the character of the juries, since it was always the common people who put themselves forward for selection as jurors, rather than the men of better position. Moreover, bribery came into existence after this, the first person to introduce it being Anytus, after his command at Pylos.[47] He was prosecuted by certain individuals on account of his loss of Pylos, but escaped by bribing the jury.

28. So long, however, as Pericles was leader of the people, things went tolerably well with the state; but when he was dead there was a great change for the worse. Then for the first time did the people choose a leader who was of no reputation among men of good standing, whereas up to this time such men had always been found as leaders of the democracy. The first leader of the people, in the very beginning of things, was Solon, and the second was Pisistratus, both of them men of birth and position. After the overthrow of the tyrants there was Cleisthenes, a member of the house of the Alcmeonidae; and he had no rival opposed to him after the expulsion of the party of Isagoras. After this Xanthippus was the leader of the people, and Miltiades of the upper class. Then came Themistocles and Aristides,[48] and after them Ephialtes as leader of the people, and Cimon son of Miltiades of the wealthier class. Pericles followed as leader of the people, and Thucydides, who was connected by marriage with Cimon, of the opposition. After the death of Pericles, Nicias, who subsequently fell in Sicily, appeared as leader of the aristocracy, and Cleon son of Cleaenetus of the people. The latter seems, more than any one else, to have been the cause of the corruption of the democracy by his wild undertakings; and he was the first to use unseemly shouting and coarse abuse on the Bema, and to harangue the people with his cloak girt up short about him, whereas all his predecessors had spoken decently and in order. These were succeeded by Theramenes son of Hagnon as leader of the one party, and the lyre-maker Cleophon of the people. It was Cleophon who first granted the two-obol donation for

[47] Pylos was recaptured by the Spartans, owing to the neglect of Anytus to relieve it, in 411 B.C. Anytus was one of the leaders of the moderate aristocratic party (ch. 34, 3), and one of the prosecutors of Socrates.
[48] Themistocles and Aristides were both of them leaders of the democracy, as is stated in ch. 23, 3. It is a mistake to regard Aristides as an aristocratic leader.

the theatrical performances,[49] and for some time it continued to be given; but then Callicrates of Paeania ousted him by promising to add a third obol to the sum. Both of these persons were subsequently condemned to death; for the people, even if they are deceived for a time, in the end generally come to detest those who have beguiled them into any unworthy action. After Cleophon the popular leadership was occupied successively by the men who chose to talk the biggest and pander the most to the tastes of the majority, with their eyes fixed only on the interests of the moment. The best statesmen at Athens, after those of early times, seem to have been Nicias, Thucydides, and Theramenes. As to Nicias and Thucydides, nearly every one agrees that they were not merely men of birth and character, but also statesmen, and that they ruled the state with paternal care. On the merits of Theramenes opinion is divided, because it so happened that in his time public affairs were in a very stormy state. But those who give their opinion deliberately find him, not, as his critics falsely assert, overthrowing every kind of constitution, but supporting every kind so long as it did not transgress the laws; thus showing that he was able, as every good citizen should be, to live under any form of constitution, while he refused to countenance illegality and was its constant enemy.

29. So long as the fortune of the war continued even, the Athenians preserved the democracy; but after the disaster in Sicily, when the Lacedaemonians had gained the upper hand through their alliance with the king of Persia, they were compelled to abolish the democracy and establish in its place the constitution of the Four Hundred. The speech recommending this course before the vote was made by Melobius, and the motion was proposed by Pythodorus of Anaphlystus; but the real argument which persuaded the majority was the belief that the king of Persia was more likely to form an alliance with them if the constitution were on an oligarchical basis. The motion of Pythodorus was to the following effect. The popular Assembly was to elect twenty persons, over forty years of age, who, in conjunction with the existing ten members of the Committee of Public Safety,[50] after taking an oath that they would frame such measures as they thought best for the state, should then prepare proposals for the public safety. In addition, any other person might make proposals, so that of all the schemes before them the people might choose the best. Cleitophon concurred with the motion of Pythodorus,

[49] Two obols was the price of a seat in the theatre; and after the time of Cleophon (the date had hitherto been placed earlier, Plutarch appearing to assign the measure to Pericles) the necessary sum was provided, for all citizens who chose to apply for it, by the state.

[50] This committee is probably the same as that which we know from Thucydides to have been appointed immediately after the news of the Sicilian disaster was received in Athens.

but moved that the committee should also investigate the ancient laws enacted by Cleisthenes when he created the democracy, in order that they might have these too before them and so be in a position to decide wisely; his suggestion being that the constitution of Cleisthenes was not really democratic, but closely akin to that of Solon. When the committee was elected, their first proposal was that the Prytanes should be compelled to put to the vote any motion that was offered on behalf of the public safety. Next they abolished all indictments for illegal proposals, all impeachments and public prosecutions, in order that every Athenian should be free to give his counsel on the situation, if he chose; and they decreed that if any person imposed a fine on any other for his acts in this respect, or prosecuted him or summoned him before the courts, he should, on an information being laid against him, be summarily arrested and brought before the generals, who should deliver him to the Eleven to be put to death. After these preliminary measures, they drew up the constitution in the following manner. The revenues of the state were not to be spent on any purpose except the war. All magistrates should serve without remuneration for the period of the war, except the nine Archons and the Prytanes for the time being, who should each receive three obols a day. The whole of the rest of the administration was to be committed, for the period of the war, to those Athenians who were most capable of serving the state personally or pecuniarily, to the number of not less than 5,000. This body was to have full powers, to the extent even of making treaties with whomsoever they willed; and ten representatives, over forty years of age, were to be elected from each tribe to draw up the list of the Five Thousand, after taking an oath on a full and perfect sacrifice.

30. These were the recommendations of the committee; and when they had been ratified the Five Thousand[51] elected from their own number 100 commissioners to draw up the constitution. They, on their appointment, drew up and produced the following recommendations. There should be a Council, holding office for a year, consisting of men over thirty years of age, serving without pay. To this body should belong the Generals, the nine Archons, the Amphictyonic Registrar, the Taxiarchs, the Hipparchs, the Phylarchs, the commanders of garrisons, the Treasurers of Athena and the other gods, ten in number, the Hellenic Treasurers

[51] This mention of the Five Thousand appears to be in direct contradiction to the statement in ch. 32, 3, that the Five Thousand were only nominally selected, which is also in accordance with the statement of Thucydides (viii. 92). There are two possible explanations: either all persons possessing the necessary qualification of being able to furnish arms were temporarily called the Five Thousand until the list of that body could be properly drawn up (thus the so-called Five thousand which took over the government after the fall of the Four Hundred actually included all persons able to furnish arms); or the Five Thousand nominated by the hundred persons mentioned at the end of the last chapter was only a provisional body, and a fresh nomination was to be made when the constitution had been finally drawn up.

(Hellenotamiae),[52] the Treasurers of the other non-sacred moneys, to the number of twenty, the ten Commissioners of Sacrifices, and the ten Superintendents of the mysteries. All these were to be appointed by the Council from a larger number of selected candidates, chosen from its members for the time being. The other offices were all to be filled by lot, and not from the members of the Council. The Hellenic Treasurers who actually administered the funds should not sit with the Council. As regards the future, four Councils were to be created, of men of the age already mentioned, and one of these was to be chosen by lot to take office at once, while the others were to receive it in turn, in the order decided by the lot. For this purpose the hundred commissioners were to distribute themselves and all the rest[53] as equally as possible into four parts, and cast lots for precedence, and the selected body should hold office for a year. They were to administer that office as seemed to them best, both with reference to the safe custody and due expenditure of the finances, and generally with regard to all other matters to the best of their ability. If they desired to take a larger number of persons into counsel, each member might call in one assistant of his own choice, subject to the same qualification of age. The Council was to sit once every five days, unless there was any special need for more frequent sittings. The casting of the lot for the Council was to be held by the nine Archons; votes on divisions were to be counted by five tellers chosen by lot from the members of the Council, and of these one was to be selected by lot every day to act as president. These five persons were to cast lots for precedence between the parties wishing to appear before the Council, giving the first place to sacred matters, the second to heralds, the third to embassies, and the fourth to all other subjects; but matters concerning the war might be dealt with, on the motion of the generals, whenever there was need, without balloting. Any member of the Council who did not enter the Council-house at the time named should be fined a drachma for each day, unless he was away on leave of absence from the Council.

31. Such was the constitution which they drew up for the time to come, but for the immediate present they devised the following scheme. There should be a Council of Four Hundred, as in the ancient constitution, forty from each tribe, chosen out of candidates of more than thirty years of age, selected by the members of the tribes. This Council should appoint the magistrates and draw up the form of oath which they were to take; and in all that concerned the laws, in the examination of official accounts, and in other matters generally, they might act according to their discre-

[52] These were the officers appointed to receive the contribution of the allied states of the Confederacy of Delos, or, as these states subsequently became, the subject-allies of the Athenian empire. After the loss of the empire by the result of the Peloponnesian war these officers were no longer required, and consequently ceased to exist.

[53] Apparently, all the rest of the Five Thousand who were over thirty years of age.

tion. They must, however, observe the laws that might be enacted with reference to the constitution of the state, and had no power to alter them nor to pass others. The generals should be provisionally elected from the whole body of the Five Thousand, but so soon as the Council came into existence it was to hold an examination of military equipments, and thereon elect ten persons, together with a secretary, and the persons thus elected should hold office during the coming year with full powers, and should have the right, whenever they desired it, of joining in the deliberations of the Council. The Five Thousand[54] was also to elect a single Hipparch and ten Phylarchs; but for the future the Council was to elect these officers according to the regulations above laid down. No office, except those of member of the Council and of general, might be held more than once, either by the first occupants or by their successors. With reference to the future distribution of the Four Hundred into the four successive sections, the hundred commissioners must divide them whenever the time comes for the citizens to join in the Council along with the rest.

32. The hundred commissioners appointed by the Five Thousand drew up the constitution as just stated; and after it had been ratified by the people, under the presidency of Aristomachus, the existing Council, that of the year of Callias,[55] was dissolved before it had completed its term of office. It was dissolved on the fourteenth day of the month Thargelion, and the Four Hundred entered into office on the twenty-first; whereas the regular Council, elected by lot, ought to have entered into office on the fourteenth of Scirophorion.[56] Thus was the oligarchy established, in the archonship of Callias, just about a hundred years after the expulsion of the tyrants. The chief promoters of the revolution were Pisander, Antiphon, and Theramenes, all of them men of good birth and with high reputations for ability and judgment. When, however, this constitution had been established, the Five Thousand were only nominally selected, and the Four Hundred, together with the ten officers on whom full powers had been conferred, occupied the Council-house and really administered the government. They began by sending ambassadors to the Lacedaemonians proposing a cessation of the war on the basis of

[54] The subject is not expressed in the original, but as it is stated that in the future the Council was to elect these officers, it seems certain that the provisional arrangement was that the Five Thousand should elect them, as in the case of the generals, the Council not being yet properly constituted.

[55] Callias' year of office began in 412 B.C., and was now within two months of its end. The date of the entry of the Four Hundred into office is consequently in May, 411 B.C.

[56] Roughly equivalent to June, the last month of the official year at Athens. The 'regular Council' means the Council which, in the ordinary course of things under the democracy, should have been elected by lot to succeed that belonging to the year of Callias.

the existing position; but as the Lacedaemonians refused to listen to them unless they would also abandon the command of the sea, they broke off the negotiations.

33. For about four months the constitution of the Four Hundred lasted, and Mnasilochus held office as Archon of their nomination for two months of the year of Theopompus, who was Archon for the remaining ten. On the loss of the naval battle of Eretria, however, and the revolt of the whole of Euboea except Oreum, the indignation of the people was greater than at any of the earlier disasters, since they drew far more supplies at this time from Euboea than from Attica itself. Accordingly they deposed the Four Hundred and committed the management of affairs to the Five Thousand, consisting of persons possessing a military equipment. At the same time they voted that pay should not be given for any public office. The persons chiefly responsible for the revolution were Aristocrates and Theramenes, who disapproved of the action of the Four Hundred in retaining the direction of affairs entirely in their own hands, and referring nothing to the Five Thousand. During this period the constitution of the state seems to have been admirable, since it was a time of war and the franchise was in the hands of those who possessed a military equipment.

34. The people, however, in a very short time deprived the Five Thousand of their monopoly of the government.[57] Then, six years after the overthrow of the Four Hundred, in the archonship of Callias of Angele,[58] the battle of Arginusae took place, of which the results were, first, that the ten generals who had gained the victory were all[59] condemned by a single decision, owing to the people being led astray by persons who aroused their indignation; though, as a matter of fact, some of the generals had actually taken no part in the battle, and others were themselves picked up by other vessels. Secondly, when the Lacedaemonians proposed to evacuate Decelea and make peace on the basis of the existing position, although some of the Athenians supported this proposal, the majority refused to listen to them. In this they were led

[57] Probably after the battle of Cyzicus, in 410 B.C., when the fleet, which was democratic in its sympathies, returned to Athens.

[58] 406 B.C. This was, however, five years after the overthrow of the oligarchy, not six, so that either Aristotle calculated from the beginning and not the end of the rule of the Four Hundred, or the numeral must be altered in the MS.

[59] This is probably inexact. Two of the generals, Conon and Leon, can hardly have been included in the accusation, as Conon was blockaded in Mytilene and Leon is never mentioned in connexion with either the battle or the trial. It is true that Aristotle says below that some of the condemned generals had not taken part in the battle, but if this had actually been the case, Xenophon could hardly have helped noticing it. Xenophon does expressly name the eight generals who were present at the battle, and states their positions in the Athenian line; and, of these eight, six stood their trial and were executed, while the remaining two declined to return to Athens and were, no doubt, condemned in absence.

astray by Cleophon, who appeared in the Assembly drunk and wearing his breastplate, and prevented peace being made, declaring that he would never accept peace unless the Lacedaemonians abandoned their claims on all the cities allied with them. They mismanaged their opportunity then, and in a very short time they learned their mistake. The next year, in the archonship of Alexias, they suffered the disaster of Aegospotami, the consequence of which was that Lysander became master of the city, and set up the Thirty as its governors. He did so in the following manner. One of the terms of peace stipulated that the state should be governed according to 'the ancient constitution'. Accordingly the popular party tried to preserve the democracy, while that part of the upper class which belonged to the political clubs, together with the exiles who had returned since the peace, aimed at an oligarchy, and those who were not members of any club, though in other respects they considered themselves as good as any other citizens, were anxious to restore the ancient constitution. The latter class included Archinus, Anytus, Cleitophon, Phormisius, and many others, but their most prominent leader was Theramenes. Lysander, however, threw his influence on the side of the oligarchical party, and the popular Assembly was compelled by sheer intimidation to pass a vote establishing the oligarchy. The motion to this effect was proposed by Dracontides of Aphidna.

35. In this way were the Thirty established in power, in the archonship of Pythodorus.[60] As soon, however, as they were masters of the city, they ignored all the resolutions which had been passed relating to the organisation of the constitution, but after appointing a Council of Five Hundred and the other magistrates out of 1,000 selected candidates, and associating with themselves ten Archons in Piraeus, eleven superintendents of the prison, and 300 'lash-bearers' as attendants, with the help of these they kept the city under their own control. At first, indeed, they behaved with moderation towards the citizens and pretended to administer the state according to the ancient constitution. In pursuance of this policy they took down from the hill of Areopagus the laws of Ephialtes and Archestratus relating to the Areopagite Council; they also repealed such of the statutes of Solon as were obscure, and abolished the supreme power of the law-courts. In this they claimed to be restoring the constitution and freeing it from obscurities; as, for instance, by making the testator free once for all to leave his property as he pleased, and abolishing the existing limitations in cases of insanity, old age, and undue female influence, in order that no opening might be left for professional accusers. In other matters also their conduct was similar. At first, then, they acted on these lines, and they destroyed the professional accusers and those mischievous and evil-minded persons who, to the great detri-

[60] The year 404–403 B.C.

ment of the democracy, had attached themselves to it in order to curry favour with it. With all of this the city was much pleased, and thought that the Thirty were doing it with the best of motives. But so soon as they had got a firmer hold on the city, they spared no class of citizens, but put to death any persons who were eminent for wealth or birth or character. Herein they aimed at removing all whom they had reason to fear, while they also wished to lay hands on their possessions; and in a short time they put to death not less than 1,500 persons.

36. Theramenes, however, seeing the city thus falling into ruin, was displeased with their proceedings, and counselled them to cease such unprincipled conduct and let the better classes have a share in the government. At first they resisted his advice, but when his proposals came to be known abroad, and the masses began to associate themselves with him, they were seized with alarm lest he should make himself the leader of the people and destroy their despotic power. Accordingly they drew up a list of 3,000 citizens, to whom they announced that they would give a share in the constitution. Theramenes, however, criticised this scheme also, first on the ground that, while proposing to give all respectable citizens a share in the constitution, they were actually giving it only to 3,000 persons, as though all merit were confined within that number; and secondly because they were doing two inconsistent things, since they made the government rest on the basis of force, and yet made the governors inferior in strength to the governed. However, they took no notice of his criticisms, and for a long time put off the publication of the list of the Three Thousand and kept to themselves the names of those who had been placed upon it; and every time they did decide to publish it they proceeded to strike out some of those who had been included in it, and insert others who had been omitted.

37. Now when winter had set in, Thrasybulus and the exiles occupied Phyle, and the force which the Thirty led out to attack them met with a reverse. Thereupon the Thirty decided to disarm the bulk of the population and to get rid of Theramenes; which they did in the following way. They introduced two laws into the Council, which they commanded it to pass; the first of them gave the Thirty absolute power to put to death any citizen who was not included in the list of the Three Thousand, while the second disqualified all persons from participation in the franchise who should have assisted in the demolition of the fort of Eetioneia,[61] or have acted in any way against the Four Hundred who had organised the previous oligarchy. Theramenes had done both, and accordingly,

[61] The Four Hundred had begun to build this fort, which commanded the entrance to the Piraeus, in the later days of their rule; but Theramenes and others of the moderate party, suspecting that it was intended to enable the oligarchs to betray the port to the Spartans, incited the populace to destroy it.

when these laws were ratified, he became excluded from the franchise and the Thirty had full power to put him to death.[62] Theramenes having been thus removed, they disarmed all the people except the Three Thousand, and in every respect showed a great advance in cruelty and crime. They also sent ambassadors to Lacedaemon to blacken the character of Theramenes and to ask for help; and the Lacedaemonians, in answer to their appeal, sent Callibius as military governor with about 700 troops, who came and occupied the Acropolis.

38. These events were followed by the occupation of Munichia by the exiles from Phyle, and their victory over the Thirty and their partisans. After the fight the party of the city retreated, and next day they held a meeting in the marketplace and deposed the Thirty, and elected ten citizens with full powers to bring the war to a termination. When, however, the Ten had taken over the government they did nothing towards the object for which they were elected, but sent envoys to Lacedaemon to ask for help and to borrow money. Further, finding that the citizens who possessed the franchise were displeased at their proceedings, they were afraid lest they should be deposed, and consequently, in order to strike terror into them (in which design they succeeded), they arrested Demaretus, one of the most eminent citizens, and put him to death. This gave them a firm hold on the government, and they also had the support of Callibius and his Peloponnesians, together with several of the Knights; for some of the members of this class were the most zealous among the citizens to prevent the return of the exiles from Phyle. When, however, the party in Piraeus and Munichia began to gain the upper hand in the war, through the defection of the whole populace to them, the party in the city deposed the original Ten, and elected another Ten,[63] consisting of men of the highest repute. Under their administration, and with their active and zealous co-operation, the treaty of reconciliation was made and the populace returned to the city. The most prominent members of this board were Rhinon of Paeania and Phayllus of Acherdus, who, even before the arrival of Pausanias, opened negotiations with the party in Piraeus, and after his arrival seconded his efforts to bring about the return of the exiles. For it was Pausanias, the king of the Lacedaemonians, who brought the peace and reconciliation to a fulfilment, in conjunction with the ten commissioners of arbitration who arrived later from Lacedae-

[62] This is quite different from Xenophon's dramatic account (ii. 3. 23-56) of the totally illegal arrest and execution of Theramenes.

[63] No other authority seems to distinguish between these two boards of Ten. Practically, the rule of the first is ignored, and only that of the second, which brought the war to a conclusion, is recognised; but the appointment of this board is assigned to the days immediately following the defeat of the Thirty, and it is not recognised that a considerable time, apparently about six months, elapsed between this event and the restoration of the democracy.

mon, at his own earnest request. Rhinon and his colleagues received a
vote of thanks for the goodwill shown by them to the people, and though
they received their charge under an oligarchy and handed in their
accounts under a democracy, no one, either of the party that had stayed
in the city or of the exiles that had returned from the Piraeus, brought
any complaint against them. On the contrary, Rhinon was immediately
elected general on account of his conduct in this office.

39. This reconciliation was effected in the archonship of Eucleides,[64]
on the following terms. All persons who, having remained in the city
during the troubles, were now anxious to leave it, were to be free to
settle at Eleusis, retaining their civil rights and possessing full and independent powers of self-government, and with the free enjoyment of
their own personal property. The temple at Eleusis should be common
ground for both parties, and should be under the superintendence of the
Ceryces and the Eumolpidae,[65] according to primitive custom. The
settlers at Eleusis should not be allowed to enter Athens, nor the people
of Athens to enter Eleusis, except at the season of the mysteries, when
both parties should be free from these restrictions. The secessionists
should pay their share to the fund for the common defence out of their
revenues, just like all the other Athenians. If any of the seceding party
wished to take a house in Eleusis, the people would help them to obtain
the consent of the owner; but if they could not come to terms, they
should appoint three valuers on either side, and the owner should receive
whatever price they should appoint. Of the inhabitants of Eleusis, those
whom the secessionists wished to remain should be allowed to do so. The
list of those who desired to secede should be made up within ten days
after the taking of the oaths in the case of persons already in the country,
and their actual departure should take place within twenty days; persons
at present out of the country should have the same terms allowed to them
after their return. No one who settled at Eleusis should be capable of
holding any office in Athens until he should again register himself on the
roll as a resident in the city. Trials for homicide, including all cases in
which one party had either killed or wounded another, should be conducted according to ancestral practice.[66] There should be a general amnesty concerning past events towards all persons except the Thirty, the
Ten, the Eleven, and the magistrates in Piraeus; and these too should be
included if they should submit their accounts in the usual way. Such
accounts should be given by the magistrates in Piraeus before a court of
citizens rated in Piraeus, and by the magistrates in the city before a

[64] Late in the summer of 403 B.C.
[65] Two ancient Athenian families, who from the earliest times had retained the duty
of superintending the Eleusinian mysteries.
[66] The reading of this passage is rather doubtful.

court of those rated in the city.[67] On these terms those who wished to do so might secede. Each party was to repay separately the money which it had borrowed for the war.

40. When the reconciliation had taken place on these terms, those who had fought on the side of the Thirty felt considerable apprehensions, and a large number intended to secede. But as they put off entering their names till the last moment, as people will do, Archinus, observing their numbers, and being anxious to retain them as citizens, cut off the remaining days during which the list should have remained open; and in this way many persons were compelled to remain, though they did so very unwillingly until they recovered confidence. This is one point in which Archinus appears to have acted in a most statesmanlike manner, and another was his subsequent prosecution of Thrasybulus on the charge of illegality, for a motion by which he proposed to confer the franchise on all who had taken part in the return from Piraeus, although some of them were notoriously slaves. And yet a third such action was when one of the returned exiles began to violate the amnesty, whereupon Archinus haled him to the Council and persuaded them to execute him without trial, telling them that now they would have to show whether they wished to preserve the democracy and abide by the oaths they had taken; for if they let this man escape they would encourage others to imitate him, while if they executed him they would make an example for all to learn by. And this was exactly what happened; for after this man had been put to death no one ever again broke the amnesty. On the contrary, the Athenians seem, both in public and in private, to have behaved in the most unprecedentedly admirable and public-spirited way with reference to the preceding troubles. Not only did they blot out all memory of former offences, but they even repaid to the Lacedaemonians out of the public purse the money which the Thirty had borrowed for the war, although the treaty required each party, the party of the city and the party of Piraeus, to pay its own debts separately. This they did because they thought it was a necessary first step in the direction of restoring harmony; but in other states, so far from the democratic parties making advances from their own possessions, they are rather in the habit of making a general redistribution of the land. A final reconciliation was made with the secessionists at Eleusis two years after the secession, in the archonship of Xenaenetus.[68]

41. This, however, took place at a later date; at the time of which we are speaking the people, having secured the control of the state, established the constitution which exists at the present day. Pythodorus was

---

[67] The exact reading of this passage also is doubtful, but the general sense appears to be that here given.

[68] 401 B.C. The date is not elsewhere definitely recorded.

Archon at the time, but the democracy seems to have assumed the supreme power with perfect justice, since it had effected its own return by its own exertions.[69] This was the eleventh change which had taken place in the constitution of Athens. The first modification of the primaeval condition of things was when Ion and his companions brought the people together into a community, for then the people was first divided into the four tribes, and the tribe-kings were created. Next, and first after this, having now some semblance of a constitution, was that which took place in the reign of Theseus, consisting in a slight deviation from absolute monarchy. After this came the constitution formed under Draco, when the first code of laws was drawn up. The third was that which followed the civil war, in the time of Solon; from this the democracy took its rise. The fourth was the tyranny of Pisistratus; the fifth the constitution of Cleisthenes, after the overthrow of the tyrants, of a more democratic character than that of Solon. The sixth was that which followed on the Persian wars, when the Council of Areopagus had the direction of the state. The seventh, succeeding this, was the constitution which Aristides sketched out, and which Ephialtes brought to completion by overthrowing the Areopagite Council; under this the nation, misled by the demagogues, made the most serious mistakes in the interest of its maritime empire. The eighth was the establishment of the Four Hundred, followed by the ninth, the restored democracy. The tenth was the tyranny of the Thirty and the Ten. The eleventh was that which followed the return from Phyle and Piraeus; and this has continued from that day to this, with continual accretions of power to the masses. The democracy has made itself master of everything and administers everything by its votes in the Assembly and by the law-courts, in which it holds the supreme power. Even the jurisdiction of the Council has passed into the hands of the people at large; and this appears to be a judicious change, since small bodies are more open to corruption, whether by actual money or influence, than large ones. At first they refused to allow payment for attendance at the Assembly; but the result was that people did not attend. Consequently, after the Prytanes had tried many devices in vain in order to induce the populace to come and ratify the votes, Agyrrhius,[70] in the first instance, made a provision of one obol a day, which Heracleides of Clazomenae,[71] nicknamed 'the king', increased to two obols, and Agyrrhius again to three.

[69] The text here is corrupt.

[70] A politician of no very great repute, who flourished at the end of the fifth century and in the early part of the fourth. It is clear from many allusions in the *Ecclesiazusae* of Aristophanes that the rate of pay had been raised to three obols shortly before the performance of that play in 392 B.C.; and the first establishment of payment for attendance at the Assembly cannot be placed many years before that date.

[71] Heracleides is only known otherwise by a mention in the *Ion* attributed to Plato, in which he is referred to as a foreigner who had held office at Athens.

42. The present state of the constitution is as follows. The franchise is open to all who are of citizen birth by both parents. They are enrolled among the demesmen at the age of eighteen. On the occasion of their enrolment the demesmen give their votes on oath, first whether the candidates appear to be of the age prescribed by the law (if not, they are dismissed back into the ranks of the boys), and secondly whether the candidate is free born and of such parentage as the laws require. Then if they decide that he is not a free man, he appeals to the law-courts, and the demesmen appoint five of their own number to act as accusers; if the court decides that he has no right to be enrolled, he is sold by the state as a slave, but if he wins his case he has a right to be enrolled among the demesmen without further question. After this the Council examines those who have been enrolled, and if it comes to the conclusion that any of them is less than eighteen years of age, it fines the demesmen who enrolled him. When the youths (Ephebi) have passed this examination, their fathers meet by their tribes, and appoint on oath three of their fellow tribesmen, over forty years of age, who, in their opinion, are the best and most suitable persons to have charge of the youths; and of these the Assembly elects one from each tribe as guardian, together with a director, chosen from the general body of Athenians, to control the while. Under the charge of these persons the youths first of all make the circuit of the temples; then they proceed to Piraeus, and some of them garrison Munichia and some the south shore. The Assembly also elects two trainers, with subordinate instructors, who teach them to fight in heavy armour, to use the bow and javelin, and to discharge a catapult. The guardians receive from the state a drachma apiece for their keep, and the youths four obols apiece. Each guardian receives the allowance for all the members of his tribe and buys the necessary provisions for the common stock (they mess together by tribes), and generally superintends everything. In this way they spend the first year. The next year, after giving a public display of their military evolutions, on the occasion when the Assembly meets in the theatre, they receive a shield and spear from the state; after which they patrol the country and spend their time in the forts. For these two years they are on garrison duty, and wear the military cloak, and during this time they are exempt from all taxes. They also can neither bring an action at law, nor have one brought against them, in order that they may have no excuse for requiring leave of absence; though exception is made in cases of actions concerning inheritances and wards of state,[72] or of any sacrificial ceremony connected

[72] When a man died leaving a daughter, but no son, his estate, though not becoming her property, was attached to her, and the nearest of kin could claim her in marriage; and the property went to the sons born of such marriage. If she was poor, the nearest of kin was obliged either to marry her or to provide her with a dowry. If there were more daughters than one, the estate seems to have been divided among them

with the family. When the two years have elapsed they thereupon take their position among the other citizens. Such is the manner of the enrolment of the citizens and the training cf the youths.

43. All the magistrates that are concerned with the ordinary routine of administration are elected by lot, except the Military Treasurer, the Commissioners of the Theoric fund,[73] and the Superintendent of Springs. These are elected by vote, and hold office from one Panathenaic festival to the next.[74] All military officers are also elected by vote.

The Council of Five Hundred is elected by lot, fifty from each tribe. Each tribe holds the office of Prytanes in turn, the order being determined by lot; the first four serve for thirty-six days each, the last six for thirty-five, since the reckoning is by lunar years.[75] The Prytanes for the time being, in the first place, mess together in the Tholus,[76] and receive a sum of money from the state for their maintenance; and, secondly, they convene the meetings of the Council and the Assembly. The Council they convene every day, unless it is a holiday, the Assembly four times in each prytany. It is also their duty to draw up the programme of the business of the Council and to decide what subjects are to be dealt with on each particular day, and where the sitting is to be held. They also draw up the programme for the meetings of the Assembly. One of these in each prytany is called the 'sovereign' Assembly; in this the people have to ratify the continuance of the magistrates in office, if they are performing their duties properly, and to consider the supply of corn and the defence of the country. On this day, too, impeachments are introduced by those who wish to do so, the lists of property confiscated by the state are read, and also applications for inheritances and wards of state, so that nothing may pass unclaimed without the cognisance of any person concerned. In the sixth prytany, in addition to the business already stated, the question is put to the vote whether it is desirable to hold a vote of ostracism or not; and complaints against professional accusers, whether Athenian or aliens domiciled in Athens, are received, to the number of not more than three of either class, together with cases in which an individual has made

under similar conditions. These heiresses were under the special protection of the Archon (see ch. 56, 6, 7), and may therefore be described as wards of state.

[73] This was the fund which provided the populace with the price of admission to the theatre.

[74] The Panathenaic festival was at the end of the first month of the Attic year (July). The other magistrates probably came into office at the beginning of that month; the Archons certainly did so.

[75] The ordinary Attic year was of 354 days, divided into twelve lunar months of thirty and twenty-nine days alternately. The deficiency was made up by inserting intercalary months, at first every alternate year, then three in eight years, and subsequently seven in nineteen. In an intercalary year the duration of the prytanies was thirty-nine and thirty-eight days, in place of thirty-six and thirty-five.

[76] The official residence of the Prytanes, supposed to represent the centre of the public life of Athens.

some promise to the people and has not performed it. Another Assembly in each prytany is assigned to the hearing of petitions, and at this meeting any one is free, on depositing the petitioner's olive-branch, to speak to the people concerning any matter, public or private. The two remaining meetings are devoted to all other subjects, and the laws require them to deal with three questions connected with religion, three connected with heralds and embassies, and three on secular subjects. Sometimes questions are brought forward without a preliminary vote of the Assembly to take them into consideration.

Heralds and envoys appear first before the Prytanes, and the bearers of dispatches also deliver them to the same officials.

44. There is a single President of the Prytanes, elected by lot, who presides for a night and a day; he may not hold the office for more than that time, nor may the same individual hold it twice. He keeps the keys of the sanctuaries in which the treasures and public records of the state are preserved, and also the public seal; and he is bound to remain in the Tholus, together with one-third of the Prytanes, named by himself. Whenever the Prytanes convene a meeting of the Council or Assembly, he appoints by lot nine Proedri, one from each tribe except that which holds the office of Prytanes for the time being; and out of these nine he similarly appoints one as President, and hands over the programme for the meeting to them. They take it and see to the preservation of order, put forward the various subjects which are to be considered, decide the results of the votings, and direct the proceedings generally.[77] They also have power to dismiss the meeting. No one may act as President more than once in the year, but he may be a Proedrus once in each prytany.

Elections to the offices of General and Hipparch and all other military commands are held in the Assembly, in such manner as the people decide; they are held after the sixth prytany by the first board of Prytanes in whose term of office the omens are favourable. There has, however, to be a preliminary consideration by the Council in this case also.

45. In former times the Council had full powers to inflict fines and imprisonment and death; but when it had consigned Lysimachus to the executioner, and he was sitting in the immediate expectation of death, Eumelides of Alopece rescued him from its hands, maintaining that no citizen ought to be put to death except on the decision of a court of law.[78] Accordingly a trial was held in a law-court, and Lysimachus was acquitted, receiving henceforth the nickname of 'the man from the drum-

[77] In the fifth century the Prytanes themselves acted as presidents at meetings of the Council and Assembly; but in the fourth century the Proedri appear to have been instituted, as here described.

[78] It should be observed that throughout the treatise a 'law-court' always means one of the large popular jury-courts, the constitutional importance of which is described in ch. 9.

head'; and the people deprived the Council thenceforward of the power to inflict death or imprisonment or fine, passing a law that if the Council condemn any person for an offence or inflict a fine, the Thesmothetae shall bring the sentence or fine before the law-court, and the decision of the jurors shall be the final judgment in the matter.

The Council passes judgment on nearly all magistrates, especially those who have the control of money; its judgment, however, is not final, but is subject to an appeal to the law-courts. Private individuals, also, may lay an information against any magistrate they please for not obeying the laws, but here too there is an appeal to the law-courts if the Council declare the charge proved. The Council also examines those who are to be its members for the ensuing year, and likewise the nine Archons. Formerly the Council had full power to reject candidates for office as unsuitable, but now they have an appeal to the law-courts. In all these matters, therefore, the Council has no final jurisdiction. It takes, however, preliminary cognisance of all matters brought before the Assembly, and the Assembly cannot vote on any question unless it has first been considered by the Council and placed on the programme by the Prytanes; since a person who carries a motion in the Assembly is liable to an action for illegal proposal on these grounds.

46. The Council also superintends the triremes that are already in existence, with their tackle and sheds, and builds new triremes or quad-riremes,[79] whichever the Assembly votes, with tackle and sheds to match. The Assembly appoints master-builders for the ships by vote; and if they do not hand them over completed to the next Council, the old Council cannot receive the customary donation—that being normally given to it during its successor's term of office. For the building of the triremes it appoints ten commissioners, chosen from its own members. The Council also inspects all public buildings, and if it is of opinion that the state is being defrauded, it reports the culprit to the Assembly, and on condemnation hands him over to the law-courts.

47. The Council also co-operates with the other magistrates in most of their duties. First there are the treasurers of Athena, ten in number, elected by lot, one from each tribe. According to the law of Solon—which is still in force—they must be Pentacosiomedimni, but in point of fact the person on whom the lot falls holds the office even though he be quite a poor man. These officers take over charge of the statue of Athena, the figures of Victory, and all the other ornaments of the temple, together with the money, in the presence of the Council. Then there are the Com-

---

[79] Quadriremes were first built at Athens a few years before 330 B.C., and in 325 B.C. they began to build quinqueremes. As the latter are not mentioned here, we seem to get a lower limit of date for the composition (or revision) of the treatise. The upper limit is fixed by ch. 54, 7 as 329 B.C.

missioners for Public Contracts, ten in number, one chosen by lot from each tribe, who farm out the public contracts. They lease the mines and taxes, in conjunction with the Military Treasurer and the Commissioners of the Theoric fund, in the presence of the Council, and grant, to the persons indicated by the vote of the Council, the mines which are let out by the state, including both the workable ones, which are let for three years, and those which are let under special agreements for [ten?] years.[80] They also sell, in the presence of the Council, the property of those who have gone into exile from the court of the Areopagus, and of others whose goods have been confiscated, and the nine Archons ratify the contracts. They also hand over to the Council lists of the taxes which are farmed out for the year, entering on whitened tablets the name of the lessee and the amount paid. They make separate lists, first of those who have to pay their instalments in each prytany, on ten several tablets, next of those who pay thrice in the year, with a separate tablet for each instalment, and finally of those who pay in the ninth prytany. They also draw up a list of farms and dwellings which have been confiscated and sold by order of the courts; for these too come within their province. In the case of dwellings the value must be paid up in five years, and in that of farms, in ten. The instalments are paid in the ninth prytany. Further, the King-archon brings before the Council the leases of the sacred enclosures, written on whitened tablets. These too are leased for ten years, and the instalments are paid in the [ninth] prytany; consequently it is in this prytany that the greatest amount of money is collected. The tablets containing the lists of the instalments are carried into the Council, and the public clerk takes charge of them. Whenever a payment of instalments is to be made he takes from the pigeon-holes the precise list of the sums which are to be paid and struck off on that day, and delivers it to the Receivers-General. The rest are kept apart, in order that no sum may be struck off before it is paid.

48. There are ten Receivers-General, elected by lot, one from each tribe. These officers receive the tablets, and strike off the instalments as they are paid, in the presence of the Council in the Council-chamber, and give the tablets back to the public clerk. If any one fails to pay his instalment, a note is made of it on the tablet; and he is bound to pay double the amount of the deficiency, or, in default, to be imprisoned. The Council has full power by the laws to exact these payments and to inflict this imprisonment. They receive all the instalments, therefore, on one day, and portion the money out among the magistrates; and on the next day they bring up the report of the apportionment, written on a wooden notice-board, and read it out in the Council-chamber, after which they

[80] This is the apparent reading of the passage, but the MS. is considerably damaged in this part.

ask publicly in the Council whether any one knows of any malpractice in reference to the apportionment, on the part of either a magistrate or a private individual, and if any one is charged with malpractice they take a vote on it.

The Council also elects ten Auditors by lot from its own members, to audit the accounts of the magistrates for each prytany. They also elect one Examiner of Accounts by lot from each tribe, with two assessors for each examiner, whose duty it is to sit at the ordinary market hours, each opposite the statue of the eponymous hero of his tribe; and if any one wishes to prefer a charge, on either public or private grounds, against any magistrate who has passed his audit before the law-courts, within three days of his having so passed, he enters on a whitened tablet his own name and that of the magistrate prosecuted, together with the mal-practice that is alleged against him. He also appends his claim for a penalty of such amount as seems to him fitting, and gives in the record to the Examiner. The latter takes it, and if after reading it he considers it proved he hands it over, if a private case, to the local justices who introduce cases[81] for the tribe concerned, while if it is a public case he enters it on the register of the Thesmothetae. Then, if the Thesmothetae accept it, they bring the accounts of this magistrate once more before the law-court, and the decision of the jury stands as the final judgment.

49. The Council also inspects the horses belonging to the state. If a man who has a good horse is found to keep it in bad condition, he is mulcted in his allowance of corn; while those which cannot keep up or which shy and will not stand steady, it brands with a wheel on the jaw, and the horse so marked is disqualified for service. It also inspects those who appear to be fit for service as scouts, and any one whom it rejects is deprived of his horse. It also examines the infantry who serve among the cavalry, and any one whom it rejects ceases to receive his pay. The roll of the cavalry is drawn up by the Commissioners of Enrolment, ten in number, elected by the Assembly by open vote. They hand over to the Hipparchs and Phylarchs the list of those whom they have enrolled, and these officers take it and bring it up before the Council, and there open the sealed tablet containing the names of the cavalry. If any of those who have been on the roll previously make affidavit that they are phys-ically incapable of cavalry service, they strike them out; then they call up the persons newly enrolled, and if any one makes affidavit that he is either physically or pecuniarily incapable of cavalry service they dismiss him, but if no such affidavit is made the Council vote whether the indi-

---

[81] All cases had to be brought before the courts by some magistrate. Several instances in which one of the Archons, or the Thesmothetae collectively, or the Arbitrators, or some other magistrate, performed this function for specific classes of cases are mentioned in the following chapters.

vidual in question is suitable for the purpose or not. If they vote in the affirmative his name is entered on the tablet; if not, he is dismissed with the others.

Formerly the Council used to decide on the plans for public buildings and the contract for making the robe of Athena;[82] but now this work is done by a jury in the law-courts appointed by lot, since the Council was considered to have shown favouritism in its decisions. The Council also shares with the Military Treasurer the superintendence of the manufacture of the images of Victory and the prizes at the Panathenaic festival.

The Council also examines infirm paupers; for there is a law which provides that persons possessing less than three minas, who are so crippled as to be unable to do any work, are, after examination by the Council, to receive two obols a day from the state for their support. A treasurer is appointed by lot to attend to them.

The Council also, speaking broadly, co-operates in most of the duties of all the other magistrates; and this ends the list of the functions of that body.

50. There are ten Commissioners for Repairs of Temples, elected by lot, who receive a sum of thirty minas from the Receivers-General, and therewith carry out the most necessary repairs in the temples.

There are also ten City Commissioners, of whom five hold office in Piraeus and five in the city. Their duty is to see that female flute- and harp- and lute-players are not hired at more than two drachmas, and if more than one person is anxious to hire the same girl, they cast lots and hire her out to the person to whom the lot falls. They also provide that no collector of sewage shall shoot any of his sewage within ten stadia of the walls; they prevent people from blocking up the streets by building, or stretching barriers across them, or making drain-pipes in mid-air with a discharge into the street, or having doors which open outwards; they also remove the corpses of those who die in the streets, for which purpose they have a body of state slaves assigned to them.

51. Market Commissioners are elected by lot, five for Piraeus, five for the city. Their statutory duty is to see that all articles offered for sale in the market are pure and unadulterated.

Commissioners of Weights and Measures are elected by lot, five for the city, and five for Piraeus. They see that sellers use fair weights and measures.

Formerly there were ten Corn Commissioners, elected by lot, five for Piraeus, and five for the city; but now there are twenty for the city and fifteen for Piraeus. Their duties are, first, to see that the unprepared corn

---

[82] This was the robe which was carried in procession at the great Panathenaic festival. It was embroidered with mythological subjects, and was woven on each occasion by a number of girls, under the superintendence of two of superior family.

in the market is offered for sale at reasonable prices, and secondly, to see that the millers sell barley meal at a price proportionate to that of barley, and that the bakers sell their loaves at a price proportionate to that of wheat, and of such weight as the Commissioners may appoint; for the law requires them to fix the standard weight.

There are ten Superintendents of the Mart, elected by lot, whose duty is to superintend the Mart, and to compel merchants to bring up into the city two-thirds of the corn which is brought by sea to the Corn Mart.

52. The Eleven also are appointed by lot to take care of the prisoners in the state gaol. Thieves, kidnappers, and pickpockets are brought to them, and if they plead guilty they are executed, but if they deny the charge the Eleven bring the case before the law-courts; if the prisoners are acquitted, they release them, but if not, they then execute them. They also bring up before the law-courts the list of farms and houses claimed as state-property; and if it is decided that they are so, they deliver them to the Commissioners for Public Contracts. The Eleven also bring up informations laid against magistrates alleged to be disqualified; this function comes within their province, but some such cases are brought up by the Thesmothetae.

There are also five Introducers of Cases, elected by lot, one for each pair of tribes, who bring up the 'monthly' cases to the law-courts. 'Monthly' cases are these: refusal to pay up a dowry where a party is bound to do so, refusal to pay interest on money borrowed at 12 per cent,[83] or where a man desirous of setting up business in the market has borrowed from another man capital to start with; also cases of slander, cases arising out of friendly loans or partnerships, and cases concerned with slaves, cattle, and the office of trierarch, or with banks. These are brought up as 'monthly' cases and are introduced by these officers; but the Receivers-General perform the same function in cases for or against the farmers of taxes. Those in which the sum concerned is not more than ten drachmas they can decide summarily, but all above that amount they bring into the law-courts as 'monthly' cases.

53. The Forty[84] are also elected by lot, four from each tribe, before whom suitors bring all other cases. Formerly they were thirty in number, and they went on circuit through the demes to hear causes; but after the oligarchy of the Thirty they were increased to forty. They have full powers to decide cases in which the amount at issue does not exceed ten drachmas, but anything beyond that value they hand over to the Arbitrators. The Arbitrators take up the case, and, if they cannot bring the parties to an agreement, they give a decision. If their decision satisfies

[83] If the rate of interest was higher, the creditor could not make use of this procedure.
[84] These are the officials elsewhere described as the local justices, who were instituted by Pisistratus (ch. 16, 5) and revived in 453 B.C. (ch. 26, 3).

both parties, and they abide by it, the case is at an end; but if either of the parties appeals to the law-courts, the Arbitrators enclose the evidence, the pleadings, and the laws quoted in the case in two urns, those of the plaintiff in the one, and those of the defendant in the other. These they seal up and, having attached to them the decision of the arbitrator, written out on a tablet, place them in the custody of the four justices whose function it is to introduce cases on behalf of the tribe of the defendant. These officers take them and bring up the case before the law-court, to a jury of 201 members in cases up to the value of 1,000 drachmas, or to one of 401 in cases above that value. No laws or pleadings or evidence may be used except those which were adduced before the Arbitrator, and have been enclosed in the urns.

The Arbitrators are persons in the sixtieth year of their age; this appears from the schedule of the Archons and the Eponymi. There are two classes of Eponymi, the ten who give their names to the tribes, and the forty-two of the years of service.[85] The youths, on being enrolled among the citizens, were formerly registered upon whitened tablets, and the names were appended of the Archon in whose year they were enrolled, and of the Eponymus who had been in course in the preceding year; at the present day they are written on a bronze pillar, which stands in front of the Council-chamber, near the Eponymi of the tribes. Then the Forty take the last of the Eponymi of the years of service, and assign the arbitrations to the persons belonging to that year, casting lots to determine which arbitrations each shall undertake; and every one is compelled to carry through the arbitrations which the lot assigns to him. The law enacts that any one who does not serve as Arbitrator when he has arrived at the necessary age shall lose his civil rights, unless he happens to be holding some other office during that year, or to be out of the country. These are the only persons who escape the duty. Any one who suffers injustice at the hands of the Arbitrator may appeal to the whole board of Arbitrators, and if they find the magistrate guilty, the law enacts that he shall lose his civil rights. The persons thus condemned have, however, in their turn an appeal. The Eponymi are also used in reference to military expeditions; when the men of military age are despatched on service, a notice is put up stating that the men from such-and-such an Archon and

---

[85] These Eponymi are unknown except from this passage and quotations from it in the grammarians. It would appear that, just as the Eponymi of the tribes were the ten heroes who gave their names to the ten tribes, so a cycle of forty-two years was arranged, to each of which the name of a hero was assigned as its Eponymus. Then, as every Athenian was liable to military service for forty-two years (eighteen to fifty-nine inclusive), each man had to go through the complete cycle before he was free from liability to serve. During the last year of his cycle, however, he was required to serve not as a soldier but as an Arbitrator; and accordingly each year the Forty took the list of those who were commencing their last year of service, and assigned to them the duties which they were to undertake as arbitrators during the year.

Eponymus to such-and-such another Archon and Eponymus are to go on the expedition.

54. The following magistrates also are elected by lot: Five Commissioners of Roads, who, with an assigned body of public slaves, are required to keep the roads in order; and ten Auditors, with ten assistants, to whom all persons who have held any office must give in their accounts. These are the only officers who audit the accounts of those who are subject to examination,[86] and who bring them up for examination before the law-courts. If they detect any magistrate in embezzlement, the jury condemn him for theft, and he is obliged to repay tenfold the sum he is declared to have misappropriated. If they charge a magistrate with accepting bribes and the jury convict him, they fine him for corruption, and this sum too is repaid tenfold. Or if they convict him of unfair dealing, he is fined on that charge, and the sum assessed is paid without increase, if payment is made before the ninth prytany, but otherwise it is doubled. A tenfold fine is not doubled.

The Clerk of the Prytany, as he is called, is also elected by lot. He has the charge of all public documents, and keeps the resolutions which are passed by the Assembly, and checks the transcripts of all other official papers and attends at the sessions of the Council. Formerly he was elected by open vote, and the most distinguished and trustworthy persons were elected to the post, as is known from the fact that the name of this officer is appended on the pillars recording treaties of alliance and grants of consulship and citizenship. Now, however, he is elected by lot. There is, in addition, a Clerk of the Laws, elected by lot, who attends at the sessions of the Council; and he too checks the transcript of all the laws. The Assembly also elects by open vote a clerk to read documents to it and to the Council; but he has no other duty except that of reading aloud.

The Assembly also elects by lot the Commissioners of Public Worship, known as the Commissioners for Sacrifices, who offer the sacrifices appointed by oracle, and, in conjunction with the seers, take the auspices whenever there is occasion. It also elects by lot ten others, known as Annual Commissioners, who offer certain sacrifices and administer all the quadrennial festivals except the Panathenaea. There are the following quadrennial festivals: first that of Delos (where there is also a sexennial festival), secondly the Brauronia, thirdly the Heracleia, fourthly the Eleusinia, and fifthly the Panathenaea; and no two of these are celebrated

[86] Every person who had held any public office had to submit himself and his accounts to examination before a jury at the end of his term of office; on which occasion any citizen might impeach his conduct during his office.

in the same place.[87] To these the Hephaestia has now been added, in the archonship of Cephisophon.[88]

An Archon is also elected by lot for Salamis, and a Demarch for Piraeus. These officers celebrate the Dionysia in these two places, and appoint Choregi. In Salamis, moreover, the name of the Archon is publicly recorded.

55. All the foregoing magistrates are elected by lot, and their powers are those which have been stated. To pass on to the nine Archons, as they are called, the manner of their appointment from the earliest times has been described already. At the present day six Thesmothetae are elected by lot, together with their clerk, and in addition to these an Archon, a King, and a Polemarch. One is elected from each tribe. They are examined first of all by the Council of Five Hundred, with the exception of the clerk. The latter is examined only in the law-court, like other magistrates (for all magistrates, whether elected by lot or by open vote, are examined before entering on their offices); but the nine Archons are examined both in the Council and again in the law-court. Formerly no one could hold the office if the Council rejected him, but now there is an appeal to the law-court, which is the final authority in the matter of the examination. When they are examined, they are asked, first, "Who is your father, and of what deme? Who is your father's father? Who is your mother? Who is your mother's father, and of what deme?" Then the candidate is asked whether he possesses an ancestral Apollo and a household Zeus, and where their sanctuaries are; next if he possesses a family tomb, and where; then if he treats his parents well, and pays his taxes, and has served on the required military expeditions. When the examiner has put these questions, he proceeds, "Call the witnesses to these facts." And when the candidate has produced his witnesses, he next asks, "Does any one wish to make any accusation against this man?" If an accuser appears, he gives the parties an opportunity of making their accusation and defence, and then puts it to the Council to pass the candidate or not, and to the law-court to give the final vote. If no one wishes to make an accusation, he proceeds at once to the vote. Formerly a single individual gave the vote, but now all the members are obliged to vote on the candidates, so that if any unprincipled candidate has managed to get rid of his accusers, it may still be possible for him to be disqualified before the law-court. When the examination has been thus completed, they proceed to the stone on which are the pieces of the victims, and on which the Arbitrators take oath before declaring their decisions, and witnesses swear to

---

[87] The reading is rather doubtful.

[88] This date (329 B.C.) gives us a limit of time after which this work must have been written, or (since the words have the air of a parenthetical or later addition) at least revised.

their testimony. On this stone the Archons stand, and swear to execute their office uprightly and according to the laws, and not to receive presents in respect of the performance of their duties, or, if they do, to dedicate a golden statue. When they have taken this oath they proceed to the Acropolis, and there they repeat it; after this they enter upon their office.

56. The Archon, the King, and the Polemarch have each two assessors, nominated by themselves. These officers are examined in the law-court before they begin to act, and give in accounts on each occasion of their acting.

As soon as the Archon enters office, he begins by issuing a proclamation that whatever any one possessed before he entered into office, that he shall possess and hold until the end of his term. Next he assigns Choregi to the tragic poets, choosing three[89] of the richest persons out of the whole body of Athenians. Formerly he used also to assign five Choregi to the comic poets, but now the tribes provide the Choregi for them. Then he receives the Choregi who have been appointed by the tribes for the men's and boys' choruses and the comic poets at the Dionysia, and for the men's and boys' choruses at the Thargelia (at the Dionysia there is a chorus for each tribe, but at the Thargelia one between two tribes, each tribe bearing its share in providing it); he transacts the exchanges of properties for them,[90] and reports any excuses that are tendered, if any one says that he has already borne this burden, or that he is exempt because he has borne a similar burden and the period of his exemption has not yet expired, or that he is not of the required age; since the Choregus of a boys' chorus must be over forty years of age. He also appoints Choregi for the festival at Delos, and a chief of the mission for the thirty-oar boat which conveys the youths thither. He also superintends sacred processions, both that in honour of Asclepius, when the initiated keep house, and that of the great Dionysia—the latter in conjunction with the Superintendents of that festival. These officers, ten in number, were formerly elected by open vote in the Assembly, and used to provide for the expenses of the procession out of their private means; but now one is elected by lot from each tribe, and the state contributes 100 minas for the expenses. The

[89] Only three tragic poets might contend at the festivals, and it was the duty of the Archon to decide what poets should be admitted to the honour. In Comedy, as stated below, five competitors were allowed, but this number applies only to the fourth century, before which time the number was limited to three. The duty of the Choregus was to defray the expense of training, maintaining, and equipping the chorus required for a play or a dithyrambic contest.

[90] If any person considered that he had been unduly saddled with one of the burdens which rich men were called upon to bear for the state (such as the equipment of a chorus or a trireme), he might require any one on whom he thought the burden should rather have been laid either to undertake it, or else to submit to an exchange of properties.

Archon also superintends the procession at the Thargelia, and that in honour of Zeus the Saviour. He also manages the contests at the Dionysia and the Thargelia.

These, then, are the festivals which he superintends. The suits and indictments which come before him, and which he, after a preliminary inquiry, brings up before the law-courts, are as follows. Injury to parents (for bringing these actions the prosecutor cannot suffer any penalty); injury to orphans (these actions lie against their guardians); injury to a ward of state (these lie against their guardians or their husbands); injury to an orphan's estate (these too lie against the guardians); mental derangement, where a party charges another with destroying his own property through unsoundness of mind; for appointment of liquidators, where a party refuses to divide property in which others have a share; for constituting a wardship; for determining between rival claims to a wardship; for granting inspection of property to which another party lays claim; for appointing oneself as guardian; and for determining disputes as to inheritances and wards of state. The Archon also has the care of orphans and wards of state, and of women who, on the death of their husbands, declare themselves to be with child; and he has power to inflict a fine on those who offend against the persons under his charge, or to bring the case before the law-courts. He also leases the houses of orphans and wards of state until they reach the age of fourteen, and takes mortgages on them; and if the guardians fail to provide the necessary food for the children under their charge, he exacts it from them. Such are the duties of the Archon.

57. The King in the first place superintends the mysteries, in conjunction with the Superintendents of Mysteries. The latter are elected in the Assembly by open vote, two from the general body of Athenians, one from the Eumolpidae, and one from the Ceryces. Next, he superintends the Lenaean Dionysia,[91] which consists of a procession and a contest. The procession is ordered by the King and the Superintendents in conjunction; but the contest is managed by the King alone. He also manages all the contests of the torch-race; and to speak broadly, he administers all the ancestral sacrifices. Indictments for impiety come before him, or any disputes between parties concerning priestly rites; and he also determines all controversies concerning sacred rites for the ancient families and the priests. All actions for homicide come before him, and it is he that makes the proclamation requiring polluted persons to keep away from sacred ceremonies. Actions for homicide and wounding are heard, if the homi-

[91] The lesser of the two chief festivals of Dionysus, held in January. Many of the plays which have come down to us were first performed at this festival, but it was not such a magnificent occasion as the great Dionysia, at which strangers from the rest of Greece were usually present in great numbers.

cide or wounding be wilful, in the Areopagus; so also in cases of killing by
poison, and of arson. These are the only cases heard by that Council.
Cases of unintentional homicide, or of intent to kill, or of killing a slave
or a resident alien or a foreigner, are heard by the court of Palladium.
When the homicide is acknowledged, but legal justification is pleaded, as
when a man takes an adulterer in the act, or kills another by mistake in
battle, or in an athletic contest, the prisoner is tried in the court of
Delphinium. If a man who is in banishment for a homicide which admits
of reconciliation[92] incurs a further charge of killing or wounding, he is
tried in Phreatto, and he makes his defence from a boat moored near the
shore. All these cases, except those which are heard in the Areopagus, are
tried by the [Ephetae] on whom the lot falls. The King introduces them,
and the hearing is held within sacred precincts and in the open air. Whenever the King hears a case he takes off his crown. The person who is
charged with homicide is at all other times excluded from the temples,
nor is it even lawful for him to enter the market-place; but on the occasion of his trial he enters the temple and makes his defence. If the actual
offender is unknown, the writ runs against 'the doer of the deed'. The
King and the tribe-kings also hear the cases in which the guilt rests on
inanimate objects and the lower animals.[93]

58. The Polemarch performs the sacrifices to Artemis the huntress and
to Enyalius, and arranges the contest at the funeral of those who have
fallen in war, and makes offerings to the memory of Harmodius and
Aristogeiton. Only private actions come before him, namely those in
which resident aliens, both ordinary and privileged, and agents of foreign
states are concerned. It is his duty to receive these cases and divide them
into ten groups, and assign to each tribe the group which comes to it by
lot; after which the magistrates who introduce cases for the tribe hand
them over to the Arbitrators. The Polemarch, however, brings up in person cases in which an alien is charged with deserting his patron or neglecting to provide himself with one, and also of inheritances and wards of
state where aliens are concerned; and in fact, generally, whatever the
Archon does for citizens, the Polemarch does for aliens.

59. The Thesmothetae in the first place have the power of prescribing
on what days the law-courts are to sit, and next of assigning them to the
several magistrates; for the latter must follow the arrangement which the

---

[92] A person who committed an involuntary homicide had to give pecuniary satisfaction to the relatives of the deceased, and he was compelled to go into exile for a
year unless they gave him leave to return earlier.

[93] This is a relic of a very primitive custom, by which any object that had caused a
man's death was put upon its trial. In later times it may have served the purpose of
a coroner's inquest. Cases of this kind, and those in which the culprit was unknown,
were tried in the court of the Prytaneum, and it is probable that the name occurred
in the treatise, but has dropped out of the MS.

Thesmothetae assign. Moreover they introduce impeachments before the Assembly, and bring up all votes for removal from office, challenges of a magistrate's conduct before the Assembly, indictments for illegal proposals, or for proposing a law which is contrary to the interests of the state, complaints against Proedri or their president for their conduct in office, and the accounts presented by the generals. All indictments also come before them in which a deposit has to be made by the prosecutor, namely, indictments for concealment of foreign origin, for corrupt evasion of foreign origin (when a man escapes the disqualification by bribery), for blackmailing accusations, bribery, false entry of another as a state debtor, false testimony to the service of a summons, conspiracy to enter a man as a state debtor, corrupt removal from the list of debtors, and adultery. They also bring up the examinations of all magistrates, and the rejections by the demes and the condemnations by the Council. Moreover they bring up certain private suits in cases of merchandise and mines, or where a slave has slandered a free man. It is they also who cast lots to assign the courts to the various magistrates, whether for private or public cases. They ratify commercial treaties, and bring up the cases which arise out of such treaties; and they also bring up cases of perjury from the Areopagus. The casting of lots for the jurors is conducted by all the nine Archons, with the clerk to the Thesmothetae as the tenth, each performing the duty for his own tribe. Such are the duties of the nine Archons.

60. There are also ten Commissioners of Games, elected by lot, one from each tribe. These officers, after passing an examination, serve for four years; and they manage the Panathenaic procession, the contest in music and that in gymnastic, and the horse-race; they also provide the robe of Athena and, in conjunction with the Council, the vases,[94] and they present the oil to the athletes. This oil is collected from the sacred olives. The Archon requisitions it from the owners of the farms on which the sacred olives grow, at the rate of three-quarters of a pint from each plant. Formerly the state used to sell the fruit itself, and if any one dug up or broke down one of the sacred olives, he was tried by the Council of Areopagus, and if he was condemned, the penalty was death. Since, however, the oil has been paid by the owner of the farm, the procedure has lapsed, though the law remains; and the oil is a state charge upon the property instead of being taken from the individual plants. When, then, the Archon has collected the oil for his year of office, he hands it over to the Treasurers to preserve in the Acropolis, and he may not take his seat in the Areopagus until he has paid over to the Treasurers the full amount. The Treasurers keep it in the Acropolis until the Panathenaea, when they

---

[94] The vases given as prizes at the Panathenaea, of which a considerable number still exist.

measure it out to the Commissioners of Games, and they again to the victorious competitors. The prizes for the victors in the musical contest consist of silver and gold, for the victors in manly vigour, of shields, and for the victors in the gymnastic contest and the horse-race, of oil.

61. All officers connected with military service are elected by open vote. In the first place, ten Generals (Strategi), who were formerly elected one from each tribe, but now are chosen from the whole mass of citizens. Their duties are assigned to them by open vote; one is appointed to command the heavy infantry, and leads them if they go out to war; one to the defence of the country, who remains on the defensive, and fights if there is war within the borders of the country; two to Piraeus, one of whom is assigned to Munichia, and one to the south shore, and these have charge of the defence of the Piraeus; and one to superintend the symmories,[95] who nominates the trierarchs and arranges exchanges of properties for them, and brings up actions to decide on rival claims in connection with them. The rest are despatched to whatever business may be on hand at the moment. The appointment of these officers is submitted for confirmation in each prytany, when the question is put whether they are considered to be doing their duty. If any officer is rejected on this vote, he is tried in the law-court, and if he is found guilty the people decide what punishment or fine shall be inflicted on him; but if he is acquitted he resumes his office. The Generals have full power, when on active service, to arrest any one for insubordination, or to cashier him publicly, or to inflict a fine; the latter is, however, unusual.

There are also ten Taxiarchs, one from each tribe, elected by open vote; and each commands his own tribesmen and appoints captains of companies. There are also two Hipparchs, elected by open vote from the whole mass of the citizens, who command the cavalry, each taking five tribes. They have the same powers as the Generals have in respect of the infantry, and their appointments are also subject to confirmation. There are also ten Phylarchs, elected by open vote, one from each tribe, to command the cavalry, as the Taxiarchs do the infantry. There is also a Hipparch for Lemnos, elected by open vote, who has charge of the cavalry in Lemnos. There is also a treasurer of the Paralus, and another of the Ammonias, similarly elected.[96]

62. Of the magistrates elected by lot, in former times some, including the nine Archons, were elected out of the tribe as a whole, while others, namely those who are now elected in the Theseum, were apportioned among the demes; but since the demes used to sell the elections, these

[95] The companies into which the richer members of the community were formed (first in 377 B.C.) for the payment of the extraordinary charges in war-time.

[96] These are the two triremes which were used for special state services. The Ammonias appears to have taken the place of the Salaminia in the time of Alexander, when the Athenians sent sacrifices to the god Ammon in it.

magistrates too are now elected from the whole tribe, except the members of the Council and the guards of the dockyards, who are still left to the demes.

Pay is received for the following services. First the members of the Assembly receive a drachma for the ordinary meetings, and nine obols for the 'sovereign' meeting. Then the jurors at the law-courts receive three obols; and the members of the Council five obols. The Prytanes receive an allowance of an obol for their maintenance. The nine Archons receive four obols apiece for maintenance, and also keep a herald and a flute-player; and the Archon for Salamis receives a drachma a day. The Commissioners for Games dine in the Prytaneum during the month of Hecatombaeon in which the Panathenaic festival takes place, from the fourteenth day onwards. The Amphictyonic deputies to Delos receive a drachma a day from the exchequer of Delos. Also all magistrates sent to Samos, Scyros, Lemnos, or Imbros receive an allowance for their maintenance. The military offices may be held any number of times, but none of the others more than once, except the membership of the Council, which may be held twice.

63. The juries for the law-courts are chosen by lot by the nine Archons, each for their own tribe, and by the clerk to the Thesmothetae for the tenth. There are ten entrances into the courts, one for each tribe; twenty rooms in which the lots are drawn, two for each tribe; 100 chests, ten for each tribe; other chests, in which are placed the tickets of the jurors on whom the lot falls; and two vases. Further, staves, equal in number to the jurors required, are placed by the side of each entrance; and counters are put into one vase, equal in number to the staves. These are inscribed with letters of the alphabet beginning with the eleventh, equal in number to the courts which require to be filled. All persons above thirty years of age are qualified to serve as jurors, provided they are not debtors to the state and have not lost their civil rights. If any unqualified person serves as juror, an information is laid against him, and he is brought before the court; and, if he is convicted, the jurors assess the punishment or fine which they consider him to deserve. If he is condemned to a money fine, he must be imprisoned until he has paid up both the original debt, on account of which the information was laid against him, and also the fine which the court has imposed upon him. Each juror has his ticket of boxwood, on which is inscribed his name, with the name of his father and his deme, and one of the letters of the alphabet up to *kappa*;[97] for the jurors in their several tribes are divided into ten sections, with approximately

---

[97] The tenth letter of the alphabet. Thus the whole body of jurors was divided into ten sections, indicated by the letters from *alpha* to *kappa*; and the courts for which jurors were required were indicated by the requisite number of letters from *lambda* onwards.

an equal number in each letter. When the Thesmothetes has decided by lot which letters are required to attend at the courts, the servant puts up above each court the letter which has been assigned to it by the lot.

64. The ten chests above mentioned are placed in front of the entrance used by each tribe, and are inscribed with the letters of the alphabet from *alpha* to *kappa*. The jurors cast in their tickets, each into the chest on which is inscribed the letter which is on his ticket; then the servant shakes them all up, and the Archon draws one ticket from each chest. The individual so selected is called the Ticket-hanger, and his function is to hang up the tickets out of his chest on the bar which bears the same letter as that on the chest. He is chosen by lot, lest, if the Ticket-hanger were always the same person, he might tamper with the results. There are five of these bars in each of the rooms assigned for the lot-drawing. Then the Archon casts in the dice and thereby chooses the jurors from each tribe, room by room. The dice are made of brass, coloured black or white; and according to the number of jurors required, so many white dice are put in, one for each five tickets, while the remainder are black, in the same proportion. As the Archon draws out the dice, the crier calls out the names of the individuals chosen. The Ticket-hanger is included among those selected. Each juror, as he is chosen and answers to his name, draws a counter from the vase, and holding it out with the letter uppermost shows it first to the presiding Archon; and he, when he has seen it, throws the ticket of the juror into the chest on which is inscribed the letter which is on the counter, so that the juror must go into the court assigned to him by lot, and not into one chosen by himself, and that it may be impossible for any one to collect the jurors of his choice into any particular court. For this purpose chests are placed near the Archon, as many in number as there are courts to be filled that day, bearing the letters of the courts on which the lot has fallen.

65. The juror thereupon, after showing his counter again to the attendant, passes through the barrier into the court. The attendant gives him a staff of the same colour as the court bearing the letter which is on his counter, so as to ensure his going into the court assigned to him by lot; since, if he were to go into any other, he would be betrayed by the colour of his staff. Each court has a certain colour painted on the lintel of the entrance. Accordingly the juror, bearing his staff, enters the court which has the same colour as his staff, and the same letter as his counter. As he enters, he receives a voucher from the official to whom this duty has been assigned by lot. So with their counters and their staves the selected jurors take their seats in the court, having thus completed the process of admission. The unsuccessful candidates receive back their tickets from the Ticket-hangers. The public servants carry the chests from each tribe, one to each court, containing the names of the members of the tribe who

are in that court, and hand them over to the officials assigned to the duty
of giving back their tickets to the jurors in each court, so that these officials may call them up by name and pay them their fee.

66. When all the courts are full, two ballot boxes are placed in the first
court, and a number of brazen dice, bearing the colours of the several
courts, and other dice inscribed with the names of the presiding magistrates. Then two of the Thesmothetae, selected by lot, severally throw
the dice with the colours into one box, and those with the magistrates'
names into the other. The magistrate whose name is first drawn is thereupon proclaimed by the crier as assigned for duty in the court which is
first drawn, and the second in the second, and similarly with the rest. The
object of this procedure is that no one may know which court he will have,
but that each may take the court assigned to him by lot.

When the jurors have come in, and have been assigned to their respective courts, the presiding magistrate in each court draws one ticket out
of each chest (making ten in all, one out of each tribe), and throws them
into another empty chest. He then draws out five of them, and assigns one
to the superintendence of the water-clock, and the other four to the telling of the votes. This is to prevent any tampering beforehand with either
the superintendent of the clock or the tellers of the votes, and to secure
that there is no malpractice in these respects. The five who have not been
selected for these duties receive from them a statement of the order in
which the jurors shall receive their fees, and of the places where the several tribes shall respectively gather in the court for this purpose when
their duties are completed; the object being that the jurors may be
broken up into small groups for the reception of their pay, and not all
crowd together and impede one another.

67. These preliminaries being concluded, the cases are called on. If it
is a day for private cases, the private litigants are called. Four cases are
taken in each of the categories defined in the law, and the litigants swear
to confine their speeches to the point at issue. If it is a day for public
causes, the public litigants are called, and only one case is tried. Water-
clocks are provided, having small supply-tubes, into which the water is
poured by which the length of the pleadings is regulated. Ten gallons are
allowed for a case in which an amount of more than 5,000 drachmas is
involved, and three for the second speech on each side. When the amount
is between one and five thousand drachmas, seven gallons are allowed for
the first speech and two for the second; when it is less than 1,000, five
and two. Six gallons are allowed for arbitrations between rival claimants,
in which there is no second speech. The official chosen by lot to superintend the water-clock places his hand on the supply-tube whenever the
clerk is about to read a resolution or law or affidavit or treaty. When,
however, a case is conducted according to a set measurement of the day,

he does not stop the supply, but each party receives an equal allowance of water. The standard of measurement is the length of the days in the month Poseideon.[98] . . . . The measured day is employed in cases when imprisonment, death, exile, loss of civil rights, or confiscation of goods is assigned as the penalty.

68. Most of the courts consist of 500 members . . . ; and when it is necessary to bring public cases before a jury of 1,000 members, two courts combine for the purpose, [while the most important cases of all are brought before] 1,500 jurors, or three courts. The ballot balls are made of brass with stems running through the centre, half of them having the stem pierced and the other half solid. When the speeches are concluded, the officials assigned to the taking of the votes give each juror two ballot balls, one pierced and one solid. This is done in full view of the rival litigants, to secure that no one shall receive two pierced or two solid balls. Then the official designated for the purpose takes away the jurors' staves, in return for which each one as he records his vote receives a brass voucher marked with the numeral 3 (because he gets three obols when he gives it up). This is to ensure that all shall vote; since no one can get a voucher unless he votes. Two urns, one of brass and the other of wood, stand in the court, in distinct spots so that no one may surreptitiously insert ballot balls; in these the jurors record their votes. The brazen urn is for effective votes, the wooden for unused votes; and the brazen urn has a lid pierced so as to take only one ballot ball, in order that no one may put in two at a time.

When the jurors are about to vote, the crier demands first whether the litigants enter a protest against any of the evidence; for no protest can be received after the voting has begun. Then he proclaims again, 'The pierced ballot for the plaintiff, the solid for the defendant'; and the juror, taking his two ballot balls from the stand, with his hand closed over the stem so as not to show either the pierced or the solid ballot to the litigants, casts the one which is to count into the brazen urn, and the other into the wooden urn.

69. When all the jurors have voted, the attendants take the urn containing the effective votes and discharge them on to a reckoning board having as many cavities as there are ballot balls, so that the effective votes, whether pierced or solid, may be plainly displayed and easily counted. Then the officials assigned to the taking of the votes tell them off on the board, the solid in one place and the pierced in another, and the crier announces the numbers of the votes, the pierced ballots being for the prosecutor and the solid for the defendant. Whichever has the majority is victorious; but if the votes are equal the verdict is for the de-

[98] i.e. December to January, when the days are shortest. A mutilated passage follows.

fendant. Then, if damages have to be awarded, they vote again in the same way, first returning their pay-vouchers and receiving back their staves. Half a gallon of water is allowed to each party for the discussion of the damages. Finally, when all has been completed in accordance with the law, the jurors receive their pay in the order assigned by the lot.

THE INDICA

By Arrian

In the Indica *Arrian redeems his promise made in the* Anabasis *to treat India in a separate treatise. The* Indica *is sometimes printed as the eighth book of the* Anabasis *but it is clear that Arrian's purpose is not strictly historical as he had conceived of history in the earlier work. The first seventeen chapters, written in the spirit of Herodotus, provide a description of the geography, customs, myths, and animals of India. Even the remaining chapters, though largely devoted to the exploits of Alexander and Nearchus, are embellished with traveller's tales. Although Arrian derived his information from older sources, the work is valuable as a manifestation of ancient observation of, and interest in, remote and foreign races.*

1. The district west of the river Indus as far as the river Cophen is inhabited by the Astacenians and the Assacenians, Indian tribes. But they are not so tall in stature or so courageous as those who dwell east of the Indus; nor are they so swarthy as the majority of the Indians. These were in ancient times subject to the Assyrians, afterwards to the Medes, and finally they submitted to the Persians, and paid tribute to Cyrus the son of Cambyses as ruler of their land. The Nysaeans are not an Indian race, but descended from the men who came into India with Dionysus; perhaps from those Greeks who were rendered unfit for service in the wars which Dionysus waged with the Indians. Perhaps also he settled with the Greeks those of the natives who were willing to join his colony. Dionysus named the city itself Nysa, and the land Nysaea, in honour of his nurse Nysa. The mountain near the city, at whose base Nysa was built, is called Meros (thigh) after the misfortune he experienced as soon as he was born. This is the story framed by the poets in regard to Dionysus, and let the writers of legends Grecian and foreign expound it. Among the Assacenians is Massaca, a large city, where also is the stronghold of the land of Assacia; and there is also another large city, Peucelaitis, not far from the Indus. These tribes have been settled west of the Indus as far as the Cophen.

2. Let me call the country east of the Indus India, and the people Indians. Towards the north of India lies Mount Taurus; but in this land it is no longer called Taurus. This range commences from the sea near

Pamphylia, Lycia, and Cilicia and extends as far as the Eastern Sea, dividing the whole of Asia. It is called by various names in different districts; in one part it is called Parapamisus, in another Emodus, in a third Imaus, and probably it has several other names. The Macedonians who accompanied Alexander's expedition called it Caucasus. But this is quite a different Caucasus from that in Scythia. They called it by this name that the report might become current that Alexander had marched even beyond the Caucasus. The river Indus bounds India on the west as far as the Great Sea, into which it discharges its water by two mouths, not near each other like the five mouths of the Ister, but like those of the Nile, by which the Egyptian Delta is formed. Thus also the river Indus forms the Delta of India, which is not smaller than that of Egypt. This delta is called in the Indian tongue Pattala. On the south India is bounded by the Great Sea itself, and the same sea bounds it on the east. The part of the country towards the south near Pattala and the outlets of the Indus was seen by Alexander and the Macedonians and by many Greeks; but into the part towards the east Alexander did not penetrate further than the river Hyphasis. A few authors have described the country as far as the river Ganges, and where are the outlets of that river and near it Palimbothra, the largest city of the Indians.

3. I consider Eratosthenes the Cyrenaean the most trustworthy authority, because he is careful to trace the circumference of the country. This writer says that the side of India has a length of 1,529 miles to one going from Mount Taurus, in which are the sources of the Indus, along that river itself as far as the Great Sea and the outlets of the Indus. And opposite this he makes another side from the same mountain to the Eastern Sea scarcely equal to this side; but he makes a peninsula stretch far into the sea to the extent of about 353 miles. Therefore according to him the side of India towards the east would extend 1,882 miles. This he considers the breadth of India. The length from west to east as far as the city of Palimbothra he says was measured in schoeni,[1] and he made a plan of it; for it was the royal road. He says that this extends to 1,176 miles. The districts beyond this have not been so accurately measured. But as many as have recorded rumours say that with the peninsula projecting into the sea it amounts to about 1,200 miles. So that the length of India upward is about 2,353 miles. Ctesias the Cnidian says that India is equal to the rest of Asia, but he talks nonsense; and so does Onesicritus, saying that it is the third part of all the earth. Nearchus says that it is a journey of four months through the plain alone of India. To Megasthenes the distance from the east to the west is the breadth of India, which others make its length. He says that where it is shortest it extends 1,882 miles, and

[1] Pliny (xii. 30) says that Eratosthenes reckoned the schoenus at 40 stades, or about 5 miles. Like the parasang it seems to have varied.

that from north to south, which is its length according to him, it extends 2,624 miles, where it is narrowest.

In the whole of the rest of Asia there are not so many rivers as in India. The largest are the Ganges and the Indus, from the latter of which the country takes its name. Both of these are larger than the Egyptian Nile and the Scythian Ister, even if their waters came together into one. To me indeed it seems that even the Acesines is larger than the Ister or the Nile, where it falls into the Indus, after having taken up into its stream the Hydaspes, the Hydraotes, and the Hyphasis, so that at this place its breadth is three and one-half miles. Perhaps also many other larger rivers flow in India.

4. I cannot be sure of the accuracy of any statements about the country beyond the river Hyphasis, because Alexander did not advance further than that river. Of the two largest rivers themselves, the Ganges and the Indus, Megasthenes has stated that the former excels much in size; and so say all other writers who mention it. He says that it rises great from its sources, and that it receives into itself the Cainas, the Erannoboas, and the Cossoanus, all navigable rivers; then the Sonus, Sittocatis, and Solomatis, which are also navigable; and besides these, the Condochates, Sambus, Magon, Agoranis, and Omalis. A great river, the Comminases, and the Cacouthis and Andomatis, which flows from the land of the Madyandinians, an Indian nation, fall into it. In addition to these the Amystis joins the Ganges, near the city of Catadoupe, as do the Oxymagis in the land of the people called Pazalaeans, and the Errenysis in that of the Mathaeans, an Indian nation. Megasthenes says that none of these is inferior to the Maeander, where that river is navigable. He says that the breadth of the Ganges in its narrowest part is about twelve miles; that in many places it forms lakes, so that the land opposite is not visible where it is flat and nowhere stands up in hills. The same is the case with the Indus. The Hydraotes, having received the Hyphasis in the land of the Astrybaeans, the Saranges from that of the Cecians, and the Neudrus from that of the Attacenians, falls into the Acesines in the land of the Cambistholians. The Hydaspes also falls into the Acesines in the land of the Oxydracians, taking with itself the Sinarus in the land of the Arispians. The Acesines joins the Indus in the land of the Mallians. The Toutapus also, a large river, falls into the Acesines. That river, with its water swollen by these, and giving its name to the united stream, itself falls into the Indus and surrenders its name to it. The Cophen falls into the Indus in the land called Peucelaitis, taking with itself the Malantus, Soastus, and Garroeas. Below these the Parenus and Saparnus, not far apart, fall into the Indus. The Soanus also falls into it, coming void of any other river from the mountainous land of the Abissarians. Megasthenes says that most of these are navigable. Therefore we ought not to

disbelieve that the Ister and the water of the Nile are not comparable with the Indus and the Ganges. We know, indeed, that no river falls into the Nile, but that canals have been cut from it through the land of Egypt. The Ister rises small from its sources, and though it receives many rivers, they are not equal in number to the Indian rivers which flow into the Indus and the Ganges. Very few of the tributaries of the Ister are navigable. Two of these, the Enus and Saus, I know, having seen them myself. The Enus mingles with the Ister on the confines of the country of the Noricans and Rhaetians, and the Saus in the territory of the Paeonians. The place where the Ister and Saus have their confluence is called Taurounus. Some one may know another navigable river which falls into the Ister, but he does not know many I am sure.

5. Whoever wishes to consider the cause of the number and size of the Indian rivers let him consider; it is sufficient for me to have recorded these statements as reports. For Megasthenes has recorded the names of many other rivers, which fall into the eastern and southern external sea, apart from the Ganges and Indus. He says that there are in all fifty-eight Indian rivers, all navigable. But even Megasthenes does not seem to me to have traversed much of the land of the Indians, though he visited more than those who went with Alexander the son of Philip. For he says that he was intimate with Sandracottus, a very great king of the Indians, and with Porus, still greater than he. This Megasthenes, indeed, says that neither do the Indians wage war with any other other men, nor any other men with them; and that Sesostris the Egyptian, having subdued most part of Asia, and having marched with his army as far as Europe, returned back home without attacking India; that Idanthyrsus the Scythian started from Scythia, and subduing many nations in Asia, advanced even into the land of the Egyptians in his victorious career; that Semiramis the Assyrian undertook an expedition into the land the Indians, but that she died before she could complete her plans; and that Alexander alone led an invading army against the Indians. The tale is current that even before Alexander Dionysus led an expedition into India, and subdued the Indians. There is also a vague story about Heracles to the same effect. Of the expedition of Dionysus, indeed, the city of Nysa is no mean monument, as also are the mountain Meros, the ivy which grows on this mountain, the Indians themselves also marching into battle to the sound of drums and cymbals, wearing speckled garments like the bacchanals of Dionysus. But of Heracles there are not many memorials. For the statement that Alexander forcibly subdued the rock of Aornus, because Heracles was not able to capture it, seems to me a piece of Macedonian boasting; just as they called the Parapamisus Caucasus, though it has no connection with it. And having observed a certain cave in the land of the Parapamisadians, they said that it was the famous cave of Prometheus,

the son of the Titan, in which he was hung for the theft of the fire. And besides, in the land of the Sibians, an Indian race, because they saw the inhabitants clothed in skins, they said that the Sibians were those who had been left behind from the expedition of Heracles. The Sibians also carry cudgels, and the figure of a club was branded upon their oxen; this too they explained to be a commemoration of the club of Heracles. If any-one gives credit to these tales, this must have been another Heracles, neither the Theban, nor the Tyrian, nor the Egyptian; but some great king of a land situated in the interior not far from India.

6. Let this be a digression on my part from the narrative, in order to show that what certain authors have recorded about the Indians on the other side of the Hyphasis does not appear credible; but those who took part in Alexander's expedition as far as the Hyphasis are not altogether unworthy of belief. For Megasthenes also says this about an Indian river, whose name is Silas, that it flows from a spring with the same name as itself through the land of the Silians, who derive their name from the river and the spring; that it supplies water of such a kind that there is nothing which it resists, that nothing either swims or floats upon it, but everything sinks to the bottom; and that that water is weaker and more murky than any other. India is visited by rain in the summer, especially the mountains, Parapamisus, Emodus, and the Imaic range, and from these the rivers flow swollen and muddy. In the summer also the plains of India are visited by rain, so that a great part of them are covered with pools; and Alexander's army had to avoid the river Acesines in the mid-dle of the summer, because the water overflowed into the plains. Where-fore from this it is possible to conjecture the cause of the similar condi-tion of the Nile, because it is probable that the mountains of Aethiopia are visited by rain in the summer, and the Nile being filled from them overflows its banks into the Egyptian country. Therefore the Nile at this season flows in a muddy state, as it would not flow from the melting of snow, or if its water were driven back by the annual winds blowing in the season of summer. Besides, the mountains of Aethiopia would not be snow-beaten on account of the heat. It is not beyond the bounds of prob-ability that Aethiopia is visited by rain as India is, for in other respects India is not unlike Aethiopia, and the Indian rivers produce crocodiles like the Aethiopian and Egyptian Nile. Some of them also produce fish and water-monsters besides, like those of the Nile, except the hippopot-amus. Onesicritus says they produce even hippopotami. The looks of the people of India and Aethiopia are not entirely dissimilar. The Indians who live towards the south are more like the Aethiopians, they are black in their faces, and their hair is black; but they are not so flat-nosed or so curly-headed as the Aethiopians. The more northern Indians would especially resemble the Egyptians in their bodies.

7. Megasthenes says that there are in all 118 Indian nations. I myself agree with him that there are many Indian nations; but I am not able to conjecture how he learned the exact number and recorded it, for he only visited a mere fraction of India, nor do many of the races have any intercourse with each other. He says that in ancient times the Indians were nomads, like that section of the Scythians who are not agriculturists, but wandering about on waggons, live at one time in one part of Scythia and at another time in another part, neither inhabiting cities nor consecrating temples to the gods. So the Indians had no cities or temples built for the gods. They clothed themselves in the skins of the wild beasts which they killed, and ate the inner bark of certain trees, which are called tala in the Indian language, and, as upon the tops of palm-trees, there grow upon them things like clews of wool. They also fed upon the flesh of the wild beasts which they caught, eating it raw, until Dionysus came into their country. But when Dionysus came and conquered them, he founded cities and made laws for them, and gave the Indians wine as he had given it to the Greeks. He also gave them seeds and taught them how to sow them in the earth; so that either Triptolemus did not come to this part when he was sent by Demeter to sow corn through the whole earth, or this Dionysus came to India before Triptolemus and gave to the inhabitants the seeds of cultivated crops. Dionysus first taught them to yoke oxen to the plough, and made most of them become husbandmen instead of being nomads, and armed them with martial weapons. He also taught them to worship the gods, and especially himself with the beating of drums and the clashing of cymbals. He taught the Indians the Satyr-dance which among the Greeks is called the cordax, and to let their hair grow long in honour of the god. He also showed them how to wear the turban, and taught them how to anoint themselves with unguents. Wherefore even to the time of Alexander the Indians still advanced into battle with the sound of cymbals and drums.

8. When Dionysus had arranged these affairs and was about to leave India, he appointed as king of the land Spatembas, one of his companions, the man most versed in the mysteries of Bacchus. When this man died his son Boudyas succeeded to his kingdom. The father reigned fifty-two years, and the son twenty years. Cradeuas, the son of Boudyas, succeeded to the throne. From this time for the most part the kingdom passed in regular succession from father to son. If at any time direct heirs were wanting, then the Indians appointed kings according to merit. The Heracles, who according to the current report came to India is said, among the Indians themselves, to have sprung from the earth. This Heracles is especially worshipped by the Sourasenians, an Indian nation, in whose land are two great cities, Methora and Cleisobora, and through it flows the navigable river Jobares. Megasthenes says, as the Indians

themselves assert, that this Heracles wore a similar dress to that of the Theban Heracles. Very many male children, but only one daughter were born to him in India, for he married many women. The daughter's name was Pandaea, and the land where she was born, and over which Heracles placed her as ruler, was named Pandaea after her. From her father she received 500 elephants, 4,000 cavalry, and 130,000 infantry. Certain of the Indians tell the following story about Heracles, that when he had passed over every land and sea and had rid them of every evil beast, he found in the sea a woman's ornament, such as up to the present day those who bring wares from India to us still buy with zeal and carry away. In former times the Greeks and now the Romans who are fortunate and wealthy with still greater zeal buy what is called in the Indian tongue the marine pearl. The ornament seemed so fine to Heracles that he collected pearls like this from all the sea and brought them to India to be an adornment for his daughter. Megasthenes says that the mussel of it is caught in nets, and that many of them live in the sea at the same place, like bees, and that the pearl-mussels have a king or queen as bees have. Whoever has the good fortune to capture the king, easily throws the net around the rest of the swarm of pearl-mussels, but if the king escapes the fishermen, the others are no longer to be caught by them. The men allow the flesh of those which are caught to rot, but they use the shell for ornament; for among the Indians the pearl is worth thrice its weight in refined gold. This metal is also dug up in India.

9. In this country, where the daughter of Heracles reigned, the women at seven years of age become marriageable, and the men live forty years at most. In regard to this the following story is told among the Indians. This girl was born to Heracles in his old age, when he perceived that his end was near. He could not find a man worthy to receive his daughter in marriage, and therefore he married her himself when she was seven years old, so that the family born from him and her might supply kings to the Indians. Heracles therefore made her marriageable at that age; and from that time all this race over which Pandaea ruled have this same gift from Heracles. To me it seems that if Heracles was able to accomplish such marvellous things, he would also have been able to make himself longer lived, so that he might marry his daughter at a mature age. But if these statements about the maturity of the girls of this country are correct, to me at any rate they seem to have some analogy with what is said about the age of the men, that the oldest of them do not live beyond forty years. For no doubt the flower of perfect manhood blooms sooner in proportion in those upon whom old age advances quicker, and death with old age; so that among them men of thirty years of age would be, I suppose, fresh, active old men, striplings of twenty years old would be past their early manhood, and the prime of early manhood would be about fifteen years

of age. Reasoning from analogy the women would thus become marriageable at seven years of age. For this same Megasthenes has recorded that in this country the fruits ripen quicker than those elsewhere, and sooner waste away.

From Dionysus to Sandracottus the Indians reckoned 153 kings, and 6,042 years. During all these years they only twice asserted their freedom; the first time they enjoyed it for 300 years, and the second for 120. They say that Dionysus was earlier than Heracles by fifteen generations, and that no other ever invaded India for war, not even Cyrus, the son of Cambyses, though he marched against the Scythians, and in other matters was the most meddlesome of the kings of Asia. However they admit that Alexander came and overcame in battle all the nations whom he visited, and that he would have conquered them all if his army had been willing. But none of the Indians ever marched out of their own country for war, being actuated by a respect for justice.

10. This also is said, that the Indians do not construct monuments for the dead, for they think that the virtues of men are sufficient to perpetuate their memory after their death, as well as the songs which they sing in their honour. It would not be possible to record with accuracy the number of their cities on account of their multiplicity. Those which are situated near the rivers or the sea are built of wood; for if they were built of brick they could not long endure on account of the rain and because the rivers overflowing their banks fill the plains with water. But those which have been founded in commanding places, lofty and raised above the adjacent country, are built of brick and mortar. The largest city in India, named Palimbothra, is in the land of the Prasians, where is the confluence of the river Erannoboas and the Ganges, which is the greatest of rivers. The Erannoboas would be third of the Indian rivers, being also larger than those elsewhere. But it yields itself up to the Ganges when it has discharged its water into it. Megasthenes says that on one side where it is longest this city extends ten miles in length, and that its breadth is one and three-quarters miles; that the city has been surrounded with a ditch in breadth 600 feet, and in depth 45 feet; and that its wall has 570 towers and 64 gates. This is a great thing in India, that all the inhabitants are free, not a single Indian being a slave. In this the Lacedaemonians and the Indians are alike. However the Helots are slaves to the Lacedaemonians and perform servile offices; but among the Indians no other Indian at any rate is a slave.

11. All the Indians have been divided into seven castes. Among them are the wise men, fewer in number than the others, but most esteemed in reputation and dignity. For no necessity is incumbent upon them to do any bodily labour; nor do they contribute anything to the commonwealth from the effects of their labour; nor in a word have they any com-

pulsory duty except to offer sacrifices to the gods on behalf of the commonwealth of India. Whoever sacrifices in his private capacity has one of these wise men as a director of the sacrifice, since otherwise he does not offer acceptable sacrifice to the gods. These also are the only Indians skilled in divination; and it is not lawful for anyone to practise the art except for a man who is a wise man. They practise divination in regard to the seasons of the year, and if any calamity befalls the commonwealth. It is not their business to practise their art in regard to the private affairs of individuals, either because the art of divination does not extend to smaller matters, or because it is not worthy of them to labour about such things. Whoever has made three errors in his practise of divination receives no other punishment except that for the future he is compelled to be silent; and there is no one who can compel that man to speak, upon whom the judgment of silence has been passed. These wise men pass their lives naked; in the winter in the sun under the open sky, but in the summer, when the sun holds sway, they live in the meadows and in the marshes under great trees, the shadow of which Nearchus says extends 500 feet all round, and 10,000 men could be shaded under one tree. So large are these trees. They feed on the fruits of the seasons and the inner bark of trees, which is both pleasant and nutritious; not less so than dates.

After these the second caste are the agriculturalists, who are the most numerous class of Indians. These have no martial weapons, nor do they care for deeds of war, but till the soil. They pay dues to the kings or to those cities which are independent. If any war happens to break out among the Indians with each other it is not lawful for them to touch the tillers of the soil, or to lay waste the country itself by destroying the crops. But while others are waging war against each other and slaying each other as they find the chance, they are ploughing in peace and quietness near them, or are gathering in the vintage, or are pruning their vines, or are reaping their crops.

The third caste of Indians are the shepherds and the cowherds, who dwell neither in cities nor in villages; but are nomads and live up and down the mountains. They pay a tax from their flocks and herds. These men also catch birds and hunt wild beasts throughout the land.

12. The fourth caste is that of the artisans and retail tradesmen. These men perform public duties at their own cost, and pay a tax upon their work, except those who make weapons of war. These receive pay from the commonwealth. In this caste are the shipwrights and sailors who sail up and down the rivers.

The fifth caste of the Indians consists of the warriors, who in number come next to the husbandmen and enjoy very great freedom and good cheer. These men practise nothing but warlike exercises. Others make the weapons for them, others provide them with horses; and others serve them in the camp, who groom the horses for them, keep their weapons bright, manage the elephants, keep the chariots in order, and drive the horses. They themselves fight, as long as it is necessary to wage war; but when there is peace, they live with good cheer; and they receive such high pay from the state that they can easily support others from it.

The sixth caste of Indians consists of men who are called overseers. These supervise what is done throughout the country and in the cities, and make reports to the king, where the Indians are ruled by a king, or to the magistrates where the people have a democratic government. It is unlawful for these men to make false reports; but no Indian has incurred the charge of falsehood.

The seventh caste consists of those who assist the king in deliberating on public affairs, or assist the officials in the cities which enjoy a democratic government. This class is small in number, but in wisdom and justice excels all the others. From them are chosen their rulers, governors of provinces, deputies, treasurers, generals, admirals, controllers of expenditure, and superintendents of agriculture.

It is not lawful for anyone to marry a woman from another caste; for example, for husbandmen to marry from the class of artisans or the reverse. It is not lawful for the same man to exercise two trades, or to exchange from one caste into another; for instance, he may not cease to be a shepherd and become a husbandman, or cease to be an artisan and become a shepherd. Only a man from any caste is allowed by them to become a wise man, because the duties of the wise men are not easy, but the most severely laborious of all.

13. The Indians hunt other wild animals like the Greeks; but the way they hunt elephants is quite different from any other kind of hunting, because these animals are like no other beasts. They choose a place that is level and exposed to the sun's heat, large enough for a great army to encamp in. They then dig a trench all round it. They make the breadth of this trench about thirty feet, and the depth about twenty-four feet. The earth which they cast up from the ditch they heap up on each bank of the trench and use it in place of a wall. In the mound upon the outer bank of the trench they dig hiding-places for themselves, leaving holes in them, through which the light may enter for them, and to enable them to observe the beasts approaching and charging into the inclosure. There, within the inclosure, they place some three or four female elephants, who are especially tame in spirit, and leave only one entrance, made by bridging over the trench. They cover this with earth and thick turf, in order that the beasts may not notice the bridge and think some trick is being played them. The men, therefore, keep themselves out of the way, lurking in the hiding-places near the trench. The wild elephants by day do not approach inhabited places, but in the night they wander in all direc-

tions and graze in droves, following the largest and bravest of their number, just as cows follow the bulls. When they approach the inclosure they hear the noise of the females and discerning them by the scent, they run at full speed towards the inclosed place. Going quite round the bank of the trench, as soon as they light upon the bridge, they rush forward into the inclosure over this. When the men perceive the entrance of the wild elephants, some of them quickly remove the bridge, others run to the neighbouring villages and tell the people that the elephants are shut up in the inclosure. When they hear this they mount the bravest and most tractable of their elephants and drive them towards the inclosure. When they arrive they do not immediately join battle, but allow the wild elephants to be severely distressed with hunger and to be cowed by thirst. As soon as they think they are in a weak state, they then place the bridge over again and advance into the inclosure. At first an obstinate battle is fought between the tame elephants and those that have been caught. Soon, as might be expected, the wild ones are overcome, being severely depressed by loss of spirit and want of food. The men, dismounting from the elephants, tie together the feet of the wild ones, which are now exhausted. Then they order the tame ones to chastise them with many blows until they fall to the ground in their severe distress. Standing near them they throw nooses round their necks and mount upon them as they lie on the ground. And in order that they may not shake off their riders, or do any other reckless thing, they cut their necks all round with a sharp knife and tie the noose round along the cut; so that on account of the wound they must keep their head and neck quiet; for if they should turn their head round through recklessness, their wound is chafed under the rope. Then at length they keep quiet, and changing their minds of their own accord, they are now led by the tame ones into imprisonment.

14. Those of them which are quite young, or through badness not worth possessing, are allowed to take themselves off to their own haunts. The captives are led into the villages and at first some green reeds and grass are given them to eat. They refuse to eat anything from loss of spirit; and the Indians stand round them and lull them to sleep by singing songs, beating drums and clashing cymbals. For, of all animals, the elephant is most naturally intelligent. Some of them have of their own accord picked up their riders who have been killed in battle and carried them away for burial; others have held the shield over them when lying on the ground; and others have incurred danger on their behalf when they have fallen wounded. One, having killed his rider in a fit of passion, died from remorse and dejection of spirit. I myself have seen an elephant playing the cymbals, while others danced. Two cymbals were fastened to the forelegs of the playing elephant, and another to the trunk. With his trunk he struck the cymbal alternately against each of his legs in

regular time, and the others moved round him as in a dance. These also walked, raising and bending their front legs alternately in regular time, just as the one who played the cymbals directed them. The female elephant copulates in the season of spring, like the cow or mare, when the air-vents near the temples of the females being opened exhale an odour. She carries her young sixteen months at the least, and eighteen at the most, and brings forth one, like the mare. This she suckles till the eighth year. Those which live longest live for 200 years; but many of them die before that age from disease. If they die from old age they reach that age. When their eyes are sore they are cured by pouring into them cow's milk, and their other diseases by giving them dark-coloured wine to drink. Pork is roasted and the fat is sprinkled upon wounds to effect a cure. The Indians adopt these cures for them.

15. The Indians think the tiger much mightier than the elephant. Nearchus says he saw a tiger's skin, but not the tiger itself; but that the Indians assured him that it is as large as the largest horse, and that no other animal can compare with it in swiftness and strength. When the tiger comes into conflict with an elephant he leaps upon his head and easily strangles him. Those which we see and call tigers are only speckled jackals, but larger than the ordinary jackals. In regard to the ants, Nearchus says that he himself did not see one like those which some other authors have described as existing in India; but that he saw many skins of these animals which had been brought into the Macedonian camp. But Megasthenes asserts that the story of these ants is correct; that these were the animals who dig up gold, not for the sake of the metal itself; but they burrow under the ground from instinct, in order that they may lie hidden in their holes, just as our small ants burrow a little under the ground. These ants are larger than foxes and therefore they burrow a distance proportionate to their size, and throw up the soil. As this contains gold ore the Indians obtain their gold from it. Megasthenes only relates hearsay, and as I myself am unable to say anything more certain than this, I willingly dismiss the story of the ants. Nearchus relates as a wonder that parrots are bred in India, and describes what kind of a bird it is and how it utters human speech; but as I myself have seen many and I know others are acquainted with the bird I shall give no description of it as of a marvel. Nor shall I speak of the size of the monkeys, or how beautiful those of India are, nor how they are caught. For these things are well known, except that monkeys are beautiful anywhere. Nearchus also says speckled serpents are caught, though they are quick in movement; and that Peithon, son of Antigenes, caught one twenty-four feet long. The Indians themselves said that the largest serpents are much larger than this. None of the Greek physicians found any cure for any one who was bitten by an Indian serpent; but the Indians

themselves healed those who had been smitten. Nearchus says, besides, that Alexander had collected around him all the Indians who were cleverest in the medical art, and had it proclaimed through the camp that whoever was bitten should come to the king's tent. These men were also curers of other diseases and infirmities. But among the Indians there are not many infirmities, because the seasons there are temperate. If anything worse than usual seized them they communicated with the wise men; who seemed to cure whatever was curable, not without the help of god.

16. The Indians use linen clothing, as says Nearchus, made from the flax taken from the trees, about which I have already spoken. And this flax is either whiter in colour than any other flax, or the people being black make the flax appear whiter. They have a linen frock reaching down halfway between the knee and the ankle, and a garment which is partly thrown round the shoulders and partly rolled round the head. The Indians who are very well-off wear earrings of ivory; for they do not all wear them. Nearchus says that the Indians dye their beards various colours; some that they may appear white as the whitest, others dark blue; others have them red, others purple, and others green. Those who are of any rank have umbrellas held over them in the summer. They wear shoes of white leather, elaborately worked, and the soles of their shoes are many-coloured and raised high, in order that they may appear taller.

The Indians are not all armed in the same way; but their infantry have a bow equal in length to the man who carries it. Placing this downward to the ground and stepping against it with the left foot, they discharge the arrow, drawing the string far back. Their arrows are little less than four and one-half feet long; and nothing can withstand one shot by an Indian archer, neither shield nor breast-plate nor anything else that is strong. They carry on their left arms targets of raw ox-hide, narrower than the men who carry them, but not much inferior in length. Others have javelins instead of arrows. All wear a sword which is broad, and not less than four and one-half feet in length. When the battle is at close quarters, a thing which very rarely happens to be the case between Indians, they bring this sword down upon the antagonist with both hands, in order that the blow may be a mighty one. The cavalry have two darts, like the darts called *saunia*, and a shield smaller than that of the infantry. Their horses are not saddled or bridled like those of the Greeks or Gauls; but a piece of raw ox-hide stitched is fastened right round the front of the horse's mouth, and in this there are brass or iron spikes not very sharp, turned inwards. The rich men have ivory spikes. In the mouth their horses have a piece of iron, like a spit, to which the reins are attached. When therefore they draw the rein, the spit curbs the horse and the spikes which are fastened to it prick him and do not allow him to do anything else than obey the rein.

17. The Indians are spare in body and tall and much lighter than other men. Most of the Indians ride camels, horses, and asses, and those who are well off, elephants. For among the Indians royal personages ride on elephants. Next to this in honour is the four-horsed chariot, third camels. It is no honour to ride on horse-back. Their women who are very chaste and would not go astray for any other reward, on the receipt of an elephant have intercourse with the donor. The Indians do not think it disgraceful for them to prostitute themselves for an elephant, and to the women it even seems an honour that their beauty should appear equal in value to an elephant. They marry, neither giving or receiving any dowry, but the fathers bring forward the girls who are of marriageable age and station them in a public place for the man who wins the prize for wrestling, boxing or running, or who has been adjudged winner in any manly contest, to make his choice. The Indians are bread-eaters and agriculturalists, except those who live in the mountains. These live upon the flesh of wild animals.

I think I have given sufficient information about the Indians. I have copied the very well-known statements made by Nearchus and Megasthenes, two esteemed authors. As my design in compiling this book was not to describe the customs of the Indians, but to relate how Alexander's fleet was conveyed from India into Persia, let the preceding portion of it be considered a digression from my narrative.

18. Alexander, when his fleet had been got ready on the banks of the Hydaspes, selected the Phoenicians, Cyprians, and Egyptians who were following him in his expedition into the interior, and from these manned the ships, choosing those who were skilled in nautical affairs for the crews and for rowers. There were also many islanders in the army, who were expert in such matters, as well as Ionians and men of the Hellespont. He appointed the following men captains of the war ships: of the Macedonians, Hephaestion, son of Amyntor, Leonnatus, son of Anteas, Lysimachus, son of Agathocles, Asclepiodorus, son of Timander, Archon, son of Cleinias, Demonicus, son of Athenaeus, Archias, son of Anaxidotus, Ophelas, son of Seilenus, and Timanthes, son of Pantiades: these were Pellaeans. From Amphipolis the following commanded: Nearchus, son of Androtimus, who wrote the account of the voyage round the coast; Laomedon, son of Larichus, and Androsthenes, son of Callistratus. From Orestis: Craterus, son of Alexander, and Perdiccas, son of Orontes. Eordaeans: Ptolemy, son of Lagus, and Aristonous, son of Peisaeus. From Pydna: Metron, son of Epicharmus, and Nicarchides, son of Simus. Besides these there were Attalus, son of Andromenes, a Tymphaean; Peucestas, son of Alexander, a man of Mieza; Peithon, the son of Cra-

teuas, a man of Alcomene; Leonnatus, son of Antipater, a man of Aegae; Pantauchus, son of Nicolaus, a man of Alora, and Mylleas, son of Zoilus, a man of Beroea; all these were Macedonians. Of Greeks were the following: Medius, son of Oxythemis, a man of Larissa; Eumenes, son of Hieronymus, from Cardia; Critobulus, son of Plato, a Coan; Thoas, son of Menodorus, and Maeander, son of Mandrogenes, the Magnesians; and Andron, son of Cabeles, a Teian. Of Cyprians, Nicocles, son of Pasicrates, a man of Soli; and Nithaphon, son of Pnytagoras, a man of Salamis. He had also a Persian, Bagoas, son of Pharnuches, as captain of one of his war ships. The steersman of Alexander's own ship was Onesicritus, a man of Astypalaea. Evagoras, son of Eucleon, a Corinthian, was secretary of the whole expedition. Nearchus, son of Androtimus, was placed over them as admiral. He was a Cretan by birth, but dwelt at Amphipolis, near the Strymon. When all things had been prepared by Alexander, he offered sacrifice to the gods of his fathers and to those who were named by the soothsayers, and especially to Poseidon, Amphitrite, and the Nereids, to Oceanus himself, to the river Hydaspes from which he was starting, to the Acesines into which the Hydaspes falls, and to the Indus into which they both fall. He also held musical and gymnastic contests, and distributed the flesh of the slaughtered animals throughout the divisions of the whole army.

19. When all things had been got ready for starting on the voyage, he ordered Craterus to march along one side of the Hydaspes with an army of foot and horse, while Hephaestion marched opposite him on the other side with another army still larger than that which was marshalled under Craterus. Hephaestion also took with him the elephants, to the number of 200. He himself took with him what were called the shield-bearing guards, all the bowmen and of the cavalry what were called the Companions, altogether 8,000 in number. Craterus and Hephaestion had been instructed to march on in advance and wait for the fleet. He sent Philip, who was his viceroy over this land, to the bank of the river Acesines, with another large army. For now, 120,000 fighting men accompanied him including those whom he had brought up himself from the Aegean sea, besides those whom the officers whom he had sent to levy an army brought back with them. He was taking with him men from all the Asiatic nations, armed in every kind of fashion. He himself starting the ships sailed down the Hydaspes as far as its confluence with the Acesines. He had altogether 1,800 ships, some ships of war, others merchant vessels, and others horse-transports and vessels conveying food with the army. But how his fleet sailed down the rivers, and what nations he subdued in the course of the voyage, how he came into danger in the land of the Mallians, how he was wounded there, and how Peucestas and Leonnatus held their shields over him after he had fallen, all this has been described

in my other book written in the Attic dialect. But this narrative is a description of the voyage which Nearchus made with the fleet, starting from the outlet of the Indus through the Great Sea as far as the Persian Gulf, which some call the Red Sea.

20. Nearchus has given the following account of this. He says that Alexander had a great wish to sail right round the sea from India as far as the Persian Sea, but was alarmed at the length of the voyage. He was afraid that his army would perish, lighting upon some uninhabited country, or one destitute of roadsteads, or not sufficiently supplied with the ripe crops. He thought that this great disgrace following upon his mighty exploits would annihilate all his success. But the desire he always felt to do something new and marvellous won the day. However, he was in perplexity whom to choose as competent to carry out his projects, and how he was to remove the fear of the sailors and of those sent on such an expedition that they were being sent out recklessly to a foreseen and manifest danger. Nearchus says that Alexander consulted him as to whom he should choose to conduct the expedition, mentioning one after another as having declined, some not being willing to run the risk of losing their reputation by failure, others because they were cowardly at heart, others being possessed by a yearning for their own land. The king accused one of making one excuse, and another of making another. Then Nearchus himself undertook the office and said, "O king, I undertake to conduct this expedition, and if God assists me, I will bring the ships and the men safely round as far as the land of Persis, at any rate if the sea in that quarter is navigable, and if the enterprise is not an impossible one for the human intellect." Alexander in reply said he was unwilling to expose any of his friends to such great hardship and such great danger; but Nearchus, all the more on this account, refused to give in, and persevered in his resolve. Alexander was so pleased with the zeal of Nearchus that he appointed him commander of the whole expedition. Then indeed the part of the army which was ordered to embark for this voyage as well as the crews had a more cheerful feeling, because they thought Alexander would never have sent Nearchus, at any rate, forward into manifest danger, unless they were likely to arrive in safety. Moreover, the magnificence of the preparations, the adornment of the ships, and the extraordinary zeal of the captains about the excellence of their rowers and crews excited those who previously were quite alarmed and reluctant, to show courage and to entertain better hopes of the entire enterprise. The fact that Alexander had himself made a start and sailed right down both mouths of the Indus into the sea, and had offered victims to Poseidon and the other sea-gods, and had presented the sea with magnificent gifts greatly contributed to the cheerfulness of the army. Trusting to Alexander's previously unparalleled success they thought there was nothing

which he would not dare, and nothing which he could not perform.

21. As soon as the annual winds were lulled to rest, they started on the twentieth day of the month Boedromion,[2] in the archonship at Athens of Cephisodorus as the Athenians reckon; but as the Macedonians and Asiatics reckoned, the eleventh year of Alexander's reign. These annual winds continue to blow from the sea to the land the whole season of summer, and thereby render navigation impossible. Before commencing the voyage Nearchus offered sacrifice to Zeus the Preserver, and celebrated a gymnastic contest. Having started from the roadstead down the river Indus, on the first day they moored near a large canal, and remained there two days. The name of the place was Stoura, twelve miles from the roadstead. Departing on the third day they sailed nearly four miles, as far as another canal, the water of which was salt. For the sea came up into it, especially with the tide, and the water mingling with the river remained salt even after the ebb. The name of this place was Caumara. Thence still sailing down the river two and one-half miles they moored at Coreestis. Starting thence they sailed not far; for they saw a reef at the mouth of the river, and the waves dashed against the shore, and this shore was rugged. But they made a canal through a soft part of the reef for half a mile and got the ships through it, when the tide reached them from the sea. Having sailed right round seventeen and one-half miles they moored at a sandy island called Crocala, and stayed there the rest of the day. Near this island lives an Indian nation called Arabians, of whom also I have made mention in my larger work, saying that they are named after the river Arabis, which flows through their land and falls into the sea, dividing their country from that of the Oreitians. From Crocala they sailed, having on their right the mountain called by them Eirus, and on their left an island lying level with the sea. The island stretching along the shore makes a narrow strait. Having sailed through this they moored in a harbour affording good anchorage. Because this harbour seemed to Nearchus large and fine, he named it Alexander's Harbour. There is an island near the mouth of the harbour, about 400 yards off, which is called Bibacta; but the whole district is called Sangada. The island lying athwart the sea has made a natural harbour. Here great and continuous winds blew from the sea; and Nearchus, fearing that some of the barbarians might band together and turn to plunder his camp, fortified the place with a stone wall. The stay here was twenty-four days. He says that his soldiers caught sea-mice, oysters, and a shell-fish called *solenes*, wonderful in size, if compared with those in this sea of ours; and the water was salt to the taste.

22. As soon as the wind ceased they put to sea, and having proceeded seven miles they cast anchor near a sandy coast: and near the coast was

[2] October, 325 B.C.

an uninhabited island, named Domae. Using this as a breakwater they anchored. But on the shore there was no water; so they advanced into the interior about two and one-half miles, and lighted on some good water. On the next day they sailed thirty-five miles to Saranga and anchored at night near the shore, about one mile from which there was water. Sailing thence they anchored at Sacala, an uninhabited spot; and sailing between two cliffs so near each other that the oars of the ships touched the rocks on both sides, they anchored at Morontobara, having advanced thirty-five miles. The harbour was large, circular, deep, and sheltered from the waves; and the entrance into it was narrow. This is called in the native tongue the Woman's Harbour, because a woman first ruled over this place. While they were sailing between the rocks, they met with great waves and the sea had a swift current; so that it appeared a great undertaking to sail out beyond the rocks. On the next day they sailed having on their left an island like a breakwater to the sea, so close to the shore that one might conjecture that a canal had been cut between it and the shore. The channel extends eight miles. Upon the shore were dense woods, and the island was covered with every sort of tree. At the approach of dawn they sailed beyond the island over the narrow surf; for the ebb-tide was still running. Having sailed fourteen miles they anchored in the mouth of the river Arabis. There was a large and fine harbour near the mouth. The water was not drinkable; for the water discharged by the river had been mixed with that of the sea. But having advanced into the interior five miles, they came upon a pond, and having got water from it they returned. Near the harbour is an elevated uninhabited island, round which oysters and every kind of fish are caught. As far as this lived the Arabians, who are the most westward of the Indian nations; beyond this the Oreitians possessed the land.

23. Starting from the outlet of the Arabis they sailed along the land of the Oreitians. After a voyage of twenty-four miles they anchored at Pagala near the beach; for the place was suitable for anchoring. Therefore the crews lay to at anchor in the ships, while the others disembarked to get water. On the morrow as soon as it was light they departed, and sailing forty-eight miles they arrived at Cabana in the evening, and anchored near a deserted shore; and because the beach was rough, they anchored in deep water. In this day's voyage a strong wind from the sea caught the ships, and during the voyage two ships of war and one light ship were lost; but the men saved their lives by swimming away, for they were sailing close to the land. Setting forth at midnight they sailed as far as Cocala, which was twenty-four miles from the shore from which they had started. The ships rode at anchor on the sea; but Nearchus disembarked the crews and they encamped on land, because they were yearning for a rest, having endured great hardship so long on the sea. He threw an

entrenchment round the camp as a protection against the barbarians. In this district Leonnatus, to whom Alexander had intrusted the operations against the Oreitians, defeated them and their allies in a great battle, in which he slew 6,000 of them and all their leaders. Of the troops of Leonnatus fifteen horsemen were slain and a few of the infantry. Apollophanes, the satrap of Gadrosia, was also slain. These events have been related in my other book; also that Leonnatus was crowned by Alexander with a golden crown in the presence of the Macedonians on account of their victory. Here, according to Alexander's instructions, corn had been stored for the victualling of the expedition; and food for ten days was placed in the ships. The ships which had been injured in the voyage to this point were also repaired. Nearchus gave to Leonnatus the sailors who seemed to him disgusted with the voyage, to be put among the infantry, and he himself filled up his naval force from the soldiers of Leonnatus.

24. Having started thence they sailed with a strong breeze, and after proceeding sixty miles they anchored in a river swollen by winter rain, the name of which was Tomerus. And at the outlet of the river was a lake. Men in stifling huts inhabited the narrow strip of land near the shore. When they saw the fleet approaching they were amazed, and extending themselves in line along the shore they formed into military array to prevent the men from landing. They carried thick spears, nine feet long; the point was not of iron, but the sharp end hardened in fire served the same purpose. They were about 600 in number. When Nearchus saw that these were waiting for him drawn up in battle array, he ordered the ships to be kept riding at anchor within range, so that his men's arrows might reach the land; for the thick spears of the barbarians seemed to be adapted for close fighting, but were not to be feared in distant skirmishing. He ordered the lightest of his soldiers and the lightest armed, who were also very expert in swimming, to swim from the ships at a given signal. Their instructions were that those who had swum ashore should stand in the water and wait for their comrades, and not attack the barbarians before their phalanx had been arranged three deep; then they were to raise the battle-cry and advance at full speed. At once the men who had been appointed to carry out this plan threw themselves out of the ships into the sea, swam quickly, placed themselves in rank, formed themselves into phalanx and began to advance at full speed shouting the battle-cry to Enyalius. Those on the ships joined in the shout, and arrows and missiles from the military engines were launched against the barbarians. They were alarmed at the flashing of the weapons and the quickness of the attack; and being struck by the arrows and the other missiles they did not turn to defend themselves even a little, but took to flight, as was natural in men half naked. Some of them were killed there in their flight, and others were captured; but some escaped into the mountains. Those who

were captured were covered with hair not only on the head but on the rest of the body; and their nails were like the claws of wild beasts. For they were said to use them as we use iron; they killed fish, splitting them up with these; with these they cut the softer kinds of wood. Other things they cut with sharp stones, for they have no iron. Some wore the skins of beasts as clothing, and others the thick skins of large fishes.

25. Here they hauled up the ships on land and repaired those that were damaged. On the sixth day they set out, and after sailing thirty-five miles they arrived at a place called Malana at the extremity of the country of the Oreitians. The Oreitians who inhabit the interior away from the sea are dressed like the Indians and are equipped with similar weapons; but their language and customs are different. The length of the voyage along the coast of the land of the Arabians from the place whence they started was about 120 miles, and along the country of the Oreitians 188 miles. Nearchus says that while they were sailing along the coast of India (for India does not extend beyond the land of the Arabians) their shadows did not act as before. For when they advanced far into the sea towards the south, the shadows themselves also were seen turned towards the south, and when the sun reached the middle of the day then they saw all things destitute of shadow. And the stars which before they used to observe far up in the sky were some of them quite invisible, and others were seen near the earth itself, and those which formerly were always visible were observed to set and rise again. These things, which Nearchus relates, seem to me not improbable. For at Syene in Egypt, when the summer solstice comes round, a well is shown in which at midday no shadow is seen. At Meroe all things are shadowless at the same season. It is therefore probable that among the Indians the same phenomena occur, as they live towards the south; and especially throughout the Indian ocean, as that sea is more inclined to the south. Let these things be so.

26. Next to the Oreitians the Gadrosians bear sway in the interior parts, through whose land Alexander with his army marched with difficulty, and suffered more hardships than in all their other expeditions put together. This I have described in my larger book. South of the Gadrosians along the sea itself live the people called Fish-eaters. Along the coast of this people's country they sailed. Having started on the first day about the second watch, they put into Bagisara after a voyage of seventy miles. There was a harbour with good anchorage, and a village called Pasira, seven miles distant from the sea. The people living near it are called Pasirians. On the next day, earlier than usual, they put to sea and sailed round a lofty and precipitous promontory which stretches far out into the sea. Having dug wells and drawn up water scanty and bad, they lay at anchor that day, because the breakers were violent on the shore.

On the next day they put in at Colta, having gone twenty-four miles. Starting then at dawn they sailed seventy miles and anchored at Calyba. The village was near the shore, and around it a few date-palms grew, the dates upon which were green. There was an island, Carnine by name, about twelve miles from the shore. Here the villagers brought sheep and fish to Nearchus as presents of hospitality. He says that the mutton was fishy like that of sea birds, because the sheep here eat fish; for there is no grass in the country. On the next day sailing twenty-four miles they anchored near the shore and a village called Cissa, three and one-half miles distant from the sea. The name of the shore was Carbis. Here they came upon some vessels which were small, as was natural, belonging as they did to some miserable fishermen. They did not catch the men, for they had fled as soon as they saw the ships were being anchored. There was no corn there, and most of the supply for the army was exhausted. But after they had thrown some goats into the ships they sailed away. Having sailed round a lofty promontory stretching out into the sea about eighteen miles, they put in at a harbour safe from the waves. There was water there, and some fishermen lived near the harbour, which was called Mosarna.

27. From this point Nearchus says a pilot sailed with them, a Gadrosian named Hydraces, who undertook to bring them with safety as far as Carmania. The course from this place was no longer difficult, and the names of the places are better known, as far as the Persian Gulf. Setting out from Mosarna in the night they sailed eighty-eight miles to the shore called Balomus, thence forty-seven miles to the village of Barna, where many palm trees were and a garden, in which myrtles and flowers as well grew. From these the villagers made garlands. Here they first, since they started, saw cultivated trees, and men living not altogether savage. Thence they sailed round twenty-four miles and stopped at Dendrobosa, the ships riding at anchor on the deep. Thence setting out at midnight they arrived at the harbour of Cophanta, having sailed about forty-eight miles. Here dwelt fishermen who had vessels both small and bad. They did not row with oars fastened to a thole, as is the custom of Greeks, but as in a river, casting a paddle upon the water on this side and on that, like men who dig the ground. In the harbour was abundance of clear water. Setting out in the first watch they arrived at Cyiza, having sailed ninety-four miles. Here the shore was deserted and there were breakers. They therefore rode at anchor, and took their dinner on board ship. Sailing thence sixty miles they arrived at a certain small city situated upon a hill not far from the shore. Nearchus considering that probably the country was sown with crops told Archias that they must capture the place. Archias was son of Anaxidotus, a Pellaean, one of the Macedonians of repute, and he was sailing with Nearchus. Nearchus said that he did not

believe they would willingly supply the army with food, and it was not possible to take the town by assault. There would therefore be the necessity of besieging it, which would involve delay. Their supply of food was exhausted. He guessed that the land was productive of corn, from the tall stalks which he observed not far from the shore. When they had decided upon this plan, he ordered all the ships but one to be got ready for sailing. Archias managed this expedition for him, while he being left with a single ship went as if to view the city.

28. When he approached the walls in a friendly manner, the inhabitants brought from the city to him as gifts of hospitality tunny-fish baked in pans, a few cakes and some dates. These men were the most westerly of the Fish-eaters and the first whom they had seen not eating the fish raw. He said that he received these things with pleasure, and should like to view their city. They allowed him to enter. When he passed within the gates, he ordered two of his bowmen to guard the postern, and he himself with two others and the interpreter mounted the wall in the direction in which Archias had gone, and gave him the signal, as it had been agreed that the one should give the signal and the other should conjecture its meaning and do the thing ordered. The Macedonians seeing the signal drove their ships aground with speed and leaped eagerly into the sea. The barbarians being alarmed at these proceedings ran to arms. But the interpreter with Nearchus made a proclamation to them that they should give corn to the army, if they wished to keep their city in safety. They denied that they had any, and at the same time began to approach the wall. But Nearchus' bowmen, shooting from a commanding position, kept them back. When they perceived that their city was already held by the enemy and on the point of being sacked, they besought Nearchus to take the corn which they had and to carry it away, but not to destroy the city. Nearchus ordered Archias to seize the gates and the part of the wall near them; while he himself sent men with the natives to see whether they were showing their corn without deceit. The natives showed them a quantity of meal made from baked fish ground to powder, but only a little wheat and barley; for they were in the habit of using the powder made from fish instead of wheat, and wheaten loaves as a dainty. When they had shown them what they possessed they victualled themselves from what was at hand and setting sail they arrived at a promontory called Bageia, which the natives consider sacred to the Sun.

29. Setting out thence at midnight they sailed 118 miles to Talmena, a harbour with good anchorage; thence they proceeded forty-eight miles to Canassis, a deserted city. Here they found a well dug, and some wild palm trees were growing near it. Cutting off the cabbages which grow on the top of these they ate them; for the food of the army was now exhausted. Being now weak from hunger they sailed a day and night, and

anchored near a deserted shore. Nearchus, being afraid that if his men landed they would desert the ships from loss of spirit on account of their distress, kept the vessels riding at anchor in deep water. Having departed thence they sailed eighty-eight miles and anchored at Canate. There were short channels running from the shore. Sailing thence ninety-four miles they anchored near the land of the Troeans, in which were small miserable villages. The people left their houses, but they found a small quantity of corn there, and some dates. They slaughtered seven camels which they caught, and ate the flesh of these. Having started at break of day they sailed thirty-five miles and reached Dagaseira, where dwelt some people who were nomadic. Having set out from thence they sailed a night and a day without stopping at all, and after proceeding 129 miles they sailed beyond the boundary of the nation called Fish-eaters, suffering much distress from lack of provisions. They did not anchor near the land because the coast for a great distance was rocky and unsafe; thus they were compelled to ride at anchor in deep water. The length of the voyage along the coast of the Fish-eaters was a little more than 1,176 miles. These people are called Ichthyophagi because they live upon fish. Only a few of them are fishermen by trade; for not many make boats for this business, or have discovered the art of catching fish. They are supplied for the most part with fish by the ebbing of the tide. Some of them made nets to catch them, mostly one-quarter of a mile in length. They construct them out of the inner bark of palm trees, which they twist as we do hemp. But when the tide ebbs and the land is left dry, most of it is destitute of fish; but where there are depressions, some of the water is left behind in them, in which are very many fishes. Most of them are small, but others are larger. These they catch by casting nets around them. The tenderest of them they eat raw as soon as they draw them out of the water; but they dry the larger and harder ones in the sun, and when they are thoroughly baked, they grind them down and make meal and loaves of them. Others bake cakes from this meal. Their cattle also live on dried fish; for the country is destitute of meadows and does not produce grass. They catch also crabs, oysters, and other shell-fish all along the coast. There is natural salt in the country.[3] From these they make oil. Some inhabit desert places, where the land is without trees, and does not produce cultivated fruits. The whole diet of these consists of fish. Few of them sow any corn in the land; and what little is produced they use as a relish to the fish; for they use fish in place of bread. The most prosperous of them collect the bones of the whales cast up by the sea, and use these instead of timber for their houses; the broad bones which they find they make into doors. The majority who are poorer make their houses of the backbones of fishes.

[3] Here there is a gap in the text.

30. Great whales live in the external sea, as well as fish far larger than those in this internal sea.[4] Nearchus says that when they were sailing from Cyiza they saw at daybreak the water of the sea being blown upward as if being borne violently aloft from the action of bellows. Being alarmed they asked the pilots what it was, and from what this phenomenon arose; and they answered that this was caused by whales rushing through the sea and blowing the water upwards. The sailors were so alarmed at this that they let the oars fall from their hands. Nearchus went to them and encouraged them, and bade them be of good cheer; and sailing past each of the vessels, he ordered the men to direct their ships straight at them as in a sea-battle, to raise a loud shout, and to row as hard as they could, making as much noise and din as possible. Being thus encouraged, at the signal given, they rowed the ships together. When they got near the beasts, the men shouted as loud as they could, the trumpets sounded, and they made as much noise as possible with the rowing. Then the whales, which were just now seen at the prows of the ships, being frightened dived to the bottom, and soon afterwards came up again near the sterns, and again blew the sea up to a great distance. Then there was loud applause among the sailors at their unexpected deliverance, and praise was given to Nearchus for his boldness and wisdom. Some of these whales are left ashore on many parts of the coast, when the ebb-tide flows, being imprisoned in the shallows; others are thrown up on the dry ground by the rough storms, and then perish and rot. When the flesh has fallen off the bones are left; which the people use for making their houses. The large bones in their sides form beams for the houses, and the smaller ones rafters, the jawbones the doorposts. For many of them reach the length of 150 feet.

31. When they were sailing along the coast of the land of the Fish-eaters, they heard a tale about a certain island, which lies twelve miles from the mainland there, and is uninhabited. The natives say it is called Nosala, and that it is sacred to the Sun, and that no man wishes to touch at it. For whoever lands there through ignorance, disappears. Nearchus says that one of their light galleys having a crew of Egyptians disappeared not far from this island; and that the pilots stoutly affirmed in regard to this occurrence that no doubt having put in at the island through want of knowledge they had disappeared. But Nearchus sent a ship with thirty oars all round the island, ordering the sailors not to land on it, but sailing along so as to graze the shore to shout out to the men, calling out the captain's name and that of any other man known to them. But when no one obeyed him, he says he himself sailed to the island, and compelled the sailors against their will to put in. He landed himself, and proved that the tale about the island was an empty myth. He heard another tale told

[4] The Mediterranean.

about this island to the effect that one of the Nereids dwelt in it; but her name was not mentioned. She had intercourse with every man who approached the island, and having changed him into a fish, cast him into the sea. But the Sun was angry with the Nereid, and ordered her to depart from the island. She agreed to depart, but besought that her disease should be healed. The Sun hearkened to her request, and pitying the men whom she had turned into fishes, he turned them back again into men. And from these, they said, the race of the Fish-eaters sprang, which continued down to the time of Alexander. I, for my part, do not praise Nearchus for spending his time and ability in proving these things false, though they were not very difficult of disproof. I know, however, that it is a very difficult task for one who reads the ancient tales to prove that they are false.

32. To the north of the Fish-eaters away from the sea the Gadrosians inhabit a barren and sandy country; on account of which Alexander and his army suffered many hardships, as I have already described in my other work. When the fleet had departed from the land of the Fish-eaters and arrived in Carmania, at the first place in that country which they reached they lay at anchor in deep water, because rough breakers stretched along into the sea. Thence they sailed not so much towards the west as before, but their prows pointed more between the west and north. Carmania is better stocked with trees and more productive of crops than the country of the Fish-eaters or that of the Oreitians; as well as more grassy and better supplied with water. They anchored at Bados, an inhabited place in Carmania, with many cultivated trees growing, but no olives. The land was fruitful in corn, and the vines were good. Starting thence and sailing ninety-four miles, they came to anchor near a deserted shore, and observed a long promontory stretching far out into the sea. The promontory seemed about a day's voyage off. Those who were acquainted with those parts said that this promontory, which stretched out, was in Arabia, and was called Maceta; and that cinnamon and such like things were carried thence to the Assyrians. From this shore where the fleet was riding at anchor, and from the promontory which they saw stretching out into the sea opposite them, the gulf runs up into the interior, which is probably the Red Sea.[5] So I think, and so did Nearchus. When they saw this promontory, Onesicritus gave orders to direct their course to it, in order that they might not suffer hardships driving their ships up the gulf. But Nearchus answered that Onesicritus was childish if he did not know for what purpose Alexander had despatched the expedition. For he did not send out the ships because he could not convey all his army by land in safety, but because he wished to explore the coast by a coasting-voyage to see what harbours and islands were there, and if any

[5] The Arabian Gulf.

gulf ran into the land to sail round it; to find out what cities were on the sea-coast, and see if any of the country was fertile, and if any was deserted. Therefore, they ought not to render their whole work futile, now they were already near the end of their labours, especially as they no longer were in want of necessaries on the voyage. He said he was afraid, because the promontory stretched towards the south, that they should meet with a country there uninhabited, waterless and fiery-hot. These arguments prevailed, and Nearchus seems clearly to me to have saved his army by this advice; for the report is current that that promontory and all the land adjacent is uninhabited and entirely destitute of water.

33. Loosening from the shore they sailed, keeping close to the land, and after voyaging eighty-two miles they anchored on another shore, named Neoptana. And again they put to sea at break of day, and sailing twelve miles they anchored in the river Anamis. The place was called Harmozeia, and was pleasant and fertile in everything; except that olive-trees did not grow there. Here they disembarked and rested with delight from all their labours, recalling all the hardships they had endured on the sea and near the land of the Fish-eaters, the desolateness of the country, and the savageness of the people. They also recapitulated their own distresses. Some of them went up far into the country away from the sea, scattering themselves about away from the camp, one in search of one thing, another of another. Here they saw a man wearing a Grecian cloak, and equipped in other respects like a Greek. He also spoke the Greek language. The men who first saw this person said that they wept; it seemed so unexpected a thing for them after so many misfortunes to see a Greek, and to hear a Greek voice. They asked him whence he came and who he was. He said he had wandered away from Alexander's camp, and that the king himself and his army were not far off. They conducted this man to Nearchus, shouting and clapping their hands. He told Nearchus everything, and that the king and the camp were distant from the sea a journey of five days. He said he would introduce the governor of this land to Nearchus, and did so. Nearchus imparted to the governor his intention of going up the country to the king. He then went back to the ships. At daybreak he drew the ships on shore, in order to repair those that had been damaged in the voyage, and likewise because he had resolved to leave most of the army in this place. Therefore he threw a double stockade round the dockyard, and made an earthen wall with a deep trench, commencing from the bank of the river and ending at the shore where his ships had been drawn up.

34. While Nearchus was arranging these matters, the governor of the country, having learned that Alexander was very anxious about this expedition, thought that he would receive a great reward if he were the first to announce to him the safety of Nearchus and his army, and he knew

that Nearchus would arrive in the king's presence in a very short time. So he drove the shortest way, and told Alexander that Nearchus would soon be with him from the ships. At that time, although the king did not believe the story, yet he rejoiced at the news, as was natural. But when one day after another passed by, the report no longer seemed credible to him, when he considered the time since he received the news. Several persons were sent one after the other to fetch Nearchus. Some after going a little distance on the journey and meeting no one returned without him, others having gone further but having missed Nearchus and his men, did not return. Then Alexander ordered that man to be arrested, as a reporter of empty rumours, and one who had made his troubles more grievous than before on account of his foolish joy. It was evident from his face and his decision that he was cast into great grief. Meanwhile, some of those who had been despatched in search of Nearchus with horses and carriages fell in with him and Archias, and five or six with them on the road; for he was coming up with so few attendants. When they met them they recognised neither him nor Archias; so much altered did they look. They had long hair, they were dirty and covered with brine; their bodies were shrivelled, and they were pale from want of sleep and other hardships. When they asked where Alexander was, they answered naming the place, but were driving past. Archias guessing the state of the case said to Nearchus, "O Nearchus, I guess that these men are driving through the desert along the same road as we, for no other reason than that they have been despatched to seek us. I do not think it a wonder that they do not know us; for we are in such a wretched state as not to be recognisable. Let us tell them who we are, and ask them why they are driving this way." He seemed to Nearchus to say what was fitting. They, therefore, asked them, whither they were driving. They replied, "To seek Nearchus and the fleet." And he said, "Here, I am Nearchus, and this is Archias. Guide us; and we will give Alexander an account of the fleet."

35. Taking them up into the carriages they drove back; and some of these men, wishing to be the first to carry the news, ran forward and said to Alexander, "Here is Nearchus and with him Archias, and five others are being brought to you." They could answer nothing about the main army. Alexander, guessing this to mean that they had been preserved in a marvellous way, but that all the rest of his army had perished, did not so much rejoice at the safety of Nearchus and Archias as grieve at the loss of the whole army. Not yet had he made all his inquiries when Nearchus and Archias approached. Alexander with very great difficulty recognised them, and because he saw them with long hair and shabbily dressed, he was the more confirmed in his grief for the fleet. Clasping Nearchus by the right hand he led him away alone from the Companions and the shield-bearing guards, and wept for a long time. At last, bearing

up, he said, "But because you at any rate and this Archias have returned
in safety to us, I should be calm at the whole calamity. In what manner
did the ships and the army perish?" Nearchus said in reply, "O king, both
your ships and army are safe; and we here are come as messengers of their
safety." Still more wept Alexander, because the safety of the army
seemed impossible for him to expect. He asked where the ships were anchored. Nearchus said, "Here at the mouth of the river Anamis they
have been drawn up and are being repaired." Alexander took an oath by
Zeus of the Greeks and Ammon of the Libyans that verily he rejoiced
more at this news than because he was coming (to Susa) as the possessor
of the whole of Asia. For he said that the grief he would have felt at the
loss of this army would have been a counterpoise to all his other successes.

36. The governor of the land whom Alexander had arrested for the
falsity of his news, seeing that Nearchus was present, fell at his knees and
said, "Here am I who brought news to Alexander that you had arrived in
safety; you see how I am situated." Then Nearchus besought Alexander
to set the man at liberty; and he was set at liberty. Alexander offered
thanksgiving sacrifices for the safety of the army to Zeus the Preserver,
Heracles, and Apollo the Warder-off-of-harm; also to Poseidon and the
other marine gods. He also celebrated a gymnastic and musical contest,
and conducted a procession of his soldiers. Nearchus marched in the front
rank of the procession, and he was pelted with garlands and flowers by
the soldiers. When this came to an end, the king said to Nearchus, "I
wish that you should no longer, O Nearchus, run the risk of danger henceforth, or suffer such terrible hardships; but another man shall conduct
the fleet from this place until he has stationed it at Susa."

But Nearchus said in reply, "O king, I wish to obey you in all things
and it is necessary for me to do so. But if you wish to confer any favour
upon me, do not act thus; but allow me to conduct the fleet to the end
of the expedition, until I have stationed the ships in safety for you at
Susa. Do not let it be the case that the difficulties of the voyage, seem-
ingly insurmountable, have been intrusted to me by you, and yet the
duties which are easy and will be closely followed by the glory of completion were taken from me and given into the hands of another." Alexander
stopped him in the midst of his remarks, and confessed besides that he
was grateful to him. So he sent him down to the coast, giving him only
a small army as escort, because he was passing through a friendly land.
But not even was his journey to the sea free from trouble to him; for the
barbarians of the surrounding districts, having gathered together, were
holding the strongholds of the land of Carmania, because the satrap who
ruled them by the appointment of Alexander had died, and Tlepolemus,
the man newly appointed, had not yet secured his power. Twice or thrice
therefore on the same day they came into conflict with various bodies of

barbarians who made their appearance. Therefore making no delay of any kind they arrived safely at the sea-coast after very great difficulty. There Nearchus offered sacrifice to Zeus the Preserver and celebrated a gymnastic contest.

37. When he had performed the duties to the gods in due order, they set out to sea; and sailing past an uninhabited and rugged island, they cast anchor at another island, which was large and inhabited. They had sailed thirty-five miles from the place whence they had started. The desolate island was called Organa, and the one at which they anchored Oaracta. Vines and palms grew in it, and it was fertile in corn. Its length was ninety-four miles. Mazenes, the governor of the island, sailed with them as far as Susa, as a voluntary pilot. In this island they said that the tomb of the first king of this country was shown. They said that his name was Erythres, from whom this sea is called Erythraean. Loosening from the island they sailed thence, and sailing along about twenty-four miles of its coast they anchored again in it, and saw another island about five miles distant from this large one. It was said to be sacred to Poseidon and inaccessible. They set forth at daybreak, and so strong an ebb tide seized them that three of the ships ran aground and they were held fast on the dry ground. The others with difficulty sailing through the breakers got safely into deep water. When the tide came up again the ships which had run aground floated off, and next day were conducted to the place where the whole fleet lay. They anchored at another island distant about thirty-six miles from the mainland, after sailing forty-eight miles. Thence they sailed at daybreak, passing a desert island, called Pylora, on the left hand; and cast anchor near Sisidone, a small town destitute of all things, except water and fish. These also are fish-eaters from necessity, because they inhabit a barren country. Having supplied themselves with water thence, they advanced to Tarsia, a promontory stretching out into the sea, after sailing thirty-six miles. Thence to Cataea, a desert island, lying level with the sea. This was said to be sacred to Hermes and Aphrodite. The voyage to it was thirty-six miles. Into this island every year sheep and goats sacred to Hermes and Aphrodite are let loose by the people living near. It was possible to see that these had got wild in the course of time and on account of the absence of men.

38. Carmania extends as far as this, but the Persians inhabit the district beyond this. The length of the voyage along the coast of Carmania was 435 miles. The Carmanians live like Persians, because they have the same boundary. They are equipped with the same weapons. Then starting from the sacred island, they now sailed along the coast of Persis, and put in at a place called Ilas, where is a harbour facing a small desert island, the name of which is Caicandrus. The voyage was forty-eight miles. At daybreak they sailed off to another inhabited island, and anchored

there. Here Nearchus says pearls are caught as in the Indian Sea. Having sailed past the end of this island, five miles, they came to anchor. Next they anchored near a lofty mountain named Ochus, in a harbour affording good mooring; and fishermen dwelt there. Having sailed thence fifty-three miles, they anchored at Apostana, where many vessels were lying moored, and a village was distant from the sea seven miles. Starting thence by night, they sailed into a gulf studded with many villages, after a voyage of forty-eight miles. They anchored near the foot of a mountain. In this place grew many palms, and all the fruit-trees besides which grow in Greece. Starting thence they sailed along about seventy miles to Gogana, an inhabited land, and anchored in the outlet of river, swollen by winter rains, called Areon. Here they had difficulty in anchoring, for the channel into the river's mouth was narrow, because the ebb-tide made the parts all round it shallow. And departing thence they anchored in the mouth of another river, after sailing ninety-four miles. Its name was Sitacus. Nor did they anchor easily in this river. The whole of this voyage along the coast of Persis was among shallows, breakers, and shoals. Here they found plenty of corn collected by the king's order, so that they might be able to victual the fleet. They remained here twenty-one days in all, and having drawn up on shore the ships which had been damaged, they repaired them. The others, too, were overhauled.

39. Starting thence they arrived at the city of Hieratis, a place inhabited. The voyage was eighty-eight miles. They cast anchor in a canal named Heratemis, made into the sea from the river. At sun-rise they sailed along to a river swollen by winter rains, named Padagrus. The whole district was a peninsula, named Mesambria, in which were many gardens, and all kinds of fruit trees grew in them. Starting from Mesambria, and sailing about twenty-four miles, they anchored at Taoce, near the river Granis; and about twenty-four miles distant from the mouth of this river, in the interior, was a palace of the Persians. Nearchus says that during this voyage a whale was seen cast up upon the shore. Some of the sailors sailed to it, and measured it, saying it was seventy-five feet long. Its skin was covered with horny scales, and as much as eighteen inches in thickness. It had many oysters and shell-fish, and much sea-weed growing on it. He says also that many dolphins could be seen near the whale, and that they were larger than those in the inland sea. Starting thence, after a voyage twenty-four miles in length, they put in at Rhogonis, a river swollen by winter rains, in a harbour affording good anchorage. Having sailed thence forty-eight miles, they anchored in a river, swollen by winter rains, called Brizana. Here they found difficulty in anchoring, because there were breakers and shallows and low rocks just rising above the sea. When the tide flowed in they lay at anchor; but when the water ebbed the ships were left on dry ground. But when the

tide came in again in due succession, they sailed away, and anchored in a river named Oroatis, the largest river, as Nearchus says, which in the course of this voyage fell into the exterior sea.

40. The Persians live as far as this point; beyond this come the Susians. Another independent nation dwells above the Susians. These are called Uxians, about whom I have said in the other book that they are robbers. The length of the voyage along the coast of Persis was 517 miles. As the report goes, the land of Persis has been divided into three parts in regard to climate. The part of it situated near the Red Sea[6] is sandy and barren, on account of the heat; the part from this toward the north enjoys a more temperate climate, the country is grassy, and the meadows moist. It bears many vines, and every other fruit tree except the olive. It blooms with all kinds of pleasure-grounds, is watered by clear rivers and lakes, and is supplied with all sorts of birds, whose haunts are near rivers and lakes. It is good for horses, and moreover beasts of burden find pasture in it; it is everywhere woody, and adapted for hunting. Going still further to the north the country is wintry and snowy. Nearchus says that certain ambassadors from the Euxine Sea, having come a very short road, met Alexander going by way of Persis, and expressed their wonder, and told him of the shortness of the road. I have said already that the Uxians are neighbours of the Susians, just as the Mardians, who are also robbers, dwell next to the Persians, and the Cossaeans next to the Medes. All these nations Alexander subdued, falling upon them in the season of winter, when they thought their country was inaccessible. He also founded cities that they might no longer be nomadic, but become agriculturalists and workers of the ground, and might possess property, on account of which they would be afraid to injure each other. Thence the fleet passed along the land of the Susians. Nearchus says that he cannot any longer give such a detailed account, except to mention the anchorages and the length of the voyage. For the coast is most of it full of shoals, and with breakers stretching out far into the sea; and this is a difficult coast to anchor on. Therefore they generally sailed out on the deep sea. They started from the mouth of the river near the boundary of Persis, where they had encamped. They took in a supply of water for five days, for the pilots said there was no water further on.

41. After sailing sixty miles they anchored at the mouth of a lake named Cataderbis, which was full of fish; and near the mouth of it was an islet named Margastana. Thence at daybreak, having sailed, they went through the shallows in single file. The shallows were indicated by stakes fixed on this side and that, just as in the isthmus between the island of Leucas and Acarnania marks have been put up for mariners in order that their ships may not run aground in the shallows. Those at

[6] The Persian Gulf.

Leucas being sandy allow the ships that have run aground to be quickly got off again; but here the mud on each side of the channel is deep and slimy; so that it was impossible for ships run aground to be got off safely by any mechanical contrivance. For poles were no use to them at all, sinking as they did in the mud; and it was impossible for men to step out to push the ships off into the channel, for they sank in the mud as far as the chest. Thus with great difficulty having sailed through the distance of seventy miles in single file, they cast anchor and there remembered their dinner. During the night and the next day until evening they continued to sail through the shallows. They travelled 106 miles, and cast anchor at the mouth of the Euphrates, near a certain village in Babylonia, named Diridotis; where the merchants bring frankincense from the country on the opposite side of the gulf, and all the other spices which the country of the Arabs produces. From the mouth of the Euphrates up to Babylon, Nearchus said, is a voyage of 388 miles.

42. Here news is brought that Alexander was marching to Susa. They therefore sailed back from thence, in order to join him by sailing up the river Pasitigris. They sailed back, having the land of Susis on their left. They sailed along the lake into which the river Tigris discharges itself. This river flowing from Armenia past the city of Nineveh, formerly great and prosperous, causes the country which lies between it and the river Euphrates to be called Mesopotamia. From the lake into the river itself is a voyage of seventy miles; here was a village of Susis which is called Aginis. This is sixty miles distant from Susa. The length of the voyage along the coast of Susis as far as the mouth of the river Pasitigris was 235 miles. Thence they sailed up the Pasitigris through a country inhabited and prosperous. After sailing eighteen miles they anchored there waiting for those whom Nearchus had despatched to see where the king was. He himself offered sacrifice to the preserving gods, and celebrated a contest and the whole fleet made merry. When it was reported that Alexander was approaching, they again sailed up the river, and moored near the bridge of boats by which Alexander was going to convey his army to Susa. Here a junction was formed, and Alexander offered sacrifices for the safety of the ships and of the men, and celebrated contests. Wherever Nearchus appeared in the army he was pelted with flowers and garlands. Here also Nearchus and Leonnatus were crowned by Alexander with golden crowns; the former for the preservation of the fleet, and the latter for the victory which he had won over the Oreitians and the neighbouring barbarians. Thus Alexander's army starting from the mouth of the Indus arrived safely.

43. The country on the right of the Red Sea (the Persian Gulf) beyond Babylonia is Arabia, most of it; part of this extends as far as the sea of Phoenicia and Palestine-Syria; but towards the west in the direction of

the inner sea the Egyptians border on Arabia. The gulf which flows from the Great Sea as far as Egypt makes it evident that on account of the external sea flowing into it, there would be a possibility of sailing from Babylon round into that gulf which extends to Egypt. But no man has ever made this voyage on account of the heat and the desolateness of the country, unless some went through the open sea. For the men of the army of Cambyses who got safely from Egypt to Susa, and the men who were despatched to Babylon by Ptolemy the son of Lagus to Seleucus Nicator went through a certain isthmus of Arabia, and travelled eight days in all over a country waterless and desert. They went, however, at full speed on camels, carrying water for themselves on the camels' backs and journeying by night. For during the day they could not keep out under the open sky on account of the heat. The country beyond this district which we show to be an isthmus extending from the Arabian Gulf to the Red Sea[7] is necessarily far from being inhabited, when the parts stretching more to the north are desert and sandy. But men starting from the Arabian Gulf near Egypt sailed round the greater part of Arabia and came into the sea near Susa and Persia, having sailed along as much of the coast of Arabia as the water put into their ships allowed; then they turned back. The men whom Alexander despatched from Babylon to sail as far as possible on the right of the Red Sea, and to discover the places there, saw some islands lying in the course of their voyage, and landed somewhere on the continent of Arabia. But there was no one who was able to pass round or to bend his course to the parts beyond that promontory which Nearchus says they saw stretching out opposite Carmania. I think that if those seas had been navigable, or if those countries could have been traversed on foot, they would have been proved to be navigable and traversable by Alexander in his fondness for searching after knowledge. Hanno the Libyan starting from Carthage sailed past the Pillars of Heracles out into the Ocean, having the land of Libya on his left. He continued his voyage towards the east for thirty-five days in all; but when he turned towards the south he met with many difficulties through lack of water, the blazing heat, and streams of fire falling into the ocean. But Cyrene in Libya, though it is situated among the more desert parts, is grassy, genial and well-watered; there are groves and meadows; and it is fertile in fruits of all kinds, and nourishes flocks and herds as far as the place where the silphium grows. Beyond the silphium the country in the interior is desert and sandy. Allow me to state I have written this book with a view to its connection with Alexander the Macedonian, the son of Philip.

[7] The Arabian Gulf is the present Red Sea, and the Red Sea is the present Sea of Arabia.

COINAGE AND PURCHASING POWER

References to money in the historians have been left untranslated and without suggested modern equivalents because it is impossible accurately to take into account the much greater purchasing power of gold and silver in antiquity. There is also evidence to show fluctuations in purchasing power, and changes in monetary standards within the period from 600 B.C. to 323 B.C. not unlike the fluctuations with which we are familiar. Consequently the usual statement, that one obol equals three cents and one drachma equals eighteen cents and so on to the talent, calculated at 1,080 dollars, is really meaningless because so many variable factors are involved.

A few calculations of wages, living costs, and known prices may be more meaningful than any table of equivalents,[1] although much of our information is from Athenian sources and it is unsafe to assume that it would apply to the whole Greek world of the Aegaean area. Certainly we know that there was a marked upward trend in wages during the period of the Peloponnesian War. The normal rate of pay for jurors, for instance, was originally two obols a day, subsequently raised to three. At the end of the fifth century one drachma a day, or even two, was the rate paid to soldiers, sailors, and artisans, whether slave or free. Tod has estimated that a single man could live in Athens on 120 drachmas a year (two obols a day) in the latter part of the fifth century, and the minimum cost for a family of four was perhaps 280 drachmas a year. For one person the cost of wheat for a year is calculated at fifteen drachmas, other food forty-five drachmas, clothing sixteen drachmas, and rent thirty-six drachmas. However, by the latter part of the fourth century the cost of living for a family of four is estimated at 450 drachmas.

Early in the sixth century a medimnus of wheat cost one drachma; this had doubled at the end of the fifth century, reached three drachmas early in the fourth century, and finally five drachmas in the latter part of the fourth century. A sheep, which brought one drachma in 590 B.C., cost ten or even twenty drachmas at the end of the fifth century.

From the standpoint of Athenian trade and revenue the budget of a Greek state seems very small by comparison with even a moderate sized

[1] Much of this material is based on the splendid discussion of M. N. Tod, "The Economic Background of the Fifth Century," *Cambridge Ancient History*, V. 1-32.

city today. The total revenue of Athens in 431 B.C. is supposed to have been about 1,000 talents, of which about 500 talents represented the tribute from the subject states. However, a trireme, the Athenian battleship, cost only about one talent to build while the wages for the crew amounted to one-half a talent a month. The total cost of pay for the Council and the very large number of jurors amounted to 150 talents a year. Since many of the ordinary expenditures of the state were borne by the wealthy citizens individually, the budget of the state was correspondingly reduced. We hear of few large fortunes, 200 talents being the largest known, but we do know of one man who spent about ten talents in ten years on public services.

The actual coinage presents considerable variation; the two basic currencies in Greece were the Aeginetan and the Euboic, to which the old Attic coinage corresponded. From the time of the Persian wars the purity of the Athenian silver coinage, combined with her naval and commercial superiority, tended to make the Attic the standard coinage in the fifth century, although the Persian gold daric circulated freely in the East. Herodotus (Book III. 95) calculates the ratio of gold to silver at 13:1 though Darius had fixed the ratio at 13.33:1. Exploitation of the silver mines at Laurium drove the ratio to 17.15:1 by 434 B.C. but the appearance of Persian gold drove the ratio down to 12:1 by 403 B.C. and the conquests of Alexander brought it to 10:1 at the end of the fourth century.

The chief Greek units of monetary exchange are as follows:

Obol	the smallest unit
Drachma	6 obols
Mina	100 drachmas
Talent	60 minas

Other units used by the historians:

Daric	Persian gold coin, 125.55 grains
Stater	Greek gold coin, 25 per cent heavier than the daric
Daric stater	20 Attic drachmas
Stater (Phocaean)	23 Attic drachmas
Stater (Cyzicene)	28 Attic drachmas (335 B. C.)
Talent (Babylonian)	60 Babylonian minas (78 Attic minas)

MEASURES AND DISTANCES

Wherever it has been possible, distances have been converted to approximate English equivalents throughout the text of all the historians, since it is seldom possible to check the distances in the original and find them so exact that we may believe them to be more than estimates. Since this is the case, the English reader can form a better impression of the author's conception of spatial relationships if the terms used are familiar to him. Herodotus, however, occasionally discusses the various measures of distance and consequently it is necessary to leave the original terms. The following table will indicate the exact distance where it is known. The two largest units, the parasang and the schoene, are the most variable since neither is in origin strictly a measure of length. The parasang was an hour's journey and the schoene, meaning a 'rope' was a rough practical measure used in estimating considerable distances. In the case of other measures, as in coinage, there were different standards and there is frequently no way of determining which standard should be applied in a particular case. It is also probable that standards of measurement were different in the same city at different times. Distances:

Foot	11.65 inches
Cubit	18.25 inches
Royal cubit	20.5 inches
Fathom	6.06 feet (or 5.8 feet)
Plethron	101 feet (or 97 feet)
Stade (Attic)	214.5 yards
Stade (itinerary)	164 yards
Parasang	30 stades (Herodotus, ü, 6); 3.4 miles (G. B. Gray, *C.A.H.*, 4.193)
Schoene	60 stades (Herodotus, ü, 6) but Strabo (804) says 30 to 120 stades.

The chief liquid and dry measures are:

Cotyle	about ½ pint
Choenix	3 or 4 cotylae, 1½ pints or 1 quart (the slave's daily corn ration)
Medimnus	48 choenices, nearly 9 gallons or 1½ bushels dry measure
Mina	15 oz. 83.75 grs.
Talent (Euboic)	57 pounds
(Aeginetan)	95 pounds
Amphora	about 9 gallons

GLOSSARY

ACROPOLIS. The upper city or citadel, especially of Athens.

AGORA. The market-place of a Greek city.

APATURIA. An Athenian festival at which grown sons were formally enrolled as citizens.

ARCHON. One of the nine chief magistrates at Athens.

ARTYNAE. Magistrates at Argos and Epidaurus.

BARATHRUM. A deep pit at Athens into which criminals were thrown.

BOEOTARCH. One of the chief magistrates of Boeotia.

CLERUCH. A citizen, especially of Athens, holding an allotment of land in a foreign country.

DECARCHY. An oligarchy of ten officials established by Lysander at the end of the Peloponnesian war.

DEME. A division of Attica roughly corresponding to the modern township.

DEMIURGOS. The name of a magistrate.

EPHOR. One of the body of five magistrates, who controlled even the kings at Sparta.

HELOT. One of the slave class among the Spartans.

HOPLITE. A heavy-armed foot-soldier who carried a spear and large shield.

INTERCALATION. The insertion of days or months into the ordinary year.

METIC. An alien allowed to settle in Athens on payment of a tax, yet without enjoying civic rights.

MINA. A sum of money, 100 drachmas; a weight, 15 oz. 83.75 grs.

NAUARCH. A subordinate naval officer whose precise duties are unknown.

NEODAMODE. A Spartan citizen of the group of emancipated Helots.

NOME. An administrative district in Egypt.

Glossary

PAEAN. A choral hymn or battle-song.

PANCRATIUM. An athletic event combining boxing and wrestling.

PARALUS. One of the two swift Athenian galleys used for official business and sacred embassies.

PELTAST. A soldier carrying a light shield and hence more mobile than the hoplite.

PERIOECI. The old inhabitants of a city state reduced to the condition of dependents but not slaves. The term is used particularly of the old Achaean stock in Lacedaemonia.

PHALANX. A compact mass of heavy infantry usually eight deep, but developed by Philip of Macedon into a more massive and more effective unit.

PHRATRY. A brotherhood or clan forming a subdivision of the tribe.

PHALLUS. The penis or an image thereof borne in Bacchic processions as an emblem of the generative power in nature.

PROXENUS. A citizen of a Greek city-state appointed because of family connections or other ties to represent the citizens of another state who happened to have dealings in the Proxenus' native state.

POLEMARCH. A general or commander. At Sparta the commander of a division. At Athens the third archon who originally commanded in battle.

PRYTANES. A committee of fifty, representing one of the ten tribes at Athens, serving as presiding officers for the Council of 500 during one-tenth of the year.

QUADRIREME. A warship with four banks of oars.

QUINQUEREME. A warship with five banks of oars.

SALAMINIA. One of the two swift Athenian galleys used for official business and sacred embassies.

SATRAP. The title of a Persian viceroy or governor of a province.

SATRAPY. The province of a Persian satrap or governor.

SCIRITAE. A division of the Spartan army consisting of 600 foot-soldiers.

SCYTALE. A Spartan staff used for sending messages in cipher. A strip of paper was rolled spirally around it, on which dispatches were written, so that they were unintelligible when unrolled; the generals had a staff of the same size on which to reroll the strip and so read the message.

TAGUS. The title of the chief or overlord of Thessaly.

TALENT. As a measure of weight the Euboic talent was about fifty-seven pounds, the Aeginetan ninety-five pounds. As an amount of money it represented these weights in silver. The talent contained sixty minas or 6,000 drachmas.

TAXIARCH. The commander of a division. At Athens the commander of the quota furnished by one tribe.

THEORI. Ambassadors sent by a state to consult an oracle.

TRIERARCH. The title of the Athenian responsible for equipping and manning a trireme for the state at his own expense.

TRIREME. A Greek warship with three banks of oars. The usual crew was 200, fifty-four oarsmen in each of the lower banks, sixty-two in the upper bank and thirty marines or reserve oarsmen.

INDEXES

INDEX TO HERODOTUS

Unimportant names are not included. References are to books (roman numerals) and chapters (arabic numerals).

coffins, at Egyptian feasts, II. 78; of crystal in Ethiopia, III. 24

coined money first used by Lydians, I. 94; coining of darics and aryandics, IV. 166

Colaeus, Samian, IV. 152

Colaxais, Scythian, IV. 5, 7

Colchis, I. 104; Colchians, I. 2, 104; II. 104, 105; III. 97; IV. 37, 40; VII. 79; Medea, VII. 62; the Phasis in Colchis, IV. 45; Aea, I. 2; VII. 193, 197; linen of Colchis, II. 105; IV. 45

Colias, in Attica, VIII. 96; Colian women, VIII. 96

collection for the return of Pisistratus, I. 61; for rebuilding the temple at Delphi, II. 180

Colophon, city, I. 14, 16, 142; men of, I. 147, 150

Colossae, city of Phrygia, VII. 30

colossal statues, I. 183; II. 91, 110, 121, 130, 149, 176

columns of temple at Ephesus given by Croesus, I. 92

Combreia, town near Pallene, VII. 123

Compsantus, river in Thrace, VII. 109

constitution of Lycurgus, I. 65; of Cleisthenes, V. 66, 69

Contadesdus, river of Thrace, IV. 90

continents, names of, IV. 45

convulsions, cure for, IV. 187

Copais, lake, VIII. 135

copper, scarce in Ethiopia, III. 23

Corcyra, III. 48, 52, 53; VII. 145; Corcyraeans, III. 48-50, 53; VII. 145, 154, 168

Coresus, near Ephesus, V. 100

Corinth, city, I. 23, 24; III. 50, 52, 53; V. 92, 93; VI. 128; VII. 202; VIII. 45; IX. 88; Corinthians, I. 14, 23, 24, 50, 51; II. 167; III. 48, 49; IV. 162; V. 75, 76, 92, 93; VI. 89, 108; VII. 137 (Aristeas), 154, 195; VIII. 1, 5 (Adeimantus), 21, 43, 61, 72, 79, 94; IX. 28, 31, 69, 95, 102, 105; Adeimantus, Aetion, Amphion, Aristeas (2), Cypselus, Lycophron, Periander, Sosicles; Corinthian women, III. 134; V. 92; Melissa, Labda; helmet, IV. 180; dress, V. 87; Bacchiadae at Corinth, V. 92; Cypselus, V. 92; Periander, I. 20, 23, 24; III. 50-53; V. 92; Corinthians against Samos, III. 48; oppose

war with Athens, V. 75, 92; help Athenians, VI. 89; at Thermopylae, VII. 202; at Artemisium, VIII. 1; at Salamis, VIII. 94; at Plataea, IX. 28, 31, 69; at Mycale, IX. 102, 105; respect for mechanic arts, II. 167

corn, in Babylonia, I. 193; trade: in Scythia, IV. 17; VII. 147; in Sicily, VII. 158

Corobius, purple-fisher of Crete, IV. 151-153

Coronea, men of, V. 79

Corsica, island, I. 165-167; men of, VII. 165

corselets, Egyptian, I. 135; VII. 89; of linen, II. 182; III. 47; VII. 63, 89

Corycian cave, VIII. 36

Corydallus of Anticyra, VII. 214

Corys, river in Arabia, III. 9

Cos, island, I. 144; IX. 76; Coans, VII. 99, 164; woman of, IX. 76; Cadmus, VII. 163; Antagoras, Hegetorides, IX. 76

cosmetics, used by Scythian women, IV. 75

cotton, III. 47, 106; VII. 65

courier, from Athens to Sparta, VI. 105; from Argives to Mardonius, IX. 12; Persian, VIII. 98

courtesans, at Naucratis, II. 135

cow, sacred to Isis, II. 41; at Sais, II. 129-132; flesh avoided by the Egyptians, II. 18, 41; by nomad Libyans and women of Cyrene and Barca, IV. 186

crafts, inherited at Sparta, VI. 60

Cranai, ancient name of Athenians, VIII. 44

Cranaspes, Persian, III. 126

Crannonian, VI. 127

Crathis (1), river of Achaea in Peloponnese, I. 145

Crathis (2), river of Sybaris, V. 45; Athene of, V. 45

Cremni (Cliffs) in Scythia, IV. 20, 110

Creston, city, I. 57; Crestonians, I. 57; V. 3, 5; VII. 124, 127; land, VIII. 116

crests on helmets invented by Carians, I. 171

Crete, I. 62, 172, 173; III. 44, 59; IV. 45, 151, 154; VII. 92, 145, 170, 171; Cretans, I. 2, 171; III. 59; IV. 151, 161; VII. 99 (Artemisia), 169-171; Minos, Corobius, Etearchus (2); Phronima, Artemisia;

Eurybiades, Spartan commander, VIII. 2, 4, 5, 42, 49, 57-64, 74, 79, 108, 124

Eurydame, second wife of Leotychides, VI. 71

Euryleon, Spartan, V. 46

Eurymachus, Theban, VII. 233

Eurypylus, Thessalian, IX. 58

Eurysthenes, king of Sparta, IV. 147; V. 39; VI. 51, 52; VII. 204

Eurystheus, king of Mycenae, IX. 26, 27

Eurytus, Spartan, VII. 229

Euxine Sea, I. 6, 72, 76, 110; II. 33, 34; III. 93; IV. 46, 90; VI. 33; VII. 36; measurement, IV. 85, 86

Exampaeus, in Scythia, IV. 52, 81

executions by night at Sparta, IV. 146

experiments of Psammetichus, II. 2, 28

expiation, ceremonies the same among Lydians and Greeks, I. 35

expounder of oracles at Delphi, VIII. 36, 37

fabulous creatures of Libya, IV. 191

Fair Strand (Cale Acte), VI. 22, 23

famine, in Lydia, I. 94; Cambyses' army, III. 25; Xerxes' army, VIII. 115; siege of Sestos, IX. 118

fatalism of Herodotus, I. 8; II. 161; IV. 79; V. 32, 92; VI. 64; IX. 109; Delphic oracle, I. 91; VI. 135; Solon, I. 33; Croesus, I. 87, 91; Croesus' advice to Cyrus, I. 207

feathers, in the air, IV. 7; gold-dust got from mud with, IV. 195

female line of descent in Lycia, I. 173

fertility of Babylonia, I. 193; of Libya, IV. 198; of Europe, VII. 5; of Aeolia, I. 149

festivals, of the Greeks, names end in the letter a, I. 148; of Apis suppressed by Cambyses, III. 29; in Egypt, II. 59-64

fifty-oared galleys used by Phocaeans, I. 163

fillet (mitra), VII. 62, 90

fine to be paid to Apollo, III. 52; imposed on Phrynichus, VI. 21; on Miltiades, VI. 136; for aggression, VI. 92

fire venerated by Persians, III. 16; abhorred by Egyptians, III. 16

"fire-bearer" in Greek fleet, VIII. 6

fire-signals, VII. 182; IX. 3

first-fruits, of inheritance offered by Croesus, I. 92; of victory by Greeks, VIII. 121, 122

fish, the only food of three Babylonian tribes, I. 200; not allowed as food for Egyptian priests, II. 37; some venerated by the Egyptians, II. 72; principal food of Egyptians, II. 77, 92; method of propagation in the Nile, II. 93; fish of Egypt, II. 72, 93, 149; of the Borysthenes, IV. 53; of lake Prasias, V. 16; revenue from fish of lake Moeris, II. 149; III. 91; prodigy of the salt fish leaping, IX. 120; Fish-eaters, I. 200, 202; II. 92; III. 19

flagellation in Egypt, II. 40, 61

fleet of Minos, I. 171; of Sesostris, II. 102; of Necos, II. 159; of Polycrates, III. 39; of Cambyses, III. 19; of the Persians at Lade, VI. 6; of the Ionians, VI. 8; of the Thasians, VI. 46, 47; of Mardonius, VI. 44; of Datis and Artaphernes, VI. 95; of the Athenians, VI. 89; VII. 144, 161; VIII. 42, 44, 61; IX. 114; of the Aeginetans, VI. 83, 92; VIII. 46; of Xerxes, VII. 44, 45, 89-100, 184; VIII. 66, 107; IX. 96; Greek fleet at Artemisium, VIII. 1, 2; at Salamis, VIII. 42-48

flesh, eaten raw by Padaean Indians, III. 99

flocks of the Phrygians, V. 49; of the Euboeans, VIII. 19, 20

food, Persian, I. 133; Massagetae, I. 216; Egyptian, II. 36, 37, 77, 92; Ethiopian, III. 23; as tribute, I. 192

foot, cut off by Hegesistratus, IX. 37

foot-pan of Amasis, II. 172

footprint of Heracles, IV. 82

foot race at Olympia, V. 22

ford over Halys made by Thales, I. 75

foreign customs adopted readily by Persians, I. 135; avoided by Egyptians, II. 79, by the Scythians, IV. 76

forgery of oracles, VII. 6

founder, honours paid to, at Abdera, I. 168; in Chersonese, VI. 38

fountain of the long-lived Ethiopians, III. 23; of Apollo at Cyrene, IV. 158; of Thestis, IV. 159; of the sun, IV. 181; Enneacrunus, VI. 137; of the Maeander and Catarracte, VII. 26; Castalia, VIII. 39; Gargaphia, IX. 49

four-yearly festivals of Athenians, VI. 87, 111, 138

foxes in Libya, IV. 192

fox-goose, II. 72

frankincense, how got, III. 107; offered to Belus, I. 183; as tribute from Arabia, III. 97; offered by Datis at Delos, VI. 97

freedom, effects of, V. 78

fringe of the Egyptian calasiris, II. 81; of the dress of women in Libya, IV. 189

full moon waited for by Lacedaemonians, VI. 108

fumes, intoxicating, I. 202; IV. 75

funerals, Persian, I. 140; III. 16; Egyptian, II. 85; III. 16; Ethiopian, III. 24; Scythian kings, IV. 71-73; other Scythians, IV. 73; Libyan nomads and Nasamonians, IV. 190; Trausi, V. 4; other Thracians, V. 5, 8; Lacedaemonian kings, VI. 58; Greeks after Plataea, IX. 85

furthest point reached by Sesostris, II. 103; by Persians in Libya, IV. 204; by Mardonius, IX. 14

Gadeira, IV. 8

Gaeson, river (?), IX. 97

Galepsus, town near Torone, VII. 122

Gallaica, region in Thrace, VII. 108

gall-fly, I. 193

games, invented by Lydians, I. 94; at Triopium, I. 144; at Agylla, I. 167; in honour of Perseus at Chemmis, II. 91

Gamphasantes, IV. 174

Gandarians, III. 91; VII. 66

Garamantians, IV. 183, 184

gardens, of Midas, VIII. 138

Gargaphia, spring, IX. 25, 49, 51, 52

garlands from hero-temple, VI. 69; worn by Persians crossing the Hellespont, VII. 55, 56

garrison posts in Egypt, II. 30

gates of Babylon, I. 179; III. 155; destroyed by Darius, III. 159; tomb over a gate, I. 187

Gauanes, brother of Perdiccas, VIII. 137

Gaumata, *see* Smerdis (2)

Gebeleizis, god of the Thracians, IV. 94

geese sacrificed in Egypt, II. 45

Gela, city, VI. 23; VII. 153, 154, 156; men of, VII. 153, 154 (Sabyllus), 155, 156

Geleon, son of Ion, V. 66

Gelo, tyrant of Syracuse, VII. 145, 153-166, 168

Gelonians, IV. 102, 108, 109, 119, 120, 136; king of, IV. 119

Gelonus (1), son of Heracles, IV. 10

Gelonus (2), city, IV. 108

genealogy of Egyptian kings and priests, II. 142, 143; of Hecataeus, II. 143; Lydian kings, I. 7; Xerxes, VII. 11; Spartan kings, VI. 53; VII. 204; VIII. 131; Macedonian kings, VIII. 139; Perseus, II. 91

geography of Herodotus, *see especially* I. 72, 202-204; II. 5-34; III. 115, 116; IV. 36-45, 99-101

geology of Herodotus, II. 8-12; VII. 129

geometry came from Egypt, II. 109

Gephyraeans, V. 55, 57, 58, 61, 62

Geraestus, in Euboea, VIII. 7; IX. 105

Gergis, Persian commander, VII. 82, 121

Gergithes, Gergith Teucrians, V. 122; VII. 43

Germanians, tribe of Persians, I. 125

Gerrhus (1), river of Scythia, IV. 19, 20, 47, 56

Gerrhus (2), place in Scythia, IV. 53, 56; Gerrhi, IV. 71

Geryones, IV. 8

Getae, IV. 93, 96, 118; V. 3, 4

gifts of honour among Persians, III. 84; VII. 106, 116; VIII. 120; as tribute to Darius, III. 97; of Scythian king to Darius, IV. 131; of Euelthon to Pheretima, IV. 162

Gigonus, town near Pallene, VII. 123

Giligamae, in Libya, IV. 169, 170

Gillus, Tarentine, III. 138

Gindanes, in Libya, IV. 176, 177

Glaucus (1), of Chios, I. 25

Glaucus (2), son of Hippolochus, I. 147

Glaucus (3), Spartan, son of Epicydes, VI. 86

Glisas, river in Boeotia, IX. 43

gnats, in the Delta of Egypt, II. 95

gnomon, II. 109

goat-footed Pan in Egypt, II. 46; men, IV. 25

goat-skins dyed red, IV. 189

goats, as sacrificial animals, II. 42, 46; intercourse with Egyptian woman, II. 46; urine as cure for convulsions, IV. 187

Gobryas, one of the seven Persians, III. 70, 73, 78; IV. 132, 134, 135

gods, "unknowable", II. 3; names of the

twelve, invented by Egyptians, II. 4;
altar of the twelve gods at Athens, II.
7; names invented by Egyptians, II. 50;
worshipped by Pelasgians without any
names, II. 52; Egyptians first assigned
days to different gods, II. 82; Egyptian
date for the last appearance of a god in
human form, II. 142; reign in Egypt,
II. 144; gods of Persians, I. 131-132;
Arabians, III. 8; Scythians, IV. 59, 62;
Libyans, IV. 188, 189

Goetosyrus, *see* Oetosyrus

gold, in Lydia, I. 93; among the Massagetae, I. 215; in Ethiopia, III. 23, 97,
114; in Siphnos, III. 57; in India, III.
102-106; in Northern Europe, III. 116;
in Libya, IV. 195; in Thasos, VI. 47, 48;
in Thrace, Scapte Hyle, VI. 47; Mt.
Pangaeon, VII. 112; Daton, IX. 75;
offerings of Gyges, I. 14; Croesus, I. 51,
52, 92; given to Lacedaemonians by
Croesus, I. 69; on the battlements of
Agbatana, I. 98; image of Belus, etc.,
I. 183; cow at Sais, II. 129, 130; statue of
Athene, II. 182; gold-dust as tribute
from Indians, III. 94; Ethiopians, III.
97; vessels of Maeandrius, III. 148; sacred gold of Scythians, IV. 5, 7; given to
Alcmaeon, VI. 125; plane-tree and vine
at Susa, VII. 27; vessels thrown into
Hellespont, VII. 54; pomegranates on
spears, VII. 41; worn by Persians,
vessels washed up near Cape Sepias,
VII. 190; gifts to men of Abdera, VIII.
120; stars offered by Aeginetans, VIII.
121; cuirass of Masistius, IX. 22; spoils
of Plataea, IX. 80; tripod at Delphi, IX.
81; reckoned by the Euboeic talent,
III. 89; value compared with silver, III.
95; tried by touchstone, VII. 10; statue,
VII. 69

Gonnus, city in Thessaly, VII. 128, 173

Gordias, son of Midas, king of Phrygia,
I. 14, 35, 45

Gorgo, daughter of Cleomenes, V. 48, 51;
VII. 239

Gorgon, II. 91

Gorgus, king of the Salaminians, V. 104,
115; VII. 98; VIII. 11

grain, in Babylonia, I. 193; in Egypt, II.
36

Greece, I. 1-3, 27, 29, 69, 92, 152; II. 44,

50, 56, 91, 104, 109, 114, 135, 146, 182;
III. 6, 39, 104, 106, 122, 130, 131, 134-
138; IV. 76, 77, 143; V. 32, 49, 58; VI.
24, 48, 49, 61, 86, 94, 98, 106, 109, 131,
138; VII. 1, 5-8, 10-13, 15, 17, 21, 25,
32, 38, 39, 46, 47, 56, 57, 82, 99, 101,
102, 105, 108, 126, 131, 138, 139, 144,
145, 147, 148, 150, 152, 157, 159, 161,
162, 168, 169, 172, 175-178, 203, 209,
235, 239; VIII. 3, 4, 15, 18, 19, 22, 30,
44, 47, 57, 60, 62, 66, 68, 72, 77, 94,
100, 101, 108, 109, 114-116, 124, 142,
144; IX. 1, 2, 7, 9, 42, 45, 60, 72, 78, 82,
95, 101, 106, 114, 121; Greek land, VII.
135; Greeks, I. 1-7, 26, 27, 35, 53, 56,
60, 65, 69, 70, 72, 74, 75, 87, 90, 94,
110, 131, 133, 135, 148, 153, 163, 170,
171, 174, 193, 202, 203, 216; II. 1, 4, 5,
13, 14, 16, 17, 20, 28, 30, 32, 36, 39, 41,
43-46, 48, 49, 51-54, 58, 59, 64, 79, 80,
82, 91, 92, 94, 105, 109, 112, 115, 118,
120, 122, 123, 134, 135, 144-146, 148,
153, 160, 167, 171, 178, 180; III. 1, 11,
25, 26, 27, 32, 38, 60, 80, 102, 103, 107,
122, 132, 139, 140; IV. 6, 8, 10, 12, 14,
18, 24, 26, 33, 45, 48, 51, 53, 76, 77-79,
85, 95, 103, 105, 108-110, 152, 158, 159,
180, 189, 190, 197, 203; V. 20, 22, 23,
28, 47, 58, 94, 97, 102; VI. 17, 29, 43,
48, 53, 54, 75, 98, 106, 112, (122), 126,
127, 134, 137; VII. 9, 10, 11, 16, 18, 37,
48, 61, 63, 74, 90, 93-95, 101-104, 106,
107, 110, 118, 130, 132, 133, 138, 139,
144, 145, 147-151, 157, 158, 161-173,
175-180, 183, 185, 189, 192, 194-196,
201-203, 205, 207, 209-214, 219, 223,
225, 233, 234, 236, 239; VIII. 1, 4, 11,
13-18, 23, 26, 29, 30, 40, 42, 44, 46, 56,
61, 65, 68, 70, 72, 75, 76, 80-87, 89, 93,
94, 96-98, 100, 102, 108, 110-112, 121-
124, 130-133, 136, 140, 142; IX. 2, 7,
15, 17, 20, 21, 22, 25, 27-29, 31-33, 36,
38, 40-43, 45, 46, 48-50, 53, 57-61, 67-
72, 76, 78, 79, 82, 85-87, 90, 92, 96, 98-
103, 105, 106, 110, 114-116, 119; in
Libya, IV. 158; in Scythia, IV. 18, 51,
78, 105; Greek Scythians, IV. 7; Greeks
about Pontus, IV. 8, 10, 24, 95; VII.
95; Greeks, of Greece, of the Greeks,
race, I. 4, 56-58, 60, 143; II. 181; VI. 53;
VII. 145; VIII. 144; tongue, II. 56, 137,
143, 144, 154; (III. 115); IV. 52, 78, 108,

lyres, IV. 192; of wild oxen, VII. 126; do not grow well in cold climates, IV. 29

horoscopes, II. 82

horses, eating serpents, I. 78; afraid of camels, I. 80, of asses and mules, IV. 129; sacrificed to Apollo, I. 216, to river, VII. 113; of Darius, III. 85-88; as tribute, III. 90; of Heracles, IV. 8-9; in Scythia, IV. 28; trained to lie down, IV. 22; round tombs of Scythian kings, IV. 72; of the Sigynnae, V. 9; of Tritantaechmes, I. 192; trained to fight, V. 111; of Zeus, VII. 40; VIII. 115; of Pharnuches, VII. 88; of Masistius, IX. 20, 22; of Mardonius, IX. 63; mares winning three times at Olympia, VI. 103

human life, misery of, V. 4; VII. 46; shortness of, VII. 46

human sacrifice, in Egypt, II. 45; Menelaus to the winds, II. 119; Tauri, IV. 103; Getae, IV. 94; Persian, VII. 114, 180; at Alus, VII. 197; Apsinthians, IX. 119

Hundred Isles, I. 151

hunting by the Scythians in Media, I. 73; accident to Darius, III. 129; method of the Iyrcae, IV. 22; Troglodytes hunted with four-horse chariots, IV. 183

Hyacinthia, festival at Sparta, IX. 7, 11

Hyampeia, peak of Parnassus, VIII. 39

Hyampolis, town of Phocis, VIII. 28, 33

Hyatae, tribe of the Sicyonians, V. 68

Hybla, city in Sicily, VII. 155

Hydarnes (1), one of the seven Persians, III. 70

Hydarnes (2), son of Hydarnes, commander of the "Immortals", VI. 133; VII. 83, 135, 136, 211, 215, 218; VIII. 113, 118

Hydrea, island, III. 59

Hyele, town in Italy, I. 167

hyenas in Libya, IV. 192

Hylleis, tribe of the Dorians, V. 68

Hyllus (1), son of Heracles, IX. 26

Hyllus (2), river, tributary of the Hermus, I. 80

Hymaeas, Persian commander, V. 116, 122

Hymettus, mountain, VI. 137

Hypacyris, river of Scythia, IV. 47, 55

Hypanis, river, IV. 18, 47, 52, 53, 81

Hyperanthes, Persian, son of Darius, VII. 224

Hyperboreans, IV. 13, 32-36; Abaris, IV. 36

Hypernotians, IV. 36

Hyperoche, Hyperborean maiden, IV. 33, 35

Hyrcanians, III. 117; VII. 62

Hyrgis, tributary of the Tanais, IV. 57

Hyria, town in Italy, VII. 170

Hyroeades, Mardian, I. 84

Hysiae, Boeotian deme of Attica, V. 74; VI. 108; IX. 15, 25

Hystaspes (1), son of Arsames, I. 209-211; III. 70; VII. 11

Hystaspes (2), son of Darius, VII. 64

Hytennians, III. 90

Iacchus, cry of, VIII. 65

Iadmon (1), Samian, II. 134

Iadmon (2), grandson of (1), II. 134

Ialysus, city, I. 144

iambic verse, I. 12

Iamidae, V. 44; IX. 33

Iapygia, III. 138; IV. 99; VII. 170; Iapygians, IV. 99; Messapians of, VII. 170

Iardanus, I. 7

Iatagoras, Milesian, V. 37

Iberia, I. 163; Iberians, VII. 165

ibis described, II. 75, 76

Icarian Sea, VI. 96

Icarus, VI. 95

Ichnae, city of Bottiaea, VII. 123

ichneumon, II. 67

Ichthyophagi, III. 19-23, 25, 30

Ida, mount, I. 151; VII. 42

Idanthyrsus, king of the Scythians, IV. 76, 120, 126, 127

Idrias, region in Caria, V. 118

Ienysus, town of the Arabians, III. 5

Iliad of Homer, II. 116, 117

Ilissus, river, VII. 189

Ilium, I. 5; II. 10, 117-120; VII. 20, 161; Ilian land, V. 94, 122; VII. 42; Athena of Ilium, VII. 43

Illyria, I. 196; Illyrians, IV. 49; VIII. 137; IX. 43

images, not worshipped by Persians, I. 131; of animals in sacrifices, II. 47; of corpse at banquet, II. 78; of heroes as auxiliaries, V. 75, 80-81; VIII. 64

Imbros, island, V. 26; VI. 41, 104

immortality, belief of Getae, IV. 94-96

war between Syracuse and Athens, VII. 32, *ib.* 33, *ib.* 58; falls into revolution, VII. 46; victory of the anti-Syracusan party, *ib.* 50.

Alcaeus, Archon at Athens, V. 19, *ib.* 25.

Alcamenes, a Lacedaemonian commander, VIII. 4; ordered to Lesbos by Agis, *ib.* 8; driven into Piraeum by the Athenians and slain, *ib.* 10.

Alcibiades, the name Lacedaemonian, VIII. 6; his extravagant character, VI. 12; had a great share in the ruin of Athens, *ib.* 15; his victories at Olympia, *ib.* 16; head of the war party at Athens, V. 43, VI. 15; irritated by the contempt of the Lacedaemonians, V. 43; negotiates an alliance with Argos, Mantinea and Elis, *ib.* 44, 46; deceives the Lacedaemonian envoys, *ib.* 45; his activity in Peloponnesus, *ib.* 52, 53, 55 [cp. VI. 16]; persuades the Athenians to declare the treaty broken and resettle the Helots at Pylos, *ib.* 56; ambassador at Argos, *ib.* 61, 76; seizes a number of suspected Argives, *ib.* 84; appointed one of the generals in Sicily, VI. 8; speech of, *ib.* 16-18; accused of mutilating the Hermae and celebrating the mysteries in private houses, *ib.* 28; begs in vain to be tried before sailing, *ib.* 29; opinion of, in a council of war, *ib.* 48; summoned home, *ib.* 53, 61; escapes at Thurii, *ib.*; condemned to death, *ib.* causes the failure of a plot to betray Messina, *ib.* 74; goes to Lacedaemon, *ib.* 88; his speech there, *ib.* 89-92; persuades the Lacedaemonians to fortify Decelea, VII. 18; supports the Chians at Sparta, VIII. 6; persuades the Spartan government not to give up the Chian expedition, VIII. 12; sent to Ionia with Chalcideus, *ib.* 12; induces the revolt of Chios, Erythrae, Clazomenae, *ib.* 14; chases Strombichides into Samos, *ib.* 16; causes the revolt of Teos, *ib.*; and of Miletus, *ib.* 17; present at an engagement before Miletus, *ib.* 26; falls into disfavour with the Lacedaemonians, *ib.* 45; retires to Tissaphernes, and endeavours to ruin the Peloponnesian cause, *ib.*; repulses the revolted cities when they beg money, *ib.*; in-

structs Tissaphernes to balance the Athenians and Lacedaemonians against each other, *ib.* 46; conspires with some Athenians at Samos to overthrow the democracy, *ib.* 47-49; opposed by Phrynichus, *ib.* 48; whom he endeavours unsuccessfully to ruin, *ib.* 50, 51; seeks to draw Tissaphernes over to the Athenian cause, *ib.* 52; persuades Tissaphernes to demand impossible terms from Peisander, *ib.* 56; recalled by the Athenians at Samos, *ib.* 81; encourages them with extravagant hopes, *ib.* 81; restrains them from sailing to the Piraeus, *ib.* 82; made commander-in-chief, *ib.*; goes to Tissaphernes, *ib.*; again restrains the people from sailing to the Piraeus, and thus performs an eminent service, *ib.* 86; sails to Aspendus, promising to keep the Phoenician fleet back, *ib.* 88; recalled by the Athenians at home, *ib.* 97; returns from Caunus, professing to have secured Tissaphernes' friendship for Athens, *ib.* 108; returns to Samos, *ib.*

Alcidas, takes command of the Peloponnesian fleet sent to Lesbos, III. 16, 26; arrives too late, *ib.* 29; determines to return, *ib.* 31; slaughters his captives, *ib.* 32; is chased to Patmos by the Athenians, *ib.* 33, 69; sails to Corcyra, *ib.* 69, 76; engages the Athenians, *ib.* 77, 78; retires, *ib.* 79-81; helps in the foundation of Heraclea, *ib.* 92.

Alcinadas, a Lacedaemonian, swears to the Treaty of Peace and the Alliance, V. 19; *ib.* 24.

Alcinous, Temple of Zeus and Alcinous at Corcyra, III. 70.

Alciphron, an Argive, makes terms with Agis, V. 59, 60.

Alcisthenes, an Athenian, father of Demosthenes, III. 91, IV. 66, VII. 16.

Alcmaeon, the story of, II. 102.

Alcmaeonidae, aid in the deposition of Hippias, VI. 59.

Alexander, the father of Perdiccas, king of Macedonia, I. 57, *ib.* 137; of Argive descent, II. 99

Alexarchus, a Corinthian commander, VII. 19.

Alexicles, an Athenian general of the

Astyochus, a Lacedaemonian admiral, VIII. 20; entrusted with the command of the whole navy in Asia, *ib.*; arrives at Lesbos, *ib.* 23; fails to save Lesbos from the Athenians, *ib.*; summoned to Chios to avert a revolution, *ib.* 24, *ib.* 31; fails to recover Clazomenae and Pteleum, *ib.* 31; enraged with the Chians for refusing to assist in the revolt of Lesbos, *ib.* 32, 33, 38, 39; narrowly escapes the Athenians, 33; he is complained of to Sparta by Pedaritus, *ib.* 38; the Spartans send out commissioners to him, *ib.* 39; at last determines to aid the Chians, *ib.* 40; hearing that reinforcements were coming, goes to meet them, *ib.* 41; defeats an Athenian squadron, *ib.* 42; receives orders from Sparta to put Alcibiades to death, *ib.* 45; betrays Phrynichus to Alcibiades, *ib.* 50; believed to have sold himself to Tissaphernes, *ib.* 50, *ib.* 83; sails to Miletus with a view to relieve Chios, *ib.* 60; offers battle to the Athenians, *ib.* 63; excites by his conduct great dissatisfaction in the fleet, *ib.* 78; offers battle to the Athenians, but declines when they offer afterwards, *ib.* 79; stoned by the sailors for offering to strike Dorieus, *ib.* 84; superseded by Mindarus, *ib.* 85.

Atalante, island off Locris, fortified by the Athenians, II. 32; inundation of the sea there, III. 89; ordered to be surrendered by the treaty, V. 18, VIII.

Atalante, in Macedonia, II. 100.

Athenaeus, a Lacedaemonian, IV. 119, *ib.* 122.

Athenagoras, a popular leader at Syracuse, VI. 35; speech of, *ib.* 36-40.

Athenagoras, father of Timagoras of Cyzicus, VIII. 6.

Athena of the Brazen House, curse of, I. 128; temple of, at Lecythus, IV. 116; at Amphipolis, V. 10; at Athens, V. 23; image of, in the Acropolis at Athens, II. 13.

Athenian Empire, foundation of, I. 14, *ib.* 18, *ib.* 74, *ib.* 93; rise of, *ib.* 19, 89-118, *ib.* 118; character of, *ib.* 19; justification of, *ib.* 75, VI. 82, 83.

Athens, once inhabited by Tyrrhenians,

IV. 109; formed by Theseus from the ancient communes, II. 15; small extent of ancient Athens, *ib.* 15; largeness of the population, I. 80; appearance of, compared to Sparta, I. 10; destruction of, in the Persian war, I. 89; building of the City Walls, I. 90, 91, 93; of the Long Walls, *ib.* 107, 108; plague of Athens, II. 47-54, 58, III. 87; resources of Athens, II. 13; the revolution at Athens, VIII. 47-72; restoration of the democracy, *ib.* 73-77, 86, 89-93, 97; the government immediately after the restoration the best within Thucydides' recollection, VIII. 97; 'the school of Hellas,' II. 41; freedom of life in, II. 37, VII. 69.

Athenians, of Ionian race, VI. 82, VII. 57; have always inhabited the same land, I. 2; their colonies to Ionia and the islands, I. 2, 12; the first Hellenes to adopt luxurious habits, I. 6; their ignorance of their own history, *ib.* 20, VI. 53, 54, 55; their activity and restlessness, especially in contrast with the Lacedaemonian character, I. 69, 70, 102, IV. 55, VI. 87, VIII. 96; treatment of their allies, I. 19, 76, 99, III. 10, VI. 76, 84, 85; general detestation of them in Hellas, I. 119, II. 8, 11, 63; their wealth and military resources, II. 13; their fondness for a country life, *ib.* 15; become sailors, I. 18; assured of empire by their naval superiority, II. 62; willing to face any odds at sea, *ib.* 88; perfection of their navy, III. 17; mode of burying the dead in the war, II. 34; their greatness and glory, II. 37-41, 63, 64; for half a century an imperial people, VIII. 68; maintain the children of the fallen at the public expense, II. 46; their mistakes in the war, *ib.* 65; their love of rhetoric, III. 38, 40; their over cleverness and suspiciousness, *ib.* 43; their fickle temperament, VII. 48; their elation at success, IV. 65; their impatience of discipline, VII. 14; 'never retired from a siege through fear of another foe,' V. 111; the most experienced soldiers in Hellas, VI. 72, VII. 61. [B.C. 510]; the Athenians governed by tyrants, I. 18, VI. 53-59; the tyrants

defeated at Salamis [in Cyprus] by the Athenians, I. 112.

Cimon, son of Miltiades, captures Eion, I. 98; conquers the Persians at the Eurymedon, *ib*. 100; commands the Athenian reinforcements at the siege of Ithome, *ib*. 102; dies in Cyprus, *ib*. 112.

Cimon, father of Lacedaemonius, an Athenian, I. 45.

Cithaeron, Mt., II. 75, III. 24.

Cities, ancient cities small, I. 2; resembled scattered villages, *ib*. 10; at first built inland, afterwards on the sea-shore, *ib*. 7; the cities of Ionia unfortified, III. 33; 'The City,' name for Acropolis at Athens, II. 15.

Citium, in Cyprus, I. 112.

Citizen, the citizen must be sacrificed to the state, II. 60, 61.

Citizenship, the Lacedaemonians deprive those who had been prisoners at Sphacteria of citizenship, V. 34.

Clarus, in Ionia, III. 33.

Classes of the citizens at Athens, III. 16, VI. 43.

Clazomenae, built on an island, VIII. 14; the Clazomenians revolt from Athens, *ib*.; fortify Polichne, *ib*.; aid in the revolt of Teos, *ib*. 16; the Peloponnesian infantry march towards Clazomenae, *ib*. 22; they are subdued by the Athenians, *ib*. 23; repulse a Peloponnesian attack, *ib*. 31.

Cleaenetus, father of Cleon, an Athenian, III. 36.

Cleandridas, father of Gylippus, a Spartan, VI. 93.

Clearchus, a Lacedaemonian commander, VIII. 8; appointed to the Hellespont, *ib*. 39, 80.

Clearidas, a Lacedaemonian, made governor of Amphipolis, IV. 132; commands with Brasidas at the battle of Amphipolis, V. 6-11; refuses to surrender Amphipolis, *ib*. 21; brings home the troops of Brasidas, *ib*. 34.

Cleinias, the father of Alcibiades, an Athenian, V. 43; another, father of Theopompus [?], II. 26; another, father of Cleopompus, *ib*. 58.

Cleippides, an Athenian commander, III. 3.

Cleobulus, ephor at Sparta, V. 36; favours the war party, *ib*.; negotiates with the Boeotians and Corinthians, *ib*. 36-38.

Cleombrotus, father of Pausanias, a Lacedaemonian, I. 94; of Nicomedes, *ib*. 107.

Cleomedes, an Athenian general in the attack on Melos, V. 84.

Cleomenes, king of Sparta, expels the 'accursed persons' from Athens, I. 126.

Cleomenes, the uncle of king Pausanias, III. 26.

Cleon, a great popular leader, III. 36, IV. 21; hostile to Nicias, IV. 27; a great enemy to peace, V. 16; his arrogance, *ib*. 7; carries the decree condemning the Mytilenaeans to death, III. 36; his speech against its repeal, *ib*. 37-40; moves and carries the slaughter of 1000 Mytilenaean captives at Athens, *ib*. 50; causes the breaking off of negotiations with Sparta, IV. 21, 22; is sent in place of Nicias to Pylos, *ib*. 27, 28; selects Demosthenes as his colleague, *ib*. 29; makes with Demosthenes an attack on Sphacteria, *ib*. 31-37; compels the surrender of the Lacedaemonians, *ib*. 38; carries a decree for the destruction of Scione, *ib*. 122; captures Torone, V. 2, 3; takes Galepsus, and attempts Stageirus, *ib*. 6; defeated and slain at Amphipolis, *ib*. 6-11.

Cleonae, in Acte, IV. 109.

Cleonae, in Argolis, in alliance with Argos, V. 67; sends troops to Mantinea, *ib*. 72, 74; a Lacedaemonian army invading Argos turns back at Cleonae in consequence of an earthquake, VI. 95.

Cleonymus, father of Clearidas, a Lacedaemonian, IV. 132.

Cleopompus, an Athenian commander, II. 58.

Cleruchi, in Lesbos, III. 50.

Clubs, the, at Athens, VIII. 48, 54, 81.

Cnemus, a Lacedaemonian commander, ravages Zacynthus, II. 66; invades Acarnania, *ib*. 80-82; defeated by Phormio, *ib*. 83, 84; receives Brasidas and two other commissioners from Lacedaemon, *ib*. 85; second defeat of, *ib*. 86-92; concerts with Brasidas an attack upon the Piraeus, *ib*. 93, 94.

to save their own power, *ib.* 90, 91; fortify Eetioneia, *ib.* 90, 91; enter into negotiations with the popular party after the destruction of Eetioneia, *ib.* 93; deposed, *ib.* 97.

Funeral, public, of those who first fell in the war, II. 34; of Brasidas, V. 11.

Future, the, the controller of events, IV. 62, 63.

Galepsus, in Thrace, a Thasian colony, IV. 107; revolts from Athens, *ib.*; stormed by the Athenians, V. 6.

Games, Delian, III. 104; Ephesian, *ib.*; Pythian, V. 1; Olympian, III. 8, V. 47, 49, 50.

Garments, offered at sepulchres, III. 58.

Gates, the Thracian, at Amphipolis, V. 10.

Gaulites, a Carian, VIII. 85.

Gela, a river in Sicily, VI. 4.

Gela, founded from Rhodes by Antiphemus and Entimus, VI. 4, VII. 57; Agrigentum founded from, VI. 4; borders on Camarina, VII. 58; conference at, IV. 58; receives and assists Gylippus, VII. 1; sends aid to Syracuse, *ib.* 33, 57.

Gelo, tyrant of Syracuse, VI. 4; expels the Megareans, *ib.*, *ib.* 94; colonizes Camarina a third time, *ib.* 5.

General, speech of a Syracusan, VI. 41.

Geraestus, in Euboea, III. 3.

Geraneia, Mount, in Megaris, I. 105, 107, 108, IV. 70.

Gerastius, a Spartan month, IV. 119.

Getae, a Sicel fort, VII. 2.

Getae, a people bordering on the Scythians, II. 96, 98.

Gigonus, in Chalcidice, I. 61.

Glauce, in the territory of Mycale, VIII. 79.

Glaucon, an Athenian commander, I. 51.

Goaxis, sons of, kill Pittacus, king of the Edonians, IV. 107.

Goddess, curse of the, I. 126.

Gods, the, portions of land dedicated to, in the confiscation of Lesbos, III. 50; the, worshipped at common altars, *ib.* 59; altar of the Twelve Gods at Athens, V. 54.

Gods, the, protect the right, I. 86, V. 104; approve the principle, 'That they

should rule who can,' V. 105; their jealousy, VII. 77.

Gold mines in Thrace worked by Thucydides, IV. 105.

Gongylus, an Eretrian, an envoy of Pausanias, I. 128.

Gongylus, a Corinthian commander, VII. 2.

Gortynia, in Macedonia, II. 100.

Gortys, in Crete, II. 85.

Graaeans, a Paeonian tribe, II. 96.

Graphe paranomon, at Athens, repealed by the oligarchy, VIII. 67.

Grasshoppers, ornaments in the form of, once worn at Athens, I. 6.

Greatness exposed to the attacks both of envy and of fear, VI. 78.

Grestonia, a district of Macedonia, II. 99, 100.

Guardians of the Law, a magistracy at Elis, V. 47.

Gulf, the Ambracian, I. 55, II. 68, III. 107; Crisaean, I. 107, II. 69, 83, 84, 90-92, IV. 76; Iasian, VIII. 26; Ionian, I. 24, II. 97, VI. 13, 30, 34, 44, 104, VII. 33, 57; Malian, III. 96, IV. 100, VIII. 3; Saronic, III. 15, VIII. 92; Terinaean, VI. 62, VII. 58.

Gylippus appointed commander of the Syracusan forces by the Lacedaemonians, VI. 93; arrives at Tarentum, *ib.* 104; fails in a mission to Thurii, *ib.*; makes his way into Syracuse, VII. 1, 2; offers battle on Epipolae, *ib.* 3; captures Labdalum, *ib.*; fails in an attack on the Athenian lines, *ib.* 4; is defeated, *ib.* 5; defeats the Athenians, *ib.* 6; goes into Sicily to collect allies, *ib.* 7; returning, he urges the Syracusans to try their fortune at sea, *ib.* 21; captures Plemmyrium, *ib.* 23; makes a diversion by land while the Syracusan fleet attacks the Athenians, *ib.* 37; goes to collect reinforcements, *ib.* 46, 50; sustains a slight defeat, *ib.* 53; exhorts the Syracusans before the battle in the harbour, *ib.* 66-68; blocks the roads against the Athenian retreat, *ib.* 74; compels the surrender first of Demosthenes', and then of Nicias' division, *ib.* 78-85; opposes the putting to death of Nicias and Demosthenes, *ib.* 86.

follow, *ib.* 100; operations in the Hellespont and battle of Cynossema, *ib.* 102-
107; Tissaphernes is annoyed on hearing that the Peloponnesians had gone
to the Hellespont, *ib.* 108, 109.

Helorine Road, near Syracuse, VI. 66,
70, VII. 80.

Helos, in Laconia, IV. 54.

Helots, murder of, at Taenarus, I. 128;
massacre of, IV. 80; intrigue with Pausanias, I. 132; revolt from the Lacedaemonians, *ib.* 101, II. 27, III. 54, IV. 56;
surrender, I. 103; settled at Naupactus
by the Athenians, *ib.* 11, 9; carry supplies into Sphacteria, IV. 26; desert to
the Messenians in Pylos, IV. 41; withdrawn from Pylos, V. 35; replaced, *ib.*
56; taken by the Athenians to Syracuse, VII. 57; Demosthenes fortifies an
isthmus in Laconia in order that the
Helots may desert there, *ib.* 26; seven
hundred sent with Brasidas, IV. 80;
afterwards settled at Lepreum, V. 34;
the Lacedaemonians send a body of
Helots and Neodamodes to Sicily, *ib.*
19, 58.

Hephaestus, the forge of, believed to be
in Hiera, III. 88.

Heraclea, in Trachis, IV. 78; founded by
the Lacedaemonians, III. 92, 100;
failure of the colony, *ib.* 93; regulated
by the Lacedaemonians, V. 12; the
Heracleans are defeated by the neighbouring tribes, *ib.* 51; Heraclea taken
over by the Boeotians, *ib.* 52.

Heraclea, in Pontus, IV. 75.

Heracles, Temple of, at Mantinea, V. 64,
66; festival of, at Syracuse, VII. 73.

Heraclidae, slay Eurystheus in Attica, I.
9; conquer the Peloponnesus, *ib.* 12;
Phalius, a Corinthian of the Heraclid
race, *ib.* 24; Archias, founder of Syracuse, an Heraclid, VI. 3.

Heraclides, one of the Syracusan generals,
VI. 73; deposed on a charge of treachery,
ib. 103.

Heraeans, of Arcadia, V. 67.

Hera, Temple of, At Argos, IV. 133; at
Corcyra, I. 24, III. 75, 79, 81; at Epidaurus, V. 75; at Plataea, III. 68.

Hermae, mutilation of the, VI. 27, 28; excitement at Athens about, *ib.* 53, 60;

confession of one of the prisoners, *ib.*
60.

Hermaeondas, a Theban, III. 5.

Hermes, Temple of, near Mycalessus,
VII. 29.

Hermione, I. 128, 131; its territory ravaged by the Athenians, II. 56; the Her-
mionians furnish a convoy to Corinth,
I. 27; supply ships to the Lacedaemonian navy, VIII. 3.

Hermocrates, speech of, IV. 59-64; second
speech of, VI. 33, 34; encourages the
Syracusans after defeat, *ib.* 72; made
general with two others, *ib.* 73, 96, 99;
speech at Camarina, *ib.* 76-80; deposed, *ib.* 103; encourages the Syracusans to prepare a fleet, VII. 21; con-
trives by a stratagem to delay the Athenian retreat, *ib.* 73; brings a fleet to
Asia, VIII. 26; remonstrates with Tissaphernes for reducing the ships' pay, *ib.*
29; again, *ib.* 45; incurs the hatred of
Tissaphernes, *ib.* 85; goes to Sparta to
expose him, *ib.*; exiled, *ib.*

Hermon, an Athenian, commander of the
Peripoli, VIII. 92.

Hermon, father of Hermocrates, a Syracusan, IV. 58, VI. 32.

Hesiod, said to have been killed at Nemea, III. 96.

Hessians, an Ozolian Locrian tribe, III.
101.

Hestiaea, in Euboea, expulsion of the
Hestiaeans by the Athenians, I. 114;
colonized from Athens, VII. 57.

Hestiodorus, an Athenian commander,
II. 70.

Hiera, one of the Liparean islands, III. 88.

Hieramenes, mentioned with Tissaphernes in the third treaty with the
Lacedaemonians, VIII. 58.

Hiereans, a Malian tribe, III. 92.

Hierophon, an Athenian commander, III.
105.

Himera, colonized from Zancle, VI. 5;
the only Hellenic city on the north
coast, *ib.* 62; the Athenians and Sicels
invade its territory, III. 115; the Hi-
meraeans aid Gylippus, VII. 1, 58.

Himeraeum, in Thrace, VII. 9.

Hippagretas, one of the Spartan commanders at Sphacteria, IV. 38.

Hipparchus, son of Peisistratus, never actually tyrant, I. 20, VI. 54, 55; slain by Harmodius and Aristogeiton, I. 20, VI. 54, 56-58; left no children, VI. 55.

Hippias, commander of the garrison at Notium, treacherously seized by Paches, III. 34.

Hippias, eldest son of Peisistratus, I. 20, VI. 54, 55; his children, VI. 55; becomes more oppressive, *ib.* 59; deposed by the Lacedaemonians, *ib.*; goes to Persia and returns to take part at Marathon, *ib.*

Hippias, father of Peisistratus, VI. 54.

Hippocles, an Athenian commander, VIII. 13.

Hippoclus, tyrant of Lampsacus, VI. 59.

Hippocrates, an Athenian general, fellow commander with Demosthenes, IV. 66; attempts Megara and captures Nisaea, *ib.* 66-69; plans with Demosthenes an invasion of Boeotia, *ib.* 76, 77; fortifies Delium, *ib.* 90; speech of, *ib.* 95; defeated and slain, *ib.* 96, 101.

Hippocrates, a Lacedaemonian commander, loses part of his fleet off Triopium by an Athenian attack, VIII. 35; informs Mindarus of the treachery of Tissaphernes, *ib.* 99; sent to Euboea, *ib.* 107.

Hippocrates, tyrant of Gela, VI. 5; refounds Camarina, *ib.*

Hippolochidas, a Thessalian, aids Brasidas in his march through Thessaly, IV. 78.

Hipponicus, an Athenian general, III. 91.

Hipponoidas, a Spartan polemarch, V. 71; banished for cowardice at Mantinea, *ib.* 72.

Homer quoted, (Il. II. 108), I. 9; (II. 570), *ib.* 13; (from the Hymn to Apollo), III. 104; the testimony of, shows the comparative smallness of the Trojan War, I. 10; his use of the name Hellenes, *ib.* 3.

Honour is ever young, II. 44; often lures men to destruction, V. 111.

Hope, the deceitfulness of, III. 39, 45, IV. 108, V. 103; the higher the hope, the greater the courage, VII. 67.

Hyacinthia, festival of, at Lacedaemon, V. 23, IV; 41.

Hyaeans, an Ozolian Locrian tribe, III. 101.

Hybla Geleatis, in Sicily, unsuccessfully attacked by the Athenians, VI. 62, 63; the Hyblaeans have their corn burnt by the Athenians, *ib.* 94.

Hyblon, a Sicel king, VI. 4.

Hyccara, in Sicily, captured by the Athenians, VI. 62.

Hylias, a river in Italy, VII. 35.

Hyllaic harbour at Corcyra, III. 72, 81.

Hyperbolus, an Athenian, ostracized, VIII. 73; murdered by the oligarchical conspirators, *ib.*

Hyperechides, father of Callias, an Athenian, VI. 55.

Hysiae, in Argos, captured by the Lacedaemonians, V. 83.

Hysiae, in Boeotia, III. 24.

Hystaspes, father of Pissuthnes, a Persian, I. 115.

Ialysus, in Rhodes, VIII. 44.

Iapygia, promontory of, VI. 30, 34, VII. 33; Iapygian mercenaries hired by the Athenians against Syracuse, VII. 33, 57.

Iasian Gulf, VIII. 26.

Iasus, in Ionia, its wealth, VIII. 28; captured by the Peloponnesians, *ib.*; Peisander accuses Phrynichus of having betrayed it, *ib.* 54.

Iberians, the Sicanians originally Iberians, VI. 2; the most warlike of barbarians, *ib.* 90.

Icarus, an island in the Aegaean, III. 29, VIII. 99.

Ichthys, promontory of, in Elis, II. 25.

Ida, mount, in the Troad, IV. 52, VIII. 108.

Idacus, in the Thracian Chersonnese, VIII. 104.

Idomene, a hill in Amphilochia, III. 112, 113.

Ilium, *see* Troy.

Illyrians hired by Perdiccas, IV. 124; desert, *ib.* 125; attack and are defeated by Brasidas, *ib.* 127, 128; the Taulantians, an Illyrian tribe, make war upon Epidamnus, I. 24; aid the Corcyraeans to besiege Epidamnus, *ib.* 26.

Imbros, colonized from Athens, VII. 57; Imbrian troops at Athens, IV. 28; Imbrians serve under Cleon at Amphip-

Leon, near Syracuse, VI. 97.

Leonidas, father of Pleistarchus, king of Sparta, I. 132.

Leontiades, father of Eurymachus, a Theban, II. 2.

Leontini, founded from Chalcis in Euboea by Thucles, VI. 3; the Leontines of Ionian descent, III. 86, VI. 44, 46, 50, 76, 77, 79; at war with Syracuse, *ib.* 86; obtain assistance from Athens, *ib.*; unsuccessfully attack Messene, IV. 25; revolution in, V. 4; the Athenians espouse their cause as an excuse for the conquest of Sicily, *ib.*, VI. 8, 19, 33, 47, 48, 63, 76, 77, 84.

Leotychides, king of Sparta, I. 89.

Lepreum, gives rise to a quarrel between the Eleans and Lacedaemonians, V. 31; the Lacedaemonians settle the Helots and Neodamodes there, *ib.* 34; they break the Olympic Truce by bringing a garrison into Lepreum, *ib.* 49; the Lepraeans do not attend the Olympic festival, *ib.* 50; the Eleans are angry with their allies for not attacking Lepreum, *ib.* 62.

Leros, [*al.* Eleus], VIII. 26, 27.

Lesbos: the Lesbians kindred of the Boeotians, III. 2, VII. 57, VIII. 4, 100; with the Chians, the only independent allies of Athens, I. 19, VI. 85, VII. 57; furnish ships to the Athenians, II. 9, 56, VI. 31; the Lesbians aid the Athenians against the Samians, I. 116, 117; revolt from Athens, III. 2; are received into the Lacedaemonian confederacy, *ib.* 15; the affairs of Lesbos set in order by Paches, *ib.* 35; the land divided among Athenian citizens, *ib.* 50; the Lesbian refugees capture Antandrus, IV. 52 [which the Athenians recover, *ib.* 75]; the Lesbians negotiate with Agis about a fresh revolt, VIII. 4; revolt and are again subdued, *ib.* 22, 23; renew negotiations with Astyochus, *ib.* 32; Pedaritus refuses them aid from Chios, *ib.*; the Athenian fleet on the way to the Hellespont puts in at Lesbos, and prepares to attack Eresus, *ib.* 100.

Leucas, a Corinthian colony, I. 30; devastated by the Corcyraeans, *ib.*;

attacked by the Athenians, III. 94, 95, 102.

Leucadian Isthmus, III. 81, 94, IV. 8; garrisoned by the Corinthians, IV. 42; naval engagement between the Peloponnesians returning from Sicily, and the Athenians, off Leucadia, VIII. 13; the Leucadians send troops to Epidamnus, I. 26; furnish ships to Corinth, *ib.* 27, 46; Corinthian fleet sails from Leucas, *ib.* 46; the Leucadians supply the Lacedaemonians with ships, II. 9; assist in the invasion of Acarnania, *ib.* 80, 81; a Leucadian vessel is sunk by an Athenian off Naupactus, *ib.* 91, 92; the Leucadians repulse an Athenian descent, III. 7; send a squadron to Cyllene to reinforce Alcidas, *ib.* 69; aid Gylippus with a fleet, VI. 104, VII. 4, 7; present before Syracuse, VII. 58; lose one ship in the battle of Cynossema, VIII. 106.

Leucimme, Corcyraeans raise a trophy on, I. 30; Corcyraean station at, *ib.* 47, 51; the Peloponnesians land there, III. 79.

Leuconium, in Chios, VIII. 24.

Leuctra, in Laconia, V. 54.

Libya, visited by the plague, II. 48; trade between Libya and Laconia, IV. 53; Phocians returning from Troy are driven to Libya, VI. 2; a Peloponnesian fleet on the way to Syracuse is driven to Libya, VII. 50; the Libyans besiege the Evesperitae, *ib.*; Inaros, king of the Libyans, I. 104, 110.

Lichas, a Lacedaemonian, victor at Olympia, V. 50; struck by the officers, *ib.*; envoy to Argos, *ib.* 22; again, *ib.* 76; goes with ten others as adviser to Astyochus, VIII. 39; objects to the treaties made with the king, *ib.* 43, 52; goes with Tissaphernes to Aspendus, *ib.* 87; rebukes the Milesians for driving out a Persian garrison, *ib.* 84; his unpopularity at Miletus, *ib.*; dies there, *ib.*

Ligurians, the, drove the Sicanians out of Iberia, VI. 2.

Limnaea, in Acarnania, II. 80, III. 106.

Lindii, the Acropolis of Gela, VI. 4.

Lindus, in Rhodes, VIII. 44.

Liparaean [or Aeolian] islands: the Lipa-
raeans colonists of the Cnidians, III.
88; invaded by the Athenians, *ib.*;
again, *ib.* 115.

Locrians [Opuntian], subjected by the
Persians, VIII. 43; allies of the Lacedaemonians, V. 64; give hostages to
the Athenians, I. 108; present at the
battle of Coronea, *ib.* 113; furnish the
Lacedaemonians with cavalry, II. 9;
Atalante, in Locris, seized by the
Athenians to prevent privateering, *ib.*
32; the Locrians defeated by the Athenians, II. 26; inundation of the sea on
the Locrian coast, III. 89; the Locrian
coast ravaged by the Athenians, *ib.* 91;
Locrian cavalry pursue the Athenians
after Delium, IV. 96; the Locrians
supply the Lacedaemonians with ships,
VIII. 3.

Locrians, [Ozolian], always carry arms,
I. 5; old inhabitants of Naupactus,
ib. 103; allied to the Athenians, III. 95,
97; subdued by the Lacedaemonians,
ib. 101; go to war with the Phocians,
V. 32.

Locris, in Italy: the Locrians in alliance
with the Syracusans, III. 86; defeated
by the Athenians, *ib.* 99; again, *ib.* 103;
cause Messene to revolt, IV. 1; join the
Syracusans in attacking the Rhegians,
ib. 24, 25; invited to Messene during a
revolution, V. 5; expelled, *ib.*; make a
treaty with Athens, *ib.*; hostile to the
Athenian expedition to Sicily, VI. 44;
send ships to the Lacedaemonians,
VIII. 91.

Loryma, in Caria, VIII. 43.

Lot, use of the lot to determine which side
should first execute a treaty, V. 21;
in the distribution of an army between
a number of generals, VIII. 30.

Lycaeum, Mount, in Arcadia, V. 16,
54.

Lycia, II. 69, VIII. 41.

Lycomedes, father of Archestratus, an
Athenian, I. 57; another, father of
Cleomedes, V. 84.

Lycophron, a Lacedaemonian, sent out
as adviser to Cnemus, II. 85.

Lycophron, a Corinthian general, IV. 43;
death of, *ib.* 44.

Lycus, father of Thrasybulus, an Athenian, VIII. 75.

Lyncus, in Upper Macedonia, II. 99;
under the rule of Arrhibaeus, IV. 83;
invaded by Perdiccas and Brasidas,
ib.; invaded a second time by them,
ib. 124; Brasidas retreats through
Lyncus, *ib.* 125-128, 129.

Lysicles, father of Habronichus, an Athenian, I. 91; another, sent to exact
money in Caria and Lycia, III. 19;
falls in battle, *ib.*

Lysimachidas, father of Arianthidas, a
Theban, IV. 91.

Lysimachus, father of Aristides, an Athenian, I. 91.

Lysimachus, father of Heraclides, a
Syracusan, VI. 73.

Lysimeleia, a marsh near Syracuse, VII.
53.

Lysistratus, an Olynthian, IV. 110.

Macarius, a Spartan commander, III.
100; falls at the battle of Olpae, *ib.* 109.

Macedonia, its early history, II. 99; kings
of Macedonia originally from Argos,
ib.; V. 80; the Athenians send an expedition against Macedonia, I. 57-61;
Macedonian troops sent by Perdiccas
too late for the Lacedaemonian expedition into Acarnania, II. 80; the Thracians invade Macedonia under Sitalces,
ib. 95-101; the military strength of
Macedonia much increased by Archelaus, *ib.* 100; Brasidas in Macedonia, IV.
78, 82, 83; second expedition of Brasidas
into Macedonia, *ib.* 124-128; the
Athenians blockade Macedonia, V. 83;
Macedonia ravaged from Methone by
the Athenians, VI. 7.

Machaon, a Corinthian commander, II.
83.

Maeander, plain of the, III. 19, VIII. 58.

Maedi, a Thracian tribe, II. 98.

Maenalia, part of Arcadia, V. 64; Maenalians at Mantinea, *ib.* 67; hostages
taken from the Maenalians by the
Argives to be given up under treaty,
ib. 77, I.

Magistrates, the good magistrate is not
always bound by the letter of the law,
VI. 14.

28; the news reaching the Peloponnesian fleet, Teutiaplus advises an immediate attack on Mytilene, *ib.* 29, 30; Paches sends Salaethus, and the most guilty of the Mytilenaeans to Athens, *ib.* 35; all the grown up citizens condemned to death by the Athenians, *ib.* 36; feeling at Athens changes, *ib.*; speech of Cleon against the recall of the decree, *ib.* 37-40; of Diodotus in favour of recalling it, *ib.* 41-48; the decree is recalled, *ib.* 49; the second ship sent to stay the slaughter arrives in time by great exertions, *ib.*; the captives at Athens put to death, their fleet and dependencies taken away, the walls of Mytilene razed, *ib.* 50; Lesbian refugees take Rhoeteium and Antandrus, IV. 52; driven out again by the Athenians, *ib.* 75; Mytilene revolts a second time, VIII. 22; recaptured by the Athenians, *ib.* 23; garrisoned by the Athenians, VIII. 100.

Myus, a city in Caria, III. 19; given by the King to Themistocles, I. 138.

Nature, human, 'always ready to transgress the laws,' III. 84; 'prone to domineer over the subservient,' IV. 61, V. 105; prompts men to accept a proffered empire, I. 76; ever credulous, *ib.* 20; jealous, II. 35; changes with the changes of fortune, I. 84, 140, II. 61, III. 39, IV. 17; prone to error, III. 45, IV. 18; misled in its judgments by hope, III. 39, IV. 108; yields when met in a yielding spirit, IV. 19; inherent vanity of, V. 68; sameness of, I. 21, 76, III. 45, 82.

Naucleides, a Plataean, invites the Thebans to Plataea, II. 2.

Naucrates, father of Damotimus, a Sicyonian, IV. 119.

Naupactus, settled by the Helots from Ithome, I. 103; allied to the Athenians, II. 9; becomes the head-quarters of an Athenian fleet, *ib.* 69, 84, 92, III. 114, IV. 13; the Peloponnesians hope to take it, II. 80; victory of the Athenians off Naupactus, *ib.* 83, 84; feigned attack of the Peloponnesians upon, II. 90; second victory of the Athenians off, *ib.* 91, 92; Phormio makes an expedition

from Naupactus into Acarnania, *ib.* 102, 103; Phormio's son, Asopius, succeeds him at Naupactus, III. 7; Nicostratus sails to Corcyra from Naupactus, *ib.* 75; the Messenians of Naupactus persuade Demosthenes to attack Aetolia, *ib.* 94-98; Demosthenes remains at Naupactus after his defeat, *ib.* 98; the Aetolians persuade the Lacedaemonians to make an expedition against Naupactus, *ib.* 100; Demosthenes, by the aid of the Acarnanians, saves the place, *ib.* 102; Athenian ships from Naupactus come to Pylos, IV. 13; the Messenians of Naupactus send a garrison to Pylos, *ib.* 41; the Athenian forces at Naupactus capture Anactorium, *ib.* 49; Demosthenes comes to Naupactus to aid Hippocrates in the invasion of Boeotia, *ib.* 76, 77; the Corinthians prepare a fleet to attack the Athenians at Naupactus, VII. 17, 19; Demosthenes and Eurymedon send reinforcements, *ib.* 31; indecisive action off Naupactus, *ib.* 34; the Messenians of Naupactus send a force to Sicily, *ib.* 31, 57.

Naval Tactics: unskilfulness of ancient tactics, I. 49; Athenian naval tactics, II. 83, 84, 89, 91, III. 78, VII. 36, 49.

Navy: Minos the first possessor of a navy, I. 4; the fleet which carried the Hellenes to Troy, *ib.* 9, 10; the early Hellenic navies, *ib.* 13, 14; progress of naval invention, *ib.* 13, 14; importance of its navy to Athens, *ib.* 93, II. 13, VII. 66, VIII. 66; the greatest number reached by the Athenian navy, III. 17; composition and number of the Lacedaemonian fleet, II. 7, VIII. 3; quick deterioration of ancient navies, VII. 14.

Naxos, subjugated by the Athenians, I. 98; Themistocles is carried to Naxos in his flight, and narrowly escapes the Athenians there, *ib.* 137.

Naxos [in Sicily], founded from Chalcis by Thucles, VI. 3; altar of Apollo the Founder at, *ib.*; the Naxians kinsmen of the Leontines, VI. 20; defeat the Messenians, IV. 25; receive the Athenian expedition, VI. 50; become allies of Athens, VII. 14, *ib.* 57; Naxos is made the winter quarters of the Athenians, VI. 72, 74, 75; they abandon it for Catana, *ib.* 88; the Naxians furnish the Athenians with cavalry, *ib.* 98.

Neapolis, a Carthaginian factory in Libya, VII. 50.

Neighbours ever enemies, IV. 95.

Nemea, in Locris, death of Hesiod at, III. 96; temple of Nemean Zeus, *ib.*

Nemea, in Argolis, V. 58-60.

Neodamodes, meaning of the word, VII. 58; settled with the Helots at Lepreum, V. 34; Neodamodes at Mantinea, *ib.* 67; sent to Syracuse with the Helots by the Lacedaemonians, VII. 19, 58; three hundred Neodamodes sent out to Agis, VIII. 4.

Nericum, in Leucas, III. 7.

Nestus, a river in Thrace, II. 96.

Nicanor, a Chaonian leader, II. 80.

Nicasus, a Megarian, swears to the one year's Truce, IV. 119.

Niceratus, father of Nicias, an Athenian, III. 51, 91, IV. 27, 42, 53, 119, 129, V. 16, 83, VI. 8.

Niciades, an Athenian, president at the passing of the one year's Truce, IV. 118.

Nicias, of Gortys, II. 85.

Nicias, father of Hagnon, an Athenian, II. 58, IV. 102.

Nicias, his religiousness, VII. 77, 86; his superstitious temper, *ib.* 50; his dilatoriness, *ib.* 42; his ill health, VI. 102, VII. 15, 77; captures Minoa, III. 51; ravages Melos, *ib.* 91; defeats the Tanagraeans, *ib.*; ravages Locris, *ib.*; yields his command at Pylos to Cleon, IV. 27, 28; leads an expedition into the Corinthian territory, *ib.* 42-45; captures Cythera, *ib.* 53, 54; swears to the one year's Truce, *ib.* 119; wounded in an attempt to take Mende, *ib.* 129; his anxiety for peace, V. 16, 43; swears to the Treaty of Peace and the Alliance, V. 19, 24; goes on an unsuccessful embassy to Sparta, *ib.* 46; designed for the command of an expedition to Chalcidice, which Perdiccas frustrates, *ib.* 83; appointed one of the generals in Sicily, VI. 8; speech of, *ib.* 9-14; second speech of, *ib.* 20-23; gives an estimate

of the forces required, *ib.* 25; argues in a council of war for an attack on Selinus, *ib.* 47; goes to Egesta, *ib.* 62; defeats the Syracusans, *ib.* 67-70; saves Epipolae, *ib.* 102; becomes sole commander after the death of Lamachus, *ib.* 103; negotiates with the Syracusans, *ib.*; fails to prevent the coming of Gylippus, VII. 1, 2; fortifies Plemmyrium, *ib.* 4; defeated by the Syracusans, *ib.* 6; sends a despatch to Athens, *ib.* 8, 10, 11-15; destroys by an ambush the Syracusan reinforcements, *ib.* 32; left in the Athenian lines while Demosthenes attacks Epipolae, *ib.* 43; swayed by information from Syracuse and fear of public opinion at home, he refuses to abandon the siege, *ib.* 48, 49; yields at last, *ib.* 50; but, an eclipse of the moon happening, decides to remain thrice nine days, *ib.* 50; exhorts the army before the battle in the harbour, *ib.* 61-64; addresses the trierarchs, *ib.* 69; endeavours to encourage his retreating soldiers, *ib.* 76, 77; commands one division in the retreat, *ib.* 78; overtaken and compelled to surrender, *ib.* 83-85; put to death by the Syracusans, *ib.* 86.

Nicolaus, a Lacedaemonian ambassador to Persia, II. 67.

Nicomachus, a Phocian, betrays to the Lacedaemonians the Athenian plan for the conquest of Boeotia, IV. 89.

Nicomedes, a Lacedaemonian, general in place of King Pleistoanax, I. 107.

Nicon, a Boeotian, commands the reinforcements to Syracuse, VII. 19.

Niconidas, a Thessalian, escorts Brasidas through Thessaly, IV. 78.

Nicostratus, an Athenian general, sails to Corcyra, III. 75; becomes the colleague of Nicias, IV. 53; assists in the capture of Cythera, *ib.* 53, 54; of Mende, *ib.* 129, 130; and in the blockade of Scione, *ib.* 131; swears to the one year's Truce, *ib.* 119; brings with Laches an expedition to Argos, V. 61; falls in the battle of Mantinea, *ib.* 74.

Nightingale, called by the Poets the 'Daulian Bird,' II. 29.

Nile, I. 104, 110.

after Pylos, VI. 89; the Lacedaemonians consider that their misfortune at Pylos was deserved, because they began the war, VII. 18; the Messenians from Pylos serve with the Athenians before Syracuse, *ib.* 57; comparison between the naval engagement at Pylos and the last battle in the Great Harbour at Syracuse, *ib.* 71; Demosthenes the greatest foe of the Lacedaemonians, Nicias their greatest friend, in the matter of Pylos, *ib.* 86.

Pyrasians, people of Pyrasus in Thessaly, II. 22.

Pyrrha, in Lesbos, III. 18, 25, VIII. 23; taken by Paches, III. 35.

Pyrrhichus, father of Ariston, a Corinthian, VII. 39.

Pystilus, joint founder with Aristonous of Agrigentum, VI. 4.

Pythangelus, a Theban Boeotarch, II. 2.

Pythen, a Corinthian, sails with Gylippus to Sicily, VI. 104, VII. 1; in command at the last fight in the harbour, VII. 70.

Pythes, of Abdera, father of Nymphodorus, II. 29.

Pythian Games, V. 1.

Pythodorus, an Athenian, archon at the commencement of the War, II. 2; supersedes Laches in Sicily, III. 115, IV. 2; sent into exile, IV. 65; swears to the Treaty of Peace and the Alliance, V. 19, 24; has a command in an expedition to Laconia, which violates the Treaty, VI. 105.

Quarries, at Syracuse, used as a prison for the Athenian captives, VII. 86, 87.

Religion, is lost amid party strife, III. 82; all religious restraint disappears during the plague, II. 53.

Reserve fund and ships set apart by the Athenians, II. 24, VIII. 15.

Revenge not always successful because just, IV. 62; sweetness of revenge, II. 42, III. 40, VII. 68.

Revenue, the Athenian, raised by tribute from the allies, I. 122, II. 13, 69, III. 13, 19, 39, 46, IV. 87, VI. 91; from mines at Laurium, II. 55, VI. 91; by a property tax, III. 19; from profits made by the land, and the law courts, VI. 91; the tribute commuted for a duty of 5 per cent. on imports and exports, VII. 28.

Revolutions, horrors of the revolution at Corcyra, III. 81, 84, IV. 46-48; growth of the revolutionary spirit in Hellas, III. 82, 83; the oligarchical revolution at Megara, IV. 74.

Rhamphias, (I) a Lacedaemonian, brings with others the last demands of the Lacedaemonians to Athens, I. 139; sets out to Chalcidice, but returns on news of Brasidas' death, V. 12, 13: (II) another [?], father of Clearchus, VIII. 8, 39, 80.

Rhegium, its important position, IV. 24; Anaxilaus, tyrant of, VI. 4; the Rhegians, Ionians, and kindred of the Leontines, III. 86, VI. 44, 46, 79; the Athenians aid them, III. 86; they sail with the Athenians against the Lipari islands, *ib.* 88; Athenian reinforcements arrive at Rhegium, *ib.* 115; the Rhegians fall into sedition and are attacked by the Locrians, IV. 1, 24, 25; refuse to receive the Athenian expedition to Sicily, VI. 44; the Athenians disappointed at this refusal, *ib.* 46; part of the Athenians stay at Rhegium till assured of a reception at Catana, *ib.* 50, 51; Gylippus puts in there, on his way to Syracuse, VII. 1; the Athenians lie in wait for a Corinthian fleet off Rhegium, *ib.* 4.

Rheiti, in Attica, II. 19.

Rheitus, in Corinthian territory, IV. 42.

Rhenea, the island near Delos, dedicated to Apollo by Polycrates, I. 13, III. 104.

Rhium, in Achaia, II. 86, 92, V. 52; the Molycreian, II. 84, 86.

Rhodes, VIII. 41; colonized from Argos, VII. 57; assists in the colonization of Gela, VI. 4, VII. 57; Rhodian troops serve in the expedition to Sicily, VI. 43, VII. 57; Rhodes revolts from Athens, VIII. 44; the Peloponnesians take up their station there, *ib.*, *ib.* 52; the Athenians make descents upon Rhodes, *ib.* 44, 55; the Peloponnesians quit Rhodes, *ib.* 60.

Rhodope, Mount, in Thessaly, II. 96.

Rhoeteum, in the Troad, VIII. 101; cap-

saeans, *ib.* 101; Dii, *ib.* 96, 98, VII. 27; Droans, II. 101; Edonians, I. 100, II. 99, IV. 102, 107, 109, V. 6; Getae, II. 96, 98; Graaeans, *ib.* 96; Laeaeans, *ib.* 96; Maedi, *ib.* 98; Odomantians, *ib.* 101; Odrysians, *ib.* 29, 96, 97, 98, 101; Paeonians, *ib.* 96, 98; Panaeans, *ib.* 101; Sinti, *ib.* 98; Tilataeans, *ib.* 96; Treres, *ib.* 96; Triballi, *ib.* 96, IV. 101;— gold mines in Thrace, I. 100, IV. 105; the Thracians prefer receiving to giving, II. 97; wanting in sense, *ib.*; their ferocity, VII. 30; once inhabited Phocis, II. 29; destroy the Athenian colonists at Ennea Hodoi, I. 100, IV. 102; march, under the leadership of Sitalces, against Perdiccas, II. 95-101. Thracian mercenaries in Athenian service at Mende, IV. 129; the Thracians are asked for aid by Cleon at Amphipolis, V. 6; the Edonian and Myrcinian Thracians serve under Brasidas, *ib.* 10; Thracian mercenaries sent home from Athens sack Mycalessus, VII. 27, 30.

Thracians, the Bithynian, in Asia, IV. 75.

Thrasybulus, an Athenian, one of the steadiest opponents of the oligarchs at Athens, VIII. 73; persuades the army and the Samians to swear allegiance to the democracy, *ib.* 75; appointed with Thrasyllus general, *ib.* 76; procures the restoration of Alcibiades, *ib.* 81; sails to Eresus which had revolted, *ib.* 100; aids Thrasyllus at Cynossema, *ib.* 104, 105.

Thrasycles, an Athenian, swears to the Treaty of Peace and the Alliance, V. 19, 24; sent with twelve ships to Chios, VIII. 15, 17, 19.

Thrasyllus, one of the steadiest opponents of the oligarchs at Athens, VIII. 73; persuades the army and the Samians to swear allegiance to the democracy, *ib.* 75; appointed with Thrasybulus general, *ib.* 76; follows Mindarus to Chios, *ib.* 100; sets about besieging Eresus, *ib.* 100, 103; pursues Mindarus to the Hellespont, *ib.*; defeats him off Cynossema, *ib.* 104, 105.

Thrasyllus, an Argive general, makes terms with Agis, V. 59, 60; attacked by the Argives, *ib.* 60.

Thrasymelidas, a Spartan, admiral in command at Pylos, IV. 11.

Thria, in Attica, I. 114, II. 19, 20, 21.

Thronium, in Locris, II. 26.

Thucles, the founder of Naxos in Sicily, VI. 3; of Leontini and Catana, *ib.*

Thucles, father of Eurymedon, an Athenian, III. 80, 91, VII. 16.

Thucydides, motives for writing his history, I. 1; its truthfulness, *ib.* 21-23, V. 26; the speeches only generally accurate, I. 22; reasons for describing the period between the Persian and Peloponnesian Wars, *ib.* 97; his reason for reckoning his history by summers and winters, V. 20; attacked by the plague, II. 48; appointed general in Thrace, IV. 104; a leading man in Thrace, *ib.* 105; fails to save Amphipolis, *ib.* 106; repulses Brasidas from Eion, *ib.* 107; exiled, V. 26; lived throughout the war, *ib.*

Thucydides, an Athenian commander at Samos, I. 117.

Thucydides, of Pharsalus, proxenus of Athens, VIII. 92; helps to prevent the panic after the destruction of Eetioneia, *ib.*

Thunder-storm, effect of, on armies, VI. 70, VII. 79.

Thuria, in Laconia, Perioeci of, I. 101.

Thurii, in Italy, Alcibiades conceals himself there, VI. 61, 88; the Thurians refuse to receive Gylippus, *ib.* 104; expel an anti-Athenian party, VII. 33, 35, 57; send ships to the Peloponnesians in Asia, VIII. 35, 61; the sailors mostly freemen, *ib.* 84; their boldness in demanding full pay from Tissaphernes, *ib.* 78, 84.

Thyamis, a river on the borders of Thesprotia, I. 46.

Thyamus, Mount, in Aetolia, III. 106.

Thymochares, an Athenian commander, VIII. 95.

Thyrea, in Laconia, given to the Aeginetans by the Lacedaemonians, II. 27, IV. 56; captured by the Athenians, IV. 57; the Argives in their treaty with Lacedaemon insert a stipulation that they and the Lacedaemonians should fight for Thyrea, V. 41; the district

mencement of the War, I. 118, II. I; lasted 27 years, as foretold by an oracle, v. 26.

End of 1st year, II. 47.
"   2nd   "   " 70.
"   3rd   "   " 103.
"   4th   " III. 25.
"   5th   "   " 88.
"   6th   "   " 116.
"   7th   " IV. 51.
"   8th   "   " 116.
"   9th   "   " 135.
"   10th   " V. 20.
"   11th   "   " 39.
"   12th   "   " 51.
"   13th   "   " 56.
"   14th   "   " 81.
"   15th   "   " 83.
"   16th   " VI. 7.
"   17th   "   " 93.
"   18th   " VII. 18.
"   19th   " VIII. 6.
"   20th   "   " 60.
"   21st   "   " 109.

War, the Persian, I. 14, 18, 23, 41, 69, 73, 74, 89, 90, 93, 95, 97, 142, VI. 82, VIII. 24; events of—Marathon, I. 18, VI. 59; Thermopylae, IV. 36; Artemisium, III. 54; Salamis, I. 73, 137; Mycale, I. 89; Plataea, *ib.* 130, III. 54, 58; capture of Byzantium, I. 128; of Eion, Scyros, Naxos, *ib.* 98; battle of the Eurymedon, *ib.* 100; Persian occupation of Sestos alluded to in, VIII. 62; dedication of the tripod at Delphi, I. 132, III. 57; its object principally the destruction of Athens, VI. 33.

War, the Sacred, I. 112.

War, Trojan, first common action of Hellas, I. 3; not equal to more modern wars, *ib.* 9-11; reason of its length, *ib.* 11; changes in Hellas after the return from Troy, *ib.* 12.

War, maxims of, 'war a matter of money,' I. 83; 'war waits for no man,' *ib.* 142; 'the battle not always to the strong,' II. 11, 89, V. 102; necessity of discipline, II. 11; courage is fortified by justifiable contempt, *ib.* 62; 'victory on the side of the greatest battalions,' *ib.* 87; much to be learned from mistakes, *ib.*; a good general is never off his guard, III.

30, V. 9; when danger has to be faced reflection is useless, IV. 10; war much a matter of chance, I. 78, 120, IV. 18, VII. 61; importance of reinforcements brought up at the right time, V. 9; 'find out an enemy's weak points,' IV. 126, VI. 91; deterioration of character caused by war, III. 82; its inscrutable nature, I. 78; no experienced man believes that war is a good or safe thing, *ib.* 80; wars are supported out of accumulated wealth, not out of forced contributions, *ib.* 141; misery of war, IV. 59.

Weak, the, must go to the wall, v. 89.

'Wells,' in Acarnania, the, III. 105, 106.

Wisdom, contemptuous wisdom brings men to ruin, I. 122.

Women, the glory of woman to restrain her weakness, and avoid both praise and blame, II. 45.

Xanthippus, father of Pericles, an Athenian, I. 111, I. 127.

Xenares, (I) Ephor at Sparta, v. 36, 46; favours the war party, *ib.* 36; negotiates with the Boeotians and Corinthians, *ib.* 36-38: (II) another, the Lacedaemonian governor of Heraclea, v. 51; slain in battle, *ib.*

Xenocleides, a Corinthian commander, I. 46, III. 114.

Xenon, a Theban commander at Syracuse, VII. 19.

Xenophanes, father of Lamachus, an Athenian, VI. 8.

Xenophantidas, a Lacedaemonian, VIII. 55.

Xenophon, an Athenian commander at Potidaea, II. 70; in Chalcidice, *ib.* 79.

Xenotimus, father of Carcinus, an Athenian, II. 23.

Xerxes, king of Persia, father of Artaxerxes, I. 137, IV. 50; his expedition against Hellas, I. 14, 118, III. 56; forewarned by Themistocles at Salamis, I. 137; his letter to Pausanias, *ib.* 129.

Zacynthus, an island opposite Elis, an Achaean colony, II. 66; its importance to the Athenians, *ib.* 7, 80; the Zacynthians assist the Corcyraeans, I. 47; be-

INDEX TO XENOPHON

(References to Books I and II of the *Hellenica* precede references to the *Anabasis*. All references to Books III to VII are preceded by the letter *H*.)

Abarnis, the promontory of Lampsacus, II. i. 29

Abrocomas, an enemy of Cyrus, posted on the Euphrates, *Anab*. I. iii. 20; some Greek mercenaries revolt from him to Cyrus, I. iv. 3; makes no defence, I. iv. 5; had burnt ships to prevent Cyrus crossing the Euphrates, I. iv. 18; arrived five days too late for the battle, I. vii. 12

Abrozelmes, Seuthes' private interpreter, *Anab*. VII. vi. 43

Abydos, I. i. 5; I. ii. 15; people of, II. i. 18; III. i. 9; IV. viii. 3; *ib*. 32; V. i. 6; *ib*. 25, the coast of, IV. viii. 35; the inhabitants of, IV. viii. 3; *ib*. 6; *ib*. 35; Philiscus of, VII. i. 27; gold mines in the neighbourhood of, IV. viii. 37

Academy, Gymnasium of, II. ii. 8; the, VI. v. 49

Acanthus, a town in the Chalcidice, v. ii. 11; *ib*. iii. 6; deputies from, v. ii. 23

Acarnania, VI. ii. 37

Acarnanians, the, IV. ii. 17; *ib*. vi. 1; *ib*. vii. 1; VI. v. 23

Achaea Phthiotis, mountains of, IV. iii. 9

Achaeans, the, I. ii. 18; with the Arcadians formed numerically the larger half of the army, *Anab*. VI. ii. 10; *H*. the Arcadians and, join in the invasion of Elis (B. C. 401?), III. ii. 26; at Nemea (B. C. 394), IV. ii. 18; occupy Calydon (B. C. 390), IV. vi. 1; their campaign against the Acarnanians, IV. vi. 3, *ib*.; allied with Lacedaemon (B. C. 371), IV. iv. 18; Epaminondas secures adhesion of (B. C. 367), VII. i. 41; in alliance with Eleians (B. C. 365), *ib*. iv. 17; at Olympia (B. C. 364), *ib*. 28; join the anti-Theban league (B. C. 362), *ib*. v. 1; *ib*. 18

Achaia, III. ii. 23; IV. viii. 10; *ib*. 23; VI. ii. 2; VII. i. 41

Acherusian Chersonese, *Anab*. VI. ii. 2

Achilleum, in the Troad, III. ii. 17; in the plain of the Maeander, IV. viii. 17

Acrisius of Sicyon, VII. i. 45

Acrocorinthus, the, IV. iv. 4

Acroreia, the cities of the, VII. iv. 14

Acroreians, the, III. ii. 30; IV. ii. 16

Adeas of Sicyon, VII. i. 45

Adeimantus, an Athenian, I. iv. 21; I. vii. 1; II. i. 30; II. i. 32

Adramytium, *Anab*. VII. viii. 8

Aeetes, *Anab*. v. vi. 37

Aegae, a town in Aeolis, IV. viii. 5

Aegina, II. ii. 19; v. i. 2; *ib*. iv. 61; VI. ii. 1

Aeginetans, the, II. ii. 3; II. ii. 9; and Athenians (B. C. 388), v. i. 2

Aeginetan obols, v. ii. 21

Aegospotami, battle of, II. i. 21

Aegosthena, town in Megaris, v. iv. 18; VI. iv. 26

Aeneas of Stymphalus killed, *Anab*. IV. vii. 13; *H*. VII. iii. 1

Aenianians, the, among the troops of Menon, *Anab*. I. ii. 6; and the Magnesians dance the Carpaea, VI. i. 7; *H*. III. v. 6; IV. iii. 15

Aeolians, the, III. iv. 11; IV. iii. 17

Aeolid, *Anab*. v. vi. 24; *H*. III. i. 10; *ib*. 16; *ib*. ii. 1; *ib*. 13; IV. viii. 33

Aeschines, an Athenian, one of the Thirty, II. iii. 2; II. iii. 13

Aeschines, an Acarnanian, *Anab*. IV. iii. 22; IV. viii. 18

Aetolia, IV. vi. 1

Aetolians, the, IV. vi. 14

Aexone, the deme, II. iv. 26

Agamemnon, III. iv. 3; VII. i. 34

Agasias of Stymphalus, an officer of the heavy infantry, *Anab*. III. i. 37; IV. i.

Andros, island of, I. iv. 21; I. v. 18

Antalcidas, the Lacedaemonian, IV. viii.
12; confers with Tiribazus (B. C. 392),
ib. 14-16; appointed navarch (B. C.
388), V. i. 6; the peace of (B. C. 387),
V. i. 31; *ib.* 36; VI. iii. 12

Antandrus, I. i. 25; I. iii. 17; II. i. 10;
Anab. VII. viii. 7; *H.* IV. viii. 35

Antigenes, an Athenian archon, I. iii. 1

Antileon, of Thurii, *Anab.* V. i. 3

Antiochus, an Arcadian, VII. i. 33-38

Antiochus, an Athenian, at Notium, I. v.
11

Antiphon, an Athenian, put to death by
the Thirty, II. iii. 40

Antisthenes, a Lacedaemonian, III. ii. 6

Anytus, an Athenian, banished by the
Thirty, II. iii. 42; II. iii. 44

Apaturia, festival of the, I. vii. 8

Aphrodision, the, temple of Aphrodite at
Megara, V. iv. 58

Aphrodite, a feast of, at Thebes, V. iv. 4

Aphytis, a town of Pallene in Macedonia,
V. iii. 19

Apollo, and Marsyas, *Anab.* I. ii. 8;
Xenophon's dedicatory offering to, *ib.*
V. iii 4; Xenophon sacrifices at Lamp-
sacus to, *ib.* VII. viii. 3; *H.* oracle of, III.
iii. 3; *ib.* V. 5; IV. vii. 2; the temple of,
VI. iv. 2; *ib.* 30; *ib.* V. 27

Apollonia, the chief town of Chalcidice,
V. ii. 11; *ib.* iii. 1

Apollonia, a town of Mysia, *Anab.* VII.
viii. 15

Apollonides, a faint-hearted officer, degraded, *Anab.* III. i. 26-32

Apollophanes of Cyzicus, IV. i. 29

Arabia, *Anab.* I. v. 1; VII. viii. 25

Aracus, a Lacedaemonian admiral, II. i. 7;
ephor at Sparta, II. iii. 10; III. ii. 6; VI.
v. 33

Araxes, the river, *Anab.* I. iv. 19

Arbaces, one of the four generals of Artaxerxes, *Anab.* I. vii. 12; governor of
Media, VII. viii. 25

Arcadia, IV. iv. 16; VI. v. 12; *ib.* 51; VII.
iv. 10; *ib.* 35; *ib.* v. 10; the Parrhasians
of, VII. i. 28; *ib.* 40

Arcadians, and Achaeans form numeri-
cally the larger half of the army, *Anab.*
VI. ii. 10; separate at Heraclea, with the
Achaeans, from the rest of the army,

VI. ii. 12; set sail first and disembark at
Calpe Haven, VI. iii. 1; get into great
danger and are rescued by Xenophon's
division, VI. iii. 17; their dance, VI. i.
11; an Arcadian blames Xenophon before the Laconian envoy, VII. vi. 8; join
in the invasion of Elis (B. C. 401?),
Hell. III. ii. 26; claim of, to Lasion, *ib.*
30; *ib.* v. 12; and Iphicrates's peltasts,
IV. iv. 16; character of, V. ii. 19; of
Orchomenus and Cleitor at war, V. iv.
36; impulse of, towards Pan-Arcadian
union and common assembly of (B. C.
370), VI. v. 6; contingents of, muster at
Asea, VI. v. 11; and unite with the
Mantineans, *ib.* 15; wise discretion of,
ib. 19; march upon Heraea (winter of
B. C. 370-369) and coalesce with the
Thebans at Mantinea, *ib.* 22; eagerness of, to invade Laconia, *ib.* 23;
enter by Oeum in the Sciritid, *ib.*
25; coalesce with the Thebans at
Caryae, *ib.* 27; unguarded behaviour
of, before Sparta, *ib.* 30; invasion of
Laconia, *ib.* 36; retire from Laconia,
ib. 50; the Thebans effect a junction
with the, Argives, and Eleians (second
invasion, B. C. 369), VII. i. 18; Lycomedes inspires the, with high thoughts,
ib. 23; brilliant exploits of, *ib.* 24; growing lukewarmness of the Thebans and
hostility of the Eleians towards, *ib.*
26; and Argives encounter Archidamus
and are defeated in battle (B. C. 368),
ib. 28; Antiochus commissioner of, at
the court of Persia (B. C. 367), *ib.* 33;
his report to the general assembly, *ib.*
38; dissension between the envoys of,
and the Thebans at the congress of
Thebes (B. C. 366), *ib.* 39; Epaminondas and the (B. C. 367), *ib.* 41-43; stress
of, between the Achaeans and Lacedaemonians, *ib.* 43; successful overtures of
Euphron to Argives and, *ib.* 43; relations of Phlius to, and Argives (B. C.
370 foll.), *ib.* ii. 2; some Phliasian exiles
and, *ib.* 5; an attack on Phlius by the
Argives and, *ib.* 10; Aeneas of Stymphalus, general of, *ib.* iii. 1; the Sicyonians and, recapture the harbour of
Sicyon (B. C. 366), *ib.* iv. 1; Lycomedes
cements an alliance between Athens

cess of (B. C. 387), become passionately desirous of peace, *ib.* 25; subscribe to the Peace of Antalcidas, *ib.* 35; Cleigenes of Acanthus on the danger to Lacedaemon of an alliance between, and Olynthus (B. C. 383), *ib.* ii. 15; assist the Theban patriots (B. C. 379), *ib.* iv. 10; nervous apprehensions of (B. C. 378), *ib.* 19; and the attempt of Sphodrias, *ib.* 21; in consequence fortify Piraeus, build a fleet (new confederacy of Delos), and display zeal in aiding the Boeotians, *ib.* 34; a detachment of Thebans and, occupy the pass on Cithaeron (Cleombrotus's expedition, B. C. 376), *ib.* 59; win the battle of Naxos, *ib.* 61; despatch Timotheus on his "periplus" (B. C. 375), *ib.* 62; and the Lacedaemonians (B. C. 374), VI. i. 1; Macedonia the timber yard of their navy, *ib.* 10; annoyed with the Thebans (B. C. 374) in reference to the maintenance of the fleet, conclude peace with Lacedaemon, *ib.* ii. 1; but hostilities speedily recommence *re* the Zacynthian exiles restored by Timotheus their general, *ib.* 4; send aid to the Corcyraeans (B. C. 373), *ib.* 9; depose Timotheus, appointing Iphicrates in his place, *ib.* 13; the Lacedaemonian troops evacuate Corcyra in fear of, *ib.* 26; alienated from Thebes *re* Plataeae and Thespiae, pass a decree to treat with Lacedaemon (B. C. 371), *ib.* iii. 1; treaty of peace between, and the Lacedaemonians, the Thebans being excluded, *ib.* 19; conscientiously carry out its terms, not so the Lacedaemonians, *ib.* iv. 1; feelings of, on receipt of the news of Leuctra, *ib.* 20; hostility of Alexander of Pherae to the Thebans and, *ib.* 35; organise a new confederacy on the basis of the King's rescript (*i.e.* the terms of the peace of Antalcidas), the Eleians alone dissenting to the principle of autonomy (B. C. 371-370), *ib.* v. 1; and the Lacedaemonian envoys in reference to the first Theban invasion (B. C. 370-369), *ib.* 33; after debate the assembly of, decrees to send assistance to Lacedaemon, *ib.* 49; Iphicrates commands, *ib.* 51; an alliance between,

and the Lacedaemonians (spring, B. C. 369), VII. i. 1; decree passed by, vesting the command in either state alternately, *ib.* 12; campaign commenced by, and Lacedaemonians, *ib.* 14; send two commissioners to the court of Persia (B. C. 368), *ib.* 33; proposed (by Pelopidas) that "Messene be independent, and, lay up their ships of war," *ib.* 37; Timomachus general of (B. C. 367, third Theban invasion), *ib.* 41; Phliasians assisted by some cavalry of (B. C. 368), *ib.* ii. 10; Euphron restored to Sicyon (B. C. 367) by, *ib.* iii. 9; forced to act single-handed *re* Oropus, are persuaded by Lycomedes to make a cross alliance with the Arcadians (B. C. 366), *ib.* iv. 1; proposal of Demotion to, concerning Corinth, *ib.* 4; the Corinthians and, *ib.* 5; four hundred cavalry of, with the Arcadians at Olympia (July, B. C. 364), *ib.* 29; the Mantineans, etc., call on, for military aid to resist the Thebans (B. C. 362), *ib.* v. 3; Epaminondas hopes to intercept, at Nemea, *ib.* 6; cavalry of, at Mantinea, behave gallantly, *ib.* 15; position and exploits of, in the battle of Mantinea, *ib.* 24

Athens, I. i. 33; burning of the old temple of Athena at, I. vi. 1; II. iii. 1; end of civil strife at (B. C. 403-402), III. i. 1; Thebans send ambassadors to, *ib.* v. 7; popular government of, and Pausanias, *ib.* 28; a squadron from, at the Oeniadae (B. C. 390-389), IV. vi. 14; Conon rebuilds a portion of the long walls of, *ib.* viii. 9; Philocrates sailing from, to Cyprus encounters Teleutias (B. C. 390), *ib.* 24; Chabrias voyaging from, to Cyprus stops at Aegina (B. C. 388), v. i. 10; rush from, to Piraeus on the occasion of Teleutias's surprise, *ib.* 20; in B. C. 387 (Peace of Antalcidas), *ib.* 35; Thebans escape to (B. C. 383), on the occasion of the seizure of the Cadmeia, *ib.* ii. 31; isolated (B. C. 379), *ib.* iii. 27; Phyllidas visits Melon at (B. C. 379), *ib.* iv. 2; Lacedaemonian ambassadors at (B. C. 378), on the occasion of the attempt of Sphodrias, *ib.* 22; Timotheus has to send to, for moneys

Elimia, in Macedonia, v. ii. 38

Elis, invaded by Agis through Achaia *via* the Larisus, III. ii. 23; and later through Aulon, *ib.* 25; the presidency of the temple of Olympian Zeus conceded to, rather than to the "villagers" of Pisa, *ib.* ii. 1; Agis and the earthquake in, IV. vii. 4; naval contingent from, levied by Lacedaemon (B. C. 374), VI. ii. 3; Iphicrates comes to moorings under Cape Ichthus in, *ib.* 31; the city of, a prey to party strife: democrats and oligarchs, VII. iv. 15; Pylos, a town in "hollow," *ib.* 16

Elymia, between Mantinea and Orchomenus, VI. v. 13

Enyalius, the god of battle, II. iv. 17; *Anab.* I. viii. 18; v. ii. 14

Epaminondas, the Theban, his object (the third Theban invasion, B. C. 367), to make the Arcadians, etc., pay better heed to Thebes by securing the adhesion of the Achaeans, which he does; on his personal authority insists that there shall be no driving of the aristocrats into exile, nor any modifications of the constitutions, and so, taking a pledge of fealty from the Achaeans, departs home; indictment of, by the opposite party in Thebes and the Arcadians; his policy reversed, with evil consequences, VII. i. 41; as head of the war department, his opinion, as to the conduct of the Theban commander at Tegea (B. C. 362), and his answer to the general assembly of the Arcadians, promising to bring an army into Arcadia and, along with those who share Theban views, to carry on the war already undertaken, *ib.* iv. 40; prosecutes his march (final invasion, B. C. 362) at the head of all the Boeotians, etc.; his calculations as to the amount of cooperation to be reckoned on within Peloponnesus; advances with rapid strides, but at Nemea slackens speed, hoping to intercept the Athenian contingent; his reflections on the importance of such an exploit; on receipt of certain news abandons his base at Nemea, and pushes on to Tegea, *ib.* v. 4; the historian's comments on the

strategy of—"in a particular combination of prudence and daring he was consummate," *ib.* 8; for certain reasons advances straight upon Sparta, and all but captures the city; cautious tactics and misadventure of, within the city of Sparta; his reason for returning with all speed into Arcadia; reaches Tegea; sends on his cavalry post-haste to Mantinea; limited success of his cavalry before Mantinea, *ib.* 9-17; the thoughts now working in the mind of (according to the historian), which determined him to deliver battle; the wonderful perfection to which he had brought his army; the alacrity with which his final orders were obeyed; his manoeuvres misleading to the enemy; his tactical formation in strengthening the attacking point of his infantry and cavalry; the complete success of his encounter, *ib.* 18-25; the strange paralysis which seized his victorious army after he himself had fallen, *ib.* 25

Eparitoi, the (select troops of the Arcadian League), successful engagement of, with the Lacedaemonians under Archidamus before Cromnus (B. C. 365), VII. iv. 22; the sacred treasures of the temple of Zeus at Olympia employed by the Arcadian League to maintain the (B. C. 363), *ib.* 33; the payment of, becomes a burning question leading to a division in the League itself; the state of Mantinea passes a resolution forbidding the use of the sacred money as pay for the, and votes a sum from their state exchequer for the purpose; some of their leading statesmen being cited to appear before the Ten Thousand, refuse to obey and shut the gates on the, sent to apprehend them; other states of the League following the example of Mantinea, the Ten Thousand forbid the use of sacred money for profane purposes, with the result that the poorer, cease to serve, and wealthier people stepping into their place, the corps tend to become an instrument in the hands of the better classes, *ib.* 34; ambassadors sent to Lacedaemon on be-

in Paphlagonia, IV. i. 15; the, heavy infantry at Nemea amounted to six thousand men, to which must be added six hundred, cavalry; the total of the forces on the, side, *ib.* ii. 16; Phliasians owing their exile to their, sympathies, as they gave out (B. C. 391), *ib.* iv. 15; Iphicrates's peltasts taught a lesson by some of the younger, troopers, *ib.* 16; the, warriors (at the Heraeum, B. C. 390) the cynosure of all beholders, *ib.* v. 6; the destruction of the, mora, *ib.* 18; garrisons placed by Praxitas in Sidus and Crommyon, *ib.* 19; the, party in Rhodes, *ib.* viii. 25; twelve of the, governors who had rallied to Abydos (after Cnidos) slain along with Anaxibius (B. C. 388), *ib.* 39; the, troops lining the road after the reduction of Mantinea (B. C. 384) exhibit proofs of discipline, v. ii. 6; the, cavalry at Olynthus under Polycharmus (B. C. 382), *ib.* 41; some, ambassadors chance to be in Athens at the date of Sphodrias's attempt (B. C. 378), *ib.* iv. 22; the men of, proclivities in Thespiae, and their opponents (B. C. 377) restrained by Agesilaus, *ib.* iv. 55; a, navy moving about Aegina, Ceos, and Andros blockades Athens, *ib.* 61; the, admiral and Timotheus off Alyzia (B. C. 375), *ib.* 65; nearly a thousand men of the total, force slain at Leuctra (B. C. 371), VI. iv. 15; the men of Tegea, led by Stasippus and others, staunch in their, proclivities, stand by Lacedaemon after Leuctra, *ib.* 18; it occurred to the Thebans (winter of B. C. 370-369) that the, forces, though disbanded, would not take long to muster, etc., *ib.* v. 24; the, ambassadors at Athens during the first Theban invasion, *ib.* 33; the Thebans surprise the, outposts on Oneion (B. C. 369, second Theban invasion), VII. i. 15; the, garrison in Asine of Laconia defeated by the Arcadians (B. C. 368), *ib.* 25; not a single, slain in the tearless battle, *ib.* 32; Euthycles the, at the Persian court, *ib.* 33; the ground of, hostility to Thebes (see Pelopidas's speech at the Persian court), *ib.* 34; sorry guard kept over Oneion by Naucles, the general commanding the, foreign brigade (B. C. 367, third Theban invasion), *ib.* 41; during the, days Euphron had been the greatest man in Sicyon, *ib.* 44; the Pellenians (in B. C. 365) had reverted to their old, alliance, *ib.* iv. 17; Agesilaus and the whole, army expected to unite with the Peloponnesian forces at Mantinea (B. C. 362), *ib.* v. 9; Epaminondas, unwilling to engage the Arcadian forces united with the whole, force in the proximity of Sparta, falls back on Mantinea, *ib.* 14; in answer to the appeal of the Hellenes in Asia send out Thibron as governor, III. i. 4; during the Asiatic campaigns the, at home were no less busily employed with other matters (*i.e.* the Eleian war), *ib.* ii. 21; the Eleians on plea of a sentence registered against the, had excluded them from the Olympian games (some years ago), *ib.*; emboldened by the first abortive attempt of Agis to invade them, the men of Elis send embassies to states known to be hostile to the, *ib.* 24; treatment of the Eleians by, *re* Epeium and the presidency of the temple of Zeus at Olympia; peace and alliance between the Eleians and, *ib.* 30; the arch-corruptress of all, young and old, at Aulon, *ib.* iii. 8; Herodas lays certain information before the (B. C. 397); his reports throw the, into a flutter of expectation and anxiety, *ib.* iv. 1; the, agree to Agesilaus's proposal and give him troops, etc., for the Asiatic campaign (B. C. 396), *ib.* 3; vexation of the army at Ephesus, including the, there present, at Tissaphernes's declaration of war (B. C. 395), *ib.* 11; the reasons which led the, to give Agesilaus absolute control over the naval (as well as the land) forces, *ib.* 27; it was clear to the leaders in Thebes that unless some one struck the first blow the, would never be brought to break the truce with the allies; on their side the, were ready to seize any pretext for marching upon Thebes, *ib.* v. 3; Pausanias at the head of the, and other Peloponnesian troops is to effect junction with

the, try to neutralise the power of Conon and Pharnabazus by working on Tiribazus through Antalcidas; offer to give up all claim to the Hellenic cities as against the king, etc. (B. C. 392), *ib.* 12; Tiribazus cannot directly adopt the cause of the, without the king's concurrence, but presents Antalcidas with money, and accepting the statement of the, as true, seizes and imprisons Conon, *ib.* 16; the, send Thibron to deal with the new satrap Struthas, a partisan of Athens (B. C. 391), *ib.* 17; the, lend a willing ear to the appeal of the Rhodian exiles (of the wealthier class) (B. C. 390), *ib.* 20; the, send out Ecdicus with too small a force and presently relieve him, *ib.* 23; the, (B. C. 389) try to neutralise the influence of the Athenians in the Hellespont and Bosporus, *ib.* 31; the, send out a new admiral (B. C. 388), Antalcidas, to Ephesus, v. i. 6; Gorgopas with the, of his force falls into the trap laid by Chabrias and is slain in Aegina, *ib.* 12; subsequently the, send out Teleutias to take command of their squadron in the Saronic Gulf once more, *ib.* 13; now that the, had procured an ally in the person of the great king, the Athenians are desirous of peace; the, were equally out of humour with the war for various reasons (B. C. 387), *ib.* 29; the, having by threat of war forced the Thebans to recognise the autonomy of the Boeotian cities, return home, *ib.* 33; the, and Athenians with their allies find themselves in the enjoyment of peace for the first time since the period of hostilities subsequent to the demolition of the walls of Athens; and the, now reach a pinnacle of glory consequent upon the peace of Antalcidas, so called, *ib.* 35; indeed late events have so accorded with the wishes of the, that they determine to go farther and dominate recalcitrant states (B. C. 386), *ib.* ii. 1; the, insist on the dismemberment of Mantinea (B. C. 385), *ib.* 5; the Phliasian exiles work on the feelings of the, *ib.* 8; the, in answer to the deputies from Acanthus and Apollonia, request the

allies to advise whether or not active measures should be taken against Olynthus; resolutions empowering the, so to do (B. C. 383), *ib.* 20; the, despatch Eudamidas at once with a portion of the troops, *ib.* 24; the hatred of Ismenias (the one polemarch at Thebes) against the, and the assiduous courtship of Phoebidas by Leontiades (the other polemarch), *ib.* 25; Leontiades (after the seizure of the Cadmeia) addresses the assembly (or select committee) at Lacedaemon in defence of the act, *ib.* 32; the, resolve to keep the citadel and to put Ismenias on his trial; constitution of the court; as the result of the whole business the, press on the combined campaign against Olynthus, *ib.* 35; disposition of the, and other troops in the first engagement (chiefly of cavalry) before the gates of Olynthus, *ib.* ii. 40; many of the, object for the sake of a handful of people (the Phliasian exiles) so to embroil themselves with that state (B. C. 380), *ib.* iii. 16; but in the end the, come round to the opinions of Agesilaus, *ib.* 17; on the death of Agesipolis the, despatch Polybiades as governor to Olynthus, *ib.* 20; the nemesis which fell upon the (in B. C. 379), when the acropolis of Thebes, wrongfully seized by them, was snatched from their hands by a handful of patriots, *ib.* iv. 1; the, put to death the governor, who had abandoned the Cadmeia instead of awaiting reinforcements, and call out the army against Thebes, *ib.* 13; fear of the, on the part of the Athenians (B. C. 378), *ib.* 19, merged into hatred when the, connive at the attempt of Sphodrias, *ib.* 34; the, again call out the army against Thebes after Cleombrotus's abortive invasion, and entrust the expedition to Agesilaus, *ib.* 35; during the next campaign (B. C. 377), Agesilaus ravages Theban territory on the east as far as Tanagra, which at that date is in the hands of a party friendly to the, *ib.* 49; the, again (for the fourth time, B. C. 376) call out the army against Thebes, Cleombrotus leading

Naupactus (mod. Lepanto), a town of the Locri Ozolae, IV. vi. 14

Nauplia, port town of Argos, IV. vii. 6

Nausicleides, and Bion, *Anab.* VII. viii. 6

Neandria, in the Troad, the men of, III. i. 16

Nemea, the stream of, between Corinth and Sicyon, site of battle, IV. ii. 14; township of Argolis, *ib.* vii. 3; VII. ii. 5; *ib.* v. 6

Neodamodes, enfranchised helots, III. i. 4; *ib.* iii. 6; *ib.* iv. 2; *ib.* 20; IV. iii. 15; V. ii. 24; VI. i. 14; *ib.* v. 24

Neon, the Asinaean, acts for Cheirisophus during his absence, *Anab.* V. vi. 36; tells tales against Xenophon, V. vii. 1; at the division of the army, advises separate action, VI. ii. 13; succeeds Cheirisophus, VI. iv. 11; at Calpe, rashly leads out a pillaging party and loses five hundred men, *ib.* 23; left to guard the camp, VI. v. 4; aspires to command the whole army, VII. ii. 2; encamps apart at Perinthus, *ib.* 11; and holds aloof from the other generals, *ib.* 17; *ib.* 29; VII. iii. 2; plays into the hands of Aristarchus, *ib.* 7

Neontichos, a Thracian fortress promised by Seuthes, with Bisanthe and Ganos, to Xenophon, *Anab.* VII. v. 8

Nicander, a Lacedaemonian puts Dexippus to death, *Anab.* V. i. 15

Nicarchus, the Arcadian, how he came riding into camp after the arrest of the generals, *Anab.* II. v. 33; (the same, or another) Arcadian officer, deserts to the Persians with twenty men, III. iii. 5

Niceratus, the son of Nicias, an Athenian, arrested by the Thirty, II. iii. 39

Nicias, the famous Athenian general, father of above, II. iii. 39

Nicolochus, a Lacedaemonian, V. i. 6; *ib.* 25; *ib.* iv. 65

Nicomachus, the Oetaean, in command of light infantry, his prowess as a volunteer, *Anab.* IV. vi. 20

Nicophemus, an Athenian, IV. viii. 3

Nicostratus, the beautiful, an Athenian knight slain before Phyle, II. iv. 6

Notium, Thrasylus sails to, I. ii. 4; after Coressus the Athenians sail to, *ib.* 11; battle of, Antiochus defeated by Ly-

sander at, I. v. 12; prestige gained by Lysander at, II. i. 6

Ocyllus, a Lacedaemonian, V. iv. 22; VI. v. 33

Odeum, the Thirty summon a meeting in the, II. iv. 9; the knights sleep out in the, *ib.* 24

Odrysians, the, a Thracian tribe, and the Athenians related, *Anab.* VII. ii. 32; Medocus, king of the, *ib.* VII. iii. 16; join Seuthes in his campaign, *ib.* VII. iv. 21; the, flock down to join Seuthes, *ib.* VII. v. 15; Teres, an ancient hero of the, *ib.* 1; a young man of the, with Medosades, *ib.* VII. vii. 1; *H.* III. ii. 2; *ib.* 5; IV. viii. 26

Oeniadae, in Acarnania, IV. vi. 14

Oenoe, betrayed by Aristarchus to the Thebans, I. vii. 28; a fortress in the Peiraeum of Corinth, IV. v. 5; *ib.* 19

Oetaeans, the, in battle with colonists of Heraclea Trachinia, I. ii. 18; Nicomachus the, *Anab.* IV. vi. 20; *H.* III. v. 6

Oeum, or Ium, in the Scriritid, VI. v. 24; the men of, *ib.* 26

Olontheus, a Lacedaemonian, VI. v. 33

Olurus, a fortress dependent upon Pellene in Achaea, VII. iv. 17

Olympia, Scillus lies on the road to, *Anab.* V. iii. 7; Temple of Zeus in, *ib.* 11; *H.* III. ii. 26; IV. i. 40; *ib.* vii. 2; VII. iv. 14; *ib.* 28

Olympian games, VII. iv. 28

Olympian Zeus, III. ii. 22; *ib.* 26; *ib.* 31

Olympic year, the, VII. iv. 28

Olynthians, in service of Menon, *Anab.* I. ii. 6; *H.* V. ii. 13; *ib.* 38; *ib.* 42; *ib.* iii. 1; *ib.* iv. 54

Olynthus, V. ii. 12; *ib.* 27; *ib.* 37; *ib.* iii. 9; *ib.* 20

Oneion, or Oneium, VI. v. 51; VII. i. 15; *ib.* 41; *ib.* ii. 5

Onomacles, ephor at Sparta, II. iii. 10

Onomacles, one of the Thirty at Athens, II. iii. 2

Onomantius, ephor at Sparta, II. iii. 10

Ophrynium, a town in the Troad, *Anab.* VII. viii. 5

Opis, a large city on the river Physcus, *Anab.* II. iv. 25

Opuntian Locrians, the, *see* Locrians

Rhoeteum, Dorieus at, *Hell.* I. i. 2

Rhoparas, governor of Babylon, *Anab.* VII. viii. 25

Sacred Mountain, *Anab.* VII. i. 14; VII. iii. 3

Salaminia, the sacred galley of the Athenians, VI. ii. 14

Salamis, Lysander pillages, II. ii. 9; the battle of, *Anab.* III. ii. 13

Salmydessus, the Hellenes with Seuthes reach, *Anab.* VII. v. 12

Samian vessels picked up by relief squadron, I. vi. 25; Hippeus a, officer, in command of, ships at Arginusae, *ib.* 29; proposition concerning the ten, vessels after Arginusae, I. vii. 30

Samius, the Lacedaemonian admiral, III. i. 1

Samolas, the Achaean, sent on an embassy to Sinope, *Anab.* v. vi. 14; in command of a brigade, VI. v. 11

Samos, Thrasylus at, I. ii. 1; Alcibiades at, I. iv. 8; the Athenians after Notium retire to, I. v. 14; Conon at, *ib.* 20; Athenian navy at, between Ephesus and Miletus, I. vi. 2; Conon pursued by Callicratidas from Methymna, fails to reach, *ib.* 15; Athenian relief squadron reach *ib.* 25; the squadron after Arginusae return to, *ib.* 38; the Athenians improve their navy at, which becomes their base of operations, II. i. 12; the men of, faithful to Athens after Aegospotami, II. ii. 6; Lysander set sails for, II. iii. 3; appoints a decarchy in, *ib.* 6; IV. viii. 23

Samothrace, the island of, v. i. 7

Sardis, Alcibiades shut up in, by Tissaphernes, escapes, I. i. 9; Lysander visits Cyrus in, I. v. 1; Cyrus collects his various armaments at, *Anab.* I. ii. 2; sets out from, *ib.* 6; Xenophon overtakes Proxenus and Cyrus at, *ib.* III. 1. 8; *H.* III. ii. 11; *ib.* iv. 25; IV. i. 27; *ib.* viii. 21; the district of, III. iv. 21

Satyr, the, and Midas, king of Phrygia, *Anab.* I. ii. 13

Satyrus, head of the Eleven, and Critias, II. iii. 54

Scepsis, in the Troad, III. i. 15

Scepsians, the, III. i. 21

Scilluntians, the, claims of Elis to (B. C. 371), VI. v. 2

Scillus, Xenophon's estate at, in Triphylia, *Anab.* v. iii. 7

Scione, painful recollections concerning, II. ii. 3

Sciritae, the, v. ii. 24; *ib.* iv. 52

Sciritid, the, of Laconia, Ischolaus posted at Oeum in (B. C. 370-369), VI. v. 24; the Arcadians enter by Oeum in, *ib.* 25; Archidamus ravages (B. C. 365), VII. iv. 21

Scolus, in Boeotia, v. iv. 49

Scopas, the Thessalian, VI. i. 19

Scotussa, in Thessaly, the men of, IV. iii. 3

Scyros, the island of, feelings of the Athenians concerning (B. C. 392), IV. viii. 15; exempted from autonomy, v. i. 31

Scythenians, the, *Anab.* IV. vii. 19

Scythes, a Lacedaemonian general, III. iv. 20

Scythians, the, bowmen, *Anab.* III. iv. 15

Selinuntian vessels, two, aid Ephesians against Thrasylus, I. ii. 8

Selinuntians, the, granted full citizenship at Ephesus, I. ii. 10

Selinus, Hellenic city in Sicily, I. i. 37

Selinus, a river, at Scillus, like the, river at Ephesus, *Anab.* v. iii. 8

Sellasia, a town in Laconian territory, II. ii. 13; ravaged (B. C. 370-369), VI. v. 27; the Lacedaemonians recover, VII. iv. 12 (B. C. 366)

Selybria, or Selymbria, Alcibiades at, I. i. 21; taken by Alcibiades, I. iii. 10; Medosades meets Xenophon at, *Anab.* VII. ii. 28; Seuthes' Hellenic army quartered above, *ib.* VII. v. 15

Selybrians, the, prefer to give money to Alcibiades, instead of admitting his troops, I. i. 21

Sestos, the Athenians at, give Mindaru the slip, I. i. 7; Alcibiades at, *ib.* 11; twelve of Clearchus's ships escape to, *ib.* 36; Thrasylus at, I. ii. 13; Athenian fleet at, before Aegosopotami, II. i. 20; distance of Aegosopotami from, *ib.* 25; IV. viii. 3

Seuthes, a Thracian prince, son of Maesades (ex-king of the Odrysians, now dead), brought up at the court of

come independent of, seems desirable to the Athenians, *ib.* 2; the Corinthians with the consent of Lacedaemon obtain peace from, *ib.* 7; the Lacedaemonian prisoners captured in Cromnus (B.C. 365) are divided between the Argives, the, the Arcadians, and the Messenians, *ib.* 27; the, on the invitation of a section of the Arcadian government prepare to open a campaign (B.C. 363), but are warned by the general assembly of the Arcadians not to advance into Arcadia unless sent for, *ib.* 35; violent proceedings of, at Tegea (B.C. 362), *ib.* 36; policy of, becomes plain to the Mantineans and one section of the Arcadians, *ib.* v. 1; fourth invasion of, under Epaminondas, *ib.* 6; valorous behaviour of the Athenian cavalry against that of, and Thessalians before Mantinea, *ib.* 16; the Arcadians inscribing clubs as the crest on their shields as though they were, *ib.* 20; after Epaminondas himself had fallen (at Mantinea), the rest of the, were not able any longer to turn their victory rightly to account, *ib.* 25

Thebans, the, Oenoe betrayed to, by Aristarchus, *Hell.* I. vii. 28; Corinthians and, urge extreme measures against Athens, II. ii. 19

Thebe, the plain of, in Mysia, *Anab.* VII. viii. 7; *H.* IV. i. 41

Thebes, Megara and, crowded with refugees from Athens during the Thirty, II. iv. 1; Thrasybulus with seventy followers sallies out from, and occupies Phyle, *ib.* 2; Timocrates the Rhodian gave gifts to Androcleidas, leader in (B.C. 395), VI. v. 1; Lysander detaches Orchomenus from, *ib.* 6; overtures of Leontiades to Phoebidas in (B.C. 383), v. ii. 25; and the rest of the Boeotian states at the feet of Lacedaemon (B.C. 379), *ib.* iv. 1; expedition of Cleombrotus into territory of (B.C. 378), *ib.* 14; state of alarm in Athens and, *ib.* 19; expedition of Agesilaus against, *ib.* 36; second expedition of Agesilaus against (B.C. 377), *ib.* 46; expedition of Cleombrotus against (B.C. 376), *ib.* 58; exempt from hostile invasion during

Timotheus's periplus (B.C. 375), *ib.* 63; the Athenians send an embassy to, before treating for peace with Lacedaemon (B.C. 371), VI. iii. 2; the seizure of the Cadmeia in, has borne evil fruit, (B.C. 371), *ib.* 11; the widow of Jason in, *ib.* iv. 37; conference of the states convened at, to listen to the king's letter (B.C. 367), VII. i. 39; Euphron of Sicyon and his opponents at, *ib.* iii. 5; Corinthian embassy at (B.C. 366), *ib.* iv. 6; a section of the Arcadian government sends an embassy to (B.C. 363), suggesting military aid, *ib.* 34; the other section sends an embassy to, with a capital indictment against the Theban harmost in Tegea, *ib.* 39; the special agreement between the Phocians and (B.C. 362), *ib.* v. 4

Theches, Mount, whence the Hellenes saw the sea, *Anab.* IV. vii. 21

Themistogenes, the Syracusan, III. i. 2

Theogenes, an Athenian, on the embassy escorted by Pharnabazus, I. iii. 13

Theogenes, one of the Thirty at Athens, II. iii. 2

Theogenes, a Locrian captain, *Anab.* VII. iv. 18

Theognis, one of the Thirty at Athens, II. iii. 2

Theopompus, a Milesian, II. i. 30

Theopompus, the Athenian, *Anab.* II. i. 12

Theramenes, the Athenian, reaches Sestos from Macedonia, I. i. 12; and Eubulus left at Chrysopolis to guard the straits, *ib.* 22; in command of a trireme at Arginusae, the duty assigned to him and Thrasybulus, I. vi. 35; with others accuses the generals before the assembly, I. vii. 4; behaviour of the party of, at the Apaturia, *ib.* 8; *ib.* 17; *ib.* 31; sent as ambassador to Lysander, and later to Lacedaemon, by Sellasia, II. ii. 16; returns to Athens with terms which he supports, *ib.* 21; chosen one of the Thirty, II. iii. 2; and Critias, at first friends, afterwards disagree, *ib.* 15; opposed to the Thirty, is accused by Critias, *ib.* 23-34; his defence, *ib.* 35-49; condemned to death by Critias, and the Thirty; springs to the altar of

generals, *ib.* I. vii. 12; *ib.* I. viii. 9; what became of, and his division in the battle, *ib.* I. x. 5 foll.; Phalinus and other heralds arrive from the king and, *ib.* II. i. 7; sent on a deputation with others, promises to conduct the army back to Hellas, *ib.* II. iii. 17; oaths and pledges exchanged between, and the Hellenes, *ib.* 26; his suspicious delay and conduct when the march commences, *ib.* II. iv. 1; hands over the villages of Parysatis to the Hellenes to plunder, *ib.* 27; interview of Clearchus with, *ib.* II. v. 2-25; entraps and puts to death five generals and twenty captains of the Hellenes, *ib.* 32; Mithridates and a relation of, present themselves at the Zapatas, *ib.* III. iii. 4; compact between Mithridates and, *ib.* III. iv. 2; abortive attack of, with a large army upon the Hellenes, *ib.* 13; hangs on the skirts of the Hellenic army with his skirmishers, *ib.* 18; his army outmarched and out-manoeuvred, witnesses the storming of a pass, and finally retires burning their own villages, *ib.* 32; the Lacedaemonians open a campaign against him, *ib.* VII. vi. 1; *ib.* 7; Thibron with the Cyreians prosecutes the war against, and Pharnabazus, *ib.* VII. viii. 24; *H.* despatched to lower Asia by the king as satrap not only of his own provinces, but those of Cyrus (B.C. 401-400); and the Ionic cities, III. i. 3; Thibron with the Cyreians ready to confront, *ib.* 6; jealousy between, and Pharnabazus, *ib.* 9; the Lacedaemonians at the instance of the Ionic cities order Dercylidas to invade Caria, the home province of, (B.C. 397); Pharnabazus visits and makes friends with, *ib.* ii. 12; shrinks from engaging Hellenes, *ib.* 14; the terms of peace agreed to by, Pharnabazus, and Dercylidas (B.C. 397-396), *ib.* 20; a fleet being fitted out by the king and, probably, *ib.* iv. 1; Agesilaus and, (B.C. 396) *ib.* 5; declares war against Agesilaus; is outwitted, *ib.* 11; is again outwitted (B.C. 395), *ib.* 21; in Sardis during the battle of the Pactolus, is thought to have betrayed the

Persians; superseded by Tithraustes and beheaded, *ib.* 25

Tithraustes, the Persian, supersedes Tissaphernes as satrap; persuades Agesilaus to quit his province, III. iv. 25; through Timagoras assists the confederate states to undertake war with Lacedaemon, *ib.* v. 1

Tlemonidas, a Lacedaemonian, in command of light troops under Teleutias, is slain by Olynthian cavalry, v. iii. 3

Tolmides, the Eleian, with Clearchus, *Anab.* II. ii. 20; III. i. 46; v. ii. 18

Torone, painful recollections concerning, II. ii. 3; in the Chalcidice, taken by Agesipolis (B.C. 380), v. iii. 18

Trachinia, see Heraclea, I. ii. 19

Tralles, a town in Caria, *Anab.* I. iv. 8; *H.* III. ii. 19

Tranipsae, a Thracian tribe, *Anab.* VII. ii. 32

Trapezus, a town of Pontus, a colony of Sinope in Colchis, *Anab.* IV. viii. 22; pays tribute to Sinope, v. v. 10

Tricaranon (a mountain with three summits bounding Phliasia to the northeast), a point of, fortified by the Argives against Phlius, VII. ii. 1; signalling from, *ib.* 5; Sicyonians and Pellenians worsted by the Phliasians under, *ib.* 11; the Argives claim and occupy (B.C. 366), *ib.* iv. 11

Triphylian, the, townships, granted autonomy (B.C. 400?), III. ii. 30

Triphylians, the, on the side of Lacedaemon at the Nemea, IV. ii. 16; Eleians protest against autonomy applying to (B.C. 371-370), VI. v. 2; claim to be Arcadians (B.C. 368), VII. i. 26

Triptolemus, VI. iii. 6

Tripurgia, in Aegina, v. i. 10

Troad, the, *Anab.* v. vi. 24; VII. viii. 7

Troezen, in southern Argolis, with Epidaurus, Hermione, and Halieis, contributes troops to Lacedaemon at the Nemea (B.C. 394), IV. ii. 16; furnishes ships (B.C. 374), VI. ii. 3; still faithful to Lacedaemon (B.C. 370-369), VII. ii. 2

Troy, III. iv. 3; VII. i. 34

Tydeus, an Athenian general, II. i. 16

INDEX TO ARRIAN

Abastanians, a tribe between the Acesines (Chenab) and Indus, VI. xv. 1

Abdera, a Greek colony, I. xi. 4

Abian Scythians, IV. i. 1

Abisares, chief of the Indian highland tribes, IV. xxvii. 7; V. viii. 3

Abissares (a tribe), IND. 4. 12

Abreas, a double-pay soldier, VI. ix. 3, x. 1

Abulites, viceroy of the Susians (Curtius, v. 8), III. xvi. 9; VII. iv. 1

Abydus, I. xi. 6

Acesines, the River Chenab, VI. iv. 1; IV. 4, xiii. 1, xiv. 5, xv. 1

Achaeans, port of, in the Troad, I. xi. 6

Achilles, I. xii. 1; VII. xiv. 4, xvi. 8

Achilleus, an Athenian envoy, III. vi. 6

Acuphis, mayor of Nysa, v. i. 3, ii. 3

Ada, Queen of Caria, I. xxiii

Addaeus, or Adaeus, a Chiliarch, at Hali-carnassus, I. xxii. 7

Admetus, a Captain of the Guards, at Tyre, II. xxiii. 2, xxiv. 4.

Adraistaeans, an Indian tribe (their city Pimprama), v. xxii. 3

Aeacus, ancestor of Alexander, IV. xi. 6

Aegae, first capital of Macedonia, I. xi. 1

Aegean Sea, VII. xx. 5

Aegospotami, battle of, I. ix. 3

Aegyptus, earlier name for River Nile, v. vi. 5

Aeolis and Aeolians, I. xviii. 1; III. xxii. 3; VII. ix. 7

Aesculapius (Asclepius), god of healing, II. iv. 8; VII. xiv. 5

Aetolians, I. vii. 4, x. 2

Africa, see Libya

Agamemnon, I. xi. 5

Agathocles, IND. 18. 3

Agenor, supposed founder of Tyre, II. xxiv. 2

Agesilaus, brother of Agis III., II. xiii. 6

Agis III., King of Sparta, opposed Alexander, II. xiii. 4, 6

Agis the Argive, a bad epic poet, IV. ix. 9

Agrianians, Alexander's light troops, a Paeonian tribe, I. i

Albanians, a tribe on west of Caspian Sea, III. viii. 4

Alcetas, commanding an infantry brigade, IV. xxii. 1, xxvii. 1, 5

Alexander the Great, *passim.*

Alexander, son of Aeropus, called Lyn-cestes, I. vii. 6, xvii. 8, xxv.

Alexander the Epirote, uncle of Alexander the Great, III. vi. 7

Alexandria, of Egypt, III. i. ii. *al.* Many other Alexandrias or Alexandreias. Near Cabul, III. xxviii. 4. Eschata (on the Jaxartes), IV. i. 3. On the Caucasus, v. i. 5

Alinda, in Caria, I. xxiii.

Amazons, IV. xv. 4; VII. xiii.

Amminaspes, a Parthian viceroy, III. xxii. 1

Ammon, in Libya, site of Temple of Zeus, III. iii., iv. Zeus Ammon, IV. ix. 9; VI. iii. 2, xix. 4; VII. viii. 3, xiv. 7, xxiii. 6

Amphion, mythical founder of Thebes, I. viii. 6

Amphipolis, I. i. 5, ii. 5, xi. 3

Amphoterus, I. xxv. 9; III. ii. 6, vi. 3

Amyntas, son of Antiochus, enemy of Alexander, I. xvii. 9, xxv. 3. Assists Dareius, II. vi. 3, xiii. 3

Amyntas, son of Andromenes, an important Macedonian officer, I. viii. 2, xiv. 2, xvii. 4; III. xvi. 10. Accused as party to the Philotas plot, III. xxvii.

Amyntas, son of Arrhabaeus, an officer, I. xii. 7, xiv. 1, xxviii. 4

Amyntas, son of Nicolaus, viceroy of Bactria, IV. xvii. 3

Amyntas, commandant at Thebes, I. vii. 1

Anaxarchus, the sophist; consoles Alexander, IV. ix; attacked by Callisthenes, xi

Anchialus, where was tomb of Sardanapalus, II. v. 2

Ancyra, now Angora, II. iv. 1

Andromachus, defeated by Spitamenes, IV. iii. 7, v. 5